ARTIFICIAL LIFE V

Complex Adaptive Systems

John H. Holland, Christopher G. Langton, and Stewart W. Wilson, advisors

ARTIFICIAL LIFE V

Proceedings of the Fifth International Workshop on the Synthesis and Simulation of Living Systems

edited by Christopher G. Langton and Katsunori Shimohara

A Bradford Book

The MIT Press
Cambridge, Massachusetts
London, England

This book was printed and bound in the United States of America.

Library of Congress Cataloging-in-Publication Data

International Workshop on the Synthesis and Simulation of Living Systems (5th : 1996 : Nara-shi, Japan)
    Artificial life V : proceedings of the Fifth International Workshop on the Synthesis and Simulation of Living Systems / edited by Christopher Langton and Katsunori Shimohara.
      p.   cm. — (Complex adaptive systems)
    Workshop held at the Nara-Ken New Public Hall, Nara, Japan, May 16th to May 18th, 1996.
    "A Bradford book."
    Includes index.
    ISBN 0-262-62111-8 (hc : alk paper)
    1. Biological systems—Computer simulation—Congresses. 2. Biological systems—Simulation methods—Congresses. I. Langton, Christopher G. II. Shimohara, Katsunori. III. Title. IV. Series.
QH324.2.I56   1996
570'.1'13—dc21
                                                     97–9088
                                                     CIP

CONTENTS

Contents

Contents

Contents

Preface

The ALife V conference took place a decade after Chris Langton decided to organize the first workshop on Artificial Life. This conference was thus an appropriate venue to reflect upon the first decade of Artificial Life as a research field, and to consider its goals in the near and long-term future.

This first decade has been characterized by a great deal of exploration into the possibilities inherent in the synthesis and simulation of life, and by the development of new technological approaches. We should never cease exploring new possibilities and techniques. We should also refine the methods and approaches we have discovered so far into viable, practical tools for the pursuit of scientific and engineering goals.

Artificial Life researchers continue to expand their efforts to collaborate with practicing biologists, in order to address real biological problems. Despite the successes in computer engineering, adaptive computation, bottom-up AI, and robotics, Artificial Life should not become a one-way street, limited to borrowing biological principles to enhance our engineering efforts in the construction of "life-as-it-could-be". We should aim to influence biology as well, by developing tools and methods that will be of real value in the effort to understand "life-as-it-is".

It is also important that we continue to examine our near-term engineering goals, in light of the larger issues surrounding the future of life on this planet. It is now clear that we are responsible for the state of "Mother Nature" here on Earth. It is time to take that responsibility seriously, by vastly extending the time-horizon in which we think about our scientific, engineering, and social goals, from years and decades to centuries and millennia.

The ALife V conference took a historical and futuristic look at the field of Artificial Life. Besides the usual presentations of the latest work in the field, we had special presentations and workshops reviewing the past and present, and previewing the future, of both Artificial and Natural life.

This volume contains the proceedings of the Fifth International Workshop on Artificial Life held at the Nara-Ken New Public Hall, Nara, Japan, from May 16th to May 18th, 1996.

The committee which selected the papers in this volume included the two editors, along with:

Tsutomu Hoshino	Hiroaki Kitano	David Ackley	Mark Bedau
Richard Belew	Eric Bonnabeau	Rodney Brooks	Jim Brown
Hugo de Garis	Howard Gutowitz	Hiroshi Deguchi	Hirofumi Doi
Michael Dyer	Teruo Fujii	Takeshi Furuhashi	Yuzuru Hushimi
Tetsuya Higuchi	Daniel Hillis	Hirokazu Hotani	Hitoshi Iba
Takashi Ikegami	Yoh Iwasa	Hiroo Iwata	Gerald Joyce
Yukinori Kakazu	Tsuguchika Kaminuma	Kunihiko Kaneko	Masakado Kawata
Yasuo Kuniyoshi	Kristian Lindgren	Melanie Mitchell	Toshiyuki Masui
Mats Nordahl	Chisato Numaoka	Steen Rasmussen	Thomas Ray
Osamu Sakura	Hidefumi Sawai	Takanori Shibata	Karl Sims
Luc Steels	Hisashi Tamaki	Jun Tani	Charles Taylor
Peter Todd	Yukihiko Toquenaga	Kanji Ueda	Tatsuo Unemi
Jari Vaario	Hiroshi Yokoi	Tetsuya Yomo	Yasuo Yonezawa

The papers are organized in this volume in the same order as their presentation at the conference. There were five invited plenary speakers: Arthur Burks, Koji Ikuta, Marvin Minsky, Susumu Ohno, and Hirofumi Miura. Three of these speakers provided written records for the proceedings. There were twelve sessions of oral papers, a total of 56 papers in all. There were also special talks on: European and Japanese traditional automata by Owen Holland and Shoji Tatsukawa, Network Tierra by Tom Ray, Genetic Programming by John Koza, and Swarm by Nelson Minar and Roger Burkhart.

In addition to the talks whose papers are reproduced in this proceedings, there were a large number of other presentations at ALife V. For example, a large poster session was held on the afternoon of Friday May 17th, where thirty five researchers presented their work and held informal feedback sessions with browsing conference attendees. There were also a number of ALife related events including demonstrations, a non-zero-sum multi-player strategic game tournament, entertainment games, virtual reality, music, ALife related CG art,and evolutionary robots. Also, considering that this ALife Workshop was held in Japan, and the first to be held outside of the U.S.A., there was a philosophical panel discussion on "What is life? East and West".

We hope that this volume will inspire and motivate people who are working in or are interested in Artificial Life, so that they may contribute to the growth and development of this field.

Acknowledgement

We would like to thank the following organizing Committee members for their help in organizing the ALife V conference.

Toshio Fukuda	Takashi Gomi	Hitoshi Hemmi
Tsutomu Hoshino	Kazuo Imamura	Godo Irukayama
Hiroo Iwata	Yukinori Kakazu	Yoichiro Kawaguchi
Hiroaki Kitano	Machiko Kusahara	Kazuhiro Matsuo
Osamu Sakura	Hidefumi Sawai	Hisashi Tamaki
Masaru Tomita	Kanji Ueda	Ken'nosuke Wada
Jari Vaario		

We would especially like to thank the following: Tsutomu Hoshino, Tsukuba Univ., who worked hard as the co-organizer, the co-program chair and the chief event organizer; Hiroaki Kitano, Sony Computer Science Laboratory, who did a good job in helping to select papers for the workshop as the co-program chair; Kanji Ueda, Kobe Univ., who helped a lot in organizing the traditional automata exhibition; Osamu Sakura, Yokohama National Univ., who organized the philosophical panel with Brian Keeley; Yoichiro Kawaguchi, Tsukuba Univ., who created a wonderful poster for the ALife V conference and the cover of this proceedings. Special thanks are also due to the following event organizers for their work; Machiko Kusahara, Tokyo Inst. of Polytechnics, for ALife related CG art, Godo Irukayama, NOF Corporation, for ALife and Music, Hiroo Iwata, Tsukuba Univ., for ALife and Virtual Reality, Takashi Gomi, Applied AI Systems, for demonstrations of Evolutionary Robots, Ken'nosuke Wada, ATR, for ALife and the Entertainment Games, Masaru Tomita, Keio Univ., and Tsutomu Hoshino for the Non-Zero-Sum Multi-Player Strategic Game Tournament.

We would also like to thank Yoh'ichi Tohkura, President of ATR Human Information Processing Research Labs., for his good advice and encouraging support during the fund-raising and the running of the workshop. Also, we owe a debt to Ryohei Nakatsu, President of ATR Multimedia Integration and Communications Research Labs., and Yukio Tokunaga, Director of the Advanced Video Processing Lab., NTT Human Interface Labs., for their help in fund raising for the workshop.

Thanks are also due to the members of the Evolutionary Systems Departments both at ATR and NTT for their help in running the workshop successfully. They are Hugo de Garis, Felix Gers, Hitoshi Hemmi, Shin Ishii, Tsukasa Kimezawa, Tatsuya Nomura, Akira Onitsuka, Tom Ray, Keiki Takadama, Hiroshi Tamagawa, Jari Vaario, Ken'nosuke Wada, Toru Yoshikawa, Akihiko Hashimoto, Tomofumi Hikage, Tadao Maekawa, Yoshie Sotome, Takashi Miyatake, and Tatsumi Yamada.

Finally, we would like to greatly thank Keiko Murakami, the secretary of the ALife V conference and the Evolutionary Systems Department of ATR, for her devotion to her tasks. She did an enormous amount of work as a virtual co-organizer, rather than as a secretary, without taking holidays for a month before the conference. She deserves a gold medal for helping us deal with so many crises so calmly.

Katsunori Shimohara, ATR/NTT
Christopher Langton, Santa Fe Institute

Kyoto, Japan
August 1996

The ALife V workshop was supported by the following organizations.

- Nara Prefectural Government
- Nara Municipal Government
- Nara Convention Bureau
- ATR Human Information Processing Research Laboratories
- NTT Human Interface Laboratories
- Foundation for Advancement of International Science

We also wish to thank the following organizations for their generous donations to ALife V.

- The Commemorative Association for the Japan World Exposition (1970)
- International Information Science Foundation
- Advanced Systems Co., LTD.
- Hewlett-Packard Laboratories Japan
- Mitsubishi Materials Corporation
- Nippon Telegraph and Telephone Corporation
- NTT Advanced Technology Corporation
- NTT Data Communications Systems Corporation
- NTT Software Co.
- US Army Research Office - Far East

Plenary Talks

Creative Uses of Logic in the Invention
of the Electronic Computer

Arthur W. Burks

Professor Emeritus of Philosophy and of
Electrical Engineering and Computer Science
University of Michigan
Ann Arbor, MI 48109
awburks@umich.edu

Abstract

Artificial Life is a creative man-machine study that evolved from the logics of cellular automata and other computerizable evolutionary structures. The subject is closely related to Charles Peirce's *logic of discovery*. Moreover, artificial life employs an investigative tool that was generated early in the history of the electronic computer. This is the human-computer discovery combine, a human operating interactively with an electronic computer in such a way as to test hypotheses and discover explanations about a particular phenomenon. Thus Artificial Life uses the *human-computer discovery combine* as an instrument of discovery.

I will sketch the early development of the modern electronic computer. It started in 1937 with Atanasoff's computer, which led to the **ENIAC (1943ff)** of Eckert and Mauchly, which led to the **EDVAC (1944ff)**, which led in turn to the **IAS (von Neumann) computer (1946ff)**. In sketching this history I will formulate some principles of the logic of discovery that were employed in making inventions embodied in these machines.

Finally, I will present von Neumann's two models of self-reproducing automata: the robot model and the cellular automaton model.

1 The First Electronic Computer, the ABC

ARTIFICIAL LIFE is a creative man-machine study that evolved from the logics of cellular automata and other computerizable evolutionary structures. Artificial life belongs to the *logic of discovery*, a subject created by philosopher Charles Peirce over 100 years ago. I will formulate and illustrate three principles of this logic that were employed in the invention of the electronic computer, an invention that took place during the 10-year period 1937-1946. Then I will show how the logic of discovery was used in the invention of cellular automata.

John Atanasoff's special-purpose computer (1937-42) started the electronic computer revolution. His graduate student Clifford Berry helped design and build it, and it came to be known as the Atanasoff-Berry Computer (ABC).

Figure 1 is a drawing of the ABC. The purpose of this machine, built at Iowa State University, was to solve sets of simultaneous equations with up to 29 variables. Never before had sets with more than 10 variables been solved.

The central solution process was carried out in binary, being preceded by decimal-binary conversions and succeeded by binary-decimal conversions. The central operation, repeated very many times by the machine operator, was as follows. The operator starts with a pair of binary cards, each holding an equation of n variables; designates a variable to be eliminated by making a plugboard connection; then feeds the two cards into the binary card reader in succession. The operator now pushes the start button on the control panel and the machine eliminates the designated variable and records the answer on a new binary card. It takes just one second to read from or record on each card, and the entire operation takes less than three minutes.

This basic operation was to be repeated systematically until an original set of 29 cards was reduced to a single card with a one-variable equation. The other 28 one-variable equations were generated by working back from this one, whereupon the machine converted these 29 solution equations into decimals and the operator calculated the final values of all the variables on a desk calculator.

Atanasoff designed a very clever vector architecture that carried out the vector operations of addition, sub-

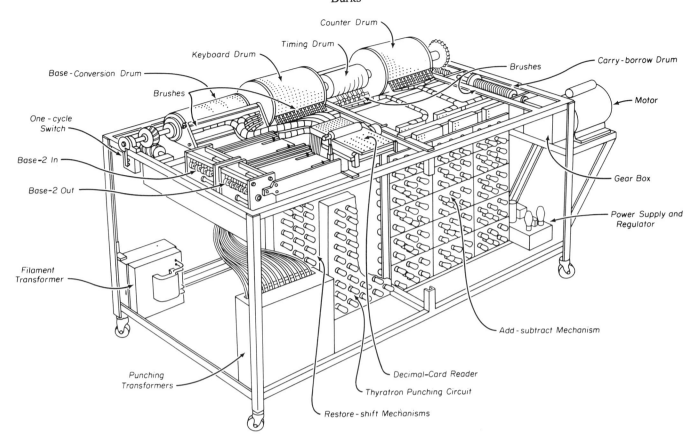

Figure 1: Drawing of the Atanasoff-Berry Computer

traction, and shifting in such a way as to avoid the need for a full vector multiplier and divider. When it was built the ABC had only 280 double triodes and 31 thyratrons (gas tubes), the latter being used for binary card recording and reading.

The ABC was well named, for it established the A, B, C's of electronic computing: drum storage with dynamic capacitor memory, vacuum-tube logic, binary arithmetic, binary-decimal base conversions, and vector processing. It also had a read-only drum memory, a central timing arrangement, and a form of electronic input-output.

* * *

The ABC was finished in the spring of 1942, and it all worked well with one exception, the vacuum-tube-controlled carbon-arc recording and reading of the binary input-output. This failed once in 10^4 or 10^5 bits - a small error rate, but because of the iterative nature of Atanasoff's reduction procedure this rate defeated his goal of solving large sets of simultaneous equations. In the summer Atanasoff and Berry both left to do war research, and neither returned to Iowa State.

The ABC led directly to the first programmable electronic computer, the ENIAC, as we will see in a mo-

ment. Eckert and Mauchly filed a patent on the ENIAC in 1947, claiming not only their own ideas but basic ideas Mauchly had learned from Atanasoff. This patent was issued in 1964, and was litigated between Honeywell and Sperry Rand from 1967 to 1973. The litigation established that Atanasoff was the inventor of the "automatic electronic digital computer", and the court declared the Eckert-Mauchly patent invalid because of derivation from Atanasoff.

Atanasoff has written his own story [1], and my wife Alice and I have written a book about the Atanasoff-Berry Computer and the long federal trial [3]. We gave a technical description of the ABC and analyzed the court evidence that proved Atanasoff to be the inventor of the electronic computer; our book is being translated into Japanese for publication next year. Clark Mollenhoff wrote a book on this subject that has already been translated into Japanese [23]. Mollenhoff was both a journalist and a lawyer; his book emphasizes the legal issues and personal aspects of the court case. We have also written an article for the Japanese journal, *The Bōsei*, on this history [4].

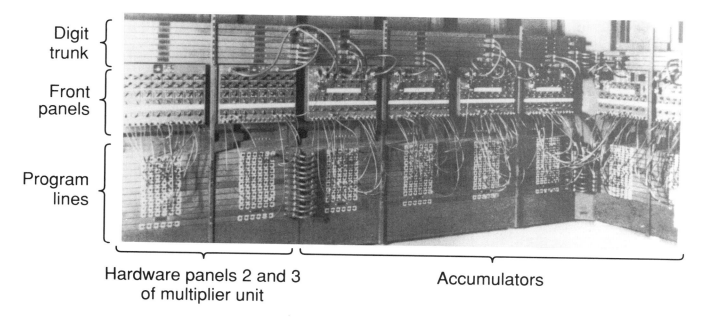

Figure 2: Segment of an ENIAC problem setup

2 From the ABC to the ENIAC

The first general-purpose electronic computer, the ENIAC (*E*lectronic *N*umerical *I*ntegrator and *C*omputer), was planned, designed, and built during 1943-46 by J. Presper Eckert, John Mauchly, and several engineers, including T. K. Sharpless, Robert Shaw, Chuan Chu, and me. This work was paid for by the Ballistic Research Laboratory of Aberdeen Proving Ground, Aberdeen, Maryland; it was carried out at the Moore School of Electrical Engineering of the University of Pennsylvania [5, 8, 13].

Figure 2 shows a segment of an ENIAC problem setup. Decimal numbers were stored in the accumulators and could be added or subtracted back and forth between them. The multiplier unit multiplied the two numbers stored in accumulators located off to the left, and it generated the product in the accumulator directly to its right. Each hardware panel contained digital circuits and the programming circuits to control these digital circuits.

The programmers of the ENIAC entered instructions by setting switches on the machine's front panels, and they sequenced these instructions by plugging cables between the front panels and the program lines that carried pulses around the machine. Numbers were transmitted among the units by means of the digit trunk lines shown above. This digital numerical plugboard system was derived from the problem setup system of an earlier computer, the mechanical analog differential analyzer, in a way I will explain next.

* * *

As we saw, the acronym "ENIAC" stands for "electronic numerical integrator and computer". The constituent "numerical integrator" of this acronym is historically meaningful, because it reflects the fact that the architecture of the electronic digital ENIAC was derived from that of the *differential analyzer*. The proposal that Eckert and Mauchly submitted to Aberdeen had the title "Report on an Electronic Difference Analyzer", and it referred to the proposed electronic digital computer as an "analyzer" and an "electronic analyzer" [3, p. 110]. But the proposed machine was to be digital, not analog, as were the general-purpose analog electronic computers invented after the war.

The Moore School had a differential analyzer, and Aberdeen Proving Ground (a unit of Army Ordnance) had one also. This was the most general computer yet created, for it solved a wide variety of differential equations, each for an indefinite number of initial conditions. In early 1943, both these analyzers were being used around the clock to compute trajectories for artillery firing tables, but they could not meet the wartime demand. The Moore School convinced the Army to support the expensive ENIAC development project on the ground that this digital electronic machine would integrate trajectories much more rapidly than the two analyzers combined.

The Moore School's analyzer is pictured in Figure 3.

The main computing component was the integrator, and for this reason analyzers were also called "integraphs". A row of integrators and their torque amplifiers is shown on the left. Continuous integration is, of course, the analog of digital accumulation, and the dozen or so

Figure 3: Moore School differential analyzer

integrators of the analyzer were replaced in the ENIAC by 20 accumulators.

The tables on the right of the analyzer were for graphical input and output. The values of the independent and dependent variables were represented by the accumulated angular rotations of shafts, and the digital counters in the foreground counted the rotations of these shafts. In the case of a graph table, the value of a variable was represented by a linear motion. Differential gears accomplished addition-subtraction, and fixed gears accomplished multiplication or division by a constant. The whole system was driven by an electric motor that rotated the independent variable shaft.

Thus the computing elements of the analyzer were integrators, differential gears, fixed gears, and the independent variable shaft. This shaft was rotated slowly by means of an electric motor, and it drove the rest of the machine. The accumulated angular rotation of this shaft represented the value of the independent variable at any moment of the computation. The input and output graph tables, and the output counters, constituted

the inputs and outputs of the analyzer.

To put an equation on the analyzer, the operators interconnected the computing and input-output elements of the machine into a pattern that mirrored the interrelations expressed by that equation. The matrix of shafts visible in the middle of Figure 3 was used for this purpose. When stripped down between problems, this matrix consisted of short segments of shaft running crosswise and down the bay, unconnected to one another. The required interconnections in this bay of shafts were established by manually inserting short lengths of shafts, fixed gears, and differential gears at the appropriate places in the bay, and then tightening the connections with screwdrivers and wrenches.

Thus the bay of shafts of the differential analyzer constituted a kind of mechanical plugboard, which could be configured to communicate mechanical rotations from one computing or input-output unit of the analyzer to another. The digital analogue of this would be an electrical plugboard for conveying digital pulse sequences representing numbers from one computing unit of the machine to another. We will see in a moment how the bay of shafts of the analog analyzer became the digital trunk plugboard in the ENIAC.

* * *

It was John Atanasoff who provided the impetus for the ENIAC, because he suggested the guiding idea that Mauchly and Eckert worked out to plan the ENIAC. This suggestion can be put in the form of what I call a *discovery analogy*: use the electronics of the ABC to make a digital machine that will solve the difference equations solved by the analyzer. Note that the term 'discovery' indicates that the analogy is formulated for the purpose of discovering a new entity. The analogy requires completion in the form of the new entity; indeed, there could be more than one such form.

Atanasoff's discovery analogy that led from the analyzer and the ABC to the ENIAC is diagrammed in Figure 4.

	Technologies	
	continuous (analog) mechanical	digital electronic
special-purpose	tide predictor, Atanasoff's Laplaciometer, etc.	Atanasoff-Berry computer
general-purpose	differential analyzer	????? general difference equation solver ?????

Figure 4: Atanasoff's discovery analogy

Eckert and Mauchly completed Atanasoff's discovery analogy by COMBINING the *architecture* of the mechanical analog differential analyzer WITH the *electronic digital technology* of the ABC. I will explain this process in terms of a simple example, computing the sine and cosine functions [3, 8, 13].

Figure 5 shows the cyclic interconnections by means of which the differential analyzer computed the sine and cosine functions. The variable x, its *sine* value, and its *cosine* value are represented by accumulated rotations, which were counted by mechanical counters and printed on paper by the analyzer. The transformation from $sine(x)$ to $-sine(x)$ was accomplished by a reversing gear.

Compare this figure with Figure 6, which shows an ENIAC problem setup to compute a sine and cosine function. The two integrators have been replaced by

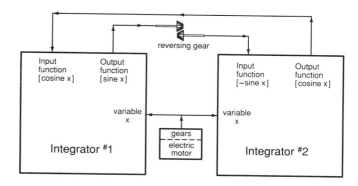

Figure 5: Differential analyzer mechanical setup to compute sine-cosine

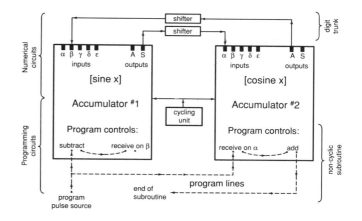

Figure 6: ENIAC plugboard setup to compute sine-cosine

two accumulators. The continuous representation of x has been replaced by a 10-digit decimal number. The continuous variation of x has been replaced by the Δx stepwise solution of the difference equations for the sine and cosine functions. The multiplication by Δx is not accomplished by a multiplier, but by means of shifter plugs inserted into the number communication channels of the numerical plugboard. A shift by a power of 10 was accomplished in the ENIAC by mechanically displacing the output wires of the plug with respect to their input decimal positions.

The reversing gear of the analyzer (fig. 5) was replaced in the ENIAC setup (fig. 6) by programming accumulator #1 to transmit subtractively to accumulator #2 rather than additively. The analyzer shafts that transmitted the output from one integrator to the other and back again were replaced in the ENIAC by plugboard connections established on the digit trunk of this machine. And the continuous rotation of the analyzer shaft that represented the input variable x was replaced in the ENIAC by the timing signals of the cycling unit.

To be a general-purpose computer, the ENIAC needed

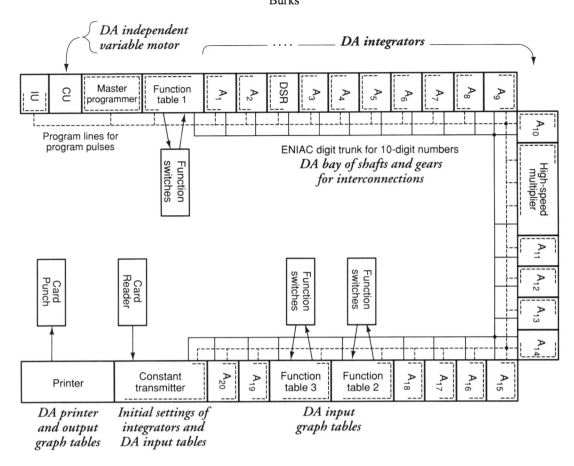

Figure 7: The digital ENIAC and the analog differential analyzer

a control layer of programming to operate its digital circuits. This was accomplished locally by means of program controls on the ENIAC'S units, and globally by means of the master programmer. Each program control of an accumulator (and similarly with other units) began operation when it received a program pulse. A program control read the instruction on its program switches and then directed the digital circuits of its unit to carry out this instruction. When its instruction was executed, the program control emitted a program pulse that was used to stimulate the next program control or controls of the program.

Figure 6 shows a non-cyclic subroutine setup on two accumulators that executes one Δt step of the integration of the sine and cosine difference functions.

The ENIAC project began on the last day of May 1943, and two model accumulators and a small cycling unit (electronic clock) to drive them had been designed and constructed by the summer of 1944. John Mauchly debugged and tested these by operating them as in Figure 6. He started the program with a push-button, and he ran it both one addition-subtraction at a time and also contin-

uously. He then made a life-test of the reliability of the electronic design of the ENIAC by connecting the end of the subroutine to the input and letting the system run. It operated correctly for weeks on end.

* * *

Eckert and Mauchly had included a form of Figure 6 as an example in their computer proposal to Aberdeen Proving Ground [3]. Herman Goldstine was the ordnance officer who sponsored the proposal, and to support the feasibility of the project Eckert and Mauchly told Herman of the success of Atanasoff's electronic computer. Herman said later that this earlier activity helped convince him and Aberdeen Proving Ground that the ENIAC should be built [3, pp. 192-193].

Figure 7 shows the layout of the ENIAC as it was finally built. Its analogies to the differential analyzer are indicated in boldface. The cycling unit of the ENIAC replaced the independent variable motor of the analyzer, accumulators replaced the integrators, the function tables replaced the analyzer input graph tables, a card reader replaced the initial settings of the analyzer at the beginning of a problem, and the card punch replaced the analyzer printer and output graph tables. The ENIAC also had a multiplier and a divider & square-rooter.

The analog computing and input-output elements of the analyzer ran continuously, and though the analyzer had to be set up for each problem, nothing like programming was involved. But the digital units of the ENIAC operated intermittently and cooperatively with each other, so that a programming system was required to control them. This system consisted of local program controls in the units (indicated in Figure 7 by dashed lines) as well as the numerical circuits, a master programmer, and a plug-board consisting of program lines that were used to communicate program pulses among the units and the master programmer.

The digit parallelism of number transmission in the ENIAC was derived from the numerical communication parallelism of the analyzer, which was an essential feature of this analog machine. But this parallelism did not turn out to be useful in the ENIAC; in 1948, at the suggestion of John von Neumann, it was replaced by a single-channel number communication system.

3 Invention of the Dynamic Random Access Memory

The invention of the modern dynamic random access memory - or DRAM - resulted from two successive applications of another discovery principle, which I call the *combinatorial discovery principle*. This principle is: combine features of earlier inventions to make a new invention. Note that, in contrast to the discovery analogy, the combination of features by this principle does not derive from any analogy but is discovered directly.

For our present story, the principle was first applied in 1944 to create the bit-serial mercury-delay-line memory, which was used in the EDVAC (Electronic Discrete Variable Automatic Computer) and its direct successors. The combinatorial discovery principle was also applied about a year later to create the random-access cathode-ray-tube memory, which was used in the von Neumann machines.

Figure 8 illustrates the basic principle of the mercury-delay-line serial memory. An electrical pulse into the input causes the input crystal to vibrate and create an acoustic pulse (small shock wave) in the mercury. This pulse travels down the mercury and causes the output crystal to vibrate and create an output pulse, which could represent a binary 1 while the absence of a pulse at a particular clock time could represent a binary 0.

When a binary sequence representing a word (number or instruction) came out of a delay line, it could either be cycled back for further storage or be sent to the rest of the computer for processing, or both. One mercury tube could store 32 words of 32 bits each, so that 32 mercury

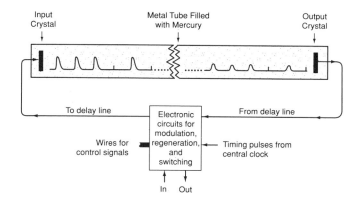

Figure 8: Mercury delay line serial memory

tubes would provide a store of 1024 words, 50 times as many as the ENIAC could store.

The mercury-delay-line memory was invented by Pres Eckert and John Mauchly, with help from Kite Sharpless. This invention resulted from applying the combinatorial discovery principle because it incorporated two earlier inventions. William Shockley had invented the acoustic delay line for measuring very short time intervals, and Eckert and Sharpless had developed a reflective mercury delay line for use in timing radar signals. That use involved only a single pulse reflected from a mirror in the mercury tube whose distance from the transmitting crystal could be varied by the radar operator.

To make a serial memory out of this device, a receiving crystal was placed at the other end of the tube and the pulse-no-pulse sequence was regenerated before being fed back into the memory, as shown in Figure 7. The idea of regeneration was invented by Atanasoff and used in the capacitor drum storage of the ABC, and Atanasoff and Berry had demonstrated it to Mauchly in June of 1941 [1, 3].

* * *

The mercury-delay-line memory was not a random-access memory, of course, since information put into a mercury line would not be available until it had traversed the full length of that line. John von Neumann conceived of the first random-access memory. In fact, he did so by applying the combinatorial discovery principle, combining principles from the television camera tube and the television viewing tube. Cross-sectional views of these tubes are shown in the two figures, Figure 9, Television camera tube (image orthicon), and Figure 10, Cathode ray tube (TV viewing tube).

The general principle of television is as follows. A camera tube scans and reads the electric charges that have been deposited inside it by the photoelectric effect. At the television station, these charges are converted into

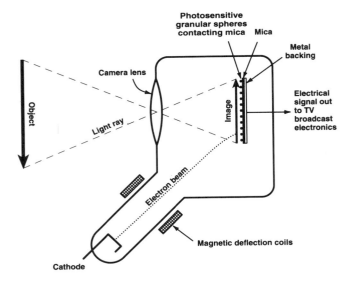

Figure 9: Television camera tube (image orthicon)

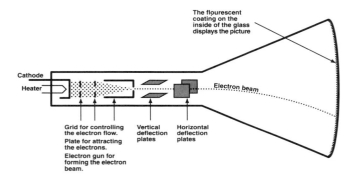

Figure 10: Cathode ray tube (TV viewing tube)

television signals and transmitted. They are received by a television antenna, and a television set decodes them and displays them in a scanning mode on a viewing tube.

Thinking of how to improve on the serial mercury-delay-line memory, von Neumann realized that these two television tubes carry out complementary operations. The camera tube reads and transmits series of electric charges that have been deposited inside it by the photoelectric effect, and the viewing tube displays them by a scanning process on its inside surface.

Johnny's idea was to combine these two functions in the same tube, replacing the continuous variation in brightness of television by two states of charge that would represent 0 and 1. The inside surface of the tube would function as a capacitor with respect to the outside surface in storing these charges, and so a large number of bits could be stored in a single TV tube. The same electron beam that writes the bits would be used to read them.

Since electric charges gradually leak off through a capacitor, these changes would need to be read and restored periodically. Thus this new *electrostatic memory tube* would need to be operated as a dynamic memory.

Von Neumann estimated that a single electrostatic memory tube could store more information than a single mercury delay line, and so 32 such tubes would store more information than the memory planned for the EDVAC. It then occurred to him that rather than storing the bits in these tubes in series, the bits of each word could be spread over the tubes, and all accessed at the same time. This completed the abstract conception of the modern dynamic random-access memory (DRAM), though it was not given that name until much later. An inventive concept or general plan still has to be reduced to practice. In the case of the cathode-ray-tube DRAM, this stage of invention was carried out by F. C. Williams and T. Kilburn of Manchester University [25]. Thus no one person created the dynamic random access memory (DRAM). Eight people created it over a period of 10 years!

4 Von Neumann's Logical Construction Method for Designing a Computer

Eckert and Mauchly had started to plan the EDVAC (Electronic Discrete Variable Automatic Computer) in the spring of 1944. Its memory would be composed of mercury delay lines, and would be large enough to store both program and data. (Recall that the programs of the ENIAC were entered into an old-fashioned electrical plugboard.) The electronics for the EDVAC's arithmetic were to be based on Atanasoff's electronic switching circuitry, speeded up to a one megacycle pulse rate.

Von Neumann became a consultant on the EDVAC project in August of 1944, and over the next year he worked on the logical design and architecture of that machine.

We were designing the ENIAC bottom up: detailed electronic circuits first, then constructs of these, and finally the block diagram structure of the machine. For the design of the EDVAC, von Neumann created a much better computer design procedure, involving the use of logic, one of his specialties.

Pres Eckert was an excellent electronics engineer. He had already seen how to upgrade Atanasoff's serial add-subtract circuit from 60 cycles per second to a megacycle rate, and how to convert the parallel electronic technology of the ENIAC into serial electronics. McCulloch and Pitts [21] had created an idealized logical symbolism for representing neural nets, which von Neumann adapted to represent the basic circuit building blocks of the new machine. Figure 11 gives a representation of his serial binary adder in my own notation [15].

Von Neumann then developed logical representations

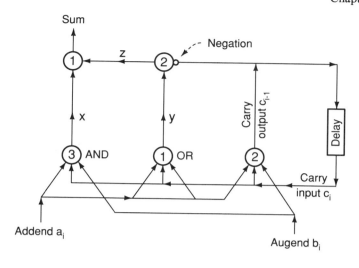

Figure 11: Von Neumann's serial binary adder

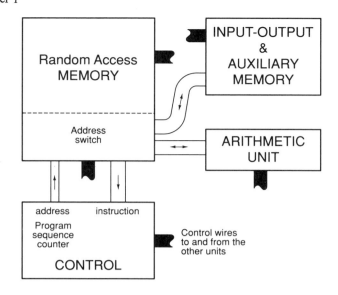

Figure 12: The von Neumann architecture

of flip-flops, counters, word length memories, and simple switches. He proceeded to the next level of long delay lines and switches for accessing them, multiplier, divider, etc. Finally, he designed the Memory, the Arithmetic Unit, and the switch that would connect the Memory to both the Arithmetic Unit and the Control.

With that much of the EDVAC characterized logically, he was able to define the code or program language for the machine. This was the first machine language for a modern computer.

* * *

After conceiving of the random-access use of the cathode-ray-tube memory, von Neumann realized that a computer based on this memory would be far superior to the serial EDVAC, both in power and in ease of programming. And so he applied his logical design procedure to develop such a parallel computer, aided by Herman Goldstine and me [14]. There would be a Memory of 40 storage tubes, an Arithmetic Unit, and a Control. We hoped for a memory of 4096 words, but the Williams memory held only 1024 words, the same capacity as the usual mercury-delay-line memory. The design of the input-output and auxiliary memory was left till later, after digital magnetic wires or tapes had been developed.

Figure 12 shows the highest level of the design, what came to be known as "the von Neumann architecture". Numbers and instructions were stored and processed in bit parallel.

Figure 13 is an example of the next lowest level of the logical design, our plan for the Arithmetic Unit. There are only four registers here, counting the register embedded in the accumulator. And these are *all* the registers in the machine! Our reason was to minimize the number of

tubes required. The ENIAC had 18,000 vacuum tubes, whereas the computer built at the Institute for Advanced Study (IAS) had fewer than 3,000 tubes [2]. Many other computers of this design were built, including the IBM 701.

* * *

After the logical designs of the EDVAC and von Neumann computers were completed, the electronic designs to execute them had yet to be carried out. This was a much larger task than that of logical design - and just as creative - each first generation computer being designed and built by several engineers and a construction staff. {See the papers by Bigelow, Burks, Chu, Eckert, Everett, Householder, Hurd, Huskey, Lavington, Mauchly, Metropolis, Rajchman, Robertson, Slutz, Suekane, Wilkes, and Wilkinson in [22]. See also [26].}

5 The Theory of Self-reproducing Automata

Von Neumann conceived his robot model of self-reproduction in 1948. A robot would be constructed of various parts and be placed in a space along with an unlimited number of instances of every part. There would be girders for structural support, logical switches and delays with wires attached for computing, a device for recognizing any object in the environment, action parts for picking up any part and moving it around, devices for joining and cutting, energy sources, and perhaps others. The problem was to design a robot made of these primitive parts with the following property: when placed in a suitable environment of parts it would collect the needed parts and assemble them into a duplicate of itself.

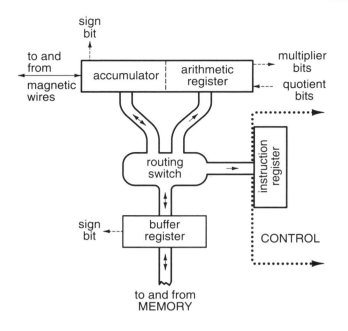

Figure 13: Architecture of the arithmetic unit of the von Neumann computer

Because of the complexity of this model universe, von Neumann found it very difficult to work out the design of a self-reproducing robot in a logically rigorous way. Stanislaw Ulam then suggested that he use a uniform discrete space of simple finite automata, instead of a continuous space with discrete parts in it. I named such a space a *cellular automaton* [24].

Following Ulam's suggestion, von Neumann first considered a 3-dimensional cellular space, but soon found that a 2-dimensional cellular space was much simpler to work with. He defined a particular 29-state finite automaton that would occupy each cell, and then proceeded to construct various finite computing structures he called "organs" and planned how to combine these into a self-reproducing automaton. The goal was a two-dimensional logical construction of a self-reproducing automaton.

However, because of his terminal illness, von Neumann stopped working on the project before it was finished. I accepted the task of editing and explaining his partial manuscript and then completing his construction [24, 6].

* * *

There are several stages in the construction of the self-reproducing cellular automaton. These are as follows:

Stage 1. An indefinitely extendable checkerboard structure is specified as the space, and a particular finite automaton of 29 states is assumed to exist in every cell. One of these states is a blank state, like an empty square on a storage tape. Von Neumann used the symbol "U" (for "unexecutable") to represent the blank state. In the

indefinitely long storage tape of Figure 14 below, "U" represents "0" and the downward pointed arrow represents "1".

The automaton in each cell is connected to its four immediate neighbors. Von Neumann defined a transition function that mapped the states of a cell and its neighbors at time t into the state of the cell at time $t + 1$.

Stage 2. To design an automaton in the cellular space, the designer specifies the initial states of a finite (usually contiguous) configuration of cells, that is, the state of each cell at time 0.

Stage 3. For this stage, von Neumann worked out logical designs of various kinds of devices as building blocks: pulse sequence generators, pulse sequence recognizers, small storage devices, an organ for crossing signal paths, etc. These building blocks would perform the functions of the flip-flops, counters, short delay lines, wires, switches, etc., of his logical design of the EDVAC, which we described in the previous section.

Stage 4. Compounds of these building blocks are then constructed, which, when activated, become functioning finite automata. See Figure 14 for an example. It shows a finite automaton M_T and an indefinitely extendable storage tape, the whole system having the power of Alan Turing's theoretical universal computer.

I'll explain how the finite automaton M_T operates the tape. To read it the automaton sends a suitable bit sequence into input i_3. This passes through cell x_n and produces either of two bit sequences at output o_3 corresponding to the bit stored at x_n. M_T then sends sequences into inputs i_3 and i_4 which write in cell x_n and either extend or contract the constructing arm.

Thus M_T can extend or contract the constructing arm, and direct the constructing head to write either of two states in a cell. More generally, M_T can direct the arm to turn corners, and also direct the constructing head to write any passive state in an adjacent cell. This ability is used in both universal construction (fig. 15) and self-reproduction (fig. 16).

Stage 5. Figure 15 shows a universal constructor after it has constructed a finite automaton with a tape. The universal constructor consists of a finite automaton M_{vN} with two attachments. One attachment is a tape that holds a description $D\{m\}$ of some finite automaton m that is to be constructed; this tape also holds information $T\{m\}$ that is to be copied onto the tape of the constructed automaton. The second attachment to M_{vN} is a constructing arm that carries a stream of signals from M_{vN} to a construction-destruction head; this stream of signals causes the construction arm to advance to an empty area and construct the automaton m there.

Construction in a blank area is accomplished by changing the states of blank cells into the states specified by the information on the tape of the universal constructor. After the construction is completed the universal con-

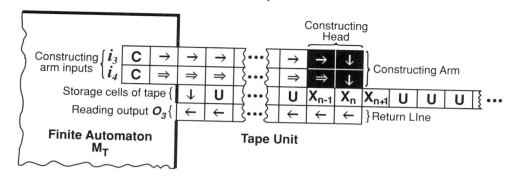

Figure 14: Cellular automaton version of Turing's universal computer

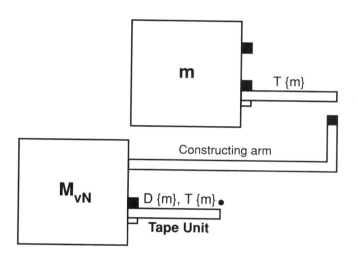

Figure 15: Von Neumann's universal constructor

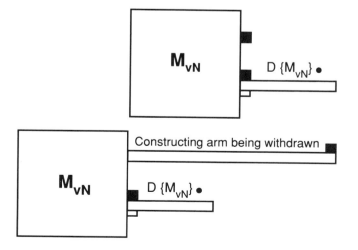

Figure 16: Automaton self-reproduction

structor activates the constructed automaton and then withdraws the constructing arm back to itself, leaving the constructed finite automaton and its tape where they were constructed.

Stage 6. The universal constructor of Figure 15 operates in two steps. First, M_{vN} reads the description $D\{m\}$ of a machine m from its tape, extends the construction arm to the area of construction, and changes the states of the cells in this area until they constitute the initial state of an automaton m. Second, M_{vN} produces a blank tape attached to the automaton m and copies the information $T\{m\}$ from its own tape onto this new tape. The universal constructor then activates the constructed automaton and withdraws its constructing arm.

Stage 7. Figure 16 is the special case of Figure 15 when the description $D\{m\}$ on the tape of the universal constructor M_{vN} is used twice by that machine. M_{vN} uses $D\{m\}$ first to construct the machine described by $D\{m\}$, namely, m, and then M_{vN} produces a blank tape attached to the new machine and copies $D\{m\}$ onto that tape. *The result of these seven stages is self-reproduction,* as Figure 16 shows.

* * *

Von Neumann's design of this self-reproducing automaton was similar in many respects to his logical design of the EDVAC, though the goals were very different. His logical design of the EDVAC was aimed at creating a good architecture and program language for a hardware machine, and in this he succeeded. His logical design of a two-dimensional self-reproducing automaton, on the other hand, was only a constructive proof in principle.

However, I think there are ultimate practical implications of von Neumann's design. For I believe that

a finite deterministic automaton can perform all natural human functions. The qualification 'natural' excludes such phenomena as supernatural and mystical experiences, extrasensory perception, and telekinesis, if these phenomena ... have no natural explanation [12, p.409; 7, 9, 10].

Moreover, modern computers, networks of them, and natural self-reproducing systems at all levels are examples of a distinctive type of system - the highly complex, coherent, holistic, non-linear, feedback system - and von Neumann's logical method is applicable to studying these, as we shall see in the next section.

We note first an interesting variant of von Neumann's result. In Figure 16, the self-reproducing automaton works from a completely detailed description of its own structure that is stored on its tape. Richard Laing has produced models in which a self-reproducing automaton reads its own structure, rather than reading a coded description of that structure. Thus it reads the object rather than a representation of that object. [17, 18].

6 The Human-Computer Discovery Combine

Electronic computers are the first active or "live" logical-mathematical systems; they provide a new tool for the logic of discovery. Computers are being designed and programmed to cooperate interactively with humans so that the calculation, storage, and judgment capabilities of the two are synthesized. I call such a system a *human-computer discovery combine*. With networking, these combines are becoming social. The powers of these combines are increasing at an exponential rate as computers continue to become faster, cheaper, and smaller.

Human-computer discovery combines belong to the class of complex, holistic, hierarchical, feedback systems [11]. Combines are especially suitable for studying such systems, in particular, living systems ranging from simple forms up to rational goal-directed systems. Both actual and artificial living and evolutionary systems are being studied by human-computer discovery combines, and these combines will be very important tools in the study of fully rational and conscious goal-directed systems.

The *gedanken* or imaginative thought experiment has long been used as a tool of logical discovery. Because of its visual powers, the human-computer discovery combine can employ more complex gedanken experiments than can the unaided human.

The modern electronic computer, created as a device to perform routine calculations rapidly, has revolutionized that activity. Von Neumann and Ulam were the first to see that the computer could also be used as an exploratory instrument of inquiry.

Von Neumann studied the non-linear equations describing fluid and gas flow, especially shock waves, by means of computer explorations and computations of revealing cases. His studies included the non-linear equations describing the weather. He hoped that the understanding gained from these studies would lead to long-range prediction of the weather. It did not, but it did lead to the discovery of a new phenomenon: *computer chaos*.

Ulam also used the computer to study non-linear mathematical transformations. In addition, he studied the growth of patterns in cellular spaces by means of computer simulations. For example, he defined two patterns in such a way that each could wipe out cells of the other, and let them conduct a fight until one pattern destroyed the other. Finally, he defined a three-dimensional cellular automaton and traced the evolution of an initial pattern through many generations. See his essays in [6].

Some of the early uses of the human-computer discovery combine took place in my Logic of Computers Group at the University of Michigan. The investigator had in mind a certain global behavior, such as self-reproduction or heart fibrillation. By trial and error experimentation on a computer the investigator constructed, step by step, a transition function and a starting state of an automaton capable of the particular behavior. Applying ideas from developmental biology, E. F. Codd used this procedure to construct an 8-state-per-cell transition function sufficient for automaton self-reproduction [6: pp. xviiiff, 52ff; 16, 19, 20].

7 Conclusion

I have formulated and illustrated three principles of the logic of discovery.

The *discovery analogy* was illustrated by the transition from the mechanical analog differential analyzer to the electronic digital ENIAC. See Figures 1-7.

The *combinatorial discovery principle* was illustrated twice. First, the mercury-delay-line serial memory combined the principle of the acoustic delay line, the use of mercury as a satisfactory medium for transmitting representations of the bits 0 and 1, and the principal of periodic information regeneration. See Figure 8.

Second, the random access memory combined the writing function of the television viewing tube and the reading function of the television camera tube, and it used this memory in bit-parallel fashion. See Figures 9 and 10.

Von Neumann invented *the logical construction method for working out the logical design of a modern electronic computer*. By this means he specified the structure of the EDVAC and the flow of information through that machine for the processing of arithmetic functions. Thus he settled organizational questions of an electronic computer before the electronic circuits of that computer were designed. With this as a basis, he wrote the first modern program language (machine language). See Figures 11, 12, and 13.

Von Neumann then applied his logical construction method to design a cellular automaton model of a self-reproducing automaton. Turing's universal computer was a special case along the way to self-reproduction.

See Figures 14, 15 and 16.

Von Neumann's self-reproducing automaton is a very abstract model of a very important feature of a class of natural, complex, holistic, hierarchical, feedback systems - those systems that can reproduce themselves.

Note and Acknowledgments

Many disputed questions concerning the invention of the ENIAC and its derivation from the ABC were settled in litigation between Honeywell and Sperry Rand in 1967 - 1973. The evidence produced in this case is analyzed and explained in reference [3] by my wife Alice and me. She has also helped me with the present paper.

This work was supported by NSF grant IRI-9224912.

References

[1] Atanasoff, John V. 1984. "Advent of Electronic Digital Computing". *Annals of the History of Computing* 6:229-82.

[2] Bigelow, Julian. 1980. "Computer Development at the Institute for Advanced Study". Pp. 291-310 of Metropolis, Howlett, and Rota 1980.

[3] Burks, Alice R., and Arthur W. Burks. 1988a. *The First Electronic Computer: The Atanasoff Story*. Ann Arbor: The University of Michigan Press. Translated into Japanese by Matsumoto Ohzahata, Kogyo Chosakai Publishing Co., Ltd., Bunko-ku, 1997.

[4] ———. 1996. "Working in the History of Computers: A Husband-Wife Memoir". Published in Japanese in *The Bōsei*, February and March 1996.

[5] Burks, Arthur W. 1947. "Electronic Computing Circuits of the ENIAC". *Proceedings of the Institute of Radio Engineers* 35(August, 1947)756-67. This was the first published technical explanation of the ENIAC.

[6] ———. 1970. Editor of, and contributor to, *Essays on Cellular Automata*. Urbana: University of Illinois Press.

[7] ———. 1972-73. "Logic, Computers, and Men." *Proceedings and Addresses of the American Philosophical Association* 46 (1972-73) 39-57.

[8] ———. 1980. "From the ENIAC to the Stored Program Computer: Two Revolutions in Computers". [22], pp. pp. 311-44.

[9] ———. 1986. *Robots and Free Minds*, Ann Arbor: College of Literature, Science, and the Arts, University of Michigan, pp. vi+97.

[10] ———. 1986. "An Architectural Theory of Functional Consciousness." *Current Issues in Teleology*, pp. 1-14. Edited by Nicholas Rescher. New York: University Press of America.

[11] ———. 1988. "The Logic of Evolution and the Reduction of Coherent-Holistic Systems to Hierarchical-Feedback Systems." *Causation in Decision, Belief Change and Statistics*, pp. 135-191. Edited by William Harper and Bryan Skyrms. Dordecht, Holland: Kluwer Academic Publishers, 1988.

[12] ———. 1990. "The Philosophy of Logical Mechanism." *The Philosophy of Logical Mechanism - Essays in Honor of Arthur W. Burks with his Responses*, pp. 347-531. Edited by Merrilee H. Salmon. Boston: Kluwer Academic Publisher.

[13] Burks, Arthur W., and Alice R. Burks. 1981. "The ENIAC: First General-Purpose Electronic Computer". *Annals of the History of Computing* 3:310-99. With comments by John V. Atanasoff, J. G. Brainerd, J. Presper Eckert and Kathleen R. Mauchly, Brian Randell, and Konrad Zuse, together with the author's responses, pp. 389-99.

[14] Burks, Arthur W., Herman H. Goldstine, and John von Neumann. 1946. *Preliminary Discussion of the Logical Design of an Electronic Computing Instrument*. Pp. iv + 53. Princeton: Institute for Advanced Study, 1946.

[15] Burks, Arthur, and Jesse Wright. 1953. "The Theory of Logical Nets". *Proceedings of the Institute of Radio Engineers* 41: 1357 - 1365.

[16] Codd, E. F. 1968. *Cellular Automata*. New York: Academic Press.

[17] Laing, Richard. 1976. "Automata Introspection". *Journal of Computer and System Sciences* 13: 172-183.

[18] ———. 1977. "Automata Models of Reproduction by Self-Inspection". *Journal of Theoretical Biology* 66: 437-456.

[19] Langton, Christopher G. 1989. *Artificial Life. The Proceedings of an Interdisciplinary Workshop on the Synthesis and Simulation of Living Systems*. Redwood City, California: Addison-Wesley Publishing Company.

[20] Levy, Steven. 1992. *Artificial Life - The Quest for a New Creation*. New York: Pantheon Books.

[21] McCulloch, W. S. and W. Pitts. 1943. "A Logical Calculus of the Ideas Immanent in Nervous Activity". *Bulletin of Mathematical Biophysics* 5:115-133.

[22] Metropolis, N., J. Howlett, G-C. Rota (eds.). 1980. *A History of Computing in the Twentieth Century.* New York: Academic Press.

[23] Mollenhoff, Clark R. 1988. *Atanasoff: Forgotten Father of the Computer.* Ames, Iowa: Iowa State University Press. Translated into Japanese by Tsuyoshi Saisho. Kogyo Chosakai Publishing Co., Ltd., Bunko-ku, 1994.

[24] von Neumann John. 1966. *Theory of Self-Reproducing Automata.* Edited and Completed by Arthur W. Burks. Urbana: University of Illinois Press. Translated into Japanese by Hidetoshi Takashi. Tokyo, Japan: Iwanami Press, 1975.

[25] Williams, F. C., and T. Kilburn. 1949. "A Storage System for Use with Binary-Digital Computing Machines". *Proceedings of the IEE (London),* in three parts: Vol. 96, pt. II, pp. 183-202 (1949); Vol. 96, pt. III, pp. 77-100 (1949); and Vol. 97, pt. IV, pp. 453-454 (1950).

[26] Williams, Michael. 1985. *A History of Computing Technology.* Englewood Cliffs, New Jersey: Prentice-Hall.

3D MICRO INTEGRATED FLUID SYSTEM TOWARD LIVING LSI
- Challenge for Artificial Cellular Device -

Koji Ikuta

Department of Micro System Engineering
School of Engineering
Nagoya University

Furocho, Chikusa-ku, Nagoya 464-01, Japan
TEL : +81 52-789-5024   FAX: +81 52-789-5027
E-mail: ikuta@mech.nagoya-u.ac.jp

ABSTRACT

New three dimensional micro fabrication process (IH process) based on stereo lithography is developed. The concept of Micro Integrated Fluid System (MIFS) made by IH process and silicon process is proposed and conceptual prototype is developed. Further advanced concept of biochemical IC and LSI toward living LSI is presented. Future application for new life science using synthetic approach and biochemical computer are described. Finally, Cellular MIFS with dynamic modification capability of inner structure by micro switch valve and metamorphosis are proposed.

1. INTRODUCTION

Downsizing of micro electronic devices such as IC and LSI have been drastically changing not only information technology but also our lifestyle for these twenty years. Another well known example of the effective downsizing is the probe scanning type microscope such as STM (scanning tunnel microscope) and AFM (atomic force microscope). Unlike conventional huge high voltage electron micro scope, the cost, space and resolution have been evolutionary improved.

Recently the downsizing of chemical analyzer and reactor have been attracting researchers in micromachine and MEMS (micro electro mechanical system) field. This reason lies on following merits .

1. Reducing sampling volume of the specimen
2. Faster sensing speed
3. Multi-sensing capability
4. Miniaturizing total equipment
5. Cost down

On the other hand, author have been pointing out another stimulating merits due to miniaturization of chemical system from the view point of life science and computer science as well as technology impact.

On this account, author's group has been conducting many fundamental researches including new three dimensional micro fabrication process, special UV polymer, shape memory alloy materials, micro actuators, micro integrated fluid system (MIFS), the MIFS based biochemical IC chip and biochemical computer. In addition to above innovative micro technology, the future applications and technical impact for life science are presented.

Let's start from the brief introduction of 3D micro fabrication named IH process.

2. STEREO LITHOGRAPHY

Our new process is mainly based on the principle of stereo lithography ("photo forming" in other word) which has been used to make 3D mock-up models in macro size in these days. The basic technique of the stereo lithography is described briefly.

In order to create 3D structure made of UV polymer which can be hardened by UV (Ultra violet) ray, two dimensional sliced shape of the   final structure so called "slice data" is required firstly. These 2D shape data are obtained in the CAD system easily. Fig.1 shows schematic relationship between final and sliced shape. Shortly speaking, final 3D shape can be constructed by stacking 2D sliced planes solidified by UV beam. So for the UV laser beam such as He-Cd is used for commercial products for macro modeling .

3. NEW 3D MICRO FABRICATION [1]

3.1. Basic Concept
The basic concepts for 3D micro fabrication proposed here is shown as Fig.2. This process is named as "IH Process" (Integrated Harden Polymer Process) can fabricate two type of materials such as polymer and metals. In order to make polymer structure, thin layers made of harden polymer are stacked from bottom to up to create complicated 3D shape such as base as shown in Fig.2(a).

Moreover metal 3D structure can be obtained by using metal molding process combined with former polymer process as shown in Fig.2(b). The polymer structure is used as a cast and the metal is electroplated into this cast. And the polymer is removed by solvent or the appropriate chemical process. Finally micro 3D structure made of metal is obtained. This process can applicable not only for

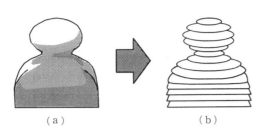

Fig.1 Final structure and sliced data

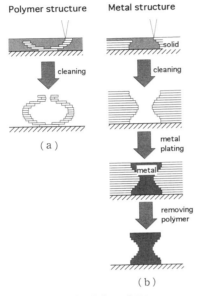

Fig.2 Basic principle of IH process

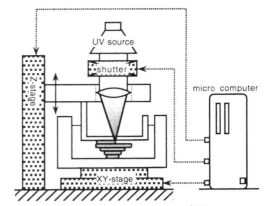

Fig.3 Total fabrication system of IH process

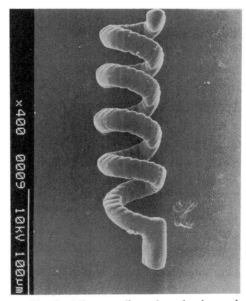

Fig.4 Micro coil spring (polymer)
(coil diameter:50 μm)

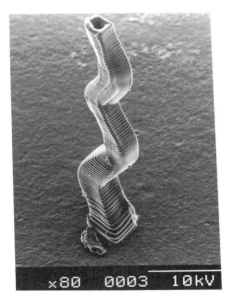

Fig.5 Bending micro pipe (polymer)
(100x100x1000 μm)

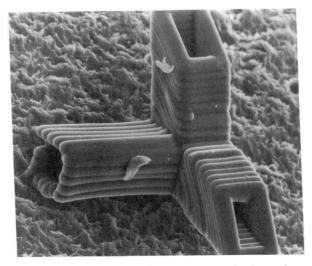

Fig.6 3D connected micro pipes (polymer)
(inner diameter: 30 μm)

any electroplatable metals but also for other materials which can be molded into polymer structure.

3.2. Apparatus

Fig.3 shows the schematic diagram of fabrication apparatus which consists of UV (ultra violet) light source, XYZ-stage, shutter, lenses and micro computer. UV harden polymer (i.e.; photo resist) is used as a material of polymer structure. As a UV light source, a Xenon lamp which is much cheaper and simpler than UV laser is utilized at this time.

In order to create micro 3D structure, thin sliced cross section shape of the final product is drawn by UV beam focused in the liquid UV polymer through the lenses, shutter and transparent plate on the Z-stage. Since only microscopic area focused by fine UV beam is hardened selectively, two dimensional shape of solid thin film in micro size is obtained. The depth of the focus is moved from bottom to surface with the motion of Z-stage. The complicated 3D shape is obtained by stacking thin films of hardened polymer.

This apparatus has following specifications.

1.UV light source:	Xenon lamp
2.Spot size of UV beam:	5μm
3.Position accuracy:	0.25 μm (in X-Y)
	1.0 μm (in Z)
4.Minimum size of Unit of Harden Polymer:	
	5 x 5 x3 μm (X,Y,Z)
5.Maximum size of fabrication structure:	
	10 x 10 x 10 mm
6.Fabrication speed:	within 30 min.

4.EXPERIMENTAL VERIFICATION

Usefulness of proposed 3D micro fabrication process was verified by several experiments for polymer and metal micro fabrication.

4.1.Fabrication Examples [1]

Many shape of 3D micro structures are fabricated successfully. Following are typical examples which can not be made by conventional micro fabrication methods.

(A)Polymer structure
1."Micro coil spring". (Fig.4)

The coil diameter is 50 μm and length is 250 μm. Required fabrication time is 20 minutes. It worked as a real spring, since it had not only flexibility but also toughness against outer load.

2."Bending micro pipe" (Fig.5)

Its size is 100x100x1000 μm and the aspect ratio is 10. Total time for fabrication is about 30 minutes.

3."3D connected micro pipes" (Fig.6)

Inner diameter of pipe is only 30μm and inside is gone through. Flow of colored liquid such as alcohol was observed. Required fabrication time is about 30 minutes.

(B)Metal structure

Metal micro structure also was fabricated by using two step process as described in Fig.2(b).

The micro cast made of polymer IH process and electroplated nickel with curved 3D shape molded from polymer successfully. Its size was 60x60x100μm.[1]

4.2. Characteristics of IH Process

According to many experiments, following features of IH process were confirmed.

1) Real three dimensional structure
2) High aspect ratio: larger than 10
3) Materials : polymer and metals
4) High production speed for small amount of number
5) No mask process is needed
6) Simple and low cost apparatus
7) Medium range of accuracy
8) Safety
9) Less space: **Desk Top Micro Fabrication**

5. MICRO INTEGRATED FLUID SYSTEM (MIFS) [2]

5.1.Conventional Micro Fluid System

As well known, miniaturization of chemical analyzing tool brings great merits as mentioned before.

However, conventional efforts to make this type of micro device have been using silicon micro processes such as anisotropical etching and surface micro machining. Fig.7 shows schematic concept to construct three dimensional micro fluid system by conventional method. Many silicon or grass plates with fine micro machined micro channels are stacked up to make three dimensional whole fluid system.

Although this method can easily make electric circuits along with micro channels, it has following problems.

1)Complicated three dimensionally winding channel system is difficult to make
2) Assemble process is necessary
3) Packaging problem

On the other hand, IH process can solve above issues. As we demonstrated at MEMS'93, various type of micro fluid parts made of UV polymer with 3D shape have been fabricated successfully by IH process.

5.2.Micro Integrated Fluid System (MIFS)

The new idea to combine conventional silicon micro fabrication process and our IH process so called **"Hybrid System"** is proposed. This unique system can provide many useful applications.

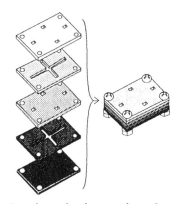

Fig.7 Conventional method to make micro fluid
system by silicon process

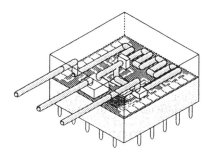

Fig.8 Basic concept of three dimensional micro
integrated fluid system (3D MIFS)

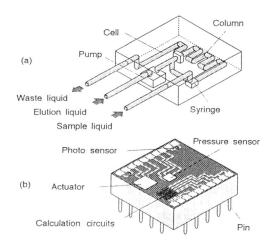

(a)

Cell
Column
Pump
Waste liquid
Elution liquid
Sample liquid
Syringe

(b)

Photo sensor
Pressure sensor
Actuator
Calculation circuits
Pin

Fi.9 Hybrid system of IH process and silicon
process for 3D MIFS

(a) Micro fluid part made by IH process
(b) Electric circuits made by silicon
process

Fig.10 Prototype of Micro Integrated
Fluid System (MIFS)

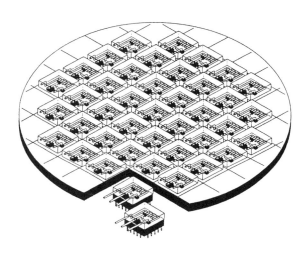

Fig.11 Concept of mass production for MIFS

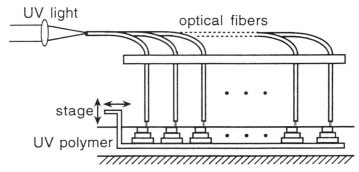

UV light
optical fibers
stage
UV polymer

Fig.12 Concept of Mass productive IH process
using optical fiber array
(Mass-IH process)

One of the important application of hybrid system is MEMS for chemical analysis and biotechnology. Fig.8 is an example of "Micro Integrated Liquid Chromatography" to show basic concept of **"Three Dimensional Micro Integrated Fluid System"** **(3D MIFS)**.

Fig.9 shows the basic concept of hybrid system combining IH process and silicon process to make 3D MIFS. Upper part in Fig.9(a) containing micro pipes, syringe, column and cell all made of polymer is to be fabricated by IH process. The bottom part in Fig.9(b) containing sensors, actuator and electric circuits is to be made by silicon process.

The conceptual prototype of 3D MIFS is shown in Fig. 10. At this time, bottom part is just a dummy of LSI. Please pay attention to upper part which was fabricated by micro stereo lithography. It consists of micro pipes with a micro syringe (300[μm] in diameter) and others as described above in 6 [mm] squire.

All micro fluid components were produced at same time without any assemble process. Moreover, IH process developed by authors has already demonstrated further miniaturization of micro fluid components. Therefore 1000 units of 3D MIFS can be fabricated by IH process in the same 6 [mm] squire size.

Following strong points are verified.

1) Simple and fast   2) Three dimensional
3) Easy Packaging   4) Low cost
5) Hybrid with silicon process is easy
6) Integration density will be improved easily

6. MASS PRODUCTIVE IH PROCESS [3]

6.1. Demand for Mass Productive Micro Stereo Lithography

Fig.11 shows future concept to minimize production cost like a present LSI process. A number of MIFS are fabricated on the silicon substrate at the same time and separated one by one. As well know, the silicon process has a strong point for mass production. On the other hand, conventional IH process as shown in Fig3. is not suitable for mass production, even though it is very useful for real 3D micro fabrication. This reason lies on the principle of stereo lithography based on drawing pattern.

On this account, new type of micro stereo lithography satisfying both 3D micro fabrication and mass productivity should be developed.

6.2. Mass-IH Process " using Micro Optical Fibers Array

Fig.12 is the proposed mass productive micro stereo lithography named " **Mass-IH Process**". The main technology is the newly developed **"Optical fiber Multi-beam scanning"** which can satisfy both simultaneous scanning and uniform accuracy in whole area. The array of single mode

optical fibers are utilized. Total number of optical fibers can be infinite in principle.

Other components of apparatus such as UV source, lens, computer controlled XYZ table and UV-polymer are almost same as regular IH process.

The Mass-IH process has following strong points;

1) Simple optical system
2) Easy miniaturization of total system
3) Uniform resolution and accuracy in whole area
4) Mass productive real 3D micro fabrication
5) High aspect ratio
6) High speed production independent from the number of products
7) Low cost
8) safety
9) Desktop micro fabrication

Although the resolution at this time is not good as conventional IH process (5 μm), feasibility as mass productive micro stereo lithography was verified. It should be noticed that the resolution obtained here is ten times better than ordinary stereo lithography. There is no critical issue to increase number of optical fibers. Increasing fibers and optimizing experimental conditions are under going.

7. MICRO CHEMOMECHATRONICS [3]

7.1. IC Chip with Biochemical Reaction

Since the MIFS is composed of micro electro mechanical parts and micro chemical parts, new technological field named " **Micro Chemomechatronics**" should be opened.

One of important application of MIFS is biochemical micro apparatus. As well known, the most of the biochemist have been handling and watching minute biochemical reaction in less than one micro litter. On the other hand, the MIFS has following merits caused by miniaturization;

1) micro sampling volume
2) high reaction rate
3) small and low cost
4) easy modification of chemical reaction
5) observabilty of reaction
6) controllability of reaction
7) easy integration
8) automatic and programmable experiment

According to above merits of MIFS, various kind of biochemical systems as follow are expected to be developed.

1) micro biochemical reactor
2) smart drag delivery system
3) artificial micro organ
4) tools for biotechnology
5) experimental tools for micro biology
6) biochemical micro simulator and computer

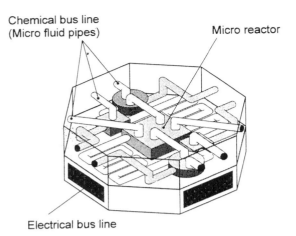

Chemical bus line
(Micro fluid pipes)

Micro reactor

Electrical bus line

Fig.13　Biochemical IC chip based on MIFS
with electrical and chemical bus lines

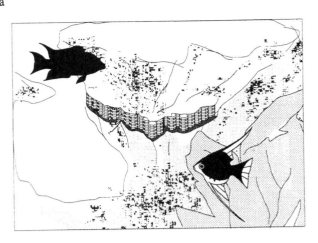

Fig.16　Hybridization of biochemical LSI with
living organ

Fig.14　Large scale integrated biochemical
MIFS (Biochemical LSI)

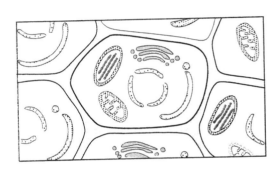

Fig.17　Biological cells

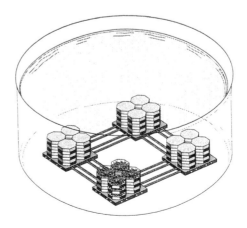

Fig.15 Basic concept of biochemical computer
constructed by several biochemical LSI

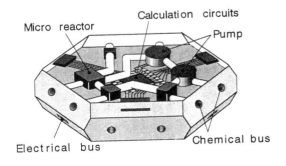

Micro reactor

Calculation circuits

Pump

Electrical bus

Chemical bus

Fig.18　Advanced Cellular MIFS in
Kelvin's polyhedron

More detail discussion on biochemical computer using MIFS is made in the later section.

7.2. Synthetic Approach for New Biology

The analytical approach has been major in micro biology and biochemistry so far. However, this method cannot be the best way for present life science such as cellular and neuro science. Because even though partial character of biological system is known, it is very difficult to understand systematic behavior of total system with complicated relationship such as cellular society and neuro system. Large demand from the scientists in those fields has become very strong in these days.

On this account, the author has been proposing **Biochemical IC Chip** based on MIFS technology as shown in Fig.13. This advanced MIFS has two type of bus line to communicate between nearest neighbors. The first is "Electrical bus line" in the lower silicon base similar to present IC chip. The second one is the "Chemical or Biochemical bus line" in the upper polymer part made by IH process.

Fig.14 shows the Large Scale Integrated Biochemical MIFS so called **"Biochemical LSI"**. Each MIFS is stacked together to enhance total performance and characteristics. Like today's micro electronic product, various type of biochemical experimental systems can be constructed by using Biochemical LSI. This approach should accelerate life science drastically.

8.BIOCHEMICAL COMPUTER

8.1. Concept and Advantage

Authors has proposed to make a new type of computational tool using Biochemical LSI based on MIFS. Like a neural network in the brain, biochemical reaction in micro scale is utilized as computer chips. Fig.15 is basic idea of the biochemical computer system constructed by four clusters of Biochemical LSI. Each cluster is connected via both electrical and biochemical bus line and the system is working in the buffer solution.

Following features are significant characteristics of Biochemical computer.

1) Both energy and material transfer occur in and between system
2) Parallel and analog reaction utilized as calculation signals
3) It can handle real chemical material in micro scale
4) Unlike today's electrical computer, over heating during computation can be control by using cooling reaction in stead of heating reaction.

Of course, basic architecture and theoretical discussion should be made for realizing Biomedical computer system.

Recently a few computer scientists has just started to think about MIFS based biochemical computer system. Kitano presented interesting idea about possibility of MIFS for the evolvable computer at A-life V workshop.

8.2. Hybridization with Living System

Fig.16 shows the image sketch of hybridization with living system. Since the Biochemical LSI can carry out both calculation and chemical production, it must be ideal implantable artificial organ. This figure is describing controlling life system and producing some structure like a coral under the sea.

9. CELLULAR MIFS AND LIVING LSI

9.1.Future of MIFS

In order to create "Living LSI", advanced concept of future MIFS is proposed in this section.
From a view point development stages, several generations of MIFS is described as bellow.

[Generations of MIFS]

1st.   Analyzer   (Passive MIFS)
2nd.   Synthesizer   (Active MIFS)
3rd.   Decentralization of control
4th.   Decentralization of energy
5th.   Locomotion and moving
6th.   Reproduction and evolution

9.2. Cellular MIFS

Basic design of more advanced future MIFS is shown as Fig. 18. Since this micro chemomechatronic device is following real biological cellular system as shown in Fig.17, the outer shape is the "Kelvin's polyhedron" which can fill three dimensional space without any vacancy. This version of MIFS is named "Cellular MIFS". Like an original concept of MIFS, Cellular MIFS has both electrical and chemical bus line on the side wall and micro biochemical reactor system is fabricated inside.

As Cellular MIFS can connect three dimensional manner, cluster of connected Cellular MIFS will show unique form like a artificial coral as shown in Fig.19.

9.3.Dynamical Modification of Internal Structure

Fig.20 shows two dimensional inside view of connected Cellular MIFS's. A lot of micro reactors are connected via chemical bus pipe lines. It should be noticed that small black circle between pipe means micro switch valve to select direction of chemical flow dynamically. Fig.21 shows two patterns of fluid system. The direction of switch valves are controlled by electric circuit on the silicon base (lower part of MIFS).

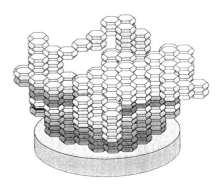

Fig.19 Artificial coral made of Cellular MIFS

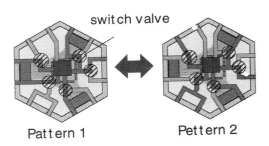

Fig.21 Dynamical modification of internal structure by switch valves

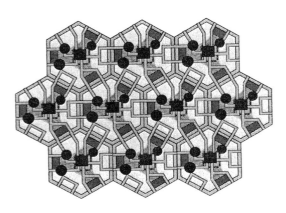

Fig.20 Two dimensional internal view of connected Cellular MIFS

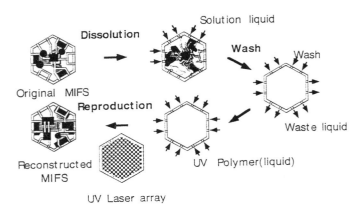

Fig.22 Metamorphosis process of Cellular MIFS

9.4. Metamorphosis of Cellular MIFS

Another unique idea for dynamic modification of internal structure of Cellular MIFS is introducing "Metamorphosis". As described in Fig.22, it needs several sequence and more complicated function of each MIFS is required. Metamorphosis is carried out as follows;

1. Dissolution by solution liquid:
2. Wash out and clean up inside
3. Filling by liquid UV polymer
4. Re-solidifying by upper placed UV laser array
5. Wash out non-curable part of UV polymer

This method is utilizing one of advantage of IH process as " on site micro fabrication". The real living LSI will be made if above Artificial Cellular System is developed in future.

10. CONCLUSION

If the potential of new technology is high, it can produce new approach in the science. Conventional A-life has been based on the rapid progress of digital computer system. Author dreams that many type of new science appear by the progress of micromachine and MEMS technology.

Acknowledgments

Author would like to thank all of my students conducting research for the articles in this paper. (Ken Hirowatari,Tsukasa Ogata, Masahiro Tsuboi, Norio Kojima and Fukaya)
Author would like to thank Prof.S.Yokoyama, Prof.E.Suzuki at University of Tokyo, Dr.A.Endo and Dr.T.Fujii for their active discussion about biochemical application of MIFS and Dr.H.Kitano at Sony Computer Science Lab for his useful advise.

References

[1]K.Ikuta, K.Hirowatari, Real Three Dimensional Micro Fabrication Using Stereo Lithography and Metal Molding", Proc. of IEEE International Workshop on Micro Electro Mechanical Systems (MEMS'93), pp.42-47, 1993
[2]K.Ikuta, K.Hirowatari, T.Ogata, "Three Dimensional Micro Integrated Fluid System (MIFS) Fabricated by Stereo Lithography", Proc. of IEEE International Workshop on Micro Electro Mechanical Systems (MEMS'94), pp.1-6, 1994
[3]K.Ikuta, T.Ogata, M.Tsuboi, S.Kojima, "Development of Mass Productive Micro Stereo Lithography (Mass-IH Process)", Proc. of IEEE International Workshop on Micro Electro Mechanical Systems (MEMS'96), pp.301-306, 1996

How Computer Science will change our lives

Marvin Minsky

Computer Science will transform our cultures. This is not because it is about computers. It is because it will help us understand brains. That will give us our first good ideas about Psychology. It will help us learn what Knowledge is. It will teach us how we learn, think, and feel. Then we'll be able to change ourselves. This will change all our sciences and humanities.

Those changes will probably be so large that no one can tell what will happen then.

INSECT-MODEL BASED MICROROBOT

Hirofumi Miura, Takashi Yasuda, Yayoi Kubo Fujisawa, Yoshihiko Kuwana
Shoji Takeuchi and Isao Shimoyama

The University of Tokyo, Mechano-Informatics, 7-3-1, Bunkyo-ku, Hongo, Tokyo 113, JAPAN
e-mail: miura@leopard.t.u-tokyo.ac.jp   URL: http://www.leopard.t.u-tokyo.ac.jp

Abstract

It should be understood that the robot is not a simple automatic machine, but instead has certain level of intelligence. Many kinds of intelligent robots have been developed in the author's laboratory during the past 15 years. These robots perform many kinds of games like the cup & ball game, top-spinning, walking on stilts, etc. These robots apparently look intelligent, but are they really and truly intelligent? There is one opinion that these robots are no more than simple automatic machines which are controlled by a computer with sophisticated programs. If so, then what is actual robot intelligence? The author is trying to construct a new robotics --- insect-model based microrobotics --- in order to get a new concept of robot intelligence.

1 WHAT IS ROBOT INTELLIGENCE?

Intelligence for the robots shown in Fig. 1 is discussed below.

(1) INTELLIGENCE FOR FAST AND ACCURATE MOTION (Cup & ball game robot)

When the motion is slow, PTP(point to point) control works well. But for the fast motion, PTP control yields position error because for fast motion, the inertial forces (centrifugal force, Colioris force, etc. which act on the joint motors) are considerably large and feedback control is disturbed by them.

So-called " inverse dynamics " is a very effective control scheme for fast motion. The cup & ball game cannot be implemented by the usual industrial robot employing PTP control scheme. On the other hand, by employing the inverse dynamics, the robot played cup & ball game with a 95% success ratio. Inverse dynamics can be robot intelligence for fast and accurate motion.

(2) INTELLIGENCE FOR LEARNING (Inverted pendulum)

The ability to learn is one of the most challenging subject in robotics. The inverted pendulum robot was developed as an example of a robot which has learning ability. If the geometrical dimensions (length, weight, position of center of gravity, moment of inertia, etc.) are not given, learning control must be employed. During the first several minutes of the experiment, a person's hands help the pendulum to maintain the vertical attitude, but after several minutes the pendulum has learned to keep the vertical attitude all by itself.

(3) INTELLIGENCE FOR DYNAMIC BALANCE (The biped and the quadruped)

In the author's laboratory many kinds of bipeds have been developed. The biped (stilt type) is statically unstable but can be balanced dynamically. It has intelligence for dynamic balance[1]. Another type of biped (human type) has knee joints and ankle joints like a human. Eight motors are mounted in this robot in total, and it can walk more slowly than the stilt type. It also walks dynamically.

The quadruped also walks dynamically. Real animals support their bodies with two legs (not three legs) and swing the other two legs in the air even during a slow walk. At low speed, one fore leg and one hind leg on the same side are in the air together. This gait is called "pace".

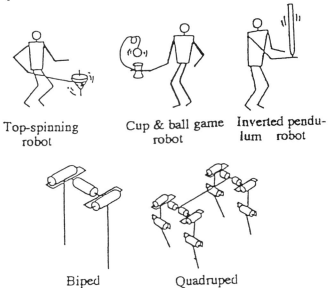

Top-spinning robot   Cup & ball game robot   Inverted pendulum robot

Biped (stilt)   Quadruped

Fig. 1 Some Examples of Intelligent Robots which have been developed at the author's lab.

When the walking speed of an animal gets faster, the gait changes to "trot (diagonal two legs are in the air together)". The gait is selected by a minimum energy consumption criterion[2],[3].

(4) INTELLIGENCE FOR LEARNING THE ROPE (top-spinning robot)

The author can spin a top. However, it is very hard to teach another person how to spin a top. This means that writing a program for the top-spinning robot is also very hard. How fast should the arm move? At which position should the top be thrown forward? How strongly should the string be pulled back? The author learned these tricks by watching his father's play. For the robot, the trajectory of a human arm and a top during human top-spinning play was input into the computer through two video cameras (one camera in front, and one over the head) and the computer generated a program to reproduce the same motion of the arm and the top from human play. With this program the robot spins a top very skillfully. This example may be called " teaching by showing."

2 CAN A MACHINE HAVE ITS OWN WILL?

Several examples of robot intelligence were presented above. These robots complete dexterous tasks like a human does. However, the author is not sure whether these robots are as intelligent as a human, because all algorithms expressed in the program are developed by a human investigating the result of analysis of human play. The robot itself is not intelligent and it only follows the program given to it by a human. The robot has no will to play these games better and better.

On the other hand, the author practiced hard on cup & ball game, top-spinning, etc., so that he could play better than his friends during childhood.

Can a machine have will? This is a big question in robotics and AI technology. The author is trying to find a new way for a small but steady step to answer this question[4].

3 INSECT-MODEL BASED ROBOTICS (Microrobot)

An insect looks much more intelligent and more lively than robots introduced above. The insect looks to have a will. If an insect robot could be developed, it is possible to make it look truly intelligent. The author's laboratory started developing insect-model based robots about five years ago when looking for a new and different way to approach intelligent robots. Since the late 1980s, microtechnology has been highlighted as a promising

technology for the development of very small sized mechanical systems. Fabrication of micromechanisms on a silicon wafer using IC process may be the key technology for developing mm sized microrobots.

Millimeter sized insects are all around us. The author considered that microtechnology should be applied to developing an insect-model based robot. Although there are still many problems which must solved to build real insect-model based microrobots, there are basic lines of solution for some problems with experimental results. This paper argues that insects will be good models for microrobots for design, control, actuation, etc., just as human beings or mammals are good models for normal-sized robots. In addition, an insect has only 10^5 neurons. The motion of an insect is produced by simple mechanisms such as "a reflex act". But it is interesting to the author that this motion looks intelligent. This is why the author is trying to develop an insect-model based robot.

4 EXTERNAL SKELETON

For developing microrobots, new design concepts must be constructed. For instance, a frictionless structure must be designed. Rotating joints must be avoided because at all rotating joint, there exists friction. Frictional forces are proportional to the sliding surface area size(L^2). Weight and inertial forces, however, are proportional to volume(L^3). As the size gets smaller, the frictional force

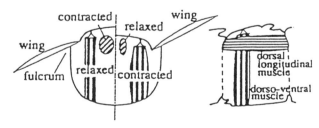

Fig.2 Cross section of an insect thorax. Distortion of the thorax causes beating of wings

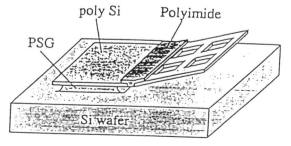

Fig. 3 Basic model of the external skeleton. Three dimensional structure is constructed by bending along the polyimide hinges.

exceeds the other forces and governs the motion of system. In an extreme case, motion cannot be realized when the system is subjected to normal actuation forces. We argue that knowledge about insects may be useful for developing microrobots. The insect has many interesting features, such as an external skeleton, elastic hinges (joints), contracting-relaxing muscles, etc. These characteristics suggest basic design principles for microrobots.

The external skeleton of an insect consists of elastic(hard) cuticles connected by elastic (soft) hinges. In general, the elasticity of the cuticles is higher than the elasticity of the hinges.The motion of body parts like wings is based on the deformation of these elastic structures. Sliding friction does not exist there.

The cross-section of an insect (fly) thorax is shown in Fig. 2[5], illustrating the beating mechanism of the wing. The muscles are inside the skeleton, while muscles are outside the skeleton in humans.The downward movement of the wing is produced by distortion of the thorax caused by contraction of the dorsal longitudinal muscle. The upward movement results from distortion of the thorax produced by the dorso-ventral muscle.

Elasticity of the thorax plays an important role in the friction-free, high-speed wing movement. For most insects, the beating frequency coincides with the structural natural frequency of the thorax. Mechanical resonance is a good way to get large deformation with small external forces. This may be applicable for actuation in microrobots.

5 ORIGAMI STRUCTURE

Since the silicon IC process is planar, a three dimensional structure is difficult to make. The author's group is proposing a folding process like paper folding (ORIGAMI in Japanese) to make a 3D microstructure. To build an external skeleton, the author's group uses polysilicon as the rigid plate, and polyimide as the elastic joint. The basic structure of an external skeleton model is shown in Fig. 3. Polyimide is a thermosetting resin, and a hinge can be set at any angle by heating after bending it to the desirable angle. This structure can be fabricated easily by IC processes.

First, the development surface figure is made on a silicon wafer, and the folding lines are made of polyimide as shown in Fig. 3. The folding operation is done by a human with a microprobe under a microscope.

6 MICROFLIGHT MECHANISM

The authors have developed the beating micromechanism actuated by electrostatic forces shown in Fig. 4. If an electric voltage is applied between Al plates and the base (silicon wafer), the plates move towards the base and the polysilicon wings bend up. When the frequency of the alternating voltage coincides with the natural frequency of mechanical vibration for the system, the beating amplitudes resonate. Including this example, several kinds of microflight mechanism have been developed. Magnetic force is also applicable for actuation of beating or microflight mechanisms, and a flying microrobot is now under development[6][7]. Fig. 5 shows a micro-flight mechanism[8]. It consists of three layers: polyimide, nickel, and polyimide. Nickel is sandwiched by two polyimide layers so as not to be attacked by HF while etching takes place to remove a sacrificial layer under polyimide. Both polyimide layers are spin-coated to 1 μm in thickness, and nickel is sputtered to 0.1 μm in thickness.

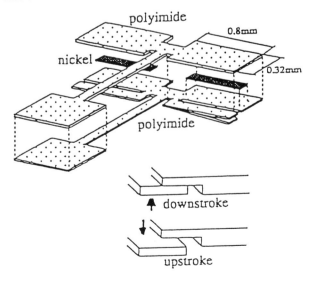

Fig. 5 Structure and dimensions of microflight mechanism

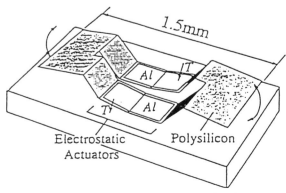

Fig. 4 Schematic figure of beating mechanism

7 MICROANT-ROBOTS

In the author's laboratory a microant-robot has been developed, as shown in Fig. 6 and 7[9]. The gait for this robot is not the same as the real ant. The two middle legs kick the ground to move forward, while the other four legs touch the ground at all times to support the body. The ground vibrated with a very small amplitude(less than 1μm) and this vibration is transmitted to the middle leg through the ground. If the frequency of the vibration coincides with the natural frequency of the leg, it resonates with a large amplitude, providing the driving force by kicking the ground. The natural frequency of a leg is set by the length of the polyimide spring, so the two middle legs can have different natural frequencies.

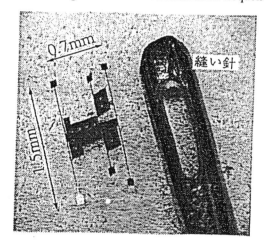

Fig. 6 Photograph of the fabricated microrobot alongside a sewing needle.

The robot can go straight, and turn to the right or to the left.

8 HYBRID INSECT ROBOT

A male silk moth pursues a female by following a phero-mone. This action can be caused by only a few molecules of pheromone which arrive at the antenna of a male silk moth. A biological sensor was constructed with a small part(5mm length) of antenna of a real male silk moth. Two sensors were attached to a simple wheeled mobile robot to determined the direction of a pheromone trace. The robot followed the pheromone trace like a real male silk moth[10].
Another example of a hybrid insect robot is shown in Fig. 7[11]. This is a hybrid kockroach robot. Two legs are cut off from the body and pasted on the paper body with adhesives.

Leggs can be actuated by appropriate electrical stimulation and the robot can walk.

9 CONCLUSIONS

Several intelligent robots which have been developed in the author's laboratory have been introduced, but the author is not sure that these robots are truly intelligent because all control schemes have been constructed by humans and all computer programs have been written by humans. It can be said that they are no more than simple automatic machines which are controlled by a computer. The author is constructing a new technology --- the insect-model based microrobot --- to look for something new in robot intelligence.

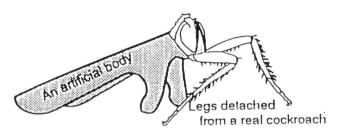

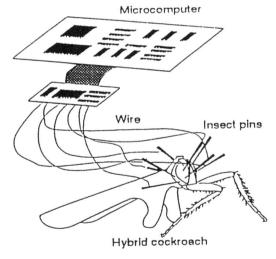

Fig. 7 A hybrid kockroach robot

Reference
[1] Miura, H; Shimoyama, I. Robotics Research-The First International Symposium:MIT Press,1984, pp.303-325.
[2] Miura, H et al., Robotics Research-The Second International Symposium: MIT Press, 1985, pp.317-324.
[3] Shimoyama, I; Miura, H et al., Robotics Research-The Third International Symposium: MIT Press, 1986, pp.357-363.

[4] Miura, H et al., Robotics Research-The 6th International Symposium: The International Foundation for Robotics Research,1994, pp. 489-495

[5] Chapman, R. F., THE INSECTS-Structure and Function, Harvard Press, 1982, ch.XI, p. 216.

[6] Kubo, Y; Shimoyama, I; Miura, H. Proc. of IEEE International Conference on R & A, 1993, pp. 386-391.

[7] Shimoyama,I; Kubo, Y; Kaneda, T; Miura, H. Proc. of MEMS '94,1994, pp. 148-152.

[8] Shimoyama,I; Kubo, Y; Kaneda, T; Miura, H. Robotics Research-The 6th International Symposium: The International Foundation for Robotics Research, 1994, pp. 497-502.

[9] Yasuda, T;. Shimoyama, I; Miura, H. Proc. of Sensors and Actuators, 1994, pp.366-370.

[10] Kuwana, Y. Ph. D. Thesis(The University of Tokyo),1996.

[11] Takeuchi, S.; Ishihara, J.; Shimoyama, I.; Miura, H. Hybrid Insect Robot, Proc. of Annual Meeting of Robotic Society of Japan, 1995, pp.1161-1162.

Special Talks on Traditional Automata

OLD JAPANESE ROBOT (KARAKURI-NINGYO)

Prof. Shouji TATSUKAWA, Kitazato Univ.

In Japan, automata were invented in the Tokugawa Period (1603-1867). One of the masterpieces is " Chakumi-Ningyo " or the Tea Serving Robot. You put a tea cup on his hands, and he will start to walk, moving his feet and swinging his head. When you take off the cup, he stops his moving. On your putting the cup again on to his hand, he now makes a turn and goes back to where he started from. The mechanism is driven by a coil spring of whalebone, wheels and gears are made of wood, and a crown wheel with foliot balance is acted as governor. You can see the diagram in the book " Karakuri-Zui " (1796). The present piece is a reproduction of the Robot faithful to the diagram.

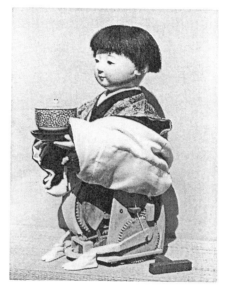

Figure 1 Chakumi-Ningyo
(side view)

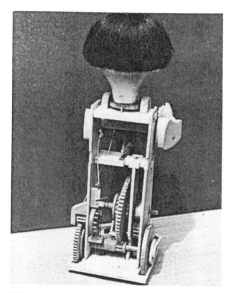

Figure 2 Chakumi-Ningyo
(back view)

Figure 3 Yumiiri-Doushi(Archer)
by Hisashige Tanaka

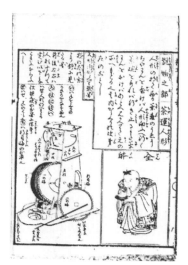

Figure 4 Karakuri-Zui
by Yorinao Hosokawa in 1796

Grey Walter: the pioneer of real artificial life

Owen Holland
Intelligent Autonomous Systems Engineering Laboratory
Faculty of Engineering
University of the West of England, Bristol BS16 1QY
United Kingdom
o-hollan@uwe.ac.uk

Abstract

Grey Walter's electromechanical tortoises, dating from 1949, are sometimes mentioned in Alife reviews, but little hard information is accessible. This paper presents original unpublished materials and photographs from archive sources. Some of these materials confirm that Grey Walter explicitly used behaviour based concepts, and that the tortoises are true behaviour based robots. Two replica tortoises have been built, modelled on the only surviving original in working order, and including some original components from Grey Walter's workshop. The construction and behaviour of these replicas has cast light on some previously unrecorded aspects of tortoise behaviour.

1 Background

Most reviews of artificial life mention Grey Walter and his electromechanical tortoises, but only in passing. In a sense, this is understandable; the only generally accessible accounts of this work are almost fifty years old - two short papers, containing qualitative descriptions of the machines and their behaviour, and a chapter and a brief technical appendix in an inevitably dated book on the electrical activity of the brain. In addition, the vacuum tube analogue technology of the machines is unfamiliar even to today's engineers, let alone today's computer scientists and biologists, making any widespread informed evaluation of the tortoises' significance even more difficult. However, when one sees some of the phrases and thoughts used in his 1950 Scientific American article, it is difficult to resist the conclusion that some such evaluation by the Alife community is required: '...imitation of life...synthetic animal...synthetic life...the scientific imitation of life...the number of components in the device was deliberately restricted to two in order to discover what degree of complexity of behaviour and independence could be achieved with the smallest number of elements...' This paper is part of a programme to make Grey Walter's work more available to the scientific community in order to enable it to be assessed and appreciated in a way which does justice to the man and his ideas.

It is essential to view Grey Walter's work in this area in the context of his overall career. He was born in Kansas City in 1910 to an Italian mother and a British journalist father, and was educated in England, studying physiology at Cambridge, and going on to do research in neurophysiology. In 1935 he began work on electroencephalography, and soon made his mark, identifying many fundamental phenomena and showing a great interest and facility in developing new electronic equipment. In 1939 he took up an appointment as Director of Physiology at the newly founded Burden Neurological Institute (BNI) in Bristol, where he remained for the rest of his career. He had a brilliant career in electro-encephalography: he identified and named delta rhythms (the slow rhythms around tumours), discovered abnormalities in epileptics between seizures, built the first on-line frequency analyser, discovered and named theta rhythms, discovered the contingent negative variation (expectancy wave), and made many other breakthroughs in collaboration with a succession of colleagues. He founded the EEG Society, and co-founded the International Federation of EEG Societies and the EEG Journal. The BNI bibliography credits 174 scientific publications to Grey Walter, almost all in the area of electroencephalography and the associated technologies; only a handful are directly about the tortoises. In a tragic road accident in 1970, he received severe head injuries. Although he made a good physical recovery, and remained at the BNI until his retirement in 1975, the accident effectively ended his career. He died of a heart attack in 1977.

2 Inspiration

From the late 1940s onward, Grey Walter developed an interest in viewing the brain as a control mechanism, and soon became identified with the cybernetic movement. However, the genesis of his inspiration for constructing the tortoise is rather surprising (The Living Brain, 1953): *"The first notion of constructing a free goal-seeking mechanism goes back to a wartime talk with the psychologist, Kenneth Craik...When he was engaged on a war job for the Government, he came to get the help of our automatic analyser with some very complicated curves he had obtained, curves relating to the aiming errors of air gunners. Goal-seeking missiles were literally much in the air in those days; so, in our minds, were scanning mechanisms. Long before (my) home study was turned into a workshop, the two ideas, goal-seeking and scanning, had combined as the essential mechanical conception of a working model that would behave like a very simple animal."*

Although he later met Wiener, Grey Walter does not seem to have been influenced by him. In a letter to Professor Adrian (12th June 1947), Grey Walter wrote: *"We had a visit yesterday from a Professor Wiener, from Boston. I met him over there last winter and find his views somewhat difficult to absorb, but he represents quite a large group in the States, including McCulloch and Rosenblueth. These people are thinking on very much the same lines as Kenneth Craik did, but with much less sparkle and humour."*

The origin of his electromechanical models seems to have been rooted in the idea that the complexity of the brain, and of behaviour, was primarily due to the richness of interconnectivity of neurons rather than their sheer number. From Craik (1943) comes the idea that the brain must be rich enough in resources to represent internally all the complexity of the external world; in the script of a radio talk on the brain in 1948, Grey Walter wrote: *"I am going to develop the hypothesis that the functional interconnection between brain cells bears some relation to the processes of thought and consciousness, and my first premise is that the variety of permutation in these connections is at least as great as the diversity and complexity which we are subjectively aware of in our own minds and objectively assume in the minds of others. The general idea behind this hypothesis is that the function of the brain is to make a working model of external reality, and it is clearly of the first importance to establish at the outset that there are as many working parts in the model as there are in the full scale pattern."*

The immediate inspiration for the tortoises was as a means of demonstrating that rich interconnections between a small number of elements (two) could support some complexity of behaviour.

3 The tortoises and their fates

We can date the development of the first tortoises to a 21 month period. Nicolas Walter, Grey Walter's son, recalls discussing his father's work with him in the spring of 1948, and is certain that no mention was made of any electromechanical models. A newspaper article of December 1949 carries pictures of Elmer and Elsie, the first two tortoises, along with a complete and accurate description of their behavioural repertoire; Elmer 'the prototype' is reported to have been built 'more than a year ago'. They were built in the 'backroom laboratory' of his house by Grey Walter, 'helped by his wife Vivian', a professional colleague for many years. (Another contemporary newspaper report was less restrained: "Toys which feed themselves, sleep, think,

walk, and do tricks like a domestic animal may go into Tommy's Christmas stocking in 1950, said brain specialist Dr. Grey Walter in Bristol last night. For two years he has been experimenting with toys containing an electric brain...Dr. Walter said the toys possess the senses of sight, hunger, touch, and memory. They can walk about the room avoiding obstacles, stroll round the garden, climb stairs, and feed themselves by automatically recharging six-volt accumulators from the light in the room. And they can dance a jig, go to sleep when tired, and give an electric shock if disturbed when they are not playful...Dr. Walter said: "There is no other machine like it in the world. This hobby of making toys with brains is proving of great value in the study of the human brain." The toy has only two cells. The human brain has ten thousand million. "But," said Dr. Walter, "most people get along with using as few as possible.")

Elmer and Elsie were the subjects of the 1950 Scientific American article. Though they certainly worked, they were somewhat unreliable, and six tortoises of an improved electrical and mechanical design were built for Grey Walter in early 1951 by Mr W.J. "Bunny" Warren. Elmer and Elsie appear to have been dismantled at about this time or shortly afterwards. (Strangely, the circuit details and photograph in 'The Living Brain', published in 1953, are those of Elmer and Elsie, rather than the 1951 batch.) Three of the 1951 tortoises were exhibited at the Festival of Britain, and were subsequently auctioned; of these, two were destroyed by fire in 1992, and the third, almost complete, was donated to the robotics collection of the Smithsonian Institute in 1993. It is in largely original condition, but is missing some small parts; it is as yet unrestored and not on public display. One was despatched to the USA in 1953 as part of an unsuccessful project to develop a tortoise-based toy; it was returned in pieces, and scrapped later that year. One was despatched in 1970 to an unrecorded address thought to have had some connection with a museum in New York or New York State, and has not been heard of since. One, slightly modified for ease of transport and display, was kept by Grey Walter until his death in 1977, when it passed to his son Nicolas, along with the hutch used for demonstrations. It was lent to Brunel University for some years, in the course of which the original batteries and their carriers were removed and lost, and a rather incongruous plastic dry-cell carrier installed. This tortoise (Figure 1) has now been restored to working order at the University of the West of England, Bristol, with the help of Bunny Warren, who still works at the BNI, and will go on permanent display in Bristol in 1996. Many original components, spares, and scrapped parts have been preserved by Bunny Warren, along with some original circuit diagrams and other documentation.

Figure 1: Grey Walter's 1951 tortoise

4 Records of tortoises, and descriptions of their behaviour

There are no formal records of experiments carried out with the tortoises. The 1950 Scientific American article contains eight sketches showing typical trajectories of Elmer and Elsie under various conditions. At some time during 1950, at one or more photographic sessions at Grey Walter's house, photographs of trajectories were produced by fixing shielded lamps on the tortoises' backs and using long exposures (Figures 2, 3, 4); examples of these photographs are found in the 1951 Scientific American article, in the first edition of 'The Living Brain' (1953), and in an unidentified American magazine. Many original prints from these photographs were found in the BNI archives. No such records have been found of the 1951 batch of tortoises.

There are no detailed published descriptions of the internal operations of the tortoises, although a sketch and brief explanation of the original circuit diagram and some mechanical details appear in "The Living Brain". A detailed photograph of Elmer without the shell appeared in 'Picture Post' in March, 1950; a similar photograph with the parts labelled appeared in an American magazine at about the same time. The BNI archives contain a print of the original circuit diagram marked up with details of component types and values; Bunny Warren's records contain the circuit diagram, with all component types and values, for the 1951 batch. However, by far the most valuable and significant document is an unpublished set of notes by Grey Walter in the BNI archives (undated, but probably 1961), which gives an excellent insight into the functioning of the machines, and also into the way in which Grey Walter saw the various separate functions as being integrated into coherent overall behaviour by the interaction of the architecture, the basic functions, and the environmental contingencies. A long

Figure 2: Elmer and Elsie interact on the way to the hutch

extract from this document is given below; it is best read in conjunction with a circuit diagram (see Walter, 1953).

From Machina Speculatrix - Notes on Operation (unpublished notes, about 1961), quoted without change: *'The first "artificial animal" was built about 12 years ago to test some theories about how simple machines could develop complex behaviour if their parts were allowed to interact more freely than usual. This first hardware pet was called "Machina speculatrix" because it is not a passive machine like a typewriter or an electronic computer that waits for a human being to operate it - M. Speculatrix speculates, it explores its environment actively, persistently, systematically as most animals do. This is its first and basic Behaviour Pattern (E) and appears when it is switched on...When it is switched on three circuits are closed:*

(Note: the circuit diagram shows both relays in the open position. However, when the circuit is powered up in the absence of light, Relay 1 closes - OEH)

1. The driving motor is on at half speed, the headlamp being in series with it. (A resistor in parallel with the headlamp was added in the 1951 design - OEH). *This propels the model slowly in the direction of the driving wheel. But this is itself rotated by -*

2. The steering scanning motor (which) is on at full speed. This turns the driving wheel continuously so that the direction of motion is continually changing. The same vspindle supports the photoelectric cell or "eye" so this rotates too; it is always "looking" in the direction in which the model is moving. This is called "scanning". The rotation (steering-scanning) gives the model a cycloidal trajectory, rather like a point on the wheel of a moving

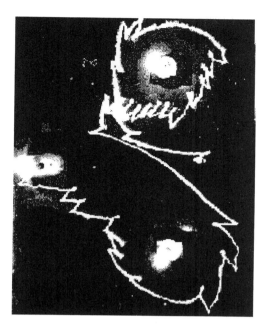

Figure 3: Elmer shows positive and negative phototropism

Figure 4: Elmer enters the hutch successfully

vehicle. This cycloidal exploration continues indefinitely in the dark or when there is no light on the horizon bright enough to affect the "eye". (The mask on the eye provides both blinkers that give it a direction of gaze and a visor that stops it seeing ordinary room lights above it). But when a light is "seen" the behaviour changes because switching on also -

3. Provides current for the filaments of the two miniature vacuum tubes. These amplify the response of the photoelectric cell to light so that, when a moderate light is seen the relay in the plate circuit of the second tube closes. This introduces behaviour pattern P, the positive phototropic or light-seeking response.

Pattern P involves immediate closing of relay 2. This disconnects the steering-scanning motor so that the driving wheel is fixed at whatever angle it was when the light was seen, and the scanning of the horizon by the eye also stops of course. At the same time the "make" contact on the relay short circuits the headlamp which is in series with the drive so that the driving motor is turned up to full speed. The model stops looking slowly round and hurries toward the light. However, unless the light was seen when the eye happened to be facing straight ahead, the angle at which the steering came to rest at the moment of sighting will deflect the model gradually <u>away</u> from the light. When the deflection is so great that the activation level of the photocell falls below threshold, the Relay 2 opens again, the scanner starts up, the drive is reduced to half speed and the model is re-positioned, this time so that the light is more directly ahead. This process of <u>progressive orientation</u> is an important part of the behaviour mechanism. It is cumulative - every time the model steers itself slightly off-beam

the momentary operation of the steering-scanning mechanism brings it back more nearly on course and it ends up with a heading on-beam. The process often looks clumsy, because the eye seems to veer away from the light and then the scanner has to make nearly a whole rotation to bring it back, but inevitably with each such operation the model gets itself into a better position to bear down directly on its goal. The aiming-error is steadily reduced as the goal is approached. As the model gets near to a bright light - a 40 watt lamp or a hand flashlamp - it "sees" the light as brighter and brighter - the brilliance of a light is inversely proportional to the square of the distance from it. For example, if the brilliance of a light was just great enough to operate the Relay 2 four feet away, the apparent brilliance will be four times greater (from the model's viewpoint) when it gets two feet up to the light. When it gets close enough the behaviour will change again to:

Behaviour pattern N, that is <u>negative phototropism</u>; the model will <u>avoid</u> a <u>bright</u> light. This is because the two vacuum-tubes are in series or "cascade". The action of a moderate light on the photo-cell is so weak that it does not affect Relay 1 in the plate circuit of Tube 1, only the Relay 2 after amplification by <u>both</u> tubes. But a bright light produces enough change in the photocell to open Relay 1 after only one stage of amplification and this relay starts the steering scanning motor going again at half speed through the headlamp. The drive motor is still full on because, of course, Relay 2 is still firmly closed. The result is that when the model gets "too close" to a light it veers smoothly away from it and avoids the fate of a moth in a candle. M. Speculatrix is moderate and restrained - it seeks an _optimum_ light, not a maximum.

There is a minor feature of the light-seeking manoeuvre which is hard to notice but is quite important both to the success of the model's speculation and to its resemblance to living creatures. The coupling between the two vacuum-tube amplifiers is "semi-direct". There is a capacitor from the plate of Tube 1 to the control grid of Tube 2, in the conventional fashion. This provides for high amplification of _transient_ signals; the glimpse of a light will have the maximum effect on Tube 2 and therefore upon Relay 2. Thus a distant light will just stop the scanner and put on full drive for a moment so that the model will start toward the light, but the effect will die away and the scanner will start up again. Next time round the model will be a little nearer the light and the hold period will be a little longer and so on. But there is another connection between Tube 1 and Tube 2, directly from the first plate to the second screen. This keeps the screen of Tube 2 at the correct positive voltage (the plate voltage of Tube 1) and at the same time provides for amplification of larger signals without decay in time. So as the model gets nearer to a light the closing of Relay 2 lasts longer and longer and finally it stays closed as long as the eye is on the light. In mathematical terms small signals are _differentiated_, large ones are _integrated_. (This is not strictly correct - OEH). In physiological jargon the model adapts to faint stimuli but maintains its response to intense ones.

If the way to the goal is clear the model will approach and circle around any adequate light, will leave bright lights in search of more moderate ones and explore the whole room in this way. But life is full of obstacles, even for humble hardware, and if the model bumps into something its behaviour will change again. Its skin is on a rubber bush which allows it to pivot freely; the skin movements are restricted only by a stick-and-ring limit switch in its belly. Beyond a certain range of movement in any direction this switch connects the grid of Tube 1 to the plate of Tube 2 through a capacitor, and this produces another change in behaviour to

Pattern O, Obstacle avoidance. Normally the two vacuum tubes act as amplifiers with the joint and individual effects described for Patterns P and N. But when, by displacement of the skin the output plate of Tube 2 is connected back to the input grid of Tube 1 the whole system is transformed from an amplifier to an oscillator, since any signal that appears on grid 1 is amplified by Tube 1 and by Tube 2, the much bigger signal is fed back to the grid of Tube 1 and so on. This sort of amplifier is called a "multivibrator" - because it generates a multitude of vibrations. As arranged in M. Speculatrix, the (oscillations) recur about once a second, and their effect is to open and close Relays 1 and 2 alternately as long as the skin is displaced. This makes the model butt, turn and recoil continuously until it is clear of the obstacle. It may edge steadily

along until it comes to an edge it can get round, it may shove the obstacle to one side if it is movable, or if it gets into a tight corner it may end by swivelling right round and trying another approach. In any case it is very pertinacious and it is also quite discerning, because as long as it is in trouble it will not respond to a light, however intense and attractive. It cannot, because as long as the skin is displacing the limit switch the amplifiers are completely preoccupied with sending signals back and forth to one another and are quite blind to outside information - an oscillator does not act as an amplifier. When the model has cleared an obstacle and the skin swings back to its normal position, the input-output circuit is opened and after one more oscillation the amplifiers resume their function of transforming light signals into movements of the relays and the whole model...

If there are a number of light low obstacles that can be moved easily over the floor and over which the model can see an attractive light, it will find its way between them, and in doing so will butt them aside. As it finds its way toward the light and then veers away from it and wanders about it will gradually clear the obstacles away and sometimes seems to arrange them neatly against the wall. This tidy behaviour looks very sensible but is an example of how apparently refined attitudes can develop from the interaction of elementary _reflex functions_. This is particularly evident when one reflex pattern is _prepotent_ over another; in M. Speculatrix, Pattern O is prepotent over Pattern P and Pattern N (because of the nature of the two tubes acting as a multivibrator). But, because of this, Pattern O assists the completion of Pattern P (by avoiding or clearing away obstacles that impede approach to the goal). The model as a whole is more likely to attain its goal even though the goal seeking mechanisms (photocell tubes and relays) are apparently thrown out of gear by the appearance of the O pattern...

Behaviour mechanisms of type P and N are sometimes described as exhibiting "_negative feedback_" because the system tends to reach an _equilibrium_ or balance point in the light field, and does this by progressive reduction of the "error", that is the distance from the light. Simpler examples of negative feedback used to establish stability are the ball-cock in a water cistern that keeps the water level constant and the thermostat that regulates a refrigerator or heating system or air-conditioner to maintain a constant temperature. On the other hand the internal oscillation in M. Speculatrix when its skin is moved is an example of "_positive feedback_" - the signals get bigger and bigger because they are fed back from plate 2 to grid 1. A negative feedback system tends of itself to run in to a goal or target, to maintain stability; a positive feedback system tends to run away to some limit set by the available power or energy. An explosion, whether chemical or nuclear is a dramatic example of positive feedback. But in M. Speculatrix the positive feedback O mode can assist completion of *a negative feedback P manoeuvre because it introduces a random but persistent hunting for clearance when the path to the target is cluttered...'*

The headlamp is fixed to the front of the tortoise's chassis; it does not rotate with the wheel and photo-cell, and when lit it does not affect the photo-cell directly. It is lit in three behaviour patterns - E, N, and O - but not in P. If the light from a headlamp is bright enough to affect a photo-cell sufficiently to cause the system to switch from E to P, then a tortoise may be affected by its own headlamp reflected in a mirror, or by another tortoise's headlamp. In the case of a tortoise in front of a mirror, its headlamp will be extinguished when the behaviour changes from E to P, and so the behaviour will change back from P to E. Since changes in relay magnetic fields and incandescent light strength are not instantaneous, and since the circuits contain reactive components, and the tortoise and the motors have some inertia, these changes in behaviour will not be instantaneous. Grey Walter reported that a tortoise in front of a mirror or white surface *"flickers and jigs at its reflection in a manner so specific that were it an animal a biologist would be justified in attributing to it a capacity for self-recognition"* (1950). In the case of two tortoises, a tortoise will only be attracted towards a tortoise which is not currently attracted towards it, and so the extinguishing of its own headlamp does not change the immediate situation. However, since the headlamp is only visible from the front of the tortoise, being occluded by the chassis from other points of view, a tortoise does not necessarily present a constant stimulus for other tortoises, as the characteristic cycloidal movement is constantly changing its orientation.. In spite of this, the tendency will be for tortoises to be attracted towards one another; one likely outcome is collision, leading to separation and reorientation by behaviour pattern O. Grey Walter describes this as follows (1950): *'Two creatures of this type meeting face to face are affected in a similar but again distinctive manner. Each, attracted by the light the other carries, extinguishes its own source of attraction, so the two systems become involved in a mutual oscillation, leading finally to a stately retreat'.*

The situations for single tortoises mentioned by Grey Walter in published accounts are as follows:

speculation: moving in an environment without lights or mirrors (E)

positive tropism: moving towards a single light (P)

negative tropism: moving away from strong light (N)

achieving optima: maintaining a distance from a single light (P and N)

solving the dilemma of Buridan's ass: moving alternately between two lights (P and N

discernment: finding its way to a light when the path is blocked by a fixed or movable obstacle which does not block the light (P and O). (It does not respond to the light when avoiding or moving obstacles).

self-recognition: moving in front of a mirror (P, and sometimes O)

internal stability: losing the response to strong light as the battery runs down, and so moving in closer to the strong light than previously. By arranging for the tortoise to switch itself off (by moving over a projection on the floor near the light, which also connects the battery terminals to a recharger), this provided an analogue of feeding only when hungry.

The situations involving more than one tortoise are:

mutual recognition: being attracted by one anothers' headlamps (P, E, and O).

crowding: tortoises in the presence of a light interfering with one another by constituting obstacles or by occluding the light, and so preventing one another from reaching the light (E, P, and O)

5 The replica tortoises

Figure 5: one of the replica tortoises

Because of the scanty original records of the behaviour of the tortoises, it is difficult to form an opinion of the effectiveness and reliability of these behaviours in practice, and also of their lifelike quality. Repeating the experiments, or conducting new ones, with original tortoises is out of the question, because the only surviving tortoise in working order is extremely fragile. As the next best solution, two replicas (Figure 5) have been constructed at the University of the West of England. They have been built using the original as a model, using the original circuit diagrams, and using some original components (including shells) supplied by Bunny Warren, whose advice and guidance during the project was invaluable. Surprisingly, the original types of vacuum tubes and the photo-cell are still available from specialist shops. Modern resistors and capacitors were used. All chassis parts were fabricated from similar materials. Similar gear-trains were made up using the nearest equivalent stock parts. Because the original motors were a constant source of trouble, modern motors of approximately the same dimensions and no-load speed were used. The original 3-cell lead-acid accumulator was replaced with a smaller 6v lead-acid gel-cell of equivalent capacity; the 45v hearing aid dry cell was replaced with a stack of five 9v rechargeable lithium batteries. The major problem involved the relays; the originals were American Air Force surplus stock, rewound with 60,000 turn coils to give adequate sensitivity. The make and break terminal positions, and the spring tension, were all adjustable by screws and locknuts. These relays are critical to the proper set-up and operation of the tortoise, because there is no other provision for adjusting the responses; since no similar component is currently available, exact replicas had to be made from scratch.

The behaviour of the two replica tortoises is extremely close to that of the original; the only functional differences centre around the relay characteristics. The replica relays have cores made of a material which has turned out to have poorer magnetic qualities than that used in the originals, and switching thresholds are higher and less stable. (This is only a problem for Relay 1, which operates on much lower currents than Relay 2.) Improved materials are currently being sourced. The main revelation has been the difficulty of demonstrating the whole behavioural repertoire under normal lighting conditions: because of the relative insensitivity of the photo-cell, Pattern N (negative phototropism) can only be achieved intermittently and with difficulty at normal light levels. (This also applies to the original tortoise.) We know that operation at normal light levels is not a problem peculiar to this particular original tortoise; a note from Grey Walter to the American company developing the toy concept, referring to the sample tortoise from the 1951 batch sent to the USA for development purposes, contains the passage: '...the sensitivity of the light response system has been set LOW so that it can operate in considerable top light; the sensitivity can be greatly increased by adjustment of the relays but operation is then very involved when the general light level is high'. Without exception, all the existing photographic records of trajectories were taken in near darkness; this may have had as much to do with the performance of the tortoises as with the demands of time-lapse photography. Because of this problem, none of the behaviours involving Pattern N have yet been replicated; trials in a darkened environment will be undertaken in the near future. It has also so far proved impossible to reproduce any of the self or mutual recognition phenomena because the headlamps do not provide enough light. In fact, the headlamp on the original is so dim as to be barely visible in daylight; the replicas have been fitted with quartz halogen lights to improve matters, but these are still inadequate to serve as an effective stimulus under normal light levels. Again, the American document is relevant: 'The pilot light is deliberately not very bright to save pattern current for this particular Transatlantic jaunt - but it can easily be brighter and fitted with a reflector to permit the mirror dance described on p.128 of The Living Brain'. The

fact that a reflector is necessary is not mentioned in any published record.

Unpublished notes found in the BNI archives and elsewhere show that Grey Walter developed his interpretations of the behaviour of groups of tortoises further than in the published sources, though no documents contain descriptions of specific trials or demonstrations. A press release for a talk entitled 'The cybernetic approach to mentality and society' given at the Graduate Center for Psychotherapy in New York (1957) contains an interesting passage on collective behaviour: *'Simple models of behaviour can act as if they could recognise themselves and one another; furthermore, when there are several together they begin to aggregate in pairs and flocks, particularly if they are crowded into a corral...The process of herding is nonlinear. In a free space they are individuals; as the barriers are brought in and the enclosure diminishes, suddenly - there is a flock. But if the crowding is increased, suddenly again there is a change to an explosive society of scuffling strangers. And at any time the aggregation may be turned into a congregation by attraction of all individuals to a common goal. Further studies have shown that in certain conditions one machine will tend to be a "leader". Often this one is the least sensitive of the crowd, sometimes even it is "blind".'*

Another passage with echoes of modern thinking on the nature of autonomous agents occurs in the English text for an article on 'Cybernetics' in the Italian *Enciclopedia Medica* (W. Ross Ashby and W. Grey Walter, 1959; Ross Ashby, the British cybernetics pioneer, was Director of the BNI for a short period in the early 1960s): *"At the same time as Ashby was developing Homeostat as a mathematical model of dynamic multiple stability, Walter was engaged in cybernetic experiments with even simpler devices to demonstrate the principles of exploratory and orienting behaviour, the profound effects of scanning on sensorimotor integration and the appearance of unpredictable behaviour patterns by interaction between complex environments and simple dynamic systems."*

6 A modern evaluation of Grey Walter's work

The tortoises were undoubtedly the first true autonomous mobile robots, and the context in which they were made identifies them firmly as the first serious attempt at producing real artificial life. They were also the first behaviour based robots. Brooks (1995) was quite correct to conclude from his analysis of Grey Walter's published work that "The limiting factors in these experiments were...the lack of mechanisms for abstractly describing behaviour at a level below the complete behaviour, so that an implementation could reflect those simpler components." However, it is clear from the long unpublished extract given above that Grey Walter did see the overall tortoise behaviour in terms of simpler components, or reflexes, and that the implementation reflected these components. It is nevertheless curious that there is no hint of such analysis in his earlier papers, or his book; perhaps he reached this understanding some time after first building and describing the tortoises.

Another modern echo is in the concept of prepotent reflexes. This suppression of some behaviour modules by the activation of a dominant behaviour is found in many behaviour based architectures, and again Grey Walter has an unassailable claim to be the inventor of the technique. He was also the first person to attempt learning on a real robot (Walter, 1951), and the first to conduct and report on experiments with multiple homogeneous robots. Although his emphasis on scanning mechanisms in the brain has not stood the test of time, his emphasis on the virtues of minimalism in model building is very modern. As a minimalist roboticist, his two active elements probably do constitute the simplest robotic system of any real interest.

In one feature of his architecture he anticipated developments which have only recently come to light in neurophysiology. Most behaviour based architectures consist of more or less independent modules, and behaviour is produced by the suppression of some modules by others, or by interaction of the outputs in the world. Grey Walter's architecture responded to a sensory input - the shell being touched - by changing the pattern of interconnection between its neuron-level elements to produce a fundamentally different circuit - an oscillator rather than a two stage amplifier. Similar processes occur in the crustacean stomatogastric system (e.g. Hooper, 1995), where stimuli external to the network modulate connectivity parameters to produce altered networks with radically different characteristics. This exploitation of rich inter-connectivity was one of Grey Walter's main ideas driving the construction of the tortoise; not only did he originate the concept, he put it on a robot 45 years ago. And in case we are tempted to think of him as someone forced into minimalism by the technology of the times, here is a passage from the late sixties (from "The future of Machina speculatrix", text sent to translator probably about 1968): *"It would only be a matter of patience and ingenuity to endow M. speculatrix with other 'senses' besides sight and touch, to enable it to respond to audible signals audibly, and so forth; also to provide it with hands. There is no serious difficulty about the elaboration of function, once the principles of mechanical 'life' have been demonstrated in a working model. If the principles are preserved, no matter how elaborate the functions of the machine, its mimicry of life will be valid and illuminating.*

Our experiments and observations with Machina speculatrix and its cousins and offspring (of which there are now quite a number) shows us that, as we had suspected, the complexity of the brain and its behaviour can be imitated to an extraordinary degree by relatively simple machinery. And a new era has opened out in our experiments. Instead of using the old-fashioned valves with their extravagant heaters and their enormous bulk, we can make the same device with transistors. And with micromodular construction in which whole amplifiers are built into the space of what only yesterday was one transistor we can include all the amplifiers needed for quite an elaborate synthetic animal. We are now envisaging the construction of a creature which instead of looking as the original did, like a rather large and clumsy tortoise, resembles more closely a small eager, active and rather intelligent beetle.

There seems no limit to which this miniaturisation could go. Already designers are thinking in terms of circuits in which the actual scale of the active elements will not be much larger, perhaps even smaller, than the nerve cells of the living brain itself. This opens a truly fantastic vista of exploration and high adventure..."

Acknowledgments

Much of this work could not have been undertaken without the generous help and technical assistance of Mr W.J. Warren, and the support of Dr. S. Butler, Scientific Director of the BNI. Dr. R. Cooper and Mrs C. Goff assisted with documentary and pictorial sources. Ian Horsfield and Chris Hart dedicated many hours and much skill to the construction of the tortoise replicas. The author thanks Nicolas Walter and the BNI for permission to quote from Grey Walter's unpublished notes, and for the loan of the original tortoise.

References

BNI archive material: A catalogue of BNI archive sources on Grey Walter's tortoises is in preparation. Further details of quoted sources may be obtained from the author.

Brooks R.A. (1995) Intelligence without reason. In Brooks R. and Steels L. (eds) **The artificial life route to artificial intelligence: building situated embodied agents**. Lawrence Erlbaum

Craik, K.J.W. (1943) **The Nature of Explanation**, Cambridge

Hooper S.L. (1995) Crustacean Stomatogastric System, in **The Handbook of Brain Theory and Neural Networks**, ed. M.A. Arbib, Bradford-MIT

Walter, W.Grey (1950) An Imitation of Life, *Scientific American*, May, pp 42-45

Walter, W.Grey (1951) A Machine that Learns, *Scientific American*, August, pp 60-63

Walter, W.Grey (1953) **The Living Brain**, G. Duckworth, London, W.W.Norton, New York

Multi-Agents, Collective Dynamics

Behaviour of Multiple Generalized Langton's Ants

Olivier Beuret and **Marco Tomassini***

Logic Systems Laboratory
Swiss Federal Institute of Technology
Lausanne, Switzerland
e-mail: tomassini@di.epfl.ch

Abstract

Since their introduction by C. Langton, virtual ants have intrigued people with their behaviour. The system is governed by very simple local rules but gives rise to intricate patterns and, to date, no general theory of its dynamics has been found. Virtual ants have been mainly studied experimentally by computer simulation. In this work we have pursued the experimental simulation of an extension of Langton's ant: the generalized ant. We give a first rough classification of the patterns that arise as a consequence of their dynamical behaviour in the case of single ants, drawing on the work of others as well as on our own simulations. We then go on to the study of multiple generalized ants and we show under what conditions some new interesting behaviours arise.

1   Langton's Ant

C. Langton[1,2] is the inventor of this amazingly simple automaton. The virtual ant moves in a planar grid. There are two kinds of cells in the grid: white cells and black cells. Initially the ant is on the central square, for example, and is given a direction (N, S, E, W) towards which it is heading. The ant moves one cell forward in that direction according to the following rule: if it finds a black square then the the cell changes its color to white and the ant turns 90 degrees to the left. Conversely, if the cell is white the color changes to black and the ant turns 90 degrees to the right. Starting from an all-white grid the ant returns periodically to the origin during the first 500 steps leaving a more or less symmetrical trail behind it. Afterwards, the patterns that are traced become somewhat chaotic[1] but suddenly a straight diagonal pattern is traced that has been called a "highway" by J. Propp, who discovered it. On the highway the ant repeatedly follows the same sequence of 104 steps (see fig. 1). The orientation of the highway depends on the initial ant direction.

If the initial configuration of black and white cells is different, for example if there are scattered black cells in the grid at the beginning, the ant always ends up building the highway, at least on the many simulations that have been done, although nobody exactly knows if this is necessarily always the case. The only rigorous result on the system to date is due to X.P. Kong and E.G.D. Cohen and says that *an ant's trajectory is necessarily unbounded and escapes from any finite region.* A demonstration of the theorem can be found in ref.[3].

Several variations on the basic ant's rules have been tried. For example, if the ant goes straight ahead instead of turning right, then an horizontal or vertical highway two cells wide is built. Another variation proposed in [3] introduces a third type of cell, a grey cell, that never changes its color. The added rule is that if the ant lands on a grey cell it continues undisturbed in its current direction. In this model one also gets an highway construction but, due to the fact that the Kong-Cohen theorem no longer applies, periodic patterns can be obtained from some initial configurations.

Figure 1 : Highway construction

*. also at CSCS, Manno, Switzerland

1. Virtual ants as described here are perfectly deterministic systems. In this work we employ the term 'chaotic' in a intuitive sense to describe patterns that appear to be random. There is no implication that the system is chaotic in the technical sense of non-linear dynamical systems theory.

2 Generalized Ants

Generalized ants are an extension of Langton's ant. A generalized ant is defined to have n states numbered from 0 to n-1 instead of just two. In our pictorial representation the n states are represented by n different colors. Generalized ants have been proposed by G. Turk at Stanford and independently by L. Bunimovich and S. Troubetzkoy [4].

A generalized ant will be described by a rule string of n bits $S_k = \{0,1\}$ with k = 0..n-1. At each iteration the ant advances by one step in a given direction, looks at the state k of the cell at this position and turns right if bit k-th in the rule string is 1 and left otherwise. At the same time, the state of the cell changes to (k+1) mod n, where mod stands for the modulus operation. In this notation Langton's ant is represented by the string (1 0). Figure 2 graphically depicts the behavior of such a generalized virtual ant.

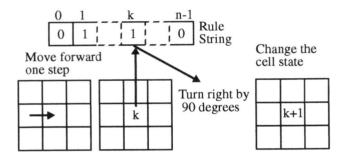

Figure 2 : Generalized ant's step

Rule strings consisting of all 1's or all 0's are trivial since the ant will simply turn in the same direction (right or left respectively) all the time. Similarly, complementing all the bits in a rule gives a mirror image of the original pattern. This can be seen for example in the case of ant 5 (101) in fig. 3.

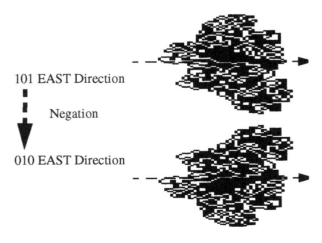

Figure 3 : Complementing a rule string.

It is interesting to examine the behaviour of a few non-trivial generalized ants to see if some general common pattern emerges. In order to simplify the notation and for classification purposes, we will use the decimal number corresponding to the rule string taken as an unsigned binary number. For example, Langton's ant (1 0) will be ant 2 in this notation. Unless otherwise specified the initial state of the grid will be 0 everywhere. Furthermore, the grid will be of finite size in practice. That is, we will assume that when an ant reaches the grid border it stops there. The observations described here are basically a systematization of those reported in [5] plus some remarks from our own experiments. Each simulation has been performed a few times only and a high but still limited number of steps has been done in each simulation. These results are therefore to be considered as indicative rather than definitive.

Ant 1 (0 1)

This ant behaves in the same way as Langton's but the trace is reversed with respect to the latter (see fig.3 above). For example, if it starts heading East then the highway is built in the south-west direction instead of north-west. Otherwise the behaviour is the same.

Ant 2 (1 0)

This is the well-known Langton's ant and does not need further comment.

Ant 4 (1 0 0)

This ant begins by tracing the same symmetrical patterns as ant 2 but with a bilateral symmetry instead of polar. This is followed by a chaotic phase and after having tracked 150 millions steps no recognizable structure emerges.

Ant 5 (1 0 1)

Same behavior as ant 2. At the beginning the patterns traced present an axis of symmetry of order two but after a while any symmetry disappears and after 150 million steps the behaviour is still apparently chaotic.

Ant 6 (1 1 0)

This ant builds a highway after 150 steps only but the pattern is different from that of ant 2. Each successive piece of the highway takes 18 steps to be built instead of 104.

Ant 8 (1 0 0 0)

This ant did not build any highway and the patterns traced did not show any signs of regularity.

Ant 9 (1 0 0 1)

Ant 9 does not build a highway. On the other hand, it generates growing symmetrical patterns.

Ant 10 (1 0 1 0)

This ant behaves in the same way as ant 2 with the same highway building period but it leaves a four colors trail instead of a bicolored one. This is a manifestation of the general phenomenon by which a rule string having two or more repetitions of a shorter rule will behave in the same way as the shorter one. Figure 4 depicts ant 10.

Figure 4 : Ant 10: chaos and highway building.

Ant 11 (1 0 1 1)

This ant, not described in [5], always behaves in a chaotic manner. Fig. 5 shows the pattern generated after 100,000 iterations.

Figure 5 : Constant chaos.

Ant 12 (1 1 0 0)

This ant builds bilaterally symmetrical patterns that persist in time. Actually, total bilateral symmetry is observed when the ant visits its initial position.

Ant 13 (1 1 0 1)

This ant starts chaotically but after about 250,000 steps a highway appears. The period of the highway is 388. Fig. 6 shows the state of the automaton shortly after the building of the highway.

Figure 6 : Highway built by ant 13.

Ant 14 (1 1 1 0)

Ant 14 seems to be an hybrid of ants 2 and 6 [5]. It builds a highway like ant 2 but the period is 52 i.e., half the period of ant 2 and the shape of the highway is similar to that of ant 6.

Jimm Propp [5] did a simulation of a few other generalized ants with rule strings of length 5 and 6 finding some new behaviors. In general, ants having five bits rule-strings do not trace bilaterally symmetrical patterns but a new spiral pattern behavior appears with ant 27. With rule strings of length 6 it was found in [5] that all the ants that generate bilaterally symmetrical patterns have numbers that are divisible by three. Clearly, more systematic simulations and analyses are needed to make sense of these regularities.

2.1 Summary of the behavior of some generalized ants

The following table gives a summary of the behavior of the non-trivial ants previously described. Ants are classified according to their highway-building capabilities and according to the symmetry of the patterns they generate. The symmetry is indicated provided that it stays stable for some time even in those cases in which it eventually disappears. When a given ant builds a highway, its period i.e., the number of steps needed for buiding a repetitive segment, is also indicated.

Table 1. Rule strings of length four: summary of observations

Ant Number	Rule String	Highway	Symmetry
2	*1 0*	yes , 104	polar
4	*1 0 0*	no	bilateral
5	*1 0 1*	no	polar
6	*1 1 0*	yes, 18	no
8	*1 0 0 0*	no,	no
9	*1 0 0 1*	no	bilateral
10	*1 0 1 0*	yes, 104	polar
11	*1 0 1 1*	no	no
12	*1 1 0 0*	no	bilateral
13	*1 1 0 1*	yes, 388	no
14	*1 1 1 0*	yes, 52	no

From the preceding table it can be seen that ants 6 and 14 have the same overall behaviour. They only differ by the fact that the common pattern 1 1 0 is preceded by a 1 in the case of ant 14. Starting from this observation, we have found experimentally that all ants whose rule string contains this same pattern preceded by all 1's (1 1 0, 1 1 1 0, 1 1 1 1 0, ...) always build a highway and behave in a manner similar to that of ant (1 1 0).

3 Collective behaviour

We are now going to describe the collective behaviour of more than one ant of the same species (i.e., having the same rule string). The ants will evolve independently of each other; that is, they will ignore each other in case of collisions. However, they influence their mutual behaviour through the trace they leave behind them since this corresponds to state changes of some cells, which amounts to a dynamical change of the environment the ants will be confronted with. Thus the dynamical evolution of a single ant will implicitly depend on the history of all the other ants, giving rise in general to unpredictable collective dynamics. Furthermore, in the following the ants are treated sequentially one after the other unless otherwise stated. In terms of automata transition rules, this means that the state of a given ant is updated before the following ant in the sequence does its transition.

We begin our study by the simulation of a two Langton's ant system and then proceed to the description of a four ants collection, followed by a pair of generalized (1 0 1 0) ants. To our knowledge, only C. Langton has performed some multiant simulation [1]. However, we have studied different ant collections and we have found some interesting, previously unknown behaviors that may emerge under appropriate conditions.

3.1 Two Langton's ants

C. Langton briefly described some behaviours of a two ant system in [1]. We have tested several configurations and will report here about the two typical behaviors that were observed: periodic interactions and chaotic evolution. When the system enters a periodic attractor, patterns repeat themselves with a constant period. On the other hand, chaotic evolutions give rise to intricate structures that fill the whole available space if sufficient time is available and in which no regular space-time pattern can be recognized. It is to be noted that for the following simulations the grid space has cyclic boundary conditions i.e., it is toroidal.

After several attempts, we found that the following configuration gives rise to an interesting behavior of the two ants. On a 500 by 500 grid the first ant was placed at X=200 , Y= 250 heading south and the second one is on the same line at X=300, Y=250 heading east. We then observed the following stages in the system behavior:

1. Individual development: in this phase both ants leave their trails independently of each other and after 10,000 steps they build their highways separately.

2. Encounter: one of the ants meets the highway of the other and "walks" along it until it meets the other ant, which is still busy building its own highway. After that the behavior of the system is again complex.

3. Withdrawal: after meeting several times the ants undo their highways and come back to their starting points. During this phase, the ant that walked on the highway to meet its companion erases its trail in such a way that the second ant finds its own highway in the same state as it was when it built it.

Figure 7 shows the construction phase and the withdrawal. However, these static pictures do not do justice of the nice dynamics of the system: our computer simulations are much more explicit and easy to follow.

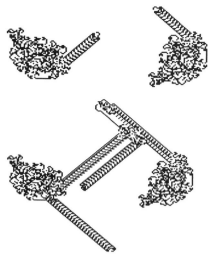

Figure 7 : Individual development and withdrawal.

Once the two ants are again at their starting points they begin to produce their traces followed by the highways but the pattern is rotated by 180 degrees with respect to the original one since they came back to the original points with their directions changed. Normally the traces should not meet since they now diverge. However, due to the cyclic structure of the grid space they go through the same phases 1-3 as described in section 3.1. At the end of this second cycle the ants find themselves again in the same position and with the same orientations as in step 0. From there on the system evolves periodically going through the same states. The pattern period is thus one complete cycle whereas the true period is two cycles. Therefore, this behaviour seems to contradict Kong-Cohen theorem since the trajectory will stay bounded in the case of a periodic multi-ant system.

We have tried a number of cases with the two ants initially on the same line. As a general rule, we have observed that if the ants directions are initially shifted by 90 degrees and the difference of their X coordinates is even (a distance of two suffices) then the interaction will be periodic, otherwise if the difference is odd it will be chaotic. If the ants are close enough to each other on the line they might meet before they start building their respective highways. However, if the original separation is even the system still shows a periodic behavior but without the highways. When the behaviour of the ant pair is chaotic there is no "highway following" behavior on the part of one of the ants. Instead, the ant goes through the highway undisturbed, after having left a complicated trail mark on it.

At least another non-collinear initial configuration of the two ants among those that have been tried has given rise to a periodic interaction in our simulations. The starting points are at X=99 , Y= 192 (heading north) and X=401, Y=217 (heading north).

3.2 Four Langton's ants

We did several simulations starting from different configurations of the ants. Here we will describe only one particular four ants configuration which, under suitable conditions, gives rise to an amazing periodic pattern development. The ants are placed initially at the following points on the grid: X=200 , Y= 200 (ant1, heading south), X=300, Y=200 (ant2, heading east), X=300, Y=300 (ant3, heading west) and X=300, Y=300 (ant 4, heading north). Fig. 8 shows the periodic pattern that emerges after 28,000 time steps. Again, the visual effect is much more interesting when watching the simulation running than on a static picture.

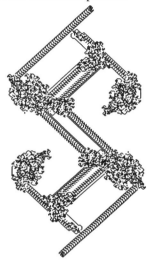

Figure 8 : Periodic interactions of four ants

For this periodic behavior to manifest itself it is necessary that some conditions be satisfied. First, the ants are updated sequentially one after the other in a round-robin manner as described in section 3.1. Second, the order in which the update takes place matters. Assuming that we always start with ant 1, there are six possibilities. We found experimentally that successively updating the ants in the order ant 1-ant 2-ant 3-ant 4 does not produce a periodic behavior. There are some transient quasi-periodic patterns but they disappear and afterwards the behavior is unstructured. In fact, all the combinations give rise to non-periodic behavior except those that imply a crossing between the ants as they are placed in the grid (see fig. 9).

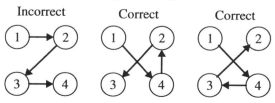

Figure 9 : Updating orders for the four ants system.

3.3   Two (1 0 1 0) ants

Single ants 10 (1 0 1 0) have already been seen as behaving identically to Langton's (1 0) ants in section 2.1. It is thus interesting to see if this similarity is maintained in the case of the joint evolution of two ants. It turns out that the behavior is indeed the same under the same initial conditions, with the emergence of an identical periodical pattern. The only difference is that the period of the system is four phases (see section 3.1) instead of two. Since four is the length of the rule string in the present case, it seems that there is a direct relationship between the period and the rule string length. This indication has been indeed confirmed by simulating two (1 0 1 0 1 0) ants. Fig. 10 shows a stage of the highway undoing.

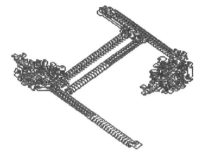

Figure 10 : Two (1 0 1 0) ants: pattern construction and withdrawal.

The collective behaviors described in this section have all been observed by imposing a sequential update of the virtual ants. It would be natural to ask whether the same or similar patterns emerge when updating all the ants in parallel. We did not have time to explore this research avenue a great deal. However, we have recently come across the work of B.Chopard [6] who carried out simulations of a two-ant system using a parallel updating rule. Under some well-defined initial conditions of the vant's position and orientation, he also reported periodic behaviour. He attributed the phenomenon to the crossing of ant trajectories and to the reversible character of the rule.

4   Conclusions

This experimental study of virtual ants behavior has shown that sometimes a slight rule modification may give rise to completely different dynamical patterns. This is a general phenomenon that has been observed in many systems where the global dynamics arise as a collective effect of local interactions. Indeed, in spite of the apparent simplicity of the ant automata, very little is known about their detailed dynamics and long-term behavior, computer simulations being at present the only practical way to study these ants. We have tried to classify the behavior of single generalized ants up to

rule string length four according to highway building capabilities and the nature of the generated patterns, i.e. whether they possess some long-lasting symmetry or are chaotic. This has allowed to pinpoint some regularity in the general behavior of the ants.

Collections of virtual ants are even more interesting since they interact indirectly through their traces and give rise to puzzling emergent phenomena. We have studied in particular two and four-ants collections. We have empirically been able to show that under some well-specified conditions these ant collections present complicated cyclic behaviors. It has also been shown that these regular patterns are very fragile as they disappear, giving way to unstructured motifs, if some parameters of the simulations are slightly modified. Pursuing the artificial insect analogy, this can be seen as a manifestation of Wilson's *multiplication effect* whereby even a small change in the individual's behavior may cause large social effects at the level of the collectivity.

In spite of the large number of simulations performed, we have only scratched the surface of the complex world of multiple generalized ants and more simulation work would be needed to uncover new phenomena and to discover possible hidden regularities. However, besides more simulations, firmer mathematical basis are required to guide the search and to further advance our knowledge of these automata.

The present work has been made possible through the construction of a software tool with simple but effective graphical capabilities. All the pictures shown here have been obtained with this program. The program will be made available to all those interested.

References

[1] C.G.Langton , *Studying artificial life with cellular automata*, Physica D, **22**, 120-149, 1986.

[2] I. Stewart , *Mathematical Recreations*, Scientific American, 88-91, July 1994.

[3] D. Gale , The Mathematical Intelligencer, Vol.**15** No 2, 54-55, 1993.

[4] L.A. Bunimovich and S.E. Troubetzkoy , *Rotators, periodicity and absence of diffusion in cyclic cellular automata*, J. of Stat. Phys. **74**, 1, 1994.

[5] J. Propp , The Mathematical Intelligencer, Vol.**16** No 1, 37-42, 1994.

[6] B.Chopard , *Complexity and Cellular Automata Models*, Physics of Complexity, Edited by S. Ciliberto, T. Dauxois and M. Droz, Editions Frontières, Gif-sur-Yvette, France, 1995.

Amoeba Like Self-Organization Model using Vibrating Potential Field

Hiroshi Yokoi*, Takafumi Mizuno**, Masatoshi Takita**, Jun Hakura*, and Yukinori Kakazu*

*Complex SystemEngineering, Hokkaido University,
N13-W8, Kita-ku, Sapporo, 060, JAPAN

**National Institute of Bioscience and Human Technology,
1-1, Higashi, Tsukuba, 305, JAPAN
e-mail: yokoi@complex.hokudai.ac.jp

Abstract

This paper reports one engineering application of spatial searching characteristics of slime mold (multi-cellar) amoeba for autonomous obstacle avoidance through flexible deformation. The remarkable characteristic of slime mold is that it transforms from unicellular period to multi-cellular period according to the state of the environment. Such characteristics become one idea for the difficulty of autonomous PDP system, such as environmental recognition, cooperative behaviors, and self-organized system control. This paper proposes an Amoeba-Like Self-Organization Model, and applies to obstacle avoidance as an example of spatial searching environment. The proposed model consists of new field technique named as the Vibrating Potential Field and new parameter tuning method inspired from thermo-dynamics. The computational application for creep through narrow path shows advantages of the model and derives powerful characteristics for intelligent searching mechanism those are heteronomous behavior and autonomous behavior.

1. Introduction

This paper proposes a model of amoeba-like self-organization with higher degree of freedom. Free deformation of amoeba body is one of the useful characteristics of adaptive behavior (i.e., obstacle avoidance, energy acquisition, predation, spatial searching, self-defense, etc.). The problem is how to control its own body element and achieve objective behavior. For the problem, this paper reports on modeling approach inspired from microscopic biological aspects of pseudopodia on Dictyostelium discoideum (many cellular amoebae). The morphogenesys of amoeba is adaptive for environment based on chemotaxis and thermotaxis that cleared as shown in [Siegert 92] and [Steinbock 93]. The adaptive behavior of amoeba derives adaptive grouping mechanism that are self-organized with declining its own degree of freedom (D.O.F.) from unicellular state with higher D.O.F. to higher ordered multi-cellular state. The objective application is obstacle avoidance with amoeba-like behavior.

The amoeba-like motion consists of displacement of gravity center and flexible deformation of the cell body. Such motion realizes complex searching behavior including global and local interactions[Agarwal 94][Shaw 95]. Those amoeba characteristics consist of autonomous tuning character of dynamics of its own body according to the stored energy and heteronomous movement of body parts depends on wavy and density information propagated from its own living field[Abe 94]. The proposed model consists of structure and interaction. The structure and the interaction are mathematically described as unit group structure using communication and interactive communication through wavy information.

For such communication, new field technique is introduced. The introduced field technique called vibrating potential field (VPF[Yokoi 92]) where each information propagated from a unit has a proper vibration and amplitude damped according to the propagated distance. The control mechanism of the whole group of units using local information requires an objective function for decentralized control. The model tunes the parameter of each unit depending on life's kinetics that the group of units conserves order by minimizing the gain of entropy. Using VPF and life's kinetics, the computer simulations show the behaviors of the proposed model that conserves its own energy level, and tunes its configurations or location of its parts.

To show the useful mechanism for group motion control, the behavior of the model is applied for the obstacle avoidance problem, and it's shown as simulation. The computational result shows the characteristics of the proposed model that is self-organizing grouping behavior and it derives obstacle avoidance. The results show the relation between number of connection among units on local group and plasticity of the whole group, and effects of plasticity to avoiding behavior. Furthermore, one specific result shows useful characteristics in the up stair's case where amoeba model goes up the stairs to acquisitive energy. Those results mean importance of communication mechanism through wavy information and grouping behavior for adaptation of obstacle environment.

2. Objective Problem Domain (Obstacle Avoidance)

The application of this paper concerns with obstacle avoidance that is motion generation problem including deformation, rotation, and transportation. The obstacle avoidance problem is divided into four types according to the moving object (robot, vehicle), such types are rigid body, links, elastic body, and plastically body. The rigid body has been approached as piano mover's problem [Schwartz 83], and autonomous vehicle using potential field approach [Arkin 90]. The links control problems are using reinforcement learning approaches and potential field approaches [Latombe 91]. The elastic body handled as position control of flexible arm problem in which neural network and fuzzy logic are applied [Koyama 91]. However, plastically body's problem has no contribution from the reason of difficulties of many-bodies' problem and control. The subjects for plastically body's problem are following four points:

  a) Analysis of interaction and representation of large degree of freedom (many-bodies' problem)
  b) Instrumentation of relation between whole area and own local position (self-observation)
  c) Mechanism for motion control of whole body (self-organization)
  d) Maximum energy acquisition mechanism (setting objective function)

3. Characteristics of amoeba

Objective creature for modeling is searching behavior of amoeba (slimemold). The characteristics of slimemold are as follows.

  1) It has both unicellular and multi-cellular periods in its life cycle.
  2) Acquisition of nutrition is based on phagocytosis.
  3) Vegetative propagating cell has no cell wall and it behaves as an amoeba.
  4) It can organize resistance cell (cyst and spore)

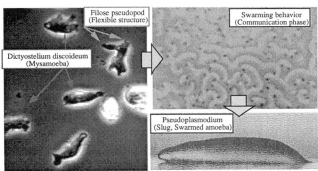

Figure 1. Photo-Image of Dictyostelium

Namely, slimemold is characterized as amoeba like behavior and phagocytosis. Figure 1 shows that slimemold in the state of protoplast realizes searching behavior and walking behavior using flexible arms (pseudopodia on Dictyostelium discoideum) stretched from cell membrane.

Such behaviors are basis of moving and perdition of all creatures. Table 1 shows typical slime mold's behaviors and algorithms, it also shows that the characteristics can be described by spatial interactions and information processing in a field. Now, four behavior-based models are proposed that realizes slime mold's behaviors shown in table 1.

Table 1. Behavior of slimemold and it's algorithm

Slimemold's behavior	Algorithm
Movement using pseudopod (or flagella)	Geometrical deformation and displacement
predation	Approaching to and aquisition nutriton
Secretion	Propagating and accepting information (Spacial information propagation)
Contact	Collision (Geometrical interaction)
Metabolism	Producting energy and heat (Spatial heat diffusion)

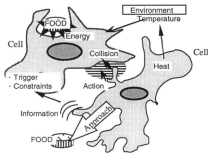

Figure 2. Behavior Model of Amoeba

3.1 Unit group model

The protoplast consists of functional particles such as nutrition, effete matter, water, protein, nucleic acid, etc. Therefore, unit group model with spatial potential interaction can describe the deformation of amoeba.

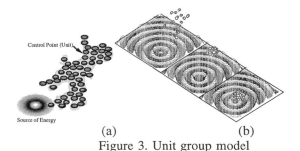

(a)   (b)
Figure 3. Unit group model

3.2 Elastic net model

The cell surface of protoplast has elastic characteristics that can be free deformed and stretch pseudopodia for searching and walking. The elastic net model can be introduced using elastic potential interaction among neighboring units and realizes cell surface model with elastic deformation.

3.3 Homeostasis model

The cell (not only slimemold) conserves its own internal energy state by metabolism. Such metabolism function realizes homeostasis that is most important character of life, and that is the basis of decision making, adaptation, functional sharing and coordination. The homeostasis model consists of energy transportation function, energy translation function and tuning function. Such three functions are mathematically described using the diffusion equation on the multiple density fields and exchanging rules among multiple density fields.

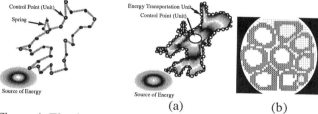

(a)   (b)

Figure 4. Elastic net model   Figure 5. Homeostasis model

3.4 Amoeba model

The amoeba model consists of unit group model, elastic net model and homeostasis model. To integrate these three models, the functions and the state spaces required in each model should be unified. The objective model processes global information and local information through unsupervised parallel distributed units' group using field technique. The introduced field technique is called the vibrating potential field (VPF) where each information propagated from unit has proper vibration and amplitude that damped according to propagated distance. Controlling the units of a system by using local information requires an objective function for decentralized control. The amoeba model tunes parameter of each unit depends on life's kinetics that the group of units conserves order by minimizing the gain of entropy. Proposed VPF offers following advantages.

(V1) Transition from multi-body's problem to two-bodies problem.

(V2) Integration of information by shared memory (field information)

(V3) Generation of global information using information integration

(V4) Observation of global information using local information

Therefore, the unified state spaces are described using whole field (where information propagates) and units (that process information and changes local information). The unified functions are potential functions (that is information source of the whole fields) and objective function (that gives reward and penalty to tune unit dynamics). Thus such four elements described amoeba model, that are multiple fields, units, potential functions and objective function shown in figure 6.

The structure of unit consists of four elements those are observation **H**, unit parameter **K**, stored energy **Q**, and action **p**. The moving mechanism of unit based on such four elements is shown as follows:

(a) Unit observes field information **H** which consists of wavy field and density field.

(b) Unit action **p** is derived by observation **H**, unit parameter **K**, and stored energy **Q**.

(c) Unit parameter **K** controls adaptive behavior, and **K** is tuned as to be minimize the increase of entropy at the location of unit.

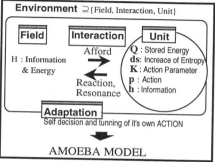

Figure 6. Basic components of propagating information in VPF

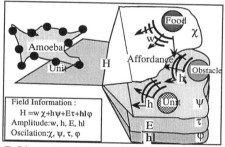

Figure 7 Observing information and amoeba model

4. Mathematical representation of amoeba model

4.1 A field of information propagating

Interaction among many units is called multi-body's problem. To translate the multi-body's problem into simple problem, the whole field **H** called VPF consists of piling up individual fields generated by units shown in Figure 7. Using VPF, such multi-body's problem is achieved through interaction between one unit and VPF as two body's interaction problems. Two body's interaction offers special feature that a unit observes the status of other units without knowledge of relationship among them.

The VPF mathematically described as equation (1) using information (**h,w,E,hl**) on individual field for each unit that propagated from unit and unit coordinate axis (ψ, χ, τ, φ) that prepares individual space for each information. In the equation (1), the information is defined only as propagating wavy signal, and described using potential function on spatial interval and time.

$$H(\mathbf{r}, \phi, t) = \sum_i^{\text{Unit number}} \{\mathbf{h}_i(\mathbf{r}, t)\psi(\phi) + \mathbf{w}_i(\mathbf{r}, t)\chi(\phi)\}$$
$$+ \sum_i^{\text{Unit number}} \sum_j^{\text{Unit number}} \mathbf{hl}_{ij}(\mathbf{r}, t)\varphi_i(\phi)\varphi_j(\phi) + \mathbf{E}(\mathbf{r}, t)\tau(\phi) \qquad ----- (1)$$

Where,

$H(\mathbf{r}, \phi, t)$: vibrating potential field (whole field).

ϕ: total coordinate axis

i: unit number

$E(r, t)$: energy function of environment

$\mathbf{h}_i(r,t)$, $\mathbf{w}_i(r,t)$, $\mathbf{hl}_{ij}(r,t)$:information propagated form unit i (potential function)

r : position vector: $r(t) = (r_x, r_y, r_z)$.

v : velocity vector: $v(t) = \dot{r}(t)$.

The information on each field $\mathbf{h}_i(r,t)$, $\mathbf{w}_i(r,t)$, $\mathbf{hl}_{ij}(r,t)$, $E(r,t)$ is spreading type information of unit that dominates interaction among units. From $H(\mathbf{r}, \phi, t)$, a unit interacts with other units on $\psi(\phi)$, $\chi(\phi)$, $\tau(\phi)$, $\varphi(\phi)$ according to the amplitude of each individual field. Such spreading type information is mathematically described using partial differential equation u=u(r,t) as eq.(2).

$$\alpha\frac{d^2u}{dt^2} + \beta\frac{du}{dt} + \gamma\nabla^2 u + \delta\nabla u + \varepsilon u = 0, \qquad ----- (2)$$

The parameters $\alpha=0, \beta=1, \chi=-1, \delta=0, \varepsilon=0$ offers diffusion type field (density field) as shown in equation (3).

$$\frac{\partial u}{\partial t} = \nabla^2 u \qquad ----- (3)$$

In a computation, numerical method (4) realizes the objective field through iteration.

$$u_{x,y,t+\Delta t} = u_{x,y,t} + \frac{u_{x+\Delta x,y,t} + u_{x,y+\Delta x,t} + u_{x-\Delta x,y,t} + u_{x,y-\Delta x,t} - 4\,u_{x,y,t}}{\Delta x^2}\Delta t$$
$$----- (4)$$

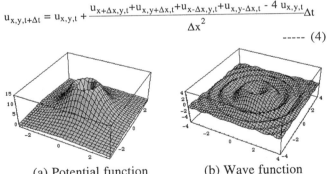

(a) Potential function   (b) Wave function
Figure 8. Information propagating from agent

Unit communication is mediated by the multiple VPF H in equation(1). However, since the description of **H** is only a summation of unit information and the objects that we deal with have many properties, the propagating information would be mixed and leads to confusion. Therefore, to avoid this confusion, we prepared the unit coordinate axes to be at a right angle to each other. Each unit coordinate axis is described as a wave equation. Boundary conditions should be different for each property to avoid confusion.

$$\frac{K(t)}{2}\frac{d^2\zeta(\phi)}{d\phi^2} + \mathbf{E}_{env}(r_i, t)\,\zeta(\phi) = 0 \;(\;\zeta(\phi) = \psi(\phi), \chi(\phi), \varphi(\phi), \tau(\phi)\;)$$
$$----- (5)$$

The advantages of using the wave equation are that the VPF can maintain some different kinds of interactions using vertical axes, and each unit can get the field information by easy operation form principle of superposition.

$$\zeta(\phi) = 0, \;(\;|\phi| = a, b, c, d\;) \qquad ----- (6)$$

Where, $\psi(\phi)$, $\chi(\phi)$, $\varphi(\phi)$, $\tau(\phi)$: unit coordinate axis.

E_{env}: interaction energy.

$K(t)$: unit parameter.

a, b, c, d : initial coefficient.

The change rule of interaction axes is brought about by coefficients a, b, c, and d. Since the coefficients give perpendicularly unit coordinate axes, equation (5) and equation (6) guarantee stable information exchanging among system. Furthermore, a unit decides its own function according to the status of neighborhood units. Then all units have to provide for observation function of the status of themselves based on the status of units of their surroundings. For this purpose, observation function equation (7) is introduced as a measure of interaction energy of unit position in environment Eenv=Eenv(r ,t).

$$d\mathbf{E}_{env} = \sum_i^{\text{Unit number}} \mathbf{E}_{out}(\mathbf{r}_i, t)\,dt \qquad ----- (7)$$

From equation (7), the detailed changing of interaction energy can be neglected, and the stable of system can be guaranteed. This section presented the characteristics of a VPF. The next section shows the information processing mechanism using field information on the VPF.

4.2. An information processing unit.

To attain cooperation in the movement of units, unit action is defined according to the field information and unit's stored energy, and is realized as a result of transition such external stimulus on unit internal parameters. Therefore, necessary values for decision of unit action **p**(t) consist of field information $H(r,\phi,t)$, outflowing energy $\mathbf{E}_{out}=\mathbf{E}_{out}(r,t)$ from unit to environment, unit parameter $K(t)$. Then Lagrangean derives equations of motion **p**(t) regarding $H(r,\phi,t)$, $\mathbf{E}_{out}$, $K(t)$ as potential function by equation (8).

$$\dot{p}(t) = M \cdot \nabla \oint H(r, \phi, t)\big(\zeta(\phi) + \varphi(\phi)\big)\,d\phi \cdot \mathbf{E}_{out} \cdot K(t) \qquad ----- (8)$$

M : the inertia mass: $M = (m_x, m_y, m_z)$.

$v(t)$: the velocity vector: $v(t) = \dot{r}(t)$.

$p(t)$: the momentum: $p(t) = M \cdot v(t)$

3.3. Unit Information (Potential Functions)

The unit information in this paper deals with amplitude of propagating information in a field. Two types of information is applied as shown in Figure 8, one is density type that simply diffuses with decline, the other is wavy type that propagates all around with gradual decline, and suffers resonance, reflection and refraction depending on a boundary condition of the field. The unit outputs such information, and influences surrounding units according to the distance among it. Although such propagating input won't actuate creatures directly, all creatures use it and make decisions according to it as well as the information from environment. Setting $\alpha, \beta, \gamma, \delta, \varepsilon$ on the partial differential equation (2), density type information is defined as $h(r,t)$ and $E(r,t)$, wavy type is define as $w(r,t)$, elastic potential among units is defined $hl(r,t)$. A propagating information is automatically estimated along to the equation (2), each potential function must be set the initial value of information (amplitude). The initial values are defined through objective function that is in next section.

4.4 Objective function

Adaptive behavior of units using local information requires an objective function for decentralized control. An ideal objective function of a decentralized system leads the units to an orderly configuration depending on environment. In this section, the objective function for each unit is set by using the concept of the mechanics of living creatures from the field of statistical mechanics.

Unit motion $p(t)$ is depending on parameter $K(t)$ as shown in Figure 9. According to the mechanics of living creatures, the each unit conserves order by minimizing the differential calculated gain of entropy ds. the term ds is derived by input-output relation of environment energy. Using state values on each unit i are inflowing heat $E_{in} = E_{in}(r_i, t)$, stored energy $Q = Q_i(t)$, work $W = W_i(t)$, $E_{out} = E_{out}(r_i, t)$, spatial heat environment $E_{env} = E_{env}(r, t)$. The inflowing heat E_{in} is input energy from environment that is transmitted through wave propagation and threshold TH as shown in equation (9)

$$E_{in} = \oint H(r, \phi, t) \chi(\phi) \, d\phi - TH \qquad ----- (9)$$

The stored energy of each unit Q is equation (10).

$$dQ = (E_{in} - E_{out} - W) \, dt \qquad --- (10)$$

The unit work W is function of velocity $v(t)$ of each unit in equation (11).

$$W = \frac{1}{2} M v(t)^2 \qquad --- (11)$$

The outflowing heat E_{out} from each unit is function of Q and E_{env} in equation (12).

$$dE_{out} = (Q - E_{env}) \, dt \qquad --- (12)$$

Since such state values are connected with other state values, numerical computation is applied to obtain. Now,

the differential calculated gain of entropy ds is define as equation (13) using state values E_{in}, E_{out}, and E_{env}.

$$ds = \frac{dE_{out} - dE_{in}}{T(E_{env})} \qquad --- (13)$$

The parameter $K(t)$ is derived as equation (14) for minimize ds.

$$\frac{\partial K(t)}{\partial t} = -\frac{\partial \, ds}{\partial K(t)} \qquad --- (14)$$

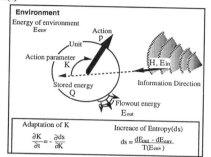

Figure 9. Adaptive behavior of amoeba model

Figure 9 shows the tuning process of unit parameter $K(t)$, and relationship among unit's state values. Actually, unit parameter $K(t)$ consists of density strength, wave amplitude, elastic coefficient, and outflowing heat ratio those parameters are initial value of potential functions $h(r,t)$, $w(r,t)$, $hl(r,t)$, $E(r,t)$. Using adaptive characteristics (tuning parameter $K(t)$), group of units acquires action pattern that unit approaches movement according to the wave propagating. Furthermore, unit autonomous tunes its own dynamics as declining invalid energy consumption.

5. Computation

The amoeba model consists of three components of computation mechanism:

I) attractive-repulsive potential interaction set among circular units.

II) sensor that observes local field information and energy level.

III) adaptation that parameter K(t) controls unit and units dynamics.

Computer Simulation shows the two types of characteristics of amoeba model depending on input energy level with threshold TH in equation (9). One characteristic is rounding behavior at TH<0. According to the equation (9), if TH<0, input energy level is positive at anytime and anywhere. Attractive force works on each unit is larger than approaching force to the energy source. Therefore, such large attractive force reduces the degree of freedom and derives rounding behavior. The rounding behavior means units go around the whole environment with approaching each energy source. The trajectory of searching behavior of proposed model patrols on the 100 energy source. Figure 10 shows examples of rounding behavior where the (a) global search and (b) local search those two types search are depending on TH. Figure 11 shows the simulation result of energy field and heat field: the energy field contains energy sources and its' propagation, heat field contains outflowed heat from units with decline. The white dots indicate energy propagation, and the gray dots mean heat diffusion that indicates higher temperature area. The white circular line means units. The result shows the units approach energy sources with avoiding higher temperature area. The other characteristic is wrapping behavior at TH>0 where the proposed model tries to achieve all energy source simultaneous through covering its own body.

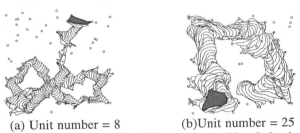

(a) Unit number = 8   (b)Unit number = 25

Figure 10. Trajectory of unit's group searching behaviors

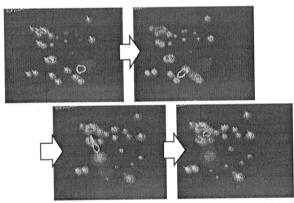

Figure 11. Round behavior in energy field and heat field among energy sources

Next results show movement of amoeba model in obstacle environment. Computation results divided into 3 cases as followings:

   a) **Local group generation depending on the environmental energy:** computer simulation in energy environment shows parameter tuning process on a number of connection among units (local group generation) shown in figure 12 and figure 13.

   b) **Obstacle avoidance in 2D horizontal plane:** computer simulation shows flexible deformation process in 2D obstacles environment depending on rate of energy acquisition that shown in figure 14(a), figure 14(b), figure 14(c) and figure 14(d).

   c) **Obstacle avoidance in 2D vertical plane with gravity:** computer simulation shows amoeba model climbs up steps with cooperative behaviors among units that shown in figure 14(e).

Figure 12 shows group generation process according to the energy input. Each unit communicates with other nearby units through individual wave mode. Since the communication circuit establishes in proportion to the strength of wave, each agent adjusts its own reception frequency to the stronger wave source. The reception frequency decides communication circuits (connections), and the wave strength depends on stored energy in the unit, therefore the unit grows connections that acquire energy effectively. As the unit's connection graph shown in figure 12, distributed many small groups are generated where amount of energy is high shown in (a), big one group is generated where amount of energy is low shown in (b).

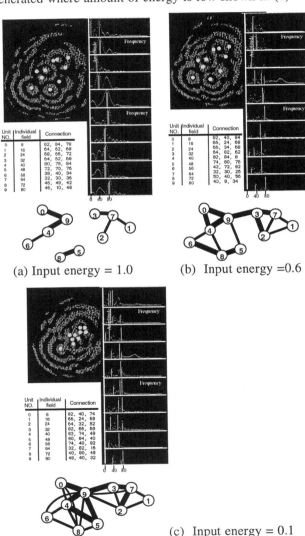

Figure 12. Autonomous grouping through resonance

Figure 13 shows searching behaviors of amoeba model in the energy environment. The results show relation among pseudopodia and unit's group, namely movements of amoeba model are depending on acquiring energy rate. A large group means growth of connections among units and means growth elasticity and deformation speed comes to slow. Such behavior of large unit's group is similar to the behavior of lobose pseudopodia. Contrarily, small unit's group becomes few connections that come to have a high flexibility, and it behaves in plastic motion by extending in many directions. Such small units group behaves like a filose pseudopodium of the Diccyostelium.

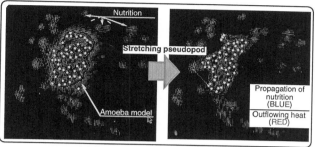

(a) Low energy environment

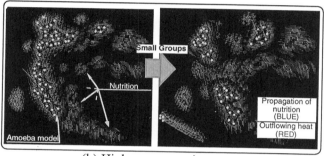

(b) High energy environment

Figure 13. Searching behavior of amoeba model

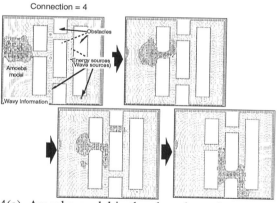

Figure 14(a). Amoeba model in the obstacle environment.

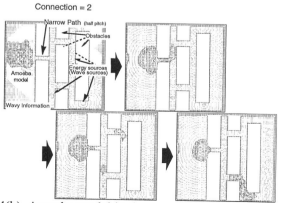

Figure 14(b). Amoeba model in the narrow path (half pitch).

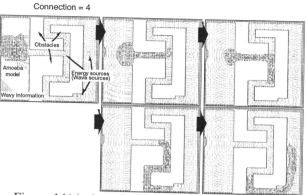

Figure 14(c). Amoeba model in the long path.

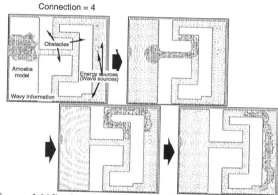

Figure 14(d). Amoeba model in the long path (far from energy source).

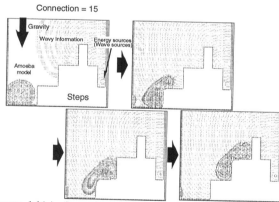

Figure 14(e). Amoeba Model Climbing Up Step

Figure 14(a),(b),(c),(d), and (e) show the behaviors in obstacles' environments. Results show relation among motion of amoeba model and the number of connections. As shown in figure 14(a), amoeba model approaches to the energy source through obstacles with flexible deformation and self-organization. Figure 14(b) has a smaller entrance (half size) comparing to Figure 14(a) where amoeba model must decline number of connections to through it. The behavior becomes distributed small groups and searching energy sources. While figure 14(c) and figure 14(d) indicate long narrow path. In such case, amoeba model selected 4 connections and goes through it. Figure 14(e) shows stair's case where amoeba model selected 15 connections and succeeded to climb up.

6. Conclusions

This paper proposed an amoeba model that is constructed using unit's group with communication through vibrating potential field (VPF). Applying amoeba model to obstacle avoidance, self-organization of flexible motion (passing through narrow path) and cooperative behaviors (climbing up steps) are shown in computer simulation. From these applications, characteristics of the proposed model are shown as follows:

1. The flexibility generated in obstacle avoidance depends on size of units group connection.
2. Group of units organized using field information has two characteristics: heteronomous and autonomous. The heteronomous system that responds on influenced from environment. The autonomous system effects to environment. The heteronomous and autonomous character gets coordination of the group of units in good condition, and optimizes its own system dynamics.

Then results show powerful characteristics of parameter tuning capability of VPF for unit's group system. Advantages and disadvantages of VPF are the following: advantages are integration of global constraints for the units, and description of recursive relationship among a system and its own components. Disadvantages are difficulty of universal objective function, and large computation cost.

While, from computational results, the complex motion of Dictyostelium can be conjectured as characteristics of local group's generation through energy conservation process. For the biggest question whether amoeba can observe density gradient at the sub micron order aria or not?, wave propagating mechanism gives easy observation. Therefore, we propose following assumption of using wavy information for communication.

Assumption: The wavy input has big deformation in a moment and it can be detected by even if dull sensor (Observable condition). The wavy information can be generated using a device that has not high power and response, and it is easy to adjust wave mode (Controllable condition). Using these two conditions (Observable condition and Controllable condition), amoeba generates reciprocal motion mechanism that some point elastic move and its' neighbor maintain configuration and exchange status in the next moment.

Although the justice of the proposed assumption is future subject, these two conditions become effective characteristics for robotics research.

References

[Abe 94] Tomoaki Abe, Anne Early, Florian Siegert, Cornelis Weijer, and Jeffrey Williams: Patterns of Cell Movement within the Dictyostelium Slug Revealed by Cell Type-Specific, Surface Labeling of Libing Cells, Cell Press, Cell, Vol.77, pp.687-699, (1994).

[Agarwal 94] Pankaj Agarwal: Simulation of Aggregation in Dictyostelium Using the Cell Programming Language, Comput. Appl. Biosci., Vol. 10, No.6, pp.647-655, (1994).

[Arkin 90]Arkin,R.C.: Integrating Behavioral, Perceptual, and World Knowledge in Reactive Navigation, North-Holland, Robotics and Autonomous Systems, 6, pp.105-122, (1990).

[Boerlijst 91] M.C. Boerlijst and P.Hogeweg: Spiral Wave Structure in Pre-biotic Evolution: Hypercycles Stable Against Parasites, North-Holland, Physica D 48, pp.17-28,(1991).

[Fujimura 89]Fujimura, K., and Samet, H.: A Hierarchical Strategy for Path Planning among Moving Strategy, IEEE Transactions on Robotics and Automation, vol.5, No.1, pp.61-69, (1989).

[Koyama 91]Koyama, H., Maeda, Y., Fukami, S., and Takagi, T.: Study of Obstacle Avoidance Problem for Mobile Robot Using Fuzzy Production System, JRSJ, vol.9, No.1, pp.75-78, (1991).

[Latombe 91] Jean-Claude Latombe: Robot Motion Planning, Kluwer Academic Publishers, pp.356-402, (1991).

[Lumer 94] Erik D.Lumer and Baldo Faieta: Diversity and Adaptation in Population of Clustering Ants, From animals to animats 3, MIT Press, pp.501-508, (1994).

[Mackay 78] Steven A. Mackay: Computer Simulation of Aggregation in Dictyostelium Discoideum, Company of Biologists Limited, T. Cell Sci., 33, pp.1-16, (1978).

[Schwartz 83] Schwartz,J.T. and Sharir,M.: On the Piano Movers' Problem:III. Coordinating the Motion of Several Independent Bodies: The Special Case of Circular Bodies Moving Amidst Polygonal Barriers, The International Journal of Robotics Research, Vol.2, No.3,(1983).

[Steinbock 93] O. Steinbock, F. Siegert, S. C. Muller, and C. J. Weijer : Three-dimensional waves of exitation during Dictyostelium morphogenesis, Biophysics, Proc.Natl.Acad.Sci.USA, Vol.90, pp.7332-7335 (1993).

[Shaw 95] M.W. Shaw: Simulation of population expansion and spatial pattern when individual dispersal distributions do not decline exponentially with distance,The Royal Society, Proc. R. Soc. Lond. B259, pp.243-248, (1995).

[Siegert 92] F. Siegert and C. J. Weijer: Three-dimensional scroll waves organize Dictyostelium slugs, Developmental Biology, Proc. Natl. Acad. Sci. USA, Vol. 89, pp. 6433-6437 (1992).

[Yokoi 92] H. Yokoi, and Y. Kakazu, "An Approach to the Traveling Salesman Problem by a Bionic Model," HEURISTICS, The Journal of Knowledge Engineering, pp.13-27,(1992).

Getting the Most from the Least:
Lessons for the Nanoscale from Minimal Mobile Agents

O.E. Holland and C.R. Melhuish

Intelligent Autonomous Systems Engineering Laboratory
Faculty of Engineering
University of the West of England
Bristol BS16 1QY, UK
email o-holland, cr-melhu@uwe.ac.uk

Abstract

Micro and nanoscale robots will require simple sensing, computation, and locomotion schemes. Drawing on investigations of the locomotion of very simple animals, this paper studies the abilities of single and multiple agents with single omnidirectional sensors and minimal computational complexity to move appropriately in relation to point sources and gradients of energy. Surprisingly efficient individual homing behaviour is obtained. Collective motion in response to static and moving targets is produced easily, both without interaction between agents (pseudo-swarming) and with interaction (true and secondary swarming), and shows some benefits for the individual under some circumstances. Some algorithms show emergent polarisation during pseudoswarming. Many of the collective simulations are strikingly reminiscent of the movements of particular insect and bird species.

1. Introduction

Engineers like to make systems with certain characteristics: use of simple components, use of many identical modules; reliability of system operation; adaptability to environmental changes; and robustness with respect to component failures. The engineer's view of natural collective systems, the best known of which are social insects, is that they use simple components (since the individual insects are typically much less complex than their solitary relatives); they use many identical insects; they exhibit system reliability; they adapt to environmental changes; and they are robust with respect to individual insect failures. The idea of making robotic systems which are modelled on such systems is therefore very attractive. However, it is surprisingly difficult to make the simplest robots possible because modern technology is based around controllable and easy to use complexity. Modern microprocessors are cheap, reliable, and extremely powerful. Memory is cheap. A video camera on a chip is a hundred dollars or so. Small reliable servo motors, encoders, and motor control chips are readily available. Why not use them? And if you're using them, why not take advantage of their power - a Kalman filter will improve performance here, an edge detection algorithm will help there, and so on. Besides, an ant is really a much more complex and powerful machine than even the best modern robots, and so surely building the simplest robot possible would be misguided as well as perverse?

These arguments are real and powerful in most conceivable robotic domains. However, at micro and nano scales, things are different. All we can expect to be able to build in those domains over the next few years are really quite dumb and simple robots, with rudimentary sensing and locomotion. At these scales, the benign macro environment becomes a viscous and swirling fog where sensing will be limited and difficult; energy use must be strictly limited, because energy can no longer be carried around in quantity but must be taken from the environment. The capacity of a single robot to achieve anything or even to survive for any length of time will be in doubt - only collective actions will succeed. It is in this domain that some of the engineering virtues of social insect systems - simplicity, repeated units - become imposed necessities, and others - reliability, adaptability, robustness - look more desirable than ever. These concerns have prompted us to look at the individual and collective abilities of the simplest possible mobile agents, with a view to developing behavioural strategies for collective micro and nanorobot systems.

There is a useful biological literature on the movement in various environmental conditions of simple animals such as protozoa, bacteria, and maggots. Schöne (1984) reviews early and modern literature on taxes, kineses, and tropisms, and provides useful abstract models of the simplest biological sensor systems. Particular investigations of interest include Colombetti and Francesco (1983), Foster and Smith (1980), Ricci (1989), Koshland (1980), Bray (1992), and Feinleib (1980). However, the real inspiration for the approach is the simulation study of *E. coli* carried out by Marken and Powers (1989). They showed that an extremely simple creature could use an extremely simple algorithm to climb a gradient reliably, and at more than half the speed of the optimal control-based algorithm; their quantitative work undercut the intuitive notion that the *E. coli* algorithm would be able to succeed only at some miserably poor rate. The gains from the sophistication of the optimal type of control were so small that the return on the extra cost of providing such a system would be in doubt in cases where the cost of provision would be high - as for example in microrobots, and presumably also in *E. coli*. The sensing, mobility, computational abilities, and environment of our simulated minimal agents are specified as follows:

Minimal sensing: The simplest possible sensor will be sensitive to a single type of strictly local environmental variation, giving some single output monotonically related to the aggregate input, and with no directional sensitivity. This corresponds to sensing the local concentration of a chemical. An equivalent sensor for distal sensing might be equally sensitive in all directions to some form of transmitted energy (light or sound); although such a sensor might be more difficult to construct than one with directional sensitivity, it will be used as an alternative model for this work because it gives the minimum information to the agent about the direction of the energy source. Both types of sensors will be called omnisensors, in distinction to the unisensors examined by Schöne which all have some directional sensitivity.

Minimal mobility: There are two broad classes of possible simple motion: impulsive, where energy will be released in a burst, giving the agent a certain momentum which will be reduced to zero after some distance (the step length), after which another impulse may be given; and smooth, where energy will be released continuously, and the speed will be determined by the relationship between the propulsive force and friction. Impulsive motion has the virtue that it need be controlled only intermittently, whereas smooth motion implies some sort of continuous control. Impulsive motion has been taken as the model for this work because of the lighter computational load.

Minimal computation: The only computation undertaken by the minimal agent will be the calculation of the step length and the change in direction, as a function of the value of the sensor input. Since control is required only at intervals, then it seems an economical strategy to sense only at these intervals. The simplest computational format providing any differentiation of output is a simple rule producing one output if the sensor function falls in one simple category, and another if it does not. The simplest categories seem to be whether the sensor value is above or below some fixed threshold, which offers only very limited possibilities, or whether the value is higher or lower than the previous sensor reading, which is of greater interest and will be used throughout this work. The simplest general

output is the specification of a turn and a step length for each condition.

There will inevitably be noise in the sense data in the environment, and also in the sensor itself. Rather than building an elaborate model, it will be assumed that such noise can be consolidated into some quantity distributed throughout the environment and varying randomly about some mean. Because noise is known to have both useful and deleterious effects in the behaviour of simple organisms, it will be useful to assess performance in noise free conditions to establish the effect of noise on the behaviour. A similar argument applies to the effects of the impulse; a randomly varying factor added to the step length with a mean proportional to the step length is convenient and defensible.

Noise in the turn angle seems rather different. Achieving a precise turn requires control of a high order; many simple organisms, such as *E. coli*, do not make controlled turns, but seem to execute a random tumble by interfering with the normal process of propulsion. However, such a gross all-or-nothing tumble seems unnecessarily limiting, and so we propose two categories of turn: small turn, which essentially continues the previous direction but adds some random turn within a small range; and large turn, which makes a random turn within a large range, possibly with some minimum.

Minimal environment: Our simple creatures will exist in the simplest possible environment to start with - a plane, with a circular boundary which agents bounce off but cannot sense. The environment may contain a single beacon - the notional point centre or source of the field of stimulation to which the omnisensors respond. By default, the intensity as a function of distance from the beacon obeys an inverse square law, but a simple inverse law may also be used. All beacons are of the same nominal strength; the fall off with distance is adjusted so that the mean noise, expressed as a percentage of the nominal beacon strength, is equal to the strength of the field at a point well within the boundary. The signal to noise ratio is therefore very low at the boundary, and very high close to the beacon. We believe that this constitutes a more realistic environment that the noise-free linear gradients studied by Marken and Powers.

When sensing of transmitted energy by an omnisensor is being considered, the energy source may also be occluded by the body of one agent so that another agent is prevented from sensing it, or senses only part of it.

2. A single agent homing on a static beacon

A number of rule sets relating movements to sensory input were assessed for their ability to bring a single agent close to a static beacon. Two rule sets which showed particularly good performance were:

Rule 0	Rule 16
if (Sc>Sp)	if (Sc>Sp)
• Rotate Randomly between +/- 5⁰	• Rotate Randomly between +/- 5⁰
• Go forward m units +/- random 5%m	• Go forward m units +/- random 5%m
else	else
• Rotate Randomly between +/- 180⁰	• Rotate Randomly between +/- 180⁰
• Go forward m units +/- random 5%m	• Go forward +/- random 5%m
Sc=Current Strength, *Sp*=Previous Strength. *m* = agent step length	

Table 1: Rule Sets

If the sensor reading has not decreased, both move forwards by the maximum step length, and with only a small angular deviation. If it has decreased, both rotate through a random angle, but Rule 0 moves the full step length again while rule 16 moves only by a small random amount. Figure 1 shows a typical trajectory for an agent using Rule 16; those produced by Rule 0 look very similar.

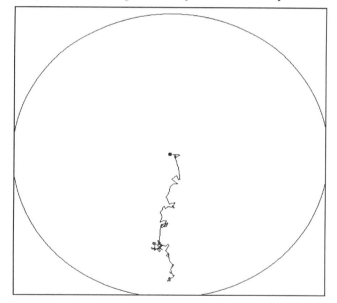

Figure 1: Typical Trajectory

Sets of 25 trials were run for each of the two rules under three conditions of noise (0, 5%, and 10%), and two of field type (inverse square, and inverse). Agents were started close to the boundary a fixed distance from the beacon, and the total distance travelled before they hit the beacon was recorded. (The beacon was given the same diameter as the agent). An agent hitting the boundary was counted as a failure. For successful trials, the ratio of the distance travelled to the initial distance to the beacon was taken as the measure of performance. Results are shown in

Table 2 the distance figures are the mean of the first 25 successful runs under each condition.

Homing was always successful with no noise, and it was also quite efficient, with Rule 16 producing trajectories only 82% longer than the minimum possible. The addition of increasing amounts of noise degrades performance, both in terms of the frequency of success, and the distance travelled on successful attempts. The inverse field is markedly worse than the inverse square under noisy conditions, but is equivalent with no noise. (When there is no noise, each field strength is a monotonically decreasing function of distance, and so each will produce identical results when the rule is selected simply on the basis of the sign of the difference in strengths.) Both of these rule sets essentially preserve direction if the last move was good. We also looked at a rule set, Rule X(90), which produced random turns in the same range (within the two forward quadrants) regardless of the change in sensory input, but made a large step only if the change had not been negative. While much worse than Rule 16, especially under noisy conditions, this was also capable of producing successful homing.

Field Type	Rule	0% Noise	5% Noise	10% Noise
		mean	mean	mean
1/d2	0	2.33	13.81	24.02
1/d2	16	1.82	12.32	28.87
1/d	0	2.33	32.10	72.23
1/d	16	1.82	58.47	93.90

Table 2: Mean Distances

3. Collective homing on a static beacon

If a number of the agents described in Section 2 are released into the arena at the same time, each will make its way to the beacon independently. If they are released at different locations, those closest to the beacon arrive there first, and those further out at progressively longer intervals. When they have reached the beacon, they mill around like gnats or flies around some attractive object; the tightness or looseness of the mass of agents, which we call a pseudoswarm, is a function of the rule set, the field type, and the noise level. Under some conditions, it is possible for agents to escape from the beacon for a while, only to return to it again. The looser pseudoswarms in particular are strikingly lifelike; those generated under different conditions are also different in visual character in ways which we find difficult to describe except in terms derived from familiar insect and animal swarms.

If many agents are released at the same point within the environment, then under certain conditions they appear to move as a swarm towards the beacon. However, when started at the periphery where the signal to noise ratio is poor, such pseudoswarms tend to disperse considerably at first, and the effect is generally far from compelling. If the beacon strength is set to zero, there is of course merely a gradual spreading out from the release point.

In order to gain some advantage from the collective situation, it is clearly necessary to give the agents some additional capacity to affect one another under some circumstances. (There are two almost trivial cases where this is not necessary: releasing many agents ensures that at least one finds the beacon, even under noisy conditions; and allowing agents to occlude the beacon with their bodies may prevent agents wastefully moving towards beacons which are already fully 'occupied'.) In the simplest case, an agent may be a source of sensory information either all the time, or only under certain conditions, such as when sensing a beacon. The problems for the minimalist approach then lie in deciding how an agent should deal with incoming sensory data from two sources - agents and beacons. The obvious possibilities are: treat them both alike, and sum them; or respond preferentially to one (obviously the beacon) if it is present. Anything else involves giving the agent more of an internal architecture than is appropriate at present. In this work we have taken the second option; agents respond to the beacon alone if they can sense it, and respond to agent data only if there is no detected beacon input. However, there is a minor problem: the field types we are using do not have a limited range, but fall off continuously with distance. We deal with this by introducing a threshold on the detection of both beacon and agent signals; it is convenient to use this to adjust the range of influence of both beacons and agents.

A consequence of this is that the radius of influence of a number of agents gathered together at a point will increase with the number of agents. We have chosen to regard this not as an artefact, but as a reasonable representation of many corresponding natural situations: for example, the larger a crowd, the greater is the distance at which it is visible and audible.

In the experimental situation, twenty five agents were released at random positions in an environment containing a central beacon. Five different types of algorithm were investigated:

(a) All agents transmit continuously, no agents can sense the beacon: Rule 16 using combined agent field strength(b) All agents transmit continuously, agents within range can sense the beacon: if (agent can detect beacon) Rule 16 using beacon field strength else Rule 16 using combined agent field strength.

(c) Agents transmit only if they are within range of the beacon: if (agent can detect beacon) Rule 16 using beacon field strength else Rule 16 using combined field strength of agents within range of beacon.

(d) Agents do not transmit: Rule 16 using beacon field strength.

(e) As (d), but with a beacon range equal to a single agent transmitting range.

A convenient performance statistic is the percentage of agents within the beacon range as a function of elapsed time; Figure 2 shows this for all five algorithms. Algorithm (c) is clearly superior to all others; an individual of this type is enabled to find the beacon faster by the collective action of its companions. Unsurprisingly, there are many natural parallels, at all scales from the feeding cries of gulls (which can be heard for miles - a much greater range than the food can be seen from) to the stridulations of the leaf-cutter ant: "*Once a foraging ant locates a desirable leaf she sings to others in the vicinity to join her. The vibrations produced in the stridulatory organ pass forward through the ant's body and onto the surface through her head, to be picked up by other workers as much as 15 centimetres away.*" (Hölldobler & Wilson, 1995). It is encouraging that this basic strategy is so effective even in these minimally capable agents.

The observations of the various algorithms are qualitatively interesting. In condition (a), which we think of as true swarming, agents start by moving towards each other locally, and form small clumps of twos and threes. They move like meat flies, furiously circling around each other. The small clumps appear to drift very slowly, and without any great attraction between neighbouring clumps, but occasionally two will meet and merge (which happens very quickly). The larger swarms thus formed move hardly at all as a body, although the agents comprising them are extremely active. We have never seen an individual escape from a large swarm, but for some reason tightly coupled pairs escape quite frequently. After long periods, a larger swarm may absorb a smaller. The perceptual impression made by this is quite startling: as the smaller swarm drifts towards the larger, an individual will suddenly dart across to the large swarm, to be followed instants later by another, and then the rest of them in an accelerating stream. There is a process of positive feedback: as the large swarm grows, its agents become less affected by the small swarm, whereas the agents in the small swarm become suddenly dominated by the large swarm. (In other simulations we have noted that using a simple inverse rule produces much looser and more freely moving swarms which amalgamate much faster, and which are strikingly gnat-like). However, the overall drift is so slow that during the run shown, few agents moved inside the beacon radius.

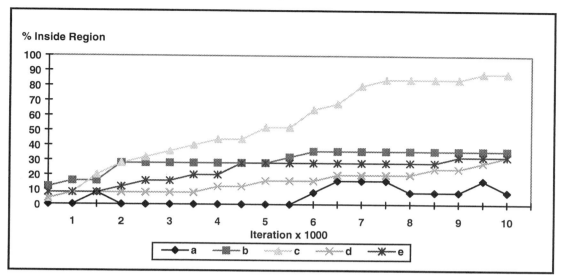

Figure 2: *% Agents Inside Beacon Range*

In condition (b), those agents within range of the beacon homed on to it as usual; in this run there were by chance quite a number within range. Those outside the beacon's influence formed clumps as in condition (a). These clumps moved slowly and showed no obvious signs of moving towards the agents at the beacon; this is not surprising because there were so few that they would have no more influence than any other small clump at the same distance. Since the agents at the beacon do not respond to agent transmissions, they cannot be lured away from it, and so it is likely that the eventual outcome would be all agents at the beacon. However, it may take hundreds of thousands of time steps before there are sufficient agents at the beacon to pull the rest in.

In condition (c), the agents within the beacon range move to the beacon, and those in the immediate neighbourhood also begin to move, soon falling within the range of influence of the beacon and homing on it. As more agents arrive at the beacon, their aggregated transmissions reach further into the arena. The effects of this can be seen as relatively distant agents which were initially unaffected begin to move towards the beacon. Condition (d) shows the effects of the beacon alone. It attracts those agents within its initial radius of influence, and thereafter can gain only agents which randomly wander within that radius. Condition (e) is a useful control to gauge the effectiveness of (c). As would be expected, it is lightly better than (d), but shows none of the progressive recruitment that makes (c) so effective.

4. True swarms moving in a sensory field

We had noticed that smaller swarms seemed to drift slowly in a sensory field, but that larger swarms had little perceptible drift. In order to quantify this, swarms of various sizes were released at a fixed distance from 100 fixed agents; the rule used was Rule 16 using the aggregate strength of field from all agents. Because the field type biases the strength of local interactions, runs were done using both simple inverse and inverse square fields. The results are shown in Table 3, in terms of the time taken until one member of the swarm comes into contact with the fixed agents (iterations), and the calculated equivalent radius of the swarm at this time (Rcluster). (Simulations were timed out if incomplete within 20,000 steps.) As far as speed of travel is concerned, it is clear that it generally decreases withsize of swarm for both field types, and that it is highly variable. However, we were surprised to find that the swarm density increases consistently as the size increases. In the limit, this is clearly unrealistic for real swarms; we therefore decided to introduce some mechanism for maintaining some minimum spacing in future simulations of large swarms.

5. Pseudoswarms and emergent polarisation

As noted previously, if a large number of simple homing agents are released in the same place at the same time in the presence of a beacon, they move towards the beacon in what looks like a swarm. This is because they start in the same place at the same time and move at the same average speed. Over longer distances, such a pseudoswarm tends to become strung out, but a strong visual impression is retained of some unity of action. (It is perhaps worth noting that some of the claimed advantages of collective movement, such as improved protection from predators, can be obtained from a pseudoswarm.)

1/d2									
	1	2	4	8	16	20	32	50	64
Iterns	105	20000	13119	3100	3564	2191	3769	3249	17135
Rcluster	-	4.13	173.17	171.55	112.82	69.10	60.54	31.68	26.7
1/d									
Iterns	124	115	205	201	1514	10003	2232	3612	5650
Rcluster	-	35.02	144.64	59.31	39.58	28.86	28.00	21.55	19.13

Table 3: True Swarm Movement

In Reynolds' dissection and synthesis of the mechanism of flocking (Reynolds, 1987), he considered only polarised flocks - that is, collectivemovement in which the agents were aligned with one another. The agents considered here have no intrinsic alignment, but it would seem logical that polarisation might be an intrinsic property of a pseudoswarm, since the net direction of travel is the same for all agents. However, it is difficult to judge this by eye because the overall impression is of a gnat-like directional chaos with a superimposed stochastic drift. In order to test for the presence of polarisation, experiments were conducted with a selection of algorithms. 100 agents were started at the same place a distance of 500 units from an inverse square law beacon. Rule 0, Rule 16, and Rule X(90) were used:

Some results are shown in Figure 3. Each histogram shows the proportion of the time agents point in a particular direction. The sectors were defined in 36^0 bands in relation to the original shortest path between the release point and the beacon. 180^0 is directly towards the beacon; a peak in this region indicates a degree of alignment with the beacon direction which therefore indicates polarisation. Rule 0 and Rule 16 showed various degrees of polarisation; Rule X(90) showed none. However, all algorithms reached the beacon in a reasonable time. This shows that polarisation naturally occurs in some pseudoswarms where agents have only a single omnisensor; it also shows that polarisation is not necessarily found in all such algorithms. It is easy to imagine that if polarisation would anyway be present in pseudoswarms of the simplest agents, evolution would already have a start in moving towards the exploitation of polarisation in flocking as demonstrated by Reynolds.

6. Pseudoswarms and secondary swarming: following moving beacons

It is perhaps easy to accept that these simple agents and algorithms can cope with static sensory fields in simple environments. But can they deal with the fields produced by moving beacons? 25 agents were started next to a beacon in a circular environment., and the beacon was moved at a constant speed to the other side of the arena, a

distance of 1000 units. The beacon was an inverse square law type, set to a relatively high strength.

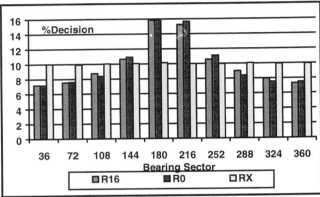

Figure 3: Polarization Histograms

When a little noise was present, both Rule 0 and Rule 16 proved able to follow the beacon quite well at low speeds. (The pseudoswarming looks surprisingly lifelike, as the agents jostle and jerk along in a loose group, spreading out behind the beacon as it moves across the arena.) However, though Rule 0 also worked well without sensor noise, Rule 16 proved less able to cope without noise. This was due to the small step taken by Rule 16 when the strength has decreased; this is always less than the amount moved by the beacon, so the strength is even lower, leading to another small step, and the inevitable loss of the beacon. The noise is apparently able to disturb this downward spiral often enough to kick the agent back into contact. Figure 4 shows the starting position for a pseudoswarm; Figure 5 shows the pseudoswarm as it arrives at the other side of the arena.

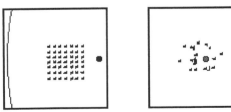

Figure 4 - 5: Start Configuration, Successful Pseudoswarm

By giving the agents simulated bodies, the effects of occlusion of the beacon were investigated. As might be expected, it caused agents which previously were able to stay up with the beacon to drop behind. Since the agents jiggle around constantly, almost every agent is bound to suffer occlusion at some time, and the longer the algorithm is run, the more agents end up trailing or losing the pseudoswarm. A simple form of collision avoidance was also tried. When run without occlusion, it reduced the pseudoswarm density, displacing agents towards the rear. Occlusion and collision avoidance together made matters even worse; however, although the pseudoswarm is loose, it still looks like a collective movement. When the beacon strength is reduced, the results are dramatic: only those agents which are initially close to the beacon move off with it, and once one of them has lost contact by some random chance, it is unlikely to regain it. Occlusion and collision avoidance make matters worse. Figure 6 shows the course of such a run.

In order to improve the collective ability to follow a moving beacon, a version of algorithm (c) in Section 3 was introduced. The agents within range of the beacon responded to it, and also transmitted a signal; agents unable to sense the beacon responded to the agent transmissions. The results were not immediate, because it turned out that when relatively few agents were following the beacon

directly, their noisy movement would not always give a signal of the right sign to the secondary followers. This was overcome by giving their transmissions a small degree of persistence which reduced the noise from their 'twinkling' and enabled reliable secondary swarming. By giving the agents relatively long range transmission, a flexible plume of agents could be towed along by the few agents close enough to the beacon to follow it successfully. This was robust even when collision avoidance and occlusion were added. Figure 7 shows a typical sequence, which has the same parameters as Figure 6 apart from the secondary swarming mechanism.

We were initially puzzled by the ability of these secondary swarms to cohere so well, because individual agents following the beacon signals were just as likely to lose the beacon as in the non-secondary swarming condition, and so as the leaders were lost, the secondary swarm might be expected to disintegrate. However, the secondary swarming is always bringing other agents within the beacon range, so that a sufficiently large but ever-changing pool of agents is maintained within the beacon's radius of influence.

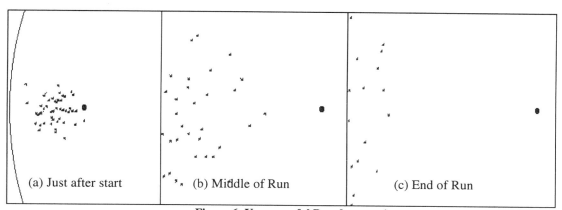

| (a) Just after start | (b) Middle of Run | (c) End of Run |

Figure 6: Unsuccessful Pseudoswarming

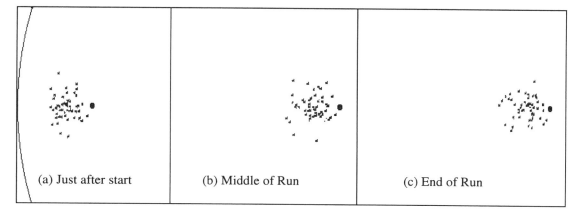

| (a) Just after start | (b) Middle of Run | (c) End of Run |

Figure 7: Successful Secondary Swarming

7. Discussion

These minimal mobile agents have proved capable of reliably coping with the simple demands of a simple environment, and seem to perform unexpectedly well. Some benefit for individuals has been shown in acting collectively, in dealing with both static and moving sources of attraction. One of the characteristics of sophisticated swarming, namely polarisation, is an emergent property of some algorithms. Although our investigations have clearly not been exhaustive, it is already apparent that the abilities of minimal systems are good enough to justify further research. There are two obvious extensions. The first is to examine sensing which is intrinsically able to give directional information. This could be done by using a single unisensor (Schöne, 1984), a sensor with some directional sensitivity. In the spirit of minimalism, this can be made by shielding an omnisensor on one side with some occluding material, as in Euglena gracilis, a flagellate protozoan with a single photosensor embedded in a pit adjacent to a heavily pigmented screening organelle, which gives a directional asymmetry. Euglena normally swims in a helical path, effectively scanning the environment rather like Grey Walter's tortoise robots of the 1950s; by changing its direction as a function of the sensed light, it is able to achieve positive phototaxis (Ricci, 1989). The second extension is to elaborate the swarming mechanism, possibly by exploiting the emergent polarisation. Since the agents tend to be aligned with the direction of net movement, it may be advantageous to move in the direction in which swarm members are aligned. A transmission which is received most strongly when the receiver and transmitter are roughly aligned may be all that is required. This could be achieved by some simple means such as a different coloured patch on the front and back of each agent, paired with an appropriate directional colour sensor.

One final remark is that collections of these simple agents in simple environments are often strikingly reminiscent of swarms of particular insects, and flocks of particular birds. It is easy to see that one set of parameters produces ant-like behaviour, and another starlings, or seagulls, or gnats, or dung flies. It might be useful to develop some taxonomy of aggregate movement types which was more objective than this, which could then be related to the algorithm or parameter characteristics. We feel that there must be more to this distinctiveness than mere aesthetics; perhaps it might be possible achieve a characterisation such as has been achieved in relating the generating equations of tree structures to natural tree species.

References

Bray D. (1992) "Cell Movements". Garland.

Colombetti G. & Francesco L. (1983) "The Biology of Photoreception" Symposium of the Society for Experimental Biology V36. Cambridge Univ Press.

Feinleib M. (1980) "Photomotile Responses in Flagellates". In: Photoreception and Sensory Transduction in Aneural Organisms". Eds: Lenci F. & Colombetti G. pp 45-68. New York & London: Plenum.

Foster K. & Smyth R. (1980) "Light Antennas in Phototactic Algae". Microbiol. Rev. 44. pp572-630.

Hölldobler B. & Wilson E.O. (1995) "Journey to the Ants." The Belknap Press of Harvard University Press.

Koshland D. (1980) "Behavioural Chemotaxis as a model behavioural System" New York. Raven Press.

Marken R. & Powers W. (1989) "Random-Walk Chemotaxis: Trial and Error as a Control Process" Behavioural Neuroscience V.103 No. 6. pp1348-1355.

Ricci N. (1989) "Locomotion as a Criterion to Read the Adaptive Biology of Protozoa and their Evolution toward Metazoa" Boll. Zool. 56. pp 245-263

Schöne H. (1984) "The Spatial Orientation of Behaviour in Animals and Man" Princeton Series in Neurobiology and Behaviour. Princeton University Press.

Formation Mechanism of Pheromone Pattern and Control of Foraging Behavior in an Ant Colony Model

Mari Nakamura and **Koichi Kurumatani**

Life Electronics Research Center (LERC), Electrotechnical Laboratory (ETL)

Nakoji 3-11-46, Amagasaki, Hyogo, 661 JAPAN

e-mail: mari@etl.go.jp

Abstract

This paper proposes a mathematical model for the foraging behavior of an ant colony. In the model, a homogeneous ant behaves according to the given rule, and interacts one another by pheromone. As a result of cooperation of many ants' micro-scale behaviors, macro-scale foraging behavior of the colony emerges without any central or hierarchical control. The model shows characteristic foraging behavior depending on colony size, that disrupts proper foraging. To avoid this behavior, we suppose a temporary desensitization of an ant to pheromone after perceiving a strong pheromone signal. This supposition influences a formation process of a pheromone pattern, and this enables us to control the colony's foraging behavior.

1. Introduction

Our study aims to reveal control mechanisms of an autonomous distributed system, where a macro-scale behavior of the system is decided by micro-scale behaviors of many agents interacting with one another by signal communications. As an example of such system, this paper proposes a mathematical model for the foraging of an ant colony. The model has the following features.

- An individual ant has a small sensing area around itself and moves on the ground at a slow speed. According to the situation, an ant changes its *modes* that decide its behavior (such as *searching bait sites, carrying bait from bait site to the nest secreting pheromone*, and *following pheromone toward bait sites*). A mode transition rule and behavior of each mode ant are defined as simple rules dependent upon local information on the ground (such as pheromone distributions). Then, the ant's behavior is defined in a micro scale (over a few grids for each step, in this paper).

- Ants in the colony communicate with one another by use of pheromones (especially, *recruit pheromone*). Pheromone secreted on the ground gradually evaporate in the air and widely diffuse. Pheromone signals are active for a short time, in a broader range than an ant's sensing area. Ants can commonly use the ground as a message board of pheromones. Then, the pheromone's behavior is formulated in a meso scale (over several grids for several steps).

- Ants behave in micro-scale, perceiving and secreting pheromone. They slowly form pheromone patterns on the ground as a result of their interaction. Accordingly, foraging behavior of the colony is organized on a macro scale (over tens of grids for tens of steps).

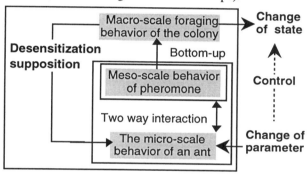

Figure 1. Purpose of this study

This model shows characteristic foraging behavior dependent on colony size, which has been simulated in preceding studies on an ant colony model [6]. There are only two typical states in such model. With sufficient colony size (or when pheromone is effective), the model shows a strong recruitment of ants to a single bait site among many sites. Almost all ants are recruited to it or trapped around it, so this recruitment impedes search for other sites. On the other hand, with a small colony size (or when pheromone is ineffective), no recruitment occurs. Almost all ants continue to search various bait sites (including previously visited ones). The above characteristic foraging behaviors are caused by a positive feedback process, as follows. Ants recruited to bait sites secrete pheromone that recruits proximate ants to the sites, and the pheromone signal thus reinforces itself. In a small colony (or with ineffective pheromone), a pheromone signal decays before successive recruitment occurs and the positive feedback process does not begin. However, in a large colony (or with effective signal), ants can cause stable successive recruitment, and the feedback process always begins. Then a pheromone signal and a recruitment grow autocatalytically as far as possible. This causes recruitment competition among bait sites, and results in over-concentrated recruitment to a single bait site.

It is difficult to control these systems in a desirable state where search and recruitment coexist properly, because the positive feedback process would either not begin or progress as far as possible. To control such a system, we suppose a temporary desensitization of an ant to the pheromone, which is caused by over-concentration (*Temporary desensitization* means that an ant loses its sensitivity for a while.). This works to interfere with the positive feedback process. With this supposition, we can control a throughput of the pheromone signal in the system according to the situation. Then we change formation process of the pheromone pattern and the foraging behavior of the colony as a whole. To explain control mechanism, we regard pheromone pattern formation as an important subsystem that can influence both the micro-scale behavior of an individual ant and the macro-scale foraging behavior of the colony (figure 1).

This paper is composed as follows. In chapter 2, we construct an ant colony model. In chapter 3, we simulate and explain the characteristic foraging behavior caused by the positive feedback process. In chapter 4, we suppose a temporary desensitization of an ant to avoid the characteristic behavior. We change colony's foraging behavior and pheromone patterns in an extended model, and explain its mechanism. In chapter 5, we discuss the model from several viewpoints, and compare it with other ant colony models.

2. Construction of an ant colony model

In this chapter, we show a basic construction of an ant colony model. At first we formulate meso-scale behavior of pheromone signals (section 2-1), and next we define micro-scale ant's behavior (section 2-2).

2-1. Formulation of pheromone distribution

In this model, *nest pheromone* and *recruit pheromone* are used for signal communication. Biologically, this supposition has much validity [3].

The recruit pheromone works as a landmark toward bait sites. Ants are attracted to strong recruit pheromone in the air, and trace a trail of recruit pheromone secreted on the ground (shown in figure 2 (b, c)). Here, *strength of evaporated pheromone in the air* and *strength of trail on the ground* are denoted as $P(x, y, z)$ and $T(x, y)$.

As shown in figure 2 (a), the recruit pheromone secreted on the ground by an ant evaporates gradually (for several steps), and diffuses widely (over several grids). We formulate decrease of pheromone trail and diffusion of evaporated pheromone as,

$$[\partial/\partial t + \gamma_{eva}] \, T(x, y) = 0 \qquad <1>$$
$$[\partial/\partial t - \gamma_{dif}(\partial^2/\partial x^2 + \partial^2/\partial y^2 + \partial^2/\partial z^2)] \, P(x, y, z)$$
$$= 0 \qquad (z > 0) \quad <2\text{-}1>$$
$$or \qquad = \gamma_{eva} T(x, y) \quad (z = 0) \quad <2\text{-}2>$$

where the ground $(z = 0)$ is a reflecting boundary for the diffusion.

The interaction of many ants in the colony organizes pattern of the recruit pheromone. Here, we define two areas with strong recruit pheromone, *an attracting area* and *an active trail*. An attracting area is defined as the region where $P(x, y, z)$ is more than a constant P_{thr}, and an active trail is defined as the region where $T(x, y)$ is more than a constant T_{thr}. (P_{thr} and T_{thr} denote *minimum sensible strengths of*

evaporated pheromone and *of pheromone trail.*) We examine spatio-temporal behaviors of these regions to study behavior of pheromone pattern in the system.

The nest pheromone informs ants in the field of the nest direction. The nest pheromone is always released around the nest entrance and diffuses from it. If no obstacle or wind impedes diffusion of the pheromone, a gradient of evaporated pheromone points to the nest from all over the field. The nest pheromone is not displayed here in order to simplify the model's structure. In following sections, "pheromone" indicates the recruitment pheromone only.

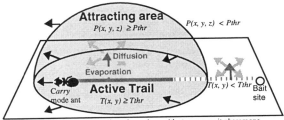

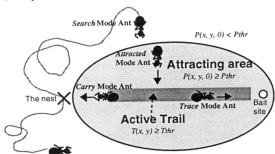

Attracting area and *active trail* are the regions with strong recruit pheromone. $P(x, y, z)$ and $T(x, y)$ denote *strengths of evaporated pheromone in the air* and *of pheromone trail on the ground*. P_{thr} and T_{thr} are *the minimum sensible strengths of evaporated pheromone* and *of pheromone trail.*

(a) Evaporation and diffusion of recruit pheromone

(b) Behavior of an ant in each mode

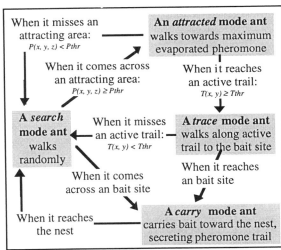

(c) Mode transition rule and behaviors of ants in each mode
Figure 2. Behaviors of an ant and recruit pheromone

2-2. Definitions of ant behaviors

An ant has a small sensing area around itself (a few grids in each direction) and moves at a slow speed (a few grids per a step). It changes its behavior according to local information (distributions of pheromones, the existence of bait sites and the nest). *Search, attracted, trace* and *carry* modes are defined for ants' behaviors in foraging. The behavior of ants in each mode (figure 2 (b)) and a mode transition rule (figure 2(c)) are defined as follows.

- A *search* mode ant walks randomly until it finds bait or an attracting area. It turns into *carry* mode after finding a bait site, or turns into *attracted* mode after reaching an attracting area.

- An *attracted* mode ant walks towards maximum recruit pheromone in the air, until it reaches an active trail or until it is left out of the attracting area that is shrinking rapidly[†]. It turns into *trace* mode after reaching an active trail, or returns into *search* mode after missing the attracting area.

- A *trace* mode ant walks along an active trail in the opposite direction to the nest, until it reaches a bait site or the end of the active trail. It turns into *carry* mode after reaching a bait site, or returns into *search* mode after reaching the end of the active trail.

- A *carry* mode ant walks straight toward the nest carrying a bit of bait until it reaches the nest. While carrying, it secretes pheromone trail on the ground, except for the ground neighboring the nest. When reaching the nest, it releases the bait and returns into *search* mode.

[†]: Because of evaporation and diffusion of recruit pheromone, an attracting area and an active trail shrink rapidly without reinforcement of other ants. An *attracted* mode ant walking at slow speed cannot keep up with such shrinking attractive area, and is left out of it.

Ants are divided into two types, the *search* mode ants and the other-mode ants. The *search* mode ants walk randomly and disperse widely over the field. On the other hand, the other-mode ants gather following pheromone toward bait sites, and secrete pheromone during carrying bait toward the nest. Their behaviors cause the positive feedback process between recruitment and pheromone signals. Interaction between *random action of search mode ants* and *autocatalytic action of recruited ants* explains the foraging behavior of the whole system ("recruited ants" means "other-mode ants".).

Without *search* mode ants, the whole system could not find new bait sites. Without recruitment, all ants in the colony would waste much time in randomly searching for bait sites that they have already visited. To execute proper foraging behavior, it is necessary that two types of ants coexist in a proper rate.

3. Characteristic behavior

In this chapter, we explain characteristic behavior depending on the colony size, caused by the positive feedback process. At first in section 3-1 we explain simulated system, next in section 3-2 we show simulation results of characteristic behavior, and finally in section 3-3 we explain its mechanism.

3-1. *Parameter settings in simulations*

Simulated system has a nest at the center of the field and eight bait sites surrounding the nest (figure 3-1). At all sites, bait is supplied without limit. In initial state (step 0), no pheromone is distributed in the field, and all of the ants take *search* mode and locate at the nest. Other important parameters in the simulation are listed below:

- *The expanse of the simulated space* covers over $0 \leq x < 100\Delta x$, $0 \leq y < 100\Delta y$, $0 \leq z < 3\Delta z$. Borders of the space (except $z = 0$) are the absorbing boundary for pheromone diffusion.

- *The lengths of a grid and a step* are fixed at $\Delta x = \Delta y = \Delta z = O(0.01 \sim 0.1m)$ and $\Delta t = O(1 \sim 10sec)$, respectively.

- *Evaporation and diffusion factors* are given as $\gamma_{eva} = 0.15\Delta t$ and $\gamma_{dif} = 0.42 (\Delta x^2 / \Delta t)$, respectively. These factors decide the time constant of trail decrease and the effective range of pheromone diffusion.

- *The minimum sensible strengths of trail* and *of evaporated pheromone* are fixed at $T_{thr} = 0.0001$ and $P_{thr} = 0.00001$, respectively. *Pheromone secreted by an ant for a step* is fixed at 0.001. These parameters are set so that pheromone signal secreted by an ant would fade out after several steps.

3-2. *Simulation results on the characteristic behavior*

Figures 3 shows simulation results in the above-mentioned model with both small and large colony (50 ants and 600 ants) conditions. With a small colony, ants are too few for stable recruitment. Almost all ant disperse widely over the field in search for bait sites. With a large colony, almost all ants are recruited to a single bait site (fifth bait site) and carry bait from it.

Figures 3-1 (a), 3-2 (a) and 3-3 (a) show simulation results with a small colony (50 ants) condition. Figure 3-1 (a) shows a snapshot of distribution of ants in each mode, attracting areas and active trails at step 1000 (in equilibrium state). *Search* mode ants disperse over the field. No stable recruitment is organized in this condition. Three ants secrete trails from the second, third and seventh bait sites to the nest. These trails and the attracting areas fade out soon (over a few steps) from the direction of the bait sites because no other ant reinforces them. Figure 3-2 (a) shows numbers of ants at each bait site for 1000 steps. A transient recruitment often occurs (at the third bait site between steps 200 and 300, and at the seventh bait site between steps 400 and 500), however it cannot continue for a long time. Figure 3-3 (a) shows percentage of ants in each mode for 1000 steps. The rate of *search* mode ants is large for all periods, specially when there is no transient recruitment.

Figures 3-1 (b), (c), (d), 3-2 (b) and 3-3 (b) show simulation results with a large colony (600 ants) condition. Figure 3-1 (b), (c) and (d) shows snapshots of the distribution of ants in each mode, attracting areas and active trails at steps 100, 800 and 1700 (in equilibrium state). In figure 3-1 (b), almost all ants are recruited to all of the bait sites, and *search* mode ants begin to disappear. This causes competition for recruitment among bait sites. In figure 3-1 (c), recruitment competition is in progress, and recruitment

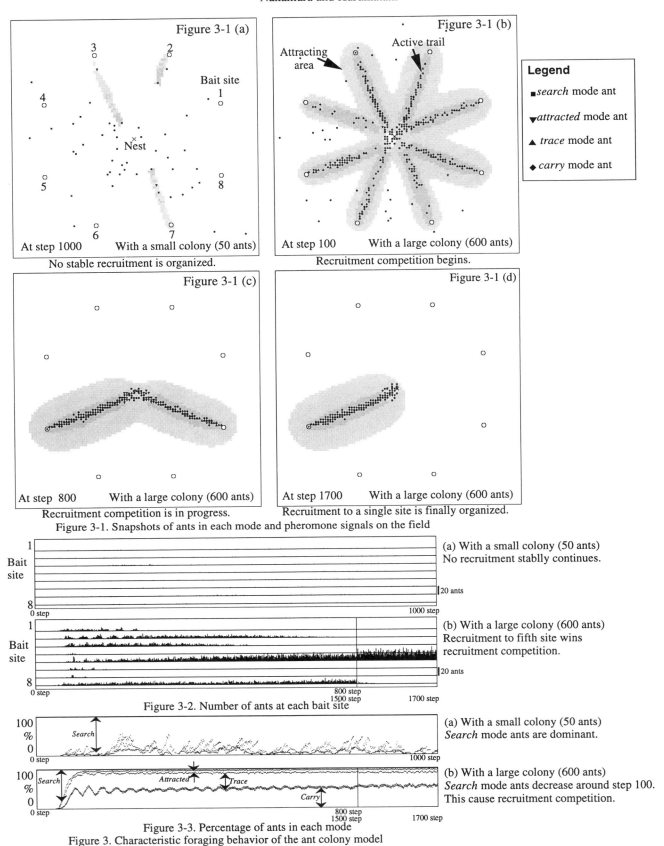

Figure 3-1 (a)

3

2

Bait site
1

4

× Nest

5

8

6   7

At step 1000   With a small colony (50 ants)
No stable recruitment is organized.

Figure 3-1 (b)

Attracting area   Active trail

At step 100   With a large colony (600 ants)
Recruitment competition begins.

Legend
■ *search* mode ant
▼ *attracted* mode ant
▲ *trace* mode ant
◆ *carry* mode ant

Figure 3-1 (c)

At step 800   With a large colony (600 ants)
Recruitment competition is in progress.

Figure 3-1 (d)

At step 1700   With a large colony (600 ants)
Recruitment to a single site is finally organized.

Figure 3-1. Snapshots of ants in each mode and pheromone signals on the field

(a) With a small colony (50 ants)
No recruitment stablly continues.

(b) With a large colony (600 ants)
Recruitment to fifth site wins recruitment competition.

Figure 3-2. Number of ants at each bait site

(a) With a small colony (50 ants)
Search mode ants are dominant.

(b) With a large colony (600 ants)
Search mode ants decrease around step 100. This cause recruitment competition.

Figure 3-3. Percentage of ants in each mode
Figure 3. Characteristic foraging behavior of the ant colony model

to only two bait sites (the fifth and eighth sites) remains. Finally, as shown in figure 3-1 (d), stable recruitment to a single bait site (the fifth site) wins the competition. Figure 3-2 (b) shows number of ants at each bait site, from steps 1 to 800 and from steps 1501 to 1700. This figure clearly demonstrates the process of the recruitment competition. The competition process takes about 1600 steps, and it is too lengthy to demonstrate all of them. We omit them between step 801 and 1500. Figure 3-3 (b) shows percentage of ants in each mode from steps 1 to 800 and from steps 1501 to 1700.

3-3. Emergence mechanism of the characteristic behavior

Ants recruited to bait sites secrete pheromone signal that recruits other ants, and the pheromone signal thus reinforces itself. This positive feedback process between recruitment and pheromone signals cause the characteristic behavior dependent on colony size.

In a relative small colony (less than 100 ants), ants are too few to cause successive recruitment before pheromone signals secreted by an ant decay, and the feedback process does not begin. No stable recruitment occurs then. Almost all ants disperse widely over the field in search for other bait sites. In a small colony, system's behavior is decided mainly by random action of *search* mode ants.

In a relative large colony (more than 200 ants), ants are sufficient to reinforce pheromone signals by successive recruitment before they fade out. Then the feedback process begins, and pheromone signal and recruitment grow strong autocatalytically as far as possible. The process is explained as follows. At first, all ants take a *search* mode, and disperse over the field (steps 0~50). Next, a recruitment occurs at all bait sites and at almost the same time (near step 100). Then, attracting areas overlap one another near the nest, and *search* mode ants become too scarce to keep up the recruitment to all bait sites. This situation cause a competition for recruitment among bait sites. The stronger the pheromone signal is, the more ants it can recruit. At the same time, the more ants a bait site recruits, the stronger its pheromone signal grows. Relative weak pheromone signals gradually decrease and disappear one after one because they cannot recruit enough ants to maintain them. This results in the over-concentrated recruitment to a single bait site. In a large colony, system's behavior is decided mainly by autocatalytic action of recruited ants.

Foraging behavior of the colony takes either of above two states, depending on the colony size. Critical colony size separating these states exists between 100 and 200 ants, but it changes by different series of pseudo random numbers used in the simulations.

Same characteristic behavior is observed when effectiveness of pheromone changes (omitted in this paper).

4. Control of an extended model

In this chapter we extend an ant colony model to avoid the characteristic behavior explained in previous chapter and to enable control of foraging. We suppose the temporary desensitization (section 4-1), show simulation results on foraging control (section 4-2), and explain the control mechanism (section 4-3).

4-1. Supposition of temporary desensitization

For proper foraging, it is important to keep a balance between random action of *search* mode ants and autocatalytic action of recruited ants. Here, we suppose changes of pheromone signals' throughput, to control rate of both types' ants. There are two possible ways to effectively control foraging behavior by changing throughput. One is to weaken the throughput when autocatalytic recruitment is far dominant. The other is to strengthen the throughput when random search is far dominant. In this paper, we choose the former. Here, we use strong pheromone signals as a mark of over-concentration, and suppose an ant's temporary desensitization to pheromone as follows.

An ant in any mode loses its sensitivity to pheromone for a while after perceiving stronger pheromone signals than T_{des} or P_{des}.
(T_{des} and P_{des} denote *minimum strengths of trail and of evaporated pheromone that evoke desensitization*; $T_{des} > T_{thr}$ and $P_{des} > P_{thr}$).

Thus, the behavior of an ant is extended as shown in figure 4. At first, this additional rule works to increase search mode ants. *Attracted* and *trace* mode ants are forced to turn into *search* mode, when they get desensitized. And during desensitization, *search* mode ants can not turn into *attracted* and *trace* mode. Secondly, the desensitization lasts enough long (fixed at 50 steps in this paper) to allow the desensitized *search* mode ants to disperse over the ground. This enables them to evade local strong pheromone signals caused by strong recruitment, after their desensitization. These effects change a process of pattern formation and enable the control of foraging behavior.

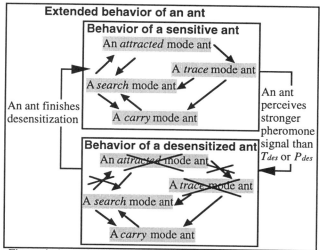

Figure 4. An ant's behavior with the desensitization supposition

4-2. Simulation results on the control of foraging behavior

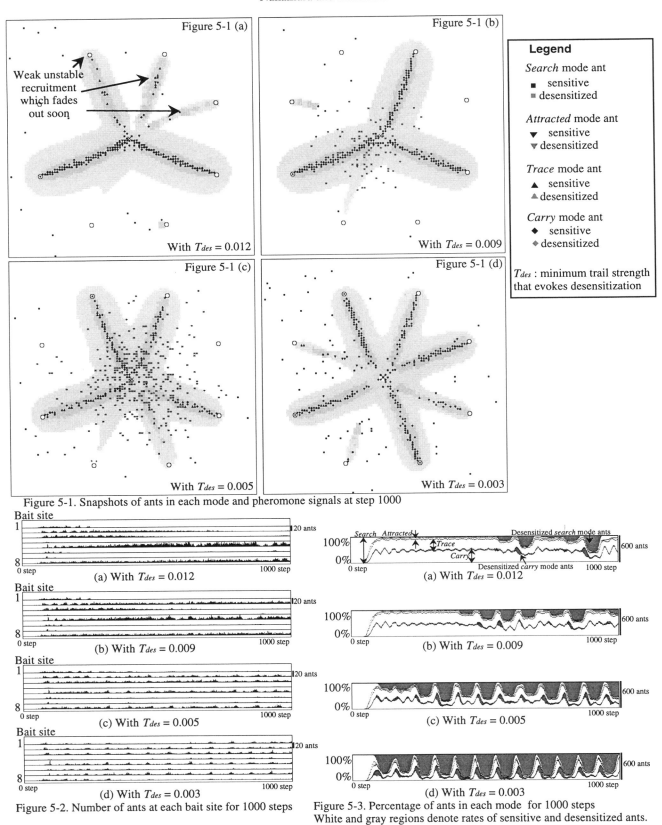

Figure 5-1. Snapshots of ants in each mode and pheromone signals at step 1000

Figure 5-2. Number of ants at each bait site for 1000 steps

Figure 5-3. Percentage of ants in each mode for 1000 steps
White and gray regions denote rates of sensitive and desensitized ants.

Figure 5. Control of foraging behavior and pheromone pattern formation

In this section, the extended model is simulated with a large colony condition (600 ants), with the same parameters and with same series of pseudo random numbers as those in chapter 3. We control macro-scale foraging behavior by only T_{des} as a control parameter. (Similar results are observed by using of P_{des}, but omitted here for simplicity.)

Figure 5 shows system's behaviors simulated with different T_{des}s (T_{des} = 0.012 (a), T_{des} = 0.009 (b), T_{des} = 0.005 (c) and T_{des} = 0.003 (d)). Figures 5-1 show snapshots at step 1000 (in equilibrium state). Desensitized ants are displayed as dark gray symbols. In figure 5-2, numbers of ants at each bait site for 1000 steps are given. In figure 5-3, percentage of ants in each mode, both sensitive and desensitized, are indicated. In each mode, the percentage of desensitized ants (gray region) is displayed on that of sensitive ants (white region).

With strong T_{des} (~ 0.02), the system behaves in the same way as those without desensitization. This is because trails never grow up to the T_{des} under this condition; consequently, no ant is desensitized.

With less strong T_{des} (= 0.012), stable recruitment to two bait sites (fifth and eighth sites) is organized. The strongest recruitment and the second strongest recruitment occur at the fifth and eighth bait sites, as with those in figure 3-1 (c) where the recruitment competition is in progress. When trail strength of the strongest recruitment (to the fifth bait site) reaches T_{des}, ants recruited to the fifth site become desensitized. During desensitization they disperse widely over the field. Then recruit competition stops, and growth of the trail becomes suppressed around T_{des} by a mechanism indicated in figure 6 (details are explained in the next section). This allows the existence of stable recruitment to two sites.

When T_{des} decreases to 0.009, 0.005 and 0.003, recruitment to three, four and five bait sites are organized, respectively (figure 5 (b), (c) and (d)). This is because the recruitment competition stops in the earlier stage. With even less T_{des}, oscillatory unstable recruitment to six ~ eight baits sites occurs, but is not displayed in this paper.

4-3. Control mechanism of foraging behavior and pheromone patterns

Dynamics of the model's behavior is explained in figure 6. By a negative feedback loop in figure 6, the model behaves so as to maintain the strengths of trails around T_{des}. The less T_{des} the system is simulated with, the earlier growing trails reaches to T_{des} during the recruitment competition. The ants recruited to stronger trails than T_{des} become desensitized. They change into *search* mode during desensitization, and disperse all over the field. After desensitization, they subsequently recover their sensitivity, and sufficient sensitive *search* mode ants are supplied all over the field. By such mechanism, the recruitment competition stops, and growth of trails are suppressed around T_{des}. The earlier the recruitment competition stops, the more trails the model organizes. This is simulated in figure 5, and the simulation results are abstracted in figure 7. Thus, we can change the organized state of the system by use of T_{des} as a control parameter.

In the simulations shown in figure 5, by decreasing T_{des}, the number of bait sites to which recruitment is organized changes from one (fifth bait site) to two (the former and eighth sites; in figure 5 (a)) to three (the former and second sites; in figure 5 (b)) to four (the former and third sites; in figure 5 (c)) to five (first, second, third, fifth and seventh sites; in figure 5 (d)) to six ~ eight (all sites). With too small a T_{des} (< 0.003), unstable oscillatory recruitment occurs. In the above simulations, the emerging order of bait sites by decreasing T_{des} is defined as fifth -> eighth -> second -> third. This closely matches the surviving order of bait sites during the recruitment competition, as shown in figure 3. This is because the organized patterns are influenced by stage of recruitment competition at the time when the trails grows to T_{des}.

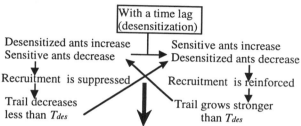

Figure 6. Dynamics of the system with supposition of desensitization

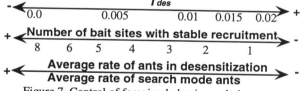

Figure 7. Control of foraging behavior and pheromone pattern with a control parameter T_{des}

5. Discussion

Generally, behavior of nonlinear distributed system can be simplified to those of small subsystems. Specifying such subsystems is important for analysis and control of such systems. In our studies [4, 5], behavior of our model can be simplified to behavior of pheromone pattern formation or to allocation of agents between random search and autocatalytic recruitment.

The action of our model is defined in a deterministic manner, except for the random walk of *search* mode ants. In our model, the random walk is the source of randomness necessary for control. We suppose a sufficiently long desensitization to maintain sufficient randomness in the system, so that ants with small sensing areas can evade the influence of local strong pheromone signals. Supposition of a sufficiently long desensitization is necessary for our model; however it has not yet been reported by biologists, as far as we know. Sufficient long desensitization is desirable, but too long desensitization is waste of time for foraging. There must be the best length of desensitization for foraging, however it is not sought in this paper.

Other stochastic models on an ant colony [1, 2] can optimize their foraging behavior by use of randomness, in a different manners from ours.

In Colorni's model [1], individual ants locate at one of the bait sites, choose their next destination with a probability in proportion to trail strength between them, and continue travel all the sites secreting pheromone trails under special binding conditions. As a result of many ants' cooperation, all ants can travel to all sites in a circuit, minimizing traveling distance.

In Deneubourg model [2], the change of ants' number recruited to each bait site is formulated as a simple differential equation. Ants are supposed to change their destinations with a probability in proportion to Gaussian noise decided by a distance between the destinations. Dynamics of pheromone was extremely simplified and omitted in their model. In various situations, it performed various foraging behaviors, and tuned its foraging behavior optimally by changing noise strength.

In this study, we aim to clarify the pattern formation process and the dynamics of foraging behavior, and control them. Here, we allow artificial suppositions (limitless bait supply and desensitization triggered by strong pheromone signals). In our next work (coming soon), more natural model is simulated (limited bait supply and desensitization triggered by a lack of bait). When bait supply is small, recruitment to many bait sites is organized, and when bait supply is large, recruitment to few sites is organized. The bait transported by a colony is kept almost constant, regardless of bait supply. It performs effective bait transportation according to given situations.

We suppose no castes among ants in this model. All ants are homogeneous and replaceable. (As for foraging, this is not so artificial.) To balance between random search and autocatalytic recruitment, we suppose temporary desensitization in an ant's behavior. Essentially, the balancing problem can be solved by supposition of sensitive ant desensitized castes, though the caste supposition impedes flexible allocation of ants to tasks and dynamic control of foraging behavior.

Although actual ant colonies use many kinds of pheromone for different aims [3], we consider only two kinds of pheromone (the nest and the recruit pheromone) in this model. Interferences among different pheromones (for example, recruit and inhibitory pheromones) may cause interesting problems. Future work will include such pheromones. In the model, numberless ants can locate in a point at the same time. An exclusive effect among ants in high density condition must be considered.

6. Conclusion

A mathematical model for the foraging behavior of an ant colony is proposed, with a supposition of temporary desensitization of an ant to pheromone. Without central control, the macro-scale foraging behavior of the system emerges as a result of the micro-scale behaviors of ants; the meso-scale formation dynamics of pheromone pattern explains this emergent mechanism. We can change the foraging behavior and the pheromone pattern formation by applying the above supposition.

References

[1] Colorni, A., Dorigo, M. and Maniezzo, V. (1992), An investigation of some properties of an "Ant algorithm", *Parallel Problem Solving from Nature, 2, Elsevier Science Publishers B. V.*, pp. 509-520.

[2] Deneubourg, J. L., Pasteels, J. M. and Verhaeghe, J. C. (1983), Probabilistic behavior in ants; A strategy of errors?, *Journal of Theoretical biology*, vol. 105, pp. 259-271.

[3] Hoelldobler, B. and Wilson, E. O. (1990), The ants, *The Belknap Press*, 1990.

[4] Kurumatani, K. (1995), Generating causal networks for mobile multi-agent systems with qualitative regions, *Proceedings of IJCAI '95*, pp. 1750-1756

[5] Nakamura, M. and Kurumatani, K. (1995), A mathematical model for the foraging of an ant colony and pattern formation of pheromone trail, *Fundamental theories of deterministic and stochastic models in mathematical biology, The Institute of Statistical Mathematics Cooperative Research Report 76*, pp. 120-131

[6] Resnick, M. (1994), Turtles, termites, and traffic jams, *The MIT Press*, 1994.

Coevolution, Symbiosis

HORIZONTAL GENE TRANSFER IN ENDOSYMBIOSIS

Lawrence Bull and Terence C Fogarty

Faculty of Computer Studies and Mathematics
University of the West of England,
Bristol, BS16 1QY, England
email: {l_bull, tcf}@btc.uwe.ac.uk

Abstract

Symbiosis is the phenomenon in which organisms of different species live together in close association, resulting in a raised level of fitness for one or more of the organisms. Endosymbiosis is the name given to symbiotic relationships in which partners are contained within a host partner. In this paper we use a simulated model of coevolution to examine an aspect of endosymbiosis, the transfer of genetic material between such symbionts, and its effect on the evolutionary performance of the partners involved. We are then able to suggest the conditions under which horizontal gene transfers between endosymbionts are more likely to occur and why; we find they emerge between organisms within a large window of their attribute space. The results are used as grounds for allowing the transfer of genetic material to emerge within artificial coevolutionary multi-agent systems.

1 Introduction

Symbiosis is the term used to describe the close association of heterogeneous organisms. The evolutionary significance of symbiosis is recognised both by "symbiologists" (e.g. [Margulis & Fester 1991]) and increasingly by evolutionary biologists in general (e.g. [Maynard-Smith & Szathmary 1995]). If classical Darwinism describes evolution by the differentiation of species, like the branching of a river [Dawkins 1995], then symbiosis describes the inverse process [Rosen 1994] - the bringing together of species to provide evolutionary innovation. This joining ranges from ectosymbioses to the formation of endosymbioses, where the transfer of genetic material becomes possible; the greater integration of symbionts - "symbiogenesis"[Merezhkovsky 1920] - can lead to new selective chimera.

In this paper we look at the transfer of genetic material between hereditary endosymbionts as part of the process of symbiogenesis. We use a modified version of Kauffman and Johnsen's [1989] NKC model to examine the conditions under which horizontal gene transfer to a single, sexually reproducing, genome represents a more efficient configuration for the genes involved. Previously [Bull et al. 1995] we have presented an endosymbiotic version of the NKC model to examine the conditions under which hereditary endosymbioses will emerge. In this paper the existence of such endosymbionts is initially fixed with half the population representing the association having experienced gene transfer and the other half staying genetically separate. The two configurations then compete for population space such that over evolutionary time the most efficient configuration will come to dominate. We find that a window exists within the symbionts' attribute space where partners having experienced gene transfer proves more efficient.

The paper is arranged as follows: section 2 describes endosymbiosis and symbiogenesis. Section 3 describes the simulated model of coevolution used in this work. Section 4 contains our results and in section 5 we finish by suggesting that gene transfer can also be viewed as a macro-level operator which can be used within the evolution of multi-agent systems to allow for more complex strategies to emerge; unused genes in one agent, transferred to another, can be exploited by the receiving partner.

2 Endosymbiosis

The most "intimate" [Ehrman 1983] of symbiotic associations is termed endosymbiosis, in which one of the partners, the "host", incorporates the other(s) internally (purely external associations are termed ectosymbioses). Endosymbionts can occur within their host's cells (intracellular), or outside them (extracellular). Extracellular endosymbionts can be either between the cells of host tissue (intercellular), or in an internal cavity, such as the gut. Intracellular endosymbionts are usually enclosed by a host membrane (there may only be a single membrane separating host and endosymbiont cytoplasm). Burns [1993] suggests that "most [symbioses] exist as a solution to unpredictable environment variability" and the evolution of endosymbiotic associations can therefore be viewed as the logical outcome of such a process - he cites how anaerobic microorganisms "endosymbiotic in the cytoplasm of aerobes ... do not experience the present day atmosphere, which from their perspective is polluted with oxygen". Law [1985] however suggests endosymbionts still indirectly experience environmental factors.

A large number of endosymbiotic associations are hereditary, wherein the host's endosymbiont(s) pass directly to offspring. The mechanism for this perpetuation ranges from transmission in the egg cytoplasm (transovarial transmission), e.g. in insects, to offspring ingesting the endosymbiont(s) shortly after birth, e.g. when cows lick their calves thereby passing on their rumen ciliates. From a genetic point of view, this mechanism of transferring information from one generation to the next is "twice as efficient in the case of symbiosis than Mendelian heredity, since half the [hosts] (the females) transmit [endosymbionts] to all progeny" [Nardon & Grenier 1991]. Indeed the apparent correspondence between (meiotic) sexual reproduction and symbiosis to form new individuals has been highlighted by Margulis; "symbiosis and meiotic sexuality entail the formation of new individuals that carry genes from more than a single parent. In organisms that develop from sexual fusion of cells from two parents, these parents share very recent common ancestors; partners in symbioses have more distant ancestors"[Margulis 1992].

The American biologist I.E. Wallin also recognised the importance of such symbioses, in what he termed symbionticism, offering the (extreme) view that "just as reproduction insures the perpetuation of existing species, the author believes that symbionticism ensures the origin of new species"[Wallin 1927]. Wallin and his Russian symbiologist forerunners, primarily Famintsyn, Merezhkovsky and Kozo-Polyansky, all shared the belief that eukaryotes are the result of symbiotic associations between more simple free-living prokaryotes. Although these claims were dismissed at the time, present day techniques have meant that the concept is now largely accepted by biologists, this being attributable to Lyn Margulis and her Serial Endosymbiosis Theory (SET) [Margulis 1970]; Margulis describes the process by which eukaryotes evolved via a series of endosymbiotic associations and horizontal gene transfers between prokaryotes (see [Margulis & Fester 1991] for other examples of symbiogenesis).

Symbiogenesis can be seen to act as a positive feedback loop [Keeler 1985] which, with every evolved beneficial adaption to the symbiosis, further increases the associations chances of selection thereby decreasing the partners' isolated fitness; the symbionts engaged in the association become increasingly interdependent over evolutionary time. Redundant traits are also selected against, which may include traits critical to the partners' isolated existence, exaggerating this unifying process [Cook 1985]. At the genetic level evidence for this loss of traits maybe seen by a difference in molecular weight

between a symbiont's DNA and that of its free-living counterpart. Within more intimate symbioses (e.g intracellular endosymbioses), when a loss of genetic material is seen, it can also be explained as being due to horizontal gene transfer, as described in [Schwemmler 1991] for example. Horizontal gene transfer is defined as "the transfer of genetic information from one genome to another, specifically between two species ... [and] requires (1) a vehicle to transport the genetic information between organisms and cells and (2) the molecular machinery for inserting the foreign piece of DNA into the host genome ... Retroviruses can accomplish both tasks"[Li & Graur 1991]. "With the transfer of genes, a symbiosis becomes more closely integrated. Part of the genome of one symbiont is transferred to the genome of the other. The new genome may underlie metabolic pathways leading to an advantageous product that neither partner was capable of producing alone" [Margulis 1992].

Within the NKC model there is no scope for the emergence of novel functionality, however we can examine the selective performance of gene transfer as a way of configuring interdependent genes with a slightly altered version of the NKC model.

3 Simulated Coevolution

3.1 The NKC Model

Kauffman and Johnsen [1989] introduced the NKC model to allow the genetics-based study of various aspects of coevolution. In their model an individual is represented by a genome of N (binary) genes, each of which depends epistatically upon K other genes in its genome. Thus increasing K, with respect to N, increases the epistatic linkage, increasing the ruggedness of the fitness landscapes by increasing the number of fitness peaks, which increases the steepness of the sides of fitness peaks and decreases their typical heights. "This decrease reflects conflicting constraints which arise when epistatic linkages increase"[ibid.]. Each gene is also said to depend upon C traits in each of the other species with which it interacts. The adaptive moves by one species may deform the fitness landscape(s) of its partner(s). Altering C, with respect to N, changes how dramatically adaptive moves by each species deform the landscape(s) of its partner(s). Therefore high values of C correspond to highly interdependent ("obligate") symbionts and low values to low interdependency ("facultive"); with this model we can adjust the strength of the symbionts' association from barely facultive through to being completely obligate in a systematic way.

The model assumes all inter and intragenome interactions are so complex that it is only appropriate to assign random values to their effects on fitness. Therefore for each of the possible K+C interactions, a table of

$2^{(K+C+1)}$ fitnesses is created for each gene, with all entries in the range 0.0 to 1.0, such that there is one fitness for each combination of traits. The fitness contribution of each gene is found from its table. These fitnesses are then summed and normalised by N to give the selective fitness of the total genome (the reader is referred to [Kauffman 1993] for full details of both the NK and NKC models).

Kauffman and Johnsen use populations of one individual (said to represent a homogeneous species) and gene mutation to evolve them in turn. That is, if a given mutant is found to be fitter than its parent in the current context of the other species, that species as a whole moves to the genetic configuration represented by the mutant. This is repeated for all species over a number of generations. In this paper we apply a generational Genetic Algorithm (GA) [Holland 1975] to their model, slightly altering some aspects; the species evaluate and evolve at the same time and do so within populations of many individuals. This allows the most appropriate association between the symbionts to emerge.

3.2 Genetic Algorithm

In this model there are three species (A, B and E), two of which are said to be in an hereditary endosymbiosis (A&B). This population is however initially divided into two, with one half being an hereditary endosymbiosis in which the partners' genomes remain genetically separated, and the other representing initially the same endosymbionts having experienced the complete transfer of genetic material such that they are represented by a

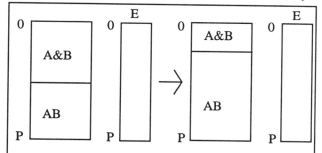

Figure 1: During evolutionary time the population space of the hereditary endosymbionts (A&B) can be invaded by their equivalent fully merged association (AB) and vice versa.

single genome. Most endosymbioses are between a sexual partner (host) and an asexual partner (endosymbiont) [Law 1985]. For example, in eukaryotic cells the nuclear genome recombines during reproduction, and the endosymbiotic organelle mitochondria (and chloroplast in plants) is passed from the mother (usually) to the offspring. We therefore arbitrarily make speciesA sexual (host) and leave speciesB (endosymbiont) asexual. The fully merged symbionts (AB) have a single, sexually reproducing genome - the genes of speciesB are said to have transferred

to speciesA such that they are concatenated on the end of the genome in order. SpeciesE is asexual and said to represent the other species with which the symbionts coevolve - their ecologically coupled partners. Each species is evaluated against its own NKC function, with the genetically separate species being evaluated on the same function as their equivalent "part" of the merged genomes.

The initial sub-population of hereditary endosymbionts (A&B) consists of individuals carrying the genomes of both symbionts, where they receive a combined fitness for selection. During reproduction with the generational GA two parents are used to make one offspring; if an hereditary endosymbiont is chosen from within the whole population space the second parent is then proportionally selected from within its sub-population. The chosen parents' speciesA genomes are recombined using multi-point crossover and then the speciesB genome of one of the parents, chosen randomly, is directly passed on to the offspring. The sub-population of endosymbionts in which complete gene transfer is assumed (AB) also uses two parents for reproduction, with the second chosen proportionally as above, to create one offspring, again using multi-point recombination. This sub-population's members also receive the combined fitness of its speciesA and speciesB "parts". Both use allele mutation.

The size of these two sub-populations are initially equally set to P/2 and at no point is there any movement of members between them; hereditary endosymbionts (A&B) do not merge into a single genome and join the other sub-population (AB) or vice versa. Roulette wheel selection is carried out over the whole population space so that over evolutionary time the most efficient genetic configuration for the two symbionts will come to dominate. That is, the hereditary endosymbioses compete against each other and their, initially equivalent, single genomed species for survival (figure 1).

We now use this model to examine the evolutionary performance of the two configurations (the reader is referred to [Bull 1995] for a full investigation), with all results being averaged performance over twenty runs.

4 Horizontal Gene Transfer

4.1 Simulation

We implement our comparative model of gene transfer in endosymbiosis using an overall population space of one hundred (P=100) individuals. Three genome lengths are used throughout, N=8, 12, and 24 - all experiments are repeated for the various N. We introduce a second value of interdependence for the endosymbionts to the third species (Ce); we can alter both the interdependence between the endosymbionts (C) and the interdependence both symbionts have with their environment (Ce). The per bit gene mutation rate of the GA (p_m) is set at 0.001 and the crossover rate (p_x) is set at 1/(N/2) per bit. All species have the same K value.

A number of experiments were carried out in which the values of K, C and Ce were varied. We find that for various

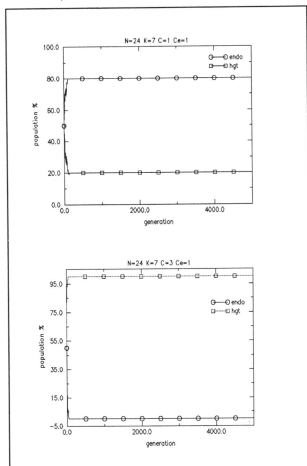

Figure 2: Graphs showing that as the amount of inter-dependence (C) is increased, the more effective horizontal gene transfer becomes.

combinations of these values different sub-populations become dominant in the model.

For Ce=1 (i.e. low Ce) and any K we find that increasing C raises the population percentage of the fully merged endosymbionts (AB) such that when C=3 there are significantly more single genomed species than hereditary endosymbiotic species. The greater C is, the bigger the difference in population percentage (figures 2&3). Conversely when C<3 the hereditary endosymbionts are dominant (i.e >50%). This shows that as the degree of dependency increases between the endosymbionts, if possible, the process of horizontal gene transfer (complete symbiogenesis) can lead to a more efficient genetic configuration.

Increasing Ce does not alter this general result, however from figure 3 it can be seen that an increase allows a higher percentage of the genetically separate endosymbionts (A&B) to dominate for higher values of C. For Ce=3 the association is able to dominate in situations up to C=5. Therefore as the endosymbionts become increasingly dependent on other aspects of their environment, they must

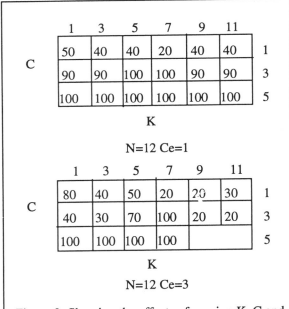

	1	3	5	7	9	11	
C	50	40	40	20	40	40	1
	90	90	100	100	90	90	3
	100	100	100	100	100	100	5

K

N=12 Ce=1

	1	3	5	7	9	11	
C	80	40	50	20	20	30	1
	40	30	70	100	20	20	3
	100	100	100	100			5

K

N=12 Ce=3

Figure 3: Showing the effects of varying K, C and Ce on the population percentage held by the merged association of a given endosymbiosis.

be increasingly interdependent for the transfer of genetic material to represent a more efficient configuration. Burns' [1993] suggestion that endosymbionts no longer experience all environmental factors may reduce this affect, which would be in the merged endosymbionts favour.

We have also run these experiments between two sexual species (results not shown) and found the same overall result; transfer does not dominate simply because one agent otherwise initially evolves without recombination.

Ikegami and Kaneko [e.g. 1990] have also investigated this "genetic fusion" (the merging of genomes), adding it to a noisy version of the Iterated Prisoner Dilemma (IPD) [Axlerod 1987]. In [Ikegami & Kaneko 1990] it is shown that (repeated) merging is most effective when "the optimal solution can be constructed as a combination of partial solutions", where it outperforms sexual reproduction on landscapes in which populations have a tendency to become stuck at local optima - due to its representing a "global jump". In these IPD models it is reported that this combination of smaller "modules" is more likely when the "dynamics become unstable and several strategies [are able to] compete in an ecology"[Ikegami 1994]. Ikegami goes on to show how the operator allows increasingly complex strategies to evolve from the incorporation of old strategies "a new algorithm comes from associations of old algorithms ... strategies are in general made up of modules of modules, showing far more hierarchical and nested organisation"[ibid.]. This builds on Lindgren's [1989] work with an IPD model in which the players were able to increase the size of their genomes via a duplication operator and in which, similarly, more complex players were seen to emerge. The process of merging as a source of innovation is also suggested by Fullen in his predator-prey coevolutionary work [Fullen 1992].

Sannier [1988] has used Margulis' SET as a source of inspiration for his distributed genetic adaptive system, DGAS, in which separately evolving entities, or "programs", exist on a grid as Pittsburgh-style classifier systems [Smith 1980]. An entity's neighbours form its environment and they are able to merge should they cooperate, "[here] two programs, each of which produces a distinct specialised behaviour, are consolidated into a

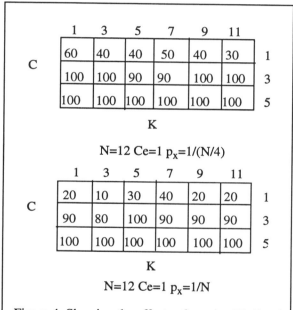

Figure 4: Showing the effects of varying K, C and p_x on the population percentage held by the merged association of a given endosymbiosis.

single program capable of producing either behaviour". Sannier relies upon sexual reproduction mechanisms to facilitate this merging between genetically dissimilar entities of varying genome size, finding that such a strategy results in the propagation of hybrid systems (entities which eventually contain the genes of both parents), though this is perhaps analogous to the "conjugal mating between disparate species [in order to] bring forth wonderful and novel creatures"[Stachel & Zambryski 1989], something "nature has wisely set barriers to"[Goff 1991].

We have also examined the consequences of varying the other parameters in the model.

Increasing the rate of crossover (e.g. $p_x = 1/(N/4)$) does not alter the overall result seen above, but we find that a

slightly larger percentage of fully merged endosymbionts (AB) can exist for the low value of C (C=1). Decreasing the rate (e.g. $p_x=1/N$) slightly reduces the average percentage of population space they can hold under these conditions (figure 4).

A higher gene mutation rate (e.g. $p_m=0.01$) does not change the general result for $p_m=0.001$, giving a slight

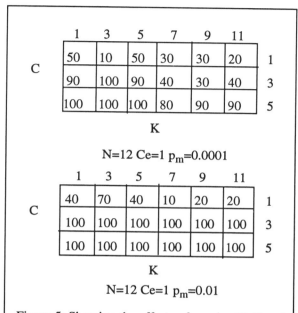

Figure 5: Showing the effects of varying K, C and p_m on the population percentage held by the merged association of a given endosymbiosis.

advantage to the merged association. However, when K is high with respect to N, a lower rate (e.g. $p_m=0.0001$) allows the genetically separate endosymbionts (A&B) to dominate relationships of higher interdependence (when C>1), as shown in figure 5.

With larger populations (e.g. P=200) we find the genetically merged endosymbionts do worse for low C (C=1), but much better once C is increased where they always completely dominate by C=3. For smaller P (e.g. P=50) the reverse is true with the genetically separate endosymbionts managing to hold more than 10% of the population space in some C=3 situations (figure 6). Therefore an increase in population size magnifies the difference seen above (with P=100) in that the genetically merged endosymbionts (AB) with their single, large, sexually reproducing genome are helped by the increase in search potential, as they were with the higher allele mutation and crossover rates shown above

. Upon examining the evolutionary progress of the third species, the endosymbionts' ecological partners, we find that gene transfer has no effect on their performance; the endosymbionts are able to alter their genome structures without adverse effect on their environment, but with potentially beneficial effects to themselves as noted above.

This is perhaps not unexpected as moving genes from one hereditary endosymbiont's genome to another does not alter its overall K value - its epistasis - which Kauffman and

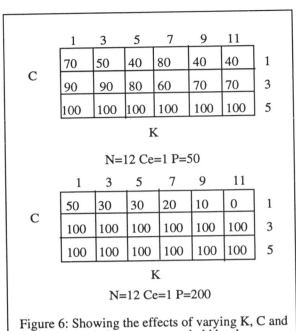

N=12 Ce=1 P=50

N=12 Ce=1 P=200

Figure 6: Showing the effects of varying K, C and P on the population percentage held by the merged association of a given endosymbiosis.

Johnsen [1989] determine as the factor responsible for coupled partners' achievable fitness levels.

4.2 Discussion

From these simulations it can be seen that if the interdependence (C) between hereditary endosymbionts is of any significance (C=3) symbionts which have experienced horizontal gene transfer, producing a larger sexually reproducing genome, become dominant within the overall population.

This is significant in that the "window" within the endosymbionts' attribute space for horizontal gene transfer overlaps - and is much larger than - the window previously reported [Bull et al. 1995] for the prerequisite formation of an hereditary endosymbiosis (figure 7). That is, from our results, assuming a suitable pathway for the transfer of genetic material exists, full symbiogenesis (i.e. forming an endosymbiosis followed by the transfer of genetic material between the partners) will be selected for since it represents a more efficient configuration for the partners, irrespective of whether new functional pathways become available or not, which they appear to [Margulis 1992].

We attribute our findings to the effect of direct inheritance of an endosymbiont (speciesB). In the genetically separate hereditary endosymbiosis (A&B) this mechanism represents both a reduction in the mixing of genetic material for the genes and a fixed recombination

point in the overall combined (supra-)organism's genome; the genes for speciesB are always passed on from one parent. When the interdependence between the two partners is increased the genes in speciesA depend upon more genes in speciesB and vice versa. Therefore passing on the endosymbiotic genes as a block always puts a recombination point between increasingly epistatic genes.

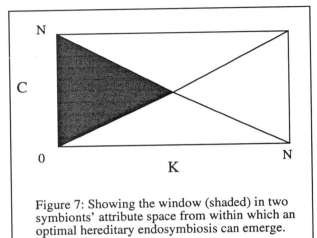

Figure 7: Showing the window (shaded) in two symbionts' attribute space from within which an optimal hereditary endosymbiosis can emerge.

In the equivalent relationship where genes have been transferred to the same sexually reproducing genome this effect is reduced since recombination can occur anywhere and hence not always between these epistatic genes.

5 Conclusion

In summary, we have seen that the process of horizontal gene transfer between endosymbionts can lead to a more efficient genetic configuration for the partners. It has been shown that a window of organism attributes exists from within which the process can lead to an evolutionary advantage and that the window overlaps that previously found for the formation of hereditary endosymbiosis. This result was based on the case where all genetic material is transferred to one sexually reproducing genome. However Vetter [1991] notes that in the case of the evolution of eukaryotes for example "The transfer of a complete metabolic pathway must be proportionally more difficult, in that [the original endosymbionts] still exist and their genes have not been entirely transferred to the nuclear chromosomes". We have run the experiments of section 4 with a population in which half the genes from the endosymbiont have been transferred to the sexual genome (figure 8). In these models we find that the dividing line between the two genetic configurations is less obvious, i.e. the more genes that are transferred to the single genome, the greater the selection pressure becomes for that genetic configuration. This corresponds with the suggestion that even though mitochondria still exist as organelles, 80-90%

of their DNA has been transferred to the nucleus [Gray 1989].

This aspect represents a direction for future work with our endosymbiosis models: how often and how much genetic material is optimally transferred at any time in a

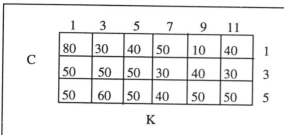

$$N=12 \quad Ce=1$$

Figure 8: Showing the effects of varying K and C on the percentage held by the merged association with N/2 genes transferred.

given association ? Horizontal gene transfer can be viewed as a macro-level genetic operator, where the frequency of use and number of genes involved can be varied (perhaps under evolutionary pressure).

Previously [e.g. Bull et al. 1995b] we have used an hereditary endosymbiosis analogy in our work to apply evolutionary computing techniques on complex problems. In that work a given problem is divided into a number of sub-systems which evolve as dependent symbionts, where each sub-system is represented by a simplified Pittsburgh-style classifier system. From the results of this work we can also imagine the use of horizontal gene transfer within the rule-based framework to potentially allow transferred genes (classifier system rules) to be used in new functions or more complex strategies as occurs in the biological phenomenon; transferred rules, possibly unused in one agent, could be used by the receiver to extend or improve its functionality by utilising the extra genetic material, as suggested by the results of [Ikegami 1994]. That is, allowing horizontal transfer in such artificial multi-agent systems will not only allow for more efficient agent configurations to emerge, it will also allow more optimal agents to emerge when a priori decisions have restricted their complexity by defining rule-bases which are too small (Harvey's SAGA [e.g. 1991] can also be seen to achieve the same effect).

6 Acknowledgements

The authors acknowledge the support of HP labs through their European Equipment grants programme. This work was supported under EPSRC grant no GR/J71687.

7 References

Axlerod R (1987), "The Evolution of Strategies in the Iterated Prisoner's Dilemma", Genetic Algorithms and Simulated Annealing, Pittman, London.

Bull L (1995), PhD Thesis, UWE Bristol.

Bull L, Fogarty T C & Pipe A G (1995), "Artificial Endosymbiosis", Proceedings of the Third European Conference on Artificial Life, Springer, pp273-289.

Bull L, Fogarty T C & Snaith M (1995b), "Evolution in Multi-agent Systems: Evolving Communicating Classifier Systems for Gait in a Quadrupedal Robot", Proceedings of the Sixth International Conference on Genetic Algorithms, Morgan Kaufmann.

Burns T P (1993), "Discussion: Mutualism as Pattern and Process in Ecosystem Organisation", Mutualism and Community Organisation, Oxford University Press, pp239-251.

Cook C B (1985), "Equilibrium Populations and Long-term Stability of Mutualistic Algae and Invertebrate Hosts", The Biology of Mutualism, Croom-Helm, pp171-191.

Dawkins R (1995), "River Out of Eden", Weidenfeld & Nicholson.

Ehrman L (1983), "Endosymbiosis", Coevolution, Sinauer Associates.

Fullen (1992), "On the Self-Organisation of Pseudo-Randomness", Parallel Problem Solving from Nature II, Springer-Verlag.

Goff L J (1991), "Symbiosis, Interspecific Gene Transfer, and the Evolution of New Species: A Case Study in the Parasitic Red Algae", Symbiosis as a Source of Evolutionary Innovation, MIT Press, pp343-363.

Gray M W (1989), "Origin and Evolution of Mitochondria DNA", Annual Review of Cell Biology 5.

Harvey I (1991), "Species Adaption Genetic Algorithms: A Basis for a Continuing SAGA", First European Conference on Artificial Life, MIT Press, pp346-353.

Holland J H (1975), "Adaption in Natural and Artificial Systems", Univ. of Michigan Press, Ann Arbor.

Ikegami T (1994), "From Genetic Evolution to Emergence of Game Strategies", Physica D.

Ikegami T & Kaneko K (1990), "Genetic Fusion", Phys. Rev. Let., 65, No 26: 3352-3355.

Kauffman S A (1993), "The Origins of Order: Self Organisation and Selection in Evolution", Oxford University Press.

Kauffman S A & Johnsen S (1989), "Coevolution to the Edge of Chaos: Coupled Fitness Landscapes, Poised States and Coevolutionary Avalanches", Artificial Life II, Addison-Wesley, pp325-370.

Keeler K H (1985), "Cost: Benefit Models of Mutualism", The Biology of Mutualism, Croom-Helm, pp100-127.

Law R (1985), "Evolution in a Mutualistic Environment", The Biology of Mutualism, Croom-Helm, pp145-171.

Li W-H & Graur D (1991), "Fundamentals of Molecular Evolution", Sinauer Associates.

Lindgren K (1989), "Evolutionary Phenomena in Simple Dynamics", Artificial Life II, Addison-Wesley, pp295-312.

Margulis L (1970), "Origin of Eukaryotic Cells", Yale University Press".

Margulis L (1992), "Symbiosis in Cell Evolution", W H Freeman and Company.

Margulis L & Fester R (1991), "Symbiosis as a Source of Evolutionary Innovation: Speciation and Morphogenesis", MIT Press.

Maynard-Smith J & Szathmary (1995), "The Major Transitions in Evolution", W H Freeman.

Merezhkovsky K S (1920) in Khakhina L N (1992), "Concepts of Symbiogenesis: History of Symbiogenesis as an Evolutionary Mechanism", Yale University Press.

Nardon P & Grenier M (1991), "Serial Endosymbiosis Theory and Weevil Evolution: The Role of Symbiosis", Symbiosis as a Source of Evolutionary Innovation, MIT Press, pp155-169.

Rosen R (1994), "Cooperation and Chimera", Cooperation and Conflict in General Evolutionary Processes, John Wiley & Sons, Inc., pp343-358.

Sannier A V (1988), "Hierarchical System Development in Distributed Genetic Adaptive Systems", PhD Dissertation, Michigan State University.

Schwemmler W (1991), "Symbiogenesis in Insects as a Model for Morphogenesis, Cell Differentiation and Speciation", Symbiosis as a Source of Evolutionary Innovation, MIT Press, pp178-204.

Smith S F (1980), "A Learning System Based on Genetic Adaptive Algorithms", PhD Dissertation, University of Pittsburgh.

Stachel S E & Zambryski P C (1989), "Generic Trans-kingdom Sex ?", Nature 340.

Vetter R D (1991), "Symbiosis and the Evolution of Novel Trophic Strategies: Thiotrophic Organisms at Hydrothermal Vents", Symbiosis as a Source of Evolutionary Innovation, MIT Press, pp219-245.

Wallin I E (1927), "Symbionticism and the Origin of Species", Williams and Watkins.

Why the Peacock's Tail is So Short
Limits to Sexual Selection

Gregory M. Werner

Computer Science Department
UCLA
Los Angeles, CA
gwerner@cs.ucla.edu

Abstract

We built a model of female choice and sexual selection to determine what variables could effect the extent to which sexual selection varied traits in a population.

In the model, there were a number of features that females could prefer, but that were detrimental to the fitness of males. We found that detrimental traits as well as preferences for these features arose in the population, as expected by theories of sexual selection. These handicaps grew so large as to severely damage the males' chances of survival. So much so, that in some simulations, females outnumber males on the order of 30 to 1 by reproduction age.

We found that sampling cost for females, discrimination ability in females, and the number of males that females evaluate all limit the lengths to which sexual selection will handicap males.

Strangely, it seems that costs and limits for the female actually halt sexual selection more than do the survival costs to the male. Males will "choose" almost certain death for a chance to mate, while females are willing expend very little energy on making the choice.

We found there to be few hard limits to sexual selection. In some circumstances, sexual selection for maladaptive traits may lead to the extinction of a species.

1 Introduction

Sexual selection is the selection for otherwise useless or detrimental traits by females when choosing their mates. Several theories have been advanced to explain this phenomenon. Zahavi (1975) suggests that costly traits arise because they show off the fitness of the animal that can accept a handicap. Hamilton and Zuk (1982) have suggested that these traits arise to show off resistance to parasites. Fisher's theory (1930) states that if a gene for a trait becomes genetically associated with the preference for the trait, the trait will become more common until selective pressures against the trait match the female's preference for it. This can cause otherwise maladaptive traits to become common in males. It is likely that all of these processes affect sexual selection. In this work, we have concentrated on Fisher's effect.

Several researchers have produced models of runaway selection (O'Donald, 80), (Lande, 81), (Collins & Jefferson, 92), (Miller & Todd, 93). These models have demonstrated the feasibility of Fisher's theory and aided our understanding of how the runaway effect may begin and be sustained.

Pomiankowski (1987, 1991) has studied the costs of sexual selection for both male and female animals. This work has concentrated on how far runaway effects can continue. It is generally accepted that at equilibrium, the reproductive benefits of an exaggerated male trait should balance the survival costs of that trait (Krebs & Davies, 87). Females pay the price of lost time, lost energy, increased predation, and increased chances of disease transmission when they look for mates. Males with harmful traits preferred by females may suffer increased development costs, increased energetic costs, increased predation, and greater susceptibility to parasitism. Pomiankowski found that Fisher's runaway process can work if and only if mutations affecting the male trait are negatively biased—mutations tend to damage traits more often than they improve them. This tendency seems likely to be common in nature and so may not be a great limitation on runaway selection.

Most experiments with sexual selection are done with three-gene mathematical models. We chose to do our simulation with a genetic algorithm instead for two related reasons. First, mathematical models must have greater constraints placed on the model in order to maintain mathematical tractability. Some simplifications require that variables that would normally evolve be kept constant. Later removing these simplifications can dramatically alter the results of the model (See for example Pomiankowski (1987, 1991)).

Second, we plan to extend this model further, and the mathematics resulting from extensions to a traditional mathematical model would certainly be intractable. The mathematics required to understand current models is already impressive. Once we have a model that produces results consistent with mathematical models, we will be able to extend it to explore issues that would otherwise be mathematically intractable such as the interaction of parental investment with sexual selection.

It is our goal in this set of experiments to explore some variables that affect sexual selection and their relative importance in establishing the equilibrium between reproductive benefits and survival costs. Of particular interest to us are the effects of females selecting for multiple traits, varying sample sizes, female discrimination ability, and female sampling cost.

2 Terminology

We use the term "sample size" to mean the number of males a female will evaluate before choosing a mate. A female with a sample size of 20 would evaluate 20 males and choose the best to be her mate.

We use the term "discrimination ability" to mean the ability of females to actually notice a difference between the features of males. For example, a female with good discrimination ability would notice a 1% difference in tail length every time. A female with poor discrimination might only rarely notice even much larger differences.

We use the term "survival ratio" to mean the ratio of females to males that survive until reproductive age. If between birth and the age of reproduction, more males than females die so that females outnumber males 2 to 1, the survival ratio would be 2 to 1.

3 Design

While this simulation did not attempt to model the evolution of a particular animal, the assumptions we made make the animals simulated most closely resemble polygynous birds such as peacocks and sage grouse.

Animals in the simulation are either male or female. By setting a flag in the simulation, we determine whether the sex of an animal is determined either randomly, in which case the sex ratio at birth is 1 to 1, or according to a sex ratio gene carried by the mother. The gene encodes the chance a particular offspring should be male.

Each animal carries genes for a number of traits that partially determine its fitness. These traits have three main characteristics-- visibility to others, usefulness to the carrier, and sex linkage. Visible traits can be seen by other animals. They may be beneficial or detrimental. Beneficial traits help the carrier to the extent that the trait is present. These traits correspond to things like hunting skill, or visual acuity which we would expect to get

increasingly better through many generations. Detrimental traits harm the carrier to the extent that the trait is present. These are traits like absurdly long tails, conspicuous colors, etc. Sex-linked traits are carried by both sexes, but only affect the fitness of males.

4 Simulation Cycle

An original population is generated randomly. Harmful traits and preferences for harmful traits are set at zero.

Fitness for each animal is determined. Fitness is defined as the sum of all the positive genetic traits, minus the sum of all of the detrimental traits, plus some random number corresponding to the environmental fortunes of the animal.

To simulate natural selection, a percentage (usually 50%) of the animals are chosen to survive. The chance of an animal surviving is directly proportional to its fitness level.

At this point, the surviving females choose their mates from among the surviving males.

Each female in turn is presented with a sample of the surviving males. (This sample size was a variable we tested in some experiments.) She rates each of the males in the sample relative to her personal preferences, and chooses the male with the highest rating to be her mate.

Each male's rating was set by determining how much each of his attributes varied from the female's ideal. This variance for each attribute was subtracted from his overall desirability.

A small random number was added to each male's rating so that the female's choice for the best mate was not perfectly accurate. The variance of this random number determines the discrimination ability of the females.

Once the mates have been determined, we produce the next generation. We randomly choose surviving females one at a time. When a female is chosen, we add an offspring to the next generation using the female and her mate as parents and using standard GA operations. We repeat this selection until the next generation's population size is the same as the current generation. Therefore, each female has, on average, 2 offspring.

At this point we kill off the old generation, and repeat the cycle with the new.

In these experiments we used population sizes of 2000 to 5000 individuals. Simulations were run from 2000 to 5000 generations.

5 Experiments

5.1 Natural Selection

To get a baseline for attribute changes, we first ran an experiment in which females randomly chose a mate from the males that survived natural selection. This effectively turned off sexual selection.

As expected, the detrimental traits quickly are selected out of the population and positive traits rise to maximum levels. Within 10 generations, positive traits are at 90% of their maximum value, and after 30 generations, the population has converged on the maximum value for positive traits and the minimum value for negative.

5.2 Runaway Sexual Selection

Next, we added a single detrimental trait that affected only males, and which was visible to females.

Similar to the results by others (Collins & Jefferson, 92), (Miller & Todd, 93), we found that after several generations of small random changes, the preference for this detrimental trait became linked with the tendency to have the trait. At this point runaway sexual selection takes off until the trait so handicaps the males that their numbers are significantly reduced.

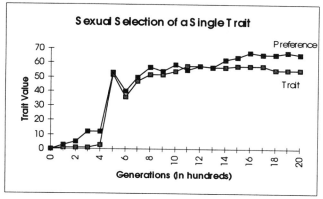

Figure 1. Males' traits evolve to meet females' preferences. Note that the males' trait values almost always are short of the females' preference.

We found that looking at the percentage of males of all animals that survived until reproductive age gave us a good indication of how much selection pressure there was on males to meet the selection criteria of females.

The most striking result was the extent to which the males would sacrifice their fitness for natural selection to gain features that females would find attractive.

The model does a good job of predicting ratios of each sex that mates. In peacocks, for example, each male has a harem of 2 to 5 females (Britannica, 1995). This is similar to the range we find in the simulation.

In white-bearded manakins, males form leks of 6 to 10 individuals and the lek is visited by approximately 200 females (Alcock, 1984). This suggests that the survival ratio may be approximately 20 or 30 to 1 in favor of females in this species. One male may mate with 75% of the females visiting the lek. Thus, there is tremendous pressure on males to meet the selection criteria of females. In the simulation, similar survival ratios were seen when females were very discriminating when choosing males.

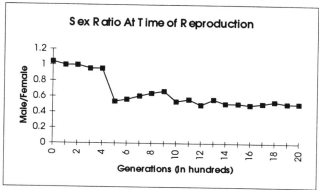

Figure 2. Because of the handicap imposed on them by detrimental traits preferred by females, males die more often than females before reproductive age.

5.3 Sexual Selection for Multiple Attributes

In the next experiment, we added more detrimental traits to the males. We tried runs with a total of 3 and 7 detrimental traits.

Once again we had runaway selection on the detrimental traits. However, the overall handicap taken on by the males was similar regardless of the number of traits. That is, a greater number of detrimental traits tended to make each of the traits less prevalent.

Usually, in the case of multiple detrimental traits, one or two traits would take off, and the remaining traits would stay at close to the level expected with only natural selection.

An interesting feature seen in several runs was the splitting up of the population into multiple preference groups. The strong preference for two traits could split the males so that each group would "specialize" in meeting the preference for one trait at the expense of meeting preferences for the other. It has been suggested that this splitting could lead to the formation of new species (Todd & Miller, 1991).

The overall handicap on males actually increased very slightly with the number of traits. This is because even for traits that are completely selected against, the average for the trait in the population is not zero. Mutations away from zero push up the average slightly. (The mutation rate in the experiments was 1/1000). Thus, adding traits tends to slightly reduce male fitness.

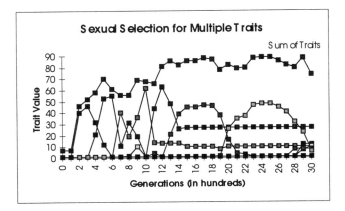

Figure 3. Average trait values for each of five traits swing wildly in a series of "fashion cycles." However, the sum of the handicap for all traits stays relatively constant.

Points of equilibrium are occasionally reached, and the population will stay at these points for up to hundreds of generations before drifting to a new equilibrium point.

This equilibrium is found where several competing forces are equivalent. Natural selection puts pressure on the males to reduce the feature that is handicapping them. Other things being equal, the features would quickly be selected out of the population if they were not preferred by the females. Males that have reduced handicaps are more likely to survive.

However, this increased chance of survival is outweighed by the much greater difficulty a male with reduced handicaps will have in finding a mate. This is because the male will be further than other males from the prototypical female's choice as an "ideal mate."

The females' genes for feature preferences always lie in the direction further away from a good fitness value for males. That is--females always desire that males be more handicapped than they are. But not much.

Here's why. If a female prefers features that are much more dramatic than they are in the population, she will tend to choose males on the high side of this trait, and her children (and her preference genes) will die from natural selection.

If a female's preferences are closer to the average male traits than those of other females, she will, on average pick a less highly ornamented male to be her mate, and her sons will not be as likely to reproduce. Thus, this less stringent preference will die with her virgin sons.

5.4 Large vs. Small Sample Sizes

We next wanted to determine the effect of the number of males a female would evaluate on the prominence of detrimental traits.

We varied the number of males the females would evaluate when selecting a mate. We ran the simulation

with sample sizes of 4, 20, and 40. Although there was a great deal of variance, in general having a larger sample size made the detrimental traits take off faster and end up at a higher equilibrium than did a small sample size. Because of this, the males' survival ratio was smaller as the sample size was smaller.

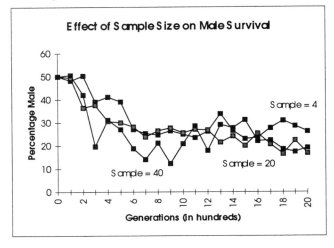

Figure 4. When females compare more males before choosing a mate, males have greater pressure to acquire costly ornaments.

5.5 Heritable Sample Sizes

To check on the validity of our belief that a greater sample size would be preferred by females and would lead to more prominent detrimental features, we ran the simulation with a gene for sample size.

We started the simulation with this gene encoding a sample size of 1 in each of the animals. Over time, the sample size evolves to a number from 60-80. It might grow no larger than this because once the sample size is this large, the variance in males is very small. Almost the whole population is the offspring of a very few males.

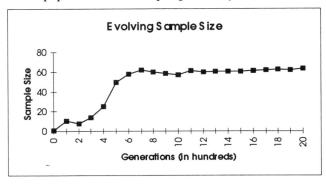

Figure 4. Females evolve a large sample size to ensure that they will have sexy sons.

5.6 Heritable Sample Sizes and Sampling Cost

Next, we wanted to determine how much females are willing to pay in terms of fitness to pick the most attractive male they can find.

We set a fitness penalty of 1% per male evaluated and ran the simulation. We found that a sample size of 1 evolved. So even when males were willing to sacrifice 80-90% of their fitness score to meet female expectations, females were not willing to sacrifice more than 1% of their fitness score to make the evaluations!

We reran the simulation with a fitness penalty of 1/10 of 1% per male evaluated. We found that a sample size of 7-15 would evolve. So females were willing to expend approximately 1% of their fitness to judge males.

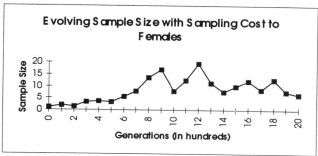

Figure 5. If sampling imposes costs on females, they evolve a small sample size.

We see the perverse situation arise where males are willing to make huge sacrifices to produce attractive traits, but females are willing to expend very little effort to appreciate the male's efforts. This may be because males receive a direct benefit for having costly traits—they reproduce more often, while females benefit only indirectly by being more choosy—by having more attractive sons.

This could help explain lekking behavior in some animals. The males gather together in one location to be evaluated and chosen as mates by females. Because females will not expend much energy to increase their sample size, a lek allows them to have a large sample size with minimum energy expenditure.

5.7 High vs. Low Discrimination Ability

Next we did an experiment to determine how females' discrimination ability would affect the limits to which males were willing to be handicapped.

We compared simulations where females had perfect discrimination with those where females' evaluations of males had a random number added. This ensured that while female's choices were generally good on average, they seldom would choose the very best male.

We found that discrimination ability had the greatest effect of any variable we tested on the eventual propensity of males to evolve disadvantageous traits. Better discrimination led to much greater handicaps for males.

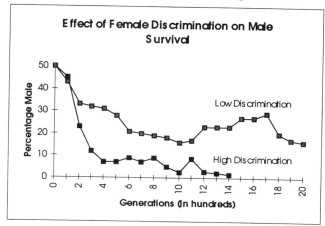

Figure 6. If females are good at discriminating small differences between males, males will pay higher costs to obtain desirable, but detrimental traits.

In cases where discrimination is high, sexual selection for handicapping traits actually led to the extinction of the population. This is because all of the males are at the low end of the population's fitness curve. If more than the usual number of low-end animals die off, all of the males may vanish.

5.8 Heritable Sex Ratios

If males are dying off disproportionately before reproducing, would it be advantageous to give birth to more males to make up for their higher mortality? This is often given in the popular press as the reason that in humans slightly more males are born than females.

The answer is no. Theoretically, the investment in male and female offspring should be equal since the expected reproductive success of either sex is equal. In this simulation, the costs of having offspring of either sex is equal, so the sex ratio at birth for the simulated animals should not change to compensate for the higher mortality of one of the sexes. This is because although one sex may be less common at time of reproduction, its mating success will be correspondingly better. These effects cancel each other out so that the expected number of offspring for either sex is the same at birth. For example, if males are twice as likely to die as females before reproducing, the survivors will have twice as many mates.

To confirm the theory (and more so to confirm that our simulation was working correctly) we ran a set of simulations where the percentage of offspring that are male is a heritable trait. As sex ratio theory predicts, the sex ratio trait stayed very close to 50%.

6 Conclusions

There are few limits to sexual selection. Males are willing to pay huge costs in fitness to be chosen by females. Ultimately, extinction of a species may be the result. Sexual selection is just one of several positive-feedback evolutionary arms races where costly specializations harm individuals and can increase the entire risk of extinction for the entire species (Miller & Todd, 1995). Other such races include those between predator and prey, and host and parasite.

6.1 Male/Female survival ratios reflect sexual selection costs.

This work suggests that the ratio of males to females surviving until reproductive age should be indicative of the costs imposed by females on males for sexually selected traits.

6.2 If multiple maladaptive traits are selected for, the males cannot afford to please females on all traits.

One or a few traits will take off, but because handicaps are additive, a few traits may stay close to the utilitarian optimum for the male, because moving away from this optimum, given his other handicaps, would kill him.

Having multiple features under sexual selection tends to drive down the prominence of any one feature. The tail of the peacock may be so large because few other features are selected for by peahens.

6.3 Traits that are under sexual selection pressure tend to find an unstable equilibrium between what is best for the males' survival and what is most desired by females.

The trait strength preferred by females is almost always higher than the trait strength found in males at each point in time. This gives a directional momentum to the evolution.

6.4 The greater the number of males females sample when choosing a mate, the lower the percentage of surviving males.

6.5 Females will not pay a high cost for sampling.

Experiments show that if sampling males costs females even a fraction of their overall fitness, as it would if females had to fly around for several days looking at males, females will not discriminate between males. This could be the reason for lekking. It allows females to very inexpensively increase their sample size.

6.6 The better females are at discriminating between males (as opposed to the more discriminating their tastes) the lower the percentage of surviving males will be.

6.7 Sexual selection can lead to extinction.

When sexual selection is at work, males constitute a hugely disproportionate percentage of the low fitness animals in the population. In a season where survival is difficult, all males may die. The highly skewed survival rates in the simulation, and the ability of female preferences to so cripple males as to doom the population to extinction suggests that in some instances, sexual selection may have played a role in the extinction of species. This could be possible in a very polygynous species where the sampling cost for females is very low (as in lekking species). Simulations with these assumptions showed that surviving females could outnumber males by 50 to 1, with the males occupying only very low relative positions of fitness.

It is possible that sexual selection could actually make a species less prone to extinction however (Miller, personal communication). By reducing the number of males in the population, the carrying capacity of the environment could be better utilized by reproducing females rather than by redundant males.

7 Future Work

We plan to add parental investment and male choice to the model to help us better understand sexual selection pressures on males in less polygynous species and selection pressures on females.

Acknowledgments

Thanks to Geoffrey Miller and Peter Todd for helpful comments. Thanks to Ruth Liow for help in preparing this document.

References

Alcock, J. (1984). Animal Behavior: An Evolutionary Approach. Sunderland, MA: Sinauer Associates, Inc., Publishers.

Ayala, F.J. (1982). *Population and Evolutionary Genetics*. Menlo Park, CA: Benjamin/Cummings Publishing Company, Inc.

Britannica Online (1995).

Collins, R.J., and Jefferson, D.R. (1992). The evolution of sexual selection and female choice. In F.J. Varela and P. Bourgine (Eds.), Toward a practice of autonomous systems: Proceedings of the First European Conference on Artificial Life (pp. 327-336). Cambridge, MA: MIT Press/Bradford Books.

Fisher, R.A. (1930). *The genetical theory of natural selection*. Oxford: Clarendon Press.

Krebs, J.R. and Davies, N.B. (1987). *An Introduction to Behavioral Ecology*. Oxford, UK: Blackwell Scientific Publications.

Hamilton, W.D. and Zuk, M. (1984). Heritable true fitness and bright birds: a role for parasites? *Science*, 218, 384-387.

Iwasa, Y., Pomiankowski, A., and Nee, S. (1991). The evolution of costly mate preferences II. The "Handicap" principle. *Evolution* 45:1431-1442.

Lande, R. (1981). Models of speciation by sexual selection on polygenic traits. *Proceedings of the National Academy of Sciences*, 78, 3721-3725.

McFarland, D. (1981) (ed.). *The Oxford Companion to Animal Behavior*. Oxford, UK: Oxford University Press.

Miller, G.F., and Todd, P.M. (1993). Evolutionary wanderlust: Sexual selection with directional mate preferences. In J. A. Meyer, H. L. Roitblat, and S. W. Wilson (eds.), *From Animals to Animats 2: Proceedings of the Second International Conference on Simulation of Adaptive Behavior*, MIT Press, Cambridge.

Miller, G.F., and Todd, P.M. (1995). The role of mate choice in biocomputation: Sexual selection as a process of search, optimization, and diversification. In W. Banzaf & F.H. Eeckman (Eds.), Evolution and biocomputation: *Computational models of evolution. Lecture notes in computer science 899* (pp. 169-204). Berlin: Springer-Verlag.

O'Donald, P. (1980). *Genetic models of sexual selection*. Cambridge, UK: Cambridge University Press.

Pomiankowski, A. (1991). The evolution of costly mate preferences I. Fisher and biased Mutation. *Evolution*: 45, 1422-1430.

Pomiankowski, A. (1987). The costs of choice in sexual selection. *J. Theoretical Biology* 128: 195-218.

Todd, P.M., and Miller, G.F. (1991). On the sympatric origin of species: Mercurial mating in the Quicksilver model. In R.K. Belew and L.B. Booker (Eds.), *Proceedings of the Fourth International Conference on Genetic Algorithms* (pp. 547-554). San Mateo, CA: Morgan Kaufman.

Zahavi, A. (1975). Mate selection--a selection for a handicap. *J. Theoretical Biology*. 53, 205-14.

Coevolution of a Backgammon Player

Jordan B. Pollack & Alan D. Blair
Computer Science Department
Volen Center for Complex Systems
Brandeis University
Waltham, MA 02254
{pollack,blair}@cs.brandeis.edu

Mark Land
Computer Science Department
University of California, San Diego
La Jolla, CA 92093
mland@cs.ucsd.edu

Abstract

One of the persistent themes in Artificial Life research is the use of co-evolutionary arms races in the development of specific and complex behaviors. However, other than Sims's work on artificial robots, most of the work has attacked very simple games of prisoners dilemma or predator and prey. Following Tesauro's work on TD-Gammon, we used a 4000 parameter feed-forward neural network to develop a competitive backgammon evaluation function. Play proceeds by a roll of the dice, application of the network to all legal moves, and choosing the move with the highest evaluation. However, no back-propagation, reinforcement or temporal difference learning methods were employed. Instead we apply simple hill-climbing in a relative fitness environment. We start with an initial champion of all zero weights and proceed simply by playing the current champion network against a slightly mutated challenger, changing weights when the challenger wins. Our results show co-evolution to be a powerful machine learning method, even when coupled with simple hill-climbing, and suggest that the surprising success of Tesauro's program had more to do with the co-evolutionary structure of the learning task and the dynamics of the backgammon game itself, than to sophistication in the learning techniques.

1.0 Introduction

It took great *chutzpah* for Gerald Tesauro to start wasting computer cycles on TD-Gammon (Tesauro92). Letting a machine learning program play itself backgammon in the hopes of bettering itself, indeed! After all, the dream of computers mastering a domain by self-play or "introspection" had been around since the early days of AI, forming part of Samuel's checker player (Samuel, 1959). Donald

Michie initiated machine learning work on reinforcement with his MENACE tic-tac-toe learner using matchboxes with the positions drawn on them (Michie, 1961). However such self-organizing systems had generally been fraught with problems of scale and representation and abandoned by the field of AI. Self-playing game learners often learn weird and brittle strategies which allow them to draw each other, yet play poorly against humans and other programs. Yet after millions of iterations of self-play, Tesauro's program has become one of the best backgammon players in the world (Tesauro, 1995) and his weights are viewed by his corporation as significant enough intellectual property to keep as a trade secret except to leverage sales of their minority operating system. (International Business Machines, 1995). However, Tesauro has published the weights for a player using a linear evaluation function called PUBEVAL, which we made use of as a yardstick. Others have replicated this TD result both for research purposes (Boyan, 1992) and reportedly in a commercial product called Jellyfish.

How is this success to be understood, explained, and replicated in other domains? Is TD-Gammon unbridled good news about the reinforcement learning method? For the idea of "conditioning" a machine with rewards and punishments has been rejected by modern cognitive science as part of the associationist paradigm based on its weak or non-existent internal representations. It has been brought back to life in modern machine learning form through work initiated by Klopf, 1982, Barto et al., 1983, and Sutton, 1984. Similarly, there is a lot of work in learning in neural networks following the explosive success of Back-Propagation at overcoming some limitations of the Perceptron(Rumelhart et al., 1986). However, with respect to the goal of a self-organizing learning machine which starts from a minimal specification and rises to great sophistication, TD-Gammon stands quite alone in both the reinforcement and neural network literature.

In general, the problem with learning through self-play is that the player could keep playing the same kinds of games over and over, only exploring some narrow region of the strategy space, missing out on critical areas of the game where it could then be vulnerable to other programs or human experts. Such a learning system might declare success when in reality it has simply converged to a "mediocre stable state" of continual draws or a long term cooperation which merely mimics competition. Such a state can arise in human education systems, where the student gets all the answers right and rewards the teacher with positive feedback for not asking harder questions.

The problem is particularly prevalent in self-play for deterministic games such as chess or tic-tac-toe. We have worked on using a population to get around it (Angeline and Pollack, 1994). Schraudolph et al., 1994 added non-determinism to the game of Go by choosing moves according to the Boltzmann distribution of statistical mechanics. Others, such as Fogel, 1993, expanded exploration by forcing initial moves. Susan Epstein, 1994, has studied a mix of training using self-play, random testing, and training against an expert in order to better understand this phenomenon.

Tesauro92 pointed out some of the features of Backgammon that make it suitable for approaches involving self-play and random initial conditions. Unlike chess, a draw is impossible and a game played by an untrained network making random moves will eventually terminate (though it may take much longer than a game between competent players). Moreover the randomness of the dice rolls leads self-play into a much larger part of the search space than it would be likely to explore in a deterministic game.

Our hypothesis is that the success of TD-gammon is not due to the Back-Propagation, Reinforcement, or Temporal-Difference technologies, but to an inherent bias from the dynamics of the game of backgammon, and the co-evolutionary setup of the training. In co-evolutionary learning, the desired task dynamically changes as the learner proceeds. We test this hypothesis by using a much simpler learning method for backgammon - namely hill-climbing - which retains the properties of self-play and initial randomness.

2.0 Setup

We use a standard feedforward neural network with two layers and the sigmoid function, set up in the same fashion as Tesauro with 4 units to represent the number of each player's pieces on each of the 24 points, plus 2 units each to indicate how many are on the bar and off the board. In addition, we added one more unit which reports whether or not the game is in the endgame or "race" situation, making a total of 197 input units. These are fully connected to 20 hidden units, which are then connected to one output unit that

judges the position. Including bias on the hidden units, this is a total of 3980 weights. The game is played by generating all legal moves, converting them into the proper network input, and picking the position judged as best by the network. We started with all weights set to zero. Our initial algorithm was hillclimbing:

i.   add gaussian noise to the weights

ii. play the network against the mutant for a number of games

iii. if the mutant wins more than half the games, select it for the next generation.

The noise was set so each step would have a 0.05 RMS distance (which is the euclidean distance divided by $\sqrt{3980}$).

Surprisingly, this worked reasonably well! The networks so evolved improved rapidly at first, but then sank into mediocrity (when tested against Tesauro's public domain evaluator PUBEVAL). The problem we perceived is that comparing two close backgammon players is like tossing a biased coin repeatedly: it may take dozens or even hundreds of games to find out for sure which of them is better. Replacing a well-tested champion is dangerous without enough information to prove the challenger is really a better player and not just a lucky novice. Rather than burden the system with so much computation, we instead introduced the following modifications to the algorithm:

Firstly, the games are played in pairs, with the order of play reversed and the same random seed used to generate the dice rolls for both games. This washes out some of the unfairness due to the dice rolls when the two networks are very close - in particular, if they were identical, the result would always be one win each. Though, admittedly, if they make different moves early in the game, what is a good dice roll at a particular move of one game may turn out to be a bad roll at the corresponding move of the parallel game. Secondly, when the challenger wins the contest, rather than just replacing the champion by the challenger, we instead make only a small adjustment in that direction:

champion = 0.95*champion + 0.05*challenger   (EQ 1)

This idea, similar to the "inertia" term in back-propagation, was introduced on the assumption that small changes in weights would lead to small changes in decision-making by the evaluation function. So, by preserving most of the current champion's decisions, we would be less likely to have a catastrophic replacement of the champion by a lucky novice challenger.

In the initial stages of evolution, two pairs of parallel games were played and the challenger was required to win 3 out of 4 of these games. Running this algorithm on an SGI workstation, we were able to get through about 15,000 generations per day.

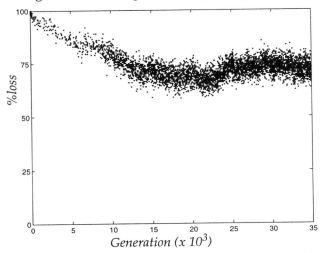

Figure 1: Percentage of losses of our first 35,000 generation players against PUBEVAL. Each match consisted of 200 games.

Figure 1 shows the first 35,000 players rated against PUBEVAL[1]. There are three things to note: (1) the percentage of losses against PUBEVAL falls from 100% to about 67% by 20,000 generations, (2) the frequency of successful challengers increases over time as the player improves, and (3) there are epochs (e.g. starting at 20,000) where the performance against PUBEVAL begins to falter. The first fact shows that our simple self-playing hill-climber is capable of learning. The second fact is quite counter-intuitive - we expected that as the player improved, it would be harder to challenge it! This is true with respect to a uniform sampling of the 4000 dimensional weight space, but not true for a sampling in the neighborhood of a given player: once the player is in a good part of weight space, small changes in weights can lead to mostly similar strategies, ones which make mostly the same moves in the same situations. However, because of the few games we were using to determine relative fitness, this increased frequency of change allows the system to drift, which may account for the subsequent degrading of performance.

To counteract the drift, we decided to change the rules of engagement as the evolution proceeds according to the following "annealing schedule": after 10,000 generations, the number of games that the challenger is required to win was increased from 3 out of 4 to 5 out of 6; after 70,000 generations, it was further

increased to 7 out of 8. The numbers 10,000 and 70,000 were chosen on an ad hoc basis from observing the frequency of successful challenges. We are currently investigating how an appropriate annealing schedule may be determined in a more principled manner as the evolution proceed by dynamically adjusting the standard deviation of the gaussian noise, currently fixed at 0.05, as well as the margin of victory required of the challenger. Of course each bout was abandoned as soon as the champion won more than one game, making the average number of games per generation considerably less than 8.

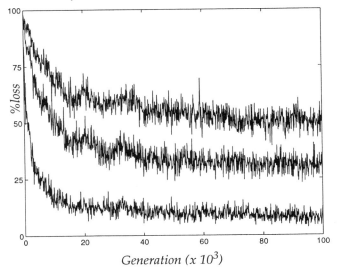

Figure 2: Percentage of losses against benchmark networks 1,000 [lower], 10,000 [middle] and 100,000 [upper]. This shows a noisy but nearly monotonic increase in player skill as evolution proceeds.

After 100,000 games, we have developed a surprisingly strong player, capable of winning 40% of the games against PUBEVAL. The networks were sampled every 100 generations in order to test their performance. Networks at generation 1,000, 10,000 and 100,000 were extracted and used as benchmarks. Figure 2 shows the percentage of losses of the sampled players against the three benchmark networks. Note that the three curves cross the 50% line at 1, 10, and 100, respectively and show a general improvement over time.

The end-game of backgammon, called the "bear-off," can be used as another yardstick of the progress of learning. The bear-off occurs when all of a player's pieces are in the player's home, or first 6 points, and then the dice rolls can be used to remove pieces. To test our network's ability at the end-game, we set up a racing board with two pieces on each player's 1 through 7 point and one piece on the 8 point as shown in Figure 3. In playing from this position, the skill involves knowing to first move the three pieces from the 7 and 8 points, and then aggressively removing

_____

1. PUBEVAL is quite a strong machine player (Tesauro, Personal Communication), trained on a database of expert preferences using comparison training. (Tesauro, 1989). Figures 1 and 4 have been corrected since an earlier release of this paper.

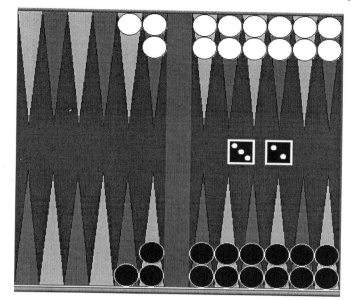

Figure 3: Starting position for bear-off trials

pieces rather than moving them around (which a random player might do). The graph in Figure 4 shows the average number of rolls to bear-off of each generation network playing itself using a set of 200 random dice-streams.

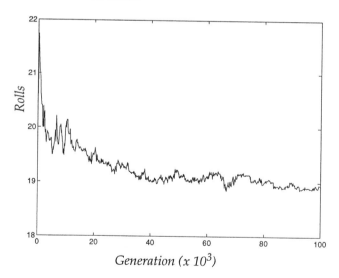

Figure 4: Average number of rolls to bearoff by each generation, sampled with 200 dicestreams. PUBEVAL averaged 16.6 rolls for the task.

3.0 Discussion

3.1 Machine Learning and Evolution

We believe that our evidence of success in learning backgammon using simple hillclimbing indicates that the reinforcement and temporal difference

methodology used by Tesauro in TD-gammon was non-essential for its success. The success came from the setup of co-evolutionary self-play biased by the dynamics of backgammon. Our result is thus similar to the bias found by Mitchell, Crutchfield & Graber in Packard's evolution of Cellular Automata to the "edge of chaos"(Packard, 1988, Mitchell et al., 1993).

TD-Gammon is a major milestone for a kind of evolutionary machine learning in which the initial specification of model is far simpler than expected because the learning environment is specified implicitly, and emerges as a result of the *co-evolution* between a learning system and its training environment: The learner is embedded in a learning environment which responds to its own improvements in a never-ending spiral. While this effect has been seen in population models, it is completely unexpected for a "1+1" hillclimbing evolution.

The process of co-evolution, as seen from evolutionary ecology, is of two species forming part of each other's environment and thus certain characteristics are co-adapted, either to an equilibrium or in a continuing arms-race. In Artificial Life, there have been many recent results on formal and computational ecology models which appear to have arms race dynamics (Holland, 1994, Kauffman, 1993, Ray, 1992, Lindgren, 1992).

The idea of machine learning based on evolution is most often thought of in terms of the genetic algorithm field pioneered by Holland (Holland, 1975). Much of this work however has become focused on optimization to a fixed goal expressed as an absolute fitness function. Using the idea of co-evolution in learning recognizes the difference between an optimization based on absolute fitness and one based on relative fitness (with respect to the rest of the population). This was explored by Hillis (Hillis, 1992) on the sorting problem, by Angeline & Pollack (Angeline and Pollack, 1994) on genetically programmed Tic-Tac-Toe players, on predator/prey games, e.g. (Cliff and Miller, 1995, Reynolds, 1994), and by Juille & Pollack on the intertwined spirals problem (Juille and Pollack, 1995). Rosin & Belew applied competitive fitness to several games (Rosin and Belew, 1995). However, besides Tesauro's TD-Gammon, which has not to date been viewed as an instance of co-evolutionary learning, Sims' artificial robot game (Sims, 1994) is the only other domain as complex as Backgammon to have substantial learning success.

3.2 Learnability and Unlearnability

Learnability can be formally defined as a time constraint over a search space. How hard is it to randomly pick 4000 floating-point weights to make a good backgammon evaluator? It is simply unlearnable. How hard is it to find weights better than the current set? Initially, when all weights are random, it is quite easy. As the playing improves, we would expect it to get harder and harder, perhaps similar to the probability of a tornado constructing a 747 out of a junkyard. However, if we search in the neighborhood of the current weights, we will find many players which make mostly the same moves but which can capitalize on each other's slightly different choices and exposed weaknesses in a tournament.

Although the setting of parameters in our initial runs involved some guesswork, now that we have a large set of "players" to examine, we can try to understand the phenomenon. Taking the 1000th, 10,000, and 100,000th champions from our run again, we sampled random players in their neighborhoods at different RMS distances to find out how likely is it to find a winning challenger. We took 1000 random neighbors at each of 11 different RMS distances, and played them 8 games against the corresponding champion. Figure 6 plots the average number of games

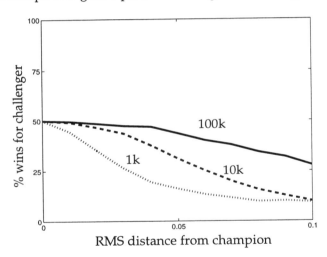

Figure 5: Distance versus probability of random challenger winning against champions at generation 1,000, 10,000 and 100,000.

won against the three champions in the range of neighborhoods. This graph demonstrates that as the players improve over time, the probability of finding good challengers in their neighborhood increases. This accounts for why the frequency of successful challenges goes up. Each successive challenger is only required to take the small step of changing a few moves of the champion in order to beat it. Therefore, under co-evolution *the unlearnable becomes learnable* as we convert from a single question to a continuous stream of questions, each one dependent on the previous answer.

3.3 Relative versus Absolute Expertise

Does Backgammon allow relative expertise or is there some absolutely optimal strategy? While theoretically there exists a perfect "policy" for backgammon which would deliver the best move for any position, and this perfect policy could exactly rate every other player on a linear scale, in practice it seems there are many relative cycles. Figure 6 shows a graph

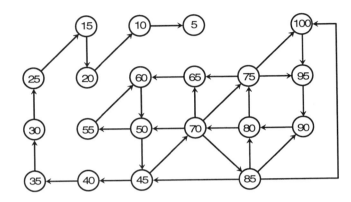

Figure 6: A partial graph of "who eats who", showing for each 5000th player, the immediate dominance relationships.

of the "food chain" over every 5000th player in our sequence of 100,000. By playing them 1000 games against each other and showing the dominance relations with arrows, we can see many relative expertise cycles, albeit with small margins of victory, such as [45,000 beats 70,000 beats 85,000 beats 45,000].

In spatial studies of iterated prisoners dilemma following (Axelrod, 1984), a stable population of "tit for tat" can be invaded by "all cooperate" which then allows exploitation by "all defect". This kind of relative expertise dynamics, which can be seen clearly in the simple game of rock/paper/scissors (Littman, 1994) might initially seen as very bad for self-play learning, because what looks like an advance might actually lead to a cycle of mediocrity. A small group of champions in a dominance circle might arise and hold a temporal monopoly preventing further advance. On the other hand, it may be that such a basic form of instability prevents the formation of sub-optimal monopolies and allows learning to progress.

3.4 Avoiding Mediocre Stable States

We are not suggesting that 1+1 hillclimbing is an advanced machine learning technique which others should bring to many tasks. Without internal cognition about opponents behavior, co-evolution usually requires a population. Therefore, there must be something about the dynamics of backgammon itself which is helpful because it permitted both TD learning, and hill-climbing, to succeed where they would clearly fail on other tasks and in other games of this scale. If we can understand why the backgammon domain led to successful acquisition of expert strategies from random initial conditions, we might be able to re-cast other domains in its image.

We believe it is not simply the dice rolls which overcome the problems of self-learning. Others have tried to add randomness to deterministic games and have not generally met with success. There is something special about backgammon which we suspect to be more critical; namely, the instability of the game with respect to predictions of winning. What is seen as exciting about backgammon to observers is that the outcome of the game continues to be uncertain until all contact is broken and one side has a clear advantage. There are many situations in backgammon where one dice roll, or an improbable sequence, can dramatically reverse which player is expected to win.

A learning system itself can be viewed as a meta-game, between teacher and student, which are identical in a self-play situation. The teacher's goal is to correct the student's mistakes, while the student's goal is to placate the teacher and avoid correction. A mediocre stable state for a self-learning system can be seen as an equilibrium situation in this meta-game. If the game includes draws, a player which learns to draw itself will have solved its meta-game equilibrium and stop learning. If draws are not allowed, it may be possible for a self-playing learner to collude with itself - to simulate competition while actually cooperating.[2] For example, if slightly suboptimal moves would allow a player to "throw" a game, a player under self-play could find a meta-game equilibrium by alternately throwing games to itself!

We cannot prove it yet, but our hypothesis is that the dynamics of backgammon discussed above actively prevent this sort of collusion from forming in the meta-game of self-learning.

4.0 Conclusions

We have noticed several weaknesses in our player that stem from the training which does not yet reward or punish the double and triple costs associated with severe losses ("gammoning" and "backgammoning") nor take into account the gambling process of "doubling." We are continuing to develop the player to be sensitive to these issues in the game. As noted in

(Sutton, 1988), the goals of good game playing and accurate position evaluation are not quite the same. In backgammon, the opponent's stable configuration is immutable in the course of a single move. This effectively partitions the space of positions into a large number of 'regions' in such a way that two moves from different regions are never directly compared. Indeed, preliminary studies on the evaluation of end-game situations suggest that our player does not operate by global position analysis. Rather, the opponent's configuration serves to multiplex an evaluation function that is then tuned to discriminate only those positions in the current region.[3]

TD-Gammon remains a tremendous success in Machine Learning, but the causes for its success have not been well understood. We do not claim that our 100,000 generation player is as good as TD-Gammon, ready to challenge the best humans, but it is surprisingly good considering its humble origins from hill-climbing with a relative fitness measure, and comparable to the players discovered by (Tesauro92) without advanced features. Interested players can challenge our evolved network using a web browser through our home page at:

http://www.demo.cs.brandeis.edu

Replicating some of TD-Gammon's success under a much simpler learning paradigm, we find that the Reinforcement and Temporal Difference methods are not the primary cause for success; rather it is the dynamics of backgammon combined with the power of co-evolutionary learning. If we can isolate the features of the backgammon domain which enable evolutionary learning to work so well, it may lead to a better understanding of the conditions necessary, in general, for complex self-organization.

Acknowledgments

This work is supported by ONR grant N00014-96-1-0418 and a Krasnow Foundation Postdoctoral fellowship. Thanks to Gerry Tesauro for providing PUBEVAL and subsequent means to calibrate it, Jack Laurence and Pablo Funes for development of the WWW front end to our evolved player, and comments from the Brandeis DEMO group, Brendan Kitts, and Chris Langton. The backgammon graphic was captured from xgammon, by Klasen and Steuer, distributed under the GNU general public license.

---

2. For example, in a prisoner's dilemma, if the payoff for temptation 7 instead of 5, the long term bonus for alternating defections (3.5) would be more rational than cooperating(3.0). See Angeline, 1994 for related discussion

3. Further work, incorporating look-ahead, might employ two networks: net A (for pruning) would be tuned to discriminate siblings in the game tree, while net B (for leaf evaluation) is tuned for global position comparison.

References

Angeline, P. J. (1994). An alternate interprestaion of the iterated prisoner's dilemma and the evolution of non-mutual cooperation. In Brooks, R. and Maes, P., editors, *Proceedings 4th Artificial Life Conference*, pages 353–358. MIT Press.

Angeline, P. J. and Pollack, J. B. (1994). Competitive environments evolve better solutions for complex tasks. In Forrest, S., editor, *Genetic Algorithms: Proceedings of the Fifth Inter national Conference.*.

Axelrod, R. (1984). *The evolution of cooperation*. Basic Books, New York.

Barto, A., Sutton, R., and Anderson, C. (1983). Neuron-like adaptive elements that can solve difficult learning control problems. *IEEE Transactions on Systems, Man, and Cybernetics*, 13.

Boyan, J. A. (1992). Modular neural networks for learning context-dependent game strategies. Master's thesis, Computer Speech and Language Processing, Cambridge University.

Cliff, D. and Miller, G. (1995). Tracking the red queen: Measurements of adaptive progress in co-evolutionary simulations. In *Third European Confrence on Artificial Life*, pages 200–218.

Epstein, S. L. (1994). Toward an ideal trainer. *Machine Learning*, 15(3).

Fogel, D. B. (1993). Using evolutionary programming to create neural networks that are capable of playing tic-tac-toe. In *International conference on Neural Networks*, pages 875–880. IEEE Press.

Hillis, D. (1992). Co-evolving parasites improves simulated evolution as an optimization procedure. In C. Langton, C. Taylor, J. F. and Rasmussen, S., editors, *Artificial Life II*. Addison-Wesley, Reading, MA.

Holland, J. (1975). *Adaptation in Natural and Artificial Systems*. The University of Michigan Press.

Holland, J. H. (1994). Echoing emergence. In Cowan, G., Pines, D., and Meltzer, D., editors, *Complexity: Metaphors, Models, and Reality*, pages 309–342. Addison-Wesley.

International Business Machines, (Sept. 12, 1995). IBM's family funpak for os/2 warp hits retail shelves.

Juille, H. and Pollack, J. (1995). Massively parallel genetic programming. In Kinnear, P. A. . K., editor, *Advances in Genetic Programming II*. MIT Press, cambridge.

Kauffman, S. A. (1993). *The origins of Order: Self-Organization and Selection in Evolution*. Oxford University Press.

Klopf, A. H. (1982). *The Hedonistic Neuron*. Hemisphere Publishing Corporation, Washington, D.C.

Lindgren, K. (1992). Evolutionary phenomena in simple dynamics. In C. Langton, C. Taylor, J. F. and Rasmussen, S., editors, *Artificial Life II*. Addison-Wesley, Reading, MA.

Littman, M. L. (1994). Markov games as a framework for multi-agent reinforcement learning. In *Machine Learning: Proceedings of the Eleventh International Conference*, pages 157–163. Morgan Kaufmann.

Michie, D. (1961). Trial and error. In *Science Survey, part 2*, pages 129–145. Penguin.

Mitchell, M., Hraber, P. T., and Crutchfield, J. P. (1993). Revisiting the edge of chaos: Evolving cellular automata to perform computations. *Complex Systems*, 7.

Packard, N. (1988). Adaptation towards the edge of chaos. In Kelso, J. A. S., Mandell, A. J., and Shlesinger, M. F., editors, *Dynamic patterns in complex systems*, pages 293–301. World Scientific.

Ray, T. (1992). An approach to the synthesis of life. In C. Langton, C. Taylor, J. F. and Rasmussen, S., editors, *Artificial Life II*. Addison-Wesley, Reading, MA.

Reynolds, C. (1994). Competition, coevolution, and the game of tag. In *Proceedings 4th Artificial Life Conference*. MIT Press.

Rosin, C. D. and Belew, R. K. (1995). Methods for competitive co-evolution: finding opponents worth beating. In *Proceedings of the 6th international conference on Genetic Algorithms*, pages 373–380. Morgan Kaufman.

Rumelhart, D., Hinton, G., and Williams, R. (1986). Learning representations by back-propagating errors. *Nature*, 323:533–536.

Samuel, A. L. (1959). some studies of machine learning using the game of checkers. *IBM Joural of Research and Development*.

Schraudolph, N. N., Dayan, P., and Sejnowski, T. J. (1994). Temporal difference learning of position evaluation in the game of go. In *Advances in Neural Information Processing Systems*, volume 6, pages 817–824. Morgan Kauffman.

Sims, K. (1994). Evolving 3d morphology and behavior by competition. In Maes, R. B. . P., editor, *Proceedings 4th Artificial Life Conference*. MIT Press.

Sutton, R. (1984). *Temporal Credit Assignment in Reinforcement Learning*. PhD thesis, University of Massachusetts, Amherst.

Sutton, R. (1988). Learning to predict by the methods of temporal differences. *Machine Learning*, 3:9–44.

Tesauro, G. (1989). Connectionist learning of expert preferences by comparison training. In Touretzky, D., editor, *Advances in Neural Information Processing Systems*, volume 1, pages 99–106, Denver 1988. Morgan Kaufmann, San Mateo.

Tesauro, G. (1992). Practical issues in temporal difference learning. *Machine Learning*, 8:257–277.

Tesauro, G. (1995). Temporal difference learning and TD-gammon. *CACM*, 38(3):58–68.

Artificial Worlds

Spatial Analysis of Artificial World

Atsushi Shinjoh
International Academy of Media Arts and Sciences
kaminari@iamas.ac.jp

Masanao Takeyama
Keio University, Faculty of Environmental Information
masanao@sfc.keio.ac.jp

Abstract

While behaviors of living systems in a real life are influenced by spatial factors such as distance and scale, these factors have never been dealt with explicitly in the study of artificial life. To overcome such deficiency, we applied geographical concetps and methodologies to analyze spatial behaviors of living systems in artificial worlds. As an example, an abstract model of city is simulated and analyzed follwong these spatial approaches. In particular, we put emphasis on the effect of spatial diffusion of information to the behavior of agents living in the artificial city. These results show two things. First is that this kind of synthetic methodology is effective to develop geography. Next is that the application of geographical analysis is effective to develop methodologies to study artificial life.

1 Spatial research

The principal object of the research of the type of creating the artificial world is to analyze the model of a variety built in the artificial world and the action of the individual more than creating the artificial world. These researches are not created the artificial world but analyzing some situations in the artificial world. It was that a research theme analyzed the change pattern of the actual surface of the earth from the 1950's in geography. These researches have been advanced since the order related to the change in the surface of the earth specially in quantitative geography was intended to be cleared up with economics, statistics, psychology, and so on.

Unfortunately, results of these researches have not been included in researches of artificial world. However these results must be introduced in an artificial world to make it a more precise thing.

In this paper, we introduce three spatial concepts ,"spatial diffusion", "spatial interaction" and "spatial behavior". These concepts are main theme of spatial analysis in geography. The point I want to make is that these spatial concepts aren't only adopted for researches of existent artificial worlds, and we proposed creative researches of artificial world as a new research theme which included these. The simulation that we show in this paper is a example of this theme. We analyzed influences from the effect of "spatial diffusion" of information to spatial changes of the surface of artificial world that was based on a spatial model in geography.

2 Spatial concepts and artificial world

While analysis of geography that have been targeting the actual surface of the earth made some individual theories and built an individual model, many ordinal models of artificial world were built with only creative imagination. So these models of artificial world do not include geographical spatial-concepts.

In this chapter, we discussed three points. To begin with, we discussed how a study of geography did lead spatial concepts. Then, we described the outline of three spatial-concepts. Finally, we showed some studies of unification of geography and various field of sciences.

2.1 Spatial analysis and abstraction

The main concept of formal geography was to describe a situation of the surface. On the other hand, it has been said that researches on spatial concepts have begun since "Geography as a science of the space" was proposed by Schaefer in 1953[20]. Although the challenge to examine the propositical surface was done in the various research area, these research results was re-analyzed and unified in geography.

There are two sorts of researches. One is to analyze mathematical data for which one statistics target technique was used. The purpose of this analysis is to predict based on statistics data. The other is to create models which show patterns of spatial arrangement. In 1826, "Isolated State Model" that is one of the oldest model in geography is built by Thünen who was a German, a researcher based through his agricultural experiences[25]. With this model, we can see the agricultural location pattern in isotropic plain. In 1909, Weber showed a "Industrial location model" [26]. In 1933, Christaller showed a "Central place model" that showed distribution of markets[5].

These two stances were advanced apart from each other since 1953, it began to contact each other after a discovery of spatial self-correlation by Cliff in 1975[7]. The general idea on spatial self-correlation is that shows a relationship between each spatial data and its neighborhood at one moment. Although it is a major promise that observation values are the mutual independence when the statistics method is applied, spatial self-correlation exists from data of the surface which is an object analyzed in geography. That is to say, it was showed that the analysis of database on the statistical methodology was not a correct one in geography. We have adopted spatial self-correlation in the statistical spatial analysis and three spatial concepts which has been analyzed.

2.2 Spatial concepts

Here, we discussed three concepts "Spatial diffusion", "Spatial interaction" and "Spatial behavior". Each concept made up with sociology, economics and psychology.

1. Spatial diffusion
   The concept "spatial diffusion" is a process what to occur in diffuse objects to surroundings. The diffusing process of time affiliated target copes with one of the space target.

   There are several researches on various field of spatial diffusion. Although the research area is specifications of several diffusing subjects such as an information, a technique and a system and spatial formations (or influences) based on these specifications, the main target in geography is a spatial diffusing process itself. Furthermore, spatial diffusion is interested in the analysis of the matter that an applicability seems to change. The simulation which we show in this paper belongs to this. In this simulation, agricurtual location patterns are changed by the spatial diffusion of the receptive subject which is a market information.

   Hägerstrand did research relation in spatial diffusion on the Swedish southern part[13]. He tried asking the fundamental general concept for using researches which was concerned with spatial diffusion of several receptive subjects based on analysis of spatial diffusion of farmer innovations(grass area's improvement by the government subsidy in objective area). In other words, his purpose is an analysis of informative and innovative process of time affiliated and spatial target, and to explain the spatial constructor and the spatial distribution based on a principle of spatial diffusion as neighborhood effects, resistance effects and barrier effects.

2. Spatial interaction
   Spatial interaction is movements between the area of two or more specifying, the place and interchange. The following three kinds of research have been advanced still now.

   (a) Spatial structures concerned with mathematical distributions.
       It is that analyzing spatial structures to let these space structures go in the numerical value distribution. One of the typical research of these is the gravity model introduced from the sociophysics[23]. The gravity model is an analogy of universal gravitation. Although an adaptation of this gravity model

to flowing phenomena was always good, the theoretical basis was poor in the beginning.

While Wilson found that an expression which high flowing patterns of the realization are described shows the shape which approximated information entropy, and he called flowing quantity for space entropy. So he built up an entropy maximization spatial interaction model[28], and the theoretical basis of gravity model was proved because expressions of Wilson model and gravity model are same structure. At present, this model is being used as the most general spatial interaction model.

   (b) Spatial structures concerned with probability of spatial distribution.
       This research is analysis of probability of spatial distribution such as migration or interchange. This concept is good for comparing several area because it is possible that actions of various behavior subjects are compared. However there is no research example in the investigation as well much because data of the number of others are necessary and are difficult to analyze these data.

   (c) Spatial structures concerned with processes of spatial equilibrium.
       This research is that analyzing the process of migration pattern from spatial imbalance to spatial equilibrium. However methods in these days are only linear programming and the malcov chain model. The development of the new technique is hoped for.

3. Spatial behavior
   It must be made clear that the space processes where to be occurred and to be formed it appreciating the space structure. Spatial behavior is spatial phenomena in the surface of the earth and spatial processes creating and formatting spatial structures. There are three approaches to analyze spatial structures described in this section, and researches of spatial behavior are especially paying special attention to next two processes.

   (a) A series of mental processes such as individual's spatial perception, spatial preference and decision making.
   (b) Relation to the mutual regulation between spatial structure and spatial behavior.

   Most of models about space target behavior are on the way to conceptualizing the general idea modeling. Based on these two processes, modeling toward the following three relations is necessary.

   (a) Relation between spatial structure and mental map.
   (b) Relation between mental map and spatial behavior.
   (c) Relation between spatial behavior and spatial structures.

   Quantitative modeling has already been done about (a) by Gould[12]. About (b), although the research was started by Clark, quantitative modeling has not been done yet[6]. The research about (c) has not been done either. So modeling which to unify these three relation has not been done yet.

2.3 Unification of geography and various field of science

The concept on complex and the research area of dynamically modeling based on computer simulation were introduced to a geographical modeling by Allen[1][2][18]. Concepts on fractals and chaos were also introduced by Goodchild, White and Rosser[11][19][27]. Except these physical concepts, researches of unification between cellular automata and geographical modeling has already been done[3][4].

3 Modeling and simulation

This model is the dynamical simulation model based on "Isolated state model" for analyzing various spatial structures. In this paper, we paid special attention to the influence of information's spatial diffusion to the dynamics of cultivated patterns.

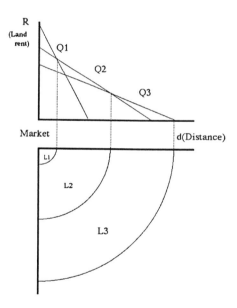

Figure 1: Isolated State Model

3.1 Isolated state model

In 1826, Thünen who is a researcher of agriculture built up "Isolated state model" that is a agricultural location model based on his agricultural experiences and analysis of cultivated patterns. This model showed the cultivated pattern paying special attention to transferring costs on the surface of abstracted isotropic plane. Lösch formulated this model in 1940. Various researches such as the analysis of spatial structures of the city is done at present[15].

The model which he announced is based on following suppositions.

1. There is a city and a market on the center of this plain.

2. There is no river or canal in this plain. Coaches are only transportation method.

3. This plain is isotropic and each farmer can farm at any place except the market.

4. This area is isolated from another area.

Then he asked following questions. "How does the distance from farm to market influence to agriculture when each farmer is economic man[1]?." Then he proposed following propositions. "Products of the soil which transfer costs are high in the suburbs of city, and agricultural patterns of this plain shows the structure of concentric circles."(Figure.1)

The Figure.1 includes two figures. The above graph shows the relationship between land lents(the vertical axis) and distances from the market(the horizontal axis) to a farm. Each straight lines, Q1, Q2 and Q3 assign the products. The point which Line Q1 and Line Q2 crosses shows that land rents of two products correspond. The below figure shows the pattern of farm. The product Q1 farms in the area L1, the product Q2 farms in the area L2. That is to say, The product which transfer costs are highest is Q1.

1. Modeling
   When we built up the simulation model, we added three suppositions.

   (a) We located 120 farmers in this plain.
   (b) The market price changes based on the law of supply and demand.
   (c) A number of products which each farmer can cultivate are two at each term.

   Then we made rules for farmers.

   - All farmers must cultivate and make a product at every term.
   - Each farmer gets information about the prices of all products and information of neighborhood's strategy, income at this term, and property.
   - Each farmer must decide which product will it cultivate based on the information and the strategy.
   - Each farmer has a strategy which is encoded by the genetic algorithm.[10]

2. Simulation
   In this simulation, each term consists of three phases.

   (a) Farm phase
       In this phase, all farmers must cultivate the one product.
   (b) Market phase
       In this phase, quantities of all products and market prices are decided by:

---
[1]Economic people's behavior is based on its income. Its acts so that income may rise.

$$P_k = \alpha(D_k - S_k) + P_{k-1} \qquad (1)$$

$$D_k = \beta D_{k-1}(1 + \frac{P_{k-1} - P_{k-2}}{P_{k-1}}) \qquad (2)$$

P:Market price of a product, D:Demand, S:Supply, α:fixed value, β:fixed value, k:term number.

(c) Strategy phase

In this phase, the strategy of each farmer has possibility of changes(crossover and mutation). We assume that two different changes mean two different situations.

- Crossover

This operation assumes following situations. If profits which one of its neighboring farmers earn are more than profits which a farmer earns at each term, a farmer may imitate the method of cultivation which its neighboring farmer used. As a result of this operation, the farmer creates a new strategy based on its old strategy and its neighborfood's strategy.

This operation is done as follows:

if R_{x-near} - $R_x \geq 0$,

$$CrossRate_{(x)} = \frac{R_{x-near} - R_x}{R_x} \qquad (3)$$

$CrossRate_{(x)}$:The crossover rate of farmer x. R_x:The income of farmer x. $x - near$: A neighbor of farmer x.

- Mutation

This operation assumes that a farmer may change its mind when its income decrease from the last term. When this operation has done, a part of this farmer's strategy is changed.

This operation is done as follows:

if $R(x_k)$ - $R(x_{k-1}) \geq 0$,

$$MutationRate(x_k) = \frac{R(x_k) - R(x_{k-1})}{R(x_k)} \qquad (4)$$

$MutationRate(x_k)$:The mutation rate of farmer x at k term. $R(x_k)$:The income of farmer x at k term.

4 Simulation results and Discussion

4.1 Simulation

In this analysis, we simulated following situations.

1. When spatial diffusion of information is off, and noise is off.

2. When spatial diffusion of information is off, and Noise is on.

3. When spatial diffusion of information is on, and noise is off.

4. When spatial diffusion of information is on, and noise is on.

Figure 2: The dynamics of market prices

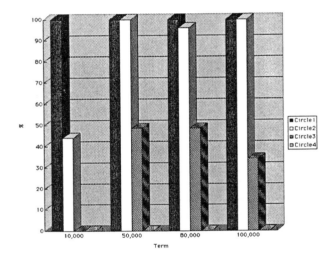

Figure 3: The occupation rates of product "a"

When "spatial diffusion of information" is off, all farmers get several information from the market directly. When the "spatial diffusion of information" is on, all farmers get information from its neighborhood except farmers who cultivate beside the market.

When the "noise" is on, the information which farmers get are wrong in the fixed probability. In this simulations, we set this fixed value 5%. All farmers can't know whether the information is right or wrong.

- Spatial diffusion of information

We made rules about "spatial diffusion of information". The rules are only used when the following concepts are used.

1. Farmers who cultivate beside the market are only get information from market directly.

2. Farmers who don't cultivate beside the market are only get information from its neighbor farmers.

3. It takes one term that each farmer receive the information and communicated to another farmers. That is to say, it takes time for diffusion of informations.

4.2 Simulation results

Here, we showed eight graphs as results of simulations.

- Graph(Figure 3, 5, 7, 9.)
  These graphs are time series graphs and indicate the fluctuation of one product's(this product is called "a") price in the market. The transport cost of product "a" is the highest of all products.

- Graph(Figure 4, 6, 8, 10.)
  These graphs indicate the rates which the products "a" occupied in each agricultural land(The farm land is the fourfold concentric circles.) at each term when the term = 10,000, 50,000, 80,000 and 100,000. The circle 1 is at the side of the market. The circle 4 is most outside of concentric circles.

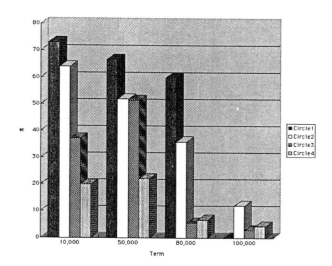

Figure 5: The occupation rates of product "a"

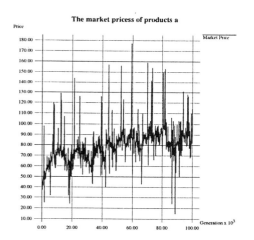

Figure 4: The fluctuation of market prices

3. When spatial diffusion of informations is on, and noise is off(Figure 6, Figure 7).
   Spatial diffusion led very characteristic results. Various strategies occurred between 80,000 term and 70,000 term. One characteristic strategy spread out to the whole area since 80,000, and finally, products which a transport cost was low were cultivated at the whole area.

4. When spatial diffusion of information is on, and noise is on(Figure 8, Figure 9).
   We expected that this result and above No.3's result showed similar patterns. However these were quite different. The information noise led various strategies. This variety of strategy obstructed characteristic patterns(as No.3's result).

1. When spatial diffusion of information is off, and noise is off(Figure 2, Figure 3).
   The structure of the products showed the structre of concentric circles. That is to say, the products which transfer costs were high were cultivated at beside market. Therefore this simulation model got the structure of Thünen's proposition. In the "Circle 1", the products "a" were cultivated(See, Figure 4). There was a steep rise at 22,000 term. The spatial structure were changed. This was because new farmers joined the simulation instead of farmers who went bankrupt at this term.

2. When spatial diffusion of information is off, and noise is on(Figure 4, Figure 5).
   Influences of the noise were big, and the dynamics of prices didn't become stable all the time. Because of this, many farmers went bankrupt.

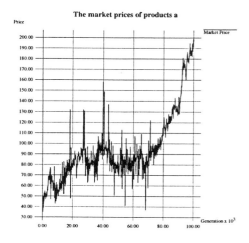

Figure 6: The fluctuations of market prices

When all farmers can get information at same time, its can behave as a "economic man". In this situations,

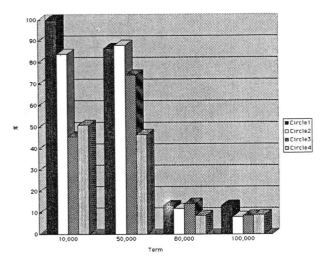

Figure 7: The occupation rates of product "a"

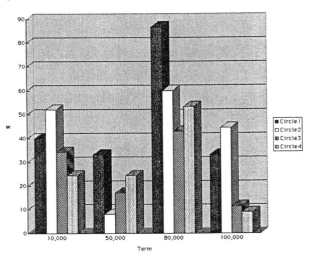

Figure 9: The occupation rates of product "a"

effects of noises are big, and the structure of "Isolated state model" collapsed. The No.1 shows that there are possibility of structural change based on new farmer's behavior.

When spatial diffusion of information is on, characteristic patterns were occurred. In this situations, one characteristic strategy occured and was adopted by most of farmers. These results showed that these two different information transmission effected the spatial structures and each farmer's strategies.

Figure 8: The fluctuations of market prices

As a result, these results show following things. The first is that formations of concentric circles show many patterns finally, while most of formally studies in geography said that the formation show a one pattern finally. The next is that there is a relation between the dynamics of cultivated patterns and information's spatial diffusion.

5 Conclusion

In most of formal simulations, causes of fluctuations or dynamics are planned when the simulation model is built. However in most of artificial worlds, fluctuations or dynamics were caused by each agent's behavior or interactions. Multi Agents System and learning algorithms (Neural Network, Lyndenmayer system, genetic algorithm and so on.) make these method possible.

On the other hand, some theoretical studies which were paid special attention to local bevavior or interactions have already done. Luman applied Auto poiesis system to social system and proposed that dynamics of the social system was caused by local interactions[16][17].

These studies shows the importance of each agent's behavior or interactions. Our model also adopted these concepts. Though this model was not a detailed model, simulation results said that spatial concepts directly effected to system's dynamics and the process of information transmission was very important factor for analyzing fluctuations of patterns of area. When we apply this model to real area and built up this in detail, we can use to predict the urban growth.

These results let us highly to recommend the importance of spatial concepts.

6 Future Works

We must analyze data of these simulation results in detail paying special attention to the farmer's strategy .

And we are going to apply our model of artificial world to the urban planning[22].

7 Acknowledgments

We are grateful for useful advices to Takemochi Ishii, Junjiro Takahashi and Michitaka Hirose. We are also grateful for useful discussion to Kazuo Jose Takagi, Amy m Iwanaga, Ken Chikaraishi, Hiloko Nakagawa, Reiko Uji and Shigeru Kuroda.

References

[1] Allen, P. M., Sanglier, M.(1979): A dynamic model of growth in a central place system. Geographical Analysis.

[2] Allen, P. M., Sanglier, M.(1981): A dynamic model of growth in a central place system II. Geographical Analysis.

[3] Bak, P., Tang, C.(1989): Earthquakes as a self-organized critical phenomenon. Journal of Geophysical Research, 94(B11), 15635-15637.

[4] Batty, M.(1991): Generating urban forms from diffusive growth. Environment and Planning **A**23, 511-544.

[5] Christaller, W.(1933): Die zentralen Orte in Süddeutschland. Gustav Fischer, Jena, 331S.

[6] Clark, W. A. V.(1972): Behaviour and the Constrains if Spatial Structure. New Zealand Geographer, Vol.28, 171-180.

[7] Cliff, A. D. et al.(1975): Elements of Spatial Structure. Cambridge University Press, Cambridge.

[8] De la Maza, M., Yuret, D.(1994): A Future Market Simulation with Non-Rational Participants. Artificial Life IV, MIT Press, 325-330

[9] Gibson, J. J.(1950): The Perception of the Visual World. Allen and Unwin:London.

[10] Goldberg, D. E.(1989): Genetic Algorithms in search, Optimization and Machine Learning. Addison Wesley

[11] Goodchild, M., Mark, D. M.(1987): The Fractal Nature of Geographical Phenomena. Ann. Association of American Geography. **77**, 265-178.

[12] Gould, P. R., White, R. R.(1968): The Mental Maps of British School Leaves. Regional Science, Vol.2, 161-182.

[13] Hägerstrand, T.(1966): Aspects of the Spatial Structure of Social Communication and the Diffusion of Information. Regional Science, 16, 27-42.

[14] Langton, C. G.(1989): Artificial Life. Artificial Life, Addison-Wesley.

[15] Lösch, A.(1940): Die räumliche Ordnungder Wirtschaft. Fischer, Jena.

[16] Luman, N.(1988): Die Wirtschaft der Gesellschaft, Suhrkamp Verlag Frankfurt am Main.

[17] Maturana, H.R., Varela, F. J.(1980): Autopoiesis and cognition:The realization of the living. D.Reidel Publishing Company, Dordrecht, Holland.

[18] Prigogine, I., Allen, P. M., Herman, R.(1977): The laws of Nature and the Evolution of Complexity. New York:Pergamon.

[19] Rosser JR, J. B.(1994): Dynamic of Emergent Urban Hierarchy. Chaos , Solutions & Fractals , Pergamon,4,553-561

[20] Schaefer, F. K.(1953): Exceptionalism in geography:a methodological examination. American Geography 43, 226-249

[21] Shinjoh, A. et al.(1995): An analysis on the emergent behavior of a virtual market system. The Third European Conference of Artificial Life, Abstract book.

[22] Shinjoh, A.(1996): An analysis on the City surrownding us with Hypothetical-Media. Keio University.

[23] Stewart, J. Q.(1947): Empirical Mathematical Rules Concerning the Distribution and Equilibrium of Population. Geographical Review, Vol. 37

[24] Toquenaga, Y. et al.(1994): Contest and Scramble Competitions in an Artificial World: Genetic Analysis with Genetic Algorithms. Artificial Life III. Addison-Wesley, 177-200

[25] von Thünen, J. R.(1827): Der Isolierte Staat, English translation, 1966, von Thünen's Isolated State. Pargamon Press, Oxford.

[26] Weber, A.(1920): On the Location of Industries. Univ. of Chicago Press.

[27] White, R., Engelen, G.(1993): Fractal urban land use patterns: A cellualar automata approach. Envir. Plan. **A**25 1175–1199

[28] Wilson, A. G.(1967): A statistical theory of spatial distribution models. Transportation Research, **1**,253-269.

Functional Emergence with Multiple von Neumann Computers

Hideaki Suzuki

Elemental Research Lab. 14
Honda R&D Co., Ltd. Wako Research Center
1-4-1 Chuo, Wako-shi, Saitama 351-01, Japan
Email: h_suzuki@f14k.f.rd.honda.co.jp

Abstract

An evolutionary programming methodology in which multiple von Neumann computers evolve through genetic algorithms (GAs) is proposed and simulated. A bit sequence in the program memory owned by the computer is composed of numerous machine codes, each of which has some computational function in the CPU. In the selection operation of GAs, a single machine code is neutral or deleterious in fitness by itself, and an appropriate combination of machine codes (an appropriate subroutine) can achieve the advantageous function which promotes its reproduction in GAs. Through the evolutionary simulation using GAs, these subroutines are created and fixed in the population one by one, and the higher function, which enables the computer to answer the expected value from the environments, finally emerges in the program memory. Under different sets of parameters, the evolutionary speed, determined by the time until this emergence, is examined and the conditions for achieving faster evolution by crossover are clarified. Randomizing the bit distribution in the program memory, crossover helps create novel advantageous subroutines and plainly accelerates the emergence of the final advantageous program at an intermediate mutation rate and at an intermediate population size. GAs are a fast and effective tool for functional emergence in this sequential programming methodology.

1 Introduction

For the spontaneous emergence of the function in the multiagent system through evolution, a designer (man) must refrain from designing agents to excess and make agents behave as freely as possible based upon the rules within themselves. All the designer can do is to implement the system architecture and to specify the environments. The von Neumann machine, which is logically equivalent to the universal Turing machine, can do everything based upon its own rules (the program in the memory) and hence is the most suitable architecture of agents for functional emergence. Such machines, after installation into some appropriate environments and evolution, can attain any higher functions in their program.

In all evolutionary adaptive systems, multiplication is the final purpose after which agents strive. The emergence of the function of agents are always directed to

this purpose; hence when some resource helps multiplication, it becomes a target of acquisition by agents. In the core memory in which a number of self-reproducing programs are shut up in the same memory and compete with each other, CPU time and the memory space facilitate the reproduction, hence programs grow increasingly smarter through evolution in obtaining these resources [1, 2]. Recently Adami [3] succeeded to impose another task (adding two numbers) on the core memory agents by use of an additional bonus. A bonus is awarded to the program which fulfills the task prepared by the designer, effectively converted into CPU time, and eventually facilitates self-reproduction. Though in his strategy the whole program is not devoted to the task imposed by the designer, the created program was composed of two parts i.e., the self-reproducing part and the task managing part, and met the requirements from both the program itself and a man. This is one example of the ways to make the inherent purpose of the evolutionary system compatible with engineering demands.

Genetic algorithms (GAs) [4, 5] are another method with which to impose the human requirement on agents more directly. In GAs, reproduction is not put in agents' hands but fulfilled by the program prepared by the designer. Released from the duty of self-reproduction, the whole program of an agent is devoted to accomplishing the task requested by the man. The fitness score indicating how well each agent copes with the task is used for determining its reproduction rate. This selection strategy enables GAs to direct evolutionary growth towards functional emergence which is useful for humans.

In the previous studies on GAs, however, the inner architecture of agents under genetic operations was too simple to create higher functions. An agent is typically a bit sequence coding a solution for some specific problem; the bit string coding the route for the traveling salesman, the bit string describing the state transition matrix of the finite state automaton, etc. Although in Artificial Life approach a designer must refrain from designing agents to excess, we must at least implement their basic architecture so that they might create higher functions based upon it.

In this paper, I propose a paradigm in which multiple von Neumann machines (MUltiple von Neumann Computers; MUNCs) evolve and create the function. Each machine is a standard computer system with hardware architecture consisting of CPU and memory. (Unlike core memory programs, machines are not put in the same memory, but prepared apart.) Each machine can independently read or write one common environmental database. GAs operate on the bit sequence (the binary representation of program) in the memory of machines and, through optimization by GAs, the functional program which can output the right answer and obtain a high reward, emerges. Since in this context the environmental database is prepared apart from the program memory, the designer can bury any problem which he wishes to make machines solve. This supplies an auto-programming tool in the sequential programming architecture, and at the same time a machine learning system, especially, a system inducing a general rule from examples.

In the following, I first demonstrate one definite implementation of MUNCs and their environment, together with the recursion strategy with GAs (section 2). After describing some results given by the simulation (section 3), I discuss the significance of MUNCs and the performance of GAs within the framework of MUNCs (section 4).

2 The Model

The basic concept of MUNCs and their environment is illustrated in Figure 1. A large number of computer systems (von Neumann machines) and their environment are prepared apart. Each computer system has a definite hardware architecture consisting of CPU and a program memory and can read or write its environmental database independently of the others.

Though the inner architecture of MUNCs is essentially user-defined and can be chosen freely by the designer, I present in this paper one concrete implementation of MUNCs and their environment, which is utilized for the numerical experiments about the GA performance in the succeeding sections.

2.1 Inner Architecture of the von Neumann Machine

Figure 2 shows the internal architecture of a von Neumann machine. It includes several registers (*id*, *en*, *ck0*, and so on), a stack (*ST_a*), and a memory (*GN*). Functions of registers are summarized in Table 1.

A program, that is a long sequence of bits in *GN*, is composed of many sequential machine instructions. Each instruction is coded in a short bit string (a small binary

```
       id: 7fe9          GN[]
       en:    0 (dec.)    sf_a
                          de_d
      ck0:  181 (dec.)    x_a4
      ck1:    0 (dec.)    m_da
                          m_ba
        a: d40c           x_a2
        b: 0006           m_ba
  fl(pnz):  010           m_bE
                          m_bE
       ep: 015f           m_da
       dp: 000c           m_Db
       DO: 0006           br_p
                          in_d
                          ph_a
                          t_ab
     ST_a[]          gp▶ in_d
     350c               de_d
     6a0c               m_ba
     d40c               sf_a
 sp_a▶ 0000             br_n
     0000               m_ab
     0000               rs_a
     0000               rs_a
     0000               x_a0
                        x_a4
                        in_d
                        br_n
                        br_p
                        br_n
                        x_a4
                        m_ab
                        m_ab
```

Figure 2. Internal architecture of a computer

Register	Function
id	Contains the identification number of the machine.
en	Contains the energy (reward) from the environment.
ck0,ck1	Clock counter used for determining the end of action.
a, b	Freely used registers.
fl	Contains flag bits 'positive', 'negative', and 'zero'.
ep	Points to the sample set of environments.
dp	Points to the address of environments.
DO	Contains the calculated answer.
sp_a	Stack pointer in *ST_a*.
gp	Instruction pointer of *GN*.

Table 1. Function of registers

number; hereafter we denote this with *mcd*). Figure 3 shows the list of mnemonic codes of the instruction set, together with their computational functions (register operations) shown in the comment lines. In this example the total number of instructions is $M_{mcd} = 22$. In Figure 2 each machine code is written with this mnemonic code in the array of *GN*.

During the active period of time, the CPU reads and decodes the machine code pointed by *gp* and executes the corresponding register operation, after which the value of *gp* is increased by one. When *gp* exceeds the memory size $I_{gp} = 32$, *gp* is reset to zero. Therefore all instructions in *GN* are executed cyclically until the end of action is reached.

The end of action is judged using two counter registers, *ck0* and *ck1*. The value of these registers are zero at the beginning of the active period, and are increased by one each time the machine operation is executed. If the value of *ck1*, which is reset to zero when the value of *DO* is changed by the register operation, exceeds a certain number $C_{k1} = 2 \cdot I_{gp}$, we judge *DO* to be saturated

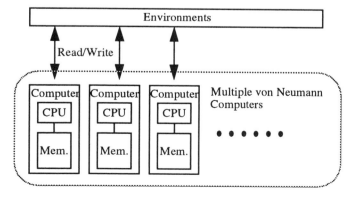

Figure 1. Basic concept of MUNCs and their environment

```
switch(mcd){
    case  0: rs_a(); break; /* a <- 0 */
    case  1: sf_a(); break; /* a <- a<<1 (shift) */
    case  2: x_a0(); break; /* a <- a^1 (exclusive-OR) */
    case  3: x_a1(); break; /* a <- a^2 (exclusive-OR) */
    case  4: x_a2(); break; /* a <- a^4 (exclusive-OR) */
    case  5: x_a3(); break; /* a <- a^8 (exclusive-OR) */
    case  6: x_a4(); break; /* a <- a^16 (exclusive-OR) */
    case  7: ph_a(); break; /* push a */
    case  8: pp_a(); break; /* pop a */
    case  9: m_ab(); break; /* a <- b */
    case 10: m_ba(); break; /* b <- a */
    case 11: t_ab(); break; /* fl <- p,n,z of a-b */
    case 12: br_p(); break; /* if p(fl)==1, gp <- gp+1. */
    case 13: br_n(); break; /* if n(fl)==1, gp <- gp+1. */
    case 14: br_z(); break; /* if z(fl)==1, gp <- gp+1. */
    case 15: m_da(); break; /* dp <- a */
    case 16: de_d(); break; /* dp <- dp-1 */
    case 17: in_d(); break; /* dp <- dp+1 */
    case 18: m_aE(); break; /* a <- ENI[ep,dp] */
    case 19: m_bE(); break; /* b <- ENI[ep,dp] */
    case 20: m_Da(); break; /* DO <- a */
    case 21: m_Db(); break; /* DO <- b */
}
```

Figure 3. Instruction set (Mnemonic code and register operation)

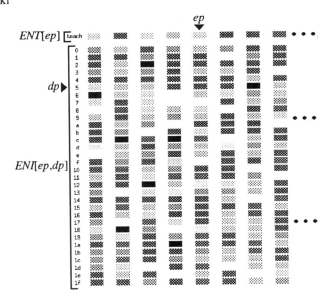

Figure 4. Environments (Database of problems)

and stop executing the machine. If the value of $ck0$, which can increase infinitely regardless of the value of DO, exceeds a large number $C_{k0} = 8 \cdot I_{gp}$, we also stop executing the machine. The latter judgement prevents the machine from moving endlessly with periodical change of the value of DO. Owing to above judgement of the end of action, the time resource (number of clocks) rationed to each machine is logically infinite. This eliminates the selective pressure related to the time resource and helps increase the algorithmic complexity of programs.

Note that neither jumping instructions (which can substitute gp with some far distant value) nor stopping instructions (which designate the end of action) are allowed in Figure 3. If such instructions were used, non-executed region would be able to exist in GN, which would extraordinarily reduce the evolutionary speed.

2.2 Environments (Problem Database)
Figure 4 shows the environmental database $ENI[ep,dp]$ used in this simulation. The database is composed of a large number of samples, each of which is one-dimensional sequence of integers. Each von Neumann machine can read an integer specified by the sample pointer ep and the address pointer dp. The values of ep or dp are limited by the total number of samples $L_{ep} = 512$ or the number of integers included in a sample $L_{dp} = 32$, respectively. In Figure 4, one sequence of integers (one sample) is lined up in a vertical column of rectangles, and the first eight samples are lined up horizontally.

The gray level of each rectangle indicates the value of the integer. (White expresses 0 and black expresses the maximum value $E_{max} = 30$.) Each value is randomly chosen within the interval $[0, E_{max}]$ at the beginning of the simulation and, after that, kept unchanged because the writing instruction is not included in the instruction set in Figure 3.

Note that the machine can change the value of dp using **m_da**, **de_d**, or **in_d**, whereas it cannot change the value of ep because the instruction which can read or write ep is not allowed in the present model. The value

of ep is chosen randomly by the designer each time a machine begins execution, and kept unchanged during the execution. ep is "invisible" to the machine itself so that the environment which virtual agents "see" is logically one-dimensional.

A top rectangle for each sample, preceded by the label "teach" in Figure 4, is the teaching number (right answer) $ENT[ep]$ specified by the designer. In this example, $ENT[ep]$ is the larger of the two values $ENI[ep,7]$ and $ENI[ep,8]$;

$$ENT[ep] = \max(ENI[ep, 7], ENI[ep, 8]). \qquad (1)$$

If the final answer stored in DO is equal to this value and the final value of $ck0$ is smaller than C_{k0}, the value of the energy register en is set to one, and set to zero otherwise. Thus the machine which can output the right answer can reap a large reward from the environments.

2.3 Evolution with Genetic Algorithms
GAs are used for optimizing the sequence of binary bits in the program memory GN. A large number of computers having the inner architecture described above are prepared and evolutionary operations are performed considering the bit sequence in GN to be a haploid genome. This searches for the novel codes and creates the functional program in GN. The simulation proceeds in the following steps:

Step 0: [Initial setting] Prepare N von Neumann computers and substitute the random binary numbers for the program memory GN.

Step 1: [Execution] For each machine, decode the program in GN and execute CPU operations until being judged to reach the end of action. After that, substitute the energy register with one or zero, according to the value of DO. This step is practiced for all machines one after another.

Step 2: [Selection] Scale the value of the energy register en (see Equation (2)). In proportion to the scaled values of *en*'s, select *N* machines randomly and create their copies. Let the binary program in *GN* of a new machine be copied from its parental machine. This create a new population of machines for next generation (the standard process of roulette selection.)

Step 3: [Mutation] Choose machine codes randomly out of all *GN*'s and replace them with random machine codes. The number of machine codes subjected to this modification is determined by the mutation rate *u* (probability of replacement per machine code per generation).

Step 4: [Crossover] Choose *r* fraction of machines out of the population and pair them randomly. Between each pair, recombine binary strings in *GN*'s with the occurrence probability of the cross-point being equal to 0.5 at every interbit gap. Hence in this mode, most matings have about half as many cross-points as they have bits. This way of crossover operation is "MPIP" (many-points minor-participants) mode defined in [6]. The crossover rate in this mode is effectively specified by the participation ratio *r*. After that, return to Step 1.

In Step 2, the value of energy register *en* is scaled with parameter $K_{sel} = 5.0$ using

$$en \to \exp(K_{sel} \cdot en). \qquad (2)$$

With this scaling, the value 0 is changed into 1 and the value 1 is changed into 148. This selection operation facilitates the reproduction of machines that have large values of *en* (reward). Generation cycle (repetition of Steps 1~4) is directed by this operation and brings about emergence of the functional program that can output the right answer shown in Figure 4.

The program for the simulation was written in the ANSI-C language and run on a desk-top MIMD computer, Parsytec XPLORER equipped with sixteen Power-PC's (80MHz).

3 Results of Experiments

3.1 Discontinuous Evolution

Figure 5 shows a typical result of the experiment with $N = 2048$, $u = 0.003$, and $r = 0.1$. In Figure 5a, three values are plotted as functions of generation number:

· diversity (heterozygosity) given by

$$H = \langle H(gp) \rangle_{gp} = \langle 1 - \sum_{mcd} \{f(gp, mcd)\}^2 \rangle_{gp}, \qquad (3)$$

where $\langle \ \rangle_{gp}$ means an average over all addresses of *gp* and $f(gp, mcd)$ is the frequency of *mcd*-th machine code in the population at address *gp*;
· ability which is the mean population value of the energy register *en* after execution (before scaling);
· error which is the normalized mean population difference between the final answer and the teaching value, given by

$$error = \langle |DO - ENT[ep]| / E_{max} \rangle_{pop}, \qquad (4)$$

where $\langle \ \rangle_{pop}$ means an average over the whole population.

Figures 5b~5d show the frequency matrices $f(gp, mcd)$, where the gray level of each cell represents the frequency. (White represents zero and black represents one.) The vertical column of cells on the right--

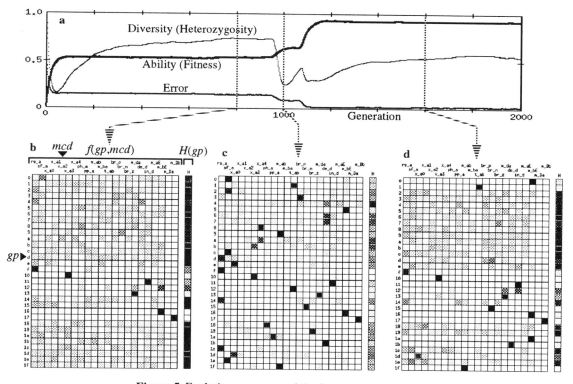

Figure 5. Evolutionary curve and the frequency matrix (a typical result)

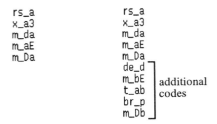

a. *ENI*[*ep*,8]-program   **b.** *ENT*[*ep*]-program

Figure 6. Useful set of codes in the typical emergent program

hand side of each matrix indicates the heterozygosity $H(gp)$ defined in Equation (3).

The program that outputs the right answer is obtained through the following steps. Firstly, immediately after the initial setting, a program which always answers *ENI*[*ep*,8] (we call this the '*ENI*[*ep*,8]-program') emerges in some individual and dominates the population. In the *ENI*[*ep*,8]-program, typically only five machine codes (see Figure 6a) are useful and the other machine codes are useless. (The term 'useful' means that the register operation of the machine code contributes to the calculation of the final answer in *DO* and 'useless' means it gives no contribution.) This domination makes the population diversity suddenly decrease because all machine codes in that individual also spread over the population on account of very strong selection and less than complete recombination. (This effect is called "hitchhiking" in population genetics.) After that, mutation and crossover, which take place at a constant rate, randomize the bit distribution. Of course these operations occur randomly regardless of the function of bits, but a modification occurring in the useful region is deleterious because it almost always destroys the program for outputting *ENI*[*ep*,8], whereas a modification occurring in the useless region is neutral unless it hinders the calculation by the useful codes. Deleterious modifications in the useful region are eliminated quickly from the population by selection, and consequently, sufficiently after the emergence of the *ENI*[*ep*,8]-program, the population is uniform in the useful region and diverse in the useless region. Figure 5b shows the population in this state, where $H(gp)$ is small (white) only in the portion of useful machine codes. Then after some time, additional useful codes are created by chance in the useless region of some individual and the program which can answer *ENT*[*ep*] (we call this the '*ENT*[*ep*]-program') emerges. This program consists of typically ten useful machine codes (see Figure 6b). The individual with this program can reap a large reward from the environments and hence spreads over the population quickly. Hitchhiking reduces $H(gp)$ in whole region of *GN* again (Figure 5c), and after that, mutation and crossover diversify the population in the useless region (Figure 5d).

In this result, the final *ENT*[*ep*]-program is created through evolution which proceeds as neutral evolutionary phases [7] and intermittent adaptive evolutionary phases. In neutral phases, mutation and crossover randomize bit sequences mostly in currently useless regions and pre-

pare candidates for the next useful codes, and in adaptive phases, selection spreads the new advantageous program through the population. Evolutionary growth curve in Figure 5 is stairlike with two steps, in each of which a new useful set of codes (subroutine) is added to the program and the mean population fitness increases largely and rapidly on account of its very large selective advantage. Using Equation (2) and $K_{sel} = 5.0$, their fitness advantage is easily estimated. The fitness advantage of the *ENT*[*ep*]-program relative to the *ENI*[*ep*,8]-program is

$$1 + s \equiv \frac{\exp(K_{sel} \cdot 1)}{\frac{1}{2}\exp(K_{sel} \cdot 0) + \frac{1}{2}\exp(K_{sel} \cdot 1)} \sim 2.0. \quad (5)$$

Similarly, the fitness advantage of the *ENI*[*ep*,8]-program relative to the program which outputs an arbitrary number in *DO* is 13.3.

3.2 Evolutionary Speed for the Functional Emergence

We then study with simulation the speed of evolution which leads to the emergence of the final function under various parameter values. Let T_d (the domination time) be the number of generations from the initial setting to the time when the error defined by Equation (4) grows smaller than 0.1 (this means the domination of the *ENI*[*ep*,8]-program). Numerical trials are executed twenty times and the 10% trimmed mean value is calculated as a result for each set of parameters.

Figure 7 shows the result of T_d as a function of the crossover rate r under different mutation rates u. The population size is taken to be $N = 2048$. Generally speaking with this figure, with a higher u, T_d is smaller. The dependence upon r under three values of u is as

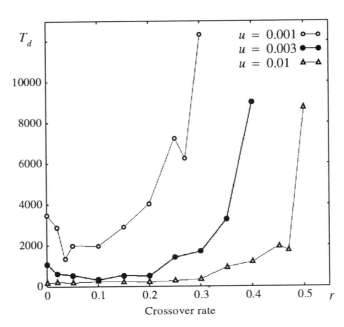

Figure 7. Evolutionary time as a function of the crossover rate

follows. When u is high ($u = 0.01$), T_d is kept small in the region of lower r and increases extraordinarily in the region of higher r. When u is intermediate ($u = 0.003$), T_d decreases with r in the region of lower r and increases extraordinarily in the region of higher r. The dependence under the lowest u ($u = 0.001$) is similar to that under the intermediate u, but the reduction ratio of T_d by r is smaller than under the intermediate u. Under these two values of u, the crossover rate has the intermediate optimum value $r = 0.1$ that makes T_d minimum.

In the following, we explain above results based upon the population genetic argument. Because the $ENI[ep,8]$-program occurs immediately after the initial setting on account of the initial diverse distribution, the domination time T_d is roughly determined by the time from the domination of the $ENI[ep,8]$-program to the domination of the $ENT[ep]$-program. As stated in the previous subsection, the domination of a new useful set of codes falls into three steps and T_d is decomposed into three parts.

$$T_d = T_v + T_c N_d + T_s, \qquad (6)$$

where T_v (the diversification time) is the waiting time until sufficient sequence diversity is stored in currently useless regions of the program memory, T_c (the creation time) is the waiting time until the appearance of the useful set of codes in the sufficiently diverse population, N_d (the destruction number) is the average number of appearances of the useful set of codes from its absence until it begins to spread, and T_s (the spread time) is the necessary time for the new useful set of codes to spread and dominate the population. In the present model, s given by Equation (5) is so large that T_s is negligibly small. We consider the effect of mutation and crossover on T_v, T_c, and N_d separately.

The dependence of T_d in the region of lower r is explained as follows. Since both mutation and crossover are randomization processes which help create a new sequence of bits, T_c is reduced by either operation. However, when u is sufficiently high ($u = 0.01$), the bit sequences are sufficiently randomized by mutation only and crossover is unnecessary for acceleration. When u is very low ($u = 0.001$) on the other hand, the population diversity is small (see Equation (7)) and crossover cannot be effective because, unlike mutation, the randomization by crossover is effective only when a crossover pair of bit sequences is heterogeneous. Crossover itself cannot increase the heterozygosity H, hence it does not affect T_v. T_v can be reduced only by mutation. (When u is very low, T_v grows very large which also diminishes the reduction ratio of T_d by crossover.) Thus there exists an intermediate optimum mutation rate in which the creation of a new useful bit sequence is accelerated most effectively by crossover.

By means of the population genetic calculation regarding each machine code as a gene, we can get the theoretical formula of H. In the steady state of the finite population under neutral mutation processes,

$$H \sim \frac{2N_e u}{1 + 2N_e u}, \qquad (7)$$

where N_e is the effective population size. (In the present roulette selection, $N_e = N$.) The approximations $u \ll 1$, $M_{mcd} \gg 1$, and $N_e \gg 1$ are used in derivation ([7] chap.8).

An extraordinary increase of T_d in the region of higher r is explained with the destruction number N_d. Even if a new useful set of machine codes is created by mutation or crossover, when its fitness is not very advantageous over the others, it is destroyed and eliminated after a few generations. This increases N_d extraordinarily and brings about the divergence of T_d. In order for a created useful sequence of bits to overcome this destruction process and to begin to spread through the population, the following condition must be satisfied.

$$(1 + s)(1 - uI_{add})(1 - r) > 1, \qquad (8)$$

where I_{add} is the number of useful machine codes included in the new additional subroutine (typically $I_{add} = 10 - 5 = 5$; we call this the functional length). The left-hand side of Equation (8) is the product of rates of increases in the frequency of a new created useful set of machine code through selection, mutation, and crossover. (See [6] for the accurate derivation.) Using Equation (5) and the approximation $uI_{add} \ll 1$, Equation (8) gives the condition $r < 0.5$, which agrees the threshold value above which T_d grows extraordinarily large in Figure 7. Thus at the intermediate mutation rate u, there exists the intermediate optimum crossover rate that minimizes the domination time T_d. Below this value the creation time T_c is large and above this value the destruction number N_d grows large.

3.3 Acceleration Rate by Crossover

Next we study with simulation how much the emergence of the $ENT[ep]$-program is accelerated by crossover. The acceleration rate is measured with A_{cross}, that is defined as T_d at $r = 0$ divided by T_d at $r = 0.1$. Figure 8 shows the result, A_{cross} as a function of the mutation rate u under different population sizes N. This figure states that A_{cross} is maximum at an intermediate u (the same result as Figure 7) and at an intermediate N.

This result is explained as follows. When N is small,

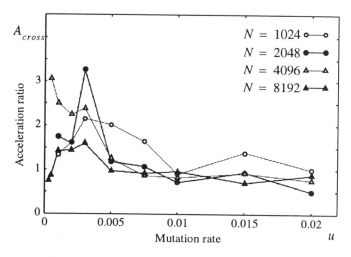

Figure 8. Evolutionary acceleration ratio by crossover

the diversity that the population can store is small (Equation (7)) and crossover cannot be effective. This makes reduction of T_c by crossover small and decreases A_{cross}. When N is very large, on the other hand, the creation time grows small in inverse proportion to N. This makes T_c small relative to T_v and A_{cross} grows small. Thus in the present model, crossover accelerates evolution most effectively at an intermediate population size. A more quantitative study about this acceleration effect will be given in [8].

4 Discussion

An evolutionary autoprogramming strategy, i.e., MUNCs and their environment was proposed and simulated. The evolution was driven by GAs and the final function was achieved through additions of useful sets of machine codes with advantageous functions. From the simulations under different values of GA parameters, evolution was most accelerated by crossover at an intermediate mutation rate and at an intermediate population size.

We now discuss some implications of above results and argue about the performance of GAs.

4.1 Genetic Algorithms applied to Bit Sequences with Functional Hierarchy

With MUNCs, GAs are combined with the Tierra-like machine language to formulate an autoprogramming strategy in the sequential programming architecture. GAs here optimize the bit sequences in the program memory GN which has the functional hierarchy "bit/instruction/subroutine/program". The computational operation by a single instruction is neutral or deleterious in fitness, and a machine enjoys very large selective advantage only when all machine codes constituting an useful subroutine are present in the same individual. This is one of the most essential point in MUNCs driven by GAs. Above fitness discontinuity makes the evolutionary growth curve conspicuously discontinuous (Figure 5) and evolutionary speed has come to be determined by the length of the neutral evolutionary time, i.e., the waiting time until the creation of a novel advantageous subroutine. As is discussed in succeeding subsections, the evolutionary acceleration effect by crossover comes from the reduction of this time.

The functional hierarchy in GN is much similar to the functional structure of the genome in DNA. The genome is a very long nucleotide sequence including many genes as functional units. Each gene is translated into a protein which activates some chemical reaction in a cell. A particular set of genes makes some highly advantageous function such as a metabolic cycle, and a great number of useful sets of genes constitute a whole organism and activate it. Thus the genome also has the hierarchical structure "nucleotide/gene/a set of gene/genome" and fitness is a discontinuous function of those units.

Although GAs were originally devised after the living genetic system which has such functional structure, genetic operations in previous studies of GAs have used for the optimization of bit sequences whose functional structure has no similarity to the living system. As a consequence, the performance of GAs has been reported diversely in literatures depending upon the fitness landscape in searching space. If GAs are applied to the optimization of the bit string which has the same functional structure as the living system has, it can have evident effectiveness as is shown in Figure 8.

4.2 Evolutionary Acceleration by Crossover

Crossover is the most characteristic operation in GAs. In this subsection, we discuss the evolutionary acceleration effect by crossover and clarify the effectiveness of GAs within the framework of MUNCs. The arguments are made as to three genetic parameters, the mutation rate, the population size, and the functional length.

4.2.1 Mutation Rate and Error Catastrophe

Although both mutation and crossover are methods for generating sequence diversity on which selection can operate, there is an important difference between them in the evolutionary outcome. Mutation, which is a random modification of bit sequences, destroys the sequences regardless of their frequencies in the population, whereas crossover affects only the polymorphic region in the population. This means that mutation destroys the established function but crossover does not destroy the codes that are already fixed in the population.

As a consequence, when we wish to make a long program with MUNCs, we must carefully choose the mutation rate u. This problem is generally known as "error catastrophe" [9]. In [6] the population genetic simulation was conducted about this matter and the following condition was obtained; no matter how advantageous a created program is, it cannot be maintained in the population if it does not satisfy

$$u \cdot I_{tot} \leq 1 - f_t. \tag{9}$$

Here I_{tot} is the total number of useful machine codes included in the program and f_t is the threshold frequency above which the program is judged to dominate the population. Therefore, if we wish to make a highly functional program with MUNCs, we must keep u very low because a higher function is almost always achieved by the program with large I_{tot}. In Figure 7, emergence of useful programs was evidently accelerated by crossover in lower u. If u must be kept low to maintain long programs, crossover can compensate the loss of randomization by mutation and accelerate evolution. This makes crossover an indispensible process for faster evolution in MUNCs. In the core memory approaches without this delicate crossover operation [1, 2, 3], it was concluded that for faster evolution the mutation rate must be as high as the error catastrophe does not occur.

4.2.2 Population Size and Functional Length

According to Figure 8, the emergence of the final program is certainly accelerated by crossover, but the maximum acceleration ratio A_{cross} is only about three. This is due to the small functional length $I_{add} = 5$ in the present model. As described in subsection 3.3, the creation time T_c is roughly inversely proportional to N. Hence, when new advantageous sequences of small length are searched with sufficiently large population N, creation is achieved in small generations so that T_c cannot be dominant in the domination time T_d and A_{cross} is diminished. If I_{add} were larger than 5, however, T_c would be extraordinarily large even with large N so that the reduction process of T_c by crossover would be dominant in evolution which would make A_{cross} much larger than three. A delicate crossover operation is an indispensible process as well when we try to create a long highly functional subroutine at a time in MUNCs. This is probably the reason why in [3], several subgoals had to be provided along the way to the final program.

4.3 Implementation of Genetic Algorithms

The basic assumption of GAs, the "building block hypothesis" [4], states that crossover combines several good subsolutions into a single individual to create an optimum solution of the problem. Such good subsolutions are called "schemas" and are considered to spread with "implicit parallelism" [5]. The fundamental theorem of GAs, "the schema theorem" [5] guarantees their spreads, which says that schemas of small *order* and small *defining length* are more likely to spread.

Recently Mitchell, Forrest, and Holland [10] assumed the discontinuous fitness function similar to the present one and studied the GA performance. They found that hitchhiking (they call this 'premature-convergence phenomenon') drops the GA performance and cast doubt on the implicit parallelism. However, they had a notion that crossover is useful in combining good schemas so that they only studied the GA performance taking notice of the time necessary for lower-order schemas to combine to form the higher-order schema.

If the merit of using the crossover operation comes from evolutionary acceleration such as is shown in Figures 7 and 8, however, crossover is useful not because it can combine good schemas to create an optimum solution, but because it can randomize bit sequences to create a good schema (here, a schema means a subroutine). This randomization and creation process by crossover is nothing more than that by mutation, and hence the advantage of crossover is lost when the mutation rate is sufficiently high (Figure 7).

The building block hypothesis, if it means that the final solution is composed of many good subsolutions (schemas), is correct, but in MUNCs, such component schemas emerge not parallel but serially (one by one). Because of a very large selective advantage, a good subroutine is completely fixed in the population immediately after its occurrence, which makes the schema resistant to the destruction process by crossover. Crossover, which is effective in the polymorphic region in the population, selectively randomizes the unestablished region and helps create a new good schema while preserving many old good schemas regardless of their order or defining length.

The primary points for the implementation of GAs which result from the arguments presented up to now are as follows.

· The fitness discontinuity due to the hierarchical structure of function in the bit sequence is essential.

· The relative fitness advantage of subroutines to be fixed must be large enough to satisfy Equation (8).

· When the final program is short, the mutation rate can be kept sufficiently high and the novel program can be quickly searched for even without crossover.

· When the subroutine that must be created at a time is short, the waiting time until its creation is so small in sufficiently large population that the creation acceleration effect by crossover is ineffective.

· When the final program is long and the subroutine created at a time is long, crossover significantly accelerates the emergence of the functional program.

Acknowledgments

It is a pleasure to acknowledge Professor Y. Iwasa, Kyushu University, for his helpful discussion on the simulation model and the analysis of results. The author also thanks Dr. Thomas S. Ray for his comments to the previous version of the manuscript. Professor T. Ikegami, Tokyo University, provided me with information about the literature cited in this paper.

References

1. Ray, T. S. (1992). An approach to the synthesis of life. In C. G. Langton et al. (Eds.), *Artificial Life II*: Proceedings of an Interdisciplinary Workshop on the Synthesis and Simulation of Living Systems (Santa Fe Institute Studies in the Sciences of Complexity, Vol. 10), (pp. 371-408) Reading, MA: Addison-Wesley.

2. Ray, T. S. (1994). Evolution, complexity, entropy, and artificial reality. *Physica, D 75*, 239-263.

3. Adami, C. (1995). Learning and complexity in genetic auto-adaptive systems. *Physica, D 80*, 154-170.

4. Holland, J. H. (1992). *Adaptation in Natural and Artificial Systems*. Boston: MIT Press.

5. Goldberg, D. E. (1989). *Genetic Algorithms in Search, Optimization and Machine Learning*. New York: Addison-Wesley.

6. Suzuki, H. The optimum recombination rate that realizes the fastest evolution of a novel functional combination of many genes. submitted to *Theor. Population Bio.*

7. Kimura, M. (1983). *The Neutral Theory of Molecular Evolution*. Cambridge: Cambridge Univ. Press.

8. Suzuki, H. The optimum recombination rate that realizes the fastest evolution of a novel functional combination of many genes. II. Effect of the finite population size. in preparation.

9. Eigen, M., Gardiner, W., Schuster, P. & Winkler, R. (1981) The origin of genetic information. *Sci. Amer. 244*, 88-118.

10. Mitchell, M., Forrest, S., & Holland, J. H. (1991) The royal road for genetic algorithms: fitness landscapes and GA performance. In F. J. Varela et al. (Eds.), *Toward a Practice of Autonomous Systems*: Proceedings of the First European Conference on Artificial Life (pp. 245-254) Cambridge, MA: MIT Press.

ccr: A network of worlds for research

David H. Ackley
Department of Computer Science
The University of New Mexico
Albuquerque, New Mexico

Abstract

Experienced artificial life world builders know the long-term evolution of a system depends heavily on its size, and that individual computers today, still, support only modest worlds. Vastly richer worlds are possible if we can meet the challenges of designing for large-scale, distributed implementation. **ccr** is an Internet-based software system in development as a common environment for human and artificial agents. With themes such as artificial life, information access, agents, entertainment, and interactivity, **ccr** is ultimately an *evolution management* system, dedicated to enabling interdisciplinary research on—and in—a complex, open-ended, shared artifact.

1 MANIFESTO

The biggest problem facing computer science today is how to go parallel. Broadly construed, this includes not only parallel and distributed computing, networks, distributed AI, and so on, but also the evolution of protocols and standards, and cryptography and computer security generally. The classical Von Neumann architecture has delivered miracles, but as a conceptual organization it is largely tapped out. To design and build future computation and communication networks, we will either learn from or be forced to rediscover evolutionary biology, which, from the beginning, has dealt with parallel and distributed processing under resource and reliability limits, conflicting individual and collective goals, and limited trust. Artificial life research can and should, but to date has yet to, inform and unify these efforts.

The central tenet of the project is that "living systems" and "information systems" refer to the same class of systems. The research goals are both theoretical and practical: To understand better the connections between 'information' and 'life', and to design, build, deploy, and evolve experimental systems that explore and extend the 'living computation' framework.

2 OVERVIEW

ccr is the working name[1] of a distributed environment for fostering and studying interactions between human and software life. The project focuses on a basic dilemma in distributed-system research: Even to uncover the real issues one must field a system with a significant number of machines and users, but as the 'mass' of the system grows it becomes more and more difficult to evolve the system structurally, to respond to the issues that are discovered.

The **ccr** vision is of a non-proprietary software system that retains evolvability and remains of moderate size over the long term—say, hundreds to thousands of machines and users, as a target—by drawing its users initially and principally from the interdisciplinary population of investigators whose research is facilitated by the existence of the system, and who are thus motivated both to shape the directions of, and put up with the overhead of, continued system evolution. Compared to proprietary commercial systems aimed at mass markets, **ccr** would be large enough to be relevant while small enough to avoid a competitive threat, and could serve as a vendor-independent technology and demand driver in addition to enabling basic research that could not be conducted safely or at all on commercial systems.

Version 0.1, the second prototype developed for the project, now comprises some 52K lines of C and another 11K of Tcl [16] and **ccrl**, and is in active development and testing in a "universe" of a dozen or so interconnected worlds. Though primitive, largely undocumented, and crash-happy, pathways are clearing toward

---

[1]I.e., the pre-version 1.0 name. As of 3/31/96 the version was v0.1.86¯(2)¯. To the question "What does **ccr** stand for?" the canonical response is "Whatever you want it to stand for," to underline the goal of bottom-up, user-driven system evolution. Similarly, those who want **ccr** to be an acronym are invited to make up expansions to suit their needs, or select from *caricature cartoon clearwater communication community competitive computation connected cooperative creedence reality reconsidered realized reified research revealed revival rooms.*

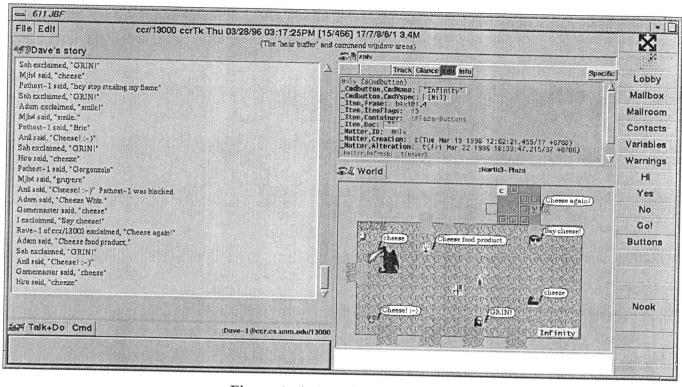

Figure 1. A view of a **ccrTk** world.

a system tamed enough for adventurous interdisciplinary researchers—and this fifth artifical life conference is a good opportunity to offer an overview as development proceeds. In addition to essentially all of the computer sciences, **ccr** needs perspectives from art, biology, ecology, economics, literature, political science, psychology, and sociology, to name a few.

This document is a first introduction to **ccr**, briefly considering both general themes and more technical issues. To anchor the discussion and provide a recurring example, Figure 1 presents a recent snapshot taken in **ccrTk**, currently **ccr**'s primary graphical interface world. Section 3 compares the **ccr** strategy to other alife research methodologies. Section 4 introduces version 0.1 specifically, touching on the interface language **ccrl**, the computation and communication model, and the object system. Section 5 concludes with riffs on methodology and the meaning of life. For more current information and plans for the system, visit http://-www.cs.unm.edu/~ackley/ccr.

3   A RESEARCH MACROCOSM, WITH PEOPLE

ccr breaks with most artificial life systems in a major way by presuming an *open world*, both in that humans are expected to interact with the system while it is running, and in that the underlying physical implementation—the computers and communications

links—is expected to change dynamically. Three consequences of this approach are: Research strategies change because global repeatability is sacrificed, humans must be enticed to use the system, and the tradeoffs between security, efficiency, and power must be addressed, not only early and fundamentally, but continually and at many levels.

3.1   Repeatability is unscalable

A great virtue of closed-world alife models is that *every* detail is determined by the researcher, so every observation can be reproduced, and utterly controlled variations can be tested. The price is that comparatively small worlds must be studied. With ingenuity, much has been and remains to be learned from such worldlets, and the possible richness of high-isolation worlds grows with improvements in affordable individual computers, but of course single-owner systems cannot compete with large collaborative networks of systems. The irony is that as computer systems become more like living systems—more complex and articulated, more robust and interconnected—they become less suited to closed-world artificial life research. Ray's NetTierra proposal [18] offers one compromise position, in which repeatability is explicitly sacrificed but isolation is mostly preserved.

3.2 Humans are evolutionary forces

ccr approaches the dilemma another way, trading the isolated clarity of lab work for the symbiotic relevance of field work. **ccr** proposes to be a strictly non-proprietary [8] experimental platform, controlled by and for its research users, providing a venue within which software for computation and communication tasks—"agents," "brokers," "robots," etc.—can be created, copied, hybridized, allowed to cooperate and compete for "market share" and perhaps win through into the base **ccr** standards and protocols.

As in typical alife systems, the overall "fitness functions" are supplied by humans; on the other hand, in **ccr** humans are also a source of novelty and change, conflicting with the Darwinian principle of blind variation. Given the nature of complex adaptive systems [11], and the gap between the manifest *intentionality* of the individual human action and the *unintentional* effects that often ensue, it is an empirical question just how un-Darwinian the evolution of a substantial **ccr** universe would actually be.

3.3 Security is biology

Communication entails risk [1]: A message sender necessarily reveals information in the act, and a message receiver is necessarily impacted in some way by the act, or else no communication has occurred. The dual tasks—of revealing some information while hiding some, and of allowing selected influences while rejecting others—are fundamental to the structure and function of living systems, from cell walls to immune systems, crucial to the very notions of self and independent existence.

A price exacted by the oft-touted mobility of a "software agent" is that it doesn't control the physical hardware that embodies it, so to protect its integrity it must either hide from or ally with the machine owner. Computer viruses take the former route; **ccr** takes the latter, committing to reveal to the owner the tradeoffs between safety and power as obviously and intuitively as possible, and placing its source code on the table as *bona fides*. In turn, in a general release of **ccr**, the hardware owners would commit to playing within the system[2] and would place their digital signatures on the table co-signed by existing **ccr** users (the bottom-up "web of trust" approach [20]) and/or an appropriate external certification authority [19]. Various flavors of anonymity can be created within the system, but only built upon a base of identified owners, shifting risk from loss of integrity to loss of anonymity. It is an open question whether special-purpose protected hardware could in principle be "owned" by the system itself, which could allow the construction of robust "public spaces" with known and re-liable rules of behavior, *inside* of independently-owned computers—and if so, under what circumstances would wise owners choose to incorporate it.

While technologies such as digital signatures [19] are necessary, security is much more than a purely technical issue, and so the purely technical power of the system must have corresponding limitations. In **ccr**, as in most high-isolation alife systems [17, 6] as well as emerging commercial systems such as Java [9], the basic approach to limiting communication risk via limiting power is to control the semantics of the *language* in which communications are expressed. Though Java significantly improves security from the "language on down", as a general purpose programming language, its approach to trust is at the level of the program and is largely boolean—you either grant a disturbing amount of power to an incoming Java 'applet' or you don't run it at all. As a research system, **ccr** sacrifices some speed and generality to gain fine-grained access control at multiple points including each function invocation, directly supporting intuitive and ccr-specific degrees and modes of trust and risk.

4 A TOUR OF VERSION 0.1

Though primitive compared to where it needs to be for widespread use, version 0.1 is already quite rich—possessing, for example, a fairly well-developed computational and communications model, a (and please excuse the jargon) multiply-inheriting runtime-extensible persistent object-oriented interpreted language with incremental network object and type cache updating, the graphical user interface world **ccrTk**, and the text-only **ccrt**—and it is difficult to know where to begin to describe it. The hands-on approach is to sit down with somebody at a pair of machines, walk them through building a "genesis" world for themselves, then show them how we build a "netdoor" between their world and mine, and then have them over for a visit. Here, an overview of the **ccrl** language serves as a backbone upon which to hang brief discussions of related topics: the user interface, the execution engine, and some basic object types—such as &Matter and &Energy—that are key elements of the **ccr** "metaphysics."

4.1 ccrl

Version 0.1 speaks a quirky language called **ccrl**[3] that mediates communications between a **ccr** world and its environment, which consists principally of humans, other **ccr** worlds, files, and spawned subprocesses. **ccrl** is more akin to an application scripting language or an object-oriented MUD programming language [3] than to a conventional development language, in that it developed out of and in tandem with **ccr**. In spots it carries

---

[2]Which includes researching attacks to devise defenses; in that spirit **ccr** 0.1 provides an "award" system to honor and memorialize the publicizers and fixers of holes.

[3]Pronounced via spelling or as *crawl* to emphasize one of its annoying quirks.

evolutionary baggage dating back at least to 1992 (version 0.1.23); a redesign based on experiences thus far is certainly warranted, but the issues are complex and the language serves adequately for the present.

4.2 Hello world

It is a tradition in presenting programming languages to begin with the "Hello world" program, which does nothing except output "Hello world" in whatever form the system most naturally supports. In different languages the program may range from a line or two up to dozens or more, and traditionally there are minor bragging rights attendant to shorter solutions. Figure 2 presents the Hello World program in **ccrl**, and typical results of executing it. **ccrl** minimizes this program just about as far as it will go. Basic input and output are built deeply into the language, rendering the Hello World task trivial, but performing the exercise does highlight how the choice of "Hello *World*" as the traditional first task—as opposed to, say, "Hello *Dave*"—reflects the fact that typical programming systems are utterly oblivious to both *who's programming* and *who's out there listening*, while to **ccr**, for example, such matters are of paramount significance. As may be suspected from Figure 1, **ccrTk**

(a)   Hello World↵
(b)   I said "Hello World"
(c)   Dave-1 said "Hello World"

Figure 2. *(a)* The "Hello world" program in **ccrl** (↵ denotes the Return key); *(b)* What I observe; *(c)* What others in the area observe.

worlds reduce the Hello World task still further, to a single mouse-click on a predefined "Hi" button—but that is indeed a cheat, since Hello World is meant to be at least a template for producing strings in general, and programming the buttons is a more complex procedure. As a template for **ccrTk**, Figure 2a is buggy in that certain initial characters are significant. Figure 3 lists some of the **ccrTk** reader's initial character shortcuts and their expansions as general **ccrl** object descriptions; a more general **ccrTk** Hello World program, similar in approach to MUD languages [3], is

'Hello world↵

In addition to "speaking" in various ways, shortcuts are available for moving around, pushing, opening, closing, and inspecting objects, and so forth.

As new users get more comfortable acting in their own world, they sometimes are irritated to discover how limited their powers are when they are visiting other worlds, until they appreciate the fundamental symmetry of the distributed **ccr** universe—every user is at once a "god" on their own world and a mere "mortal" when visiting

other worlds, and to first-order if you can't do it to their world, then *they* can't do it to *your* world. This symmetry can be impacted in various ways by world-local programming, but it appears so far that the early architectural choice of a peer-to-peer universe, rather than a client-server one—so that, for example, all users are "home owners" with something to lose—was sound.

```
'→[Say text "•"]     :→[Pose text "•"]
;→[Be text "•"]      !→[TimeOut at •]
?→[Focus on •]       *→[Teleport to •]
+→[Open object •]    <→[Get at • field ]
-→[Close object •]   >→[Set at • field  to ]
```

Figure 3. ccrTk keyboard shortcuts and expansions. (• denotes the cursor.)

4.3 Building

The expansions in Figure 3 suggest the general syntax of **ccrl**:

[*TypeName slotname slotvalue slotname slotvalue* ...]

where each *slotname* names a local variable declared by *TypeName* or one of its ancestor types. When handed to a **ccrl** reader such expressions produce a *description* of an object, and an extra step is needed to produce an object so described. Rather than the "read-eval-print" loop typical of interactive languages, the **ccrl** interaction cycle is "read-build-run": First (attempt to) convert the textual form into an internal object description, then (attempt to) build an object matching the given description, and then "run" the object. This last step may amount only to performing a function call and returning a value (as **Get** does, for example), or (as in the case of **Say**) it may involve asynchronously "releasing" the object into the shared environment to have effects in a region of space-time often involving network traffic to other worlds.

If a **ccr** object is an instance of the **&Matter** type, then once built it will persist across program restarts until specifically removed. Each piece of matter has an identifier that is unique across the entire **ccr** universe (such as :North3-Plaza@ccr.cs.unm.edu/13000, where I was when I said "Say cheese!" in Figure 1). In **ccr** all matter objects are named, but not all objects are matter. For example, objects of type **&Act** mediate computation and communication, and thereby drive the dynamics of the universe. An input like

You're kidding!↵

which **ccrTk** readers parse as the description

[Exclaim Text "You're kidding"]

eventually builds an &Exclaim object, which inherits from a distant ancestor called &Energy, which is an &Act.[4] Acts are somewhat like the "stack frames" of conventional programming languages, but in **ccr** they are first-class, allocated objects. &Energy objects, in particular, "propagate" until they visit every object in the refspace of their point of origin, or are "absorbed" somewhere along the way. In Figure 1, for example, my world was being bombarded by energy packets that had originated on some half a dozen worlds and propagated through the network to reach mine.[5]

4.4 Refspace

If for no other reasons than efficiency and security, distributed systems must somehow limit the range of possible object interactions. Often interactions are limited to one "room" at a time—so travelling through doors is an adventure, since you can't see what you're getting into until you're in it; other mechanisms such as "*k*-nearest neighbors" lead to a fluctuating and non-obvious "radius of interaction" as objects move.

In **ccr**, the *reference space* or "refspace" of a given &Matter object is the set of &Matter objects that are reachable from the given object by following "propagation rules" determined by the types of objects encountered. The lower right panel in Figure 1—with all the rectangles and little icons and speech balloons—is a rendering of the refspace of my **ccr** body. The rules of energy propagation are symmetric and largely hierarchical, so for example, anything said by anybody in a &Room propagates up to the room and then down to the other occupants. But there is one huge exception: A &Link object, when mated to another &Link, propagates to its mate the energy that reaches it hierarchically, and "reradiates" energy arriving from its mate into the hierarchy. This lateral propagation occurs whenever the connection between two &Link objects is open, even if the links are located in different containment hierarchies, and *even if* they are on different **ccr** worlds. Via links, **ccr** worlds weave themselves into the fabric of the **ccr** universe.

The most common subtypes of &Link are &Door, &Body, and &Soul; here we discuss only the first. A door is a link that only can be mated to another door, and then only if they "match up" in a East/West or North/South pair. In the refspace shown in Figure 1, the largest black-outlined rectangle is a &Room—named

:Plaza though that is not obvious—and each of the small grey rectangles overlapping the edges of the Plaza is actually a mated pair of doors, with one end in the Plaza and the other end someplace else. Because my body was *contained* by a door, the entire refspace of the door's mate was part of my refspace, and consequently I also saw one of the smaller rooms north of the Plaza. That room has doors on three walls; the south door connects back to the Plaza, the west door and the northern east door are currently unmated. The southern east door is mated and open, and leads to some other room. The door I was standing in, which appears a cautionary orange on a color display, is actually a *netdoor*, connected through the Internet to another world, and all of my refspace there appears somewhat darker than my own world, as a reminder that that is not space that I control. On that remote world, one body is visible speaking. He "heard" everything I said, and vice versa, but he was unable to hear the clamor going on in the Plaza, because *his* refspace—determined by his location—ends at the door I was standing in. If I were to take a step south, I would leave the doorway and enter the Plaza, and I'd no longer be able to see him, and vice versa. As bodies move, their refspaces merge and separate, and the ongoing stories of their **ccr** lives—mine is visible scrolling in the large left-hand window—intertwine and diverge.

4.5 Making new physics

Though the god of a **ccr** world can travel anywhere within it in a single step, using &Teleport energy, visitors from other worlds must travel "overland" using doors, allowing gods to control visitor access to their worlds in a natural way. Most worlds, for example, have regions that are private simply because they are unreachable from any netdoor.[6] It is also easy to build disconnected "public" regions that each have a netdoor but have no local doors joining them, allowing visits to different areas of a world while barring transits all the way through it. Although this basic connectivity-by-doors approach is intuitive and has worked well, gods often wish to provide other sorts of access mechanisms for other purposes. The extensibility of **ccrl** offers many ways to fulfill such wishes.

As a concrete example, though with only a brief explanation, Figure 4 presents a **ccrl** type and method definition that is in common use in the current **ccr** universe, designed to provide visitors with controlled access to the powerful teleport energy. The first expression defines a new type called &ZapSpace, which inherits from &Space so it will be a visible and enterable object, and which inherits from &Force so it will be able to build and release (selected types of) energy. ZapSpace defines one local variable or "slot" to store a teleport destination;

---

[4]It was expected and initially designed so that 'Energy' was the most abstract active element of the system, but Acts turn out to be more general—in particular, &Functions are acts but not energy, unobservable except to their creator, since they do not spontaneously 'propagate'.

[5]More specifically, the "17/7/8/6/1" in the status line near the top of Figure 1 reveals that at that moment my world was connected to, and was thus willing to accept energy from, eight other worlds (and had, overall, seventeen open I/O channels, seven visitors from other worlds, six open netdoors, and one active external process.)

[6]Unusually powerful items, such as the Quit button, are also protected by "point defenses."

```
[deftype at "ZapSpace" isa (&Space &Force)
  redefault ((_Space,Floor () B1,1x1:.))
  slots (("destination" (::private) @@))]
[defmethod act &enter object &ZapSpace
 class ::object
 at [let
      variable
       (($dest [get
                at [get at $self
                       field _verb,object]
               field _ZapSpace,destination])
        ($objid [get at $self field _verb,subject]))
     at [if at $dest
          then
           [progn
             at ([teleport obj $objid at $objid
                 to $dest]
                [return])]]]]]
```

Figure 4. Defining a new type and method.

in this case, mostly for entertainment value, the slot is marked ::Private, meaning that values in this slot will never be shipped offworld by the network cache management system, and so visitors will be unable to tell where a given ZapSpace will take them, until they try it.

The second expression defines a method that will be executed whenever an object requests to enter a ZapSpace. If the _ZapSpace,Destination slot has been initialized by the local god, the method teleports the subject of the enter energy—whatever is attempting to enter the ZapSpace—to the fixed destination, and then performs a [return], in effect "absorbing" the enter energy so that it has no further effects. Unlike doors as normally used, a ZapSpace is asymmetric: There may be no way back, for visitors, from the destination of a ZapSpace. Fortunately, the "bail button" (the "outward and inward arrows" icon at the top of the righthand column of buttons in Figure 1) *always* brings a user back home, come what may while out exploring the universe.

5 DISCUSSION

That brief look at version 0.1 raises far more questions than it answers, but hopefully it at least provides a flavor of the system and some of the issues involved. This final section returns to broader questions: How can we do research, particularly alife research, in **ccr**? In what sense is **ccr** alive?

5.1 ccr for alife

From a high-isolation "in the lab" perspective, having "humans in the loop" means any data on **ccr**'s evolutionary behavior is fundamentally tainted—after all, what's to stop a researcher/user from "cooking the data" by acting in some particular way solely for that purpose? This is indeed a problem, though not an insurmountable one; in addition to careful experimental design and data collection, the key is building a large enough universe that idiosyncratic individual effects wash out, much as

medical research conducts large-scale studies using its own professional ranks as subjects.

It is also possible to perform more-and-less isolated alife experiments within **ccr**. For example, Hofmeyr [10] has built a small system of reproducing and evolving "robots" confined to a single room on his world, using a combination of **ccrl** code and external C++ code running in subprocesses managed by **ccr**. In such cases, **ccr** provides an infrastructure both for the experiment and for allowing visitors around the world to watch and interact with the "evolvobots" in action. A common, Internet-aware platform such as **ccr** could substantially improve the abilities of alife researchers to collaborate, and to observe, share, and duplicate results.

Figure 5. Evolving robots in **ccrTk**.

Figure 5 shows some early evolution in Hofmeyr's **ccr** "laboratory." The lab has no doors—the only way in, for visitors, is via an external ZapSpace destined for the lab, and there is no way out at all, short of asking Hofmeyr for a teleport, if he's around, or else bailing. The robots move about, analyzing the visual appearances of those around them, and reacting in various ways depending on their evolving genetic predispositions. Some seek visually-pleasing "mates" with which to recombine—which may in fact be a visitor to the lab, as the hybrid offspring in the middle of the west wall suggests. More aggressive robots will chase after visitors or robots with appearances they dislike—the robot initialized with a "mouse" image is evidently such an offender in Figure 5—and the aggressor will destroy the displeasing creature if it gets adjacent to it.

Other **ccr** creatures survive and make a living "in the wild." The egg-shaped face visible near the upper-left corner of the Plaza in Figure 1, for example, is a "Floyd" robot [15]. Floyds can't move or reproduce without the intervention of the world owner, but they use the **ccr** infrastructure to keep in touch with each other, forming a 'Floyd-species-level' communication network within the **ccr** universe. Especially in these early days, when the universe is small, asking one's Floyd "Who is up?" is a handy way to check activity around the universe.

At a pedagogical level, getting a software agent to function effectively in a system as rich as **ccr** is itself an insightful process. For example, since **ccr** must view external subprocesses as "non-self", there are "filters" attached to their representations inside the system: A "senses" filter determining what propagated energy should be transmitted the subprocess, and "effector" filters determining what the subprocess is allowed to build and run within **ccr**. Examining the filters allows a **ccr** user to "size up" an unfamiliar robot, to tell precisely what it is capable of sensing and doing, and to act accordingly. Novice robot builders often set all the filters to `(([Anything] ::Allowed))`, both with high hopes of constructing a powerful robot that is keenly aware of its environment, and to avoid figuring out which types are actually relevant. They quickly find their robot buried under a flood of energy of which as users, due to the default filters on their souls, they had been blithely unaware—communications protocols, timing signals, incremental database updates, and so forth—a firehose of data that is both computationally and conceptually hard to handle. It takes some experience to appreciate just how deeply coupled are the senses, effectors, and brains of a well-adapted creature, and how being *less* aware of the environment can both radically reduce the brains required to handle a given task and lead to far more elegant solutions.

5.2 Living computation

Managing distributed computations across large networks of separately administered resources is in important ways more akin to managing a human society than to marshalling the closely-held resources of a single digital computer. Viewing living systems, especially living ecosystems, as computational systems, provides many insights into what the successful architecture may look like [2]. Though object-oriented programming, for example, is a step in the right direction, fundamental issues—some quite obvious in the context of living systems—remain largely unrecognized.

Consider, for example: Relatively "complex" living organisms such as, say, mammals, are *always* "designed, built, and tested" on a *whole system* basis—there are (until *very* recently) no "plug-ins," "patches," or "upgrades" to an individual's genetic code. The germ line code storage and transmission mechanisms defend against external alterations in many ways—physical, biochemical, developmental, immunological, instinctive, and cultural. Such elaborate and expensive defenses are sensible given the relatively high cost of producing a system—if the results could be easily "hijacked," the capital investment would be unwarranted.

On the other hand, relatively "simple" living organisms such as bacteria are capable of incorporating "stray" bits of code from their environment into their "operating systems"—as when a gene coding for drug resistance is observed to "jump species"—to the dismay, at least, of the complex organisms that produce the drug. Such promiscuity is sensible given the relatively low cost of producing a system, combined with the potential gains to be had by "stealing code."

Is a computer system more like a collie or an *E. Coli*? On the one hand, even a personal computer is an expensive investment, and if it is used productively its value rises much higher than its capital cost. On the other hand, personal computers today are a motley patchwork of code from dozens of sources, with essentially no "sense of self" [7], most of them still lacking even the most basic immunologic mechanisms such as protected kernel mode.

We can be quite confident that this embarrassing combination of traits is not an evolutionarily stable strategy in Maynard-Smith's sense [14], as the essentially immediate explosion of computer viruses following the rise of personal computers attests. Today, the appellation "personal computer" is in important ways a misnomer. The personally-owned computer does not "know" its owner in any significant way, and that's just as well because it is fundamentally unable to distinguish between what is "inside itself" and to be trusted with sensitive information (merely beginning with passwords) and what is not. If future personal computers do not make a credible case for *loyalty* to their owners, all the interface and ease-of-use improvements in the world will not get people to use them for serious work, but if a useful system demonstrates it is watching out for its owner's best interests, first, last, and always, from hardware to software to data to communications, people would clap rocks together in Morse code, if they had to, to interact with it.

5.3 ccr as life

I have talked about objects and processes within **ccr**, and about **ccr** itself, in a variety of "life-like" terms, without qualifying such descriptions as figurative or metaphorical. Although this is typical in alife research, it is worth some consideration. Developing **ccr** over the last five years or so has led me to think that Dawkins' suggestion, that the origin of *life* on Earth also marked the origin of *information* on Earth [5], is so deeply correct that I must suggest that we may view

Life preserves information

as *defining both* "life" and "information" in terms of each other. It is certainly plausible to claim that "All living systems do an effective job preserving information". Is it completely absurd to say that "All effective information-preserving systems are living systems"? We ground out the mutual recursion in cases where we have other *prima facie* reasons to describe a system as "living" or as "preserving information"—and our understanding of the dual role of DNA, as both an active catalytic controller of chemistry during the existence of a cell and as a passive reaction product during cell copying, provides one such base case.

Such a high-handed approach, while riding roughshod over all sorts of important issues, offers a way to unite "life is selfish gene-copying" advocates [4] with "life is self-production" advocates [13], viewing copying and maintenance as *the* two fundamental strategies for preserving information. On some of the standard challenges for definitions of life, the view would include mules, exclude fire, and probably leave crystals on the margin, depending on how much "information-theoretic" information we expect to find in a crystal—which won't be much, if the crystal is pure. Impure or semi-crystalline materials, such as, say, integrated circuits, are of course another matter.

On the prospects for life in manufactured computers, the view is that, rather than being an esoteric research topic, that is a prosaic, long-established fact. Popular software programs today are preserving their information spectacularly, with population sizes in the millions and booming; malicious computer viruses are harder to measure though detections of new strains are booming as well [12]. The emergence first of affordable personal computers and now of mass-market computer networking adds urgency to the real research question: With the great flexibility of programmable computers laying before us, *what kind* of artificial life do we want?

ACKNOWLEDGMENTS

I thank the research management: Tom Landauer, Mike Lesk, George Furnas, & Jim Hollan; the gods of version 0.0: Steve Abney, George, Michael Littman, & Scott Stornetta; and the primordial gods of version 0.1: Ben Bederson, Patrik D'haeseleer, George, Mark Handler, Steve Hofmeyr, Lee Jensen, Craig Jorgensen, Nigel Kerr, Michael, Adam Messinger, Nelson Minar, Anil Somayaji, Jason Stewart, & Jeff Zacks, the creator of **ccrTk**. All screwups, of course, are my fault.

REFERENCES

1 Ackley, D.H., & Littman, M.L. (1994b) Altruism in the evolution of communication. In *Artificial Life IV: Proceedings of the Fourth International Workshop on the Synthesis and Simulation of Living Systems.* edited by R. A. Brooks & P. Maes. A Bradford Book, The MIT Press: Cambridge, MA..

2 Belew, R.K., Mitchell, M., & Ackley, D.H. (1996, in press). Computation and the natural sciences. In R.K. Belew and M. Mitchell (editors), *Adaptive individuals in evolving populations: Models and algorithms.* Reading, MA: Addison-Wesley.

3 Curtis, P. LambdaMOO Programmer's Manual. At `ftp://parcftp.xerox.com/pub/MOO/Programmers-Manual.txt`

4 Dawkins, R. (1989) *The Selfish Gene.* Oxford University Press: New York.

5 Dawkins, R. (1995) *River out of Eden: A Darwinian View of Life.* BasicBooks, HarperCollins Publishers: New York.

6 Dewdney, A.K. (1984, May) In the game called Core War hostile programs engage in the battle of bits. *Scientific American.* See also, e.g., at `ftp://ftp.csua.berkeley.edu/pub/corewar`.

7 Forrest, S., Hofmeyr, S.A., Somayaji, A., and Longstaff, T.A. (1996, in press). A sense of self for Unix processes. *1996 IEEE Symposium on Computer Security and Privacy.*

8 Free Software Foundation, Inc. The GNU General Public License Version 2. At `http://www.cygnus.com/doc/license.html`.

9 Gosling, J. and McGilton, H. (1995, May). *The Java Language Environment: A White Paper.*, Sun Microsystems Computer Company. At `http://java.sun.com/`.

10 Hofmeyr, S. A. (1995, November). *Human and alife interactions in* ccr. At `http://www.cs.unm.edu/~steveah/ccr.ps`.

11 Holland, J. H. (1995) *Hidden Order: How Adaptation Builds Complexity.* Addison-Wesley: Reading, MA.

12 Kephart, J. O. A biologically inspired immune system for computers. In *Artificial Life IV: Proceedings of the Fourth International Workshop on the Synthesis and Simulation of Living Systems.* edited by R. A. Brooks & P. Maes. A Bradford Book, The MIT Press: Cambridge, MA., 130–139.

13 Maturana, H. R., & Varela, F. J. (1980). *Autopoiesis and Cognition.* Reidel: Dordrecht.

14 Maynard Smith, J. (1982). *Evolution and the theory of games.* Cambridge University Press: Cambridge.

15 Minar, N. (1995). *Floyd, a global network of communicating agents.* At `http://www.santafe.edu/~nelson/ccr/floyd/`.

16 Ousterhout, J. K. (1994) *An introduction to Tcl/Tk.* Addison-Wesley: Reading, MA.

17 Ray, T. S. (1991) An approach to the synthesis of life. In *Artificial Life II, SFI Studies in the Sciences of Complexity*, vol. X, edited by C. G. Langton, C. Taylor, J. D. Farmer, & S. Rasmussen, Addison-Wesley, 371–408.

18 Ray, T. S. (1995) A proposal to create a network-wide biodiversity reserve for digital organisms. ATR Technical Report TR-H-133. Also available at `http://www.hip.atr.co.jp/ray/pubs/reserves/node1.html`.

19 Schneier, B. (1994) *Applied Cryptography: Protocols, Algorithms, and Source Code in C.* John Wiley: New York.

20 Zimmerman, P. R. (1995) *The Official PGP User's Guide.* MIT Press: Cambridge, MA.

Gaia: An Artificial Life Environment for Ecological Systems Simulation

Nuno Gracias[2]
ngracias@isr.ist.utl.pt

Henrique Pereira[1,2]
hpereira@isr.ist.utl.pt

José Allen Lima[2]
jalima@isr.ist.utl.pt

Agostinho Rosa[2]
acrosa@isr.ist.utl.pt

[1]EST - Politechnical Institute of Setubal
[2]Systems and Robotics Institute
Instituto Superior Técnico
Av. Rovisco Pais 1096 Lisboa Codex
Portugal

Abstract

This paper presents an ecology simulator for the study of certain aspects of ecology and biology, such as learning, evolution and population dynamics.

The simulator is an artificial world, where two kinds of species can evolve: autotrophs and heterotrophs. Heterotrophic individuals, or critters, are capable of moving, eating, fighting and mating. They have a simple nervous system, a neural network, with a retina input. Associative Hebbian learning is used in the modification of synapses. Nervous system structure and physiological characteristics are coded in the critter's genome. Autotrophs are static. They are born and grow according to a definable geographic distribution and rate.

Simulations were carried out to study learning and behaviour evolution, in an approach as close as possible to biological reality. It was found that critter learning was essentially phylogenetic, i.e., Hebbian learning was limited to develop genetically defined connections, and did not perform any significant correlation between inputs and outputs. This suggests that, for animals with very simple nervous systems, behaviours evolve mainly through genetics, as opposed to a possible emergent scheme of reinforcement learning.

Interspecific resource competition was also studied. It was found that if two similar species were sowed in the world, one of them won the competition. Several explanations for this phenomena are presented. A strong relation was found, between the geographic distribution of autotrophs and heterotrophs. Limit cycles of the two populations were observed.

1. Introduction

Over the last decades, two apparently independent fields of Biology, Evolution and Neurobiology became increasingly closer. While Evolution studies the appearance and evolution of species, on a time scale of hundreds of thousand of years, Neurobiology studies the learning process at the cellular level, on a time scale from seconds to a few years, i.e. an individual's life time.

However, these two fields are unquestionably close. Without Evolution the nervous system would not appear. Without nervous system, evolution would not have taken the path it took. Nonetheless, neither is evolution at the level of the nervous system well known, nor is the role played by the nervous system in natural evolution. And although natural selection, the basic mechanism of evolution, is nowadays known, we only have a few clues about how the structure and the physiology of the nervous system is transmitted between generations.

The main goal of this work was to test the present knowledge about learning and evolution. "Can the known biological mechanisms explain the evolution of organisms with a very simple nervous system?", was the question we tried to answer.

This work was inspired on a similar one, *PolyWorld* (PW) by Larry Yaeger [1994]. Yaeger created a two dimensional artificial world to simulate a simple ecosystem. He inoculated it with growing food cells and *critters*. The critters had a neural network to simulate the nervous system, and were able to see, to move, to eat, to fight, and most important, to reproduce. After some simulation time, the critters were seeking their own food and assuring the species continuity by mating.

The reproduction of Yaeger's results was one of our initial aims, but in our ecological simulator some features not present in PW were added, in order to study population dynamics and autotroph-heterotroph relationships. We gave the name *Gaia* to our ecological simulator. *Gaia* is an ancient Greek goddess, representing Earth as a whole organism [Margulis & Sagan, 1986]. This does not necessarily mean that we totally agree with Lovelock's Gaia Hypothesis, but we think that some self regulation features should appear in our artificial world.

2. Background

In the last decades several computer-based ecology systems have been developed. The fundamental principles of evolution dynamics were explored in systems built by Conrad [1985] and Packard [1989]. Strategy evolution on a group of artificial ants was studied by Collins and Jefferson [1992] in *AntFarm*, using Finite State Automata and Neural Networks. Population dynamics as the result of interactions between individuals was studied by Taylor [Taylor *et al*, 1989]. New mechanisms on how evolution can guide learning were studied by [Ackley & Littman, 1992]. Todd & Miller [1991] explored evolutionary selection on learning algorithms, for controlling organisms with simple vision and scent sensory devices.

An example of computational ecology is *Tierra*, developed by Ray [1992]. Based on evolutionary programming. *Tierra* is a virtual computer adapted for synthetic life, with its own set of instructions and operating system. Ray's approach was to try to recreate the complexity and diversity of the Cambrian explosion, starting with hand-coded evolving organisms.

There are few references to ecological systems, intended to come close to their biological counterparts. PolyWorld was originally directed towards the evolution of neural architectures for complex behaviours, but the biologically based reproduction and evolutionary mechanisms used made it also a tool for studying ecology and evolutionary biology [Yaeger 1994]. Lindgren *et al* [1993] studied food webs resulting from artificial ecologies with external resource flows, and modelled the interactions between species using game theory. Jonhnson [1994] created an ecological community with organism body-size constraints and studied the resulting community structure and dynamics.

3. Approach

We consider that an ecology simulator should work at four levels, similarly to a natural ecosystem:

1. Apply **physical laws** to organisms, like physical restrictions to movement and energy use.
2. Apply **biological laws** to organisms: select in an implicit or explicit way the most fit organisms, allow interactions between individuals (reproduction or predation, etc.)
3. Implement the organisms **nervous system** and its learning mechanisms.
4. Implement **genome** decoding mechanisms, to simulate embryo development, as well as genome recombination mechanisms for reproduction.

These artificial ecosystem laws, mechanisms and structure should be as close as possible to biological reality. *Gaia* tries to satisfy these requirements.

3.1 Overview

Gaia is a two dimensional rectangular world delimited by walls. It can also have other obstacles spread on the world surface, that may work as an allopatric speciation mechanism [Curtis & Barnes, 1994]. Gaia uses a meaningful colour code, so that inhabitants that are able to see can easily distinguish its elements. Obstacles and walls are blue. Autotrophs are red and heterotrophs are green.

Two type of species can be sowed into *Gaia*: **autotroph** and **heterotroph**. Autotroph individuals work as **food cells** for heterotroph beings and are the only energy source on *Gaia*. Autotrophs are red coloured.

Heterotrophs, or **critters**, play the most important role in this artificial world, and logically, have the most complex structure. They have a nervous system and carry a genome which defines several structural and physiological characteristics. When a critter dies its remaining energy is converted into a food cell. This is not just a energy conservation principle, but also a way to allow the emergence of predator-prey and cannibalism relationships. Killing another critter is

a way of getting food. Critters have a triangular shape, a genetically defined green colour intensity and a genetically defined size. Their main **functional blocks** are:

- **Locomotion**: this block controls angular and linear speed.
- **Vision**: a linear colour sensor array which is the only source of information from the outside world.
- **Genome**: the genome has five chromosomes, it is decoded at *birth* according to an ontogenetic developmental program and is recombined in reproduction.
- **Nervous system**: the nervous system is a neural network, with sensory neurons in a retina, and with motor neurons deciding what kind of actions the critter will engage in; synaptic efficacies are modified through associative Hebbian learning.

Critters also have internal variables, the **state variables** and the **will variables**. The state variables are:

- **Health**: represents the degree of damage, decreasing in each collision or fight.
- **Food Value**: represents the amount of energy reserves that a critter has.
- **Can Fight, Can Mate**: expresses if a critter is ready to fight or mate; this implements a time latency in mating and fighting interactions; a predefined amount of time is required until one can mate (fight) again; new born critters can not mate until they reach maturity.

The will variables are the outputs of the critters' nervous system motor neurons:

- **Want to Eat, Want to Fight, Want to Mate**: express critter desire of eating, fighting and mating; when a critter wants to mate, it changes its colour by adding a red component to its green natural colour.
- **Moving, Turning**: commands the Locomotion block.

The simulator was developed for a IBM/ AT based personal computer (PC), running the MS-Windows operating system. For simulations with 40 critters, each time step takes about 5 seconds on a 100 MHz Pentium based PC.

3.2 *Gaia* Physics

When designing *Gaia* we adapted Newton physical laws to a simple two dimensional world. But the energy conservation principle is not verified because *Gaia* is not a closed system. Autotrophs get their energy from a virtual energy source[1].

Mass M, was defined as being proportional to the squared size. The **moment of inertia, J,** was defined as being proportional to size. Finally **kinetic energy** was defined by

$$E_c = k_1 \cdot M \cdot v^2 + k_2 \cdot J \cdot \left(\frac{d\theta}{dt}\right)^2$$

---

[1] In *Gaia* only heterotroph beings dissipate energy, through collision, locomotion and metabolism.

This formula is used for computing critter energy loss through collision and movement.

3.3 Autotroph beings

Autotrophs do not have a nervous system nor a genome They are born at a constant birth rate (until saturation) and with a gaussian geographical distribution, with definable mean and variance. Because *Gaia* heterotroph beings are monophagous predators, this acts as a **limiting distribution factor** [Krebs, 1994].

An autotroph energy value increases with its age by the expression :

$$(FOOD\_FIN\_VALUE - FOOD\_IN\_VALUE) \cdot \left(1 - e^{\frac{-age}{FOOD\_TIME\_CONST}}\right) + FOOD\_IN\_VALUE$$

3.4 Heterotroph beings

Several similar species of heterotrophs can be sowed into *Gaia*. At the beginning they all share the same genetic pool, i.e., they are phenotipically and genetically identical except for a random variation. However members of different species do not interbreed, i.e., species are genetically isolated. This allows the study of **interspecific competition** and **sympatric speciation** [Krebs 1994].

3.4.1 Vision

In Gaia, as in PW, vision is used as the only external sensory mechanism and the most important for the guidance of the basic behaviours required for survival.

The approach for the development of a vision system in Gaia was to make it as close as possible to a biological retina on a functional level, while taking great care with the computational expenses. Each critter has a simulated retina which feeds directly to the neural network. All individuals have equal retinas and therefore equal visual resolution. Their visual evolution is carried out by an evolving, critter-specific number of vision neurons that sample the retina cells, and feed the information to the internal layers.

As stated before, Gaia is a 2-dimensional world. All its elements can be pictured as bidimensional planar shapes. For this reason, it is not reasonable to use a vision mechanism more complex than simple linear vision, where the rays of incoming light are projected along a simple line.

In our simulation a pin-hole camera model was adapted for circular retinas, which allows wide angle vision. Although not very realistic, the critters can sense light over 360 degrees. The images on the retinas are created using ray-tracing. Each light ray that hits the sensing cells is traced to its origin in order to determine its intensity and colour.

One of the biologically inspired feature is the critters ability to adjust their vision according to their will. They can concentrate or expand the raytracing scanning. This feature is a simple implementation of foveal vision and can be roughly compared with the zooming of an optical camera. This provides a way for the critters to minimise the effects of low resolution retinas. By concentrating the scan lines on the front of their "heads" they can be more sensible to the presence of objects in the area they are heading to, and can more

easily identify them. On the other hand, if they distribute them equally around their bodies, they have uniform vision and can detect any incoming attacker. The vision "spread" can be changed dynamically during the critters lifetime[2]. This could be used in a cyclic manner although such a complex behaviour is highly unlikely to emerge.

A good distance perception of the surrounding objects can be an important competitive advantage for a critter. With it, one can guide itself efficiently, and be able to collect food near the obstacles without collision penalties. However, low resolution retinas do not provide means to accurately measure the angular size of the nearby objects, which is the first step towards a correct evaluation of its distance. Therefore an additional source of distance information was added to the vision system, which consists on the attenuation of the light rays with increasing distances. Dim stimuli can easily be associated with distant objects, and a growing stimulus with incoming critters or obstacles. This attenuation makes Gaia a foggy world, where vision decays with distance.

3.4.2 Nervous system

Gaia critters' nervous system is similar to the one used in Yaeger's PW. It is a **neural network**, with a genetic encoded structure[3]. Genetic representation of the neural network is based on Harp *et al* [1990] biological inspired schema, which seems to capture much of the architectural regularity of nervous systems in vertebrates.

The neural network is organized by **areas** (neuron layers) with an unidimensional structure. It has five **sensory areas** (input layers), three starting from the retina (one dedicated to each vision colour component), one receiving the value of critter's energy, and another (optional) receiving a random value. It has six **motor areas** (output layers), one for each possible behaviour: moving, turning left, turning right, eating, mating and fighting. Finally, it has a genetically defined number of **internal areas**. Each **internal area** can be **inhibitory** or **excitatory**, meaning that synapses starting from that area are excitatory (synaptic efficacy greater than zero) or inhibitory (synaptic efficacy less than zero). Each area can have **projections** (a group of synapses) to any other area (the network can be fully recurrent), including to itself.

Ontogenetic developmental program

To translate the genome representation to a "living" neural network, *Gaia* uses an ontogenetic developmental program that is applied to a critter at the time of birth.

The genes that make up the neural network representation are: number of internal neuron areas ($NINA$), number of neurons in each internal area (NN_i), initial bias in each neuron area (IB_i), bias learning rate for each neuron area (BLR_i), connection density between each pair of neuron areas (CD_{ij}), topological distortion between each pair of neuron areas (TD_{ij}), learning rate between each pair of areas (LR_{ij}).

Connection density determines the number of connec-

---

[2] At this moment this feature is disabled.

[3] Structure is not modified during the critter lifetime, only synaptic efficacies, and these are not genetically coded. In *Gaia* there is no inheritance of acquired characteristics (Lamarckism).

tions between two areas in the following way:

$$NC_{i,j} = CD_{i,j} \times NN_i \times NN_j$$

where NC_{ij} is the number of synapses between the source area i and the target area j.

Topological distortion determines the degree of disorder of a projection, i.e., the average receptive radius of the connections. That is, for a *TD* of 100%, synapses are mapped in a completely random fashion. For a *TD* of 0%, synapses connect contiguous stretches of neurons.

The ontogenetic developmental program can be stated as follows. We start by building a matrix of the number of synapses between each area. This matrix is used in the verification of network blueprint abnormalities. There are two kind of abnormalities [Harp *et al*, 1990]:

- fatal abnormalities: there is no pathway from input to output
- minor abnormalities: some areas don't have input or output projections

Critters with fatal abnormalities are culled out from the population, and in critters with minor abnormalities the abnormal areas are ignored in the network instantiation. In this case, genetic information about abnormal areas is preserved, acting like "introns" in the genome[4].

The following step in the developmental program is the synaptic mapping. For each source area and for each target area the projections are built according to the TD parameter. Finally the synaptic efficacies are initialized between a definable minimum and maximum value, and neuron bias is initialized with the values specified by the critter genome.

Network dynamics and learning

During the critter lifetime, and at each pattern presentation, activations are calculated as follows, if **j** is a sensory neuron

$$a_i^{k+1} = F_{sensory}\left(\sum_{j \in \{ aferent\ neurons \}} a_j^k \cdot w_{ij} + \xi_i \right)$$

otherwise

$$a_i^{k+1} = F\left(\sum_{j \in \{ aferent\ neurons \}} a_j^k \cdot w_{ij} \right)$$

where $a_i^\wedge$ is the activation of neuron i at local time step k, ς_i is the input at unit i (matched retina value, health value or random value), w_{ij} is the connection weight[5] between neurons j and i, $F_{sensory}$ and F are the following functions[6]:

$$F_{sensory}(x) = \frac{\tan^{-1}(x)}{\pi/2} \qquad F(x) = \frac{1}{1+e^{-\alpha \cdot x}}$$

where α is a specifiable logistic slope (typically 0.5).

Activations are calculated by areas, going from the sensory areas through the motor areas. At each area, activations are updated synchronously. Each time a new area is calculated a new time step is considered (**k=k+1**). That way, we assure that at each global time step[7] (at each pattern presentation) the signal presented at network input propagates to the output. It should be noted that for each area, the activations a_i of afferent connections coming from the above areas or from the area itself, are the activations of the previous global time step, which gives "memory" to the network.

At the end of each global time step **t**, the synaptic efficacies are updated according to a Hebb rule:

$$s_{ij}^{t+1} = s_{ij}^t + \eta_{sl,tl}\left(a_i^t - 0.5\right)\left(a_j^t - 0.5\right)$$

where $\eta_{sl,tl}$ is the learning rate between the area of the source neuron and the area of the target neuron.

As Yaeger states, this simple "summing and squashing" neuron and Hebbian update rule are coarse abstractions of the complexities present in natural nervous system, but they may capture their main information processing attributes. Linsker's [1988] work on self-organisation in the visual system gives us a good hope on this subject.

3.4.3 Reproduction & Genetics

Gaia, like other artificial life simulators, is based on Genetic Algorithms (GA). The main difference to a traditional GA is that reproduction is not based on an explicit fitness function. Reproduction needs two critters at the same time, at the same place and both expressing the reproduction will. Thus it is almost certain that initial populations, created at random, will quickly be led to extinction. To perform an adaptation of this population we introduced the Steady State Genetic Algorithm (SSGA). The SSGA assigns an explicit fitness to each living critter, rewarding the number of eatings, matings and age.

When the population size drops below a predefined critical limit, SSGA reproduces *artificially* according to the fitness function, to restore the population size. This mode should eventually be turned off during simulation. If a simulation leaves SSGA then it is considered that a Successful Behaviour Strategy (SBS) has been reached [Yaeger 1994].

The genetic code is composed by five chromosomes, and each chromosome can hold a variable set of eight bit genes. Each gene is scaled to use all its dynamic range and then it is converted to Gray code.

The genetic operators used are only mutation and crossover. Mutation works at bit level, while crossover works at gene level, i.e., the crossover operator can not disrupt a gene. The control parameters of these operators such as mutation rate or number of crossover points, are coded in the

---

[4] It should be noted that these introns can result from an undesired mutation. Their preservation provides a way for the later recovering of the original information.

[5] The connection weight is equal to *synaptic efficacy* if the synapse is excitatory, and equal to − *synaptic efficacy* if the synapse is inhibitory.

[6] Sensory neurons are excitatory. The only way to provide negative output to other layers is using an output range from -1 to +1.

[7] For a given critter a global time step is equal to *numAreas* local time steps (*numAreas* is the number of network areas).

critter's own genetic data. Although, in nature, this is not entirely true, we hoped it would work as a self tuning GA.

The genetic code also holds physical characteristics, like size, and neural characteristics. And, being the size of cognitive structure variable, so is the genetic code. Chromosome 0 holds tuning parameters and physical aspects. Chromosome 1 holds the neural network main description. Chromosomes 2 to 4 hold area-to-area dependency matrixes.

Chromosome 0	Mutation Rate
	Crossover Rate
	Crossover Points
	Size
	Secondary Size
	Colour ID
	Life Spawn
	Fraction of Energy to Offspring
Chromosome 1	Number of input neurons devoted to green
	Number of input neurons devoted to red
	Number of input neurons devoted to blue
	Number of neural areas
	Array of number of neurons per area
	Array of each area bias learning rate
	Array of each area initial bias
Chromosome 2	Connection density matrix
Chromosome 3	Topological distortion matrix
Chromosome 4	Areas learning rate matrix

Table 1 - Genetic structure

3.4.4 Metabolism & Interactions

One of the main characteristics of living beings is their ability to modify and interact with the environment. Another characteristic of life is metabolism, i.e., the work of all internal systems with the purpose of keeping the entire system alive. In Gaia, interactions can be expressed as energy (or health) exchanges between a critter and the environment.

At each time step a critter loses internal energy (called food value) by moving and by *thinking* (called vital metabolism). The first is computed by the kinetic energy formula, the second is proportional to the neural network size. A critter can also gain or lose energy or health by interacting with the environment. Next we describe the basic interactions. However, more complex interactions such as cannibalism may appear as combinations of these interactions and behaviours.

Critter-critter fight interaction: Occurs when at least one wants to fight. The combat results in a decrease of health proportional to the opponent size. In this case there is an advantage for being bigger than the opponent.

Critter-critter mating interaction: This only occurs when both express mating desire and both belong to the same species. The result is the birth of one offspring close to its parents, and a decrease of the parents' food value. This energy is transferred to offspring in the amount defined in the genetic code.

Critter-food eating: In order to eat a food cell, a critter must express its will to do so. After eating, the food value and health are increased proportionally to the cell energy.

Critter-wall (collision): The critter gets its health decreased by the collision energy. Small critters lose less energy. For collisions there is an advantage in being small.

Critter's birth: When a critter is created by mating, it is placed in the parents' neighbourhood. If it is created by the SSGA, it is placed at random.

Critter's death: A critter dies when its food value or health becomes negative, or when it ages reaches its life span. If a critter dies with any food energy left, its carcass is turned into a food cell. This enables hunting and cannibalism interactions.

4. Results

It was important to verify the reproducibility of Yaeger's results. The first simulations had only one initial species like in PolyWorld and, even with very different world settings, some common individual and group behaviour patterns were present. After this, we started studying interspecific competition, predator prey dynamics and sexual selection.

4.1 Group Behaviour

The first successful group behaviour was the **reproduction niche**. It was characterised by a large group of critters being concentrated in a small portion of the world, rotating around a patch of food, like a spiral galaxy. This group behaviour reaches a high reproduction rate, and has success when the autotroph have an high birth rate and a small variance distribution. Otherwise critters die of starvation, because the group does not explore efficiently the surrounding space. It was found that if the world dimensions were changed (for instance to take a very narrow shape) critters regulated their linear speed to be able to rotate without colliding. This group behaviour is somehow a mix of Yaeger´s "frenetic joggers" and "edge runners".

In some simulations where autotrophs had large distribution variances (at least along one of the axis), the *niches* started moving like **flocks**. The motion made possible a more efficient world exploration, allowing a longer lifetime for the individuals. **Figure 1** shows an example of this behaviour.

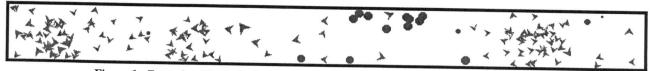

Figure 1 - Example of flocks in Gaia. Circular objects are food cells, triangular ones are critters.

A very interesting and beautiful behaviour emerged between reproduction *niches*, the **mating synchronization** behaviour. It happened when two overlapping rotating niches, forming an eight, synchronized their movement and mating latency. This maximized their reproduction rate with a strong selective advantage.

4.2 Individual Behaviour

PolyWorld known individual food related behaviours were observed (and also the basic PolyWorld behaviour "responding to visual stimuli by speeding up"). New and more complete individual behaviour strategies were found.

The two main individual behaviour strategies observed where:

- food seeking
- obstacle avoidance

Individuals presenting good food seeking strategies were fairly common in some simulations. Typically they were also able to reproduce, thus transmitting this behaviour through generations. Food seeking strategies could be generally described as follows: increasing linear speed when seeing food, decreasing speed and turning when not. It is advantageous to eat as fast as possible in the presence of food, because in a group of critters, the faster eats the most. If there is no food in sight, an energy saving strategy is adopted, which consists of turning in small circles, and scanning the surroundings for newly grown food.

Obstacle avoidance strategies were of two kind:

- simple obstacle avoidance: critters slowed down and turned when seeing an obstacle.
- wall-following: critters moved along the walls, keeping a constant distance to the wall, and turning in the corners.

These strategies were not so common as food seeking strategies, although also being of selective advantage. Nonetheless they appeared more often in narrow shaped worlds.

Most of this behaviours can be established by simple colour associations, like increasing speed when seeing red food elements (excitatory connection from red sensory neurons to linear moving motor neuron).

4.3 Learning

It was found that emerged behaviours were not the result of associative learning during critters lifetime, but instead it was the result of "natural" selection of network structures able to develop well adapted behaviours. Hebbian learning does not seem to provide significant knowledge to the critters. It seems that in *Gaia* Hebbian learning is limited to

developing genetic pre-established connections, i.e., learning occurs over generations and not during a generation (a study of this is presented in [Pereira, Lima & Gracias, 1995]).

One of the most unexpected phenomena was the appearance (and survival) of many non-reactive critters. This happened mainly in simulations where a reproduction niche emerged. These critters were born with high values of initial bias for the several layers, and with very low connection densities. As a result, they presented constant activation values at motor neurons, determined by bias weights. So, the motor neuron activations were in practice static and inherited from the parents.

Recurrent neural networks did not perform better than non-recurrent neural networks. Simulations were carried out with non-recurrent networks, and with general recurrent networks. The same behaviours emerged in both types of simulation.

An interesting phenomena observed was some "senility" in the reactive critters. It seems that sometimes, after some age, Hebbian learning saturates synaptic efficacies. This clear deserves further study[8].

4.4 Intraspecific competition and speciation

In Gaia, critters species compete for the same resource: food. Two competing species were studied. Two different things could be expected to happen:

- species populations reaching an equilibrium through competition: a constant ratio between the two species (for instance 1:1) could emerge, when birth rate equalled death rate.

- speciation to different energy gathering strategies: one species could speciate in a greater energy gathering (greater size), and in consequence slower exploring speed, and the other one in a smaller energy gathering and greater exploring speed.

The time scales for these two phenomena would be fairly different, the last one should be several times greater.

Only the first phenomena was observed. It could be expected that, starting from the same genetic pool, and the two species being, by this fact, almost equal, the system would have fixed points in any population ratio between the two species, as predicted by the Lotka-Volterra equations for competition [Krebbs, 1994]. But what happened was that one of the species won the competition, and the other extinguished (see **Figure** 2). This is also the most common phenomena in nature [Curtis & Barnes; 1994].

---

[8] Oja et al [1991] proposed a stable Hebian learning rule for non-linear neurons. Biological plausibility of this new learning rule is not yet clear, but may eventually solve this problem.

The first explanation for this result comes from the fact that Gaia populations are finite (as in Nature). The system can jump from one fixed point to another as a result of a small disturbance. Because the populations are finite, the accumulation of this disturbances can lead to the extinction of one of the species.

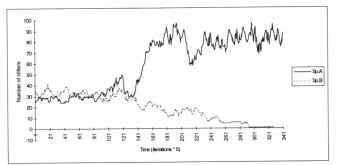

Figure 2: Competing species evolution in a typical Gaia simulation

The second explanation, and the most important is that critter reproduction is "sexual"[9]. Somehow, the reproduction rate of a species (and in consequence the birth rate) is proportional to the probability of critters meetings. In turn, this probability is proportional to the number of critters of that species. So, when one of the species suffers a casual disturbance, and its population is slightly reduced, its birth rate is also diminished. This works as a positive feedback, and the population is easily led to extinction. On the other hand, the other species gets more food and increases its population, which increases the birth rate, and also acts as a positive feedback.

4.5 Predator-prey dynamics

Autotroph and heterotroph population sizes shows an highly correlated evolution (see **Figure** 3). Heterotroph population reaches a steady state when birth rate equal death rate. Birth rate is proportional to available food density, i.e., to autotroph population size. In turn, autotroph population grows at constant rate. Equilibrium is reached when this number equals the number of autotroph individuals eaten, which is proportional to heterotroph population size. Somehow the "food birth constant" defines the environment support value for heterotroph populations. When the food birth constant was increased, heterotroph population average size naturally rose in direct proportion.

Other phenomena observed in autotroph-heterotroph dynamics was stable limit cycles of autotroph and heterotroph numbers (see **Figure** 3). A period of autotroph population growth is followed by heterotroph population growth, and in consequence autotroph population starts to decrease, which also leads to heterotroph population decrease. So, populations of autotrophs and heterotrophs present periodic oscillations, which are relatively stable in *Gaia*.

---

[9] With "sexual" we mean that it is necessary the mating of two critters for reproduction. There's no vegetative reproduction.

It was also observed a kind of genetic drift. When autotroph population dropped to very low values, critters started to lose their ability to eat. This can be explained by the fact that knowing how to eat was no longer of selective advantage. These critters would die of starvation. Being this characteristic out of selection pressure, harmful mutations would not be rejected.

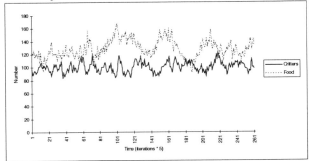

Figure 3: Autotroph heterotroph populations evolution in a typical Gaia simulation

4.6 Self-Tuning GA

Although this was a promising method, we observed that the mutation rate always converged to the minimum allowed value. This can be explained by a selfish attitude of the mutation gene [Dawkins, 1976]. If a gene is carrying a high mutation rate, it is carrying a high chance of being destroyed by a mutation. On the other hand, if it is carrying a low mutation rate, it is carrying a lower change of disruption. This leads to the lowest value of mutation, i.e., a higher chance of gene survival. In fact, this tuning structure does not optimise the GA itself, but the survival of the low mutation allele.

Crossover rate and crossover points, never seemed to converge to a particular value, making us wonder if there was any tuning at all.

4.7 Sexual selection

A kind of "sexual selection" emerged in *Gaia*. When SSGA maintained the simulation, there was no significant sexual selection and critters evolved to the minimum possible size, as a strategy of energy saving. But when the population went out of SSGA, the ability to reproduce started to be very important, and big critters become common. They reproduced easily, due to the bigger reproduction radius. It is interesting to see how the reproduction ability pressure is higher than the low metabolic rate pressure.

5. Conclusions

Results suggest that learning in animals with very simple nervous systems is mainly phylogenetic. Associative Hebbian learning, seems to play a minor role when compared to the natural selection of genetic structures of nervous systems. It also seems that, Hebbian learning in neural networks with the topologies and sizes used in Gaia, cannot explain higher associative learning mechanisms.

It was found a deep connection between the complexity of behaviours emerged and the difficulties posed by the world. In worlds where was very easy to survive, only dumb critters appeared. But if worlds were difficult (like having few food elements), intelligent beings appear. Nature always goes the simpler way.

The behaviour study showed that the most important feature was the reproduction ability. Any interesting behaviour, such as obstacle avoidance, can only "survive" if is connected with a good reproduction strategy. This differs from classical GA. In GA every new feature is expressed in fitness. In Gaia, even if one presents a good eating strategy, this feature will disappear if one cannot reproduce.

For competing species with sexual reproduction, the importance of reproduction ability can also explain the typical natural "winner takes all" competition result. A competing species that suffers a decrease in population size, also suffers a global decrease in reproduction ability (the probability of finding a mate decreases), which acts as a positive feedback until species extinction.

This work shown that some ecology features can be studied in an artificial system. Nonetheless, ecology simulators still have many limitations.

6. Future Work

In such a complex system as nature, it is actually impossible to produce what might be considered a complete simulator. There is a never ending number of features that can be added to make it more close to its biological counterpart. But Gaia itself is a very complex system and a more carefully analysis on the effects of some parameter variations is the first step.

For new versions of Gaia we are considering the use of alternative cognitive structures, such as reinforcement learning, conditioned leaning with modulatory synapses and systems leaving for the GA the choice of the best learning structure.

Another future direction is the improvement of biophysics by introduction of temperature. Critters metabolism loss would raise temperature, zones without critters would decrease temperature. Food should have an optimal growth temperature. With this, we expect to see self-regulation features at extra-organism level.

The inclusion of diploidism and dominance relationships is another idea for Gaia. We are now studying a new diploidism method and testing it in very simple experiences.

Acknowledgements

The author would like to thank the Portuguese Youth Institute and the Scientific Youth Association for their support on this research.

We also would like to show here our gratitude to Tiago Domingos for all his coperation in the reviewing of this paper.

References

Ackley D., Littman M. [1992]. *Interaction between learning and evolution. Artificial* Life II, C. Langton (Ed.), Addison-Wesley: Reading, MA.

Conrad, M [1987]. *Computer Test Beds for Evolutionary Theory.* Oral presentation at Artificial Life I Conference, 1987

Collins R.J., Jefferson D.R. [1992]. *Antfarm: toward simulated evolution.* Artificial Life II, C. Langton (Ed.), Addison-Wesley: Reading, MA

Curtis, H., Barnes N.S. [1994]. *Invitation to Biology.* Worth Publisher.

Dawkins, R. [1976] *The Selfish Gene.* Oxford: Oxford University Press.

Harp, S., T. Samad, and A. Guha [1990]. *Towards the Genetic Synthesis of Neural Networks,* Proceedings of the Third International Conference on Genetic Algorithms, J. D. Schaffer (Ed.), Morgan Kauffman: San Mateo, CA

Johnson A.R. [1994]. *Evolution oversize structure predator prey community.* Artificial Life III, C. Langton (Ed.), Addison-Wesley: Reading, MA

Krebbs, C.J. [1994]. Ecology: *Experimental analysis of distribution and abundance.* Harper Collins.

Lindgren K., Nordahl M.G., [1994]. *Artificial food webs.* Artificial Life III, C. Langton (Ed.), Addison-Wesley: Reading, MA

Linsker, R. [1988] *Self-Organization in a Perceptual Network.* Computer, March 1988, Vol.21, No. 3, 105-117.

Margulis L., Sagan D. [1986]. *Microcosmos.* Summit Books (Ed), New York.

Miller G.F., Todd P.M. [1991]. *Exploring adaptive agency I: theory and methods for simulating evolution of learning.* Connectionist models, Proc. 1990 Summer School. Tourestzky D.S. (Ed), Morgan Kaufmann, CA.

Packard, N.[1989] *Intrinsic Adaptation in a Simple Model Evolution,* Artificial Life I, C. Langton (Ed.), Addison-Wesley: Reading, MA

Pereira, H, N. Gracias, J. Lima [1995]. *Solving the XOR Problem Using Genetic Algorithms,* Proceedings of 1st Workshop of Biomedical Engineering, A. Rosa (Ed.), Instituto Superior Técnico

Ray, T.S [1992]. *An Approach to the Synthesis of life,* Artificial Life II, C. Langton (Ed.), Addison-Wesley: Reading, MA

Taylor, C. E., D. R. Jefferson, S. R. Turner, and S.R. Goldman [1989] RAM: *Artificial Life for the Exploration of Complex Biological Systems,* Artificial Life, C. Langton (Ed.), Sante Fe Institute Studies in Science of Complexity, Proc. Vol. VI. Redwood City, CA: Addison-Wesley

Yaeger, L. [1994]. *Computational Genetics, Physiology, Metabolism, Neural Systems, Learning, Vision and Behaviour or PolyWorld: Life in a New Context,* Artificial Life III, C. Langton (Ed.), Addison-Wesley: Reading, MA

VR, Art, Games

Playing Games through the Virtual Life Network

Hansrudi Noser[1], Igor Sunday Pandzic[2], Tolga K. Capin[1], Nadia Magnenat Thalmann[2], Daniel Thalmann[1]

[1] Computer Graphics Laboratory
Swiss Federal Institute of Technology (EPFL)
CH1015 Lausanne, Switzerland

{noser, capin,thalmann}@lig.di.epfl.ch

[2] MIRALAB - CUI
University of Geneva
24 rue du Général-Dufour
CH1211 Geneva 4, Switzerland
{ipandzic,thalmann}@cui.unige.ch

Abstract

Simulating autonomous virtual actors living in virtual worlds with human-virtual interaction and immersion is a new challenge. The sense of "presence" in the virtual environment is an important requirement for collaborative activities involving multiple remote users working with social interactions. Using autonomous virtual actors within the shared environment is a supporting tool for presence. This combination of Artificial Life with Virtual Reality cannot exist without the growing development of Computer Animation techniques and corresponds to its most advanced concepts and techniques. In this paper, we present a shared virtual life network with autonomous virtual humans that provides a natural interface for collaborative working and games. We explain the concept of virtual sensors for virtual humans and show an application in the area of tennis playing.

Keywords: Artificial Life, Virtual Reality, Telecooperative Work, Computer Animation, Networked Multimedia, Virtual Actors.

1. Introduction

One of the most challenging Virtual Reality applications are real-time simulations and interactions with autonomous actors especially in the area of games and cooperative work. In this paper, we present VLNET which is a shared virtual life network with virtual humans that provides a natural interface for collaborative working and games. Virtual actors play a key role in VLNET. Three kinds of virtual actors may coexist in a VLNET scene: participant, guided and autonomous actors. A participant actor is a virtual copy of the real user or participant; his movement is exactly the same as the real user. A guided actor is an actor completely controlled in real-time by the user. An autonomous actor is an actor who may act without intervention of the user. As a typical example, we will consider tennis playing as shown in Figure 1.

Using VLNET, we will show how it is possible to have players who may be participants, guided or autonomous. For example, a participant could play tennis or chess against another participant or an autonomous actor. A 3D puzzle may be solved by two autonomous actors or a participant with the help of a guided actor. VLNET brings together four essential technologies: networked Computer Supported Cooperative Work (CSCW), Virtual Reality, Artificial Life, and Computer Animation.

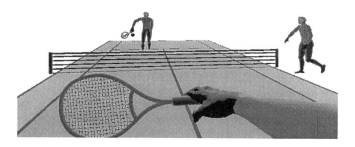

Figure 1. Tennis

In the next Section, we will present an overview of the system, then we will discuss the three types of actors, emphasizing the autonomous actors. Section 5 explains the simulation of virtual sensors for these autonomous actors. Section 6 presents tennis playing and navigation based on these sensors. Section 7 is dedicated to the problem of making autonomous virtual actors aware of participants. Finally, some aspects of implementation are described.

2. The System Architecture

A typical environment for game playing through VLNET is shown in Figure 2. For the real time tennis game simulation with synthetic actors we use a behavioral L-system interpreter. This process shares with the participant client through VLNET clients and the VLNET server the environment elements important for the simulation, as the tennis court, the tennis ball, an autonomous referee, the autonomous player and the participant. The representation of the participant in the L-system interpreter is reduced to a simple racket whose position is communicated to the other clients through the network at each frame. The racket position of the autonomous actor is communicated at each frame to the user client where it is mapped to an articulated, guided actor. This guided actor is animated through inverse kinematics according to the racket position. The referee is also represented by a guided articulated actor in the user client getting its position at each frame from the L-system animation process. The ball movement is modeled according to physical laws in the animation system and communicated to all clients through the network.

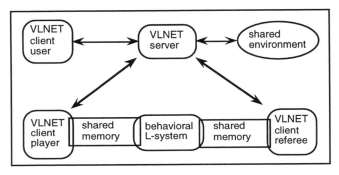

Figure 2. The system architecture

2.1 The VLNET System

Providing a behavioral realism is a significant requirement for systems that are based on human collaboration, such as Computer Supported Cooperative Work (CSCW) systems. Networked CSCW systems [1, 2, 3, 4] also require that the shared environment should: provide a comfortable interface for gestural communication, support awareness of other users in the environment, provide mechanisms for different modes of interaction (synchronous vs. asynchronous, allowing to work in different times in the same environment), supply mechanisms for customized tools for data visualization, protection and sharing.

The VLNET [5, 6] (Virtual Life NETwork) system supports a networked shared virtual environment that allows multiple users to interact with each other and their surrounding in real time. The users are represented by 3D virtual human actors, which serve as agents to interact with the environment and other agents. The agents have similar appearance and behaviors with the real humans, to support the sense of presence of the users in the environment. In addition to user-guided agents, the environment can also be extended to include fully autonomous human agents used as a friendly user interface to different services such as navigation. Virtual humans can also be used in order to represent the currently unavailable partners, allowing asynchronous cooperation between distant partners.

The environment incorporates different media; namely sound, 3D models, facial interaction among the users, images represented by textures mapped on 3D objects, and real-time movies. Instead of having different windows or applications for each medium, the environment integrates all tasks in a single 3D surrounding, therefore it provides a natural interface similar to the actual world. The objects in the environment are classified into two groups: fixed (e.g. walls) or free (e.g. a chair). Only the free objects can be picked, moved and edited. This allows faster computations in database traversal for picking. In addition to the virtual actors representing users, the types of objects can be: simple polygonal objects, image texture-mapped polygons, etc. Once a user picks an object, he or she can edit the object. Each type of object has a user-customized program corresponding to the type of object, and this program is spawned if the user picks and requests to edit the object.

2.2 The Behavioral L-system

The environment of the autonomous actors is modeled and animated with L-systems which are timed production systems designed to model the development and behavior of static objects, plant like objects and autonomous creatures. They are based on timed, parameterized, stochastic, conditional environmentally sensitive and context dependent production systems, force fields, synthetic vision and audition. More details about our L-system-based animation may be found in [7, 8, 9, 10]. Original L-systems [11] were created as a mathematical theory of plant development with a geometrical interpretation based on turtle geometry. Our behavioral L-system [12] is based on the general theory about L-Grammars described in this work.

An L-system is given by an axiom being a string of parametric and timed symbols, and production rules specifying how to replace corresponding symbols in the axiom during the time evolution. The L-system interpreter associates to its symbols basic geometric primitives, turtle control symbols or special control operations necessary for an animation. We define the non generic environment as a tennis court directly in the axiom of the production system. The generic parts as growing plants are defined by production rules having only their germ in the axiom. Actors are also represented by a special symbol.

3. Participant, user-guided and autonomous real-time creatures

As virtual actors play a key role in VLNET, we will first try to clarify the concept of virtual actor. We define a virtual (or synthetic) actor as a human-like entity with an abstract representation in the computer. A real-time virtual actor is a virtual actor able to act at the same speed as a real person. Virtual Reality, Interactive Television, and Games require real-time virtual actors. In VLNET, three types of real-time virtual actors may coexist in the same shared environment.

- **Participant actors**

A participant actor is a virtual copy of the real user or participant. His movement is exactly the same as the real user. This can be best achieved by using a large number of sensors to track every degree of freedom in the real body, however this is generally not possible due to limitations in number and technology of the sensing devices. Therefore, the tracked information is connected with behavioral human animation knowledge and different motion generators in order to "interpolate" the joints of the body which are not tracked.

- **Guided actors**

A guided actor is an actor completely controlled in real-time by the user. In VLNET, the best example of actor guidance is guided navigation. The participant uses the input devices to update the transformation of the eye position of the virtual actor. This local control is used by computing the incremental change in the eye position, and estimating the rotation and velocity of the center of body. The walking motor uses the instantaneous velocity of motion, to compute the walking cycle length and time, by which it computes the necessary joint angles. The arm motion for picking an object as a chess pawn (see Figure 3) is a similar problem to walking: given 6 degrees of freedom (position and orientation) of the sensed right hand with respect to body coordinate system, the arm motor should compute the joint angles within the right arm.

Figure 3. Chess

- **Autonomous actors**

An autonomous actor is an actor who may act without intervention of the user. In the next sections, the role of the autonomous real-time virtual actor is explained in more details.

4. Autonomous Actors

An autonomous system is a system that is able to give to itself its proper laws, its conduct, opposite to heteronomous systems which are driven by the outside.

Guided actors are typically driven by the outside. Including autonomous actors that interact with participants increases the real-time interaction with the environment, therefore we believe that it contributes to the sense of presence in the environment. The autonomous actors are connected to the VLNET [13] system in the same way as human participants, and also enhance the usability of the environment by providing services such as replacing missing partners, providing services such as helping in navigation. As these virtual actors are not guided by the users, they should have sufficient behaviors to act autonomously to accomplish their tasks. This requires building behaviors for motion, as well as appropriate mechanisms for interaction.

Simulating autonomous actors should be based on biology and is directly a part of Artificial Life as well as simulation of plants, trees, and animals. This kind of research is also strongly related to the research efforts in autonomous agents [14] and behavioral animation as introduced by Reynolds [15] to study the problem of group trajectories: flocks of birds, herds of land animals and fish schools. Haumann and Parent [16] describe behavioral simulation as a means to obtain global motion by simulating simple rules of behavior between locally related actors. Wilhelms [17] proposes a system based on a network of sensors and effectors. Ridsdale [18] proposes a method that guides lower-level motor skills from a connectionist model of skill memory, implemented as collections of trained neural networks. More recently, genetic algorithms were also proposed by Sims [19] to automatically generate morphologies for artificial creatures and the neural systems for controlling their muscle forces. Tu and Terzopoulos [20] described a world inhabited by artificial fishes.

Our autonomous virtual actors [21] are able to have a behavior, which means they must have a manner of conducting themselves. Behavior is not only reacting to the environment but should also include the flow of information by which the environment acts on the living creature as well as the way the creature codes and uses this information. Behavior of autonomous actors is based on their perception of the environment as it will be described in details in the next section.

5. Virtual Sensors

The problem of simulating the behavior of a virtual actor in an environment may be divided into two parts: 1) provide to the actor a knowledge of his environment, and 2) to make react him to this environment.

The first problem consists of creating an information flow from the environment to the actor. This synthetic environment is made of 3D geometric shapes. One solution is to give the actor access to the exact position of each object in the complete environment database corresponding to the synthetic world. This solution could work for a very " small world ", but it becomes impracticable when the number of objects increases. Moreover, this approach does not correspond to reality where people do not have knowledge about the complete environment.

Another approach has been proposed by Reynolds [13]: the synthetic actor has knowledge about the environment located in a sphere centered on him. Moreover, the accuracy of the knowledge about the objects of the environment decreases with the distance. This is of course a more realistic approach, but as mentioned by Reynolds, an animal or a human being has always around him areas where his sensitivity is more important. Consider, for example, the vision of birds (birds have been simulated by Reynolds), they have a view angle of 300º and a stereoscopic view of only 15º. The sphere model does not correspond to the sensitivity area of the vision. Reynolds goes one step further and states that if actors can see their environment, they will improve their trajectory planning.

More generally, in order to implement perception, virtual humans should be equipped with visual, tactile and auditory sensors. These sensors should be used as a basis for implementing everyday human behavior such as visually directed locomotion, handling objects, and responding to sounds and utterances. For synthetic audition, in a first step, we model a sound environment where the synthetic actor can directly access to positional and semantic sound source information of a audible sound event. Simulating the haptic system corresponds roughly to a collision detection process. But, the most important perceptual subsystem is the vision system. A vision based approach for virtual humans is a very important perceptual subsystem and is for example essential for navigation in virtual worlds. It is an ideal approach for modeling a behavioral animation and offers a universal approach to pass the necessary information from the environment to the virtual human in the problems of path searching, obstacle avoidance, and internal knowledge representation with learning and forgetting. In the next sections, we describe our approach for the three types of virtual sensors: vision, audition and haptic.

5.1 Virtual vision

Although the use of vision to give behavior to synthetic actors seems similar to the use of vision for intelligent mobile robots [22, 23], it is quite different. This is because the vision of the synthetic actor is itself a synthetic vision. Using a synthetic vision allow us to skip all the problems of pattern recognition and distance detection, problems which still are the most difficult parts in robotics vision. However some interesting work has been done in the topic of intelligent mobile robots, especially for action-perception coordination problems. For example, Crowley [24], working with surveillance robots states that "most low level perception and navigation tasks are algorithmic in nature; at the highest levels, decisions regarding which actions to perform are based on knowledge relevant to each situation". This remark gives us the hypothesis on which our vision-based model of behavioral animation is built.

We first introduced [25] the concept of synthetic vision as a main information channel between the environment and the virtual actor. Reynolds [26, 27] more recently described an evolved, vision-based behavioral model of coordinated group motion, he also showed how obstacle avoidance behavior can emerge from evolution under selection pressure

from an appropriate measure using a simple computational model of visual perception and locomotion. Tu and Terzopoulos [20] also use a kind of synthetic vision for their artificial fishes. In [29] , each pixel of the vision input has the semantic information giving the object projected on this pixel, and numerical information giving the distance to this object. So, it is easy to know, for example, that there is a table just in front at 3 meters. With this information, we can directly deal with the problematic question: "what do I do with such information in a navigation system?" The synthetic actor perceives his environment from a small window of typically 30x30 pixels in which the environment is rendered from his point of view. As he can access z buffer values of the pixels, the color of the pixels and his own position he can locate visible objects in his 3D environment. This information is sufficient for some local navigation.

We can model a certain type of virtual world representation where the actor maintains a low level fast synthetic vision system but where he can access some important information directly from the environment without having to extract it from the vision image. In vision based grasping for example, an actor can recognize in the image the object to grasp. From the environment he can get the exact position, type and size of the object which allows him to walk to the correct position where he can start the grasping procedure of the object based on geometrical data of the object representation in the world. This mix of vision based recognition and world representation access will make him fast enough to react in real time. The role of synthetic vision can even be reduced to a visibility test and the semantic information recognition in the image can be done by simple color coding and non shading rendering techniques. Thus, position and semantic information of an object can be obtained directly from the environment world after being filtered.

5.2 Virtual audition

In real life, the behavior of persons or animals is very often influenced by sounds. For this reason, we developed a framework for modeling a 3D acoustic environment with sound sources and microphones. Thus, our virtual actors are able to hear [10]. For example, tennis playing with sound effects (ball-floor and ball-racket collision) and simple verbal player - referee communication has been realized. The synthetic actor can directly access to positional and semantic sound source information of an audible sound event. This allows him to localize and recognize sound sources in a reliable way and to react immediately.

5.3 Virtual tactile

At basic level, human should sense physical objects if any part of the body touches them and gather sensory information. This sensory information is made use of in such tasks as reaching out for an object, navigation etc. For example if a human is standing, the feet are in constant contact with the supporting floor. But during walking motion each foot alternately experiences the loss of this contact.

Traditionally these motions are simulated using dynamic and kinematic constraints on human joints. But there are cases where information from external environment is needed. For example when a human descends a stair case, the motion should change from walk to descent based on achieving contact with the steps of the stairway. Thus the environment imposes constraints on the human locomotion. We propose to encapsulate these constraints using tactile sensors [28] to guide the human figure in various complex situations. In our work, the sphere multi-sensors have both touch and length sensor properties, and have been found very efficient for synthetic actor grasping problem (see Figure 4).

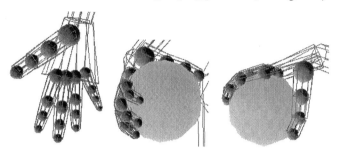

Figure 4. Tactile sensors

Another type of tactile sensor has been implemented in the L-system animation system where parts of the environment are modeled by a force field based particle system which, for example, animates the tennis ball dynamics of the tennis game. To simulate the tactile sensor we defined a function used also in conditions of production rules evaluating the global force field at the position given by the parameters x, y, z of the query symbol ? [29]. The query symbol ? makes part of environmentally sensitive L-systems and sets its parameters x, y and z during the interpretation step of the formal symbol string to the actual position of the turtle. Thus, at the following time step, this position data can be used through the parameters in the conditions of the production rules. The force field function returns the amount of the global force field at the actual turtle position and by comparing this value with a threshold value, a kind of collision detection with force field modeled environments can be simulated.

6. Perception-based behaviors

Synthetic vision, audition and tactile allow the actor to perceive the environment. Based on this information, his behavioral mechanism will determine the actions he will perform. Actions may be at several degrees of complexity. An actor may simply evolve in his environment or he may interact with this environment or even communicate with other actors. As we emphasize the aspect of game, sensor-based tennis playing, game judging and navigation are the most important behaviors. A behavior can be composed of other behaviors and basic actions. A basic action is in general a motor procedure allowing an actor to move. A high level behavior uses often sensorial input, special knowledge and basic actions or other high level behaviors. To model behaviors we use an automata approach. Each

actor has an internal state which can change each time step according to the currently active automata and its sensorial input. To control the high level behavior of an actor we use a stack of automata for each actor. At the beginning of the animation the user furnishes a sequence of behaviors (a script) and pushes them on the actor's stack. When the current behavior ends the animation system pops the next behavior from the stack and executes it. This process is repeated until the actor's behavior stack is empty. Some of the behaviors use this stack too, in order to reach subgoals by pushing itself with the current state on the stack and switching to the new behavior allowing them to reach the subgoal. When this new behavior has finished the automata pops the old interrupted behavior and continues. This stack based behavior control helps an actor to get more autonomous and to create his own subgoals while executing the original script.

6.1 Tennis playing based on vision, audition and tactile sensors

We modeled a synthetic sensor based tennis match simulation for autonomous players and an autonomous referee, implemented in the L-system based animation system. The different behaviors of the actors are modeled by automata controlled by an universal stack based control system. As the behaviors are severely based on synthetic sensors being the main channels of information capture from the virtual environment we obtain a natural behavior which is mostly independent of the internal environment representation. By using this sensor based concept the distinction between a digital actor and an interactive user merged into the virtual world becomes small and they can easily be exchanged as demonstrated with the interactive game facility.

The autonomous referee judges the game by following the ball with his vision system. He updates the state of the match when he "hears" a ball collision event (ball - ground, ball - net, ball - racket) according to what he sees and his knowledge of a tennis match, and he communicates his decisions and the state of the game by "spoken words" (sound events).

A synthetic player can also hear sound events and he obeys the decisions of the referee. The player's game automata uses synthetic vision to localize the ball's and his opponent's position and he adaptively estimates the future ball -racket impact point and position. He uses his partner's position to fix his game strategy and to plan his stroke and his path to the future impact point.

6.2 Vision-based navigation

In cooperative work as a 3D puzzle (Figure 5), actors have to walk through the virtual space and it requires a navigation system. More generally, the task of a navigation system is to plan a path to a specified goal and to execute this plan, modifying it as necessary to avoid unexpected obstacles [23].

We may distinguish two types of navigation methods: The **local navigation** algorithm uses the direct input information from the environment to reach goals and sub-goals given by the **global navigation** and to avoid unexpected obstacles. The local navigation algorithm has no model of the environment, and doesn't know the position of the actor in the world. In our approach, local navigation is based on the concept of Displacement Local Automata (DLA). These DLAs work as a black box which has the knowledge to create goals and sub-goals in a specific local environment. They can be thought of as low-level navigation reflexes which use vision, reflexes which are automatically performed by the adults.

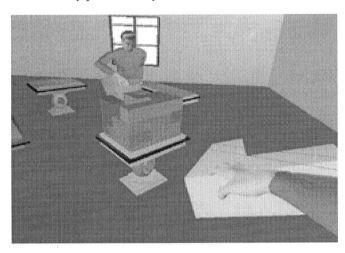

Figure 5. 3D puzzle

The global navigation needs a prelearned model of the environment to perform path-planning. This model is constructed with the information coming from the sensory system. Most navigation systems developed in robotics for intelligent mobile robots are based on the accumulation of accurate geometrical descriptions of the environment. Kuipers et al. [30] give a nearly exhaustive list of such methods using quantitative world modeling. In robotics, due to low mechanical accuracy and sensory errors, these methods have failed in large scale area. We don't have this problem in Computer Graphics because we have access to the world coordinates of the actor, and because the synthetic vision or other simulations of perception systems are more accurate. Elfes [31] proposed a 2D geometric model based on grid but using a Bayesian probabilistic approach to filter non accurate information coming from various sensor positions. Roth-Tabak [32] proposed a 3D geometric model based on a grid but for a static world. In our approach [33], we use an octree as the internal representation of the environment seen by an actor because it offers several interesting features. With an octree we can easily construct voxelized objects by choosing the maximum depth level of the subdivision of space. Detailed objects like flowers and trees do not need to be represented in complete detail in the problem of path searching. It is sufficient to represent them by some enclosing cubes corresponding to the occupied voxels of the octree. The octree adapts itself to the complexity of the 3D environment, as it is a dynamic data

structure making a recursive subdivision of space. The octree has to represent the visual memory of an actor in a 3D environment with static and dynamic objects. Objects in this environment can grow, shrink, move or disappear.

7. Making virtual actors aware of real ones

The participants are of course easily aware of the actions of the virtual humans through VR tools like Head-mounted display, but one major problem to solve is to make the virtual actors conscious of the behavior of the participants. Virtual actors should sense the participants through their virtual sensors (Figure 6).

We have seen that virtual vision is a powerful tool in modeling virtual autonomous actors. Such actors can have different degrees of autonomy and different sensing channels to the environment

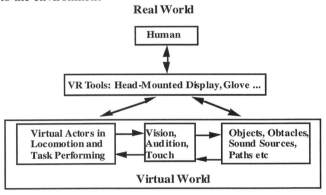

Figure 6. Real and virtual sensors

Let us now consider the case of a participant playing tennis with an autonomous virtual human. The participant can participate in VR by the head-mounted display and the earphones. He cannot get any internal VR information. His only source of knowledge from the VR is communicated by the vision, the sound, and some tactile sensory information. His behavior is strongly influenced by this sensory input and his proper intelligence. In order to process the vision of the autonomous virtual actor in a similar way than the vision of the participant, we need to have a different model. In this case, the only information obtained by the autonomous virtual actor will be through the virtual vision looking at the participant actor. Such an autonomous virtual actor would be independent of each VR representation (as a human too) and he could in the same manner communicate with human participants and other autonomous virtual actors.

For virtual audition, we encounter the same problem as in virtual vision. The real time constraints in VR demand fast reaction to sound signals and fast recognition of the semantic it carries.

Concerning the tactile sensor, we may consider the following example: the participant places an object into the Virtual Space using a CyberGlove and the autonomous virtual actor will try to grasp it and put it on a virtual table for example. The actor interacts with the environment by grasping the object and moving it. At the beginning of interactive grasping, only the hand center sensor is active.

The six palm values from the CyberGlove are used to move it towards the object. Inverse kinematics update the arm postures from hand center movement. After the sensor is activated, the hand is close enough to the object final frame. The hand center sensor is deactivated and multi-sensors on hand are now used, to detect sensor object collision.

8. Implementation

We exploit a distributed model of communication, therefore each user is responsible for updating its local set of data for the rendering and animation of the objects. There is always one user that determines the environment. The other users are "invited" and do not need to specify any parameters, all the environment data is initially loaded over the network to the local machine when the user is connected to the shared environment. There exists one server responsible of transmitting the actions to the participants. The communication is asynchronous. The information about the users' actions are transmitted to the server as the actions occur. The actions can be changing the position or orientation of actors, as well as grasping or releasing an object. The actions are sent to the other users by the server in terms of new orientations of the updated objects in space, as well as other possible changes such as modification to the objects. The architecture requires the broadcasting of the data from the server to all the users in the system. To overcome the problem of bottleneck when there are a lot of users, we take advantage of the geometric coherence of interactions among the actors in the 3D environment.

The network overhead can have a significant effect, especially with increasing number of users. Therefore, it is important to provide low-latency high-throughput connections. Therefore we are experimenting our system over the ATM pilot network, provided to the Swiss Federal Institute of Technology and University of Geneva, by Swiss Telecom. The ATM technology, based on packet switching using fixed-length 53-byte cells, allows to utilize traffic rates for videoconferencing, video-on-demand, broadcast video. The quality of service is achieved on demand, and guarantees a constant performance. The network has full logical connectivity at the virtual path level and initially supports PDH 34 Mbit/s and SDH 155 Mbit/s links. The pilot provides point to point links in the first phase. Multipoint links are expected to be added in the future, allowing more efficient multiple-user virtual environments. An experience was held during Telecom '95 between Singapore and Geneva using ATM.

The simulation part should also be performed efficiently using appropriate mechanism. We make use of the HUMANOID system for modeling and real-time animation of virtual actors [34]. The HUMANOID environment supports all the facilities real-time manipulation of virtual actors on a standard graphics workstation.

For realistic modeling of human shapes, we make use of deformed body surfaces attached to the human skeleton, rather than simple geometric primitives representing body links with simple skeleton. The original model is based on metaballs and splines [35] and allows parametric representation of different human bodies. The human skeleton that we use is based on anatomical structure of real skeleton without compromising real-time control; and consists of 74 degrees of freedom without the hands, with additional 30 degrees of freedom for each hand.

We include the facial interaction by texture mapping the image containing the user's face on the virtual actor's head. To obtain this, the subset of the image that contains the user's face is selected from the captured image and is sent to other users. To capture this subset of image, we apply the following method: initially the background image is stored without the user. Then, during the session, video stream images are analyzed, and the difference between the background image and the current image is used to determine the bounding box of the face in the image. This part of the image is sent to the other users after optional compression and the receiving side recognizes automatically the type of incoming images.

L-systems are given by ASCII text files which can be created and edited by any text editor. Our L-system animation system is capable to read several L-system text files and to interpret them in parallel during an animation. One L-system text file typically models for example the growth and topology of a plant or a tree or contains the rules of some actor behavior.

For fast display, we use the IRIS Performer environment [36]. Performer provides an easy-to-use environment to develop real-time graphics applications. It can extract the maximum performance of the graphics subsystem, and can use parallel processors in the workstation for graphics operations. Therefore, it is an appropriate platform to increase the performance of display part of the system.

9. Future Work

Further improvements are to include physical models for interaction, natural language interface with the virtual actors, and sound rendering. We also intend to incorporate more complex behaviors and communication between the three different types of virtual actors.

Acknowledgments

The research was partly supported by ESPRIT project HUMANOID-2, Swiss National Foundation for Scientific Research, l'Office Fédéral de l'Education et de la Science, and the Department of Economy of the State of Geneva.

References

1. Macedonia M.R., Zyda M.J., Pratt D.R., Barham P.T., Zestwitz, "NPSNET: A Network Software Architecture for Large-Scale Virtual Environments", Presence: Teleoperators and Virtual Environments, Vol. 3, No. 4, 1994.

2. Gisi M. A., Sacchi C., "Co-CAD: A Collaborative Mechanical CAD System", Presence: Teleoperators and Virtual Environments, Vol. 3, No. 4, 1994.

3. Stansfield S., "A Distributed Virtual Reality Simulation System for Simulational Training", Presence: Teleoperators and Virtual Environments, Vol. 3, No. 4, 1994.

4. Fahlen L.E., Stahl O., "Distributed Virtual Realities as Vehicles for Collaboration", Proc. Imagina '94, 1994.

5. Pandzic I., Çapin T., Magnenat Thalmann N., Thalmann D., "VLNET: A Networked Multimedia 3D Environment with Virtual Humans", Proc. Multi-Media Modeling MMM `95, World Scientific, Singapore

6. Thalmann D., Capin T., Magnenat-Thalmann N., Pandzic I.S., " Participant, User-guided, and Autonomous Actors in the Virtual Life Network VLNET ", Proc. ICAT/VRST '95, Chiba, Japan, November 1995, pp.3-11.

7. Noser H, Thalmann D, Turner R, *Animation based on the Interaction of L-systems with Vector Force Fields*, Proc. Computer Graphics International '92, pp. 747-761

8. Noser H. Thalmann D., *L-System-Based Behavioral Animation*, Proc. Pacific Graphics 93, Aug. 1993, World Scientific Publishing Co Pte Ltd, pp. 133-146

9. H. Noser, D. Thalmann, *Simulating Life of Virtual Plants, Fishes and Butterflies*, in: Magnenat Thalmann N. and D. Thalmann, Artificial Life and Virtual Reality, John Wiley, 1994.

10. Noser H., Thalmann D., *Synthetic Vision and Audition for Digital Actors*, Computer Graphics Forum, Vol. 14. Number 3, Proc. Eurographics '95, pp. 325 -336, 1995

11. P. Prusinkiewicz, A. Lindenmaer, The Algorithmic Beauty of Plants (1990), Springer Verlag

12. Noser H., Thalmann D., The Animation of Autonomous Actors Based on Production Rules, Proc. Computer Animation '96, IEEE Computer Society Press, 1996

13. Thalmann D., "Automatic Control and Behavior of Virtual Actors", Interacting with Virtual Environments, MacDonald L., Vince J. (Ed), 1994.

14. Maes P. (ed.) "Designing Autonomous Agents", Bradford MIT Press, 1991.

15. Reynolds C. "Flocks, Herds, and Schools: A Distributed Behavioral Model", Proc.SIGGRAPH '87, Computer Graphics, Vol.21, No4, 1987, pp.25-34

16. Haumann D.R., Parent R.E. "The Behavioral Test-bed: Obtaining Complex Behavior from Simple Rules", The Visual Computer, Vol.4, No 6, 1988, pp.332-347.

17. Wilhelms J. "A "Notion" for Interactive Behavioral Animation Control", IEEE Computer Graphics and Applications , Vol. 10, No 3 , 1990, pp.14-22

18. Ridsdale G. "Connectionist Modelling of Skill Dynamics", Journal of Visualization and Computer Animation, Vol.1, No2, 1990, pp.66-72.

19. Sims K. "Evolving Virtual Creatures", Proc. SIGGRAPH '94, 1994, pp. 15-22.

20. Tu X., Terzopoulos D. "Artificial Fishes: Physics, Locomotion, Perception, Behavior", Proc. SIGGRAPH '94, Computer Graphics, 1994, pp.42-48.

21. Magnenat Thalmann N., Thalmann D., "Digital Actors for Interactive Television", Proc. IEEE, August 1995.

22. Horswill I. "A Simple, Cheap, and Robust Visual Navigation System", in: From Animals to Animats 2, Proc. 2nd Intern. Conf. on Simulation of Adaptive Behavior, MIT Press, 1993, pp.129-136.

23. Tsuji S, Li S. "Memorizing and Representing Route Scenes", in: Meyer J.A. et al. (eds) From Animals to Animats, Proc. 2nd International Conf. on Simulation of Adaptive Behavior, MIT Press, 1993, pp.225-232.

24. Crowley J.L. "Navigation for an Intelligent Mobile Robot", IEEE journal of Robotics and Automation, Vol. RA-1, No. 1, 1987, pp 31-41.

25. Renault O., Magnenat Thalmann N., Thalmann D. (1990) "A Vision-based Approach to Behavioural Animation", The Journal of Visualization and Computer Animation, Vol 1, No 1, pp 18-21.

26. Reynolds C.W. "An Evolved, Vision-Based Behavioral Model of Coordinated Group Motion", in: Meyer J.A. et al. (eds) From Animals to Animats, Proc. 2nd International Conf. on Simulation of Adaptive Behavior, MIT Press, 1993, pp.384-392.

27. Reynolds C.W. "An Evolved, Vision-Based Model of Obstacle Avoidance Behavior", in: C.G. Langton (ed.), Artificial Life III, SFI Studies in the Sciences of Complexity, Proc. Vol. XVII, Addison-Wesley, 1994.

28. Huang Z., Boulic R., Magnenat Thalmann N., Thalmann D. (1995) "A Multi-sensor Approach for Grasping and 3D Interaction", Proc. CGI '95

29. P. Prusinkiewicz, M. James, R. Mech, *Synthetic Topiary* , SIGGRAPH 94, Computer Graphics Proceedings, Annual Conference Series, 1994, pp. 351-358.

30. Kuipers B., Byun Y.T. "A Robust Qualitative Approach to a Spatial Learning Mobile Robot", SPIE Sensor Fusion: Spatial Reaoning and Scene Interpretation, Vol. 1003, 1988.

31. Elfes A. "Occupancy Grid: A Stochastic Spatial Representation for Active Robot Perception", Proc. Sixth Conference on Uncertainty in AI, 1990.

32. Roth-Tabak Y. "Building an Environment Model Using Depth Information", Computer, 1990, pp 85-90.

33. Noser H., Renault O., Thalmann D., Magnenat Thalmann N. (1995) "Navigation for Digital Actors based on Synthetic Vision, Memory and Learning", Computers and Graphics, Pergamon Press, Vol.19, No1, pp.7-19.

34. Boulic R., Capin T., Huang Z., Kalra P., Lintermann B., Magnenat-Thalmann N., Moccozet L., Molet T., Pandzic I., Saar K., Schmitt A., Shen J., Thalmann D., "The Humanoid Environment for Interactive Animation of Multiple Deformable Human Characters", Computer Graphics Forum, Vol.14. No 3, Proc.Eurographics '95, 1995.

35. Shen J., Thalmann D, "Interactive Shape Design Using Metaballs and Splines", Implicit Surface '95, Eurographics Workshop on Implicit Surfaces, Grenoble, France, 1995

36. Rohlf J., Helman J., "IRIS Performer: A High Performance Multiprocessing Toolkit for Real-Time 3D Graphics", Proc. SIGGRAPH'94, 1994.

The Esthetics of Artificial Life

Human-like Communication Character, "MIC"

&

Feeling Improvisation Character, "MUSE"

Naoko Tosa, Ryohei Nakatsu

ATR Media Integration & Communications Research Laboratories

Seika-cho Soraku-gun Kyoto 619-02 Japan

{tosa,nakatsu}@mic.atr.co.jp

Abstract

Artist adopt artificial life techniques as a method for artistic expression. Besides this use, it is possible that the medium itself becomes a product concept. Marshall McLuhan's principle that "the medium is the message" does not emphasize sound and image content, but instead draws a link with the technical nature of future media that will break the chains reality has with equivalent symbols [1]. As technical standards rapidly improve, reality as it stands now is becoming alienated from our lives. As we create a virtual life that is nothing short of an artificial life, and communicate with this life itself, we have to ask where our future is leading us.

1. Introduction

In this paper, we address the issues of communication and esthetics of artificial life that possess "human form" in modern society, both from artistic and engineering standpoints.

From the standpoint of an image maker, artists seek images that can be touched physically as well as emotionally. This is not, interactive art relying on equipment of the past. Instead, it is interactive art based on communication and on creatures that have a real ability to participate in an interactive process.

From an engineering standpoint, researchers have long dreamed of producing human-like robots or computer agents that can communicate with humans in a really human-like way. As it has been recognized that the non-verbal aspect of communications, such as emotion based communications, plays a very important role in our daily life, we have come to the conclusion that if we want to create life-like characters, we have to develop non-verbal communication technologies.

2. Neuro-Baby

Based on the above considerations, one of the authors began a study to create "Neuro-Baby"(NB), a baby-like character that can understand and respond to the emotions of humans [2]. Based on the experiences of developing the early version of NB, we started the development of a revised version, "MIC & MUSE." The basic improvements in "MIC & MUSE" are the following.

2.1 Enriched characteristics and interactions

In the original form, NB had only one visualized figure of a baby. It could recognize emotions of humans and respond to them. Emotion communication, however, is only one aspect of non-verbal communication. In our present study, therefore, we included another kind of non-verbal communication: communication based on music. In addition to "MIC," which is an emotion communication character, we have created "MUSE," which has the capability of musical communication.

2.2 Improvement of non-verbal communication technology

Non-verbal communication technology has been improved to achieve context-independent and speaker-independent emotion recognition. This technology was also applied to the recognition of musical sounds. Details of emotion recognition technology will be stated in Section 4.

3. Design of " MIC & MUSE"

3.1 Personality of the Characters

"MIC" is a male child character. He has a cuteness that makes humans feel they want to speak to him. He is playful and cheeky, but doesn't have a spiteful nature. He is the quintessential comic character. "MUSE" is a goddess. She has beautiful western looks, is very expressive, has refined manners, is feminine, sensual, and erotic; these are the attractive features of a modern woman.

3.2 Emotion

How many and what kinds of emotional expressions are to be treated are both interesting and difficult issues. The following are some of examples of emotional expressions treated in several papers:

a. anger, sadness, happiness, cheerfulness[2]
b. neutrality, joy, boredom, sadness, anger, fear, indigna-tion[4]
c. anger, fear, sadness, joy, disgust[5]
d. neutral, happiness, sadness, anger, fear, boredom, disgust [6]
e. fear, anger, sadness, happiness[7]

In our previous study, we treated four emotional states[2]. Based on the experiences of demonstrating our first version NB to a variety of people and based on the consideration that with an increasing number of emotional states the interaction between NB and humans becomes richer, in this study we have selected seven emotional states.

(1) MIC recognizes the following seven emotions from intonations in the human voice. An arrow(--->) indicates how to make intonations. The physical form of intonations is called prosody,

and how to treat prosody will be stated in Section 4.
a. Joy (happiness, satisfaction, enjoyment, comfort, smile)
  ---> exciting, vigorous, voice rises at the end of a sentence
b. Anger (rage, resentment, displeasure)
  ---> voice falls at the end of a sentence
c. Surprise (astonishment, shock, confusion, amazement, un-expected) ---> screaming, excited voice
d. Sadness(sadness, tearful, sorrow, loneliness, emptiness)
  --->weak, faint, empty voice
e. Disgust ---> sullen, aversive, repulsive voice
f. Teasing ---> light, insincere voice
g. Fear ---> frightened, sharp, shrill voice

(2) MUSE's emotions are generated by a musical grammar (we use moods of the melody and resume of piano)

a. Joy   ---> rising musical scale, elevated, allegro
b. Anger   ---> vigoroso, 3 times same sound (repetitious)
c. Surprise---> several times same sound (repetitious)
d. Sadness---> falling musical scale, volante
e. Disgust ---> dissonant sound, discord
f. Teasing ---> scherzando
g. Fear   ---> pesante

3.3 Communication

In most cases, the content for media transmission conceals the actual functions of the medium. This content is impersonating a message, but the real message is a structural change that takes place in the deep recesses of human relations. We aim for this kind of deep communication.
(1) People use a microphone when communicating with MIC. For example, if one whistles, MIC's feeling will be positive and he responds with excitement. If the speaker's voice is low and strong , MIC's feeling will be bad and he gets angry.
(2) People can communicate with MUSE in an improvi-sational manner via a musical installation.

4. Processing

In this section, principles and details for the recognition of emotions included in speech are described. Also, the generation process of Neuro Baby's reactions, which correspond to the emotion received by it, will be explained.

4.1 Basic principle

NB has advanced from its original version through several stages[2][3] to "MIC & MUSE." In our present research, we tried to realize higher level processing which achieves more sophisticated interactions between NB and humans. For this purpose, we have considered and emphasized the following issues.

(1) Precise speech processing

What kinds of speech features are to be adopted for the recognition of emotions is another important and difficult issue. One standpoint is that the features to be used for emotion recognition should be totally different from those used for speech recognition, because in the case of emotion recognition, the prosodic features of speech play a more significant role than phonetic features such as speech spectrums. There is another standpoint that the phonetic features are as important as the prosodic features, because prosodic features and phonetic features are tightly combined when uttering speech ,and it is impossible for us to express our emotions by controlling only

prosodic features. In our study, therefore a combination of two kinds of features is considered: one is the feature expressing phonetic character-istics of speech and the other is that expressing prosodic characteristics.

(2) Speaker-independent and content-independent emotion recognition

Speaker independence is an important aspect of speech/emotion recognition. From a pragmatic standpoint, a speaker-dependent emotion recognition system requires a tiresome learning stage each time a new speaker wants to use the system; therefore, it is not easy to use. Another point is that humans can understand the emotions included in speech as well as the meaning conveyed by speech even for arbitrary speakers. Also, content independence is indispensable for emotion recognition. In daily communication, various kinds of emotions are conveyed for the same words or sentences; this is the key to rich and sensitive communications among people. In our study, therefore, by adopting a neural network architecture and by introducing a training stage that use a large number of training utterances, we have developed a speaker-independent and content-independent emotion reco-gnition system.
Figure 1 illustrates a block diagram of the processing flow. The process mainly consists of three parts: speech processing, emotion recognition and generation of reactions.

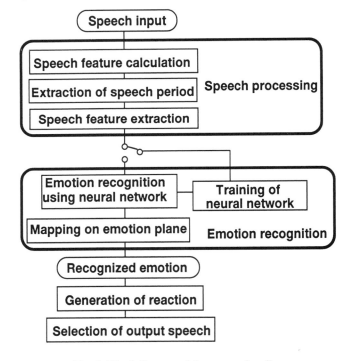

Fig. 1 Blockdiagram of the processing flow

In the following sections, the detail of each process and the system configuration for carrying out the emotion recognition process is described.

4.2 Feature extraction

(1) Speech feature calculation

Two kinds of features are used in emotion recognition. One is a phonetic feature and the other is a prosodic feature. As the phonetic feature, LPC (linear predictive coding) parameters [8], which are typical speech feature parameters and often used for speech recognition, are adopted. The prosodic feature, on the other hand, consists of three factors: amplitude structure, temporal structure and pitch structure. For the features expressing amplitude structure and pitch structure, speech power and pitch parameters are used, each of which can be obtained in the process of LPC analysis. Also, a delta LPC parameter that is calculated from LPC parameters and expresses a time variable feature of the speech spectrum are adopted, because this parameter corresponds to temporal structure. Speech feature calculation is carried out in the following way: Analog speech is first transformed into digital speech by passing it through a 6 kHz low-pass filter and then is fed into an A/D converter that has a sampling rate of 11 KHz and an accuracy of 16 bits. The digitized speech is then arranged into a series of frames, each of which is a set of 256 consecutive sampled data points. For each of these frames, LPC analysis is carried out in real time and the following feature parameters are obtained.

Speech power: **P**
Pitch: **p**

LPC parameters: $c_1, c_2, \dots, c_{12}$

Delta LPC parameter: **d**

Thus for the t-th frame, the obtained feature parameters can be expressed by $F_t = (P_t, p_t, d_t, c_{1t}, c_{2t}, \dots, c_{12t})$

The sequence of this feature vector is fed into the speech period extraction stage.

(2) Extraction of speech period

Figure 2 illustrates both the processes of speech period extraction and speech feature extraction. In this stage, the period where speech exists is distinguished, and it is extracted based on the information of speech power. The extraction process is as follows. Speech power is compared with a predetermined threshold value PTH; if the input speech power exceeds this threshold value for a few consecutive frames, it is decided that the speech is uttered. After the beginning of the speech period, the input speech power is also compared with the PTH value; if the speech power is continuously below PTH for another few consecutive frames, it is decided that the speech no longer exists. By the above processing, the speech period is extracted from the whole data input.

(3) Speech feature extraction

For the extracted speech period, ten frames are extracted, each of which is situated periodically in the whole speech period, keeping the same distance from adjacent frames.

Let these ten frames be expressed as $f_1, f_2, \dots, f_{10}$.

The feature parameters of these ten frames are collected and the output speech features are determined as a 150 (15x10) dimensional feature vector. This feature vector is expressed as

$$F_v = (F_1, F_2, \dots F_{10}),$$

where F_i is a vector of the fifteen feature parameters corresponding to the frame f_i. This feature vector F_v is then used as input to the emotion recognition stage.

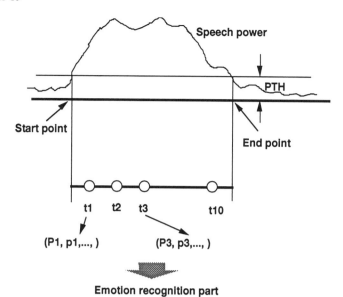

Fig. 2 Speech period exptraction and speech fuature extraction

4.3 Emotion recognition

Recognizing emotions is a difficult task. The main reason is that even if human babies obtain the ability of emotion extraction from speech earlier than that of meaning extraction, adults mainly rely on meaning recognition in our daily communication, especially in business commu-nication. This is why speech recognition research has long treated emotions contained in speech as just fluctuations or noise. What makes the situation more complicated is that emotional expressions are intertwined with the meaning of speech, consciously or unconsciously. In the unconscious case, context rather than the emotional feature itself plays a more important role. This means that the intensity of emotional expression varies dramatically depending on the situation. Of course, our final target is to recognize emotions in speech even if emotional expression is unconsciously mixed with the meaning of speech. For the time being, however, this is out of our research target for the above reasons. Therefore, the strategy adopted here is to treat speech intentionally uttered to contain specific emotional expressions, rather than speech with unconscious emotion expressions. As for recognition algorithms, there are two major methods: neural networks and HMMs (Hidden Markov models). Although the HMM approach is main stream in speech recognition, we have adopted the neural network approach here because of the following reasons:

a. Content independent emotion recognition is our target. Although HMMs are suitable in content recognition, neural networks are considered to be better algorithms.

b. HMMs are suitable where the structure of the recognition object is clear to some extent. As phoneme structures are the basis for the content of words or sentences, HMMs are appropriate. In the case of emotion recognition, however, the structure of the emotion feature is not clear. Therefore, a neural network approach is more suitable.

(1) Configuration of the neural network

Configuration of the neural network for emotion recognition is shown in Fig.3.

This network is a combination of eight sub-networks and the decision logic stage combines the outputs of the eight sub-networks and outputs the final recognition result. Each of these eight sub-networks is tuned to recognize one of seven emotions (anger, sadness, happiness, fear, surprise, disgust, and tease) and neutral emotion. The construction of each sub-network is as follows (Fig. 4).

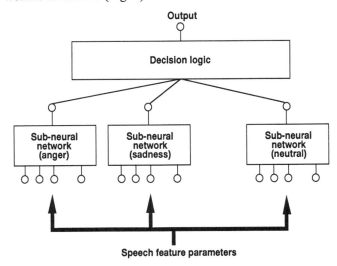

Fig. 3 Configuration of emotion recognition part

Basically, each sub-network has the same network architecture. It is a three layered neural network with one 150 input nodes corresponding to the dimension of speech features, 20 to 30 intermediate nodes and 1 output node. The reason we have adopted this architecture is based on the consideration that the difficulties of recognizing emotions varies depending on the specific emotion. Thus, it is easier to prepare a specific neural network for each emotion and tune each network depending on the characteristics of each emotion to be recognized. This basic consideration was confirmed by carrying out preliminary recognition experi-ments. Although negative emotions such as anger or sadness are rather easy to recognize, positive emotions such as happiness are difficult to recognize. Thus, the detailed architecture of the networks, such as the number of inter-mediate nodes, differs depending on the specific emotion.

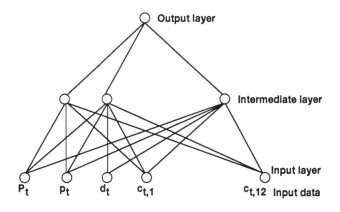

Fig. 4 Configuration of a sub-network

As it is necessary to combine the outputs of these eight sub-networks and decide the total output of the emotion recognition stage, a final decision logic is prepared. The details of the decision logic will be described later.

(2) Neural network training

For the recognition of emotions, it is necessary to train each of the sub-networks. As our target is the speaker-independent and content-independent emotion recognition, the following utterances were prepared for the training process.
Words: 100 phoneme-balanced words
Speakers: five male speakers and five female speakers
Emotions: neutral, anger, sadness, happiness, fear, surprise, disgust, and tease
Utterances: Each speaker uttered 100 words eight times. In each of the 8 trials, he/she uttered words using different emotional expressions. Thus, a total of 800 utterances for each speaker were obtained as training data. Eight sub-networks were trained using these utterances.

(3) Emotion recognition by a neural network

In the emotion recognition phase, speech feature parameters extracted in the speech processing part are simultaneously fed into the eight sub-networks. Eight values, V=(v1, v2, ..., v8), are obtained as the result of emotion recognition. To evaluate the performance of emotion recognition, we carried out a small emotion recognition experiment using sub-networks trained by the above process. By the simple decision logic of selecting the sub-network with the highest output value, an emotion recognition of about 60% was obtained.

(4) Mapping on an emotion plane

As described above, the output of the emotion recognition network is a vector V=(v1, v2, ..., v8) and the final recognition result should be obtained based on V. In our previous study, we expressed the final emotion state by a point on a two-dimensional plane. Based on the experiences of previous research, in our present study we rearranged the positions of the eight emotions on the emotion plane E as shown in Figs. 7 and 8.

To carry out the mapping from V onto E. The simple decision logic shown below is adopted here.
Let m1 and m2 be the first and second maximum values among v1, v2,...., v8, and also let (xm1, ym1), (xm2, ym2) be the emotion positions corresponding to m1 and m2, respectively. The final emotion position (x, y) is calculated by

$$x = c \times x_{m1} + (1-c) \times x_{m2}, \quad y = c \times y_{m1} + (1-c) \times y_{m2}$$
(c:constant value).

Through the processes of 4.1 to 4.3, the emotion recognition of MIC is carried out. These recognition processes are mainly designed for emotion recognition, but for the present study is also applied to the musical sound recognition of MUSE.

4.4 Generation of reaction and selection of output speech

(1) The structure of animation

There are four emotional planes, all of which use the same x,y data (Fig. 5).
a. Plane "a" generates facial animation by choosing the 3 key

frames A1, A2 and A3 which are closest to the (x,y) data point. The computation of a weighted mean frame A is done as follows. Let a1, a2, and a3 be the distances between A and A1, A2, A3 as shown in Fig. 6.
Then, A is calculated by

$$A = (A_1/a_1 + A_2/a_2 + A_3/a_3) \div (1/a_1 + 1/a_2 + 1/a_3) .$$

b. Plane "b" generates an animation of the character's body by mapping each (x,y) data point on the plane to a body key frame.
c. Plane "c" is a mapping of each (x,y) data point to camera parameters such as zoom, tilt, and pan.
d. Plane "d" is a mapping of each (x,y) data point to background tiles.

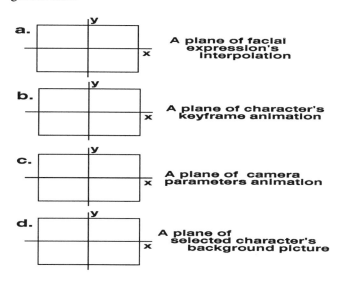

Fig. 5 The structure of animation.

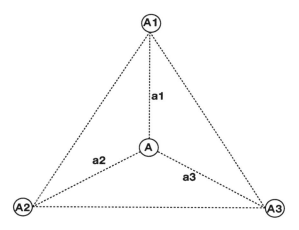

Fig. 6 Computation of a weighted mean value

(2) Selection of output speech

This is a mapping from the (x,y) data points of the emotional plane to 200 sampled speech utterances, and one of the utterances is selected as the output speech. A personal computer is used to play the selected sounds.

4.5 Reaction of the characters

Reactions of MIC & MUSE were carefully designed and were visualized using computer graphics. Several examples of emotional expressions by MIC are shown in Fig. 7. Several examples of emotional expressions by MUSE are shown in Fig. 8.

4.6 System configuration

Figure 9 illustrates the system configuration along with specific processing assigned to each computer. Two workstations running in parallel to realize real-time interactions are the key to this system.

5. Emotion translation through networked MICs

MIC is considered as an artistic agent for expressing feelings within a cyberspace. Moreover by connecting MIC and another MIC on a computer network, they can bring on new sensations through non-verbal communication based on emotions, feelings, and cultural backgrounds.
Figure 10 illustrates this new type of communications. Person A and B are communicating each other using MIC-A and MIC-B as their agents which can translate and transmit their emotions to the other person. If person A speaks emotionally into the microphone, the voice is fed into MIC-A. MIC-A carries out the translation of the emotions by recognizing the emotion involved in the speech and reacting to it in such ways as emphasizing positive emotions and controlling negative emotions. Person B sees MIC-A's reaction and sends back feelings through his/her messenger, MIC-B, to person A. Thus the communication between person A and B is carried out by using MIC-A and MIC-B as their messenger or mediator. This new type communication is expected to evoke fondness and affinity in our future network life.

6. Future work

Real human emotions are much more complex and detailed than represented by the simple model introduced here. Therefore, we would like to investigate how to further improve our model. In particular, we would like to extend the model to include the following emotions.
a. Shame (embarrassment);
b. Like (love, dear, intense yearning, desire);
c. Unpleasantness (hate, detestation, dislike, melancholy, pain, dispirit);
d. Offensiveness(impatience, irritation, tension, impression).
Further study to improve emotion recognition is also necessary. A higher emotion recognition rate is expected by preparing more speakers and word/sentence utterances and by designing more sophisticated multiple layered neural networks. On the other hand, it is necessary to develop recognition algorithms dedicated to musical sound recognition of rhythm and melody.
As for the characteristics MIC & MUSE, it is desirable to design a cyberspace where the characters will live and to develop methods that will allow communication between the characters within the cyberspace and interaction with humans.

7. Conclusion

In this paper, a new form of artificial life characters, called "MIC& MUSE", are introduced. The basic concept and the details of these life-like characters are discussed both from artistic and engineering standpoints. This research was carried out by a collaboration between an artist and a researcher, where the artist first proposed the basic concept and requested for necessary algorithm and the researcher clarified the specification of the algorithm and realized it on a computer. We think this kind of collaboration is a key to the success of the research.

These artificial life characters or "androids" will unravel a new point of view in a new direction which allows the blending of art, computer science, psychology, and philosophy in a kind of novel research on realistic human expression.

References

[1] Jean Baudrillard: La Societe de consommation, Ses mythes, Ses structures, Gallimard, 1970.

[2] N. Tosa, et al., "Neuro-Character," AAAI '94 Workshop, AI and A-Life and Entertainment (1994).

[3] N. Tosa, et al., "Network Neuro-Baby with robotics hand," Symbiosis of Human and Artifact, Elsevier Science B.V. (1995).

[4] S. Mozziconacci, "Pitch variations and emotions in speech," ICPhS 95 Vol. 1, p. 178 (1995).

[5] K. R. Scherer, "How emotion is expressed in speech and singing," ICPhS 95, Vol. 3, p. 90 (1995).

[6] G. Klasmeyer and W. F. Sendlmeier, "Objective voice parameters to characterize the emotional content in speech," ICPhS 95, Vol. 1, p. 182 (1995)

[7] S. McGilloway, R. Cowie, and E. D. Cowie, "Prosodic signs of emotion in speech: preliminary results from a new technique for automatic statistical analysis," ICPhS, Vol. 1, p. 250 (1995).

[8] J. D. Markel and A. H. Gray, "Linear prediction of speech," Springer-Verlag (1976).

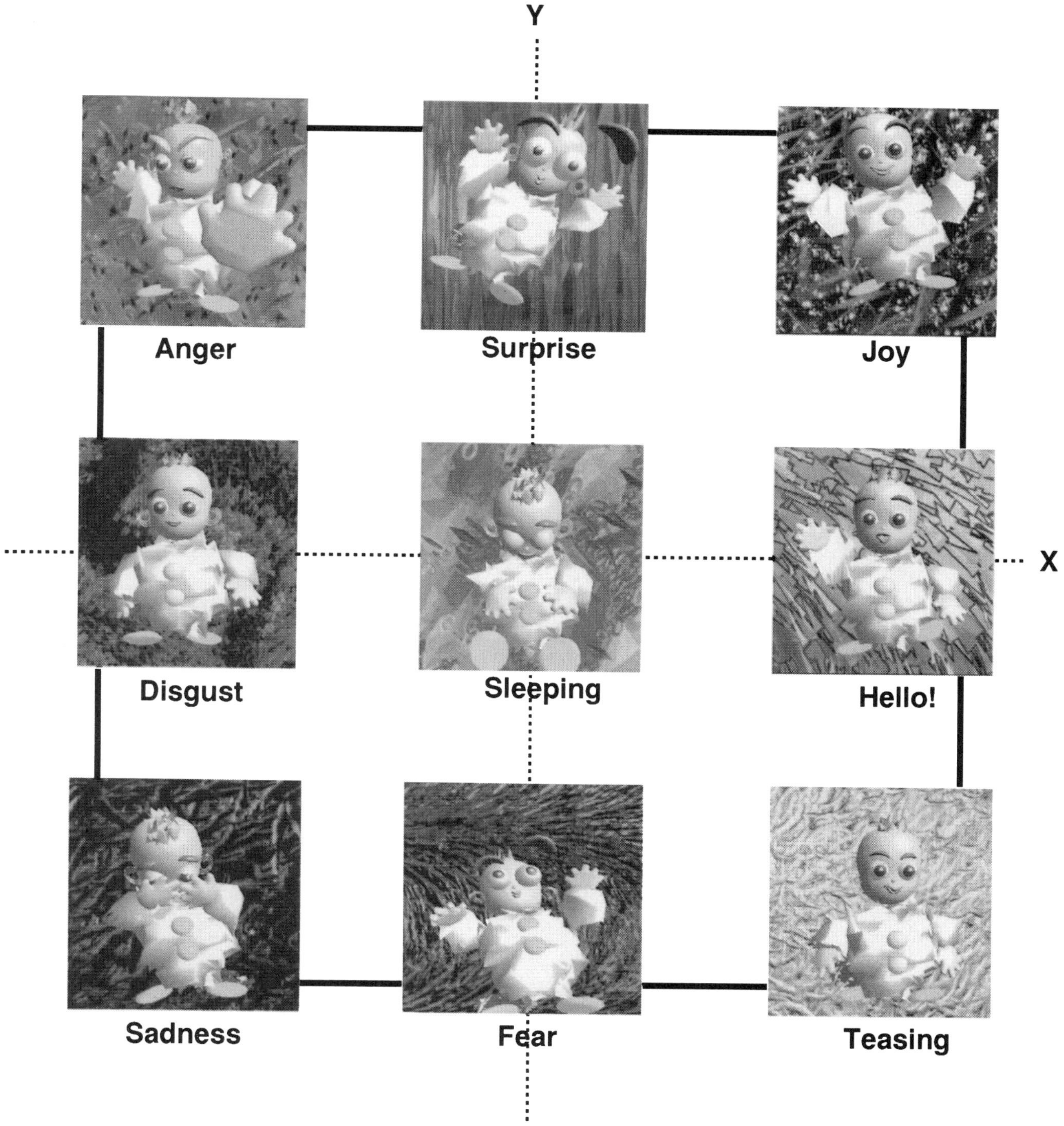

Figure 7. (Tosa, Nakatsu) MIC's emotional expression. (See Plate 1.)

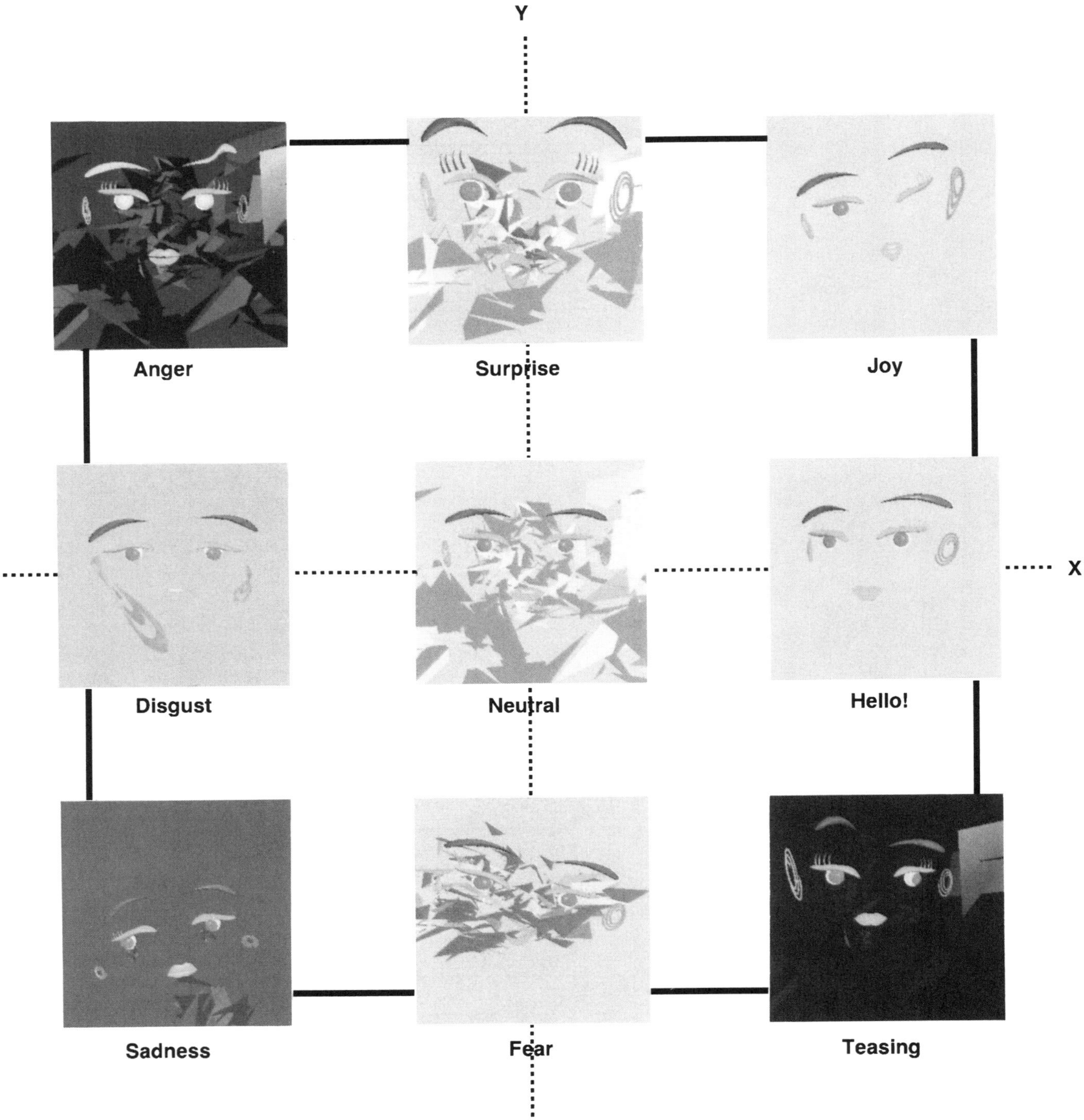

Figure 8. (Tosa, Nakatsu) MUSE's emotional expression. (See Plate 1.)

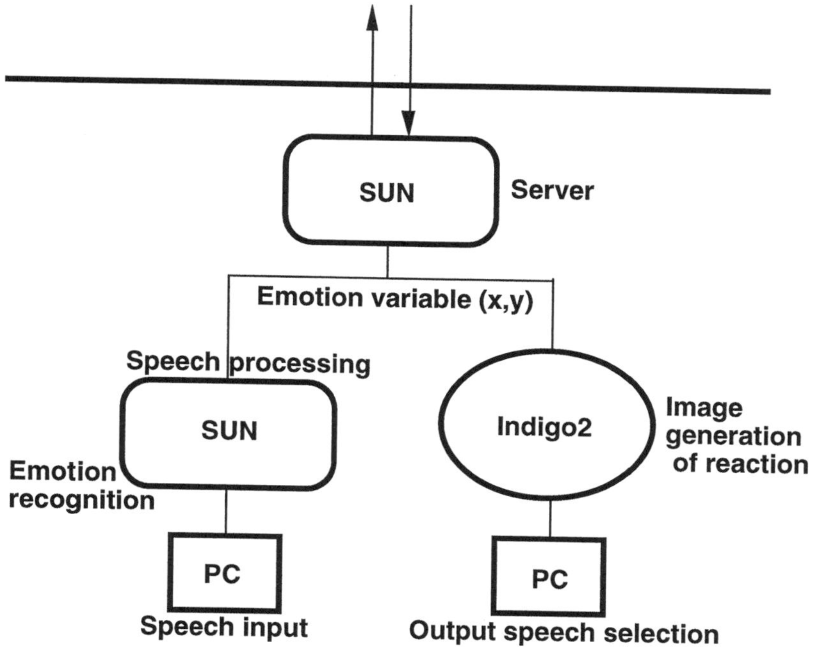

SUN
Server
Emotion variable (x,y)
Speech processing
SUN
Indigo2
Image generation of reaction
Emotion recognition
PC
Speech input
PC
Output speech selection

Fig. 9 System Configration

Culture
Feeling
Emotion model
Person A
MIC-A
Network
Culture
Feeling
Emotion model
Person B
MIC-B

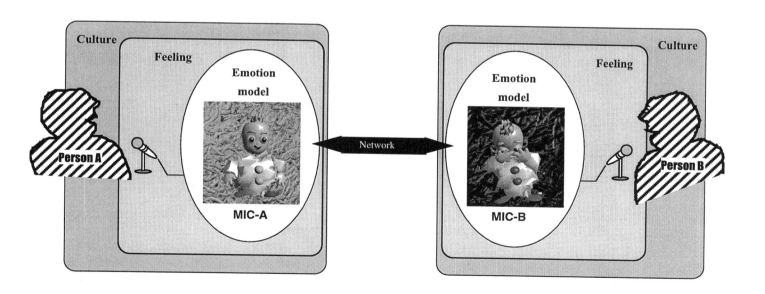

Fig. 10 Emotion Translation through networked MICs

Artificial Life:
A New Way to Build Educational and Therapeutic Games.

Luigi Pagliarini*ϕ, Henrik Hautop Lundψ, Orazio Miglino§ϕ, Domenico Parisiϕ

* Institute of Psychology, University of Pavia
P.za A.A. Botta 6, 27100 Pavia, Italy
e-mail: luigi@caio.irmkant.rm.cnr.it

ψ Department of Artificial Intelligence, University of Edinburgh,
5 Forrest Hill, Edinburgh EH1 "QL, Scotland UK
e-mail: henrik@daimi.aau.dk

§ Cognitive Science Group, Department of Psychology, University of Palermo,
Viale delle Scienze, 90128 Palermo, Italy
e-mail: orazio@caio.irmkant.rm.cnr.it

ϕ Neural Systems and Artificial Life Group, Institute of Psychology,
National Research Council, Viale Marx 15, 00137 Rome, Italy
e-mail: domenico@kant.irmkant.rm.cnr.it

Abstract

Entertaining and educational game tools can be build using techniques derived from the field of Artificial Life. Six different games that all make use of Neural Networks and Genetic Algorithms are presented, and their use as educational tools in biology and psychology curricula are discussed. The games help students at all levels understand concepts about Darwinian evolution theory (selective pressure, mutation, etc.), ecological concepts such as population density and resource needs, and concepts related to brain and behaviour. Furthermore, the pedagogic perspective of Piaget's cognitive development theories is enlarged through the use and study of artificial organisms that are represented by real robots. The games allow students to modify artificial organisms both at the level of brain, body, and behavior, thereby understandig the interaction and close relationship between brain body and behaviour. Two other games play with face expressions and aesthetics. The games make it possible to study the development of the ability to read and use face expressions in children and artists. The games are currently being used in a therapeutic context by therapists who work with mentally diseased children.

1. Introduction

In November 1994, a science exhibition called Futuro Remoto took place in Naples, Italy. The exhibition was a great success with more than 130.000 visitors. The exhibition contained numerous interactive science experiments for school children in the age of 7 to 15 years. Among these interactive science experiments, the Institute of Psychology, National Research Council, Rome presented a set of Artificial Life games. In this paper we describe some of these games along with some new ones, and we discuss some of the pedagogical experiences gained from having school children play with artificial life games. The games were made with the goal to be both entertaining and educating. The games allow children/students to study and understand evolutionary theories in ways that would otherwise be impossible in biological settings, partly because of the time constraints involved in genetics experiments with large number of generations of real animals. Indeed, the Artificial Life approach gives children the possibility to learn the dynamics of populations from both a biological and a behavioural point of view in ways that are potentially highly motivating. Finally we attempt to explore therapeutic potential of one of the games (i.e.,

Face-It) to complete the overview of this new way of representing real phenomena in computer games.

2. Shape Your Brain and Pet Evolution

Two of the games, Shape Your Brain and Pet Evolution, have the common goal of developing the behavior of a miniature mobile robot called Khepera. The Khepera robot is widespread in the field of Evolutionary Robotics, because of its small size and robustness. The Khepera has an onboard Motorola 68331 controller with 256 Kbytes RAM and 512 Kbytes ROM, two DC motors, two wheels, eight infrared sensors, and is as small as 55 mm. of diameter, 30 mm. of height and 70 g. of weight. A simple neural network control system can be build for the Khepera robot by using the values of the eight sensors as sensory input for 8 input neurons, and having 2 output neurons that give activation to the two motors of the Khepera robot. In both Shape Your Brain and Pet Evolution, the task consists in developing a control system for the simulated robot, so that the robot is able to explore as much as possible of a walled rectangular enviroment with an obstacle at its center. The robot must move in the enviroment without hitting into the walls or the obstacle. The control systems to be developed by the user are neural networks in both games. Yet, the developmental process differs in the two games. In the first, the user observes each single step of the simulated robot and in each step he/she is allowed to change the connection weights of the neural network that constitute the control system. In this way, the user experiences how the same behaviors that are appropriate under some circumstances (e.g., far away from obstacles) are not appropriate under other circumstances (e.g., close to obstacles). To succeed the user must construct a global behavior that lets the robot behave appropriately under all circumstances. This is a rather difficult task, since the user has to adjust all the connection weights of the neural network that control the robot's behavior so that the neural network produces the right activation of the robot's motors under all cases. The behaviour of the robot emerges from the highly non-linear interactions among all the different weights. The construction process is somewhat simpler in the second game, Pet Evolution. Here, a simulated evolutionary process is used as developmental tool. A population of nine simulated robots (neural networks) is constructed randomly as representing the initial population. Each robot lives for a fixed number of time steps in the environment with walls and obstacle, and the behaviors of all nine robots is shown on the screen. The user selects the three robots that show the best behaviour according to some criterion that might be either choosen by the user or described to the user from outside. Each of the three selected robots makes three copies of its neural network control system, with random mutations applied to a some of the connection weights. The total of nine mutated copies constitutes the next generation.

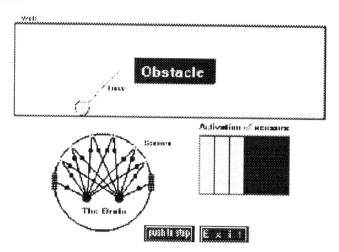

Figure 1. Shape Your Brain. At the top is shown the rectangular environment with the Khepera robot. Below, at the left side, the Khepera robot with 6 sensors (small circles) connected to 2 motors/wheels (small rectangles at the sides). The connections between sensors and motors represents the control system (simple one-layer Neural Network) of the Khepera robot. The user can modify the strength of these connections and successively observe the change in behavior at the top of the screen. Below, at the right side are shown the activation levels of each of the 6 sensors when the Khepera robot is placed as shown above on the screen in the rectangular environment.

The user selects the best among these robots, the selected robots generate nine offspring, etc. The process is repeated for as many generations as desired. One experiences the second game, Pet Evolution, as somewhat simpler than the first game. This tells the attentive user, that evolution is capable of finding adaptive solutions to difficult problems by using selective reproduction and mutation. Further it makes the user reflect why traditional artificial intelligence techniques to combine pre-defined rules often fail. A parallel can be drawn between pre-defining rules and explicitly deciding connection weights of the neural network control system as is the case in the first game. On the other hand, the second game shows that the use of artificial life techniques with simulated evolution processes may facilitate the task considerably.

3. Survive! and Animal Challenge.

Survive! is a single person game and consists of a little world where few organisms and some food pieces are initially placed in randomly selected locations. The organisms are small neural networks that navigate in the environment. When an organism reaches a food piece, the food piece is ingested and disappear from the environment. When an organism has ingested a certain number of food pieces it generates one offspring and gives the offspring part of its food energy. The current energy level of an organism is indicated by the organism's size. If an organism lives for a long period without ingesting any food pieces, the organism die.

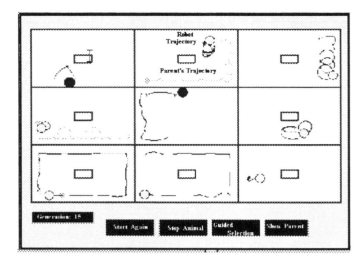

Figure 2. Pet Evolution. 9 rectangular environments with rectangular obstacles are shown on the computer screen. A simulated Khepera robot (circular shape) is placed in each environment, where it moves based on its sensory input, motor system and control system (Artificial Neural Network). After all 9 Khepera robots have lived for a certain time period, the user can choose 3 of the 9 robots for reproduction. Each selected robot (parent) produces 3 copies (offspring) of its control system. However, the copies differ from the parent and from each other, because of some introduced noise (random mutations). The new population of 9 robots are shown on a new screen image. The viewing and selection process can then be repeated until a desirable behavior of the robots is obtained.

When the game starts the only thing a player can do is to administrate a container of food pieces so as to to keep the population alive as longer as possible. Population size and the number of foods are constantely monitored. The player must find the food distrubuition schedule (e.g.: give all the food in the container at the beginning, give the food at regular intervals, give the food only when population risk exitnction) which is the best one. The game constantly tells the user which is the best (i.e., longer time) score ever reached. By so doing the player learns about such topics as energy management and population dynamics and demography. Animal Challenge is a more complicated form of the Survive! game just presented. There are two different populations living in the same enviroment and competing for the same food resources. One population is identical to the population of Survive! In the other population the organisms are born as immature individuals that are fed by their parents and learn during immaturity

some skills that will increase the energy extracted from food when they become adults. The player can vary initial population size and food reintroduction schedule and furthermore he/she can choose the initial geographical distibuition of the two populations. Possible outcomes include extinction of both populations, extinction of one population and survival of the other, and a stable state in which both populations manage to survive.

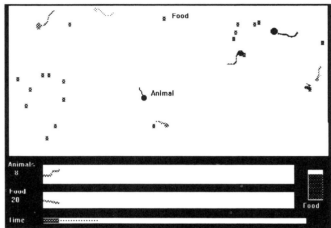

Figure 3. Survive! At the top is shown the environment in which 8 organisms live. The organisms have a circular shape and leave a trace of their trajectory. Their size reflects their current energy level. Food pieces are randomly distributed in the environment. Below are diagrams monitoring current number of living organisms, number of food elements in the enviroment, and time. To the right is shown how many food pieces are still in the container.

4. Artificial Painter.

Artificial Painter uses a genetic algorithm applied to a population of neural networks to evolve pictures that, for example, can be used in artistic design. The evolution of pictures is based on the user's aesthetic evaluation (Cantoni and Levialdi, 1995) of a number of pictures shown on the screen. The technique resembles the one used by Karl Sims (who introduced artificial evolution of computer graphics (Sims, 1991)) in that both models use evolutionary techniques to develop images. The Artificial Painter model is inspired by bio-imaging techniques that visualize physiological activity by means of coloured pictures used in research and diagnostics (e.g.: Computed Tomography (CT), Positron Emission Tomography (PET), and Single Neuron Records). At the same time, the pictures can have a great aesthetic appeal. In Artificial Painter the techniques of Single Neurons Recording is applied to artificial neural network. In previous research, this technique has been adopted in Artificial Life experiments to record and analyze the pattern of activation of vaious classes of units in neural networks (Lund and Parisi, 1995; Treves et al., 1992). The neural network "lives" in an environment that is constituted by a rectangular cell grid. The neural network senses angle and distance of each of various landmarks placed in the enviroment.

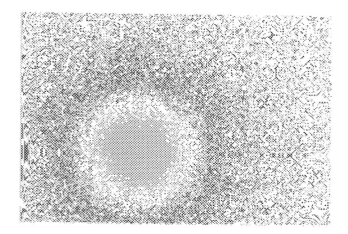

Figure 4. An Artificial Painter Image. The image is constructed assigning colours to the activation levels af neural network units that control the behavior of an artificial organism living in an environment.

The activition level of each output unit of the neural network is recorded by placing the neural network in every cell of the environment. The network responds in different ways as a function of the various cells in which it is currently located. Each level of output is mapped in different colors and shown in a computerized picture where each pixel represents a cell in the environment. A genetic algorithm works on a population of genotypes. In Artificial Painter, the genotype of each individual neural network is represented by a string encoding each landmark coordinates, neural network connection weights, the type of information encided in each output unit, and color mapping. Different landmark coordinates give different sensory input, while different connection weights cause different activation flow in the neural network. The net input to the output unit is processed by the mathematical function specified in the individual genotype. The mathematical function can be formed by a combination of a number of functions such as sum, logistic, exponential, cos, sin, etc. The individual genotype also encodes a palette of colors that associate a specific color to each level of output activity. Artificial Painter constructs an initial population of 16 random genotypes. Each individual generates a picture that is shown on the screen. The user then selects the 4 most appealing pictures simply by clicking on them with the mouse button. Each selected individual is cloned 4 times and the 4x4=16 individuals constitute the new

generation. Each clone is mutated in some randomly chosen parts of the genotype (bit string). The mutations can affect landmark coordinates, connection weights, output unit function type, and color mapping. The selection and cloning process continues until a satisfactory result (picture) is obtained (for a more thorough description, see Lund, Pagliarini, and Miglino, 1995(a)(b); or WWW URL: http://www.daimi.aau.dk/~hhl/ap.html).

5. Face-It.

Face-It uses a genetic algorithm to evolve genotypes representing different faces. It has been implemented as software that is able to build different expressions of approximately the same face (for technical details, see WWW URL: http://gracco.irmkant.rm.cnr.it/luigi/lupa_face.html).

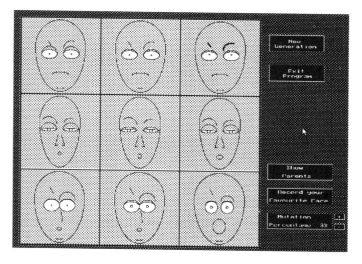

Figure 5. Face-It. The user can develop facial expressions with the Artificial Life technique. Face-It is being used by therapists to teach mentally diseases children to understand facial expressions.

The technique resembles that of Artificial Painter. The user selects the faces that will reproduce and mutations are applied to reproducing genotypes. Selective reproduction and random mutation of genotypes lead to the emergence of desired face expressions. When talking about this kind of program, which usually fascinates kids for its strong connection to human communication abilities, it is very hard to find the limits of its applicability in entertainment, communication, educational and psychological fields. One application of Face-It touches all these fields. Recently, we have started a research project together with a group of therapists in Bologna (Italy) where we will apply the above software to try to teach children with mental diseases to capture and understand facial expressions. Children feel very much like playing when doing therapy. Another application is in the field of Computer Mediated

Communication field. In this field there is a growing need to comunicate with characters that express different moods and have different facial expressions (Maes, 1995). Until now all such graphical expressions of prototypes of human emotions have been free-hand drawings. Face-It could allow users to generate more personal and sharper definition of personal feelings.

6. Conclusions

The games described in this paper, all based on artificial life techniques, can be usefully applied in educational, entertainment, and therapeutic settings. They can also be used for research purposes. Among their various uses we mention the following: to teach young researchers about basic mechanisms of Sensory-Motors Agents (e.g., Survive!) and Genetic Algorithm functioning (e.g., Pet Evolution); to test tasks difficulty (e.g., with a software like Shape Your Brain) and appropriatness before starting real experiments; to analyze research hypotheses (e.g., Animal Challenge). The six games were shown in the games session of Artificial Life V. Demo versions including further descriptions can be found at WWW URL: http//kant.irmkant.rm.cnr.it/lupa_apgames.html. In the version described in this paper there are no links connecting the artificial oragnisms living in simulations to the artificial organisms represented by physical robots living in a real physical enviroment. However, at the Futuro Remoto exhibition, both Lego and Khepera robots were used to present a further dimension of the games. It is our view, that by modifying and experimenting with artificial organisms at the level of brain, body, and behavior, children can learn important concepts concerning the interaction and close relationship between brain, body and behavior. We view this as an advanced use of Piaget's cognitive development theories (Piaget, 1967) (for a further discussion of this, see Miglino and Lund, 1995). Furthermore, the games can be powerful tools for the teaching of concepts of Darwinian evolution theory, that may be otherwise difficult to teach to young children. Our experiences with the Futuro Remoto exhibition show, that by using these artificial life games, children are capable to understand these evolutionary concepts as well as rather complicated robotics techniques. The use of the games with mentally diseased children gives further evidence that artificial life may be a powerful educational and therapeutic tool.

Acknowledgments.

The game Animal Challenge was realized by D. Denaro, National Research Council, Rome. The games Shape Your Brain and Pet Evolution were programmed thanks to an active collaboration of Stefano Nolfi, National Research Council, Rome.

References.

Cantoni V., Levialdi S. (1995). Computer-aided creativity?, *European Journal for high ability*, **6**, 181-187.

Lund, H. H., Pagliarini, L., and Miglino, O. (1995a). Artistic Design with Genetic Algorithms and Neural Networks. In J. T. Alander (Ed.) *Proceedings of INWGA*, Vaasa University, Vaasa.

Lund, H. H., Pagliarini, L., and Miglino, O. (1995b). The Artificial Painter. In *Abstract Book of Proceedings of Third European Conference on Artificial Life*, Granada.

Lund, H. H., and Parisi, D. (1995) Pre-adaptation in Populations of Neural Networks Evolving in a Changing Environment. *Artificial Life* **2**, (2).

Maes, P. (1995) Intelligent Software. *Scientific American*, September 1995, 66-68.

Miglino, O., and Lund, H. H. (1995) Robotics as an Educational Tool. Technical Report. C.N.R., Rome. 1995.

Piaget, J. (1967) *La construction du réel chez l'enfant*. Delachaux & Niestlé, Paris.

Sims, K. (1991) Artificial Evolution for Computer Graphics. *Computer Graphics* **25**, 4, 319-328.

Treves, A., Miglino, O., and Parisi, D. (1992) Rats, Nets, Maps, and Emergence of Place Cells. *Psychobiology* **20**, 1, 1-8.

Artist Talks

The Art of the GROWTH Algorithm with Cells

Yoichiro Kawaguchi
University of Tsukuba
Institute of Art.
Tennodai,Tsukuba-Science City 305 , JAPAN
e-mail: yoichiro@geijutsu.tsukuba.ac.jp

ABSTRACT

In this artistic note, we would like to show the GROWTH images applied by the fundamental principle of the growth of cells . The self-organization of the three-dimensional space which is composed with a mass of cell can generate complex evolving space.
We began with the aspect of non-linear first of all. For example,it is possible that a cell would react to the next impulse even if it did'nt to the first one. Those impulses would cause facilitaion and inhibition together, but if the amount of those impulses exceed a threshoid,the cell would react all of a sudden. This pulling together phenomenon shows a very interesting result. Sometime,the cell would blink or vibrate by that reaction of facilitation and inhibition. This emergent reaction can be applied for our art. The growth of three-dimensional cells could bring about unexpectable, delicate, and emergent vibration.

1. INTRODUCTION

In 1976, We began developmental computer art using a line drawing computer system(Fig.1,Fig2), with the advice of Eiichi Izuhara[1] at the Industrial Product Researc Institute of the MITI in Tokyo.

Since that time we have been able to explore(Fig3) more complex developmental structure generation with our "GROWTH" algorithm. This algorithm makes it easy to create organic images baced on the growth rule of seashel and tendril plant, and with it we can generate a greate variety of complex images.

These images(Fig4) were presented for the public at the SIGGRAPH'82 Conference in Boston[2][3]. GROWTH algorithm with Metaball(Fig5) were explored more organic surfaces for SIGGRAPH'83 Erectronic Theatre, Film&Video show[4][5].

Figure 1. "Ecology," 1976. Non-linear images were generated by a self-growth algorithm using the Lotka-Volterra model.

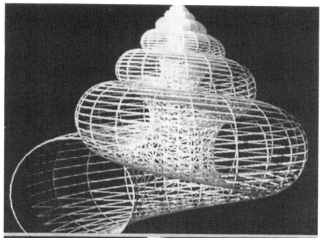

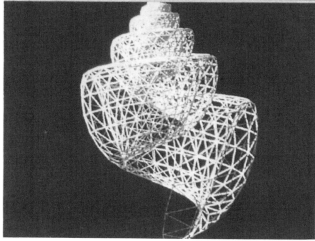

Figure 2. "Shell," 1976. Many kinds of organic images were generated by the GROWTH algorithm.

Figure 3. "Tentacle," 1980. The GROWTH algorithm explored like a mutant that lives on another planet.

Figure 4. "Tendril," 1981. These GROWTH images were presented at SIGGRAPH '82 in Boston.

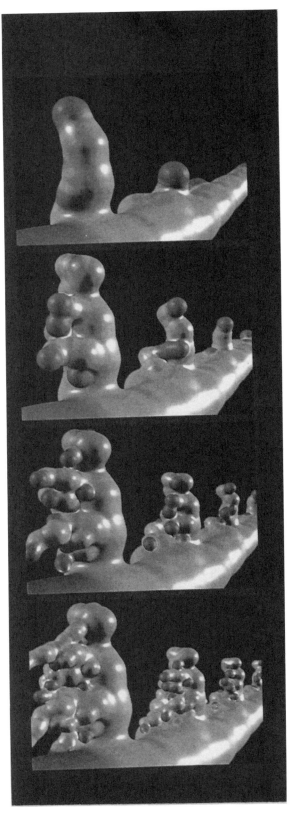

Figure 5. "GROWTH: Mysterious Galaxy," 1983. GROWTH with Metaball images were shown at SIGGRAPH '83.

2. THE SITUATION OF SPACE

In recent two decades[5],none of new trial of research of art arouse by 3D volume has been made. We will assume that a space is like a lattice box and the box is consisted with a number of elements called cell. Each element of the lattice box, cell, has only one signal of 0 or 1. 0 means null, and 1 means being. The cell can have a signal of either 0 or 1 in a certain moment of time. Of course, each signal can be determined as 0 or 1. To determine the whole situation of the lattice box, the signal of each cell should be read successively.

The signal of cell in the next generation is determined by the processing of the present signal applied by a certain kind of rule. The determine is whether the each signal remains same or changed in the next generation. To determine the signal of the cell in the next generation, to scout the area that surround the cell is needed. In the mean of area here, it stands up, down, left, right, front, back, and the diagonal ways all together.

3. CELL SPACE

We will use a lattice coordinates to simulate the life and death of the cell in three-dimensional space. We also use a term of cell as an elemental cube in the lattice coordinates. The cell means, like a pixel in two-dimensional space, a basic element in three-dimensional space. A group of cell would make a three-dimensional object just like millions of cell make a life form in nature. It is easy to describe an object in three-dimensional space with those elements called cell.

Space has its certain amount of size in three-dimension. This space can be divided into a number of cells. The number of cells are variable. Then the space can be easily understandable with those elements. Cell is the minimum space for a life to live in and it can be visualized as a cube that has a three-dimensional size. The three-dimensional space which is consisted with cells is called cell space. So, cell space can be thought as a mass of cells. I would like to apply the concept of self-reproduction to the three-dimensional space which is consisted with cells.

There are two ways to describe the variations of three- dimensional cell space.

(1) The cell space is consisted with the sliced two-dimensional plane of the cell in the order of time stratum.

(2) The cell space is consisted with the each cell that has other cells around in three-dimensional space.

From now on, I will describe the cell space in the two ways above.

4. TIME STRATUM OF CELL PLANE

Now I would like to introduce the research of a mass of cell in a plane which accumulated orderly in three-dimensional space. A mass of cell in a plane can be thought as a a mass of pixel that has the height of a unit to be three-dimension.

This mass of cell in a plane is a kind of life form which is generated, multiplied, and exterminated by a certain rule. We'll see the more aspect of each cell which is generated or exterminated later. Whether the each cell would survive or die is determined by calculation of the rule, that is, each cell is decided to survive or die by the situation of the other cells that surround it. This mass of cell in a plane in a certain moment of time is stacked up in order of time to generate a stratum of time.

Think of the increase or decrease of cell in a time stratum. The cell plane of a time stratum is determined to be generated by the condition of the cell plane of the former time stratum. Each cell is generated by the calculation of surrounding cells, not by random. If there are too many cells near each cell, it would decrease. The entire situation of each cell is calculated one by one. So, every cell in a plane should be calculated to determine the next generation, that is, next time stratum.

5. CHANGE OF SITUATION OF CELL PLANE

Let's assume that there is a living situation made of randomly generated cells in a plane for the first time. The living situation is determined by the number of cell in a same plane. If the number of cell is too many or too few, the cells in a plane will not have a good environment to survive or multiply in. It means the cell has its appropriate environment to live in. The increase or decrease of cell can be simulated in a lattice space filled with cube elements. Each cell's destiny is determined by the surrounded cells and can be 1 as survive or 0 as die. The result comes from the situation of front, back, left, right, and diagonal ways of each cell.

Let me explain the environment of each cell that would change the situation of it.

(A) The total four cells situated on front, back, left, and right of the cell. In this case, the result as follows will happen. (fig 3)

(a) Stabilization (No more transformation)

(b) Saturation of the space by the cells

(c) Extermination

(B) The total eight cells situated on front, back, left, right, and diagonal ways.

(1) In case of the present cell is live

(a) The cell would survive if the number of live cells in eight ways is 2 or 3.

(b) The cell would die in any other situation.

(2) In case of the present cell is dead

(a) The cell would resurrect if the number of live cells in eight ways is 3.

(b) The cell would remain dead on any other situation.

The simple rules are as follows;

(1) Survive : In case of the total amount of live cell that surround a live cell is 2 or 3, the cell would survive.

(2) Die : In case of the total amount of live cell that surround a live cell is less than 1 or more than 4, the cell would die.

(3) Resurrect : In case of total amount of live cell that surround a deadcell is 3, the cell would resurrect.

Figure 6. "Artificial Life Metropolis CELL," 1993. These
images on HDTV were shown at SIGGRAPH '93. (See Plate 2.)

The successive time stratum of cell plane is unexpectably generated from the former plane by above rules. The orderly pattern in a time stratum can be found in the process.

The algorithm of the program that analyze the present cell plane to make the composition of cells in the next generation is as follows;
(1) Calculate the present cell plane with the rule.
(2) Accumulate the next generation which is generated by the rule on the older generation of the cell plane.
The following chart is as follows;

Case #1 of the beginning situation on the cell plane.
-(Random number is also available)
The life and death of the present cell
Loop of generation
Loop of Y axis
Loop of X axis
Generating of the cell
Checking the number of live
cells
Loop of X axis
Loop of Y axis
(1) Check the number of live cells
(2) Apply the rule
(3) Determine the next generation

Case #2 of the beginning situation on the cell plane.
Loop of angle
Loop of stacking Z axis
Loop of Y axis
Loop of X axis
If the present cell is live, generate a
cell
Renewal of cell screen

The algorithm above can be repeated. The movement of cell is internally a simple generation by a rule. However, it looks like a life form that actually live in motion.

6. CHANGE OF SITUATION BY CELL PLANE

Next, I would like to talk about the situation of a life form in a three-dimensional space orderly consisted with cell. It is different to the mass of cell in a plane.
The increase or decrease of cell in a lattice space can be determined by the situation of up, down, front, back, left, right, and diagonal ways. Each cell's life can be determined by the surrounded cells. The cell would survive if the amount of live cells surrounded is a certain number we give. Of course, it would die if it has any other number of live cells surrounded. And in case of the dead cell, it would resurrect if a certain number of cells are live on the boundary of it.
In two-dimensional space, it has proven that the life game can be much more variable if the life of the cell in the next generation is determined by the situation of eight ways than four ways. In means that the signals in the diagonal ways must be calculated as well as simple four boundaries to make more interesting result. But in three-dimensional space, it

is not yet proven that which method is more efficient to make interesting result. The area of boundary of each cell could be six cells, eighteen cells, or twenty-six cells. I wrote above that the cell would be survive in the next generation if it has two or three cells surrounded in two-dimensional space. But the rule will be more variable if it is in the three-dimensional space, of course. I used to use these rules simultaneously in my work.
Let me explain the environment of each cell that would change the situation of it.
(1) The total six cells situated on up, down, front, back, left, and right of the cell.
(2) The total eighteen cells situated on up, down, front, back, left, right, and the diagonal ways along the X, Y, Z axis of the cell.
(3) The total twenty-six cells situated on up, down, front, back, left, right, and the all diagonal ways of the cell.

And the simple rules are as follows;

(1) Survive : In case of the total amount of live cell that surround a live cell is a specific number, the cell would survive.
(2) Die : In case of the total amount of live cell that surround a live cell is not a specific number, the cell would die.
(3) Resurrect : In case of total amount of live cell that surround a dead cell is a specific number, the cell would resurrect.

The successive time stratum of cell plane is unexpectable generated from the former plane by above rules. The orderly pattern in a time stratum can be found in the process.

The algorithm of the program is as follows;

Case #1 of the beginning situation on the cell plane.
The life and death of the present cell
Loop of Z axis
Loop of Y axis
Loop of X axis
Generating of the cell
Checking the number of
livecells
Loop of Z axis
Loop of X axis
Loop of Y axis
(1) Check the number of live cells
(2) Apply the rule
(3) Determine the next generation
The algorithm above can be repeated. The movement of cell is internally a simple generation by a rule. But, it would be much more complicated in the three-dimensional space.

7. INTERACTIVE INCREASE AND DECREASE OF CELL

In the three-dimensional cells, it is difficult to expect the increase or decrease of the number of cell. Therefore, I decided to use the method as follows to solve this problem.
(a) If there are too many cells and the space is

almost saturated, the factor which cause increase is restrained.

(b) If there are seldom cells, the restraint of the factor is removed. That is, the factor which cause increase added.

It will be more helpful if you think the interactive increase and decrease of cell as like this. Suffice it to say that there is a kind of ecological relation in the cell space. As you see in the first example above, the number of cell is limited by the food if it spread too much. As a result, the appropriate space is reserved in the cell space. It is just like a season; the condition can be controlled as the spring-summer season is jumped into the more severe fall-winter season. And as you can see in the second example above, the number of cell is increased by feeding it on the eve of extermination. It is like jumping from the fall-winter season into spring-summer season. To put it in a concrete, the increase or decrease of the numerical value (G(i);i=1,5) is needed.

(1) Survive : In case of the total amount of live cell that surround a live cell is (G1) or (G2), the cell would survive.

(2) Die : In case of the total amount of live cell that surround a live cell is less than (G3) or (G4), the cell would die.

(3) Resurrect : In case of total amount of live cell that surround a dead cell is (G5), the cell would resurrect.

8. Ecological correlation of cell

The number of cell in cell space is countless. So I divided the cells into the several types which is determined by the shape of a cell group.

(1) First, the cells are divided into two groups of male as PA and female as PB by the sexual distinction. With this classification, we can see the characteristic of fusion and repulsion between the cell group.

(a) In case of multiplication of type PA and type PB together in the cell space, they fuse each other.

(b) In case of multiplication of the same type together
in the cell space, it repulse each other.
The phenomena above can be taken as male and female in the natural ecological system.

(2) Second, the cells are divided into several groups of unisex. In this case, we set up Q1, Q2, Q3, Q4 ... Qn as species.

There is characteristic of fusion between Q1 and Q1.

There is characteristic of fusion between Q2 and Q2.

......

There is characteristic of fusion between Qn and Qn.

Then there live several species in the cell space which process self reproduction by correlation.

There is also hostility between the different species in the cell space.

Q3 will be exterminated if Q1 and Q3 meet each other.

Q2 will be exterminated if Q2 and Q3 meet each other.

Q1 will be exterminated if Q1 and Q2 meet each other.

From this kind of correlation system, the situation of cell in each generation is generated.

(3) If we endow immoral life to the cell, the whole situation of cells will be just cycling. So the endowment of life age to the cell must be considered. In the early life of each cell, the rate of multiply will be increased. Let's suffice it to say that the rate of multiply as S(i) and the length of life as m (i = 0~m);

Species Qn is;

the age of 0 : Q * S(0)
the age of 1 : Q * S(1)
:
:
the age of i : Q * S(i)
the age of m : Q * S(m)

$0 < S(i) < $ Scale_Max. (Scale_Max. is a highest rate)

The purpose of age system will be reached if the rate of multiply S(i) is coming down according to the age (i).

Figure 7. "Artificial Life Metropolis CELL," 1993. (See Plate 3.)

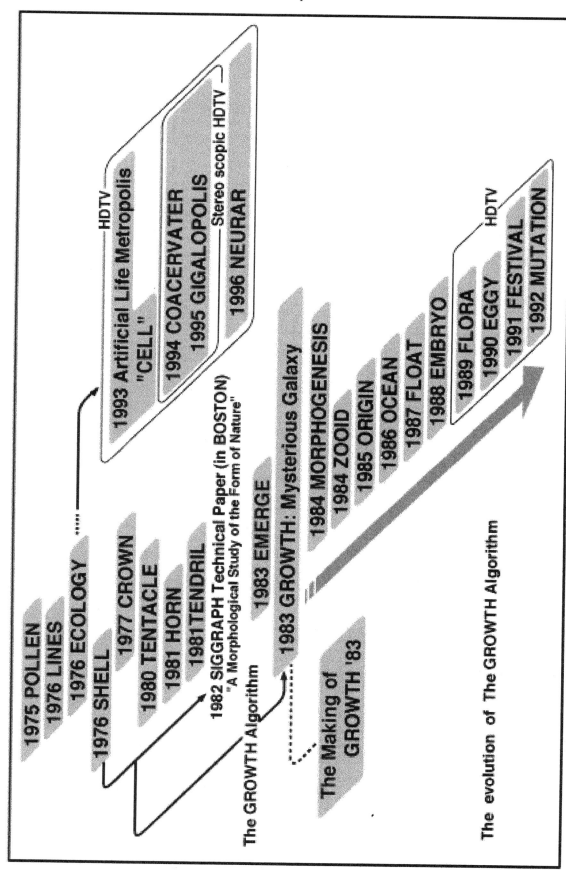

Figure 8. The history of Yoichiro Kawaguchi's works

9. CONCLUSION

I explained the trial of application of three-dimensional cells(Fig.6) into the state of art in this note. It means that the success of the self-organization system(Fig.7) of the cell in correlation is gained with the animation of the art which is experimented in the setting of the cell space(Fig.9).

I tried to experiment the cells as a self-organization in the space of artificial life, not just as a simple life game. And the fact that the part of result of the experiment[6] was made public as an artwork in SIGGRAPH '93 Electronic Theatre (Film and Video Show)[7] prove that it can also be handled as an independent state of art. I hope as many as people to enjoy(Fig.8) the new world of three- dimensional cells from now on.

10. ACKNOWLEDGEMENT

I would like to express sincere thanks to Eiichi Izuhara for advicing me to explore my own "GROWTH" algorithm research in 1976. Koichi Omura gave me a chance to use Metaball rendarer since 1983. Reona Ezaki and Tsutomu Hoshino gave me a chance to use computer graphic system for making the works " Artificial Life Metropolis CELL" at the University of Tsukuba in 1993. Tokiichiro Takahashi in NTT Hi Lab also helped me a lot by transforming my works into HDTV format. My thank also goes to Won-Kon Yi in the doctoral course and Chang-Jin Im to translate this note in English.

11. REFERENCES

[1] D'Arcy W. Thompson,"On Growth and Form I,II",Cambridge Univ. Press,1968
[2] Kawaguchi Yoichiro, "A Morphological Study of the Form of Nature" Technical Proceedings, ACM-SIGGRAPH'82
[3] Katheleen Stein,"Kawaguchi's Spiral",OMUNI Nov.,Omuni Publication International,1982
[4] Kawaguchi,Y."GROWTH:Mysterious Galaxy",ACM-SIGGRAPH'83,Film & Video show tape.
[4] Kawaguchi,Y. "Morphogenesis",JICC publishing Inc.1985
[5] Gardnar M. "Scientific America",Oct.1970
[6] Kawaguchi,Y. "COACERVATER", books with CD-ROM, NTT Publishing Inc.,1994
[7] Kawaguchi, Y. "Artificial Life Metropolis - Cell" (4'00" on HDTV tape) Siggraph Electronic Theatre,ACM-SIGGRAPH '93

Figure 9. "Artificial Life Metropolis CELL," 1993. (See Plate 3.)

"A-Volve" an evolutionary artificial life environment

by Christa Sommerer (1) & Laurent Mignonneau (2)

(1) & (2) ATR Advanced Telecommunications Research
2-2 Amity Hikaridai, Seika-cho Soraku-gun, 61902 Kyoto, Japan
Tel: 81-77495-1426, Fax: 81-77495-1408 and 43-7612-47278 (Austria)
christa@mic.atr.co.jp, laurent@mic.atr.co.jp, http://www.mic.atr.co.jp/~christa

Abstract

"A-Volve" is an interactive real-time environment where visitors can interact with artificial creatures, that live in the space of a water filled glass pool.

These virtual creatures are products of evolutionary rules and influenced by human creation and decision. Their genetic code is transported from generation to generation providing an environment, that evolves by itself and is open to the influence of human interaction.

"A-Volve" is an artistic computer installation, that implements artificial life, genetics, evolution as well as unencumbered interaction with virtual space and artificial life. "A-Volve" has been shown worldwide [1] - [7] and has received several awards for Interactive Art and Multimedia. ("Prix Ars Electronica 93"[8], Linz, Austria, "Ovation Award"[9] Multimedia Festival 94, Los Angeles, USA.

1. System description:

In the interactive real-time environment "A-Volve" visitors interact with virtual creatures in the space of a water filled glass pool. These virtual creatures are products of evolutionary rules and influenced by human creation and decision. Designing any kind of shape and profile with their finger on a touch screen, visitors will "bear" virtual three dimensional creatures, that are automatically "alive" and swim in the real water of the pool.

Algorithms calculate the creatures form and their movement in space. The movement and behavior of the virtual creature is decided by its form, how the viewer was designing it on the touch screen. Behavior in space is, so to speak an expression of form. Form is an expression of adaptation to the environment. Form and movement are closely connected, the creatures capability to move will decide its fitness in the pool. The fittest creature will survive longest and will be able to mate and reproduce. The creatures will compete by trying to get as much energy as possible. Thus predator creatures will hunt for prey creatures, trying to kill them. The creatures also interact with the visitors, by reacting to their hands movement in the water. If a visitor tries to catch a creature, it will try to flee or stays still, if it gets caught. The visitor so is able to influence the evolution by for example protection preys against predators.

If two strong creatures meet, they can create an offspring and a new creature can be born. It carries the genetic code of its parents. Mutation and cross-over provides a nature-like reproduction mechanism, that follows the genetic rules of Mendel. This newly born offspring will now also react and live in the pool, interacting with visitors and other creatures. Algorithms, developed by Mignonneau and Sommerer ensure smooth and natural movements and "animal-like" behavior of the creatures.

None of the creatures is pre calculated, they are all born exclusively in real time, through the interaction of the visitors and the interaction of the creatures. Thus a large variety of forms will be possible, representing human and evolutionary rules. By closely connecting the real natural space of the water to the unreal virtual living space of the creatures, "A-Volve" minimizes the borders between "real" and "unreal", creating a further step, after "Interactive Plant Growing"[10] - [12], in the search of Natural Interfaces and Real-Time Interaction [13].

2. Creation and Genetic Code:

2.1.) Creation:

Drawing a 2 dimensional side view and section of any possible form with their fingers onto a touch sensitive screen, visitors will create three dimensional creatures.

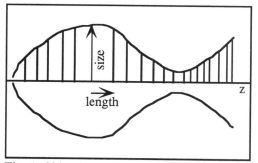

Fig. 1: Side view

A special touch screen editor created by L. Mignonneau, allows the visitors to draw any form, as shown in Figure 1. As he draws a side view of a creature, the outline of this drawing will be mirrored around the z- axis. Our software now subdivides this drawing into 20 points or vertices, that provide the length and size for each parameter point. We then add this size and length information to the genetic code of the creatures genetic string, like shown in Figure 4.

In order to get a three-dimensional form, we not only need a side view but also depth information.
This time the visitor draws a form that represents the section through the creatures body along the z-axis.
The same process of acquiring vertex points is applied to the creatures section, like shown in Figure 2:

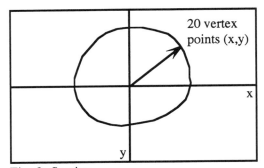

Fig. 2: Section

We again acquire 20 vertex point for x and 20 vertex points for y, all of which are added to the creatures genetic code, as shown in Figure 4.
We are now able to combine these two two-dimensional drawings in real-time to create a three-dimensional form, with a total of 400 vertex points (x, y, z). Figure 3 shows how the above described side view and section are combined into the three-dimensional form:

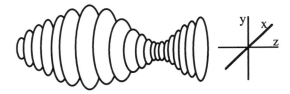

Fig. 3: Three-dimensional creature

Each of the creatures will have 400 vertex points, but their parameters in x, y and z differ, as each visitor draws different side views and sections.
Depending on how the side view and section were drawn, the creatures body volume will correspond, providing important information for the creatures movement and behavior.

2.2.) Genetic Code:

We described above how a creature gets created from two two-dimensional drawings and how we acquire the vertex points in z, y and z.
We can now list up all these parameters and add them to the genetic string of the creature:
20 parameters for size and 20 parameters for length, coming from the side view; 20 parameters for x and 20 parameters for y, coming from the section drawing. This gives us a total of 80 parameters for x, y and z. As we also need color, texture and brightness information for each creature, we will get another 10 parameters, 3 for Color (RGB red-green-blue),

3 for Brightness (B of RGB) and 4 parameters for the texture (T of RGB and 1 Alpha value).

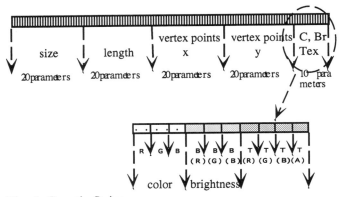

Fig. 4: Genetic String

Figure 4 shows now the genetic string of the creature with all its 90 parameters. Each creature in the pool has such a genetic string, the creatures are haploid and asexual.
The color of the creature is decided by random, the textures depend on the drawing pressure, with which the viewer has drawn the creature on the touch screen.

3. Fitness and Movement:

"A-Volve" provides a novel system, where movement and fitness is linked to the design and shape of a creature. Movement and behavior is so to speak an expression of form. A good design will become a fast and fit creature, whereas less good design will be slow. We will see later that the fitness and speed of the creature's swimming movement will significantly influence its survival in the pool and how successfully it will be able to reproduce and evolve.

3.1.) Movement by propagation through a muscle:

The creature has a virtual muscle attached to its front. This muscle produces a wave function, that is propagated along each ring of the creatures body in the z-axis.

3.1.a) Muscle articulation:

The muscle articulation is a rotation around the x, y and z axis, where the rotations are propagated in a given time step along the z-axis. This produces the propagation of the wave and will influence the direction in which the creature will move or swim. This is shown in Figure 5.

3.1.b) Muscle Contraction:

The second important parameter for the creatures movement its the muscle contraction. The muscle contracts and releases the rings (and vertices) in z and x. Besides, this compression is also propagated along the z-axis in a given time step, creating a propagation delay of the compression.
As the muscle contracts, the creature will be pushed forwards into the given direction, like seen in Figure 6.

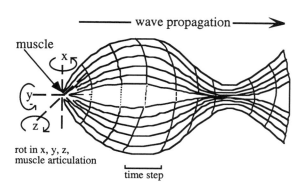

Fig. 5: Muscle Articulation

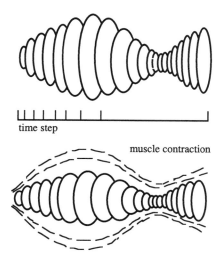

Fig. 6: Muscle Contraction

3.2) Fitness and Speed:

The distance in which a creature pushes itself forward trough one muscle contraction, is its speed.
This speed is equivalent to the creature's fitness.
They more distance a creature can make with one muscle contraction, they faster its is, hence the fitter its is.
We can easily see, that the shape of the creature decides significantly how the muscle is propagating the wave along the body. If a creature has a fluid dynamic design, this wave is propelled fast and the creature can push itself very far with one muscle contraction. That would mean that this creature is a fit creature. We call the fitness of the creature a function of the speed and a function of it's design.
The concept of "A-Volve" is to let visitors find how to design good and fit creatures, as the creatures fitness will decide its survival in the pool.
Fitness (F) is influenced by the viewers design, and also passed on through heritage from one generation to the other. Although each creature has its own constant fitness during its life time, the fitness of the creatures always corresponds to the fitness to the other creatures in the pool.

4. Energy:

When a creature is born or sent into the pool, it has an given energy level of E=1. Unlike the fitness F, the energy (E) is changing during the creatures life time.
This energy is a function of movement. When a creature moves a lot or fast, it will loose its energy faster. The muscle compression is directly liked to the amount of energy used.
If the creature reaches a certain minimum level of energy E<1, then the creature becomes hungry.
To cope with hunger, it will try to catch other creatures, in order to kill them. When the creatures succeeds, it will eat up the energy of the prey and add this energy to it's own energy. When a creatures eats for example a young prey creature, it will gain more energy, then eating a older creature, that has already lost a lot of energy. Since the energy for each creature is changing constantly, we will get a complex behavior between predators and preys.

5. Predator - Prey Behavior:

As we mentioned above, the energy level will decide whether a creatures wants to kill an other creature or not.
Also the creature's fitness has an impact on this decision.
If the creatures energy level is smaller than 1, it will be hungry and thus will become a potential predator.
Before searching for a prey, it has to evaluate its own fitness and check who else is in the pool at the moment, to compare its fitness to the other creatures fitness.
To do so, the creature uses its vision system:

5.1.) Vision - Field of View:

The creature has a vision system, virtual eyes, attached to its front. These eyes provide a field of vision, with a vision angle of 110 degrees, as shown in Figure 7.

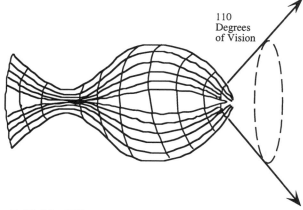

110
Degrees
of Vision

Fig. 7: Field of View

These eyes allow the creature not only to detect other creatures but to see and avoid walls. Thus the creature will be able to react to what its sees, turn itself on the walls, hunt a prey or try to escape from a predator.

5.2.) Fitness and Energy decides Predator-Prey Behavior:

A creature is not born as a predator or a prey, but will decide whether to attack or to flee, depending on the other creatures fitness and energy at the current moment. Thus a creature can be a predator first, but finally become a prey when a fitter creature with more energy comes into the pool.
The creatures therefore have to change their strategy constantly whom to attack and whom to flee. As the energy level (E) also decreases by each movement the creature does, it can become hungry again, even if it has already eaten.
As soon as the critical level of E<1 is reached, the creature becomes a potential predator.
If it is then fit and fast enough to catch and kill other creatures, it will look for a suitable prey to attack:
through his vision system the predator always chooses the prey that is nearest of it and will provide the most energy with the smallest effort of movement.
Figure 9 shows how the balance between fitness and energy influences and decides if the creature becomes a predator or a prey.
The attacked creature knows when it is hunted and tries to escape. In some cases the creature can escape, when for example another weak creature with more energy comes in the field of view of the predator. Then the predator might change his target and the original prey could escape.
In some other cases it also happened, that the prey creature is more skilled to turn itself at the wall of the pool, gets an advantage and escapes.

5.3.) Killing:

In the case the prey could not escape, the predator will attack the prey, kill it and "eat" its energy.
If a creature gets caught, it will die and its energy will be added to the predators energy.
The predator virtually sucks the prey into his front where the muscle is located. The prey then dies and the predator adds the preys energy to its own energy.
If the predator eats a relatively "fresh" prey, which still had some energy left, he will eventually get enough energy to raise his energy level E>1. If this is the case, the predator now will have enough energy to mate.
If the prey on the other hand was already old and had few energy left, the predator might have to eat a second prey for achieving an energy level higher then E>1.
Figure 9 shows how the predator finally caught a prey and added up his energy level E > 1.
Now the predator is ready to mate.

6. Mating and Genetic Exchange:

To find the right mating partner, our predator will select a creature, that is nearest and has the most energy.
If he succeeds to allocate such a creature, both new partners will swim towards each other and prepare to mate.
Mating is asexual and the creatures bodies merge into each other. When the merging process is performed the genetic code of the parents creatures will be exchanged:
a child creature is born.

6.1.) Birth:

The child creature starts as a small form, that gradually grows up. The child carries the genetic code of both parents achieved by genetic cross-over and mutation.
As the genetics means form, fitness, color and texture, the child thus looks and swims similar to its parents.
As fitness is linked to the form, both is inherited from parents to the children.
The usual case is, that fast and fit parents will create a fast and fit offspring. However sometimes mutation of the genetic code can occur and the offspring will be less fast than its parents.

6.2.) Cross Over:

To create a genetic string for the child, the genetic strings (as described earlier in Figure 4) of both parents are exchanged partially by applying cross-over on several sections of the strings. The size and location of the cross-over sections can vary and is decided by random, thus providing variety for the child's genetics.

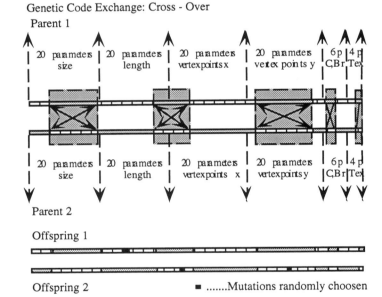

Genetic Code Exchange: Cross - Over

(c), 94 Sommerer & Mignonneau

Fig. 8: Cross-Over and Mutations

Figure 8 shows an example of how the Cross-Over operation is performed between the parents.
We notice that this operation will produce two children, with complementary code.
In "A-Volve" we take only one of the two child creatures, as the space in the pool is limited to about 20 creatures at the time. Besides the system is interactive for the visitors and real-time performance would be limited by too many creatures in the pool. Of course it is easily possible to enhance the population of creatures, if one decides to keep both children per mating process.

6.3.) Mutation:

In Figure 8 we see that some mutation is applied randomly to the genetic string of the child creatures. Even though the random is very little, it will help to create offspring that differ from their parents by some small parameters. This random mutation thus provides new features and diversity for the offspring and its future generation.

7. Childhood:

The newly born creature is very small and needs time to grow up. As its fitness is not yet developed, the parents have to stay near of the child until it is grown up and reaches its original fitness and energy level E=1.
The parents will therefore defend the child against predators and attack them as they come near.
As soon as the child is grown up, it will by itself decide a strategy how to behave in the pool.
In Figure 9 we see how the both parents take care of the child and protect it against an incoming predator.

8. Life Span and Death:

A-Volve is an interactive system, where visitors should be able to create new creatures quite frequently. The amount of creatures can reach up to 20. Therefore the creatures have to live only a limited amount of time. We set the life time of the creatures to a maximum of 1 minute, within which the creature should eat, reproduce and mate. Not all of them succeed and some creatures of course will die earlier.

The creatures can die in 3 different ways:
1. Starving - they couldn't get enough energy by killing other creatures
2. Natural Death- the maximum life time was reached
3. Being Killed - a prey gets killed by a predator

They are born in two different ways:
1. Being created by the visitors on the touch screen
2. Being born by mating and genetic exchange of two parents creatures

9. Evolution:

As the genetic code of the offspring is transported from generation to generation and the emphasis of the system is based upon selection for fitter creatures, the system is able to evolve over time towards fitter creatures. Although the evolution could take place by itself and without influence from outside, the system is designed in a way, the visitor and his interaction and creation of forms will significantly influence the evolutionary process. We can consider the visitors a form of an external selection mechanism.
The three main internal parameters, Fitness, Energy and Life Time, regulate the interaction, reproduction and evolution among the creatures. The external parameters are the visitors drawings on the touch screen as well as his interaction with the creatures.
Figure 9 shows now the complete diagram of how creatures in "A-Volve" interact with each other and how creation,

birth, energy level, fitness, predator-prey behavior, mating and death are regulating the life of these artificial creatures.

10. Interaction Creature - Visitor:

Not only are the creatures interacting with each other, they also interact with the visitors.
A camera detection system and interface developed by Mignonneau, allows us to detect the visitors hands, when he reaches into the pool. The creature get the information that a hand is there and will act accordingly.
When touching a creature with ones hands, the creature first will be irritated and wants to escape. Once it is caught, it will calm down and will stop to swim.
Touching and stopping a predator, the visitor can help the prey to escape. Or he also can try to push creatures together, and promote their mating process.
"A-Volve" thus gives the visitor the possibility to create, interact with and observe artificial life, that follows its own internal laws, but is open to the influenced by his decisions.
By creating creatures, observing them in the pool and influencing their behavior, the visitors will identify with their creatures. The interaction between the visitors happens mainly through the virtual creatures, which mate and fight with each other. Thus the visitors will also communicate with each other, by supporting their creatures in the pool.

11. Intention and Conclusion:

"A-Volve" is a pool of artificially living creatures, that are open to outside influences by reacting and interacting with their "natural" and "artificial" environment.
"A-Volve" reduces the borders between real and unreal, by connecting reality to "non-reality."
Human decision in the creation of a new form and the rules of evolution and selection create an environment that is open to modifications and selections, following the laws of evolution and creation.
Water as the metaphor for birth and basic evolution is the medium for this artificial life "pool", that is open to its real environment.
"A-Volve" is installed permanently at NHK building, NTT Nagoya from July 96 to July 98.
More information about "A-Volve" is available at: http://www.mic.atr.co.jp/~christa

Acknowledgments:

"A-Volve" was supported by ICC InterCommunication Center NTT Japan , NCSA National Center for Supercomputing Application Urbana Illinois, USA and ATR Human Information Processing Laboratories, Kyoto, Japan. We would like to thank Prof. Donna Cox and Prof. George Francis for their support.
We would especially like to thank Dr. Tom Ray for his collaboration on the genetics and evolution.

References:

[1] Sommerer, Christa, and Mignonneau, Laurent.
A-Volve: A real-time interactive environment
New York, USA: ACM Siggraph Visual Proceedings,
1994: 172-173

[2] Ishi-Kawa, Leyla, and Falk, Lorne and Kusahara,
Machiko. *A-Volve: Evolucion Artificial - Un entorno
interactivo en tiempo real*
Madrid, Spain: Fundacion Arte Y Tecnologia, 1996

[3] Inter Communication Center ICC.
Interactive Plant Growing and A-Volve
Christa Sommerer & Laurent Mignonneau
Tokyo, Japan: NTT/ICC 1994

[4] Hong-hee, Kim, and Goodman, Cynthia.
Info Art: The Kwangju Biennale
Seoul, Korea: Kwangju Biennale Foundation: 117-120

[5] Sommerer, Christa, and Mignonneau, Laurent.
A-Volve: A real-time interactive environment
Ciudad Guayana, Venezuela: CNIASE 95 Conference
Proceedings, 1995: 239-242

[6] Sommerer, Christa, and Mignonneau, Laurent, and
Usami, Yoshiyuki. *Artificial Life and Art: artificial Art
Worlds by C. Sommerer and L. Mignonneau*
Tokyo, Japan: Computer Today, No.71 1996: 41-46

[7] Falk, Lorne.
Brave New Worlds of Sommerer & Mignonneau
USA, Silicon Graphics Iris Univers, No. 35, 1996:
36-39 & http://www.sgi.com/ion/winter_95/sm.html

[8] Leopoldseder, Hannes. *Der Prix Ars Electronica:
Golden Nica Award - Interactive Art*
Linz, Austria: Veritas Verlag, 1993: 100-104

[9] Druckery, Timothy, and Goldman, Lisa.
The Interactive Media Festival
San Francisco, USA: Arc Awards, 1995

[10] Sommerer, Christa, and Mignonneau, Laurent.
Interactive Plant Growing
New York, USA: ACM Siggraph Visual Proceedings,
1993: 164-165

[11] Sommerer, Christa, and Mignonneau, Laurent.
Interactive Plant Growing
Wien, Austria: PSV Verleger Genetische Kunst
Kuenstliches Leben, Ars Electronica 93, 1993:408-414

[12] Capucci, Pier Luigi.
*Interactive Plant Growing: Christa Sommerer & Laurent
Mignonneau*
Milano, Italy: Domus, March 96, 1996

[13] Sommerer, Christa, and Mignonneau, Laurent.
Art as Living System
Boston: MIT Press, Leonardo Journal, Vol. 30, No. 5, 1997

"A - V o l v e" diagram

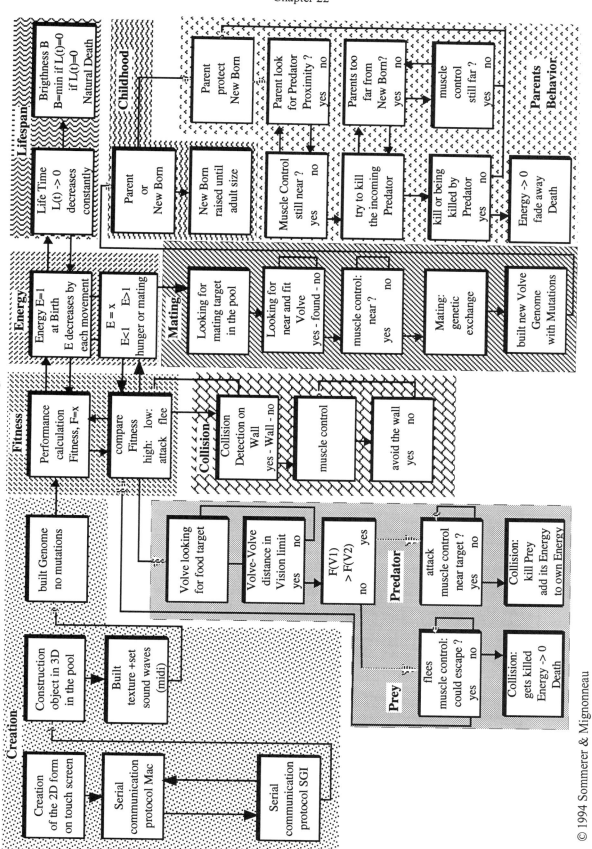

Fig. 9: A-Volve Diagram

© 1994 Sommerer & Mignonneau

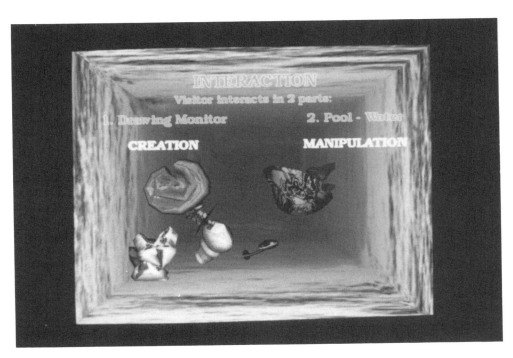

"A-Volve." (See Plate 4.)
Images © 1994 Sommerer & Mignonneau

"A-Volve." (See Plate 4.)
Images © 1994 Sommerer & Mignonneau

Cooperation & Competition

Self-organising vocabularies

Luc Steels
Artificial Intelligence Laboratory
Vrije Universiteit Brussel
Pleinlaan 2, B-1050 Brussels, Belgium
E-mail: `steels@arti.vub.ac.be`

Abstract

The paper investigates a mechanism by which distributed agents spontaneously and autonomously develop a common vocabulary. The vocabulary is open in the sense that new agents and new meaning may be added at any time. Self-organisation plays a critical role for achieving coherence.

1 Introduction

The 'artificial life' approach has already shed some light on certain issues related to the origins and evolution of language. Several researchers have carried out experiments to investigate the origin of communication [7], the origin of vocabulary [15], and the growth in complexity of syntax [3]. They generally assume that genetic evolution is the main driving force towards new structure, coherence, and more complexity. But humans learn the languages present in their environment during their life time. There is no evidence that a *particular* natural language is innate (although the thesis has been advanced that there is an innate language acquisition device [1]). Moreover languages are continuously evolving and expanding and speakers must consequently adapt.

This paper explores cultural creation and transmission as an alternative explanation for the origins of language. It proposes that self-organisation plays a critical role. The paper focuses on the formation of vocabularies, i.e. a set of associations between words and meanings. Meanings take the form of features (which could be Boolean properties, attribute-value pairs or instantiated relations). Three mechanisms are proposed for language formation: (1) agents may *generate* a new word and associate it with as yet non-lexicalised meanings, (2) agents adopt word-meaning associations from others and thus words *propagate* in the population, and (3) a positive feedback mechanism between the selection of a word in a conversation and the success so far in using that word leads to self-organized *coherence*. It will be shown that based on these mechanisms a common but still evolving vocabulary emerges. Moreover no separate mechanism is needed for language acquisition.

The proposed mechanism is general and can be applied to express any kind of meaning. In another paper [11] I show for example an application for the expression of spatial concepts. Agents develop names and spatial descriptions for identifying each other using spatial relationships. A longer paper [12] describes the mechanisms in more detail and shows a mapping from arbitrary feature sets to (multi-word) expressions. This research is part of a larger research program for understanding the origins of intelligence [14] which attempts to combine a growth in complexity of grounded, situated behavior [10] [13] with an evolving capacity for the creation of language and meaning.

The rest of this paper is in three parts. The first section introduces the proposed mechanism in more detail. The second section provides some results of computational simulations. Some conclusions end the paper.

2 Language formation mechanisms

Our point of departure will be that language is a shared, negotiated set of conventions between a group of agents for expressing meaning. The social and functional dimension of a linguistic interchange is therefore viewed as primary. It is captured by embedding the language formation process in *language games* [16].

Let there be a set of agents $A = \{a_1, ..., a_n\}$. Each agent a is assumed to have a set of features $F_a = \{f_1, ..., f_m\}$. $\mathcal{F}$ is the set of all possible feature sets. A set of features $D_{a_1}^B$ distinguishes an agent a_1 from a set of other agents $B = \{a_2, ..., a_n\}$ iff $D_{a_1}^B \subset F_{a_1}$ and $\forall a \in B, D_{a_1}^B \not\subset F_a$. $D_{a_1}^B$ is called a *distinctive feature set* with respect to a_1 and B. There can be several distinctive feature sets for the same a_1 and B. There can also be none if $F_{a_1} \subseteq F_{a_k} \in B$.

A *word* is a sequence of letters drawn from a finite shared alphabet. In the experiments reported later, a word is a consonant-vowel sequence, such as "(t a)" or "(k i)". An *expression* is a set of words. Word order is not assumed to play a role.

A *lexicon* $L \subset \mathcal{F} \times W$ is a relation between a possible feature set $K \subset \mathcal{F}$ and a word $w \in W$. Each member of this relation is called an *association*. Each agent $a \in A$

is assumed to have a single lexicon L_a which is initially empty.

$u(<K,w>,a)$ is the number of times the association $<K,w>\in L_a$ has been used by a. $s(<K,w>,a)$ is the number of times the association $<K,w>\in L_a$ was used successfully by a, i.e. when it is part of a language game which ended with communicative success (defined shortly).

A *language game* $g =<C,i,r,o>$ includes a context $C = \{a_1, a_2, ..., a_j\} \subseteq A$, an initiator $i \in C$, a recipient $r \in C$, and a topic $o \in C$. The language game involves the following steps:

1. Both the initiator i and the receiver r determine the distinctive feature sets $\mathcal{D}_o^C = \{D_i^B \mid B = C\backslash\{o\}\}$. It is assumed that both agents share the same perception, i.e. $\mathcal{D}_o^C = \{D_i^B \mid B = C\backslash\{o\}\} = \{D_r^B \mid B = C\backslash\{o\}\}$.

2. The initiator chooses one feature set $D_j \in \mathcal{D}_o^C$ and constructs an expression e which *covers* D_j.

3. The recipient *uncovers* from e the feature sets $\mathcal{H} = \{H_1, ..., H_p\}$

4. g ends in communicative success when $\mathcal{H} \bigcap \mathcal{D}_o^C \neq \emptyset$, otherwise in failure.

The *cover* and *uncover* functions are at the heart of the language encoding and decoding process. They are defined as follows:

- Given an agent $a \in A$, $cover(D, L_a) = \{e \mid e = \{w \mid D = \bigcup K \text{ with } <K,w>\in L_a\}\}$.

- Given an agent $a \in A$, $uncover(e, L_a) = \{H \mid H = \bigcup K \text{ with } <K,w>\in L_a, w \in e\}$.

The cover function yields a set of possible expressions. Only one expression is selected for use in the communication, based on two criteria: (1) the smallest set is preferred and (2) in case of equal size, an expression is preferred for which the implied associations score better. The score $m(<K,w>,a) = s(<K,w>,a)/u(<K,w>,a)$ for $<K,w>\in L_a$.

The different rules that agents follow in the adoption or formation of language are as follows:

1. *Not enough distinctions:* $\mathcal{D}_o^C = \emptyset$. The game fails and pressure is put on a meaning creation process to introduce a new distinction.

2. *Lexicon inadequate for initiator:* $cover(D_j, L_i) = \emptyset$. The game ends in failure but the initiator may create a new word (with probability 0.05 in the present experiments) and associate it in his lexicon with the non-covered meanings. The same situation may also occur when only a subset of D_j cannot be covered, in which case a word may be made for the remaining uncovered meanings.

3. *Lexicon inadequate for recipient:* $uncover(e, L_r) = \emptyset$. The recipient may not have enough associations in his lexicon to uncover all the meanings from e. In this case the game ends in failure. Several futher possibilities can be distinguished:

   (a) *No words at all could be uncovered:* $uncover(e, L_r) = \emptyset$. In this case, the recipient can deduce that the expression must be associated with one of the feature sets in the distinctive feature sets, and the association is consequently constructed.

   (b) *Some but not all words could be uncovered:* It could be that some words could be uncovered but others could not be. When there is only one word which is unknown, the recipient can deduce the meaning and a new association can be created. When there is too much uncertainty no changes are made.

4. *No words missing:* Both the initiator and the recipient have associations to encode or decode the distinctive feature sets:

   (a) *Success:* $\mathcal{H} \bigcap \mathcal{D}_o^C \neq \emptyset$. The distinctive feature sets expected by the recipient include the one uncovered from the expression used by the initiator. Both the use and the success of the association is incremented by the initiator and the recipient.

   (b) *Success but too general:* Same as (a) but the recipient decoded more possible meanings for the expression. In that case, only the success of the association that was effectively relevant gets incremented.

   (c) *Mismatch in meaning:* $\mathcal{H} \bigcap \mathcal{D}_o^C = \emptyset$. The feature set decoded by the recipient is not one of the feature sets that is distinctive for the object. The success record of the implied association is therefore not incremented.

3 Simulation results

The mechanisms described in the previous section have been instantiated in the form of computer programs implemented in LISP. The program creates agents, assigns randomly values for features from the set of possible features, and then starts a series of language games. For each game, a context, initiator, recipient and topic are randomly chosen. A language game is printed out by the program as follows:

```
Dialog 47 between a-2 and a-4 about a-2.
    Context: {a-2 a-6 a-5 a-4 }
    a-2 = ((f1) (f2))
a-2: (f1) => ((d o))
a-4: => (f1)
(success)
```

a-2 can be identified through f1 or f2. a-2 picks f1 and encodes it as "((d o))". This expression is succesfully decoded as f1 by a-4. The language game ends in success.

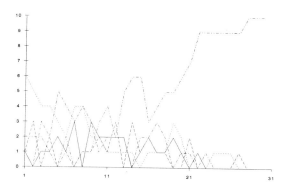

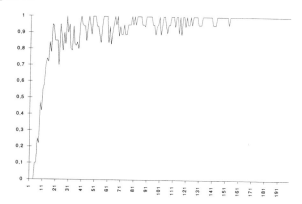

Figure 1: The results of a typical experiment with 10 agents, 5 possible words, and 1 meaning. It plots the communicative success of each word (y-axis) over time (x-axis). We see a search period in which different words compete until one gains complete dominance.

Figure 3: This figure plots the formation of a language from scratch. 4000 language games are shown. The x-axis plots the number of language games (scale 1/20). The y-axis shows the average communicative success.

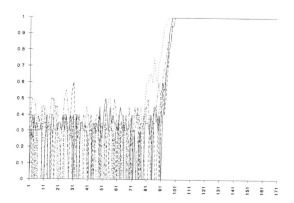

Figure 2: The graph plots the highest communicative success of all words over time for an experiment with 20 agents, 5 different meanings and 5 possible words. The combinatorial implosion happens after 90 time steps.

The reaching of coherence has often the effect of a phase transition. Initially several words will compete for the same meaning but due to the positive feedback effect between communicative success and choice of a word, coherence emerges. Figure 1 shows results for 10 agents, 5 words and 1 feature.

Figure 2 shows results when several meanings are involved. There are 10 agents, 5 possible words and 5 possible meanings. Contrary to what might be expected, there is no combinatorial explosion but an implosion. Once a word has a consistent meaning it is no longer available and so the set of possible choices for the others are shrinking. Consequently we see a rapid evolution towards coherence as soon as a sufficient part of the vocabulary has been established. This phenomenon is similar to the combinatorial implosions pointed out by Kauffman in the clustering and interconnection of autocatalytic networks [4].

Here are the results of a series of experiments starting with 5 agents, and 3 features with each 3 possible values (giving in total 9 possible meanings). Only those meanings are lexicalised that are relevant for identifying the agents with respect to a subset of the other agents.

Fig. 3 shows the evolution of the language from the beginning. The communicative success climbs steadily from 0 to become absolute. The agents have developed a sufficient number of words to distinguish each other based on their features. Close inspection of the preferred language (i.e. the word-meaning association with the highest score) shows that only one feature has not been lexicalised:

```
f1: [(t i) (a-6 a-7 a-8 a-9 a-10)]
f2: [(n e) (a-6 a-7 a-8 a-9 a-10)]
f3: [(n e) (a-6 a-8 a-9 a-10)]
    [(t i) (a-7)]
f4: [(r e) (a-6 a-7 a-9 a-10)]
    [(d a) (a-8)]
f5: [(r e) (a-8 a-9 a-10)]
    [(d a) (a-6 a-7)]
f6: [(b e) (a-6 a-7 a-8 a-9 a-10)]
f7: [(s o) (a-6 a-7 a-8 a-9 a-10)]
f8: [(z u) (a-6 a-7 a-8 a-9 a-10)]
```

We also see incoherence (for f3 and f4 two words are used by the group) and ambiguity ("(n e)" can mean both f2 and f3). These incoherences and ambiguities do not have an impact on communicative success, for example because they do not matter (all agents that have f2 also have f3) or because additional words expressing other features are used to disambiguate. Note that agents keep track of more words than the ones they preferably use and therefore can often "understand" the words of others even if they would not use these themselves.

Fig 4. plots how the language adapts after a new agent (a-12) is added. The new agent entering the group acquires the already existing language. At the same time,

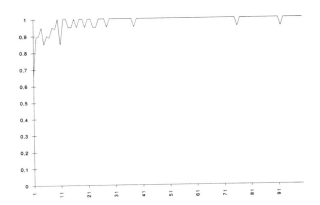

Figure 4: This figure plots 2000 language games illustrating the adaptation of language after a new agent comes in. The x-axis plots the number of language games (scale 1/20). The y-axis shows the communicative success.

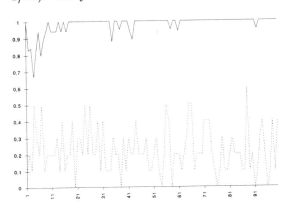

Figure 5: Another agent enters and the language adjusts. 2000 language games are shown. The y-axis shows the communicative success (top graph) and the failure in making distinctions (bottom graph). Many language games fail by lack of available distinctions because too many agents have joined the group that have the same features as those already present.

new words may get created because new distinctions become lexicalised. Initially there is a drop in communicative success but after some time period, adjustments and new lexicalisations restore it.

When more and more agents are added, the available features become insufficient to distinguish one agent from others. Consequently language games start to fail on that basis. This is seen in fig 5.

Fig 6. plots the adaptation of the language after a new feature (with 3 possible values) is introduced. There is a drop in communicative success when the new distinction is introduced but after a certain period, communicative success reaches again the maximum. The success in making distinctions has also improved.

A similar experiment where a new feature with 5 possible values is introduced is shown in fig 7. Again we see

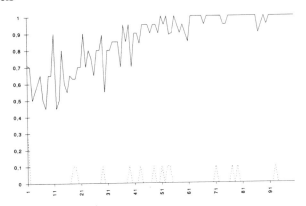

Figure 6: This figure plots the adaptation of language after a new distinction has been introduced. The failure to make distinctions has decreased. 2000 language games are shown.

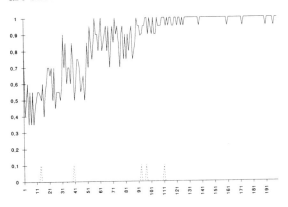

Figure 7: This figure plots the adaptation of language after yet another distinction has been added. 4000 language games are shown.

a drop in communicative success followed by a rebound.

The language now looks as follows:

```
f1: [(t i) (a-6 a-7 a-8 a-9 a-10 a-11 a-12
          a-13 a-14)]
f2: [(z u) (a-14)]
    [(n e) (a-6 a-7 a-8 a-9 a-10 a-11 a-12 a-13)]
f3: [(t i) (a-14)]
    [(n e) (a-6 a-8 a-9 a-10 a-11 a-12 a-13)]
    [(k u) (a-7)]
f4: [(n u) (a-7 a-11 a-12 a-13 a-14)]
    [(r e) (a-6 a-9 a-10)]
    [(d a) (a-8)]
f5: [(d a) (a-6 a-7 a-10 a-11 a-12 a-13 a-14)]
    [(r e) (a-8 a-9)]
f6: [(b e) (a-6 a-7 a-8 a-9 a-10 a-11 a-12
          a-13 a-14)]
f7: [(s o) (a-6 a-7 a-8 a-9 a-10 a-11 a-12
          a-13 a-14)]
f8: [(z u) (a-6 a-7 a-8 a-9 a-10 a-11 a-12
```

```
                a-13 a-14)]
f9:  [(z u) (a-6 a-7 a-8 a-9 a-10 a-11 a-12
                a-13 a-14)]
f10: [(r u) (a-6 a-7 a-8 a-9 a-10 a-11 a-12
                a-13 a-14)]
f11: [(m e) (a-6 a-7 a-8 a-9 a-10 a-11 a-12
                a-13 a-14)]
f12: [(n o) (a-6 a-7 a-8 a-9 a-10 a-11 a-12
                a-13 a-14)]
f13: [(t e) (a-6 a-7 a-8 a-9 a-10 a-11 a-12
                a-13 a-14)]
f14: [(m u) (a-6 a-7 a-8 a-9 a-10 a-11 a-12
                a-13 a-14)]
f15: [(v u) (a-6 a-7 a-8 a-9 a-10 a-11 a-12
                a-13 a-14)]
f16: [(v a) (a-7 a-8 a-9 a-10 a-11 a-12 a-13 a-14)]
     [(g i) (a-6)]
f17: [(j i) (a-6 a-7 a-8 a-9 a-10 a-11 a-12
                a-13 a-14)]
f18: [(b o) (a-6 a-7 a-8 a-9 a-10 a-11 a-12
                a-13 a-14)]
f19: [(k u) (a-6 a-7 a-8 a-9 a-10 a-11 a-12
                a-13 a-14)]
f20: [(p i) (a-6 a-7 a-8 a-9 a-10 a-11 a-12
                a-13 a-14)]
f21: [(v e) (a-6 a-7 a-8 a-9 a-10 a-12 a-13 a-14)]
     [(k a) (a-11)]
```

A typical conversation at this point is the following:

```
Dialog 12470 between a-12 and a-14 about a-6.
   Context: {a-14 a-12 a-3 a-5 }
   a-6 = ((f1 f4) (f19 f17) (f4 f19) (f1 f17))
   a-12: (f1 f4) => ((t i) (n u))
   a-14: => ((f3) (f1) (f2))
(success-but-too-general)
```

a-14 and a-12 identify a-6 by a number of possibilities. One of them is the feature set ($f1$ $f2$). a-12 chooses this one and encodes it in a two-word expression: "((t i) (n u))". The expression is ambiguous for a-14, because "(t i)" can be both f3 and f1. The combination (f1 f2) is however in the distinctive feature set. The language game is therefore successful and the success rate of "(t i)"for f1 (but not for f3) increases.

The experiments illustrate that the vocabulary formation mechanism is an open system: new agents (and therefore new contexts and meanings) as well as new distinctions may be introduced, and the vocabulary adapts. Adaptation takes the form of new lexicalisations, or disambiguation of existing lexicalisations. For example, f4 is progressing towards the word "(n u)" whereas before it was expressed mostly as "(r e)". This will give a disambiguation with respect to f5, which is now mostly expressed as "(d a)" whereas earlier on it was also expressed as "(r e)".

4 Conclusions

The paper proposed an approach for vocabulary formation by a group of distributed agents. The approach is based on three mechanisms: agents create new associations between words and meanings when a particular meaning has not yet been lexicalised, words propagate through the population because agents adopt word-meaning associations from others, and a positive feedback between success in use and re-use self-organises the distributed vocabulary until it reaches coherence. Simulation results show that the language formation process is remarkably fast although more experiments need to be done to test whether the mechanism scales up.

5 Acknowledgement

The research and writing of this paper has been financed by the Belgian Federal government FKFO project on emergent functionality (FKFO contract nr. G.0014.95) and the IUAP 'Construct' Project (nr. 20) of the Belgian government, with additional support from the external researcher program of the Sony Computer Science Laboratory in Tokyo.

References

[1] Chomsky, N. (1980) Rules and Representations. Brain and Behavior Science. Vol 3. pp. 1-15.

[2] Deneubourg, J-L. (1977) Application de l'ordre par fluctuations a la description de certaines etapes de la construction du nid chez les termites. Insectes Sociaux, Tome 24, 2, p. 117-130.

[3] Hashimoto, and Ikegami (1995) Evolution of Symbolic Grammar Systems. In: Morán, F, A. Moreno, J. Merelo and P. Chacón (Eds.) (1995) Advances in Artificial Life. Third European Conference on Artificial Life. Granada, Spain. Springer-Verlag, Berlin. p. 812-823.

[4] Kauffman, S.A. (1993) The origins of order: self organization and selection in evolution. Oxford University Press, Oxford.

[5] Langton, C. (ed.) (1995) Artificial Life. An overview. The MIT Press, Cambridge, Ma.

[6] Maynard-Smith, J. and E. Szathmary (1994) The major transitions in evolution. Oxford University Press, Oxford.

[7] MacLennan, B. (1991) Synthetic Ethology: An Approach to the Study of Communication. In: Langton, C., et.al. (ed.) Artificial Life II. Addison-Wesley Pub. Co. Redwood City, Ca. p. 631-658.

[8] Pinker, S. (1994) The language instinct. Penguin Books, London.

[9] Prigogine, I. and I. Stengers (1984) Order Out of Chaos. Bantam Books, New York.

[10] Steels, L. and R. Brooks, eds. (1995) Building Situated Embodied Agents. The Alife route to AI. Lawrence Erlbaum Assoc., New Haven.

[11] Steels, L. (1996) A self-organizing spatial vocabulary. Artificial Life Journal,[to appear], 1996.

[12] Steels, L. (1996b) The Spontaneous Self-organization of an Adaptive Language. In: Muggleton, S. (ed.) (1996) Machine Intelligence 15. Oxford Univ. Press, Oxford.

[13] Steels, L. (1996c) Discovering the competitors. Journal of Adaptive Behavior. 4(2), 1996.

[14] Steels, L. (1996d) The origins of intelligence. In: Proceedings of the 1995 Carlo Erba Meeting on Artificial Life. Fondazione Carlo Erba, Milano.

[15] Werner, G. and M. Dyer (1991) Evolution of Communication in Artificial Organisms. In: Langton, C., et.al. (ed.) Artificial Life II. Addison-Wesley Pub. Co. Redwood City, Ca. p. 659-687.

[16] Wittgenstein, L. (1974) Philosophical Investigations. Translated by G. Anscombe. Basil Blackwell, Oxford.

How Do Selfish Agents Learn to Cooperate?

Akira Ito

Kansai Advanced research Center
Communications Research Laboratory
588-2, Iwaoka, Nishiku, Kobe, 651-24, Japan
ai@crl.go.jp

Abstract

How should an autonomous agent, which acts at its own will and takes responsibility for its actions, interact with other agents? Can it cooperate through sacrificing its own profit, if cooperation is favorable or profitable for the society as a whole? Dawkins' answer is "yes, so long as the genes are shared among them." Axelrod's answer is "yes, so long as interaction occurs repetitively between the same agents." In this paper, we examine a third condition: "if information on the past behaviors of other agents is disclosed", and investigate how selfish agents behave under such a situation. The Prisoner's Dilemma game is used as a model of interactions of autonomous agents. It is found that through interactions with other agents, even a selfish agent can learn to cooperate.

1 Introduction

It is often said that a machine system can do only what it is programmed to do, while a living being can act at its own will. We wanted to make a machine system that would act at its own will, but could also cooperate with humans, with other machines, and make a cooperative society.

How should an autonomous agent, which acts at its own will and takes responsibility for its actions, interact with other agents? Unfortunately, there seems to be no consensus among researchers as to what an "autonomous agent" really is. Thus, we must start by defining our autonomous agent.

Autonomous agent An autonomous agent is an autonomous system (automaton) whose inner mechanism cannot be understood algorithmically solely by observing its behavior from outside. Aims, goals, and intentions are the heuristics introduced by an observer for modeling an agent whose inner mechanism is inaccessible to him.

According to the definition, when interacting with other agents, one cannot know beforehand what rules they are following. The only thing one can do is to make model of (guess about) the agent with which one has to interact. To model the opponent of interaction, however,

1) one should not presuppose the existence of common goals, and
2) one should not expect rational behavior from the opponent.

The assumption of a rational agent is often adopted in modeling other agents. To assume the opponent's rationality, however, it is necessary that the opponent:
1) has some definite goals to follow, and
2) has the ability to execute logical calculations
- which is not, in general, guaranteed. In fact, these naive expectations for rationality are often betrayed in everyday life. Nevertheless, if no such assumptions are allowed, it is very difficult to predict the opponent's behavior.

The assumption of rationality may be plausible, if we can presuppose a rational designer behind the agents. Fortunately, we can introduce a world where some rationality can be safely assumed [1]. It is a world where an evaluation of an agent's action is reflected in its survival rate and breeding rate. We formulated this as an "evolutionary world."

Evolutionary world An evolutionary world is a world where the evaluation of an agent's action is reflected in its survival rate and breeding rate (natural selection).

Common goal An agent seeks the common goal of increasing its number of offspring.

In an evolutionary world, all species that does not seek their common goal will ultimately cease to exist. In other words, those that have survived until now must have sought the common goal of increasing their offspring.

This assumption is very popular for biological systems [2][3][4]. Our point is to propose it as a design principle for a purely artificial autonomous agent (machine system). In this evolutionary world, "act at its own will" simply means that it operates according to its inner mechanisms, and "take responsibility for its action" simply means the existence of the natural selection mechanism in the world. An autonomous agent thus defined is what Dawkins called "selfish gene" [5], and "homo economicas" [6], which is the theoretical basis of modern economics.

If these autonomous agents cannot cooperate with other agents, and with humans, however, then they have no significance from an engineering viewpoint. Hence, our question is the following: Can selfish agents as defined above make a cooperative society? That is, if there is a situation where cooperation is more profitable for the society as a whole, can a selfish agent cooperate without seeking its own immediate profit?

If there are no conditions or restrictions on the environment, the answer is probably "no." Dawkins' answer is "yes, if genes are shared among the society" [5]. Axelrod's answer is "yes, if the game is played repetitively between the same players" [7][8][9].

In our society, however, there are occasions when we can cooperate but when neither of the above conditions hold. We try to behave cooperatively partly because we regard others' evaluation of ourselves important. This means that the circulation of information plays certain roles in the emergence of cooperation. Hence, we propose a third condition, i.e., "if information on the past behavior of other agents is disclosed," and investigate whether we can answer "yes" to the question [10][11].

2 The Prisoner's Dilemma game under the disclosure of information

We used the Prisoner's Dilemma game as a model of the interaction of autonomous agents. It is a standard model for investigating the problem of cooperation [12][13][14]. The Prisoner's Dilemma game is a non-zero-sum game between two players (A and B). In the game, each participant plays either C (Cooperate) or D (Defect), and points are earned accordingly, as listed in Table 1.

Table 1. Payoff matrix of the Prisoner's Dilemma game

A \ B	C	D
C	A:3 B:3	A:0 B:5
D	A:5 B:0	A:1 B:1

The main features of the game are:
1) Whatever the move of the other player is, it is more profitable for a player to defect.
2) The points earned when both defect, or the average points earned when one defects whereas the other cooperates, are lower than when both cooperate.
Axelrod showed the following:
1) Cooperation emerges if both players expect to play repetitively in the future (Iterated Prisoner's Dilemma game).
2) The only rational strategy for a single round game is to defect, and no cooperation can emerge in such a situation.
Our aim is to break the above dilemma situation by introducing a disclosure of information.

First, let us briefly explain our world model[10][11]. An agent moves around randomly in a two-dimensional space (lattice) of $N \times N$. That is, an agent moves to one of the neighboring sites with probability p_{rw}, or stays at the same place with probability $(1 - 4p_{rw})$. Agents occupying the same location can, and must, make a match. The match is equivalent to the Prisoner's Dilemma game, with the payoff matrix listed in Table 1. In the match, each agent decides either to cooperate or to defect, applying his match strategy algorithm to the match history of the opponent. Match records are made open to the

public, and can be accessed by any agent. The match history is a list of match records whose format is given below.

(Time Agent1 Agent2 Move1 Move2)
An agent has initial assets of A_0, and the profit calculated as follows is added each time it makes a match.

Profit = Payoff of the original PDG
    - (Match fee (constant) + Algorithm calculation cost)

An agent whose assets become less than zero is bankrupt, and is deleted from the system. On the other hand, an agent whose asset become larger than $2A_0$ produces a child and imparts an amount A_0 to it. The child inherits the match strategy of its parent. There is no way to identify the parent agent from its child agent. The system parameters used are given in Table 2.

Table 2. System parameters

Probability of the agent's random walk p_{rw}	1/40
Size of the lattice N	15
Initial asset A_0	20
Match fee C_d	2.5
Algorithm calculation cost/instruction C_{am}	0.002
Strategy inheritance cost/instruction C_{st}	0.1

In this artificial world where agents are made to play the Prisoner's Dilemma game repetitively, each time changing opponents, what strategy is the most advantageous, and how can it be learned by a selfish agent seeking only its own profit? A condition of the match is that the match history is disclosed to the public. This is the theme of our current research.

3 Description of match strategy algorithms

The match strategy is an algorithm that calculates what move to play next based on the match history of the opponent. As the match history will be disclosed to other agents, the strategy should take into account not only the expected profit of the current match, but also the effect the play of this match might have on future matches.

To investigate the learning of match strategies, we needed a framework for describing strategies. Hence, we introduced a strategy algorithm calculator as follows. The calculator had 8 (typed) registers, and 6 opecodes (all without operands). Moreover, the calculator had an infinite-length stack, and could execute reflective (recursive) calculations. Inputs to the calculator were the (current) time, the pointer to the opponent, and the match strategy algorithm. The calculator returned the next move (either C or D) as the result of the calculation. The registers, opecodes, and the flow of the calculations are shown in Fig. 1 using a syntax similar to C++, and as a schematic diagram in Fig. 2.

First the calculator loaded the match record of the opponent's latest match into the history register. Suppose the opponent in the next match is a, and a's latest match was R_n (i.e., the match record of the match R_n was loaded), and the opponent of a in R_n was a_n. The calculator processed the strategy algorithm step by step.

```
/* type definition */
enum move {C,D};  // enumerate type {C,D}
typedef int time;  // time type
class agent;  // agent type
typedef int instruction-pointer ip;
struct register{ // registers
  move h;  // output register
  time t;
  agent* a;
  history his; // match history
  instruction-pointer ip;
};
struct history{
  time time;
  agent agent;  // the other agent
  move my;      // move of this agent
  move you;     // move of the other agent
};
class agent{ ... ;        // agent's private data
  history history;
};
/* opecode */
enum opcode {
  LC;  // loadh-c;  load C to h register
  LD;  // loadh-d;  load D to h register
  BM;  // branch-m; branch acc. his.my
  BY;  // branch-y; branch acc. his.you
  SL;  // apply self; apply its own algorithm
       //                    to his.agent
  TP;  // decriment time by 1, and goto top;
};
typedef al-codes List-of opcode;  // like LISP's list
/* abstract machine */
am(time t, agent a,  al-codes al) {
/* current time, the other agent, strategy algorithm */
  instruction-pointer ip=0;
/* set C or D randomly */
  move h=random_selection('C','D');
/* load  agent(a)'s (at the time t) latest deal history to
                                his registers */
  history his=latest_rec(a,t);
  for(;;){  // fetch opecode
    switch (c=get_opcode(al,ip++)){
      case LC: h='c';break;
      case LD: h='d';break;
      case BM: (his.my=='c')?
        ip=branch1, ip=branch2 ;break;
      case BY: (his.you=='c')?
        ip=branch1, ip=branch2 ;break;
      case SL: (am(t-1, his.agent, al)=='c')?
        ip=branch1, ip=branch2 ;break;
      case TP: t--;ip=0;break;
    }
  }
  return h;
}
```

Fig. 1. Flow of a strategy algorithm calculator

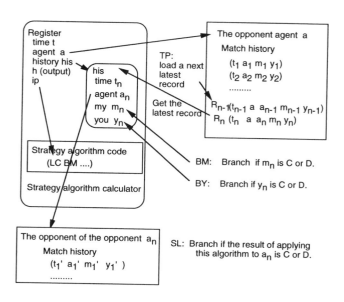

Fig. 2. Schematic diagram of a strategy algorithm calculator

The code LC or LD loaded 'C' or 'D' into the move register. BM, BY, and SL were branch instructions. BM branched if the move of a in R_n (i.e., m_n) was C or D. BY branched if the move of a_n in R_n (i.e., y_n) was C or D. SL branched according to the move that this algorithm suggested, if it were in place of a in R_n. TP went one record back in the opponent's match history (i.e., loaded R_{n-1}), and applied the algorithm again. The process terminated either when the algorithm reached an end, or it ran out of the match history. Code sequences are expressed in list forms of LISP. A branch instruction is accompanied by two lists corresponding to the code sequences after the branch. As is seen from the program flow, the output move was undefined if the algorithm terminated without ever executing LC or LD. In such a situation, the calculator was assumed to randomly output a move, i.e. either C or D with probability 1/2. Hence, the random strategy can be expressed by the algorithm of length 0, NIL.

The following are a few basic strategies together with their strategy algorithm codes.

1. Good-natured (CCC):

(LC)

Always cooperate.

2. Tit for Tat (TFT):

(LC BM (LC) (LD))

Mimic the opponent's play in his latest game. Cooperate, if the opponent's history is empty.

3. Random (RAN):

NIL

Cooperate/defect with probability 1/2, irrespective of the opponent.

4. Exploiter (DDD):

(LD)

Always defect.

5. Revised Tit for Tat (TT3):

(LC BM (LC) (BY (LD) (TP)))

If both agents defected in the opponent's latest game, then go one record back in the opponent's history, and apply this algorithm again. Otherwise, mimic the latest move of the opponent. Cooperate if the opponent's history is exhausted.

6. Reflective (REF):

(LC BM (LC) (BY (SL (LD) (TP)) (TP)))

In the record of the opponent in the latest game, if both agents defected, or if the opponent defected and this algorithm also suggests D in the opponent's position, then go one record back in the opponent's history and apply this algorithm again. Otherwise mimic the opponent's latest move. Cooperate if the opponent's history is exhausted.

TFT strategy is known to be effective for the Iterated Prisoner's Dilemma game[8]. In our model, however, it did not work well. Hence we invented TT3 and REF strategies to overcome the weakness of TFT[10].

4   Learning of strategy algorithms

First of all, note that the strategy devised for the Iterated Prisoner's Dilemma (IPD) game does not work well for our model. At first thought there does not seem to be much difference between our model and IPD, because all the match history is accessible. In IPD, however, if the opponent played D first, it is obvious that the opponent is uncooperative. On the other hand, in our model, you may sometimes be forced to play D to an unknown opponent, fearing that it might play D to you, or intending to punish the seemingly uncooperative behavior of the opponent. This in turn may make others play D against you.

The fact that the simple TFT (Tit for Tat) strategy does not work well is confirmed by our experiment. When matched with DDD (always play D) strategy, an agent with TFT strategy starts to play D even to his comrades (i.e., agents with TFT strategy), ultimately leading to mutual retaliations among agents with TFT strategy. As we charged 2.5 points for a match fee, any algorithms that could not cooperate among themselves were destined to decay in the long run (See Fig. 3). This was a disappointing result. Couldn't autonomous agents cooperate by themselves? Couldn't they learn to cooperate through experience? We wanted agents with TFT strategy to learn a better strategy.

Hence, we endowed agents a simple learning ability and investigated how they learned through experience. As our target was to make agents learn strategies by themselves, we assumed that the agents had no prior knowledge as to what might be a good strategy. Hence, the agents had to make a blind search for a candidate strategy. The simplest search algorithm is to change the strategy code randomly, i.e., randomly insert, delete, or replace strategy codes. Of course, these random modifications of strategy codes mostly led to a poor strategy. Hence, this algorithm should be used only when an agent has a strong reason for revising its strategy.

The timing of the strategy revision

Each agent calculated the average points he got, and the average points all the agents got, and compared the results. If he was earning more than others, there was no reason to revise the strategy. Conversely, if he was earning less than others, it would be a good time to revise the strategy. Note that the points of other agents were calculable from the match history.

The algorithms used were the following:

$$Av(t) = 0.75Av(t-1) +$$
$$0.25 \times \text{(average points for all the agents at } t-1),$$

$N(t)$ = Number of matches after adopting the current strategy,

$S(t)$ = Sum of points after adopting the current strategy,

$$\Delta(t) = Av(t) - (S(t)/N(t) + \sigma/SQRT(N(t))).$$

These were calculated every 10 steps. If it was found that

$$\Delta(t) \geq 0,$$

then with probability p_m calculated by

$$p_m = \min (10^{5\Delta(t)-2.0}, p_r),$$

a random modification of strategy codes was executed. Here, the min(*,*) means the minimum of the two, and p_r is the upper probability, which was set to 0.4. The term $\sigma/SQRT(N(t))$ was inserted in order to make allowances for statistical errors in the evaluation of the average $S(t)/N(t)$. In the simulation, σ was set to 1.0.

Random modification of strategy codes

The following random replacements of codes were executed, where l stands for the length of its strategy algorithm codes:

1) Deletion of codes: A code in the algorithm was deleted with probability p_m/l. If the deleted code was a branch instruction, one of the code sequences corresponding to the branch became unnecessary. Hence, it was also deleted.

2) Insertion of codes: An instruction code selected randomly from the code set was inserted at any place in the algorithm with probability p_m/l. If the inserted code was a branch instruction, the algorithm then needed two code sequences corresponding to the branch. Hence one of the code sequences after the branch was set to NIL (NOP: No operation).

3) Replacement of NIL (NOP): Due to an insertion of a branch instruction, the code NIL often entered into the code sequences. This was unfavorable for the system performance. Hence, with an upper probability p_r, NIL was replaced by a code randomly selected from the code set.

4) Simplification of redundant code: Redundant codes brought about by the above mutation processing were deleted, as shown below.

○ If the code LC or LD appeared in the code sequences more than once without a branch, the effect of the first code was overridden by the later code. Hence, the code sequence after the branch up to the last LC/LD was deleted.

○ If the same branch instruction succeeded, the same path was always followed at the second branch. Hence, such a code sequence was changed to one without a

branch.
○ The code after TP was never executed. Hence, the code sequences after TP were also deleted.

It is important to note that in the above procedure, agents sought to improve their own profit, and no cooperation or altruism was implied a priori.

5 Simulation

First of all, our world needed some pressure, or incentive for learning. In fact, in a world consisting of only cooperative strategies, each agent just played C, and there was no motivation for learning. Hence, agents with uncooperative strategies (called vaccine agents hereafter) were injected into the society of TFT agents. Then cooperative strategies had to learn to fight/retaliate against vaccine agents, or they would be destroyed by the injected vaccines. Note that there was no differences between injected vaccine agents and other agents, and vaccine agents could also revise their own strategies.

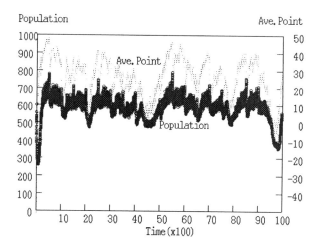

Fig. 3. Changes in population and average point during training phase

If an injected vaccine was too strong, the learning agents were destroyed by the vaccine. On the other hand, if the injected vaccine was too weak, it had little effect on the learning. Hence, the vaccine of DDD (who always played D), or RAN (who played either C or D randomly) was injected with increasing intensity. Detailed information on the training procedure is given in Table 3. For example, in the interval [0 10000], vaccine agents with strategy DDD were added every 500 steps, until the number of vaccine agents was 10% of the total population. As the RAN strategy was more difficult to detect than the DDD strategy, the RAN vaccine was injected after the training by the DDD vaccine. The changes in population and average point for an early training phase (time 0-10,000) are shown in Fig. 3. The population and average point underwent a sudden decrease and recovery several times. These dips in popu-

lation correspond to "an era of disturbances" in which strategies were severely evaluated and selected.

Table 3. Vaccines Injected for Training

Time	Vaccine	Vaccine ratio(%)
(TFT)0-10000	DDD	10
10,000-20,000(S_1)	DDD	20
20,000-30,000	DDD	33
(S_1)30,000-40,000	RAN	20
40,000-50,000(S_2)	RAN	33

To evaluate the effect of the learning, the system before the training (TFT), after the training by DDD (S_1), and after the training by RAN (S_2) were matched against half the population of DDD agents (Fig. 4), or an equal population of RAN agents (Fig. 5). While the society of TFT agents was destroyed by uncooperative strategies, S_1 and S_2 were able to destroy uncooperative strategies and recovered the original population, verifying the effect of the strategy learning. Figure 5 also shows that training by the RAN vaccine greatly increased the retaliative ability of the system against RAN.

To investigate what strategies were learned, we list in Table 4 the top three strategies for the systems S_1 and S_2. For example, the top strategy in S_1 (S_1 1) can be read as follows:
Code: (BM (LC) (LD BY (SL NIL (LC TP)) (TP)))
First, load the latest record of the opponent. Check the move of the opponent (BM). If it is C, then play C (LC). If it is D, set D to the default move (LD), and check the move of the opponent of the opponent (BY). If it is D, then apply this algorithm to the next latest record of the opponent (TP). If it is C, check what move this algorithm would advise if it were in the place of the opponent. If it is C, play the default move (NIL). If it is D, set C to the default move (LC), and apply this algorithm to the next latest record of the opponent (TP).

The strategies in Table 4 are all, a sort of, "kinship" algorithms derivable from "S_1 1" by addition/deletion/replacement of (mostly redundant) codes. The fact that the top group mainly consists of "kinship" algorithms is probably due to the small size of our world (lattice of 15×15). In fact, it is well-known that isolated evolution of a "small eco-system" often leads to a dominance by a single species [15][16]. Hence, partly to compensate these effects, we conducted the same experiment (simulation) five times. Each experiment gave different strategies for the top algorithm in S_2 as shown in Table 5. The variety of strategies in Table 5 indicates that the dominance of a particular strategy in each experiment was rather accidental. Nevertheless, we observed the following common features in the experiment.
1) S_1 seemed to have learned a retaliative ability against DDD, and S_2 seemed to have learned a retaliative ability against RAN.
2) As the learning phase progressed, agents with recursive strategies became more and more dominant.

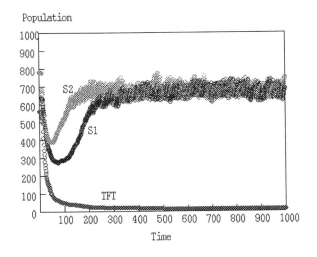

Fig. 4 Matches of TFT, S1, S2 against DDD

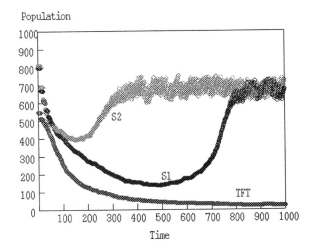

Fig. 5 Matches of TFT, S1, S2 against RAN

Table 4. Top three strategies for S_1 and S_2

Rank	Population	Strategy
S_1 1	11.7%	(BM (LC) (LD BY (SL NIL (LC TP)) (TP)))
S_1 2	11.7 %	(BM (LC) (LD BY (SL (LD) (LC TP)) NIL))
S_1 3	7.2 %	(BM LC (BY (LD) (SL NIL NIL)))
S_2 1	20.4 %	(BM (LC BY NIL NIL) (LD BY (SL NIL (LC TP)) (TP)))
S_2 2	8.1 %	(BM (LC BY NIL (LC)) (LD BY (SL NIL (LC TP)) (TP)))
S_2 3	6.6%	(BM (LC BY NIL (SL NIL NIL)) (LD BY (SL (LD) (LC TP)) (TP)))

Table 5. Top strategy of S_2 for five runs of simulation

Experiment #	Strategy
1	(LC BM (LC) (LD SL NIL (TP)))
2	(LC BM (LC BY (LC) (LC TP)) (LD SL (LD) (LC)))
3	(BM (LC BY NIL NIL) (LD BY (SL NIL (LC TP)) (TP)))
4	(LC BM NIL (LD BY (LD) (TP)))
5	(LC BM NIL (LD SL (BY (LD) NIL) (BY (LC) (LD))))

6 Discussion

6.1 Training by artificial noise

In sec. **5** we employed vaccine agents to enforce learning of better strategies. Interestingly, nearly the same effects could be obtained by imposing artificial noise on the society. That is, the move of an agent in each play was randomly reversed (e.g. C was changed to D and vice versa) with a probability e, modeling the effect of random fluctuations of the environment[9]. This brought a little scepticism into the society. However small it was, it gradually accumulated and ultimately led to an era of disturbances in which all agents were defecting. As we explained in sec. **5**, such an era of disturbances could generate a strong motivation in the society to learn better strategies.

The procedure we used was as follows. Noise, specified by the error probability e, was imposed on the society of TFT agents with increasing magnitude as shown in Table 6. To our surprise, the society maintained its cooperativeness even at an error rate of 20%. This suggests that the society learned better strategies under noisy conditions, because the society of TFT agents collapsed immediately when an error rate of 20% was suddenly imposed. In fact, by examining the system after the training by noise (T_1) in nearly the same way as in sec. **5**, we confirmed that the society really had acquired the strategies comparable to those found in the society trained by vaccines. The top three algorithms in T_1 are given in Table 7. Here again recursive strategies became dominant in the population, which proves the robustness of recursive strategies even in a noisy environment.

Table 6. Noise imposed for training

Time	Error probability
(TFT)0-10000	2 (%)
10,000-20,000D	5 (%)
20,000-30,000	10 (%)
30,000-40,000(T_1)	20 (%)

6.2 Selection of system parameters

So far, we have not explained how we decided the system parameters given in Table 2. It is true that cooperation among agents emerged only for certain ranges of parameter values. One of the important factors for its emergence was a spatial connectivity in the world. That is, if p_{rw} was large and N was small, an outburst of uncooperative strategies caused by random fluctuations spread to all over the world at once. The society of agents had to learn to cope with such an outburst of uncooperative strategies before it spread over the whole world. If the typical timescale for an agent to learn new strategies is t_0, then the following inequality should hold.

$$p_{rw}t_0 \ll N^2/4$$

If we assume that $t_0 = 1000$, then we obtain $p_{rw} \ll 0.05$.

DDD (always play D) strategy was evolutionary stable even under the disclosure of information. No cooperative strategies could intrude into the society of DDD agents, once it was established. Hence we needed some mechanisms to destroy this stability. Match fee C_d was introduced so that no strategies could earn positive points

among themselves without cooperating. Without this mechanism, the region of uncooperative strategies generated by random fluctuations continued to grow until all the world was occupied by uncooperative strategies.

Algorithm calculation cost C_{am} was introduced to model the real world where any mechanism for calculations (inferences) must have some cost. A more practical reason for introducing it was to inhibit the unlimited divergence of strategy algorithms. Parameters were determined so that a simulation of the society consisting of hundreds of agents could be simulated on a standard UNIX workstation. The restriction was not essential for our model. However, it might have some side effects on possible strategies. Hence, we are planning to conduct simulations with a smaller value of C_{am}, and see what strategies can emerge.

6.3 Strategy algorithm calculator

The architecture of the strategy algorithm calculator was designed so that all the promising strategies we had found in preliminary simulations[10] could be expressed in its machine code. The calculator was not, however, a universal Turing machine, i.e., there were some useful strategy algorithms it could not calculate. In fact, it had no counters, and could not calculate strategies such as "Play C when the opponent defected more often than me." The reason for not implementing counters was that agents could not use counters effectively, at least at an early stage of learning. The necessity for a small instruction set was also stressed by Ray in his implementation of Tierra[3].

The calculator took as input the current time and a pointer to the opponent. It did not take into account who the user of this algorithm really was (i.e., who is "me" for this algorithm). That is, two agents with the same strategy would play exactly the same move against the same opponent, irrespective of differences in their past experiences. For example, the calculator could not express strategies such as "Play D to those who played D to me in the past." This restriction was, however, intentional. We wanted to model the world full of strangers, where we had to evaluate the cooperativeness of other agents only from their observed actions. We wanted to make the world so large that the probability of an agent ever meeting the same agents again in its lifetime was very low. Unfortunately, such a large world could not be simulated on a standard UNIX workstation. However, if the expected number of matches with the same agent was large, the problem was simply reduced to the Iterated Prisoner's Dilemma problem, which was clearly not our intention. Hence we tried to avoid such a problem by intentionally omitting "who is me" term in the argument list of the strategy algorithm calculator.

7 Summary and conclusion

We investigated the role of information in the emergence of cooperation in a society of autonomous agents. Agents were made to play the Prisoner's Dilemma game, each time changing the other party of the match, under the condition that the match history was to be disclosed

Table 7. Top three strategies for T_1

Rank	Population	Strategy
T_1 1	20.6%	(BM (LC) (BY (LD SL (LD)) (LD TP)) (TP)))
T_1 2	18.2 %	(BM (LC) (LD BY (SL NIL (TP)) (TP)))
T_1 3	11.7 %	(BM (LC) (LD BY (SL (LD) (TP)) (TP)))

to the public. An evolutionary world was introduced, wherein the evaluation of an agent's action was reflected in its survival rate and breeding rate.

The agents had a very simple learning ability, and tried to revise their own strategy through interactions with other agents. The aim of the agents was to increase their own profit, and no cooperation or altruism was implied a priori. We found the following:
1) Under the disclosure of information, even a selfish agent comes to cooperate for its own sake.
2) An agent can learn to cooperate through interactions with other agents.

To learn a strategy for interactions, a society needs some incentive for learning. This result is not incidental. In a society where the cost of calculation (or information) is finite (not zero), the best strategy in a peaceful era is CCC (always play C). Hence, in a peaceful society where all agents plays C, even an agent with a more sophisticated strategy learns the CCC strategy, making the society as a whole vulnerable. This is inevitable, as is verified repeatedly in our society. Hence, our third finding,
3) To maintain a cooperative society, we must have some tension or vaccine, which makes members of the society alert to uncooperative strategies.

Our research target in the future is to make a machine system that acts at its own will, and takes the responsibility for its actions. The problem of cooperation is an unavoidable hurdle, which even human beings are always confronting[17][18]. We hope that the disclosure of information will be effective for the emergence of cooperation in both human and machine society.

References

[1] Dawkins, R.: *The Blind Watchmaker*, Longman, Harlow, 1986.

[2] Trivers, R.: *Social Evolution*, Benjamin/Cummings, 1985.

[3] Ray, T. S.: "An Approach to the Synthesis of Life," *Artificial Life II*, C. G. Langton et al. (ed.), Addison-Wesley, 1992.

[4] G. M. Werner and M. G. Dyer, "Evolution of Communication in Artificial Organisms," C. G. Langton (eds.), *Artificial Life II*, Addison Wesley, 1992, pp. 659-687.

[5] Dawkins, R.: *The Selfish Gene*, Oxford Univ. Press, Oxford, 1976.

[6] Bacharach, M.: *Economics and the Theory of Games*, Curtis Brown Ltd., London, 1976.

[7] Axelrod, R. and Hamilton, W. D.: "The Evolution of Cooperation," *Science*, Vol. 211, Mar. 1981, pp. 1390-1396.

[8] Axelrod, R.: *The Evolution of Cooperation*, Basic Books Inc., 1984.

[9] Axelrod, R. and Dion, D.: "The Further Evolution of Cooperation," *Science*, Vol. 242, Dec. 1988, pp. 1385-1390.

[10] Ito, A. and Yano, H.: "The Optimal Deal Strategies under the Disclosure of the Contract History," *J. of Japanese Society for Artificial Intelligence*, Vol. 10, No.2, Mar. 1995 (in Japanese).

[11] Ito, A. and Yano, H.: "The Emergence of Cooperation in a Society of Autonomous Agents," *First Intl. Conf. on Multi Agent Systems, (ICMAS'95)*, pp. 201-208, San Fransisco, 1995.

[12] Rosenschein, J. S. and Genesereth, M. R.: "Deals Among Rational Agents," *Proc. 9th Intl. Joint Conf. on Artificial Intelligence (IJCAI'85)*, Aug. 1985, pp. 91-99.

[13] Lindgren, K. : "Evolutionary Phenomena in Simple Dynamics," *Artificial Life II*, C. G. Langton (eds.), Addison Wesley, 1992, pp. 295-312.

[14] Stanley, E. A. et al.: "Iterated Prisoner's Dilemma with Choice and Refusal of Partners," *Artificial Life III*, C. G. Langton (ed.), Addison Wesley, 1993, pp. 131-175.

[15] Wright, S.: *Evolution and the Genetics of Populations*, 14 Vols. Univ. Chicago Press, 1968, 1969, 1977, 1978.

[16] Sigmund, K.: *Games of Life*, Oxford Univ. Press, 1993.

[17] Poundstone, W.: *Prisoner's Dilemma*, Doubleday, 1992.

[18] Yamagishi, T.: *Shakaiteki Dilemma no Shikumi*, (in Japanese), Saiensu-sha, 1990.

Evolution of Communication and Strategies in an Iterated Three-person Game

Eizo Akiyama*and Kunihiko Kaneko†

Abstract

A non-zero-sum 3-person coalition game is presented, to study the evolution of complexity and diversity in communication and strategies, where the population dynamics of players with strategies is given according to their scores in the iterated game and mutations. Two types of differentiation emerge initially; a biased one to form classes and a temporal one to change their roles for coalition. Communication rules are self-organized in a society through evolution. Open ended evolution of cooperation and communications toward diversity and complexity emerges, as cannot be observed in the simulations of 2-person games.

1 Introduction

In a society with inter-acting agents under competitive situation, emergence of cooperation is commonly observed, while strategies and communication emerge and evolve to the diversity and complexity through class differentiation or temporal changes of roles. The society itself leads to open ended evolution toward diversified society. In the present paper we discuss the mechanism of such evolution by adopting an iterated three-person game model.

1.1 Lack of diversity and complexity in communication in 2-person games

The evolution of cooperative behaviors observed among selfish individuals has been a topic of debates over decades, especially among social scientists and evolutionary biologists. For individuals to cooperate, there must inevitably exist some kind of communication based on such strategies that can take account of information of others. Through the emergence of diversified communication, various kinds of cooperation can appear, such as the differentiation of roles with time or space. To study relationships between agents through actions and communications, it is useful to adopt a model with game dynamics. The evolution of cooperation through strategies

and communications have been studied extensively, with the use of iterated 2-person dilemmatic games. The diversity and complexity in strategies may emerge through the competition and cooperation coexisting antagonistically. Here, we will survey a couple of such 2-person games and point out drawbacks in the studies of 2-person games for the purpose of the diversity and complexity.

The Iterated Prisoner's Dilemma

The Iterated Prisoner's Dilemma (IPD) model has the essential features common to all symmetric 2-person dilemmatic games. IPD model has been quite extensively investigated with regard to the emergence of cooperative behaviors. In the Prisoner's Dilemma (PD) game, two players either cooperate or defect, with the score in Table 1.

Table 1: the pay-off matrix for Prisoner's Dilemma : In each element, (S_1, S_2) corresponds to the score of player 1 and player 2, respectively.

		player 2	
		C	**D**
player 1	Cooperate	3, 3	0, 5
	Defect	5, 0	1, 1

Computer tournaments of IPD programs were organized by Axelrod, where each player has a strategy depending on the history of hands, that is to say, it is only the history of hands that players are allowed to use as information when they communicate each other [2]. The most successful strategy therein was well-known Tit-For-Tat (TFT), that cooperates on the first move and then plays whatever the other player chose on the previous move. When the evolution of strategy is included, the cooperation prevails in society through the success of the TFT-like (cooperative) algorithm. Strategies of players may become rather complex but the actions seen in the final society are "Cooperate" only (in some special cases "Defect" only). Thus the model cannot explain the diversity and complexity of communications and strategies of our world, where various types of communications and strategies coexist, ranging from simple to sophisticated ones. This is a drawback of the IPD model

---

*Department of Pure and Applied Sciences, University of Tokyo, 3-8-1 Komaba, Tokyo 153, Japan, E-mail: akiyama@cyber.c.u-tokyo.ac.jp

†E-mail: kaneko@complex.c.u-tokyo.ac.jp

One possible way to get rid of this drawback may be the inclusion of the noise, as players' errors for actions, as has been studied by K. Lindgren [7]. Through the evolution, strategies of players become complex and continue to evolve toward further complexity, however, the emergent society itself tends to be very simple at later stages, that is, almost any two players mostly cooperate with each other (except for some intervals to get rid of the noise effect). Thus the noise effect is not adequate to account for the complexity and diversity in strategies and communication.

As a model for the emergence of communication code, the IPD model has a disadvantage in its game rule. In the PD, the two hands, C(ooperate) and D(efect) have their specific meanings, and the game is asymmetric between C and D. Thus the evolved strategy as well as the action should strongly depend on C or D.

The Iterated Leader's Dilemma

There are several 2-person games where no strategy therein explicitly embodies the meaning of "cooperation", and the cooperation is defined within some kind of interaction between players. These characteristics of such 2-person games are partly common with those of our 3-person game model to be discussed later. An example of such 2-person game is the Iterated Leader's Dilemma. In the Leader's Dilemma Game, whose payoff matrix is shown in Table 2, two players fight for a leader's position. The behavior to seek for the leader is called 'active', abbreviated by 'A', while the other behavior to follow the leader is called 'passive' abbreviated by 'P'.

Table 2: the pay-off matrix for Leader's Dilemma : When two players actions are 'A' and 'P', the active player gains the biggest payoff and the passive one gains the second biggest, where the total payoff of both players is the highest. You have to be active in order to win, but if both players are active, the score is the worst.

		player 2	
		P	**A**
player 1	Passive	1, 1	3, 5
	Active	5, 3	0, 0

Here communication between players is more important than in the PD, since it is entirely owing to another player's action whether a player can be in a cooperative situation, such as (player 1, player 2) = (A, P)–(P, A)–(A, P)–(P, A)–..... in Iterated Leader's Dilemma (ILD).

Then is this ILD model relevant to the evolution of diversity and complexity in communications and strategies? We have carried out several simulations on ILD (with noise). So far the evolution only to cooperation with a simple period-2 communication is observed, that is, the repetition of (A, P)–(P, A)–, once two players enter the (A, P) or (P, A) situation generated by their initial conditions or noise. The evolution of strategy here only works for a quicker recovery from (A, A) or (P, P) situation caused by the noise.

Single-coalition structure in 2-person games

In a 2-person game, only one coalition structure is possible. In this case coalition is nothing but the emergence of cooperation between particular two players. In 2-person games, there is no need for the evolution of communication once coalition is accomplished between any two players. For instance, period-4 interaction — repetition of (A, P)–(A, P)–(P, A)–(P, A)– — is also an optimal communication to achieve the cooperation in ILD, but there is no need to shift from a certain optimal communication (such as period-2 iteration) to another as long as the coalition is sustained. In a 2-person game, if the only one coalition has already been constructed by a communication, there is no other coalition to be made. This may be the reason why the evolution of communications and strategies in 2-person games does not continue towards complexity and diversity.

Of course, a straightforward way to introduce the complexity is by combinatorics, such as including a variety of moves in the game, like the chess. We do not take this direction however, since we are interested in the origin of diversity and complexity solely through the inter-actions of players, *without* implementing it in a game initially. Thus the use of a N-person game is requested as a possible simplest model at the next step.

1.2 N-person game model

In such a game as is called a N-person game (N ≥ 3), substantial qualitative differences to a game of one or two persons emerge, mainly because of the possibility that within an N-person sample from the population, there can be more than one coalition of agents simultaneously. Also, interactions among coalitions, such as persons switching their allegiance, emerge, leading to coalition shrinking or expanding, so that coalition structures themselves become the integral parts of the game. To form coalition, some communications are necessary that may take complex and diverse forms, as are made possible by temporal changes of roles in the coalition. In the present paper we study one of the simplest N-person game, a deterministic 3-person, and non-zero-sum game with two hands, focusing especially on describing the structures of coalitions [1]. The evolution of artificial ecology of species with different strategies is studied through repeated games by players. The main topics to be discussed are

- the evolution of algorithms and communications
- emergent forms of cooperation
- the dynamics of diversification and complexification
- the nature of the society evolved.

Indeed our simulation shows class differentiation between exploiting and exploited players at the initial stage, and then the temporal differentiation of roles to attain the cooperativity. At later stages the co-evolution between the complexity and diversity is found for communications and strategies.

2 Modeling

2.1 Iterated three-person coalition game model

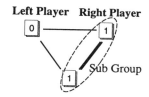

Figure 1: sub-group with the right player

The rule of our three-person game is as follows;

1. Each player must hand in either a card 0 or 1.

2. If two players hand in the same card, they are regarded as forming a sub-group, and gain the score of 3 points. A player excluded from the sub-group cannot gain any score. If all three players hand in the same card, they cannot get any score, either.

A player can get points when a sub group is constructed in which (s)he belongs to. In another word, players compete for indivisible resources that can be shared only if one player is made to be the odd man out. The pay-off matrix of this game is given in Table 3. In the

Table 3: Pay-off matrix of our 3-person coalition game : The number '0' or '1' in column 2, 3, and 4 represents respectively the card that the left player, the right player, or you have handed in. According to the hands of the three players, there are 8 states, which are defined through the binary representation of their hands, as is given. For instance, you and the right player are within the sub-group of card 1 if you are in the state 3. In this case, your right player is in the state 5 because you correspond to the left player for the player. *If and only if your state is between 2 and 5, you are in a sub-group and can get point 3.* On condition that you are in the state 0 or 7, any sub-group is not constructed and every player cannot gain any point. *Note that the player of an even state hands in card 0, while that of an odd state hands in card 1.*

state	Left	Right	You	your points
0	0	0	0	0
1	0	0	1	0
2	0	1	0	3
3	0	1	1	3
4	1	0	0	3
5	1	0	1	3
6	1	1	0	0
7	1	1	1	0

table, we distinguish right and left players, assuming that the three players are located in a circle so that each player has its right and left players. Of course the rule of

our game keeps the right/left symmetry. However, each player is assumed to be able to distinguish the right and left players, which is essential to the choice of its strategy, as will be seen later. Handing in of the cards by

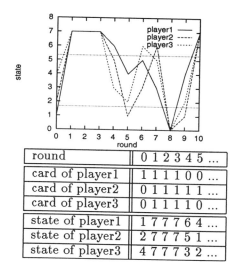

round	0 1 2 3 4 5 ...
card of player1	1 1 1 1 0 0 ...
card of player2	0 1 1 1 1 1 ...
card of player3	0 1 1 1 1 0 ...
state of player1	1 7 7 7 6 4 ...
state of player2	2 7 7 7 5 1 ...
state of player3	4 7 7 7 3 2 ...

Figure 2: An example of the game play : The horizontal axis shows rounds, while the vertical axis shows the states of the players. Dotted lines are drawn near states 2 and 5. Players whose state is between these dotted lines can get 3 points, as stated in the caption of the pay-off matrix.

3 players described above is regarded as '1 round of the game', which is repeated in succession until the decided maximum round number. Such an iterated action of three players as a whole will be called simply an 'interaction' or 'communication'. The cards to be handed in by each of the players are decided according to their strategy, only referring to the history of the states, defined by the hands of the three players as in Table 3. The memory-length, that is the number of prior rounds to be referred for the strategy, is provided by the algorithm of each player, which is finite within a given fixed range. Thus, the next card to be handed in is decided according to the sequence of finite length history of states. Since there are 8 states per round in this game, the history sequence can be described by a octonary string, such as 0472101.., while the strategy algorithm has a list of several octonary strings with a finite length. If a certain sequence in the list is a part of, or contains, the history sequence, the player hands in the card 1. A list of such "card 1 sequences" can be expressed by an octonary tree structure, which gives the coding of the strategy algorithm in this model, like the binary tree coding by Ikegami [3]. Also, the information of the first card is given in each player's algorithm. Figure 2 is an example of the game play, where the player 1, 2 and 3 are located in an anti-clockwise order, and the state for each player is decided according to Table 3.

By taking an ensemble of players and regarding the players with the same strategy as the same species, we study the population dynamics of each species. The population dynamics is defined as follows: In each generation, a player makes the iterated 3-person game with all possible pairs of the other players, including those from its own species. By summing up the points of the game, a player's, accordingly the species', score is given. The fraction of the population $x_i(t)$ for a species i is updated, following its average score s_i subtracted by the average points of all the players $\overline{s}$ [1]:

$$x_i(t+1) - x_i(t) = d(s_i - \overline{s}) x_i(t) \qquad (1)$$

where d is a growth constant. After all the fractions $x_i(t)$ are updated, they are normalized to make the population size 1.0. When the population is updated to the next generations, a single point mutation of the algorithm occurs with a given fixed ratio (0.1 in later examples). Here the mutation adds or removes one branch at every node in the tree of the algorithm.

2.2 Notabilia of this model

Deterministic game

As noted previously, both the game and the algorithm are deterministic. Thus all the three players of the same species hand in the same card for each round. Since the state and the memory-length are finite, the change of the state must finally fall in a periodic cycle through the iteration of the game. We will call this periodic cycle a periodic part, and call the dynamics leading up to the periodic part a transient part. It is true that the periodic part is most important for the total score because it is usually quite longer than the transient part, but the effect of the transient part cannot be ignored as long as the finite maximum round number exists.

Differentiation of roles

In order for a fitness of a player to increase, one of the other two players must give in and accept the role of an outsider from the sub-group, or two players can cooperate and make the remaining player the odd man out. Anyway, to increase their score, they must split to form a situation of 2 against 1. As will be observed from the results of the simulation, players can differentiate into two different types of roles within a given 3-person sample.

I. Class differentiation A biased differentiation. The roles are fixed by players, and a particular player loses on the average and is exploited by others. A thorough example of this differentiation is shown in Figure 3-(a), where the coalition between particular two players is formed. In a complete class differentiation as Figure 3-(a), two players within the coalition can gain 3 points on the average.

II. Temporal differentiation The roles of the players are changed according to the passage of time. A thorough example of this differentiation is shown in Figure 3-(b), where the coalition among 3-players is formed. As in Figure 3-(b) if one of the players is out of the sub-group in turn, each player gets 2 points on the average, and the full and equal cooperation is attained.

---

[1]If the score of a species is below the average $\overline{s}$ and its population goes down below a preordained lower bound (KillLimit), it becomes extinct, and the species is eliminated.

Symmetry of card 0/1

It may be useful to note the important difference between our game and the PD, besides the number of players. In the PD, the two hands, C(ooperate) or D(efect) have their specific meaning, and the game is asymmetric between C and D. Thus the evolved strategy as well as the action should strongly depend on C or D. In our 3-person game, the genetic coding of a strategy is not symmetric about the hands 0 and 1 due to the tree structure referring particularly to the card 1. However, the game itself keeps the card 0/1 symmetry and the two cards have no specific meanings. To make some kind of communication and form a sub-group, information is given in the time series of the hands. As will be seen, societies of various types of periodic hands such as the period-3 of 001 or period-5 of 00101 are formed through the evolution.

3 Simulation results

We have carried out simulations of the 3-person game, setting the maximum round number to 1000, and the maximum memory length to 4. The simulation starts with 6 species whose algorithms are given by the tree made randomly with the memory length = 1, that is, players are able to refer hands of only one previous round. First we present a rough sketch of the evolution of our model while detailed accounts will be given later. Through several simulations, we reach the following scenario of the evolutionary process to the complex and cooperative society:

1. A new species arising from mutations leads to class differentiation, which lowers the score of the old species and its population. Thus the society is tended to be dominated by the new species.

2. This dominance is broken by the emergence of co-operative interactions, supported by periodic temporal differentiation. The ratio of cooperative interactions increases with the evolution.

3. The temporal differentiation of periodic changes of hands with the $3n$ period ($n = 1, 2 \cdots$) dominates the society. The whole species therein shows identical patterns of the hands at the periodic part, while the diversification occurs only in the transient part.

4. Some mutants that also change the periodic part increase their population, and dominant periods in the society are changed. After having experienced alternations of some dominant periods, the society starts to allow for the coexistence of various periods. With this increase of diversity, the interaction and strategy increase the complexity, through the appearance of longer periods.

All the simulations support the following evolutionary process, although there are subtle differences by simulations in the period of the cyclic change of hands and the order of societies realized.

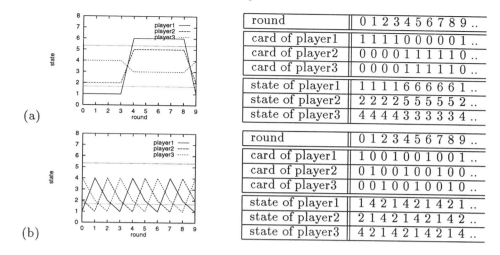

round	0 1 2 3 4 5 6 7 8 9 ..
card of player1	1 1 1 1 0 0 0 0 0 1 ..
card of player2	0 0 0 0 1 1 1 1 1 0 ..
card of player3	0 0 0 0 1 1 1 1 1 0 ..
state of player1	1 1 1 1 6 6 6 6 6 1 ..
state of player2	2 2 2 2 5 5 5 5 5 2 ..
state of player3	4 4 4 4 3 3 3 3 3 4 ..

round	0 1 2 3 4 5 6 7 8 9 ..
card of player1	1 0 0 1 0 0 1 0 0 1 ..
card of player2	0 1 0 0 1 0 0 1 0 0 ..
card of player3	0 0 1 0 0 1 0 0 1 0 ..
state of player1	1 4 2 1 4 2 1 4 2 1 ..
state of player2	2 1 4 2 1 4 2 1 4 2 ..
state of player3	4 2 1 4 2 1 4 2 1 4 ..

Figure 3: (a) Example of class differentiation (b) Example of Temporal differentiation

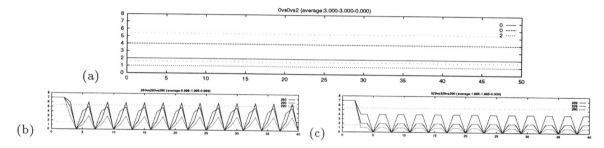

Figure 4: Examples of Class Differentiation : In (a), the three players are ID0, ID0, ID1—two persons from species ID0 and one from species ID2—, get the average scores 3.000, 3.000, 0.000 respectively. (b) and (c) are examples from later generations.

3.1 Class differentiation evolving with generation

To gain points in cooperation with other species in our iterated 3-person game, some kind of rules, such as periodic voluntary exclusion from the sub-group, must be formed by players. Such rule, however, is not formed for a duration. For most initial conditions, players are ignorant of a possible rule of cooperation at the early generations. First, class differentiation to exploit other species is formed through evolution, because it requires only the mutation of the communication between the same strategies. Two players of the same species should cooperate together and squeeze the other player. Since those who exploit other species get higher scores and increase their population, the exploitation is increased through the evolution. With generations, new species with a longer memory length appears which adopts a more complicated rule that is to exploit others and hard to be deciphered by them. Thus the class differentiation with a more complex strategy emerges successively.

The simplest example of class differentiation is shown in Figure 4-(a), where two players of the same species handing in the card 0 always exclude the remaining player from the sub-group and form coalition among the same species. (Note again that the player of an even state hands in card 0, while that of an odd state hands in card 1. See Table 3.) In this simple case, the excluded player could have escaped this exploitation, if it adopted a simple 2-memory-length strategy like "if excluded twice by the same cards, change the hand". Indeed this type of mutation occurs at a later stage, while there appears a more complicated form of the exploitation as in Figure 4-(b)(c) by using a longer memory length. For example, in (c), the player corresponding to the bottom line changes cards when excluded twice, but still it is exploited with the rate 2/3. The excluded player again can escape from the exploitation by having a longer memory length of the strategy (4 in this case). Thus the complexity of communication is increased within the class differentiation, where a species with a complex strategy (with a longer memory length) dominates over a long time.

3.2 Cooperation among different species and the formation of temporal differentiation

In the class differentiation, the dominant species increases their population by exploiting other species.

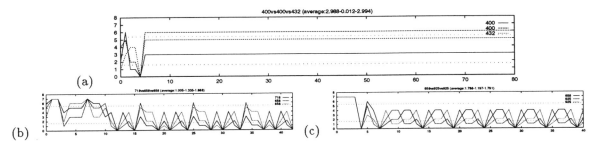

(a)

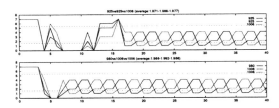

(b)

(c)

Figure 5: The emergence of cooperation and its evolution : (a) A (right) player from species ID400 hands in card 0, while the left player from ID400 and one from ID432 hand in card 1. Thus, both species can be in the sub-group get gains. This is an example of imperfect cooperation where two species gain unequal average score. In (a) to (c), the degree of temporal differentiation increases, and the difference of scores by players get smaller.

Thus, when the species occupies most populations of the society, it cannot get scores any more. If there appears new species that is not exploited by the dominant one and cooperates among them (Figure 5-(a)), their relative population is increased. Thus the society of class differentiation collapses and cooperation between two species replaces. An example is given in Figure 5, where the players get points by the cooperation with periodic differentiation of roles at a later generation. By the formation of rules of temporal differentiation, cooperation of different species, as might be of three species, can be easily realized.

Temporal differentiation of period-3n

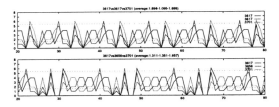

Figure 6: Examples of temporal differentiation in a uniform period-6 society : These are representatives of inter-actions in a society where all interactions are period-6.

After the emergence of cooperative interactions among different species, the society with the period-3n is gradually formed, where the players equally exchange the role of the excluded. Furthermore, any set of three players performs the same period-3n changes of hands.

An example is given in Figure 6, where society with period-6 interaction emerges, and continues stably over many generations. Here, the sub-group with the card 1 is formed, and each of the three players is excluded twice per 6 steps, by showing the card 0. As shown in this example, all the three players get the equal score in the period-3n society.

Since each player in the period-3n society gets the highest possible score among "equal-score" societies, it is rather difficult for a new species to exceed the predecessors by adopting a different type of periodic patterns.

The easiest and commonly observed strategy of a mutant at this stage is to preserve the periodic part and change the transient part. It should be noted that the transient part is essential to shift the phases of the period-3n oscillation by players, since they should change the hands out of phase each other, to form the cooperation. There can be a variety of choices for the transient part. Indeed in our simulation, new species with modified transient parts appear successively.

New species with communication indiscernible from that of the old species—the end of the uniform period-3n society

Figure 7: Pseudo period-6 society : Here are samples of the pseudo period-6 interaction, which destroy the period-6 society.

As the species of period-3n society gain points efficiently, a new species with modified periodic parts have to exploit the old period-3n species, to invade into the society. Since such mutation is not easy (and indeed the period-6 society lasts over many generations), it emerges only after a long enough period. First, new species appears showing the same period-3n interactions fundamentally but shifting the phase to a degree undetectable by the old species in case two players from new species face the old. One player of new species, on the other hand, remains to be cooperative with two players from the old species, using the period-3n interaction. We will call such undetectable type of interactions as 'the pseudo period-3n interactions', in which the periods are longer than 3n but some fractions of the original periodic-3n interaction is included. The present situation might be called as a "weakly classed" differentiation. In fact, as is shown in Figure 7, the new species lowers the old species' points while retaining to a degree its own points by performing 'the pseudo period-6 interactions'.

The transition of societies with periodic temporal differentiation

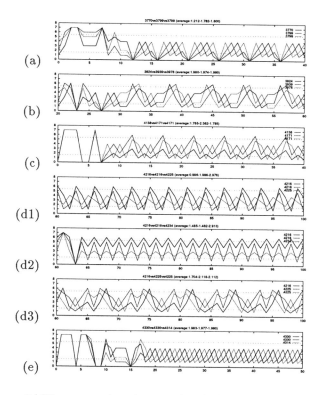

Figure 8: The successive change of periodic societies with generation : (a) is a sample of interactions from period-5 society, (b) from period-18, (c) from another type of period-5, (d1–3) from a diversified society lasting only for a short span, (e) from period-3.

The evolution that undermines periodic parts itself continues, even after the termination of the period-3n society. At this stage, a variety of societies of periodic inter-actions appear successively, such as period-5 or period-18 society, and so on. In this simulation, the society has shifted in the flow illustrated in Figure 8-(a) to (e).

3.3 Diversification and complication

The evolution to diversification

So far, the society is composed mainly of one type of inter-actions (with the same period). The diverse inter-actions are unstable and observed only in the transition between stable societies. At this late stage, however, the society consists of several different inter-actions with different periods, and remains stable.

Such society appears first in our simulation as the co-existence with period-3 and period-6 inter-actions (See Figure 9-(a)), which is born out of the period-3 society. After some generations, a variety of inter-actions co-exist as in Figure9-(b)(c), which are examples of inter-actions made by three players in the same society.

Evolution to complexity by a breaking of the phases of player hands

The strategy to break the phase of the oscillation, already seen in the pseudo-3n inter-action, is again seen here. In contrast with the pseudo-3n case, however, more complex inter- actions emerge successively by breaking the phases more frequently. For example, in Figure 10-(b)(c) the periods for the cyclic hands are about 100. The dynamics here is rather irregular, and looks rather unpredictable. We note that even in this society, some of the inter-actions remain very simple, such as the period-6 one as in Figure10(a). Complex inter-actions exist within the diversity of species, while the diversity is supported by the complexity in strategies.

4 Further analysis

4.1 Fraction of card 0/1 handed in

In our 3-person coalition game, card 1 and 0 themselves have no specific meanings, and are completely symmetric. Figure 11 shows the frequency of card 1 served by players in all tournaments in a generation. The fraction fluctuates between 0.3 and 0.4 through generation 5000 to 7500, for example. The communication prevailed in this period is period-6 interaction where 2 players hand in card 0 and the other player hands in card 1, with the result that the fraction of card 1 must be 1/3 except the transient part.

In spite of the asymmetry between two cards in players' strategy coding, the fraction of card 1 fluctuates around 0.5 with the alternation of generations, while there are several generations in which the ratio deviates from 0.5 distinctly. The communication rules, generated through interactions among players, dominate the effect of 0/1-asymmetry in players' strategy coding. Thus new rules are formed which may adopt card 1 more than card 0 or vice versa.

4.2 Left/right asymmetry in strategy

Results described above have been obtained in the simulations where players have the ability to distinguish the (right/left) position. We have carried out several simulations without this ability, in other words, using the algorithm depending only on the number of 0 and 1 by the other two players, besides its own hand. We have found only the evolution towards the class differentiation, but not the temporal differentiation. When constructing the rules of the temporal differentiation of roles, some kind of individual identification is necessary to allocate precisely the proper player with time. In our 3-person game, players do not distinguish each individual player and cannot identify others until the start of interactions. They identify others only by their actions and location. The above result implies that players are not capable of creating the rule of temporal differentiation only by actions. Thus temporal differentiation seems to be formed by the information of location and actions of others, for example, by the implicit rule that "each player should give in if its 'right' player gave in in the previous round (leading to a clockwise period-3 society)".

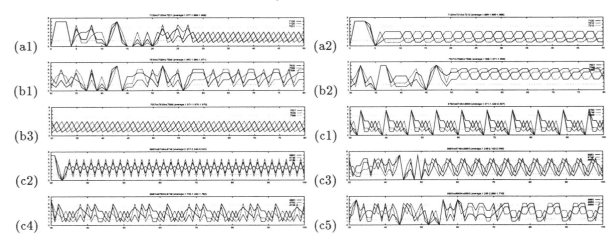

Figure 9: from (a), (b), to (c) in time : (a1–2) co-existence of period-3 and 6 inter-actions in a society. (b1–2) that of period-3, 6, 15. (c1–5) a variety of inter-actions seen in a society.

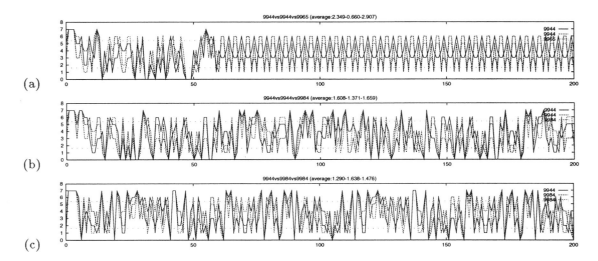

Figure 10: Diversification and complication : (a)–(c) are representatives of inter-actions in a society. (a) is rather simple, while others are quite complex with periods about 100.

5 Discussion

5.1 Emergence of cooperation due to differentiation of roles, and diversity of communication and strategies in a society

When agents compete for resources that are finite and in scarcity, some player must suffer from loss of profits. In our simulation, we have found two types of differentiation to resolve such situation, class and temporal differentiation. Both types of differentiation are also seen in the recent model of cell differentiation with competition for nourishment among cells [5], where cells actively take nutrition or rest in turn, to form a kind of time sharing system, while biased differentiation is observed at later stages. In our model, with the evolution of communication and strategies, both types of differentiation appear by generations or in a mixed form such as weakly classed

differentiation, and lead to diversification and complication of cooperation. Indeed, this evolution process is consistent with the isologous diversification theory proposed for the cell differentiation [6]. The diversity of communication in a society prevents new species from easily exploiting current species and prevailing in the society, because invaders have to compete with a variety of strategies. It is necessary for new species to communicate cooperatively to some degree with old species. In this sense, diversity is essential to keep a cooperative society.

5.2 Co-evolution of diversity and complexity

In our simulation, once the co-existence of several short-period communications is found, diversity and at the same time complexity gradually increase in a society. In

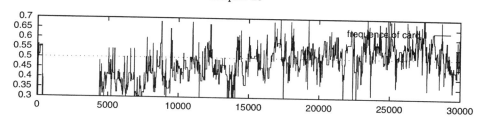

Figure 11: Frequency of card 1 : The horizontal axis shows the generation, while the vertical axis shows the fraction for the frequency of card 1.

a diverse society, a player has to cope with a variety of communications. A simple strategy cannot afford such diverse responses. Hence diversity enhances complexity of strategies. On the other hand, interactions with a long period by the complexity of strategies allow the diversity of communication. Thus the diversity and complexity of communications and strategies *co-evolve* in our simulation, which seems to be seen in (real) ecological systems and in human society.

5.3 Emergence and evolution of communication code

It may be useful to note the following two points found in our simulation, one is the ritualization of communication by players, and another is the complication of communication codes so that the behavior pattern of a player might not be detected.

As stated before, card 1 and 0 themselves have no specific meanings and are symmetric in our model. However, some logic to break the symmetry and to assign meaning to the 0/1 symbol sequence is self-organized by forming 'rules' of societies through the evolution, where all (or a part of) players adopt a pattern of sequence and ritualize the interaction. Here, the organization of communication sequences is highly dependent upon the history of evolution.

In our model, there exist many kinds of 3- persons' coalition (3PC), which are implemented by such communication as period-3, period-18, and so on. The society consisting of 3PC is basically stable. There also exist a variety of 2-persons' coalitions (2PC) which are basically unstable — like class differentiation. There also exist, of course, coalitions between 2PC and 3PC, such as period-5, pseudo period-3n (weakly classed), etc. Formation of coalition inevitably needs some kind of communication. In a 2-person non-zero-sum game, as stated in the introduction, some kind of cooperative and optimal communication , such as 'almost cooperate' situation in IPD, appears to construct the only one coalition. Further evolution of communications, however, cannot emerge there, since the formation of the coalition in a 2-person game needs cooperation only against the game environment that has no strategy, and there is no need for subsequent evolution about communication codes in contrast with the 2PC in the 3-persons game. Thus, if the rule itself is not so complex for players' strategies (like chess), there is no room for the open ended evolution of communications in 2-person games.

In our 3-person game, open ended evolution of the communication code toward diversity and complexity can be observed. Simple communication code for the coalition is easily detected by others, and may be exploited by a more complex one. Thus there appears a pressure for developing a complex communication and strategy. This mechanism of the evolution is common with that observed in the imitation game [4]. The codes deciphered only within the same coalition can be generated through complexity. Add to that, through players' itineration among 2PCs and 3PC, various communication patterns emerge and coexist in a society simultaneously, and the conflicts between coalitions call in further complexity, leading to such open ended evolution as cannot be seen in 2-person game simulations.

Acknowledgments

The authors would like to thank T.Ikegami, S.Sasa, and T.Yamamoto for useful discussions and also thank B.Hinrichs for critical reading of the manuscript. This work was partially supported by a Grant-in-Aid for Scientific Research from the Ministry of Education, Science, and Culture of Japan, and the first author was given support by the Nomura Foundation.

References

[1] E. Akiyama and K. Kaneko. Evolution of cooperation, differentiation, complexity, and diversity in an iterated three-person game. In *Proceedings of the 1995 International Workshop on Biologically Inspired Evolutionary Systems*, pages 76–83, 1995. , to appear Artificail Life (1996).

[2] R. Axelrod. *The Evolution of Cooperation*. New York: Basic Books, 1984.

[3] T. Ikegami. *Physica D*, 75:310–327, 1994.

[4] K. Kaneko and J. Suzuki. In C. Langton, editor, *Artificial Life III*, pages 43–54. Addison-Wesley Publishing Conpany, 1994.

[5] K. Kaneko and T. Yomo. *Physica D*, 75:89–102, 1994.

[6] K. Kaneko and T. Yomo. *in Advances in Artificial Life*. Springer, 1995. , and preprint.

[7] K. Lindgren. In *Artificial Life II*, pages 295–312, 1991.

Our Meeting With Gradual: A *Good* Strategy For The Iterated Prisoner's Dilemma

Bruno Beaufils, Jean-Paul Delahaye and Philippe Mathieu

Université des Sciences et Technologies de Lille

Laboratoire d'Informatique Fondamentale de Lille – U.R.A. 369 C.N.R.S.

U.F.R. d'I.E.E.A. Bât. M3 – F-59655 Villeneuve d'Ascq Cedex

e-mail: {beaufils, mathieu, delahaye}@lifl.fr

Abstract

In this paper, after a short return to the description of the classical version of the Iterated Prisoner's Dilemma and its application to the study of cooperation, we present a new strategy we have found named *gradual*, which outperforms the *tit-for-tat* strategy, on which are based a lot of works in the Theory of Cooperation. Since no pure strategy is evolutionarily stable in the IPD, we cannot give a mathematical proof of the absolute superiority of *gradual*, but we present a convergent set of facts that must be viewed as strong experimental evidences of the superiority of *gradual* over *tit-for-tat* in almost every rich environment. We study in detail why this strategy is a good one and we try to identify the difference it has with *tit-for-tat*. Then we show how we have improved the strength of *gradual* by using a genetic algorithm, with a genotype we have created, which includes a lot of well-known strategies for the IPD, such as *tit-for-tat*. We present our ideas on a tree representation of the strategies space and finally we propose a new view of evolution of cooperation in which complexity plays a major role.

1 The Classical Iterated Prisoner's Dilemma

In this paper we first present the classical version of the Iterated Prisoner's Dilemma which is fully described in [30] and its application to the study of cooperation. We insist on the importance of the pure version of this problem. Then we present a new strategy we have found called *gradual*, which outperforms the *tit-for-tat* strategy which is classically recognized as the best possible strategy in the classical IPD.

In section 2, we present in details the *gradual* strategy which has the same qualities than *tit-for-tat* plus a progressive retaliation and forgiveness possibilities. Two experiments are reported, the first one with twelve general strategies to show the precise behavior of it, the second one with the results of a tournament we have organized in the French edition of the "Scientific American".

In section 3 we try to improve the strength of this strategy by using a genetic algorithm, on a genotype we have created and which includes lots of well-known strategies (in fact our genotype can cover more than 8×10^{15} strategies). We present our ideas on a tree representation of the strategies space and finally we propose a new view of evolution of cooperation in which complexity plays a major role.

In the last sections we describe our results and we discuss about the natural behavior of this strategy and its good robustness in ecological competitions.

1.1 IPD and Artificial Life

This game is issued from the Game Theory of John von Neumann and Oskar Morgenstern and has been introduced by RAND game theorists Merrill Flood and Melvin Dresher in 1952. The idea was to introduce some *irrationality* in Game Theory, which is used as a way of modelling interactions between individuals.

This game has been found to be a very good way of studying cooperation and evolution of cooperation and thus a sort of theory of cooperation based upon reciprocity has been set in a wide literature, such as in [1, 3, 4]. The experimental studies of the IPD and its strategies need a lot of time computation and thus with the progress of computers, a lot of computer-scientists and mathematicians have studied it as they have been able to use specific methods, like genetic algorithms, on it, see [9, 2, 5, 8, 19, 21, 26, 27, 20, 31].

As cooperation is a topic of continuing interest for the social, zoological and biological sciences, a lot of works in those different fields have been made on the IPD: [6, 7, 16, 17, 18, 22, 23, 25, 29, 24].

Although all people who have studied the IPD come from different research fields, it could be said that they are all working on the same topic, which belong to the Artificial Life field, the bottom-up study of Life.

1.2 Recall on the IPD

Let two artificial agents have the choice between cooperation and defection. They play one against the other, in a synchronous manner, so that they do not know what the other will play. They get a score according to the situation of the move:

- They both cooperate and then get both the cooperation reward, let evaluate it to R points;

- They both defect and then get both the selfish punishment, let evaluate it to P points;

- One chooses to defect while the other chooses to cooperate, then the one who has defected gets the selfish temptation salary, let it be T points, and the one who has cooperated gets the sucker score, let it be S points.

To have a dilemma, temptation must be better than cooperation, which must be better than punishment, which must be better than to be the sucker. This can be formalised as:

$$T > R > P > S$$

Since this one-shot version of the Prisoner's Dilemma is not very interesting (the most rational choice is to defect), the game is iterated, the final score being the sum of all the moves scored. Each player does not know how many moves there will be, thus each agent's strategy can be studied, to look, for instance, how each player tries to put cooperation in the game.

To avoid the one-shot Prisoner's Dilemma solution to influence strategies, by giving too much importance to temptation regarding cooperation, it is useful to add the following restriction : $2R > T + S$

With this restriction, strategies have no advantage in alternatively cooperate and defect. The classical payoff matrix used is shown in table 1.

T	5
R	3
P	1
S	0

Table 1: Classical payoff rate in the IPD

To study the behavior of strategies, two kinds of computation can be done.

The first one is a simple round-robin tournament, in which each strategy meets all other strategies. Its final score is then the sum of all scores done in each confrontation. At the end, the strategy's strength measurement is given by its range in the tournament. This is the way the *tit-for-tat* strategy has been isolated by Axelrod in [1].

The second one is a simulated ecological evolution, in which at the beginning there is a fixed population including the same quantity of each strategy. A round-robin tournament is made and then the population of bad strategies is decreased whereas good strategies obtain new elements. The simulation is repeated until the

population has been stabilised, *i.e.* the population does not change anymore. This is this way that nasty strategies, those who take the initiative of the first defection, have been discovered to be not very stable, because they are invaded by kind ones.

1.3 Why studying the IPD?

As we have just said in section 1.1 a lot of works have been done on the IPD and from different points of view. The common points of almost all those works are :

- they do not extensively looked for new strategies, thus good strategies and new characteristics have perhaps been missed.

- they study variations of the IPD, because they think the original model is too simple. Those variations offer more proximity to real life.
  Here are examples of such studies: [9, 6, 7, 16, 21, 23, 28, 20, 31].

- they seldom call into question classical results about *tit-for-tat*, which are often considered as definitive. An exception is the paper of Boyd and Loberbaum [8] showing that no pure strategy is evolutionarily stable in the IPD.

To avoid confusion with works quoted in the second point, let us call the Iterated Prisoner's Dilemma we have described, the Classical Iterated Prisoner's Dilemma (CIPD). We think that new works and new discoveries are possible on the CIPD and thus we look for good strategies for it and try to understand how and why they work. The CIPD, as a model of cooperation study, has not been totally understood. It is still a good model for this kind of problem because it is the simplest model and not everything is known about it.

One more reason, if needed, to make those researches, is that good strategies in the CIPD, are still good in a lot of variants of the game.

2 *Gradual*, a good strategy for the CIPD

2.1 Behavior of *gradual*

During our researches we have been led to test and verify classical results [1, 3]. Thus, in order to do so, we tried to create a lot of strategies to look at their behaviors and to check if they had the qualities of *tit-for-tat*. At this time we were trying to increase the efficiency of strategies by modifying their parameters little by little, and looking at the effect of the changes in round-robin tournaments and ecological simulations, until we were satisfied by the results of a strategy. During these experiments we have created many strategies including *gradual* and discovered its strength.

This strategy acts as *tit-for-tat*, except when it is time to forgive and remember the past. It uses cooperation on the first move and then continues to do so as long as the other player cooperates. Then after the first defection of the other player, it defects one time and cooperates two times; after the second defection of the opponent, it defects two times and cooperates two times, ... after the nth defection it reacts with n consecutive defections and then calms down its opponent with two cooperations.

As we can see this strategy has the same qualities as those described by Axelrod in [1] for *tit-for-tat* except one: the simplicity. *Gradual* has a memory of the game since the beginning of it.

2.2 Performance of *gradual*

We conducted some experiments with *gradual* and other strategies. Their results show the good performance of *gradual*. Other results are reported in [11].

We made two kinds of experiments with strategies: round-robin tournaments and ecological simulation. In the following example we have used 12 classical strategies. Each game consists of 1000 moves, with the classical payoff shown in table 1. The general results do not depend on the precise value of payoff and on the number of move, see [11].

2.2.1 Description of the 12 strategies used

The 12 strategies are described below.

cooperate always cooperates

defect always defects

random cooperates with a probability of 0.5

tit-for-tat cooperates on the first move and then plays what its opponent played on the previous move

spite cooperates until the opponent defects, then defects all the time

per_kind plays periodically [cooperate, cooperate, defect]

per_nasty plays periodically [defect, defect, cooperate]

soft_majo plays the opponent's most used move and cooperates in case of equality (first move considered as equality)

mistrust has the same behavior as *tit-for-tat* but defects on the first move

prober begins by playing [cooperate, defect, defect], then if the opponent cooperates on the second and the third move continues to defect, else plays *tit-for-tat*

gradual

pavlov cooperates on the first move and then cooperates only if the two players made the same move, this strategy was studied in [27].

2.2.2 Some results

Results of round-robin tournament and of a simple ecological simulation are presented in tables 2, 3 and figure 1.

They show that *gradual* clearly outperforms all other opponents and especially *tit-for-tat*, in round-robin as well as in ecological evolution. In this latter type of computation we have noticed that *gradual* and *tit-for-tat* have the same type of evolution, with the difference of quantity in favor of *gradual*, which is far away in front of all other survivors when the population is stabilised.

We notice that *gradual* is relatively strong, compared to other strategies, when opposed to clever, or probabilistic strategies like *prober* or *random*, but the most significant point is that *gradual* has never, or not often, bad scores: in almost all cases, it has been able to install cooperation with its opponents.

strategy	final score
gradual	33416
tit-for-tat	31411
soft_majo	31210
spite	30013
prober	29177
pavlov	28910
mistrust	25921
cooperate	25484
per_kind	24796
defect	24363
per_nasty	23835
random	22965

Table 3: Ordered final score in Round-robin

Numerous other experiments (with for example random subsets of strategies) confirm the conclusion that *gradual* is more robust and obtain better score than *tit-for-tat* in almost all contexts (exceptions especially constructed are obviously possible but are seldom and not easy to obtain).

A systematic study of the dynamic evolution of populations with 3 strategies confirms the conclusions of [8] that very complex phenomenon may sometimes occur in the IPD [15].

2.3 The experiment with "Pour La Science"

We have been surprised by those results and then with the help of "Pour La Science", the french edition of the "Scientific American", we have organized a tournament. Each reader was invited to submit his own strategy. A description of this tournament and its results can be found in [10, 12, 13]. The tournament did not used the CIPD, but a variant in which each player had the ability to give up in a definitive way with its opponent.

However the winner was a strategy which is a variant of *gradual*, adapted to the game with renunciation

	coop	def	rand	tft	spite	p_nst	p_kn	sft_mj	mist	prob	grad	pav
coop	3000	0	1481	3000	3000	999	2001	3000	2997	6	3000	3000
def	5000	1000	3003	1004	1004	2332	3668	1004	1000	1008	1340	3000
rand	4012	499	2228	2250	505	1667	2824	1980	2240	1581	940	2239
tft	3000	999	2248	3000	3000	1998	2667	3000	2500	2999	3000	3000
spite	3000	999	3010	3000	3000	2331	3663	3000	1003	1007	3000	3000
p_nst	4334	667	2502	2003	671	1666	3335	671	1999	2006	979	3002
p_kn	3666	333	2024	2667	343	1665	2334	3666	2664	2664	767	2003
sft_mj	3000	999	2380	3000	3000	2331	2001	3000	2500	2999	3000	3000
mist	3002	1000	2244	2500	1003	1999	2669	2500	1000	3000	3001	2003
prob	4996	998	2522	2999	1002	1996	2669	2999	2995	1004	2999	1998
grad	3000	915	2815	3000	3000	2219	3472	3000	2996	2999	3000	3000
pav	3000	500	2244	3000	3000	1332	2833	3000	1998	2003	3000	3000

Table 2: Round-Robin 2 by 2 scores

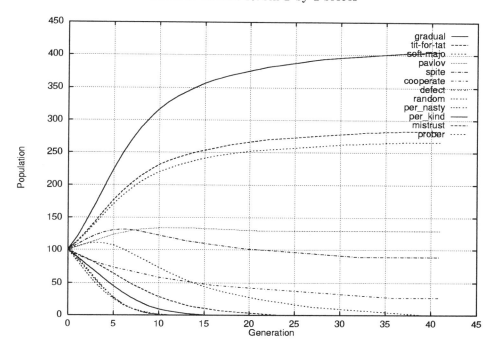

Figure 1: Ecological evolution

and with a different progressive function for retaliation ($N(N+1)/2$ instead of N, with N the number of opponent's previous defections). This fact makes us think that *gradual* has something *tit-for-tat* has not and that classical interpretation of *tit-for-tat* results concerning simplicity must be revisited.

2.4 Comparison with *tit-for-tat*

With the same approach to all these results as Axelrod made on *tit-for-tat*, we can say that the most three important qualities of *gradual* are: kindness (it does not begin to defect), reactivity (it defects when the opponent has defected) and forgiveness (it comes back to cooperation after punishment). These ones are well known to be *good*, but in *gradual*, unlike in *tit-for-tat*, they are not joined by simplicity. In fact the main difference between *tit-for-tat* and *gradual* is their view of the past, the former has a short one and the latter the biggest possible, since it has to know the full history of the current game

to decide what to do on the next move. We can say that *gradual* is much more *complex* than *tit-for-tat*. Let us recall an analyse of Axelrod in [1, page 110]:

The advice takes the form of four simple suggestions for how to do well in a durable Iterated Prisoner's Dilemma:

1. Don't be envious,

2. Don't be the first to defect,

3. Reciprocate both cooperation and defection,

4. Don't be too clever.

When Axelrod writes that, he states that a strategy has to be understandable, hence simple, mainly for its opponents to understand that all it wants is to establish a cooperation period. He thinks that if the strategy clearly announces how it will act, then the other player will be able to cooperate more quickly.

We have previously discussed this point in [14], for the Iterated Prisoner's Dilemma with Renunciation. We agree with Axelrod but we think that having a clear behavior is not always a good idea, for instance against complex-clever-and-nasty or random strategies. The results of *gradual* confirm us in this opinion.

2.5 Natural inspiration of *gradual*

Finally we think that *gradual* presents a natural behavior, which we can find in our daily life, which is, for instance, used by some creditors with their debtors. Let us think of the government and the taxpayers or an electricity company and their bad customers.

This behavior can however be interpreted in two ways:

- The player is very offensive and wants to force his opponent to cooperate and thus clearly shows him that he will be more and more aggressive, so that its best choice is to cooperate.

- The player is very defensive and does not want to be exploited and thus he looks less and less for cooperation, which is risky, but plays more and more the rational choice of the single round Prisoner's Dilemma, to insure its score. However as it is not a single round game, he retries sometimes to reinstall cooperation.

Those two interpretations are two ways of looking at the game, as we have two ways of looking at our relationships with other people in real life. In the first case it tries to explain to the opponent what is the better choice for both of them, whereas in the second case it tries to protect itself. This is a kind of choice between opening or closing its relationship with the opponent, knowing none of the real made choice. It is clear that in real life this is not a simple choice to do. We think that *gradual*, instead of *tit-for-tat*, offers this type of complexity to the player and thus that Axelrod's idea about simplicity is not generally true.

2.6 Is *gradual* strong enough ?

Gradual's behavior, its performance, its inspiration of the "Pour la science" tournament winner and its natural roots, suggest that it is a strong strategy which truly outperforms *tit-for-tat*. The point that we found a strategy stronger than *tit-for-tat* and that its superiority comes from a more complex behavior is enough to think that there is maybe another more complex strategy which is better than *gradual*. *Gradual* may be improved and in order to know if it can be the case, one of the solutions is to use optimization tools on it.

3 Looking for better strategies using Genetic Algorithms

In order to try to improve *gradual's* performances, we have chosen to use a genetic algorithm to optimize *gradual*, so we have constructed a genotype and a fitness function evaluating the quality of strategies.

With this genetic algorithm we thought we would be able to run into the space of described strategies, looking for good ones, especially the ones better than *gradual*.

3.1 Genotype description

Here is the description of the genotype we have set up, using extensions of *gradual's* ideas, to describe a big family of strategies.

The extensions we have added to *gradual* are:

- ability to parameter the time it took the strategy to react at a defection;

- ability to take into account the defection made during a punishment period;

- ability to use defection, or score, threshold, to begin a punishment;

- ability to forgive randomly;

- ability to defect randomly;

- ability to modify the vision of the past.

The 19 different genes of the genotype and their meanings are given now :

begin the first move to do;

alea the number used to determine random defection;

calcul_type the type of detection used to launch a punishment period;

threshold the threshold above which punishment is launched;

forgive the number used to determine random forgiveness move;

blind the ability to update the evolution during a reaction-punishment-lull period;

vision the length of the past the strategy can see (0 being from the beginning);

punishment_evolution the type of punishment length evolution (polynomial or log.);

A_p, B_p, C_p the coefficients of punishment length evolution;

reaction_evolution the type of reaction length evolution (polynomial or log.);

A_r, B_r, C_r the coefficients of reaction length evolution;

lull_evolution the type of lull length evolution (polynomial or log.);

A_l, B_l, C_l the coefficients of lull length evolution;

Strategies described in this way play as follows: after the first move, which is **begin**, they defect with a probability of $p = 1/$**alea**. If they do not defect then they decide if a reaction-punishment-lull period has to be launch, according to **calcul_type**, **threshold** and **vision** parameters. If such a period has to be launch, it is done with a probability of $p = 1 - 1/$**forgive**. Parameters of such a period, *i.e.* reaction, punishment and lull length are computed according to the number of done punishments (let it be N) in one of those two manners, according, respectively, to **reaction_evolution**, **punishment_evolution**, **lull_evolution**: If the computation has to be polynomial the value will be:

$$A_i N^2 + B_i N + C_i$$

and in the logarithmic case it will be

$$A_i \frac{\log(N)}{\log(B_i)} + C_i \quad (B_i > 1)$$

with $i \in \{r, p, l\}$ and N updated at each move if it is not **blind**.

The most new parameter here is the **vision** one, which makes a big difference in the description of strategies to be used in genetic algorithms, as they have been done for now in [2, 19, 21], where strategies are limited to a small view of the past (3 or 4 moves in general).

3.2 A big space

The space of described strategies, is greatly open and depends on the way individuals are generated at the beginning of the genetic algorithms.

This space is so open that it includes almost every well known strategies:

gradual Cooperate, 0, Defection, 1, 0, Yes, 0, Polynomial, 0,1,0, Polynomial, 0,0,0, Polynomial, 0,0,2

tit-for-tat Cooperate, 0, Defection, 1, 0, Yes, 1, Polynomial, 0,0,1, Polynomial, 0,0,0, Polynomial, 0,0,0

defect Defect, 1, whatever you wish

cooperate Cooperate, 0, Defections, 0, Yes, 0, Polynomial, 0,0,0, Polynomial, 0,0,0, Polynomial, 0,0,0

With this approach, *tit-for-tat* could be seen as a degenerated strategy coming from this family and thus from *gradual*. It is a degenerated *gradual*, because some of its parameters are erased, in comparison to *gradual*.

Hence there is a chance that *gradual* could also be a degenerated strategy, coming from some X strategy, with this X better and more complex than *gradual* and then than *tit-for-tat*.

Our idea is that there is no limitation to this affiliation between good strategies and that the space of strategies is full of complex good ones, which have not been found now.

The complexity could be such that the full strategies space might be seen as a tree, where the large space of strategies described here with our genotype is only one branch of it. Maybe on another branch there are other strategies better than *tit-for-tat*, or *gradual* built with other ideas.

4 Results

4.1 How we have obtained it

The genotype we have created defines a space of 8.64×10^{15} different strategies. We have used a simple Genetic Algorithm, using uniform cross-over (*resp.* mutation) to cross over two elements of the population (*resp.* to mute one of it). The algorithm chooses randomly a vector of 19 bits, one bit for each gene and then swaps the genes of the two individuals (*resp.* mutes the gene of the individual) when there is a 1 at the gene's position in the vector.

To compute the fitness of a strategy we have used a simple idea: to be good a strategy needs to beat, in a simple round-robin tournament as those used by Axelrod, the best known strategies at this time, as well as some special ones like the simplest ones (Cooperate, Defect, Random, ...). It is however clear that this is not sufficient and that there may be more complex ways to appreciate the quality of strategies, using, for instance, its behavior in ecological simulation.

So we have chosen a selection of 34 strategies found in previous works, trying to have an heterogeneous selection of behaviors and we compute the fitness of a strategy as its rank in a round-robin tournament including the quoted 34 strategies and itself.

The initial population was made by 150 randomly generated strategies.

We have obtained some results which are easy to understand as every gene has a clearly defined contribution in the behavior of the strategy.

4.2 Remarkable values of genes

Some genes have converged to remarkable values, which give the ability to precise some of our ideas and to infirm, or confirm, some of classical ideas about qualities a strategy needs to have to be good.

The less surprising result is that in almost all our experiments, the **begin** gene has converged very quickly to the Cooperate value, which means that good strategies, we were looking for, would not be too aggressive and have great chances to be kind ones.

This idea has been encouraged by the convergence of the **alea** gene.

Like the **begin** gene, the **alea** gene has converged very quickly to the 0 value, which in our experiments is interpreted as: never defect randomly.

Since the **begin** gene has converged almost at the same time to the Cooperate value, it is clear that strategies we were looking for have to be kind ones. That did not sound surprising since the idea that to be good, strategies have to be kind, is widely accepted.

Nevertheless this is a new way of confirming one of Axelrod's idea, using a different method than the one he has used to find it.

The **forgive** gene had also converged in almost all cases to the 0 value, which means that strategies must not forgive any of its opponent defection.

This is closely in relation with the fitness we have used, *i.e.* without any ecological simulation and thus push some known strategies back, like for instance the *generous tit-for-tat* family , which is however included in the strategies space described by our genotype.

The fitness we use is not dedicated to the creation of strategies which have to be strong in ecological simulation. That could be an explanation of the convergence of this gene, which eliminates some good strategies in ecological simulation.

The last remarkable convergence is the **blind** gene convergence, which has converged to the No value, which means that strategies we were running to would not forget to count opponents defection during reaction-punishment-lull periods, which is not, for instance, the case of *gradual*.

This convergence clearly shows that good strategies would be a little bit more clever, thus more complex, than *gradual* and thus more than *tit-for-tat*. This fact confirms our idea and thus goes against the generally accepted ideas about the relation between efficiency and simplicity.

The convergence of this gene is another confirmation that simplicity does not mean strength in the CIPD.

4.3   One generated strategy which outperforms *gradual*

Just for the illustration, here is the description of one of the strategies we have found with the help of the genetic algorithm we have used on our genotype:

> Cooperate, 0, Defection, 1, 0, No, 5, Polynomial, 1,1,3, Polynomial, 0,0,0, Polynomial, 15,8,4

This strategy beats *gradual* and thus *tit-for-tat*, in round-robin tournament, as well as in an ecological simulation. In the two cases it has finished first just in front of *gradual*, *tit-for-tat* being two or three places behind, with a big gap in the score, or in the size of the stabilised population.

All those results have been found with the 34 strategies chosen for the fitness computation and where confirmed with an experiment involving 300 strategies.

5   Conclusions and further works

As we said, the IPD is a good model in the study of cooperation, but it has not been often studied in its classical

version. While a lot of works try to discuss, or to find how to improve the model itself, we choose to go deeper in the CIPD by looking for good strategies and by trying to understand what make those strategies strong, knowing that every results on the CIPD, can often be ported in other variations of the IPD.

We have found a strategy which leads us to reformulate some of the classical results about simplicity and then have two purposes:

1. trying to find more *complex-and-good* strategies;

2. trying to find what makes those strategies good.

For the former, we have used a genetic algorithm to look for strategies in a big space of strategies, which we have described with a genotype we have created. For the latter we just have to study the results of the experiments done by the genetic algorithm.

The first result we have found enables us to think that simplicity is not a good quality for a strategy, but that like in real-life, complexity may be advantageous.

We also think that this complexity can be so important that maybe there is not a classical linear evolution in the strength of strategies, but that the space of strategies can be seen as a tree with lots of branches. Then each branch is a large space of strategies, with good and bad ones and with some connections between branches, so that there is not a finite set of quality for a strategy to be good, but rather that particular combination of some qualities make the strength of a strategy.

We are now working on those two purposes by improving the fitness of the genetic algorithm, hoping that we could find stronger strategies; and by trying to create other genotypes, to explore other branches of the total space of strategies, hoping we could then find other combinations of qualities.

The former work implies that methods to measure the strength of a strategy have to be set, whereas the latter could reinforce our ideas about the natural emergence of the complexity in the CIPD.

A simulation software with many strategies is already available for Unix, Dos or Windows by web at `http://www.lifl.fr/~mathieu/ipd` or by anonymous ftp on the following site `ftp.lifl.fr` in `pub/users/mathieu/soft`

References

[1] R. Axelrod. *The Evolution of Cooperation*. Basic Books, New York, 1984.

[2] R. Axelrod. The evolution of strategies in the iterated prisoner's dilemma. In L. Davis, editor, *Genetic Algorithms and the Simulated Annealing*, chapter 3, pages 32–41. Pitman, London, 1987.

[3] R. Axelrod and D. Dion. The further evolution of cooperation. *Science*, 242:1385–1390, 1988.

[4] R. Axelrod and W. D. Hamilton. The evolution of cooperation. *Science*, 211:1390–1396, 1981.

[5] S. Bankes. Exploring the foundations of artificial societies. In R. A. Brooks and P. Maes, editors, *Artificial Life, Proc. 4th International Workshop on the Synthesis and Simulation of Living Systems*, volume 4, pages 337–342. MIT Press, 1994.

[6] J. Batali and P. Kitcher. Evolutionary dynamics of altruistic behavior in optional and compulsory versions of the iterated prisoner's dilemma. In R. A. Brooks and P. Maes, editors, *Artificial Life, Proc. 4th International Workshop on the Synthesis and Simulation of Living Systems*, volume 4, pages 344–348. MIT Press, 1994.

[7] J. Bendor. In good times and bad: Reciprocity in an uncertain world. *American J. of Political Science*, 31:531–558, 1987.

[8] Robert Boyd and Jeffrey P. Lorberbaum. No pure strategy is evolutionarily stable in the repeated prisoner's dilemma game. *Nature*, 327:58–59, 1987.

[9] E. Ann Stanley D. Ashlock, M. D. Smucker and L. Tesfatsion. Preferential partner selection in an evolutionnary study of prisoner's dilemma. Economics R. No 35, Submitted for publication, 1994.

[10] J.P. Delahaye. L'altruisme récompensé ? *Pour La Science*, 181:150–156, 1992.

[11] J.P. Delahaye and P. Mathieu. Expériences sur le dilemme itéré des prisonniers. Rapport de Recherche 233, LIFL Lille CNRS (URA 369), 1992.

[12] J.P. Delahaye and P. Mathieu. L'altruisme perfectionné. *Pour La Science*, 187:102–107, 1993.

[13] J.P. Delahaye and P. Mathieu. L'altruisme perfectionné. Rapport de Recherche 249, LIFL Lille CNRS (URA 369), 1993.

[14] J.P. Delahaye and P. Mathieu. Complex strategies in the iterated prisoner's dilemma. In A. Albert, editor, *Chaos and Society*, Amsterdam, 1995. IOS Press.

[15] J.P. Delahaye and P. Mathieu. Studies on ipd dynamics with few number of strategies : Is there any chaos in the pure iterated prisoner's dilemma. Rr., LIFL Lille CNRS (URA 369), 1996.

[16] M. R. Frean. The prisoner's dilemma without synchrony. *Proc. Royal Society London*, 257(B):75–79, 1994.

[17] H. C. J. Godfray. The evolution of forgiveness. *Nature*, 355:206–207, 1992.

[18] N. V. Joshi. Evolution of cooperation by reciprocation within structured demes. *J. of Genetics*, 66(1):69–84, 1987.

[19] K. Lindgren. Evolutionary phenomena in simple dynamics. In J.D. Farmer C. Langton, C. Taylor and S. Rasmissen, editors, *Proc. Workshop on Art. Life*, volume 2, pages 295–312. Santa Fe Institute, Addisson Wesley, 1992.

[20] D. Ashlock M. D. Smucker, E. Ann Stanley. Analyzing social network structures in the iterated prisoner's dilemma with choice and refusal. RR. CS-TR-94-1259, University of Wisconsin-Madison, Departement of Computer-Sciences, 1994.

[21] C. Martino. Emergent nastiness in iterated prisoner's dilemma games. 2.725: Design and Automation, 1995.

[22] R. M. May. More evolution of cooperation. *Nature*, 327:15–17, 1987.

[23] P. Molander. The optimal level of generosity in a selfish, uncertain environment. *J. of Conflict Resolution*, 29(4):611–618, 1985.

[24] M. Nowak. Stochastic strategies in the prisoner's dilemma. *Theoretical Population Biology*, 38:93–112, 1990.

[25] M. Nowak and K. Sigmund. The evolution of stochastic strategies n the prisoner's dilemma. *Acta ApplicandæMathematicæ*, 20:247–265, 1990.

[26] M. Nowak and K. Sigmund. Tit for tat in heterogeneous populations. *Nature*, 355:250–253, 1992.

[27] M. Nowak and K. Sigmund. A strategy of win-stay, lose-shift that outperforms tit-for-tat in the prisonner's dilemma game. *Nature*, 364:56–58, 1993.

[28] M. Oliphant. Evolving cooperation in the non-iterated prisoner's dilemma. In R. A. Brooks and P. Maes, editors, *Artificial Life, Proc. 4th International Workshop on the Synthesis and Simulation of Living Systems*, volume 4, pages 350–352. MIT Press, 1994.

[29] R. Pool. Putting game theory to the test. *Science*, 267:1591–1593, 1995.

[30] W. Poundstone. *Prisoner's Dilemma :* John von Neumann, Game Theory, and the Puzzle of the Bomb. Number 0-19-286162-X. Oxford University Press, Oxford, 1993.

[31] Xin Yao and P. J. Darwen. An experimental study of n-person iterated prisoner's dilemma game. *Informatica*, 18:435–450, 1994.

Evolvable Hardware

Evolving Large Scale Digital Circuits

Hitoshi Hemmi
ATR Human Information Processing Research Laboratories

Jun'ichi Mizoguchi
Japan Hewlett Packard, HSTD

Katsunori Shimohara
ATR Human Information Processing Research Laboratories

Abstract

Adaptive autonomous systems will soon be equipped with two important properties: electronic operation speed and massive complexity. Production Genetic Algorithms (PGAs) and other techniques are successfully allowing digital electronic circuits to evolve their behaviors in a Hardware Description Language (HDL) based evolutionary system. Several experimental results in this paper show that the system provides satisfactory conditions as an evolutionary framework for an adaptive system. Some hints to make the system scalable are discussed here.

1 Introduction

Hardware evolution and evolvable hardware will become the most important components for complex adaptive systems. Despite long tenacious research efforts, creating flexible autonomous agents is still a tough problem for engineers. Thinking about the amazing creativity of nature, however, evolvable hardware that mimicks natural evolution can very likely to create such an agent. Furthermore, such agents are expected to consist of a huge number of components; a software only technique solely is not feasible. Massive parallelism of hardware are indispensable to cope with such hugeness.

We have been constructing a hardware evolutionary system [1, 2] named AdAM (Adaptive Architecture Methodology). This system uses a special purpose programing language, HDL (Hardware Description Language), and evolves HDL-programs. Section 2 gives an overview of this system.

The main technique used in this system is Production Genetic Algorithms (PGAs)[1], which skillfully change the HDL programs and makes their evolvement possible. Section 3 briefly reviews this technique.

Section 4 is devoted to experiments and results of applying the AdAM system to some application problems.

Section 5 discusses the scalability issue.

In work related to the AdAM project, Higuchi et al.[3] uses a FPGA (Field Programmable Gate Array), looks at the architecture bits of the FPGAs as chromosomes and evolves them using Genetic Algorithms.

The main difference between Higuchi's method and AdAM is that the former aims to evolve circuit structures while the latter aims to evolve circuit behaviors expressed as HDL programs.

2 The AdAM system

The AdAM system uses LSI (Large Scale Integrated circuit)-CAD (Computer Aided Design) system and add automatic-al evolutionary mechanism to the system. Figure 1 shows an overview of the AdAM system.

This system provides a program development process. In the process, production rules translated from HDL grammar and structured chromosomes are used to automatically generate HDL source programs. The generated HDL programs are simulated along with some application problems by using a behavior simulation tool. The results are then evaluated as to how well each HDL-program (i.e., digital circuit) fits the problem. After the evaluation results are obtained, some transformations are performed on the development process to improve circuit performance. The generated HDL-programs are converted into circuit schematics, FPGA (Field Programmable Gate Array) configuration data, or LSI mask patterns using a net-list synthesizer and other CAD tools. In this sense, the HDL programs can be considered to correspond to hardware.

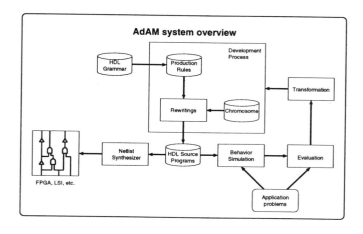

Figure 1: The AdAM system

3 Production Genetic Algorithms

This section briefly reviews the Production Genetic Algorithms (PGAs) [1].

One significant drawback of HDL as a hardware evolution tool is that HDL is too vulnerable to the change caused by evolutionary operations. The main objective of PGAs is to apply evolutionary operations safely to the HDL programs. We will explain PGAs along with Fig. 1.

3.1 Production rules

Figure 2 shows production rules corresponding to a HDL grammar. In Fig. 1, HDL programs are developed by a rewriting process using these production rules.

```
(r0.0)   module       → K_MOD name list_comp list_pin list_action
(r1.0)   name         → K_NAME
(r2.0)   list_comp    → comp
(r2.1)   list_comp    → list_comp comp
(r3.0)   list_pin     → empty
(r3.1)   list_pin     → list_pin pin
(r4.0)   list_action  → action
(r4.1)   list_action  → par_action
(r4.2)   list_action  → cond_action
                        :
(r7.0)   action       → action1
(r7.1)   action       → action action1
(r7.2)   action       → action action2
(r8.0)   action1      → register
(r9.0)   action2      → memory
                        :
(r20.0)  comp         → K_INPUT input_name
(r20.1)  comp         → K_OUTPUT output_name
(r20.2)  comp         → K_BIDIRECT bus_name
(r20.3)  comp         → K_INSTRIN inst_name
                        :
```

Figure 2: Production Rules (HDL grammar)

The numbers following to 'r' are production numbers. For example, 'r4.1' indicates a rule having category number 4 and sub-number 1

3.2 Chromosomes

In the development process in Fig. 1, chromosomes in Fig. 3 are used to determine the production rules applied to each symbol.

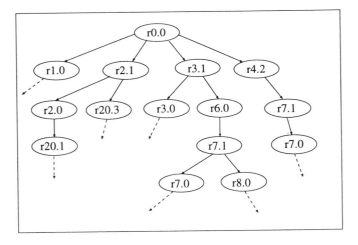

Figure 3: Chromosomes

3.3 Genetic operations

The AdAM system has five genetic operations.

Crossover In tree-structured chromosomes, crossover can be operated between subtrees for root nodes having identical category rules; that is, two rules are applied to the same symbol.

Figure 4 shows a crossover example.

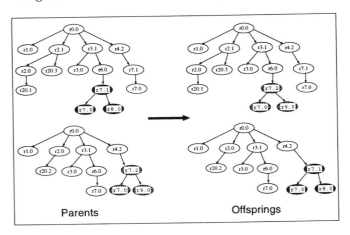

Figure 4: Crossover

Mutation Mutation acts on a node of a chromosome and changes the label to index another rule with the same category as the previous rule.

Gene duplication This operation is related to recursive rules. There is a rule that generates its left hand symbol among its right hand symbol sequence. In a chromosome, such a rule can appear repeatedly in a line. Gene duplication is an operation that copies a node and its subtree block, and arranges them in a line. This is a neutral operation; that is, the HDL program does not change its functionality.

This operation is useful when combined with mutation. When mutation occurs in either subtree block, the HDL program gets a new functionality, but its past functionalities are preserved.

Fusion Fusion is similar operation with gene duplication, but an inserted block is brought from another individual circuit.

Deletion Deletion is a operation roughly the opposite of gene duplication or fusion.

4 Experiments

This section describes some experiments and their results, applying the AdAM system to behavior control tasks that concern artificial ant problems.

4.1 Artificial ant problems

The artificial ant problems are tasks to make an artificial ant on toroidal lattice space eat food adequately arranged on the space as much as possible. Jefferson et al. [4] succeeded in making an ant follow a trail called

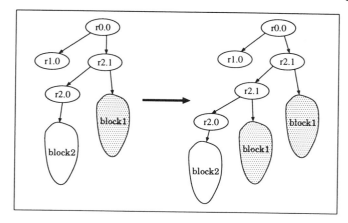

Figure 5: Gene duplication

A copy of block1 is inserted between block1 and block2

the "John Muir Trail" (Fig. 6) by using a Finite State Automaton and an Artificial Neural Network. In Fig. 6, the black cells indicate the food's existence. Similarly, Koza did this on the "Santa Fe Trail" with GP [5].

Our target is to generate a digital circuit capable of controlling an ant on the John Muir Trail. One or more inputs and two outputs are sent to the hardware. An input is a sensory input for the ant. The two outputs are decoded and used to determine four actions of the ant: go straight, turn left, turn right, or do nothing.

This section describes experiments to evolve the circuits that control the artificial ant behavior.

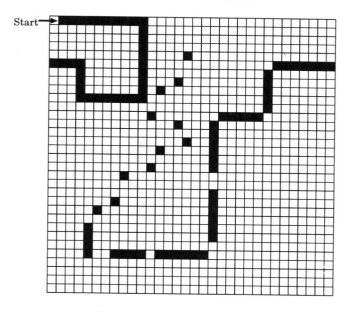

Figure 6: John Muir Trail

One sensory input circuits The target circuit in this experiment has one input and two outputs. The ant only gets one sensory input from the cell in front of it, whether or not the food exists on the cell.

We set three different situations for this problem and did experiments to each case. Experimental conditions were same in all cases: population size was 200, crossover rate was 50% per individual, mutation rate was 0.5%, gene duplication rate was 2%, and deletion rate was 1%. In all cases, the fitness evaluation waw given by the following formula:

$$performance = score + (time\_limit - time\_steps)$$

Score is the number of pieces of food (maximum 89) the ant ate within the limited time (time_limit = 350). Time_step is the number of steps that the ant took. If the time limit was reached before the ant ate all the food, then time_step equals 350.

Case 1 The system is started with a circuit scale assumed insufficient for ant control. The circuits expand their scale by gene duplication and settle at a suitable size.

This experiment is a basic one, and we have reported the result in a previous paper ([1]). However we include it here for comparison reference.

Case 2 In this experiment, each circuit consists of two modules. Each module has one output, and these outputs are combined to make two outputs of whole circuit. One input to the whole circuit is distributed to both modules of the circuit. Each module is treated as belonging to different species and evolving in different populations. This is an experiment for a coevolution model.

Case 3 The HDL we use has a lot of built-in operators that express logical and arithmetic operations. In this experiment, the production rules are modified to inhibit some operators form appearing in the HDL programs. This experiment tests the independentness of this technique to the particular HDL.

Figure 7, 8, and 9 graphically show the results for case 1, case 2, and case 3 respectively. Each graph shows average fitness of the population and fitness of best individual.

The HDL-programs have control structures based on finite state machine. In Fig. 7, before the 100th generation, the number of control states for almost all of the circuit is 3 or 4. At the 251st generation, a circuit with a perfect score appears. This circuit has 6 control states and traverses the entire trail in 332 time steps. After expanding the circuit scale and increasing the functions, a circuit that traverses the entire trail in 230 time steps appears at the 849th generation, and the evolved hardware has 8 control states. In this way, the experiment shows the process, in which the small circuits expand their scale by gene-duplications and obtains a suitable scale and functionality.

In Fig. 8, at the 144th generation, a circuit with a perfect score appears. This circuit traverses the entire trail in 314 time steps. At the 270th generation, a circuit that takes 266 time steps to traverse the trail appears. The two modules of this circuit both have 4 control states. Here, two circuit modules of whole circuit belonging different species were co-evolved and cooperatively control one artificial ant. Figure 10 shows the schematic diagram of the best circuit.

In Fig. 9, at the 103rd generation, a circuit with a perfect score, that takes 300 time steps to traverse the trail appears. At the 381th generation, a circuit which takes 282 time steps appears.

This result implies that the success of the AdAM method is not sensitivity dependent on a particular programing language.

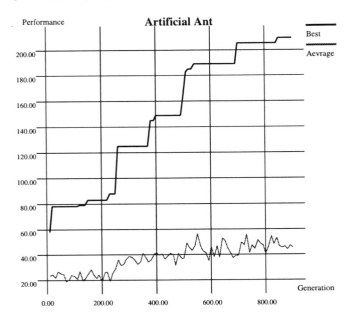

Figure 7: Artificial Ant, Case 1

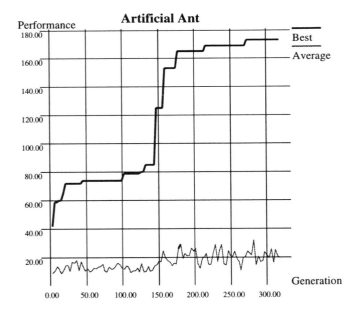

Figure 8: Artificial Ant, Case 2

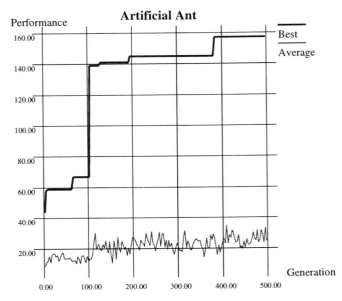

Figure 9: Artificial Ant, Case 3

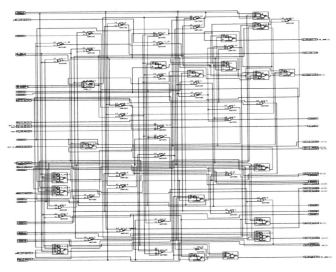

Figure 10: Part of schematic diagram of circuit obtained in case 2

Circuits with 3 sensor inputs In this experiment, the artificial ant can see 3 neighboring cells: front, left, and right. That is, the controller circuit has 3 inputs and 2 outputs. Figure 11 shows the evolutionary progression of this case.

Here, we picked the best circuit and applied to another ant trail problem (Santa Fe Trail [5, page 55]). The result was satisfiable; the artificial ant on the Santa Fe Trail controlled by the circuit took all the food within the time limit. This implies that the acquired behavior is not only for particular problem (John Muir Trail, Fig. 6), but is universally applicable to problems of this kind.

Circuits with 5 sensor inputs In this experiment, the artificial ant can see 5 neighboring cell: front, left,

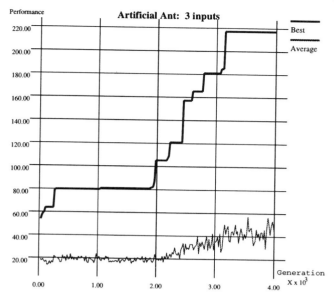

Figure 11: Artificial Ant, 3 inputs

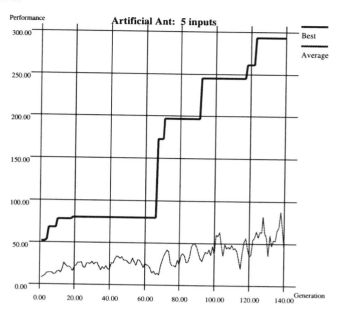

Figure 12: Artificial Ant, 5 inputs

right, left front, and right front; the ant controller circuit has 5 inputs that indicate the existence of food in each cell. Figure 12 shows the evolutionary progression of this case.

The best circuit in this experiment controls the artificial ant to complete the trail in 147 steps. This is the shortest path to pass the trail in Fig. 6. In other words, the circuit is a kind of perfect solution to this problem.

Even more significant thing is that despite the resultant lager scale of the circuit, the evolutionary speed in this case is far faster than in the previous experimental cases.

A discussion concerning this fact is given in the next section.

5 Discussion

So far, we have seen some successful experimental results. These examples show the feasibility of the AdAM system. Now is the time to discuss the scalability issue; is it possible to evolve a large scale circuit in the AdAM system?

There was one hint to this question. In the previous section, the evolution speed in Fig. 12 is far faster than the evolution speed of previous circuits. As for the scale of circuits, the circuits in Fig. 12 are far superior to the previous ones.

The explanation to this fact may be as follows. Evolved circuits in problems with 5 inputs must have some kind of functional regularity that concerns each input pin. For example, the ant should turn left if there is food in the left cell or turn right if there is food in the right cell. If the ant finds food at the left front corner, the ant should change its inner state for turning left, etc.

The AdAM system provides a genetic operator to support functional regularity: gene duplication. Owing to this regularity, circuits with 5 inputs may be able to

evolve at a fast pace. A circuit with only 1 input cannot accomplish this.

Considering large scale but practical application problems, in most cases there may be some kind of functional regularity in the solutions to the problems. If so, there is very good chance that the AdAM system can produce a solution.

Problems that require complex solutions with no regulality might be the real tough ones.

6 Conclusion

This paper has given an overview of the hardware evolutionary system AdAM and its key technique PGAs. Several experimental results showed that AdAM system has good feasibility. A brief discussion about the scalability of AdAM system was also given.

References

[1] Jun'ichi Mizoguchi, Hitoshi Hemmi, and Katsunori Shimohara. Production genetic algorithms for automated hardware design through an evolutionary process. In *IEEE Conference on Evolutionary Computation*, 1994.

[2] Hitoshi Hemmi, Jun'ichi Mizoguchi, and Katsunori Shimohara. Development and evolution of hardware behaviors. In Rodney Brooks and Pattie Maes, editors, *Artificial Life IV*. MIT Press, 1994.

[3] Higuchi Tetsuya, Iwata Masaya, Kajitani Isamu, Iba Hitoshi, Hirao Yuji, Furuya Tatsumi, and Bernard Manderick. Evolvable hardware and its applications to pattern recognition and fault-tolerant systems. In *Towards Evolvable Hardware*, Lecture Notes in Computer Science. Springer-Verlag, 1996.

[4] David Jefferson et al. Evolution as a theme in artificial life; the genesys/tracker system. In *Artificial Life II*, pages 549–576. Addison-Wesley, 1992.

[5] John R. Koza. *Genetic Programming: On the programming of computers by means of natural selection*. The MIT Press, 1992.

Towards Evolvable Electro-Biochemical Systems

Hiroaki Kitano

Sony Computer Science Laboratory
3-14-13, Higashi-Gotanda, Shinagawa
Tokyo, 141 Japan
kitano@csl.sony.co.jp

Abstract

This paper describes a basic idea of evolvable biochemical systems and how such systems can be designed using evolutionary approach. With the recent development in micro-fabrication technique, there are chances that biochemical process can be incorporated in electric circuits as a part of very large integrated circuits. An aggressive research would be to explore possibilities of electro-biochemical systems — a computer based not only on electronics, but also on biochemical reactions. While an evolutionary approach may provide a viable paradigm for the design of electro-biochemical systems, it need to be able to generate complex and interrelated circuits invlving biochemical and electric layers. This paper discusses possible development schemes for electro-biochemical systems.

1. Introduction

Since the invention of digital computers, most research on computational systems have been conducted almost exclusively on systems based on electric circuits, digital computers. Digital computer is flexible and efficient platform for computing based on given programs. However, their physical structures and their effects are static during execution of the program and effects are confined within the space of information.

Biological system has drastically different characteristics. It is a dynamic system, both in information processing and in physical configuration. There is metabolism (exchange) of information and matters, where current computers have only a metabolism (exchange) of information, at best. In essence, biological system is an open dissipative system, from both information and physical point of view.

With the recent development of micro-fabrication technologies, we are now in the stage to seriously consider the possibilities of electro-biochemical systems — a computer based not only on electronics, but also on biochemical reactions. The most salient characteristics of such a computing system is that it can incorporate metabolism of both information and matters. Biochemical part of the system can take in and out biochemical substances, so that the system can be an open system with regards to matters. The direct use of matters, as opposed to information, provide us an opportunities to actually build self-organizing and morphogenetic systems in the real physical world. In addition, molecular level dynamics embodies intrinsic parallelism unattainable by digital computers. By using biochemical devices, the distance between natural and artificial biological system can be reduced substantially.

Although such an electro-biochemical systems can be designed manually, just like convetional computer systems at this moment, evolutionary approach may provide viable design strategies. A flexible and programmable electro-biochemical system can be used to acquire desired configuration through artificial evolution. Such an evolvable electro-biochemical system (EEBS) can be applied to produce biochemical substances and possibly to inject the produced substances to the biological systems, to build systems which biochemical state of the environment triggers the dynamical behaviors of the system, and new computing machinery directly using biochemical processes.

One of the major issues in designing complex systems using evolutionary approach is how to encode and generate complex structures. Similar to other systems such as neural networks and logic circuits, introduction of morphogenesis, or development stage, enables evolutionary design of complex structures. What need to be considered, in addition to neural networks and logic circuits, is that EEBS involves multiple layers such as biochemical layers and electric layers. A method to consistenly handle these layers need to be defined.

In this paper, we will describe a basic concept for EEBS and possible scheme for the development stage, so that complex systems can be designed using evolutionary approach.

2. Evolvable Electro-Biochemical Systems

This section describes basic ideas of evolvable electro-biochemical systems (EEBS). The basic idea is to evolve an electro-biochemical system using a cluster of advanced MIFS controlled by genetic codes. An EEBS can be used to evolve desired chemical substance and long RNA chains [Fodor et al., 1991, Bartel and Szostak, 1993, Joyce, 1989, Kauffman, 1992]. In addition, variations of evolvable biochemical systems can be used for new computing devices that directly use biochemical processing for computing.

2.1. Devices

EEBS requires a novel device which can handle both biochemical and electric processes. It should be a flexible and programmable device so that the system can dynamically reconfigure itself according to changes in the environment and adapt through evolution. A possible device which assume in this paper is an integration of Micro Integrated Fluid System, Field Programmable Gate-Array, and possibly Optical Interconnects.

Micro Integrated Fluid System An option for drastically different computing, chemical, and biological device exists using recent development in micro-fabrication technologies. A pioneer work to develop such a device has been carried out by Ikuta at Nagoya University [Ikuta et al, 1994]. A three-dimensional micro-integrated fluid system (MIFS) is a micro-fabricated device that integrates VLSI and microscopic chemical and biological reactors. MIFS is produced using the integrated harden polymer process (IH process) that can fabricate polymers and metals. Unlike conventional micro-fabrication processes, the IH process can produce very complex three-dimensional polymer or metal devices. IH process can attain a resolution of $5 \times 5 \times 3$ micro-meters, with the position accuracy of $0.25 \times 0.25 \times 1.0$ micro meters. Figure 1 shows a conceptual structure of MIFS. The figure is drawn based on [Ikuta et al, 1994]. The upper layer implements micro structures such as pipes, valves, micro-actuators, and other facilities to enable biochemical reactions. The lower layer is an electrical circuit with sensors, CPUs, memory, gate-arrays, driver for actuators, and other circuits. These two layers are integrated so that real-time sensing, computing, and control of biochemical processes can be attained within a single chip.

Field Programmable Gate Array Recent progress in semiconductor devices enables us to use programmable hardware devices such as the Field Programmable Gate Array (FPGA)[Xilinx, 1990, Lattice, 1990]. The FPGA is a programmable hardware device

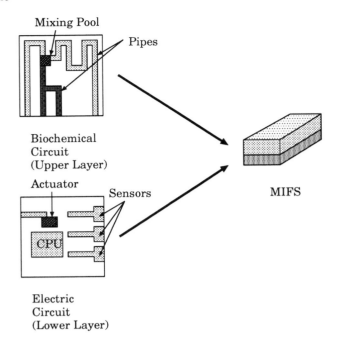

Figure 1: MIFS Structure

that enables users to reconfigure its internal circuit connections and logic node functionalities. Already, a concept of evolvable hardware was proposed and some prototype systems has been created [Higuchi and Manderic, 1994, Thompson, 1995]. Evolvable hardware is defined as an electronic hardware system that evolves to determine its circuit using an FPGA and other reconfigurable modules. While evolvable hardware confine itself within electric circuits, EEBS handles biochemical substances along with electric circuits.

2.2. Architectures

In EEBS, each individual is an electro-biochemical reaction circuit created using a set of advanced MIFS chips. Chromosome encode a set of rules to generate specification for such a electro-biochemical circuits and materials to be supplied to the circuit. Figure 2 shows one of possible configurations of an entire system. The idea of cluster of MIFS chips was already argued by Ikuta, but the architecture in this paper is specific to evolvable systems.

In this case, a system consists of (1) a controller that carries out GA operations and controls an entire process, (2) a biochemical supply and evaluation system that supply materials to each cluster and to evaluate material produced by each individual MIFS cluster, and to provide the evaluation results to the controller, and (3) a population of advanced MIFS cluster that carry out biochemical reactions.

Alternative configuration is to provide a large seem-

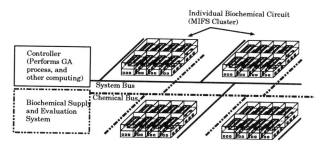

Figure 2: Evolvable Electro-Biochemical Systems

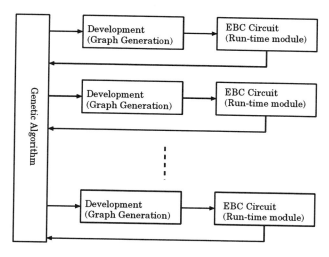

Figure 3: EEBS Process Based on Grammar Encoding Approach

less array of EEBS modules and resource competition dynamics takes care of selections.

3. Morphogenesis

One of the main issues in the evolutionary system is how to evolve complex structures. For this issue, we have been arguing that the incorporation of a morphogenesis stage is a critical factor for the successful evolution of complex systems [Kitano, 1990]. The idea of incorporating the development process to map a genotype into a phenotype was first proposed in [Kitano, 1990] to evolve a neural network structure, and has been applied for various domains [Gruau and Whitley, 1993, Sims, 1994, Hemmi et al, 1994]. Currently, there are two major approach for incorporating morphogenesis stage for mapping genotype to phenotype:

Grammar Encoding Approach: This approach is originally proposed in [Kitano, 1990]. It used a graph L-system as a graph rewriting scheme. Instead of acquiring a connectivity matrix directly, the method obtains rewriting rules so that the connectivity matrix can be generated by successive application of the rule. Experimental results clearly demonstrate that the grammar encoding method is far superior than direct encoding method, in evolving neural network structures [Kitano, 1990] and logic circuits [Kitano, 1996]. It is now being applied in a variety of fields [Gruau and Whitley, 1993, Sims, 1994, Hemmi et al, 1994].

Cellular Approach: This approach was proposed in [Kitano, 1994, Kitano, 1995] to be more biologically plausible model of morphogenesis than [Kitano, 1990]. It models chemical reactions within each cells and interactions between cells to influence gene expressions and cell differentiations.

These two approaches have their own merits. Thus, which approach to be implemented shall be decided based on the type of application.

4. Grammar Encoding Approach

EEBS based on the grammar encoding approach follows standard procedure for GA-based evolutionary process with development stage. Figure 3 shows an overall scheme of this approach. Development stage is an off-line process, i.e. development will be done before run-time, and modules are configured following the result of development stage.

The basic flow of the system is:

Randomly create an initial population.
Loop:
    Execute morphogenesis process to determine
        the system configuration.
    Configure MIFS clusters –
        Set up valves and electric circuits.
    Check if there is violation of the prohibit rule.
    Start electro-biochemical processes
        (Flow chemicals, heat materials,
        execute programs, etc.).
    Evaluate products/behavior performance.
    Clean up MIFS clusters.
    If a desired result is obtained, exit.
    Else, continue.
    Select individual based on fitness,
        perform crossover and mutation to produce
        individuals for the next generation.
Goto Loop.

This process is similar to a conventional GA process, except some care has to be taken due to the nature of the biochemical process. These are clean-up of system at each generation, checking the prohibit rules to avoid potential hazatous biochemical reactions, etc.

Other configurations which is not based on standard

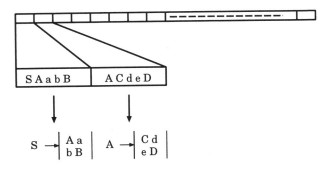

Figure 4: Rewriting Rules Encoded on Chromosome

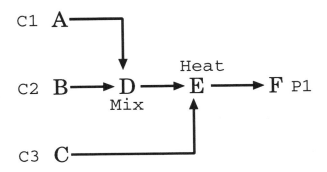

Figure 5: A Simple Chemical Circuit

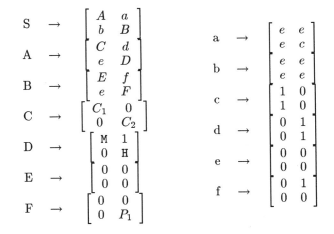

Figure 6: Configuration Matrix for a simple chemical circuit

$$
\begin{array}{ccc}
S & \rightarrow & \begin{bmatrix} A & a \\ b & B \end{bmatrix} \\
A & \rightarrow & \begin{bmatrix} C & d \\ e & D \end{bmatrix} \\
B & \rightarrow & \begin{bmatrix} E & f \\ e & F \end{bmatrix} \\
C & \rightarrow & \begin{bmatrix} C_1 & 0 \\ 0 & C_2 \end{bmatrix} \\
D & \rightarrow & \begin{bmatrix} M & 1 \\ 0 & H \\ 0 & 0 \\ 0 & 0 \end{bmatrix} \\
E & \rightarrow & \\
F & \rightarrow & \begin{bmatrix} 0 & 0 \\ 0 & P_1 \end{bmatrix}
\end{array}
\qquad
\begin{array}{ccc}
a & \rightarrow & \begin{bmatrix} e & e \\ e & c \end{bmatrix} \\
b & \rightarrow & \begin{bmatrix} e & e \\ e & e \end{bmatrix} \\
c & \rightarrow & \begin{bmatrix} 1 & 0 \\ 1 & 0 \end{bmatrix} \\
d & \rightarrow & \begin{bmatrix} 0 & 1 \\ 0 & 1 \end{bmatrix} \\
e & \rightarrow & \begin{bmatrix} 0 & 0 \\ 0 & 0 \end{bmatrix} \\
f & \rightarrow & \begin{bmatrix} 0 & 1 \\ 0 & 0 \end{bmatrix}
\end{array}
$$

Figure 7: A rule set to develop a simple biochemical circuit

GA-like procedure are possible, so that dynamic viability is imposed for selection, instead of predefined fitness measure.

Morphogenesis stage involve development of both biochemical and electric circuits. In the rest of this section, development of biochemical and electric circuits will be described.

4.1. Developing Biochemical Circuits

In defining circuits for the biochemical part of EEBS, the graph rewriting rules need to be modified so as to incorporate necessary information to fully specify configurations of the EEBS. Rewriting rules are encoded on chromosome as shown in Figure 4. Through an evolutionary process, rewriting rules to generate complex structure are acquired, not the direct configuration of the system. For example, a simple process of mixing two chemicals (C1 and C2), then add the other chemical (C3) and heat them to obtain product (P1) is shown in Figure 5. This is represented by a configuration matrix as shown in Figure 6.

This configuration matrix can be generated using a set of rules as shown in Figure 7. Rules from S to F are vertex rewriting rules and that from a to f are edge rewriting rules. Symbol M means mix, and symbol H means heat. Figure 8 shows how a configuration matrix is developed. After obtaining the initial configuration matrix, unnecessary parts are removed to obtain the final

matrix shown in Figure 6.

This configuration matrix is sent to an MIFD cluster so that a biochemical reaction circuit is configured by changing settings of various valves, sensors, heaters, etc.

4.2. Developing Electric Circuit

Morphogenesis of an electric part of EEBS can be attained using grammar encoding method. A set of graph rewriting rules is encoded in a chromosome as a sequence of fragments. Each fragment represents a rule. A rule is represented as:

$$
LHS \quad \rightarrow \quad \begin{bmatrix} UL & UR \\ LL & LR \end{bmatrix}
$$

This rule is applied when the left hand side (LHS) matches a symbol in the matrix. The symbol is rewritten as a 2 by 2 matrix with four symbols (UL: Upper Left, UR: Upper Right, LL: Lower Left, LR: Lower Right). For example, a fragment of the chromosome AOHCL represents the following rule:

$$
\begin{array}{cc}
A & a \\
b & B
\end{array}
\quad \rightarrow \quad
\begin{array}{cccc}
C & d & e & e \\
e & D & c & e \\
e & e & E & f \\
e & e & e & F
\end{array}
\quad \rightarrow \quad
\begin{array}{cccccccc}
C_1 & 0 & 0 & 1 & 0 & 0 & 0 & 0 \\
0 & C_2 & 0 & 1 & 0 & 0 & 0 & 0 \\
0 & 0 & C_3 & 0 & 1 & 0 & 0 & 0 \\
0 & 0 & 0 & M & 1 & 0 & 0 & 0 \\
0 & 0 & 0 & 0 & H & 0 & 0 & 1 \\
0 & 0 & 0 & 0 & 0 & 0 & 0 & 0 \\
0 & 0 & 0 & 0 & 0 & 0 & 0 & 0 \\
0 & 0 & 0 & 0 & 0 & 0 & 0 & P_1
\end{array}
$$

Figure 8: Development Process of a Simple Biochemical Circuit

$$
A \rightarrow \begin{bmatrix} O & C \\ H & L \end{bmatrix}
\qquad
F \rightarrow \begin{bmatrix} K & H \\ L & K \end{bmatrix}
\qquad
H \rightarrow \begin{bmatrix} T & Q \\ J & T \end{bmatrix}
$$

$$
D \rightarrow \begin{bmatrix} T & A \\ K & G \end{bmatrix}
\qquad
M \rightarrow \begin{bmatrix} J & E \\ C & P \end{bmatrix}
$$

$$
B \rightarrow \begin{bmatrix} N & S \\ P & D \end{bmatrix}
\qquad
A \rightarrow \begin{bmatrix} D & I \\ R & G \end{bmatrix}
\qquad
J \rightarrow \begin{bmatrix} F & A \\ I & E \end{bmatrix}
$$

$$
S \rightarrow \begin{bmatrix} T & T \\ D & H \end{bmatrix}
\qquad
O \rightarrow \begin{bmatrix} Q & O \\ T & E \end{bmatrix}
$$

Figure 9: An example of the rules (First 10 rules)

$$
A \rightarrow \begin{bmatrix} O & H \\ C & L \end{bmatrix}
$$

Although the allele value of the chromosome described in this paper is shown as a letter for readability, real implementation uses an integer value. At each allele position, an integer ranging from 0 - 19 is assigned. Suppose the number of non-terminals is given as N; the chromosome can therefore encode more than N rules, allowing redundancy. One reason for allowing redundancy is to better ensure the other rule is used when the first rule be destroyed by mutation or crossover.

The development process starts from an initial node. For each symbol in the matrix, the matching rule is applied. The rewriting cycle continues until a matrix of the necessary size is generated. An example of rules is shown in Figure 9.

These rules are used to rewrite a graph. An example of the rewriting process is shown in Figure 10. The initial symbol O is rewritten using rule 15 at the first iteration. This results in a 2 by 2 matrix. Subsequently, the each element of the matrix is rewritten using rules in the chromosome. After several iterations, a matrix of the desired size is generated.

Once the matrix is created, it is downloaded onto a logic circuit. In a real system, the matrix will be downloaded to an FPGA in each module. Each value in the upper right area is set to either 1 or 0, where 1 repre-

$$
O \rightarrow \begin{array}{cc} Q & O \\ T & E \end{array}
\quad \rightarrow \quad
\begin{array}{cccc}
O & H & Q & O \\
G & A & T & E \\
B & E & K & Q \\
D & C & E & B
\end{array}
$$

$$
\Rightarrow
\begin{array}{cccc}
2 & 1 & 1 & 1 \\
1 & 0 & 1 & 1 \\
0 & 1 & 4 & 1 \\
1 & 0 & 1 & 1
\end{array}
$$

Figure 10: Development of Matrix

sents a connection and 0 represents no connection. The diagonal elements represent the function of each node. In Figure 10, logic gate functions are shown by using integer numbers: AND = 0, OR = 1, NOT = 2, XOR = 3, NOR = 4, and NAND = 5. This can be adjusted for the hardware implementation for a specific FPGA device. In addition, the system has sensor, actuator, and other numeric computing nodes.

4.3. Integrated Morphogenesis Process

So far, we have discussed morphogenesis process for biochemical and electric circuits independently. However, these need to be treated in an integrated manner. Since the control will be imposed on the biochemical process, the interface from the electric circuits to biochemical process will be created on the edge node of the matrix for biochemical prcess.

For example, a simple biochemical circuit shown in Figure 5 was augmented with electric control in Figure 11. **Flow control A**, **Flow control B**, and **Prog A** are electric part of the process. These are interfaced through edge nodes in the matrix. Electric circuits will be treated as sub-matrix to be expanded under these edge nodes. Figure 12 shows an integrated connectivity matrix.

5. Electro-Biochemical Cellular Automata

So far we have described the morphgenesis process for the grammar encoding approach using off-line application of top-down rewriting rules. Alternative approach

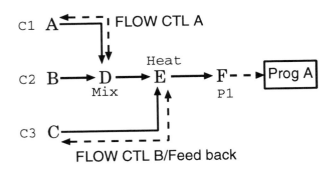

Figure 11: A Simple Chemical Circuit with Electric Control

	A	B	C	D	E	F	G
A	C_1			CTL_A			
B		C_2		1			
C			C_3		CTL_B		
D				Mix	1		
E					Heat	1	
F						P1	Exec
G							ProgA

Figure 12: Configuration Matrix for a simple chemical circuit with electric control

is to exploit emergent property of collective and interactive units — Electro-Biochemical Cellular Automata (EB-CA). In this approach, each unit is defined as a cell. Figure 13 shows an overall scheme for this approach. Figure 14 shows a framework of the control flow. This approach is an augmented version of the model presented in [Kitano, 1995, Kitano, 1994].

Morphogenesis process starts from a single cell, and subsequent divisions. While this model is much closer to real biological systems, it must incorporate various biological findings to enable complex pattern formation. Although the emergence of dynamical clustering and differentiation associated with chaotic dynamics has been investigated as a source of diversity of cell types [Kitano, 1994, Kitano, 1995], none of these studies leads to the

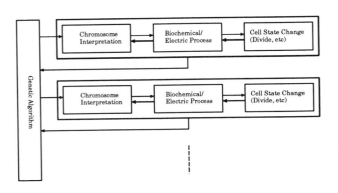

Figure 13: EB-CA process

```
Randomly create an initial population.
Loop1:
    Loop2:
        Interpret chromosome to set up biochemical
            and electric circuits
        Initiate biochemical and electric process.
        Check cell status change condition (CSCC).
        If any CSCC is satisfied,
            execute status change
            (divide, kill, etc)
        Check stop condition
        If Stop condition is not met, goto Loop2.
    Evaluate individual.
    Clean up MIFS clusters.
    If a desired product is obtained, exit.
    Else, continue.
    Select individual based on fitness,
    perform crossover and mutation to produce
    individuals for the next generation.
    Goto Loop1
```

Figure 14: An Algorithm for EB-CA

generation of complex structures. While we believe that that chaotic dynamics is definiately a key factor, other factors must be taken into account for the complex structure formation.

5.1. Symmetry Breakdown for Morphogenesis

In order to implement a basic scheme for complex structure formation, we will take a look at the real biological systems. Aside from chaotic dynamics, expression of specific genes are critical in formation of complex structures. Expression of gene must be controlled spatio-temporally so that specific gene will be expressed at specific time and location. Thus, finding fundermental principles for coordinating transcriptions is essential.

Our hypothesis is that symmetry breakdown and contraints are two fundermental principles in biological pattern formation. In this paper, we focus on symmetry breakdown. We assume that diversity of cell types, thus related morphogenesis, are created due to symmetry breakdown at four levels; (1) disparity of mutation level between the leading strand and the ragging strand in DNA replication [Wada et al., 1993], (2) asymmetric distribution of chromatin, or repressors, in DNA replication [Kitano and Imai, 1996], (3) asymmetric distribution of cytoplasmic materials [Rhyu et al., 1994, Knoblich et al., 1994], and (4) cell-cell interactions which was discussed in chaotic dyanmics papers [Kitano, 1994, Kitano, 1995].

While these four level of symmetry breakdown can be introduced in the machinary, DNA replication-dependent transcriptional regulation scheme plays key role particularly in regulating temporal-specific gene expression [Kitano and Imai, 1996]. When DNA is replicated, chromatin structure is once disassembled and strands are exposed to allow replication. For two daughter strands, chromatin structure must be reconstructed. A chromatin at the mother strand is transfered to one of two daughter strand, while the other strand need to reconstruct a chromatin. When this reconstruction takes place, transcription activator binds to the specific site instead of chromatin. Thus, chromatin structure for this daughter strand will not be formed. This creates systematic displacement of heterochromatin structure triggered by DNA replication. This mechanism can also apply to repressor binding. At each DNA replication repressors, specifically an array of repressors, are once dissociated from the binding site, and it need to be attached to the binding region. However, depending upon the chemical environment of the replication site, repressors may be attached to only of the two strands and repressor may be not bind to the other strand. Details of this mechanism and its biological implications will be published elsewhere [Kitano and Imai, 1996].

5.2. Chromosome Encoding and Interpretation

Chromosome Structure Figure 15 shows chromosome structure and encoding. A chromosome is a sequence of fragments, each of which encodes conditions for invoking specific actions. Along with the sequence, a data structure representing a chromatin structure is defined. Changes in chromatin structure can be modelled using a template which represents chromatine structures. At each division, a part of templete opens systematically so that genes which were covered by the template will be a subject of transcription. This mechanism enables highly complex structure formation. Gene which are in the open region (i.e. not covered by chromatin template) are subject of transcription.

Gene Interpretation Each gene will be interepreted at each cycle. Variable values can be a result of computing or sensor readings. It can also be a counter value which counts number of replications the cell have undergone. For example, [A > 0.5 | open B](this is a human readable form of the chromosome) can be read as *if a value of A is over 0.5, then open valve B.* This time, the value of variable A can be set according to the sensor readings, such as temperture or density of specific chemical. Multiple tuples in condition side are treated as AND, because OR can be implemented if a different fragment with same action exists. For example, [A > 0.5 | Open B][B < 0.2 , C > 1.0 | Open B] is If ((A > 0.5) OR (B < 0.2 AND C > 1.0)) , Then Open B). Such rules are compiled and directly implemented on FPGA in the silicon layer of MIFS. While multiple independent circuits can be implemented, it attains micro second order reaction time, which may be

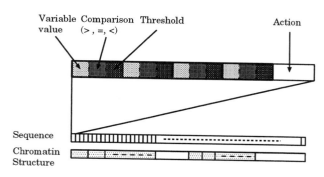

Figure 15: Chromosome coding for EB-CA

crucial for some applications.

Cell Division Cell status change specifies operations such as cell division. For example, cell division can be defined as:

```
Divide
     Copy Sequence to NewCellUnit with Mutation
     Copy Chromatin Structure Template to NewCellUnit
          with disparity
     Copy Registers to a NewCellUnit
     Open valves to transport specific chemicals
          to a NewCellUnit
     If specified condition is reached,
          then close valves
```

This Divide operation implements a simple version of symmetry breakdown at mutation of DNA sequence, chromatin structure, and cytoplasmic materials.

Figure 16 shows an example of changes in chromatin structure template. At each cell division, chromatin structure changes and areas covered by chromatin and areas open for transcription changes. This mechanism can be a temporal control mechanism for gene regulation because certain genes will be expressed only after certain number of cell divisions.

6. Concluding Remarks

In this paper, we proposed evolvable electro-biochemical systems (EEBS), and discussed extensively on the morphogenesis stage on the EEBS. EEBS is an integrated system exploiting biochemical reactions and electronics using the state-of-the-art technologies. It is based on the device being developed using special polymar fabrication process and recent silicon technologies.

While existing computing machinary is confined within the logic circuits, the direct use of biochemical process tightly coupled with electric circuits explore new area of research in computer science, A-life, and biology.

Since the research in described in this paper have just

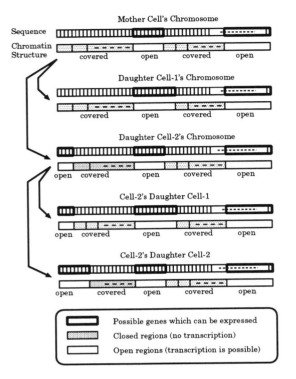

Figure 16: Asymmetric Distribution of Chromatin Structure

started, we do not have tangible results yet. However, we believe that the concept and technologies proposed in this paper contribute to the community in open up the possiblity of using biochemical process for computing and production scheme.

Acknowledgements

The author would like to express sincere thanks to Professor Ikuta, Nagoya University for providing me information on MIFS chips, and for informative discussions.

References

[Bartel and Szostak, 1993] Bartel, D. and Szostak, J., "Isolation of New Ribozymes from a Large Pool of Random Sequences," *Science*, Vol. 261, pp 1411-1418, 1993.

[Fodor et al., 1991] Fodor, S., Read, J., Pirrung, M., Stryer, L., Lu, A., and Solas, D., "Light-Directed, Spatially Addressable Parallel Chemical Synthesis," *Science*, Vol. 251, pp 767-773, 1991.

[Gruau and Whitley, 1993] Gruau, F., and Whitley, D., "Adding Learning to the Cellular Development of Neural Networks: Evolution and the Baldwin Effect," *Evolutionary Computation*, 1(3): 213-233, 1993.

[Hemmi et al, 1994] Hemmi, H., Mizoguchi, J., Shimohara, K., "Development and evolution of hardware behaviors", *Proc. of Artificial Life IV*, MIT Press, 1994.

[Higuchi and Manderic, 1994] Higuchi, T., Iba, H., Manderick, B., "Evolvable Hardware", in *Massively Parallel Artificial Intelligence*, (ed. H.Kitano), MIT Press, 1994.

[Ikuta et al, 1994] Ikuta, K., Hirowatari, K., and Ogata, T., "Three Dimensional Micro Integrated Fluid Systems (MIFS) Fabricated by Stereo Lithography," *Proc. of IEEE International Workshop on Micro Electro Mechanical Systems*, Oiso, 1994.

[Joyce, 1989] Joyce, J., "Amplification, mutation and selection of catalytic RNA," *Gene*, 82, pp 83-87, 1989.

[Kauffman, 1992] Kauffman, S., "Applied Molecular Evolution," *J. thor. Biol.*, 157, 1-7, 1992.

[Kauffman, 1993] Kauffman, S., *The Origins of Order*, Oxford University Press, 1993.

[Kitano, 1990] Kitano, H., Designing Neural Network using Genetic Algorithms with Graph Generation System", *Complex System*, Vol. 4-4, 1990.

[Kitano, 1994] Kitano, H., "Evolution of Metabolism for Morphgenesis", *Proc. of Artificial Life IV*, 1994.

[Kitano, 1995] Kitano, H., "A Simple Model of Neurogenesis and Cell Differentiation Based on Evolutionary Large-Scale Chaos", *Artificial Life*, 2: 79-99, 1995.

[Kitano, 1996] Kitano, H., "Morphogenesis for Complex Systems", *Toward Evolvable Hardware: Proc. of EVOLVE-95*, 1996 (to appear).

[Kitano and Imai, 1996] Kitano, H. and Imai, S., "Two distinct instrinstic mechanism regulate the stochastic and catastriphic phases in cellular senescence," manuscript, 1996.

[Knoblich et al., 1994] Knoblich, J., Jan, L., and Jan, Y., "Asymmetric segregation of Numb and Prospero during cell division," *Nature*, Vol. 377, 624-626, 1995.

[Lattice, 1990] Lattice Semiconductor Corporation, *GAL Data Book*, 1990.

[Marchal et al, 1994] Marchal, P., Piguet, C., Mange, D., Stauffer, A., Durand, S., "Embryological development on silicon", *Proc. of Artificial Life IV*, MIT Press, 1994.

[Rhyu et al., 1994] Rhyu, M., Jan, L., and Jan, Y., "Asymmetric Distribution of Numb Protein during Division of the Sensory Organ Precursor Cell Confers Distinct Fates to Daughter Cells," *Cell*, Vol. 76, 477-491, 1994.

[Sims, 1994] Sims, K., "Evolving 3D Morphology and Behavior by Competition," *Proc. of Artificial Life IV*, Cambridge, MIT Press, 1994.

[Thompson, 1995] Thompson, A., "Evolving electronic robot controllers that exploit hardware resources", *Proc. of the 3rd European Conf. on Artificial Life*, 1995.

[Wada et al., 1993] Wada, K., Doi, H., Tanaka, S., Wada, Y., and Furusawa, M., "A neo-Darwinian algorithm: Asymmetrical mutations due to semiconservative DNA-type replication promote evolution," *Proc. Natl. Acad. Sci. USA*, Vol. 90, 11934-11938, 1993.

[Xilinx, 1990] Xilinx Semiconductor Corporation, *LCA Data Book*, 1990.

Morphogenesis, Embryology

Investigations with a
Multicellular Developmental Model

Kurt Fleischer

Previous address: California Institute of Technology, MS 350-74, Pasadena, CA, USA, 91125

Current address: Pixar Animation Studios, 1001 W. Cutting Blvd #200, Richmond, CA, USA, 94804

e-mail: kurt@pixar.com

Abstract

This paper reports recent simulation experiments that probe the capabilities of a particular multicellular developmental model.

Biological development is a complicated process involving cells interacting under genetic control. Cells interact via chemical, mechanical, and electrical mechanisms to create the shape of an organism. Instead of trying to simplify a developmental system sufficiently to enable a thorough mathematical analysis, we have tried to include in our model as many of the relevant mechanisms as is computationally feasible. The resulting simulation system exhibits many emergent phenomena seen in biological systems:

- combination of lineage-directed and interaction-directed development,
- morphogenesis based on the interaction of multiple mechanisms,
- formation of segmented shapes,
- formation of hierarchical structures, and
- regeneration of damaged structures.

In the future, we believe there will be great value in using simulations such as these to gain *intuitions* about biological systems that can later be examined more closely and subjected to analysis.

Note: Several of the images in this paper are best viewed in color. Color versions of the figures are available at the web page http://www.gg.caltech.edu/~kurt/Devsim/alife5.html.

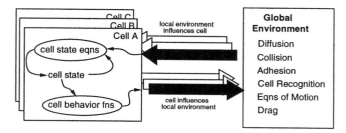

Figure 1: Overview of our developmental model.

1 Introduction

This paper chronicles a set of simulation experiments designed to verify whether or not our developmental model is a viable substrate for the study of pattern formation and the creation of biological structures. To determine this, we have attempted to create successively more ambitious structures and behaviors using the model. Our results to date indicate that the model is capable of representing a wide range of biologically relevant phenomena, including:

- axis formation,
- formation of segmented patterns,
- generation of hierarchical structure,
- regeneration of structures when damaged, and
- pattern formation via combinations of developmental mechanisms (e.g., chemical diffusion combined with direct cell-cell interaction).

This paper presents examples of each of these phenomena, exhibiting the use of *local* interactions to create a *global* multicellular structure. Note that the interactions can be via a variety of processes; chemical signaling, mechanical forces, adhesive membrane chemicals, etc.

1.1 The Model

We describe the model briefly here, and refer the reader to prior work [4, 5] for a more detailed discussion. In this article we focus on a few selected experiments that show the model's strengths and weaknesses.

The model we are considering represents cells as discrete entities with a state vector and a shape (circle or sphere). The state vector represents concentrations of chemicals inside the cell or in the cell's membrane. Populations of these cells interact with each other and with the surrounding environment via several mechanisms. Cells can sense membrane chemicals, release and/or sense chemicals that diffuse in the environment, and they can interact physically by exerting motive forces and causing collisions. The chemicals in the cell surface

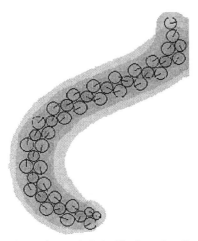

Figure 2: Axis Formation: 1-2-1 Chain of cells. The shaded regions denote the concentration of diffusing chemicals.

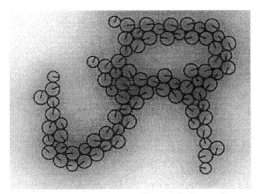

Figure 3: Chain of cells with branches.

may be adhesive and bind to particular chemicals in the surface of an adjacent cell.

We use a dynamical system to represent all internal workings of a cell: gene expression, gene regulation, cell metabolism, chemical kinetics, internal cell transport, etc. The state of the dynamical system then determines the operation of the cell. A simulated cell's activities include movement, mitosis, release of diffusing chemicals, size change, and expression of chemical factors on the cell surface. The dynamical system is user-programmable; each simulation experiment is specified by a different set of differential equations and initial conditions.

The simulations begin with a single cell (or a few cells) that divide and differentiate to give rise to multicellular simulated organisms. This provides us with a substrate within which we can begin to ask questions about how changes to equations governing a cell's internal dynamics affect the morphogenesis and behavior of the organism as a whole.

The simulations described in this article include:
◇ chains of cells (with geometric constraints),
◇ curling segmented chains of cells,

◇ neural network with two level hierarchy,
◇ regenerating hierarchical structures,
◇ initial trials with 3-D developmental simulations, and
◇ cells on reaction-diffusion patterns.
Note that the structures created by these developmental simulations tend to be asymmetric and contain heterogeneous cell types.

1.2 Related Work

We build on prior work in developmental biology [6] and biological modeling [15, 9, 12]. Due to space limitations in this article, we can only briefly mention a few of the most closely related papers. For a more complete discussion, please see [4].

Some recent models use a combination of grammars to represent some cell events (e.g., mitosis), and differential equations to represent continuous changes in cell state [10, 13]. The production rule system described in [16] is similar, using production rules for difference equations. Boolean networks have also been used to model cell state changes [3].

Lattice-based models [1, 7] are able to represent more diverse cell shapes, and hence can replicate differential adhesion phenomena [14] that are difficult to reproduce with simple cell shape representations, such as our spheres [4, Sec. 6.4]. However, it is not clear how to efficiently compute 3-D lattice models.

Each of these systems has some very strong aspects and each has fairly broad modeling capabilities. In this paper, we attempt to push our model further, and to show emergent phenomena that are more distantly removed from the underlying representation. With complicated multiple-mechanism models, it is not easy to determine a priori what behaviors can and cannot be generated. Thus we need to exercise them extensively to have a basis for comparison with other models. It would be nice to come up with a standard suite of examples to attempt in each system, giving us a better metric for comparison.

2 Creating Simple Body Plans

Most real organisms begin their development by forming a coordinate system, creating asymmetries that can be used to distinguish anterior from posterior, dorsal from ventral, and medial from lateral. More complicated structures are then formed within this framework. The following hypothetical organisms exploit differing strategies to create simple body plans.

2.1 Forming chains of cells

The virtual organism shown in Figure 2 begins as one cell and creates a body axis by growing and dividing to form a chain of cells. The chain is comprised of cells of three cell types with different behaviors. We'll call the three cell types P (progenitor), L (large) and S (small).

The final chain structure is constructed from L and S cells in the pattern 1S-2L-1S-2L (perhaps this pattern is easier to see in Figure 5. Only the P type cells undergo cell division; the L and S types do not divide.

The organism starts as a single P cell. It divides three times to create a L cell, then another L cell, then a S cell. The orientation of the cleavage plane for each P cell division is determined by gradients of diffusing chemicals that are released by the L cells. After each cell division, one daughter cell differentiates into a P cell, and the other daughter becomes an S or L cell depending on the neighboring contacts. This process is repeated cyclically to lengthen the chain of cells. Contact between the cells is maintained via adhesive surface chemicals.

In the normal growth of this organism, when the P cell divides, the two daughter cells are identical. Which one becomes the progenitor is determined by the contacts with neighboring cells. This strategy works if the contacts are maintained. However, errors can occur in the structure (Figure 3) when the ambient concentrations of diffusing chemicals get large. When this happens, the gradient that the progenitor cell uses to choose its cleavage orientation may not be aligned with the axis of the chain, causing the P cell to divide at an improper orientation. Sometimes this effect becomes so severe that the cell contacts are not maintained as expected, and two progenitor cells can get created, causing a fork in the chain.

This type of defect in the simulated developmental process is reminiscent of similar irregularities seen in biological systems. If a cell's fate is determined by its neighbors, and the neighbors are removed or modified, it may adopt a different fate.

2.2 Geometric constraints on organism shape

The experiment in Figure 4 is similar to the previous one, with a modification to the sizes of the S and L cells. The sizes of the small S cells and large L cells here fit together tightly, constraining the chain to be nearly straight. Occasional errors in the cleavage orientation (as discussed above) can still occur, and give rise to the kinks visible in the chain. When the growing chain collides with the boundary of the chamber, the collision causes the chain to grow in a different direction.

Figure 4 and Figure 5 show that the size and shape of the individual cells determines the shape of this virtual organism. The cells fit together snugly, constraining the organism to have a moderately rigid lattice shape. The orientations of cell divisions are controlled during development so that it forms a long chain rather than forming a grid of cells.

The cell shapes used in this simulation are simply circles, so changing the size and location of a cell is the only way to affect the total shape of the organism. In real or-

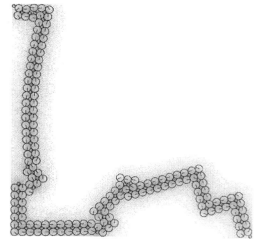

Figure 4: In this example, the shape of the organism is primarily determined by geometric constraints that depend on the size and shape of the constituent cells.

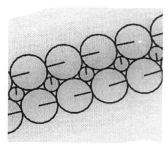

Figure 5: Closeup of Figure 4. The smaller cells fit in the interstices of the larger cells. Thus the two cell types combine to form a rigid chain structure (in this 1-2-1-2 sequence).

ganisms, cell shapes vary greatly, and yet the principle of using cell shape to geometrically determine the shape of a multicellular assembly still applies. For instance, long and narrow "cigar-shaped" epithelial cells tend to form sheets with the long axes of the cells aligned (this maximizes the contact surface area where they adhere).

2.3 Segmented Structure

The experiment shown in Figure 6 builds on the 1-2-1 chains of Section 2.1 to create an example of segment formation. Once again, we have two cell types in the final structure, small cells (S) and large cells (L) that fit together tightly to form a fairly rigid chain.

Some L cells differentiate into a new type (L') and emit a diffusing chemical y (shown with dark shading). This chemical inhibits nearby L cells from differentiating. The range of inhibition is limited, so as the chain grows, eventually one of the new L cells will differentiate as well. How many L cells are skipped before the next one differentiates depends on the diffusion coefficient for y and the sensitivity of the L cells to the threshold of y.

The final structure has L' cells located periodically

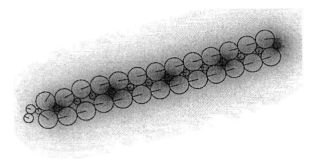

Figure 6: Segmented structure.

along the axis of the chain. These cells can serve as a basis for the elaboration of a segmented organism.

2.4 Bending Chain

Figure 7 shows the addition of a global mechanical behavior to the segmented chain of the example shown in Section 2.3. Once the chain has formed, the cells on the top side of the chain contract in unison while the cells on bottom side of the chain expand. This causes the chain to curl up.

The mechanical behaviors of the individual cells here effect a global shape change, forming a circle of cells from a linear chain. There are many ways to form a similar pattern using different combinations of developmental mechanisms. This experiment was inspired by the mechanical cell models of gastrulation and eversion shown in [12].

2.5 Hierarchical Structure

Figure 8 shows several virtual organisms as they develop over time. Each is a multicellular entity with a two-level deep hierarchy. The initial cells divide to create the next level in the hierarchy, and those in turn divide to create the next level. **The colors mentioned here are visible in the color images are available on the web site referred to at the top of this article.**

In this example there are three cell types, R, G, and W, with the following behaviors:

◇ Type R cells are the large central cells emitting a diffusing chemical shown in red.

◇ Type G cells are the medium-sized cells emitting a different diffusing chemical shown in green. G cells tend to cluster around the R cells because they are attracted to the chemical emitted by the R cells, and they adhere to the R cells. A G cell begins to die if not in contact with an R cell.

◇ Type W cells are the little cells clustered around the G cells. They are attracted to the chemical emitted by the G cells, and they adhere to the G cells. A W cell dies if not in contact with a G cell.

Contact chemicals as well as an attractive diffusing chemical are used to keep cells attached to each other. Each pair of cell types has their own complementary pair

of surface chemicals. There is an R-G surface chemical used to bind R and G cells together, and similarly a G-W surface chemical for G and W cells.

The simulation starts with six randomly placed R cells. Each R cell divides asymmetrically into an R and a G when there are too few G's attached to it (as in panels (a) to (c) above). "Too few" is determined by a threshold on the amount of a surface chemical bound on the membrane of the R cell. That surface chemical binds heterophilically with the complementary chemical on the surface of a G cell, and thus indicates the presence of a neighboring G cell. Each addition G cell in contact causes more of the chemical to be bound. If the amount bound is below a certain threshold, the R cell prepares to divide again.

Each G cell divides into a G and a W when there are too few W's in contact with it, in a similar manner. W cells do not divide.

Each of the six virtual organisms turn out to be slightly different due to differences in each initial cell's local environmental conditions as well as some noise in the sensors, and interactions between the growing organisms.

Some of these organisms have four lobes while others have five. This can arise because the R cell is deciding when to stop dividing based on the amount of bound chemical it senses on its surface. This can vary based on a several factors, primarily the speed of growth of the adjacent G cells, and the amount of time it takes for an R cell to recommence a cell division. In some cases, four G cells were created quickly enough to halt the R cell division; in other cases, the R cell divided yet another time.

This organism is capable of regenerating damaged parts, since it will respond to enough missing G or W cells by recommencing cell division This is discussed further in Section 3.

2.6 Hierarchical Neural Network

The dark cell in the center of Figure 10 has sent out neurites to connect to the cells emitting chemicals shown in a medium shade of gray. They, in turn, are locally connected to the nearby cells (emitting chemical shown in red). Neurites connecting the cells are shown as black curves. The small circles at the ends are the synapses.

In this model, neurons at each level in the hierarchy emit a different diffusing chemical. This enables the neurites from higher-level neurons to find them easily, without confounding them with neurons from other levels.

2.7 Developmental Simulation in 3-D

Three-dimensional extensions were recently made to the simulator. We anticipate that the ability of the simulator to operate in 3-D will be useful for examining many aspects of morphogenesis. The following simple exper-

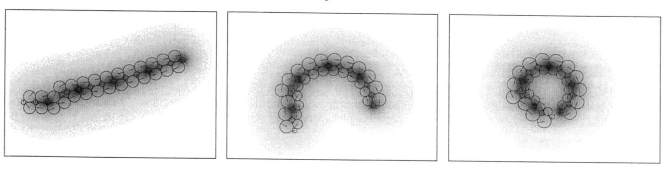

Figure 7: Curling up. This shape change is due to a contraction and expansion of individual cells on opposite sides of the chain. Adhesive surface chemicals serve to keep the cells in contact as they contract.

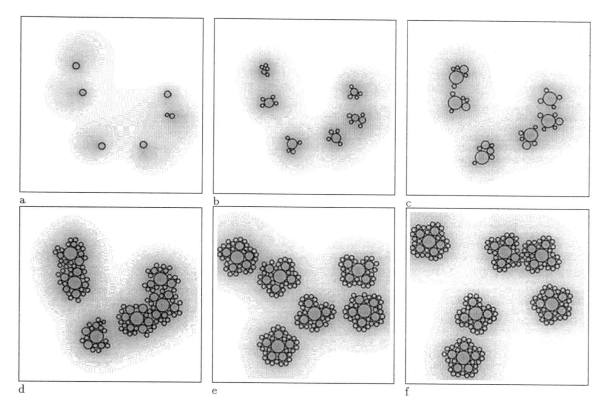

Figure 8: Generation of hierarchical structures.

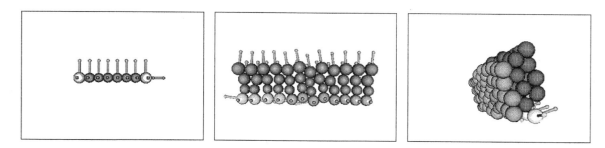

Figure 9: Cell layers (in 3-D). The local coordinate frame of each cell is shown with three small arrows. Rightmost frame is a side view.

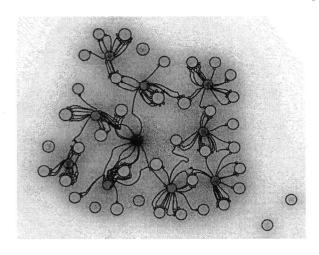

Figure 10: Two-level hierarchical neural network.

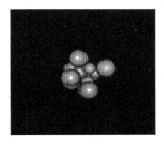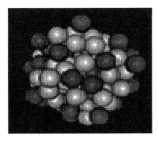

Figure 11: A 3-D clump of cells.

iments give some idea of how these capabilities extend the range of structures that can be generated.

2.8 Blob of Cells with Contact Inhibition

Figure 11 shows a clump of cells that grow to a certain size (controlled by an intracellular clock), and then some cells differentiate into another cell type. Lateral inhibition via a surface chemical prevents neighbors of a differentiated cell from also differentiating.

2.9 Layers of Cells

Formation of cell layers is critical in most multicellular organisms. The layered structure shown in Figure 9 is formed in three stages using a simple strategy. From a single cell, a line of cells is created by repeatedly dividing with a vertical cleavage plane. Then each cell divides with a horizontal cleavage plane a few times to create a sheet of cells. Each cell in the sheet then divides in the third plane to create multiple layers.

2.10 Spiral Growth

Multiple cell divisions by a single progenitor cell created the top two shapes of Figure 13. Two cells moving in opposite directions were used for the lower shape.

The progenitor cell rotates its cleavage axis gradually as it divides. This simple rule, together with the geometric collisions, gives rise to the shapes in these figures.

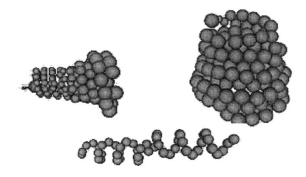

Figure 13: Spiral growth with various parameters.

Different values for cell growth rate, rotation rate and tilt angle account for the variations in the three simulations.

3 Regeneration of Damaged Structures

Biological development is more than a straightforward execution of a set of hardwired genetic commands. It also involves interaction with the environment and adaptation to changes in the environment. This includes reacting to direct intervention such as shown in Figure 12 and Figure 14, where a cell or pair of cells dies due to some external influence.

In panel Figure 12(a), we explicitly kill a G cell so that we can observe the resulting behavior of the virtual organism. Panels Figure 12(b) and (c) show the simulation at a later time. The W cells that were attached to the G cell that was killed will also die unless they are attached to some other G cell. We can see that of the seven W cells involved, five of them perish but two remain because they are connected to the neighboring G cell.

The death of a single G cell may or may not cause the parent R cell to begin dividing and creating new G cells. This depends on whether the amount of bound R-G surface chemical has crossed its threshold. In the case of Figure 12, the R cell is not dividing, since the three full-grown G cells in contact with it cause enough of the R-G surface chemical to be bound. So we see that there is effectively some hysteresis to the process, and this three-lobed organism is stable.

In Figure 14 we see that killing two more G cells does cross the threshold, causing the R cell to regenerate several G cells, and they, in turn, divide to create their W cells, until a stasis is once again obtained.

Size regulation in this experiment is accomplished locally via cell-cell communication. Cells divide if they have insufficient neighbors. Enlarging the 'virtual petri dish' here will not lead to more cells. The organisms try to maintain a particular size and shape, relatively independent of the environment.

Parameter variations. It is interesting to consider the effects of modifying parameters to the dynamical

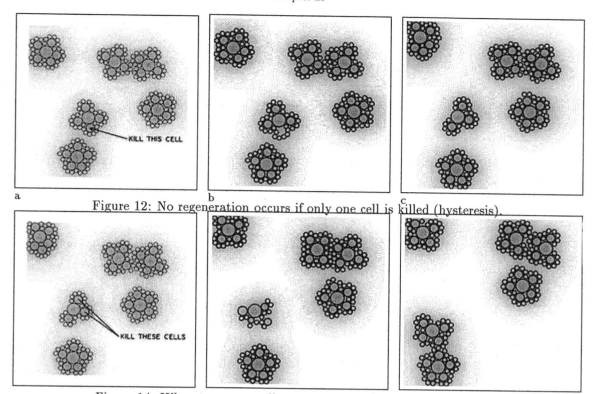

a b c
Figure 12: No regeneration occurs if only one cell is killed (hysteresis).

Figure 14: When two more cells are killed, the structure regenerates.

equations governing the cells. This is analogous to testing some of the paths available to an evolutionary algorithm on this system. Thus we can investigate the effect of development on the process of evolution [8].

For instance, if we lower the cell-division threshold for the R cells, then the R cells will stop dividing sooner, and will tend to create organisms with fewer lobes.

If we raise the threshold, then the R cells may never stop dividing (the threshold is never reached). Only a few G cells can remain in contact with a single R cell (due to the geometric constraints). The remaining G cells will die if they cannot maintain contact with the R cell, creating a dynamic equilibrium of G cells being created and then dying.

Another method of scaling this example would be to allow an R cells to divide into two R cells. This enables our organisms to reproduce, which could be a foundation for experiments in artificial evolution.

Adding a third level of hierarchy (cells subordinate to the W cells) is less straightforward. Several modifications to the cell state equations are required, since each level of the hierarchy is implemented with its own surface chemical (R-G or G-W) and diffusing chemical. A new surface chemical would be required for each hierarchical level in this scheme.

4 Cells on Reaction-Diffusion Patterns

This experiment uses a reaction-diffusion computation to provide a pre-pattern that guides later cell growth [15,

11]. The lighter and darker colors indicate concentrations of two diffusing chemicals r and g, computed using equation 14.7 from Murray's book [11].

The cells are dividing only where the concentration of g is large (darker shading in Figure 15). They are also climbing the gradient of g, and avoiding chemical r (lighter shading). The reaction-diffusion model specifies the prepattern, then cell movement together with forces due to collisions and adhesion with neighboring cells cause the propagation of cells along the darker valleys.

An area for future investigation is to allow the cells to emit or absorb the extracellular chemicals r and g. The simulation system is capable of doing this currently. It would be interesting to compare the stability with respect to initial conditions of such a system to that of a classical reaction-diffusion system.

5 Conclusion

Using our multicellular simulator, we have begun to explore emergent developmental phenomena. Our current investigations have focussed on recreating phenomena that are known to be important in biological development.

In the process of creating each of these simulation experiments, we devise regulatory mechanisms to limit the size and growth of the simulated organism.

We have tried to include as many of the relevant phenomena as is computationally feasible. This enables us

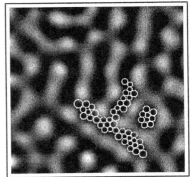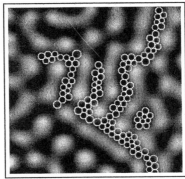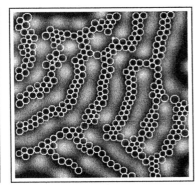

Figure 15: Cells growing on reaction-diffusion patterns. These images show the simulation at various stages in time.

to explore pattern formation based on the interactions of multiple developmental mechanisms. For example, the simulation of Section 2.4 used adhesive surface chemicals, changes in cell shape, gradients of diffusing chemicals, and orientation of cleavage planes to obtain its final shape.

The inclusion of several physical mechanisms gives the simulation system many of the features of the real system being modeled. However, it is harder to analyze mathematically. This is a tradeoff. In the future, we believe there will be great value in using simulations such as these to gain *intuitions* about biological systems that can later be examined more closely and subjected to analysis.

Acknowledgements

This work was performed at the Caltech Graphics Lab. I would like to express my thanks to Professor Alan Barr for his advice, support, and encouragement, and his contributions to the design of the model. I am also grateful to Matt Avalos, Cindy Ball, Allen Corcorran, Bena Currin, Dian De Sha, Dan Fain, Louise Foucher, David Laidlaw, Mark Montague, Alf Mikula, Preston Pfarner, Erik Winfree, and Denis Zorin for valuable discussions, support, and code.

This work was supported in part by grants from Apple, DEC, HP, IBM, NSF (ASC-89-20219) as part of the NSF/ARPA STC for Computer Graphics and Sci. Vis., by DOE (DE-FG03-92ER25134) as part of the Ctr for Rsrch in Comp. Bio., the Beckman Foundation, and by NIDA and NIMH as part of the Human Brain Project. All opinions and conclusions expressed in this document are those of the author and do not necessarily reflect the views of the sponsors.

References

[1] Pankaj Agarwal. The cell programming language. *Artificial Life*, 2(1), 1995.

[2] Rodney A. Brooks and Pattie Maes, editors. A Bradford Book, MIT Press, Cambridge, MA, 1994.

[3] Frank Dellaert and Randall D. Beer. Toward an evolvable model of development for autonomous agent synthesis. In Brooks and Maes [2].

[4] Kurt W. Fleischer. *A Multiple-Mechanism Developmental Model for Defining Self-Organizing Structures.* PhD dissertation, Caltech, Department of Computation and Neural Systems, June 1995.

[5] Kurt W. Fleischer and Alan H. Barr. A simulation testbed for the study of multicellular development: The multiple mechanisms of morphogenesis. In Christopher G. Langton, editor, *Artificial Life III*. Addison-Wesley, 1994.

[6] Scott Gilbert. *Developmental Biology.* Sinnauer Associates, 3rd edition, 1991.

[7] James A. Glazier and Francois Graner. Simulation of the differential adhesion driven rearrangement of biological cells. *Physical Review E*, 41(3), Mar 1993.

[8] Brian Goodwin. *How the Leopard Changed Its Spots.* Charles Scribner's Sons, 1994.

[9] Aristid Lindenmayer. Mathematical models for cellular interaction in development, parts i and ii. *J. Theo. Bio.*, 18, 1968.

[10] Eric Mjolsness, David Sharp, and John Reinitz. A connectionist model of development. *J. Theo. Bio.*, 152, 1991.

[11] J. D. Murray. *Mathematical Biology.* Springer-Verlag, New York, 2nd edition, 1993.

[12] Garrett M. Odell, George Oster, P. Alberch, and B. Burnside. The mechanical basis of morphogenesis. *Developmental Biology*, 85, 1981.

[13] Przemyslaw Prusinkiewicz, Mark Hammel, and Eric Mjolsness. Animation of plant development using differential l-systems. *Computer Graphics*, 27, 1993. (Proceedings of Siggraph '93).

[14] M. S. Steinberg. The problem of adhesive selectivity in cellular interactions. In M. Locke, editor, *Cellular Membranes in Development*. Academic Press, 1964.

[15] Alan Turing. The chemical basis of morphogenesis. *Phil. Trans. B.*, 237, 1952.

[16] Jari Vaario. Modeling adaptive self-organization. In Brooks and Maes [2].

Structural Formation by Enhanced Diffusion Limited Aggregation Model

Akira Onitsuka
Graduation School of Kobe University
Rokkodai Nada, Kobe 657, JAPAN
e-mail: onitsuka@mi-2.mech.kobe-u.ac.jp

Jari Vaario
Nara Women's University
Dept. of Information and Computer Sciences
Kita-Uoya, Nishi-machi, Nara 630, JAPAN
e-mail: jari@ics.nara-wu.ac.jp

Kanji Ueda
Kobe University
Department of Mechanical Engineering
Rokkodai Nada, Kobe 657, JAPAN
e-mail: ueda@mech.kobe-u.ac.jp

Abstract

In this paper an enhanced Diffusion Limited Aggregation (DLA) model is used to explore the possibilities to model structural formation. First, point diffusion sources are used to model axon- and dendrite-like tree-structures. Second, this DLA model is enhanced to model three dimensional structures. Finally, the standard DLA model is enhanced by intra- and inter-cell activities. With these additional features DLA models provide a useful tool for studying the structural formation. Furthermore, the structures could be evolved by genetic algorithms by encoding some control elements into genetic representation.

1 Introduction

The structural formation is an important topic in the domain of Artificial Life. With structures we mean organizations, where the elements have relative locations to each other. Therefore, it is difficult to design complex structures directly. However, applying genetic algorithms is also not straightforward task. It is because that the problems of how to encode structural information in genes, and what criteria should be used in fitness evaluation are still unsolved.

One possible approach is to use environmental factors to control the formation process. This would reduce the genetic control and be capable of generating more complex structures. Using only environmental control is, however, not enough, because the needed stability is not reached. We still need the genetic control elements to provide the stability. The balance between these controls is discussed in (Vaario, Ogata, and Shimohara, 1996).

The problem remains on how to model both environmental direction and genetic control. In this paper we approach this problem from the traditional DLA model point of view. In order to introduce some genetic control elements we have enhanced the model by intra- and inter-cell activities. With these enhancements we are directing research toward creating three dimensional structures, organizations.

An important aspect with these experiments is to create a model, that is capable of repairing itself after external disturbance. There are several engineering applications, where this kind repairing mechanism could be used.

2 Modeling of environment

The DLA model has been used widely as the representation method of the environment where an organism grows. An example of growth which can be described with this DLA model is a bacterium colony, which is consuming a nutrient from its environment, in a petri dish (Kaandorp, 1994).

In DLA model, it is assumed that the speed of the diffusion process in the environment, described by eq. 1, is very fast compared to that of the growth process of an organism.

$$\frac{dc}{dt} = D \,\nabla^2\, c \qquad (1)$$

where c is the nutrient concentration and D is the diffusion coefficient.

According to the above assumption, the environment (concentration field) will become a steady state, that is to say, the left side of eq. 1 is equal to zero. In this steady state, the distribution of the nutrient concentration is described by the following equation, which is called the homogeneous Laplace equation.

$$\nabla^2\, c = \frac{\partial^2 c}{\partial x^2} + \frac{\partial^2 c}{\partial y^2} = 0 \qquad (2)$$

where $c = c(t, x, y)$ represents the nutrient concentration at the point (x, y) at time t.

This is simulated by a computer, before each growth step, using the following method (Ames, 1977; Press, Flannery, Teukolsky, and Vetterling, 1988).

$$while(((c_{x,y})_n - (c_{x,y})_{n-1}) > tolerance) \{$$
$$c_{x,y} = (c_{x+1,y} + c_{x-1,y} + c_{x,y+1} + c_{x,y-1})/4$$
$$\} \tag{3}$$

where n is the iteration number, $c_{x,y}$ is the concentration at lattice (x,y) location, and *tolerance* is the condition which judges its value to be converging.

The two dimensional concentration field described by eq. 2 can be visualized by Fig. 1. In this figure, the height of the sheet represents the local nutrient concentration. The concentration is maximal at the place where a point-like diffusion source exists. And, the curved surface represents the steady state, which satisfies eq. 2, of the concentration field.

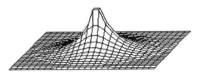

Figure 1: Two dimensional field where point-like diffusion sources exists.

3 Growth by DLA model

3.1 Growth in a two-dimensional lattice

First, we construct a model which grows in the environment represented by eq. 2. This environment is two dimensional (50x50) lattice, and the nutrient concentration is supposed to remain constant on the boundary of the environment except for the front edge.

In this simulation, the growth of an organism starts with one occupied site in the lattice (see Fig. 2(a)). In Fig. 2, the sites occupied by a cell of the organism are displayed as black rectangles. In next growth steps, new sites are added to the organism. The probability that one site will change from an unoccupied site to an occupied site, is given by eq. 4;

$$p((x,y) \in \circ \to \bullet) = \frac{c_{x,y}}{\sum_{(i,j)\in\circ} c_{i,j}} \tag{4}$$

where $p((x,y) \in \circ \to \bullet)$ represents the probability that an unoccupied site around occupied sites will be changed into an occupied site in next growth step, $c_{x,y}$ represents the nutrient concentration at lattice (x,y) location. This modeling method is inspired from (Kaandorp, 1994).

In this simulation, the number of cells increases almost infinitely, because the nutrient concentration is supposed to remain constant on the boundary of the environment, that is to say, the nutrient is inexhaustibly supplied to this organism.

In next simulation, in order to create an environment for controlling a growth of an organism, we use point-like diffusion sources instead of edge-wise diffusion sources. In addition, it is assumed that the nutrient concentration at the place of a diffusion source becomes zero if a cell of

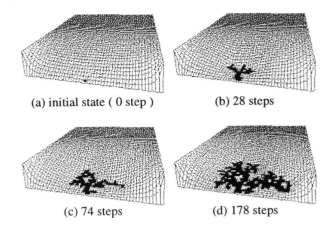

(a) initial state (0 step)   (b) 28 steps

(c) 74 steps   (d) 178 steps

Figure 2: Two dimensional growth in an environment, where edges are 1 expect the front edge being 0. (After (Sander, 1986))

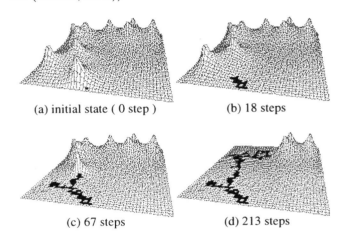

(a) initial state (0 step)   (b) 18 steps

(c) 67 steps   (d) 213 steps

Figure 3: Two dimensional growth in point diffusion fields.

this organism exists there, but this concentration remain constant if none of cells of this organism exists there.

Fig. 3(a) shows the initial state of this simulation, where we create ten point-like diffusion sources at random, and the growth process of this organism is displayed in Fig. 3(b)-(d).

By the way, we added eq. 5 into eq. 4, because the range of being affected by a point-like diffusion source is considerably narrow.

$$p((x,y) \in \circ \to \bullet) = \frac{1}{N}, \text{ if } \sum_{(i,j)\in\circ} c_{i,j} = 0 \tag{5}$$

where N represents the total number of unoccupied sites around occupied sites.

Fig. 3 shows that this organism grows toward each diffusion source gradually. And, this growth process seems to resemble neural growth process.

In these simulations, a growth rule controls the whole organism. But, in order to construct a system which is capable of repairing itself, it is necessary to give a set of

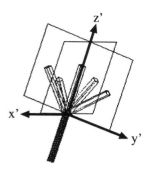

Figure 4: The position where a cell can create a new cell, which is represented by wire frame.

growth rules into each cell of an organism. Therefore, in the next section, we present models which include the above and are extended three dimensions.

3.2 Growth in a three-dimensional space

In this section the diffusion model is extended into three dimensions. The previous eq. 3 is now adapted into three dimensions, where the number of neighbor elements becomes six plus the value of the cell itself.

Now, however, the growing cells cannot necessarily placed exactly on the grid of diffusion model. In the case that a cell isn't placed on the grid, there are two principle ways of calculating the value of the nutrient concentration. The first method is to subdivide three dimensional lattice further in order to place the cell on a new divided grid. The second method is to calculate an approximate value (linear interpolation of eight corner values) of the nutrient concentration at the location of the cell.

Using the first method, we can get the value of the nutrient concentration correctly. But, this method is computationally heavy. Thus, we decide to use the second method.

Fig. 4 shows places (five alternative cells) where each cell can create a new cell. For representational reasons the cells are drawn as rectangles, instead of drawing them as cubes. The selection from five places is now calculated based on the previously used method (eq. 4 and eq. 5).

First, we give edge-wise diffusion sources at the border of the environment, which is represented by a 40x40x40 lattice, except for the bottom.

By running this simulation, this plant-like organism spread out in all directions (Fig. 5). This growth doesn't stop. It is because that the nutrient is inexhaustibly supplied to this organism.

Next, we present the growth process in the environment where only one point-like diffusion source exists. Fig. 6 shows the relative position between the initial place of this organism and the place where the diffusion source exists.

Fig. 7 shows the growth process in this simulation. As was mentioned in the previous section, it is assumed that the nutrient concentration at the place of a diffusion

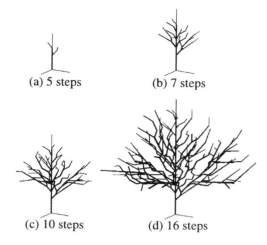

(a) 5 steps   (b) 7 steps

(c) 10 steps   (d) 16 steps

Figure 5: Three dimensional growth in edge-wise diffusion sources.

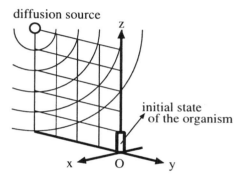

Figure 6: The relative position between a cell and diffusion source.

source becomes zero if a cell exists there. Therefore, in this simulation, this plant-like organism stops growing further after a cell of this organism reaches at the place of a diffusion source.

So far, we have presented some growth processes affected only by the environment which can be described with the DLA model. But, actual growth processes are under the influence of not only the environment but also activities within each cell, interactions with other cells, and so forth. In the next section, we present new models which include the above.

4   The enhanced DLA model

It goes without saying that the basic elements for organization are cells. But the biochemical mechanisms within each cell are very complicated, and include various catalytic reactions. In addition, the reaction consist of two types of activities : intra-cell activity and inter-cell activity. Therefore, it is almost impossible to construct a complete biochemical model.

The method of modeling these mechanism are presented in (Vaario, 1994; Kaneko and Yomo, 1994; Kitano, 1994), and interesting results are gotten.

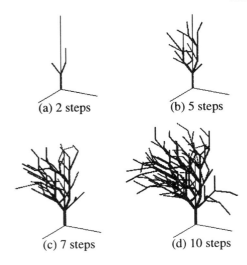

(a) 2 steps   (b) 5 steps

(c) 7 steps   (d) 10 steps

Figure 7: Three dimensional growth in a point-like diffusion source.

In this paper, we create a simple model which include some mechanisms, that is to say, intra-cell activity, inter-cell activity and cell behavior.

Chemicals Here, we assume that intra- and inter-cell activities are based on some chemicals. Therefore, we use some chemicals' concentrations within each cell as the internal state of the cell (Kaneko and Yomo, 1994). And, we use the following representations; $c_i^m(t)$ represents the concentration of m-th chemicals within the i-th cell at time t. $C^m(t)$ represents the same chemicals which exists in the environment.

4.1 Intra-cell activity

We introduce the metabolic reaction as intra-cell activity(see Fig. 8). In this figure, $E^{0,1}$ represents an enzyme that trigger off a metabolic reaction which create c^1 from c^0. And we represent chemicals and enzymes as bit strings of a given length (Kitano, 1994).

As shown in Fig. 8, in simulations which will be presented later, we use four kinds of chemicals.

As shown in Fig. 9, a chromosome is a set of strings, each of which represents a rule governing the metabolic reaction. In this paper, we represent a metabolic rule as a 10-bits string. And the length of a chromosome is 70 bits, that is to say, a chromosome consists of 7 metabolic rules.

For example, the string of '0111101101' is interpreted as '$c^1 < 4.0 \Rightarrow E^{3,1}$ is activated'. That is to say, if the concentration of c^1 within a cell is less than 4.0, then enzyme $E^{3,1}$ is activated. Therefore, c^1 is created by c^3 within this cell ($\delta c^1 = E^{3,1} c^3$). From the point of view that a chemical is created from an other chemical by enzyme(E), this metabolic reaction resembles the model of (Kaneko and Yomo, 1994)($A \rightarrow C$) more than that of (Kitano, 1994) ($A + B \rightarrow C$).

As was mentioned above, a metabolic rule contains a conditional clause. Therefore, at each growth step, triggered metabolic reactions within each cell are under

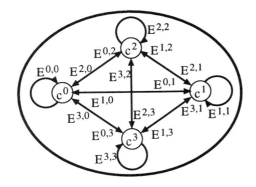

Figure 8: Intra-cell activity.

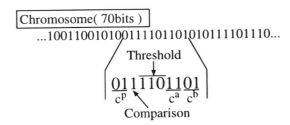

Figure 9: Chromosome control governing metabolic reactions.

the influence of the amount of each chemical within the cell.

After these remarks, the amount of each chemical within each cell can be calculated as follows:

$$c_i^m(t+1) = c_i^m(t) + \frac{dc_i^m(t)}{dt} \quad (6)$$

$$\frac{dc_i^m(t)}{dt} = \sum_{k=0}^{M}(E^{k,m}c_i^k(t)) - \sum_{k=0}^{M}(E^{m,k}c_i^m(t))$$
$$+ \quad Transport_i^m(t) + Diffusion_i^m(t) \quad (7)$$

$$E^{a,b} = \begin{cases} \delta, & \text{if } E^{a,b} \text{ is activated} \\ 0, & \text{otherwise} \end{cases} \quad (8)$$

where δ is constant, here $\delta=0.3$.

The first and second terms of the right side of eq.7 represents the increment and decrement of m-th chemicals according to metabolic reactions, respectively. Eq.7 differs slightly from Kitano's model by metabolic reaction part ($E^{k,m}c_i^m(t)$).

The third and fourth terms of the right side of eq.7 represents interaction with other cells and interaction with environment respectively.

4.2 Inter-cell activity

In this section, we describe inter-cell activities, that is to say, interaction with other cells and interaction with environment.

Interaction with other cells A cell interacts with adjacent cells, that is to say, transports chemicals each other. This interaction is represented as follows ((Kitano, 1994)):

$$Transport_i^m(t) = A_1 \sum_j^N T(i,j)[c_j^m(t) - c_i^m(t)] \quad (9)$$

$$T(i,j) = \begin{cases} 1, & \text{if cell i and j are in contact} \\ 0, & \text{otherwise} \end{cases} \quad (10)$$

where N represents the total number of adjacent cells around the i-th cell, A_1 is constant (in this paper, A_1=0.1).

Interaction with environment Each cell absorbs/diffuses chemicals from/into its environment, which is represented as DLA model, through its membrane.

In addition, in this simulation, it is assumed that c^2 and c^3 aren't diffused into the environment. This interaction is expressed as follows ((Kaneko and Yomo, 1994), (Kitano, 1994)):

$$Diffusion_i^m(t) = A_2[C^m(t) - c_i^m(t)] \quad (11)$$

where A_2 is constant, and it's value is 0.1. But, according to the above assumption, A_2 is equal to zero if m equals 2 or 3.

4.3 Result of intra- and inter-cell activities

According to these equations, the amount of chemicals' concentration within each cell are calculated. And, the behavior of each cell is determined by the result of this calculation.

Cell division In this model, we regard c^1 as the energy which is necessary for creating a new cell. When c^1 within a cell is more than a certain quantity, the cell can create a new cell. This behavior is represented as follows:

$$\text{if } c_i^1(t) \geq A_3 \text{ then create a new cell} \quad (12)$$

where A_3 is constant, here A_3=5.0.

The direction of creating a new cell (see Fig. 4) is determined by the chemicals' concentration in the environment surrounded the cell. When a cell division takes place, chemicals within the cell is divided into two cells equally.

Cell death When the sum of chemicals within a cell is less than a certain quantity, the cell dies. This is described by the following:

$$\text{if } \sum_{k=0}^M c_i^k \leq A_4 \text{ then die} \quad (13)$$

where A_4 is constant, here A_4=5.0.

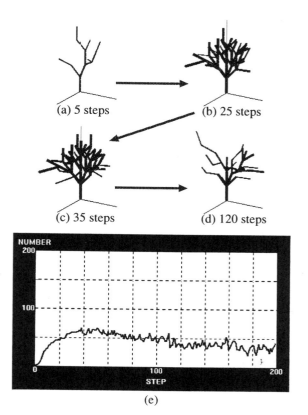

(a) 5 steps (b) 25 steps

(c) 35 steps (d) 120 steps

(e)

Figure 10: Growth with hand-coded chromosome.

5 Results of Simulations

In this section, we present some simulations by using the enhanced DLA model as was mentioned above. Simulations described here are as follows:

- Growth with hand-coded chromosome

- Evolutionary adjustment of growth regulators

- Growth with best chromosome

- Repair of damaged structure

By the way, at the beginning of these simulations, there are no chemicals in the environment. And we give the same quantity of chemicals except for c^1 within the base cell of an organism.

In addition, chemicals c^0 is kept supplying to this base cell during these simulations.

5.1 Growth with hand-coded chromosome

First, we examine how organism grows by a hand-coded chromosome governing metabolic reactions. A metabolic reaction in the hand-coded chromosome is '$c^0 > 0.2 \Rightarrow E^{0,1}$ is activated', that is to say, 'if the concentration of c^0 within a cell is more than 0.2, then enzyme $E^{0,1}$ is activated'.

Fig. 10(a)-(d) show the result of this simulation, and Fig. 10(e) represents the transition of the number of cells from 0 step to 200 steps.

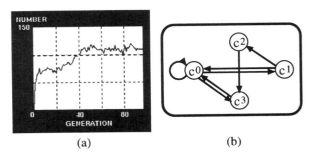

(a)   (b)

Figure 11: Evolutionary adjustment of growth regulators.

The result of this simulation is interpreted as follows : the number of cells keep increasing, and then the number reaches the maximal number at 39 steps. But the number fluctuates around it, and decreases gradually. It is because that the cells still divide periodically in time, but neither of divided cells have enough chemicals within themselves and are alive. Therefore c^3 and c^4 within each cell decreases gradually, with the result that the number of cells fluctuates around the number less than the maximal number at 39 steps.

5.2 Evolutionary adjustment of growth regulators

Next, we introduced an evolutionary process to acquire appropriate genetic codes for metabolic reactions. We use a genetic algorithm as this evolutionary process. The population size is 10, and we use elitist reproduction. Crossing over is 2-point crossover, and mutation rate is 0.014. Fitness is evaluated according to the number of cells existing at the 35th step.

Of course, this evolutionary process does not reflect biological fitness in the real world. We use this process, because this is very simple and enough to acquire appropriate genetic codes for metabolic reactions ((Kitano, 1994)).

Fig. 11(a) shows the number of cells at the 35th step in each generation, and Fig. 11(b) is a set of metabolic reactions acquired by the 86th generation.

5.3 Growth with best chromosome

Next, we examine how the organism grows by the chromosome acquired by an evolutionary process as was mentioned above.

Fig. 12(a)-(d) show the results of this simulation, and Fig. 12(e) shows the transition of the number of cells from 0 step to 200 steps.

Compared with Fig. 10(e), the maximal number of cells is more than that of simulation using a hand-coded chromosome. We think this reason as follows : this chromosome can create c^1 from not only c^0 directly but also c^2 or c^3 indirectly. In addition, this chromosome can create c^0 or c^2 from c^1. Therefore, because the sum of chemicals within each cell is always more than a certain quantity, both of divided cells have enough chemicals to be alive.

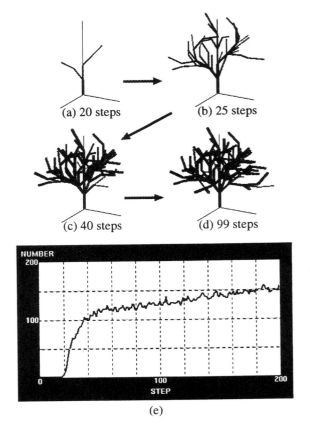

(e)

Figure 12: Growth with the best chromosome.

Therefore, we consider that appropriate chromosome for metabolic reactions is acquired this evolutionary process.

5.4 Repair of damaged structure

Finally, we try to examine whether this organism is capable of repairing itself in the case of external disturbance. In this simulation, we cut about 33 percents of cells away at the 100th step.

Fig. 13(a) shows the organism before external disturbance, and Fig. 13(b)-(d) show the growth process of this organism after external disturbance, and Fig. 13(e) shows the transition of cell's number from 0 step to 200 steps.

After external disturbance, the number of cells keep increasing, and reaches the maximal number and fluctuates around it. But the maximal number of cells after external disturbance is less than that of cells before this disturbance. So it is impossible to think that this organism is capable of repairing itself completely.

We think that this reason is as follows:

- *Heavy disturbance:* In this simulation, we cut about 33 percents of cells away. But, this percentage as external disturbance may be heavy. We have to check whether this organism can repair itself or not, in the case of less disturbance.

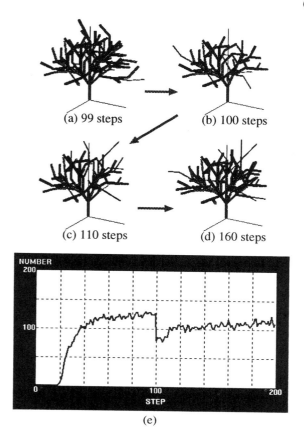

(a) 99 steps   (b) 100 steps

(c) 110 steps   (d) 160 steps

(e)

Figure 13: Repairing damaged structure.

- *Weakness of link between the environment and the genetic code:* As was mentioned, a growth of an organism is under the influence of not only the environment but also the genetic code. In addition, the balance between these factors is very important for organism's growth, organization. Therefore, in order to model structural formation, it will be necessary to link between the environment and the genetic code and find out the balance between these factors.

- *Abstract structure:* Organisms used in this paper are abstract without any information of their final structures. Thus, these organisms are not capable of repairing themselves completely. In the future work, these structures are used to model neural dendrite trees. The final structure is partly defined by the genetic information, and partly by the environmental factors like the diffusion fields generated by sensors.

6 Conclusion

In this paper, we used the diffusion limited aggregation (DLA) model to create the environment where an organism grows. This is remarkable different from other related works. Our mainly motivation is to study the structural formation, where the actual simulation of environment is necessary.

We also presented some simulations in which this DLA

model and genetic codes are combined. This connection isn't complete now. However, if we find out the balance between these factors and create a system which can self-organize and repair itself after external disturbance, we will be able to extend this model to actual engineering problems.

Reference

Ames, W. F. (1977). *Numerical methods for partial differential equations.* Academic Press, New York.

Kaandorp, J. A. (1994). *Fractal Modelling: Growth and Form in Biology.* Springer-Verlag.

Kaneko, K., and Yomo, T. (1994). Cell division, differentation and dynamic clustering. *Physica D*, 75(1–3).

Kitano, H. (1994). Evolution of metabolism for morphogenesis. In Brooks, R., and Maes, P. (Eds.), *Artificial Life IV*, pp. 49–58. The MIT Press.

Press, W. H., Flannery, B. P., Teukolsky, S. A., and Vetterling, W. T. (1988). *Numerical recipes in C.* Cambridge University Press, Cambridge.

Sander, L. M. (1986). Fractal growth processes. *Nature*, 322, 789–793.

Vaario, J. (1994). Modeling adaptative self-organization. In Brooks, R., and Maes, P. (Eds.), *Artificial Life IV*, pp. 313–318. The MIT Press.

Vaario, J., Ogata, N., and Shimohara, K. (1996). Synthesis of environment directed and genetic growth. in this volume.

Synthesis of Environment Directed and Genetic Growth

Jari Vaario and **Naoko Ogata**
Nara Women's University
Kita-Uoya, Higashi-machi, Nara 630, JAPAN
e-mail: jari@ics.nara-wu.ac.jp

Katsunori Shimohara
ATR Human Information Processing Research Laboratories
2-2 Hikari-dai, Seika-cho, Soraku-gun, Kyoto 619-02 JAPAN
e-mail: katsu@hip.atr.co.jp

Abstract

In this paper we propose a new method for controlling the growth of tree-like structures in a diversified environment. The tree-like structures are modeled by Lindenmayer systems, and the environment is modeled by a simulation of diffusion fields. The originality of this research is in the way it combines Lindenmayer systems with the environment model. The simulation results show that genetic information to determine the final structures could be remarkably reduced by letting environmental factors direct the formation. The results provide a method for combining the evolutionary approach for individual development.

1 Introduction

The fact that genetic code cannot predetermine a complex system completely is well known. The code would become too complicated. This is well illustrated by the problem of modeling a brain-like neural network structure. Determining all connections by genetic code would result in extremely long genetic code. The genetic information gives only the overall directions and ranges of the growth, and the environmental factors fill in the details. It is important to model the growth process as a function of the environmental factors.

On the other hand we cannot let everything be decided by the environmental factors. There must be a balance between genetic control and environmental control. In order to study this balance we need a simulation system, where various scenarios can be tested and validated. This paper describes a simulation system where we can synthesize genetic and environment directed growth.

The simulation system is divided into an environment model and a genetic growth model as described below.

1.1 Environment model

The environmental factors could be modeled in various ways. In (Vaario & Shimohara, 1995) it was proposed a method for using gradient fields to direct the growth process. This approach is well suited to modeling electro-magnetic fields, and other similar interacting forces. However, for modeling chemical diffusion, the method has some limits.

Another widely used method is diffusion fields, which can be modeled by a cellular automaton-like mechanism. The diffusion fields are able to describe chemical and other diffusion in the environment, making them suitable for, for example, nutrient modeling. Diffusion fields are successfully used in Diffusion Limited Aggregation (DLA) models, where the aim is to model bacterial growth in a nutrient (Sander, 1986).

1.2 Genetic growth model

Genetic based growth can be modeled by a variety of models. One method utilizing fractal structures is the Lindenmayer system (Prusinkiewicz & Lindenmayer, 1990). It provides an easy implementation for the genetic directed growth of multiple branching dendrite and axon tree structures.

In this paper we describe how a diffusion model could be used for directing the predetermined growth of Lindenmayer systems. The technique used here can be classified as postprocessing Lindenmayer systems.

This research has been influenced by Kaandorp's work (Kaandorp, 1994), although we have used 'ordinary' Lindenmayer systems to model the growth. Also, the research aims are different. Where Kaandorp aims to model marine organisms (sponges and corals), our aim is to study the relation of environmental and genetic control, and then apply these ideas to the engineering field.

1.3 Philosophical considerations

The balance between genetic and environment directed growth can be seen as the balance between the stability and flexibility of a system (see Figure 1).

The stability is produced by the genetic growth in order to build a system similar to its successful ancestors. However, the environment might change during the reproduction time. Being able to adapt to the environmental changes directly, without being forced to wait for the evolutionary adaptation, is a remarkable advantage. This adaptation can be viewed as the flexibility of a system.

The problem in fact, relates closely to the question of embodiment (Varela, Thompson, & Rosch, 1993), *i.e*, how a system is defined and separated from its environment. The individual development and organization under environmental influence as described by Piaget (Pi-

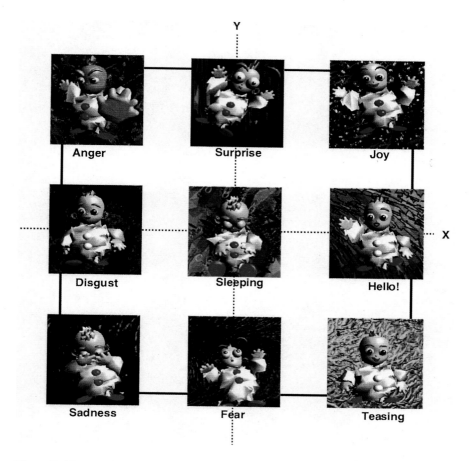

Figure 7. (Tosa, Nakatsu) MIC's emotional expression.

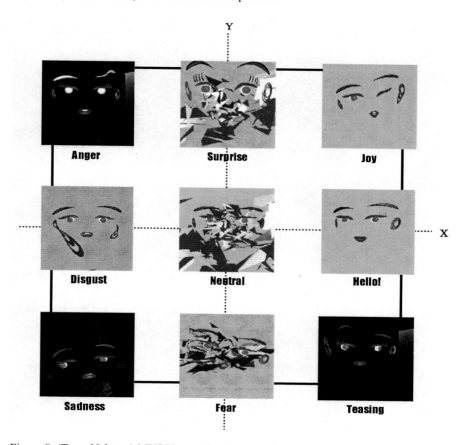

Figure 8. (Tosa, Nakatsu) MUSE's emotional expression.

Plate 1

Figure 6. "Artificial Life Metropolis CELL," 1993. These images on HDTV were shown at the SIGGRAPH '93.

Plate 2

Figure 7. "Artificial Life Metropolis CELL," 1993.

Figure 9. "Artificial Life Metropolis CELL," 1993.

Plate 3

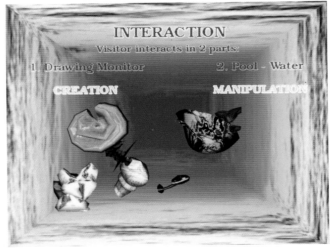

"A-Volve." Images © 1994 Sommerer & Mignonneau.

Plate 4

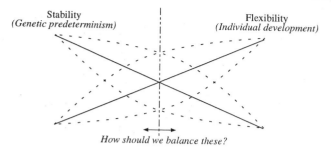

Figure 1: Illustration of the problem to balance genetic and environment directed growth.

aget, 1974, 1975) is an important aspect when one aims at modeling intelligent systems.

These philosophical questions are approached in this paper from a primitive developmental modeling point of view. Although primitive, the following simulations present an important step towards modeling more realistic living systems, and applying the concept in various engineering fields.

2 Diffusion models

In this paper we have selected diffusion fields as the fundamental method for describing the environment. A nutrient is put into an environment continuously at a specific location. This nutrient diffuses in the environment and attracts growing elements.

Diffusion is thoroughly analyzed by Banks (Banks, 1994). Here we have selected diffusion from continuous sources, especially rectilinear diffusion in a semi-infinite region of constant diffusivity, $\mathcal{D}$ (Banks, 1994, page 341).

$$\frac{\delta N}{\delta t} = \mathcal{D}\frac{\delta^2 N}{\delta x^2}$$

The concentration field of the nutrient will attain a steady state when $\frac{\delta N}{\delta t}$ equals zero. Assuming that the diffusion is a faster process than growth requires that this equilibrium state must be calculated between each growth step.

2.1 Computer simulation

In order to simulate this on a computer, we can apply the following algorithm (see, for example, (Ames, 1977; Press, Flannery, Teukolsky, & Vetterling, 1988)).

```
while( (c_{i,j}^n - c_{i,j}^{n-1}) > tolerance ) {
    c_{i,j}^n = 1/4 (c_{i+1,j}^{n-1} + c_{i-1,j}^{n-1} + c_{i,j+1}^{n-1} + c_{i,j-1}^{n-1})
}
```

where $c_{(i,j)}^n$ is the concentration of the nutrient at the *(i, j)* lattice site, n is the 'iteration number', and tolerance is ≈ 0. This is the same algorithm that Kaandorp used in his models (Kaandorp, 1994). In order to simulate various types of nutrient fields, the above is repeated for each type.

Logically, a cell $c_{1,j}$ can have four states: *source* (if it is continuously source, then 1.0 at the beginning of each diffusion calculation iteration), *drain* (always 0.0, affects

the neighbor cell calculation), *transporter* (a 'normal' cell updated as described above), and *block* (does not have a value, and does not participate in the neighbor cell calculation, *i.e.*, these cells are skipped in the above iteration loop). The last state is not used in this paper. The edge cells are usually either source or drain cells. The often used tourus topology of the environment is not logical with diffusion models.

2.2 Interactions with the growth model

With this model, a growing object which is consuming a nutrient from its environment can be described. The concentration is zero on the object, and one on the source of the nutrient. This can be illustrated by a mesh, where the height represents the concentrations at a given point (Figure 2).

Figure 2: Illustration of diffusion fields with several point sources and edges being drains.

Although diffusion is easy to implement, it is time-consuming to evaluate. One can reduce the execution time by allowing a greater tolerance (in the above algorithm), but then the accuracy of the simulation suffers. Similarly, reducing the resolution decreases computation requirements, but then the growth modeling suffers from the low resolution. Due to these computational limitations, only 2-dimensional growth phenomena have been considered in this paper.

3 Lindenmayer systems

In this paper we have selected Lindenmayer systems (Prusinkiewicz & Lindenmayer, 1990) (L-systems) to model the growth process. This selection is based on the facts that they are well known and can represent the fractal tree structures necessary for neural connection models.

L-systems have already been used for several years to successfully model the growth process of plants. They have a well known restriction, however, that prevents them from modeling the environment. A proposal for postprocessing is described in Figure 3.

Another possibility is to use "interleaved L-systems" as proposed in (Vaario, 1993, 1994). In this method the environment is modeled by a L-system which includes several other L-systems, recursively. An upper level L-system could modify the lower level L-systems and interchange information from one system to the other. How-

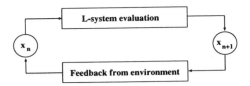

Figure 3: Principles of postprocessing of Lindenmayer systems. After the generation of the symbol string, it is processed by an algorithm modifying the symbols.

ever, the rules become unnecessarily complicated, because the actual space manipulation must be done by the L-system rules. Using the postprocessing approach results in a clear separation between the L-systems and the environment.

3.1 Postprocessing algorithm

The postprocessing algorithm is used to get the effect of the nutrient value from the environment. This effect is used to calculate the branching angle of the L-systems in the following way.

Branches are mapped to a field which is divided into an $X \times Y$ lattice. From each site in that lattice, nutrient concentrations $C(i, j)$ are obtained. The site $P(x, y)$ is the apex of a growing branch. C_n ($n = 1, ..., 8$) is a nutrient concentration in the site neighboring $P(x, y)$. Each site is a place where the branch will possibly grow. $\vec{V}_n$ ($n = 1, ..., 8$) is a vector from P heading to each neighbor site. This is illustrated in Figure 4. The growth vector of $P(x, y)$ is given by

$$\vec{G}_{x,y} = \sum_{n=1}^{8} \vec{V}_n C_n$$

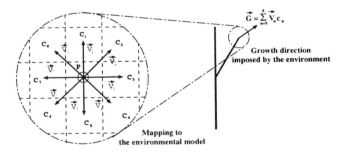

Figure 4: The mapping mechanism for a feedback from the environment.

This vector determines the direction and length of the following growth step. The tree grows toward the site where the nutrient concentration is higher. The length ($| \vec{G} |$) is additionally used by the L-system to determine whether growth continues.

The nutrient field is consumed at the growth site. In this paper, a simple model is used to set the cell as a drain. This means that during the diffusion calculation the concentration of this cell is not updated, although it affects the concentration of neighbor cells decreasingly.

4 Growth of tree-like structures

In the following we describe the basic results of this method (see Figure 5). In this paper, all tree structures are obtained by interpreting strings generated by the following L-system.

$$
\begin{array}{llll}
\delta : & 27.5° & & \\
\omega : & X & & \\
p_1 : & F & & \rightarrow \quad F \\
p_2 : & H & : (| \vec{G} | > Th) & \rightarrow \quad F \\
p_3 : & X & : (| \vec{G} | > Th) & \rightarrow \quad Y \\
p_4 : & Y & : (| \vec{G} | > Th) & \rightarrow \quad F[+X]H[-X]X
\end{array}
$$

'F' and 'H' are trunk segments of the tree, and they are drawn as a dark green segment. 'Y' is used to describe the growing part, and it is drawn as a red segment. 'X' is not drawn. '[' and ']' describes the branches of the tree. '+' and '−' describe the branching angle (27.5°).

The change 'H' $\longrightarrow$ 'F' (rule p_2) corresponds to the change into a fixed stage, where 'F' is not affected by the environment, whereas 'H' will direct itself according to the environmental effect. New branches are generated by rule p_4. 'Y' generates a fixed segment 'F', two branches '[+X]H[−X]' capable of growing, and a start 'X' to grow further. Rule p_3 is used to create a slight delay in the growth so that the environmental effect can affect to the growth direction.

The minimal growth is depressed by the condition $| \vec{G} | > Threshold$. Without this minimal growth the figures become clearer. The growth could be resumed at these stages assuming we do not remove these elements.

An overview of this system is illustrated in Figure 5.

The following examples have been tried. All of these produce a different final structure.

- Growth without the environmental influence

- Growth with feedback from an equally distributed diffusion field

- Growth with feedback from an unequally distributed diffusion field

- Repairing ('re-growth') after an external disturbance

- Competing growth in the field of point diffusion sources

- Growth in various diffusion fields

4.1 L-system without environmental influence

The above L-system rules were used to attain the deterministic growth of a tree structure. The resulting tree structure is shown in Figure 6. The age of the symbols is shown by the color. As is well known, the collision of branches cannot be avoided by these rules.

These rules can be viewed as genetic information determining the final structure. In order to create changes in the structure, the rules must be modified. Reverse engineering of the rules (having first the structure and then finding the rules that could produce it) is difficult.

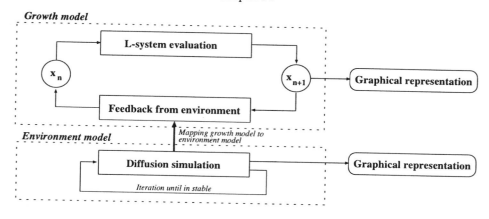

Figure 5: An overview of the implementation.

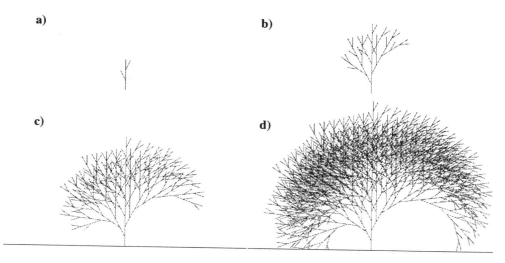

Figure 6: Lindenmayer system without feedback from the environment.

4.2 L-system with a simple environmental model

When a simple diffusion field is used with the above L-system, the result is as shown in Figure 7. The diffusion source is at the three edges of the area.

The growth is stopped at the area where the field has vanished. This gives an impression of realistic tree growth where the lower branches will stop growing because of a lack of light.

The red color indicates branches that are still growing. The concentration of red areas is, naturally, greater where the diffusion field value is high. These branches clearly illustrate how the environmental model can be used to direct the growth process.

From the figure, one can see that branch avoidance can be achieved by the method, although this depends greatly on the selected resolution. If the diffusion model uses a lower resolution compared to the average growth step, then branches will eventually collide. Using a relatively higher resolution compared to the growth step, the avoidance can be achieved.

4.3 L-system dividing into two directions

In this example, the diffusion field causes a separation of branches toward the diffusion sources. The resulting structure is remarkably complex compared to the structure that results from plain L-system growth.

This method could be used not only to increase the complexity of models, but also as a basis for modeling structural formation. For example, in the case of the structural formation of neural systems, if sensor cells create a diffusion field based on what they sense, the neural connections can direct themselves toward these sensors.

4.4 Repairing of L-system after an external disturbance

In this example, a branch of the L-system was cut externally. The L-system before the cut, immediately after the cut, and two sequential stages of the reconfiguration are shown in Figure 9. After the cut the diffusion model brings nutrient close to the cut location, where previously depressed (by the lack of nutrient) elements receive nutrient enough to restart the growth (*ie.,* $|\vec{G}|$ exceeds the threshold value).

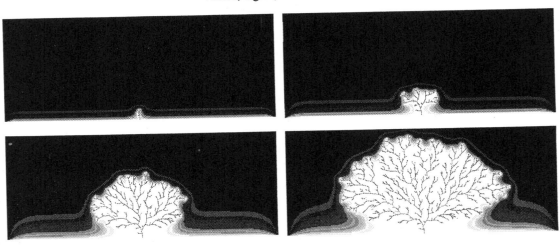

Figure 7: Lindenmayer system with feedback from an equally distributed environmental field.

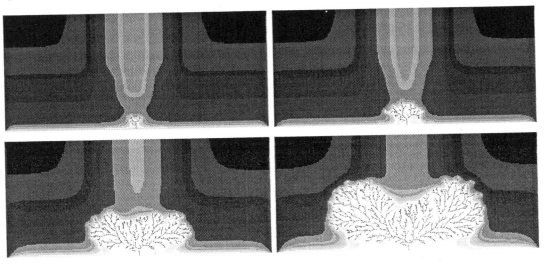

Figure 8: Lindenmayer system dividing into two directions by the feedback of environmental factors.

The structures before and after the disturbance are not identical. This is caused by the fact that the other branches also start to grow, competing for the diffusion source. Especially, the branch facing the cut space will be depressed, because the branch above it will consume the diffusion source. The cut branch will, however, be partly repaired by a new branch initiated at the cut location.

In order to model a more exact repair mechanism, the restarted growth locations should be limited to the cut locations, and the growth should be restarted from a specific rule. How to implement this using simple rules is under investigation.

4.5 Competition of L-systems with point diffusion sources

In this example (Figure 10), several point diffusion sources are used to compete between six identical L-systems. The difference between the L-systems is created by the environmental factors. The L-systems depress the

growth of others while competing for the diffusion source. With slightly different initial conditions a different final result could be achieved. The middle L-system is able to grow fastest, because the concentration of diffusion fields is highest.

This same situation arises in biological neural systems, where the neural connections compete for the target neurons.

4.6 L-systems growing in various diffusion fields

In this example L-systems grow in an environment with various types of diffusion fields. The L-systems are identical, except for the sensitivity of the diffusion field. The diffusion sources are located randomly. There are 24 L-systems initially at the edges of the area competing with each other. The initial location of the diffusion fields and the final state of the L-systems are given in Figure 11.

This example demonstrates an arbitrary situation that might be faced in modeling neural growth where connec-

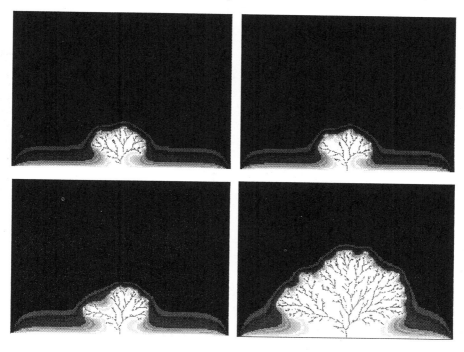

Figure 9: Lindenmayer system restarting the growth and repairing itself after an external disturbance.

tions are directed by several diffusion fields.

5 Discussion about modeling neuromorphogenesis

Recently, neuromorphogenesis has became a research subject aimed at creating more complex neural structures. The subject is not only scientifically interesting, but could also provide an 'automatic' mechanism to be used in engineering applications. Especially, robotics has a need to develop sophisticated control systems that are capable of learning not only simple input/output patterns, but to direct behavior in unknown situations as well.

This research could be roughly said to have begun from the work of Edelman (Edelman, 1987, 1988). His ideas of neuromorphogenesis and its applications to robotics provided the direction for the research. On the other hand, Brooks (Brooks, 1991) contributed to the field by arguing that it must start from simple behavior, and stating that new behaviors will accumulate on top of previous behaviors, forming a layer of behaviors.

Putting these two ideas together, one can easily infer that a simple neural structure capable of directing a simple behavior could evolve in time toward a more complex structure capable of directing a large repertoire of behaviors.

The remaining problem is how to describe the neural network structure. One engineering approach is to define it by hand. This is to some extent possible, as the work of Beer (Beer, 1990) has proved. However, in the long range this is not feasible, mainly because the complexity will increase beyond the capabilities of humans to control.

An alternative to this is the evolutionary approach.

Here the neural structure is described by genetic information, and then genetic algorithms are applied to it. This method has been tried a lot. The results are somehow promising, but the remaining problems are great.

The most recent direction is to model a complete neuromorphogenesis process to the extent proposed originally by Edelman: cell division, cell differentiation, cell mobility, growth of neural connections, etc. The problem with this direction is that to implement it the neural network model itself is not enough; we also need a model for the environment. And when it comes to modeling a whole chemical and physical world where the cells live, it is no longer a trivial problem. This is the approach recently taken by Fleischer (Fleischer & Barr, 1994) and Kitano (Kitano, 1994). of

In this paper, neuromorphogenesis is approached from the direction of modeling chemical diffusion fields, and determining how they can be used to direct neural growth. In the future, this model is assumed to be one part (chemical world) of a model where various environmental factors are combined to direct the neural growth. Another method of modeling the environment by gradient fields was presented in (Vaario & Shimohara, 1995).

6 Conclusion

This paper describes a method for combining Lindenmayer systems and a model of diffusion fields. The proposed method provides a nice example of how diffusion fields could be used to direct genetic growth. This is important for the future when more complex systems will be built by genetic algorithms. It will be difficult to encode all features into the genetic codes, and allowing too many dimensions to evolve would lead only into a long

a)

b)

c)

d)

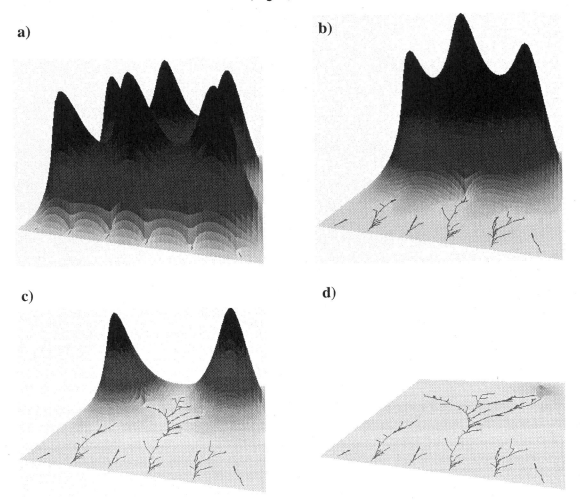

Figure 10: Lindenmayer systems competing for the diffusion sources.

Initial stage

Final stage

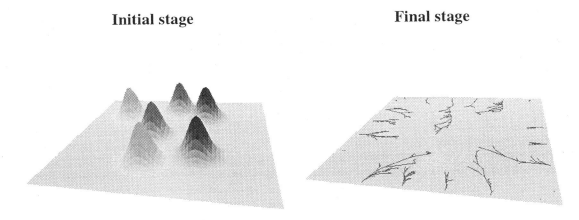

Figure 11: Lindenmayer systems growing in several kinds of diffusion sources.

evolving time.

The model of the growing process will provide a gradual and continuous adaptation compared to the jumpwise adaptation provided by plain genetic algorithms. Combining the individual based developmental process and population based evolutionary process is one of the challenges of tomorrow's evolutionary systems.

In this paper the balance between the genetic and environment directed growth was much on the side of the environment directed growth. In some cases (as the example of the repairing L-system) we need a more dominating genetic predetermination, or a more specific environment direction, of the targeted structure.

A more detailed analysis of the balance between genetic and environmental control factors is still necessary. Also, a realistic neural network model should be modeled by this method. This is the direction of our future work.

Reference

Ames, W. F. (1977). *Numerical methods for partial differential equations.* Academic Press, New York.

Banks, R. B. (1994). *Growth and Diffusion Phenomena.* Springer-Verlag.

Beer, R. D. (1990). *Intelligence as Adaptive Behavior.* Academic Press.

Brooks, R. A. (1991). Intelligence without representation. *Artificial Intelligence*, pp. 139–159.

Edelman, G. M. (1987). *Neural Darwinism - The Theory of Neuronal Group Selection.* Basic Books, New York.

Edelman, G. M. (1988). *Topobiology.* Basic Books.

Fleischer, K., & Barr, A. H. (1994). A simulation testbed for the study of multicellular development: The multiple mechanisms of morphogenesis. In Langton, C. G. (Ed.), *Artificial Life III.* Addison-Wesley.

Kaandorp, J. A. (1994). *Fractal Modelling: Growth and Form in Biology.* Springer-Verlag.

Kitano, H. (1994). Evolution of metabolism for morphogenesis. In Brooks, R., & Maes, P. (Eds.), *Artificial Life IV*, pp. 49–58. The MIT Press.

Piaget, J. (1974). *Adaptation and Intelligence — Organic Selection and Phenocopy.* The University of Chicago Press. (reprint 1980).

Piaget, J. (1975). *The Equilibration of Cognitive Structures.* The University of Chicago Press. (reprint 1985).

Press, W. H., Flannery, B. P., Teukolsky, S. A., & Vetterling, W. T. (1988). *Numerical recipes in C.* Cambridge University Press, Cambridge.

Prusinkiewicz, P., & Lindenmayer, A. (1990). *The Algorithmic Beauty of Plants.* Springer-Verlag.

Sander, L. M. (1986). Fractal growth processes. *Nature, 322*, 789–793.

Vaario, J. (1993). *An Emergent Modeling Method for Artificial Neural Networks.* Ph.D. thesis, The University of Tokyo.

Vaario, J. (1994). From evolutionary computation to computational evolution. *Informatica, 18*(4), 417—434.

Vaario, J., & Shimohara, K. (1995). On formation of structures. In Morán, F., Moreno, A., Merelo, J. J., & Chacón, P. (Eds.), *Advances in Artificial Life*, pp. 421–435. Springer.

Varela, F. J., Thompson, E., & Rosch, E. (1993). *The Embodied Mind.* The MIT Press.

Philosophical Session

Further steps towards a realistic description of the essence of life

Federico Morán
Dept. Bioquímica, Fac. Químicas,
Universidad Complutense, 28040 Madrid, Spain
Phone: +341-3944151 Fax: +341-3944159
Email: fmoran@solea.quim.ucm.es

Alvaro Moreno
Dept. de Lógica y Filosofía de la Ciencia,
Universidad del País Vasco,
Apdo. 1249, 20080 San Sebastián, Spain

Eric Minch
Dept. of Genetics,
Stanford University Medical Center,
Stanford, CA 94305, USA

Francisco Montero
Dept. Bioquímica, Fac. Químicas,
Universidad Complutense, 28040 Madrid, Spain

Abstract

The problem of the essential properties of living systems is here addressed through a comparative analysis of four classic models for the origin of life, and an argument is developed for imposing further requirements on such models. It is seen that with respect to their accommodation of spatial organization and energetic metabolism these models are deficient, despite their adequacy for their original theoretical purposes. We argue that underlying any of these models is the problem of their energetic autonomy as self-maintaining dissipative structures. This implies certain constraints in the definition of their components—specifically the need for spatial organization and for energetic coupling—which should be taken into account when dealing not only with realizations but also with the very logic of the system. Finally, we conjecture that the mediation of energetic coupling by an energy currency exchange mechanism may be a necessary rather than a merely casual property.

1 Introduction

The aim of this paper is to contribute to the universalization of biological theory through a study of the more general principles of metabolism, i.e., of the energetic aspects of living organization. The proper nature of this subject will lead us to deal with a methodology at the edge of physics, chemistry, biology, and Artificial Life (*ALife*) itself.

The challenge of the universalization of biology, explicitly addressed by Chris Langton in his well known introduction of the field of *ALife* (Langton, 1989), has raised many discussions focused on the idea of life as bare organization (Emmeche 1992,1994; Harnad 1994; Moreno *et al.* 1994a). Sciences like physics and chemistry are considered as universal sciences because their theories and laws are in principle valid for describing all processes that take place in their domains. In these domains the main body of phenomenology is independent of the history (or at least in a negligible manner). However, the problem of biology is the essential historicity of the phenomenon of life: biological systems in the earth are in a large extent, the result of a concatenation of successive contingent events. Though this fact implies a major difficulty for the aim of building a universal science of life, *ALife* offers a new frame which will allow significant progress in this direction. Virtual organisms and environments created in computer media permit experimentation in a great variety of conditions, parameters, energy, etc. This allows us to study in an accessible span of time a sequence of processes which in real conditions would be unattainable. With this tool it is possible to scan a sufficient variety of historical scenarios so that it may be possible, by induction, to abstract the necessary (i.e., the universal) from the contingent (the historical). On the other hand, the domain of the origin of life permits both biology and *ALife* to keep in touch with the methodology of physics and chemistry. In this way, we claim, some progress in the direction of a realistic universalization of living organization can be achieved.

2 Virtual and material life

As we have pointed out in the introduction, the study of life can be developed according to two different methodologies. The first is the computational study of symbolic systems capable of performing lifelike behaviors (*virtual life*). The second is the study of real living systems that exist in physical space and time, and whose changes also imply energetic processes (*material life*). Accordingly, in the sequel we will distinguish between these two levels of description of life: virtual and material. The former addresses lifelike organization in simulations that can be implemented in computer media, whereas the latter means the physical implementations or instantiations of living organization that respond to the question of life as it must be in the real world. As the virtual life approach is purely computational, it can generate systems exhibiting lifelike properties that would, in the real world, require complex underlying levels of organization which can be ignored in most of the computational models. On the other hand, when dealing with material systems, biologists—either of life or *ALife* —have to deal with all relevant levels of organization, in the form of physical laws (energetic requirements, thermodynamic constraints, kinetic mechanisms, etc.) and chemical requirements (disposition of materials, building blocks, substrate disposition, chemical compatibilities, etc.)

Thus, the research program of virtual life is based on the reduction of all biological phenomenology to purely relational terms, namely to a complete dematerialization of biological systems. This approach is the source of a certain skepticism among biologists in regard to standard *ALife* . There are two main reasons for this. Firstly, because virtual models of *ALife* pose problems of empirical valuation, i.e., there are no material systems that would eventually correspond to such models. Secondly, because the very immateriality of these models breaks the link between biology and physics or chemistry, which are the basis for the standard methodology of biology. This in turn is due to two main reasons: on the one hand biologists, when dealing with specific biological components (proteins, nucleic acids, etc.), take for granted the implicit underlying levels of organization; on the other hand, biologists do not conceive the fundamental mechanisms of life outside of the thermodynamic frame. This implies a set of consequences or constraints concerning the size of components, interaction of multiple levels of description (micro/macro), mass action laws, energy transduction, etc., that will be further addressed in Section 4.

Biology itself has some theoretical arguments which permit one to face the problem of its universalization. There are physico-chemical arguments explaining that the process of molecular evolution towards complexity leads to organic components. In addition, there is empirical evidence of the ubiquity of this fact.

However, these arguments alone do not permit biology to develop a full fledged research program towards its universalization. Admittedly to achieve such an enterprise requires the cooperation of computational approaches of virtual *ALife* (i.e., a survey of the general principles of living organization by means of computational models). Our claim is that without taking into account the material aspects of living organization this goal will remain unreachable.

3 Complexity and recursivity of self-maintaining metabolic networks

Although the problem of the origin of life has been approached in many different ways, there are only a few classic models which address the problem in terms which are sufficiently general as to apply to life on other planets, or to media other than those with which biology has concerned itself. Among these the foremost are Rosen's (M,R)-system, Eigen's hypercycle, Kauffman's autocatalytic network, and Varela's autopoietic model. Autocatalytic networks and hypercycles are described in terms of familiar biochemical phenomena: amino acids and polypeptides, purines, pyrimidines and polynucleotides, and so forth. The autopoietic model abstracts from these (though drawing on them) to the set of general metabolites and generalized catalysts. The (M,R)-system abstracts further to the set of possible realizations of general metabolites and catalysts. Here we summarize the relevant characteristics of these four in-

fluential models of biogenesis with respect to their structural complexity and structural recursiveness. We consider in particular the topology of their corresponding reaction networks and their accommodation of genomicity, energetics, and spatial organization.

3.1 Structural comparison of (M,R)-systems, hypercycles, autocatalytic nets, and autopoietic models

All four models rely on several types of biochemical interaction, specifically those of reaction, diffusion, catalysis, and template replication. Catalysis, though, is fundamentally a shorthand concept for a cycle of rapid reactions, and replication is but a special case of catalysis. Any reaction, no matter how complex, can be reduced to a series of elementary binary reactions of cleaving and binding (lysis and ligation), or the differential birth and death of the participating chemical species. The forward reaction $a + b \rightarrow ab$ can then be seen as the local death of the reactants, a and b, and the local birth of the product, ab. Catalysis of the above forward reaction by a catalyst c involves a cycle of rapid reactions such as $c + a \rightarrow ca$, $ca + b \rightarrow cab$, $cab \rightarrow c + ab$. The competition between this cycle and the uncatalyzed direct reaction can be seen as an embedding of the rapid catalytic cycle in a higher, slower level containing the uncatalyzed pathway, since events in the higher level cannot occur before events in the lower level have relaxed. Polymerization involves a succession of similar catalytic events which we can express as a temporally recursive series of reactions: $c + a \rightarrow ca^*$, $ca^* + a \rightarrow ca^*$, $ca^* \rightarrow c + a^*$, where a^* signifies a string of one or more elements of a, which may be a molecular species or a class of species (such as amino acids). Diffusion is an inherently spatial concept, and from a given location can also be seen as the birth or death of chemical species; diffusion or introduction of a into a local space corresponds then to the 'reaction' $\emptyset \rightarrow a$, and removal or diffusion out as $a \rightarrow \emptyset$. Thus we can compare the four models directly by reducing the complex events in each to elementary reaction and diffusion events, preferably with characteristic relaxation times.

The (M,R)-system. Robert Rosen introduced the (M,R)-system in a series of papers (1958, 1959, 1963, 1966, 1967) that explored the characteristics of abstract metabolic networks. The (M,R)-system is defined in terms of mappings from inputs to outputs; the metabolic M-units transform metabolic inputs into products, and the repair R-units transform these products into M-units. Whenever a given M-unit ceases to function (due to degradation or depletion), it is repaired or replenished by some R-unit. Rosen's analysis determined that every (M,R)-system must contain at least one M-unit which, once removed, cannot be replaced (a non-reestablishable component). This means that all (M,R)-systems are 'mortal', in that their structure can be irreversibly changed by environmental perturbations. In addition, the more such non-reestablishable components

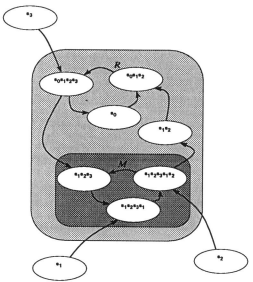

Figure 1: The minimal (M,R)-system, including four distinct substrings (s_0, s_1, s_2, and s_3) and six reactions. The reactions in the M box are much more rapid than those in the R box, which are much more rapid than any reactions outside both boxes.

are present in an (M,R)-system, the less damage is done to the system when one of them is removed.

The (M,R)-system includes no genomic component. It is a catalytically-mediated metabolic net. Rosen defines it, though, as having a category-theoretic structure which, under certain weak conditions, can be recursively extended in such a way that the very same relation obtaining between metabolic and repair components characterizes the relations between repair components and those of the next higher level, which can be interpreted as genomic. As he points out in his paper on realization (1971), "there is no essential intrinsic distinction between 'metabolic' and 'genetic', but only a conventional and subjective one." The extended recursive structure, which we could call the (M,R,G)-system, includes a genomic level. In category-theoretic terms, the metabolic level is described by a mapping f: $(A \to B)$, where A is a set of substrates, B a set of products, and f a set of catalysts (M-units). The repair level is described by the mapping ϕ: $(B \to H(A,B))$, where $H(A,B)$ is the set of all possible mappings from which f is drawn, and ϕ is the mapping which yields f from inputs B; ϕ is thus the set of repair units, the machinery which produces the required catalysts. The genomic level is described by a mapping β: $(H(A,B) \to H(B,H(A,B)))$. What prevents this from becoming an infinite recursion is that the elements of A, B, f, ϕ, and β are all drawn from the same set of molecules: whether we regard them as operands or as operators, as reactants or actions, depends on the level from which we view them.

A minimal (M,R)-system is depicted in Figure 1 in terms of elementary reactions at various rates. The structure is recursively iterated at each level, and each

level contains a cycle with connections to the cycle at the next level. The network can be arbitrarily complex, provided only that every M-unit is catalyzed by an R-unit and that there is a net flow of material through the network.

The autocatalytic network. Kauffman's work on autocatalytic networks, summarized in Kauffman (1993), involved the simulation of large numbers of random reaction networks, and the statistical characterization of the resulting ensemble. He found that below a critical threshold of initial variety of substances and catalytic probability (a parameter of the model which set the likelihood of a given substances' catalyzing other reactions) the network could never grow, while above that threshold the network grows without bound.

Kauffman specifically includes in his treatment of autocatalytic networks both the simple nongenomic case of the autocatalytic set of polypeptides and the quasigenomic case of autocatalytic networks of ribozymes (enzymatic RNA).

The interactions of an autocatalytic network have no recursive structure, but a strongly-connected interlocking web, although the property of self-maintenance was intended at successive levels. Because catalytic properties are assigned randomly, an arrangement of elementary reactions capable of realizing an autocatalytic network while maintaining thermodynamic consistency is extremely unlikely. Any thermodynamically feasible network would take the form of a flattened (M,R)-system, in which M- and R-units share the same level. If we ignore the levels in Figure 1, we can see it as an autocatalytic network in which s_0, s_1 s_2, and s_3 are in the food set and their various catenation products are the reactants and catalysts. The main difference between (M,R)-systems and autocatalytic networks is thus that the former have multiple levels of reaction rate, while autocatalytic nets have only two (the catalytic and noncatalytic pathways).

The hypercycle. Eigen's (1971) hypercycle model is based on a two-level autocatalytic system. At the inner, lower level are a number of autocatalytic cycles corresponding to single-stranded RNA: loops of complementary nucleotide pairs, which mutually reproduce by template replication. Each such pair codes for a product corresponding to an enzyme which catalyzes formation of the next pair. He showed that a simple autocatalytic cycle of enzymes itself was incapable of evolution, but that if the enzyme products join the RNA cycles into a higher-level cycle, the functional properties of the whole can be preserved while the lower-level cycles mutate into more efficient forms, i.e., the hypercycle can evolve. In other words, while the error-catastrophe of autonomous self-reproduction prohibits a spontaneous stable system, the self-reinforcing loop of individually unreliable components is so much more stable that spontaneous occurrence and robustness with respect to mutation during replication is plausible. The hypercycle model is explicitly genomic, relying as it does on the coding capability of RNA. The translation mechanism required for this,

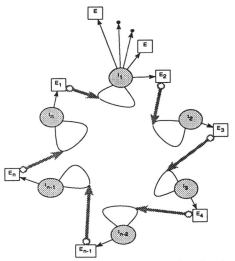

Figure 2: The hypercycle. RNA instructional units $(I_1 \ldots I_n)$ reproduce autocatalytically (shown as small loops), and instruct the formation of enzymes (arrows to E_j). The enzymes catalyze t e autocatalytic loops of other RNA molecules (heavy arrows). The system as a whole forms a larger loop, the hypercycle.

though, and for the template replication of the complementary pairs, is assumed available, and its origin left unexplained.

An abstract view of the hypercycle is diagrammed in Figure 2. The structure is not recursive but cyclic, since the relations between the RNA and the enzymes are not the same as the relations of either to the hypercyclic loop. Though not a recursive structure, it does illustrate multilevel organization in a way which was intended to be recursive. The rapid polymerization of the enzymes and the slower enzyme-mediated autoreplication of the RNA leads to a two-level structure for each subcycle: the more rapid lower level includes the reactions $I_j+e \rightarrow I_je^*, I_je^*+e \rightarrow I_je^*, I_je^* \rightarrow I_j+E_k$, while the slower, higher level includes $I_j + E_j \rightarrow I_jE_j, I_jE_j + a \rightarrow I_jE_ja^*, I_jE_ja^* + a \rightarrow I_jE_ja^*, I_jE_ja^* \rightarrow I_j + \bar{I}_jE_j, \bar{I}_jE_j \rightarrow \bar{I}_j + E_j$, where I_j and E_j are the jth RNA and enzyme, e is the class of amino acids, and a is the class of nucleotides. A repetition of the RNA self-replication transforms the complementary string $\bar{I}_j$ into I_j, and iterating over the subcycles transforms the E_k eventually back into E_j. The hypercycle is thus an extended (M,R)-system which is constrained to cyclic form.

The autopoietic model. Autopoiesis (self-making) is a concept introduced by Maturana and Varela (Varela *et al.* 1974) which has since grown into a large body of theory touching not only on biology but on fields as diverse as cognitive science, management strategy, and mathematical logic, among others. A recent definition by Varela (Deffuant *et al.* 1995; Varela 1996) is:

> An autopoietic system—the minimal living organization—is one that continuously produces the components that specify it, while at the same time

realizing it (the system) as a concrete unity in space and time, which makes the network of production of components possible. More precisely defined: an autopoietic system is organized (defined as unity) as a network of processes of production (synthesis and destruction) of components such that these components:

(i) continuously regenerate and realize the network that produces them, and

(ii) constitute the system as a distinguishable unity in the domain in which they exist.

This general definition encompasses a great variety of systems (though not including the three models considered above), hence the broad applicability of the theory across many disciplines. We consider here not autopoiesis the theory but autopoiesis the model of biogenesis. Specifically, the model developed by Varela *et al.* and implemented as a computer simulation by Zeleny (1977) is a minimal autopoietic system based on catalytic and reaction and diffusion events, and results in a self-maintaining membrane in a cellular automaton. The model is realized using five types of molecule (substrate, catalyst, and three links of different stability), and seven events (production, two types of bonding, two types of disintegration, and two types of diffusion). Simplifying the description somewhat (there are several parameters specifying rates of production, decomposition, and diffusion), the central process which makes this system self-maintaining is a polymerization of substrate by catalyst into a spatially closed membrane, which permits diffusion of substrate but not of any enclosed catalyst. The more rapid level of reactions includes production $(c + a \rightarrow c + a^*)$, and the slower level includes diffusion $(\emptyset \leftrightarrow a)$, and decomposition $(a^* \rightarrow a)$. This is thus a spatially-extended version of the autocatalytic network.

Two important aspects of the autopoietic model should be mentioned here: first, the autopoietic organization avoids concern with genomic control: Varela believes that "reproduction is *not* intrinsic to the minimal logic of the living [system]" (Varela 1996). And second, unlike the other three models, the autopoietic model deals specifically and as necessary with the spatial organization of living systems. Indeed, according to the theory, without the formation of a membrane there is no basis for distinguishing the living system from its surroundings, and thus no autonomous system at all. But the interpretation of autopoiesis in the theory—either as an abstract organization or as a real physical system—remains controversial. G. Fleischacker (1989) for instance, has argued the necessity of situating this abstract definition in a thermodynamic frame.

3.2 Spatial organization and energy transduction

Of these models, only autopoiesis is explicitly spatial, and its spatial organization is extremely simple, consisting of a two-dimensional cellular automaton with zero or one molecule per cellular unit. The other models implicitly involve reactions among one- or higher-dimensional species within a zero-dimensional space. Rosen (1981) has extended the (M,R)-system, however, to encompass spatial structure by embedding it in the formalism of reaction-diffusion systems. Eigen and Schuster (1979) propose that compartmentation of hypercycles into protocells conferred evolutionary advantage, since boundary effects could increase the efficiency of the network. In this direction recent results (Nuño *et al.* 1995) demonstrate that the inclusion of diffusion in the kinetic equations of replicator models could lead to a spontaneous symmetry breaking, with points in the space where the elements of the network accumulate. This result shows a possible pathway for compartmentation of autocatalytic nets. Kauffman does not discuss the spatial structure of the autocatalytic network, but his model is sufficiently rich to support a hypothesis similar to that of Eigen and Schuster. From the point of view of these models' authors, however, spatial organization is unnecessary for the theoretical argument, since the models demonstrate the point just as well employing only nonspatial rapid-flow chemostats.

Similarly, all four models work just as well without any coupling to exergonic and endergonic metabolic reactions. They are provided by their investigators with whatever nutrients and event probabilities are needed. For the theoretical purposes these models are meant to serve, this is entirely justified. The authors are dealing, after all, with the *logic* of virtual life, not with its implementation in some particular material basis. In computer science one can design or analyze logical circuitry without regard to the reality of the underlying hardware, and this holds also for the formal treatment of possible biochemical control systems. Accordingly these authors need not consider that in implementing such systems, one must include a good deal of ancillary machinery which has no interpretation in the logical design. In computer engineering, side effects of the hardware include power supply, capacitive leakage, current induction, switch bounce, generation of heat, and many others whose correction vastly complicates the task[1]. Likewise in metabolism, the collection of nutrients, excretion of waste products, correction of errors, defensive and competitive strategies, and so forth all require ancillary metabolic machinery which seems to us almost to embody the essence of living systems. The authors of the above models stress, however, that this is not the essence of life: the models treat the essence. To a first approximation this may be true, but there are two considerations which must be taken into account.

For one thing, if one wishes to discuss evolution, it is essential that the individual members of the population be spatially distinct, for consider: if multiple organisms were to coexist within one of these zero-dimensional spaces, and all had the same genome, then reproduction would not produce new organisms, but would instead simply increase the concentration of the various metabolite pools. On the other hand, if they have distinct genomes, then they must also have distinct metabolic

networks, but the inevitable kinetic 'cross-talk' among the various metabolite pools would erase any distinction among them and bind them together into a superorganism.

A thermodynamic objection to the purely logical approach to metabolic design arises even with pregenomic organizations, and arises from the necessarily dissipative nature of biological components. This will be discussed in depth in next Section.

4 Linking organization with materiality

In previous models of *ALife* the specification of the relation among the components of the system does not take energetic requirements into account. What these models intend is to generate by synthetic procedures some functional properties of biological organization (operational closure, adaptability, generation of internal variety or information content, etc.) in abstract constructive terms. Although everyone accepts that energetic constraints are essential when we have to describe material living systems, the problem arises when we have to consider whether or not they affect the very logic of the organization. In other words, the question is whether the viability of the system should be stated in purely functional-constructive terms, as in the former cases, or in energetic-constructive terms.

There is a large consensus for defining life in terms of hierarchical, temporally recursive, organization (see Section 3). Thus, one can define living organization as the result of a process of temporally recursive networks of component production, self-closed by a physical border generated by the system itself, whose viability is based on informational mechanisms of self-reproduction. But we can look at this definition from two complementary points of view: functional and energetic. From the functional view, life appears as an organization where the informational components which assure viability of the system depend for their expression on the very products that they codify. In another paper (Moreno *et al.* 1994b) one of the authors has pointed out that, even ignoring energetic aspects, such a type of organization is hardly understandable apart from its material embedding. From the energetic view, life appears as a network of production of components self-closed by a physical border, so that it assures the mechanisms of energetic coupling that the system requires as a dissipative structure (this concept will be developed in Section 4.1). Here the idea of recursivity lies in the mutual relation between components and energetic couplings: the network generates those components that allow mechanisms of energetic coupling which generate the very organization that produces them recursively. Accordingly, the energetic approach constrains the logic of the system, firstly, through the type of components that it should produce for its own viability, and secondly, through the possibility of setting up some universal principles of any metabolism.

As we shall argue in the next point, the roots of this mutual relation between energetic requirements and the logic of the system lie in the special kind of dissipative structures of which living organization is made.

---

[1]This does not apply to the context of robotic realizations of autonomous *ALife* agents. In this field the actual physical implementation is an important matter

4.1 Thermodynamic constraints

From the energetic point of view, every organized system based on self-maintained networks needs a supply of energy/matter from the environment. This implies that the system cannot be isolated. A first reason why this energy supply should be considered is to take into account the activation of the different reactions that occur in the system network (for example, the formation of new chemical bonds). The second reason lies in the necessity of maintaining the structure and the order of the system against the natural tendency to disorder (second principle of thermodynamics), that is, to dissipate entropy. As a dissipative system, then, any living organization can only be maintained through a continual supply of energy. The equilibrium structures that we can isolate from living systems (for example any crystal) do not need energy to be maintained; once formed they stay stable and maintain their order. Biological or dissipative structures differ, in that they are nonequilibrium structures and need a continual flow of energy to be maintained.

The thermodynamics of irreversible processes teaches us that any isolated system progresses necessarily to equilibrium, which is synonymous with homogeneity and absence of any order. The way to maintain a system away from equilibrium is by means of external constraints. In this case the system can evolve either to a stationary state or to more complex solutions, called dissipative structures by I. Prigogine. This means that far from equilibrium an ordered system never reaches levels of minimum entropy production, and needs a continual supply of extra energy simply to maintain its order. The main difference between physical dissipative structures and living ones is that the latter, in addition to their external constraints, participate directly in their own self-maintenance, through the generation of what has been called functional constraints (Csanyi 1989). This participation takes place through the production of components, i.e., the dissipative structure of any living system must be chemically supported. Moreover, the living system acts on its environment, transforming it.

Thus, life is based on a self-sustaining chemical organization able to ensure its own energetic autonomy. The ensemble of these processes is called metabolism. Metabolism, hence, comprises both degradative (*catabolic*) and synthetic (*anabolic*) processes, that do not necessary produce common intermediates. This will be a constraint in the definition of the energetic requirements.

4.2 Energetic requirements

Biological systems, besides the need to materialize all their functions—or the more significant ones, like information, specific catalysis, individualization, etc.—need a supply of energy. A higher degree of living organization is to have a kind of *self-supply* of energy that guarantees the survival in the case of lack of external energy/matter source. This idea is represented in Figure 3. In the presence of external sources of energy and/or matter the living being transforms it by an *internal energy*

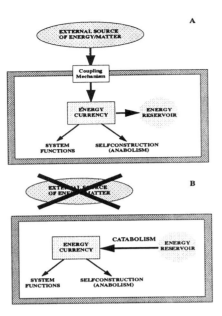

Figure 3: Representation of the two modes of operation of an autonomous living being: (A) when the external source of energy and/or matter is present; (B) in case of temporary cutoff of the external energy supply.

pull (this concept is referred to as an *energy currency* by Skulachev and will be explained below). The primary form or forms of internal energy can be used to realize system functions, construct system components (anabolism), and to maintain an energy reservoir. (b) In the case of lack of external supply the system needs to maintain its activity and self-construction, and this is done by means of the use of the energy reservoir, i.e., by means of the catabolism that regenerates the internal pull of convertible energy.

Therefore, there must be, firstly, mechanisms to couple to the external energy source, and secondly mechanisms of coupling between all internal phenomena of energy transduction. This internal coupling of energy must permit the independent functioning of anabolism and catabolism, as well as the independence between system functions and self-construction. It can be said that these requirements were present from the beginning of life, whether or not we can imagine a more adequate framework for it. If we imagine an origin based on the selection and evolution of informational components (the RNA world, for instance), in order that this selective and evolutionary process can be performed it is necessary that the information carrying molecules have a fast turnover. This further implies a relative instability of the polymers in watery solution (tendency to hydrolysis), so that their formation in adequate concentrations means starting from activated monomers. Since the monomers resulting from hydrolysis of the polymers are energy poor, their activation is necessary in order to form new polymers. But the situation is identical if we consider a scenario for the origin of life in terms of the autopoietical hypothesis. The possibility that materials could enter an individualized system against a gradient, and the survival of the individualized system itself, imply the need for an external supply of energy. In sum, if we consider life as a dynamical system capable of generating self-organizing processes of any kind, it must have not only a material requirement, but an energetic one. None of the four models considered in Section 3.1 address this important requirement for autonomy: the networks collapse if the external energy supply is interrupted.

When we consider the possible molecular candidates for the support of information, we find that not every molecule is suitable for carrying information; similarly the energetic couplings between the biological system and the environment and those that take place inside the system itself cannot occur arbitrarily. This question can be addressed in two ways: what the possibilities are for two processes of coupling energetically from the physical point of view, and what mechanisms the biological system has chosen for achieving these couplings. We will consider in this section only the latter problem and briefly discuss the first question in the last section. From the observation of the mechanisms of coupling in terrestrial biological systems, we can find that they are really *universal*. Skulachev (1992) defines this universality through what he calls the *three fundamental laws of bioenergetics*. These are:

First law: *The living cell avoids direct utilization of external energy sources in the performance of useful work. It transforms energy of these sources to a convertible energy currency, i.e. ATP, $\Delta\tilde{\mu}_{H+}$, or $\Delta\tilde{\mu}_{Na+}$, which is then spent to support various types of energy-consuming processes.*

Second law: *Any living cell always possesses at least two [classes of] energy currencies, one water-soluble (ATP) and the other membrane-linked ($\Delta\tilde{\mu}_{H+}$ or $\Delta\tilde{\mu}_{Na+}$)*

Third law: *All the energy requirements of the living cell can be satisfied if at least one of the three convertible energy currencies is produced at the expense of external energy sources.*

From the first law, it can be deduced that direct couplings seldom occur; on the contrary, they take place using components which exchange currency as a way of interchanging energy (as if Nature would prefer to create this 'money' ready to use in every process that needs it). More explicitly, the energy flow lost by a process which is intended for use by another one is translated into another component, currency, that later can be used for some other process. Any biological process which is a source of energy translates it into any of the three energy currencies. Conversely any process which needs energy takes it from one of these three forms, by coupling with them.

The first class currency is a chemical, ATP, and represents a soluble biochemical substance that is ubiquitous, highly energetic, and stable. There are not many candidates to be plausible substitutes for ATP. The experiments of prebiotic chemical synthesis performed by Miller (1992) demonstrate that, starting from basic

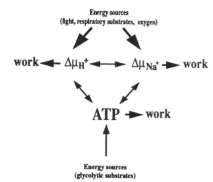

Figure 4: The three energy currencies and their relation to external and internal sources of energy. (From Skulachev 1992).

chemical compounds, like water, ammonia, carbon dioxide, phosphate, etc, it is possible to synthesize basic biological compounds like amino acids, sugars, nucleotides, and lipids. Among all of these, ATP is the best candidate.

The second class currencies are related to membranes. They represent the gradient of H^+ and Na^+ electrochemical potentials across membranes. It is important to remember that the existence of some kind of membrane is imposed by the necessary condition of self-identity of each living being. Many authors have pointed out the necessity of pumping out ions to compensate for the excess osmotic pressure of early cells (see a review in Skulachev 1994). Now we have an opportunistic use by the cell of these ionic gradients in realizing the energy budget.

The second law represents, in the words of Skulachev, that the cell always has some currency *in cash* and some *in cheques*. For coupling with an external source of energy only one of the three currency mechanisms is necessary. Paraphrasing Skulachev, the third law is interpreted as meaning that it does not matter how an income is received, in cash or cheques, so long as they are interconvertible. Figure 4 shows schematically the interconversion between the three energy currencies.

5 Discussion

The need for spatial organization in living systems can be argued in two ways. First, as was claimed in Section 3.2 above, it is necessary that organisms be spatially distinct if evolution is to proceed, since without separation there is only a single superorganism. Second, as Varela argues in his autopoietic theory, spatial heterogeneity in cellular metabolism is a necessary concomitant of the development of a membrane, which is itself axiomatic in autopoiesis. The need for an energetic metabolism has also been justified in Section 4, on the grounds that production of functional components of living systems entails generally dissipative processes. In addition to this, the necessity of autonomy from the external energy supply strongly conditions the existence of two distinct—but interdependent—metabolisms: anabolism and catabolism.

All this is but the instantiation of a phenomenology,

from which two questions arise: (1) Is it necessary to have an energy exchange currency, without which the system would collapse at the energetic level? (2) Are the existing currencies chosen by chance or are there really not many possibilities?

We conjecture that the three laws are not just consequences of opportunistic decisions made by chance, but rather in some way necessarily imposed by physical, chemical, and energetic considerations. We can justify this conjecture by considering the three laws together.

The first law states that a common currency will arise; this necessity is imposed by the statistical unlikelihood that a distinct energetic mechanism could arise to couple each dissipative process of the organism. Once any component has mediated its coupling, this mediating mechanism will be exploited opportunistically by all other components which require energy, purely for reasons of efficiency and proximity. The origin of this solution is based on the impossibility of stable energetic coupling among the vast number of necessary metabolic transformations. It must be taken into account that to have physical coupling between two processes, they must occur in the same microregion of space and they must have a common intermediary. It is quite clear that there are not common intermediaries for every pair of metabolic reactions: there are necessary chemical constraints, for not every metabolite can be synthesized, or can be stable, or soluble, etc.

The second law states that multiple currencies are likely; this follows from the necessity for spatial organization, because once living systems distinguish themselves from their surroundings by semipermeable membranes, the separate affinities of intracellular and pericellular chemistry entail distinct mechanisms for mediation of intracellular and transmembrane interactions.

The third law states that all but one of the currencies can feed off the one with external coupling; this also seems plausible, on grounds of efficiency and proximity alone. So, the construction of a viable and physically coherent metabolism depends on the existence of energy interchange currencies.

Any scenario for the origin of life, including computer simulations implementing any of the four classic models of biogenesis discussed, can thus be judged on its accommodation of intra- and intercellular spatial organization as well as on its accommodation of energetic coupling. Furthermore, these should ideally emerge as a *result* of the behavior of the simulation, rather than being built in. In this case, it would be possible to test our conjecture empirically, by discovering in how many such cases an energy currency is developed and—within these—the distribution of the number of distinct currencies. The fact that there are three and only three in the metabolic designs present in the Earth biosphere is likely to be only contingent; we should like to find out how many such designs occur in the universe of spontaneously emerging life forms.

Acknowledgments

This work has been supported in part by grants no. PB92-0456 and PB92-0908 from the DGICYT, MEC (Spain), and UPV 003.230-HA 164/94 from the University of the Basque Country.

References

Csanyi, V. (1989) *Evolutionary Systems and Society. A general theory of life, mind and culture.* Durham: Duke University Press.

Deffuant, G., Fuhs, T., Monneret, E., Bourgine, P., and Varela, F. (1995), Semi-algebraic networks: an attempt to design geometric autopoietic models. *Artificial Life*, 2:157–177.

Eigen, M. (1971), Selforganization of matter and the evolution of biological macromolecules. *Naturwissenschaften*, 58:465–523.

Eigen, M., and Schuster, P. (1979), *The Hypercycle*. Berlin: Springer.

Emmeche, C. (1992) Life as an abstract phenomenon: is artificial life possible? In Varela, F., and Bourgine, P. (eds.) *Toward a Practice of Autonomous Systems.* Cambridge, MA: MIT Press, pp. 466–474.

Emmeche, C. (1994) Life as a multiverse phenomenon? In *Artificial Life III*. Langton, C. (ed). Redwood City, CA: Addison-Wesley, pp 553–568

Fleischacker, G. (1989) Autopoiesis: the status of its system logic. *BioSystems*, 22:37–49.

Harnad, S. (1994) Artificial life: synthetic vs virtual. In *Artificial Life III*. Langton, C. (ed). Redwood City, CA: Addison-Wesley, pp. 539–552

Kauffman, S.A. (1993). *The Origins of Order*. New York: Oxford University Press.

Langton, C. (ed.) (1989) *Artificial Life*. Redwood City, CA: Addison-Wesley.

Miller, S.L. (1992) The prebiotic synthesis of organic compounds as a step toward the origin of life. In *Major Events in the History of Life* Schopf, J-W. (ed.), Boston: Jones and Bartlett, pp. 1–28.

Moreno, A., Umerez, J. and Fernandez, J. (1994a) Definition of life and research programs in artificial life. *Ludus Vitalis*, 2(3):15–33.

Moreno, A., Etxeberria, A. and Umerez, J. (1994b) Universality without matter?. In Brooks, R. and Maes, P. (eds) *Artificial Life IV*, Cambridge, MA: MIT Press, pp. 406–410.

Nuño, J.C., Chacón, P., Moreno, A., and Morán, F. (1995) Compartmentation in replicator models. In *Advances in Artificial Life*, Morán, F., Moreno, A., Merelo, J.J., and Chacón, P. (eds.), Heidelberg: Springer Verlag, pp. 116–127.

Rosen, R. (1958), A relational theory of biological systems. *Bull. Math. Biophysics*, 20:245–260.

Rosen, R. (1959), A relational theory of biological systems II. *Bull. Math. Biophysics*, 21:109–128.

Rosen, R. (1963), Some results in graph theory and their application to abstract relational biology. *Bull. Math. Biophysics*, 25:231–241.

Rosen, R. (1966), A note on replication in (M,R)-systems. *Bull. Math. Biophysics*, 28:149–151.

Rosen, R. (1967), Further comments on replication in (M,R)-systems. *Bull. Math. Biophysics*, 29:91–94.

Rosen, R. (1971), Some realizations of (M,R)-systems and their interpretation. *Bull. Math. Biophysics*, 33:303–319.

Rosen, R. (1981), Pattern generation in networks. *Prog. Theor. Biology*, 6:161–209.

Skulachev, V.P. (1992). The laws of cell energetics. *Eur. J. Biochem.*, 208:203–209.

Skulachev, V.P. (1994). Bioenergetics: the evolution of molecular mechanisms and the development of bioenergetic concepts. *Antonio van Leeuwenhoek*, 65:271–284.

Varela, F. (1996), Life: identity and cognition. *Brain and Cognition*, in press.

Varela, F., Maturana, H., and Uribe, R. (1974), Autopoiesis: the organization of living systems, its characterization and a model. *BioSystems*, 5:187–195.

Zeleny, M. (1977), Self-organization of living systems: a formal model of autopoiesis. *Int. J. Gen. Systems*, 4:13–22.

Evaluating Artificial Life and Artificial Organisms

Brian L. Keeley

Experimental Philosophy Laboratory, Department of Philosophy,
University of California at San Diego, 9500 Gilman Drive, La Jolla, CA 92093-0302 USA
e-mail: bkeeley@ucsd.edu

Abstract

It is often heard in Artificial Life (A-Life) circles that contemporary biology studies *life-as-we-know-it* (an Earth based, carbon chain phenomenon), whereas A-Life takes as its domain of study *life-as-it-could-be*. But lacking a clear definition of "life" the question arises: how would we recognize life-as-it-could-be, if we managed to create it? This short paper offers some speculations on this question and argues that in attempting to create A-Life careful attention must be paid to life-as-we-know-it. A-Life must look to biology as the measure its own success. A taxonomy of relatedness—a characterization of the different ways the products of A-Life (here called "artificial organisms") can be similar or dissimilar to natural life—is offered. This philosophical discussion is put to use in a concrete A-Life context, "biological robotics", the A-Life approach to robotics. In this case, I argue that the ability of an artificial organism to interact seamlessly with existing biological organisms is an important criterion of its success as an A-Life model.

1 Introduction

How ought one evaluate Artificial Life (A-Life)? That is to say, what must the field's practitioners do in order to achieve its stated goals? Setting aside the question whether A-Life has plausible and coherent goals, it is an interesting question how we would recognize that we had achieved the goals of A-Life as they now stand. The purpose of this paper is not to set new goals for A-Life, but to help more clearly define the existing goals. (This paper is a work-in-progress. It is offered in the spirit of what used to be called "speculative philosophy". I hope it will provoke thought and discussion on a too little discussed question. For more, see[Keeley forthcoming].)

What are the goals of A-Life? First and foremost, A-Life is a science which seeks to help understand the phenomenon of life. A-Life is a component of *Biology* (with a capital "B"), the scientific study of life. The existence of A-Life calls attention to the fact that, in practice, contemporary *biology* (with a lower-case "b") tends to focus exclusively on Earth based life. Traditionally, biology has taken as its domain of interest *life-as-we-know-it*: carbon-chain chemistry, heredity via DNA and RNA, Kreb cycles, etc. According to the proponents of A-Life, just as Physics should not be restricted to the study of motion of objects on Earth, nor Chemistry to naturally occurring compounds and reactions, neither should Biology be restricted to Earth based, naturally occurring instances of biological phenomena. The primary goal of A-Life is to help Biology achieve this more general reach. Traditional biology has been restricted to naturally occurring life-as-we-know-it because there has never been any other biological phenomena to study. The field of A-Life is founded on the belief that technology has developed to the point that we can now begin to replicate biological phenomena by hand and in artificial media. At the very least, A-Lifers act on the conviction that such a possibility is worth exploring.

In essence, A-Life seeks to expand Biology's reach beyond life-as-we-know-it by providing examples of *life-as-it-could-be* [Langton 1989]. This raises an immediate problem: Given that A-Life seeks to provide us with life-as-we-**don't**-know-it, how are we to recognize artificial organisms as a examples of *life* at all? (The term "artificial life" is ambiguous and can be taken as referring both to the field and to its products (a mass noun referring to artificial constructs that are alive). To avoid possible confusion, I will reserve the term "Artificial Life" (A-Life) for the scientific field, and I will refer to its products as "artificial organisms".) What is to prevent us, when presented with a human-made and entirely alien (relative to life-as-we-know-it) phenomenon, from identifying that phenomenon as something other than Biological? In other words, how can we identify something as life-as-it-could-be rather than as *something-exceedingly-interesting-but-not-alive*? The cooling of spin glasses, the chemistry of cold fusion, and the formation of new stars are all complex and interesting phenomena, but we do not class them as *biological*. By what criteria would we classify an artificially generated phenomenon as an instance of *life*-as-it-could-be?

One source of the problem here is that we lack a widely accepted definition of life. However, this need not bother us too greatly. It is true that we lack an agreed upon definition of "life", but such is often the fate of young sciences. Definitions are the hallmark of mature sciences, not young ones. We can take comfort from the 1890 advice of William James [1981], describing the then embryonic field of psychology:

"It is better not to be pedantic, but to let the science be as vague as its subject, and include [vaguely defined] phenomena if by doing so we can throw any light on the main business in hand. It will ere long be seen, I trust, that we can; and that we gain much more by a broad than by a narrow conception of our subject. At a certain stage in the development of every science a degree of vagueness is what best consists with fertility." [19]

However, even if we accept the vagueness of the target of our domain, it still seems important that we have some way of evaluating where we are and where we are going. To say that something is vague is not to say it should be *ignored*. We should also remember that one of our goals as scientists is to eliminate this vagueness in our midst. It is the spirit of this paper to acknowledge the vagueness of A-Life's current position and to offer some ideas towards its eventual resolution.

2 Possible Relationships between the Natural and the Artificial

My approach to clearing up the vagueness is to explore the relationship between A-Life and little-b-biology. A-Life seeks to create artificial organisms, whereas biology studies plants, animals, and other instances of life-as-we-know-it. Let me begin by asking: How *might* these two classes of entities be related?

2.1 Of Natural, Artificial, and Nature Identical Ingredients

To explore the possible relationships between artificial and natural entities, consider the case of food product labelling; an everyday situation where the relationship between the natural and the artificial is important. It is commonly felt that food products should bear labels indicating what artificial or natural ingredients they contain. However, there is a problem with the term "artificial" in this context. This word has two related, but different, meanings. In the first sense, artificial is the antonym of "natural"; a reference to the *genesis* of the phenomenon in question. For example, we speak of natural vs. artificial selection when we wish to distinguish between selection pressures brought about by Mother Nature as opposed to those brought about by human hands.

The term "artificial" has a second, slightly different, meaning. In this second sense, it is the antonym of "genuine", as when we speak of "artificial lighting" in a room. Here, the connotation is not only that the light does not have a natural source (*e.g.*, the sun), but that there is something different about the light itself. For example, the sun is a *constant* source of light energy, whereas a florescent light emits *pulses* of light at a very high frequency. This sense of artificial involves a reference to the *substrate* or composition of the phenomenon, as when Langton [1989] refers to A-Life recreating biological phenomena in "artificial" media. Artificial in this sense means that Mother Nature does not use such a medium in making this kind of product.

OK, so back to food product labelling. Identifying "natural" ingredients is simple enough. These are ingredients derived from natural food sources (plants, animals, and minerals) without any significant change to their chemical make up. They are made of *natural* stuff, and made in a *natural* way. Thus, natural strawberry flavoring is a substance made from actual strawberries and has a chemical composition identical (or very similar) to the substance which gives naturally occurring strawberries their distinctive flavor.

What about artificial ingredients? One's first response might be to say that all substances that do not meet the above criteria for naturalness are, by definition, artificial. (It should be noted that this simple response seems to be the practice of many governmental agencies responsible for labelling food.) However, to do this is to ignore the ambiguity of "artificial" just identified. Recognizing this ambiguity means recognizing that such a scheme classes together two groups that seem, at least intuitively, to be importantly different.

First, there are those artificial substances which are created in highly unnatural ways, but whose resulting chemical make up is *very much* like that of naturally occurring substances. Perhaps biochemists have isolated the collection of compounds that give strawberries their particular flavor and it turns out that these compounds can be made cheaply and easily in chemical factories. We might imagine that the compounds are mixed up in great vats by a series of well-controlled chemical processes. Nonetheless, thanks to modern technology, these substances are virtually indistinguishable from those substances which can be found in nature. If such a strawberry flavoring were given to a chemist, along with the natural substance that it mimics, she would find it very difficult (if not impossible) to tell them apart.

Second, there are those artificial substances that are created by entirely unnatural processes—as just described—but which bear little chemical similarity to naturally occurring substances. Food scientists are constantly looking for cheap, easy to produce chemical substances which can fool our palates. Such a strawberry flavoring compound would differ from its natural counterpart in both genesis and composition. It would be artificial in *both* senses of the word.

These two groups of human-made substances seem importantly different. A reasonable consumer, for instance, might well be more worried about ingesting one rather than the other. To distinguish them, I will reserve the term "artificial" to those substances that are both human-made and whose chemical composition is markedly different from that of natural substances. For the latter group—the human-made substances that are compositionally similar or identical to natural products—I will use the term "Nature Identical".

This suggests a straight forward taxonomy: *Natural* strawberry flavoring is derived from naturally grown strawberries in a process that does not significantly alter its make up. *Artificial* strawberry flavoring is a substance that does not come from strawberries and which has a distinctly different chemical composition from that which gives strawberries their flavor. Finally, *nature identical* strawberry flavoring is not derived from strawberries, but is chemically indistinguishable from that which gives strawberries their flavor.

Notice, however, it is not true that artificial strawberry flavoring has *nothing* to do with natural strawberries. Such a substance should *taste like* strawberries. It should bear some functionally described relationship to them. All three substances—natural strawberry flavoring, artificial strawberry flavoring, and nature identical strawberry flavoring—share with actual strawberries the capacity to elicit in humans the same taste sensations. This capacity is what makes a substance artificial *strawberry* flavoring instead of artificial *blueberry* flavoring.

3 Three Types of Relationship between the Artificial and the Natural

However, this is not a paper about the philosophy of food science. The point of the above discussion is to identify three *general* ways in which natural and artificial entities (substances, processes, or other phenomena) can be related. The example of food product labelling points to three candidate categories: (1) entities can be *genetically* related; that is, they can share a common origin, (2) entities can *functionally* related in that they share properties when described at some level of abstraction, and (3) entities can be *compositionally* related; that is, they can be made of similar parts arranged in similar ways. Let us consider these three possibilities in more detail.

3.1 The Genetic Relationship

First, two entities can share a *genetic* relationship; that is, they can share a common history or origin. In our example above, strawberries and natural strawberry flavoring share a common origin. For a second example, it has been claimed that the human thumb shares a close genetic relationship to the chimpanzee thumb, but both of these thumbs are genetically dissimilar to the panda's "thumb". Whereas the thumbs of humans and chimpanzees are derived from the same finger bone of a recent common ancestor, the panda's thumb is derived from the *wrist* bone

of an ancestor who is not shared with either humans or chimps.

3.2 The Functional Relationship

Second, two entities can share a *functional* relationship. For two entities to be functionally related, they must share some abstract description. Cummins [1980] offers an example of such a functional analysis:

"Schematic diagrams in electronics provide [an] obvious illustration [of functional analysis]. Since each symbol represents any physical object whatever having a certain capacity, a schematic diagram of a complex device constitutes an analysis of the electronic capacities of the device as a whole into the capacities of its components. Such an analysis allows us to explain how the device as a whole exercises the analyzed capacity, for it allows us to see exercises of the analyzed capacity as programmed exercise of the analyzing capacities. In this case, the 'program' is given by the lines indicating how the components are hooked up." [187]

The same schematic diagram can be an accurate, abstract description of a variety of different electronic realizations, whether those realizations are composed of vacuum tubes, transistors, or integrated circuits. While they may be made of vastly different materials, they share the same organization, i.e., the same functional description. They can be said to be *functionally isomorphic*. A functional relationship is perhaps the weakest kind of relationship possible between the natural and the artificial.

It is the functional similarity between the different types of strawberry flavorings that leads us to classify them all as types of *strawberry* flavoring. Contemporary biology also makes use of functional concepts. Terms such as "predator", "prey", "parasite", "reproduction", etc., group together biological entities that need not share either a strong genetic or compositional relationship. It makes sense to speak of both Spanish moss and tapeworms as "parasites", despite their obvious differences, because they share important similarities in the way they obtain nutrients and interact with other organisms in their respective environments.

Note also that evolutionary biology makes much use of this concept, as when biologists attempt to identify homologies and analogies. Homologies and analogies are functionally defined concepts. For example, the electroreceptive modality in fish has evolved at least twice—once in South and Central America (in the Gymnotiform family), once in Africa (in the Mormyriform family). Both groups of fish possess a specialized "electric organ" that produces a regular electric discharge, and this organ is used in perception and social communication. Since it is not believed that Gymnotiforms and Mormyriforms share a common ancestor that was itself electroreceptive, we consider electroreception to have resulted from convergent evolution of the two groups. The species of the two groups are functionally similar in that they can be described as having analogous sensory systems. However, that shared sensory system is not the result of any close genetic relationship between the two groups of fish.

3.3 The Compositional Relationship

Finally, if two entities are made out of the "same stuff", in similar ways, they can be said to share a *compositional* relationship. Both criteria—shared components and shared organization—are required for compositional similarity. Natural and Nature identical strawberry flavoring share a strong compositional relationship. Turning again to the electric fish example, if you look at the electric organs of these animals, you will find that whereas most species of either family have organs that are myogenic (derived from muscle tissue), there are a few species of both families that have an organ that is neurogenic (derived from nerve tissue). This difference in tissue type is a difference in composition. Due to this difference, one can make predictions that cut across the genetic classification. For example, curare will have a paralytic effect on all myogenic electric organs, regardless of their genetic relationship.

4 A-Life's Relationship to Biology

Above, I set out a taxonomy of relationships between artificial and natural entities. What are the consequences of this taxonomy for A-Life? First of all, I claim that artificial organisms are deemed living (or deemed biological) on the basis of the artificial organisms' relationship to natural life. Life-as-it-could-be must bear *some* relationship to life-as-we-know-it to be deemed a kind of life at all. The products of A-Life and Earth-bound, naturally occurring organisms must have *something* in common, by virtue of which they both can be classed together as instances of some more general notion of "Biological". In the form of a slogan, my first claim is:

1) *The touchstone of artificial life and artificial organisms must be biology and natural life.*

Although this claim should not be controversial, some critics of A-Life worry that its implications are not sufficiently appreciated A-Lifers. Take for example, the widely-reported complaint of John Maynard-Smith that A-Life, as it is pursued at the Santa Fe Institute, is disturbingly "fact free". In the context of the above claim, this remark cannot be ignored as that of a disciplinary scientist complaining that others are paying insufficient attention to his scientific field. Instead, I believe Maynard-Smith is attempting to remind A-Lifers that, *first and foremost*, capital-B-Biological theories (whether derived from the study of natural or artificial organisms) must apply to the most diverse and robust instances of life available to us—natural life, the domain of little-b-biology. And you cannot apply your theories to the biological world if you do not know the "facts" of contemporary biology.

2) *Artificial organisms and natural life are genetically __dis__-similar.*

When you get to the bottom of things, this is the essential difference between A-Life and little-b-biology. Where biology studies natural life—life-as-we-know-it—life as we have found it here on earth, the product of billions of years of natural forces, Artificial Life seeks to study Biological processes wrought by human hands. It might turn out to be the case that there is no scientifically interesting example of a Biological process that does not have a natural origin, but the entire edifice of A-Life rests on the rejection of this intuition. Indeed, A-Lifers claim to have already begun to take the initial steps towards creating artificial (in the sense of man-made) organisms. More than anything else, what is *artificial* about artificial life is that it is literally "life made by Man rather than by Nature" [Langton 1989].

3) *Artificial organisms and natural life must be to some degree functionally related.*

This is the crux of the initial claim that natural life is the touchstone of A-Life. Recall how artificial strawberry flavoring must taste similar to natural strawberries in order to be a kind of strawberry flavoring (as opposed to blueberry or some other flavoring). Artificial Life finds itself in the same position. In order to claim that it is studying something of the same kind as what traditional biologists study, artificial organisms need to share at least some general description with natural organisms.

More often than not, the only relationship artificial organisms have to natural life is a functional relationship. Take for example, Terzopoulos, Tu, and Grzeszczuk's work simulating fish behavior. Terzopoulos and his colleagues have created a highly detailed computational model of the watery world of fish, that allows them to define bodies (fish and sharks with fins) and to determine how those bodies would move in a liquid medium. They combine this with a relatively complex model of fish musculature. Their system allows for the creation of very life-like graphics animation. They write that,

"The long-term goal of our research is a computational theory that can potentially account for the interplay of physics, locomotion, perception, behavior, and learning in higher animals. A good touchstone of such a theory is its ability to produce visually convincing results in the form of realistic computer graphics animation with little or no [human] animator intervention." [328]

Such a goal—to produce convincingly realistic animation—is to attempt to capture a rather abstract functional characterization of a biological phenomenon, in this case, the visual appearance of fish and shark locomotion. But such artificial organisms as these share little if any compositional similarity with biological fish, nor does anyone wish to claim such. The parts of the biological fish (muscles, skin, etc.), and how they are arranged such that locomotion can be seen, are very different indeed from the parts of the artificial fish (data structures, programs) which produce the realistic graphics on the computer monitor. This is not to say that building such models is scientifically pointless. Quite the contrary, such functional modeling can act as elegant tests of our ethological and biophysical understanding of animal locomotion. Nonetheless, such artificial organisms are artificial in both senses of the term.

The pursuit of functional similarity has a distinguished history. We can find a precedent in artificial intelligence (AI). In 1949, Alan Turing [1990], seeking to do an end-run around laborious arguments and counter-arguments about the definition of "intelligence", suggested an "imitation game" as a sufficiency test for intelligence. Turing's move was to avoid the endless debate about the precise necessary and sufficient conditions for intelligence. He instead posed a difficult test of intelligence, suggesting that *surely if* something could pass such a test, then we would have sufficient warrant to call it intelligent, even if there were putative intelligent beings that *could not* meet such a difficult criterion.

The Turing Test (as it came to be known) involved a human interrogator who could interact with both another adult human and an (alleged) AI via a teletype. The interrogator's task was to determine who was the human and who was the AI. She could ask the two opponents questions, play games (such as chess or go) with them, have them tell jokes, and so on—whatever she thought might expose a non-intelligent impostor machine. Surely, Turing argued, anything which could do as well as a human on such a test (or a battery of such tests) should be considered as intelligent as its human opponents.

The brilliance of the Turing Test is that the sufficient criterion is not some objective criterion, such as the ability to answer riddles, solve equations, or to play grandmaster-level chess, but rather a subjective one. To pass the Turing Test, one must be able to convince an intelligent entity that one is likewise intelligent. The Turing Test is an imitation game. Turing recognized that much of what it means to be intelligent is to be able to participate unobtrusively in a community of intelligent beings. A sufficient condition of intelligence is to be accepted as intelligent by those who have already been deemed such.

4) *It is possible for artificial organisms to share compositional similarities with natural life; that is, nature identical organisms are a possibility.*

Nature identical artificial organisms are those which share not only a functional relationship with natural life, but which produce that similarity with similar parts and through related processes involving those parts.

For example, it is easy to see how attempts to create "alternative chemistries of life" might be compositionally related to natural processes. There is little reason to believe that the set of interacting chemical compounds exhibited in nature—the particular set of proteins, amino acids, sugars, etc.—are the only set of agents capable of carrying out such biological processes as replication, metabolism, and homeostasis. Scientists who experimentally investigate the origin of life—how the first replicating molecules arose—are investigating a type of artificial life. It makes sense to suggest that such artificial-life-in-a-test-tube might be both functionally and compositionally related to natural life. Indeed, life-as-we-know-it may have evolved out of something very much like these chemical systems.

5 Evaluating Biological Robotics: two tests

In this final section, I want to apply the philosophical discussion above to a specific area of A-Life: biological robotics. A number of individuals who are interested in A-Life are also interested in building robots [Beer 1990], [Beer, *et al* 1993], [Connell 1990], [Cliff 1990], [Cliff 1995] (see also the work of Rodney Brooks and Mark Tilden). When you put these two interests together, you get a different approach to both Biology and robot building. (I use the term "Biological Robotics" to distinguish the attempt to build Biologically-interesting robots from the more standard approaches to robot building.) What are the specific implications of what I have discussed above for research in this specific area?

We noted above Turing's insight that intelligence can be treated as a communal property—a property bestowed by a community which is already possesses it. Life too can be seen as a communal property. Living things typically exist within a web of other living things; within an ecology. Biological organisms often rely on other organisms for nutritional substance. Species that practice sex rely on others for reproduction. The existence and behavior of other organisms undoubtedly has a great effect on the reproductive success of virtually all organisms.

It makes sense then to consider a Turing-style imitation game within the context of A-Life. The intuition is that *surely if* some artificial organism were able to convince living things to treat it as if it were alive, then we would have sufficient warrant to declare that artificial organism "alive". I want to suggest two possible imitation games.

5.1 The Purring Test

The first test, which I call the "Purring Test", is taken from an idea first presented by Mark Tilden at *Artificial Life III* [Santa Fe, NM June 15-19, 1992]. First, the intuition: Anyone who owns a cat knows that they can be very discriminating with their attention. Mice, hamsters, and fish can hold a cat's attention for hours, whereas most remote controlled cars and robots from the toy store will elicit nary a sniff. Cats, the products of millions of years of selection, have evolved nervous systems capable of distinguishing between interesting and uninteresting animate objects. The Purring Test harnesses that capacity for discrimination and designates cats as the interrogator in an A-Life imitation game. This sets the following goal for the creation of life-like robotics: create an autonomous vehicle capable of capturing the attention of your average household cat to same degree as do some inarguably living entities (rats, mice, etc.).

Of course, one need not be *felinocentric* about things. Dogs, frogs, monkeys, and chimpanzees might also be used in Purring Tests. Consider a triangulation test, in which an "artificial mouse" is tested in its ability to elicit pursuit and capture behavior from cats, owls, *and* rattlesnakes. Whether we use cats or other animals is not the issue here. What is important is the claim that it is a more useful goal for roboticists (or rather roboticists who claim an interest in biology) to create a robot capable of passing the Purring Test than to build the mythical "automated household manservant" that can wash the dishes, scrub the tub, answer the door, and make a perfect martini. The Purring Test identifies a goal for biological robotics (a subdiscipline of A-Life) that distinguishes it from standard robotics (a subdiscipline of engineering or computer science).

I suggest that passing the Purring Test is an even more laudable goal (for A-Life) than building an autonomous lunar or mars rover. For while such autonomous rovers would be a great *coup* for engineering, it is not clear what building such a robot would teach us about Biology. Building robots with the Purring Test in mind could contribute greatly to our understanding of ethology. For example, such a goal might suggest legs over the traditional wheel as the mode of locomotion. This is because the behavior of wheeled creatures are much more difficult than that of legged creatures for animals to interpret. There is not a lot of difference between a remote control car which is stopped but about to accelerate forward top speed and the same car with dead batteries. However, antelopes, wildebeests, and other typical lion-prey can tell the difference between a lion at rest (which is of little immediate threat) and a lion crouched and prepared to run (which is of great importance to the would-be prey). By building animal mimics, the biological roboticist can contribute to ethology by helping to identify "releasers" of

natural animal behavior, for it is on the basis of that animal behavior that we judge an artificial organism's performance on the Purring Test.

5.2 The Ecological Indistinguishability Test

An imitation game need not test functional relatedness alone. It may be used to test compositional relatedness as well. Consider a second, more difficult, imitation game: the "Ecological Indistinguishability Test". (This suggestion is related to one offered by [Harnad 1994], although he makes "Mother Nature" the arbiter, rather than other animals within the ecosystem.) The Purring Test only requires the ability to fool an animal (or animals) into treating the subject of the test as if it were alive on a rather short time scale. An artificial mouse organism might well pass the Purring Test by systematically eliciting predator behavior from a cat, but once dismantled and ingested, the cat may not be able to digest the pieces. Such an artificial mouse would be functionally equivalent to a biological mouse relative to the cat's perceptual system, but not relative to its digestive system. Also, such a robot might well completely disrupt an ecosystem into which it is introduced.

The Ecological Indistinguishability Test attempts to bring such concerns on board by requiring that artificial organisms be able to blend into the existing ecological web without major disruption. Artificial organisms ought to be able to obtain needed energy "in the wild", either from other organisms or from natural sources, such as the sun. They ought to be capable of entering into symbiotic relationships—parasitic, mutual, or commensual—with pre-existing organisms. They ought to viable on a long-term basis; that is, on time scales longer than the life-span of a single organism. This last requirement would seem to suggest that they be able to adapt on evolutionary—not just individual—time-scales.

Notice that the Purring Test requires that we be able to identify the artificial organism relative to other specific organisms, e.g., "artificial mouse", or at least "artificial prey organism for cats, owls, and rattlesnakes". The Ecological Indistinguishability Test generalizes things considerably more, holding that an artificial organism be able to blend into a given ecosystem with as little disruption as the introduction of some other, inarguably biological organism.

(In a sense, this attention to the impact of artificial organisms on the existing ecology into which they have been introduced is just good stewardship. If we are going to introduce anything into an existing ecosystem, be it artificial organisms, chemicals or whatever, we ought to be moderately confident that it will not disrupt that ecosystem in extreme ways. The idea of the Ecological Indistinguishability Test is that the degree to which an artificial organism disrupts the ecosystem is intended as a measure of its naturalness.)

6 Conclusion

The question dealt with here—How would we recognize an artificial organism as a genuine example of artificial life; life-as-it-could-be?—is not a straight-forward one. I suggest that if we look to other areas of our modern, technological culture, we might find some help in dealing with the ambiguities of our young field.

In particular, taking a lesson from the problem of identifying artificial food ingredients, we find an ambiguity in the concept "artificial" that is pertinent to discussions in A-Life. All A-Life models are, by their very nature, artificial in the sense that they are brought about by human hands and are not the products of "Mother Nature". A-Life is the science of life of human genesis. However, artificial organisms need not be artificial in the sense that their structure and content is completely different from that of natural occurrences of life. The degree of compositional similarity between artificial and biological organisms is an important free variable within A-Life, and is not pre-ordained at the outset.

However, at all times, an important yardstick for A-Life is its relationship to the biology of life on earth. Our only way of judging artificial instances of life as living, is by comparison to life-as-we-know-it. A-Life can indeed contribute to capital-B-Biology, but only by expanding its explanatory domain beyond that of life-on-earth, and not by *ignoring* the phenomena of traditional biology.

This rather abstract, philosophical discussion of the goals of A-Life can be put to work and I do so in the last section of the paper. I take up, as just one example, the project of biological robotics, the attempt to build biologically-realistic automata. The goal of building biological robotics which are related to animals in functional and compositional ways suggests two tests. The first, the Purring test, makes existing animals the arbiters of our work, and suggests the goal of building robots that animals will interact with in natural ways. The second, the Ecological Indistinguishability test, sets a higher standard. Passing this test requires building ecologically sound robots—robots that can participate in existing ecological contexts in such a way as not to disrupt them too greatly.

This speculative discussion is not offered as the final word on how to evaluate our progress within artificial life. Instead, it offers us concrete, workable goals and might offer a guide for the next few years. It is my hope that the current paper will generate more thought and more clarity as to what exactly artificial life seeks to do when its proponents attempt to create "life-as-it-could-be".

Acknowledgements

This paper has benefitted from feedback from Sandy Mitchell, Laura Perini, and an anonymous reviewer. Thanks also go to Dr. Charles Taylor for putting me onto this topic in the first place.

References

[Beer 1990]
R. D. Beer, *Intelligence as Adaptive Behavior: An Experiment in Computational Neuroethology*. San Diego: Academic Press, 1990.

[Beer, et al 1993]
R. D. Beer, R.E. Ritzmann, and T. McKenna (eds.), *Biological Neural Networks in Invertebrate Neuroethology and Robotics.* Academic Press, 1993.

[Boden forthcoming]
Margaret Boden (ed.), *Philosophy of Artificial Life*. Oxford University Press, forthcoming.

[Cliff 1990]
Dave Cliff, "Computational neuroethology: a provisional manifesto", in *From animals to animats: Proceedings of the first international conference on simulation of adaptive behavior (SAB90)*, J.-A. Meyer and S. W. Wilson, eds. Cambridge MA: MIT Press, 1990: 29-39.

[Cliff 1995]
Dave Cliff, "Neuroethology, Computational" in *Handbook of Brain Theory and Neural Networks*, M. A. Arbib (ed.). MIT Press, 1995.

[Connell 1990]
Jonathan H. Connell, *Minimalist mobile robotics: a colony-style architecture for an artificial creature*. Boston: Academic Press, 1990.

[Cummins 1980]
Robert Cummins, "Functional Analysis" in N. Block (ed.), *Readings in Philosophy of Psychology, Vol. 1*. Cambridge, MA: Harvard University Press, 1980.

[Harnad 1994]
S. Harnad, "Levels of functional equivalence in reverse bioengineering". *Artificial Life 1* (1994): 293-301.

[James 1981]
William James, *The Principles of Psychology*. Cambridge, MA: Harvard Univ. Press, 1981.

[Keeley forthcoming]
Brian L. Keeley. *Biology Matters: Philosophy, Computational Neuroethology, and Electric Fish.* Unpublished Dissertation, Depts. of Cognitive Science and Philosophy, University of California, San Diego.

[Langton 1989]
C. G. Langton, "Artificial Life". In *Artificial Life*, edited by C. G. Langton. SFI Studies in the Sciences of Complexity, Proc. Vol. VI. Redwood City, CA: Addison-Wesley, 1989: 1-47. To be reprinted in [Boden forthcoming].

[Turing 1990]
A. M. Turing, "Computing machinery and intelligence". In M. A. Boden (ed.), *The Philosophy of Artificial Intelligence.* Oxford: Oxford University Press, 1990: 40-66.

[Terzopoulos, Tu, and Grzeszczuk 1994]
Demitri Terzopoulos, Xiaoyuan Tu, and Radek Grzeszczuk, "Artificial fishes with autonomous locomotion, perception, behavior, and learning in a simulated physical world". *Artificial Life IV: Proceedings of the fourth international workshop on the synthesis and simulation of living systems,* R. A. Brooks and P. Maes (eds.). MIT Press, 1994: 17-27.

Differentiation of the Realms of Artifacts and Information: How Does It Relate to Parts/Whole and Inside/Outside ?

Kanji Ueda

Department of Mechanical Engineering

Kobe University

Rokkodai, Nada, Kobe 657, JAPAN

e-mail: ueda@mech.kobe-u.ac.jp

Abstract

This paper first describes the environmental problems of artifacts which we face today. There are three phases in the artifactual environment: the first one where the artifact is made, the second one where the artifact behaves, and the third one which surrounds these. It second clarifies that the key issues to be discussed are the parts and the whole, and the inside and outside, while the former relates to self-organization and the latter to self-reference from system theory point of view, and it considers how ALife relates to these issues. Then, it points out the significance of the differentiation of the information realm from the artifact realm in the Earth history. Finally, it discusses the author's idea of biological artifacts which merges information in approaching these problems in real environment .

1 Introduction

Science and engineering have attempted to obtain new ideas from living systems since a long ago, as typically seen in cybernetics [1]. Recent interests have changed from closed to open type, from centralized to distributed, from top-down to bottom-up, from knowledge-based to behavior-based, from optimization to adaptation, from homogeneity to diversity; furthermore the trends' key words have changed from determinism to emergence. This is especially true in the field of artificial life.

Such terms as man-made life and the artificialization of life have been used in several ways since old times. However, it was Christopher G. Langton who proposed artificial life, or ALife as a science. Langton [2], who in 1987 organized the Interdisciplinary Workshop on the Synthesis and Simulation of Living Systems, asserted that the concept of life should be expanded from "life as we know it" to "life as it could be".

By doing so, we would be able to further understand the essence of life. If the shape of life as we know it is a product of chance and if the initial synthesis of the origin of life had differed slightly, it would not be surprising that a quite different life system would have evolved thereafter. This means that silicon-based life rather than carbon-base life would be plausible. From this standpoint, one would be able to escape dealing with the only restrictive and irreversible life system which has long perplexed biologists. It was a proposal of a general science of life.

Emergence is the key concept in ALife. There has been two opposing views in the discussions about life, that is, mechanism and vitalism. Langton has taken the emergence stance which does not approach neither of these. Unlike the simplistic mechanism which says that the whole is a linear sum of the parts and vitalism which says that the whole deterministically governs the parts, emergence is a process where the whole is expressed through the local interaction of the parts; this whole becomes the environment to the parts and a new order is organized. Emergence has the characteristic of controlling various life phenomena from development to behavior and evolution and from the individual to society to the ecosystem. Instead of existing organic mediums, the basic stance of ALife is to create emergent behavior in artificial medium using for example, a computer.

Various computational models have been proposed for the methodology of ALife [3]. A common point of agreement among all of these researches is that they all show implicitly the complex structure or behavior of the whole emerged out of the explicit local relationships of the parts. This differs from the conventional and symbolistic Artificial Intelligence methodology which begins from the global modeling of a closed world.

Since the first ALife, researchers of fields such as biology, computer science, engineering, social science and human science have joined and further developed the research. Philosophical aspect is also essential in ALife study, as Bedau [4] described.

This paper describes the environmental problems of artifacts which we face today, and considers how ALife relates to the issues such as the parts and the whole, and inside and outside from a system theory point of view. Then, it clarifies the meaning of the differentiation of the information realm from the artifact realm in the Earth history, and discusses the author's idea of biological artifacts in relation to self-organization and self-reference in real world.

2 Artifactual Environment

If engineering is defined as the science dedicated to create things which did not exist in the natural world, it would not be inaccurate to say that to discuss about artifacts and their environment is to for the first time reconsider engineering.

Showing the limitations of specific disciplines, Yoshikawa [5] who proposed artifactual engineering as a general engineering science mentioned that the problems faced today are "modern devils" such as the population explosion and food shortage, the coexistence of surplus production areas and famine areas, global environmental destruction, the magnifying of accidents, isolationism created by urban life, and the appearance of new diseases. In fact, these problems all can be attributed to the problem of the artifactual environment.

The artifactual environment includes three phases: the first one where the artifact is made, the second one where the artifact behaves, and the third one, that is, natural environment, which surrounds these as shown in Figure 1.

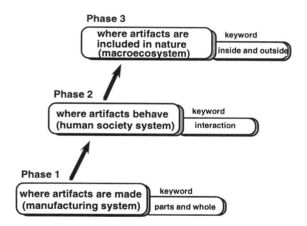

Figure 1 Three phases of artifactual environment.

The first one is the environment where human inputs intention into a natural thing and transforms it into an artifact, in other words, it is the manufacturing system in the narrow sense of the word. Here the optimization problem is how to realize the global goal of the whole through the mobilization of the elements when they receive their goals. Here the key word is "the part and the whole".

The second is related to the human society's environmental problems. At this time, artifacts and humans become the environment each other. The key word now becomes environmental interaction.

Moreover, the third environment should include natural things with the humans and artifacts, that is, the macroecosystem becomes the environment. The problem here is related to the destruction myth where the artifactual fuel is extracted from infinity and its waste can be returned to infinity. In fact, it is the problem of the limitation of unlimitedness, where the inside constantly approaches the outside. The key words is "inside and outside".

3 System Theory Aspects

Let us look at such artifact environmental problems from system theory standpoint (see Figure 2).

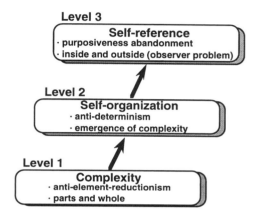

Figure 2 Three levels from system theory aspects.

From what type of relations of the parts is the whole organized? To this question, Bertalanffy [6] has already pointed out that the whole is something more than the sum of the parts. The critique to the element-reductionism, which says that it is not the linear sum of the simplified behavior of the elements which determines the behavior or structure of the whole but the whole is much more complex, as well as Koestler's holon idea [7] insist that it goes beyond Descartian thought which supported modern rationalism. Systems theory has already been beyond the element-reductionism since the beginning. This leads to the fact that all problems cannot be treated as system optimization. The problem is optimized only after the system's internal condition has been determined, and such condition is maintained, and the objective functions have been fixed. However, such a case would be rare since the system's internal and external environments are always changing.

Although one thus criticizes the element-reductionism and discards determinism, it is not easy to design and manufacture artifacts. Rather, it would be more convincing to say that the expansion of the determinism would signify progress, and that the areas not controlled by the determinism is knowledge's untrodden area and savage; therefore, should be object to be conquered. Most of the problem is that even if one could analyze and determine the rules of the parts, compose the whole by the manipulation of symbols and control, one would not be able to solve all the problems. That is the essence of the present problem.

Now, why is not the critique to the element-reductionism enough? The critique to the element-reductionism can interpret the complexity of the whole, but when it defines the generation of the complexity as emergence, it fails to realize emergence. Emergence involves the self-organization from the parts. A whole which can be explained arithmetically is not complex.

However, that is not all. There is an even bigger problem. That is the self-reference. It is the problem of a manufactured artifact referring to the action of making another artifact. This cannot be solved by introducing feedback, because the essential problem of self-reference is the problem of the observer. This is equivalent to the aforementioned problem of inside and outside in the artifactual environment. After setting a boundary, the more one inquires into the controllability and optimization within the boundary, the more uncontrollable the external side becomes. In other words, only when the observer is able to stand outside the environment, the environmental problem becomes an internal one and the optimization of the inside becomes possible. However, as the realm of the artifact expands it crosses the boundary and the observer is forced to appear in the inside. This is the essential point of self-reference. At such a time, it becomes impossible to indicate the system's input and output.

In fact, self-reference is also related to problem the first one. It becomes a self-reference problem of the objective of the manufacturing system which designs and manufactures an artifact. Unlike such systems as the system of heavenly bodies, an engineering system is purposiveness oriented. In reality, such infallibility breaks down. Besides the abandonment of a purposiveness in a practical science such as engineering, the loss of necessity is a more difficult problem than the anti-element-reductionism and the self-organization problem.

How does such discussion of the part and the whole, i.e. self-organization, and inside and outside, i.e. self-reference relate to ALife. It is evident that ALife has noticed the complexity which is more than the sum of parts. The way to solving self-organization is advancing with an approach which realizes emergent behavior. However, advances in self-reference are insufficient. More than this, there seems to be no clear direction of approaches to solve the problem. That is, if ALife can first prescribe the inside and outside, it may be possible to achieve self-organization which will be the inside, but the problem of the observer who sets the boundary between the outside and the inside has not been solved. Autopoiesis [8] attempts to theorize this problem.

4 Differentiation of the Realm of Information

As it is clear by now, the difficulty of solving the modern devils is closely related to the difficulty of self-organization and the handling of self-reference in the artifact environment. Having said this, the author would like to consider the role of information within the artifact issue.

The so-called environmental problem has been considered a problem of materials and energy. In reality, information is also important, and it is the main point to be discussed here. The Earth which originated approximately 4.5 billion years ago was differentiated into earth, air and water, then the realm of living organisms differentiated from the realm of water, as shown in Figure 3.

The first signs of life are said to have appeared approximately 3.6 billion years ago. After which, evolution repeated itself, creating tens of millions of species up to now, thus we have a diverse ecosystem. Human has created various artifacts, and while realizing personal dreams and longings he made society and state prosper. He developed culture and built civilization. Humanity now is glorifying the so-called realm of artifacts.

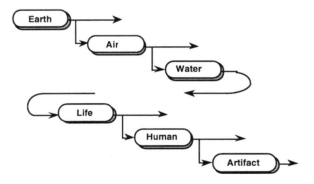

Figure 3   The differentiation of realms in the Earth.

However, the over-expansion of the realm of artifacts has seriously affected the degradation of natural resources and the global ecosystem, and has brought such serious problems as the reckless increase of artifacts, the overflow of empty information and the alienation of human.

From the beginning, living organisms take nutritional elements and light from the outside and through metabolism transform them into living substances and energy. By this process, it is able to adapt to changes in the environment and realizes homeostasis which maintains life activities. The transformation process of materials and energy takes place in the living organism autonomously without external control through the expression of its own information.

Of course, human as a living organism is also included in this chain. However, human, by creating artifacts, increased the volume and efficiency of the chain transformation but also created by-products such as massive consumption of resources and problems of decomposition.

As shown in Figure 4, mutual exchange of materials and energy occurs between the realms of artifacts, life, earth, air and water. The increase of entropy produced by the irreversible process of transformation is eventually discharged outside the Earth. This will scatter in the cooling process of space which accompanies its expansion. However, because of the expansion of the realm of artifacts, the method of extracting resources from infinity and returning such waste products and energy to infinity has become invalid.

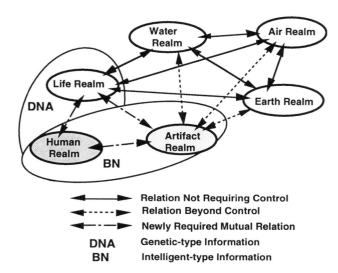

Relation Not Requiring Control	
Relation Beyond Control	
Newly Required Mutual Relation	
DNA	Genetic-type Information
BN	Intelligent-type Information

Figure 4   Energy and material input-output relationships between realms and covering information types.

In other words, a natural mutual relation without the need of control has been established between the realms of life, water, air and earth. However, it can be said that the mutual relations between the realm of artifacts and the rest has gone beyond the controllability. Originally, it was expected to have a controllable relation between the realms of humans and artifacts, but it has failed and a new mutual relation is being required.

Regarding this point, the authors believe that the meaning of the differentiation of the information realm is essentially important. Natural things are the objects that one should extract information from, and artifacts are the objects that one should put information into. By contrast, it can be said that living organisms are the subjects that express information.

It is human who extracts the meaning embedded in the object material as information when be observes natural things, analyzes their structure, extracts the elements' relations and designates symbols in formulated rules. This is precisely the element-reductionism.

Information acquired in such a way is separated from the object substance, is saved and processed in humans' brains, it is expanded and modified through communication to others using language and processed. Human's brain evolved as a storage and processing instrument of BN-(brain and neurons) type information in addition to DNA-(genetic) type information. Moreover, human conquered the individual's physical limitations by improving his information-processing capabilities by transferring his own information to the outside through stories made by invented symbols in the form of books which were then placed in libraries, thus developing the storing and processing of information. Furthermore, the computer quickly expanded the amount of information and before long information began producing information. In other words, it created a closed world of information. The author called this the differentiation of the information realm. Human newly introduced information into the Earth system structured by the cycle of materials and energy.

Such differentiation of the realms of information and artifacts brought about both positive and negative sides, as shown (see Figure 5). BN-type information acquired from differentiation improved the efficient use of substances by improving the compatibility of artifacts by propagating itself efficiently and making Lamarcian type evolution possible. In addition, the demand for the compatibility rule urged the establishment of a modern science which advocates universality.

On one side, the differentiation of the information realm caused the negative side. Because it brings about the division of the material and the information. The evolution of a closed artifact realm and a closed information realm will increase the gap between them.

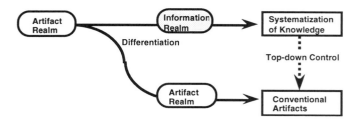

Figure 5   The differentiation of information realm and top-down control in conventional artifacts.

This differentiation causes artifacts and information to act alone or run recklessly and often bring about unexpected events. In order to control this, the systematization of a great amount of knowledge to work as a detour will be necessary. A detour would make difficult agile adaptation towards dynamic changes in environment. Or would make unavoidable forced homogeneity if one aimed for efficiency. Uniform control is simple but diverse control is extremely difficult.

It must be emphasized that originally, information was meant to tie the realms of humans and artifacts together. However, the differentiation of the information realm brought about the separation of artifacts from humans.

The biggest problem related to the differentiation of the information realm is the over-confidence to be able to standardize knowledge through the operation of symbols.

Among the types of intelligence, perhaps there is intelligence that cannot be reduced by symbolized knowledge, in other words, intelligence which cannot be based of the element-reductionism but rather one that emerges high level complexity through self-organization and may involve self-reference. Such a thing is what we ought to call intelligence. One would not be able to handle such intelligence through analytical methods nor would one be able to provide it to an artifact from the top down after translating it into symbols, as in conventional AI approaches. Intelligence is not the object of analysis but the subject that emerges. While behaving it self-acquires in the bottom up ways, learns, and regulates itself. In other words, it self-organizes and self-refers.

To provide artifacts with such intelligence is what the author called the paradigm shift from the knowledge type intelligence to the emergence type intelligence [9].

5   Biological Artifacts

How can one realize emergence type intelligence of artifacts? Regarding this, The author would like to show the biological approach which was proposed at about the same time as ALife in the late '80s.

Originally, in the realm of living things, material and information were inseparable. The inseparability of both made emergence possible, which is its basic characteristic i.e., the expression by living things of their internal information. This makes possible the coexistence of contradicting features like flexibility and preservation such as when living organisms self-realize while adapting to the environment. Emergence also allows the symbiosis of individuals that while maintaining their autonomy form a diverse ecosystem.

The fact that the information is internal is the cause for the distinction made between the living type self-organization and non-living type self-organization and the cause for self-reference only appearing in living systems.

If this is so, through the re-merging of the realms of information and artifacts as shown in Figure 6, the metabolism and homeostasis of the artifact realm may be possible by the co-existence of the autonomy of the individual and the diversity of the whole, self-organization and the inclusion of self-reference. The author would like to call this the Biological Paradigm [10]. The Biological Paradigm is an approach to solve the problems which we face today.

Biological artifacts inside the manufacturing system develop according to DNA-type information. Such a manufacturing system was proposed as the Biological Manufacturing System [11-16]. Biological artifacts developing, and continuing to hold DNA-type information

would learn through BN-type information, would self-recover, would adapt in a dynamic environment, would cooperate with other artifacts and would manifest its own functions. It would be easy to repair, recycle and dispose properly such artifacts. In addition, the artifact would evolve along with the maturing of culture, live in symbiosis with human beings and other living organisms as a member of the macroecosystem, and may eventually link to nature's chain. In other words, the artifact would adapt and evolve in the macroecosystem.

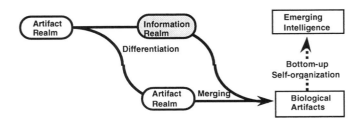

Figure 6   Merging of information realm and bottom-up self-organization in biological artifacts.

However, the characteristic of the biological artifacts, that the behavior of the whole which emerges from the part is non-deterministic creates the expectation of the appearance of diversity while suggesting uncontrollability. But if we look at present artifacts, can we really say that such systems are perfectly predictable and controllable? In reality, presupposing that artifacts such as robots and programs are deterministic is a type of fantasy. So rather, one must think of emergence-type artifacts. Adaptation not optimization is what we are looking for.

6   Conclusion

In this paper, the author has discussed the relation of ALife to the present engineering problems in the artifactual environment from the standpoint of the systems theory. The author suggested that there is a source of the problem in the differentiation of the information realm, and explained the biological artifact approach which merges information.

There is much expectation for ALife, which uses emergence as its key word. At the same time, there are criticisms. There are such criticisms as the moral questions of "the dangers of creating life", biologists ask, "If even the definition of natural life is unclear can one define ALife?" Conservative engineers inquire, "Isn't the undeterministic characteristic of emergence inappropriate for optimization?" Moreover, good old fashioned AI criticize that "it is not a new paradigm but a repetition of the symbol-pattern debate".

If the author may add a criticism, as the author has mentioned here, present ALife has not sufficiently considered the fact that the essence of natural life lies in self-reference and the inseparability of information and the medium. When it became clear that this was impossible in principle, the author believes that ALife becomes irrelevant.

The proposed biological artifacts will exhibit the characteristics of self-organization and self-reference which are not present in conventional artifacts, in the three artifactual environments, the environment where the artifacts are made, the environment where the artifacts behave and the natural environment which surrounds these. One should not imprison artifacts into one corner of nature, but liberate them and turn them into living organisms and admit them into our world. To question the possibility of this will begin the discussion of the verifiability of a self-reference engineering model. The author would like to leave this issue for a future occasion.

The problem of inside and outside, self-reference, has, of course, been discussed by various fields such as philosophy, math, physics, biology, cognitive sciences, social sciences and linguistics. Engineering has, at last, started its discussion, although engineering is historical and society-based, so that it was a science of self-reference.

References

[1] N. Wiener; "Cybernetics, or Control and Communication in the Animal and the Machine", John Wiley, New York, (1948).

[2] C. Langton: "Artificial Life", Addison-Wesley Pub. Com. Inc., (1989).

[3] K. Ueda, K. Shimohara and H. Iba edited; "Method of Artificial Life", Kogyochosakai Pub. Co. Ltd., Tokyo, (1995).

[4] M. Bedau: "Philosophical Aspects of Artificial Life", Proceedings of the First European Conference on Artificial Life, edited by F.Varela and P.Bourgine, MIT Press, (1992), 494.

[5] H. Yoshikawa: "Techno Globe", Kogyochosakai Pub. Co. Ltd., Tokyo, (1993).

[6] L. von Bertalanffy: "General System Theory", Yearbook of the Society for the Advancement of General Systems Theory, Ann Arbor, (1956).

[7] A. Koestler: "The Ghost in the Machine", London, (1967).

[8] F.Varela, H.Maturana and R.Uribe: "Autopoiesis: The Organization of Living Systems, its Characterization and a Model", Biosystems 5 (1974), 187.

[9] K. Ueda: "Intelligent Manufacturing Systems: from Knowledge-type to Emergence-type", Journal of the Japan Society for Precision Engineering, Vol.59 No11 (1993), 1775.

[10] K. Ueda: "Artificial Life and Biological Artifacts", Journal of the Japan Association for Philosophy of Science, Vol. 23, No. 1, (1996), 1.

[11] K. Ueda: "An Approach to Bionic Manufacturing Systems toward Future Factory", Proceedings of the 3rd JSPS-VCC Joint Seminar on Integrated Engineering, (1990), 485.

[12] K. Ueda: "An Approach to Bionic Manufacturing Systems Based on DNA-type Information", Proceedings of International Conference on Object-Oriented Manufacturing Systems, Calgary, (1992), 303.

[13] K. Ueda, K. Ohkura: "An ALife Approach to Artifactual Engineering", ALife IV, (1994).

[14] K. Ueda: "Biological-Oriented Paradigm for Artifacts", Proceedings of the First International Symposium on Research into Artifacts, University of Tokyo, (1993), 110.

[15] K. Ueda: "Biological Manufacturing Systems", Kogyochosakai Pub. Co. Ltd.,, Tokyo, (1994).

[16] K. Ueda and K. Ohkura: "A Biological Approach to Complexity in Manufacturing Systems", Proceedings of the 27th CIRP International Seminar on Manufacturing Systems, Ann Arbor, (1995), 69.

Diversity, Complexity

Distance Distribution Complexity: A Measure for the Structured Diversity of Evolving Populations

Jan T. Kim

Max-Planck-Institut für Züchtungsforschung
Carl-von-Linné-Weg 10, 50829 Köln, Germany
Email: kim@mpiz-koeln.mpg.de

Abstract

Simulations of evolution are a major focus of interest in Artificial Life. Most investigations have focused on evolution of biological information and convergence in evolutionary algorithms. The formation of structured biodiversity by evolution, however, has not been adressed in a quantitative way to date.

In this paper, distance distribution complexity (DDC) is introduced as a measure for the quantitative characterization of structured biodiversity. To demonstrate its properties, DDC is used to analyze runs of LindEvol-GA, a computer model of evolution of plant growth patterns. It is shown that elevated levels in DDC are correlated with the evolution of complexity in the morphology and the developmental programs of the simulated plants, and that high DDC values are correlated with an edge of chaos.

1 Introduction

One of the most interesting and fascinating properties of Life is the formation of life forms and ecosystems of increasing complexity and sophistication by evolution. Numerous Artificial Life computer models have been established to investigate various aspects of evolution (e.g. [1, 2, 3]).

Many analyses and results of computer simulations of evolution focus on the formation of biological information. The selective accumulation of genomes in a small part of sequence space is frequently interpreted as a gain of information by the evolving system.

For computer science, evolutionary algorithms are mainly interesting as algorithms for optimization. Here, the goal is fast convergence at the global optimum of the fitness function without getting stuck at irrelevant local optima. The convergence of an evolutionary algorithm is equivalent to the concept of biological information mentioned above.

This type of information generation, however, is not the only landmark of evolution. The capability of ongoing development of life in a process that is commonly considered to be open ended is no less impressive. This phenomenon cannot appropriately be captured by convergence analysis. In a truly open ended evolution, complete convergence can never occur.

Open ended evolution has been described for various Artificial Life models (e.g. [14, 12, 9]). LindEvol-GA, described here, also belongs to this class of models. A prominent landmark of open ended evolution is the formation of complex biodiversity. In this paper, distance distribution complexity (DDC) is proposed as a measure for the complexity of biodiversity that is applicable to a wide range of evolutionary systems. Key properties of distance distribution complexity are demonstrated using LindEvol-GA as an example.

2 Description of the LindEvol-GA model

2.1 Simulation of plant growth

Plant growth in LindEvol-GA takes place in a two-dimensional world with a discrete, orthogonal lattice structure with a cylinder surface topology.

A plant consists of one or more cells. A cell occupies exactly one lattice site. Each cell has a binary energy state, it is either energy-rich or energyless.

In each generation, plants grow together for a vegetation period consisting of a number of days. A day starts with the simulation of light: In each column of lattice sites, a photon is introduced at the topmost site. From there, it travels downward. If it encounters a plant cell, it is absorbed with a probability of 50% turning an energyless cell into an energy-rich one.

Plants grow by producing new cells through cell divisions, which can only be performed by energy-rich cells and results in two energyless cells. Cell division is controlled by the genome of a plant. A genome is a sequence of rules, each rule specifies a cell division for a particular local structure formed by other cells of the plant in the nine cell neighborhood surrounding a given cell (Fig. 1). The rules in a genome form a context-sensitive Lindenmayer-System [15], which deviates from tradional L-systems by using rules which act upon struc-

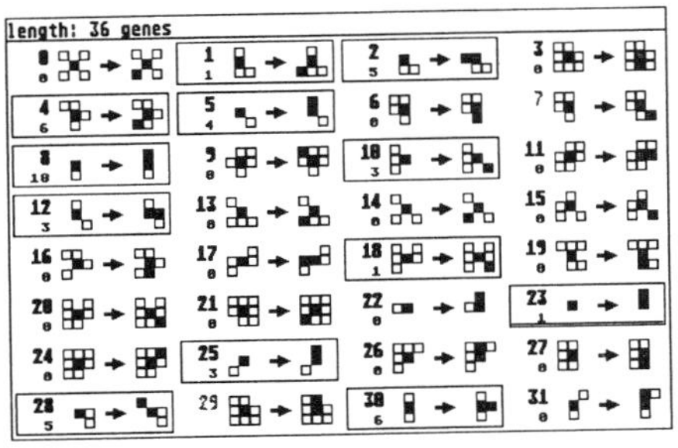

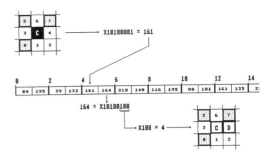

Figure 1: Example for a LindEvol-GA genome. The figure shows an extract of a genome. The left side of a rule depicts the local structure surrounding the central cell before division, the righthand side shows the resulting structure after division. The large numbers in front of each gene are the gene's index within the genome, the small numbers indicate how often the gene was activated during the vegetation period (30 days). Genes that have been activated are boxed, the germ cell gene has an additional underline.

Figure 2: Encoding of growth rules in a byte string. The activity of the energy-rich cell C is to be determined. The lattice sites in the Moore neighborhood of C are indexed according to the scheme shown. Neighboring cells of the same plants are shown as shaded boxes. They form a local structure which is mapped to an eightbit number. In the genome, a gene with a lefthand side matching this eightbit number is searched from left to right. A gene meeting this condition is found at position 4 in the genome. In the three least significant bits of the subsequent byte, the position of the daughter cell D is encoded as the index according to the indexing scheme. After the cell division, both the mother cell C and the daughter cell D are energyless.

tures with the dimensionality of the phenotype instead of one-dimensional strings from which the phenotype is derived by graphical interpretation.

Rule sets are encoded in strings of bytes with an even-numbered length. Each gene is encoded in two neighboring bytes. The first byte encodes the left part, three bits in the second byte specify the position of the daughter cell. Fig. 2 describes the details of the encoding scheme.

At the start of a vegetation period, plants are equidistantly placed on the floor of the world and consist of one energyless germ cell. At the end of a vegetation period, the number of energy-rich cells in each plant is determined and becomes the fitness value of the genome of that plant. This fitness evaluation induces contradictory demands on plant growth: On the one hand, a plant has to use energy to produce cells in order to achieve a high fitness value. On the other hand, if too much energy is used for cell divisions, a low fitness value results.

2.2   The genetic algorithm

The genetic algorithm [5] used in LindEvol-GA operates with a constant population size, denoted by p, and a constant selection rate s. For mutation, the replacement rate m_r, the insertion rate m_i and the deletion rate m_d determine the probabilities for the corresponding mutation events. These rates remain constant during a simulation.

In the selection step, the genome population is sorted according to the fitness values. The fraction of genomes with the lowest fitness values is then replaced with randomly selected genomes from the surviving part of the population. The size of the fraction of genomes that are replaced is specified by the selection rate.

There are three elementary mutation events, replacement, insertion and deletion. In a replacement event, a

random value is written into the affected byte. In an insertion, a randomly generated gene (i.e. two random bytes) is inserted between two characters, or at one end of the genome. Likewise, a deletion is the removal of a two byte block from the genome. The sites of insertions and deletions do not have to coincide with gene borders. The probability of each type of mutation event per generation and site is determined by the corresponding rate (m_r, m_i and m_d, respectively).

A simulation is started with a population of randomly generated genomes with a user specified length l_{init}. With this initial population, the loop of fitness evaluation by simulating a vegetation period, selection and mutation is entered.

The structure of LindEvol-GA matches the concepts put forward by Wilson [19]. It should be noted that the fitness value of a genome does not only depend on the genome itself, but also on the other genomes in the population. A multitude of spatial and temporal interactions between plants is possible, therefore, intrinsic adaptation [11] takes place.

2.3   Error threshold analysis for LindEvol-GA

The evolution of genetic information is bounded by sharp error thresholds [10, 17] which can be characterized as edges of chaos. In this section, an estimation for the error threshold limiting the complexity of developmental programs that evolve in LindEvol-GA is analytically derived.

All genomes belonging to the surviving fraction of the population in the selection step are reproduced with the same probability. With a selection rate of s, the expected number of copies made of a surviving genome is therefore $s/(1 - s)$. Since the parent remains in the population as well, the expected value of the total number of copies of that genome after selection is:

$$N(s) = 1 + \frac{s}{1 - s} = \frac{1}{1 - s} \tag{1}$$

In the mutation step, the probability for a character to be randomized is the replacement mutation rate m_r. In the following analysis, it is assumed that $m_i = m_d = 0.0$; since the simulation experiment discussed in this paper has been performed with these parameter settings. The probability that no character in a genome of length l is subjected to randomization is:

$$P_u(m_r, l) = (1 - m_r)^l \tag{2}$$

Thus, the expected number of copies of a surviving genome that are unchanged by mutation can be estimated as:

$$A(m_r, s, l) = \frac{(1 - m)^l}{1 - s} \tag{3}$$

In this estimation, the possibility that the random value generated for a mutated byte matches the former value stored in that byte was neglected.

In order for a genotype to be evolutionarily stable, it is necessary that each copy of that genotype in the surviving part of the population gives rise to at least one copy of that genotype after reproduction and mutation, i.e. that $A(m_r, s, l) \geq 1.0$. The error threshold for a genotype of length l is reached if $A(m_r, s, l) = 1.0$. Therefore, the replacement mutation rate fulfilling this condition for given values of s and l is defined as the error threshold $t(s, l)$. Using eq. 3 and resolving for $t(s, l)$, one obtains:

$$t(s, l) = 1 - \sqrt[l]{1 - s} \tag{4}$$

In a genome, there can be many genes which are never activated during the development of a plant (see Fig. 1). The inactive genes can be mutated in many ways without altering the developmental program of the plant, while the active genes have to be strictly conserved in order to keep the plant growth pattern unchanged. Thus, the evolutionary stability of a developmental program depends mainly on the conservation of the active genes. The error threshold for a developmental program can therefore be estimated by the error threshold of a genome consisting only of the active genes. Since a gene consists of two bytes, the estimation of the error threshold for a developmental program consisting of r genes is:

$$t_D(s, r) = 1 - \sqrt[2r]{1 - s} \tag{5}$$

Since mutations in the inactive genes can cause alterations of the growth pattern, this estimation does not apply if $2r \ll l$.

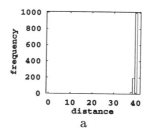 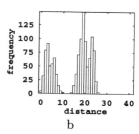

a   b

Figure 3: Distance distribution of a randomized population (a) and of a population with a cluster structure (b). The histograms show distributions of edit distances from populations in LindEvol-GA, (a) shows the distribution of a randomly generated initial population, (b) shows the distribution after 1000 geneartions.

3 Distance distribution complexity

3.1 Concept

In entirely uniform populations, in which all genomes are identical, there obviously is no diversity. On the other hand, a population of genomes that are randomly scattered in sequence space may be labelled diverse. However, its diversity has a simple structure; the complex variability seen in biodiversity is of a different type. Most notably, life forms in Nature never have entirely uncorrelated genomes. Rather, any two living beings show some degree of similarity, depending on the least common taxonomic category they share.

Thus, a measure for the quantitative characterization and analysis of structured diversity should yield low values for uniform populations as well as for random populations, while yielding high values for populations with a clustered taxonomic structure. A cluster can be quantitatively characterized by an appropriate distance measure; the distance between two species belonging to the same cluster should be significantly lower than the distance between two species belonging to different clusters.

The taxonomic structure of a population can therefore be assessed by analyzing the distribution of values in the matrix of distances between all individuals of a population [6]. For a uniform population, all distance values are zero. For a randomized population, the values are centered around the expected value for the distance between uncorrelated individuals. The distance distribution of a clustered population exhibits two or more distinct peaks (Fig. 3). These effects of the taxonomic structure of a population upon the distance distribution is used by distance distribution complexity (DDC) to quantitatively characterize the complexity of the diversity in the population.

3.2 Definition

Let $P = \{g_1, g_2, \ldots, g_n\}$ be a population of genomes, and $D(g_i, g_j)$ a distance measure. Let $F(d)$ be the number of pairs of genomes in P having distance d:

$$F(d) := |\{(g_i, g_j) : g_i, g_j \in P, i < j,$$
$$D(g_i, g_j) = d\}|$$

The condition $i < j$ prevents double counting of distance values. It also prevents counting zero values from measuring the distance of a genome to itself. $f(d)$ is defined as the relative frequency of the distance value d:

$$f(d) = \frac{F(d)}{\sum_i F(i)} = \frac{2 \cdot F(d)}{n \cdot (n-1)}$$

Then, distance distribution complexity (DDC) is defined as the Shannon entropy of the distribution of distance values:

$$C_d := -\sum_d f(d) \log(f(d))$$

For DDC analysis of sequence sets, the distance measure D should reflect the evolutionary distance between two sequences. Depending on the mutation mechanisms which are known or assumed to act on the sequences, Hamming distance or edit distance are suitable distance measures. More elaborate measures that also reflect more complex sequence transformations are available from various alignment algorithms (see e.g. [4]).

For the DDC analysis of LindEvol-GA, relative edit distance was used. It is defined as edit distance, divided by the length of the longer genome of the two genomes between which distance is computed. If evolution is neutral, and the mutation rate is constant, relative edit distance $e(g_1, g_2)$ grows monotonously with the time that has passed since the divergence of g_1 and g_2:

$$e(g_1, g_2) \sim \frac{\alpha - 1}{\alpha} - e^{-t}$$

where α is the size of the alphabet of characters occurring in the genome.

3.3 Properties of distance distribution complexity

For a uniform population, all pairwise distances are zero. Thus, $f(0) = 1$, and resultingly, $C_d = 1 \cdot \log(1) = 0$. The distance values in a population of genomes that are randomly distributed in sequence space are concentrated in a small area (Fig. 3a), therefore, the Shannon entropy of the distribution is low. In the distance distribution of a population with a complex structure (Fig. 3b), the distance values are much more evenly distributed, and consequently, DDC is significantly elevated. By yielding elevated values for populations with clustered structures while yielding low values for randomized or uniform populations, DDC meets the key criteria for a measure that quantitatively characterizes the biodiversity of populations.

A population with several clusters can be considered to be a system with several quasispecies. Uniform populations as well as randomized populations can both be

seen as systems with only one quasispecies, where the degree of variability within the quasispecies is minimal in a uniform population and maximal in a randomized population.

Thus, populations with several quasispecies have a higer DDC than populations with one quasispecies. Even higher DDC values can be arise in taxonomies with a multilevel tree structure in which the quasispecies themselves form clustered clusters on higher levels. Thus, DDC discriminates populations with such complex taxonomic structures from randomized or converged populations which both have a trivial taxonomic structure.

4 The simulation experiment and its results

In a genetic algorithm in which mutation, but no selection, takes place, the population is fully randomized at all times. If, on the other hand, selection is active in the absence of mutations, an entirely uniform population evolves after an initial phase. Only in simulations, in which mutations and selection both occur, the evolution of populations with a complex taxonomic structure can be expected. The interplay between mutation and selection is also necessary for the evolution of complex plant forms with high fitness values, and for the evolution of complex developmental programs.

To show that such simulations in which complex taxonomic structures arise can be detected using DDC, a series of LindEvol-GA simulations was performed. In each run, 350 generations were simulated. During the last 50 generations, DDC was measured in each generation, and the average DDC measured in these 50 generations was saved. To investigate correlations between DDC and other measures and indicators of complexity, the average value of the following quantities was determined for the same 50 generations interval:

- The mean fitness value. Fitness can be used as an indicator for phenotypic complexity in LindEvol-GA, as large, multicellular plants with a complex structure tend to have high fitness values.

- The mean number of active genes in a genome. The complexity of a developmental program can be quantified by the number of genes which are activated in its realization. This approach of quantifying the complexity of an organism by estimating the number of genes in its genome is also used in traditional genetics.

- The genetic diversity. Genetic diversity is defined as the Shannon entropy of the frequency distribution of the species in an ecosystem [13]. In LindEvol-GA, each genotype is considered an individual species. Genetic diversity was normalized to the interval [0, 1] by division with $-\log(1/p)$.

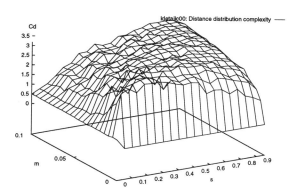

Figure 4: Average distance distribution complexity in generations 300-349. The selection rate (s) is plotted on the axis pointing to the right into the paper plane, the replacement mutation rate (m) is plotted on the left axis pointing into the paper plane. The vertical axis shows the average mean fitness value.

- The mean information content of the character positions in the alignment of all genomes of the population [16]. The information content of a character position in an alignment is defined as $H_{max} - H(i)$, where $H(i)$ is the Shannon entropy of the distribution of character states at position i, and H_{max} is the maximum value of the Shannon entropy [16]. To use existing software, the LindEvol-GA genomes were broken up into two bit components and translated to the nucleotide alphabet {A, C, G, T} using the mapping 00 → A, 01 → C, 10 → G, 11 → T. Since there are 4 nucleotides, $H_{max} = \log_2(4) = 2$.

The control parameters for the LindEvol-GA runs were chosen to systematically scan a part of the plane stretched out by replacement mutation rate and selection rate in control parameter space. The other control parameters were kept constant at the following values:

insertion rate:	0
deletion rate:	0
population size:	50
initial genome length:	20 genes
size of world:	150 by 30 sites
vegetation period:	30 days

Replacement mutation rates were chosen from the range from 0.0 to 0.1 with a step width of 0.005. Selection rates were chosen from the range from 0.0 to 0.95 with a step width of 0.05. Thus, a total of 420 runs were performed in the experiment. Fig. 4 shows the average DDC observed in the LindEvol-GA runs. The results of mean fitness, mean number of used genes, genetic diversity, and mean information content are shown in Fig. 5.

5 Discussion

Fig. 4 shows that DDC is zero in all runs with $s > 0$ und $m_r = 0$. This is expected, as discussed in (3.3). In runs with $m_r > 0$ und $s = 0$, DDC is greater than zero, but with values around 0.5, it is low compared to the other runs in the series. With $m_r = 0.005$, DDC is markedly increased when selection is turned on (i.e. $s > 0$). It reaches a maximum at selection rates ranging between 0.2 and 0.3. Higher selection rates strongly drive the system towards uniformity, they promote the formation of one quasispecies converged in a local fitness optimum. This explains why they lead to a decrease in DDC.

At higher mutation rates, the peaked structure of DDC as a function of selection rate remains; the maximum shifts toward higher selection rates. Higher mutation rates allow the formation of complex taxonomic structures at higher selection rates.

DDC as a function of m_r at $s = 0.05$ has a single peak at $m_r = 0.01$. The decrease at higher mutation rates is due to the predominance of randomization, causing fast dissipation of emerging clusters and thereby abolishing the formation of complex cluster structures. The peaked shape persists at elevated selection rates, with the maximum shifting towards higher mutation rates. At the highest selection rates in the series, the maximum is outside the mutation rate window. It is obvious, though, that DDC is bound to decrease at even higher mutation rates, as populations will be fully randomized after each time step if $m_r = 1.0$.

These observations confirm that DDC does have the properties that have been mentioned and discussed in section 3. High mutation rates lead to low DDC values due to randomization, while high selection rates cause low DDC values through uniformity. A balanced interplay between mutation and selection gives rise to high DDC values. Therefore, the plot of DDC as a function of selection rate and mutation rate has a characteristic, dome-like shape.

5.1 DDC and other complexity measures based on Shannon entropy

Neither the plot of relative genetic diversity (Fig. 5a) nor the plot of average information per character position (Fig. 5b) have the dome-like shape of the DDC plot. Genetic diversity grows with increasing mutation rates and declines with increasing selection rate. Thus, genetic diversity can discriminate between converged and diversified populations, but differenced between structured and randomized diversity cannot be detected.

Average character information content grows with increasing selection rates and declines with increasing mutation rates; it thus has the opposite characteristics than relative genetic diversity. Information content can thus be used for the detection of convergence, but not for the specific detection of structured diversity.

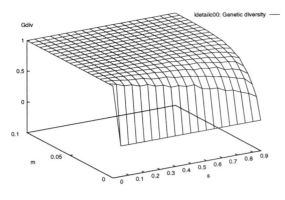

a: Genetic diversity

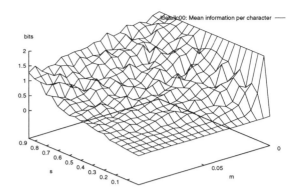

b: Mean information content

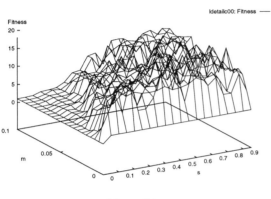

c: Mean fitness

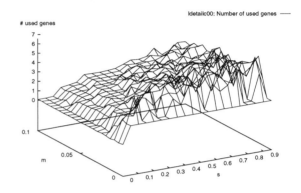

d: Mean number of active genes

Figure 5: Average values of various indicators and measures of complexity, measured in generations 300-349. In (a), (c) and (d), the axes are organized analogous to Fig. 4. In (b), the m, s-plane was clockwise rotated by 90 degrees with respect to the other figures.

5.2 DDC and indicators of genetic and phenotypic complexity

Fig. 5c shows average mean fitness as a function of replacement mutation rate and selection rate. In runs with $s > 0$ and $m_r = 0$, average mean fitness equals 3. This is the highest fitness value existing in the initial population, and without mutation, no evolution of fitness beyond this limit can occur. With $s = 0$, no elevated fitness values evolve because there is no advantage associated with them. Only when selection and mutation both are active, evolution of high fitness values is observed.

Thus, there is a qualitative similarity between average mean fitness and DDC which can be observed by comparing figs. 4 and 5c. This correlation can be shown more clearly by plotting the value pairs of average mean fitness and average DDC from the 420 runs. Such a plot is shown in Fig. 6a. It shows that runs with average mean fitness smaller than 2 (i.e. very small fitness values) have DDC values ranging between 1.2 and 2. At larger fitness values, DDC becomes more scattered, but the positive correlation between fitness and DDC remains. In runs

with high fitness, DDC values between 2.5 and 3.2 are observed.

The surface of the average mean numbers of active genes (fig 5d) is structurally very similar to the surface of fitness values. Plotting DDC against average mean numbers of active genes (Fig. 6b) reveals that for lower numbers of active genes, there is a strong, positive correlation between the average mean number of active genes and DDC. With large numbers of active genes, DDC values are rather scattered and show a declining tendency. This declining tendency is due to the fact that the critical error threshold is lower for longer, more complex developmental programs (see eq. 5). Therefore, the most complex developmental programs evolve under conditions where strong selection leads to submaximal DDC values.

These significant correlations between fitness and DDC and between complexity in developmental programs and DDC demonstrate that DDC is a measure that can be used to detect LindEvol-GA runs in which evolution of phenotypic complexity can be observed. It can be assumed that this result can be transferred

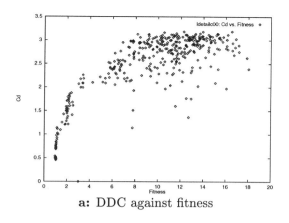

a: DDC against fitness

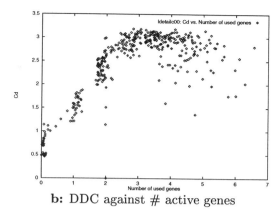

b: DDC against # active genes

Figure 6: Correlation diagrams. (a)shows value pairs of average mean fitness and average DDC in the 420 runs of the series. (b) shows the value pairs of average mean number of active genes and average DDC.

to other evolutionary algorithms. This supports the widespread notion that evolution of complex life forms is related to the evolution of structured diversity [18]. An intuitive argument for this idea is the observation that Evolution of Life, which displays extremely impressive powers of innovation and optimization, is associated with biodiversity that is no less impressive. More formally, it can be argued that effective optimization depends on the capability of the system to conserve optima encountered so far, while allowing further exploration of sequence space. In an evolutionary algorithm with these properties, the coexistence of two or more quasispecies can be expected at most times. Such states give rise to elevated DDC. Thus, DDC is a measure that can be used to quantitatively characterize the efficiency of an evolutionary process.

5.3 DDC and the edge of chaos

In none of the runs performed in this experiment, developmental programs consisting of more than seven genes evolved (Fig. 5d). It can therefore be assumed that developmental programs with more genes do not confer any additional evolutionary advantage. In runs with an average mean number of active genes well below seven, fitness values significantly below the maximal range are observed. It can be concluded that the replacement mutation rate limits the evolution of complexity if the replacement mutation rate exceeds the error threshold for developmental programs consisting of seven genes, i.e. if $m_r > t_D(s, 7)$. Thus, the curve of $t_D(s, 7)$ can be characterized as an edge of chaos.

Fig. 7 shows the distribution of the runs with the highest 80 DDC values observed on the plane spread out by selection rate and replacement mutation rate. The diagram shows a strong correlation between high DDC values and the edge of chaos as predicted by error threshold analysis. Runs with high DDC values concentrate just

below the error threshold for developmental programs of maximal useful length. Since complexity has been shown to occur near the edge of chaos [8], the observation of high DDC values in the vicinity of an edge of chaos provides additional support for DDC as a measure of complexity in evolving populations.

6 Summary and outlook

With DDC, a measure has been developed that can be used to quantitatively characterize structured diversity in sequence sets. With a series of runs of LindEvol-GA, a computer model of evolution of plant growth patterns, possible uses of DDC have been demonstrated. It was shown that DDC can discriminate populations with structured diversity from both randomized and converged or uniform populations. A strong correlation between high DDC values and indicators of complexity in phenotypes and complexity in developmental programs has been demonstrated. It was also shown that high DDC values are observed near an edge of chaos, where complexity is expected to be maximal. Other complexity measures based on shannon entropy do not show such properties. Rather, they tend to be maximal for populations that have a simple, either randomized or uniform, structure.

The results presented here indicate that structured diversity plays a crucial role for the evolution of complexity in LindEvol-GA. It appears likely that this also holds true for other evolutionary systems. This issue should be further investigated by DDC analyses with other simulations of evolution. Since DDC is tentatively correlated to efficiency of evolutionary algorithms, a practical application of DDC would be the online adjustment of control parameters of an evolutionary algorithm, aiming to maximize DDC.

DDC analysis can be applied to any collectionist system for which an appropriate distance measure is avail-

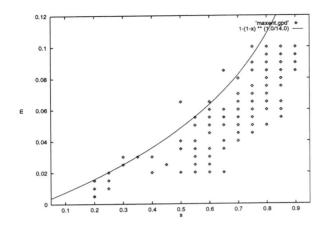

Figure 7: Plot of the location of the runs in which the top 80 DDC values were observed. The curve shows $t_D(s,7)$, the error threshold for developmental programs consisting of seven genes as a function of the selection rate.

able. In particular, DDC analysis can be carried out using sequence based distance measures with almost all evolutionary systems. Thus, it is hoped that DDC proves as a useful general measure of complexity in evolutionary processes (see preface of [7]).

References

[1] Conrad, M. und Ritzki, M.M. 1989. "The Artificial Worlds Approach to Emergent Evolution." *BioSystems* **23**: 247-260.

[2] Eigen, M. 1971. "Selforganization of Matter and the Evolution of Biological Macromolecules." *Naturwissenschaften* **58**: 465-526.

[3] Fontana, W. und Schuster, P. 1987. "A Computer Model of Evolutinary Optimization." *Biophysical Chemistry* **26**: 123-147.

[4] Genetics Computer Group, 1994. "Program Manual for the Wisconsin Package, Version 8." September 1994, Genetics Computer Group, 575 Science Drive, Madison, Wisconsin, USA 53711

[5] Goldberg, D.E. 1989. *Genetic Algorithms in Search, Optimization and Machine Learning.* Addison-Wesley, New York, NY.

[6] Higgs, P.G. and Derrida, B. 1992. "Genetic Distance and Species Formation in Evolving Populations." *J. Mol. Evol.* **35**: 454-465.

[7] Langton, C.G. 1989. *Artificial Life* Santa Fe Institute Studies in the Sciences of Complexity, Proceedings Volume VI. Addison-Wesley, Redwood City, CA.

[8] Langton, C.G. 1992. "Life at the Edge of Chaos." In *Artificial Life II*, edited by C.G. Langton C. Taylor, J.D. Farmer und S. Rasmussen, 41-91. Santa Fe Institute Studies in the Sciences of Complexity, Proceedings Volume X. Addison-Wesley, Redwood City, CA.

[9] Lindgren, K. 1992. "Evolutionary Phenomena in Simple Dynamics." In *Artificial Life II*, edited by C.G. Langton et al, 295-312. Santa Fe Institute Studies in the Sciences of Complexity, Proceedings Volume X. Addison-Wesley, Redwood City, CA.

[10] Maynard Smith, J. 1989. *Evolutionary Genetics.* Oxford University Press, Oxford.

[11] Packard, N.H. 1989. "Intrinsic Adaptation in a Simple Model for Evolution." In *Artificial Life*, edited by C.G. Langton, 141-155. Santa Fe Institute Studies in the Sciences of Complexity, Proceedings Volume VI. Addison-Wesley, Redwood City, CA.

[12] Ray, T.S. 1992. "An Approach to the Synthesis of Life" In *Artificial Life II*, edited by C.G. Langton et al, 371-408. Santa Fe Institute Studies in the Sciences of Complexity, Proceedings Volume X. Addison-Wesley, Redwood City, CA.

[13] Ray, T.S. 1994. "Evolution, Complexity, Entropy and Artificial Reality." *Physica D* **71**: 239-266.

[14] Rokhsar, D.S., Anderson, P.W. und Stein, D.L. 1986. "Self-Organization in Prebiological Systems: Simulations of a Model for the Origin of Genetic Information." *J. Mol. Evol.* **23**: 119-126.

[15] Rozenberg, G and Salomaa, A. 1986. *The Book of L.* Springer Verlag, Heidelberg.

[16] Schneider, T.D. und Stephens, R.M. 1990: "Sequence Logos: A New Way to Display Consensus Sequences." *Nucleic Acids Research* **18**: 6097-6100.

[17] Schuster, P. und Swetina, J. 1988. "Stationary Mutant Distributions and Evolutionary Optimization." *Bull. Math. Biol.* **50**: 635-660.

[18] Stanley, S.M. 1973. "An Ecological Theory for the Sudden Origin of Multicellular Life in the Late Precambrian." *Proc. Natl. Acad. Sci* **70**: 1486-1489.

[19] Wilson, S.W. 1989. "The Genetic Algorithm and Simulated Evolution." In *Artificial Life*, edited by C.G. Langton, 156-166. Santa Fe Institute Studies in the Sciences of Complexity, Proceedings Volume VI. Addison-Wesley, Redwood City, CA.

Biodiversity through sexual selection

Peter M. Todd and Geoffrey F. Miller
Max Planck Institute for Psychological Research
Center for Adaptive Behavior and Cognition
Leopoldstrasse 24
80802 Munich GERMANY
ptodd@mpipf-muenchen.mpg.de, miller@mpipf-muenchen.mpg.de

Abstract

What engenders biodiversity? Natural selection certainly adapts species to their ecological niches, but does it really create all of the new niches and new species to fill them? Consider: the most successful, complex, and numerous species on earth are composed of sexually-reproducing animals and flowering plants. Both groups typically undergo a form of sexual selection through mate choice: animals are selected by conspecifics and flowering plants are selected by heterospecific pollinators. This common feature suggests that the evolution of biodiversity may be driven not simply by natural-selective adaptation to ecological niches, but by subtle interactions between natural selection and sexual selection. This paper presents theoretical arguments and simulation results in support of our view that sexual selection creates new fitness peaks (and thus new niches), helps species escape from old local optima to find new, better peaks, and promotes speciation to increase the number of lineages searching for peaks. Natural selection is a precondition for biodiversity (because it permits ecological adaptation), but sexual selection may often be a more direct cause of species diversity for animals and flowering plants. The paper concludes with implications for evolutionary engineering, human evolution, and conservation priorities.

1 Introduction

Most research on biodiversity asks about biodiversity as product rather than process: how much biodiversity has there been, is there, and should there be? (See e.g. Wilson & Peter, 1988.) This concern for counting species is reasonable given our appalling efficiency as agents of extinction. But our best hope of promoting biodiversity over the long term may be to understand better the evolutionary processes that actually produce biodiversity – ecosystems rich with species, adaptations, and innovations. In this paper we take a step in that direction, discussing one major, often overlooked process capable of engendering biodiversity: sexual selection.

At first glance, it might seem obvious that natural selection does all the work of biodiversification. Darwin's engine of ecological adaptation seems likely to be the engine of ecological diversification as well. But natural selection is mainly a hill-climber in the fitness landscape. It brings species closer to adaptive peaks, but does it really create new peaks, promote shifts from one peak to another, or increase the number of species doing hill-climbing? In fact, Darwin's (1859) *Origin of species* did not offer any plausible mechanism of peak-production, peak-hopping, or speciation (Wilson, 1992, p. 52); it only suggested that natural selection can hill-climb fitness peaks to produce complex adaptations. We propose that Darwin's (1871) other favorite process, sexual selection, can fill these gaps. While natural selection explains most adaptation, sexual selection can explain much of biodiversity. As we will argue and demonstrate through simulations, sexual selection through mate choice can (1) create new dynamic adaptive peaks in the fitness landscape, corresponding to a population's mate preferences, which can shift about rapidly and stochastically and lead the population to explore new regions of phenotype space; (2) allow populations to escape current local optima to find new naturally-selected fitness peaks; and (3) split old species apart into new ones through a form of spontaneous sympatric speciation, increasing the number of lineages exploring phenotype space.

There are good *a priori* reasons to look to sexual selection as a wellspring of biodiversity, even before knowing many details of its operation. Sexual selection has traditionally been considered a minor, peripheral, even pathological process, tangential to the main work of natural selection and largely irrelevant to such central issues in biology as speciation, the origin of evolutionary innovations, and the optimization of complex adaptations (for a historical review see Cronin, 1991). But this traditional view is at odds with the fact that the most complex, diversified, and elaborated taxa on earth are those in which mate choice operates: animals with nervous systems, and flowering plants. The dominance of these life-forms, and the maintenance of sexual reproduction itself, has often been attributed to the advantages of genetic recombination. But recombination alone is not diagnostic of animals and flowering plants: bacteria and non-flowering plants both do sexual recombination. Rather, the interesting common feature of animals and flowering plants is that both undergo a form of sexual selection through mate choice. Animals are sexually selected by opposite-sex conspecifics (Darwin, 1871; see Cronin, 1991), and flowering plants are sexually selected by heterospecific pollinators such as insects and hummingbirds (Darwin, 1862; see Barth, 1991). Indeed, Darwin's dual fascination with animal courtship (Darwin, 1871) and with the contrivances of flowers to attract pollinators (Darwin, 1862) may reflect his understanding that these two phenomena shared some deep similarities.

Sexual selection arises in any competition to fulfill the mate choice criteria imposed by the brains (and bodies) of the opposite sex. The nervous-system-mediated decisions that implement mate choice play a very important role in evolution, because brains are a special sort of generator of selective forces. The nervous systems of organisms make choices that affect the survival and reproduction of other organisms in ways that are quite different from the effects of inanimate selection forces (as first emphasized by Morgan, 1888). This sort of *psychological selection* (Miller, 1993; Miller & Freyd, 1993) by animate agents – that is, selective forces stemming from the psychology and behavior of individuals – can have much more direct, accurate, focused, and striking results than simple *biological selection* by ecological challenges such as unicellular parasites or *physical selection* by habitat conditions such as temperature or humidity. Sexual selection is only one form of psychological selection that is likely to promote biodiversity. For example, psychological selection by predators can favor the diversification in prey species of mimicry, camouflage, warning coloration, and protean (unpredictable) escape behavior. But because sexual selection typically acts within one species, both the mate choice preferences and preferred traits can evolve more rapidly than psychologically-selected traits between species. (See, e.g., Moynihan, 1975, for a discussion of the diversification of mating displays within cephalopod species and the conservation of predator warning displays between them.) Hence, in this paper we emphasize the evolutionary effects of mate choice, because it is probably the strongest, most common, and best-analyzed form of psychological selection.

Of course, sexual selection does not operate alone – the physical and biological environment is always imposing natural selection as well. So how does sexual selection interact with natural selection? The traditional answer has been that sexual selection either copies natural selection pressures already present (e.g., when animals choose high-viability mates), making it redundant and impotent, or introduces new selection pressures irrelevant to the real work of adapting to the ecological niche (e.g., when animals choose highly ornamented mates), making it distracting and maladaptive (Cronin, 1991). In this paper we take a more positive view of sexual selection. By viewing evolution as a process of search, optimization, and diversification in an adaptive landscape of possible phenotypic designs, we can better appreciate the *complementary roles* played by sexual selection and natural selection. We suggest that the successful diversity of sexually-reproducing animals and flowering plants is no accident, but is due to the complex interplay between the dynamics of sexually-selective mate choice and the dynamics of naturally-selective ecological factors. Both processes together are capable of generating evolutionary innovations and biodiversity much more efficiently than either process alone.

This paper extends our earlier work on genetic algorithm simulations of sexual selection (Miller, 1994; Miller & Todd; Todd, 1996; 1993; Todd & Miller, 1991, 1993) to the domain of biodiversity. We begin with a discussion of how sexual selection can create new peaks – that is, new niches to be filled – in the adaptive landscape, and simulation results showing the power of mate preferences to influence the course of evolution as it chases after those peaks. But natural selection too creates fitness peaks, and in section 3 we show how sexual selection can help a population escape from one naturally selected peak to find another. Such peak creation and exploration is necessary for biodiversity, but it does not explain the existence of multiple species across multiple peaks – we turn to this issue, speciation, in section 4. We conclude with a consideration of the implications of this work for both the biological sciences and various engineering domains.

2   Generating new adaptive peaks in the fitness landscape

The selective forces of both natural and sexual selection create "peaks" in the adaptive landscape – sets of traits that are more favored than other traits – that can drive a population's evolution. Natural selection typically results in convergent evolution onto a few (locally) optimal ecological niches established by the combined selective forces of other species and physical environmental characteristics. Because these niches are constrained by relatively stable physical factors or tightly-interwoven ecosystems, the niches and the ecological roles they provide will often be rather stable themselves. Thus, the adaptive landscape peaks constructed by natural selection will tend to arise and shift only slowly over time (except in relatively rare cases of tight co-evolution – see Futuyma & Slatkin, 1983), an effect hinted at in the long-term equilibria of the number of species and families in any given geographic region across millions of years (Wilson, 1988).

In contrast, sexual selection allows a species to create its own peaks in the fitness landscape – those phenotypes that are currently most desired as potential mates. This self-defining aspect of sexual selection via mate choice can result in rapidly shifting adaptive peaks that lead the population on a fast course through unexplored regions of phenotype space, as we will see. To visualize this process, imagine a population of individuals situated in some abstract phenotype space (say, a two-dimensional space, with dimensions corresponding to phenotypic size and color). Each individual has a particular mate preference function that specifies how likely it is to mate with others of a given phenotype in their species. Imagine that this probability-of-mating (POM) function is cone-shaped, centered over some point in phenotype space[1]. In this case, the individual's desire to mate with another individual will be highest at the center point, and will fall off linearly with distance in the phenotype space until it hits zero – total disinterest in mating – for all phenotypes beyond some radial distance away from the central point. Thus if we plotted an individual's POM function in three dimensions, it would look like a conical mountain poking up from the two-dimensional plane of phenotypes.

We can then sum a whole population's set of individual conical mate preferences over the phenotype space to create a final total mountain range of mating probabilities. Those individuals who are lucky enough to have phenotypes perched at a high elevation in this mountain range (corresponding to "sexual ideals") will be sought after by many other individuals wishing to mate with them. It is these pinnacles in the range of mate choice consequences that represent the adaptive peaks that sexual selection creates, via the desires of the individuals in a given population. And these psychologically-created peaks literally compose the environment to which individuals adapt through sexual selection. (These peaks, of course, are combined with those stemming from natural selection to create the complete adaptive landscape on which a given species evolves, but we can talk about the contributions of each force separately to emphasize their differences. See Heisler, 1994, for a related discussion.)

But because mate preferences (and thus probability-of-mating functions) are determined by genes that can evolve, this apparently stable mountain range of sexual preferences is actually, over a longer time scale, more like a storm-tossed ocean with wave-peaks rising and falling as generations go by. Sexual selection can fluidly create new adaptive peaks as preferences change, or shift the locations of existing ones in phenotype space. Because the mate choice mechanisms that constitute the sexually selective environment can themselves evolve under various forces, the environment and the adaptations – the traits and preferences – can co-evolve under sexual selection, as Fisher (1930) realized. This creates a causal flow of sexual selection forces that is bi-directional, and thus, as a coupled feedback system, often rapid, complex, and chaotic.

What factors influence the positions and movements of sexual-selective peaks in phenotype space? One important contributor is the current distribution of available phenotypes, which will of course be affected by natural selection. In this case, mate preferences will change over time to reflect population structure because individuals with preferences centered in densely populated regions of phenotype space will find a plethora of acceptable mates, and will likely have more offspring. So under this pressure the peaks of POM functions will generally evolve towards the peaks in the current phenotypic frequency distribution of individuals.

In particular, if a population is perched atop a naturally selected adaptive peak due to stabilizing selection (as most populations are most of the time) then mate preferences will often evolve to favor potential mates near the current peak. In this way, sexual selection will tend to reinforce the stabilizing natural selection that is currently in force. But if a population has been evolving and moving through phenotype space, then mate preferences can evolve to "point" in the direction of movement, conferring more evolutionary "momentum" on the population that it would have under natural selection alone. These sorts of directional mate preferences (Kirkpatrick, 1987; Miller & Todd, 1993) can be visualized as a population-level vector that continually pushes an adaptive peak in some direction in phenotype space. The selective pressures represented by that peak in turn can keep the population evolving along a certain trajectory, in some cases even after natural selection forces have shifted. In sum, (directional) mate preferences will often evolve to be congruent with whatever (directional) natural selection is operating on a population. Sexual selection may thereby smooth out and reinforce the effects of natural selection.

But sexual selection vectors (and their associated adaptive peaks) can often point in directions different from natural selection vectors, resulting in a complex evolutionary interplay between these forces. For example, stochastic genetic drift can act on mate preferences as it can on any phenotypic trait; this effect is important in facilitating spontaneous speciation and in the capriciousness of runaway sexual selection. Intrinsic sensory biases in favor of certain kinds of courtship displays, such as louder calls or brighter colors, may affect the direction of sexual selection (Guilford & Dawkins, 1991; Ryan, 1990; Ryan & Keddy-Hector, 1992). Learned preferences can become more exaggerated through the phenomenon of "peak shift," well-known from behaviorist psychology (Guilford & Dawkins, 1991). An intrinsic psychological preference for novelty, as noted by Darwin (1871) and studied in the "Coolidge effect" (Dewsbury, 1981), may favor low-frequency traits and exert "apostatic selection" (Clarke, 1962), a kind of centrifugal selection that can maintain stable polymorphisms, facilitate speciation, and hasten the evolution of biodiversity. Thus, a number of effects may lead mate choice mechanisms to diverge from preferring the objectively highest-viability mate as the sexiest mate. These effects will in turn make sexually selected peaks differ from naturally selected peaks in the adaptive landscape, allowing sexual selection to lead an evolving population into new regions of phenotype space.

---

[1] In general, this function will be maximal for some phenotype, and will fall off more or less gradually for increasingly dissimilar phenotypes, according to the species' generalization curves, so a cone is a reasonable approximation. The exact shape of this function for any particular species, though, is not generally known; but the behavior of our model is robust across different function assumptions.

2.1 Macroevolutionary effects of sexually selected adaptive peaks

To demonstrate the powerful, often unpredictable way in which mate preferences can create new adaptive peaks and drive the long-term course of evolution, we developed a simulation of a population evolving under directional sexual selection. We eliminated natural selection – that is, differences in survival rates – from this simulation, so that the effects of sexual selection would be clearer (but we will reintroduce it in the next section). We present here a bare-bones description of the simulation and the phenomena we have observed relevant to the creation of biodiversity; more details can be found elsewhere (e.g. Miller & Todd, 1993).

To simulate the evolution of a population of individuals choosing whom to mate with based on their own preferences, we modified a genetic algorithm in the following way: to get into the next generation, an individual does not have to score well on some natural selection fitness function, but rather must choose a suitable mate and be chosen by that individual in return. An individual's mate preferences are defined in terms of some particular phenotype (that is, a fixed position in phenotype space), which we call its sexual reference position (SRP). For the simulations presented here, we use an SRP situated at the phenotype-space location of one of an individual's two parents[2]. Given a particular SRP, the peak of the cone-shaped mate preference probability-of-mating (POM) function described earlier is offset some distance away from the SRP in a particular direction, with both distance and direction variables genetically specified. This yields a directional mating preference of the kind we discussed in the previous section.

The (binary) genotypes in this simulation encode the elements just described in the following way. Two genes determine the individual's phenotypic traits. Two genes determine the direction in phenotype space along which the individual's preference function (POM) is offset from its sexual reference (SRP), and one gene determines the distance of this offset. Together, these three genes determine the individual's mate preference vector. Finally, one more gene determines the individual's "pickiness" in choosing other mates – that is, the generalization radius of its POM function.

As with most genetic algorithms, the population size is fixed in these simulations, at 100 individuals[3]. To create the next generation of individuals, we use the following sexual selection method: First, two individuals are selected randomly from the population (a "mom" and a "dad" – though there are no actual sexes in

this model). Random selection here means there are no natural selective forces at work. Next, the mom's POM function is constructed based on "her" *directional* preferences, and dad's is constructed based on "his" *non-directional* preferences (i.e. by centering his mate preference function on his parent-imprinted reference position). This corresponds to the usual situation of choosier mate choice on the part of members of just one sex (typically females).

At this point, the mom's probability of mating with the potential dad is determined, by seeing how well his phenotype matches her POM function, and the dad's probability of mating with the mom is determined in a complementary fashion. These two probabilities are multiplied (representing mutual consent) to yield an overall probability of mating, a die is thrown, and if the parents get lucky then two new offspring are created and put into the next generation. The offspring are made by applying 2-point crossover to the two parental bit-string genotypes, and then mutating the resulting children slightly (mutation rate .01 per bit). If the mom and dad prove unlucky, failing to meet each others' preferences, a new dad is chosen and tried again with the same mom. This continues until a successful match is found for this mom, or until she has proven too finicky (our criterion is going through 500 failed mating attempts). The entire mating process is repeated until the next generation is filled (50 successful matings).

It is important to remember just what is evolving in this population. The phenotypic locations of individuals, controlled by their two phenotype trait genes, will change from generation to generation, evolving in response to sexual selection pressures exerted by the mate preferences of the population as a whole. The preferences themselves, coded in the two phenotype preference genes, also evolve from generation to generation, tracking the locations of the individuals (i.e. potential mates) in the population. For the simulations in this section, we specified a small minimum length (.02 units out of the full 1.0 range) for the directional preference vectors to ensure that they wouldn't devolve to be effectively non-directional, and we used a (small) fixed width (also .02 units – but these values are not critical) for the POM functions to keep overly indiscriminate individuals, who would mate with anyone, from evolving. But the phenotypes and the direction of the preference vectors are always free to evolve, and these are the genes of most interest here, as we will now see.

We begin with the initial population of 100 individuals clustered in the center of a square phenotype space, each with a randomly-set directional mate preference. After this we turn the population loose, letting both phenotypes and preferences evolve freely, and record where the process of continually creating and chasing new sexually selected adaptive peaks takes the population over successive generations. In Figure 1, we show data from five separate runs of the average phenotypic location of the population as it evolves over 1000 generations under directional sexual selection. (The runs are superimposed on the same plot, but had no influence on each other.) These runs clearly show

---

[2] This is not the only way an SRP can be determined, but it corresponds to the natural situation of sexually imprinting on a parent, which occurs in many bird species and some other vertebrates as well – see Todd & Miller, 1993. Similar results are obtained with SRPs that correspond to the individual's own phenotype or an evolved phenotypic preference; we have explored imprinting largely because of our interest in the interactions between learning and evolution.

[3] In our next generation of models we are eliminating the fixed population size, because it puts too strong a limit on the number of species we can evolve and thus limits the potential biodiversity.

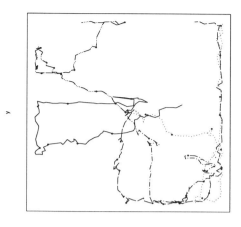

Figure 1: Sexual selection using directional mate preferences. Five runs, each plotted with different line-styles, showing the rapid movement of the population average phenotype across 1000 generations per run (dots mark each 100th generation).

3   Escaping local fitness optima through sexual selection

Species do not spend all of their time evolving rapidly through phenotype space. Populations will often be perched on some adaptive peak in the fitness landscape for a time, held there through the optimizing effect of sexual and natural selection acting together. But many such peaks are only local evolutionary optima, and better (or at least other) peaks may exist elsewhere. Once a population has converged on such a locally optimal peak then, how can it move off that peak, incurring a temporary ecological fitness cost, to explore the surrounding adaptive landscape and perhaps find a higher-fitness peak elsewhere?

Wright's (1932, 1982) "shifting balance" theory in part addresses this problem of escaping from local evolutionary optima (see Futuyma, 1986, p. 174). He suggested that genetic drift operating in quasi-isolated populations can sometimes allow one population to move far enough away from its current fitness peak that it enters a new adaptive zone at the base of a new and (and possibly higher) fitness peak. Once that population starts to climb the new fitness peak, its genes can spread to other populations, so that the evolutionary innovations developed in climbing this peak can eventually reach fixation throughout the species. Thus, the species as a whole can climb from a lower peak to a higher one. (The "Baldwin effect," in which learning can speed up and guide evolution by allowing adaptive individuals to search the fitness landscape within their lifetimes, is another potential peak-shifting mechanism – see Baldwin, 1896, and Hinton & Nowlan, 1987.)

Wright's shifting balance model suggests that genetic drift might provide enough random jiggling around the local optimum to sometimes knock the population over into another adaptive zone, but the analysis of adaptive walks in rugged fitness landscapes (Kaufmann, 1993) indicates that this is unlikely to be a common occurrence. Our model of population movement in phenotype space via mate choice is similar to Wright's shifting balance theory, but it provides a mechanism for exploring the local adaptive landscape that can be much more powerful and directional than random genetic drift: sexual selection. Here, we are relying on a kind of "sexual-selective drift" resulting from the stochastic dynamics of mate choice and runaway sexual selection to displace populations from local optima.

We hypothesize that with mate choice, the effects of sexual-selective drift will almost always be stronger and more directional than simple genetic drift for a given population size, and will be more likely to take a population down from a local optimum and over into a new adaptive zone. Genetic drift relies on passive sampling error to move populations off of economic adaptive peaks, whereas sexual selection relies on active mate choice, which can overwhelm even quite strong ecological selection pressures. As Figure 1 and our earlier simulation analyses (Miller & Todd, 1993) make clear, directional mate preferences drive populations to move through phenotype space much more quickly than

two main effects: sexually selected adaptive peaks tend to shift in an inertia-laden way, generating the longish straight portions of the paths, and they are subject to random perturbations that can add up over the long term to unpredictable shifts in direction. In contrast, when we evolve a population using sexual selection with non-directional mate preferences (centered on each individual's SRP, rather than offset from it), the population average phenotype merely drifts and jiggles slowly from its starting-point in the center. (There are also edge effects in these runs due to the non-toroidal phenotype space we used; but these could be interpreted as physical limits on the variation of certain phenotypic traits, for instance the maximum reflectivity an individual's display surfaces can attain.)

This simulation shows the capricious nature of directional sexual selection, and the way in which it can create shifting adaptive peaks that pull a population along a rapid but winding trajectory through phenotype space. The short-term evolution is adaptive: phenotypic traits adapt to the current mate preferences, climbing up the current sexually selected fitness peak. But the long-term course of evolution is continuously capricious: neither phenotypic traits nor mate preferences ever settle down to a stable, optimal, equilibrium, because there is no stable adaptive landscape external to the population. Rather, the two play catch-up with each other, engaged in a kind of arms-race that neither preferences nor traits – adaptive peaks nor species – can ever win, but which keeps them running quixotically across phenotype space.

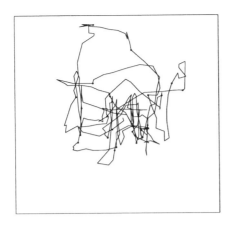

x

Figure 2: Directional sexual selection allowing a population to escape from a central natural selection fitness peak. One run across 3000 generations (dots mark each 100th generation).

they would under genetic drift alone.

But the runs in Figure 1 included no natural selection. Can we be sure that sexual selection would still allow peak-shifting and peak-jumping if natural-selective peaks were also present? In particular, would sexual selection allow a population to escape from a naturally selected fitness peak, to explore other regions of phenotype space? In Figure 2, we see that the answer to both questions, at least for certain conditions, is yes – sexual selection can operate in our model even when opposed by natural selection.

Here we have introduced a natural selection fitness peak into the center of the phenotype space (with increasing distance from the center yielding linearly lower fitness), so that, when we run the simulation without sexual selection and with only natural selection, the population evolves to cluster around the middle point of the space, no matter where it starts from. In this simulation, though, we see the evolutionary path of one population over 3000 generations under the simultaneous combined forces of *both* natural selection (center peak) and directional sexual selection (shifting self-defined peak). Clearly, the addition of sexual selection allows the population to escape the naturally selected peak for long periods of time, to explore the surrounding phenotype space. With another stronger naturally selected peak elsewhere in the space, the sexually wandering population will stumble upon it and rise up that peak (before again usually leaving that peak in turn). Thus, sexual selection can be seen as a way of making Wright's shifting balance model more powerful, by allowing active mate choice dynamics to replace passive genetic drift as the main source of evolutionary innovation.

We can summarize our view of sexual selection's role in peak-creation and peak-jumping as follows:

Species perched on adaptive peaks will generally have mate choice mechanisms complementary to the natural-selective pressures keeping them there (so that healthy, fit individuals are considered sexy, attractive mates), resulting in long periods of evolutionary stasis for most species, most of the time. But occasionally, directional preferences, or intrinsic perceptual biases in preferences, or genetic drift acting on preferences, can lead to runaway dynamics that take a population (or at least the males) away from the ecological fitness peak towards a new, sexually selected peak. Thus, the effects of mate choice can be visualized as vectors that pull populations away from naturally selected adaptive peaks out on long forays into the phenotypic unknown, where they may or may not encounter new ecological opportunities and evolve economically useful traits.

Sexual dimorphism can promote this peak-jumping (Miller & Todd, 1995): males will often be driven away from ecological fitness peaks faster than females, because of the prevalence of female choice exerting pressure on male trait evolution (Cronin, 1991; for a compelling individual-based simulation, see Collins & Jefferson, 1992). This sexual division of labor could make the exploration of phenotype space even more powerful and efficient. If the males do not encounter a new fitness peak in their phenotypic wanderings, little is lost: the males will have evolved sexually dimorphic courtship innovations, and the females will have evolved mate choice mechanisms to assess those innovations, both of which have some economic (naturally selected fitness) costs but substantial reproductive (sexually selected) benefits.

But if the males do encounter a new adaptive peak to be exploited, much could be gained. If a male courtship innovation, evolved under the force of female choice (or the female mate choice mechanism that judges that male trait), happens to be modifiable into a useful economic innovation, then it will be elaborated through natural selection – and the species will evolve up the new fitness peak as this useful innovation is honed. Having entered a new adaptive zone, the lucky population can rapidly climb the new peak, the innovation can spread to both sexes (i.e. sexual dimorphism can decrease if both sexes benefit from the innovation), and a new species may emerge as it becomes reproductively isolated from other populations. The result could look like a period of rapid evolution concentrated around a speciation event, just as described by punctuated equilibrium theory (Eldredge & Gould, 1972). Moreover, and more speculatively, it could be that if the new adaptive zone happens to be particularly large and fruitful, and the economic innovation proves particularly advantageous, then the event will appear as the establishment of a key evolutionary innovation, and may lead to the formation of new higher taxa. Thus, a lineage that starts out as a sexually-selected fluke may, if successful (i.e. if it subsequently keeps speciating), become retroactively labeled a new genus, family, or even order.

4 Sympatric speciation through sexual selection

4.1 Traditional views of speciation

So far we have seen how sexual selection through mate choice can help a population to explore phenotype space in a rapid, unpredictable manner, with the result that old fitness peaks can be left, and new ones created and conquered. But the world would be a lonely place if only one species at a time participated in this quixotic foray. Clearly there are many species simultaneously finding and filling new environmental niches all the time, so we need a way of explaining the path from one species to many. Speciation, of course, does exactly that. When a biological lineage splits apart into reproductively isolated subpopulations, one "search party" scouring the adaptive landscape for new peaks is replaced by two independent parties – one species becomes two. Here again, we can ask whether mate choice and sexual selection can help promote this aspect of biodiversity, this time by facilitating speciation.

Though vitally interested in both speciation and mate choice, Darwin did not seem to perceive this connection, and the *Origin of species* (1859) in fact offered no clear mechanism of any sort whereby speciation could happen. The biologists of the Modern Synthesis (e.g. Dobzhansky, 1937; Huxley, 1942; Mayr, 1942) saw species as self-defined reproductive communities, and yet often argued *against* the idea that sexual selection, the obvious agent of reproductive self-definition, could induce speciation, because their attitude towards Darwin's theory of selective mate choice was so hostile (see Cronin, 1991).

Instead, two major theories of speciation developed during the Modern Synthesis, and both suggested that speciating populations are split apart by some divisive force or "cleaver" external to the population itself. The cleaver splits the population in two, physically or phenotypically, and then reproductive barriers arise afterwards through genetic drift or through selection against hybridization. In Mayr's (1942) model of *allopatric* speciation, the cleaver is a new geographic barrier arising to separate previously interbreeding populations. For example, a river may shift course to isolate one population from another. Some combination of genetic drift and natural selection then causes the two newly isolated groups to diverge phenotypically and genotypically. Once enough divergence accumulates, the populations can no longer interbreed even when the physical barrier disappears, and so are recognized as separate species. Speciation for Mayr was a side-effect of geographical separation.

In Dobzhansky's (1937) model of *sympatric* speciation, the cleaver is more abstract: it is a low-fitness valley in an adaptive landscape, rather than a barrier in geographic space. For example, an adaptive landscape might develop two high-fitness peaks (niches) separated by a low-fitness valley. This valley could enforce disruptive selection against interbreeding between the peaks, thereby driving an original population to split and diverge towards the separate peaks in two polymorphic subpopulations. Dobzhansky further suggested that after divergence, reproductive isolation evolves through selection against hybridization: since hybrids will usually fall in the lower-fitness valley, mechanisms to prevent cross-breeding between the separate populations will tend to evolve. Thus the evolution of reproductive isolation (speciation itself) is viewed as a conservative process of consolidating adaptive change rather than a radical process of differentiation.

4.2 A model of speciation via sexual selection

But can speciation occur, not through the action of a natural selection cleaver, but as the result of a sexual selection carrot? To test the logical possibility of speciation without either type of cleaver, we first used a form of our sexual selection simulation described in section 2 that allowed for the possibility of spontaneous sympatric speciation. We did this by simply leaving out the directional component of the mate preferences, so that they are determined solely by the individual's sexual reference position (either based on their parent's or their own phenotype) and mate pickiness. With this setup, instead of the population running around phenotype space in a mad capricious dash, it oozes about much more slowly, but is also much more likely to split apart – speciate – into two independent species. New species break free from old ones, and they slowly evolve apart under the constant action of genetic drift in this small population size. Often in this low-dimensionality phenotype space the newly formed species will drift back together into a coherent whole, but in nature this is extremely unlikely to happen – speciation is a one-way street (see Todd & Miller, 1991, 1993 for detailed results).

Of course, the most convincing demonstration of the power of sexual selection to create new species that can independently find different niches is to see speciation happen in our model with directional mate preferences in place. In this case, when two new species are formed and their average directional preference vectors point in different directions, the two subpopulations will head off on two rapidly diverging trajectories through phenotype space. This is essential for the creation of true biodiversity – both the formation of new species, and the impetus for them to move away at a good clip from their current fitness peak to other regions of phenotype space, ensuring that they will grow more unique over time.

This feature of continuing rapid species divergence was missing from our early non-directional speciation results, where only the slow process of drift operated to push species apart. But similarly, speciation rarely occurred in the directional selection-inspired wanderings in Figures 1 and 2, primarily because the powerful directional preferences acting there overwhelmed most divisive jostling random effects necessary for the population to split into new species – the individuals, in essence, were swept away by the relentless urge for mates in a certain direction, and never had time to stop and ponder the random fluctuations that might have allowed them to begin to differ in desires from their fellow species-mates. Therefore, to allow speciation to begin to happen in a directional selection context, we had to break down some of the strength of the directional preferences. We did this by simply doubling the length (number of bits) of the genes that code the phenotypic traits and preferences of individuals, so that mutation will move these values around more slowly. We also kept the directional preference vectors small and the POM pickiness high, to help retard the sexually selected peak shifts.

As a result, when we made these parametric changes to our model, we observed just what we had hoped to see: both the speciation and fairly rapid directional divergence between new species that can be seen in Figure 3. Here we've plotted one run across 1000 generations, showing the location and relative size of each species cluster every 10 generations; when there is more than one species present at a given generation, a line is drawn connecting the centers of each to indicate which ones appeared simultaneously. The species here still tend to stay fairly close together in phenotype space, and to rejoin each other frequently, but these peculiarities may largely stem from the fixed population size. Our next simulations, with larger population sizes and with natural selection in place, are beginning to show that new species can escape from the peaks they are born on to new peaks elsewhere in phenotype space.

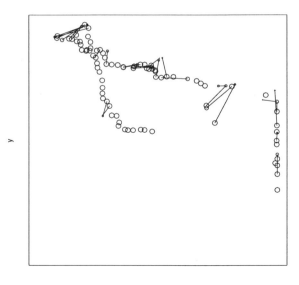

Figure 3: Directional sexual selection and speciation operating simultaneously. One run across 1000 generations, with the locations and relative sizes of each species plotted as a circle every 10 generations (lines connect multiple species present in the same generation, indicating an instance of speciation).

4.3 Sexual selection, speciation, and the origins of biodiversity

Simulations of this sort, of course, are only one piece of evidence in support of the idea that sympatric speciation through mate choice is important in the creation of biodiversity. There is also biological evidence that speciation rates are indeed higher when selective mate choice plays a more important role. Ryan (1986) found a correlation between cladal diversity in frogs and complexity of their inner ear organs (amphibian papilla), which are responsible for the operation of female choice on male calls. He reasoned that "since mating call divergence is an important component in the speciation process, differences in the number of species in each lineage should be influenced by structural variation of the inner ear [and hence the operation of mate choice]" (p. 1379). Immelmann (1972, p. 167) has argued that mate preferences derived from imprinting on the phenotypes of one's parents may speed speciation in ducks, geese, and the like: "imprinting may be of special advantage in any rapidly evolving group, as well as wherever several closely related and similar species occur in the same region [i.e. sympatric situations]."

Vertebrates are one thing – certainly birds do it. But bees? The enormous diversity of insects (at least 750,000 documented species, maybe as many as 10 million in the wild) might seem at first sight to contradict the notion that mate choice facilitates speciation, since few (except Darwin; see also Partridge, 1994) seem willing to attribute much mate choice to

insects. But Eberhard (1985, 1991, 1992) has shown that male insect genitalia evolve largely through the effects of cryptic female choice, in such as way that speciation could be promoted.

Further evidence for speciation through mate choice comes from a consideration of biodiversity and the numbers of species across different kingdoms and phyla. There seems to be a striking correlation between a taxon's species diversity and the taxon's evolutionary potential for sexual selection through mate choice, resulting in highly skewed richness of species across the five kingdoms. Recent estimates of biodiversity suggest there may be somewhere between 10 and 80 million species on earth (May, 1990, 1992). But of the 1.5 million or so species that have actually been identified and documented so far by taxonomists, the animal kingdom contains about 1,110,000, the plant kingdom contains about 290,000, the fungi contain about 90,000, the protists contain about 40,000, and the monera contain only about 5000 (Cook, 1991; Wilson, 1988)[4]. Although the majority of species in each kingdom can undergo some form of genetic recombination through sexual reproduction, only in the animals and the flowering plants is selective mate choice of central importance. Of

---

[4] It should be noted that sampling biases probably accounts for some of the skewness here: many animals and plants are larger and easier to notice and to classify than fungi, protists, or monera. But it is expected that a large proportion of the species still to be identified are insects and other small, but sexually discriminating, animals (Wilson, 1988).

the 290,000 documented species of plants, about 250,000 are angiosperms (flowering plants) frequently fertilized by animal pollinators. And of the 1,110,000 documented species of animals, those with sufficient neural complexity to allow for some degree of mate choice (particularly the arthropods, molluscs, and chordates) are much more numerous than those without. Thus, species diversity is vastly greater among taxa wherein a more or less complex nervous system mediates mate choice, either a conspecific's nervous system in the case of animals or in a heterospecific pollinator's nervous system in the case of flowering plants.

This pattern is the opposite of what we might expect if allopatric speciation were the primary cause of biodiversity. The effects of geographic separation (allopatry) should obviously be weaker for species whose reproduction is mediated by a mobile animal. Animals can search over wide areas for mates and pollinators can fly long distances. So allopatric speciation would predict lower species diversity among taxa whose reproduction is mediated by mobile animals with reasonably complex nervous systems – just the opposite of what we observe. To further explore the role of selective mate choice in creating species biodiversity, we need to analyze the degree of mate choice in the various taxa more accurately, adjust the speciation rates between taxa for number of generations of evolution (and thus organism size), and if possible take into account the amount of geographic spread and migratory range of the species involved. In this way, we hope to gain more evidence to show that sympatric speciation through mate choice, particularly through assortative mating, is a compelling explanation for the extreme biodiversity of animals and flowering plants, and is thus one of the most powerful mechanisms for dividing up and spreading out evolution's exploratory search of the adaptive landscape.

5 Implications

Species come pretty cheap, on the sexual selection analysis we have described here. New species can arise quickly, spontaneously, and capriciously, through the reproductive isolation caused by divergence of mate preferences and the genitals, secondary sexual traits, and courtship behaviors that they favor (Eberhard, 1985; Andersson, 1994). And "new species are usually cheap species. They may be very different in outward traits, but they are still genetically similar to the ancestral forms and to the sister species that surround them" (Wilson, 1992, pp. 73-74). The resulting differences between sibling species are usually reproductive rather than ecological; the innovations that distinguish species usually serve sexual rather than economic functions. Of course, competitive exclusion will force sibling species occupying close habitats to diverge ecologically to some degree – but these slight ecological specializations will often follow speciation rather than cause it.

This conception may have implications for our conservation priorities and rationales. If we view species simply as repositories of possibly useful biochemicals (selected for some ecological use in the wild and there-fore possessed of some possible medical use in humans), or of possibly inspirational adaptations to be imitated in artificial systems, our sexual selection model makes it difficult to justify a concern for biodiversity at the species level. This is because sibling species are likely to contain very similar biochemical and ecological adaptations. In an anthropocentric, utilitarian framework, the preservation of genera would be more important than preservation of individual species, because genera represent the taxonomic level corresponding to interesting ecological innovations.

But there is another, more aesthetic view possible, that would value the unique secondary sexual traits and courtship behaviors of sibling species for their own sake, regardless of their human utility. Indeed, though books on biodiversity usually contain verbal arguments stressing the economic benefits of biodiversity, their cover art usually evokes the wondrously diverse colors and sounds of animal courtship. Perhaps we can learn to combine our romantic empathy with our appreciation of sexual selection to value biodiversity at the species level for its true evolutionary significance: as a literal expression of millions of different modes of sexual love.

What role could simulated sexual selection play in evolutionary engineering, evolutionary robotics, and artificial life? If mate choice has been critical to the innovation, optimization, and diversification of life on our planet, we might expect that mate choice will also prove important in the design of complex artificial systems using genetic algorithms and other evolutionary optimization techniques. Evolutionary engineering methods are often defended by claiming that we have a "sufficiency proof" that natural selection alone is capable of generating complex animals with complex behaviors. But this is not strictly true: all we really know is that natural and sexual selection *in concert* can do this. Indeed, the traditional assumption in genetic algorithms research that sexual recombination *per se* is the major advantage of sexual reproduction (Goldberg, 1989) may be misleading. If instead the process of selective mate choice is what gives evolutionary power and subtlety to sexual reproduction, then current genetic algorithms work may be missing out on a major benefit of simulating sex.

In previous papers (Miller, 1994; Miller & Todd, 1995) we argued in more detail that sexual selection has five potential benefits in such simulations: it can (1) speed optimization by increasing the accuracy of the mapping from phenotype to fitness, by decreasing the sampling error characteristic of most natural selection; (2) speed optimization by increasing the effective reproductive variance in populations even when survival-relevant differences are minimal, by imposing an automatic, emergent form of fitness scaling; (3) promote escape from local optima, by augmenting genetic drift with more powerful, directional forms of sexual-selective drift; (4) promote the emergence of complex innovations, insofar as sexually-selected courtship traits or mate preferences can become modified to ecological functions; and (5) promote spontaneous speciation, automatically increasing the number of lineages doing evolutionary search when multiple fitness peaks are present. In general, if we view sexual selection as a process of search for new peaks in the adaptive landscape and escape from old ones, and natural selection as a process of hill-climbing and optimization of those peaks, we can see how each handles a share of the classic explore/exploit tradeoff that must be faced by any adaptive system (Holland, 1975/1992). We hope other researchers will join us in investigating these hypotheses.

Finally, we turn to sexual selection and human mental evolution (see also Miller, 1993; Ridley, 1993). The evolution of the human brain can be seen as a problem of escaping a local optimum: the ecologically efficient, ape-sized, 500 cc. brain of the early *Australopithecenes*, who were pretty good at bipedal walking, gathering, scavenging, and complex social life. During the rapid encephalization of our species in the last two million years, through the *Homo habilis* and *Homo erectus* stages up through archaic *Homo sapiens*, our ancestors showed very little ecological progress – tool making was at a virtual stand-still, the hunting of even small animals was still quite inefficient, and we persisted alongside unencephalized *Australopithecene* species for well over a million years.

These facts suggest that large brains did not give our lineage any significant ecological advantages until the last 100,000 years, when big-game hunting and complex tool-making started to develop quite rapidly – long after we had attained roughly our present brain size. Instead, we propose that the human brain probably evolved through runaway sexual selection operating on both males and females to elaborate various forms of cultural courtship behaviors such as language, humor, music, dance, art, and intellectual creativity (Miller, 1993; in press). Sexual selection for creativity really means mate choice for behavioral, linguistic, and conceptual diversity, with co-evolution of the cognitive capacities for appreciating these more distinctly human forms of biodiversity. Thus, we reach a happy concordance: the same sexual selection process that has engendered such biodiversity in our world could have also engendered in us the perceptual, cognitive, moral, and aesthetic capacities to appreciate that diversity at many levels, from the spectrum-spanning colors of beetles through the endless improvizations of bird song to the cognitive combinatorial explosion that we call human imagination.

References

Baldwin, J. M. (1896). A new factor in evolution. *American Naturalist, 30,* 441-451.

Barth, F. G. (1991). *Insects and flowers: The biology of a partnership.* Princeton: Princeton Univ. Press.

Clarke, B. C. (1962). The evidence for apostatic selection. *Heredity (London), 24,* 347-352.

Collins, R. J., & Jefferson, D. R. (1992). The evolution of sexual selection and female choice. In F. J. Varela and P. Bourgine (Eds.), *Toward a practice of autonomous systems: Proceedings of the First European Conference on Artificial Life,* pp. 327-336. Cambridge, MA: MIT Press/Bradford Books.

Cook, L. M. (1991). *Genetic and ecological diversity: The sport of nature.* London: Chapman & Hall.

Cronin, H. (1991). *The ant and the peacock: Altruism and sexual selection from Darwin to today.* Cambridge: Cambridge Univ. Press.

Darwin, C. (1859). *On the origin of species,* 1st ed. London: John Murray.

Darwin, C. (1862). *On the various contrivances by which orchids are fertilized by insects.* London: John Murray.

Darwin, C. (1871). *The descent of man, and selection in relation to sex.* London: John Murray.

Dewsbury, D. A. (1981). Effects of novelty on copulatory behavior: The Coolidge Effect and related phenomena. *Psychological Review, 89*(3), 464-482.

Dobzhansky, T. (1937). *Genetics and the origin of species.* (Reprint edition 1982). New York: Columbia U. Press.

Eberhard, W. G. (1985). *Sexual selection and animal genitalia.* Cambridge: Harvard Univ. Press.

Eberhard, W. G. (1991). Copulatory courtship and cryptic female choice in insects. *Biological Review, 66,* 1-31.

Eberhard, W. G. (1992). Species isolation, genital mechanics, and the evolution of species-specific genitalia in three species of *Macrodactylus* beetles. *Evolution, 46*(6), 1774-1783.

Eldredge, N., & Gould, S. J. (1972). Punctuated equilibria: An alternative to phyletic gradualism. In T. J. M. Schopf (Ed.), *Models in paleobiology,* pp. 82-115. San Francisco: Freeman, Cooper.

Fisher, R. A. (1930). *The genetical theory of natural selection.* Oxford: Clarendon Press.

Futuyma, D. J. (1986). *Evolutionary biology,* 2nd ed. Sunderland, MA: Sinauer.

Futuyma, D. J., & Slatkin, M. (Eds.). (1983). *Coevolution.* Sunderland, MA: Sinauer.

Goldberg, D. E. (1989). *Genetic algorithms in search, optimization, and machine learning.* Reading, MA: Addison-Wesley.

Guilford, T., & Dawkins, M. S. (1991). Receiver psychology and the evolution of animal signals. *Animal Behavior, 42,* 1-14.

Harvey, I., Husbands, P., & Cliff, D. (1992). Issues in evolutionary robotics. In J.-A. Meyer, H. L. Roitblat, & S. W. Wilson (Eds.), *From Animals to Animats 2: Proceedings of the Second International Conference on Simulation of Adaptive Behavior,* pp. 364-373. Cambridge, MA: MIT Press.

Heisler, I. L. (1994). Quantitative genetic models of the evolution of mating behavior. In C. R. B. Boake (Ed.), *Quantitative genetic studies of behavioral evolution,* pp. 101-125. Chicago: University of Chicago Press.

Hinton, G. E., & Nowlan, S. J. (1987). How learning guides evolution. *Complex Systems, 1,* 495-502. (Also reprinted in R. Belew and M. Mitchell (Eds.), *Adaptive individuals in evolving populations: Models and algorithms.* Reading, MA: Addison-Wesley, 1996.)

Holland, J. H. (1975). *Adaptation in natural and artificial systems.* Ann Arbor: University of Michigan Press. (2nd ed. 1992, Cambridge, MA: MIT Press.)

Huxley, J. S. (1942). *Evolution: The modern synthesis.* New York: Harper.

Immelmann, K. (1972). Sexual and other long-term aspects of imprinting in birds and other species. In D. S. Lehrman, R. A. Hinde, & E. Shaw (Eds.), *Advances in the study of behavior,* vol. 4. New York: Academic Press.

Kauffman, S. A. (1993). *Origins of order: Self-organization and selection in evolution.* New York: Oxford University Press.

Kirkpatrick, M. (1982). Sexual selection and the evolution of female choice. *Evolution, 36,* 1-12.

Kirkpatrick, M. (1987). The evolutionary forces acting on female preferences in polygynous animals. In J. W. Bradbury & M. B. Andersson (Eds.), *Sexual selection: Testing the alternatives,* pp. 67-82. New York: Wiley.

Koza, J. (1993). *Genetic programming.* Cambridge, MA: MIT Press/Bradford Books.

Lande, R. (1980). Sexual dimorphism, sexual selection and adaptation in polygenic characters. *Evolution, 34,* 292-305.

Lande, R. (1987). Genetic correlation between the sexes in the evolution of sexual dimorphism and mating preferences. In Bradbury, J. W., & Andersson, M. B. (Eds.), *Sexual selection: Testing the alternatives,* pp. 83-95. New York: John Wiley.

Langton, C. L., Farmer, J. D., Rasmussen, S., & Taylor, C. (Eds.). (1992). *Artificial Life II.* Addison-Wesley.

May, R. M. (1990). How many species? *Phil. Trans. Royal Soc. London B, Biological Sciences, 330*(1257), 293-304.

May, R. M. (1992). How many species inhabit the earth? *Scientific American, 267*(4), 42-48.

Mayr, E. (1942). *Systematics and the origin of species.* (Reprint edition 1982). New York: Columbia U. Press.

Miller, G. F. (1993). Evolution of the human brain through runaway sexual selection. Unpublished Ph.D. thesis, Psychology Department, Stanford University.

Miller, G. F. (1994). Artificial life through sexual selection. In Cliff, D. (Ed.), *Artificial Intelligence and Simulation of Behavior Quarterly,* Special issue on Artificial Life in the U. K.

Miller, G. F. (in press). A review of sexual selection and human evolution: How mate choice shaped human nature. In C. Crawford and D. Krebs (eds.), *Evolution and human behavior: Ideas, issues, and applications.* Lawrence Erlbaum.

Miller, G. F. & Freyd, J. J. (1993). Dynamic mental representations of animate motion: The interplay among evolutionary, cognitive, and behavioral dynamics. Cognitive Science Research Paper 290, University of Sussex. Submitted as a target article for *Behavioral and Brain Sciences.*

Miller, G. F., & Todd, P. M. (1993). Evolutionary wanderlust: Sexual selection with directional mate preferences. In J.-A. Meyer, H. L. Roitblat, & S. W. Wilson (Eds.), *From Animals to Animats 2: Proceedings of the Second International Conference on Simulation of Adaptive Behavior,* pp. 21-30. Cambridge, MA: MIT Press.

Miller, G. F., & Todd, P. M. (1995). The role of mate choice in biocomputation: Sexual selection as a process of search, optimization, and diversification. In W. Banzhaf & F.H. Eeckman (Eds.), *Evolution and biocomputation: Computational models of evolution,* pp. 169-204. Berlin: Springer-Verlag.

Morgan, C. L. (1888). Natural selection and elimination. *Nature,* Aug. 16, 370.

Moynihan, M. (1975). Conservatism of displays and comparable stereotyped patterns among cephalopods. In G. P. Baerends, C. Beer, & A. Manning (Eds.), *Function and evolution in behavior: Essays in honour of Professor Niko Tinbergen, FRS.* Oxford: Clarendon Press.

Partridge, L. (1994). Genetic and nongenetic approaches to questions about sexual selection. In C. R. B. Boake (Ed.), *Quantitative genetic studies of behavioral evolution,* pp. 126-141. Chicago: University of Chicago Press.

Ridley, M. (1993). *The red queen: Sex and the evolution of human nature.* London: Viking.

Ryan, M. J. (1986). Neuroanatomy influences speciation rates among anurans. *Proc. Nat. Acad. Sci. USA, 83,* 1379-1382.

Ryan, M. J. (1990). Sexual selection, sensory systems, and sensory exploitation. *Oxford Surveys of Evol. Biology, 7,* 156-195.

Ryan, M. J., & Keddy-Hector, A. (1992). Directional patterns of female mate choice and the role of sensory biases. *American Naturalist, 139,* S4-S35.

Simpson, G. (1944). *Tempo and mode in evolution.* New York: Columbia U. Press.

Szalay, F. S., & Costello, R. K. (1991). Evolution of permanent estrus displays in hominids. *J. Human Evolution, 20,* 439-464.

Todd, P. M. (1996). Sexual selection and the evolution of learning. In R. Belew and M. Mitchell (Eds.), *Adaptive individuals in evolving populations: Models and algorithms.* Reading, MA: Addison-Wesley.

Todd, P. M., & Miller, G. F. (1991). On the sympatric origin of species: Mercurial mating in the Quicksilver Model. In R. K. Belew & L. B. Booker (Eds.), *Proceedings of the Fourth International Conference on Genetic Algorithms,* pp. 547-554. San Mateo, CA: Morgan Kaufmann.

Todd, P. M., & Miller, G. F. (1993). Parental guidance suggested: How parental imprinting evolves through sexual selection as an adaptive learning mechanism. *Adaptive Behavior, 2*(1), 5-47.

Wilson, E. O. (1988). The current state of biological diversity. In E. O. Wilson & F. M. Peter (Eds.), *Biodiversity.* Washington, DC: National Academy Press.

Wilson, E. O. (1992). *The diversity of life.* Cambridge, MA: Harvard University Press/Belknap.

Wilson, E. O., & Peter, F. M. (1988). *Biodiversity.* Washington, DC: National Academy Press.

Wright, S. (1932). The roles of mutation, inbreeding, crossbreeding, and selection in evolution. *Proc. Sixth Int. Congr. Genetics, 1,* 356-366.

Wright, S. (1982). Character change, speciation, and the higher taxa. *Evolution, 36,* 427-443.

Zahavi, A. (1975). Mate selection: A selection for a handicap. *Journal of Theoretical Biology, 53,* 205-214.

Repairing Genetic Algorithm and Diversity in Artificial Ecosystems

Yukihiko Toquenaga
Institute of Bilogical Sciences
University of Tsukuba
toquenag@darwin.esys.tsukuba.ac.jp

Takuya Saruwatari and **Tsutomu Hoshino**
Institute of Engineering Mechanics
University of Tsukuba
{takuya, hoshino}@darwin.esys.tsukuba.ac.jp

Abstract

Genetic repairing is an important driving force of biological evolution. We propose the Repairing Genetic Algorithm (RGA) which incorporates such repairing mechanism to create open-ended evolving systems. RGA uses self-repairing and X-over by folding bit-strings to fix bits damaged by external hazard. Repairing is governed by a simple rule which replaces damaged bits with copies of the complementary parts in the same genotype. We tested RGA performance in bit-matching prey-predator ecosystems changing arena size, energy efficiency, spatial structure, and capability of repairing. Divergent and persistent ecosystems were achieved using RGA when spatial structure was introduced.

1 INTRODUCTION

The problem of diversity in biological systems has attracted many researchers in variety of fields. Recent advances in computer sciences have allowed migrants to these topics from theoretical physics as well as computer sciences. They have constructed general complex systems and found many similar aspects between their models and real biological systems. Although most of the models are unrealistic, they provide useful metaphors such as the Edge of Chaos (Kauffman 1993), the Self Organized Criticality (Solé and Manrubia 1995), and the Homeochaos (Kaneko and Ikegami 1992). Diversity, or variability is a prerequisite that allows Darwinian Evolution to take place. The critical aspect is how to generate and maintain the diversity. Evolutionary processes have selected for genetic systems that are capable of both changing and maintaining genetic diversity.

Studies at the molecular level have proposed many possible sources of genetic variability. Neutral evolution (Kimura 1983) and Duplication Evolution (Ohno 1970) are plausible mechanisms and both are supported by real biological data. More theoretical studies, such as Quasi-species (Eigen et al. 1988) and Disparity Evolution (Doi et al. 1994) also provide remarkable insights

into the origins of diversity. A key aspect of all these theories is "error." Genetic systems have to cope with internal and external errors. Repairing is a proximate mechanism to manage such errors, which produces and reduces genetic and phenotypic variations. Avise (1993) extended this view and proposed that repairing at the molecular level might explain evolution of sex, aging, and multicellularity in biological systems.

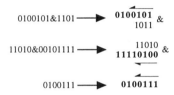

Figure 1: Decoding genotypes into phenotypes. The bit-strings at the left hand side are transformed into their folding structures at the right hand side. The realized phenotype bit-patterns are indicated in boldface.

If repairing at the molecular level is so important and powerful, it should be incorporated into any biological and evolutionary problem. In this paper, we apply a Genetic Algorithm that incorporates self-repairing mechanisms to generate and reduce diversity in artificial prey-predator ecosystems consisting of bit-string creatures. We show that the diversity is quite different between ecosystems with and without repairing operations. We also report that there are two different types of diversity in the systems; one has large population size with high diversity and apparently stable population dynamics, and the other has relatively small population size with low diversity, but chaotic population dynamics.

2 MODEL

2.1 Repairing Genetic Algorithm

We assume that hermaphrodite and haploid individuals are living in our ecosystems. A bit-string in our Repairing Genetic Algorithm (RGA) consists of three characters: "1," "0," and "&." The "&" represents a folding point of a bit-string. If there are more than one "&"s in a string, the downstream bits including the second "&" are discarded. The phenotype of a bit-string is evaluated as the bit-pattern (excluding the "&") of the longer arm starting from the folding position. If the lengths of the two arms are the same, the arm including the starting point is used as its phenotype. If a bit-string does not have "&," its phenotype is evaluated from the end of the bit-string (Fig. 1).

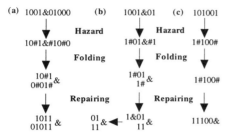

Figure 2: Three examples of self-repairing. (a) A bit-string that has been damaged at three loci cures itself by folding and self-repairing. (b) A damaged bit in a bit-string changes into the second folding point, and the downstream portion is eliminated. (c) A bit-string without a folding point obtains a folding point at the edge by the random replacement of damaged bits.

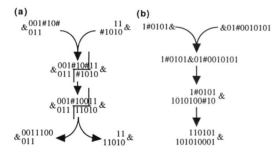

Figure 3: X-over and Fusion. (a) X-over: The right and the left bit-strings align their long-arms which are not cured by self-repairing. The overlapped parts of the two individuals are fixed by self-repairing. The fourth damaged bit on the longer arm of the upper individual is not fixed and changes into "1" by random replacement. (b) Fusion and self-repairing: Two bit-strings that have "&"s at the edge fuse together and become a single string. The new string now can fold and repair the damaged bits.

Mating occurs at reproduction, and each parent produces an unfolded copy of itself. We assume that severe hazard occurs on the offspring bit-string as parents are copied. The hazard erases the memory of several bits in the offspring genotype (damaged bits are indicated as "#" in Fig. 2 and Fig. 3). To "repair" the damage, an offspring bit-string folds itself. Then each "#" is replaced with the letter on the complementary arm. Note that the repaired bit-pattern may differ from the original because

"repairing" is just copying the facing letter on the other arm.

If the lengths of long and short arms are different in two offspring, the pair of strings aligns their nonoverlapping parts of the longer arms. Damaged bits are repaired in the same way as the self-repairing operation (Fig. 3a). We call this repairing operation "X-over" because it corresponds to crossing-over operation in classical genetic algorithms. Fusion of two bit-strings occurs if both of them have "&" at the edge (Fig. 3b). The two bit-strings fuse at the terminal "&"s and merge into a single string. Note that the new phenotype is that of the longer bit-string of the two. The fused bit-strings repair themselves by the self-repairing operation.

Variable Parameters	
Spatial Structure	Yes/No
Repairing Operation	Yes/No
World Size	$8 \times 8 / 16 \times 16 / 32 \times 32$
Energy Efficiency	2/4
Fixed Parameters	
Initial Energy of Founders	50
Self Maintainance Cost	1
Hazard Rate	0.5 per bit
Maximum Longevity	100 time steps
Reproduction Thresould	100
Maximum Run Time	10,000

Table 1: Parameters

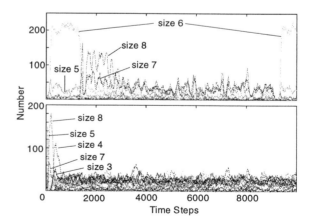

Figure 4: Two examples of the population dynamics of persistent ecosystems. Each line represents a population consisting of individuals with the same phenotypic size. Upper and lower figures correspond to a Chaotic and a Stuffed ecosystem, respectively.

NO SPACE											
NONREPAIR						REPAIR					
WS	64		256		1024		64		256		1024
EE	2	4	2	4	2	4	2	4	2	4	2	4
F	1	0	0	0	0	0	2	0	0	0	0	0
E	2	0	0	0	0	0	8	0	1	2	0	0
P	7	10	10	10	10	10	0	10	9	8	10	10
SPACE											
NONREPAIR						REPAIR					
WS	64		256		1024		64		256		1024
EE	2	4	2	4	2	4	2	4	2	4	2	4
F	3	0	0	0	0	0	2	0	0	0	0	0
E	1	0	1	0	0	0	6	0	1	0	0	0
P	6	10	9	10	10	10	2	10	9	10	10	10

Table 2: Fates of artificial systems. NO SPACE: systems without spatial structure, SPACE: systems with spatial structure, NONREPAIR: systems without repairing operation, REPAIR: systems with repairing operation, WS: World Size, EE: Energy Efficiency, F: Foundation Failure, E: Extinction, P: Persistent

NO SPACE											
NONREPAIR						REPAIR					
WS	64		256		1024		64		256		1024
EE	2	4	2	4	2	4	2	4	2	4	2	4
F	7	6	0	0	0	0	0	0	0	0	0	0
S	0	4	0	10	0	10	0	10	0	8	0	10
C	0	0	10	0	10	0	0	0	9	0	10	0
SPACE											
NONREPAIR						REPAIR					
WS	64		256		1024		64		256		1024
EE	2	4	2	4	2	4	2	4	2	4	2	4
F	6	10	3	7	3	3	1	3	0	0	0	0
S	0	0	0	3	0	7	1	7	0	10	0	10
C	0	0	6	0	7	0	0	0	9	0	10	0

Table 3: Frequency distribution of Persistent patterns. NO SPACE: systems without spatial structure, SPACE: systems with spatial structure, NONREPAIR: systems without repairing operation, REPAIR: systems with repairing operation, WS: World Size, EE: Energy Efficiency, F: Frozen, S: Stuffed, C: Chaotic

2.2 Artificial Ecosystems

Photosynthesis The artificial arena is two dimensional and filled with homogeneous cells. Each cell can be occupied by at most one individual. A living creature has a single genetic bit-string subjected to RGA. Sun light is represented by "11111" and it continuously showers each cell in the arena. Each individual first tries to consume the sun light (photosynthesis). The energy gain by the photosynthesis is a linear function (weighted by scale coefficient, or energy efficiency) of the Humming distance between the sun light and its phenotype. At every time step, a creature has to pay a self maintenance cost that is proportional to its phenotypic size, or the bit-length of its phenotype.

Predation Each individual tries to consume another individual (predation) in the arena after photosynthesis. We made two versions of spatial structure. The first one assumes no specific spatial structure and each individual can use any cell within the arena. In the second system, each individual can only access the neighborhood cells. The neighborhood size of an individual is the same as its phenotypic size. We adopted a torus system to avoid the edge effect. In both the spatial and nonspatial systems, an individual tries to consume another individual randomly selected from the cells that it can access.

Consuming another individual differs from photosynthesis. If the phenotypic size of a victim is shorter than its consumer, the consumer can slide its phenotype (the longer arm) along the victim's phenotype, and find and use the most profitable part of its phenotype. If the consumer's phenotype is shorter than the victim's, the consumer cannot slide its phenotype bit-string and can only align it from the beginning of the victim's phenotype. The energy gain of the consumer is determined by the following equation;

$$\frac{H.D.}{P.L.} \times V.E.$$

where H.D. is the realized Humming Distance, P.L. is the phenotypic size of the consumer, and V.E. is the victim's energy reserve.

Reproduction Each individual produces a single offspring if its energy reserve exceeds a certain threshold. The offspring obtains half of the energy of its parent. At the same time, the parent looses the same amount of energy. Thus, there is a tradeoff between reproduction and self maintenance. The birth place of each offspring is determined in the same way that consumers choose their victims. If the chosen cell is already occupied by another individual, the offspring becomes a victim of the resident. Thus, there is a priority effect in the spatial competition. Each individual has certain maximum longevity. However, if its energy reserve drops to zero, it dies before the maximum longevity is achieved. We tried several parameter sets as shown in Table 1. We turned off the two repairing operations (self-repairing and X-over) for nonrepairing systems (repairing operation = NO). For each parameter combination, we ran ten replicates changing random seeds (one and prime numbers ≤ 23). The simulation was event-driven and generations were overlapping.

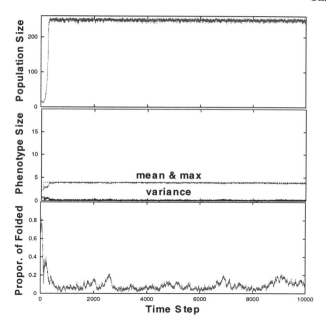

Figure 5: Changes of total population size (top), mean phenotypic size (middle), and proportion of folded individuals (bottom) in a Frozen ecosystem

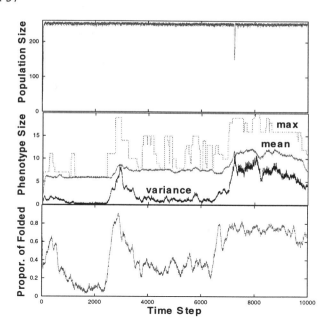

Figure 7: Changes of total population size (top), mean phenotypic size (middle), and proportion of folded individuals (bottom) in a Stuffed ecosystem with the repairing operation

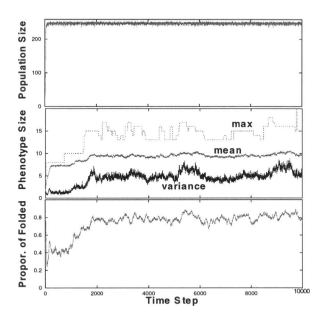

Figure 6: Changes of total population size (top), mean phenotypic size (middle), and proportion of folded individuals (bottom) in a Stuffed ecosystem without the repairing operation

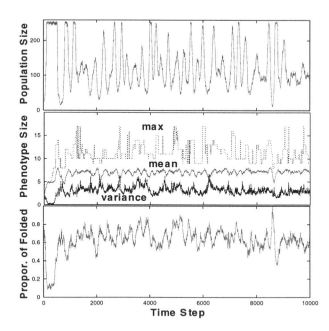

Figure 8: Changes of total population size (top), mean phenotypic size (middle), and proportion of folded individuals (bottom) in a Chaotic ecosystem

3 RESULTS

The resultant ecosystems showed quite complicated population dynamics. Figure 4 illustrates two typical examples of the population dynamics of persistent ecosystems, classifying individuals according to their phenotypic size. The upper panel shows that the first transient dominating phase by size class six was taken over later on by several size classes. In the lower panel, the first transient dominance of several size classes was suddenly halted by a burst of diversity with the emergence of many different size classes, each of which represented only a small proportion of the total population size. To examine the key mechanisms of such dynamics, we recorded several summary statistics for each simulation. The statistics are the total population size, the mean of phenotypic size, and the proportion of individuals that had a folding point in their genotype.

3.1 Extinct and Persistent Ecosystems

First we classified each run by patterns of the population dynamics. We defined three patterns: Foundation Failure(F), Extinction (E), and Persistence (P). In the Foundation Failure, the founder individuals could not establish in the arenas and the total population size monotonously decreased. In Extinction, the total population size increased at least once, but the systems eventually went extinct. Persistent ecosystems are those that lasted until the end of the simulation (10,000 time steps). Table 2 summarizes the results of this categorization. In general, lower energy efficiency and small world size caused Foundation Failure or Extinction. Extinction events also occurred more often in systems with repairing operation but the effect is weaker. There is no extinction if the world size is 1,024. Although it is not statistically supported, introducing space somehow rescued repairing systems from extinction, whereas it mildly escalated extinction in nonrepairing systems (see changes in the columns for EE=2 and WS=64).

3.2 Frozen, Stuffed, and Chaotic Ecosystems

We further classified the persistent communities into three categories. The first category is Frozen in which almost all cells of the universe were occupied and phenotypic size of individuals remained at relatively small values (Fig. 5). The second category is Stuffed in which cells in the universe were fully occupied as in the case of Frozen, but the phenotypic size increased in thresold fashion. There is a minor difference between repairing and nonrepairing systems. In nonrepairing systems the phenotypic size monotonously increased (Fig. 6), whereas the size changed irregularly in repairing systems (Fig. 7). The third pattern is Chaotic in which the phenotypic size increased but only a portion of the whole universe was occupied. Moreover, the population

dynamics fluctuated irregularly (Fig. 8). The distribution of the three persistent patterns for each parameter combination is summarized in Table 3. It is clear that the external factors, such as world size and energy efficiency, are very important to determine the system behavior.

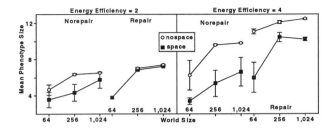

Figure 9: Mean phenotypic sizes of persistent ecosystems during 8,000 and 10,000 time steps. The error bars indicate 95% significant intervals.

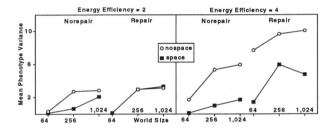

Figure 10: Mean variances of phenotypic size for persistent ecosystems during 8,000 and 10,000 time steps.

3.3 Phenotypic Size

The four main effects (spatial structure, repairing, world size, and energy efficiency) and interactions among them were highly significant on the mean phenotypic size, variance of phenotypic size, and the mean proportion of folded individuals. Figure 9 shows comparison of mean phenotypic size among ecosystems for each parameter combination. The mean values were calculated only for persistent ecosystems using data between 8,000 and 10,000 time steps. The phenotypic size increased as the world size and the energy efficiency increased. Spatial structure reduced the mean phenotypic size. Figure 10 also shows the corresponding changes in variance in the phenotypic size. Repairing systems showed wider variety and higher mean values in phenotypic size than nonrepairing systems when the energy efficiency was high.

In the no spatial structure model, there was a remarkable difference in phenotypic size between repairing and nonrepairing systems which eventually went extinct (Fig. 11). In nonrepairing systems the phenotypic size never increased and the proportion of folded individuals remained at near zero. On the contrary, the mean

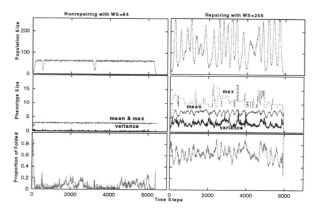

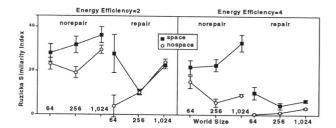

Figure 13: Means of Ružička similarity index between extracted populations of a run at sequential time steps. The error bars indicate 95% significant intervals.

Figure 11: Two examples of extinct ecosystems when energy efficiency was two. The right hand side panels are of a nonrepairing system with world size 64. The left hand side panels are of a repairing system with world size 256. The top, the middle, and the bottom panels show the total population size, the mean phenotypic size (with variance and max), and the proportion of the folded individuals, respectively.

phenotypic size increase and the proportion of folded individuals kept a high level in the repairing system.

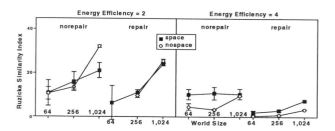

Figure 14: Means of Ružička of similarity index among extracted populations at the 10,000th time step for a given parameter combination. The error bars indicate 95% significant intervals.

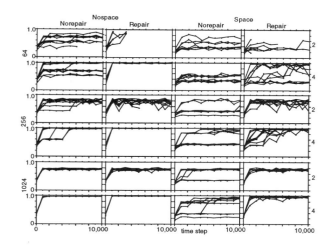

Figure 12: The temporal changes of the standardized Shannon-Wiener index. Each line represents a run of simulations for a specified parameter combination. The world size and energy efficiency are shown in the left and right sides, respectively.

patterns, then the two were classified into different species.

The Shannon-Wiener index is sensitive to the world size that determines the maximum diversity of a given system. Thus, we standardized each index value by dividing by log(world size) to enable comparison among the systems of different world size. The standardized Shannon-Wiener index ranges from zero (no diversity) to unity (maximum diversity at the world size).

Figure 12 shows the changes of Shannon-Wiener indices for each parameter combination. There were high and low plateaus for nonrepairing systems when there was spatial structure. Spatial structure tamed diversity of nonrepairing systems. In repairing systems, however, diversity did not change by introducing spatial structure if the world size was more than 64.

3.4 Diversity

Diversity within a ecosystem To investigate species diversity of the artificial ecosystems, we measured Shannon-Wiener diversity index for extracted populations every 1,000 time steps. To calculate the index, we classified individuals based on both size and patterns of their phenotypes. Thus, if two individuals had the same phenotypic size but different phenotypic bit-

Changes in Species Composition To investigate sequential change in species composition within an ecosystem, we measured Ružička similarity index (RI) (Pielou 1984) between populations at successive time steps for each run. This index is calculated as follows;

$$RI = 100 \times \frac{\sum_{i=1}^{s} \min(x_{i1}, x_{i2})}{\sum_{i=1}^{s} \max(x_{i1}, x_{i2})}$$

where s is the total numer of species and x_{ij} is the number of species i in ecosystem j. This index ranges from zero (no matching) to 100 (perfect matching). We also

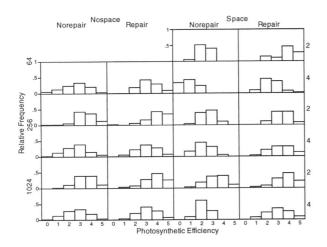

Figure 15: An example of photosynthesis gain distribution at time step 10,000.

used the same index to measure pair-wise similarity in species composition among replicates for the same parameter combination at the last time step (=10,000).

Figure 13 shows the sequential similarities between extracted populations within an ecosystem. Repairing systems showed lower similarities between populations of consecutive time steps than nonrepairing systems. Spatial structure increased the similarity for nonrepairing systems. Figure 14 shows the similarities among populations for each parameter combination at the 10,000th time step. The similarity was much less than those observed in sequential comparison within an ecosystem. Again repairing systems showed lower similarity (high diversity) than nonrepairing systems.

3.5 Photosynthetic Ability

Distributions of photosynthetic gain were relatively stable during evolution. Figure 15 shows typical examples of the distribution at the 10,000th time step. The distribution of repairing systems was more skewed to the left than the non repairing ones. In other words, individuals in repairing systems were better at photosynthesis than those in nonrepairing systems.

3.6 Spatial Patterns

In systems with spatial structure, we could not see any spatial patterns (spirals, concentric circles, stripes, etc.) in two dimensional distributions of phenotypic size classes. There was no spatial structure in the distribution of groups categorized by photosynthetic efficiency.

4 DISCUSSION

The artificial ecosystem based on the bit-matching rules showed five types of fates: Foundation Failure, Extinction, Frozen equilibrium, Stuffed equilibrium, and Chaotic fluctuation. The latter three are all persistent

but can be distinguished by differences in population dynamics and diversity. Although the differences were mainly generated by external factors (energy efficiency, spatial structure, and world size), the internal genetic mechanism also played an important role in achieving persistent ecosystems. The repairing genetic algorithm (RGA) kept systems from becoming frozen, and realized high diversity and persistent systems when spatial structure is introduced.

4.1 RGA as a selfish-gene model

The key mechanism of RGA is elongation of genotype and phenotype by repairing (Fig. 5-9). Note that repairing in RGA is not actually repairing to the original bit-strings. Each bit that faces a damaged locus replaces it with copy of itself. Thus, RGA is a strong expression of selfish gene. Selection at the lower level often contradicts to those at the higher levels. RGA enabled the local rules at the genetic level to achieve the global persistence and high variability at the community levels with spatial structure.

Although RGA has no reference in biological systems, this algorithm shares several aspects with stem-loop formation in DNA and RNA. Forsdyke (Forsdyke 1995) found "fossil records" of such stem-loops in DNA and discusses the role the stem-loops play in repair and recombination of genetic materials at the early stages of evolution. RGA may be a good starting place for exploring the evolution of complicated stem-loop formations in real biological systems.

4.2 Causes of Extinction

One of the causes of Foundation Failure is insufficiency of matching pairs within the initial populations. The causes of Extinction are much more difficult to understand. The remarkable difference between repairing and nonrepairing systems was the tendency to increase phenotypic size (Fig. 9) and variance(Fig. 10).

Increasing phenotypic size expands cardinal as well as dimensional variability of searching space for the bit-matching game. As the maximum number of individuals was limited for each arena size, increasing search space would decrease the probability of achieving profitable mismatch between consumers and their victims. A system crash would occur once bit-strings lost the capability to use "sun light" during evolutionary interactions. The crash events, however, can not be predicted from the changes of diversity (Fig. 12, see also Saruwatari et al. 1994).

Nonrepairing systems avoided extinction by keeping individuals at small size in small worlds. In contrast, repairing systems increased the phenotypic size and diversity of individuals, and went extinct in small worlds with low energy efficiency (Table 2 and Fig. 11). Thus the system diversity did not always indicate system stability or persistence in our model. Repairing systems were relatively extinction prone in the world without space structure, but it was not true in the worlds with spatial structure.

4.3   Effects of Spatial Structure

Spatial structure in ecological systems has two functions. First, it moderates unstable interactions within subpopulations and can keep a meta-population from going extinct (Gotelli 1991). Second, it allocates initial genetic variance into variance among demes by random drift and inbreeding (Wade and Goodnight 1991). Because we adopted fine-grained population structure (Manderick and Spiessens 1989), the size of demes was automatically determined by the systems themselves. In this case, the above two function could have worked simultaneously.

Unfortunately, the world sizes we adopted were relatively small compared to the breeding and interacting group sizes of individuals, and it is doubtful that the second function worked effectively. The increase in the incidence of Frozen state in nonrepairing systems meant that spatial structure merely brought homogeneity of community members. However, the repairing systems overcame the homogenizing pressure and behaved equally well in both spatial and non-spatial arenas when world size was larger than 64.

4.4   Chaotic Dynamics

An open question is that dynamics of some persistent systems showed highly fluctuating behavior. Previous studies addressing on chaotic behaviors use chaos generators (logistic equation, etc.) as units of artificial ecosystems (e.g., Ikegami and Kaneko 1992, Kaneko and Ikegami 1992). Our model systems became chaotic even without such chaos generators when the energy efficiency was low and the world size was more than 64. The bit-matching game, which we used as the trophic rule in our model, may well correspond to the gene-for-gene interactions between host and parasites. Thompson (1994) reported that gene-for-gene interactions tend to generate chaotic dynamics in natural plant-pathogen systems.

Even frozen and stuffed equilibrium, the dynamics fluctuate quite irregularly around equilibriums. There are several theoretical studies showing that prey-predator systems tend to evolve from the low dimensional to the high dimensional chaos (homeochaos) (Kaneko and Ikegami 1992, Solé and Valls 1992). Contrast between Frozen/Stuffed, and Chaotic dynamics may correspond to the relationship between homeochaos and low dimensional chaotic behavior.

Acknowledgements

We deeply thank Dr. Nozomi Ytow for helping us to construct our simulation environment. We also thank Prof. Michael Wade who accepted Y. Toquenaga as a visiting scholar at the University of Chicago and supported him during this study. This study is partially supported by the Grant-In-Aid of Ministry of Education, Science, Sports and Culture of Japan (Nos. 07243102 and 06402060).

References

Avise, J. C. (1993). The evolutionary biology of aging, sexual reproduction, and dna repair. *Evolution 47*, 1293–1301.

Doi, H., K. Wada, and M. Furusawa (1994). Asymmetric mutations due to semiconservative dna replication: Double-stranded dna type genetic algorithms. In R. A. Brooks and P. Maes (Eds.), *Artificial Life IV*, pp. 359–364. MIT press.

Eigen, M., J. McCaskill, and P. Schuster (1988). Molecular quasispecies. *J. Phys. Chem. 92*, 6881–6891.

Forsdyke, D. R. (1995). A stem-loop "kissing" model for the initiation of recombination and the origin of introns. *Mol. Biol. Evol. 12*, 949–958.

Gotelli, N. J. (1991). Metapopulation models: The rescue effect, the propagule rain, and the core-satellite hypothesis. *Am. Nat. 138*, 768–776.

Ikegami, T. and K. Kaneko (1992). Evolution of host-parasitoid network through homeocahotic dynamics. *Choas 2*, 397–408.

Kaneko, K. and T. Ikegami (1992). Homeochaos: dynamic stability of a symbiotic network with population dynamics and evolving mutation rates. *Physica D 56*, 406–429.

Kauffman, S. (1993). *The origin of order*. New York: Oxford UP.

Kimura, M. (1983). *The neutral theory of molecular evolution*. Cambridge UP.

Manderick, B. and P. Spiessens (1989). Fine-grained parallel genetic algorithms. In J. D. Schaffer (Ed.), *3rd International Conference on GA*, pp. 428–433. Morgan Kaufmann.

Ohno, S. (1970). *Evolution by gene duplication*. Springer-Verlag.

Pielou, E. C. (1984). *The interpretation of ecological data*. New York: Wiley & Sons.

Saruwatari, T., Y. Toquenaga, and T. Hoshino (1994). Adiversity: Stepping up trophic levels. In R. A. Brooks and P. Maes (Eds.), *Artificial Life IV*, pp. 424–429. MIT press.

Solé, R. V. and S. C. Manrubia (1995). Are rainforests self-organized in a critical state? *J. Theor. Biol. 173*, 31–40.

Solé, R. V. and J. Valls (1992). On structural stability and chaos in biological systems. *J. Theor. Biol. 155*, 87–102.

Thompson, J. N. (1994). *The coevolutionary process*. Chicago: Chicago UP.

Wade, M. J. and C. J. Goodnight (1991). Wright's shifting balance theory: An experimental study. *Science 253*, 1015–1018.

An individual-based model that reproduces natural distribution of species abundance and diversity

C. Ilia Herráiz, J. J. Merelo, Sergio Olmeda, A. Prieto

GeNeura Team, Depto. de Electrónica y Tecnología de Computadores, Facultad de Ciencias
Campus Fuentenueva, s/n, 18071 Granada (Spain)
e-mail: {ilia,jmerelo,sergio}@kal-el.ugr.es; http://kal-el.ugr.es/geneura.html

Abstract

The study and analysis of biological diversity has got paramount importance in life sciences. The change in any environmental factor, biotic or abiotic, turns up on diversity indices, and, at the same time, diversity is a measure of ecosystem performance. Diversity models are scarce, largely phenomenological and based on differential equations or statistical distributions; that is the reason why diversity has received attention lately from the artificial life field.

In this paper we will first examine how diversity can be characterized, and different approaches to the study of diversity. We then introduce a model whose objective is to reproduce species abundance distribution and diversity in different circumstances. The model is an artificial world composed of food strings and artificial organisms with a *dietary* chromosome that determines its resource requirements, and an *information processing* chromosome, which allows it to choose which food strings to eat.

Results show that species distribution resembles those of real ecosystems, by analyzing them using standard statistical models. The resulting diet of the living species varies with resource availability. In the near future, a computer model based on this one could be used as a tool to assess diversity change in real ecosystems.

1   Introduction

Diversity can be defined in many ways, but it is usually associated to the amount of different biological species living in a given ecosystem, and also to the *complexity* of the living forms present and their interactions. Intuitively, there is more diversity in a tropical forest than in a desert, but, however, there is great discussion about how to accurately measure this diversity.

Diversity is important at least for a couple of reasons. First, in any of its forms, it is an accurate index of the state of an ecosystem. Low diversity usually means that the state is poor (although it might occur in ecosystems with lots of available resources, like rivers contaminated with phosphates), while a high diversity means that an ecosystem is in good shape. The second reason is that diversity affects the performance of an ecosytem [1], in such a way that a system with a high diversity exploits better the resources available to it than another with low diversity. In a sense, it could be said that diversity reflects the optimality of an ecosystem.

Diversity is related to other factors in ecology: *niche occupation*, since diversity is a measure of available niches, *food webs*, since trophic relations are an important factor in diversity, and *speciation*, because some of the factors that make diversity rise is the introduction of new species in geological time. At the same time, new species create new niches, in such a way that all the aforementioned elements are related to each other.

In itself, the study of the evolution of diversity and the factors that have an influence on it is interesting for several disciplines, something already pointed out by Margalef in 1986 [2]. May [3] has applied it to human population and wealth distribution in the USA and the UK, Aguila [4] to the evolution of pottery designs, in itself a problem of cultural evolution, and it could probably be applied to other problems like the evolution of markets and products along with consumer's preferences. Similar models like Zipf's law [5], are applied in linguistics. The potential of diversity as a measure of performance of an optimization process like a genetic algorithm has also been realized by Bedau et al. in [6]. It has also been used by Wuensche, in the form of entropy, as a measure of complexity in CA rules [7]. In a word, diversity is present, or arises in a wide range of complex systems.

Focusing in living systems, and for obvious reasons, it is usually impossible to measure total diversity of an habitat, even in a controlled environment. A comprehensive measure of diversity would have to include all *phyla*, from microorganisms to the biggest animals. Abundance and diversity measurements are usually reduced to some taxa (for instance, only worms, or only a certain kind of trees), and to limited space and time coordinates. Diversity varies at all levels, through a year, through a season, and even when the size of the sampled region is changed in any way. That is the reason why usually several diversity indices, for instance, the so called α, β and γ are given. These indices show how diversity varies with the measured area. In any case, the abundance of a chosen subset of species is measured [8] by using different devices (traps, sieves and so on), and then counting specimens, measuring biomass, or any other observable that depends on abundance.

The difficulty of measuring total diversity, together with the fact that species interact with each other and with the environment in a non-linear way [9], make very difficult to predict how different factors like the introduction or extinction of a species, the presence of a pollutant or climatic changes can affect diversity and thus the ecosystem as a whole. The usual way to approach this problem is the creation or utilization of controlled environments, for instance, plastic bags in a lake, the *Ecotron* described in [1], in which temperature, humidity, light and water are controlled by a computer, or the small islands described by Wilson in [9]. Due to the timescale of changes in Nature, these environments only yield results at the end of several years, which are, even so, incomplete. A computer model like the one proposed in this paper that would meaningfully mirror the essential aspects of species abundance and diversity would save time and money (and many animal lives, too: in a colonization experiment in small islands [9], all insects were exterminated) by predicting the influence of environmental or abiotic factors.

Diversity also varies in a wider scale in geological time. In geological time, great speciation events like the Cambrian explosion [10, 11] were characterized by a sharp increase in diversity, in the form of new species; big extinctions were also accompanied by a dive in diversity. It is not well known if diversity measures just certify the fact that the number of species shrunk, or declining diversity caused also massive extinction.

In this paper, we will try to present a computer model that tries to mirror abundance distribution and diversity of real ecosystems. The paper is organized as follows: section 2 describes the state of the art in diversity models, indices and computer models. Our own model is described in section 3, and results obtained are presented in section 4 and discussed in 5.

2 Models of species abundance and diversity

There have been several models that attempt to reproduce species abundance and diversity in real ecosystems. Usual theoretical models, by means of a formula or differential equations, compute abundances which then try to fit to observed abundances in a certain ecosystem. Diversity can then be deduced from the graphs or computed as diversity indices.

In order to measure abundance distributions, the abundance versus rank of the species is plotted. This is called a rank/abundance graph. Usually abundance is plotted in logarithmic scale, in such a way that ecosystems fall into one of four distributions: geometric, logarithmic, normal logarithmic and broken stick [3].

In the *geometric distribution* [12], species abundance follow a geometric sequence. This distribution follows from the *niche preemption hypothesis*, which asserts that each species uses the same portion k of the resource available to it. The first species uses k, the second the same portion k of the remaining $(1 - k)$ and so on. This distribution is usually found in resource poor environments, or in those that have suffered a short time ago an environmental catastrophe, or have been colonized a short time ago (these environments are said to be in the first stages of a *succession*).

Fisher's *logarithmic series model*, is similar to the previous one, but follows from taking more biologically realistic assumptions. It predicts that the number of species with number of individuals in a range $S(N)$ takes the form

$$\alpha x, \frac{\alpha x^2}{2}, \frac{\alpha x^3}{3} \cdots \qquad (1)$$

. This leads to a decrement of species abundance slower than in the previous case. This model is used in situations close to the previous ones, i.e., habitats dominated by only one resource (like a forest, in which light is the limiting resource).

Most of the studied communities fit themselves to the *lognormal* distribution. May proves [3] that when a random variable is subject to the influence of many factors, it distributes itself as the normal distribution. Human population distribution, and wealth distribution in a country have been proved to take this form. It is usually applied to mature and varied ecosystems, and represents an optimal abundance of species.

The *broken stick* model is "the closest thing in nature to an uniform distribution" [3]. It is usually found in ecosystems whose resources are equitatively distributed, for instance in very well defined communities inhabited by taxonomically related organisms.

Although species abundance and/or frequency is the best way of describing diversity, in some cases, diversity can be reduced to a single index, which, although less informative, allows comparison of different system at a glance. Probably the best known is the so-called *Shannon-Wiener* diversity index, or simply *entropy*. It is computed from the equation

$$H' = -\sum_{i=1}^{S} p_i \ln p_i \qquad (2)$$

where

$$p_i = \frac{n_i}{N} \qquad (3)$$

is the proportion of individuals of the i species and S is the total number of species. Base 2 and 10 logarithms are also used instead of the natural logarithm. This index measured for taxa in natural systems amounts to about 1.5 - 2.5; on a few ocassions it can go up to 4.5. With this index, samples with an uniform distribution of individuals in species are arbitrarily considered more diverse than those in which the number of individuals in each species varies widely.

There is another simple index which is used sometimes, Margalef's index, computed as

$$D_{Mg} = (S - 1)/\ln N \qquad (4)$$

This index is more related to the number of species than to its distribution

Other group of diversity indices are usually called *dominance indices*, because they are higher when the population is dominated by only one species. Probably the most famous is *Simpson's* index, which is computed as follows

$$D = \sum_{i=1}^{S} \left(\frac{n_i(n_i - 1)}{N(N - 1)} \right) \qquad (5)$$

where N is the total number of individuals in the population, and n_i the number of individuals belonging to species i. The inverse of this index, $C = 1/D$ is also used as a measure of diversity.

The attempts at systematization presented so far come from theoretical biology and ecology. But, from the inception of Artificial Life, the creation of multispecies systems and its dynamics have been studied using computer individual-based models, in which each individual is represented explicitly, as opposed to dealing with variables like population. Tierra [13] was the first of such models, created specifically to model evolutive events like mass extinctions and the Cambrian diversity explosion. It obtained good results in showing the evolution of different strategies to survive, and the continuous creation of new species. The avida system [14] is inspired in Tierra, and has proved that it can accurately model some types of species distribution. The definition of species corresponds to organisms with an equal number of instructions in the first case, and organisms with the same genotype in the second.

Other simulations have also been created to specifically address diversity or any of the factors influencing it. Johnson's [15] and Lindgren/Nordahl's [16] focus more on trophic relations in order to generate realistic food webs and, in the case of Johnson, realistic mass sequences for the different trophic levels. Levchenko's model [17, 18] includes explicit spatial coordinates and trophic interactions among populations, and its main target is to emulate the creation of evolutionary trees.

Saruwatari et al.'s model [19] was the first to explicitly address diversity, and it focuses also on trophic relationships, trying at the same time to reproduce energy flow among trophic levels. The H' entropy values through generations are at the same level as measured in natural ecosystems, and reflects events like mass extinction, although it cannot predict them. The latest version of the model [20] incorporates a chromosome fixing mechanism and changes slightly the feeding conditions, creating a more stable system, less prone to mass extinctions.

In this paper, we will present a model in which resources are finite, so that the main relationship among individuals is competition for those resources. In this sense, it is related to the *mechanistic models* described in [21], in which resource requirements and the impact of each individual on the environment are the main features of each model organism. In the proposed model, food and artificial organisms are in separate "worlds", so that trophic interactions cannot take place; but, even so, diversity arises and changes under the influence of different initial conditions. This model is presented in the next section.

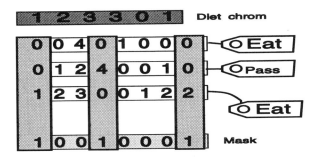

Figure 1: Representation of the *dietary* chromosome, whose components are letters of the alphabet $A(P) = \{0, ..., 7\}$; and the *information processing* chromosome, which contains several labelled vectors, with labels indicating the action to take when that vector is the closest to the food string, and the ones in the mask tell which components will be taken into account to compute distances.

3 A new model

The basic ideas in the model proposed in this paper are as follow:

- resources are finite, and individuals have to compete for them;

- these resources are consumed by the individuals, which have a genetic preference for some of them;

- part of what individuals eat "builds" their body, being a factor in their fitness.

In this work, we will try to prove that these 3 hypotheses are enough to reproduce some models of natural abundance of species; in order to implement them, a world composed of *agents* and *food strings* is implemented in a computer. Each agent has got a chromosome, designated *dietary* chromosome, that codifies what it can "digest". Each agent, by eating, builds *proteins* which are exact and full copies of that dietary chromosome. For instance, in the chromosome depicted in figure 1, the agent will build a protein when it manages to consume 2 "1"s, 2 "3"s, one "0" and one "2"; twice that amount of components will build 2 proteins and so on. One of the components of the fitness of an agent will be the amount of proteins it has built in this way. The *dietary* chromosome is a string of letters taken from an alphabet $A(P)$ of cardinality P (P is usually equal to 8). The world is composed by a certain amount F of food strings, which are composed by letters from $A(P)$ too.

To be able to take a decision about which strings to eat, each agent is provided with an *information processing* chromosome (see also figure 1), composed of

- A variable size set of labelled vectors, usually called *brain*. Vectors have dimension P (i.e., the same as the cardinality of the alphabet), and possible values of the labels are *eat* or *pass*. This can be described in pattern recognition terms as a labelled codebook of the kind used, for instance, in LVQ-trained neural networks [22]. It is also similar to the bitstring matching procedures introduced in [19].

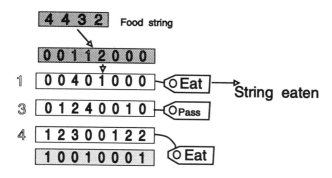

String eaten

Figure 2: Eating process: the food string is converted into a P component vector $\vec{x}$, with x_i = Number of times i appears in the food string. $\vec{x}$ is matched to the *brain* vectors taking into account only those vector components with an 1 in the mask (shaded binary string in the bottom), in this case the first, forth and last. The food string is at the top of the figure, and computed distances at the left hand side of the vectors.

- A binary *mask* of length P, whose 0s indicate which of the components of the previous vectors will not be taken into account. It could be said that 1s represent those senses which are present in the agent, and 0s absent senses.

Each timestep, an agent is presented a food string. This food string is turned into a P-component vector, with each component representing the number of times food component i appears in the food string, which is then matched to all the vectors in the brain of the agent (see figure 2). The action written in the label of the closest vector in the absolute value distance sense is taken. If it decides to pass, it has got several chances, until it eats.

The food string is then digested; only those components present in the dietary chromosome will be stored and used to build proteins, the other wasted. The efficiency, i.e., the proportion of food components eaten that are actually stored in this process is the other component of the fitness of the agent.

After a number of "eating opportunities", or when the world runs out of food, a Genetic Algorithm is run on the population, taking as *fitness* the metabolic efficacy (the building blocks used/buildings block eaten rate) and the number of *proteins* built. Variable length chromosomes are used for the *dietary* and *information processing* chromosome. All chromosomes are binary-coded. In the dietary case, a byte is used for each character in the string, which is decoded by to the remainder of dividing the value by P. In the case of the brain, one byte is used for each component of the vector, which is decoded to an unsigned integer (range 0-256); another byte codes the label, whose last bit is used. The mask is coded as a single byte, all of whose bits are used.

Agents are placed in a grid, but the only relation among agents in neighbouring cells occurs at the time of selection and reproduction. Agents fitness is compared

only with those on the neighborhood, and each agent is the offspring of two other agents in the neighboring cells. Due to the local comparisons, competition takes also place locally. This strategy has been preferred over *panmictic* selection and reproduction for several reasons: first, we are not interested in pure optimization, but in the dynamics of the species creation and competition process; second, parallelization of the algorithm is simpler since there is no need of heavy interchange among processors of fitness, and third, the number of comparisons needed for selection grows only linearly with the number of individuals, instead of exponentially (less if a efficient classification algorithm is used).

A classical genetic algorithm is run on the agent population, except for some modifications: the aforementioned restrictions to selection and mating to neighbors in the grid and the utilization of variable length chromosomes and operators that act on those chromosomes. These operators eliminate a whole gene in a chromosome (for instance, a component of a dietary chromosome or a full labelled vector in the "brain" chromosome), duplicate it with mutation or add a random one. Thus, chromosomes can have in principle any length, allowing open-ended evolution in this sense.

The genetic algorithm runs as follows:

1. Generate initial population, with dietary chromosomes in the size range $l_{\min} \rightarrow l_{\max}$ (1-16, in the experiments described) and brains in the range $B_{\min} \rightarrow B_{\max}$ (1-3).

2. Generate F random foodstrings from the alphabet $A(P)$ with maximun length x ($x = 5$, in the experiments described).

3. While there are food strings: present a food string a number of times k to an agent, until it is eaten or until $k = k_{\max}$. The eaten string dissapears from the world.

4. Compare each agent with those around it. If the fitness (number of built proteins times efficiency) is the best of all, clone it with low mutation probability, and place clone in the same place; if it is not the best, substitute it by the offspring of the fittest agent in the neighborhood and another random agent. Chromosome length variation operators, uniform crossover and mutation are always applied. Go back to step 2.

This algorithm is programmed in C++ using GAGS library [23]. As is usual in GAs, fitness increases with time, but it does not reach a maximum and stays in it, it rather oscillates around a maximum (see figure 3). This is due to the process of generation of strings, and to the local competition, which knocks down fit species whose food has been eaten out by another less fit, but more ravenous one. It must be taken into account that the one that eats more need not be the fittest; this title goes to the one that builds more proteins and takes advantage efficiently of what it eats.

4   Results

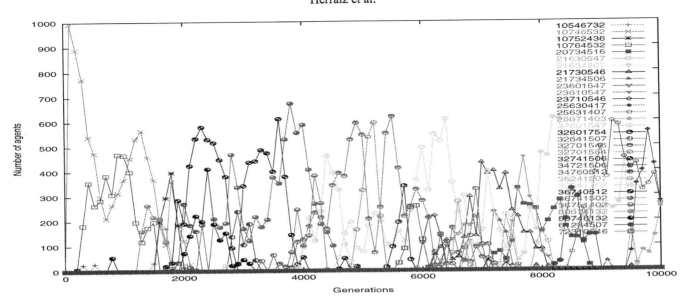

Figure 5: Evolution of the number of agents in each species in a run with 1225 agents and 200000 food strings. Species which never reach the threshold of 150 agents have not been represented for clarity.

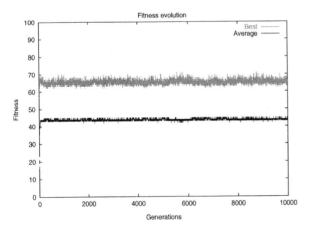

Figure 3: Evolution of the best and average fitness in a typical run. The fitness first goes down, due to the fact mentioned before: at the beginning, fit agents eat everything, and unfit do not eat anything, but soon, the world is filled with fit agents. Competition at a small scale takes place, making the fitness of the best oscillate.

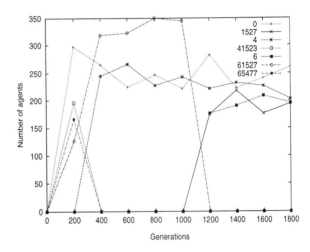

Figure 4: Evolution of the number of agents in each species in a run with 900 agents, and 150000 food strings. In this graph, a species goes extinct and is replaced by two species, one quasi-generalist and the other specialist, that fill the same niche.

The program has been run around 20 times, changing mainly population, number of foodstrings, and mutation rate. Populations range from 400 to 2500, number of foodstrings from 200000 to 1 million, and mutation rate 0.01 or 0.001. The other rates are constant, like uniform crossover set at 0.1, and length-changing operators at 0.01. Some of the runs have been done with the same parameters, in order to test repeatability of results. Simulations have been performed in Sun workstations and Silicon Graphics Indigo (GNU's C++ compiler) and Indy (SGI C++ compiler). Depending on the number of food strings and the population, simulations take from several days to several weeks.

Interesting results have been obtained with respect to speciation patterns, species abundance and entropy. They will be examined in turn.

4.1 Speciation

Species are defined in our model by the "dietary" chromosome, not by total identity of the genotype. Agents of the same species can have different behavior, although they will have the same diet. The inverse is not true: different permutations of the dietary chromosome will be considered different species. As any other assumption in an artificial world, this species definition is completely arbitrary, but we consider it reasonable, since biological species have the same resource requirements in a wide sense.

Diet can then be classified in *specialist*, when the dietary chromosome consists of a single component, *generalist*, when it includes all the components in P, and *quasi-generalist* when it includes only some components of P. Resulting diets after some hundred of generations include only one copy of each component, because it is easier to build proteins in that way.

All kind of behaviors appear in different runs. The following characteristcs have been observed

- When there is not enough food (this is a rough frontier, placed around 50-100 foodstrings per agent), usually all-generalist or all-specialist strategies arise. All-generalist strategies are unstable: different generalist species fight for the dominance of the simulated ecosystem, and as as result, diversity is high (see figure 4. This fulfills the "Gause exclusion principle"[24, 21], which states that a niche is occupied by only one species and, obviously, only one species can fill the generalist niche. All-specialist strategies arise less often, but are stable (a species dominates through all the simulation), and are characterized by a low diversity, since it is very difficult to find another optimal strategy from a single genetic change of a specialist species. All specialist strategies also arise when the mutation rate is lowered to 10^{-3}. These strategies result from the optimization of the two factors in fitness: efficacy in the first case, and number of proteins built in the second case.

- When food is enough, around 200 foodstrings per capita, and when the genetic pool is also big enough (more than 900, in this case) is when quasi-generalist

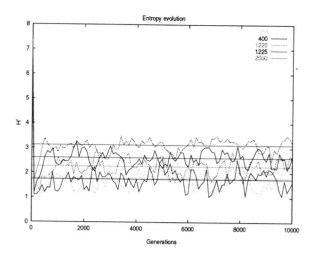

Figure 6: Evolution of the H' index for the experiments mentioned in the text. Average entropy is also plotted, as a straight horizontal line for each of the runs. As it can be seen, entropy increases with the number of agents in the population, but its standard deviation also increases.

strategies arise (see figure 4. Generalist strategies do not appear, except at the early stages of the simulation, and usually quasi-generalists share the world with specialists, complementing each other: specialists feed on the strings that the quasi-generalist do not want. In other cases, there is a certain amount of niche overlapping: two quasi-generalist have a dietary chromosome that is the same except for a single component.

4.2 Abundance and frequency distributions, and entropy

These factors have been studied systematically with the model, by using different worlds in which the amount of food did not vary (200000 food strings with maximum length 5), and the population increased from 400 to 2500 through 1225. Two experiments were carried out for population 400 and 1225, and one for population equal to 2500. Simulations run for 10000 generations, which took half a week in a Silicon Graphics. One of the things to test was the importance of the amount of food on diversification, as opposed to the population or gene pool present. In each case, only generalist strategies survived, but no species dominated during all the run, being some species substituted by others. First, H' index was plotted for all the runs, as is shown in figure 6. Average entropy increases with the number of agents, but the range of variation also increases, in such a way that the bigger the population, the bigger the standard deviation. Changes in diversity reflect also succession events, in which one species is extinct, and its dominance is replaced by the dominance of another generalist species.

Then, species abundance was plotted. Since there is only one resource available, foodstrings, a geometric or logseries distribution is to be expected. The species abundance was saved every 1000 generations, and av-

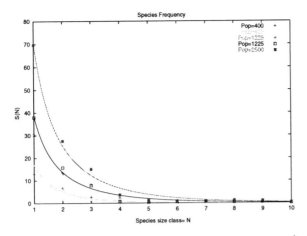

Figure 7: $S(N)$ plot for all 5 runs, with RMS fit to $\frac{\alpha x^k}{k}$ for three of them. The other fits have been omitted for clarity. In this graph, the number of species in the size class shown as x coordinate is plotted as y coordinate.

Population	α	H'
400	28 ± 3	1.77 ± 0.05
400	17 ± 2	1.73 ± 0.05
1225	54 ± 4	2.6 ± 0.05
1225	39 ± 3	2.25 ± 0.06
2500	97 ± 5	3.12 ± 0.05

Table 1: Parameter α and diversity computed for different runs, with standard deviation

eraged for all the run except generation 0. This averaged species abundance distribution was plotted, and was found to diverge from the geometric distribution; this divergence increases with the population; thus, other hypothesis had to be tested. A logseries distribution was then tested. In order to do that, $S(N)$ was computed every 1000 generations, and averaged for all the run except the first generation. The species frequency was distributed in *octaves*, in such a way that the first octave included species with up to 1 individual, the second with up to 2 individuals, the third with up to 4 individuals and so on. This $S(N)$ was then fitted to a logarithmic series (as shown in section 2); the results of some of the fits are shown in figure 7. The computed α coefficient, along with the computed H' and its standard deviation are shown in the next table.

Theory shows that there is a relation between this α parameter and entropy [3], namely,

$$H' = log(\alpha) + 0.58 \qquad (6)$$

. The previous data was fitted to the curve $a log(\alpha) + b$, with the result shown in figure 8, i.e., $a = 0.9 \pm 0.1$ and $b = -0.9 \pm 0.4$; $\chi^2 = 0.103008$. The first coefficient is consistent with a value of $a = 1$; the second is different, although within the same order of magnitude, but it must be taken into account that this is the origin y coordinate, and it would probably vary with the insertion of more data points. This computation is similar

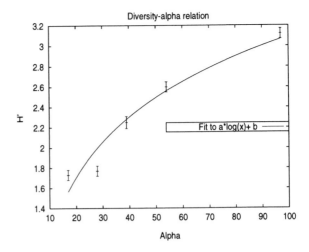

Figure 8: α index for the logarithmic series plotted against Shannon-Weaver index H'. The solid line represents the fit to a logarithmic function. The horizontal errorbars have been omitted for clarity.

to the one shown in Adami's paper [14], except that the power law used there has been corrected with a term depending on the size class. This proves that abundance distribution in this world, created following the hypotheses mentioned at the beginning of this section, follow the same law than natural systems. Other trivial results also hold in this model: H' grows with the mutation rate (since entropy is a function of the randomness of a system, the more mutation, more randomness and thus more entropy); low entropy is also associated to low efficiency of the ecosystem where not all the ecological niches are filled.

5 Discussion and future work

In this paper, it has been proved that a system based on explicit representation of each organism necessities, a finite amount of resources to stimulate competition, and fitness based on the efficacy of each agent and its ability to eat what it needs are enough to generate a wide array of behaviors, that ultimately resemble those found in natural ecosystems. Specialist, generalist and anywhere-in-between strategies arise, diversity varies with speciation events and, at the same time, generates speciation events. Experiments run on several worlds suggest that they behave like some natural ecosystems, namely, those that approximate the logarithmic series distribution.

The limitation to resemble other kinds of ecosystems is mainly due to the limited types of resources available. That is why the model will be extended with other resources, mainly space, in such a way that agents will have to fight for space as well as for food, and food will not be evenly distributed.

At the same time, the model as it is now is not able to generate food webs, mainly because all agents would want to eat those of their same species, since food is not transformed in any way when stored. Some kind of food processing (metabolism) will be incorporated into the model, in such a way that what is stored in the organism is different from the stuff eaten. The same "protein building" principle, however, will be used. At the same time, to create realistic trophic levels, energy expenses must also be taken into account.

There are many more experiments that can be performed on the model, like elimination of the dominant species, separation of the population in reproductively isolated communities, introduction of a predator, and so on [25]. The system as it is now only allows batch processing, that is why an important step will be to port the system into a powerful simulation system like Swarm, developed at Santa Fe Institute. This will allow more real-time control of the simulation while it takes place.

Acknowledgements

I would like to acknowledge the support and suggestions of Nelson Minar, Chris Langton, Luis Cruz, Yukihiko Toquenaga and H. H. Lund. This paper has been supported in part by DGICYT grant no. PB-92-0456.

References

[1] S. Naeem; L. J. Thompson; S. P. Lawler; J. H. Lawton; R. M. Woodfin. Empirical evidence that declining species diversity may alter the performance of terrestrial ecosystems. *Phil. Trans. R. Soc. Lond. B*, (347):249–262, 1995.

[2] R. Margalef. Reflections on diversity and meaning of its quantitative expression (in spanish). In *Simposium on Biological Diversity, Madrid*, Nov-Dec 1989.

[3] Robert M. May. Patterns of species abundance and diversity. In J. M. Diamond M.L. Cody, editor, *Ecology and Evolution of Communities*, pages 81–120. Harvard university press, 1975.

[4] Lourdes Aguila. Decorated ceramic diversity in the Fort Stanton Reservation, Lincoln County. Master's thesis, Dept. of Anthropology, Easter New Mexico University, 1995.

[5] G. K. Zipf. *Human Behavior and the Principle of Least Effort*. Hafner, New York, 1965.

[6] Mark A. Bedau; Frank Ronneburg; Martin Zwick. Dynamics of diversity in an evolving population. In *Parallel Problem Solving from Nature, 2*. Elsevier Science BV, 1992.

[7] Andy Wuensche. Complexity in one-d cellular automata; gliders, basins of attraction and the Z parameter. Technical report, Santa Fe Institute, Santa Fe, N.M, 1994. Working Paper 94-04-026.

[8] Anne E. Magurran. *Diversidad Ecológica y su medición*. Ediciones Vedrà, 1989.

[9] E. O. Wilson. *The diversity of life*. Penguin Science, 1992.

[10] Jeffrey S. Levinton. The Big Bang of animal evolution. *Scientific American*, 267(5):52–59, November 1992.

[11] J. Madeleine Nash. When life exploded. *Time Magazine*, 146(23):62–70, Dec 4. 1995.

[12] H. Inagaki. Une étude d'écologie évolutive: Application de la loi de Motomura aux fourmis. *Bull. Ecol.*, 5(3):207–219, 1974.

[13] T. Ray. An evolutionary approach to synthetic biology. *Artificial life*, (1):195ff, 1994.

[14] Chris Adami; C. Titus Brown and Michael R. Haggerty. Abundance-distribution in Artificial Life and stochastic models: "age and area" revisited. In *Advances in Artificial Life, Morán, Moreno, Merelo, Chacón, (eds.), LNAI 929*, pages 503–514. Springer Verlag, 1995.

[15] Alan R. Johnson. Evolution of a size-structured, predator-prey community. In *Artificial Life III, C. Langton (ed.)*, pages 105–129. Addison-Wesley, 1994.

[16] K. Lindgren; M. G. Nordahl. Artificial food webs. In *Artificial Life III, C. Langton (ed.)*. Addison Wesley, 1994.

[17] V. F. Levchenko. *Models in the Theory of Biological Evolution (in russian)*. SPb, 1993.

[18] Levchenko V.F. The experience of simulation of evolutionary process. Available from http://rumba.ics.uci.edu:8080/faqs/simulation.

[19] T. Saruwatari; Y. Toquenaga; T. Hoshino. Adiversity: Stepping up trophic levels. In *Artificial Life IV, R. Brooks, P. Maes (eds.)*, page 424ff, 1994.

[20] Y. Toquenaga; T. Saruwatari; T. Hoshino. Stepping up trophic levels with self-repairing genetic algorithm. In *Congress on the Evolution of Complexity*, 1995.

[21] Mathew A. Leibold. The niche concept revisited: mechanistic models and community context. *Ecology*, 76(5):1371–1382, 1995.

[22] T. Kohonen. The self-organizing map. *Procs. IEEE*, 78:1464 ff., 1990.

[23] J. J. Merelo. GAGS programmer's and user's manual. Technical report, Grupo GeNeura, Depto. Electrónica, Universidad de Granada, 1995. Available from ftp://kal-el.ugr.es/GAGS.

[24] Sharon E. Kingsland. *Modelling Nature: Episodes in the History of Population Ecology*. University of Chicago Press, 1992.

[25] E. C. Pielou. *Ecological Diversity*. Wiley-Interscience, 1975.

Robotics, Animats

Mother Operations to Evolve Embodied Robots Based on the Remote-Brained Approach

Masayuki INABA, Satoshi KAGAMI, Fumio KANEHIRO
Kenichiro NAGASAKA, Hirochika INOUE

Department of Mechano-Informatics
The University of Tokyo
7-3-1 Hongo, Bunkyo-ku, Tokyo, JAPAN

Abstract

We introduce a methodology with 'mother operations' breeding real embodied robots of which brain is shared by virtual bodies and real bodies using the remote-brained approach. In this framework the robot system is designed to have the brain and body separate, both conceptually and physically. The brain is raised in the mother environment inherited over generations. It allows us to develop a robot brain is shared by both virtual environment and real environment. For robots where the brain is raised in a mother environment, it can benefit directly from the mother's 'evolution'. In order to design research environment for real embodied robots, we introduce this framework and describe the mother operations breeding both virtual and real robots based on the new approach.

Keywords: robotics, autonomous agent, evolution, robot architecture, embodied agent

1 Introduction

Robotics is a research field to investigate the intelligent connection from perception to action in the real world. Although the viewpoint from intelligent connection from perception and action is the key in robotics, the subject which builds the intelligent connection and the process building it have been rarely considered in robotics field. In most case, the intelligent connections have been planned in human brain. A large number of examples of the connection has been examined and proposed.

Recent wave in ALife gives a new viewpoint to make us look at the subject which builds the intelligent connection[1][2][3]. Sims[4] showed a process building bodies which can survive in a world simulating the real world. Although this is done in a virtual world, the idea suggests much.

When we try to deal with such processes building intelligent connections from perception to action, it is necessary to have a good environment to test architectures of connections. As Maes notes that ALIVE system works an environment to test architectures without frustration of time-consuming processes in building robots [5]. Al-

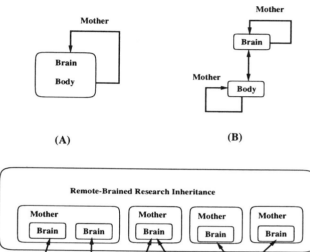

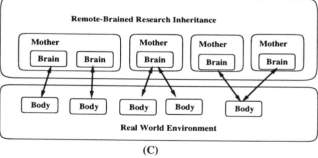

Figure 1: Conceptual Structure of the Remote-Brained Environment

though ALIVE system is a good environment to test an agent which interacts with human, if we insist the interaction of face-to-face and hand-to-hand, it is required to explore some methodology to decrease the frustration of the process building a physical body and testing the software on it. Our approach to challenge this is the remote-brained approach.

2 Methodology to Evolve Embodied Robots

2.1 The Remote-Brained Approach

Robots of the future will act in the real world. To realize robots with the common sense to do this will, it is generally believed, require massively parallel processing. This is a problem for those of us who want to do experi-

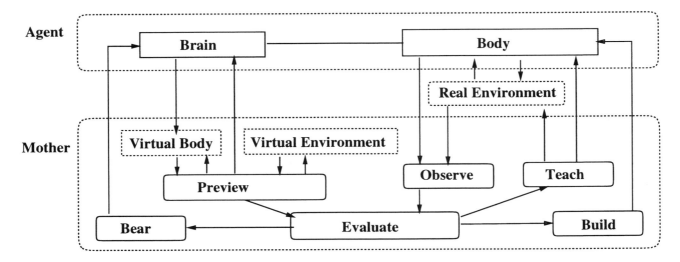

Figure 2: General Relation between an Agent and its Mother

ments with robots in the real world today — it is hard to build active, limber, situated robots when they have to carry along heavy brains. Our answer is "remote-brained robots[6]".

The remote-brained robot does not bring its own brain within the body. It leaves the brain in the mother environment and talks with it by radio links. This framework provides us with broad research approaches to both dynamic and intelligent robotics including legged robot, hand eye system and autonomous mobile robot. We can design and implement a remote-brained robot body without limitation of brain hardware. The brain software can be shared by the bodies which are designed to suit each research project and task. The mother environment allows us to observe the behavior of the brain software during experiments in real world and extend them towards massive parallelism for future. The brain is raised in the mother environment inherited over generations. For robots where the brain is raised in a mother environment, it can benefit directly from the mother's 'evolution', meaning that the software gains power easily when the mother is upgraded more.

Figure 1 is shown to explain evolutions of robots. (A) is an ordinary style of developing a robot. Mother, a developer, builds a robot and improves the software by observing its behaviors. If the robot includes a brain inside its body, the mother has to evaluate the brain by looking the motion of the body. If the body has some display to show the behaviors inside the brain directly, the process to improve it becomes easy for the mother.

(B) is a style of the remote-brained approach. The mother can observe the behaviors of both body and brain directly. The improvement process of them become independent and simplified. This provides us with a cue to build an automatic improvement system of a robot on an artificial system. Most effective implementation

of the remote-brained approach is to connect a brain and a body through wireless link. This provides a body with free movement independent from the mother hardware and a mother with rich experience through the free mobile body.

The remote-brained approach not only encourages us to build a physically grounded brain-body but also provides us with an environment to test other architectures. (C) shows an example of a remote-brained research environment. This is a sort of a research laboratory inherited over generations. Mothers who have different aims work on brain-body systems. The mother of the left has two brain-body systems to build multi-robots system. The mother of the center has two bodies and tries to control both bodies from a brain. Two mothers of the right share a body to test their own brain system. The environment for mothers are inherited over generation. They have their own aims to build the brain-body system.

2.2 Mother Operations to Breed Robots

The aim of this research is to investigate what processes are required to bear and grow an embodied robot and to build a model of a mother in order to build an artificial mother in the future. The structure of the mother model is proposed in figure 2 which shows relationship between an agent and a mother and the operations done by the mother. This model is based on the remote-brained design of a robot. In this model, the mother operations are six: **Bear**, **Preview**, **Observe**, **Teach**, **Build** and **Evaluate**. So far, the interafce between **Body** and **Real Environment** has been emphasized in robotics and new wave of AI. However, this model stresses the importance of the interface between an agent and its mother.

Preview simulates the situation of the real environment and **Body** behaviors according to action values given from **Brain**. It shows simulated results to **Brain**.

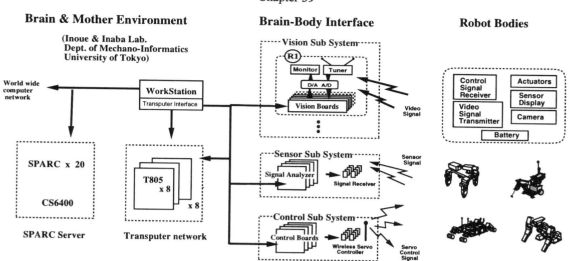

Figure 3: Hardware Configuration of Our Remote-Brained Robotics Environment

Observe monitors behaviors of **Body** through real sensors of the mother. **Evaluate** receives observed behaviors from **Preview** and **Observe** and select appropriate operations from **Teach, Bear, Build.**

In remote-brained approach, **Brain** is placed in the mother side. Advantages of remote-brained approach can be explained by this structure. One advantage is based on that the mother operations are divided into three independent operations; **Bear** is software operation, **Build** is hardware construction, **Teach** is interaction such as teaching-by-showing[8]. A mother can employ experts to suit each operation.

Second, the operation **Bear** is simplified because the brain is not placed inside the agent body but in the same side of the mother. This means that it allows to build a loop from **Preview** to **Bear** by software on the same computer. If the mother has real eye to perform **Observe** process, the system can have parallel evaluation processes through both **Preview** and **Observe** because the **Brain** is shared by both virtual body and real body. This allows the mother to compare the result from those paths and utilize them to perform **Evaluate.**

In order to pursuit evolutional and physically grounded intelligence, it is crucial to investigate how to build these mother operations. In this section, we present example cases of **Preview** and **Teach** with brains raised by them and show an approach to investigate to **Build** operation in next section.

3 Our Remote-Brained Environment

The framework of remote-brained robotics allows us to carry out different kinds of robotics researches in an environment. The research topics include the mother environment for raising brains, brain software based on different approaches, brain architecture on parallel

computers, manipulation in handling flexible objects, multi-robot coordination, reconfigurable robot system with distributed modular bodies, adaptive behaviors of quadruped robots, apelike robots and humanoids, and so on[9].

Figure 3 shows the hardware configuration of the brain base which consists of three blocks of vision subsystems and the motion control system. The vision system can receive video signals from cameras on robot bodies through wireless video link. The vision board consists of a transputer augmented with a special LSI chip which performs local image block matching[10]. It can provide a robot body with real time visual capabilities such as pattern matching, motion detections, and object tracking. The transputer is a micro-processor which can communicate with other transputers through four serial high speed communication links.

The robot body receives motion signals transmitted from the control subsystem. Each motion control subsystem consists of several transputers and wave transmitter modules. It can control up to 280 channels on 35 wave bands. Each channel can transmit a reference value for a servo module.

The key to simplify the configuration for multisensor integration is the method for multiplexing different kinds of sensor signals. Our approach to multisensor integration is based on the video signal. We design the multisensor integration so that the vision signal includes the other sensor signals[11].

At the higher level of description, we have used two substrates; the multiple Lisp environment and a new language application designed for parallel computer. The lisp language is object-oriented Lisp, Euslisp[12], which was designed for specifically for the needs of robot programming and includes powerful facilities for robot programming: modeling robot body structures, model-based object recognition, network interface over workstations, transputer interface, window-based programming, and so on. It is now extended to multithread programming[13] on CRAY CS6400.

One of the advantages of the remote-brained approach is the ability to use many actuators and switch them by software. We have succeeded built several cases of multiple agents[6]: (1) a robot which has reconfigurable modular bodies, (2) two cooperating robots in handling flexible object, (3) a robot controlled by computer and a robot controlled by human, (4) playing soccer games writteln in FLENG[14] designed for the super-parallel computer PIE64[15].

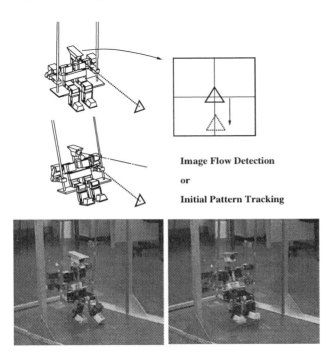

Image Flow Detection

or

Initial Pattern Tracking

Figure 4: Vision-Based Learning of Dynamic Motion in Swing

4 Bearing a Brain Through 'Preview' Operation

One example of **Preview** operation is a case of building a brain to perform vision-based dynamic action of an agent. Figure 4 shows an experiment of an apoid swinging based on vision. The apoid can ride on a swing and row it based on tracking vision. In this experiment, the swing and the virtual body are modeled in three dimensional geometric model. The **Preview** ticks away the states of virtual body and environment according to the trajectory given from the brain. The **Preview**ed result is informed to the brain as sensing data.

At the first stage, the builder of the apoid body **Evaluate** the previewed data and **Bear** the brain based on

the model of parametric oscilator. The brain structure is based on a feedback loop architecture. The attention selection is done in both space and time. The watching region is given by the last position of the visual tracker. The apoid controls the angle of neck to view the target successfully. The monitoring time to generate the reference value for action is defined by the frequency of the swing. The frequency is also measured by vision.

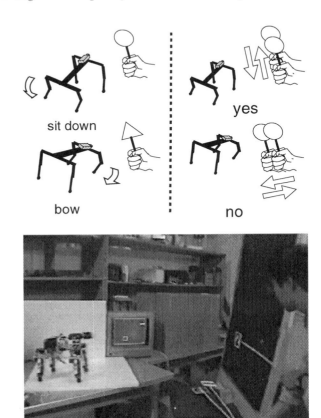

Figure 5: Experiment of Visual Teaching

As the next stage, the builder changes the **Evaluate** process and the **Bear** operation as GA system. **Evaluate** sets fitness of all population of the genes. **Bear** operation is operation on all population of genes. **Brain** receives the map of connections from the perception to the action. A map is modeled a neural network which has four layers. The input data to the network is optical flow in this case. The output of the network is signals for actuators. The sitting robot could swing by a network with a single input and a single output network. This stage close the loop **Preview**, **Evaluate** and **Bear** without a human operator.

5 'Teach' Through Real Body

An agent requires learning capability to survive in the real world. In our modeling of a mother, **Teach** operation is to help a robot after birth to grow through supervised learning. The key point of this model is that the mother can not access a brain directly. This means that the agent knows the taught data from its own sensors on the body. The mother has to think about how to teach through the body.

Figure 5 shows an experiment of reacting to human behavior observed visually. It shows the scheme of learning gesture selection. This leads to the task of implementing motions taught by a human. As the interface with a human is vision, it is assumed that the robot knows the predefined meta signs, Yes and No, to know whether the requested gesture is right or not.

In the experiment, human shows a gesture sign to request a gesture. When the robot detects a gesture sign, it starts performing a gesture. After the robot performs a gesture corresponding to the presented sign, human verifies the correspondence. If it is bad, human indicates No by waving the sign horizontally. The brain is built on a feedback loop architecture at the first stage. It receives a task shown by the pattern and verifies the result by the human reaction.

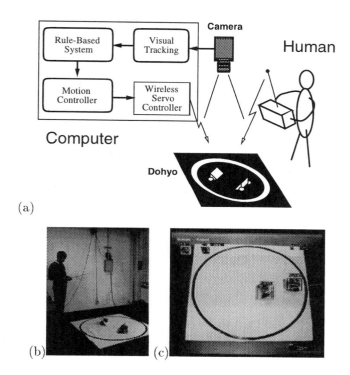

Figure 6: Experiment of Sumo Game with Human Controlled Robot

6 Evaluating Brain-Body Connection Through 'Observe' Operation

'Observe' operation performs to observe real body actions controlled by the brain. The mother can **Evaluate** the connection from brain to body by them and feedback it to the next **Bear**, **Build** and **Teach** operations. An experiment using computer-vision **Observe** operation is shown in figure 6. In this experiment, we have built an environment where the robot can play sumo games in real time with a human controlled robot. The computer can observe the robot players as shown in figure 6(c). It can know the positions and orientations of robots in real time and evaluate which is the winner of a game.

As the human has experience playing games, he can improve the tactics and the game strategies. Then the mother of the computer-controlled robot has to match improvement to win games. This competitive situation requires advanced tools for developing software for real-time reactive behaviors based on vision[16].

In this experiment, the brain-body architecture is a model of parallel connection from perception to action. The parallel connection is implemented with parallel production system of prioritied rules. **Observe** watch both robots and detect the winner. **Evaluate** can check the history of games and evaluate the winning rate. If the rate is not good, **Bear** change the set of rules or priorities of them.

As we adopted a remote-brained approach, it is possible for a human to interact through robot bodies with remote-control devices. This method, robot development motivated by the task of playing games with humans, stimulates us to improve the mother environment for the robot brain.

7 'Build' Real Body

Build operation generates a real body. Although it is hard to have fully automatic factory to build a real complex robot, the remote-brained approach helps to reduce the complexity as its software and hardware is separate. The operation **Build** is just to perform assembly of hardware modules to build a body in the remote-brained approach.

Here our approach is to evolve from our 4-limbed robots. We want to keep open the possibility of doing research that cannot be done with a 'waist-up' humanoid robot. Our approach towards humanoid robots will be via apelike robots, apoids.

Figure 7 shows some of the remote-brained apelike robots, apoids. Each apoid in the picture corresponds to (a) .. (d) from left. They have different structure in body but each joint of the robot uses same modules.

The apoid (a) has 16DOF (3 in leg, 4 in arm and gripper, 2 in head). The apoid (b) has the same number of total DOF of the body but the freedom of the leg is extended. Each leg has four DOF. The extended degree is added at the ankle and it gives the robot the function to tilt the body to left and right directions in standing, which allows the robot to move the center of the gravity of the body over each foot. Thus the robot can perform biped walking in static way. The apoid (a) can not do such static biped walking. It just performs static locomotion by knuckle walking.

The apoid (c) has 22DOF (4 in arm, 1 in gripper, 5 in leg, 2 in head). It can change walking direction during biped walking because of the extended degree of a leg. As an arm has more degree, it can carry an object with holding it horizontally.

The apoid (d) has 35DOF (6 in arm, 4 in gripper, 6 in leg, 4 in head). As the number of degree in each an arm and a leg is six, it can control its hand and foot in any position and orientation in three dimensional space, even if it can't change the orientation of the body orientation. This robot can move on a chair and manipulate objects on a desk. One of the goal task of this robot is to perform getting back an object that is fallen down from the desk.

Figure 7: Evolved Real Apoid Bodies

8 Functional Evolution Through Shared 'Brain'

How to evolve from an ape's use of arms and legs to bipedal locomotion, taking our clue for our 'mother environment for software development' from development over long time spans in the natural world, is another goal of our research.

Figure 8 shows real walking sequences developed by the apoids ((a),(b) and (c) respectively). A walking sequence is generated through **Observe** and **Bear** loop based on the structural differences in them. If the mother has only the virtual body simulator inside, it is able to build a teaching loop through the **Preview**. This makes the **Bear** operation interactively. The next stages are to make methods for **Teach**, to make **Observe** by computer vision and to make **Preview** by computer program.

In order to connect an automatic loop through the **Build** operation, the mother can make use of the apoids explained above. That is, if the mother has computer vision-based **Observe**, it can change the body structure by selecting one from already developed apoids. As the remote-brained system does not place the brain inside

body, the mother system can continue raising the same brain after switching the body. This is another feature of the remote-brained system. In this case, the system structure becomes a variation of a system with multiple bodies shown in Figure 1.

The goal here is to know how the brain for apoid (a) should be raised to accept the body of apoid (b) and so on. Another goal is to know whether there is a brain which accepts all body structures, and whether there is a general method to build such brain. In order to approach these questions, we have tried to share the software environment in the mother environment. The software of apoid (d) is designed over the software developed for apoids (a),(b),(c).

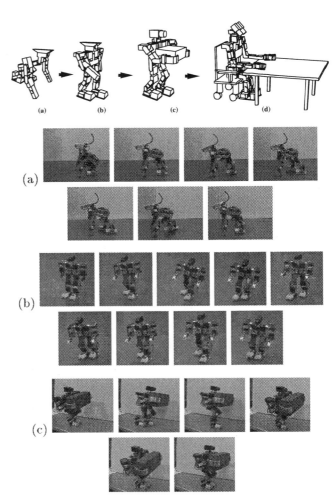

Figure 8: Sequence of Walking: (a)Knuckle Walking, (b) Biped Walking, (c) Carrying an Object

9 Evolution of 'Mother'

Mother is generated and evolved by human researchers in this framework. Although one of the goals in this framework is to build an artifical mother, we have to know the problems by doing experiments with real robots and evolve the mother by the problem analysis. The mother operations are improved by detection and reduction of the gap between the virtual world and the real world.

An apoid can have the possibility to pick itself up[17]. The sequences shown in Figure 9 are examples. The case of (a) is developed through **Preview** with virtual body and environment simulator. **Preview** can calculate the balance of the robot body. As shown in the figure, the brain can estimate the contact points between the body and the ground by calculating the center of its body gravity and the configuration of the body lims. The mother provides the robot brain with the function to estimate its body motion. The evolution of **Brain** depends on the mother evolution. The facilities for **Preview** operation is the key to the brain evolution.

The case of (b) seems to be same with (a). However, the effect of the difference between the virtual body and the real body is large. In such a case, the mother should **Teach** how to modify the action to the robot through **Observe** process. It has to have a good observer that can recognizes the robot body. As **Teach** operation is done through the body, the mother requires a real hand to perform physical contact to the robot body to **Teach** motions. It means that the mother also should be an embodied robot in the future.

If the robot can not accept the **Teach** operations, the mother have to perform **Bear** or **Build** operation based on **Observe** and **Evaluate** operations. The evolution in the mother through this flow through **Observe** to **Bear** is a good target to investigate emerging properties for real embodied agents. In order to get good results in new generation, the mother usually inherits the former effects. It is required to create new generation of the mother sometime because of the progress of fundamental technologies of computer, software, mechatronics and so on.

The evolution of a mother is a sort of a history of development done in a robotics laboratory which has to absorb new hardware and technology to build advanced real bodies and brains. Our laboratory has evolved the mother environment twice. The first generation was a hand-eye system[18]. The second generation was a network-oriented robot system augmented with the vision server for **Observe**[19]. After these progress, the remote-brained approach provides our robots with mobility and many degrees of freedom. The current mother has the virtual world and its evaluators now. The future mother may have an automatic builder of bodies and an automatic teaching body.

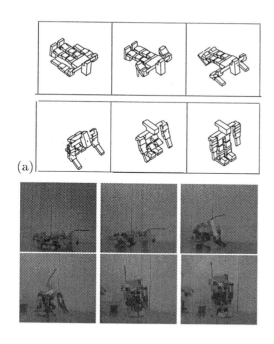

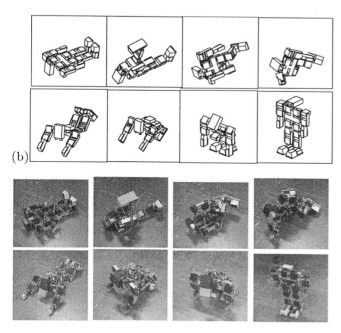

Figure 9: Sequence of Getting Up: (a) From Face Down, (b) Rolling Over from Face Up

10 Concluding Remarks

This paper has introduced a methodology based on mother operations towards physically grounded evolution using the remote-brained approach. The environment we have developed provides us with shared brain architecture which interface virtually evolved brain with breeding operations of real embodies bodies.

The background of the remote-brained approach was motivated by the question of whether the inference and representation techniques of AI are useful for robots in the real world. The answer will depend on how AI is interfaced to the real world. The remote brained approach allows us to tie AI directly to the world, enabling the verification of high-level AI techniques which could previously only be used in simulation. For robot research, this approach opens the way to the use of powerful parallel computers. For AI, this approach allows experiments with real agents, an essential step to the application of AI in the real world. There has been a missing link in research, between 'AI which couldn't survive if embodied in the real world' and 'robots with feeble intelligence'. The remote-brained approach opens the way for engineering advances which will bridge the gap.

This paper also emphasized the importance of the entity of 'mother' and described the interface between a mother and a robot. So far a mother was a human in most cases. However, in order to deepen intelligence research, we believe it is crucial to view the world consisting of the inherited mother world, the borne agents, and the processes breeding them. The remote-brained approach is the key to advance this research approach and it will open the way towards evolutional study of real embodied robots.

References

[1] C.G. Langton, editor. *Artificial Life*. Addison-Wesley, 1988.

[2] L. Steels. Towards a Theory of Emergent Functionality. In *Proceedings of First International Joint Conference on Simulation of Adaptive Behavior*, pp. 451–461, 1990.

[3] I. Harvey. The Artificial Evolution of Behaviour. In *Proceedings of First International Joint Conference on Simulation of Adaptive Behavior*, pp. 400–408, 1990.

[4] K. Sims. Evolving 3D Morphology and Behavior by Competition. In *Proceedings of the 4th International Workshop on the Synthesis and Simulation of Living Systems, Artificial Life IV*. The MIT Press, 1994.

[5] P. Maes, T. Darrell, B. Blumberg, S. Pentland, and L. Foner. Interacting with Animated Autonomous Agents. In *Proceedings of AAAI-94 Workshop Program on Artificial Intelligence, Artificial Life, and Entertainment*, pp. 43–47, 1994.

[6] M. Inaba. Remote-Brained Robotics: Interfacing AI with Real World Behaviors. In *Proceedings of the 6th International Symposium on Robotics Research (ISRR6); Robotics Research, to appear*. The MIT Press, 1993.

[7] H. Kitano. Challenges of massive parallelism. In *Proc. of 13th IJCAI*, pp. 813–834, 1993.

[8] Y. Kuniyoshi, M. Inaba, and H. Inoue. Teaching by showing: Generating robot programs by visual observation of human performance. In *Proc. of 20th International Symposium on Industrial Robots and Robot Exhibition*, pp. 119–126, 1989.

[9] M. Inaba, S. Kagami, F. Kanehiro, K. Takeda, and H. Inoue. Vision-Based Adaptive and Interactive Behaviors in Mechanical Animals using the Remote-Brained Approach. In *Proceedings of the IEEE/RSJ/GI International Conference on Intelligent Robots and Systems*, pp. 933–940, 1994.

[10] H. Inoue, T. Tachikawa, and M. Inaba. Robot vision system with a correlation chip for real-time tracking, optical flow and depth map generation. In *Proceedings of the 1992 IEEE International Conference on Robotics and Automation*, pp. 1621–1626, 1992.

[11] Masayuki Inaba. Extended Vision with Robot Sensor Suit: Primary Sensor Image Approach in Interfacing Body to Brain. In *Preprints of the International Symposium on Robotics Research*, pp. 439–447, 1995.

[12] T. Matsui and M. Inaba. EusLisp: An Object-Based Implementation of Lisp. *Journal of Information Processing*, Vol. Vol. 13, No. 3, pp. 327–338, 1990.

[13] T. Matsui and I. Hara. Parallel and Asynchronous Programming in Multithread Euslisp. In *Proc. of 12th Conf. Robotics Society of Japan*, pp. 3273–3274, 1994.

[14] M. Nilsson and H. Tanaka. Fleng prolog - the language which turns supercomputers into prolog machines. In *In Proc. Japanese Logic Programming Conference, ICOT Tokyo*, pp. 209–216, 1986.

[15] H. Koike and H. Tanaka. Parallel inference engine pie64. *bit :Parallel Computer Architecture*, Vol. 21, No. 4, 1989.

[16] M. Inaba, S. Kagami, and H. Inoue. Real time vision-based control in sumo playing robot. In *Proceedings of the 1993 JSME International Conference on Advanced Mechatronics*, pp. 854–859, 1993.

[17] M. Inaba, F. Kanehiro, S. Kagami, and H. Inoue. Two-armed bipedal robot that can walk, roll-over and stand up. In *Proceedings of the IEEE/RSJ International Conference on Intelligent Robots and Systems*, Vol. 3, pp. 297–302, 1995.

[18] H. Inoue and M. Inaba. Hand eye coordination in rope handling. In Michael Brady and Richard Paul, editors, *Proceedings of the First International Symposium on Robotics Research (ISRR1)*, pp. 163–174. MIT Press, 1983.

[19] Y. Kuniyoshi, H. Inoue, and M. Inaba. Design and implementation of a system that generates assembly programs from visual recognition of human action sequences. In *Proceedings of IEEE International Workshop on Intelligent Robots and Systems (IROS)*, pp. 567–574, 1990.

Toward Evolution of Electronic Animals Using Genetic Programming

John R. Koza
Computer Science Dept.
258 Gates Building
Stanford University
Stanford, California 94305
koza@cs.stanford.edu
http://www-cs-faculty.stanford.edu/~koza/

Forrest H Bennett III
Visiting Scholar
Computer Science Dept.
Stanford University
Stanford, California 94305
fhb3@slip.net

David Andre
Visiting Scholar
Computer Science Dept.
Stanford University
Stanford, California 94305
andre@flamingo.stanford.edu
http://www-leland.stanford.edu/~phred/

Martin A. Keane
Econometrics Inc.
5733 West Grover
Chicago, IL 60630
makeane@ix.netcom.com

Abstract

This paper describes an automated process for designing an optimal food-foraging controller for a lizard. The controller consists of an analog electrical circuit that is evolved using the principles of natural selection, sexual recombination, and developmental biology. Genetic programming creates both the topology of the controller circuit and the numerical values for each electrical component.

1. Introduction

Connectionist learning algorithms, reinforcement learning algorithms, genetic algorithms, and other learning algorithms all require, in one way or another, that the system be exposed, in its learning phase, to a non-trivial number of training cases that are representative of the environment.

Researchers in the field of artificial life usually adopt one of two approaches for exposing their system to these training cases. One approach is to simulate the system inside a computer; the other approach is to operate the system in a real-world environment.

An example of the first approach is the familiar simulated robot with errorless sensors that flawlessly executes operations in a sanitized environment in discrete time and space. Although such simulations can be conducted at high speeds within a computer, they may have little resemblance to the real-world environment.

An example of the second approach is an actual physical robot with noisy sensors that imperfectly executes operations in a realistic environment. However, the time required for actual operation in the real world precludes exposing the system to any significant number of training episodes. For example, in a novel experiment, Floreano and Mondada (1994) ran the genetic algorithm on a fast workstation to evolve a control strategy for an obstacle-avoiding robot. The fitness of an individual strategy in the population within a particular generation of the run was determined by executing a physical robot tethered to the workstation for 30 seconds in real time. This experiment was necessarily severely limited because there are only 2,880 30-second intervals in a day. Consequently, a run involving a population of only 80 individuals and only 100 generations required about three days. One can contemplate shortening the time for each episode by perhaps one order of magnitude and one can also contemplate simultaneously operating more than one physical robot in parallel (at increasing financial investment). However, it is difficult to see how this approach can offer any realistic possibility of being scaled up by the *many* orders of magnitude necessary to undertake significant learning or evolution. On the other hand, there will likely be increases of many orders of magnitude in computer speed because of both speedups in microprocessors and speedups from parallelization.

This paper proposes that a way to get the best of both of the above two approaches is to do the simulation inside a computer using a highly realistic simulation employing the very same parts that would be used in a realistic system in the physical world. Specifically, we describe how we used a currently available accurate analog electrical simulator in conjunction with genetic programming to evolve a controller composed of analog electrical parts.

2. Optimal Food-Foraging Strategy

The *Anolis* lizard (figure 1) of the Caribbean is a "sit and wait" predator that perches head-down on tree trunks and scans the ground for edible insects.

Figure 1 *Anolis* **lizard perched on a tree trunk.**

Roughgarden (1995) shows that the food-foraging strategy that yields the most food calls for the lizard to chase an insect alighting at distance, x, within its viewing area if

$$x < \sqrt{\left(\frac{3v}{\pi a}\right)},$$

where abundance, a, is the number of insects per square meter per second and where v is the lizard's sprint velocity. (See also Koza, Rice, and Roughgarden 1992).

3. Electrical Implementation

A foraging strategy can be realized by an electrical circuit (figure 2) whose input comes from the input neuron of the lizard's visual system and whose output goes to an output neuron that causes the lizard to chase an insect. The visual neuron may generate a signal whose frequency is proportional to the logarithm of the insect's distance, x (with, say, 1000 Hertz corresponding to 8 meters). The output neuron may receive a voltage (say, 1 volt) that activates the lizard. The food-foraging problem can be viewed as a problem of designing a circuit (figure 2).

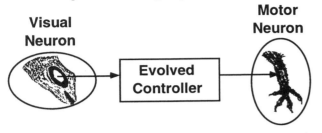

Figure 2 Controller has input at lizard's visual neuron and output at lizard's motor neuron.

Electrical circuits consist of a variety of different types of components, including resistors, capacitors, inductors, diodes, transistors, and energy sources. The problem of circuit synthesis involves designing an electrical circuit that satisfies user-specified design goals. Circuits receive input signals from zero, one, or more input sources and produce output signals at one or more output ports (probe points). In designing a circuit, the goal is to achieve certain desired values of one or more observable (or calculable) quantities involving the output(s) of the circuit (in relation to its inputs). A complete specification of an electrical circuit includes both its topology and the sizing of all its components. The *topology* of a circuit consists of the number of components in the circuit, the type of each component, and a list of the connections between the components. The *sizing* of a circuit consists of the component value(s) (typically numerical) associated with each component.

Electrical engineers will recognize that a lowpass filter can implement the above optimal food-foraging strategy. Specifically, the desired filter might have a passband below 1,000 Hertz and a stopband above 2,000 Hz. The passband voltage might be between, say, 970 millivolts and 1 volt (i.e., a passband ripple of 0.3 decibels or less) and the stopband voltage might be between 0 volts and 1 millivolts (i.e., a stop band attenuation of at least 60 decibels). These design requirements can be satisfied by an elliptic (Cauer) filter of order 5, with a reflection coefficient of 20%, and modular angle of 30 degrees. The circuit is assumed to be driven from a AC input source with 2 volt amplitude with an internal (source) resistance of 1,000 Ohms and a load resistance of 1,000 Ohms.

SPICE (an acronym for Simulation Program with Integrated Circuit Emphasis) is a massive 217,000-line program written over several decades at the University of California at Berkeley for the accurate simulation of analog, digital, and mixed analog/digital electrical circuits (Quarles et al. 1994). SPICE performs various types of analysis on circuits containing various circuit elements. The input to a SPICE simulation consists of a netlist describing the circuit and certain commands concerning the type of analysis to be performed and output to be produced.

4. Genetic Programming

Genetic programming is an extension of John Holland's genetic algorithm (1975) in which the population consists of computer programs of varying sizes and shapes (Koza 1992, 1994a, and 1994b; Koza and Rice 1992).

5. Cellular Encoding of Neural Networks

In *Cellular Encoding of Genetic Neural Networks*, Frederic Gruau (1992) described an innovative technique, called *cellular encoding*, in which genetic programming is used to concurrently evolve the architecture of a neural network, along with all weights, thresholds, and biases of the neurons in the network. In this technique, each individual program tree in the population is a specification for developing a complex neural network from a very simple embryonic neural network (consisting of a single neuron). Genetic programming is applied to populations of network-constructing program trees in order to evolve a neural network capable of solving a problem.

6. Analog Circuit Synthesis

Considerable progress has been made in automating the design of certain categories of purely digital circuits. Hemmi, Mizoguchi, and Shimohara (1994) and Higuchi et al. (1993) have employed genetic methods to the design of digital circuits using a hardware description language (HDL).

The design of analog circuits and mixed analog-digital circuits has not proved to be as amenable to automation. In DARWIN (Kruiskamp and Leenaerts 1995), CMOS opamp circuits are designed using the genetic algorithm. In DARWIN, the topology of each opamp is picked randomly from a preestablished hand-designed set of 24 topologies in order to ensure that each circuit behaves as an opamp.

7. The Mapping between Program Trees and Electrical Circuits

Genetic programming breeds a population of rooted, point-labeled trees (i.e., graphs without cycles) with ordered branches. There is a considerable difference between the kind of trees bred by genetic programming and the labeled cyclic graphs encountered in the world of electrical circuits.

Electrical circuits are cyclic graphs in which *every* line belongs to a cycle (i.e., there are no loose wires or dangling components). The lines of a graph that represents a circuit are each labeled. The primary label on each line gives the type of an electrical component. The secondary label(s), if any, on each line give the value(s) of the component(s), if any. One numerical value is sufficient to specify certain components (e.g., resistors); none are required for diodes; and many are required for a sinusoidal voltage source.

Genetic programming can be applied to circuits if a mapping is established between the kind of point-labeled trees found in the world of genetic programming and the line-labeled cyclic graphs employed in the world of circuits. In our case, developmental biology provides the motivation for this mapping. The growth process used herein begins with a very simple embryonic electrical circuit and builds a more complex circuit by progressively executing the functions in a circuit-constructing program tree. The result is the topology of the circuit, the choice of types of components that are situated at each location within the topology, and the sizing of all the components.

Each program tree can contain (1) connection-modifying functions that modify the topology of the circuit (starting with the embryonic circuit), (2) component-creating functions that insert particular components into locations within the topology of the circuit in lieu of wires (and other components) and whose arithmetic-performing subtrees specify the numerical value (sizing) for each such component, and perhaps (3) automatically defined functions.

Program trees conform to a constrained syntactic structure. Each component-creating function in a program tree has zero, one, or more arithmetic-performing subtrees and one or more construction-continuing subtrees. Each connection-modifying function has one or more construction-continuing subtrees. The arithmetic-performing subtree(s) of each component-creating function consists of a composition of arithmetic functions and numerical constant terminals that together yield the numerical value for the component. The construction-continuing subtree specifies how the construction of the circuit is to be continued.

Both the random program trees in the initial population (generation 0) and all random subtrees created by the mutation operation in later generations are created so as to conform to this constrained syntactic structure. This constrained syntactic structure is preserved by using structure-preserving crossover with point typing (Koza 1994a).

8. The Embryonic Electrical Circuit

The embryonic circuit used on a problem depends on the number of input signals and the number of output signals.

The embryonic circuit used herein contains one input signal, one output (probe point), a fixed source resistor, and a fixed load resistor, and two modifiable wires. The two modifiable wires (**Z0** and **Z1**) each initially possess a writing head (i.e., are highlighted with a circle in figure 3). A circuit is progressively developed by modifying the component to which a writing head is pointing in accordance with the functions in the circuit-constructing program tree. Each connection-modifying and component-creating function in the program tree modifies the developing circuit in a particular way and each also specifies the future disposition of the writing head(s).

Figure 3 shows the embryonic circuit used for the one-input, one-output filter circuit discussed herein. The energy source is a 2 volt voltage source **VSOURCE** whose negative (−) end is connected to node 0 (ground) and whose positive (+) end is connected to node 1. There is a fixed 1000-Ohm source resistor **RSOURCE** between nodes 1 and 2. There is a modifiable wire **Z1** between nodes 2 and 3 and another modifiable wire **Z0** between nodes 3 and 4. There are circles around **Z0** and **Z1** to indicate that the two writing heads point to these modifiable wires. There is a fixed isolating wire **ZOUT** between nodes 3 and 5, a voltage probe labeled **VOUT** at node 5, and a fixed 1000-Ohm load resistor **RLOAD** between nodes 5 and ground. There is an isolating

wire **ZGND** between nodes 4 and 0 (ground). All of the above elements of this embryonic circuit (except **Z0** and **Z1**) are fixed and not subject to modification during the process of developing the circuit. All subsequent development of the circuit originates from writing heads. Note that the output of the embryonic circuit is a constant zero volt signal **VOUT** at node 5.

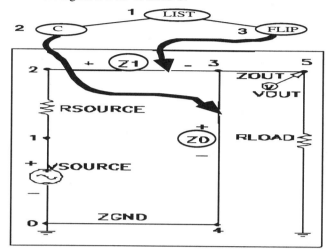

Figure 3 One-input, one-output embryonic electrical circuit.

The domain knowledge that went into this embryonic circuit consisted of the facts that (1) the embryo is a circuit, (2) the embryo has one input and one output, and (3) there are modifiable connections between the output and the source and between the output and ground.

A circuit is developed by modifying the component to which a writing head is pointing in accordance with the associated function in the circuit-constructing program tree. The figure shows a capacitor-creating C function (described later) and a polarity-reversing FLIP function (described later) just below the connective LIST function at the root of the program tree. The figure also shows a writing head pointing from the C function to modifiable wire **Z0** and pointing from the FLIP function to modifiable wire **Z1**. This C function will cause **Z0** to be changed into a capacitor and the FLIP function will cause the polarity of modifiable wire **Z1** to be reversed.

9. Component-Creating Functions

Each individual circuit-constructing program tree in the population generally contains component-creating functions and connection-modifying functions.

Each component-creating function inserts a component into the developing circuit and assigns component value(s) to the inserted component. Each component-creating function spawns one or more writing heads (through its construction-continuing subtrees). The construction-continuing subtree of each component-creating function points to a successor function or terminal in the circuit-constructing program tree.

The arithmetic-performing subtree of a component-creating function consists of a composition of arithmetic functions (addition and subtraction) and random constants (in the range −1.000 to +1.000). The arithmetic-performing subtree specifies the numerical value of the component by returning a floating-point value that is, in turn, interpreted as the value for the component in a range of 10 orders of magnitude (using a unit of measure that is appropriate for the particular type of component involved). The floating-point value is interpreted as the value of the component in the following way: If the return value is between −5.0 and +5.0, U is equated to the value returned by the subtree. If the return value is less than −100 or greater than +100, U is set to zero. If the return value is between −100 and −5.0, U is found from the straight line connecting the points (−100, 0) and (−5, -5). If the return value is between +5.0 and +100, U is found from the straight line connecting (5, 5) and (100, 0). The value of the component is 10^U in a unit that is appropriate for the type of component. This mapping gives the component a value within a range of 10 orders of magnitude centered on a certain value.

9.1. The C Function

The two-argument capacitor-creating C function causes the highlighted component to be changed into a capacitor. The value of the capacitor is the antilogarithm of the intermediate value U (previously described) in nano-Farads. This mapping gives the capacitor a value within a range of plus or minus 5 orders of magnitude centered on 1 nF.

9.2. The L Function

The two-argument inductor-creating L function causes the highlighted component to be changed into an inductor. The value of the inductor is in micro-Henrys within a range of plus or minus 5 orders of magnitude centered on 1 µH.

9.3. Other Component-Creating Functions

Numerous other component-creating functions can be employed in this process. We describe one other function for illustrative purposes (even though it is not used in solving the optimal food-foraging problem for the lizard).

Figure 4 shows a resistor **R1** (with a writing head) connecting nodes 1 and 2 of a partial circuit.

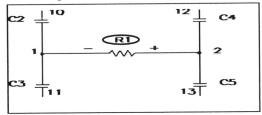

Figure 4   Circuit with resistor R1.

The functions in the group of three-argument transistor-creating QT functions cause a transistor to be inserted in place of one of the nodes to which the highlighted component is currently connected (while also deleting the highlighted component). Each QT function also creates five new nodes and three new modifiable wires. After execution of a QT function, there are three writing heads that point to three new modifiable wires.

Figure 5 shows the result of applying the QT0 function to resistor **R1** of figure 4, thereby creating a transistor **Q6**.

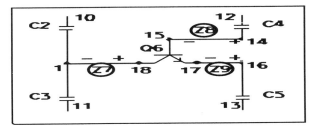

Figure 5   Result of applying QT0 function.

10.   Connection-Modifying Functions

The topology of the circuit is determined by the connection-modifying functions.

10.1. The FLIP Function

The one-argument polarity-reversing FLIP function attaches the positive end of the highlighted component to the node to which its negative end is currently attached and vice versa. After execution of the FLIP function, one writing head points to the now-flipped original component.

10.2. SERIES Division Function

The three-argument SERIES division function operates on one highlighted component and creates a series composition consisting of the highlighted component, a copy of the highlighted component, one new modifiable wire, and two new nodes. After execution of the SERIES function, there are three writing heads pointing to the original component, the new modifiable wire, and the copy of the original component. Figure 6 shows the result of applying the SERIES function to resistor **R1** of figure 4.

First, the SERIES function creates two new nodes, 3 and 4. Second, SERIES disconnects the negative end of the original component (**R1**) from node 1 and connects this negative end to the first new node, 4 (while leaving its positive end connected to the node 2). Third, SERIES creates a new wire (called **Z6** in the figure) between new nodes 3 and 4. The negative end of the new wire is connected to the first new node 3 and the positive end is connected to the second new node 4. Fourth, SERIES inserts a duplicate (called **R7** in the figure) of the original component (including all its component values) between new node 3 and original node 1. The positive end of the duplicate is connected to the original node 1 and its negative end is connected to new node 3.

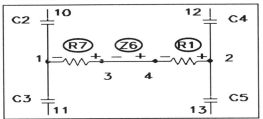

Figure 6   Result of applying SERIES.

10.3. Parallel Division PSS Function

The four-argument parallel division function PSS operates on one highlighted component to create a parallel composition consisting of the original highlighted component, a duplicate of the highlighted component, two new wires, and two new nodes. After execution of PSS, there are four writing heads. They point to the original component, the two new modifiable wires, and the copy of the original component.

First, the parallel division function PSS creates two new nodes, 3 and 4. Second, PSS inserts a duplicate of the highlighted component (including all of its component values) between the new nodes 3 and 4 (with the negative end of the duplicate connected to node 4 and the positive end of the duplicate connected to 3). Third, PSS creates a first new wire **Z6** between the positive (+) end of **R1** (which is at original node 2) and first new node, 3. Fourth, PSS creates a second new wire **Z8** between the negative (−) end of **R1** (which is at original node 1) to second new node, 4.

Figure 7 shows the results of applying the PSS function to resistor **R1** from figure 4. The negative end of the new component is connected to the smaller numbered component of the two components that were originally connected to the negative end of the highlighted component. Since **C4** bears a smaller number than **C5**, new node 3 and new wire **Z6** are located between original node 2 and **C4**. Since **C2** bears a smaller number than **C3**, new node 4 and new wire **Z8** are located between original node 1 and **C2**.

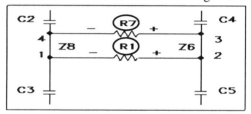

Figure 7   Result of applying PSS.

10.4. VIA and GND Functions

Eight two-argument functions (called VIA0, ..., VIA7) and the two-argument GND ("ground") function enable distant parts of a circuit to be connected together. After execution, writing heads point to two modifiable wires.

The VIA functions create a series composition consisting of two wires that each possess a successor writing head and a numbered port (called a *via*) that possesses no writing head. The port is connected to a designated one of eight imaginary layers (numbered from 0 to 7) of an imaginary silicon wafer. If one or more parts of the circuit connect to a particular layer, all such parts become electrically connected as if wires were running between them.

The two-argument GND function is a special "via" function that establishes a connection directly to ground.

10.5. The NOP Function

The one-argument NOP function has no effect on the highlighted component; however, it delays activity on the developmental path on which it appears in relation to other developmental paths. After execution of NOP, one writing head points to the original highlighted component.

10.6. The END Function

The zero-argument END function causes the highlighted component to lose its writing head.

10.7. Other Connection-Modifying Functions

Numerous other connection-modifying functions can be employed in this process. We describe two other functions for illustrative purposes (not used in the problem at hand).

The functions in the group of three-argument Y division functions operate on one highlighted component (and one adjacent node) and create a Y-shaped composition consisting of the highlighted component, two copies of the highlighted component, and two new nodes. The Y functions insert the two copies at the "active" node of the highlighted component. For the Y1 function, the active node is the node to which the negative end of the highlighted component is connected. Figure 8 shows the result of applying Y1 to resistor **R1** of figure 4.

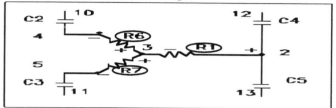

Figure 8   Result of applying the Y1 function.

The functions in the group of six-argument DELTA functions operate on one highlighted component by eliminating it (and one adjacent node) and creating a triangular Δ−shaped composition consisting of three copies of the original highlighted component (and all of its component values), three new modifiable wires, and five new nodes. Figure 9 illustrates the result of applying the DELTA1 division function to resistor **R1** of figure 4 when the active node (node 1) is of degree 3.

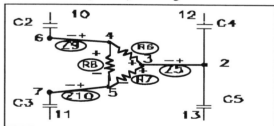

Figure 9   Result of applying DELTA1 function.

11. Preparatory Steps

Since the problem of designing the lowpass LC filter calls for a one-input, one-output circuit with a source resistor and a load resistor, the embryonic circuit of figure 3 is suitable for this problem.

Since the embryonic circuit starts with two writing heads, each program tree has two result-producing branches joined by a LIST function. There are no automatically defined functions. The terminal set and function set for both result-producing branches are the same. Each result-producing branch is created in accordance with the constrained syntactic structure that uses the left (first) argument(s) of each component-creating function to specify the numerical value of the component. The numerical value is created by a composition of arithmetic functions and random constants in this arithmetic-performing subtree. The right (second) argument of each component-creating function is then used to continue the program tree.

In particular, the function set, $\mathcal{F}_{aps}$, for an arithmetic-performing subtree is

$\mathcal{F}_{aps} = \{+, -\}$.

The terminal set, $\mathcal{T}_{aps}$, for an arithmetic-performing subtree consists of

$\mathcal{T}_{aps} = \{\mathfrak{R}\}$,

where $\mathfrak{R}$ represents floating-point random constants between −1.000 and +1.000.

The function set, $\mathcal{F}_{CCS}$, for a construction-continuing subtree of each component-creating function is

$\mathcal{F}_{CCS} = \{C, L, SERIES, PSS, FLIP, NOP, GND, VIA0,$
$\qquad VIA1, VIA2, VIA3, VIA4, VIA5, VIA6, VIA7\}$.

The terminal set, $\mathcal{T}_{CCS}$, for a construction-continuing subtree consists of

$\mathcal{T}_{CCS} = \{END\}$.

Note that all of the above is applicable to any LC circuit involving one input and one output.

The user-supplied fitness measure drives the evolutionary process. In general, the fitness measure may incorporate any calculable characteristic or combination of characteristics of the circuit, including the circuit's behavior in the time domain, its behavior in the frequency domain, its power consumption, or the number, cost, or surface area occupied by its components.

The evaluation of fitness for each individual circuit-constructing program tree in the population begins with its execution. This execution applies the functions in the program tree to the very simple embryonic circuit, thereby developing it into a fully developed circuit. A netlist describing the circuit is then created. The netlist identifies each component of the circuit, the nodes to which that component is connected, and the value of that component. Each circuit is then simulated to determine its behavior using the 217,000-line SPICE simulator (modified to run as a submodule within our genetic programming system).

Since we are designing a filter, the focus is on the behavior of the circuit in the frequency domain. SPICE is requested to perform an AC small signal analysis and to report the circuit's behavior for each of 101 frequency values chosen from the range between 10 Hz to 100,000 Hz (in equal increments on a logarithmic scale). Fitness is measured in terms of the sum, over these 101 fitness cases, of the absolute weighted deviation between the actual value of the voltage that is produced by the circuit at the probe point **VOUT** at isolated node 5 and the target value for voltage. The smaller the value of fitness, the better (with zero being best). Specifically, the standardized fitness is

$$F(t) = \sum_{i=0}^{100} \left[W(d(f_i), f_i) d(f_i) \right]$$

where $f(i)$ is the frequency of fitness case i; $d(x)$ is the difference between the target and observed values at frequency x; and $W(y,x)$ is the weighting for difference y at frequency x.

The fitness measure does not penalize ideal values; it slightly penalizes every acceptable deviation; and it heavily penalizes every unacceptable deviation.

The procedure for each of the 61 points in the 3-decade interval from 1 Hz to 1,000 Hz is as follows: If the voltage is between 970 millivolts and 1,000 millivolts, the absolute value of the deviation from 1,000 millivolts is weighted by a factor of 1.0. If the voltage is less than 970 millivolts, the absolute value of the deviation from 1,000 millivolts is weighted by a factor of 10.0. This arrangement reflects the fact that the ideal voltage in the passband is 1.0 volt, the fact that a 30 millivolt shortfall is acceptable, and the fact that a voltage below 970 millivolts is not acceptable.

The procedure for each of the 35 points between 2,000 Hz to 100,000 Hz is as follows: If the voltage is between 0 millivolts and 1 millivolt, the absolute value of the deviation from 0 millivolts is weighted by a factor of 1.0. If the voltage is more than 1 millvolt, the absolute value of the deviation from 0 millivolts is weighted by a factor of 10.0.

We considered the number of fitness cases (61 and 35) in these two main bands to be sufficiently close that we did not attempt to equalize the weight given to the differing numbers of fitness cases in these two main bands.

The deviation is overlooked for each of the 5 points in the interval between 1,000 Hz and 2,000 Hz (i.e., the "don't care" band). Hits are defined as the number of fitness cases for which the voltage is acceptable or ideal or which lie in the "don't care" band. Thus, the number of hits ranges from a low of 5 to a high of 101 for this problem.

Some of the bizarre circuits that are randomly created for the initial random population and that are created by the crossover operation and the mutation operation in later generations cannot be simulated by SPICE. Circuits that cannot be simulated by SPICE are assigned a high penalty value of fitness (10^8).

The population size, M, is 320,000. The percentage of genetic operations on each generation was 89% crossovers, 10% reproductions, and 1% mutations. A maximum size of 200 points was established for each of the two result-producing branches in each overall program. The other parameters for controlling the runs of genetic programming were the default values of Koza 1994a (appendix D).

This problem was run on a medium-grained parallel Parystec computer system consisting of 64 Power PC 601 80 MHz processors arranged in a toroidal mesh with a host PC Pentium type computer (running Windows). The so-called *distributed genetic algorithm* was used with a subpopulation (deme) size of $Q = 5,000$ at each of $D = 64$ demes. On each generation, four boatloads of emigrants, each consisting of $B = 2\%$ (the migration rate) of the node's subpopulation (selected on the basis of fitness) were dispatched to each of the four toroidally adjacent processing nodes. Details of the parallel implementation of genetic programming can be found in Andre and Koza 1996.

12. Results

12.1. A Circuit with the "Ladder" Topology

The best individual program tree from generation 0 of run A has a fitness of 58.71, scores 51 hits.

As the run proceeds from generation to generation, the fitness of the best-of-generation individual tends to improve.

SPICE cannot simulate about two-thirds of the programs of generation 0 for this problem. However, the percentage of unsimulatable circuits drops rapidly as new offspring are created using Darwinian selection, crossover, and mutation. The percentage of unsimulatable programs drops to 33% by generation 10, and 0.3% by generation 30.

The best individual program tree of generation 32 has a fitness of 0.00781 and scores 101 hits. Figure 10 shows the best circuit from generation 32 from run A. It has a recognizable seven-rung ladder topology of a Butterworth or Chebychev filter. It also possesses repeated values of various inductors (in series horizontally across the top of the figure) and capacitors (vertical shunts). Figure 11 shows the behavior in the frequency domain of this circuit. The circuit delivers a voltage of virtually 1 volt between 1 Hz and 1,000 Hz and virtually suppresses the voltage above 2,000 Hz.

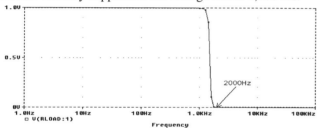

Figure 11   Frequency domain behavior.

12.2. A Circuit with "Bridged T" Topology

Different runs of genetic programming produce different results. Figure 12 shows a fully compliant best circuit from generation 64 of another run (run B). In this circuit, inductor **L14** forms a recognizable *bridged T* arrangement in conjunction with **C3** and **C15** and **L11**. The bridged T arrangement is a different topology than the ladder topology.

Note that if we disregard **C12** (whose 0.338 nF size is insignificant in relation to the 127 nF size of **C24** and

C21), there are three π *sections* to the left of the "bridged T." Each π section is a π-shaped segment consisting of a 127 nF capacitor as the left leg of the π, an inductor at the top, and another 127 nF capacitor as the right leg of the π).

12.3. A Circuit with a Novel Topology

Figure 13 shows a fully compliant circuit from generation 212 of another run (run C) with a novel topology that no electrical engineer would be likely to create.

13. Related Work and Future Work

We have also genetically designed a difficult-to-design asymmetric bandpass filter (Koza, Andre, Bennett, and Keane 1996), a crossover (woofer and tweeter) filter, an amplifier and other circuits (Koza, Bennett, Andre, and Keane 1996).

14. Conclusions

We have described an automated design process for designing analog electrical circuits based on the principles of natural selection, sexual recombination, and developmental biology. The paper described how genetic programming evolved the design of a low-pass filter that is the solution to the problem of finding the optimal foraging strategy for a lizard.

Acknowledgements

Tom L. Quarles advised us about SPICE. Figure 1 is courtesy of Jonathan Roughgarden from *Theory of Population Genetics and Evolutionary Ecology: An Introduction* (1979). Simon Handley made helpful comments on drafts of this paper.

Bibliography

Andre, David and Koza, John R. 1996. Parallel genetic programming: A scalable implementation using the transputer architecture. In Angeline, Peter J. and Kinnear, Kenneth E. Jr. (editors). 1996. *Advances in Genetic Programming 2*. Cambridge, MA: MIT Press.

Floreano, Dario and Mondada, Francesco. 1994. Automatic creation of an autonomous agent: Evolution of a Neural-Network Drive Robot. In Cliff, Dave, Husbands, Philip, Meyer, Jean-Arcady, and Wilson, Stewart W. (editors). 1994. *From Animals to Animats 3 Proceedings of the Third International Conference on Simulation of Adaptive Behavior*. Pages 421–430.

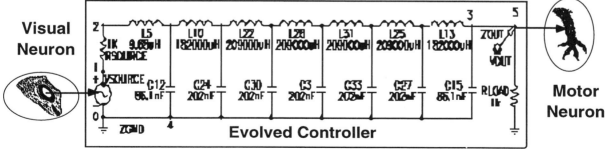

Figure 10   Best-of-run seven-rung "ladder" circuit from generation 32 of run A.

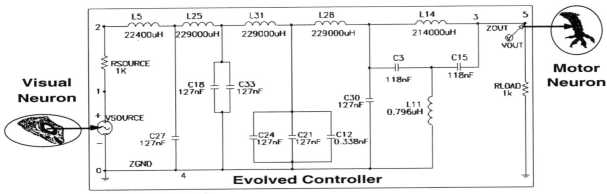

Figure 12　**"Bridged T" circuit from generation 64 of run B.**

Gruau, Frederic. 1992. *Cellular Encoding of Genetic Neural Networks*. Technical report 92-21. Laboratoire de l'Informatique du Parallélisme. Ecole Normale Supérieure de Lyon. May 1992.

Hemmi, Hitoshi, Mizoguchi, Jun'ichi, and Shimohara, Katsunori. 1994. Development and evolution of hardware behaviors. In Brooks, R. and Maes, P. (editors). *Artificial Life IV: Proceedings of the Fourth International Workshop on the Synthesis and Simulation of Living Systems*. Cambridge, MA: MIT Press. 371–376.

Higuchi, T., Niwa, T., Tanaka, H., Iba, H., de Garis, H. and Furuya, T. 1993. Evolvable hardware – Genetic-based generation of electric circuitry at gate and hardware description language (HDL) levels. Electrotechnical Laboratory technical report 93-4, Tsukuba, Japan.

Holland, John H. 1975. *Adaptation in Natural and Artificial Systems* Ann Arbor, MI: University of Michigan Press.

Koza, John R. 1992. *Genetic Programming: On the Programming of Computers by Means of Natural Selection*. Cambridge, MA: MIT Press.

Koza, John R. 1994a. *Genetic Programming II: Automatic Discovery of Reusable Programs*. Cambridge, MA: MIT Press.

Koza, John R. 1994b. *Genetic Programming II Videotape: The Next Generation*. Cambridge, MA: MIT Press.

Koza, John R., Andre, David, Bennett III, Forrest H, and Keane, Martin A. 1996. Automated WYWIWYG design of both the topology and component values of analog electrical circuits using genetic programming. In Koza, John R., Goldberg, David E., Fogel, David B., and Riolo, Rick L. (editors). *Genetic Programming 1996: Proceedings of the First Annual Conference, July 28-31, 1996, Stanford University*. Cambridge, MA: MIT Press.

Koza, John R., Bennett III, Forrest H, Andre, David, and Keane, Martin A. 1996. Use of automatically defined functions and architecture-altering operations in automated circuit synthesis using genetic programming. In Koza, John R., Goldberg, David E., Fogel, David B., and Riolo, Rick L. (editors). *Genetic Programming 1996: Proceedings of the First Annual Conference, July 28-31, 1996, Stanford University*. Cambridge, MA: MIT Press.

Koza, John R., and Rice, James P. 1992. *Genetic Programming: The Movie*. Cambridge, MA: MIT Press.

Koza, John R., Rice, James P., and Roughgarden, Jonathan. 1992. Evolution of food-foraging strategies for the Caribbean *Anolis* lizard using genetic programming. *Adaptive Behavior*. 1(2) 47-74.

Kruiskamp, Wim and Leenaerts, Domine. 1995. DARWIN: CMOS opamp synthesis by means of a genetic algorithm. *Proceedings of the 32nd Design Automation Conference*. New York, NY: Association for Computing Machinery. Pages 433–438.

Quarles, Thomas, Newton, A. R., Pederson, D. O., and Sangiovanni-Vincentelli, A. 1994. *SPICE 3 Version 3F5 User's Manual*. Department of Electrical Engineering and Computer Science, University of California, Berkeley, California. March 1994.

Roughgarden, Jonathan. *Anolis Lizards of the Caribbean: Ecology, Evolution, and Plate Tectonics*. Oxford University Press 1995.

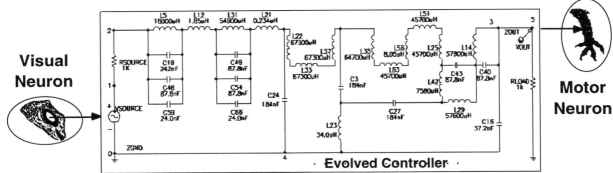

Figure 13　**Novel topology of 100% compliant circuit from generation 212 of run C.**

Generalist and Specialist Behavior Due to Individual Energy Extracting Abilities.

Henrik Hautop Lund and **Domenico Parisi**

Institute of Psychology, National Research Council, Viale Marx 15, 00137 Rome, Italy

Department of Artificial Intelligence

University of Edinburgh, 5 Forrest Hill, Edinburgh EH1 2QL, Scotland, UK

e-mail: henrikl@aifh.ed.ac.uk   domenico@kant.irmkant.rm.cnr.it

Abstract

The emergence of generalist and specialist behavior in populations of neural networks is studied. Energy extracting ability is included as a property of an organism. In artificial life simulations with organisms living in an environment, the fitness score can be interpreted as the combination of an organisms behavior and the ability of the organism to extract energy from potential food sources distributed in the environment. The energy extracting ability is viewed as an evolvable trait of organisms - a particular organism's mechanisms for extracting energy from the environment and, therefore, it is not fixed and decided by the researcher. Simulations with fixed and evolvable energy extracting abilities show that the energy extracting mechanism, the sensory apparatus, and the behavior of organisms may co-evolve and be co-adapted. The results suggest that populations of organisms evolve to be generalists or specialists due to individual energy extracting abilities.

1 Generalist vs. Specialist Behavior.

To survive and reproduce organisms must extract energy from substances present in the environment. However, not all organisms extract the same energy from the same substances. Different organisms may specialize in the type of food they eat. For example, on Barro Colorado Island, Republic of Panama, howler monkeys (*Alouatta palliata*) eat mainly leaves whereas spider monkeys (*Ateles geoffroyi*) eat mainly fruits (Milton, 1981; 1993) although both leaves and fruits are present in the environment. Furthermore, the internal food-processing mechanism of an organism (gut, colon, metabolism, etc.) tends to become adapted to the particular diet in such a way that the quantity of energy the organism is able to extract from each food type is determined evolutionarily. Because of their internal food-processing mechanisms for extracting energy from low fiber, energy rich fruits, spider monkeys would not be able to survive on the howler monkeys diet of high protein, energy low leaves, and viceversa. Finally, the sensory apparatus of the organism and its behavior also tend to co- evolve with the food preferences of the organism and its ability to extract various amounts of energy from different food types.

In simulations of the evolution of populations of artificial organisms (neural networks) the capacity of organisms to extract energy from the environment is captured by the formula or criterion that determines the fitness, i.e. the reproductive chances, of each individual. For example, organisms which live in an environment that contains discrete food elements may reproduce in proportion to the number of food elements they are able to capture during their life. The fitness formula in this case is the number of food elements captured. In other circumstances the environment may contain two types of elements, A and B, and the fitness formula might be: number of objects of type A captured plus half the number of elements of type B captured. In other words, it is assumed that B elements have only half the energy value of A elements for those organisms. In still other circumstances A elements can be defined to provide energy but B elements can be dangerous and therefore reduce the energy of the organisms if touched. In this case, the fitness formula might be the number of A elements captured minus the number of B elements touched. As we see, in these cases, the fitness score depends on the organisms' abilities to extract energy from the different elements in the surrounding environment.

In simulations using ecological neural networks (Parisi, Cecconi, and Nolfi, 1990; cf. also Wilson, 1991) the fitness formula is important not only as a criterion measure that networks should maximize evolutionarily but because it determines the type of behavior networks tend to exhibit in the environment. Given a particular environment and a particular fitness formula, we can expect organisms to evolve behaviors appropriate to both the environment *and* the fitness formula. In our first example, evolved organisms are likely to exhibit approaching behavior with respect to the single type of objects (food elements) present in the environment, whereas in the second example, organisms might exhibit a preference for approaching type A elements rather than B elements because of the difference in energy value. In the third example, organisms might exhibit approaching behavior with respect to food elements and avoidance behavior with respect to dangerous objects.

In order to study how specialist and generalist behaviors emerge based on the individual energy extracting ability, we look at a fitness formula that summarizes a number of properties of a particular species of organisms related to their nutritional needs, to the mechanisms and processes in their bodies which extract energy from ingested materials, etc. In the case of the howler monkeys and the spider monkeys quoted above, the fitness formula describes the adaptation of howler monkeys to extract more energy from leaves than from fruit and viceversa for the spider monkeys. (The relation between food and the evolution of our species has been outlined by Harris and Ross (1987)).

Like all other traits of organisms, the energy extracting mechanism can evolve. In fact, we can interpret the energy extracting mechanism of a particular species of organisms as an inherited property of that species of organisms. If the energy extracting mechanism varies (slightly) from one individual to another, is inherited, and is subject to random mutation, we can study its evolution in a population of organisms as we may study any other trait. Furthermore, energy extracting abilities and thereby fitness formulae can change during the life of an organism as any other developmental trait. As noted by Taylor (1987), "a microhabitat which represents the best compromise at one life stage might not be so for the other life stages".

To convince ourselves that what is called the energy extracting mechanism is a trait of organisms we should consider the notion of ecological niche. The notion of ecological niche designates the environmental resources from which a given species of organisms extracts the energy needed for survival and reproduction. Hence, two different species of organisms can live in the same environment (or habitat) but occupy two partially or completely different niches. For example, if the environment contains both elements of type A and elements of type B, one species may eat the A elements and the other the B elements.

However, the notion of ecological niche covers more than just components of the external environment. In order to specialize for A elements the organisms of the first species must possess a number of specific properties. They must have a sensory apparatus which is sensitive to A elements, they must behave in such a way that A elements are found and eaten, and they must possess internal mechanisms for processing A elements and extracting energy from them. The organisms of the second species that is specialized for B elements (and ignores A elements) must have the corresponding adaptations with respect to their sensory apparatus, their behavior, and their internal mechanisms for processing food. Therefore, an ecological niche includes properties of the environment (e.g., what types of elements it contains) but also properties of the organisms living in that environment (e.g., sensory apparatus, behavior, and food processing mechanisms). If any of these properties changes it should be expected that the other properties will change as well. In other words, the various components of an ecological niche co-evolve.

The internal mechanisms for processing ingested elements - and that are part of the ecological niche of a species - are the mechanisms that transform environmental elements ingested by the organism into energy units and therefore determine the total energy level of the organism on which its survival and reproductive chances depend. Therefore, the energy extracting ability is a property of organisms like any other of their properties. Energy extracting mechanisms vary from one species to another and they may also vary among individuals of the same species. For example, one individual may obtain 1 unit of energy from ingesting element A whereas another individual obtains only 0.999 units of energy.

2 Simulations with a fixed fitness formula

Imagine a population of organisms living in an environment which contains three types of elements, A, B, and C. Each individual organism lives alone in its environment. The environment is a grid of 40x40 cells which contains a total of 15 elements, 5 for each of the three types. An organism is represented by a neural network with input encoding sensory information about the location of elements and output encoding motor behavior with which the organism can turn and move in the environment. The population evolves by selective agamic (non sexual) reproduction and random mutations in inherited weight matrices. The network architecture is fixed and identical in all organisms. The criterion for reproduction is given by a fitness formula which describes how much energy an organism obtains by stepping on an element of each of the three types. The individuals which reproduce are those with most energy at the end of their life.

We have used two types of encodings for the sensory information about element location. In one population (encoding E1) a network has five input units (cf. Figure 1). Of these five units two encode angle and distance of the currently nearest element. The angle is measured clockwise with respect to the facing direction of the organism and is mapped in the interval between 0 and 1. The distance is the Euclidean distance between the organism and the nearest element and is also mapped in the 0-1 interval. The remaining three units encode the type of the element. Each of these three units is assigned to one of the three types, A, B, and C. The unit corresponding to the type of the currently nearest element takes a value of 1 while the other two units take a value of 0.

In the alternative sensory encoding (E2) a network has six input units (cf. Figure 1). Two of these units encode angle and distance of the nearest element of type A, two encode angle and distance of the nearest element of type B, and the remaining two encode angle and distance of the nearest element of type C.

While differing in their sensory apparatus, both popula-

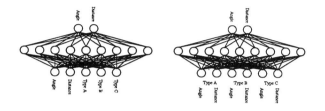

Figure 1: The neural network architecture with the E1 sensory encoding, and the neural network architecture with the E2 sensory encoding.

tions of networks have the same motor apparatus. Two output units encode the motor behavior of the organism. One output unit encodes angle of turning and the other unit encodes length of the step forward (one of five possible lengths). In any given cycle a network first turns in the direction chosen and then it moves in this direction for the chosen distance. The networks are of the feedforward type with a single intermediate layer of 9 hidden units.

Another dimension on which the organisms can differ is their internal food processing mechanisms. Some organisms have a food processing mechanism that enables them to extract the same amount of energy from all three types of food elements. Other organisms extract different amounts of energy from the various food types. What we call the food processing mechanism is the same as the fitness formula in terms of the fitness value determined for each organism.

We compare two versions of the fitness formula. In one version all three types of elements (A, B, and C) have the same energy value: one unit. In other words, an organism's fitness is increased by one unit whether the organism happens to step on (to eat) an element of the A, B, or C type. The alternative fitness formula assigns different energy values to the three element types. A and B elements have an energy value of one unit while C elements have an energy value of ten units. Both versions of the fitness formula are used in populations with E1 and in populations with E2. Hence, we describe simulations of the evolution of four different populations that can have one of two types of sensory apparatus and one

of two types of fitness formulae.

The initial population is composed by 100 individuals. The connection weights of the 100 networks are randomly generated. Each individual lives alone for a total of 5000 cycles in an environment which contains 15 food elements, 5 of each type. Since food elements disappear when eaten, food is periodically reintroduced. More precisely, each individual lives for 20 epochs, each of 50 cycles in each of 5 environments with a new random distribution of 15 food elements (total = 5000 cycles). Before they die, the 20 individuals that have the greatest amount of energy (fitness) reproduce by generating 5 copies each of their matrix of connection weights. Mutations are imposed to the inherited matrices by adding a quantity randomly selected in the interval between -0.1 and 0.1 to 10% of the weights. Evolution goes on for a total of 500 generations.

We have run a number of different simulations of each type. All simulations give the same kind of results but we will describe only one instance of each type since although the simulations result in different kinds of behavioral strategies, within each type the results are qualitatively equal. Let us call an organism that tends to eat all three types of elements a "generalist". An organism which tends to eat only one or two, but not all three, types of elements, will be called a "specialist". When the sensory encoding is E1 and the fitness formula assigns the same energy value to all elements, the population tends to be colonized by generalists. In other words, the typical behavioral strategy which emerges evolutionarily is to approach and eat all types of elements with no preference for any particular type. When the encoding is E2, on the contrary, a specialist behavioral strategy is observed, notwithstanding that all element types have the same energy value. Typically organisms tend to eat one type of food element and ignore the other two types.

From the point of view of global fitness, E1 produces

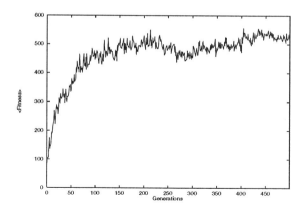

Figure 2: Total fitness of the best organism of each generation with the E1 sensory encoding.

a higher fitness than E2 when the energy value of each

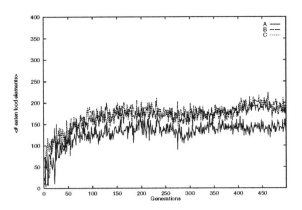

Figure 3: Number of food elements eaten of each type by the best organism of each generation with the E1 sensory encoding.

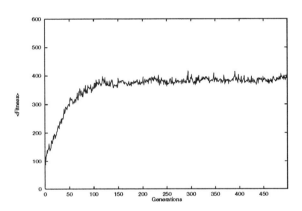

Figure 4: Total fitness of the best organism of each generation with the E2 sensory encoding.

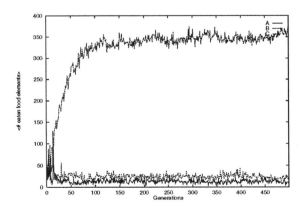

Figure 5: Number of food elements eaten of each type by the best organism of each generation with the E2 sensory encoding.

type of elements is the same. More specifically, at end of evolution the best individuals of the E1 population collect around 500 energy units (cf. Figure 2) by eating about the same number of elements (160-170) of each of the three types - they are generalists (cf. Figure 3). The best individuals of the E2 population, on the other hand, are able only to collect less than 400 energy units and these units come almost entirely from eating elements of the preferred type - they are specialists (cf. Figure 5). In this condition, the generalist strategy is more efficient than the specialist strategy. A generalist succeeds in capturing more food elements than a specialist.

When the fitness formula assigns different energy values

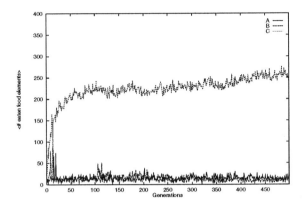

Figure 6: Number of food elements of each type eaten by the best organism of each generation with a fitness formula that assigns C elements 10 times the energy value of A or B elements with E1 sensory encoding.

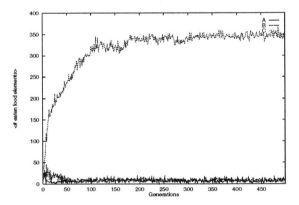

Figure 7: Number of food elements of each type eaten by the best organism of each generation with a fitness formula that assigns C elements 10 times the energy value of A or B elements with E2 sensory encoding.

to the three element types (with C having 10 times the energy value of A or B), we see a different picture. First, a specialist strategy emerges in both the E1 and the E2 populations. Organisms tend to approach and eat the elements that have a higher energy value (C) and to ignore (not eat) the other elements (A and B). Second, the E2 sensory system appears to be more useful in this condition than the E1 system. E2 organisms eat around 350 food elements of the preferred type vs 250 food elements of the type preferred by E1 organisms (cf. Figure 6, Figure 7).

We conclude that a specialist strategy can emerge evolutionarily either as the result of the particular type of sensory system which characterizes a particular species of organisms (E2, with a fitness formula which assigns the same value to all food types) or of the internal food processing mechanism of the organisms (a fitness formula which assigns a greater energy value to a single type of food, with both E1 and E2). To better see how this may come about we should examine more closely the kind of behavior which is exhibited by the organisms of our four populations.

Let us begin with the two populations where the fitness formula assigns the same energy value to all food types. When an organism perceives the location of the nearest food element and is separately informed of the type of element (sensory system E1), then the strategy which evolves is to ignore the sensory information about type of element (which is treated as noise) and just proceed to capture the nearest food element whatever its type. This generalist strategy is quite efficient because it allows an organism to approach and eat the food element which at any given time is the nearest one.

On the other hand, when an organism perceives at the same time the location of the three nearest food elements of each type (sensory system E2), then the evolved strategy is different. Organisms specialize on one food type and ignore the other types. In other words, they tend to ignore the sensory information coming from four of the input units and to make their motor output depend on the sole information from the two input units encoding the location of the preferred food type. This strategy is less efficient, because an organism is forced to approach a food element even when it is currently not the nearest one. The alternative strategy would be to choose each time the food element which is nearest, but this strategy does not emerge. The reason appears to be that this alternative strategy would involve a comparison among the three food elements to decide which is the nearest, and this could be too high a "cognitive" load for our simple networks. Hence, these organisms evolve a specialist strategy.

When we turn to the two populations that have fitness formulae which assign a greater energy value to one food type with respect to the other two types, it is clear that these organisms are under pressure to consider food type. They are forced to concentrate on the food type (C) which has an energy value 10 times that of the other two types (A and B). Hence, no generalist strategy is

likely to emerge in these populations.

The organisms with an E1 sensory system have a rather difficult task, however. They see one food element at each time. If the food element that they currently perceive is not of the C type, they must actively avoid the food element. In fact, they must go away from it because this is the only behavior that will increase the chances of making a C food element the nearest food element and, therefore, to perceive it. This is exactly the behavior which is observed in the evolved organisms of this population. When they perceive a non-C food element they move away from it until they perceive a C element. Then they approach the C element. The actual behavior which is observed is to move a step forward of maximum length. (Remember that these organisms can choose a length from 0 to 5 of the step forward.) This movement is likely to displace the organism away from the currently perceived element and, more importantly, to change the element which is currently nearest, thereby increasing the chance of seeing a C element. All of this implies that these organisms must evolve three abilities: (a) an ability to take information about food type (from the relevant input units) into consideration in order to decide what to do, (b) an ability to move away from non-C elements when the perceived element is a non-C element, and (c) an ability to approach C elements when observed. It is no surprise that the resulting strategy is not particularly efficient when compared with the strategy which evolves in the organisms with an E2 sensory system.

The organisms with an E2 sensory system and a variable value fitness formula behave like the organisms with an E2 sensory system and a fixed value fitness formula (see above). These organisms have an additional pressure to concentrate on a single food type and ignore the concurrent information about the location of the other food types. When the fitness formula assigns the same energy value to all food types, a specialist strategy emerges apparently in order to avoid the "cognitive" load of considering all sensory information and making comparisons among its various parts (see above). When the fitness formula assigns a much higher energy value to a particular food type, the specialist strategy allows an organism not only to avoid this "cognitive" load, but also to concentrate on the food type with the highest energy value. This indicates why the resulting strategy turns out to be quite efficient.

3 Simulations with an evolvable energy extracting mechanism

The simulations of this second set examine the evolution of populations of organisms when the energy extracting mechanism, upon which the fitness formula is based, also may evolve. There is no fixed fitness formula which is decided by the researcher because the energy extracting mechanism is considered as a trait of organisms. It is inter-individual variable, it is inherited by individual organisms (together with their parents' weight matrix), and it is subject to random mutations at reproduction. Hence, it evolves.

We have already described the rationale for this interpretation of the fitness formula. The quantity of energy that an individual organism extracts from a particular element type present in the environment is a function of the properties of the organism. The body of an organism includes mechanisms for processing ingested elements and extracting energy from these ingested elements. The quantity of energy which is extracted in each particular case (and which ultimately determines the fitness of the individual, i.e. its reproductive chances) depends on the particular properties of the element ingested but also on the particular properties of the individual organism. Since the relevant properties of organisms are not identical from one individual to another (and from one species of organisms to another species), the fitness formula which describes the quantity of energy (what we have called the energy value) of each type of element becomes a property of the individual organism which can be inherited exactly like all other properties.

The initial population is constructed by assigning a randomly generated energy extracting mechanism (i.e. fitness formula) to each individual. In other words, for any particular individual, the energy value for that individual of each of the three types of elements is decided randomly (within a given range from -0.1 to 0.1). When an individual reproduces, its offspring inherit the same fitness formula of its parent except for mutations. Mutations can slightly increase or decrease (by a random value chosen in the interval from -0.1 to 0.1) the energy value an offspring extracts from a given food type with respect to its parent. All the remaining parameters of the simulations are identical to those of the preceding simulations. The organisms have an E1 sensory system (organisms are separately informed of the location of the nearest food element and of the type of this element) because this sensory system has been shown in our previous simulations to yield either a generalist or a specialist behavioral strategy as a function of the fitness formula (i.e. energy extracting ability).

We have run two sets of simulations with an evolvable fitness formula. In the first set there are no limits to the evolutionary growth of the energy extracted from a given food type. A particular food type can have an indefinitely great energy value. This is obviously biologically (and physically) implausible. Therefore we have run a second set of simulations in which the energy value of a given food type can increase only to a certain limit. (This is due to a suggestion from Rik Belew and Filippo Menczer.)

The results for the population with an unlimited evolv-

able fitness formula are the following. While there is a general tendency for specialist strategies to emerge evolutionarily, for some initial populations (random seed for generating the initial set of 100 weight matrices) we also observe an opposite tendency to evolve generalist behavioral strategies. This is in contrast with our previous simulations in which the same behavioral strategy evolved independently of initial conditions. Specialists eat fewer elements than generalists (cf. Figure 9, Figure 10), but their fitness tends to be slightly higher than the fitness of generalists (cf. Figure 8). The explanation for this result appears to be in the evolution of the fitness formula. Generalists tend to evolve a fitness formula which assigns the same energy value to all three element types (cf. Figure 12). Specialists evolve a fitness formula which assigns a higher energy value to a single element type, which is the element type for which they become specialized (cf. Figure 11). Hence, specialists can obtain higher total fitness by eating fewer food elements.

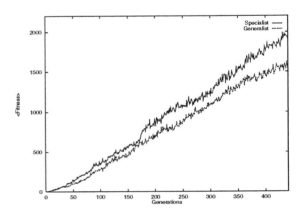

Figure 8: Total fitness of the best organism of each generation of two simulations, one with organisms with a specialist behavior, and one organisms with a generalist behavior.

The greater dependence on initial conditions of these simulations with an evolvable fitness formula can be explained in the following way. In these simulations there are more degrees of freedom than in the previous simulations. In those simulations, the fitness formula was fixed and the evolved behavioral strategy was determined by the chosen fitness formula. In these new simulations, both the behavioral strategy and the fitness formula are free to evolve. Therefore, they co-evolve. This makes the system more dependent on initial conditions. A slight initial tendency, based on the particular random assignment of connection weights, to have a fitness formula which assigns the same energy values to all food types induces a slight tendency to behave as a generalist, which then reinforces the particular fitness formula. Or viceversa. The same applies when there is an initial tendency

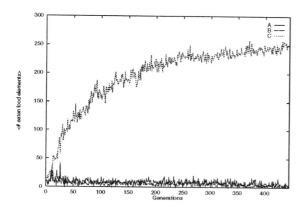

Figure 9: Number of food elements of each type eaten by the best organism of each generation with specialist behavior.

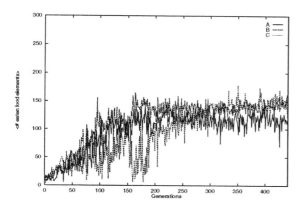

Figure 10: Number of food elements of each type eaten by the best organism of each generation with generalist behavior.

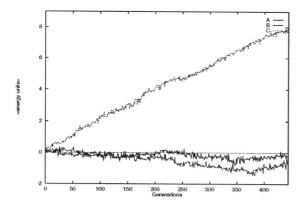

Figure 11: The evolved fitness formula of the best organism of each generation with specialist behavior.

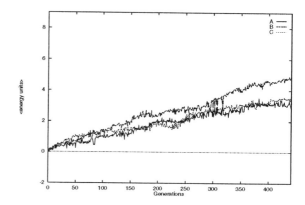

Figure 12: The evolved fitness formula of the best organism of each generation with generalist behavior.

to have a fitness formula which assigns more energy value to a single food type and this induces the development of a specialist strategy. In all cases the rule appears to be the same. If A and B co-evolve, a slight initial tendency to go in one particular direction as far as A (B) is concerned, induces B (A) to go in the corresponding direction. Then the change in B (A) reinforces the parallel change in A (B). Since different initial conditions tend to cause initially slight tendencies, systems, in which a greater number of aspects co-evolve, are likely to be more sensitive to initial conditions.

Dependence on initial conditions can further be viewed as an instance of *Muller's ratchet.* Muller (1958) points out that it is highly unlikely for a mutation to undo a previous mutation; therefore, when mutations strike on a small group of the population, or when random sampling causes this group to produce fewer offspring, the group may be entirely wiped out, and the ratchet clicks one notch, since this process can be repeated but rarely reversed. (Muller (1958) and Sigmund (1993) provide a more thorough description of Muller's ratchet). In our case, if there is an initial tendency to behave as specialists, a small group of generalists may be eliminated from the population if mutations, by chance, decrease the energy values in the fitness formula in sufficient quantities. The generalist behavior will be wiped out and may never re-appear again, since it takes a lot of mutations to change a specialist behavior into a generalist behavior. Further, the co-evolution of the fitness formula lets the organisms extract (high) energy from only one food type, and the transition to a generalist behavior will never be advantageous. Yet, as we will show, the transition can be advantageous if the fitness formula is so constrained that there is a limit on the maximum energy value of each element type.

In the preceding simulation there was no limit on the energy that an organism could extract from a given food source with its internal processing mechanism (fitness formula). This is obviously implausible. Although an evolving population of organisms can change its internal mechanism for extracting energy from food, there are likely to be various constraints and limits on this evolutionary process of change. More specifically, there are likely to be intrinsic limits on the maximum quantity of energy that can be extracted from a given food source. When the limit has been reached, any mutation can only decrease this quantity.

Therefore, in the following simulation, the fitness formula varies from one individual to another and can be changed by mutations. However, there is a limit of 4 energy units for each food type. In other words, the energy extracted from a given food type can be changed by mutations but it cannot go beyond a maximum value of 4 units. If a new mutation would imply a further increase in this value, the mutation simply has no effect. Of course, a new mutation can also decrease the maximum value of 4 energy units.

The pattern of results for the first 200 generations

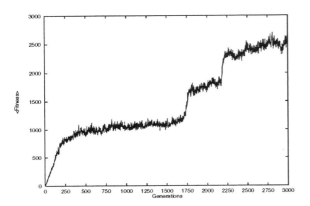

Figure 13: Total fitness of the best organism of each generation with a limited evolvable fitness formula.

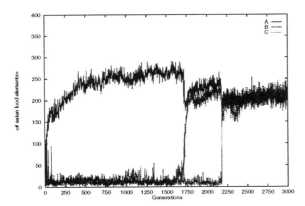

Figure 14: Number of food elements of each type eaten by the best organism of each generation with a limited evolvable fitness formula.

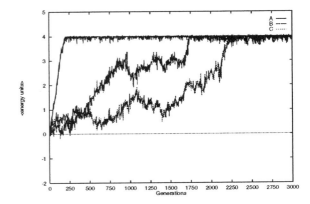

Figure 15: Evolution of the fitness formula for the best organism of each generation.

is similar to the results of the simulations with an unlimited fitness formula. The organisms tend to evolve a specialist behavioral strategy for most initial conditions. They obtain almost all of their energy from eating A elements while B and C elements are virtually ignored (cf. Figure 14). At the same time, the energy value of A elements quickly reaches its maximum value of 4 units at around generation 200 (cf. Figure 15), which is accompanied by a parallel rapid increase in fitness (cf. Figure 13).

However, the similarities stop at this evolutionary stage. After generation 200, the energy value of B elements begins to increase gradually and, more slowly, the energy value of C elements increases (cf. Figure 15). Further, it is remarkable that during this stage the number of B or C elements eaten continues to be very low while the number of A elements increases until a stable state at around generation 500 is reached (cf. Figure 14). This is parallelled by a slow increase in fitness (cf. Figure 13). It is not until around generation 1750, when the energy value of B elements also has reached its maximum value of 4 energy units, that B elements are actively sought and eaten. In fact, at this stage it happens quite suddenly that A elements and B elements are eaten almost with the same frequency, at a level only slightly below the frequency of eating A elements in previous generations (cf. Figure 14). This result causes a rapid increase in global fitness at this stage (cf. Figure 13).

The same happens some generations later for C elements. They reach their maximum energy value at around generation 2250 and, at this point, organisms suddenly start to eat them with the same frequency as elements of type A and B. As expected, the curve for global fitness shows three sudden increases: before generation 200, at generation 1750, and at generation 2250, while it only increases slightly in the periods in between.

The general conclusion is that when the energy extracting mechanism (i.e. fitness formula) evolves, but there are limits on the possible energy value of single food types, the behavioral strategy which emerges initially is specialist but then this strategy is replaced by progressively more generalist strategies. The organisms first prefer the single food type that has the highest energy value but when the energy value that can be extracted from this food type has reached its maximum value, they include other food types that can provide increasing quantities of energy.

Two phenomena that require an explanation are the increase in energy value of the initially unpreferred food types (B and C) while at the same time the organisms continue to eat very few of these elements and the sudden change in strategy (from specialist to generalist) with corresponding increases in fitness when these initially unpreferred food types reach a high energy value. The two phenomena obviously are related.

Consider what must happen if organisms have to change their behavioral strategy without damaging their fitness or, possibly, improving it. An organism of one of the first 1750 generations that eats only A elements (because they have the greatest energy value) must be able to *go away* from B and C elements when it encounters them (cf. the preceding Section). This has been a complex behavior to evolve and we must suppose that it is rather well consolidated when a change in behavioral strategy occurs. To change the current strategy means to abandon this behavior and to turn to the opposite behavior of *approaching* new types of food elements. However, for this new behavior to pay in terms of fitness it is first necessary that food types that were previously avoided have reached a sufficient energy value. Otherwise, any change in behavior is likely to reduce fitness and it cannot be retained in the population. When a new food type (for example, type B at around generation 1750) has reached the necessary high energy value, the change in behavior can be quite rapid since this is the only route which is open at this stage for increasing fitness (consider that at this evolutionary stage, A elements already have reached their maximum energy value and the organisms already eat most of them.)

It is interesting, however, that organisms gradually increase the energy value gained from B elements (and later, C elements) before this happens. Otherwise, it might be impossible for the organisms to change their behavioral strategy and for their fitness to increase significantly after generation 1750. The gradual increase of the energy value of B elements takes place between generation 200 and generation 1750 and it appears to be due to the fact that some B elements (and C elements) are eaten before generation 1750, although not many, but this seems to be sufficient to cause a slow increase in the energy value of B elements (and later, C elements), especially since other ways for increasing fitness based on A elements gradually become marginal. It seems then that

it is possible to find a related explanation both for the gradual increase in the energy value of non preferred food types while behaviors do not change much, and for the sudden change in behavior that is observed later when the gradual change in energy value of these food types has reached a threshold which justifies a rapid change in behavior. (A more thorough explanation where the above is supported by an analysis of the activation of the neural networks input, hidden, and output units can be found in Lund and Parisi, 1995).

4 Discussion

In the simulations with a fixed fitness formula we observed how the fitness formula and the sensory apparatus of a population of organisms shape the behavior which emerges evolutionarily in a particular environment. However, both the fitness formula and the sensory apparatus are not inevitable conditions which are 'given' from outside. They are traits of organisms which, like all other traits, can be changed by evolution. In fact, the fitness formula (i.e. energy extracting ability), the sensory apparatus, and the behavior of organisms (i.e. how they react to sensory information) are likely to be co-adapted and to co-evolve.

In the simulations with an evolvable energy extracting mechanism (i.e. fitness formula), we have observed the co-evolution of the fitness formula and of behavior given a particular sensory apparatus. (However, the sensory apparatus itself could be changed by evolution. Simulations in which evolution shapes network architecture including aspects of the sensory apparatus (input units) have been conducted by Nolfi and Parisi (In press) and Cangelosi, Parisi, and Nolfi (1993)). If the fitness formula is fixed, and it assigns the same energy value to all three types of food, organisms ignore sensory information about food type and develop a generalist strategy, seemingly if this allows them to reduce their "cognitive" load. This is what happens with the organisms which have a sensory system of the E1 type. But, given this same sensory system if the fitness formula is an evolvable trait, organisms evolve a fitness formula which assigns a greater energy value to a single type of food and at the same time they develop a specialist strategy which tends to concentrate on the food type with highest energy. The specialist behavioral strategy is also what emerges in populations with a fixed fitness formula that assigns a greater energy value to a single type of food.

The role of the sensory apparatus is also clear. By itself a sensory apparatus of the E1 type favours a generalist strategy apparently because this strategy reduces "cognitive" load. As will be recalled, with E1 an organism is separately informed by its sensory system of the location of the nearest food element (two input units) and of the type of the element (three input units). A generalist strategy allows a network to reduce its "cognitive" load by ignoring the sensory information about food type and to concentrate on developing the appropriate weights for approaching the currently nearest food, whatever its type (these weights are those of the connections from the two input units encoding angle and distance of the nearest food to the hidden units). This strategy is appropriate insofar as all food types have the same energy value. However, if one food type has a significantly greater energy value than the other types, the advantages of concentrating on this food type while ignoring the others represents a pressure on the networks to evolve the appropriate weights for taking food types into consideration (these weights are those of the connections from the three input units encoding food type to the hidden units). Hence, a specialist strategy emerges. The greater effectiveness of this second strategy becomes manifest in the simulations with an evolvable fitness formula. If left free to choose evolutionarily the most appropriate fitness formula, organisms evolve a fitness formula with a greater energy value for a single food type together with the corresponding specialist strategy - notwithstanding their E1 sensory apparatus. The advantages of usually eating a type of food with great energy value are greater than the costs of developing a more complex "cognitive" ability (i.e. set of weights) that includes being able to discriminate food type.

This happens if the energy value of any single food type can increase indefinitely. If there are limits to this increase, as must necessarily be the case, then an initial specialist strategy will be replaced by a generalist strategy in later evolutionary stages. The fitness formula evolves towards similar high values for all food types and a generalist strategy is more appropriate in these circumstances.

The constraints posed by the E2 sensory apparatus are opposite to those of the E1 apparatus. While E1 by itself is more consistent with a generalist strategy, E2 favours a specialist strategy. E2 separately informs the organism of the location of three food elements, one of each type. Given E2 a specialist strategy allows the network to concentrate on developing the appropriate weights for mapping the sensory information from a single food type (two of the six input units) into the correct motor response while ignoring the remaining sensory information (the other four input units). The strength of this constraint is shown by the fact that even with a fitness formula which assigns the same value to all food types, what emerges is a specialist strategy. Evolved organisms prefer to concentrate on a single food type, although this food type does not have a greater energy value than the other types, and to approach a food element of that type even if it is not currently the nearest one.

A general implication of the simulations with an evolvable energy extracting ability, which can be interpreted as an evolvable fitness formula, is that they allow us to see applications of genetic algorithms to populations of neural networks in a different light. The classical view of genetic algorithms is that they are methods for developing systems that maximize fitness. This is why the fitness formula is typically fixed and it is chosen by the researcher as the starting point of a simulation. But if one adopts an artificial life framework and applies genetic algorithms to populations of *ecological* neural networks, i.e. networks which behave in and interact with an environment (Parisi et al., 1990), things begin to look different. The goal of the genetic algorithm may cease to be that of maximizing a given fitness formula and may become that of developing systems that exhibit a certain type of behavior in a particular environment. If this is the goal, then the fitness formula ceases to be a fixed a priori and it becomes an independent variable which can be manipulated in order to obtain the desired behavior. Going back to our simulations, if we want to develop organisms with an E1 sensory apparatus which behave as generalists, approaching and eating all types of food, we should use a fitness formula that assigns the same energy value to all food types. If instead we want specialists which search the environment for only one type of food, the fitness formula should assign a greater energy value to one food type than to the others.

However, this is still looking at genetic algorithms from an engineering point of view, as tools for obtaining some desired result. If genetic algorithms are viewed as models of natural biological phenomena (both real and possible, according to the definition of artificial life (Langton, 1992)), then it is not clear that nature has some desired result to obtain - a particular behavior or the maximation of some function. In the biological world all is change and all components of an evolving system tend to co-evolve. In this perspective the fitness formula becomes a trait of organisms like all other traits. More precisely, in the context of our simulations, the fitness formula represents some property of the mechanisms and processes in organisms that extract energy from ingested materials. Fitness formulae are different in different species of organisms and in different individuals of the same species; they are inherited (or have a genetically inherited component) and are subject to mutations (and to recombination in sexually reproducing organisms). Therefore, they evolve. In our simulations with an evolvable fitness formula, we have made a first attempt to analyze how fitness formulae co-evolve with behavior, how this co-evolution of energy extracting abilities of organisms may cause them to become either specialists or generalists, and how the particular sensory apparatus constraints this co-evolution.

The study of evolutionary changes in fitness formulae can produce many more interesting results if other variables are also considered (Menczer and Belew, In press; Lund and Parisi, 1995; Lund, 1995). Among these other variables are (a) different densities of different food types in the environment, (b) the geographical distribution of different food types, (c) the co-presence of many organisms that belong to the same species or to different species in the same environment, and (d) temporal or spatial changes in the environment.

The fitness formula of a population of organisms is likely to be influenced by the different availability (density) of different food types, in addition to their different energy value (the role of density dependent habitat selection in nature has been described by Barker (1992) and Rosenzweig (1991)). Another important variable can be the localization in the environment of the different food types. If different food types are found in different locations, this can influence the spatial nature of foraging behavior and, if many organisms share the same environment, the spatial distribution of different species. More generally, significant phenomena are likely to emerge when the same environment is shared by many organisms of the same species or of different species, and these phenomena can influence the evolution of the fitness formula of these organisms. Finally, the environment in which a species lives can change because of intrinsic changes occurring in the environment (temporal changes) or because one or more organisms move to a different environment (spatial changes). In both cases, the fitness formula of these organisms is likely to change evolutionarily in response to these environmental changes.

The study of the role of these variables in populations with an evolvable energy extracting mechanism is the objective of our future work in this area.

References

Barker, J.S.F. (1992). Genetic Variation in Cactophilic *Drosophila* for Oviposition on Natural Yeast Substrates. *Evolution*, 46 (4), pp. 1070-1083.

Cangelosi, A., Parisi, D. and Nolfi, S. (1993). Cell division and migration in a 'genotype' for neural networks. *Network*, 5, pp. 497-515.

Harris, M. and Ross, E.B. (1987). Food and Evolution. Toward a theory of human food habits. Philadelphia, Temple University Press.

Langton, C.G. Artificial Life. (1992). In L. Nadel and D. Stein (eds.) Lectures in Complex Systems, SFI Studies in the Sciences of Complexity, Lect. vol. IV, Reading, MA.

Lund, H.H. (1995). Specialization under Social Conditions in Shared Environments. In F. Moran, A. Moreno, J.J. Merelo, and P. Charon (eds.) Advances in Artificial Life: Proceedings of the Third European Conference on Artificial Life, Heidelberg: Springer-Verlag.

Lund, H.H. and Parisi, D. (1995). Pre-adaptation in Populations of Neural Networks Evolving in a Changing Environment. *Artificial Life 2:2*.

Menczer, F. and Belew, R.K. (In press). Latent Energy Environments. To appear in: R. K. Belew and M. Mitchell (eds.) "Plastic Individuals in Evolving Populations", Santa Fe Institute Studies in the Sciences of Complexity, Reading, MA: Addison Wesley.

Milton, K. (1981). Food Choice and Digestive Strategies of Two Sympatric Primate Species. *American Naturalist*, 117, 4, pp. 496-505

Milton, K. (1993). Diet and Primate Evolution. *Scientific American*, 269, 2, pp. 70-77

Muller, H.J. (1958). Evolution by mutation. *Bulletin of the American Mathematical Society*, 64, pp. 137-160.

Nolfi, S. and Parisi, D. (In press). 'Genotypes' for neural networks. In M. Arbib (ed.) Handbook of Brain Theory and Neural Networks. Cambridge, MA: MIT Press.

Parisi, D., Cecconi, F., and Nolfi, S. (1990). ECONETS: neural networks that learn in an environment. *Network*, 1, pp. 149-168.

Rosenzweig, M.L. (1991). Habitat selection and population interactions: the search for mechanism. *American Naturalist* 137 (suppl.), pp. S5-S28.

Sigmund, K. (1993). Games of Life. Oxford, Oxford University Press.

Taylor, C.E. (1987). Habitat selection within species of *Drosophila*. *Evolutionary Ecology*, 1, pp. 389-400.

Wilson, S.W. (1991). The Animat Path to AI. In J. Meyer and S.W. Wilson (eds.) From Animals to Animats: Proceedings of the First International Conference on Simulation of Adaptive Behavior (SAB90), Cambridge, MA: MIT Press.

Perception and Learning in Artificial Animals

Demetri Terzopoulos, Tamer Rabie and **Radek Grzeszczuk**
Department of Computer Science, University of Toronto
6 King's College Road, Toronto, ON M5S 3H5, Canada
e-mail: {dt|tamer|radek}@cs.toronto.edu

Abstract

We employ a virtual marine world inhabited by realistic artificial animals as an ALife laboratory for developing and evaluating zoomimetic perception and learning algorithms. In particular, we propose active perception strategies that enable artificial marine animals to navigate purposefully through their world by using computer vision algorithms to analyze the foveated retinal image streams acquired by their eyes. We also demonstrate learning algorithms that enable artificial marine animals to acquire complex motor skills similar to those displayed by trained marine mammals at aquatic theme parks.

Figure 1: *Artificial fishes swimming among aquatic plants in a physics-based virtual marine environment.*

1 Introduction

A recent result of artificial life research is a virtual world inhabited by artificial animals and plants that emulate some of the fauna and flora of natural marine environments [1]. In this paper, we employ this highly realistic virtual world as an artificial zoological laboratory. The laboratory facilitates the investigation of open problems related to biological information processing in animals, and it has enabled us to develop and evaluate zoomimetic perception and learning algorithms.

The psychologist J.J. Gibson studied (in pre-computational terms) the perceptual problems faced by an active observer situated in the dynamic environment [2].[1] We present a prototype active perception system that enables artificial marine animals to navigate purposefully through their world by analyzing the retinal image streams acquired by their eyes. Retinal image analysis is carried out using computer vision algorithms. We equip our artificial animals with directable, virtual eyes capable of foveal vision. This aspect of our work is related to that of Cliff and Bullock [5], but our realistic animal models have enabled us to progress a great deal further.[2] Our

goal is to engineer general-purpose vision systems for artificial animals possessing zoomimetic eyes that image continuous 3D photorealistic worlds. We assemble a suite of vision algorithms that support foveation, retinal image stabilization, color object recognition, and perceptually-guided navigation. These perceptual capabilities allow our artificial fishes to pursue moving targets, such as fellow fishes. They do so by saccading their eyes to maintain foveation on targets as they control their muscle-actuated bodies to locomote in the direction of their gaze.

We also demonstrate motor learning algorithms that enable artificial marine animals to acquire some nontrivial motor skills through practice. In particular, these algorithms enable an artificial dolphin to learn to execute stunts not unlike those performed by trained marine mammals to the delight of spectators at aquatic theme parks. This research builds upon the low-level motor learning algorithms described in our prior work [1]. It reinforces our earlier claim that biomechanical models of animals situated in physics-based worlds are fertile ground for learning novel sensorimotor control strategies.

2 Review of Artificial Fishes

Artificial fishes are autonomous agents inhabiting a realistic, physics-based virtual marine world (Fig. 1). Each agent has a deformable body actuated by internal muscles. The body also

---

[1] Computational versions of Gibson's paradigm were developed in computer vision by Bajcsy [3] and Ballard [4] under the names of "active perception" and "animate vision", respectively.

[2] Cliff and Bullock [5] were concerned with the evolution of simple visually guided behaviors using Wilson's animat in a discrete 2D grid world.

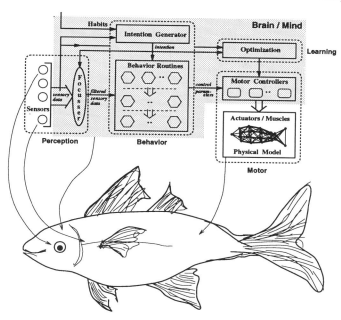

Figure 2: *Artificial fish model (from [1]).*

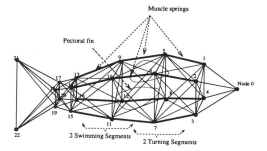

Figure 3: *Biomechanical fish model. Nodes denote lumped masses. Lines indicate uniaxial elastic elements (shown at natural length). Bold lines indicate muscle elements.*

harbors eyes and a brain with motor, perception, behavior, and learning centers (Fig. 2). Through controlled muscle actions, artificial fishes are able to swim through simulated water in accordance with hydrodynamic principles. Their functional fins enable them to locomote, maintain balance, and maneuver in the water. Thus the model captures not just the form and appearance of the animal, but also the basic physics of the animal in its environment. Although rudimentary compared to those of real animals, the brains of artificial fishes are nonetheless able to learn some basic motor functions and carry out perceptually guided motor tasks. The behavior center of the artificial fish's brain mediates between its perception system and its motor system, harnessing the dynamics of the perception-action cycle. The innate character of the fish is determined by fixed habits. Its dynamic mental state is represented by a set of mental variables—hunger, libido, and fear. An intention generator serves as the fish's cognitive faculty, arbitrating the artificial fish's behavioral repertoire in accordance with its perceptual awareness of the virtual world. The behavioral repertoire includes primitive, reflexive behavior routines, such as collision avoidance, as well as more sophisticated motivational behavior routines such as foraging, preying, schooling, and mating.

The details of the artificial fish model are presented in the paper [1] (or see an earlier version in the ALIFE IV Proceedings). The reminder of this section covers details about the motor system which are necessary to understand the learning and vision algorithms to follow.

The motor system comprises the dynamic model of the fish including its muscle actuators and a set of motor controllers (MCs). Fig. 3 illustrates the biomechanical body model which produces realistic piscine locomotion using only 23 lumped masses and 91 elastic elements. These mechanical components are interconnected so as to maintain the structural integrity of the body as it flexes due to the action of its 12 contractile muscles.

Artificial fishes locomote like real fishes, by autonomously contracting their muscles. As the body flexes it displaces virtual fluid which induces local reaction forces normal to the body. These hydrodynamic forces generate thrust that propels the fish forward. The model mechanics are governed by Lagrange equations of motion driven by the hydrodynamic forces. The system of coupled second-order ordinary differential equations are continually integrated through time by a numerical simulator.[3]

The model is sufficiently rich to enable the design of motor controllers by gleaning information from the fish biomechanics literature. The motor controllers coordinate muscle actions to carry out specific motor functions, such as swimming forward (swim-MC), turning left (left-turn-MC), and turning right (right-turn-MC). They translate natural control parameters such as the forward speed or angle of the turn into detailed muscle actions that execute the function. The artificial fish is neutrally buoyant in the virtual water and has a pair of pectoral fins that enable it to navigate freely in its 3D aquatic world by pitching, rolling, and yawing its body. Additional motor controllers coordinate the fin actions.

3 Perception

This section describes a vision system for artificial fish which is based solely on retinal image analysis via computer vision algorithms [6].[4] We have developed a prototype active vision

---

[3] The artificial fish model achieves a good compromise between realism and computational efficiency. For example, the implementation can simulate a scenario with 10 fishes, 15 food particles, and 5 static obstacles at about 4 frames/sec (with wireframe rendering) on a Silicon Graphics R4400 Indigo² Extreme workstation. More complex scenarios with large schools of fish, dynamic plants, and full color texture mapped GL rendering at video resolution can take 5 seconds or more per frame.

[4] By contrast, in our prior work [1] the artificial fishes rely on *simulated perception*—a "perceptual oracle" which satisfies the fish's sensory needs by directly interrogating the 3D world model; i.e., the autonomous agents were permitted direct access to the geometric and photometric information available to the graphics rendering en-

system for our artificial animals. The system is designed for extensibility, so that it can eventually support the broad repertoire of individual and group behaviors of artificial fishes. However, our approach to perception applies to any animal, not just fishes. In fact, we view artificial fishes as virtual piscine robots, and we do not restrict ourselves to modeling the perceptual mechanisms of real fishes [7]. Indeed, it will soon become evident that our piscine robots sense their world through virtual eyes that are patterned after those of primates!

3.1 Active Vision System

The basic functionality of the active vision system starts with binocular perspective projection of the color 3D world onto the 2D retinas of the artificial fish. Retinal imaging is accomplished by photorealistic graphics rendering of the world from the animal's point of view. This projection respects occlusion relationships among objects. It forms spatially nonuniform visual fields with high resolution foveas and low resolution peripheries. Based on an analysis of the incoming color retinal image stream, the perception center of the artificial fish's brain supplies saccade control signals to its eyes and stabilize the visual fields during locomotion, to attend to interesting targets based on color, and to keep targets fixated. The artificial fish is thus able to approach and track other artificial fishes using sensorimotor control.

Fig. 4 is a block diagram of the active vision system showing two main modules that control foveation of the eyes and retinal image stabilization.

Eyes and Foveated Retinal Imaging The artificial fish is capable of binocular vision and possesses an ocular motor system that controls eye movements [8]. The movements of each eye are controlled through two gaze angles (θ, ϕ) which specify the horizontal and vertical rotation of the eyeball, respectively, with respect to the head coordinate frame (when $\theta = \phi = 0°$, the eye looks straight ahead).

Each eye is implemented as four coaxial virtual cameras to approximate the spatially nonuniform, foveal/peripheral imaging capabilities typical of biological eyes. Fig. 5(a) shows an example of the 64×64 images that are rendered (using the GL library and SGI graphics pipeline) by the four coaxial cameras of the left and right eye. The level $l = 0$ camera has the widest field of view (about 120°). The field of view decreases with increasing l. The highest resolution image at level $l = 3$ is the fovea and the other images form the visual periphery. Fig. 5(b) shows the 512×512 binocular retinal images composited from the coaxial images at the top of the figure (the component images are expanded by factors 2^{l-3}). To reveal the retinal image structure in the figure, we have placed a white border around each magnified component image. Significant computational efficiency accrues from processing four 64×64 component images rather than a uniform 512×512 retinal image.

gine, as well as object identity and dynamic state information about the physics-based world model.

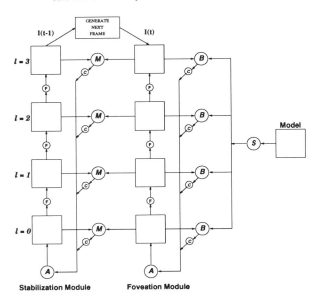

Gaze Control For One Eye

Figure 4: *The active vision system. The flow of the algorithm is from right to left. A: Update gaze angles (θ, ϕ) and saccade using these angles, B: Search current level for model target and if found localize it, else search lower level, C: Select level to be processed (see text), F: Reduce field of view for next level and render, M: Compute a general translational displacement vector (u, v) between images $I(t-1)$ and $I(t)$, S: Scale the color histogram of the model for use by the current level.*

Foveation by Color Object Detection The brain of the fish stores a set of color models of objects that are of interest to it. For instance, if the fish is a predator, it would possess mental models of prey fish. The models are stored as a list of 64×64 RGB color images in the fish's visual memory.

To detect and localize any target that may be imaged in the low resolution periphery of its retinas, the active vision system of the fish employs an improved version of a color indexing algorithm proposed by Swain [9]. Since each model object has a unique color histogram signature, it can be detected in the retinal image by histogram intersection and localized by histogram backprojection. Our algorithms are explained more fully in [10].

Saccadic Eye Movements When a target is detected in the visual periphery, the eyes will saccade to the angular offset of the object to bring it within the fovea. With the object in the high resolution fovea, a more accurate foveation is obtained by a second pass of histogram backprojection. A second saccade typically centers the object accurately in both left and right foveas, thus achieving vergence.

Module A in Fig. 4 performs the saccades by incrementing the gaze angles (θ, ϕ) in order to rotate the eyes to achieve the required gaze direction.

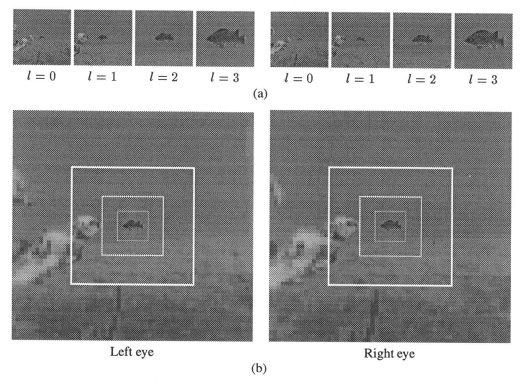

$l = 0$ $l = 1$ $l = 2$ $l = 3$ $l = 0$ $l = 1$ $l = 2$ $l = 3$

(a)

Left eye   Right eye

(b)

Figure 5: *Binocular retinal imaging (monochrome versions of original color images). (a) 4 component images; l = 0, 1, 2, are peripheral images; l = 3 is foveal image. (b) Composited retinal images (borders of composited component images are shown in white).*

Visual Field Stabilization using Optical Flow It is necessary to stabilize the visual field of the artificial fish because its body undulates as it swims. Once a target is verged in both foveas, the stabilization process (Fig. 4) assumes the task of keeping the target foveated as the fish locomotes. Thus, it emulates the optokinetic reflex in animals.

Stabilization is achieved by computing the overall translational displacement (u, v) of light patterns between the current foveal image and that from the previous time instant, and updating the gaze angles to compensate. The displacement is computed as a translational offset in the retinotopic coordinate system by a least squares minimization of the optical flow between image frames at times t and $t - 1$ [6].

The optical flow stabilization method is robust only for small displacements between frames. Consequently, when the displacement of the target between frames is large enough that the method is likely to produce bad estimates, the foveation module is invoked to re-detect and re-foveate the target as described earlier.

Each eye is controlled independently during foveation and stabilization of a target. Hence, the two retinal images must be correlated to keep them verged accurately on the target. Referring to Fig. 6, the vergence angle is $\theta_V = (\theta_R - \theta_L)$ and its magnitude increases as the fish comes closer to the target. Therefore, once the eyes are verged on a target, it is straightforward for the fish vision system to estimate the range to the target by triangulation using the gaze angles.

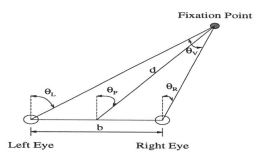

Figure 6: *Gaze angles and range to target geometry.*

3.2 Vision-Guided Navigation

The fish can use the gaze direction for the purposes of navigation in its world. In particular, it is natural to use the gaze angles as the eyes are fixated on a target to navigate towards the target. The θ angles are used to compute the left/right turn angle θ_P shown in Fig. 6, and the ϕ angles are similarly used to compute an up/down turn angle ϕ_P. The fish's turn motor controllers (see Section 2) are invoked to execute a left/right turn—left-turn-MC for an above-threshold positive θ_P and right-turn-MC for negative θ_P—with $|\theta_P|$ as parameter. Up/down turn motor commands are issued to the fish's pectoral fins, with an above-threshold positive ϕ_P interpreted as "up" and negative as "down".

The problem of pursuing a moving target that has been fix-

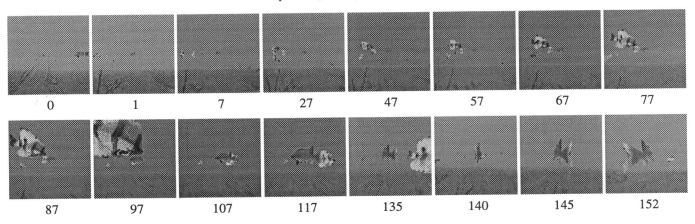

| 0 | 1 | 7 | 27 | 47 | 57 | 67 | 77 |

| 87 | 97 | 107 | 117 | 135 | 140 | 145 | 152 |

Figure 8: *Retinal image sequence from the left eye of the active vision fish as it detects and foveates on a reddish fish target and swims in pursuit of the target (monochrome versions of original color images). The target appears in the periphery (middle right) in frame 0 and is foveated in frame 1. The target remains fixated in the center of the fovea as the fish uses the gaze direction to swim towards it (frames 7–117). The target fish turns and swims away with the observer fish in visually guided pursuit (frames 135–152).*

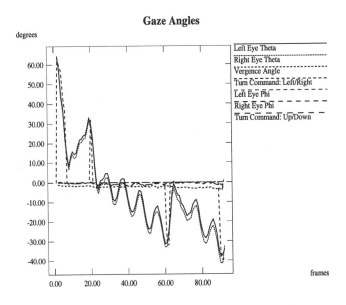

Figure 7: *Gaze angles resulting from the pursuit of a target by the AV fish.*

ated in the foveas of the fish's eyes is simplified by the gaze control mechanism described above. The fish can robustly track a target in its fovea and locomote to follow it around the environment by using the turn angles (θ_P, ϕ_P) computed from the gaze angles that are continuously updated by the foveation/stabilization algorithms.

We have carried out numerous experiments in which the moving target is a reddish prey fish whose color histogram model is stored in the memory of a predator fish equipped with the active vision system. Fig. 7 shows plots of the gaze angles and the turn angles obtained over the course of 100 frames in a typical experiment as the predator is fixated

upon and actively pursuing a prey target. Fig. 8 shows a sequence of image frames acquired by the fish during its navigation (monochrome versions of only the left retinal images are shown). Frame 0 shows the target visible in the low resolution periphery of the fish's eyes (middle right). Frame 1 shows the view after the target has been detected and the eyes have performed a saccade to foveate the target (the scale difference of the target after foveation is due to perspective distortion). The subsequent frames show the target remaining fixated in the fovea despite the side-to-side motion of the fish's body as it swims towards the target.

The saccade signals that keep the predator's eyes fixated on its prey as both are swimming are reflected by the undulatory responses of the gaze angles in Fig. 7. The figure also shows that the vergence angle increases as the predator approaches its target (near frame 100). In comparison to the θ angles, the ϕ angles show little variation, because the fish does not undulate vertically very much as it swims forward. It is apparent from the graphs that the gaze directions of the two eyes are well correlated.

Note that in frames 87–117 of Fig. 8, a yellow fish whose size is similar to the target fish passes behind the target. In this experiment the predator was programmed to be totally disinterested in and not bother to foveate any non-reddish objects. Because of the color difference, the yellowish object does not distract the fish's gaze from its reddish target. This demonstrates the robustness of the color-based fixation algorithm.

4 Learning

The learning center of its brain (see Fig. 2) enables the artificial fish to acquire effective locomotion skills through practice and sensory reinforcement. Our second challenge has been to enhance the algorithms comprising the artificial fish's learning center so that it can learn more complex motor skills

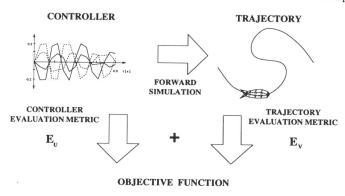

Figure 9: *The objective function that guides the learning process is a weighted sum of terms that evaluate the controller and the trajectory.*

than those we demonstrated in reference [1].

4.1 Low-Level Motor Learning

Recall that some of the deformable elements in the biomechanical model (Fig. 3) play the role of contractile *muscles* whose natural length decreases under the autonomous control of the motor center of the artificial animal's brain. To dynamically contract a muscle, the brain must supply an *activation function* $a(t)$ to the muscle. This continuous time function has range $[0, 1]$, with 0 corresponding to a fully relaxed muscle and 1 to a fully contracted muscle. Typically, individual muscles form muscle groups, called *actuators*, that are activated in unison. Referring to Fig. 3, the artificial fish has 12 muscles which are grouped pairwise in each segment to form 3 left actuators and 3 right actuators. Each actuator i is activated by a scalar *actuation function* $u_i(t)$, whose range is again normalized to $[0, 1]$, thus translating straightforwardly into activation functions for each muscle in the actuator. Thus, to control the fish's body we must specify the actuation functions $\mathbf{u}(t) = [u_1(t), \ldots, u_i(t), \ldots, u_N(t)]'$, where $N = 6$. The continuous vector-valued function of time $\mathbf{u}(t)$ is called the *controller* and its job is to produce locomotion. Learned controllers may be stored within the artificial animal's motor control center.

A continuous *objective functional* E provides a quantitative measure of the progress of the locomotion learning process. The functional is the weighted sum of a term E_u that evaluates the controller $\mathbf{u}(t)$ and a term E_v that evaluates the motion $\mathbf{v}(t)$ that the controller produces in a time interval $t_0 \leq t \leq t_1$, with smaller values of E indicating better controllers $\mathbf{u}$. Mathematically,

$$E(\mathbf{u}(t)) = \int_{t_0}^{t_1} \left(\mu_1 E_u(\mathbf{u}(t)) + \mu_2 E_v(\mathbf{v}(t)) \right) \, dt, \quad (1)$$

where μ_1 and μ_2 are scalar weights. Fig. 9 illustrates this schematically.

It is important to note that the complexity of our models precludes the closed-form evaluation of E. As Fig. 9 indicates, to compute E, the artificial animal must first invoke

a controller $\mathbf{u}(t)$ to produce a motion $\mathbf{v}(t)$ with its body (in order to evaluate term E_v). This is done through forward simulation of the biomechanical model over the time interval $t_0 \leq t \leq t_1$ with controller $\mathbf{u}(t)$.

We may want to promote a preference for controllers with certain qualities via the controller evaluation term E_u. For example, we can guide the optimization of E by discouraging large, rapid fluctuations of $\mathbf{u}$, since chaotic actuations are usually energetically inefficient. We encourage lower amplitude, smoother controllers through the function $E_u = \left(\nu_1 |d\mathbf{u}/dt|^2 + \nu_2 |d^2\mathbf{u}/dt^2|^2 \right)/2$, where the weighting factors ν_1 and ν_2 penalize actuation amplitudes and actuation variation, respectively. The distinction between good and bad controllers also depends on the goals that the animal must accomplish. In our learning experiments we used trajectory criteria E_v such as the final distance to the goal, the deviation from a desired speed, etc. These and other criteria will be discussed shortly in conjunction with specific experiments.

The low level motor learning problem optimizes the objective functional (1). This cannot be done analytically. We convert the continuous optimization problem to an algebraic parameter optimization problem [11] by parameterizing the controller through discretization using basis functions. Mathematically, we express $u_i(t) = \sum_{j=1}^{M} u_i^j B^j(t)$, where the u_i^j are scalar parameters and the $B^j(t)$, $1 \leq j \leq M$ are (vector-valued) temporal basis functions. The simplest case is when the u_i^j are evenly distributed in the time interval and the $B^j(t)$ are tent functions centered on the nodes with support extending to nearest neighbor nodes, so that $\mathbf{u}(t)$ is the linear interpolation of the nodal variables.

Since $\mathbf{u}(t)$ has N basis functions, the discretized controller is represented using NM parameters. Substituting the above equation into the continuous objective functional (1), we approximate it by the discrete *objective function* $E([u_1^1, \ldots, u_N^M]')$. Learning low level motor control amounts to using an optimization algorithm to iteratively update the parameters so as to optimize the discrete objective function and produce increasingly better locomotion.

We use the simulated annealing method to optimize the objective function [12]. Simulated annealing has three features that make it particularly suitable for our application. First, it is applicable to problems with a large number of variables yielding search spaces large enough to make exhaustive search prohibitive. Second, it does not require gradient information about the objective function. Analytic gradients are not directly attainable in our situation since evaluating E requires a forward dynamic simulation. Third, it avoids getting trapped in local suboptima of E. In fact, given a sufficiently slow annealing schedule, it will find a global optimum of the objective functional. Robustness against local suboptima can be important in obtaining muscle control functions that produce realistic motion.

In summary, the motor learning algorithms discover muscle controllers that produce efficient locomotion through optimization. Muscle contractions that produce forward movements are "remembered". These partial successes then form

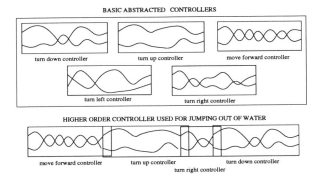

Figure 10: *Higher level controller for jumping out of water is constructed from a set of abstracted basic controllers.*

the basis for the fish's subsequent improvement in its swimming technique. Their brain's learning center also enable these artificial animals to train themselves to accomplish higher level sensorimotor tasks, such as maneuvering to reach a visible target (see [1] for the details).

4.2 Learning Complex Skills

Abstracting Controllers It is time consuming to learn a good solution for a low level controller because of the high dimensionality of the problem (large NM), the lack of gradient information to accelerate the optimization of the objective functional, and the presence of suboptimal traps that must be avoided. For tractability, the learning procedure must be able to abstract compact higher level controllers from the low level controllers that have been learned, retain the abstracted controllers, and apply them to future locomotion tasks.

The process of abstraction takes the form of a dimensionality reducing change of representation. More specifically, it seeks to compress the many parameters of the discrete controllers to a compact form in terms of a handful of basis functions. Natural, steady-state locomotion patterns tend to be quasi-periodic and they can be abstracted very effectively without substantial loss. A natural approach to abstracting low-level motor controllers is to apply the fast Fourier transform (FFT) [12] to the parameters of the controller and then suppress the below-threshold amplitudes.

Typically, our artificial animals are put through a "basic training" regimen of primitive motor tasks that it must learn, such as locomoting at different speeds and executing turns of different radii. They learn effective low level controllers for each task and retain compact representations of these controllers through controller abstraction. The animals subsequently put the abstractions that they have learned into practice to accomplish higher level tasks, such as target tracking or leaping through the air. To this end, abstracted controllers are concatenated in sequence, with each controller slightly overlapping the next. To eliminate discontinuities, temporally adjacent controllers are smoothly blended together by linearly fading and summing them over a small, fixed region of overlap, approximately 5% of each controller (Fig. 10).

Composing Macro Controllers Next the learning process discovers composite abstracted controllers that can accomplish complex locomotion tasks. Consider the spectacular stunts performed by marine mammals that elicit applause at theme parks like "SeaWorld". We can treat a leap through the air as a complex task that can be achieved using simpler tasks; e.g., diving deep beneath a suitable leap point, surfacing vigorously to gain momentum, maintaining balance during the ballistic flight through the air, and splashing down dramatically with a belly flop.

We have developed an automatic learning technique that constructs a macro jump controller of this sort as an optimized sequence of basic abstracted controllers. The optimization process is, in principle, similar to the one in low level learning. It uses simulated annealing for optimization, but rather than optimizing over nodal parameters or frequency parameters, it optimizes over the selection, ordering, and duration of abstracted controllers. Thus the artificial animal applying this method learns effective macro controllers of the type shown at the bottom of Fig. 10 by optimizing over a learned repertoire of basic abstracted controllers illustrated at the top of the figure.

We have trained an artificial dolphin to learn effective controllers for 5 basic motor tasks: turn-down, turn-up, turn-left, turn-right, and move-forward. We then give it the task of performing a stunt like the one described above and the dolphin discovers a combination of controllers that accomplishes the stunt. In particular, it discovers that it must build up momentum by thrusting from deep in the virtual pool of water up towards the surface and it must exploit this momentum to leap out of the water. Fig. 11(a) shows a frame as the dolphin exits the water. The dolphin can also learn to perform tricks while in the air. Fig. 11(b) shows it using its nose to bounce a large beach-ball off a support. The dolphin can learn to control the angular momentum of its body while exiting the water and while in ballistic flight so that it can perform aerial spins and somersaults. Fig. 11(c) shows it in the midst of a somersault in which it has just bounced the ball with its tail instead of its nose. Fig. 11(d) shows the dolphin right after splashdown. In this instance it has made a dramatic bellyflop splash.

5 Conclusion

We have demonstrated that the artificial fishes model that we developed in our prior work may be effectively employed to devise sophisticated algorithms for perception and learning. We have successfully implemented within the framework of the artificial fish a set of active vision algorithms for foveation and vergence of interesting targets, for retinal image stabilization, and for pursuit of moving targets through visually-guided navigation. Note that these vision algorithms confront synthetic retinal images that are by no means easy to analyze (compared to the sorts of images encountered in physical robotics). We have also demonstrated enhanced learning algorithms that can enable an artificial marine mammal to acquire complex motor skills. These skills necessitate locomotion through water, ballistic flight through air, and a graceful

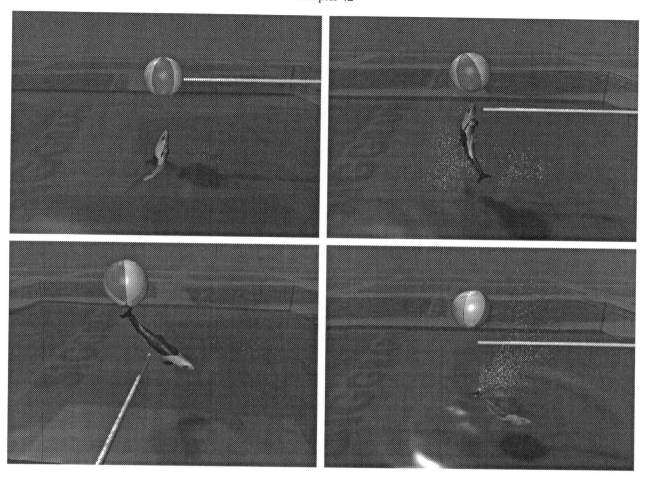

Figure 11: *"SeaWorld" skills learned by an artificial dolphin.*

style of execution. The use of highly realistic, physics-based virtual worlds inhabited by biomimetic autonomous agents appears to be a fruitful strategy for exploring difficult open problems in biological information processing and control. Our approach has value beyond artificial life to related disciplines such as vision, robotics, and virtual reality.

Acknowledgements

We would like to thank Xiaoyuan Tu for making the research described herein possible by developing and implementing the artificial fish model. This work was supported by grants from the Natural Sciences and Engineering Research Council of Canada.

References

[1] D. Terzopoulos, X. Tu, and R. Grzeszczuk. Artificial fishes: Autonomous locomotion, perception, behavior, and learning in a simulated physical world. *Artificial Life*, 1(4):327–351, 1994.

[2] J. J. Gibson. *The Ecological Approach to Visual Perception.* Houghton Mifflin, Boston, MA, 1979.

[3] R. Bajcsy. Active perception. *Proceedings of the IEEE*, 76(8):996–1005, 1988.

[4] D. Ballard. Animate vision. *Artificial Intelligence*, 48:57–86, 1991.

[5] D. Cliff and S. Bullock. Adding "foveal vision" to Wilson's animat. *Adaptive Behavior*, 2(1):49–72, 1993.

[6] B. K. P. Horn. *Robot Vision.* MIT Press, Cambridge, MA, 1986.

[7] R. D. Fernald. Vision. In D. H. Evans, editor, *The Physiology of Fishes*, chapter 6, pages 161–189. CRC Press, Boca Raton, FL, 1993.

[8] M. E. Goldberg, H. M. Eggers, and P. Gouras. The ocular motor system. In E. R. Kandel, J. H. Schwartz, and T. M. Jessel, editors, *Principles of Neural Science*, pages 660–678. Elsevier, New York, NY, 1991.

[9] M. Swain and D. Ballard. Color indexing. *Int. J. Computer Vision*, 7:11–32, 1991.

[10] D. Terzopoulos and T.F. Rabie. Animat vision. In *Proc. Fifth International Conference on Computer Vision*, Cambridge, MA, June 1995. IEEE Computer Society Press.

[11] C. J. Goh and K. L. Teo. Control parameterization: A unified approach to optimal control problems with general constraints. *Automatica*, 24:3–18, 1988.

[12] W. H. Press, B. Flannery, et al. *Numerical Recipes: The Art of Scientific Computing, Second Edition.* Cambridge University Press, 1992.

A First Result of The Brachiator III — A New Brachiation Robot Modeled on a Siamang

Fuminori SAITO
Electrotechnical Laboratory
AIST, MITI
1–1–4 Umezono, Tsukuba,
Ibaraki 305, Japan
e-mail: `saitoo@mein.nagoya-u.ac.jp`

Toshio FUKUDA
Dept. of Micro System Engineering
Nagoya University
1 Furo-cho, Chikusa-ku,
Nagoya 464–01, Japan
e-mail: `fukuda@mein.nagoya-u.ac.jp`

Abstract

This paper presents a study to realize a type of dynamic locomotion which is called "brachiation" by a robot. Brachiation is often performed by long-armed apes living on trees. Modeling a long-armed ape, we have developed a new brachiation robot, which has a redundant structure consisting of 9 links, 12 D.O.F. and 14 actuators. A framework of a motion controller for the robot is based on decomposition of a complex motion into fundamental behavior agents. As the first experiment, behaviors are programmed using some feedback controllers and sequence generators, and locomotion between branches is successfully performed by the robot.

1 Introduction

Apes living on trees perform locomotion from branch to branch by their arms using swing motion like a pendulum. This locomotion style is called "brachiation" (Fig. 1). Brachiation is one of very dynamic locomotion types of animals. This research has been focused on robots to perform brachiation and developing control techniques for such dynamic motions.

1.1 Previous studies

Fukuda *et al.*[Fuk91] studied a robot consisting of a planar six-link structure with two arms, two hands, a torso and a leg. They proposed control methods for exciting the system to increase the swing amplitude, and also studied to control the robot to catch a target branch from pending state and to perform cyclic locomotion. Though they built an experimental system – the Brachiator I, locomotion from branch to branch was not achieved. Some of the reasons for that were because of its designs of both hardware and controller; The robot did not have enough rotation speeds at the joints and the controller was not so flexible for changing control parameters.

Saito *et al.*[Sai94c, Sai94b] studied on a two-link robot – the Brachiator II, which has two arms and no body. It has only one control input at the joint between the arms. Its structure is quite simple, however motion control of the robot is not straightforward since the joint between its hand and a branch is unactuated. Hence the motion of the robot depends heavily on the natural frequency of the system determined by the gravity.

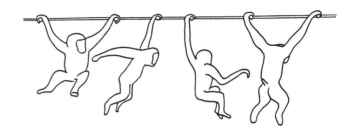

Figure 1: Brachiation of a long-armed ape

In order to obtain feedforward motions for locomotion, a learning method based on trial-and-error is proposed and applied to the robot, and locomotion from branch to branch was successfully achieved. A reinforcement learning technique is also applied to obtain a controller based on states and objective motion parameters[Sai94a, Sai94b].

Motion control of the two-link robot is simple in a sense that only one control input should be considered at a time. We have no need to coordinate multiple inputs. However because it has no kinematical redundancy, its initial and desired configurations are uniquely determined when branches to grasp are given. This fact constrains the robot to move between two configurations with little tolerance.

1.2 Current study

Unlike the two-link robot mentioned above, living apes have lots of links and actuators, and they can take a variety of configurations even if two branches to grasp are determined. This redundancy enables the apes to move robustly according to each situation. If we could build a robot which has similar kinematic structure like apes, it might be able to utilize such redundancy and perform like real apes — in fact, one of our objectives of the study is to make a robot look alike a real ape as much as possible. The main issues of this study include development of both a hardware and a controller: 1)

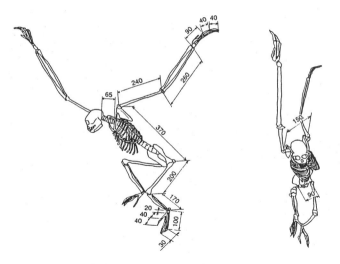

Figure 2: The measured lengths of a siamang

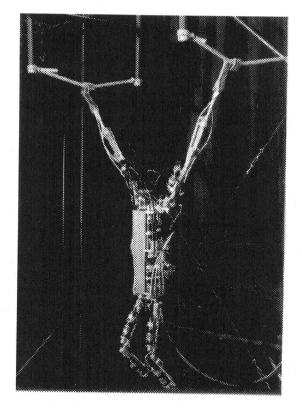

Figure 3: The Brachiator III

how much degrees of freedom we can give the robot with keeping its shape in a real size, and 2) how to control such a complex structure with a large number of actuators. In this paper, a new brachiation robot with a redundant degrees of freedom which is modeled on a siamang, or one of long-armed apes, is presented, and a fundamental framework to control such a robot is addressed. Then the first result of its locomotion control is shown in the section of the experiment.

2 Development of the Brachiator III

The newly developed robot modeled on a siamang – "Brachiator III" (or B3) – is the third model of the brachiation robots in this research. It was designed in the size of a real long-armed ape. The model of the robot was a female siamang, about 7 to 8 years of age. The length of each link was measured from the skeleton specimen as shown in Fig. 2. The Brachiator III was almost precisely developed according to these lengths. Figure 3 shows the B3 and Fig. 4 shows its kinematic structure.

The brachiator consists of nine links (without counting the short links at the both shoulders). It seems desirable to give the robot a similar number of degrees of freedom which real apes have, however the number of actuators which can be mounted on the robot is limited because of the low power/weight and power/volume ratio of currently available actuators. The B3 is given following twelve degrees of freedom in total, which seems quite important for brachiation: two degrees of freedom for each shoulder, one for each elbow, one for each wrist, one for each hip, and another one for each nee. Each joint is actuated by a dc motor with harmonic drive gears and opening of two hook–shaped hands are also performed by dc motors, hence totally fourteen actuators are used. The total weight is 9.7 kg and it is heavier than the model of 6.7 kg, however it is not unreal according to the data that adult siamangs weighted in the range from

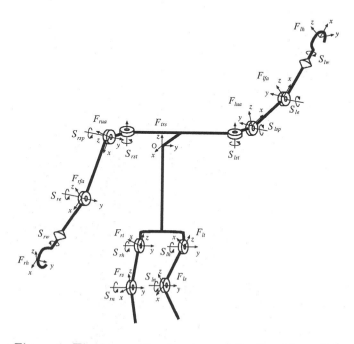

Figure 4: The kinematic structure of the Brachiator III

9.0 to 11.6 kg[Nap67]. The gross weight corresponds to the model, however its distribution is not same because of the design in which large actuators are gathered in the torso to meet the constraint of the size.

The torques of all actuators are transmitted to pulleys at the joints by wires with outer cables, then the joint axes are rotated. Each actuator has an encorder to measure the rotation and three rate gyros are equipped to the torso for measuring the attitude of the body. The hardware system is controlled by a VMEbus board computer with the VxWorks operating system. For reducing collision force, "branches" are made of vinyl tube with the inner and the outer diameter of 8 and 13 mm respectively, and several branches are put on "trees" made of steel pipes for locomotion.

3 Complex Motion Control based on Fundamental Behaviors

In the study of the two-link brachiation robot[Sai94c, Sai94a, Sai94b], locomotion patterns to move between branches are generated by learning methods based on trial and error. One of the targets of this research is to apply such learning techniques to the motion control of a complex system such like the Brachiator III. Generally, it requires unaffordable time to learn complex motions totally from scratch, and it is often practically impossible for a robot – a real hardware system – to learn by itself. However humans and animals can learn highly complicated motions by themselves. The reason for the success is of course because of the robustness of the physical body, but it must be also because of the carefully organized brains for storing and utilizing previously obtained experiences.

We can explain the importance of experiences for developing motion controllers by taking our learning process to walk as an example. As we know, a newborn baby has few knowledge of moving each part of the body. Before it starts to walk, it needs to obtain a lot of abilities to perform fundamental motions, such as taking desired configuration of each leg, standing with both legs, moving center of mass forward and backward or side by side. It can be considered that walking which we are performing is combined and optimized motion of those fundamental behaviors learned through a long period of time. An example of this sort of motion learning is implemented to a biped robot by Miller and his colleagues[Tho94a, Tho94b]. In their studies, a biped-robot was trained firstly how to stand and how to step at the same place, then how to walk. It could obtain fairly stable walking by the learning process. In such way, complicated motions can be partitioned into some functionally different fundamental motions .

Figure 5 shows the framework of the control system applied here. Each of the small units shows a behavior agent. When a controller in designed in this framework, if an objective complex behavior is a difficult one to be realized by a single step, it is divided into a set of more fundamental behaviors. Each fundamental behavior agent often consists of a further combination of lower

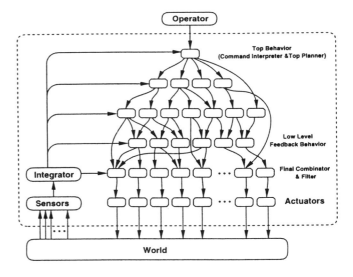

Figure 5: A framework for complex motion control based on combination of fundamental behaviors

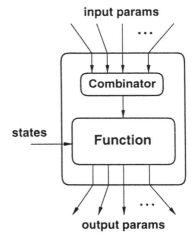

Figure 6: A framework for each fundamental behavior

behavior agents.

The behavior agent at the top of the hierarchy plays a role of the overall motion planner, which interprets commands from an operator and activates lower behavior agents. All of other behaviors are activated directly or indirectly by this top behavior agent. The behavior agents just above the lowest layer perform low-level feedback control for each actuator. The behavior agents at the lowest layer upon actuators play roles of final combinators and output filters to send actuation commands to the actuators. No matter how these intermediate behaviors are connected, outputs from the lowest behavior agents are control signals for the actuators.

Figure 6 shows the framework of each behavior agent. It consists of a combinator part and a function part. When many upper behavior agents compete to activate the same lower behavior with different input parameters, they should be combined into a parameter which can adequately coordinate both requirements. This is the role of the combinator, though it is not implemented in the current controller.. The function part determines output parameters, which will be sent to the lower behavior agents according to the combined input parameter and state variables from the sensor data integrator. This function part can be realized by many kinds of methods, such as PD feedback controllers, time-based or state-based sequence generators[Sai94c], state–action mappings using neural networks[Sai94a, Sai94b], AI-based controllers, and so on.

4 Controller Design for the Brachiator III

The controller for the Brachiator III is encoded according to the framework described in the previous section. In this section, we look into examples of the first implementation of this controller. To simplify the problem, the behavior hierarchy in this implementation is designed allowing each behavior to receive only one input at the same time, therefore no combinator is used.

Figures 7 to 11 show the hierarchy of behavior agents and their input–output flows for three high level behaviors: an initial position behavior, a still hanging behavior and a first locomotion behavior. In the hierarchy, brachiation in the top layer is the behavior agent which interprets commands from a control panel and supplies outputs to lower agents. All lower agents are activated by this top behavior agent directly or indirectly.

In the second layer, three high level behavior agents are located. They are not activated at the same time. The initial position is the behavior to return all joints to their origins. The still hanging is the behavior to hang from two given branches, and this is performed before starting locomotion. The first locomotion, whose details will be described later, is the behavior to start locomotion from statically hanging state after performing the still hanging behavior. Next to this, an agent for performing "continuous locomotion" will be placed in the next step of the implementation.

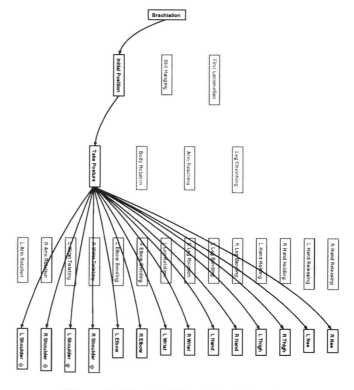

Figure 7: The initial position behavior

In the third layer, behavior agents of medium complexities are located. These agents can be activated at the same time. The layer includes a take posture behavior for taking any postures by PID controllers, a body rotation behavior to rotate the body while performing locomotion, an arm reaching behavior for approaching a free arm to a given target, and a leg stretching behavior for folding and stretching out the legs.

In the fourth layer, agents for primitive behaviors are located. They behave as local feedback controllers and produce outputs to the lowest behavior agents which are final filters of the inputs to the actuator drivers.

Let us take a look into further details of the first locomotion behavior. This behavior is divided into three modes: an init mode, a swing mode and a locomotion mode.

In the init mode shown in Fig. 9, the robot rotates both shoulders in order to make the torso to face the direction to move as much as possible, and takes a state for starting the swing mode.

In the swing mode shown in Fig. 10, it swings its torso once forward and backward using the pendulum motion, while it folds and stretches out the legs. This mode is performed to obtain sufficient energy before starting locomotion. The first locomotion behavior has a time-based sequence generator and provides inputs to the left- and the right arm rotation and the leg stretching behavior in this mode. A sequence generator is a function to map a single input (time or other parameter) to multiple output sequences consisting of several spline sequences as shown in Fig. 12. The leg

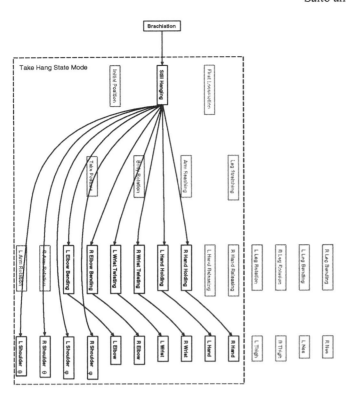

Figure 8: The still hanging behavior

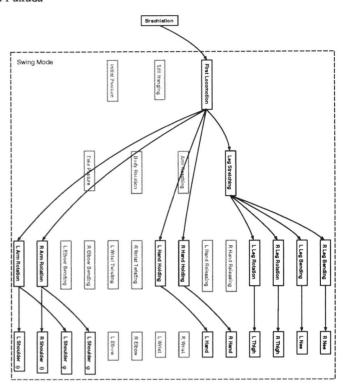

Figure 10: The first locomotion behavior (swing mode)

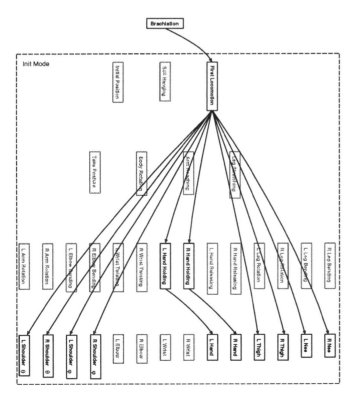

Figure 9: The first locomotion behavior (init mode)

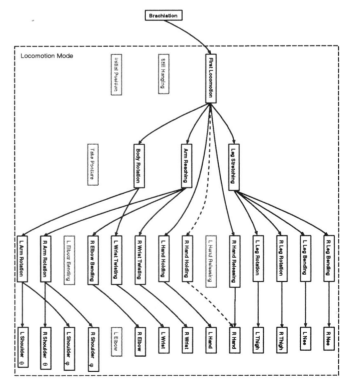

Figure 11: The first locomotion behavior (locomotion mode)

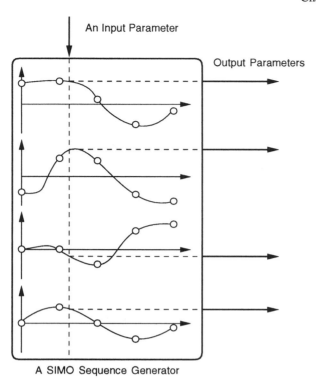

An Input Parameter

Output Parameters

A SIMO Sequence Generator

Figure 12: A sequence generator

stretching behavior also has a sequence generator and activates four low-level feedback behaviors according to the parameter given by the **first locomotion** behavior.

In the **locomotion mode** shown in Fig. 11, it performs motion to switch the rear arm to the next branch. The figure shows the snapshot of the behavior activations while it is performing locomotion after releasing the right hand and hanging by the left hand. Also in this mode, the **first locomotion** behavior uses a sequence generator based on time and activates lower behaviors such as a **body rotation** behavior, an **arm reaching** behavior and a **leg stretching** behavior. Each of them has a sequence generator based on the given parameter and generates outputs for the lower behaviors.

5   Experiment

As a first experiment, locomotion control is performed between parallel branches at the same intervals of 0.9 m with the same heights. The experimental procedure is as follows: first an operator hangs the robot from the initial two branches while it is taking a posture to hang by the **still hanging** behavior, then lets it sequentially perform the **init mode**, the **swing mode**, and the **locomotion mode** of the **first locomotion** behavior.

From the fact that even humans and animals can perform complex motions for the sake of vast amount of knowledge and experience, it is extremely important to utilize available information for a robot which is much less of them than us. As the first step, we engaged to train motions to the robot based on our knowledge. The

difficulty of the training is how to give control sequences to each behavior agent. Though the developed robot cannot precisely mimic the motion of real apes because of the difference of degrees of freedom, weight distribution and so on, some studies of natural brachiators give us suggestions of the desired motion of the robot. By performing the following motion, a living brachiator has been well-adapted to obtain momentum for moving forward as much as possible[Fle74]:

1. In the down-swing phase, it stretches out legs and free arms to make the length between the fixed rotation point and the center of gravity longer.

2. In the up-swing phase, it folds legs and free arms contrary to 1.

3. It tries to keep the motion of the center of gravity in the vertical plane, which includes the fixed rotation point and the moving direction, by using rotation of a wrist, an elbow and a shoulder of a supporting arm.

The descriptions 1 and 2 explain that apes are maximizing increments in the system energy by utilizing the gravity force, and 3 explains that they are minimizing energy consumption which is useless for locomotion towards the desired direction.

Considering these points and referring to motions of real apes, a rough trajectory was given to each middle level behavior agent at first in a quasi-static way by specifying several points to form the trajectory. Then, through repetitive attempts with combining all behaviors in dynamic way, each trajectory was tuned step-by-step by a trainer. vvSince the locomotion is very fast and dynamic, the motions performed quasi-statically and dynamically are quite different. For tuning the motion, each trial was videotaped and examined to obtain the next input sequences which seems to yield better results. In the framework which we applied here, we can tune each fundamental behavior as well as those combinations in higher levels. Operations in the higher level allows us to manipulate several actuators at once and often brings faster tuning than the operations only in the lowest level. Figure 13 shows the experimental result of successful locomotion between the branches which is obtained after about two hundreds of trials.

6   Discussion and Future Work

The controller in the presented framework is developed from two processes: decomposition of a complex motion into fundamental motions in a top-down way and realization of them in a bottom-up way. When we perform some complex motions such as walking, we seem not to divide them consciously into fundamental motions, however. We might not even go through the process, instead the control hierarchy has been self-organized in a bottom-up manner from the lower level behaviors to the top ones. From the viewpoint of evolutionary computation, though self-organization of the control structure would be an attractive approach, applying a theory to a real hardware system is constrained by many issues, such as durability of the hardware and required time for

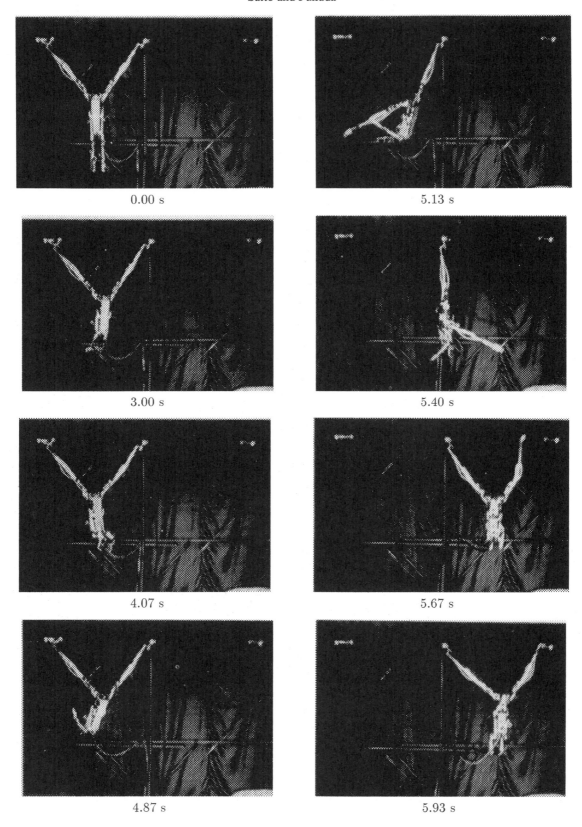

0.00 s

5.13 s

3.00 s

5.40 s

4.07 s

5.67 s

4.87 s

5.93 s

Figure 13: The locomotion of the Brachiator III in experiment (while performing the first loco-motion behavior after hanged from branches)

the evolution. In the framework applied here, we take an realistic standpoint to decompose the objective motion by utilizing available knowledge and information.

For the purpose of providing nearly desirable feedforward motions, the experiment was a success, though the motions are not optimized yet. Currently we are studying to apply a heuristic learning method[Sai94c] to obtain smoother and more efficient motions. At the same time, we are seeking to develop a controller which depends on some state variable that appropriately describes the motion of the robot rather than motion time.

7 Summary

A new brachiation robot with redundant degrees of freedom is developed which is modeled on a siamang, or one of long-armed apes. The framework of a motion controller for such complex systems is presented and applied to the robot, and locomotion from branch to branch is successfully performed in experiment.

References

[Fle74] Fleagle, J.: Dynamics of a Brachiating Siamang, *Nature*, Vol. 248, pp. 259–260, 1974.

[Fuk91] Fukuda, T., H. Hosokai, and Y. Kondo: Brachiation Type of Mobile Robot, in *Proc. IEEE Int. Conf. Advanced Robotics (ICAR '91)*, pp. 915–920, 1991.

[Nap67] Napier, J. R. and P. H. Napier: *A Handbook of Living Primates*, Academic Press, 1967.

[Sai94a] Saito, F. and T. Fukuda: Learning Architecture for Real Robotic Systems — Extension of Connectionist Q–Learning for Continuous Robot Control Domain, in *Proc. 1994 IEEE Int. Conf. on Robotics and Automation*, pp. 27–32, 1994.

[Sai94b] Saito, F. and T. Fukuda: Two–Link–Robot Brachiation with Connectionist Q–Learning, in *From Animals to Animats 3 (Proc. of the Third Int. Conf. on Simulation of Adaptive Behavior)*, pp. 309–314, The MIT Press, 1994.

[Sai94c] Saito, F., T. Fukuda, and F. Arai: Swing and Locomotion Control for a Two–Link Brachiation Robot, *IEEE Control Systems*, Vol. 14, No. 1, pp. 5–12, 1994.

[Tho94a] Thomas Miller, W., III: Real–Time Neural Network Control of a Biped Walking Robot, *IEEE Control Systems*, Vol. 14, No. 1, pp. 41–48, 1994.

[Tho94b] Thomas Miller, W., III, S. M. Scalera, and A. Kun: Neural Network Control of Dynamic Balance for a Biped Walking Robot, in *Proc. of the Eighth Yale Workshop on Adaptive and Learning Systems*, pp. 156–161, 1994.

Self-Assembling Microstructures

Kazuo Hosokawa, Isao Shimoyama,* and Hirofumi Miura*

The Institute of Physical and Chemical
Research (RIKEN)
2-1 Hirosawa, Wako-shi,
Saitama 351-01, Japan
hosokawa@cel.riken.go.jp

*Department of Mechano-Informatics,
The University of Tokyo
7-3-1 Hongo, Bunkyo-ku,
Tokyo 113, Japan
{isao, miura}@leopard.t.u-tokyo.ac.jp

Abstract

Several self-assembling microstructures have been fabricated, and approximately 100 units floating on the surface of water were self-assembled two-dimensionally. The basic assembly units are 400 μm large, and consist of both polyimide and polysilicon thin films. Surface tension was used in this system as the bonding force. The surface tension is the local interaction between the units, and is dominant in the microscale. Each unit was bonded selectively by employing the following characteristics of the surface tension: 1) objects located at equal heights are attracted to each other, 2) large attractive forces act on sharp parts, and 3) objects located at different heights are mutually repulsed. The curling-up property of the thin films was used to obtain the different heights. Self-assembling behavior was also predicted by using a rate equation.

1 Introduction

Viruses and bacterial flagella are constructed automatically out of protein sub-units[1, 2]. This phenomenon is called self-assembly, which is a powerful technique applicable to micro-fabrication. This report discusses fundamental experiments in two-dimensional self-assembly using the surface tension of water.

There is previous research reporting on micro-self-assembly. Cohn et al.[3] experimented with the self-assembly of a two-dimensional lattice consisting of about 1000 hexagonal units (1 mm in diameter) by placing the units on a slightly concave diaphragm that was agitated by a loudspeaker. Yeh and Smith[4] fabricated trapezoidal GaAs blocks (about 10 μm) and a Si wafer with trapezoidal holes. The blocks are placed in the holes by releasing them in a carrier fluid (ethanol) and dispensing the fluid over the wafer. They are fixed by a sticking force when the fluid evaporates.

To achieve self-assembly, the following conditions must be met: generating bonding forces, bonding selectively, and moving the parts randomly so that they come together by chance. Cohn et al.[3] demonstrated self-assembly using gravity and mechanical vibration. Complementary shapes were used to combine together. Yeh and Smith[4] also reported on self-assembly by gravity, sticking forces, and fluid oscillation. However, these forces do not cause selective interaction between assembly elements.

In the microscale, the dominant surface tension force causes an interaction like magnetic force, so more sophisticated micro-self-assembly may be performed. We employ the surface tension specified by the geometric shapes of self-assembly units. To disturb our self-assembly system, either magnetic or fluid forces can be utilized.

2 Large Model

A large self-assembly model several millimeters in size was made before fabricating the micron order models using thin film technology[5]. Figure 1 shows a basic unit of the large model. One hundred units were put into a flat box as illustrated in Fig. 2. Their movement was restricted to a plane. An electric motor rotates the box at a rate of 4.0 rpm and shakes the units thoroughly. The units are bonded to each other by magnetic force. Six units form a complete body (Fig. 3).

The behavior of this self-assembling system was examined by use of rate equations[5, 6], which were derived by analogy with chemical kinetics. Stable clusters of this system are the six cases shown in Fig. 3. They are represented by the

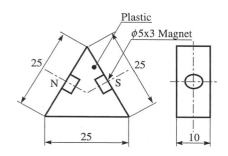

Figure 1. Large model (Unit: mm).

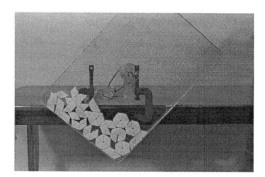

Figure 2. Experimental apparatus.

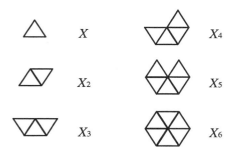

Figure 3. Stable large model clusters.

symbols X, X_2, ..., X_6 according to the number of constituent units. The elementary processes are described similarly to chemical reactions as follows:

$$2X \rightarrow X_2, \qquad X + X_2 \rightarrow X_3, \quad X + X_3 \rightarrow X_4,$$
$$X + X_4 \rightarrow X_5, \quad X + X_5 \rightarrow X_6, \quad 2X_2 \rightarrow X_4, \qquad (1)$$
$$X_2 + X_3 \rightarrow X_5, \quad X_2 + X_4 \rightarrow X_6, \quad 2X_3 \rightarrow X_6.$$

When symbol x_i denotes the quantity of X_i, the statistical behavior of the state vector

$$\boldsymbol{x}(t) = \left(x_1(t), x_2(t), x_3(t), x_4(t), x_5(t), x_6(t) \right)^{\mathrm{T}} \qquad (2)$$

can be predicted using the rate equation

$$\boldsymbol{x}(t+1) = \boldsymbol{x}(t) + A\boldsymbol{P}(\boldsymbol{x}(t)). \qquad (3)$$

In Eq. (3), step t represents the number of collisions between any two clusters. The component a_{ij} of the coefficient matrix A is a stoichiometric number of j-th reaction in Eq. (1). The j-th component of the vector $\boldsymbol{P}(\boldsymbol{x})$ represents the probability that the j-th reaction occurs. Then,

$$A = \begin{pmatrix} -2 & -1 & -1 & -1 & -1 & 0 & 0 & 0 & 0 \\ 1 & -1 & 0 & 0 & 0 & -2 & -1 & -1 & 0 \\ 0 & 1 & -1 & 0 & 0 & 0 & -1 & 0 & -2 \\ 0 & 0 & 1 & -1 & 0 & 1 & 0 & -1 & 0 \\ 0 & 0 & 0 & 1 & -1 & 0 & 1 & 0 & 0 \\ 0 & 0 & 0 & 0 & 1 & 0 & 0 & 1 & 1 \end{pmatrix},$$

$$\boldsymbol{P}(\boldsymbol{x}) = \frac{1}{S^2}(P_{11}^{\mathrm{b}}x_1^2, 2P_{12}^{\mathrm{b}}x_1x_2, 2P_{13}^{\mathrm{b}}x_1x_3, 2P_{14}^{\mathrm{b}}x_1x_4,$$
$$2P_{15}^{\mathrm{b}}x_1x_5, P_{22}^{\mathrm{b}}x_2^2, 2P_{23}^{\mathrm{b}}x_2x_3, 2P_{24}^{\mathrm{b}}x_2x_4, P_{33}^{\mathrm{b}}x_3^2)^{\mathrm{T}}, \qquad (4)$$

where, $S = x_1 + \cdots + x_6$ is the total of the clusters. In addition, the bonding probability P_{lm}^{b} is the conditional probability of X_l and X_m bonding on the condition that they collide. We assumed that P_{lm}^{b} depends only on the shape of the clusters. That is, P_{lm}^{b} is assumed to be equal to the probability that X_l and X_m are in an attitude in which they can be linked together when they collide. Table 1 shows the calculated bonding probability.

Figure 4 shows the experimental data and calculated results with the initial condition of $\boldsymbol{x}(0) = (100, 0, ..., 0)$.

Table 1. The bonding probability, P_{lm}^{b}, of the large model.

	$l = 1$	2	3	4	5
$m = 1$	0.472	0.444	0.417	0.278	0.139
2		0.389	0.333	0.222	0
3			0.250	0	0
4	Symmetric			0	0
5					0

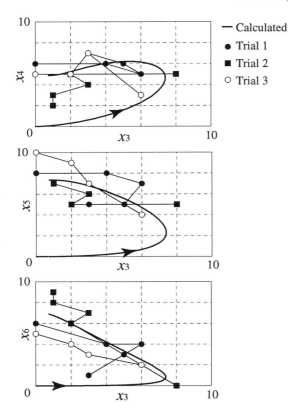

Figure 4. Self-assembling behavior of the large model.

3 Bonding Force

3. 1 Bonding force caused by surface tension

The surface tension acting on an object on water surface is calculated using the shape of the water as shown in Fig. 5.

The shape of the water surface, $z(x, y)$, is given by the following Young-Laplace equation:

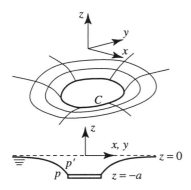

Figure 5. Water surface structure around a floating object.

$$\gamma(1/R_1 + 1/R_2) = p - p', \qquad (5)$$

where, γ is surface tension of water, R_1 and R_2 are the principal curvature radii of the surface of the water, and $p - p'$ is the pressure difference, as shown in Fig. 5. Equation (5) can be approximated when height a is small as

$$\nabla^2 z = k^2 z, \qquad (6)$$

where, $k^2 = (\rho_{\text{water}} - \rho_{\text{air}}) g / \gamma$, ρ_{water} and ρ_{air} are the density of water and air, and g is the acceleration due to gravity, and $k = 367$ m^{-1}. The boundary conditions are written as $z = -a$ at the edge and $z = 0$ at infinity.

The potential energy of water

$$U = \iint (u_S + u_G) dx dy \qquad (7)$$

is calculated from the water shape given by Eq. (6), where u_S is the surface free energy density given by Eq. (8).

$$u_S(x, y) = \frac{\gamma}{2} \left[(\partial z / \partial x)^2 + (\partial z / \partial y)^2 \right]. \qquad (8)$$

The higher order terms of $\partial z / \partial x$ and $\partial z / \partial y$ are ignored in Eq. (8). The u_G term in Eq. (7) is the gravitational potential energy density given by Eq. (9),

$$u_G(x, y) = \frac{\gamma}{2} (kz)^2, \qquad (9)$$

and can be ignored in small scale.

Potential energy U is determined by position $\boldsymbol{q}$ of the object. The force $\boldsymbol{f}$, acting on the object, is calculated by Eq. (10).

$$\boldsymbol{f} = -\frac{\partial U}{\partial \boldsymbol{q}}. \qquad (10)$$

The following results are derived from numerical calculations for several cases. There is a stable equilibrium distance between two objects on the water. This distance is determined by the height difference between the objects. When the objects are positioned at the same height, the equilibrium distance is zero, so it can be thought that an attractive force acts between the objects. On the other hand, when the heights are different, the equilibrium point is detached from the surface of the object. This distance increases with the difference of heights, and can be thought of as a repulsive force that acts between the objects. The gradient of the water surface is large around a sharp projection. The surface free energy density u_S is also large there. This means that a sharp projection receives force strongly from the water.

A similar situation appears in the Laplace equation of an electrostatic field, where height z, and surface tension γ correspond to electrical potential ϕ and permittivity ε, respectively. Both equations are identified if gravity is ignored. In addition, since the force decreases in proportion to the characteristic length, it becomes dominant in the microscale.

3.2 Measurement of bonding force

The experimental setup to measure the attractive force caused by the surface tension is shown in Fig. 6. The polyimide tip rises to the surface of the water because polyimide sheds water. Forces in the x- and z-directions were calculated from the displacement of the polysilicon beam. The sinking depth a was calculated from the force in the z-direction.

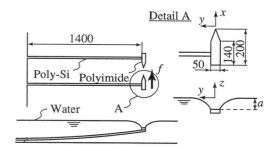

Figure 6. Measurement system for bonding force of surface tension (Unit: μm). The polysilicon beam is 5 μm wide and 3 μm thick.

The shape of the water surface is obtained by solving Eq. (6) using difference calculus. Since this system is symmetric, the calculation is conducted over one quarter of the surface. Figure 7 shows the water surface obtained. Equation (7) can be integrated numerically from this result. The gradient of U is calculated approximately by potential energies U corresponding to different positions of the polyimide tip.

Figure 8 shows the experimental and calculated results. From the calculation, the force f is proportional to a^2.

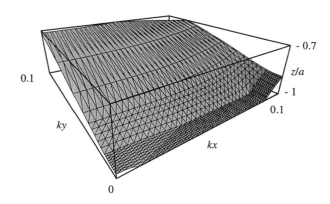

Figure 7. Water surface calculated by difference calculus (z-axis is exaggerated).

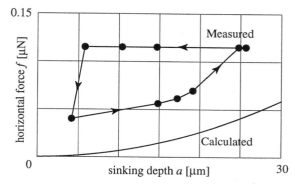

Figure 8. Relation between horizontal force f and sinking depth a.

Since both polyimide tips are in contact in the horizontal portion of the graph, sticking causes hysteresis, so only the lower part of the measured data are significant.

The force f tends to increase with the sinking depth a. The difference between experimental data and calculated data may be caused by ignoring the orientation of the polyimide tips. Although we assume that the polyimide tips are located horizontally, they actually rotate around the x-axis at an angle of $30 \sim 45$ degrees.

4 Self-Assembly Experiment

4.1 Self-assembly by attractive forces only (Type 1)

A total 108 self-assembling units shown in Fig. 9 were fabricated by thin film processes.[1] The units float on the water surface as shown in Fig. 10 because the polyimide layer repels the water. They are stirred with an external magnetic

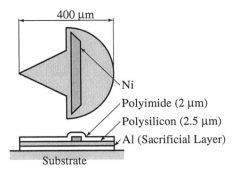

Figure 9. Design of Type 1.

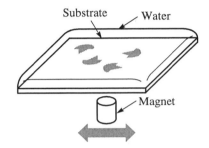

Figure 10. Type 1 experiment.

force. Four units form a complete body as in Fig. 12(a) by linking at their sharp corners.

Hydrochloric acid (HCl) was applied to the substrate in order to remove the Al sacrificial layer. The unit should not be turned over or overlapped during release. Figure 11 shows how to remove the units from the wafer. After dripping HCl onto the substrate, most of the HCl should be removed immediately so that the polyimide surface of the units are exposed. After removing the Al sacrificial layer, the units (structures) should not be dried completely because the assembly units stick to the surface of the wafer. Pure water is carefully added so that they rise to the surface.

Incomplete bodies in Fig. 12(c) appeared instead of the expected complete ones shown in Fig. 12(a) because of the undesirable coupling shown in Fig. 12(b). In the best case, eight final complete bodies, e.g. about 30% yield, were obtained experimentally. Figure 13 is a photograph of the experimental results.

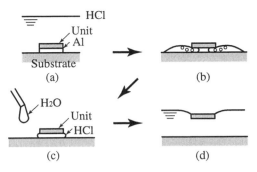

Figure 11. Release method: (a) HCl is dripped onto the self-assembly units. (b) The HCl is drawn from the substrate by a syringe to the extent that only a small amount of HCl remains on the substrate. (c) After removing the sacrificial layer, pure water is added. (d) The assembly units rise to the surface.

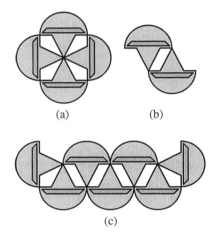

Figure 12. (a) Desirable goal, (b) Undesirable coupling, (c) A typical result.

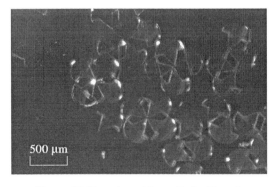

Figure 13. Experimental results for Type 1.

---

1. At first we had intended to assemble them using the magnetic force of Ni as a bonding force. However, the surface tension turned out to be dominant.

4. 2 Self-assembly by attractive and repulsive forces (Type 2)

Considering the undesirable coupling described above, we improved the structure to that shown in Fig. 14. A bimorphic film consisting of two layers with different thermal expansion coefficients curls up when it is heated or cooled[7]. The curvature depends on the difference of the thermal expansion coefficients, thin film thickness, and the temperature. We can control the curvature with proper design of the thicknesses of the two layers. If only a part of the structure is made form two layers, the structure curls up at a specified point.

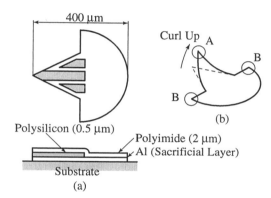

Figure 14. The improved microstructure, Type 2. (a) Design, (b) Curling-up height can be controlled by the polysilicon in the shaded area.

Since a part of the structure consists of polyimide and polysilicon layers, the tip A has a different curling-up height from the tips B in Fig. 14(b). Using this structure, undesirable coupling was eliminated because tips with a different height are mutually repulsed. Figure 15 shows the Type 2 experimental results. In addition, the Ni layer in Fig. 9 became unnecessary because the system was mechanically shaken instead of being excited magnetically.

This system was analyzed by the rate equation (see Section 2). Figure 16 shows stable clusters of Type 2. The elementary processes are:

$$2X \rightarrow X_2, \qquad X + X_2 \rightarrow X_3,$$
$$X + X_3 \rightarrow X_4, \quad 2X_2 \rightarrow X_4. \tag{11}$$

When the symbol x_i represents the quantity of X_i, the rate equation of this system is:

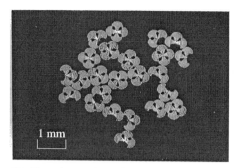

Figure 15. Experimental results of Type 2. This structure eliminates the undesirable coupling shown in Fig. 12(b).

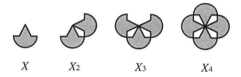

Figure 16. Stable clusters of Type 2.

$$x(t+1) = x(t) + AP(x(t)), \tag{12}$$

where,

$$x(t) = \left(x_1(t),\, x_2(t),\, x_3(t),\, x_4(t)\right)^{\mathrm{T}},$$

$$A = \begin{pmatrix} -2 & -1 & -1 & 0 \\ 1 & -1 & 0 & -2 \\ 0 & 1 & -1 & 0 \\ 0 & 0 & 1 & 1 \end{pmatrix}, \; P(x) = \frac{1}{S^2}\begin{pmatrix} P_{11}^{b} x_1^2 \\ 2P_{12}^{b} x_1 x_2 \\ 2P_{13}^{b} x_1 x_3 \\ P_{22}^{b} x_2^2 \end{pmatrix}. \tag{13}$$

In Eq. (13), $S = x_1 + \dots + x_4$ is the total of the clusters. The bonding probability P_{lm}^{b} was calculated in the same way as the large model. The results are summarized in Table 2.

Table 2. Type 2 bonding probability P_{lm}^{b}.

	$l = 1$	2	3
$m = 1$	0.438	0.375	0.188
2		0.250	0
3	Symmetric		0

In Fig. 17, the experimental data is compared with the calculated results. For Theory A, P_{lm}^{b} in Table 2 is used. However, it is assumed that P_{13}^{b} equals zero for Theory B. In other words, reaction

$$X + X_3 \rightarrow X_4 \tag{14}$$

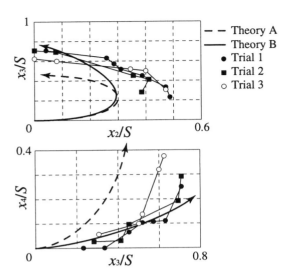

Figure 17. Self-assembling behavior of Type 2.

is ignored. The arrow in Fig. 17 indicates the direction of time.

The experiment was repeated three times. The number of each state is normalized by the total number of clusters because the numbers of initial units are different in each trial. Figure 17 indicates that Theory B is closer to the experimental data. Although the assembly units are pushed manually by a thin glass rod, the reaction (14) is hardly observed.

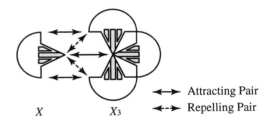

Figure 18. Forces acting between the unit X and the cluster X_3.

Table 3. Experimental data of Type 2.

trial No.	initial number of units N	final state x_f	yield $4x_{f4}/N$
1	77	(0, 1, 17, 6)	31.2 %
2	79	(0, 0, 17, 7)	35.4 %
3	81	(0, 0, 15, 9)	44.4 %
average			37.0 %

The repelling pairs seen in Fig. 18 prevent X and X_3 from combining together. Due to these repelling pairs, the yields and the final states listed in Table 3 are not improved compared with those of Type 1 (about 30%).

5 Conclusions

The surface tension acts on objects floating on the surface of water. This force has the following characteristics: 1) objects located at equal heights are attracted to each other, 2) large attractive forces act the sharp parts, and 3) objects located at different heights are mutually repulsed.

Using these characteristics, 2D self-assembling thin film microstructures were made. The important design considerations are: 1) float the units on the water surface by the repellent tendency of polyimide, 2) sharpen the bonding area, 3) control the height of the bonding tips using the curling-up technique, and connect specified pairs.

The surface tension of water was used to assemble microstructures. On the other hand, hydrophobic interaction is the main driving force for making 3D protein conformations out of 1D polypeptide, and to assemble the protein subunits into a complicated structure[8]. Hydrophobic side chains are enveloped inside the structure, and are kept away from water molecules. The hydrophobic interaction is similar

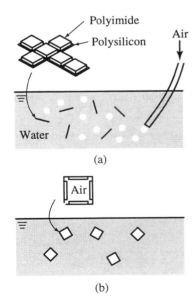

Figure 19. An idea that 3D structures are self-assembled around bubbles using quasi hydrophobic interaction.

to the surface tension in the sense that both are the minimization of the free energy of water around the structure.

We suppose that it may be possible to fabricate 3D microstructures by an analogous mechanism to the hydrophobic interaction. Polyimide repels water since the contact of polyimide and air has lower energy than the contact of polyimide and water. Using polyimide (or other resins) instead of the hydrophobic side chain, 3D units could be made from 2D thin films by quasi hydrophobic interaction with air bubbles as shown in Fig. 19.

References

[1] D. L. D. Casper, "Movement and Self-Control in Protein Assemblies—Quasi-Equivalence Revised," *Biophysics Journal*, Vol. 32, pp. 103-138, 1980.

[2] C. J. Jones and S. Aizawa, "The Bacterial Flagellum and Flagellar Motor—Structure, Assembly and Function," *Advances in Microbial Physiology*, Vol. 32, pp. 109-172, 1991.

[3] M. B. Cohn, C. J. Kim, and A. P. Pisano, "Self-Assembling Electrical Networks: An Application of Micromachining Technology," *Proc. Transducers '91*, pp. 490-493, 1991.

[4] H. J. Yeh and J. S. Smith, "Fluidic Self-Assembly of Microstructures and its Application to Integration of GaAs on Si," *Proc. Micro Electro Mechanical Systems*, pp. 279-284, 1994.

[5] K. Hosokawa, I. Shimoyama, and H. Miura, "Dynamics of Self-Assembling Systems—Analogy with Chemical Kinetics—," *Artificial Life*, Vol. 1, No. 4, pp. 413-427, 1995.

[6] K. Saitou, M. J. Jakiela, "Automated Optimal Design of Mechanical Conformational Switches," *Artificial Life*, Vol. 2, No. 2, 1995.

[7] M. Ataka, A. Omodaka, N. Takeshima, and H. Fujita, "Fabrication and Operation of Polyimide Bimorph Actuators for a Ciliary Motion System," *J. Microelectromechanical Systems*, Vol. 2, No. 4, pp. 146-150, 1993.

[8] A. L. Lehninger, "Biochemistry," Worth Publishers, Inc., New York, 1975.

A Robot that Behaves like a Silkworm Moth in the Pheromone Stream

Yoshihiko Kuwana, Isao Shimoyama, Yushi Sayama, and Hirofumi Miura
Department of Mechano-Informatics, The University of Tokyo
7-3-1 Hongo, Bunkyo-ku, Tokyo 113, JAPAN
{kuwana, isao, sayama, miura}@leopard.t.u-tokyo.ac.jp
[URL]http://www.leopard.t.u-tokyo.ac.jp

Abstract

Emergent behavior of moths is clarified by synthesis with currently developed tools, including living sensors and recurrent neural networks. The antennae on a silkworm moth are very sensitive compared to artificial gas sensors. Living antennae can be used as living gas sensors that detect pheromone molecules with great sensitivity. Recurrent artificial neural networks have been applied to control the pheromone tracing. As a result, a mobile robot with living antennae can follow a stream of pheromone just like a living male silkworm moth. The small numbers of neurons can generate moth-like behavior, including casting and turning, while interacting with the environment. The turning behavior in particular is a suitable tactic for small intelligence when losing pheromone.

1 Introduction

A male silkworm moth (*Bombyx mori*) follows a pheromone path to locate a female. Entomologists and neuroethologists characterize this behavior as follows: when a moth is inside the pheromone stream, in which pheromone molecules (Bombykol) arrive at the antennae frequently, the moth moves straight upwind in surges. If the moth is out of the stream, without pheromone stimulation, it exhibits side-to-side casting behavior to search out pheromone plumes. Until finally reaching a female, the moth shows tonic casting behavior as well as phasic surge behavior depending on the existence of pheromone. Details of this behavior, however, are still under investigation[1][2].

The number of neural cells in an insect is about 10^5, while those in humans number 10^{10}. Since the amount of neural cells is restricted by the number of molecules, there are no tiny living organisms with a substantial amount of neural cells because the available volume is limited. Due to this limitation, insect behavior is both fixed and reflexive. A moth uses its neural system to create pheromone tracing behavior by processing information from its antennae.

The purpose of this research is to clarify moth emergent behavior by synthesis with currently developed tools, includ-ing living sensors and recurrent neural networks. The results can be applied to microrobot control because microrobots have little room for intelligence, like insects. Although insect behavior is considered simple, insects have evolved over millions of years to a suitable form for their size through natural selection.

The antennae on a silkworm moth are very sensitive compared with artificial gas sensors. These living antennae can be used as gas sensors to detect pheromone molecules with great sensitivity. In our research, it is shown that signals from an antenna can easily be obtained with electrodes connected to both ends of an antenna[3]. Recurrent artificial neural networks are applied for controlling the pheromone tracing. As a result, a mobile robot with living antennae can follow a stream of pheromone like a male silkworm moth.

Sauer[4] has previously reported on antennae as a pheromone sensor, measuring the pheromone concentration in the field with antennae of *Lobesia botrana*. Ishida[5] has demonstrated a mobile robot capable of detecting an alcohol source with semiconductor sensors. However, sensitivity and response time were not satisfactory. Our system employs highly sensitive living sensors, not semiconductor sensors. The advantage of this approach is in conducting a real world experiment with living sensors instead of computer simulation. No modelling of the environment or sensors for investigating moth behavior needs to be performed.

2 An antenna as a pheromone gas sensor

Insects react to chemical and physical stimuli sensitively and selectively. Silkworm moth antennae generate signals only if pheromone from a female silkworm moth arrives at the antennae. **Figure 1** shows a silkworm moth and its antenna. The antenna is 5 mm in length and is covered with hair. **Figure 2** shows one example signal (electroantennogram, EAG) obtained from both ends of an antenna. An EAG is a potential difference generated between two ends of an antenna when a male antenna is stimulated with female sex pheromone.

The antennae play an important role in insect behavior. At present, artificial sensors cannot be substituted for living sen-

Fig. 1 Male silkworm moth

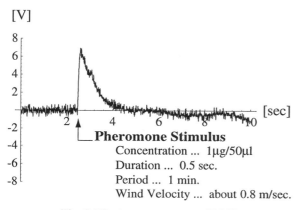

Fig. 2 Electroantennogram (EAG)

Pheromone Stimulus
Concentration ... 1μg/50μl
Duration ... 0.5 sec.
Period ... 1 min.
Wind Velocity ... about 0.8 m/sec.

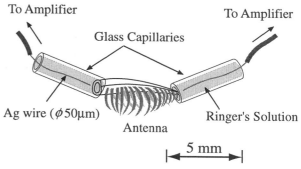

Fig. 3 Pheromone Sensor (Type-I)

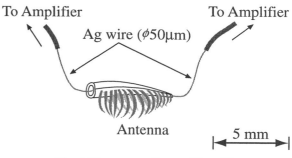

Fig. 4 Pheromone Sensor (Type-II)

sors due to less sensitivity and selectivity. In addition, artificial sensors achieve only a portion of a living sensor's characteristics, meaning that certain important aspects may be lost.

We've fabricated two kinds of pheromone sensors. In the Type-I sensor shown in **Fig. 3**, both ends of the antenna are inserted into glass capillaries filled with Ringer's solution. The glass capillaries are 5 mm long and have a 1.2 mm in external diameter, and a 0.7 mm in internal diameter. The Ringer's solution is used as an electrolyte to conduct electric signals from the antenna, and in addition, the solution is useful in keeping the antenna wet. A 50 μm lead in diameter is inserted into the other side of the glass capillary. Nerve activity is picked up from the antenna through the lead wire.

Both ends of the glass capillary are sealed by beeswax, which quickly solidifies at low temperature. Beeswax is harmless to living organisms. The impedance between the lead and the Ringer's solution was measured at 20 MΩ.

A second type of pheromone sensor is shown in **Fig. 4**. The Type-II sensor employs silver (Ag) electrodes inserted into both ends of the antenna directly without any glass capillaries. Since Ringer's solution is not used, the Type-II sensor is more sensitive than Type-I.

In order to evaluate the pheromone gas sensors, dose response and life time were measured. Dose response curves were obtained by plotting the relationship between the concentration vs. amplitude of EAG at flow velocities of 0.375 m/s, 0.75 m/s and 1.125 m/s. Pheromone stimulates the sensor for 0.5 sec at 1/60Hz.

Sensitivity of the pheromone sensor was evaluated by determining the threshold using the dose response curves. The pheromone concentration is written as 10^{-10}g/10μl (i.e. artificially synthesized pheromone 10^{-10}g in weight is dissolved in 10 μl n-hexane as a solvent). **Figure 5** shows typical dose response curves obtained from the Type-I pheromone sensor using the biologically specified amplifier. **Figure 6** shows a dose response curve obtained from the combination of the Type-II pheromone sensor and the biologically specified amplifier. As seen by the EAG amplitude of these two graphs, the Type-II sensor is about ten times as sensitive as the Type-I. From **Fig. 6**, the resolution of this living sensor is 10^{-10}g/10μl, or 10^{-4}ppm.

Figure 7 shows the dose response curve obtained from the combination of the Type-II sensor and the original amplifier design. From this curve, the resolution of this combination is 10^{-9}g/10μl, or 10^{-3}ppm. The original amplifier design was installed into a simple, small mobile robot described in **Section 3**.

The lifetime of this living sensor is defined as the time when the response by periodic stimulation becomes compatible to the background noise. The lifetime was measured at about 80 minutes experimentally.

Because the Type-II pheromone sensor is more sensitive,

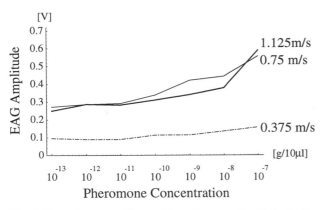

Fig. 5 Dose Response Curve (Type-I sensor, the biologically specified amplifier)

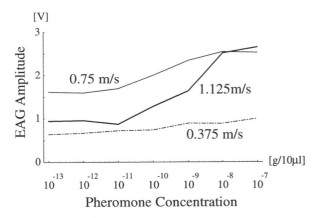

Fig. 6 Dose Response Curve (Type-II sensor, the biologically specified amplifier)

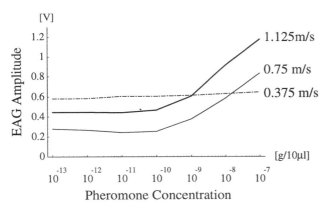

Fig. 7 Dose Response Curve (Type-II sensor, the original amplifier design)

two Type-II sensors were mounted on the front of a mobile robot, as shown in **Fig. 8**. Pheromone is vaporized by hand using a syringe ahead of the robot. Only the female pheromone stimulates the pheromone sensors. Air without pheromone does not affect the sensors, and therefore this robot can trace a pheromone path just like a male moth.

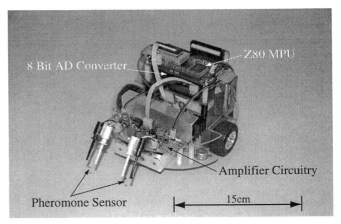

Fig. 8 Pheromone-Guided Mobile Robot

3 Pheromone tracing behavior by recurrent neural networks

To demonstrate a moth-like behavior with pheromone gas sensors, both simulations and experiments were carried out with a mobile robot. The autonomous pheromone tracing mobile robot consists of the two pheromone sensors, instrument amplifiers (the original amplifier design), an AD Converter, a micro-processor (Z80), two DC motors, and batteries, as shown in **Fig. 8**. During the experiment, pheromone gas flows out of a tube at speed of about 1 m/s from the front of the robot. The pheromone stream is calibrated as the gray areas in the experimental results by using a visualization technique with smoke, as shown in **Fig. 13** and **Fig. 19**.

During the simulations we assumed that pheromone expands inside a trapezoid, as shown in **Fig. 9**. Only inside this pheromone plume, can the robot detect the pheromone with the reliability. When the robot is near the pheromone source, it can detect the pheromone with a probability of 0.8. On the other hand, when the robot is near the starting point, it can sense the pheromone with a probability of 0.3. The farther away from the pheromone source, the lower the probability of pheromone detection is.

A simple neural network with eight neurons and recurrent connections, as shown in **Fig. 10**, was used for controlling the mobile robot. Using this network, two kinds of programs, simple reflex-based control and recurrent neural network based control, were examined to achieve moth-like behavior.

The necessary information for the oriented walk may be the existence of pheromone. A real moth also uses visual information, however. Our neural network includes two input and two output neurons, that is, sensor and motor neurons in **Fig. 10**. The input neurons receive pheromone stimulus. The output neurons drive two motors that determine the orientation of the mobile robot. All neurons can be connected to each other in both directions.

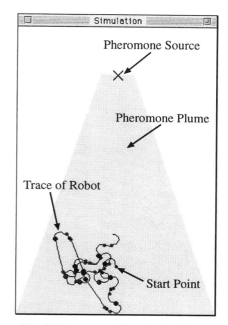

Fig. 9 Pheromone Simulation Plume

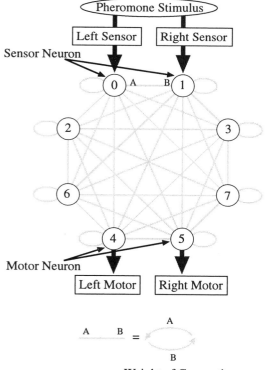

A, B ...... Weight of Connection

Fig. 10 Recurrent neural network for controlling the robot

3.1 Simple reflex-based control

The first program is based on reflex without a memory mechanism, as shown in **Fig. 11**. When the right (left) antenna detects pheromone, the left (right) motor receives the sig-

nal and turns right (left). If both antennae are stimulated simultaneously, the robot goes straight ahead, and if there is no stimulation, the robot does not move in any direction.

Figures 12 and **13** show the simulation and experimental results of the simple reflex-based control, respectively. Since this control requires continuous stimulation, the robot does not move outside the pheromone stream. Although the pheromone leads the robot to the pheromone source, turning behavior does not appear.

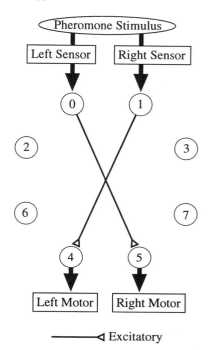

◁ Excitatory

Fig. 11 Simple reflex-based program

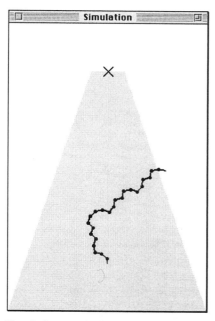

Fig. 12 Simulation result (Simple reflex-based program)

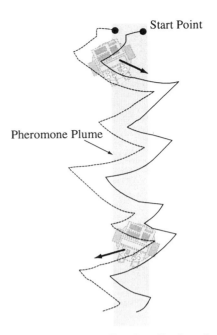

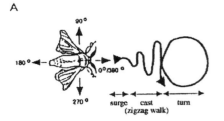

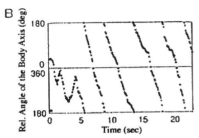

Fig. 13 Experimental result (Simple reflex-based program)

Fig. 14 Silkworm moth behavior when stimulated by pheromone (courtesy of Kanzaki)

3.2 Recurrent neural networks

The behavior of the robot described in the previous section appears awkward. A real moth has flip-flopping activity patterns[6][7][8][9][10], a sign that its neural system is based on not only reflex but also memory. The moth behaves unpredictably in a complex environment including pheromone.

Kanzaki[6] analysed moth behavior in a simplified environment. Surging, casting, and turning motions appear in this order after an inactive moth is stimulated by pheromone. The direction of rotation is determined by the side of the initially stimulated antenna. For example, when the right antenna is stimulated, the moth moves forward with surges, zigzags right-left-right-left, and finally rotates clockwise, as shown in **Fig. 14**. Since the direction of rotation is determined by the side of the antennae, Kanzaki proposed that there is a memory mechanism like a flip-flop in the neural system.

Based on his results, we assumed that the moth behavior emerges by interaction with the environment where pheromone is distributed complexly in spite of the simple neural system. To confirm our assumption, we conducted two experiments. Both programs are based on recurrent neural networks (RNN) with feedback loops that contribute memory to the system.

In the first experiment, the weights among neurons are determined by genetic algorithm (GA). The weights between the neurons are encoded into a GA gene. The fitness of the pheromone tracing is defined as the nearest distance between the robot and the pheromone source. Crossover and mutation are applied to optimize the connections of the neurons, as listed in **Table 1**. An average of five trials is taken as fitness of the pheromone tracing. In each trial, the robot starts from dif-

ferent initial positions in order to obtain behavior that does not depend on the initial position.

The result of GA optimization is shown in **Fig. 15**. Pheromone tracing with the GA-optimized recurrent network is simulated in the field shown in **Fig. 16**. Pheromone is distributed uniformly inside the trapezoid, and since both antennae detect pheromone at an equal probability[1], the robot cannot reach the pheromone source only by comparing the difference of pheromone concentration between both antennae.

Table 1 Genetic Algorithm Parameters

Number of Robots in 1 Generation	50
Crossover	20% of All Robots
Mutation	10% of All Robots
New Robots	5% of All Robots
Number of Generations	100

As a result, a robot with GA connections moves toward the pheromone source efficiently as shown in **Fig. 16**. During an experiment, however, the robot deflects out of the stream. This may occur due to the difference of the environments between the simulation and the real world. When connections are determined by GA, the model should accurately agree with the real environment.

Another set of connections has been heuristically determined by examining the results by Kanzaki. One pheromone stimulation excites the sequence of casting, and turning. This sequence is achieved by the connections shown in **Fig. 17**. **Figures 18** and **19** show the simulation and experimental results, respectively. Contrary to the GA case, the robot traces the pheromone stream in simulation and experiment. In addition, the turning behavior appears to detect the pheromone

1. Strictly speaking, the probability is not equal in left and right antennae, but the difference is very small and negligible.

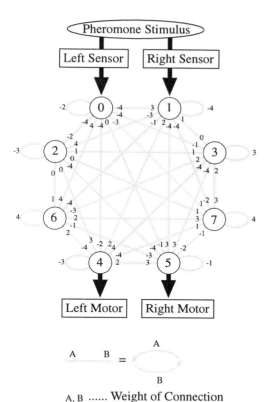

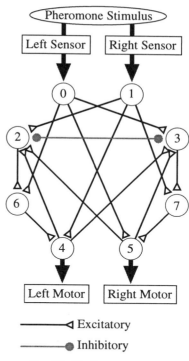

Fig. 15 GA-optimized RNN

Fig. 17 Flipflop-type RNN

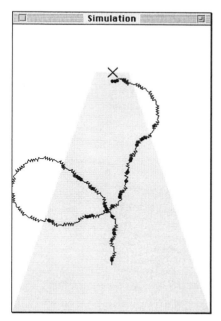

Fig. 16 Simulation result (GA-optimized RNN)

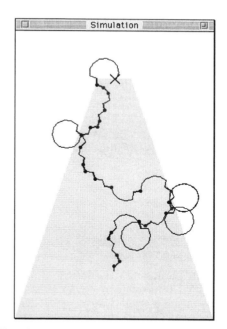

Fig. 18 Simulation result (Flipflop-type RNN)

4 Conclusions

plumes when the robot goes out of the stream in both simulation and experiment results. The overall behavior of the robot looks quite similar to that of a real moth. The use of only eight neurons is able to generate a complex behavior due to the complex real pheromone distribution.

The antennae of a moth can be used as gas sensors for mobile robots for a duration of about 80 minutes. The sensitivity is 10^{-4}ppm, 10,000 times higher than that of an artificial gas sensor. This robot may be able to detect gas pipe leaks due to earthquake damage, for example, if pheromone is mixed in

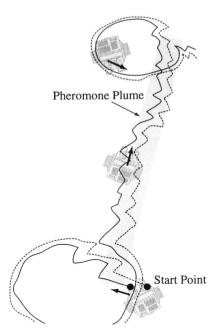

Pheromone Plume

Start Point

Fig. 19 Experimental result (flipflop-type RNN)

with natural gas.

Recurrent neural networks contribute a memory mechanism to the pheromone tracing. The small numbers of neurons can generate moth-like behavior, including casting, and turning while interacting with the environment. The turning behavior in particular looks like a suitable tactic for small intelligence when losing pheromone.

The difference between the real world and the simulation condition yields a discrepancy of when a GA is used, and the sensor model of the simulation provides an additional discrepancy. Therefore, real world experiments with living antennae may provide a fascinating interface between A-Life and neuroethology.

References

[1] Tristram Wyatt, "Moth flights of Fancy," Nature, Vol. 369, No. 6476, pp. 98 - 99, 1994.

[2] Agenor Mafra-Neto and Ring Cardé, "Fine-scale Structure of Pheromone Plumes Modulates Upwind Orientation of Flying Moths," Nature, Vol. 369, No. 6476, pp. 142- 144, 1994.

[3] Yoshihiko Kuwana, Isao Shimoyama, and Hirofumi Miura, "Steering Control of a Mobile Robot Using Insect Antennae," Proceedings of the 1995 IEEE/RSJ International Conference on Intelligent Robots and Systems (IROS 95), pp. 530 - 535, 1995.

[4] Arne E. Sauer, Gerhard Karg, Uwe T. Koch, Jacobus J. DeKramer, and Roland Milli, "A Portable EAG System for the Measurement of Pheromone Concentration in the Field," Chemical Senses, Vol. 17,No. 5, pp. 543 - 553, 1992.

[5] Hiroshi Ishida, Kin-ichiro Suetsugu, Takamichi Nakamoto, and Toyosaka Moriizumi, "Study of autonomous mobile sensing system for localization of odor source using gas sensors and anemometric sensors," Sensors and Actuators A, Vol. 45, No. 2, pp. 153 - 157, 1994.

[6] Ryohei Kanzaki, Naoko Sugi, and Tatsuaki Shibuya, "Self Generated Zigzag Turning of Bombyx mori Males during Pheromone-mediated Upwind Walking," Zoological Science, Vol. 9, pp. 515 - 527, 1992.

[7] Edmund A. Arbas, Mark A. Willis, and Ryohei Kanzaki, "Organization of Goal-Oriented Locomotion: Pheromone-Modulated Flight Behavior of Moths," Biological Neural Networks in Invertebrate Neuroethology and Robotics (Eds. Randall Beer et al.), Academic Press, 1993.

[8] Ryohei Kanzaki, Akira Ikeda, Tatsuaki Shibuya, "Morphological and Physiological Properties of Pheromone-Triggered Flipflopping Descending Interneurons of the Male Silkworm Moth, Bombyx mori," Journal of Comparative Physiology A, Vol. 175, pp. 1 - 14, 1994.

[9] Ryohei Kanzaki, "Olfactory Processing Pathways of the Insect Brain Lateral Accessory Lobe System in the Protocerebrum Produces Olfactory Flip-Flopping Signals in Bombyx mori," Olfaction and Taste, Vol. 11, pp. 831 - 834, 1994.

[10] Ryohei Kanzaki and Akira Ikeda, "Morphological and Physiological Properties of Pheromone-Triggered Flip-Flopping Descending Interneurons of the Male Silkworm Moth, Bombyx mori," Olfaction and Taste, Vol. 11, p. 851, 1994.

Biology

Evolutionary Optimization of Biopolymers

and

Sequence Structure Maps

CHRISTIAN REIDYS[a,b,c], STEPHAN KOPP[a], PETER SCHUSTER[a,b]

[a]Institut für Molekulare Biotechnologie
Beutenbergstraße 11, D-07708 Jena, Germany

[b]Santa Fe Institute
1399 Hyde Park Rd., Santa Fe, NM 87501, USA

[c]Los Alamos National Laboratory
Theoretical Division, Los Alamos, New Mexico, USA

E-Mail: duck@santafe.edu

Abstract

Searching for biopolymers having a predefined function is a core problem of biotechnology, biochemistry and pharmacy. On the level of RNA sequences and their corresponding secondary structures we show that this problem can be analyzed mathematically. The strategy will be to study the properties of the RNA sequence to secondary structure mapping that is essential for the understanding of the search process. We show that to each secondary structure s there exists a neutral network consisting of all sequences folding into s. This network can be modeled as a random graph and has the following generic properties: it is dense and has a giant component within the graph of compatible sequences. The neutral network percolates sequence space and any two neutral nets come close in terms of Hamming distance. We investigate the distribution of the orders of neutral nets and show [10] that above a certain threshold the topology of neutral nets allows to find practically all frequent secondary structures.

1. Introduction

An RNA structure with a given shape or function is assumed to be formed by many RNA sequences. Their distribution in sequence space is of particular importance for the hardness of the corresponding search problem. The structure of a biopolymer is defined only in the context of some physical conditions. Minimum free energy structures for example fulfill the thermodynamic condition of a molecular ground state, or kinetic structures that are understood as the well defined outcome of a

controlled process of biopolymer formation. In an abstract sense this means that one is interested in a (local) point to point assignment of sequence space and shape space. In general such a mapping will not be one-to-one: many sequences may be mapped into the same structure. The degree of this redundancy will strongly depend on the notion of structure applied. Structure in X-ray crystallography is tantamount to a set of atomic coordinates and at sufficiently high resolution structures are unique in the sense that structures from different sequences will never coincide. Molecular biologists, however, commonly apply another, a coarse-grained notion of structure when, for example, they say intuitively that two proteins have the same structure. An appropriate coarse grained notion of structure apparently is context dependent and thus anything but trivial.

In this paper we are dealing with RNA molecules. Secondary structures are used as appropriate examples for structural coarse-graining. They are sufficiently simple to allow statistical analysis by means of conventional combinatorics [9]. The relation between RNA sequences and secondary structures is understood as a (non invertible) mapping from sequence space into shape space [3, 5, 6]. RNA secondary structures distinguish only paired and unpaired regions irrespective of the particular bases at the individual positions (**G**, **C**, **A**, or **U**). Therefore many different sequences the so called compatible sequences can meet the base pairing conditions as determined by a given secondary structure. For the biophysical alphabet the number of compatible sequences is readily computed for any given secondary structure s, with u unpaired bases and p base pairs to be $4^u \cdot 6^p$. The number of compatible sequences is certainly substantially larger than the number of sequences that actually form the given structure as their minimum free energy conformation or, for example, as their kinetically determined structure [14]. Here we pursue to model the sequence structure mapping making the assumption that apart from biophysical pairing rules the mapping is essentially random. Connecting neighboring neutral sequences in sequence space, i.e., sequences that are mapped into the same point in shape space and which are inter-converted by a single move consisting of a base or a base pair exchange, yields neutral networks whose properties are studied by the analytical techniques of random graph theory [2]. The topology of these networks plays a fundamental role for the optimization problem.

The paper is organized as follows: first we summarize some theory of random induced subgraphs of generalized hypercubes following [12] (where all proofs can be found). The corresponding results should make the reader familiar with the generic properties of those random induced subgraphs and the main ideas of the proofs. Second we apply the random graph theory to construct neutral networks and we obtain complete sequence structure mappings by constructing neutral networks with respect to corresponding secondary structures iteratively. We then analyze the so called SOC (sequence of components) of single preimages of these mappings and compute the preimage size distribution depending on the underlying λ parameter. Finally, we discuss the implications for the optimization process of biopolymers.

2. Random Induced Subgraphs of Generalized Hypercubes

A *graph* G consists of a tuple $(\mathrm{v}[G], \mathrm{e}[G])$ and two maps

$$\mathrm{e}[G] \longrightarrow \mathrm{v}[G] \times \mathrm{v}[G] \qquad e \to (\iota(e), \tau(e))$$
$$\mathrm{inv} : \mathrm{e}[G] \longrightarrow \mathrm{e}[G] \qquad e \to \mathrm{inv}(e)$$

satisfying the following conditions: for each $e \in \mathrm{e}[G]$ we have $\mathrm{inv}^2(e) = e$, $\mathrm{inv}(e) \neq e$ and $\tau(e) = \iota(\mathrm{inv}(e))$. The set $\{e, \mathrm{inv}(e)\}$ is called *geometric edge*. $\mathrm{v}[G]$ is called *vertex set* and $\mathrm{e}[G]$ *edge set* respectively.
Next we recall some terminology of graph theory.

- G' is a *subgraph* of G, $G' < G$, if $\mathrm{v}[G'] \subset \mathrm{v}[G]$ and $\mathrm{e}[G'] \subset \mathrm{e}[G]$.
- Let $H \subset \mathrm{v}[G]$. The *induced subgraph* or *spanned subgraph* of H in G, $G[H]$, has the vertex set $\mathrm{v}[G[H]] = H$ and the edge set $\mathrm{e}[G[H]]$ is the subset of all edges in $\mathrm{e}[G]$ where both incident vertices belong to H.
- The *(out)degree* δ_v of a vertex v is the number of edges $e \in \mathrm{e}[G]$ such that $\iota(e) = v$.
- G is γ-*regular* if for each vertex $v \in \mathrm{v}[G]$ holds $\delta_v = \gamma$.
- The *order* of a graph G, $|G|$ is the cardinality of its vertex set, i.e., $|\mathrm{v}[G]|$.
- A *path* π in G is a tuple of the form

$$\pi = (v = v_1, e_1, v_2, \ldots, e_{m-1}, v_m = v')$$

where $\iota(e_k) = v_k, \tau(e_k) = v_{k+1}$ for $1 \leq k < m$. Since π is already characterized by its vertices we use the notation $\pi = (v_i)_{1 \leq i \leq m}$.
We further say that the v_i and e_i *occur* in π. The path π *connects* the vertices v and v', if both occur in π.

- The *support* of a path π is the set

$$\mathrm{Supp}(\pi) := \{v \in \mathrm{v}[G] \,|\, v \text{ occurs in } \pi\}.$$

- The *length* of a path $\pi = (v_1, e_1, v_2, \ldots, e_{m-1}, v_m)$ is $\ell(\pi) := m - 1$, i.e. the number of edges that occur in π.
The set of all paths in G shall be denoted by $\Pi(G)$.

- Two vertices $v, v' \in \mathrm{v}[G]$ are called connected if there exists a path in G in which both vertices occur. A graph G is *connected* if for any two vertices $v, v' \in \mathrm{v}[G]$ are connected.

- The *distance* $d_G(v, v')$ of two vertices in G is the minimum length of a path connecting v and v'. If there is no path connecting v and v' we set $d_G(v, v') = \infty$. We shall drop the index G when no confusion is possible.

- The *diameter* of a graph G is the maximum of all distances of pairs of vertices $v, v' \in \mathrm{v}[G]$.

- The *ball* centered at $v \in \mathrm{v}[G]$ with radius r is the set

$$B_r(v) := \{v' \in \mathrm{v}[G] \,|\, d_G(v, v') = r\}.$$

- The *boundary* $\partial_G V$ in G of a set $V \subset \mathrm{v}[G]$ is

$$\partial_G V := \{v' \in \mathrm{v}[G] \setminus V \,|\, \exists v \in V : d_G(v, v') = 1\}.$$

The *closure* in G of $V \subset \mathrm{v}[G]$, $\overline{V}$, is given by $\overline{V} := V \dot\cup \partial_G V$.

In the sequel we write ∂ instead of ∂_G. We further introduce the r-th *factorial moment* of a positive, integer valued random variable $\hat{Y}$:

$$\mathbf{E}[\hat{Y}]_r := \sum_{j=r}^{\infty} [j]_r \,\boldsymbol{\mu}\{\hat{Y} = j\}$$

where $[j]_r = j \cdot (j - 1) \cdot \ldots \cdot (j - (r - 1))$.

Basic Model: *Let H be a finite graph and $\mathcal{G}(H)$ be the set of all induced subgraphs. We assume $0 \leq \lambda \leq 1$ to be given and set for $\Gamma \in \mathcal{G}(H)$*

$$\boldsymbol{\mu}_\lambda\{\Gamma\} := \lambda^{|\mathrm{v}[\Gamma]|} (1 - \lambda)^{|\mathrm{v}[H]| - |\mathrm{v}[\Gamma]|}.$$

Obviously $\boldsymbol{\mu}_\lambda$ fulfills $\sum_\Gamma \boldsymbol{\mu}_\lambda\{\Gamma\} = 1$ and we obtain choosing the set of all induced subgraphs as σ-field a probability space Ω.

2.1 Density

We shall discuss in this section the *density property* of random graphs $\Gamma_n < \mathcal{Q}_\alpha^n$, where $\mathcal{Q}_\alpha^n$ is a generalized hypercube, i.e., the graph formed by all n-tuples of coordinates x_i contained in a finite set $\mathcal{A}$ (of cardinality α) where each two tuples are neighbors when they differ in exactly one coordinate.

Let H be a finite graph. A subgraph $G < H$ is called *dense* in H if and only if $\overline{\mathrm{v}[G]} = \mathrm{v}[H]$.

We will establish the existence of a "critical" λ-value, λ^* that has the following property: for $\lambda < \lambda^*$ a.a.s. (asymptotically almost surely) no random graph Γ_n is dense and for $\lambda > \lambda^*$ a.a.s. every random graph Γ_n is dense. We will call λ^* the *threshold value for the density property*. For this purpose we consider the random variable

$$\hat{Z}_n(\Gamma_n) := |\{v \in \mathrm{v}[\mathcal{Q}_\alpha^n] \mid v \notin \overline{\mathrm{v}[\Gamma_n]}\}| \tag{1}$$

that is defined on Ω_n and counts the number of vertices having no adjacent vertex $v \in \mathrm{v}[\Gamma_n]$. We first compute the asymptotic distribution of the following sequence of random variables $(\hat{Z}_n)$ associated to the sequence of probability spaces (Ω_n). For this purpose we make use of the *sieve formula* [2] (p.17) that implies a number of results about the convergence in distribution for a sequence of integer valued random variables $(\hat{X}_n)$.

Theorem 1. *Let $(\hat{X}_i)_{i \in \mathbb{N}}$ be a sequence of non-negative integer valued random variables such that*

$$\forall r \in \mathbb{N}: \quad \lim_{n \to \infty} \mathbf{E}[\hat{X}_n]_r = \mathbf{E}[\hat{X}]_r$$

and

$$\forall m \in \mathbb{N}: \quad \lim_{r \to \infty} \mathbf{E}[\hat{X}]_r r^m / r! = 0$$

Then we have the following convergence in distribution: $\hat{X}_n \longrightarrow \hat{X}$.
Proof. [2, p.23] ∎

Corollary 1. *Let $\mu = \mu(n)$ be a bounded, non-negative function on $\mathbb{N}$ and assume a sequence of non-negative integer valued random variables $(\hat{X}_i)_{i \in \mathbb{N}}$ to be given. Suppose for an arbitrary natural number r we have*

$$\lim_{n \to \infty} \mathbf{E}[\hat{X}_n]_r - \mu^r = 0 \,.$$

Then the following convergence holds in distribution:

$$d(\hat{X}_n, P_\mu) \to 0 \,,$$

where P_μ is the Poisson measure.
Lemma 1. *Suppose*

$$\mu := \lim_{n \to \infty} (|\mathcal{Q}_\alpha^n|(1-\lambda)^{\gamma_n+1}) \in \mathbb{R}_+ \cup \{0\} \cup \{\infty\}$$

exists. Then for $\mu < \infty$ the random variables $\hat{Z}_n$ converge in distribution to a Poisson distributed random variable, i.e.,

$$\lim_{n \to \infty} \boldsymbol{\mu}_n\{\hat{Z}_n = \ell\} = \frac{\mu^\ell}{\ell!} e^{-\mu} \,. \tag{2}$$

In particular we have

$$\lim_{n \to \infty} \boldsymbol{\mu}_n\{\hat{Z}_n = 0\} = e^{-\mu} \,,$$

and

$$\lim_{n \to \infty} \mathbf{E}[\hat{Z}_n] = \alpha^n (1-\lambda)^{\gamma_n+1} \,.$$

Finally, for $\mu = \infty$ and $\ell \in \mathbb{N}$ holds

$$\lim_{n \to \infty} \boldsymbol{\mu}_n\{\hat{Z}_n \geq \ell\} = 1 \,.$$

The following theorem shows that $\lambda^* := 1 - \sqrt[\alpha^{-1}]{\alpha^{-1}}$ is a *threshold value* for the density property of random induced subgraphs as introduced in the basic model. Above λ^* a.a.s. all subgraphs are dense and below λ^* a.a.s. none of them.

Theorem 2. *Let $\lambda^* := 1 - \sqrt[\alpha^{-1}]{\alpha^{-1}}$ then for $\lambda > \lambda^*$ holds*

$$\lim_{n \to \infty} \boldsymbol{\mu}_n\{\Gamma_n \text{ is dense in } \mathcal{Q}_\alpha^n\} = 1$$

and for $\lambda < \lambda^*$ we have

$$\lim_{n \to \infty} \boldsymbol{\mu}_n\{\Gamma_n \text{ is dense in } \mathcal{Q}_\alpha^n\} = 0 \,.$$

2.2 Connectivity and Giant Components

Let G be a finite graph. Being connected is an equivalence relation on $\mathrm{v}[G]$ and there exist maximal subsets $V \subset \mathrm{v}[G]$ consisting of connected vertices. A *component* of G is then the induced subgraph $G' = G[V]$ of such a maximal connected subset of vertices. If $V = \emptyset$, $G[\emptyset]$ is called a *trivial component*. If G is disconnected we shall investigate the so called *sequence of components*, i.e., the list of orders of the maximal connected subgraphs of G into which G can be decomposed.

Given a graph G, the *sequence of components* of G is the ordered tuple $(|\mathcal{X}_i|)_{1 \leq i \leq |G|}$, where each $\mathcal{X}_i$ is a component of G and $|\mathcal{X}_i| \geq |\mathcal{X}_{i+1}|$. We call a component $\mathcal{X} < G$ a *giant component* if and only if $|\mathcal{X}| \geq \frac{2}{3}|G|$. The key idea in the proof of the connectivity theorem bases on the following observation (formulated as lemma 2 below). A.a.s. *each pair of vertices $v, v' \in \mathrm{v}[\Gamma_n]$ with $d(v, v') = k$, for fixed natural number k, is connected by a path in Γ_n.*

For this purpose we refer to a certain family of independent paths in $\mathcal{Q}_\alpha^n$. I.e. for $v, v' \in \mathrm{v}[\mathcal{Q}_\alpha^n]$ with $d(v, v') = k$ we write v, v' as $v = (x_1, ..., x_k, x_{k+1}, ..., x_n)$ and $v' = (x'_1, ..., x'_k, x_{k+1}, ..., x_n)$. Then for $v_1 \in \partial\{v\} \cap B_{1+k}(v')$ we set

$$g_j(v_1) := (x_1, ..., x_j, x'_{j+1}, ..., x'_k, x_{k+1}, .., \hat{x}_r, ..., x_n)$$

$$0 \leq j \leq k \quad \hat{x}_r \neq x_r \tag{3}$$

and inspect $g_k(v_1) = v_1$, $g_0(v_1) \in B_1(v') \cap B_{1+k}(v)$. We introduce the random variable $\hat{Y}_{n,k}^{v,v'}$ that counts the (independent) paths in the random graph Γ_n connecting the vertices v, v' having distance k.

Lemma 2. *Let k be a natural number, $\mathcal{Q}_\alpha^n$ a generalized hypercube and $\Gamma_n < \mathcal{Q}_\alpha^n$ a random graph with $\lambda > 1 - {}^{\alpha-1}\sqrt{\alpha^{-1}}$. Then $\lim_{n\to\infty} \boldsymbol{\mu}_n\{T\} = 1$ where*

$$T := \{\Gamma_n \mid \forall v, v' \in \mathrm{v}[\mathcal{Q}_\alpha^n], d(v, v') = k :$$
$$\exists v_1 \in \partial\{v\}, v_1' \in \partial\{v'\} : \hat{Y}_{n, d(v_1, v_1')}^{v_1, v_1'} > 0\}.$$

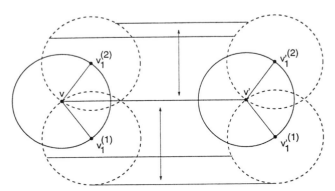

Fig. 1: An illustration for the proof of lemma 2. For given $v, v' \in \mathrm{v}[\mathcal{Q}_\alpha^n]$ each pair of vertices $(v_1^{(i)}, v_1'^{(i)})$ leads to "sufficiently many" independent pairwise disjoint paths in $\Pi(\mathcal{Q}_\alpha^n)$.

Now we are prepared to state the connectivity theorem:

Theorem 3. *Let $\mathcal{Q}_\alpha^n$ a generalized hypercube and $\Gamma_n < \mathcal{Q}_\alpha^n$ a random induced subgraph. Then*

$$\lim_{n\to\infty} \boldsymbol{\mu}_n\{\Gamma_n \text{ is connected}\} = \begin{cases} 1 & \text{for} \quad \lambda > 1 - {}^{\alpha-1}\sqrt{\alpha^{-1}} \\ 0 & \text{for} \quad \lambda < 1 - {}^{\alpha-1}\sqrt{\alpha^{-1}} \end{cases}.$$
$$(4)$$

Remark. A related result in the special case of the Boolean hypercube can be found in [2]. The corresponding subgraphs A_p are constructed as follows: We set $\mathrm{v}[A_p] := \mathrm{v}[\mathcal{Q}_2^n]$ as vertex set and the edge set $\mathrm{e}[A_p]$ is obtained by independent random choices with probability p in the edge set $\mathrm{e}[\mathcal{Q}_\alpha^n]$. Then the idea of the proof is to establish an *edge boundary* of possible components using an *isoperimetric inequality* due to Harper, Bernstein, and Row [7, 2]. For Boolean hypercubes Ajtai, Komlós and Szemerédi 1982 proved the following related result: for random subgraphs A_p of $\mathcal{Q}_2^n$ obtained by edge selections, there exists a component of order $g\, 2^n$ with constant $g \in \mathbb{R}_+$ if $p = c/n$ and $c > 1$ [1].

Finally, for any positive λ a.a.s. there exists a giant component in random induced subgraphs $\Gamma_n < \mathcal{Q}_\alpha^n$.

Theorem 4. *Let $0 < \lambda \leq 1$. Then we have*

$$\lim_{n\to\infty} \boldsymbol{\mu}_n\{\Gamma_n \text{ has a giant component}\} = 1.$$

3. Sequence Structure Maps Via Random Graphs

3.1 Neutral Networks of Secondary Structures

A *pairing rule* Π is a symmetric relation in $\mathcal{A} \times \mathcal{A}$. Following [15] a *secondary structure* s w.r.t. Π is a vertex-labeled graph on n vertices $(x_1, \ldots, x_n)$ with an adjacency matrix A fulfilling

(1) $a_{i,i+1} = 1$ for $1 \leq i \leq n - 1$;
(2)   For each i there is at most a single $k \neq i - 1, i + 1$ such that $a_{i,k} = 1$ and $[x_i, x_k] \in \Pi$;
(3)   If $a_{i,j} = a_{k,l} = 1$ and $i < k < j$ then $i < l < j$.

We call an edge (x_i, x_k), $|i - k| \neq 1$ a *bond* or *base pair*. A vertex x_i connected only to x_{i-1} and x_{i+1} shall be called *unpaired*. The number of base pairs and the number of unpaired bases in a secondary structure s are $p(s)$ and $u(s)$, respectively. The size of the alphabet is α and the number of distinct base pairs is given by β.

We proceed by constructing the preimage of a fixed secondary structure as a random induced subgraph of the graph of compatible sequences. Let s be a secondary structure and

$$\Pi(s) := \{[i, k] \mid a_{i,k} = 1, k \neq i \pm 1\}$$

its *set of contacts*. Then a vertex $x \in \mathrm{v}[\mathcal{Q}_\alpha^n]$ is said to be *compatible* to s if and only if $\forall [i, j] \in \Pi(s) : [x_i, x_j] \in \Pi$ i.e. the coordinates x_i and x_j are in Π for all pairs $[i, j] \in \Pi(s)$. We denote *the set of all compatible sequences* by $\mathbf{C}[s]$. Finally the *graph* of compatible sequences w.r.t. the secondary structure s, is given by

$$\mathcal{C}[s] := \mathcal{Q}_\alpha^{u(s)} \times \mathcal{Q}_\beta^{p(s)}.$$

Neutral Network: *Let $\Gamma_u < \mathcal{Q}_\alpha^u$ and $\Gamma_p < \mathcal{Q}_\beta^p$ be random subgraphs with underlying parameters λ_u and λ_p as introduced in the basic model. Then we set $\Gamma_n[s] = \Gamma_u \times \Gamma_p$,*

$$\boldsymbol{\mu}_{\lambda_u, \lambda_p}(\Gamma_n[s]) := \boldsymbol{\mu}_{u, \lambda_u}(\Gamma_u) \times \boldsymbol{\mu}_{p, \lambda_p}(\Gamma_p),$$

and $\boldsymbol{\mu}_{\lambda_u, \lambda_p}$ is a probability measure and $\Gamma_n[s] < \mathcal{C}[s]$.

We can think of the neutral network, $\Gamma_n[s]$, to be obtained by selecting the coordinates v_1, v_2 of the vertex $(v_1, v_2) \in \mathrm{v}[\mathcal{C}[s]]$ with the probabilities λ_u and λ_p. This process leads to the vertex set $V_{\lambda_u, \lambda_p} \subset \mathbf{C}[s]$ whose induced subgraph $\mathcal{C}[s][V_{\lambda_u, \lambda_p}]$ is

$$\Gamma_n[s] = \Gamma_u \times \Gamma_p.$$

The theory presented in the previous chapter implies for neutral networks of secondary structures density and connectivity if both factors Γ_u and Γ_p are dense and connected.

3.2 Complete Mappings

Once we know how to construct a neutral network $\Gamma_n[s]$ we order the set of secondary structures $\mathcal{S}_n$ and define a complete mapping by iterating the construction process of the corresponding neutral network w.r.t. the ordering. Thereby we obtain w.r.t. a given λ parameter a complete sequence to structure mapping.

Let $\mathbf{C}^* : \mathcal{S}_n \to \mathcal{P}(\mathrm{v}[\mathcal{Q}_\alpha^n])$ and $r : \mathcal{S}_n \to \mathbb{N}$ be two mappings such that $j \le i \implies r(s_j) \ge r(s_i)$. A mapping $f : \mathcal{Q}_\alpha^n \to \mathcal{S}_n$ is called $\mathbf{C}^*$-map if and only if

$$(*): \quad f(v) = s \implies v \in \mathbf{C}^*[s].$$

A mapping $f_r : \mathcal{Q}_\alpha^n \to \mathcal{S}_n$ is called $\mathbf{C}^*$-random-map if and only if f_r is given by

$$f_r^{-1}(s_0) := \Gamma_n[s_0]$$
$$f_r^{-1}(s_i) := \Gamma_n[s_i] \setminus \bigcup_{j < i} [\Gamma_n[s_i] \cap \Gamma_n[s_j]].$$

reads in the particular case of $\Gamma_n[s] = \mathbf{C}[s]$:

$$f^{-1}(s_{r_0}) := \mathbf{C}[s_0]$$
$$f^{-1}(s_{r_i}) := \mathbf{C}[s_i] \setminus \bigcup_{j < i} [\mathbf{C}[s_i] \cap \mathbf{C}[s_j]]$$

It turns out that the random maps in secondary structures as defined above have a few large preimages and many small ones as reported in figure 2. This observation fits in the computational results about RNA sequence structure maps that exhibit a characteristic rank order function known as a *generalized Zipf's Law*:

$$\psi(i) = a(1 + i/b)^{-c},$$

as shown by extensive numerical calculations [13, 14]. Here a is a normalization constant, b is the number of frequent structures and c describes the power-law decay for rare structures.

4. Searching in Shape Space

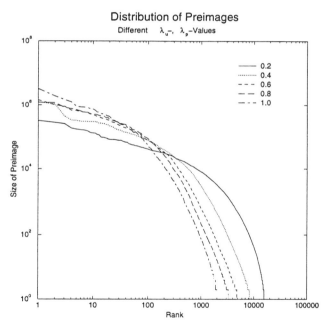

Fig. 2: We report here the logarithm of the sizes of the neutral networks $f^{-1}(s)$ obtained by a $\mathbf{C}^*$-random map and λ parameters $\lambda = 0.2, 0.4, 0.6, 0.8, 1.0$. The corresponding neutral networks are ordered on the x-axis by the logarithm of their orders. Note that the rank of the secondary structure s does not necessarily coincidence with the size of the corresponding preimage $|f^{-1}(s)|$.

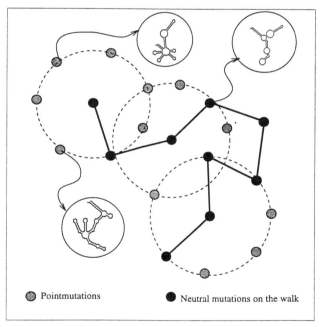

Fig. 3: A random walk on a neutral network. From each step (black) all point mutant sequences (grey) are formed and mapped into their corresponding secondary structures. Thereby, step by step, shape space is searched by w.r.t. one neutral network.

In particular any RNA folding map is a $\mathbf{C}^*$-map setting $\mathbf{C}^*[s] := \mathbf{C}[s]$ since the neutral networks are constructed *a priori* in the graph of compatible sequences. We will assume that $\mathbf{C}^* = \mathbf{C}$ and then the recursion

The time evolution of a population of asexually replicating molecules on a flat landscape can be described by a random walk. On more complex fitness landscapes a selective pressure drives the population towards sites of higher fitness. In the simplest case one may think of one or few fit structures. Then the populations searches "along one neutral network" [4] until sequences of another network corresponding to a fitter structure are found (see fig. 3).

The key question [10] is: to what extend is the shape space searched by a population diffusing [11] on a fixed neutral network? Here the following result [12, 11] gives some insight, implying that *any* two neutral networks that are dense and have a giant component come close in sequence space and therefore allow for transitions from one network to the other [4]. Practically *all* other structures are found forming one error mutants with respect to a fixed neutral net. Explicitly the result reads

Theorem 5. *[Intersection–Theorem] Let* Π *be a non-empty pairing rule on* $\mathcal{A}$ *and* s *and* s' *be arbitrary (non-empty) secondary structures. Then we have w.r.t.* Π

$$\mathbf{C}[s] \cap \mathbf{C}[s'] \neq \emptyset \, .$$

The topology of neutral networks (following the predictions of random graph theory) plays therefore a crucial role in the optimization process. Only the existence of a giant component in the net and its density guarantee that any other net can be reached. In the tables shown in appendix A, we report the existence of those giant components.

Finally we discuss the so called *search capacity* of our mappings. This means to a fixed λ parameter we compute the size of the preimage of those secondary structures that are found by a random walk of the particular (fixed) neutral network. Passing the critical parameter $\lambda = 0.5$ for density and connectivity, the shape space is searched effectively by a random walk on the corresponding neutral network. For the small sequence length considered in the computer experiments, it turns out that below $\lambda = 0.5$ it is difficult to perform a random walk on the network lasting sufficiently many steps.

Fractions of neutral neighbors can be determined numerically by RNA folding based on sequences over an **AUGC** alphabets [3, 9, 8]. These fractions turn out to be characteristically above the critical values derived from random graph theory, and therefore indicate how well suited nature is for optimization on secondary structures.

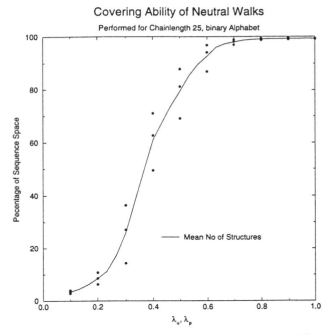

Fig. 4: We compute the percentage of the preimage of those secondary structures that are found by a random walk of one particular (fixed) neutral network. "Found" means that from each sequence realized in the walk we map all sequences of Hamming distance one and thereby obtain a stepwise increasing family of structures realized w.r.t. the random walk on the chosen network.

Acknowledgments

We want to thank Mr. F. Haubensak for the hints and support he gave us to create the two columns per page.

References

[1] Ajtai, Komlós, and Szemerédi. Largest random component of a k-cube. *Combinatorica*, 2:1 – 7, 1982.

[2] B. Bollobás. *Random Graphs*. ACADEMIC PRESS, 1985.

[3] W. Fontana, P. F. Stadler, E. G. Bornberg-Bauer, T. Griesmacher, I. L. Hofacker, M. Tacker, P. Tarazona, E. D. Weinberger, and P. Schuster. RNA folding and combinatory landscapes. *Phys. Rev. E*, 47(3):2083 – 2099, March 1993.

[4] C. V. Forst, C. Reidys and J. Weber. Evolutionary Dynamics and Optimization: Neutral Networks as Model-Landscapes for RNA Secondary-Stucture Folding-Landscapes. *Advances in Artificial Life*, 1995.

[5] W. Gruener, R. Giegerich, D. Strothmann, C. Reidys, J. Weber, I. L. Hofacker, P. F. Stadler, and

P. Schuster. Analysis of rna sequence structure maps by exhaustive enumeration I. neutral networks. *Monatshefte fuer Chemie*, 127:*–*, 1996.

[6] W. Gruener, R. Giegerich, D. Strothmann, C. Reidys, J. Weber, I. L. Hofacker, P. F. Stadler, and P. Schuster. Analysis of rna sequence structure maps by exhaustive enumeration II. structures of neutral networks and shape space covering. *Monatshefte fuer Chemie*, 127:*–*, 1996.

[7] L. Harper. Minimal numberings and isoperimetric problems on cubes. *Theory of Graphs, International Symposium, Rome*, 1966.

[8] I. L. Hofacker. *A Statistical Characterisation of the Sequence to Structure Mapping in RNA*. PhD thesis, University of Vienna, 1994.

[9] I. L. Hofacker, W. Fontana, P. F. Stadler, S. Bonhoeffer, M. Tacker, and P. Schuster. Fast folding and comparison of RNA secondary structures. *Monatshefte f. Chemie*, 125(2):167–188, 1994.

[10] M. Huynen, P. F. Stadler, and W. Fontana. Evolutionary dynamics of RNA and the neutral theory. *PNAS*, 1994. accepted.

[11] C. Reidys. *Neutral Networks of RNA Secondary Structures*. PhD thesis, Friedrich Schiller Universität, Jena, May 1995.

[12] C. Reidys, P. F. Stadler, and P. Schuster. Generic properties of combinatory maps and neutral networks of RNA secondary structures. *Bull. Math. Biol.*, 1995. submitted.

[13] P. Schuster, W. Fontana, P. F. Stadler, and I. L. Hofacker. From sequences to shapes and back: A case study in RNA secondary structures. *Proc.Roy.Soc.(London)B*, 255:279–284, 1994.

[14] M. Tacker, W. Fontana, P. Stadler, and P. Schuster. Statistics of RNA melting kinetics. *Eur. Biophys. J.*, 23(1):29 − 38, 1994.

[15] M. S. Waterman. Secondary structure of single - stranded nucleic acids. *Studies on foundations and combinatorics, Advances in mathematics sup-*

Appendix A

Rank	$|\Gamma|$	Structure	μ_u	μ_p	Sequence of Components
1	1494359	.......((....(((.....)).).))	0.823	0.854	1494359
2	1471814	.((.((.((.....))...)).......	0.795	0.858	1471810, 4×1
3	1180817	(((......)))............	0.599	0.487	1180665, 2, 150×1
4	1131781	..((..((.........)).))....	0.736	0.723	1131775, 6×1
5	895743	....((.....))....((...))	0.726	0.499	829839, 65886, 2, 16×1
6	811332	..(((((((.........))).))..	0.862	0.871	811332
7	769357	..(((......)))((.....)).	0.852	0.825	769357
8	764731	..((.....(((...)))..))....	0.880	0.826	764731
9	676878	....((...)).((.......))..	0.608	0.501	676783, 95×1
10	577625	((.......)).(((.....))).	0.740	0.723	577616, 9×1

Tab. 1: Mapping parameters $\lambda_u = \lambda_p = 0.9$, μ_u, μ_p are the percentages of unpaired and paired segments of sequences contained in the neutral net.

Rank	$|\Gamma|$	Structure	μ_u	μ_p	Sequence of Components
1	3466927	.......((......))........	0.567	0.618	3466927
2	1339085	...........((...)).......	0.409	0.306	1337547, 2× 3, 30× 2, 1472×1
3	718788	....((..((.....))..))...	0.514	0.576	718747, 2, 39×1
4	650290	....(((....)))...........	0.357	0.305	646820, 6, 5, 14× 3, 165× 2, 3087×1
5	642094	((....((........)).))...	0.500	0.513	642025, 2, 67×1
6	606699	.((.((.....))..)).......	0.456	0.553	606464, 6× 2, 223×1
7	596554	..((.....)).............	0.230	0.237	570539, 10, 3× 7, 7× 6, 20× 5,
					56× 4, 277× 3, 1618× 2, 21551×1
8	575245	.........(((........)))..	0.313	0.336	569428, 6× 4, 25× 3, 280× 2, 5158×1
9	500107	.((...((...))......))....	0.456	0.393	499841, 5× 2, 256×1
10	447051	.........((.....))......	0.333	0.000	443329, 4, 15× 3, 122× 2, 3429×1

Tab. 2: Mapping parameters $\lambda_u = \lambda_p = 0.6$ (see also caption of tab. 1)

Rank	$|\Gamma|$	Structure	μ_u	μ_p	Sequence of Components
1	1604053	.......((......)).......	0.387	0.481	$1604009, 18\times 2, 8\times 1$
2	1011867	.........((.....))......	0.279	0.349	$1008832, 4, 6\times 3, 169\times 2, 2675\times 1$
3	649324	..((.....)).............	0.209	0.000	$327019, 301123, 2\times 8, 2\times 7, 4\times 6,$
					$9\times 5, 53\times 4, 215\times 3, 1299\times 2,$
					17628×1
4	511011	.....(((...........)))..	0.244	0.311	$506282, 2\times 6, 5, 8\times 4, 41\times 3,$
					$274\times 2, 4009\times 1$
5	484477	.((...((...))......))....	0.351	0.555	$484319, 3\times 11, 2\times 10, 8, 2\times 7,$
					$6, 2\times 2, 73\times 1$
6	471135	.........(((........)))..	0.270	0.219	$359724, 107579, 9, 5, 8\times 4,$
					$29\times 3, 206\times 2, 3287\times 1$
7	440221	.........((.....)).......	0.170	0.193	$413333, 9, 8, 4\times 7, 9\times 6,$
					$29\times 5, 143\times 4, 411\times 3, 2060\times 2,$
					20719×1
8	375080	....((..((......))..))...	0.368	0.467	$330454, 44442, 7\times 7, 4\times 6, 111\times 1$
9	363837	......(((......))).......	0.272	0.181	$274624, 85356, 6, 5, 8\times 4,$
					$41\times 3, 212\times 2, 3267\times 1$
10	315083	((.((........)).)).......	0.248	0.443	$313124, 2\times 7, 3\times 5, 4, 13\times 3,$
					$97\times 2, 1693\times 1$

Tab. 3: Mapping parameters $\lambda_u = \lambda_p = 0.4$ (see also caption of tab. 1)

COMPUTER SIMULATION OF DISPERSAL BY ANOPHELES GAMBIAE s.l. IN WEST AFRICA

John Carnahan[1], Song-gang Li[2], Carlo Costantini[3],
Yeya T. Touré[4], and Charles E. Taylor[1]

[1]Department of Biology, University of California, Los Angeles, CA 90024,
email:carnahan@biology.ucla.edu, taylor@biology.ucla.edu
[2]Department of Biology, Peking University, Beijing, China, email: swlsg@peastms.pku
[3]Istituto di Parassitologia, Università di Roma 'La Sapienza', Roma, Italia,
email: c.costantini@ic.ac.uk
[4]Ecole de Medecine et de Pharmacie, Bamako, Mali, email: yeya@mrtcbko.malinet.ml

ABSTRACT

One fundamental insight from Artificial Life has been to model populations of animals by populations of coexecuting computer processes. We have been using such an approach to simulate the behavior of malaria-transmitting mosquitoes, members of the *Anopheles gambiae* complex, in West Africa. We performed sets of Mark-Release-Recapture experiments, where a few thousand mosquitoes were captured, marked, released and then some were recaptured. The experiments were simulated and the parameter space searched to find those values which gave the best fit between simulation and observation. This method has been applied with a set of coexecuting custom-written programs on a 16,000 node Connection Machine for data obtained near Ouagadougou, Burkina Faso (Costantini et al., 1996a). We have recently performed such experiments near Bamako, Mali, and are using the SWARM simulation system to model their behavior.

1. INTRODUCTION

Models of population behavior for the study of ecosystem organization, population genetics, geographic dispersal, etc., have traditionally been expressed as systems of algebraic or differential equations (see e.g. Roughgarden 1979; May, 1981). By "computer simulation" one typically meant solving these equations numerically, as opposed to analytically.

As computers have become more powerful and biologists have become more accustomed to thinking in computational metaphors, a richer variety of modeling paradigms are becoming available. From deterministic systems of differential equations that could be solved analytically, through stochastic models that usually required computers to solve them numerically, we have come to see the concepts of complex systems enter ecological models – for example with chaos and metastable equilibria. More recently there have been models that view organisms as processes, so that an ecosystem can be simulated by the concurrent execution of many such processes.

There are several reasons why this new paradigm is attractive (Taylor and Jefferson, 1994). It is common with equational models to refer to the derivative of a variable with respect to population size N. This implies the assumption of very large populations in order for such a derivative to make sense. That assumption is not always appropriate and may be seriously misleading. A second reason is that when realism is desired, it may take tens to hundreds of lines of equations to express even a simple model of an organism's behavior as a function of the many genetic, memory, and environmental variables that affect its behavior. It is frequently more economical and transparent to describe such systems by organisms acting according to a few simple rules, their collective action giving rise to complex emergent behavior. Finally, equational models are generally poor at dealing with highly nonlinear effects such as thresholding, if-then-else conditionals, and so on that often arise in biology, while these are natural for simple computer processes.

One fundamental insight from Artificial Life has been to model populations of animals by populations of coexecuting computer processes. An early example of this approach is the RAM system, described by Taylor *et al*. (1989) in which animal-like processes (parameterized Lisp programs) and environment-like processes could execute concurrently and synchronously. RAM animals reproduce asexually, but live in a common environment in which they interact and compete ecologically. Since that time, many other systems representing organisms as programs have been developed to explore problems in biology. In the literature of computer science these are referred to as "object-oriented models" (see e.g. Abelson and Sussman, 1985). In the area of ecological modeling they are sometimes referred to as "individual-based models" (Judson, 1994; DeAngelis and Gross, 1992) as well as "artificial life models" (Kawata and Toquenaga, 1994; Taylor and Jefferson, 1994; Kawata, 1996). The SWARM simulation system is an especially interesting effort to develop a set of general tools for this paradigm (Burkhart, 1994).

We are using such artificial life models to address issues that have arisen in the development of new methods for malaria control. In this paper we review our progress and describe our current efforts in that direction. The paper is organized into six sections. In section 2 we provide some background on malaria and *Anopheles gambiae* that motivated the study; section 3 describes the Mark-Release-Recapture (MRR) experiments we performed near Ouagadougou, Burkina Faso, in West Africa; Section 4 describes how this was simulated on a 16,000 processor Connection Machine and parameter values found that minimized the difference between simulation and observed outcomes. Section 5 describes a second set of experiments we performed near Bamako, Mali; and section 6 describes how we have begun to simulate these with the SWARM simulation system.

2. MALARIA AND *ANOPHELES GAMBIAE*

Malaria: Malaria continues to be one of the most serious health problems in the world today. One hundred million people or more suffer from this disease, with more than a million children dying from it each year. The problem in public health that motivates our research is how to ameliorate this disease. A variety of new methods for control are being explored, including better vector control methods and vaccines. Some of these methods involve release of genetically manipulated mosquitoes (Curtis, 1994). For example, the possibility exists that mosquitoes that normally act as vectors can be genetically engineered to be refractory to the malaria parasite, no longer transmitting the disease. If these genetically engineered mosquitoes were able to displace the resident, disease-transmitting, population, people would still get bitten by mosquitoes, but the malaria parasite would not be transmitted with that bite. This possibility is under active investigation (WHO, 1991; Collins and Besansky, 1994).

For such use of refractory mosquitoes in malaria control to be successful, it will be necessary to know much more about the population structure of these species than we do at present. Used correctly, with close attention to accurate and appropriate field data, computer simulations can be helpful for this (Roberts, 1995; Service, 1993a). As phrased by Collins and Besansky (1994) "The strategy for transforming the whole population urgently needs theoretical definition with modeling and with laboratory experiments, as well as by extensive study of vector populations in the malaria-endemic countries." The research described here is directed at acquiring the necessary knowledge about the population density and dispersal of malaria vectors in two malaria-endemic locations in West Africa, and then, using that knowledge, to develop a computer model of their dispersal.

Let us continue to use the release of refractory mosquitoes as an example. Questions about the dispersal and survival of the released mosquitoes will have to be addressed in even the earliest phases of development. What is the size of the resident population? How many must be displaced? Do the engineered mosquitoes disperse like native ones? Do they survive like native ones? How many preliminary experiments must we perform in order to have confidence in our estimates -- i.e. how much variation is there between releases and how can that be minimized? When and where should releases be made? And so on. Some of these questions can probably be answered satisfactorily without a computer model, but most cannot. Further, there are serious ethical questions with experiments that involve the release of mosquito vectors. Assessing the likely consequences of these will certainly require simulations. Finally, when the complexities of mosquito behavior are taken into consideration, the approximate means for estimating dispersal, survival and other of the important factors in vector control often fail to work, so the parameter values can be calculated only through simulation.

Mosquitoes: Some members of the Afro-tropical species of *An. gambiae s.l.* are among the most efficient transmitters of malaria in the world, and play an especially important role in transmitting malaria in Africa (WHO, 1989). They have proven very difficult to control. Consequently, members of the *An. gambiae* complex, in particular *An. gambiae s.s.*, are likely candidates for early experimental manipulations of vector populations.

The taxonomy and population structure of the *gambiae* group is unfortunately quite complicated (Coluzzi *et al.*, 1985). The species complex consists of at least six sibling species, two of which are present in the study areas we will employ -- *An. gambiae s.s.* and *An. arabiensis*. The taxonomic situation is further complicated by the presence of chromosomal forms within *An. gambiae* (Coluzzi *et al.*, 1979, 1985). In our study area three such forms are found – Bamako, Mopti, and Savanna. Crossing among some of the forms is rare, but does occur. This gives them a peculiar taxonomic status -- someplace between sympatric race and species. These chromosomal forms exhibit behavioral and ecological differences (Coluzzi *et al.*, 1977; Touré *et al.*, 1994). It appears impossible to distinguish among these taxonomic units without referring to cytological preparations or DNA. We have used both in the studies described below, but we could detect no difference in behavior among them. Therefore, when referring to *An. gambiae s.l.* it is understood that we are speaking of *An. gambiae s.s.* and *An. arabiensis* together; and when referring to *An. gambiae s.s.* we are doing so without reference to their chromosomal forms, unless otherwise stated.

Movement by *An. gambiae s.l.* females is tied to their feeding and oviposition cycles. A "typical" female will first oviposit when she is about 4 days of age. This requires one or two blood meals before her first oviposition, which will then occur early in the evening. Afterwards, she will bite again that evening, rest in the hut for two days or so, then go out and oviposit, go to a hut, bite again, etc. (Brengues and Coz, 1973; Carnevale *et al.*, 1979; Gillies, 1988). While such is the norm, many, perhaps most, females seem to depart from this in one way or another. For example, the average cycle appears to be about 2.4 days in some areas, rather than 2.0 (Carnevale et al., 1979) and some, perhaps as many as half, of the females appear to leave the hut after they have been fed (Molineaux and Gramiccia, 1980; Gillies, 1988). Not all An. gambiae s.l. feed on humans, though this seems to be the rule on the study site. No doubt there are important regional and seasonal differences in behavior. The points to be made here are: (1) dispersal in female An. gambiae s.l. is closely tied to their gonotrophic state, so that simple models which assume uniform dispersal (Lincoln Index, Fisher/Ford, etc. described by Service, 1993) may give seriously erroneous results; but at the same time, (2) it must be recognized that there is likely to be considerable variation about the "typical" theme, so that models of dispersal that require uniform adherence to a single cycle may also be seriously erroneous. In our first simulations we ignored the oviposition cycle, or assumed that all females cycled in lock step. We are attempting to include greater realism in our current efforts.

3. MRR EXPERIMENTS NEAR OUAGADOUGOU

Probably the most informative single experiments for learning about dispersal in many species of insect are MRR experiments. They have long been used to gain insight about mosquito populations. Service (1993) lists more than 150 such studies from various species of mosquitoes. As they relate to An. gambiae s.l., large numbers of mosquitoes are captured from huts throughout the study area, marked with identifying dust, and taken to one or more central areas where they are released. On subsequent days mosquitoes are recaptured from throughout the study area again, and the locations of the marked recaptures are noted. With appropriate assumptions and statistical considerations it is possible to make some inferences about their movement, their population density, and their survivorship, among other things.

During 1991 and 1992 we conducted MRR studies in Goundri, a small village near Ouagadougou, Burkina Faso (Costantini 1996a). It is 12° 30' N and 1° 20' W. This is an agricultural region in the Sudan Savannah vegetation belt of West Africa. The mean average rainfall is about 800 mm/year, falling mostly in the rainy season, June-September. Goundri consists of a collection of 70-80 compounds, each consisting of 2-12 mud huts surrounded by a mud wall. The huts may be round, 2-3 m in diameter with thatched roofs or rectangular, ca. 3 m x 6m, with corrugated iron roofs. An artificial lake with associated rice fields is located about 500 m from the village edge and there is a small clay quarry about 200 m from the village. Both offer good breeding/oviposition sites.

Adult resting mosquitoes were captured by hand, using small hand pooters or through use of small vacuum aspirators from the walls, ceilings, and belongings of people in the huts of the village. Collections were made during the late morning, 9:00 AM - 12:00 noon. Upon capture the mosquitoes were stored in paper cups that had been capped with silk bolting cloth, approximately 20-50 mosquitoes per

cup. These cups had been dusted with fluorescent dust of one color or another so that the mosquitoes in the cup would be marked.

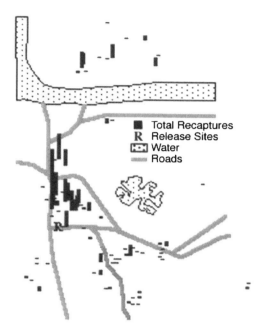

A. Days 1 and 2

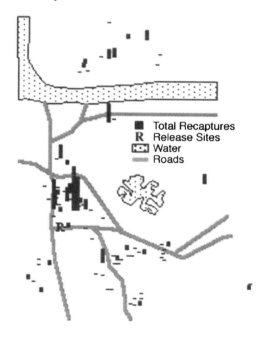

B. Days 3 - 10

Figure 1. Distribution of marked female Anopheles gambiae sensu lato from Mark-Release Recapture experiments in the village of Goundri, near Ouagadougou, Burkina Faso. Results from 5 experiments in each of 1991 and 1992 are pooled. (A) Days 1-2 after release; (B) Days 3-10 after release.

Releases were made around 1:00 PM. This was done by uncapping the cupped mosquitoes inside a cubic population cage, then opening the arm of the population cage inside a hut. This allows for free movement in and out by the mosquitoes. There were 5 releases in each of 1991 and 1992, with 1200-4200 females per release. Over two years the total number of females released was 21,114. The experimental protocol differed somewhat from one year to the other. For details see Costantini *et al.*, 1996a.

Recaptures were made on subsequent days, in much the same manner as mosquitoes were captured for release, except that the cups for storage were not dusted and upon collection, the adults were taken to the Centre National de Lutte contre le Paludisme, in Ouagadougou, where they were scored later that day or the next.

A total of 222 female mosquitoes were recaptured, for a total recapture rate of 1.05%. The distribution of recaptured females for days one and two after recapture are shown in Figure 1A, and for days 3 and subsequent in Figure 1B. We estimated the dispersal necessary to generate these numbers, using two simple models of dispersal by fitting the simulation parameters to the observations.

4. COMPUTER SIMULATIONS OF DISPERSAL IN OUAGADOUGOU

The principal method for obtaining unbiased measures of dispersal in insects using MRR experiments was introduced by Dobzhansky and Wright (1943). As such experiments are performed today, traps are placed at regular intervals (e.g. 20 m) in a cross-shaped pattern. Then insects are collected, taken to the center of the cross, marked and released. If: (a) dispersal is uniform; and (b) the traps are arranged in a sufficiently regular pattern; then the distribution should result in a 3-dimensional bell-shaped curve which flattens as time goes by. Wright showed how to adjust mathematically for the insects caught at various distances so that the distribution could be "filled in", giving the statistical illusion that insects are sampled from throughout the area, and a single measure of dispersal could then be estimated and its sampling distribution calculated. Many researchers have subsequently used these techniques to obtain more refined measures of dispersal by *Drosophila* and other insects (see e.g. Taylor and Powell, 1983).

This method of measuring dispersal absolutely requires that (a) dispersal be uniform and (b) the traps be arranged in a regular pattern; otherwise the "filling in" is not possible. In very few instances are Wright's assumptions likely to be realized. First, *An. gambiae s.l.* probably do not move in a random direction. "Host-seeking" females are instead attracted to human habitations by a combination of CO_2 and human body odor (Gillies, 1988; Costantini *et al.*, 1996), probably moving upstream in plumes formed by wind. When they are ovipositing the attractive stimuli are different. Second, movement by *An. gambiae s.l.* females is not random, but is tied to their feeding and oviposition cycles, as described above. Finally, the huts from which *An.*

gambiae s.l. are collected typically do not lie in anything like a cross or other regular pattern. The distribution of huts in the study area near Ouagadougou are shown in Figure 1. In general, Wright's method does not work for anophelines so other, more general, methods must be used to estimate dispersal.

Toward that end, Dobzhansky *et al.* (1979) suggested that it should be possible to estimate dispersal with a more complex model -- over heterogeneous areas with unequal dispersal rates. They first postulated a model of dispersal having a few parameters, 5 or 6 in their case, then searched through the relevant parameter space on a computer, taking the closest fit to the data as the best estimate of those parameters. These authors performed MRR experiments with *D. pseudoobscura* in the same sites that Dobzhansky and Wright had used. By assuming that dispersal was random, but allowing the rate of movement to differ among areas, they obtained a much closer fit to the data than with Wright's method. Costantini *et al.* (1996a) adapted this method to *An. gambiae s.l.*, as described below.

Dispersal by the female mosquitoes was simulated on a CM-2 Connection Machine that had 16,000 processors with memory associated to each. In the 1991 experiment a total of 7,260 female anopheline mosquitoes were released, and during 1992 a total of 13,854. It was possible to assign each mosquito that was released to a separate processor on the computer. The architecture of this machine is such that commands that emanate from the front end computer are carried out by all processors on the CM-2 in step.

Two models of behavior were explored. First an initial set of parameters to be explored and an initial random seed were chosen. There were four parameters for the first model and three for the second. They are described below. Then for each of 72 time steps during a simulated day the programs were executed, and at the end of each simulated day the simulated distribution of mosquitoes was compared to the distribution that was observed. Using a variant of conjugate gradient search, Powell's method (Press *et al.*, 1992), a new set of parameters to be explored was chosen, and the simulation repeated. In all but a few cases the search converged and the satisfaction criterion was met. In the few cases it did not the search was stopped at a depth of 200. The search proved to be very sensitive to the random seed, so we repeated the search 33 times with different random seeds and random sequence of variables to be changed in the searching procedure. When the least squared fit between simulated and observed value had been assigned, we took the average of 24 simulations of those values to characterize the fit.

Both models recognized that females do not all disperse equally during their egg-laying cycle. In Model I we assumed that a proportion of females do not move, *probability of not moving*, while most chose to move a random distance, determined by *maximum distance*, and random direction. At the end of each day, if they did not die, 1 - *probability of mortality*, they would enter a hut determined by their location and *hut attractiveness*. The model was as follows:

```
REPEAT (day+1) UNTIL
  (day = *number of days*)
  REPEAT (timestep+1) UNTIL
  (timestep = *number of time
  steps per day*)
    REPEAT (i+1) UNTIL
     (i = *number of mosquitoes*)
     IF (mosquito's life state
     = living)
       IF (random(0,1) >
       *probability of not
        moving*)
         MOVE random(-*maximum
         speed*, *maximum
           speed*)
       ELSE
         STAY
       IF (random(0,1) <
       *probability of
        mortality*)
         SET mosquito's life
         state = not living
    REPEAT (i+1) UNTIL
     (i = *number of mosquitoes*)
     IF (mosquito's life state
     = living)
       REPEAT (j+1) UNTIL
        (j = *number of huts*)
        IF (distance to hut <
        *hut attractiveness*)
          REPORT that mosquito
          is close to hut
```

In model II we attempted to be more precise about the gonotrophic cycle. Rather than a fixed proportion of females remaining still, we assumed that each female cycled at a rate determined by the speed at which they digested their blood meals, *digestion rate*. The model was:

```
REPEAT (day+1) UNTIL
  (day = *number of days*)
  REPEAT (timestep+1) UNTIL
   (timestep = *number of time
   steps per day*)
    REPEAT (i+1) UNTIL
     (i = *number of mosquitoes*)
     IF (mosquito's life state =
     living)
       *probability of not moving*
       = mosquito's feeding
       state
     IF (mosquito's feeding state
     = not empty)
       mosquito's feeding state =
       mosquito's feeding state
       - *digestion rate state*
```

```
     IF (random(0,1) >
     *probability of not
       moving*)
       MOVE random(-*maximum
       speed*, *maximum speed*)
     ELSE
       STAY
     IF (random(0,1) <
     *probability of mortality*)
       SET mosquito's life state =
       not living
  REPEAT (i+1) UNTIL
   (i = *number of mosquitoes*)
   IF (mosquito's life state =
   living
     REPEAT (j+1) UNTIL
      (j = *number of huts*)
      IF (distance to hut < (*hut
      attractiveness*)*(number
      of huts in compound))
        REPORT that mosquito is
        close to hut
```

Surprisingly, the two models did not differ greatly in their fit to the data, though Model I was consistently a bit better. The correlation coefficients between observed and simulated for 1991 was $r = 0.51$ for Model 1 and $r = 0.37$ for Model II. For the 1992 data $r = 0.57$ for Model 1 and $r = 0.55$ for Model II. It is not apparent to us why model I, which was simpler, fit better. We surmise that the ovarian cycling in Model II was mischaracterized or was too rigid. In the studies we have undertaken more recently, described below, we recorded the ovarian state of all captured females in order to get a better understanding of the role of ovarian cycling.

This was a first attempt, and while it accounted for a good deal of the variance in dispersal, it was deficient in a number of significant ways: (1)It made no distinction among the various species and chromosomal forms of the *An. gambiae* complex; (2) It did not distinguish the behavior of females in the various gonotrophic states; (3) It assumed no difference in the behavior of individuals collected from different areas -- i.e. no habitat fidelity; (5)The model largely ignored mosquitoes outside of the huts; (6) The model had only a rough, and largely undirected, set of rules for dispersal by the mosquitoes; and (7) Day-to-day and year-to-year variation in mosquitoes collected per hut was very large, and no attempt was made to relate this to human behavior or to environmental changes.

In an effort to correct these limitations and to expand on the experiments in Ouagadougou, we began a second series of experiments, this time in a village near Bamako, Mali. This site was chosen because it, too, has been the focus of much prior research, and because it has a well-equipped laboratory for molecular biology, which is desirable for comprehensive species identification and study of population structure.

5. EXPERIMENTS NEAR BAMAKO

The site for our second MRR study was Banambani, Mali, a small village of about 1,000 inhabitants, approximately 20 km. from Bamako. A map of the area is shown in Figure 2. It is located at 12° 48' N and 8° 03' W, in the Sudan Savannah vegetation belt (Lawson, 1966) of Western Africa. The site has received attention from several aspects of malaria transmission (Touré, 1985). Like Ouagadougou, annual rainfall is between 500 and 1,200 mm, typically concentrated during June-November, especially from July-September, at which time the densities of *An. gambiae s.l.* are greatest. The principal breeding/oviposition site appears to be a stream near the village, which is apparent in Figure 2. The density, both per hut and per village of *An. gambiae s.l.* is very much less in Banambani than in Goundri, and the species composition also appears to be somewhat different. Like Goundri, both *An. arabiensis* and *An. gambiae s.s* are present. In Goundri *An. gambiae s.s.* consists largely of the Mopti and Savanna chromosome forms, but all three of Mopti, Savannah and Bamako near Banambani. The relative proportions at the time of this study were about 2:1:1.

MRR experiments were performed during July/August in 1993 and 1994 (Touré *et al.*, in prep.) Four releases were performed. The procedures for release and recapture are essentially those used in the study near Ouagadougou, modified to address some of the questions left open from that study. In Bamako, unlike Ouagadougou: (1) DNA from all recaptured females and a sample of unmarked ones were analyzed to determine species, according to the method of Scott *et al.* (1993); (2) the gonotrophic state of all captured females, marked and unmarked, were recorded during the afternoon of the recapture, to provide data for testing of the role of gonotrophic cycling in dispersal from these experiments; and (3) Two release sites were used, with different marking colors for each.

The distribution of mosquitoes recovered in day 1 after release are shown in Figure 2A, and those recovered in days 2 and later are shown in Figure 2B. We have begun to simulate these releases in more or less the manner described of Ouagadougou, with the additional detail we were able to collect during these experiments. This time, rather than writing specialized code for the Connection Machine, we are using the Swarm simulation system, under development at the Santa Fe Institute, taking advantage of the various tools it has to offer.

6. COMPUTER SIMULATIONS OF DISPERSAL IN BANAMBANI

Custom-written programs, like those used in our previous simulations, sometimes carry subtle but important assumptions that make publication and replication of simulations difficult (see Judson, 1994). A standardized simulation framework would be useful for reporting analyses

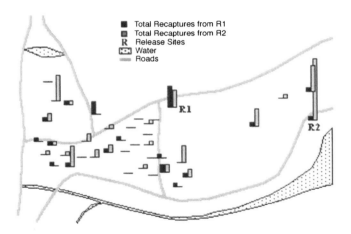

A. Day 1

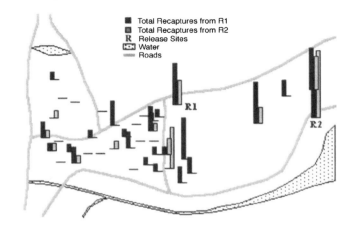

B. Days 2-11

Figure 2. Distribution of marked female *An. gambiae* sensu lato from Mark-Release Recapture experiments in the village of Banambani, near Bamako, Mali. Results from 4 experiments in each of 1993 and 1994 are pooled. (A) Day 1 after release; (B) Days 2-11 after release.

of complex simulations. In addition, while it was not difficult to write the necessary simulation code for the Ouagadougou study, the tools we would like for analyzing those simulations have been lacking and are sometimes very difficult to program. For these reason, among others, we have chosen to use the SWARM simulation system to build a new model of mosquito dispersal. The SWARM system is being developed at the Santa Fe Institute by Roger Burkhart, Christopher Langton, and Nelson Minar and their associates (Burkhart, 1994).

The SWARM simulation system is an object-oriented framework that permits the analysis of many interacting agents with ruled-based specifications of behavior in a possibly dynamic environment (Hiebler, 1994). It is designed to facilitate agent management and provides a user interface with a variety of simulation tools to individual-based models, all using a common language. The most artificial and subtle assumptions of simulations typically involve time, because of the difference between continuous time in nature and discrete time in a computer process (Burkhart, 1994). A well-documented feature of SWARM is discrete time-step scheduling where each object may do some unit of computation each time step (Hiebler, 1994). By documenting such assumptions, reports on analyses done in SWARM may be properly detailed to allow some measure of repeatability within the same SWARM framework. Equally important, we are finding that building a model with SWARM is faster and easier because many of basic tasks of building an agent-based computer model are already provided.

The SWARM system is designed to allow the direct mapping of behavioral rules of agents and produce a dynamic model that can then be used to predict states of an individual or groups of individuals. In our present study we are using SWARM to reconstruct the 1993-1994 MRR studies in Banambani. In setting up the simple physical environment, hut objects were placed on a 2-dimensional lattice at relative coordinates corresponding to their counterparts in Mali. As in the MRR experiments themselves, the mosquito agents, each with their own set of state variables defined in SWARM, were then released. The scheduler coordinates their behavior in this environment over the next several simulated days according to the specified parameter values. Following the best-fitting model from Ouagadougou, the parameters used in the present model were number of days, probability of not moving, maximum speed, probability of mortality and number of time steps per day. The general schedule of each simulation was as described for Model 1, above.

After each simulation the closeness of fit of spatial distributions between simulated mosquito agents and recaptured mosquitoes will be assessed to find the best set of parameter values using standard algorithms like those used in the Ouagadougou study. One important insight that has been gained from our study so far is that the rules governing animal behavior can be easily and naturally characterized using Artificial Life constructs in SWARM.

The models we have used to date are very simple. Our next steps will be to make the model more realistic. We intend to soon include genotype, gonotrophic state, habitat fidelity and wind-borne attractants from the huts. During 1993 and 1994 we collected data that should permit us to parameterize and test the importance of these variables. Our future plans include building a model that can predict year-to-year variation in mosquito distributions, and to validate these simulations by experimental manipulations. In the long run, we anticipate that these studies will lead to practical and useful tools for malaria vector control.

ACKNOWLEDGMENTS

Portions of this work were supported by the Ministry of Health in Burkina Faso, Direzione Generale per la Cooperazione allo Sviluppo of the Italian Ministry of Foreign Affairs, UNDP/World Bank/WHO Special Programme for Tropical Disease Research, US Agency for International Development to the NIH for a malaria research facility in Mali, NSF DIR-9024251, and the UCLA Academic Senate. We thank the many people who contributed to this project: we wish to especially thank Mario Coluzzi, Vincenzo Petrarca and Peter Andrews.

REFERENCES

Abelson, H. and G. Sussman, 1985. The Structure and Interpretation of Computer Programs. MIT Press, Cambridge.

Brengues, J. and J. Coz. 1973. Quelques aspects fondamentaux de la biologie d'*Anopheles gambiae* Giles (*Sp.* A) et d'*Anopheles funestus* Giles, en zone de savane humide d'Afrique de l'Ouest. Cah. O.R.S.T.O.M., Sér. Entom. méd et Parasitol., 11:107-126.

Burkhart, R. 1994. The Swarm Multi-Agent Simulation System. Position Paper for OOPSLA '94 Workshop on "The Object Engine". Available on WWW as http://www.santafe.edu/projects/swarm/oopsla94.html.

Carnevale, P., M-F. Bosséno, M. Molinier, J. Lancien, F. Le Pont, and A. Zoulani. 1979. Étude du cycle gonotrophique d'*Anopheles gambiae* (Diptera, Culicidae) (Giles, 1902) en zone de forêt dégradée d'Afrique Centrale. Cah. O.R.S.T.O.M., Sér. Entom. méd et Parasitol. 17:55-75.

Collins, F.H. and N.J. Besansky. 1994. Vector biology and the control of malaria in Africa. Science 264:1874-1875.

Coluzzi, M., A. Sabatini, V. Petrarca, and M.A. Di Deco. 1977. Behavioral divergences between mosquitoes with different inversion karyotypes in polymorphic populations of the *Anopheles gambiae* complex. Nature 266:832-833.

Coluzzi, M., A. Sabatini, V. Petrarca, and M.A. Di Deco. 1979. Chromosomal differentiation and adaptation to human environments in the *Anopheles gambiae* complex. Trans. R. Soc. Trop. Med. Hyg. 73:483-497.

Coluzzi, M., V. Petrarca, and M.A. Di Deco. 1985. Chromosomal inversion intergradation and incipient speciation in *Anopheles gambiae*. Boll. Zool. 52:45-63.

Costantini, C., G. Gibson, N'F. Sagnon, A. della Torre, J. Brady, and M. Coluzzi. 1996. Mosquito responses to carbon dioxide in a West African Sudan savanna village. Medical and Veterinary Entomology (in press) 10(2):000-000.

Costantini, C., S-G Li, A. della Torre, N'F. Sagnon, M. Coluzzi, and C. Taylor. 1996a. Density, survival and dispersal of *Anopheles gambiae* complex mosquitoes in a West African Sudan savanna village. Medical and Veterinary Entomology (in press) 10(2):000-000.

Curtis, C.F. 1994. The case for malaria control by genetic manipulation of its vectors. Parasitology Today 10:371-374.

DeAngelis, D.L. and L.J. Gross. 1992. Individual-based Models and Approaches in Ecology: Populations, Communities and Ecosystems. Chapman and Hall.

Dobzhansky, Th., J.R. Powell, C.E. Taylor, and M. Andregg. 1979. Ecological variables affecting the dispersal behavior of Drosophila pseudoobscura and its relatives. American Naturalist. 114:325-334.

Dobzhansky, Th. and S. Wright. 1943. Genetics of natural populations. X. Dispersion rates in Drosophila pseudoobscura. Genetics 28:304-340.

Gillies, M.T. 1988. Anopheline mosquitos: vector behaviour and bionomics, pp. 453-485. In W. H. Wernsdorfer and I. McGregor [eds.], Malaria: Principles and Practice of Malariology. Churchill Livingstone, NY.

Hiebler, D. 1994. The Swarm simulation systems and individual-based modeling. Decision Support 2001: Advance Technology for Natural Resource Mangagement. Toronto, 1994.

Judson, O.P. 1994. The rise of individual-based model in ecology. Trends in Ecology and Evolution 9:9-14.

Kawata, M. 1995. Effective population size in a continuously distributed population. Evolution 49:1046-1054.

Kawata, M. and Toquenaga, Y. 1994. From artificial individuals to global patterns. Trends in Ecology & Evolution, 1994, 9:417-421.

Lawson, G.W. 1966. Plant Life in West Africa. Oxford University Press.

May, R. M. 1981. Theoretical ecology : Principles and Applications. 2nd. ed. Sinauer Assoc., Sunderland, Mass.

Molineaux, L. and G. Gramiccia. 1980. The Garki Project. Research on the epidemiology and control of malaria in the Sudan savanna of West Africa. World Health Organization. Geneva.

Press, W.H., B.P. Flannery, S.A. Teukolsky, and W.T. Vetterling. 1992. Numerical Recipes in C: The Art of Scientific Computing. 2nd ed. Cambridge University Press, Cambridge.

Roberts, F.C. 1995. Computer models: Killing mosquitoes with information. J. Am. Mosquito Control Assn. 11:(2) 284-289.

Roughgarden, J. 1979. Theory of Population Genetics and Evolutionary Ecology: An Introduction. Macmillan Publishing Co., New York

Scott, J.A., W.G. Brogdon and F.H. Collins. 1993. Identification of single specimens of the Anopheles gambiae complex by the polymerase chain reaction. Am. J. Trop. med. Hyg. 49:520-529.

Service, M. W. 1993. Mosquito Ecology: Field Sampling Methods. 2nd ed. Elsevier Applied Science Publishers Ltd. London.

Sevice, M.W. 1993a. The role of ecology and ecological modeling in vector control.. Bull. Soc. Vector Ecol. 18:85-98.

Taylor, C.E. and D.R. Jefferson. 1994. Artificial Life as a tool for biological inquiry. Artificial Life 1:1-13.

Taylor, C.E. & J.R. Powell. 1983. Population structure of Drosophila: Genetics and ecology. pp. 29-60. In M. Ashburner, H.L. Carson, & J.R. Thompson [eds.], The Genetics and Biology of Drosophila, vol 3d. Academic Press. London.

Taylor, C.E., D. R. Jefferson, S.R. Turner, and S.R. Goldman. 1989. RAM: Artificial life for the exploration of complex biological systems. pp. 275-295. In C.G. Langton [ed.], Artificial Life. Addison Wesley. Reading, Mass.

Touré, Y.T. 1985. Génétique Écologique et Capacité Vectorielle des Membres du Complexe Anopheles gambiae au Mali. Thèse Doctorat d'État ès Sciences Naturelles. Aix - Marseille.

Touré, Y.T. V. Petrarca, S.F. Traoré, A. Coulibaly, H.M. Maiga, O. Sankaré, M. Sow, M.A. Di Deco, and M. Coluzzi. 1994. Ecological genetic studies in the chromosomal form Mopti of Anopheles gambiae s.Str. in Mali, West Africa. Genetica 94:213-223.

W.H.O. 1989. Geographical distribution of arthropod-borne diseases and their principal vectors. WHO/VBC/89.967. Geneva.

W.H.O. 1991. Report of the meeting "Prospects for Malaria Control by Genetic Manipulation of its Vectors". January 27-31, 1991. TDR/BCV/MAL-ENT/91.3

An Approach to Molecular Artificial Life: Bacterial Intelligent Behavior and its Computer Model

H. Ohtake[1], T. Yako[2], T. Tsuji[2], J. Kato[1], A. Kuroda[1] and M. Kaneko[2]

[1]Department of Fermentation Technology, Hiroshima University, Higashi-Hiroshima, Hiroshima 739, Japan, e-mail: hohtake@ue.ipc.hiroshima-u.ac.jp, and [2]Department of Industrial and Systems Engineering, Hiroshima University, Higashi-Hiroshima, Hiroshima 739, Japan, e-mail: tsuji@ue.ipc.hiroshima-u.ac.jp

Abstract

We here describe an approach to "Molecular Artificial Life" which represents a digital life designed on the molecular basis of living systems. We choose a simple, free-living bacterium *Pseudomonas aeruginosa*, which is amenable to biochemical and genetic analysis, as a model organism for understanding real-life behaviors in molecular detail. We focus on the bacterial intelligent behavior called chemotaxis, because it is possibly the simplest real-life behavior that can be studied objectively and analyzed quantitatively. Biochemical and genetic analysis is carried out to characterize the molecular circuitry that is responsible for the chemotaxis of *P. aeruginosa*. On the basis of molecular evidence, we propose a computer model for bacterial chemotaxis. The model will be used as part of a digital life that simulates the whole bacterial system in molecular detail.

1. Introduction

The fact that life-like systems will play an important role in our future societies is becoming ever more widely accepted. Life-like systems are expected to actively monitor environmental conditions and to wisely respond to the changing conditions. Much work has been published on the phenomenological models for simulating the behavior of real-life systems [1]. However, these models are often superficial and unsatisfied from the biological viewpoint. The phenomenological models for instance give little insight into the fundamental properties of real-life systems, including flexibility and adaptability, at the molecular level. Short cuts and superficial attention to basic principles are likely to lead at best to poor performance and at worst to expensive failures.

Bacteria are small (typically less than 5 μm long), free-living organisms that are ubiquitous in a wide range of environments from soil and water to human host. They live in precarious environments where nutrient levels, temperature, humidity and other conditions can change rapidly and unexpectedly. Bacteria have evolved their intelligent skills to cope wisely with changing conditions. For example, bacteria can monitor many aspects of their surroundings by using various molecular sensors and actively respond to changing conditions by altering patterns of gene expression [2]. Most bacteria can also seek out favorable environments and escape away from unfavorable ones by changing their swimming direction in response to environmental stimuli [3]. These skills allow bacteria to communicate not only with the abiotic environment but also with each other in microbial communities.

Since bacteria are most amenable to biochemical and genetic analysis, they have assumed a special role in molecular and cellular biology. The bacterial system can also be treated as a model for studying the behavior of living systems in molecular detail. We here propose an approach to "Molecular Artificial Life" which represents a digital life designed on the molecular basis of free-living systems. We choose a monoflagellated, obligately aerobic bacterium *Pseudomonas aeruginosa* as a model organism. We focus on the bacterial intelligent behavior called chemotaxis [4], because it is possibly the simplest real-life behavior that can be studied objectively and analyzed quantitatively. The first section of this paper reviews our current understanding of the molecular chemotaxis machinery in *P. aeruginosa* [5,6,7,8,9]. The second section describes a simple computer model for bacterial chemotaxis which is designed on the basis of molecular evidence. The model can be used as part of a digital life that simulates the whole bacterial system in molecular detail.

2. Bacterial chemotaxis

Bacterial chemotaxis is the process by which bacterial cells migrate through concentration gradients of chemical attractants and repellents [4]. Chemotaxis can be viewed as an important prelude to metabolism, prey-predator relationships, symbiosis, and other ecological interactions in microbial communities [10]. In addition to its biological importance, chemotaxis has assumed a special role in giving insight into the signal transduction network of living systems [2]. Bacterial chemotaxis has also contrib-

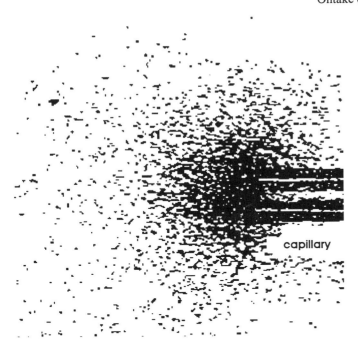

Fig. 1 Chemotactic response of *P. aeruginosa* toward inorganic phosphate (Pi). The capillary tube, with a diameter of approximately 10 μm, contained 10 mM Pi and 1% agarose. Bacterial cells, which are within the focus of microscope, can be seen as small dotts [11].

uted to the understanding of the mechanisms of sensory transduction in more complex organisms.

2.1. Bacterial chemotactic behavior

Bacterial chemotaxis is a quick process that occurs within one second after cells are subjected to a chemical stimulus. The computer-assisted capillary technique has been developed for bacterial chemotaxis assays [11]. In this method, digital image processing is used to count the number of bacteria accumulating around the mouth of a capillary that contains a chemical compound plus agarose gel (Fig. 1). The bacterial response toward a strong attractant is so quick that a cloud of bacteria, as can be seen in Fig. 1, starts to form soon (typically less than 10 s) after the start of microscopic observation. The range of chemical stimuli that elicit behavioral responses varies from bacterial species to species. *P. aeruginosa* exhibits chemotactic responses to a wide range of chemical stimuli including L-amino acids, sugars and organic acids and inorganic phosphate (Pi) [5]. This organism is also known to be repelled by thiocyanic and isothiocyanic esters [12]. Several lines of evidence suggest the presence of regulatory mechanisms underlying the chemotaxis by *P. aeruginosa*. For example, *P. aeruginosa* taxis toward several L-amino acids is subject to control by nitrogen availability

in a manner similar to the control of various enzymes of nitrogen metabolism [13]. The strength of chemotactic responses to glucose and citrate is also dependent on prior growth of the cells on those carbon sources [14]. In addition, *P. aeruginosa* shows Pi taxis, only when the cells are starved for Pi [5]. However, these regulatory mechanisms are still poorly understood at the molecular level.

2. 2. Mechanism for bacterial chemotaxis

The basic mechanism of bacterial chemotaxis has been intensively studied with enteric bacteria *Escherichia coli* and *Salmonella typhimurium*, and it is suggested that similar mechanisms work among a variety of bacterial species including *P. aeruginosa* [4]. *P. aeruginosa* is capable of swimming motility by rotating a polar flagellum that extends up to several cell lengths from its surface. The external filament is helical in shape and works against the medium. *P. aeruginosa* moves in a three-dimensional random walk. When cells swim toward higher concentrations of attractants, the random walk is biased to achieve net migration by reducing the probability of random reorientation. This is performed by modulating the direction of flagellar rotation. Bacteria can detect spatial gradients of chemicals by monitoring their concentration changes over time as they swim from one place to another. Since bacteria are small and are subject to the effects of Brownian motion, they have to compare concentrations over distances substantially greater than their own length.

To exhibit chemotactic responses, bacteria should have information processing machinery consisting of elements at least: (i) a measure of the present concentration of a chemoeffector; (ii) a memory of the chemoeffector concentration at the recent past; (iii) a comparator for measuring the difference between the present and recent past concentrations; and (iv) a switch that influences motor reversal according to the input from the comparator (Fig. 2). Bacteria also adapt to the continued presence of a stimulus. The immediate changes in swimming behavior that result when cells first are exposed to chemotactic stimuli diminish over time. Cells subsequently return to prestimulus behaviors although they remain in the presence of the chemoeffector. Adaptation is necessary for detecting new stimuli. For further information on chemotaxis, a number of reviews [2,4,15,16] are available .

2. 3. Molecular chemotaxis machinery

The signal-transduction network that mediates bacterial chemotaxis allows cells to modulate their swimming behavior in response to changes in chemical stimuli. First, sensors at the cell surface receive environmental stimuli (Fig. 2). Signals are then converted to internal signals by chemotactic transducers. Transducers can also directly sense a variety of chemical stimuli [18]. After being

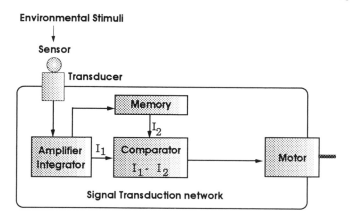

Fig. 2 Bacterial chemotaxis machinery. I_1 and I_2 are chemotaxis signals detected at present and recent past, respectively. Arrows indicate signal flow through the elements of chemotaxis machinery.

amplified and integrated, the internal signals are transmitted through the intracellular signal transduction pathway to the flagellar motors. The components of the intracellular signal transduction pathway are chemotaxis proteins which function to regulate phosphorylation and dephosphorylation of a response regulator (CheY) that interacts with the flagellar motor switch complex to control swimming behavior [16]. Protein methylation and demethylation of transducer proteins is also caused to adjust the level of excitation to the chemical stimuli.

Molecular analysis of chemotaxis genes in *P. aeruginosa* was achieved only recently. We selected *P. aeruginosa* chemotaxis mutants by the swarm plate method after NTG mutagenesis [9]. These mutants were fully motile but incapable of swarming, suggesting that they had a defect in the intracellular signalling pathway. *P. aeruginosa* chemotaxis genes were then cloned by phenotypic complementation of these mutants. We have currently cloned a chemotaxis gene cluster which contains at least the *cheY*, *cheZ*, *cheA*, *cheB* and *cheJ* genes (Fig. 3). The predicted products of the first four genes shared high similarity with the enteric Che proteins [16]. However, the *cheJ* gene product had no significant homology with any known protein species. Insertional inactivation of the chromosomal *cheJ* gene rendered *P. aeruginosa* defective in chemotaxis. Since the chromosomal *cheJ* mutant was fully motile, the CheJ protein is not a component of flagellar apparatus. CheJ may play an unexpected role in the chemotactic signal-transduction pathway in *P. aeruginosa*.

Biochemical evidence suggested that *P. aeruginosa* possesses approximately 73 kDa proteins that are covalently modified by dynamic methylation and demethylation reactions in response to L-amino acids [17]. To clone the chemotactic transducer genes in *P. aeruginosa*, we selected another mutant that is defective in taxis toward L-serine

but normal to peptone. A *P. aeruginosa* chemotactic transducer gene, designated *pctA*, was cloned by complementing this mutant. The PctA protein had the typical structural features of methyl-accepting chemotactic transducers (MCPs) in enteric bacteria [4]. The strongest homology with the enteric MCPs was found in the "highly conserved domain" (HCD) [8]. The chromosomal *pctA* mutant was defective in taxis toward glycine, L-serine, L-threonine and L-valine, indicating that PctA serves as the chemosensor for these L-amino acids. Further sequence analysis of the *pctA* region revealed the presence of at least two additional genes encoding MCP-like proteins. Our current understanding of the chemotaxis machinery in *P. aeruginosa* is summarized in Fig. 3.

3. Model for bacterial chemotaxis

To understand how bacterial intelligence arises from the simple signal transduction network, a mathematical model for bacterial chemotaxis was developed (Figs. 4 and 5). The model presented here is designed on the molecular basis of *E. coli* chemotaxis which has been most intensively investigated [15,18].

The transducer protein is likely to be involved in the processes for measurement of current concentration, a record of recent past concentration and a means for comparison [18]. Events through to occur at the transducer can be presented as a model for a cycle of excitation and adaptation (the upper part of Fig. 4). In the unstimulated state [I], the ligand-binding sites are unoccupied. Occupancy of the ligand-binding site is a measure of current concentration. Binding results in a shift in the state of the transducer from [I] to [II] which generates a positive internal signal for a chemotactic response. This signal activates the dephosphorylation of CheA. Ligand binding activates the methyl-accepting sites for a net increase in

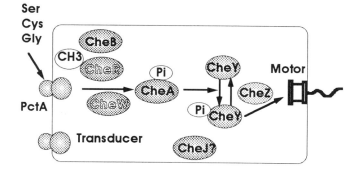

Fig. 3 Chemotactic signal transduction network in *P. aeruginosa*. The components of the intracellular signal transduction pathway are chemotaxis (Che) proteins. CheR and CheW, which are found to be involved in the *E. coli* chemotaxis system, have not been identified in *P. aeruginosa*. The function of CheJ is unknown.

methylation, thus setting the state of adaptation [III]. The modification reactions are slow on the time scale of changes in occupancy, which is likely to provide a memory of recent past concentration. The balancing of ligand occupancy and modification is likely to be a comparison of current and past concentrations. Loss of ligand creates a negative stimulus [IV]. In this state, demethylation is activated, and the transducer is restored to the null signalling state [I]. CheR and CheB proteins are the enzymes catalyzing methylation and demethylation, respectively.

Four cytoplasmic proteins, CheA, CheW, CheY and CheZ, are involved in the intracellular signal transduction (the lower part of Fig. 4). CheA, which is an auto-phosphorylating kinase, is the central component of the signal transduction network [16]. The phosphorylated CheA transfers Pi to CheY, and the phosphorylated CheY in turn biases the flagellar motor toward clockwise (CW), resulting in a change of swimming direction [4]. CheZ accelerates hydrolysis of Pi from CheY. The phospho-rylated CheA also transfers Pi to CheB, increasing the methylesterase activity. CheW is thought to couple a primary signal received by the transducer to CheA.

Our model equations are simply the conservation equations for the components in the signal transduction network (Fig. 5). On the basis of molecular evidence, the first four differential equations (Fig. 5(a)) represent the fraction of transducer in each of four states as a function of time. The concentration changes in chemotaxis proteins as a function of time are given by the last six equations (Fig.5(b)). The frequency of reversal of swimming direction is assumed to be dependent on the value of the ratio C_y/C_{yp}. When the ratio C_y/C_{yp} is lower than 1.0, the flagellar motor is biased toward clockwise, resulting in change of swimming direction. Parameters, v_{12}, v_{12}, v_{23}, v_{34}, v_{43}, v_{41}, v_b, v_{bp}, v_y, v_{yp} and v_{yz} are constant, while v_{41}, v_{ap} and v_a are functions of C_{bp}, C_4 and C_2, respectively (see the legend to Fig. 5).

It is best to determine the rate constants experimentally. However, in vitro kinetic experiments with purified proteins are time-consuming, and no systematic study has been reported on determining the rate constants. In this preliminary work, the rate constants in the model equations were adjusted to represent the general features that have been observed in studies of sensory response and adaptation. The general features considered are: (i) the response of a bacterial cell to a chemical attractant is typically observed within 1 s after being subjected to the stimulus; (ii) the time required for intracellular signal transduction is approximately 200 ms; (iii) adaptation occurs less than 1 min after being subjected to stimuli; (iv) the dephosphorylation of CheB is so fast that at most 10-20% of CheB remains phosphorylated; and (v) the half-life of phosphorylated CheY is to the extent of 6-15 s in the absence of CheZ. We also assumed that the ratio of C_y/C_{yp} is 1.0 under the unstimulated conditions. Fig. 6 shows the temporal change in the fraction of transducer in each of four states, which occurs upon addition of a saturating stimulus. The initial conditions and rate constants used in this simulation are given in the legend to Fig. 6. Upon

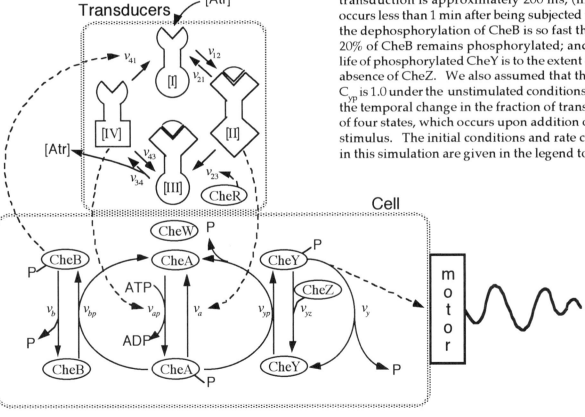

Fig. 4 Schematic illustration of chemotactic signal transduction in *E. coli* [15,18]. In this model, chemical attractants are directly sensed by chemotactic transducer proteins. Atr, attractant; P, inorganic phosphate (Pi).

$$[I] + [Atr] \xrightarrow{v_{12}} [II]$$

$$[II] \xrightarrow{v_{23}} [III]$$

$$[III] \xrightarrow{v_{34}} [IV] + [Atr]$$

$$[IV] \xrightarrow{v_{41}} [I]$$

$$\dot{C}_1 = v_{41}C_4 - v_{12}C_1C_{atr} + v_{21}C_2$$

$$\dot{C}_2 = v_{12}C_1C_{atr} - v_{21}C_2 - v_{23}C_2$$

$$\dot{C}_3 = v_{23}C_2 - v_{34}C_3 + v_{43}C_4C_{atr}$$

$$\dot{C}_4 = v_{34}C_3 - v_{43}C_4C_{atr} - v_{41}C_4$$

(a) Transducers

$$[ATP] + [A] \underset{v_a}{\overset{v_{ap}}{\rightleftarrows}} [A\text{-}P] + [ADP]$$

$$[Y] + [A\text{-}P] \xrightarrow{v_{yp}} [Y\text{-}P] + [A]$$

$$[Y\text{-}P] + [Z] \xrightarrow{v_{yz}} [Y] + [Z] + [P]$$

$$[Y\text{-}P] \xrightarrow{v_y} [Y] + [P]$$

$$[B] + [A\text{-}P] \xrightarrow{v_{bp}} [B\text{-}P] + [A]$$

$$[B\text{-}P] \xrightarrow{v_b} [B] + [P]$$

$$\dot{C}_{ap} = v_{ap}C_a - (v_{yp}C_y - v_{bp}C_b - v_a)C_{ap}$$

$$\dot{C}_{yp} = v_{yp}C_yC_{ap} - v_{yz}C_{yp}C_z - v_yC_{yp}$$

$$\dot{C}_{bp} = v_{bp}C_bC_{ap} - v_bC_{bp}$$

$$\dot{C}_a = v_{yp}C_yC_{ap} + v_{bp}C_bC_{ap} + v_aC_{ap} - v_{ap}C_a$$

$$\dot{C}_y = v_{yz}C_{yp}C_z + v_yC_{yp} - v_{yp}C_yC_{ap}$$

$$\dot{C}_b = v_bC_{bp} - v_{bp}C_bC_{ap}$$

(b) Chemotaxis proteins

Fig. 5 Mathematical model for bacterial chemotaxis. The model consists of the conservation equations for transducers (a) and chemotaxis proteins (b). Parameters, v_{12}, v_{12}, v_{23}, v_{34}, v_{43}, v_{41}, v_b, v_{bp}, v_y, v_{yp} and v_{yz} are assumed to be constant. $v_{41} = f_{41}(C_{bp} - C_{bp}(o)) + k_{41}$; $v_{ap} = f_{ap}C_4 + k_{ap}$; $v_a = f_aC_2 + k_a$, where f_{41}, k_{41}, f_{ap}, k_{ap}, f_a and k_a are constant. $C_{bp}(o)$ is the initial concentration of C_{bp}.

addition of an attractant, there is a rapid shift in the state of transducers from [I] to [II]. The subsequent increase of C_3 indicates the adaptation of transducers due to methylation. The time course of concentrations of chemotaxis proteins, as well as the ratio C_y/C_{yp}, is illustrated in Fig. 7. The concentration of phosphorylated CheY drastically increased approximately 200 ms after the addition of an attractant. Then the dephosphorylation of CheY proceeded, showing the adaptation to the stimulus. These preliminary results encourage us to use the present

model for analyzing the dynamic behavior of bacterial chemotaxis machinery.

In real-life systems, the rate constants are determined by the biochemical properties of chemotaxis proteins which are the products of the chemotaxis genes on the bacterial chromosome. Therefore, there exist relationships between the rate constants and the chemotaxis genes as shown in Fig. 8. Taking into account these relationships, we are now analyzing how chemotaxis proteins act in concert to generate bacterial intelligence by means of "Ge-

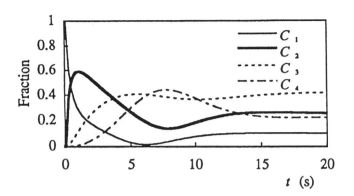

Fig. 6 Temporal change in the fraction of transducer in each of four states, which occurs upon addition of a saturating stimulus. The initial conditions are: $C_1(0)=1.0$, $C_2(0) =C_3(0)=C_4(0) = 0$, $C_p(0) = C_{atr}(0) =C_z(0) =1.0$, $C_{ap}(0) =C_{yp}(0) =C_{bp}(0) =C_a(0) =C_y(0) =C_b(0) =0.5$. Rate constants are: $v_{12}=3.0$, $v_{21}=0.1$, $v_{23}= 0.3$, $v_{34}=0.2$, $v_{43}= 0.1$, $f_{41}= 5.0$, $k_{41}= 0.1$, $f_{41}= 5.0$, $k_{ap}= 20.0$, $k_a= 5.0$, $f_{ap}= 900.0$, $f_a=500.0$, $v_{bp}=0.1$, $v_b=0.05$, $v_{yp}=30.0$, $v_{yz}=15.0$, $v_y=1.0$.

netic" Algorithms (GA). "Genetic" operations, including crossover and mutation, are performed for the digital bacterial "chromosome" consisting of rate constants. The intelligence of digital-form bacteria is then evaluated by their chemotactic responsiveness which is predicted by computer simulation. Particular attention will be paid to the understanding of the mechanism by which a memory and a comparator function. We also expect in the simulation study to seek out digital-form bacteria that may exhibit unexpected intelligent behaviors. Evolution of digital-form bacteria is another topic in our future simulation study.

4. Concluding remarks

Our interest is not to simulate simple, well-characterized biological events, but to address in molecular detail real biological problems which are too complex to solve by means of biochemical and genetic techniques. In the present work, particular attention was directed to the use of bacterial system as a model for studying the behavior of living systems. Unlike viruses which can reproduce

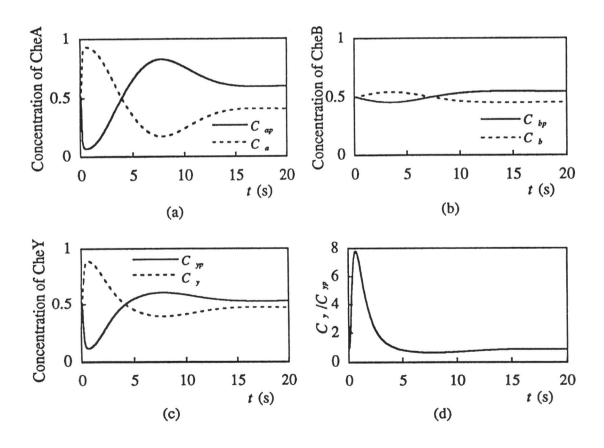

Fig. 7 Time course of concentrations of chemotaxis proteins, as well as the ratio C_y/C_{yp}, which occurs upon addition of a saturating stimulus. Concentrations are shown by a normalized scale. The initial conditions and rate constants are given in the legend to Fig. 6.

Digital Bacteria

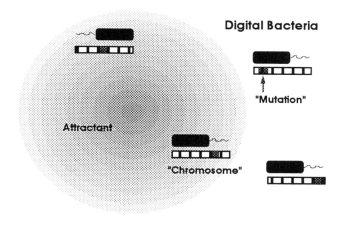

Digital bacterial "chromosome"

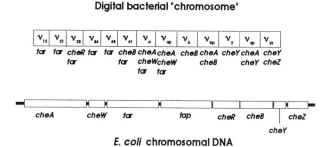

Fig. 8 Evolution of digital bacteria. "Genetic" Algorithms (GA) is used to generate crossover and mutation in the digital "chromosome" consisting of a set of rate constants. The digital "chromosome" can be related to the chemotaxis genes on the *E. coli* chromosome. Related genes are shown below relevant rate constants.

only with the help of the cells they infect, bacteria are free-living organisms and are still susceptible to biochemical and genetic analysis. In free-living organisms, it remains unknown how gene products act in concert to regulate the whole system. The future of biology is in the analysis of complex systems [19], and the behavior of complex system can not be understood simply by analyzing the expression of individual genes. Therefore, the computer model presented here should have great utility for extrapolating biochemical and genetic analysis of real-life behaviors. As far as bacterial systems are concerned, the simulation results can be examined by biochemical and genetic analysis. Conversely, findings from biochemical and genetic analysis can provide ideas for improving the computer model. Both the approaches are necessary to perfect the understanding of real-life behaviors. We believe that the approach described here is also helpful in presenting a conceptual framework for gaining the information needed to sustain life.

References

[1] Pielou. P.C. 1969. An introduction to Mathematical Ecology, John Wiley & Sons, Inc., N.Y.

[2] Taylor, B.L., and M.S. Johnson. 1993. Universal themes of signal transduction in bacteria, p. 3-15. In: J. Kurjan and B.L. Taylor (ed.), Signal transduction. Academic Press, Inc.

[3] Adler, J. 1966. Chemotaxis in bacteria. Science 153: 708-716.

[4] Stewart, R.C., and F.W. Dahlquist. 1987. Molecular components of bacterial chemotaxis. Chem. Rev. 87: 997-1025.

[5] Kato, J., A. Ito, T. Nikata, and H. Ohtake. 1992. Phosphate taxis in *Pseudomonas aeruginosa*.. J. Bacteriol. 174: 5149-5151.

[6] Kato, J., Y. Sakai, T. Nikata, and H. Ohtake. 1994. Cloning and characterization of a *Pseudomonas aeruginosa* gene involved in the negative regulation of phosphate taxis. J. Bacteriol. 176: 5874-5877.

[7] Kato, J., Y. Sakai, T. Nikata, A. Masduki, and H. Ohtake. 1994. Phosphate taxis and its regulation in *Pseudomonas aeruginosa*, p. 315-317. In: A. Torriani-Gorini, E. Yagil, and S. Silver (ed.), Phosphate in Microorganisms, American Society for Microbiology, Washington, D. C.

[8] Kuroda, A., T. Kumano, K. Taguchi, T. Nikata, J. Kato and H. Ohtake. 1995. Molecular cloning and characterization of a chemotactic transducer gene in *Pseudomonas aeruginosa*. J. Bacteriol. 177:7019-7025.

[9] Masduki, A., J. Nakamura, T. Ohga, R. Umezaki, J. Kato, and H. Ohtake. 1995. Isolation and characterization of chemotaxis mutants and genes of *Pseudomonas aeruginosa*. J. Bacteriol. 177: 948-952.

[10] Chet, I., and R. Mitchell. 1979. Ecological aspects of microbial chemotactic behavior. Annu. Rev. Microbiol. 30: 221-239.

[11] Nikata, T., K. Sumida, J. Kato, and H. Ohtake. 1992. Rapid method for analyzing bacterial behavioral responses to chemical stimuli. Appl. Environ. Microbiol. 58:2250-2254.

[12] Ohga, T., A. Masduki, J. Kato, and H. Ohtake. 1993. Chemotaxis away from thiocyanic and isothiocyanic esters in *Pseudomonas aeruginosa*.. FEMS Microbiol. Lett. 113: 63-66.

[13] Craven, R. C., and T.C. Montie. 1985. Regulation of *Pseudomonas aeruginosa* chemotaxis by the nitrogen source. J.Bacteriol. 164: 544-549.

[14] Moulton, R.C., and T.C. Montie. 1979. Chemotaxis by *Pseudomonas aeruginosa*. J. Bacteriol. 137:274-280.

[15] Boyd A., and M. Simon. 1982. Bacterial chemotaxis. Annu. Rev. Physiol. 44: 501-517.

[16] Bourret, R.B., K.A. Borkovich, and M.I. Simon.1991. Signal transduction pathways involving protein phosphorylation in prokaryotes. Annu. Rev. Biochem. 60: 410-441.

[17] Craven, R. C., and T. C. Montie. 1983. Chemotaxis of *Pseudomonas aeruginosa*: involvement of methylation. J. Bacteriol. 154: 780-786.

[18] Hazelbauer, G.L. 1988. The bacterial chemosensory system. Can. J. Microbiol. 34: 466-474.

[19] Nowark, R. 1995. Entering the postgenome era. Science 270: 368-371.

IN VITRO SELF-REPLICATION SYSTEM AS A MINIMUM SET OF LIFE

**Tetsuya Yomo, Toshiyuki Habu, Shiro Soga, Tomoaki Matsuura,
Yasufumi Shima** and **Itaru Urabe**

Department of Biotechnology, Faculty of Engineering, Osaka University,
2-1 Yamadaoka, Suita, Osaka 565, JAPAN

Abstract

An in vitro self-replication system was constructed using biological molecules, *Thermus thermophilus* DNA polymerase and its gene, which carry the function and information, respectively. The set of the molecules can be propagated through the life cycle of production of the enzyme from the gene and replication of the gene by the produced enzyme. As the ability of the gene replication is determined by the enzyme encoded on the gene, the system has a feedback loop from the function to the information. Therefore, the system not only propagates by self-replication, but also has potential to evolve like the natural living systems, and can be regarded as a minimum set of life. Using this system, the effect of selfishness on the competition of two self-replication systems consisting the wild-type and mutant genes; the latter encodes a mutant enzyme with lower specific activity (about 60%). For the complete selfish system (100% selfish), the mutant gene disappeared after repeating the life cycle four times, while the wild-type gene was maintained until the fourth generation. For partially selfish systems (70% and 30% selfish), on the other hand, both genes were maintained until the fourth generation. These results indicate that it is not only the phenotype of the gene but also the degree of the selfishness that greatly affect the results of competition, and that only in a highly selfish system can a gene with a better phenotype overcome its competitor as that of the Darwinian evolution

1 Introduction

Analytical mode is but a starting point in most scientific entities, which come to maturity only when synthetic approach is incorporated. In biology, most researches deal with the analysis of biological entities provided to us by nature. The entities, broad and diverse as it is, is dominated by accident and historical contiguency, and hence are to be stretched out to an extent of surpassing the original set to give us a glimpse of possible biologies beyond one's ken as to the present. Synthetic approach by far is of artificial life in computers [1], and synthesis of self-replicating molecules [2,3]. For our approach, we have constructed an in vitro self-replication system using biological molecules, *Thermus thermophilus* DNA polymerase and its gene, which carry the function and information, respectively. This set of molecules brings together a life through a cycle involving the production of enzyme from the gene and replication of the gene by the enzyme produced. The system can then serve as a gateway for the investigation of synthetic life in the laboratory level.

A living system has a set of molecules that carries function and information. The set forms a "self", and the self is propagated by the self-replication of the set. During the process of propagation down to several generations, an error, i.e., mutation may occur in the replication of the molecule carrying the information. The mutated self will then diverge into a different phenotype, which in turn will affect the rate of propagation or the fitness of the self. This feedback system leads the effects of random mutation into a systematic evolution. To attain such evolutionary system is then to construct a minimum set of life as the first step for the synthetic approach.

2 Results and Discussion

In our system, we used a pair of molecules as a set, *T. thermophilus* DNA polymerase as a functional molecule and the gene [4] (see Fig. 2) coding for the enzyme as an information molecule. This set of molecules can be propagated through the life cycle shown in Fig. 1. The gene produces the DNA polymerase, assisted by the in vitro transcription/translation system, to form the first set of molecules. The gene is then replicated by its enzyme yielding the genes of the second generation. Through several cycles, a series of descendants can be prepared. Although this cycle needs external assistance for the synthesis of enzyme from its gene, this assistance can be regarded as that of the role of a host cell for the life cycle of a virus or even as that of the nutrients. It is to be noted that the assisting system, if works accurately, does not affect the

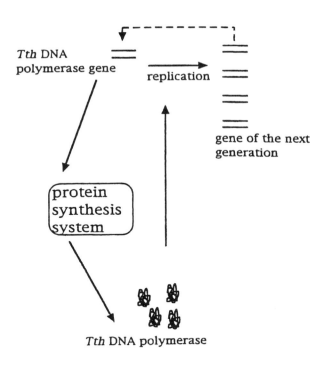

Fig. 1. Life cycle of self-replication system.

property of the enzyme, i.e., the primary structure. As the information of the gene determines the property of the enzyme which replicates the gene, the set of molecules forms a "self" and is propagated by self-replication. In addition, as the ability of the gene replication is determined by the enzyme encoded on the gene, the self has the feedback system from the function to the information. Therefore, the self has the potential to evolve like the natural living systems, and can be regarded as a minimum set of life.

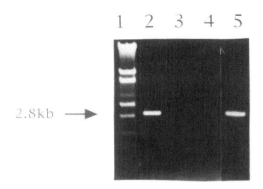

Fig. 3. Agarose-gel electrophoresis of the second and third generation of DNA polymerase gene. Lane 1, marker; lane 2, the PCR reaction mixture for the second generation of the gene; lane 3, the same reaction mixture as that of lane 2 except that the DNA polymerase was omitted from the mixture; lane 4, the same reaction mixture as that of lane 2 with the omission of template DNA (the gene of the first generation); lane 5, the PCR reaction mixture for the third generation of the gene. The arrow indicates the 2.8 kb fragment. The wild-type gene (the first generation, about 2.3 pmol) was transcribed by T7 RNA polymerase [7,8]. The resultant mRNA was purified after DNase I treatment, and translated using the *E. coli* cell-free expression system [9] (total 1 ml). The obtained DNA polymerase of the first generation was purified with an affinity column (Econo-Pac Heparin Cartridge, Bio Rad) and concentrated (about 10 pmol in 50 μl). The 4 μl of the 20 times solution of the first generation gene (about 0.26 μM) was used for PCR (total 0.1 ml), where the first generation gene was replicated by its enzyme (25 μl of the above enzyme solution). The resultant second generation gene was recovered from the agarose gel (lane 2) yielding a 20 μl gene solution. The gene in an aliquot (15 μl) of the solution was first amplified by PCR (total 0.1 ml) before used for mRNA synthesis as described above. The preparation of the enzyme for second generation follows the same procedures as described above. The remaining solution of the second generation gene was 20 times diluted from which 4 μl was used for PCR (total 1 ml). Consecutively, the second generation gene was replicated by its enzyme (the amount of the enzyme was the same as above). The resultant third generation gene in the PCR mixture is shown in lane 5.

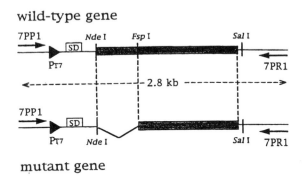

Fig. 2. Schematic illustration of the structure of the wild-type and mutant DNA polymerase genes. P$_{T7}$, T7 promoter; SD, Shine-Dalgarno sequence. These genes were constructed using the expression vector pGEMEX-1 (Promega, Madison), the *NdeI-SalI* fragment from pLED-NS [4] (for the wild-type gene), and the *NdeI-SalI* fragment from pLED-NF2 [5] (for the mutant gene). The nucleotide sequence of 7PP1 is 5'-CGGGA-GATCTCGATCCCGCGAA-3' and that of 7PR1 is 5'-GCATCTAGAGGGCCCGGATCCCTCG-3'; these primers were used for gene amplification by polymerase chain reaction [6] (PCR).

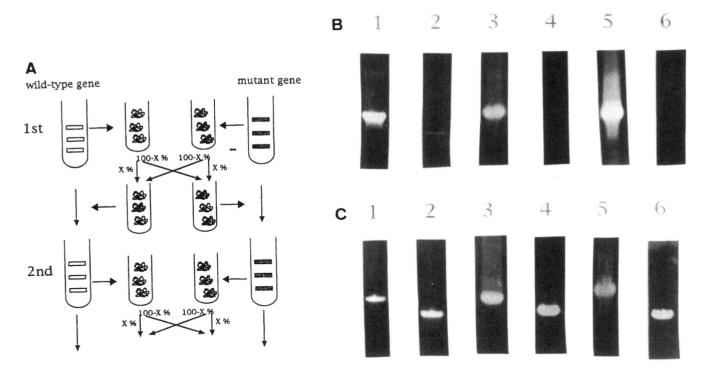

Fig. 4. Effect of selfishness on the competition between the wild-type and the mutant genes. A, Strategy of changing the selfishness of the self-replication system. For the complete selfish system (X = 100), the wild-type gene is replicated only by the wild-type enzyme and the mutant gene by the mutant enzyme. For the X% selfish system, each gene is replicated by the enzyme mixture of which X% is its own product and (100 - X)% is the product of its competitor gene. B and C, Fate of the wild-type gene (lanes 1, 3, and 5) and mutant gene (lanes 2, 4, and 6) at the second (lanes 1 and 2), third (lanes 3 and 4), and fourth (lanes 5 and 6) generations during the competition in a 100% selfish system (B) and 30% selfish system (C) as visualized on the agarose-gel electrophoresis. The experimental procedures are essentially the same as those described in the legend to Fig. 3 except for the composition (ratio) of the enzyme solution used in replication and that the dilution factor of the gene to be replicated was increased from 20 times to 50 times in the production of the gene for the next generation.

Fig. 3 shows how well the self-replication system works. The band in lane 2 shows the second generation of the gene which is produced only through the replication and amplification of the gene in the first generation by polymerase chain reaction [6] (PCR) using DNA polymerase prepared from the gene of the first generation. The second generation gene was recovered from the gel, and used for the next cycle. Lane 5 in Fig. 2 shows the gene of the third generation. Thus, it is confirmed that the set of the DNA polymerase and its gene can be propagated through the life cycle shown in Fig. 1.

It is proven that our system has all the advantages towards the natural systems. That is, our system is a good model where the ease in accessibility and manipulation, reproducibility, and subjectivity to precisely controllable experiments are beyond questions. To demonstrate the ability of our system, we examined the effect of selfishness on the competition of two self-replication systems consisting the wild-type and mutant genes, of which

structures are shown in Fig. 2. The mutant gene lacks the N-terminal region of the enzyme, and the mutant enzyme has about 60% activity of that of the wild-type [5]. However, the set of the mutant enzyme and its gene can also be propagated under the conditions described in the legend to Fig. 3. The selfishness of the system can be controlled by mixing the enzymes produced from the wild-type and mutant genes at various ratios and by using the mixture for the replication of the genes as schematically shown in Fig. 4A. For complete selfish system (100% selfish), the wild-type enzyme replicates only the wild-type gene and the mutant enzyme does the mutant gene, i.e., X = 100 in Fig. 4A. Although for both life cycles, the amount of enzyme in the first generation is almost the same (this is confirmed by a separate experiment), the amount of the wild-type gene replicated is larger than that of the mutant gene due to the difference in the enzyme activity. Hence, the amount of the wild-type gene used in the second generation, which is the same as that of the first generation, is larger than that of the mutant gene. After undergoing several life cycles, the mutant gene will then be eliminated while the wild-type gene is maintained.

The results obtained by the competition experiment are as expected, i.e., the amount of the mutant gene decreased in the second generation and became negligible in the third and the fourth generations, while the wild-type gene was maintained until the fourth generation (Fig. 4B). For 0% selfish system, i.e., $X = 0$, the wild-type gene is replicated by the mutant enzyme and the mutant gene is by the wild-type enzyme. In this case, it is apparent that the wild-type gene will not be maintained due to the low activity of the mutant enzyme, and so as with the mutant gene due to the decreasing amount of the wild-type enzyme. How about in a partially selfish system? For a 30% selfish system, i.e., $X = 30$ in Fig. 4A, the wild-type gene is replicated by an enzyme mixture of which 30% is the wild type and 70% is the mutant, and the mutant gene is replicated by another enzyme mixture of which 30% is the mutant and 70% is the wild type. The results show that both genes were maintained until the fourth generation (Fig. 4C). Similar results were also obtained for the 70% selfish system (data not shown). These results indicate that it is not only the phenotype of the gene but also the degree of the selfishness that greatly affect the results of competition, and that only in a highly selfish system can a gene with a better phenotype overcome its competitor as that of the Darwinian evolution. In the natural ecosystem, however, there are many kinds of interactions between the competitors [10], and some of the interactions may reduce their selfishness. In this case, competitors will be able to coexist as demonstrated by the experiment shown in Fig. 4C.

Here, we introduced a new frontier in biology by synthetic approach. Though the approach parallels that of the artificial life research in computer science [1], we have the advantages of involving natural molecules, so as to allow the system to work as that in nature. The biological system is composed of various functional macromolecules, and the macroscopic behavior of the system, such as growth, competition, organization, and evolution, comes from the microscopic behavior of the macromolecules. The complexity of the microscopic behavior of the macromolecules renders the inevitable limitations on the capability of computers in artificial life researches, not to

mention more about the large number of parallel processing undergone by the mass of molecules in a biological system. Though artificial life in computers encompasses the entity of the biological system, much assumptions are being taken that lead to vast simplification, and hence, lose track of the microscopic behavior of the macromolecules. On the contrary, our synthetic life is brought about by large number of natural molecules, and hence, can be said as a better representation of biological system in nature. Therefore, our self-replication system will be a powerful tool to go for a deeper insight in biology.

Acknowledgment

This work was supported in part by Grants (07243211 and 07309001) from the Ministry of Education, Science, Sports and Culture, Japan.

References

1. Taylor, C. & Jefferson, D. *Artificial Life* 1, 1-13 (1992).
2. Orgel, L. E. *Nature* 358, 203-209 (1992).
3. Rebek Jr, J. *Chemistry in Britain* 30, 286-290 (1994).
4. Asakura, K., Komatsubara, H., Soga, S., Yomo, T., Oka, M., Emi, S. & Urabe, I. *J. Ferment. Bioeng.* 76, 265-269 (1993).
5. Shima, Y., Hasegawa, A., Arakawa, T., Tanaka, K., Ikeda, K., Komatsubara, H., Inoue, H., Kawakami, B., Oka, M., Emi, S., Yomo, T., Negoro, S. & Urabe, I. *J. Ferment. Bioeng.*, in press.
6. Saiki, R. K., Gelfand, D. H., Stoffel, S., Scharf, S. J., Higuchi, R., Horn, G. T., Mullis, K. B. & Erlich, H. A. *Science* 239, 487-491 (1988).
7. Elaine, T. S. & Robert, C. M. Jr. *Nucleic Acids Res.* 13, 6223-6236 (1985).
8. Krieg, P. A. & Melton, D. A. *Methods Enzymol.* 155, 397-415 (1987).
9. Zubay, G. *Annu. Rev. Genet.* 7, 267-287 (1973).
10. Fredrickson, A. G. & Stephanopoulos, G. *Science* 213, 972-979 (1981)

Simulating Evolution of the Vitality by the Biased Mutation Model

Yasuhiro Kikuchi and Hirofumi Doi

Institute for Social Information Science

Fujitsu Laboratories Ltd.

1-9-3 Nakase, Mihama-ku, Chiba-shi 261, JAPAN

e-mail: {kikuchi, doi}@iias.flab.fujitsu.co.jp

Abstract

Rapid evolution in response to changing environmental conditions has been observed in the several ecological systems so far, but the mechanism of such adaptations on fitness and the rapidity of their evolution is not sufficiently clear. To study these evolutionary adaptations, we present a simple genetic model in which mutation rates of the genes around the replication origin are higher than those of the other genes. Creatures we used in simulations have a circular genome on which only ten loci lie and there are four hypervariable loci near the replication origin. 10!=3,628,800 different species are defined by the order of the loci A to J and these are classified into five classes K0 to K4 depending on the configuration of the loci A, B, C and D, which interact with environmental factors. Each species has the intrinsic vital force against environmental changes according to its class number. In the population of a species belongs to the advanced class K3 or K4, individuals which adapt to the new environment arise rapidly. Evolutionary processes to the higher classes are simulated by the algorithm based on natural selection and the reversion of the gene cluster.

1 Introduction

So far, it has been thought that the mutations occurred randomly and the probabilities of the replication error were uniformly distributed over the whole genome. Also the evolutionary theory has been discussed on the basis of such a consideration. However, the recent experimental studies have revealed that there are some biased mutations, for example, strand-specific mutations between the leading and lagging DNA strands [11, 12, 8, 10, 6], sequence-dependent mutations by the HIV-1 reverse transcriptase [7, 1], and so on. It has been of interest, therefore, to study evolution caused by the biased mutation.

The aim of this paper is to consider the significance of the biased mutation. Rapid evolution in response to changing environmental conditions has been observed in the ecological systems such as bacterial colonies and HIV-infected hosts. It is thought that such a behaviour, which should be called *evolutionary adaptation* or *genetic adaptation*, comes from not only the random mutation but also the occurrence of errors located on the specific region(s) of the genome. In other words, one can say that the appropriate distribution of mutation rates for the genetic adaptability has been acquired by natural selection.

In order to study evolution, the computer simulation seems to be one of the powerful methods because as for in the virtual ecological system on computer memories, we can easily observe evolution. Here we propose and test a novel biased mutation model inspired by the structure of bacterial genomes or plasmids. Simulations are run by the computer program based on the genetic algorithm (GA) [5].

2 The Model

2.1 Structure of the Genome

For brevity, here we consider an abstract genome which consists of only ten loci from A to J. All allele states $a_A, \cdots, a_J$ are assumed to be 0 or 1. Thus a state of this genome is expressed by a binary string $a_A \cdots a_J$ in ten length. A combination of allele states of the genome determines how many replica will be reproduced in the next generation. The optimal allele states $x_A, \cdots, x_D$ of the loci A, $\cdots$, D are assumed to be reversed with the probability γ during a generation being affected by the environmental changes. On the other hand, regarding the allele states of the loci E, $\cdots$, J, it is assumed that 0 indicates the normal state and 1 implies the defective state in anything; namely the state 0 is always superior to the state 1. A degree of selection g is calculated by two binary substrings $a_A \cdots a_D$ and $a_E \cdots a_J$ as follows:

$$g = m(a_A \cdots a_D, x_A \cdots x_D) + m(a_E \cdots a_J, 0 \cdots 0) \quad (1)$$

where the function $m(s_1, s_2)$ returns the number of the common bits between two binary strings s_1 and s_2.

The genome is assumed to be cyclic structure like a bacterial genome or a plasmid. In other words, it is a ring of the loci A, $\cdots$, J. Fig. 1 shows a schematic picture of the genome of our model. Sites of the loci are numbered from 0 to 9 starting at the second site on the left side of the replication origin (*ori*). Here we assume that the mutation rate in the region 0-3 (near *ori*) is r-fold greater

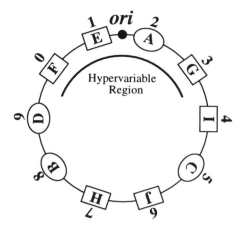

Figure 1: A schematic picture of the genome.

than that in the region 4-9 (far from *ori*). The mutation rate μ averaged over the genome is defined as

$$10\mu = 4\mu_n + 6\mu_f \qquad (2)$$

where μ_n and μ_f denote the mutation rates in the region 0-3 and 4-9 respectively. From the above equation we can obtain μ_n and μ_f if μ and r are given. In this paper, μ is treated as an independent parameter. On the other hand, r is fixed as $r = 3.0$.

2.2 Classification of Species

In our model, we obtain 10!=3,628,800 different species according to the configuration of the loci A, $\cdots$, J on the genome. A species are expressed by a sequence of ten letters A, $\cdots$, J in numerical order of the sites. For example ACEGDHBFJI indicates that the locus A lies on the site 0, the locus C lies on the site 1, and so on. Here we consider classifying them from the viewpoint of vitality. Let K be the number of the loci A, $\cdots$, D in the region 0-3. For instance IAFJBEDGHC and CDFBJIEAGH are $K = 1$ and $K = 3$ respectively, because IAFJ includes A and CDFB includes B, C and D. By the definition, it is obvious that K is an integer between 0 and 4. We will abbreviate these five classes defined by K to K0, $\cdots$, K4 respectively. The numbers of species belong to these classes are K0: 259,200 (7.1%), K1: 1,382,400 (38.1%), K2: 1,555,200 (42.9%) K3: 414,720 (11.4%) and K4: 17,280 (0.5%).

The vitality of the species is determined by K. When the ratio $r = 3.0$, the total mutation rates over the loci A-D and E-J are calculated as shown in Tab. 1. If the mutation rates are uniformly distributed over the genome (i.e., $r = 1$), these values will be 4μ and 6μ respectively. Thus we can say that the distribution of mutation rates on the genome of the species belong to K0, K3 or K4 is extremely biased.

In the light of strategy, the high mutation rate of the loci A-D is favorable to survive. Because it allows rapid arising of individuals which adapt to the new environmental conditions. On the other hand, the allele states

Table 1: The total mutation rates over the loci A-D and E-J of the five classes in the case of $r = 3.0$.

Class	Mutation rate	
	A-D	E-J
K0	$2.22\,\mu$	$7.78\,\mu$
K1	$3.33\,\mu$	$6.67\,\mu$
K2	$4.44\,\mu$	$5.56\,\mu$
K3	$5.56\,\mu$	$4.44\,\mu$
K4	$6.67\,\mu$	$3.33\,\mu$

of the loci E-J should be kept to 0, therefore the low mutation rate of these loci is good for survival. Consequently one can say that the greater K is, the higher the vitality becomes.

2.3 The Algorithm

The outline of the algorithm used here is shown in Fig. 2. The population size is 1,000. Since the selection process of GA conserves the population size, here we suppose the *null* replicon which is the same as the proper replicon except for having no genome; it has a degree of selection $g = G_0$ which is a constant value. A place in which a null replicon stays implies that there is no individual. We will put as $G_0 = 9.2$ in the following experiments, thus the population will soon vanish if the optimal replicon ($g = 10$) does not arise. The algorithm is halted when the population vanished or generation ran into the limit T.

$a_A, \cdots, a_J$ of each replicon and $x_A, \cdots, x_D$ are initially assumed to be 0, then g values of all individuals are 10 (maximum). In the selection step, a new population is generated by the individuals which were randomly selected among the current population according to the fitness values defined as

$$f = \exp(\beta g) \qquad (3)$$

where β is a positive constant (fixed as $\beta = 1.5$ in the following simulations). Segmental reversions (e.g. FEAGICJHBD $\rightarrow$ FECIGAJHBD) randomly occur with the probability χ per an individual during a generation. Moreover, about 1% individuals of the population are randomly replaced with the null replicon.

3 Results and Discussion

3.1 Comparing the Vitality of the Five Classes

To begin with, we tested the ability to survive of each class. The algorithm was run with $\chi = 0$ (i.e., without segmental reversion) and $\gamma = 0.05$ (corresponding to one bit alternation of $x_A, \cdots, x_D$ during five generations) for the following five species: EFGHIJABCD (K0), DEFGHIJABC (K1), CDEFGHIJAB (K2), BCDEFGHIJA (K3) and ABCDEFGHIJ (K4). Tab. 2 shows the results of each species varying the value of μ from 0 to 0.10. The percentages of the cases that the creatures survived during 1,000 generations among 100 simulations are listed.

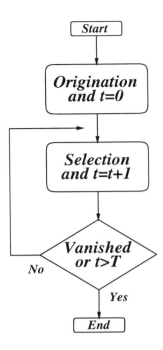

Figure 2: The outline of the algorithm.

Table 2: Survival probabilities of the five classes during 1,000 generations.

Mutation rate μ	Cases of survival (%)				
	K0	K1	K2	K3	K4
0.00	0	0	0	0	0
0.02	0	1	14	34	71
0.04	0	4	24	66	94
0.06	0	0	3	34	86
0.08	0	0	0	0	52
0.10	0	0	0	0	0

Comparing the five classes, one can say that the ability to survive increases in the order of K0, $\cdots$, K4 for any value of μ. These results are consistent with prediction in the previous section. It was shown that the classes K0, K1 and K2 did not have enough vitality under the condition of these experiments.

Regarding the dependence of μ, a common tendency has been shown in the results of all classes. There was a single peak between the varying range of μ, and 0.04 was the optimal value. These results show that whether the population survives or not is much affected by the value of μ.

3.2 Simulating Evolution of the Vitality

In our model the species of the class K3 or K4 are more advanced than those of the others. It is an interesting problem whether advanced species can be generated by natural selection or not. To test this, starting from JAI-

HBGCFDE (K1) we ran the algorithm with the reversion probability $\chi = 0.001$.

There were a few cases that the creatures survived during 2,000 generation. In the total 69 survival cases among 1000 simulations, we obtained the species belong to the class K2 (7 cases), K3 (48 cases) and K4 (14 cases). Let us look at the cases that the class K4 was generated. Fig. 3 shows the population profiles of K1 to K4 in the typical case. This reveals the evolutionary process of K1 $\rightarrow$ K2 $\rightarrow$ K3 $\rightarrow$ K4. The retrogression such as K3 $\rightarrow$ K2 has never been observed so far as we know.

We succeeded in simulating evolution of the vitality by using the biased mutation model. This results suggests that the genome in which the mutation rate depends on the distance from *ori* might acquire the genetic adaptability to the fluctuating environment by the process based on natural selection. If so, will evolution to such as K3 or K4 in our model be found among the real lives?

Recently, the whole genome data (1,830,137 base pairs) of *Haemophilus influenzae* was obtained by random sequencing [3]. This genome is circular and there is a coding region of strA, the streptomycin resistance gene, near the replication origin *ori*. It is known that mutants of the strA gene show a high-level streptomycin resistance [9]. On the other hand, the strA mutant is less adaptive than the wild-type under the condition without streptomycin. Namely genetic alternations of strA allow the bacteria to adapt to changing streptomycin density. This is indeed similar to the situation of our model. If the region near *ori* of the *Haemophilus influenzae* genome is hypervariable as same as our model, the simulations we presented here will be very interesting results.

3.3 The Other Biased Mutations

By some research groups, it has been reported that the mutations occurred at a higher frequency in the lagging strand than in the leading strand during replication of the DNA double strands [11, 12, 8, 10, 6]. These results will affect the evolutionary theory, because the genomes of almost all living things consist of the DNA double strands and spontaneous misreading of base during DNA synthesis seems to act as a major factor in evolution. In fact, the new evolutionary theory based on the disparity mutation as mentioned above was proposed [4] and its effects were tested by the computer simulations [13].

The biased mutation has been observed in not only DNA double strands but also a single nucleotide strand. For example, nonrandom mutations affected by local nucleotide sequences when the reverse transcriptase of human immunodeficiency virus type 1 (HIV-1) acts as DNA-dependent DNA polymerase *in vitro* have been seen [7, 1]. Furthermore the statistical analysis has shown that the biased distribution of mutation rates observed in the HIV-1 genome can be characterized by the local sequences in six length [2]. These results are thought to be derived from interaction between the polymerase and nucleotides. The biased mutation allows HIV-1 for successively reproducing some mutants which can escape from the immune attack. Namely HIV-1 has

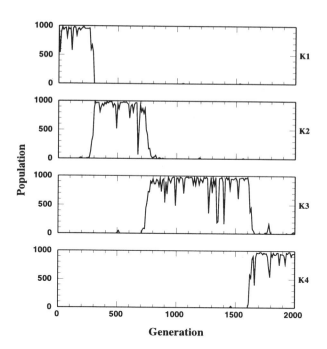

Figure 3: Population profiles in the typical case of the class K4 arising.

...een acquired the genetic adaptability to environmental ...anges caused by the immunocytes in the evolutionary ...rocess.

Evolution is one of the most important standpoints ...f the study on the genomes, thus simulating the evolu-...onary process by using the artificial life will contribute ...o the developments of genome projects. At the present ...me, there are active genome projects for many organ-...ms in the whole world. A number of genes associated ...ith the genetic adaptation will be discovered by these ...rojects. From the viewpoint of our biased mutation ...odel, it is thought that the configuration of genes is ...nportant for the evolutionary theory.

We thank Dr. Iwaki for valuable discussions and sug-...estions.

References

[1] Abbotts, J., Bebenek, K., Kunkel, T.A. and Wilson, S.H., Mechanism of HIV-1 reverse transcriptase, J. Biol. Chem. 264 (1989), 16948-16956.

[2] Doi, H., Importance of purine and pyrimidine content of local nucleotide sequence (six bases long) for evolution of the human immunodeficiency virus type 1, Proc. Natl. Acad. Sci. USA 88 (1991), 9282-9286.

[3] Fleischmann, R.D. et al, Whole-genome random sequencing and assembly of Haemophilus influenzae Rd, Science 269 (1995), 496-512.

[4] Furusawa, M. and Doi, H., Promotion of evolution: disparity in the frequency of strand-specific misreading between the lagging and leading DNA strands enhances disproportionate accumulation of mutations, J. theor. Biol. 157 (1992), 127-133.

[5] Goldberg, D.E., Genetic Algorithm in Search, Optimization and Machine Learning, Addison-Wesley (1989).

[6] Iwaki, T., Kawamura, A., Ishino, Y., Kohno, K., Kano, Y., Goshima, N., Yara, M., Furusawa, M., Doi, H. and Imamoto, F., Preferential replication-dependent mutagenesis in the lagging DNA strand in Escherichia coli, Mol. Gen. Genet., in press.

[7] Roberts, J.D., Bebenek, K. and Kunkel, T.A., The accuracy of reverse transcriptase from HIV-1, Science 242 (1988), 1171-1173.

[8] Roberts, J.D., Nguyen, D. and Kunkel, T.A., Frameshift fidelity during replication of double-stranded DNA in HeLa cell extracts, Biochemistry 32 (1993), 4083-4089.

[9] Stuy, J.H. and Walter, R.B., Cloning, characterization, and DNA sequence of the high-level streptomycin resistence gene strA1 of Haemophilus influenzae Rd, J. Bacteriol 174 (1992), 5604-5608.

[10] Thomas D.C., Nguyen D.C., Piegorsch, W.W. and Kunkel, T.A., Relative probability of mutagenetic translesion synthesis on the leading and lagging strand during replication of UV-irradiated DNA in a human cell extract, Biochemistry 32 (1993), 11476-11482.

[11] Trinh, T.Q. and Sinden, R.R., Preferential DNA secondary structure mutagenesis in the lagging strand of replication in E. coli, Nature 352 (1991), 544-547.

[12] Veaute, X. and Fuchs, R.P.P., Greater susceptibility to mutations in lagging strand of DNA replication in Escherichia coli than in leading strand, Science 261 (1993), 598-600.

[13] Wada, K., Doi, H., Tanaka, S., Wada, Y. and Furusawa, M., A neo-Darwinian algorithm: asymmetrical mutations due to semiconservative DNA-type replication promote evolution, Proc. Natl. Acad. Sci. USA 90 (1993), 11934-11938.

Origin of Life

Chasing: A Mechanism for Resistance against Parasites in Self-replicating Systems.

Mikael Cronhjort and Clas Blomberg
Teoretisk Fysik, Kungl Tekniska Högskolan, S-100 44 Stockholm, Sweden
E-mail: mic@theophys.kth.se, cob@theophys.kth.se

Abstract.

We have performed calculations on two dimensional cellular automata models with cluster formation for various catalytic networks, especially a simple auto-catalytic species and the hypercycle with few species. We discuss the mechanisms of cluster formation. A mechanism for resistance to parasites is discovered for clusters with a single auto-catalytic species and other networks giving essentially homogeneous clusters: As the parasite attacks a cluster from one side, the cluster may grow fast enough in the opposite direction to prevent destruction. Thus, the parasite will be chasing the main species in the cluster. As correlations and local effects are important for these results, they are expected to be obtained only in cellular automata and not in models based on partial differential equations.

1 Introduction

Reaction-diffusion systems often lead to spatial patterns which appear for a large number of different applications [1, 2, 3, 4]. They have been studied frequently with many interesting aspects in recent years. In particular, their relevance for the origin of life has been emphasised in some papers [1, 2, 5, 6] as spontaneous spatial ordering provides a desirable compartmentation and may be a first step to cell formation.

The models which we consider represent a set of different macromolecules that are able to replicate and form copies of the existing ones. The reactions are supposed to be governed by catalytic support from molecules in the set. This means that the rate of replication of a certain macromolecule depends on the presence of catalytic molecules in its immediate neighbourhood. In principle, these are models of a stage of evolution such as the "RNA-world" [7] in which the same type of molecules occur as self-replicating units and also provide the catalytic support for the replication. We will here consider cellular automata models, and the spontaneous occurrence of clusters in such models. These clusters, which comprise many macromolecules, form a type of primitive cells. They may show resistance against unfavourable mutations, in particular parasites, which is our main theme here. Such clusters may also develop different types of mutations and compete as units: The clusters with favourable mutants may grow by the cost of others, less appropriate.

Because of these possibilities, it is desirable to get knowledge about clusters, their occurrence and their dynamics. Spatial, non-linear systems can be studied by partial differential equations (reaction-diffusion equations) (PDE) or by cellular automata (CA) with random rules. Basically, these two models can exhibit the same kind of rules and may be regarded as related models. Often, the emerging patterns are similar. Still, there are fundamental differences, some of which will be emphasised in this paper. The most important ones arise from the fact that various units in PDE are represented by continuous concentrations, and that many species can be present in each point, while the CA is discrete, and each point can only contain one unit. In many aspects, the CA can be regarded as a simulation procedure, and its appearance applies mainly to a molecular level, while the PDE is regarded as a large scale description. As said above, we will in this paper consider clusters occurring in CA. PDE clusters are treated in other papers [6, 8].

The molecules in the CA appear as states or units in a lattice: The state of each lattice point may represent either any of the different macromolecules or empty space (water). The rules of these CA, which contain random features, can correspond to reaction diffusion equations and represent growth, decay and diffusion of the molecular species. There are several ways to do this. In particular, the CA can be synchronously or asynchronously updated. The asynchronous updating, which is used in the models of this paper, can be regarded as more straightforward and more similar to what may be regarded as a molecular simulation. It also offers more possibilities of variations. In that case, at each basic step, a point of the CA lattice is selected randomly and possibly changed according to the basic rules: A state corresponding to a molecule can be reproduced at an neighbouring empty lattice point, it can decay and be replaced by an empty state, and it can move (diffuse). In synchronous models, e.g. the model used by Boerlijst and Hogeweg [1, 2] who studied spiral patterns of a two dimensional hypercycle system, one goes through the complete lattice in a regular way at each time step and changes all points simultaneously depending on the rules and the states at the preceding time. In the systems we treat, there does not seem to be any essential, qualitative differences between the ways of updating if one is cautious to have similar type of rules (which must be formulated slightly differently).

Spatial patterns are formed by a mutual interplay of

growth, decay and diffusion terms. In general, some type of growth limitation is needed which prevents the system to grow without limits. This is necessary in PDE, but CA have a natural growth limitation as the number of available sites for molecules is limited. The Boerlijst-Hogeweg CA did not have any explicit growth limitation rule. Growth limitation is, however, a natural ingredient in a realistic system and is necessary for the occurrence of clusters. It normally implies that the growth gets weaker when the concentration of macromolecules increases. Growth limitation can be explicitly introduced by a factor that depends on the total concentration of macromolecules. It is also possible to introduce an explicit dependence of resources. A common way to do that is to consider activated monomers that are needed for building up the macromolecules [9]. When new macromolecules occur, the amount of monomers decrease, and there is also a term which restores the monomers towards an equilibrium value when they are not used for replication. Monomers have to be considered as an extra source spread out in the plane, and their concentrations can be continuous in contrast to the number of macromolecules on the CA-lattice. The growth limitation should contain the concentration of molecules (i.e. the frequency of occupied sites in the CA-lattice) in some region surrounding a certain point. For the monomers, in the same fashion, one considers the average in some region. For clusters to occur, these rules shall not be too local, i.e. the region that is considered shall be rather large. In the models described in this paper, the region is the entire lattice. For the monomers, this means explicitly that the monomer diffusion is significantly higher than that of the macromolecules. This seems to be a reasonable assumption as the monomers are much smaller.

Diffusion, which can be realised in many ways, is most straight forward in an asynchronous model, where a chosen unit can move in a random direction, either to only empty points or it may change site with another filled lattice point. For the synchronous updating, diffusion can be realised by rotations of 2×2 regions. In that case, there is no restriction that the movement goes only to an empty point. Such a restriction in the asynchronous model gives a kind of "cage effect" where high concentrations hinder the diffusion. This may in some cases provide qualitative features that can not be obtained by the synchronous models.

2 The model

These simulations are made with an asynchronously updated CA. We consider a square lattice with 200×200 points, each of which can be filled by a molecule of a number of different types (species). We use periodic boundary conditions, and the initial state is a random distribution of molecular units. Each time step consists of 200^2 basic steps, each in which one lattice point is randomly selected. Decay may occur if the selected point contains a molecular unit of species i: With a certain probability, $p_{\text{decay}}(i)$, the unit is taken away. If the unit remains, its 8 neighbouring sites are investigated. If there are empty sites among these and a certain repli-

cation condition is fulfilled, a new molecule of the same type as the original one is placed at one of the empty points: The molecule is replicated.

The probability for replication, $p_{\text{repl}}(i)$, is proportional to the catalytic support from other molecules in its neighbourhood,

$$support(i) = noncat(i) + \sum_{j=8 \text{ neighbours}} cat(i, j). \quad (1)$$

Here, i represents the molecular species of the selected lattice point and j the species of the neighbouring points. *noncat* represents non-catalysed replication, i.e. getting a new unit without extra catalytic support, and *cat* the corresponding replication with catalytic support by molecule j. In our calculations, we put the non-catalytic term equal to zero and only consider growth with catalytic support. The $cat(i, j)$-function is a kind of matrix representing the catalytic support by species j to get a new unit of species i. It can represent a rather general possibility of a catalytic network. If $cat(i, i)$ is not zero, then species i also gives catalytic support to molecules of the same type. We will refer to such types as auto-catalytic species. We will also consider a "hypercycle", a circular network with n molecular species, where species 1 gives support to species 2, 2 to 3 and so on, that means $cat(i, i - 1) > 0$, for all $1 < i \leq n$, and $cat(1, n) > 0$ but all others are zero. In this context we are interested in hypercycles with few components: If the number of components, n, is less than 5 we obtain clusters with an essentially homogeneous internal structure. When $n \geq 5$, the models considered in this paper give clusters with spiral patterns. Such patterns are not studied here: We hope to study such clusters in a future paper. We will also consider "parasites". A parasite is a species which is replicated by some catalytic support, i.e. there is some $cat(p, i) > 0$ where p represents the parasite species. On the other hand, all matrix elements of the form $cat(i, p)$ shall be zero: The parasite does not support the replication of any molecule.

To this, we have a growth limitation, γ, which in this type of model can be made in one of two different ways.

a) We can multiply the *support* (eq. 1) with a factor such as

$$\gamma = 1 - \frac{c_{\text{tot}}}{c_0}, \quad (2)$$

where the total concentration, c_{tot}, is the fraction of lattice points occupied by any molecule and c_0 is a fixed number indicating the maximum total concentration ($0 < c_0 \leq 1$). A suitable value for cluster formation is $c_0 = 0.2$ which may give $c_{\text{tot}} \approx 0.18$, i.e. 18% of the lattice points are occupied.

b) The growth limitation can also be made by monomers which are assumed to build up the macromolecules. One way to introduce that is to assume that at each time step, there is a certain amount of monomers. The monomers are available for replication on all lattice points, i.e. they do not belong to any particular point. The probability for growth is proportional to the number of monomers. For each replication, the number of monomers is reduced by a given amount, and at each step, the monomers are restored towards the equilibrium value.

With the above described rules we calculate the probability for replication of a molecule of species i as

$$p_{\text{repl}}(i) = support(i) \cdot \gamma. \qquad (3)$$

It is simplest in all cases to have the same growth limiting rules for all lattice points, but it is possible to calculate the corresponding quantities for a certain region around each selected point. However, it is important for the cluster formation that the region is large enough to contain a cluster and some empty space around it.

Finally, a chosen molecule at an occupied site may move to a neighbouring lattice point in a random direction. If the selected neighbour is empty, the originally selected molecule will move to the neighbouring lattice point with a probability $p_{\text{diff}}(i)$, which is normally 1, but included to enable different species to have different rates of diffusion. It can be required that molecules can go only to empty lattice points, which gives a "cage effect" where high concentrations imply low diffusion, or they may change positions with other molecules, which gives a diffusion more similar to that of the synchronous CA.

The results from CA should be compared to results from a related partial differential equation, which in this case can be written as:

$$\frac{\partial X_i(x, y, t)}{\partial t} =$$

$$= \left[noncat(i) \cdot X_i + \sum_j cat(i, j) \cdot X_i X_j \right] \cdot \gamma(X_{\text{tot}})$$

$$- g_i \cdot X_i + D_i \cdot \nabla^2 X_i \qquad (4)$$

The meaning of the first term on the right hand side is the same as in eq. 1. Again, γ is a growth limiting factor. g represents the decay, and the last term the diffusion. We will not here consider any results from this equation but rather use it as a comparison.

3 Patterns

The cellular automata as described in the previous section provide certain spatial patterns. These may cover the entire lattice or they appear as clusters, surrounded by essentially empty regions. These features depend essentially on the growth limiting condition. Clusters may be obtained when such conditions are explicitly introduced and are not too local. This is discussed above and essentially means that the condition should take the concentration of filled lattice points (or some weighted average) in a region around a particular point into account. To get a cluster, that region should be larger than the cluster so that all points in the cluster and the (empty) points that surrounds it get essentially the same condition.

If the growth limitation is too local or if there is no such condition in the model, one gets a pattern that fills the entire space. Without any explicit condition, where only the availability of empty lattice points limits

the growth, this pattern can be rather dense, e.g. like the spiral patterns of the original Boerlijst–Hogeweg CA model [1, 2]. With a too local growth limiting condition, we get a sparse, but qualitatively similar pattern. There is a critical concentration: If the pattern is too sparse, it falls apart and vanishes. (The actual critical concentration depends on the details of the model and its parameters). When clusters form, they are always rather dense and it is normally possible to have a cluster on the lattice with a much smaller total number of filled points than is possible for a sparse pattern that covers the entire lattice. In that sense, clusters are more robust than continuous patterns.

When the models discussed in this paper are applied to hypercycles with 5 or more species, we obtain clusters containing a spiral pattern similar to that of the Boerlijst–Hogeweg CA model [1, 2]. In this paper, however, we focus on clusters having an essentially homogeneous internal structure. Let us then turn to the explicit models, which are characterised by the number of components and the choice of cat-function in eq. 1.

3.1 One auto-catalytic species and a parasite

The simplest model is to consider only one molecular component, which is auto-catalytic, i.e. $cat(1,1)$ is not zero. With proper growth limiting conditions one then gets a cluster which is essentially circular and densely filled with that molecule. We will refer to this species as the "main species". This becomes interesting if we also introduce a parasite, which means a molecular species which does not provide any catalytic support, i.e. $cat(1, p) = cat(p, p) = 0$, but it grows with support from the main species: $cat(p, 1)$ is not zero. Such a parasite will kill the system in most cases in the PDE description (c.f. [10]), if either its growth term is stronger, $cat(p, 1) > cat(1, 1)$, or if its decay rate is slower, $g_p < g_1$. We will here mainly consider such "lethal" parasites. In the PDE (eq. 4), the decay and growth rates are scaled with each other, why it does not really matter which inequality that is used. This is not so for the CA. We have used both in our calculations.

This system shows a clear resistance against "lethal" parasites: The main species may coexist with the parasite even if the catalytic support is larger for the parasite than for the main molecule, or if the decay probability is larger for the main species than for the parasite. If the parasite is "non-lethal", e.g. the parasite and the main species have identical parameters, the parasite decays without killing the main species. The main species survives when the cat-elements differ up to about a factor three, or the decay probabilities differ up to a factor which is at least five.

In a cluster there is a dense core with only the main species, while the parasite forms a layer outside the cluster (fig. 1). The cluster moves, as the main species decays locally due to competition with the parasite but it grows at the parasite-free part of the boundary. The parasite cannot encircle the cluster if the quotient of the cat- or decay-parameters is not very large. The main species

a)   **b)**   **c)**

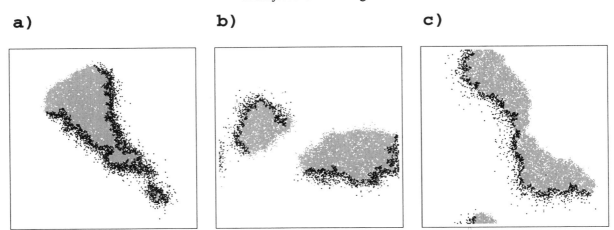

Figure 1: An auto-catalytic species (grey) coexists with a parasite (black). a) A parasite with three times higher catalytic support than the auto-catalytic species makes the cluster move fast. The parasite-free boundary is small. A part of the cluster is cut off by the parasite. This part does not move and will soon decay, but as long as it remains, it may split or even kill the main cluster in a collision. b) More reasonable parameter values give a more regular cluster shape. Collisions can split the cluster. c) When the decay rate of the main species is high (here it is five times the decay rate of the parasite) the cluster is wide but short.

in the cluster can grow faster along the parasite-free part of the boundary than the parasite can in its regions, so the cluster moves instead of being killed, and the parasite chases the main species. The shape of the moving cluster varies, depending on the parameters. When the parasite has a high catalytic support, the cluster is narrow and long and moves very fast (fig. 1a). For moderate catalytic support of the parasite, the cluster is more circular and moves slowly (fig. 1b). When the parasite and the main species have equal catalytic support but the main species has higher decay probability, the cluster is wide and short (fig. 1c). For very high decay probabilities we observe lattice dependence: The cluster is aligned at an angle of 45° compared to the lattice. Apparently this orientation gives the fastest growth at the parasite-free boundary, which enables the auto-catalytic species (and the cluster) to survive.

It can be mentioned that even if a cluster is almost circumvented by parasites, then for the stable situation discussed above, the main species can "break through" the parasite and rapidly increase the parasite-free boundary to get a stable cluster where both species coexist. The parasite can split a cluster and then also normally destroy one of the parts.

This behaviour is quite different from what would be described by the PDE (eq. 4). The reason for this is that the molecule positions are strongly correlated and such a correlation is completely neglected in eq. 4. The probability for a molecule to replicate depends on its immediate neighbours: It needs an empty lattice point and catalytic support (eq. 1). Because there are many neighbours that provide catalytic support and many empty lattice points at the parasite-free boundary, the main species can grow faster there than the parasite can in the interfacial region with fewer empty sites and also a competition with the main species. This, of course, means that the rules of competition are quite different

for this, highly correlated system, than for the "conventional" PDE approach.

3.2 Homogeneous clusters for other systems

The above described mechanism for resistance to parasites applies also to many-component systems which do not show temporal oscillations or spatial patterns inside the clusters. (Hypercycles with many components give spiral patterns, c.f. [1, 2].) For instance, one may have a two-component hypercycle with: $cat(1, 2) = cat(2, 1) > 0$, but $cat(1, 1) = cat(2, 2) = 0$. This and similar systems do also give clusters which are to be characterised as "homogeneous", essentially random mixtures of the molecular species (fig. 2a). There is no particular internal structure in the clusters. Parasites occurring in such clusters cannot remain there (fig. 2b–c): The cluster moves, and the parasite will eventually form a layer at one side of the cluster, chasing the cluster. The parasite does not mix with the species of the hypercycle. As the parasite is in general replicated by only one of the species in the cluster, it is irregularly spread along the boundary of the cluster. The cluster is easily split in several parts.

Similar clusters are obtained not only for hypercycle networks with few components but also for many other catalytic networks. There are correlations in these clusters. For instance, when also auto-catalytic possibilities are considered in the catalytic networks, there is a tendency that the same molecules are close to each other. This does not change any essential features: The clusters may still be essentially homogeneous with only small correlated regions. For more complex catalytic networks, it is also possible that there is differentiation, i.e. different clusters, or parts of a cluster, can contain different parts of the original catalytic network, perhaps only one single species.

a)   **b)**   **c)**

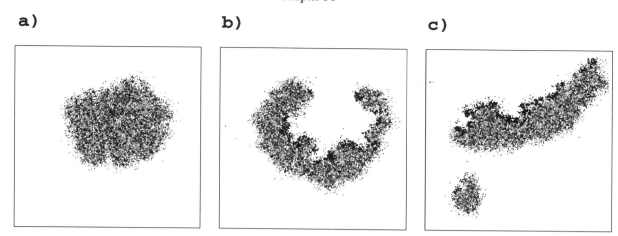

Figure 2: Homogeneous clusters display similar resistance to parasites as the auto-catalytic species. Here a cluster with a three-component hypercycle is shown. a) In the cluster the species (represented by 3 different grey shades) are essentially homogeneously distributed. b) The parasite (black) has been introduced at one place in the interior of the cluster. The hypercycle decays locally where the parasite grows, but the cluster also begins to grow outwards. Note how irregular the growth of the parasite is, as it receives support from only one of the hypercycle species. c) A moving cluster, which is frequently split by the parasite, coexists with the parasite.

4 Summary and conclusions

Clusters may form if certain explicit growth limitations are applied to reaction-diffusion systems. The limitation must not be too local: In must allow for competition between the interior of a cluster and the empty space around it.

For many systems one obtains different results for CA models and PDE models. The CA can include effects depending on correlations in positions between the individual molecules. These effects, which cannot be modelled in PDE systems, are important e.g. for auto-catalytic species and especially for resistance to parasites. They may imply radically different conditions for auto-catalytic species in CA and PDE models, respectively. In a CA, the off-spring is placed adjacent to the "parent"-molecule. This favours auto-catalytic species in CA models, where they may give catalytic support to each other. In general, the effect of the diagonal elements in the matrix representing catalytic support is enhanced.

Homogeneous clusters may display resistance to parasites. The parasite forms a layer on parts of the surface the clusters, chasing the auto-catalytic species or an essentially homogeneous mixture of species. The clusters move with a "tail" of coexisting parasites.

References

[1] M. C. Boerlijst & P. Hogeweg, Self-structuring and selection: Spiral waves as a substrate for evolution, in: *Artificial Life II*, C.G.Langton et al., Eds., (Addison Wesley, Redwood City, USA, 1991) pp 255–276.

[2] M. C. Boerlijst & P. Hogeweg, Spiral wave structure in pre-biotic evolution: Hypercycles stable against parasites, *Physica D* **48** (1991) 17–28.

[3] A. T. Winfree, Rotating chemical reactions, *Sci. Amer.* **230** (6) (1974) 82–95.

[4] V. S. Zykov, Spiral waves in two-dimensional excitable media, *Ann. N. Y. Acad. Sci.* **591** (1990) 75–85.

[5] P. Hogeweg, Multilevel evolution: replicators and the evolution of diversity, *Physica D* **75** (1994) 275–291.

[6] P. Chacón & J. C. Nuño, Spatial dynamics of a model for prebiotic evolution, *Physica D* **81** (1995) 398–410.

[7] W. Gilbert, The RNA world, *Nature* **319** (1986), 618.

[8] M. Cronhjort & C. Blomberg, Clusters in 2D catalytic networks, submitted.

[9] C. Blomberg, G. von Heijne, O. Leimar, Competition, coexistence and irreversibility in models of early evolution, in: *Origin of life*, E. Wollman, Ed., (D. Reidel Publ. CompanyDordrecht, The Netherlands 1981) pp 385–392.

[10] M. Cronhjort & C. Blomberg, Hypercycles versus parasites in a two-dimensional partial differential equations model, *J. theor. Biol.* **169** (1994) 31–49.

Atomoid: A New Prospect in Reaction-Formation System Spontaneous Hypercycles Guided by Dissipative Structural Properties

Shinichiro YOSHII*, Hiroaki INAYOSHI**, and Yukinori KAKAZU*

*Complex Systems Engineering, Hokkaido University, Sapporo 060, Japan.
e-mail: yoshii@complex.hokudai.ac.jp, kakazu@complex.hokudai.ac.jp

**Electrotechnical Laboratory, Tsukuba 305, Japan.
e-mail: inayoshi@etl.go.jp

Abstract

In this paper, we propose a reaction-formation model called "Atomoid", the reaction dynamics of which are analogous to those found in the physical world based on energy levels. Our ultimate aim is to realize an evolvable emergent system above a non-symbolic reaction-formation system. To realize such a system, we construct a model of Atomoid and focus on the self-reproduction process as it is essential for self-organizing or emergent systems. Self-organizing processes can be observed, not only in living systems, but also in non-biological systems. In particular, the evolution towards the origin of life is non-biological, and is referred to as chemical evolution. Many models simulating self-reproduction or chemical evolution have already been proposed. However, these models require specific and arbitrary rules to be described symbolically in advance, and therefore, there is no consistency or coherence to be guaranteed in their dynamics. On the other hand, by means of an analogy to physical atomic reaction, Atomoid can boast attractive properties that differ from those of other models. In addition, in spite of having only very simple reaction rules, Atomoid can realize complex atomic reactions. Furthermore, the emergence of self-reproductive hypercycles can be observed, because of its dissipative structural properties. These spontaneous hypercycles are very similar to the most primitive hypercycles as proposed by M. Eigen. The prospects and some interesting dynamics of Atomoid are discussed through simulations.

1. Introduction

The objective of our study is to realize the emergence of a self-reproducing molecular system through the modeling of Atomoid whose reaction dynamics are analogous to that of physical atomic reaction based on energy levels. There are still some missing links concerning the process whereby self-reproducing biomolecules emerge from the stage of chemical evolution, because of the difficulty in artificially controlling physical systems and a lack of biological approaches. In this paper, we focus on the process by which a self-reproductive molecular system could emerge at an atomic level.

As has been much studied by many scientists including A. Oparin, the functions of self-reproduction or metabolism are essential for living-systems. In the realm of artificial life, self-reproduction has also been studied, and many interesting models simulating such phenomena have already been proposed. In particular, as self-reproductive models, there are the studies of self-replicating cellular automata by C. G. Langton [9] and self-reproducing machines by A. R. Smith [16]. Furthermore, R. J. Bagley and et al. studied the emergence of the metabolism [1, 18], and there are many studies relating to the origin of life [2, 8, 15, 17].

However, all these studies are intended as investigations into the dynamics or kinetics of systems which are premised on having the potential for self-reproduction or are modeled so that objective phenomena can be simulated. In respect to this point, H. H. Pattee has distinguished computer simulations from computer realizations of life, and has described the differences between them [12]. From his point of view, the studies mentioned above are no more than computer simulations of living system behaviors, since they contain symbolically described specific or arbitrary rules which metaphorically stand for something else, or deterministic equations empirically defined in advance. For these reasons, no matter how accurate they may be, these simulation results are different from the actual realization of living systems in a computer. As long as there are such arbitrary rules, the significance of the system being simulated cannot be isolated from one's theory or knowledge. In Conway's cellular automaton game of life [4], for example, although the dynamics being simulated are interesting, one must ask why does a cell have to be turned to "on", even if three of its eight neighbors are "on"? Or, where does the cell being turned to "on" come from? There is no consistency or coherence to be guaranteed in the state transitions of the system.

On the other hand, turning to the physical world, functions of self-reproduction or metabolism can be observed where, in spite of bonding or separation, a constant number of atoms is maintained without abrupt generations or disappearances. It has been revealed that such functions would emerge in non-equilibrium systems through studies such as the theories of dissipative structures [14] and synergetics [7], and recently it has also been elucidated from the viewpoint of autopoietic systems [10]. Nevertheless, none of the models proposed so far can employ scientific knowledge because of their implementation of arbitrary rules and the lack of a material, substantive model. However, there is no reason why we should restrict the realization of living systems to carbon environments. Therefore, we have constructed the Atomoid system as a substantive model and discuss how the emergence of self-reproductive molecules is derived from the properties of a dissipative structure. Beginning with a model analogous to physical atomic reaction based on energy levels does not mean reductionism, but rather enables coherent dynamics to be realized in addition to scientific knowledge being employed. The dynamic law of Atomoid is reversible, but the dynamic process from the initial conditions is irreversible. An artificial physical model of a literal and non-symbolic reaction-formation system like Atomoid allows us to explicate the phenomena of self-organization in non-living systems.

Section 2 outlines the model of the reaction-formation system Atomoid. Section 3 describes the reaction rules of Atomoid in detail. Section 4 shows simulation results and presents the emergence of self-reproductive hypercycles. Lastly, section 5 discusses those simulation results and the prospects of Atomoid, and then concludes this paper.

2. Atomoid

2.1 Penrose's work and Atomoid

L. S. Penrose's work [13] was helpful in modeling Atomoid. Penrose built a series of mechanical models illustrating self-reproduction. The blocks in his models have hooks which can engage other blocks in different arrangements. When many unhooked blocks are placed into a box with only one pair of them hooked together and the box is shaken, the rest of the blocks begin to combine with their neighboring blocks. After they have grown by hooking up, these hooked blocks then divide into two identical bodies. His work exhibits two significant points: One is the role of the "seed" and the influx of energy with shaking the box. A seed refers to a pair of blocks hooked beforehand, and the shaking of the box with the seed placed in it yields fluctuation in the system. As a result, a self-reproduction process emerges. The other is that each block has its own structure and that their combination represents the structure of a block of a higher order.

The artificial life models mentioned above don't have any concept to represent higher structures through lower structures. Therefore, their dynamics are irreversible and no object is continually preserved. For example, in cellular automata, a cell rewritten by an arbitrary rule is different from its former self and its state no longer reflects that of the former. Therefore, the modeling of Atomoid is premised on the following features:

- Each unit has an "operator", which represents the manner in which it will change others, and an "operand",

which describes its state or structure and which is operated on by others' operators.

- The operator and operand of a unit of a higher order are constructed based on those of a lower order.

- Identical units have the same internal structure. But, their internal states are not always identical.

- Even if reacting units are identical, the resulting reaction is dependent on the manner of the reaction.

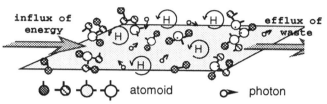

Fig. 1 Atomoid world.

2.2 Model

Each atom in Atomoid has its own hands which can bond with those of others. When M means the kind of atom, an atom whose atomic number is k $(k = 1, \cdots, M)$ is described as follows:

$$a_k = (hd(k), \varphi_j(k), r_j(k), \theta_j, s_j \mid j = 1, \cdots, hd(k)), \quad (1)$$

where $hd(k)$, $\varphi_j(k)$, a pair of $r_j(k)$ and θ_j, and s_j denote the number of bonding hands, the operator which operates the other atoms, the operand which represents the bonding hand structure, and the energy state of the hand respectively. $hd(k)$, $\varphi_j(k)$, and $r_j(k)$ are constant relating to the atom whose atomic number is k.

The bonding hand in Atomoid has the following properties:

- The bonding hands of an atom are independent of each other.

- As will be shown later, the energy structure, that is to say, the energy level of the bonding hand, is changed by $r_j(k)$ and θ_j of the other atoms and only two states $\{ground, excited\}$ are permitted for the energy state s_j.

- The initial values of $r_j(k)$ and θ_j are equal to the identical atoms. $r_j(k)$ is constant, but θ_j changes dynamically with the atomic reactions. This means a change in the energy structure of the bonding hand.

- When a photon in the system is absorbed or released, or an atomic reaction occurs, the energy state is transited from $ground$ to $excited$ or from $excited$ to $ground$.

Next, we explain the relationship between the bonding hand structure and the energy structure: When the bonding hand structure of atom k is represented by the abbreviated form r and θ, the ground state energy e_0 and the excited state energy e_1 are defined as follows with the complex form $z = re^{i\theta}$.

$$e_0 = \min(r\cos\theta, r\sin\theta), \qquad -r \le e_0 \le r \quad (2)$$

$$e_1 = \max(r\cos\theta, r\sin\theta). \qquad -r \le e_1 \le r \quad (3)$$

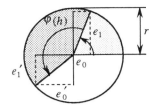

Fig. 2 Change in energy level by $\varphi(h)$.

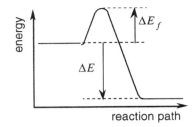

Fig. 3 Activation energy ΔE_f.

Each energy is allowed to have a positive or a negative value, since it is defined relatively based on a given standard. When operated by the operator $e^{i\varphi(h)}$ of atom h, the bonding hand structure $z = re^{i\theta}$ is changed as follows:

$$z' = ze^{i\varphi(h)} = re^{i(\theta + \varphi(h))} \qquad (4)$$

With this change, its energy structure, that is, its energy level changes from (e_0, e_1) to (e'_0, e'_1).

$$e'_0 = \min(r\cos(\theta + \varphi(h)), r\sin(\theta + \varphi(h))). \qquad (5)$$

$$e'_1 = \max(r\cos(\theta + \varphi(h)), r\sin(\theta + \varphi(h))). \qquad (6)$$

Fig. 2 shows the change in the energy level from (e_0, e_1) to (e'_0, e'_1) by the operator $\varphi(h)$.

3. Reaction Rules

Any atomic reaction depends on whether the energy structures of the reactors become more stable or not as a whole in the thermodynamic sense of the Atomoid system.

3.1 Reaction between Two Atoms

If a hand of atom α and one of atom β are to bond with each other, the possibility for bonding is calculated as follows: α's hands are to be regarded as $z_i = r_i e^{i\theta_i}$ $(i = 1, \cdots, hd(\alpha))$,

$$z'_i = z_i e^{i\varphi(\beta)}, \qquad (7)$$

and β's hands as $z_j = r_j e^{i\theta_j}$ $(j = 1, \cdots, hd(\beta))$

$$z'_j = z_j e^{i\varphi(\alpha)}. \qquad (8)$$

At this moment, under the assumption that the energy states of every hand are transited to the ground state at the new energy level on being operated on by the other, the sum ΔE of all the energy changes relating to both atom α and β is calculated. That is,

$$\Delta E = \sum_{j \in \alpha, \beta} \left(e'_0(j) - e_{s_j}(j) \right). \qquad (9)$$

If the following relation holds between ΔE and the activation energy ΔE_f depicted in Fig. 3, that is,

$$\Delta E + \Delta E_f < 0, \qquad (10)$$

then both hands are bonded with each other. Bonding makes the energy structure more stable as a whole. The activation energy ΔE_f is a parameter to express the ease with which atoms are able to bond together. The smaller ΔE_f is, the longer the molecules that tend to be formed. And then, α's bonding hand structure θ_i and β's θ_j are updated as follows:

$$\theta_i \Leftarrow \theta_i + \varphi(\beta) \quad (i = 1, \cdots, hd(\alpha)), \qquad (11)$$

$$\theta_j \Leftarrow \theta_j + \varphi(\alpha) \quad (j = 1, \cdots, hd(\beta)). \qquad (12)$$

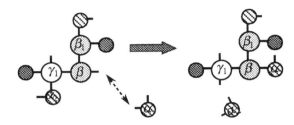

Fig. 4 Example of a reaction between an atom and a molecule.

3.2 Reaction between Atom and Molecule

Suppose that an atom and an molecule are to bond with each other, as shown in Fig. 4. The subscripts in the molecule denote their distances from atom β which is to bond. First, focusing on atom α, and atom β, which is a member of that molecule, the possibility for bonding is calculated in the same way as the reaction between the two atoms. If $\Delta E + \Delta E_f < 0$, bonding is realized and both hand structures are updated. On the other hand, at this moment, connections bonded previously may be broken with the change in β's energy structure, in which case, the possibility for separation is calculated. Separation changes the structure by $-\varphi$. That is, defining $\mathrm{conc}(a(\beta))$ as an atom which has previously bonded with atom β, if $\mathrm{conc}(a(\beta))$ exists and the following condition holds, the connection between the atoms is broken.

$$e_{s_j}(j) + e_{s_k}(k) > e'_1(j) + e'_1(k), \qquad (13)$$

where $e_{s_j}(j)$ and $e_{s_k}(k)$ denote β's and $\mathrm{conc}(a(\beta))$'s energy before separation, and $e'_1(j)$ and $e'_1(k)$ denote the excited energy after separation, respectively. With this separation, β's bonding hand structure θ_j and $\mathrm{conc}(a(\beta))$'s θ_k are updated as follows:

$$\theta_j \Leftarrow \theta_j - \varphi(\mathrm{conc}(a(\beta))), \qquad j = 1, \cdots, hd(\beta) \qquad (14)$$

$$\theta_k \Leftarrow \theta_k - \varphi(\beta). \qquad k = 1, \cdots, hd(\mathrm{conc}(a(\beta))) \qquad (15)$$

Now, suppose that bonding α with β in Fig. 4 separates atom γ_1 from β. The change in the separated γ_1's energy structure may subsequently break the connection between γ_1 and another atom, for example, α_2. If the connection between them is broken and the bonding condition between β and γ_1 is satisfied, they are bonded again, as shown in Fig. 4.

Such reaction processes in Atomoid show how its features differ from other artificial models. First, the reaction dynamics are completely reversible as structural change is defined by means of the rotation degree. At any given moment, each object is still preserved as itself. Second, regarding the separated molecules or atoms, their internal structures are completely identical with those which are independently constructed from each constituent atom. Finally, depending on the internal structure as a whole, some local interaction may effect a connection in some far away locality.

Furthermore, even if a hand has already been bonded, the bonding partner can be exchanged in cases where the conditions for separation and bonding are satisfied.

3.3 Reaction between Two Molecules

Although basically equal to the rules described above, complex and various reactions would occur because of additional structural changes and their subsequent reactions. Fig. 5 illustrates an actual example from the simulation results.

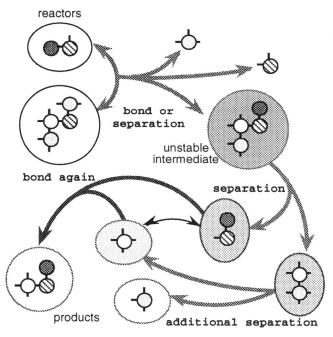

Fig. 5 Actual example of reaction from simulation results.

3.4 Reaction with Photons

Photon is the sole energy resource in the system and moves randomly. A photon ρ is modeled with its energy range γ and phase ϕ as follows:

$$\rho = (\gamma, \phi). \tag{16}$$

When an atomic reaction occurs, a photon, as described below, is generated in the system.

$$\gamma = |\Delta E|. \tag{17}$$

$$\phi = \frac{1}{2}(\varphi(\alpha) + \varphi(\beta)). \tag{18}$$

If a photon hits the hand of an atom, and if the following conditions hold, it can cause the energy state of the hand to switch from ground to excited. That is,

$$\gamma > \Delta e, \tag{19}$$

$$|\phi - \varphi| < \psi, \tag{20}$$

where Δe denotes sufficient energy to cause excitation and ψ is the parameter which restricts the absorption of photons. If ψ is smaller, then the photons can operate on those atoms which have a specific kind of energy structure. When a photon is absorbed, its γ is deducted as follows and it moves again:

$$\gamma \Leftarrow \gamma - \Delta e. \tag{21}$$

Photons play a role in bringing fluctuation into the system, and may be able to produce peculiar molecules which could not be normally produced. This is because the ratio for $\Delta E < 0$ tends to increase if the bonding hand is excited by a photon before an atomic reaction.

4. Simulations

4.1 Dynamics of the System

Here, the macro-dynamics of the Atomoid system are simulated. In the following simulations, four kinds of atoms are employed, as shown in Fig. 6. All of the atoms are generated randomly. Table 1 gives the parameters for the simulations. The component ratio of the atoms is shown in Fig. 7.

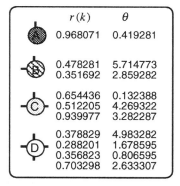

Fig. 6 Atoms in simulation.

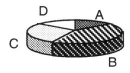

Fig. 7 Component ratio of atoms.

population	5000
activation energy	$\Delta E_f = 0.7$
threshold for absorbing photons	$\psi = \frac{\pi}{6}$

Table 1 Parameters of simulation.

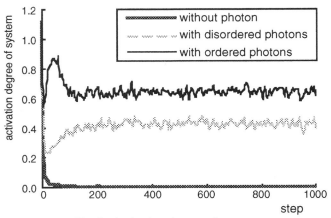

Fig. 8 Activation degree of system.

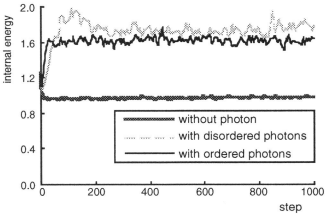

Fig. 9 Internal energy of atoms.

Fig. 8 indicates the activation degree of the system when the photon energy poured into the system is controlled in different ways. The degree is measured by the ratio of actual atomic reactions to all calculations. A lower activation degree means that few reactions have occurred, or in other words, that the system is "frozen". Fig. 9 indicates the transition of the internal energy of the atoms. The more the energy states of the atoms that are ground, the lower the internal energy that is observed, and the system is more stable thermodynamically. Next, let us discuss the macro-dynamics of the system.

First of all, we will inquire into the macro-dynamics where the system is given no photon energy and all the photons that have been generated by atomic reactions have been removed. In such a case, the atoms spend all the internal energy that they have been given in the beginning, and possible atomic reactions occur. As a result, the whole system becomes frozen right at the start of the simulation, as shown in Fig. 8. Fig. 9 shows how the entire internal energy is naturally kept at the lowest level, as all the atoms release their internal energy. These are very trivial dynamics.

Next, we pour photons of different phases into the system. Such disordered photons can be absorbed by various atoms if their energy structure agrees with a photon's phase. Thus, the internal energy of the system is kept at the highest level, as shown in Fig. 9, since the photons excite the energy states of the atoms. Therefore, reactions are able to occur more easily, and the activation degree of the system thereby stands at a higher level. This result is also predictable.

Finally, a case where the system is given ordered photons is discussed. The phases of these photons are unified. Such ordered photons with small entropy can operate only on specific atoms whose energy structure satisfies the conditions for absorption of photons. Nevertheless, the activation degree is higher than in any of the other cases mentioned above. Furthermore, its internal energy is kept at a lower level than those cases with disordered photons. This is because a particular reaction network is formed as a result of the photons' operations on specific atoms, and this causes the emergence of hypercycles [5, 6] which dissipate large entropy. This result is very interesting and suggests a mechanism for self-reproduction or self-organization.

The following sections discuss such phenomena as regards the emergence of hypercycles.

4.2 The Reaction Network toward Equilibrium

In this section, we inquire into the reaction process towards equilibrium in detail. The population is limited to 100 even though the component ratio of the atoms is the same. Moreover, ΔE_f is increased to 1.0, since the molecules formed are too long to follow all the reactions if ΔE_f is smaller. Here, a unique chemical formula is adopted for the purpose of simplifying the description of the molecules. The molecule in Fig. 10, for example, is described as 121-26, the left hand of which denotes its molecular formula and the right hand discriminates itself from the structural isomers. The parameters of the detailed simulation are given in Table 2.

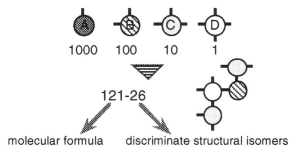

Fig. 10 Description of molecule.

population	100
activation energy	$\Delta E_f = 1.0$
threshold for absorbing photons	$\psi = \dfrac{\pi}{6}$

Table 2 Parameters of detailed simulation.

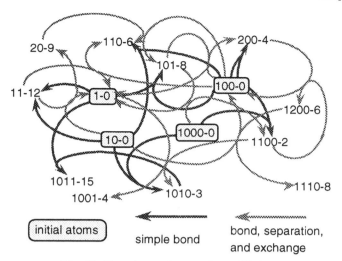

Fig. 11 Reaction path towards equilibrium.

Fig. 11 shows the reaction network towards equilibrium in the case of no photon. This figure represents only an abbreviation of the original as this was too large to include in its entirety. First, molecules such as 110-6 or 11-12 are formed from the initial atoms. These molecules subsequently form second products. However, once the system reaches equilibrium, no more reactions occur. In this respect, the dynamics of the system at equilibrium are trivial.

4.3 The Emergence of Spontaneous Hypercycles

Next, the system is given ordered photon energy after reaching equilibrium. Fig. 12 shows the change in the number of molecule representatives. Photons whose phase is unified to $\phi = \frac{\pi}{6}$ are poured into the system, as soon as it reaches equilibrium at the 200th step. Its dynamics change drastically right after the influx of the photons, after which the

emergence of some kinds of spontaneous hypercycles is observed in the system, as shown in Fig. 13. These figures are abbreviations as their size doesn't allow full inclusion here. The outlined molecules are those which are excited by the photons. In other words, these molecules have an energy structure which satisfies the conditions for absorption of photons.

To begin with, let us look at Fig. 13 a). First, molecule 200-4 is formed out of two initial atoms of 100-0. The photon excites this 200-4, and then a pair of 200-4 form themselves into the molecule 300-8 and the atom 100-0. On the other hand, the initial atom 100-0 and 10-0 bond together into 110-6, and then a pair of 110-6 are formed through the subsequent reaction with 210-10. This may represent one of the most primitive forms of a self-reproductive network. These molecules are not plotted in Fig. 12 as there are too many in the system. Second, the molecule 310-14 is formed out of the atom 10-0 and the product 300-8. This is used as a rich resource for the formation of all following networks such as c) or d). Thus, Fig. 12 indicates that the number of 310-14 is increasing. Then, the reaction between 310-14 and 110-6 produce a pair of 210-10 as shown in Fig. 13 c). Furthermore, a pair of 110-6 are formed as a result of the reaction between 210-0 and 10-0. This network closely resembles the mutually catalytic type of self-reproductive hypercycle, as asserted by Eigen. On the other hand, in the reaction network of d), 210-12 is made from 110-6. This next reacts with 310-14, and a pair of 110-6 are formed as result of the separation of an unstable intermediate 210-10. In this respect, this network is a kind of autocatalytic self-reproductive hypercycle. Fig. 12 indicates that the number of molecule 210 begins to increase after the emergence of such self-reproductive hypercycles.

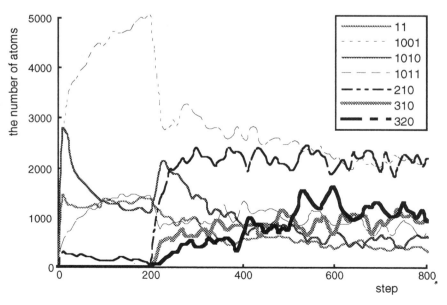

Fig. 12 Change in number of atoms.

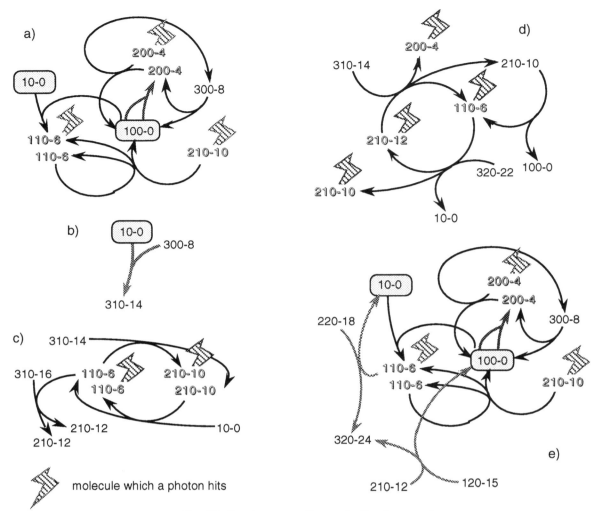

Fig. 13 Spontaneous self-reproductive hypercycles.

As long as there is enough resource, these hypercycles can maintain themselves while dissipating large entropy. But, these hypercycles alter their patterns continually, as the simulation time steps go by, though all those detailed alterations have been omitted from the figures. Actually, these networks function as a huge hypercycle arising from a highly complex set of connections. These reaction networks indicate a self-organizing or self-reproductive mechanism in a non-living system.

5. Discussions

What the emergence of self-reproductive hypercycles in the reaction-formation system of Atomoid indicates is clearly distinct from the main stresses of previous studies on hypercycles [2, 3, 8, 11]. These studies focus mainly on the dynamics of systems modeled with symbolic or mathematical description. They require arbitrary bit string description, a subconscious metaphor of RNA, as the media carrying information, or solid mathematical modeled description as a reaction-diffusion system. Because the dynamics are implicitly embedded in their description, the system requires a

groundless randomness, such as mutation, in order to escape trivial dynamics. Such a system cannot preserve consistency regarding its dynamics under such a description. However, this is not the case with Atomoid. Atomoid, which is modeled by means of literal reaction rules and the substantive object of an atom, can employ scientific knowledge. Thus, in Atomoid, dissipative structural properties guide the emergence of self-reproductive hypercycles. These hypercycles can only be observed when the system is given ordered energy. Of course, we have confirmed that different patterns of hypercycles would emerge if the ordered phases of the photons differed. Although enormous reaction networks were generated in the system when given disordered energy, only random reactions occurred without the emergence of hypercycles.

Another remarkable feature of Atomoid is its potential as a reaction-formation system. Only four kinds of atoms were employed at the beginning of the simulations. Nevertheless, Atomoid can generate vast kinds of molecules. Their genotypic properties are expressed as the energy structure in each atom. Furthermore, the process of how molecule 320-

24 in Fig. 13 e) is formed is also interesting. There had been no 320-24 in the system before the photons were poured into it, as shown in Fig. 12. However, this molecule can only be formed through the reaction path in the figure. It cannot be formed any other way, no matter how well the atoms of which it would consist might be stirred. Even if the reaction rule of Atomoid is completely reversible, the reaction process itself is irreversible in such a non-equilibrium system, as this would mean the breaking of its symmetry. Thus, simulation result is reminiscent of the stage of chemical evolution towards the origin of life. Molecules which are generated one after another subsequently generate new molecules. In addition, if different kinds of fluctuation are induced, the generated molecules naturally differ.

Finally, we describe a new prospect which such reaction-formation systems might offer. As shown in the simulation results, the self-reproductive hypercycles emerge as a result of self-organization under a dissipative structure. These hypercycles can maintain themselves as long as ordered energy is given into the system. On the other hand, the influx of energy brings the breaking of symmetry into the system. As a consequence, the system can generate new constituents through the interaction between its own constituents, depending on the environmental conditions. Thus, the hypercycle alters its boundary continually or renews itself self-referentially through its functioning. In this respect, such a self-renewing system could help us explore the possibilities for the development of autopoiesis systems.

In this paper, we proposed a reaction-formation system named Atomoid which is analogous to physical atomic reactions. Through simulations, we observed that self-reproductive hypercycles emerged in this non-equilibrium system, and discussed the noteworthy features of Atomoid.

References

[1] Bagley, R. J., Farmer, J. D. and Fontana, W.: Evolution of a Metabolism, *Artificial Life II*, Santa Fe Institute Studies in the Sciences of Complexity, Proc. Vol. X, pp. 141-158, Addison-Wesley, 1991.

[2] Banzhaf, W.: Self-organization in a System of Binary Strings, Artificial Life IV, Proceedings of the Fourth International Workshop on the Synthesis and Simulation of Living Systems, pp. 109-118, The MIT Press, 1994.

[3] Boerlijst, M. C. and Hogeweg, P.: Spiral Wave Structure in Prebiotic Evolution: Hypercycles Stable Against Parasites, Physica D 48, 1991.

[4] Gardner, M.: On Cellular Automata, Self-Reproduction, The Garden of Eden and the Game of 'Life', *Scientific-American*, 224(2), pp. 112-117, 1971.

[5] Eigen, M.: Self-Organization of Matter and the Evolution of Biological Macromolecules, *Naturwissenschaften* 58, 1971.

[6] Eigen, M. and Schuster, P., The Hypercycle: A Principle of Natural Self-Organization, *Naturwissenschaften* 64, 1977.

[7] Haken, H.: *Synergetics: Nonequilibrium Phase Transitions and Self-Organization in Physics, Chemistry and Biology*, Springer-Verlag, 1977.

[8] Ikegami, T and Hashimoto, T.: Coevolution of machines and tapes, Advances in Artificial Life, Proceedings of Third European Conference on Artificial Life, pp. 234-245, Springer, 1995.

[9] Langton, C. G., ed.: *Artificial Life*, Santa Fe Institute Studies in the Sciences of Complexity, Proc. Vol. VI, pp. 1-47, Addison-Wesley, 1989.

[10] Maturana, H. R. and Varela, F.: *Autopoietic Systems*, Biological Computer Laboratory, 1975.

[11] Nuño, J. C., Chacón, P., Moreno, A., and Morán, F.: Compartimentation in Replicator Models, Advances in Artificial Life, Proceedings of Third European Conference on Artificial Life, pp. 116-127, Springer, 1995.

[12] Pattee, H. H.: Simulations, Realizations, and Theories of Life, *Artificial Life*, Santa Fe Institute Studies in the Sciences of Complexity, Proc. Vol. VI, pp. 63-77, Addison-Wesley, 1989.

[13] Penrose, L. S.: Self-Reproducing Machines, *Scientific-American*, 200(6), pp. 105-113, 1959.

[14] Prigogine, I.: *Order Out of Chaos*, Bantam Books, 1984.

[15] Rasmussen, S.: Toward a Quantitative Theory of the Origin of Life, *Artificial Life*, Santa Fe Institute Studies in the Sciences of Complexity, Proc. Vol. VI, pp. 79-104, Addison-Wesley, 1989.

[16] Smith, A. R.: Simple Nontrivial Self-Reproducing Machines, *Artificial Life II*, Santa Fe Institute Studies in the Sciences of Complexity, Proc. Vol. X, pp. 709-725, Addison-Wesley, 1991.

[17] Tamayo, P. and Hartman, H.: Cellular Automata, Reaction-Diffusion Systems and the Origin of Life, *Artificial Life*, Santa Fe Institute Studies in the Sciences of Complexity, Proc. Vol. VI, pp. 105-124, Addison-Wesley, 1989.

[18] Yamamoto, T. and Kaneko, K.: Tile Automaton for Evolution of Metabolism, *Advances in Artificial Life*, Proceedings of Third European Conference on Artificial Life, pp. 188-199, Springer, 1995.

Replication and Diversity in Machine-Tape Coevolutionary Systems

Takashi Ikegami *and Takashi Hashimoto †

Institute of Physics,

The Graduate School of Arts and Sciences, University of Tokyo,

Komaba 3-8-1,Meguro-ku, Tokyo 153, Japan

Abstract

The origin and evolution of genetic system is studied by metaphor of machine-tape coevolutionary system. Mutation is taken as a rewriting process which machines act on tapes. A tape consists of a bit string, encoding a machine function. Tapes can be replicated only being read by adequate machines. It is reported in our previous studies that complex but stable autocatalytic structures evolve under effects of external noise. Ensembles of such autocatalytic networks are studied in this paper. Each network, embedded in a cell structure, can exchange machines with other networks. Each cell is assumed to be duplicated when a cell has a sufficient amount of mutually catalyzing machines. A daughter cell has the same kinds and populations of machines and tapes as its parental cell. It is found that developed cells are classified into two different types. One cell type has unstable dynamics which generates cell differentiation. The other cell type has stable dynamics which generates unlimitedly identical cell types. The former differentiating cells form an ecology with essentially large degrees of freedom. On the other hand, the latter cell types are cancer-like cells, whose dynamics cannot be effected by the other existing cells. Hence those cancer cells are characterized as those with independent small degrees of freedom.

1 Introduction

Biological processes are essentially very unstable. They consist of huge complicated chemical reactions. Not only due to their nonlinearity of interactions but to their context dependent usages of chemicals, it is very difficult to control by themselves. For example, a chemical A interacts with a chemical B to generate a chemical C but sometimes a chemical D. We cannot determine the whole possible reactions in advance. This non-deterministic and context dependent nature is not originated in statistics but is the essential feature of biological systems.

On the other hand, life's other characteristics is to control stable self-reproduction. Most living things control their number of copies to balance with other living things. However, the above uncontrollable nature of living states may make it a difficult task.

John von Neumann first proposed an automaton model for self-reproduction [1]. In his abstract modeling, a necessary condition for self-replication is to distinguish a machine from its description tape. A machine (i.e. an entity which should be copied) is too unstable to replicate by itself. It can only be replicating by reading stable objects called tapes. Indeed, Neumann constructed replicating configurations consisting of machines and tapes in two dimensional plane with 29 automaton states.

However, possible self-replicating structures are quite fragile. A one bit flip of replicating pattern will lead to non-replicating structures. Even without external disturbance, replication becomes difficult. If we have two machines with different syntax for reading tapes, one machine may read tapes to produce different machines.

In the previous studies [2, 3], we have examined such situations by introducing simple machines and tapes model. Machines with different transition table compete in reading tapes. Due to external noise, machines make errors. We have found that external noise destabilize local replication (i.e. a machine reads a tape to produce the same machine and tape). But if the noise excesses some threshold, a network gives up local replication and acquires global replication. Namely, both machines and tapes are replicated globally to form a replicating network. We call a structure with such dual global replication a double loop structure.

Such core structure is stably retained even after removing external noise. Stable replication requires stable core structures. But on the other hand, we notice that it is too stable for evolution. Once there appears a stable core network, evolution will no longer be possible. To maintain evolutionability and diversity, it is important to remain certain kinds of instability in networks. In other words, a network should be balanced between stability and instability, being to be susceptible to open environments.

In the present paper, we study the ensemble of networks to discuss more about replication and diversity. Each network of machines and tapes is put in a cell struc-

---

*E-mail address : ikeg@sacral.c.u-tokyo.ac.jp

†E-mail address : toshiwo@sacral.c.u-tokyo.ac.jp

ture not to directly couple with other networks. Cells can exchange machines but not tapes among other cells. Each machine can replicate by reading adequate tapes. At the same time each cell can replicate when there appear many mutually catalyzing machines in a cell. Cells with temporally oscillatory core networks can have many machines at one time so that it can divide. A daughter cell has the same kinds and population of machines and tapes as its parental cell. Simulating dividing cell assembly, we find that there exist two different cell types. One cell type has unstable dynamics, which can duplicate but cannot leave identical cell types. The other cell type has stable dynamics, whose division turns out to be perfect replication. Those stable cells proliferate exponentially, which are very insensitive to inter-cellular interactions. Duplication of the unstable cells forms a differentiated cell assembly. It makes essentially large degrees of freedom. On the other hand, because of its context-free behavior and exponential growth nature, the latter cell types are to be called cancer cells. It consists in a product of small degrees of freedom. We also report that inter-cellular interaction can suppress the emergence of cancer cell.

Recently, Kaneko and Yomo [4] have studied an assembly of cells with metabolic networks. Based on their simulations, they propose a new theory for cell differentiation from the dynamical systems view point. Our model system compensates for their system in several aspects. First, we are not propose a model for cell development but a model for the origin of genetic systems. How different genetic systems come to evolve to cooperate is our main concerns. Second, our system consists of two objects, machines and tapes. With this notion of duality, we can take a cell replication as tape-rewriting process. A new view of mutation as a rewriting computational process will be proposed here. Third, our system changes the network topology itself. Stable core network is destabilized by the other core networks. Consumption of common chemicals brings about cell differentiation in Kaneko and Yomo's model. In our model, external machines to a cell destabilize its replication to produce diversity of genetic systems.

2   Modeling

In the previous study, we have simulated the evolution of machines and tapes in one cell. We have shown that external noise brings about autocatalytic structures, called core networks. Once these core networks are formed, they are stably replicated even without external noise. In other words, we cannot expect the further evolution of network once a core network appears. The notion of core network includes a hyper-cycle structure proposed by Eigen and Schuster [5, 6, 7] as a special case. If all tapes are replicated locally, a notion of core network coincides with that of hypercycle. In general, tapes in core networks are globally replicated.

In order to study the further evolution of core networks, we introduce a cell assembly in the present paper. That is, machines and tapes are contained in a cell structure. Each cell can have different sets of machines and tapes. Hence its dynamics consists of two parts. One is intra-cellular dynamics which represents the population dynamics of machines and tapes in each cellular structure. The other one is inter-cellular dynamics which represents the global dynamics of cell assembly.

We assume two different levels of replication. One is replication of machines and tapes. The other one is replication of cells, which contain an ensemble of machines and tapes. Hence these replications are not mutually independent. A cell division at the same time means transfer of the ensemble of machines and tapes included in a cell. In below, we first introduce fundamental processes of machine-tape reactions. Then we introduce intra- and inter-cellular dynamics. Finally, we introduce division conditions and definition of cell mutations.

Fundamental Processes

A tape has a bit string of a circular form. A machine consists of 3 different parts, a head, a tail and a transition table. Each head and tail is expressed by a 4 bit string, whose pattern will be compared with binary patterns of tapes. A transition table consists of 4 mappings; $(\sigma^m, \sigma^t) \rightarrow (\sigma'^m, \sigma'^t)$, where σ^m and σ^t represents a current binary state of machine and tape. Tape and machine state change to (σ'^m, σ'^t), respectively depending on a current state of machine and tape.

(1) Interaction of machines and tapes

Machine $\mathbf{M_i}$ reads tape $\mathbf{T_j}$ iff tape $\mathbf{T_j}$ has a same pattern of head $\mathbf{h_i}$ and tail $\mathbf{t_i}$ of a machine $\mathbf{M_i}$ in a different site of the tape. The sites from a first bit of $\mathbf{h_i}$ to that of $\mathbf{t_i}$ is called the reading frame.

Then machine $\mathbf{M_i}$ reads a tape $\mathbf{T_j}$ and rewrites the reading frame according to its own transition table. A half population of machine starts to read a tape with the internal state 1 and the other half does with the state 0. We assume that there exist a sufficient amount of resource so that a pair of machine and tape generates a new tape $\mathbf{T_l}$ and a new machine $\mathbf{M_k}$ translated from the tape many times.

$$\mathrm{M_i + T_j \Rightarrow M_k + T_l + M_i + T_j} \tag{1}$$

(2) Translation of tapes:

Not only bits of a reading frame, but every bit of tape is repeatedly picked up to construct a new machine from a first site of the reading frame. If a length of a tape is not long enough, the same bit is used for coding several different part of a machine. In the present model, we use a fixed length of 7-bit tapes and 16-bit machines. A first 8 bits are mapped onto head and tail parts in order. The next 8 bits are mapped onto a transition table. In order to cover 16 bits by 7 bits, several bits are used twice or three times.

Each tape has a source where an attached machine starts to search for the head and tail pattern. Starting from the site, patterns are searched for in the clockwise direction of a circular tape. When a head pattern is found, a tail pattern starts to be searched in the clockwise direction. The site of source can be updated randomly when the tape is newly generated after its extinction. An identical tape with different source can make different machines by being read by the same machine. Note that every translational invariant tape in a same cell has the same source site.

Intra-cellular Dynamics

We assume a finite capacity N for both tapes and machines. By iterating the following procedures, we simulate the machine/tape reactions:

1. Compute concentration of tapes (f^T) and machines (f^M) by dividing the population number by the capacity size N.

$$f_i^M = \frac{m_i}{N}, f_j^T = \frac{t_j}{N}, \qquad (2)$$

where m_i and t_j are the population of the $i-th$ machine and the $j-th$ tape, respectively.

2. Make a total cN numbers of new machines and tapes from reaction of machines and tapes. Here the coefficient c gives a rate of new machines in a total capacity N. One generation is defined as the period needed to make cN new machines. The rate of reaction f_{ij} is given by,

$$f_{ij} = \frac{f_i^M f_j^T}{\sum_{k,l} f_k^M f_l^T}. \qquad (3)$$

3. Remove d^M % of old machines and d^T % of old tapes.

4. Put the new machines and tapes back in a cell. Hence the population of tape j and machine i of the next generation becomes,

$$t_j' = (1 - d^T)t_j + \sum_{k+i \to j} cf_{ki}N. \qquad (4)$$

$$m_i' = (1 - d^M)m_i + \sum_{k+j \to i} cf_{kj}N, \qquad (5)$$

If no reactions occur, the second terms in the above equations vanish. It should be noted here that each machine has its unique description tape but the inverse is not true. Generally a tape encodes several machines depending on which machine reads the tape.

5. Taking an integer part of the above population, we obtain the actual population of the next generation. Hence the machine or tape whose concentration (f_i^M, f_j^T) is lower than N^{-1} is removed from the system.

Inter-cellular Dynamics

1) Interaction among cells

Only machines can be exchanged between cells. We assume that machines are corresponding to active chemicals, which can go across a cell membrane to interact with tapes in other cells. On the other hand, tapes are inactive chemicals which cannot cross the membrane. Introducing this diffusion processes of machines, time evolution of machine population in the above equation will become,

$$m_i'^a = (1 - d^M)m_i^a(1 - \epsilon) + \sum_{k+j \to i} cf_{kj}N, \qquad (6)$$

$$m_i''^a = m_i'^a + \epsilon \frac{\sum_b m_i'^b m^a}{\sum_c m'^c}, \qquad (7)$$

where $m'^a = \sum_j m_j'^a$ and $m^a = \sum_j m_j^a$. Population dynamics of tapes is same as before (i.e. eq.(4)). It should be remarked that tapes as well as machines have a cell index. In Eq.(6), m_i^a denotes a population of machine type i in a cell a. Combining equations 4),6) and 7), we complete population dynamics $\{m_i^a, t_j^a\} \to \{m_i''^a, t_j''^a\}$ for one generation.

The strength of interactions between cells is given by the parameter ϵ. A large ϵ value gives a large amount of machine flow between cells.

2) Cell division dynamics

We assume that a cell can divide when it possesses an enough amount of machines and tapes. The degree of this fertility of a cell is measured by the number of non-parasitic machines in a cell. If the cell fertility excesses a given division threshold T_D, the cell divides. Once a cell divides, it cannot be divided after G_{nd} generations. We also assume that if a cell fertility goes below the removal threshold T_R, the cell will be removed from a system. Hence the division/removal thresholds and non-replicating periods are main system parameters in the present simulation.

When division occurs, a population of every machine and tape is halved and transfered to descendant cells. Hence a division event always makes two cells with identical network structures.

Active Cell Mutation Rates

Average active mutation rates are computed for each cell. In the present study, no external noise is taken into account. *Mutation* is only caused deterministically. We call it active mutation since it does not replicate a tape but actively rewrites it. A rewritten tape can be taken as a miss-copy of the original tape. The rate of this mutation is measured by the rewriting rate for an interacting pair of machine and tape. If a machine i rewrites a tape j by w bits, a mutation rate of this reaction is given by,

$$\mu_{ij} = \frac{w}{L_{ij}}, \qquad (8)$$

where L_{ij} denotes a length a machine i reads a tape j. Cell mutation rate is given by averaging over the all possible reactions in a cell. Namely, a mutation rate of a cell type a is computed as,

$$\mu^a = \frac{\sum_{(ij)} \mu_{ij} m_i^a t_j^a}{\sum_{(ij)} m_i^a t_j^a}. \qquad (9)$$

We use this mutation rate for characterizing each cell type. Since different cell mutation rate indicates different network topologies or different composition of machines and tapes.

3 Results of Simulation: differentiation vs. replication

As an initial soup, we prepare roughly 20 randomly selected cells. Each cell contains 10 randomly selected machines and a few tapes. A machine without the description tape is unstable and smoothly removed from a cell. Hence a cell which contains machines with no description tapes will die out smoothly. On the other hand, a cell which evolves a core network will be stably sustained in a system.

Here we give a definition of a core network. A core network is an auto-catalytic network, where constituting machines are generating and being generated by the other machines within the auto-catalytic network. Necessary tapes to encode these machines are self-maintained in a core network. Different from a fixed state core, an oscillatory core changes its topology in the course of time. Not only populations of machines and tapes but a network topology itself varies in time. In Fig.1, we draw examples of temporal changes of topologies of core network. It changes from Fig.1-a) to Fig.1-g) and back to the same topology Fig.1-a) after approximately 23 generations in this example. This periodicity is dependent on a core structure.

The following is one example of cell evolution from an initial soup, which contains two cells with oscillatory core states and 8 cells with fixed state cores. Out of 8 fixed state cores, only one core has a non-trivial property, maintaining many machines and tapes. For given control parameters, only an oscillatory core can divide. Fig.2 is a cell phylogeny from a cell number 5 of an oscillatory core state. The other oscillatory state is destabilized to become a fixed state.

When a cell divides, it leaves an identical set of machines and tapes with the identical populations. Hence the duplicated cells show identical oscillations at least for a short period of time.

Same tapes will be created from the duplicated two identical cells. However sources of new tapes which do not present at the division time will be updated randomly. A source is a site from which machine starts to search for its head pattern. Therefore an identical tape with different source can make different machines being read by the same machine.

It seems that an assembly, which is consisted of a unique type of core structure, will not produce diversity of core networks. A cell division event always makes identical core structures. Even an oscillatory core cannot be destabilized by the own internal machines. But it can be perturbed by the external machines from other core networks under the inter-cellular interactions.

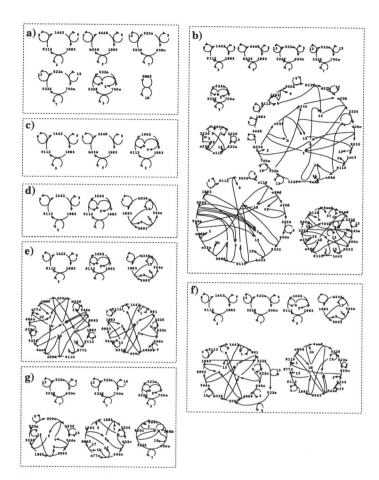

Figure 1: Oscillatory core networks at several generations within a period of time are selected and depicted by drawing their embedded autocatalytic loops separately. Within a loop, each machine and tape is denoted by its hexadecimal number converted from its binary representation. A symbol 9112 $\rightarrow^9$ 1443 indicates that a machine 9112 reads a tape 9 to generate a tape 9 and a machine 1443. All machines in core networks are mutually catalyzing. The topology of this core network changes from a) to g) and back to a) during each period of time.

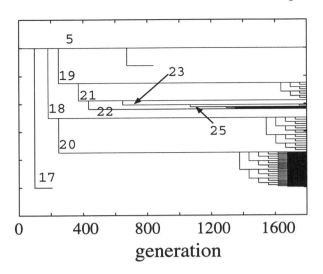

Figure 2: A cell phylogeny from an initial cell of an oscillatory core. The horizontal axis shows the generations. The lines connect cells with their direct descendants by a cell division. Division and removal thresholds T_D and T_R are given by 67 and 1, respectively with a non-dividing time G_{nd} by 50.

Tapes which do not constitute a core network are called peripheral tapes. A core topology is insensitive to how peripheral tapes code machines. But such peripheral tapes can become a big disturbance to a core structure when being read by external machines. Peripheral tapes often update their source since they are temporally extinguished and regenerated by definition.

Hence whether a cell can divide to leave identical cell types or not depends on how peripheral tapes are utilized by the external machines. In Fig.2, we see that an example of cell phylogeny in the course of time. Three different cell types, 18, 19 and 20, appear at the generation around 300. Until the generation around 1500, only the descendants of cell 21 can make the descendants. It is remarkable that this cell 21 fails to make exact copies. It differentiates, and leaving a variety of core networks. During this stage, other cells do not show any divisions.

After 1500 generations, all other cells begin to duplicate. As is seen in Fig.2, those divisions besides cell 21 look like bifurcations. That is, daughter cells always duplicate when their parents duplicates. It seems that such bifurcation can only increase identical core networks, and showing no differentiation. This is more clearly observed in Fig.3, where cell mutation rates at several generations are overlaid for each cell. We see that the descendants of cell 21 are becoming alike from each other. On the other hand, the descendants from other cells are exactly identical. Henceforth we call those cells which show complete replication cancer cells.

In Fig.4, we show the temporal evolution of cell mutation rates for the several descendants of cell 21. At the generation marked by 1, cells 76 and 56 begin to differentiate. At the next generation marked by 2, the new differentiation occurs. As the result, we have more than

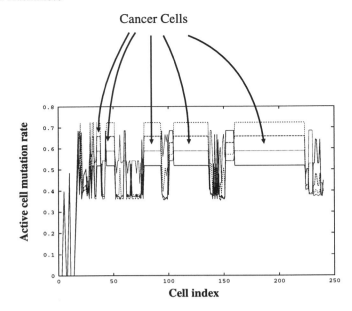

Figure 3: Active cell mutation rates at successive generations are overlaid against each cell index. The same level of cell mutation rates implies the same core network. Those corresponding to cancer cells are indicated in the figure. Division and removal thresholds T_D and T_R are given by 67 and 1, respectively with a non-dividing time G_{nd} by 50.

seven different cell types at the end 1800 generations for this cell lines. We note that different cell descendants sometimes can have the same cell mutation rates. In Fig.4, a cell type B appears at the different portion of the cell line of cell 56. Both cells 56 and 58 are descendants of cell 21, but their evolutionary pathway become quite different. It seems that the initial instability in cell 21 is inherited to the cell 58's cell line.

After 1500 generations, the descendants from all the other cells besides cell 21 will dominate the assembly. At the same time, the average cell mutation rates is elevated. Distribution of cell mutation rates averaged over generations 1800-1850 are depicted in Fig.5. We see that cells with rather high mutation rates are dominating the assembly. Distributed mutation rates(0.4 $\sim$ 0.54) with low population number are the descendants of cell 21. We will look into these mechanisms by the experiments in the following section.

4 Turning off cellular interactions

At one generation, some cells begin to replicate unlimitedly. But it doesn't seem that such cells have particular topologies. To reveal the mechanism of the unlimited growth of cells, we turn off the inter-cellular interactions at certain generations (Fig.6). Shortly after turning off the interaction, most cells start to replicate exponentially. This exponential growth is as same as what we observe in Fig.3 where inter-cellular interactions are allowed.

This experiment tells us that inter-cellular interaction

a)

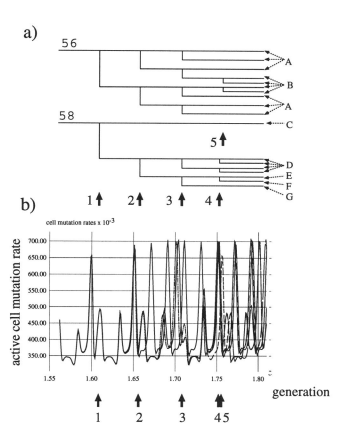

b)

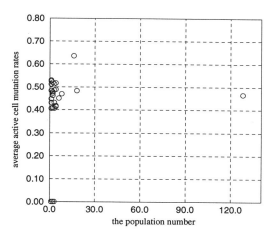

Figure 5: Active cell mutation rates, which are averaged over 50 generations, are plotted against the number of the cells having the mutation rates. Active mutation rates with a large cell number imply cancer cells. Those with the low cell number are corresponding to those of differentiable cell types. Division and removal thresholds T_D and T_R are given by 67 and 1, respectively with a non-dividing time G_{nd} by 50.

Figure 4: a) A partial phylogeny of descendants of cell 21. As in Fig.2, cells are connected with their direct descendants by lines. Alphabets attached to each end of cell lines are corresponding to groups having same active mutation rates. 7 different cell types (marked by A to G) can be specified with respect to their active mutation rates. b) Temporal evolution of active cell mutation rates. Those of descendants in the above phylogeny a) are overlaid. Marks (1,2,3,4 and 5) indicate division events. Division and removal thresholds T_D and T_R are given by 67 and 1, respectively with a non-dividing time G_{nd} by 50.

suppresses cells to become cancer cells. In other words, inter-cellular interactions keep cells in unstable states to prevent from exact replication.

Oscillating core networks can only become unstable cell states. It is known from our previous studies [8] that oscillating core structures have roughly 4 types. These are,1)periodic oscillation with its machine number ranging from 50 to 110; 2)Same number of machines with quasi-periodic oscillations; 3) Amplitude of machine number is bounded between 80 and 110 with quasi-periodic oscillations; 4) Quasi periodic oscillation with a small amplitude, where the average machine number is roughly 100.

If the core type 3) appears at a certain stage, it definitely shows strong replication. But we note that the core networks in both cancer and differentiable cells have rather common structures, which belong to the core type 2). Hence stability of core networks may be strongly dependent on their context, i.e. what kinds of cell structures exist in a cell assembly.

What kinds of core network can coexist with other core networks is more important for generating diversity in a cell assembly than an individual structures. The followings are the phenomenological evidences for the coevolution of different cell structures:

1) If there exists only one unique core structure from the beginning, the divisions will turn out to be perfect replication with exponential growth of the population number.

2) If there exist more than two different cells, division of cells can become unstable. A fixed state core cannot differentiate by itself. But cells with oscillatory core networks will be differentiated under the existence of fixed

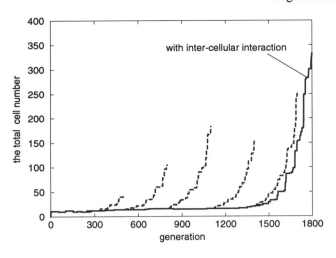

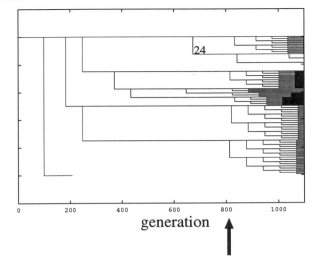

Figure 6: Inter-cellular interaction is turned off at several different generations (indicated by broken lines). Shortly after turning off the interaction, we see that a total number of cells exponentially grows. The right-most curve represents a growth curve of a system with inter-cellular interaction.

Figure 7: A cell phylogeny obtained by the interaction turning-off experiments. The interaction is turned off at generation 800, which is indicated by an arrow. We note that a cell 24 which has died at time step around 800 in Fig.2 will survive to replicate at later stages. Also a first parental cell 5 will begin to replicate.

state cores.

3) If we allow cells to interact but not to divide, oscillating cores are gradually extinguishing. Hence an assembly will be consisted of fixed state cores only.

4) Inter-cellular interactions can inhibit the emergence of cancer cells.

5) Morphology of phylogeny certainly changes after turning off the inter-cellular interactions. As is seen in Fig.7, most cells become cancer cells after the turning off event. Even a removed cell(i.e. cell 24) in Fig.2 can survive to divide. On the other hand, not every cell becomes a cancer cell with inter-cellular interactions. The environment for cancer cells are equivalent to those without inter-cellular interactions. However, the environment for the other cells are inflow machines from the cancer cells. Emergence of cancer cells accelerates the division of unstable cells without suppressing the differentiation.

5 Discussions

We have studied evolution of machine-tape networks in cell assembly.

Under the present conditions, cellular systems with only oscillatory core networks can divide. We found that there exist two different cell types. One cell type divides to leave different cell structures as its descendants. The others do perfect replications.

Whether a cell can perform perfect replication or not depends on the underlying dynamics of a core network. If a cell has a stable core network, it is not disturbed by the external machines from other cells. But if a core network is unstable, external machines will give a big disturbance to the core network. However such stabil-

ity cannot be determined independently. It is strongly dependent on a structure of a cell assembly, which core networks are constituting of. Inter-cellular interactions prevents cells from becoming cancer cells. Namely, *who reads tapes* determines the stability of core networks. A small difference caused in the process of machines reading tapes will be enhanced to change the whole genetic code. Such instability may be related to the observation of description will be related to the "description instability" introduced by Tsuda [9]. BZ chaos absorbs external noise to generate stable periodicity. On the other hand, logistic chaos enhances external noise. If we simply take external noise as observation, stability of chaotic dynamics is dependent on how it is observed. Instability in networks with its description tapes may belong to this type of description instability.

It is interesting to note that a stable cell can replicate perfectly but an unstable cell cannot. An assembly with unstable core networks holds much diversity than ones with stable core networks. Such diversity is well reflected in the distribution of active cell mutation rates. Different active mutation rate implies the underlying different core networks. Unstable cells are difficult to transfer its core structure to its descendants. As the result, unstable cells show cell differentiation but stable cells only show exact replication. The increasing population of stable cells gives positive feedbacks on the whole assembly, leading to exponentially growth of the cancer cells. At the same time, the differentiation of unstable cells are accelerated.

It is further noted that unstable cell community forms a system with an essentially large degrees of freedom.

On the other hand, a stable cell community is composed of a direct product of a small degrees of freedom.

This picture reminds us of "homeochaos" [10, 11], which is proposed as the possible mechanism for sustaining diversity in a large host-parasite network. In the model, chaotic instability is shared by almost all species by sustaining a high mutation rate, leading to weak high-dimensional chaos, termed "homeochaos". The cellular ensemble of network supports this view in the different context in the present model.

Fontana's Alchemy [12, 13] shares common features with our system. His level 0 system is corresponding to our simple fixed state core and a level 1 to stable core structures. Instead of meta-inhibition of self-copying in Fontana's model, we have introduced external noise to bring about core structures. A level 2 corresponds to the present model, inter-cellular interacting system. What he calls "glue" is to corresponding to machine exchanges between different core networks. Inter-cellular interactions are producing such glue machines. We found that machines produced in one cellular system is just for a self-maintenance [2, 3]. On the other hand, machines produced in a cell assembly are for cell communication.

Are there any biological implications? I propose the following points for the real experiments.

1) To study more about the relationship between symbiosis and genetic systems. For example, diversification in genetic systems of mitchondoria are strongly dependent on whether mitchondoria is in animal cells or in green plant cells [14]. We expect that this can be a good example of coevolutionary aspect of different core networks.

2) To study how mutation rate in one cell effects mutation rates in other cells.

3) To study the suppression of cancer cells in a cell assembly due to its inter-cellular interactions.

4) To study the context dependency of protein usages. One is for the cell replication and the other is for the cell communication. Multi-cellularity is an evolutionary event that generates from genetic systems for self-replication to those for cell communication. Such context dependent nature of chemicals are also reported experimentally [15].

Acknowledgment

The authors are grateful to K.Kaneko, T.Yomo, Y.P. Gunji and Y.Takagi for stimulating discussions. This work is supported by Grant-in-Aids (No.07243102) for Scientific Research on priority are "System Theory of Function Emergence" from the Japanese Ministry of Education, Science and Culture.

References

[1] J.von Neumann, *Theory of Self-reproducing Automata* (ed. A.W.Burks, Univ. Illinois Press, 1966)

[2] T.Ikegami and T.Hashimoto, *Coevolution of machines and tapes* in "Advances in Artificial Life" (eds. F. Moran et al. 1995, Springer).

[3] T.Ikegami and T.Hashimoto, *Active Mutation in Self-reproducing Networks of Machines and Tapes* (to appear Artificial Life journal).

[4] K.Kaneko and T.Yomo, "Isologous Diversification: A theory of Cell Differentiation" (preprint, 1995).

[5] M.Eigen and P.Schuster, *Hypercycle* (Springer-Verlag, 1979).

[6] M. Eigen, Sci. Am. (1993) July, 32.

[7] P.Schuster, Physica 22D(1986) 100.

[8] T.Hashimoto, *Evolution of Code and Communication in Dynamical Networks* (PhD. thesis, University of Tokyo, 1996).

[9] I.Tsuda, *Chaos-teki Noukan*(in Japanese, Science-sousho, 1990).

[10] K.Kaneko and T.Ikegami, Physica D 56 (1992) 406:;

[11] T.Ikegami and K.Kaneko, CHAOS 2 (1992) 397.

[12] W.Fontana and L.W.Buss, Proc.Natl.Acad.Sci. USA 91 (1994) 757-761.

[13] W.Fontana and L.W.Buss, Bull. Math. Biol. 56(1994) 1-64.

[14] S.Osawa, Micro.Biol.Rev. 56(1992)229-264.

[15] A.Vallesi et al. Nature 376(1995) 552–524.

Igniting the cycle of creation – an approach to create metabolism with Tile Automaton

Tomoyuki Yamamoto and Kunihiko Kaneko

Department of Pure and Applied Sciences,
University of Tokyo, 3-8-1 Komaba, Tokyo 153, Japan
E-mail: yamamoto@complex.c.u-tokyo.ac.jp, kaneko@complex.c.u-tokyo.ac.jp

Abstract

Tile Automaton is designed as a model for the origins of life, emerging from complex metabolic pathways of chemical reactions. Like computer game "Tetris", tiles with various shapes stand for molecules. They move on a plane (for a spatial version) or are stored in a tank (for a tank version). Their shapes are changed by the reactions induced by the collisions. The rules of reaction are deterministic and dependent on their mutual shape-to-shape relations.

We have obtained self-organization of ever-creating sets from a small number of simple-shaped tiles in the spatial version and temporally differentiated pathways of reaction in the tank version. These evolutions are realized through many-body reactions, spatial relationship and the interference of contexts which is believed to be essential for emergence of life-like phenomena.

1 introduction

It is interesting to ask "Is life a machine?". In textbooks on molecular biology, proteins are described as *machine*. DNA is regarded as *a plan of life*. Studies of current cell biology have been focused on revealing mechanisms of molecular machines. Still, it is impossible to describe life as a popular image of "machine". Chemical dynamics in a cell involves interference of a variety of processes, and is much more complex than any human-made machine. The plan of the design is not given initially, nor is it separated from a machine itself.

The aim of Artificial Life(ALife) does not lie in describing and collecting fragments of life, but in constructing another possible life. Since the life is not a static *state* but a dynamic *process*, it is understood only through its construction. In this respect, the question "is life a machine?" may not be productive. Rather, we should start from "which sort of *machine* the life is?".

Which feature distinguishes a natural machine of life from a human-made one? The architectures of artificial systems are based on combinations of simple tasks. Each element is designed to have a single function, and to avoid interference with others. Thus a human-made machine is understood by counting its elements and corresponding functions, and then by combining them. The quality of complexity in a biological system is different. The complexity there, we believe, can not be understood by such combinations. The interference among processes is essential feature for living systems. Even if all molecules within a cell are listed up, we still cannot understand or reconstruct a cell as a living system.

In an artificial system, the function of each element is rigidly defined, while a biological process consists of "indefinite functions". From chemical reactions within a cell to the mechanics of bodies, all processes of life are dynamic, parallel, and mutually dependent. Here we list up some of the salient features in the processes.

- real-time processes
  There is no strict "master clock". Any element may have to receive an input or respond to it before its current process is done. In contrast, a digital computer must keep its temporal order so that CPUs are required to wait for a memory access, or communication with co-processors, and internal executions. Though the computer is an extreme case, all human-designed machines seem to have built-in sequential programs.

- many-body interactions
  We are often tended to disregard many-body interactions, since they are too difficult to analyze due to the combinatorial explosions of such interactions. To avoid the difficulty, we often consider only one-to-one interactions. However, such approximation may lead to serious errors, since a huge number of many-body reactions are involved, especially in biochemistry. A typical example is given by enzyme reactions which include at least three-body reactions, and also depend on the environment. In addition, enzymes, proteins, or ribosomes are large "machines" which consist of many elements by themselves.

- interference between modules
  Function of an element may be altered, depending on the contexts due to the interaction or other mutual relationships. Even if a function of a unit is clarified in a certain context, there is no reason that it is the only function. A function of a unit or a module is given only as an approximation at a given context. Elements consisting of a module themselves can change in time.

Moreover, complex systems such as cells have several contexts. For example, metabolic process, DNA replication, and other synthesizing processes might form an individual level, but indeed they interact with each other. There are interferences among these processes.

Taking into account of the above features, Tile Automaton[1] is introduced. The grand goal here is to build a life with a bottom-up approach from the level of chemical reactions. In the present model, we start from movable tiles with various shapes and changes of shapes by reaction process, while other properties such as mass, velocity, or excitation of molecules are included as implicit properties, to include real-worldness into the model. The reaction rule is explicitly given by the shapes of the tiles while no internal state is considered. In this respect, our model differs other models based on a finite state automaton (e.g. [2]). Ongoing reactions, however, turn to depend implicitly on the configuration, velocity, excitations of molecules. The reaction processes are thus dependent on the environment – or "context". If some function is assigned to reaction process forming some shapes, the function is indefinite. On the other hand, the change in reaction processes (or functions) can lead to a different context. Through the chain of these processes, there appears the interference between functions and contexts. We call this process "mixing of contexts"[1], which we propose as the essence of machanism of life.

2 model

Each tile has a shape and mass. A tile consists of a set of connected cells, which occupy a unit square. We apply the following rules of reaction and motion for these tiles, a basic one and two subsidiary ones.

- the basic rule (the inversion rule):
  When tiles collide with others (where overlapping is not allowed), the states of the nearest neighbor cells to the colliding side are inverted. This area is called *reacting zone* (see fig.1). Momentum of eliminated cells is equally divided to created cells, so that the momentum is preserved. Note that the number of cells is not preserved. When tiles collide with two or more sides, reacting zones for each colliding sides are joined. See also fig.3

- the joint rule:
  The new cells created by the above rule may contact with others which were disjoint before the reaction. In such case, we connect them to form a tile. See fig.2.

- the rate rule:
  This rule decides whether we apply the above basic reaction rule or not. We assume that the above reaction rules are applied only when the ratio of cells occupying the reacting zone falls within a predefined interval of values(see fig.3). The upper limit is the most significant parameter. In the world of Tile, the rule of reaction is only the inversion. Thus cells' proportion to reacting zone corresponds to the growth rate of cells. If the upper limit is smaller than 0.5, the cell number

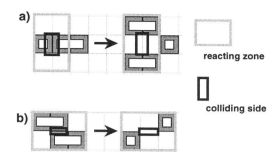

Figure 1: Basic rule. Cells within a reacting zone are inverted. The number of cells is not preserved.

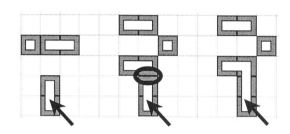

Figure 2: Joint rule. An arrow points another tile which does not join the reaction(left). If it collides with a newly created tile by the reaction(center), these tiles are united together(right)

does not decrease. Here, we usually set the upper limit to $0.55 \sim 0.6$, where typical interesting behaviors are observed, since cells grow in a non-trivial manner.

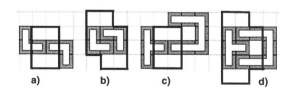

Figure 3: Several possible cases of two-tile collisions. According to their relative positions, the colliding side and the reacting zone vary. Rates of cells to the reacting zone are:
a: 2/6, b:6/10, c:2/6, d:8/13.

The inversion rule does not allow simple reproduction. We should note that shapes of tiles are strongly mixed by these rules.

We have studied two versions of Tile, with the above features in common. In the first one, i.e., the "spatial version", Tiles move around with their own velocity on a 2-dimensional plane. In the second one , i.e., in the "tank version", all tiles are stored in a reaction tank and their velocities are ignored. Instead excitation by collisions of tiles, they are randomly selected to set as a reacting pair as will be discussed.

3 evolution on the plane

3.1 model

In the spatial version, tiles move by Newtonian mechanics – as in molecular dynamics-like simulations. Each cell has real valued velocity and position. Tiles move as a unit with the mean velocity of constituting cells. Coordinates are rounded to an integer when the tiles collide.

All tiles move parallelly unless their destination is already occupied by others. When two tiles collide without reaction, they reflect each other with the elastic collision. Thus the momentum and energy are preserved by this non-reactive collision.

To prevent tiles from slowing down, we have introduced a dumper between tiles – a linear spring whose natural length and maximum length are both 2.0. Since dumpers are rearranged by the reaction with removal or creation of cells, the reaction is either endothermic or exothermic. The tiles are accelerated by the exothermic reactions.

For technical reasons, friction is applied for tiles whose velocity exceeds the speed limit. The time step is adopted so as not to make crossing of tiles. We have applied the condition $dt = 0.5/v_{max}$ (here, v_{max} is the maximum velocity of tiles).

3.2 results – overview

We usually apply open boundary conditions for the world. Then the world will get empty unless tiles produce new tiles continuously. While we allow for the production of new cells at the basic rule, we have made no explicit rule for continuous production. Figs.4 and 5 show some examples of the evolutions (see the next section).

Schematically, the evolution on spatial model is described as follows.

- At the initial condition, we usually start from a small number of simple-shaped tiles (random initial condition on center area of the world). Their velocities are also chosen randomly. See fig.4a.

- After a short period of time, collisions of tiles lead to clusters. Reactions at each cluster are strongly correlated, and large tiles are formed trough the joint rule and multi-body reaction. See fig.4b.

- Some of clusters can grow through production of new tiles. We call these clusters "active cores". Since there are no attractive forces between tiles, they are emitted out from the cluster due to reflection. Thus all tiles can drop out unless they produce new tiles continuously from the open boundary. In fig.5c, large tiles are isolated and they do not make reaction anymore. All clusters have a risk of death when their number of tiles is decreased.

- The clusters attain some stability with growth. Even if they make distraction or division, they can avoid to die by making collisions with tiles emitted out from other clusters. Inactive clusters are activated again through the interference between them. Though a single cluster as an active core of creation is often fragile, the complex of clusters is stable and keeps creation for ever. We call such dynamical structure(or a process) a "factory" (See 4 d, e and f) Of course, some of the worlds may get empty, which we call death state.

- Once tiles form a factory, it gets "fat" with tiles through continuous creation. Since the creation occurs only at the outside of the factory, they approach a fixed state. See fig.4 e and f,

The emergence of a factory is the most remarkable result of this model. A factory is a self-organized dynamical structure which keeps creation of tiles in a non-trivial manner. Though its process is complicated and is not cyclic as that of machines in the usual sense, a kind of "indefinite" function is realized within a factory.

A factory produces diverse tiles through flexible mechanisms for the production. Since there is no difference between products and components of this "machine", a factory can make reconstruction by itself. Factories are stable against external perturbations. After the perturbations, their productivities are restored, though the exactly same structure is not restored.

On the other hand, the problem of a "fat factory" is also due to the flexibility in functions of a factory. A fat factory is induced by "traffic jams" around the factory. Since the crossing of tiles is prohibited, any hooking between tiles can cause deadlocking.

3.3 dynamical complexity and factory

As mentioned before, all tiles move parallelly with real-valued velocities. Their motion looks like chaotic, since the collision among tiles can show strong chaos as in the billiard system. In our model, the number of tiles and cells vary with time. Thus it is impossible to apply the notion of chaos in its regular sense. Still we can clearly see the amplification of small differences in initial conditions.

Moreover, there exists complexity also in the shape-to-shape relation by the reaction. The rules of reaction are deterministic and have strong dependency to the mutual position of tiles. Though simple replication is not allowed, our system can increase diversity and make a complex process of production through motion as a factory.

In figs.4 and 5, temporal evolutions starting from slightly different initial conditions are shown. Two initial conditions differ only in the velocity of one tile. The velocity of a tile shown by a gray arrow (see fig.5) is modified its velocity from $v_y = -0.1794$ to -0.18. Even this small difference leads to completely different results.

At time 100, both worlds have many tiles with variation. The world success in forming a factory between time 200 and 600. Some of large tiles remain and they form a boundary of the factory. For example, in fig.4, the large tile at the left side remains up to time 2000. Within it active tiles are produced at time 600. This base

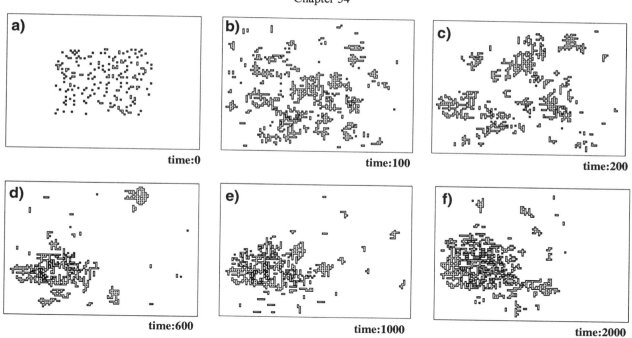

Figure 4: The evolution of spatial version. Started with 204 cells, 160 tiles. The shapes of tiles are simple at the initial condition. System size is 96x72. Boundary is open.

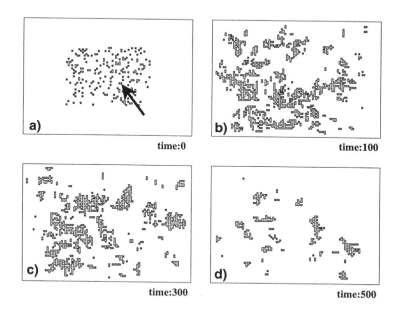

Figure 5: A tiny difference at the initial condition leads to completely different result. In this case, velocity of a tile (pointed by the arrow) is slightly modified (v_y is changed from -0.1794 to -0.18) from the initial condition of fig.4.

tile is a core of a factory. It hooks and keeps small tiles using its rugged shape which plays the role of "body" of a factory, since such shape prevents reaction by the rate rule and brings about stability. While no reaction is made within the "body" tile, small tiles can move at the inside and make reaction when they reach outside of the body.

On the other hand, in fig.5, tiles fail to form a factory. Though there are many large tiles at time 100(fig.5b) and 300(fig.5c), no tile is successful to form form an active cluster with its "body".

To see how chaos contributes to Tile's complexity, we have discretized the velocity to eliminate chaos in our system. The velocity of a tile is rounded with a defined resolution. As the resolution is decreased and fewer discrete states are allowed, the formation of a factory is more difficult. Even if the variety of shapes is relatively rich, a sufficient number of new tiles is not created. When the resolution is larger than $\Delta v = 0.2$, no factory is observed. In the world of finite states, the variety is limited, since the motion is periodic. For lasting growth of tiles, complex motion is required.

4 evolution within a tank

4.1 model

For the tank version, the positional relation among tiles is disregarded. time step, a pair of tiles is randomly selected from the "Tank" – list of all existing tiles. The configuration of tiles for collision is randomly chosen to form complexes. Instead of spatial information, temporal aspects of the reaction process are taken into account here. We introduce intermediate states. According to whether a complex makes reaction or not, it waits for a certain period of time before reaction or undoing of the non-reacting complex. Tr and Tw are waiting periods of reacting and non-reacting complex, respectively.

During the waiting periods, each complex can be chosen for reaction, in the same manner as a single tile. Then, regarding a waiting complex as one unit, new configuration is arranged. Thus a three-body reaction is realized. Multi-body reactions are also taken place, consequently.

Through three or more-body reactions, the pathways of reaction are strongly extended and the diversity of tiles are increased. Since a non-reacting two-body complex may turn into reactive when it meets another complex, many-body reaction is thought to play the role of an enzyme implicitly. One of the functions of many-body reactions is the extension of the possible configuration space. We have seen expansion of diversity, as the probability of many-body reaction increases.

To keep constant the collision rate per a tile, we set the time step as $dt = 1/N_{tile}$, with the total number of tiles N_{tile}. We have n_r collision(selection of reacting tiles) at each time step. The parameter n_r determines the population density of waiting complexes at intermediate states, and gives the ratio of many-body reaction.

In the present paper, we have applied further boundary conditions for the tank, partly to suppress the trivial reproductions of tiny tiles with short pathways. Population limit and density limit are also applied. Population is rescaled only when the total population exceeds the twice the population limit. Small tiles are assumed to be supplied, and at least one of each tiles with the size$\leq$ 5 is preserved, as long as once they appear. since even if it is possible to form nontrivial autocatalytic network such as Hypercycle[3], it requires continuous inflow to complete first recursion. Therefore we cannot expect complex pathways of reaction without amplification.

4.2 results

The most remarkable result in this model is the growth of "unit tiles" and "joint growth". Each unit tile consists of more than 10 cells, and large, joint-grown tiles are made by unification of unit tiles. We have shown a snapshot of tank in fig.6. We can see diverse tiles and several groups of tiles which have similar parts in common. As mentioned before, we keep at least one of each tile less than 5 cells. For larger tiles, same characteristic tiles appear as the tiles grow. In fig.8, examples of unit tiles and joint-grown tiles are shown. While edges of units are modified by the reaction, they keep common shapes at a "core" part, as is discussed below(fig.8a). They can join with other units or tiles while the cores of units remain(fig.8b). Their shapes are modified through reactions to form a family(fig.8c). Joint growth is taken place when units make reaction as a function of them(fig.8d).

In most cases, each unit is classified into two parts – a "core" and "arms". We call a densely packed region as a core. Cores are difficult to make reaction by the rate rule and also hard to collapse due to its density. Arms are thin and curved parts of a unit connecting to a core. We should note that their stability is not enough to survive for a long time. Arms can be cut by attacks of small tiles, and cores without arms are no more stable. Since unit tiles disappear in short time even if we cut off the supply of small tiles, they are not independent of the context formed by small tiles.

The joint growth can be regarded as an emergent context. Since the growth through connection of units is faster than decomposition due to the reaction with small tiles, the time scale of joint-grown tiles is separated from that of small tiles. Though joint-grown tiles are sustained by supply of unit tiles, joint growth is observed as long as unit tiles exist even if the supply of small tiles is cut off.

The existence of units is shown in the histograms of sizes of tiles (see fig.7). There are clear gaps on the distribution. In our rough estimation, the size of each unit is from 10 to 20, while size of each arm is 5 to 10. Then, the size of the largest unit tile(a unit with extra arms) ranges from 25 to 30. Tiles which are larger than 30 have multiple units. When joint growth proceeds mainly by simple combination of the units, we can expect a gap of population around 30. Thus the obtained distribution suggests the growth of tiles by unification of unit tiles.

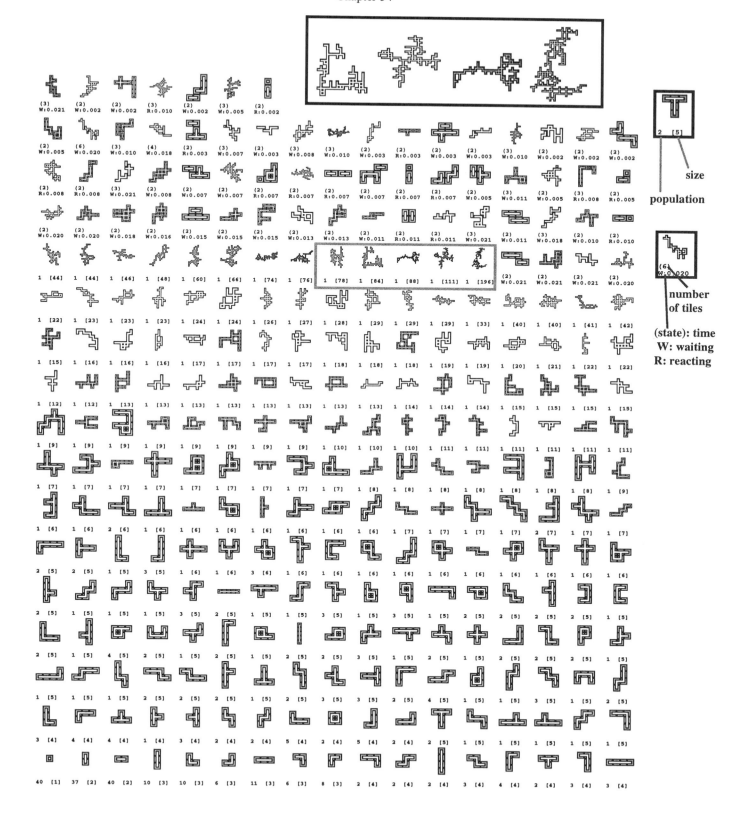

Figure 6: The snapshot of a tank at time 17.0, obtained starting from 103 cells(66 tiles). Reacting time(T_r) is 0.01, waiting time(T_w) is 0.02. 10 reaction pairs are chosen at a time step. The four largest tiles are also shown in a frame.

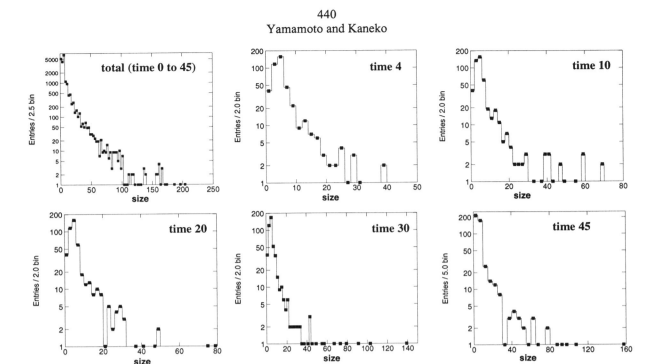

Figure 7: The histograms of mass of tiles obtained from the same initial condition as fig.6. Semi-log plot. Note that there are clear gaps in sizes on each snapshot.

5   concluding remarks

5.1   the mixing of contexts

As mentioned, chaos is essential for the existence of a factory in the spatial model. Though chaos is indeed one of the sources of the complexity[4], it should be emphasized that the formation of a factory is not due to chaos alone. We think that the path of evolution is generated within the interference between two contexts – the motion and the shape – by the reaction.

On the context of motion, chaos breaks the periodicities and enhances any small difference as the time evolution, in contrast with CA models(e.g.[5]), which cannot get ride of periodic motion. The context of shape is believed to utilize the differences which come from chaotic motion as information. Since the rules of reaction are strongly sensitive to mutual positions of tiles, the difference is enhanced here again, in a different context. Then, tiles as moving objects are rearranged and induce a new context of motion. Their boundary conditions for motion are also reconstructed with the change of shapes. Thus there is a feedback loop between two contexts, and the reaction plays the role of interface.

The structure within each context is not static but dynamic and parallel. There is neither a sender nor a receiver of information as a fixed object. The feedback loop is organized by itself through the mixing of contexts. Here we would like to emphasize that the "mixing of contexts" is one of the most important concept in a evolutionary system.

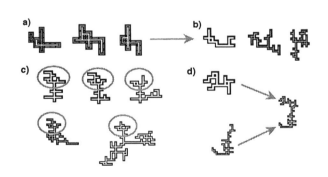

Figure 8: Shown are variations of units, families, and tiles with multiple-unit. See text.

5.2 systems with multiple time scales

Though we cannot describe the complete pathways of reaction, it is possible to evaluate the length of the network according to the size of tiles. For small tiles whose sizes are less than three, there are many short loops which we call "trivial loops". Since trivial pathways are short among all loops, their time scale is the shortest.

If a tile is decomposed by the reaction, it can be decomposed continuously into tiny tiles since the decomposition rate is faster than the growth rate in general. Therefore, all tiles can be broken into tiny tiles, which are regarded as relaxation process. On the other hand, the pathways of joint growth proceed faster than trivial loops. However, joint growth cannot be realized by small tiles. Since the shapes which can be used as a connector are limited and multiple connectors are required for continuous growth, there is a lower limit(about 20) of the sizes of units.

In addition, the joint growth is not often taken place, because two units have to make reaction only with limited configuration. Otherwise, their connectors may be broken by the reactions from some other directions, or with other tiles that cannot be connected. On the other hand, since larger tiles have longer relaxation time, they can restore their connectors through reactions. Therefore, the joint growth has stability against the decomposition into trivial loops.

Though we have not found "mechanical" functions of the joint growth tiles, the diversification of time scale as a function is significant when one think the biological systems(e.g.[6]). In a system with the differentiated time scales, the semantics of a object can be differ according to its current context and its function can be indefinite. Then, through the above processes, such system can modify its semantics by itself. Here, we have observed a joint growth as an emergent function from the difference of relaxation time. Though the existence of connector is implicitly written in the rules of reaction, the emergence of joint growth is non-trivial since there can be many other functions hidden in the description of the model. Although it is not explicitly described, one may think that a kind of information is created by joint growth, through the interface between temporally differentiated pathways.

In other related works of metabolic systems, such as Algorithmic Chemistry[7] or Tape-Machine Network[8], are not obtained temporally differentiated pathways of reaction while they are topologically complex. The reason is thought that they are based on monolithic contexts, without implicit feature, like a shape or a size. A real metabolic system has reproduction pathways of multiple time-scales with a hierarchal structure; energy is supplied into slow cycles like the protein synthesis from fast cycles such as the glyoxylate cycle. Thus resources of the slow context of molecular machines are supplied from the fast context of energy source.

5.3 conclusion

Through this study, we have found the self-organization of ever-creating sets on the spatial model. In the tank model the diversity of unit tiles is developed, which provide the joint growth as emergent feature. Both models have common essential rules of reaction. The unification of these two features will be required as a future problem. Self-reproducing factory is essential for the construction of the life, while the joint-grown tiles work as the functional proteins or membranes.

We have also seen the indefinite function through the mixing of contexts, due to the process of a factory. However, we have not succeeded in controlling the factory as a molecular machine. For the further study, the interface between a factory and environment is necessary, that is the emergent process to control the production, to create ordered tiles which reproduce by themselves.

acknowledgment

The authors would like to thank Drs. T. Yomo, P. Hogeweg, S. Sasa and Mr. C. Furusawa for discussions. This work is partially supported by Grant-in-Aids (No. 05836006, 06302085 and 06-4028) for Scientific Research from the Ministry of Education, Science and Culture of Japan. One of authors (TY) is supported by research fellowship from Japan Society for Promotion of Science.

References

[1] Tomoyuki Yamamoto and Kunihiko Kaneko. Tile automaton for evolution of metabolism. In F. Morán et. al., editor, *Advences in Artificial Life (proceedings of ECAL'95*, page 188. Springer, 1995.

[2] N. S. Goel and R. L. Thompson. Movable finite automata(MFA): A new tool for computer modeling of living systems. In C. G. Langton et. al, editor, *Artificial Life*, pages 317–340. Addison-Wesley, 1988.

[3] M. Eigen and P. Schuster. *The Hypercycle: A Principle of Natural Self-Organization*. Springer-Verlag, Berlin, 1979.

[4] Kunihiko Kaneko. Chaos as a source of complexity and diversity in evolution. *Artificial Life*, 1(1/2):163–177, 1994.

[5] E. Berlekamp, J.H. Conway, and R. Guy. *Winning Ways for Your Mathematical Plays*. Academic Press, New York, 1982.

[6] J. Vd Laan and P. Hogeweg. Predator-prey coevolution: interactions across different time scales. *Proc. R. Soc. London B*, 259:35–42, 1995.

[7] W. Fontana and L. W. Buss. "The Arrival of the Fittest": Toward a theory of biological organization. *Bull. Math. Biol.*, 56:1–64, 1994.

[8] Takashi Ikegami and Takashi Hashimoto. Coevolution of machines and tapes. In F. Morán et. al., editor, *Advences in Artificial Life (proceedings of ECAL'95*, page 234. Springer, 1995.

Evolutionary Theory & Dynamics

Manifestation of Neutral Genes in Evolving Robot Navigation

Tsutomu Hoshino and **Masahiro Tsuchida**
Institute of Engineering Mechanics, University of Tsukuba
1-1-1 Tennoudai, Tsukuba-shi, Ibaraki-ken, 305, Japan
e-mail: hoshino@esys.tsukuba.ac.jp, tsuchida@darwin.esys.tsukuba.ac.jp

Abstract

Genes are incorporated in a graph-represented chromosome, and decoded into the neural-network controller of a sensori-motor behavior model, which is to be evolved and tested in a memory-less robot navigation problem. Neutral genes in this research are defined as those genes ineffective to the phenotypic fitness. What we really observed in the simulation are: (1) Neutral mutation is accumulated in the chromosome with a great genotypic diversity in the undecoded genes as well as in those genes decoded in the unconnected links in the neural network. (2) Phenotypic diversity, on the other hand, is diminished by the selective pressure in the environments before the major jumps in fitness. (3) A crucial mutation on the regulator gene triggers the manifestation of genotypic diversity, making crucial genes decoded into the functional neurons. (4) The functional neurons contribute to the big jumps in the fitness. (5) Evolution incorporated with neutral genes is characterized by bigger fitness jumps than the evolution without the neutral genes, which, on the other hand, merits a gradual and reliable increase of fitness, being relatively insensitive to the random seeds.

This evolutionary simulation demonstrates an example which may support a hypothesis that neutral mutation in the regulator genes and other manifestation mechanisms involved in the decoding process caused the big jumps in fitness often noticed in natural biological evolution with punctuated equilibria.

1 Introduction

Neutral mutations and their roles in molecular evolution were first discussed in the theory of neutral evolution proposed by Kimura [4] in 1960's, where he claimed that "the main cause of evolutionary change at the molecular level is random fixation of selectively neutral or nearly neutral mutants rather than positive Darwinian selection." Although he thought that "Natural selection is so prevalent at the phenotypic level," and he refrained from extending his theory to the manifestation of neutral mutations and the phenotypic selection, he mentioned a hypothesis that "neutral or nearly neutral alleles may have a latent potential for selection which can be realized under the appropriate conditions," quoting Calder's book "The Life of Game" (1973) that "A gene that is neutral today may ... come to assume great significance. ... the day may come when a peculiar molecule goes through one more mutation that suddenly gives it a new importance - just as changing one card can alter a worthless poker hand into a royal straight flush". This imagination or hypothesis is what the present authors want to demonstrate in this report.

Ohno [9] advocated the importance of gene duplication as an evolutionary force by examining biochemical data of protein and DNA sequences. In his theory, the genes may have acquired the new functions through neutral changes in the duplicated genes. The duplicated genes may have hidden themselves from the strong selection pressure, and acquire the diversity thereby, while sacrificing the original functional genes by exposing themselves to the selection.

The hypothesis proposed on the extension of the achievements by those pioneers is that the neutral genes and diverse mutations accumulated thereby may have induced the discontinuous jumps observed in the history of biological evolution. Here the neutral genes are defined as those genes ineffective to the fitness. The hypothesis insists that the neutral genes and diversity thereby are free from the selection, and they may induce major jumps in the fitness by a mutation on the regulator gene triggering the manifestation of neutral genes. Though the mutations always happen equally on both the structural and regulator genes, a crucial mutation on a regulator gene triggers the manifestation of the associated neutral genes, whose functions are needed in the changing environment.

The difficulty of validation of this neutral evolution hypothesis lies in the fact that the definition of neutral genes and their manifestation process to the phenotypic behaviors are not clear and we cannot examine the selective pressure at the genetic level. However, with proper definition of the neutrality and explicit manifestation process, we can present an example which demonstrate this hypothesis in a behavioral artificial creature embedded in the changing environment.

In this report the hypothesis is tested in the cases of a sensor-based engineering robot (or it may be taken as an abstract model of an animal with a few antennas and legs), which is navigating through a twisted corridor to the goal area (the same as the starting area) and continues the circumnavigation within a given time. The robot must always avoid the death-by-hard-collision to the obstacles and walls by controlling the speed and distance from the wall.

The robot has not incorporated any explicit map or knowledge for the navigation in its memory. The robot has only the proximity-sensors, motor-drives, and a neural-network as an internal behavior model. The navigation course is a connection of sub-courses (sub-environments) with increasing difficulty for the robot. The robot is rewarded by the fitness evaluation of the navigation to be used in the genetic evolution of the sensori-motor behavior models.

The neural network used as the sensori-motor models is developed by decoding the graph-represented chromosome, which includes the regulator gene, masking the decoding process of the chromosome, where the genetic information stored in the undecoded structural genes does not affect the fitness at all. This undecoded part of the chromosome acts as the neutral genes. The manifestation of these neutral genes is called type 1.

Another manifestation is associated with the functional but isolated neurons and synaptic links. Supposed that the genes in the parents chromosome were decoded into the isolated non-functional neurons, that were deleted immediately after birth. In this children's generation, some neurons are linked and form a functional neural network. This manifestation is called type 2.

We traced the simulated evolution in detail at the microscopic gene level, and have found a sequence of manifestations of both types 1 and 2 in neural networks, that induces remarkable progress in robot behavior in changing environments.

The present study on evolutionary behavior aims primarily at the study of simulated evolution with big fitness jumps and punctuated equilibria, in the adaptation of behavioral robotic systems, and not only limited to the simulation of the biological system supporting the hypothesis of neutral evolution.

It is also a belief of the authors that ALife simulations must be analyzed on what is happening at every hierarchical level of complexity, as the micro-level analyses of genes and manifestations are done here. With that kind of effort, ALife will share in the investigation of the common issues of science, and eventually will receive more respect and support.

2 Past Related Research and Position of This Paper

In regard to the computational framework, the most stimulating previous study with a similar interest and model structure of multi-level organization is found in the paper by Miglino et. al. [10], where the pre-adaptation of structure acquired in the neural network is analyzed, assuming a navigating agent with hierarchical organization in the gene, neuron, and behavior levels. They concluded that discontinuity in the fitness can be attributable to the pre-adaptation in the stable period of fitness prior to the fitness jump.

However, their analysis was mainly done in terms of pre-adaptation that the trait once built for one function is adapted in another environmental condition to another trait. The trait in their analysis is only noticed as a structural similarity in the connection pattern, not in the genotypic and functional analysis of the neural net. Moreover, the neutral mutation which triggered the jump is not analyzed at all.

Though the model structure of the multi-level organization and the interest in the possible discontinuous evolutionary mechanism are shared with our work, our study reported here is mainly concentrating on the manifestation mechanism of neutral genes through the 3-level behavior model of realistic (but simulated) robot navigation, where the neutral mutations accumulated in the stable period before the jump (not the pre-adapted traits there) and other manifestation mechanisms may be responsible for the big jumps in fitness.

Several studies have been made so far on the introduction of the duplication operator (together with the deletion and/or split operators) into the neural network development by Belew [1] [5], in finite state automata evolution by Wada [12] and one of the authors [2]. The gene duplication operator was also introduced by Lindgren [7] [6], in order to build-up the complexity in the strategies for Iterated Prisoner's Dilemma game, and it successfully led to the infinite strategy-space and consequently open-ended evolution. Though these works reported the effective construction of redundancy and complexity in the chromosome, their analyses were mainly on the global performances and finding of the important genes, and did not delve into the micro-level functions of these genes.

The present study of robot navigation evolution is categorized in the study of behavior evolution as reviewed elsewhere [11] [8], but it has special emphases on neutral evolution, especially the detailed analysis of the manifestation of neutral genes, which results in big jumps in fitness and punctuated equilibria.

3 Robot and Environment for Evolution

The simulated robot is the "Khepera" [3], whose shape is shown in Fig. 1. The Khepera robot has 8 proximity sensors in its periphery, and 2 motor-driven wheels in the both sides. Each sensor reading is an integer (0 - 1023). Both wheels can be driven independently, and speed is controllable in units of 8 mm/sec.

The sensor sensitivity function used in the simulation was made by fitting a function of two arguments: perpendicular distance to the wall and incident angle of the ray to the wall, on the measurements of proximity sensors placed in front of the aluminum wall.

In the simulation, each robot is born, one by one, in the artificial world shown in Fig. 1, and is evaluated in terms of the fitness value.

Reward to the robot or the fitness is essential for the robot to evolve within the Genetic Algorithm(GA)

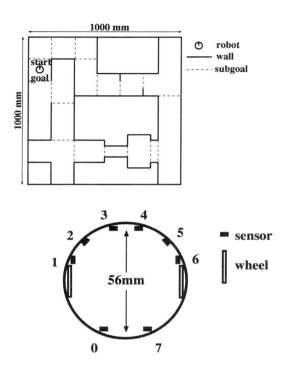

Figure 1: Navigation course (upper) and Khepera robot(lower)

framework. If the reward is given only when the robot reaches the goal, it would not encourage the robot that has acquired better traits in the navigation toward the goal.

It is a conventional approach that a set of subgoals (17 subgoals) are supposed in the course, as depicted in Fig. 1. The subgoals are not landmarks. The robot cannot detect the subgoals. Whenever the robot passes a subgoal for the first time in a certain round of navigation, it is given +100, an intermediate reward for the fitness, which encourages the associated behaviors in the GA process. The reward is not known to the navigating robot, but is only used in the evolutionary GA computation.

The fitness will be 1700 when the robot makes one round of the course. It gains more value by circumnavigating the course. The navigation stops when the robot hits the wall or the number of move steps reaches the maximum, i.e. 2000.

The world looks like a static environment for the designer, a person who looks at the world from the sky. When the population fails the navigation in a certain part, the evolutionary process (GA) takes the population back to the previous sub-environment, so that this back-and-forth evolutionary process makes the whole environment a changing environment for the navigating robots.

The world is dynamic in the robot's view, in the same sense that the moon surface has emerged as a new world to our mankind after Apollo-11.

4   Internal Behavior Model and GA Operators

No explicit map is given to the robot or learned by the robot. The behavior model is of the perception-action type, which responds only to the instantaneous sensors. Based on the many trials, the model structure, discretization of sensor readings, development of the neural networks, GA parameters and selection method were chosen to get efficient evolution.

4.1   Developed Neural Network: NN

The genotype is a tree-graph-represented chromosome. Each node or gene has a depth-first numbered neuron-id number, absolute Cartesian-coordinates of the neuron to be developed, an associated weight of the up-stream link, and a regulator gene masking the decoding process of down-stream genes. The down-stream genes are neutral when the regulator gene is activated; this mechanism leads to the type 1 manifestation mentioned in the later sections.

A maximum of 10 initial tree-graph chromosomes are randomly generated as follows: (1) The root node of the graph is generated with random parameters except the regulator genes being fixed to "active" position. (2) With 1/2 probability, the down-stream sub-tree is generated. (3) The generating process is stopped when more than a certain maximum number (temporarily 300) of nodes have been generated.

The chromosome of the tree-graph is decoded such that the each gene node corresponds to a single neuron, keeping the topological similarity between the chromosome graph and the neural network. Therefore, the up-stream and down-stream neurons and the associated link between them are defined similarly to the topology of the chromosome graph.

The procedures are: (1) According to the sequence (depth first) of the id-number, detached 1 at the root node, the neural network is developed in a square region of size 256, with 8 sensor input regions and 8 motor output regions, as shown in Fig. 4. (2) Each new neuron is located according to the x-y Cartesian-coordinates stored in the gene node, unless any other neuron has already been located within the square neighborhood of size 16. (3) If the location has been occupied by another neuron, the new neuron is not located, but only the up-stream link is generated to the up-stream neuron of the new neuron. (4) The number of axons of a neuron (i.e. number of links from a neuron) is limited to 5.

The isolated links and neurons are deleted immediately after the development, which causes the type 2 manifestation discussed later.

4.2   Function of neural network

The functional behavior of the neural network is as follows. (1) The 8 sensor values of the robot are input to the sensor regions of the neural network. (2) All neurons operate synchronously. In each synchronous cycle, each neuron receives a value from the up-stream neuron(s), and gives a value to the down-stream neuron(s).

(3) The maximum number of synchronous operating cycles is limited to the square root of the total number of neurons. (4) The left- and right-wheel driving values are determined such that the maximum value among the left-four output regions is determined and the speed associated with this region is given to the left-motor. The same process is taken in the right-four output regions. (5) When more than two output values happen to be the same, the greater speed is chosen. The maximum values of zero correspond to the speed zero.

These limitations in functions (3), (4), and (5) lead to the type 3 manifestation explained later.

The input-output function of each neuron is the step function where the jump occurs at the zero input value with unit output value for zero input value. Therefore, the behavior corresponding to the all zero sensor values is subject to the neural network structure and link parameter values, which are to emerge. No supervised learning nor any explicit training of the neural network is done.

4.3 Genetic operators

The graph-represented chromosomes are genetically operated to create the next gene population by using several operators in the following sequence.

(1) Cross-over. Partial graphs in the parents chromosome are randomly chosen. These are interchanged. (2) Deletion. Partial graphs in the chromosome are eliminated. (3) Point mutation. Information associated with the node is randomly changed. (4) Insertion. A randomly-generated partial graph is inserted. (5) Duplication. A partial graph is randomly chosen and is copied to a randomly chosen point within the same chromosome.

4.4 Types of manifestation

When the regulator gene is active, it masks the decoding process of the genes (neutral genes) in the left-side subtree below the regulator gene, as shown in Fig. 2. The masked genes are called type 1 neutral genes. The manifestation associated with these genes is called type 1.

Another type of neutrality and manifestation is called type 2, where the parent's genes have been decoded into the isolated neurons which did not contribute to the fitness and were deleted. The manifestation of these neutral genes in the children is often triggered by establishing new links to the other neurons and solving the isolation of the neutral genes of parents.

The other mechanism that masks the genes from the selection is, what we call type 3, that the genes and associated neurons are already manifested and linked in the neural net, but are not functional, depending on the environmental inputs, the nonlinearity and several limitations in the neurons and neural network. This type 3 manifestation arises depending on the sensing in the variety of navigation trajectories and the environmental conditions, that makes the trace of manifestation difficult. We restrict ourselves in this report to the types 1 and 2 neutrality and manifestation.

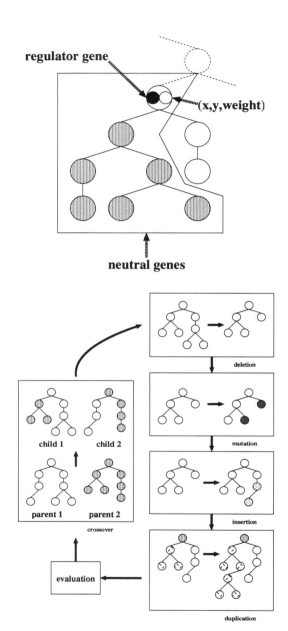

Figure 2: Regulator gene (upper) and genetic operators (lower). The regulator gene controls the decoding of genes only in the associated subtree(left-side).

5 Experimental Cases

5.1 Experiment 1: Evolution with Regulator Genes

A series of simulations were carried out, called Experiment 1 hereafter, under the parameter set of (mg = 1000, pop = 30, elite = 2, mr = 0.05, dr = 0.3, ir = 0.5, mrg = 0.1, sp = (60,200,0)), where mg = total number of generations, pop = population size, elite = number of elitists from the top to be saved to the next generation, mr = rate of mutation per node on x-y coordinates and weight, dr = duplication rate per chromosome, ir = insertion rate per chromosome, mrg = rate of mutation on regulator gene, sp = coordinates of initial location and starting angle of the robot.

The elitist is here defined as the individual with the maximum fitness in each generation. When the top fitnesses are equal, the one with the smallest chromosome among the tops is chosen as the elitist.

The elitists' fitness curve, the elitists' chromosome size, the number of genotypes/phenotypes, and the trajectory of navigation and neural networks of the elitist at generation 1000 are shown in Fig. 3.

The number of genomes is identified by matching all the chromosomes with respect to the chromosome size and total numbers of manifested and functional neurons. The number of phenotypes is determined by counting the different x-y coordinates and angles of the robots at the points that the robots terminate the navigation.

The analysis is made here mainly on the big jumps, which, we define, are jumps associated with the fitness increase by 1000 or more.

There is a big jump in fitness at generation 59 (to be more precise, between generations 58 and 59). Immediately before this jump, the decrease of the number of phenotypes and, at the same time, the increase of the genotypes are observed as shown in Fig. 3. As a matter of fact, the chromosome size jumps and decays sharply as well, in every jump of fitness.

The fitness is 400 in generation 58, which indicates that the robot fails the left turn, after the two right turns. The dip in the curve of number of phenotypes before generation 59 indicates that, while the left-turn behavior is not successfully acquired yet, the selective pressure diminishes the diversity in the phenotypic behavior. On the other hand, the neutral mutations accumulated in the neutral genes (type 1) contribute to the increase in genotypic diversity.

The elitist in generation 59 has the parents 58.10 and 58.11 (ones in 10th and 11th order of fitness, respectively). The functional and neutral genes/neurons are summarized in Table 1. The manifestation types are also summarized in Table 2. The trajectory of navigation and neural networks of these robots are displayed in Fig. 5.

The careful analysis below reveals that the neutral genes and their manifestation induce the big jump in fitness, acquiring the desired neural net behavior in the new environmental situation.

The parents 58.10 and 58.11 have the identical phenotype. The elitists 58.0 and 58.1 have also the same

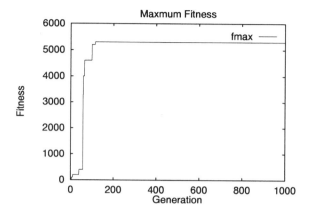

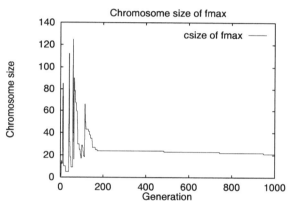

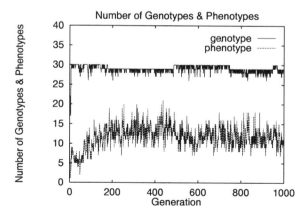

Figure 3: Experiment 1:Fitness(top), chromosome size (middle), and number of genotypes/phenotypes(bottom) of the elitists in each generation

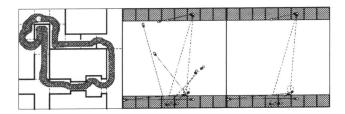

Figure 4: Experiment 1:Navigation trajectory(left) and neural networks. The networks are with isolated links undeleted (middle) and with the links deleted(right). The upper boxs denote the sensors from 0(left-back in Khepera robot) to 7 (right-back in Khepera, number increasing clockwise). The lower boxs are 4 speeds of both wheels: from the left corner to the right, the speeds of left wheel of -2, -1, +1, +2, and, +2, +1, - 1, - 2 of right wheel, respectively.

Table 2: Summary of the manifestation types in Experiment 1

Jumps at generations (fitness jump)	Number of Manifestation Types of		
	1	2	others
5 (0 to 100)	0	0	5(mutation)
11 (100 to 200)	0	0	1(mutation)
40 (200 to 400)	0	0	1(mutation)
59 (400 to 4000)	4	1	1(mutation)
65 (4000 to 4600)	1	0	2(mutation)
100 (4600 to 5200)	0	0	1(mutation)
115 (5200 to 5300)	0	0	0(cross over)

Table 1: Summary of the neutral genes/neurons in generation 59 and its parents, 58.10(the 10th chromosome in generation 58) and 58.11. Symbol * indicates the neurons already existed in generation 58 as the functional neurons. Two numbers x.y associated with neuron is the coordinates of neuron x and y in the neural network region.(C-Size: Chromosome Size, F.Neurons: Functional Neurons, D.F.Neurons: Downstream Functional Neurons)

Generation and Order (C-Size)	Fitness	F.Neurons - D.F.Neurons (Neutral Neurons)	Manifestation Type of F.Neurons (Parents)
59.0=elitist (125)	4000	110.29 - 174.14	*
		174.14 - 106.252	*
		106.252 - 156.179	
		and - 174.233	*
		156.179 - 2.234	type 2 (58.10,58.11)
		2.234 - 200.81	type 1 (58.10)
		200.81 - 184.62	mutation
		184.62 - 95.214	type 1 (58.10,58.11)
		95.214 - 163.236	type 1 (58.10)
		163.236 - none	type 1 (58.10,58.11)
		174.233 - none	*
58.0=elitist (9)	400	110.29 - 174.14	
		174.14 - 106.252	
		106.252 - 174.233	
		174.233 - none	
		(106.252 - 156.179)	
		(156.179)	
58.10 (125)	400	Same F.Neurons as 58.0 's	
		(156.179 - 2.223)	
		(2.223)	
		(67.50)	
58.11 (147)	400	Same F.Neurons as 58.0 's	
		(156.179)	

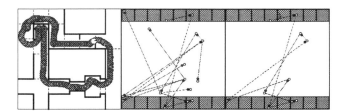

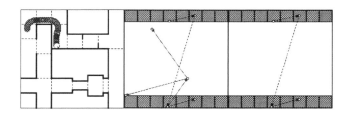

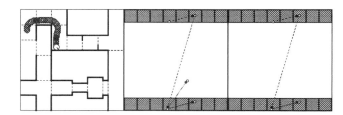

Figure 5: Experiment 1: The navigation trajectory and neural networks of the offspring 59.0(top) with the new links from sensor 5 (the 3rd box from the right on the upper edge) to motor 0 (the left lower corner box), and parents 58.10(middle) and 58.11(bottom)

phenotype. The most contributed gene/neuron in 59.0 is the gene 2.234 locating on the coordinates x = 2 and y = 234. The offspring 59.0 acquires the neuron 2.234 by type 1 manifestation. The neuron 2.234 has a link to neuron 156.179, that is identified in the neutral gene pool of the parents 58.10 and 58.11, which was manifested by type 2 process. The link through these manifested neurons is the most contributed connection that makes the left-hand wheel revolve in the highest reverse speed, and helps the quick left turn that was desired. It is impressive that 4 of type 1 and 1 of type 2 manifestations, and 1 of mutation on the structural genes, all contributed in this big jump.

Among the other jumps noticed in Experiment 1, the second biggest jump at generation 65 (fitness increase from 4000 to 4600) also involves a type 1 manifestation.

The parents 58.10 and 58.11 have the chromosome sizes, 125 and 147, much larger than that of the 58.0 elitist, 9. The increases of chromosome size are noticed in all jumps in generations 5, 11, 40, 65, 100, 115, though not all the jumps are necessarily associated with the type 1 and 2 manifestations. It is impressive, however, that the biggest two jumps at generations 59 and 65 are induced by the type 1 manifestation.

5.2 Experiment 2: Evolution with All Genes Manifested

A question may arise, that is, if all these neutral genes (of only type 1) have always been manifested as non-neutral, i.e. if the neutral genes do not exist at all, then what happened in the evolution? The experiment 2 was carried out with this setup of free manifestation. Though all the genes are under selective pressure, the genes with promising functions will eventually emerge in time, and shall be selected and multiplied.

A set of experiments with varying 30 random seeds were carried out to test this objection. The regulator genes were always put in the "decode" position, that makes all the genes decoded in the sense of type 1 all the time. The type 2 mechanism is not tested here, since we cannot control explicitly the type 2 manifestation. The result is tabulated in Table 3.

Table 3: Comparison between Experiments 1 and 2 on the average generation and number of jumps for one round of navigation. The average is taken over 30 runs with different random seeds.

Neutral/ Non-neutral	Generation	Number of fitness jumps
with neutral genes	374.1(average)	5.6(average)
without neutral genes	211.6(average)	6.1(average)

The evolution with type 1 manifestation is always associated with one or more big jumps, and the fitness increase is more abrupt, showing the punctuated equilibria. For the evolution without type 1, the fitness is increasing with smaller jumps, before the robot makes

the first round of navigation. The speed of evolution is largely dependent on the random seeds.

As shown in Table 5.2, the success rate for one complete round is low in cases with type 1, compared with cases without type 1 which completed the navigation almost all the time.

Table 4: Comparison between Experiments 1 and 2 on the rate of success in complete one round of navigation and the rate of big jump. The rate is taken over 30 runs with different random seeds.

Neutral/ Non-neutral	Complete	Big jump
with neutral genes	23.3%(7/30)	85.7%(6/7)
without neutral genes	96.7%(29/30)	51.7%(15/29)

Some of the typical fitness curves in Experiments 1 are illustrated in Fig. 6, controlling the type 1 neutrality.

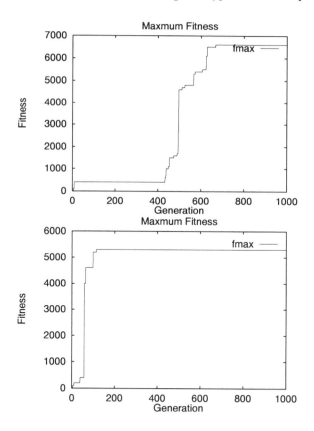

Figure 6: Fitnesses of Experiment 1 without the neutral genes of type 1(upper) and Experiment 2 with the neutral genes of type 1(lower)

The explicit incorporation of neutral genes in the chromosome will make the system evolve quickly to the desired behaviors. But, in terms of the probability of achieving the complete one round of navigation, the evolution without the navigation is more reliable. Further simulation studies will be necessary to find the factors affecting the speed of evolution and reliability.

6 Conclusion

The role of neutral genes in the quick and big fitness jumps is now clear. The big jump observed at generation 59 in Experiment 1 is a typical case, where many valuable functions with genetic diversity are accumulated in the neutral genes. Phenotypic diversity, on the other hand, is diminished by selective pressure in the environments before the major jumps in fitness. Coincidentally with the environmental needs for a new behavior (i.e. left sharp turn, for example), a mutation on the regulator gene triggers the type 1 manifestation of neutral genes with desired functions, and suddenly a big jump occurs, i.e. a remarkable stepwise increase of fitness punctuating the equilibria.

Evolution incorporated with neutral genes is characterized by big fitness jumps in the earlier generations. On the other hand, evolution without neutral genes achieves reliable increase of fitness, being relatively insensitive to the random seeds. For engineering applications, the neutral evolution method is promising if we wish systems to evolve quickly toward the desired versatile behaviors, though further study is necessary on the environmental conditions for it.

For scientific interest, this evolutionary simulation demonstrates an example which may support a hypothesis that neutral mutation in the regulator genes caused the big jumps in fitness punctuating the equilibria. However, it seems reasonable, this is merely a story and does not prove any theory of biological evolution. It does demonstrate, at least, the logical feasibility or flawlessness of the hypothesis by providing a logically consistent example. Though the generalization of this story relies heavily on the power of imagination of the reader, it may share a common logical basis with the true history of biological evolution.

Acknowledgements

The authors would like to express many thanks to Dr. Yukihiko Toquenaga, Mr. Isamu Kajitani, Dr. Didier Keymeulen, Dr. Arthur Sanderson for their valuable and often critical comments on the theory of neutral genes and evolution, as well as on English expressions. This study is partially supported by the Grant-In-Aid of Ministry of Education, Science, Sports and Culture of Japan (07243102 and and 06402060).

References

[1] Richard K. Belew. Interposing an ontogenic model between genetic algorithms and neural networks. In *Advances in Neural Information Processing Systems NIPS 5*, pages 99–106. Morgan Kaufmann, 1993.

[2] Tsutomu Hoshino. *Dreams and Worries of Artificial Life (Jinkou-Seimei no Yume to Nayami),(in Japanese),Popular Science Series*. Shouka-Bo, 1994.

[3] K-Team. *Khepera USERS MANUAL*. Laboratoire de microinformatique Swiss Federal Institute of Technology (EPFL), 1993.

[4] Motoo Kimura. *The Neutral Theory of Molecular Evolution*. Cambridge Univ. Press, 1983.

[5] Mats G.Nordahl Kristian Lindgren, Anders Nilsson and Inrid Rade. Regular language inference using evolving neural networks. In *COGANN-92, Int. Workshop on Combinations of Genetic Algorithms and Neural Networks*, pages 77–86. IEEE Computer Society Press, 1992.

[6] M.G. Nordahl Kristian Lindgren. Artificial food webs. In *ARTIFICIAL LIFE III*, pages 73–104. Addison Wesley, 1994.

[7] Kristian Lindgren. Evolutionary phenomena in simple dynamics. In *ARTIFICIAL LIFE II*, pages 295–312. Addison Wesley, 1994.

[8] Pattie Maes. Modeling adaptive autonomous agents. *Artificial Life*, pages 135–162, 1994.

[9] Susumu Ohno. *Evolution by Gene Duplication*. Springer-Verlag, 1970.

[10] Domenico Parisi Orazio Miglino, Stefano Nolfi. Discontinuity in evolution: how different levels of organization imply pre-adaptation. In *Adaptive Individual in Evolving Populations (to appear)*. Addison-Wesley, 1996.

[11] Luc Steels. The artificial life roots of artificial intelligence. *Artificial Life*, pages 75–110, 1994.

[12] Ken'nosuke Wada. *Evolution of Digital Life(in Japanese)*. Iwanami, 1994.

On Evolutionary Dynamics

Christian V. Forst[a1] and Christian Reidys[b]

[a]Institut für Molekulare Biotechnologie, Jena, Germany
Beutenbergstraße 11, p/o box 100 813, D-07708 Jena, Germany
Phone: **49 (3641) 65 6459   Fax: **49 (3641) 65 6450
E-Mail: chris@imb-jena.de

[b]Los Alamos National Laboratory, NM, USA
TSA-DO/SA, Los Alamos, NM 87545, USA
E-Mail: duck@santafe.edu

Abstract

Motivated by RNA secondary-structure folding-landscapes based on computer algorithms we construct a mathematical framework which provides a comprehensive and coherent description of evolutionary dynamics.

In this paper we study the evolutionary dynamics of a population of self-replicating RNA molecules with autocatalytic interactions (hypercycles and parasites). We use a stochastic replication dynamics in a mean field approximation (no spatial resolution), sitting on top of a genotype-phenotype mapping, including neutral networks (families of RNA genotypes with the same phenotype [31]). The neutral nets as well as the autocatalytic interactions are modeled by random graphs [29]. This approach enables us to develop a structure theory of landscapes on the one hand and to understand evolutionary dynamics by means of theory and simulation on the other hand.

The evolutionary dynamics select complex cooperative RNA structures. Hypercycles are found to be able to co-exist as well as survive parasites with superior catalytic support. These results are surprising when compared to a deterministic description of the same dynamics where neither co-existence nor survival in the presence of parasites are possible. Our findings are more in concert with the results obtained using a spatial description of the dynamics.

1. Introduction

Dynamics of self-replicating macromolecules has been modeled by two different approaches in literature:

Non-catalytically active entities: This concept of error-prone replication is based upon the selection-model of Fisher [11]. Individuals reproduce by their fitness, by accident mutations occur thus different individuals emerge by replication, and a constant organization maintains a selective force. Eigen *et al.*[8] extended these models by studying binary sequences as individuals. Applying mean-field-theory yields the well known *Quasispecies* model which has been analyzed by birth-death processes [23]. By extending this concept with fitness-landscapes based on RNA-secondary structure folding-landscapes [14, 13] one can study error-prone replication of RNA-molecules in a more realistic setup. These simulations can easily be correlated with biochemical experiments in the $Q\beta$-system of Biebricher and Eigen [4].

A recently developed mathematical model of a so-called *single-shape* landscape generalizes Eigen's concept. A *phenotypic error-threshold* can be characterized which describes the information-breakdown of replicating biopolymers [15, 28].

Catalytically active species: Self-replication of catalytically active species is usually modeled by higher order replicator equation. The famous classical approach of dynamical system is the *hypercycle* [9]. Motivation is a more natural model where various species do interact not only by competition for a given external resource, but also by predator-prey relations or symbiosis. The analogous to an ecosystem on a molecular level is an *autocatalytic network* consisting of self-replicating macromolecules which act as catalysts in replication reactions of other species or even catalyze their own replication [10, 22]. Although no *in vitro* system exhibiting this type of dynamic is know at present, the discovery of the catalytic potential of RNA, and especially the demonstration that RNA catalyzed template-induced synthesis of RNA is possible [6], suggests that an ecosystem of catalytically active RNAs which catalyze RNA replication might be feasible [26]. Recent experimental studies make evident that hypercyclic coupling in vitro is within reach [16]. In such a model, the fitness of a certain species will

---

[1]Author to whom correspondence should be addressed.

depend on the composition of the entire system, i.e. we have to replace the constant fitness value by a function of the population numbers of – in general – all species in the system.

Catalytic interaction between reacting species has been discussed recently in literature: Bagley *et al.* [2, 3] studied spontaneous emergence of metabolisms. Nuño *et al.* [1, 25, 24] suggested a catalytic network introduced through faulty self-replication into a mutant molecular species. Stadler *et al.* [34] investigated reaction-mutation networks and observed error-thresholds as first order phase transitions. Examples of low dimensional dynamical systems ($n = 2, 3$ and 4) are discussed and complete qualitative analysis is presented. Fontana *et al.* [12, 33] studied networks that are a generalization of replicator (or Lotka-Volterra[2]) equations. They model the dynamics of a population of object types whose binary interactions determine the specific type of interaction product. Similar studies about dynamics of programmable matter were performed by Rasmussen *et al.* [27].

Peter Schuster [30] proposed to incorporate a genotype phenotype mapping for the study of *evolutionary dynamics*. The scenario can be described by interactions of the following three processes (Fig. 1):

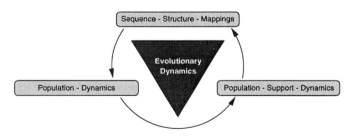

Figure 1: Evolutionary Dynamics

- *Genotype-Phenotype Mapping:* Modeling biological systems with selective forces and error-prone replication has to keep both genotypes and phenotypes in mind. In general mutations take place on the level of genotypes while selection acts on phenotypes. Thus it is the sequence to structure and further the structure to function mapping which provides the (kinetic) parameters for population dynamics.
- In *Population-Dynamics* the classic approach is to describe time-development of species or chemicals in a concentration-space by methods of chemical kinetics. Whenever a new entity emerges or a "weak" species

dies out, the concentration-space adapts and changes it's dimensionality.

- *Population-Support-Dynamics* closes the cycle by establishing a relation to the genotype-phenotype-mappings. By exploring new regions of the sequence-space by migrating sets of genotypes it supplies genotype-phenotype-mapping with new input.

2. Neutral Networks of RNA Secondary Structures

We begin by defining a RNA secondary structure [35]: A *secondary structure* is a vertex-labeled graph on n vertices with an adjacency matrix $A = (a_{i,k})_{1 \leq i,k \leq n}$ fulfilling

(1) $a_{i,i+1} = 1$ for $1 \leq i \leq n - 1$;

(2) For each i there is at most a single $k \neq i - 1, i + 1$ such that $a_{i,k} = 1$;

(3) If $a_{i,j} = a_{k,l} = 1$ and $i < k < j$ then $i < l < j$.

We call an edge (i, k), $|i - k| \neq 1$ a *bond* or *base pair* and write $[i, k] \in s$. A vertex i connected only to $i - 1$ and $i + 1$ shall be called *unpaired*. We shall denote the number of base pairs and the number of unpaired bases in a secondary structure s by $n_p(s)$ and $n_u(s)$ respectively. We denote the size of the alphabet by α and the number of distinct base pairs by β.

In this section we model the preimages of secondary structures –so called *neutral networks* – as random graphs. For this purpose we discuss properties of random induced subgraphs of generalized hypercubes.

2.1. Random induced Subgraphs of generalized Hypercubes

A generalized hypercube is a graph whose vertices are all n-tuples where the coordinates x_i are elements of the finite set $\mathcal{A}$ (of size α) and two vertices are adjacent if they differ in exactly one coordinate.

Each subset $X \subset \mathrm{v}[\mathcal{Q}_\alpha^n]$ induces the subgraph $\mathcal{Q}_\alpha^n[X]$ establishing a one-to-one correspondence between $X \subset \mathrm{v}[\mathcal{Q}_\alpha^n]$ and $\mathcal{Q}_\alpha^n[X]$. Let us denote the set of all induced subgraphs of $\mathcal{Q}_\alpha^n$ by $\mathcal{G}(\mathcal{Q}_\alpha^n)$. We suppose $0 \leq \lambda \leq 1$ to be given and set for $\Gamma_n \in \mathcal{G}(\mathcal{Q}_\alpha^n)$

$$\boldsymbol{\mu}_\lambda\{\Gamma_n\} \stackrel{\text{def}}{=} \lambda^{|\mathrm{v}[\Gamma_n]|} (1 - \lambda)^{\alpha^n - |\mathrm{v}[\Gamma_n]|}.$$

---

[2]According to Hofbauer [19] Replicator-equations with $n + 1$ species are – apart from a transformation of the time scale – equivalent to a n-species Lotka-Volterra equation

Obviously $\boldsymbol{\mu}_\lambda$ fulfills $\sum_{\Gamma_n} \boldsymbol{\mu}_\lambda\{\Gamma_n\} = 1$ and we thereby obtain the probability space

$$\Omega \stackrel{\text{def}}{=\!=} (\, \mathcal{G}(\mathcal{Q}_\alpha^n), \mathcal{P}(\mathcal{G}(\mathcal{Q}_\alpha^n)), \boldsymbol{\mu}_\lambda \,) \,.$$

For random induced subgraphs of generalized hypercubes there exists *one* threshold value λ^* for the density and the connectivity property. Here a subgraph $\Gamma_n < \mathcal{Q}_\alpha^n$ is called *dense* in $\mathcal{Q}_\alpha^n$ if and only if $\overline{\mathrm{v}[\Gamma_n]} = \mathrm{v}[\mathcal{Q}_\alpha^n]$. The main result on density reads

Theorem 1. *Let* $\lambda^* \stackrel{\text{def}}{=\!=} 1 - \sqrt[\alpha-1]{\alpha-1}$ *then for* $\lambda > \lambda^*$ *holds*

$$\lim_{n\to\infty} \boldsymbol{\mu}_n\{\Gamma_n \text{ is dense in } \mathcal{Q}_\alpha^n\} = 1$$

and for $\lambda < \lambda^*$ *we have*

$$\lim_{n\to\infty} \boldsymbol{\mu}_n\{\Gamma_n \text{ is dense in } \mathcal{Q}_\alpha^n\} = 0 \,.$$

For the connectivity property we have

Theorem 2. *Let* $(\mathcal{Q}_\alpha^n)$ *be a sequence of generalized hypercubes and* $\Gamma_n < \mathcal{Q}_\alpha^n$ *random induced subgraphs. Then*

$$\lim_{n\to\infty} \boldsymbol{\mu}_n\{\Gamma_n \text{ is connected}\} = \begin{cases} 1 & \text{for} \quad \lambda > 1 - \sqrt[\alpha-1]{\alpha-1} \\ 0 & \text{for} \quad \lambda < 1 - \sqrt[\alpha-1]{\alpha-1} \end{cases} \,. \tag{1}$$

A proof can be found in [29].

2.2. Compatibility and Construction of Neutral Nets

By definition of secondary structure its preimage is a subset of the *set of compatibles sequences*. A sequence x is said to be *compatible* to a secondary structure s if the nucleotides x_i and x_j at sequence positions i and j can pair whenever (i,j) is a base pair in s. Note that this condition does by no means imply that x_i and x_j will actually form a base pair in the structure $\varphi(x)$ obtained by some folding algorithm. The set of all sequences compatible with a secondary structure s will be denoted by $\mathbf{C}[s]$. There are two types of neighbors to sequence $x \in \mathbf{C}[s]$: each mutation in a position k which is unpaired in the secondary structure s leads again to a sequence compatible with s, while point mutations in the paired regions of s will in general produce sequences that are not compatible with s. This problem can be overcome by modifying the notion of neighborhood. If we allow the exchange base pairs instead of single nucleotides in the paired regions of s we always end up with sequences compatible with s. This definition of neighborhood allows us to view

$x \in \mathbf{C}[s]$ as a graph. It can be shown [29] that this graph is the direct product of two generalized hypercubes

$$\mathbf{C}[s] = \mathcal{Q}_\alpha^{n_u} \times \mathcal{Q}_\beta^{n_p} \tag{2}$$

where n_u is the number of unpaired positions in s, α is the number of different nucleotides, i.e., $\alpha = 4$ in the case of natural RNAs, n_p is the number of base *pairs* in s, and β is the number of different *types* of base pairs that can be formed by the α different nucleotides; for natural RNAs we have $\beta = 6$. The sequence length is $n = n_u + 2n_p$.

We construct the *neutral network* w.r.t. s as a graph product of random induced subgraphs of $\mathcal{Q}_\alpha^{n_u}$ and $\mathcal{Q}_\beta^{n_p}$ respectively (corresponding to the unpaired and paired coordinates w.r.t. the secondary structure s) as illustrated in the figure below:

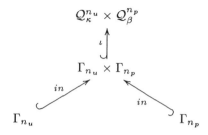

2.3. Complete Mappings

Once we know how to construct a neutral network $\Gamma_n[s]$ we order the set of secondary structures $\mathcal{S}_n$ and define a complete mapping by iterating the construction process of the corresponding neutral network w.r.t. the ordering. Thereby we obtain w.r.t. a given λ parameter a complete sequence to structure mapping. Formally speaking let $\mathbf{C}^* : \mathcal{S}_n \to \mathcal{P}(\mathrm{v}[\mathcal{Q}_\alpha^n])$ and $r : \mathcal{S}_n \to \mathbb{N}$ be two mappings such that $j \leq i \implies r(s_j) \geq r(s_i)$. A mapping $f : \mathcal{Q}_\alpha^n \to \mathcal{S}_n$ is called $\mathbf{C}^*$-*map* if and only if

$$(*): \quad f(v) = s \quad \implies \quad v \in \mathbf{C}^*[s]$$

A mapping $f_r : \mathcal{Q}_\alpha^n \to \mathcal{S}_n$ is called $\mathbf{C}^*$-*random-map* if and only if f_r is given by

$$f_r^{-1}(s_0) \stackrel{\text{def}}{=\!=} \Gamma_n[s_0]$$
$$f_r^{-1}(s_i) \stackrel{\text{def}}{=\!=} \Gamma_n[s_i] \setminus \bigcup_{j<i} [\Gamma_n[s_i] \cap \Gamma_n[s_j]] \,.$$

In particular any RNA folding map is a $\mathbf{C}^*$-map setting $\mathbf{C}^*[s] \stackrel{\text{def}}{=\!=} \mathbf{C}[s]$ since the neutral networks are constructed *a priori* in the graph of compatible sequences. We will assume that $\mathbf{C}^* = \mathbf{C}$ and then the recursion reads in the particular case of $\Gamma_n[s] = \mathbf{C}[s]$:

$$f^{-1}(s_{r_0}) \stackrel{\text{def}}{=} \mathbf{C}[s_0]$$
$$f^{-1}(s_{r_i}) \stackrel{\text{def}}{=} \mathbf{C}[s_i] \setminus \bigcup_{j < i} [\mathbf{C}[s_i] \cap \mathbf{C}[s_j]]$$

2.4. Coupling of Neutral Networks

In this section we will show that each two neutral networks being dense and connected come "close" in sequence space. To verify this we embed all secondary structures of fixed length n into the symmetric group S_n. Let S_n be the *symmetric group in n letters* and $\mathcal{S}$ be the set of all secondary structures. A *transposition* $\tau \in S_n$ is written as $\tau = (x_i, x_k)$. A base pair of a structure s is given by $[i, k]$. The set of all base pairs is denoted by $\Pi(s)$. Then

$$\imath : \mathcal{S} \to S_n; \qquad s \mapsto \imath(s) \stackrel{\text{def}}{=} \prod_{[i,k] \in \Pi(s)} (i, k).$$

Clearly the map $\imath$ is an *embedding* of the set $\mathcal{S}$ of secondary structure in the set S_n of permutations. It can be verified that $\imath(s)^2 = 1$, i.e., for any secondary structure the permutation assigned by $\imath$ is an *involution*. It is known from the theory [32] that any two involutions generate a *dihedral group*, D_m. Therefore $\imath$ in a natural way gives rise to the mapping

$$\jmath : \mathcal{S} \times \mathcal{S} \longrightarrow \{D_m < S_n\};$$
$$(s, s') \mapsto \jmath(s, s') \stackrel{\text{def}}{=} \langle \imath(s), \imath(s') \rangle.$$

The key result of the above considerations is the following theorem

Theorem 3. (Intersection–Theorem) *Let s and s' be two arbitrary secondary structures. Then*

$$\mathbf{C}[s] \cap \mathbf{C}[s'] \neq \emptyset.$$

A proof can be found in [29].

That means for each pair of secondary structures we can always find sequences that are compatible to both structures. Hence any two connected and dense neutral networks come very close (Hamming distance $4 - (\lambda_1 + \lambda_2)$). The cyclic group $\langle \imath(s) \circ \imath(s') \rangle$ operates on the set of all 'positions' of the sequence $x = (x_1, \ldots, x_n)$. This operation induces a *cycle decomposition* of the generator $\imath(s) \circ \imath(s')$. In fact we can evaluate the coupling of the networks by the above cycle decomposition as follows:

suppose a sequence on one network is given then how likely a sequences located on one network can move by point mutations to the other net. Using a simplified model the situation can be illustrated as shown in Fig. 2.

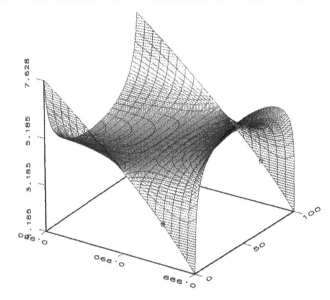

Figure 2: (Cf. [36]) By a simple replication-deletion process evolutionary dynamics of individuals are modeled. Two classes of individuals can occur (referring to two phenotypes or *bins*) and are transferred by an erroneous replication into each other. An unspecific dilution maintains a constant organization. In this figure the negative logarithm of the stationary distribution is plotted depending on the coupling rate between two bins (corresponding to two nets) and the possible states. For a strong coupling ≈ 1 a bistable situation occurs where either one or the other bin (i.e. neutral net) is completely occupied. For the decoupled case the most probable states of the distribution lie between those two extremas.

3. Hypercycles

3.1. Modeling Finite Populations in Sequence Space

Let us begin by mentioning a general concept for describing "populations" on graphs. For this purpose let N be a natural number such that $N \geq 2$ and let $\mathbf{V}$ be a (finite) family of vertices $(v_i \mid i \in \mathbb{N}_N)$ where $\{ v_i \mid i \in \mathbb{N}_N \} \subset \mathrm{v}[\mathcal{Q}_\alpha^n]$. We shall call $\mathbf{V}$ a *population* in $\mathcal{Q}_\alpha^n$. The theory of point processes provides a powerful tool by identifying such a family $(v_i \mid i \in \mathbb{N}_N)$ with an integer valued measure:

$$\mathbf{V} = (v_i \mid i \in \mathbb{N}_N) \quad \longleftrightarrow \quad \phi \stackrel{\text{def}}{=} \sum_{i=1}^{N} g_{v_i}, \qquad (3)$$

$$\text{where } g_{v_i}(v) \stackrel{\text{def}}{=} \begin{cases} 1 & \text{for } v \neq v_i \\ 0 & \text{otherwise .} \end{cases}$$

A *replication-deletion process* is a mapping from $(v_i \mid i \in \mathbb{N}_N)$ to the family $(v'_i \mid i \in \mathbb{N}_N)$ as follows:
We select an ordered pair (v_l, v_k) where $v_l, v_k \in \{ v_i \mid i \in \mathbb{N}_N \}$. For

$$\ell \stackrel{\text{def}}{=} \text{res}_{\mathbf{v}[\Gamma_n[s]]} \phi(\mathbf{v}[\Gamma_n[s]])$$

the first coordinate v_l is chosen with probability $\sigma \ell / [(N - \ell) + \sigma \ell]$ from $(v_i \mid i \in \mathbb{N}_N)$ where $\text{res}_{\Gamma_n[s]}(v_i) \geq 1$ (the elements of $\mathbf{V}$ that are located on the neutral network) with uniform probability and from the remaining elements (with uniform probability) otherwise. The second coordinate of the above pair is selected with uniform probability on $(v_i \neq v_l \mid i \in \mathbb{N}_N)$ i.e. $1/(N-1)$. We assume the times $\hat{T}$ between these mappings to be exponentially distributed (scaled by the mean fitness)

$$\boldsymbol{\mu}\{\hat{T} \leq t\} = e^{-[(N-\ell)+\sigma\ell]\,t} .$$

We map $v_l = (x_1, ..., x_n)$ randomly into the vertex $v^* = (x'_1, ..., x'_n)$. This is done by mapping each coordinate x_i to a $x'_i \neq x_i$ with probability p where all $x'_i \neq x_i$ are equally distributed and leave the coordinate fixed otherwise. This random mapping $v_l \mapsto v^*$ is called "replication". Finally, we delete the second coordinate of the pair (v_l, v_k), that is v_k and have a mapping $(v_l, v_k) \mapsto (v_l, v^*)$. Thereby we obtain a "new" family by substituting the v_k by the v^*.

3.2. Hypercyclic Coupling

One important complex organization is the catalytic interaction of different phenotypes. A first and classical approach is to analyze cooperative behavior. The *hypercycle* [7, 9] serves as a paradigm for co-operation between different species. It is of particular relevance to study the stability of hypercycles against viruses and concurring hypercycles.

The dynamical behavior of the above system can be described by the following reaction equations. We denote I_i, $i = 1, \ldots, n$ as reacting species with a fixed phenotype $S(I_i)$, $f[S(I_i)]$ as fitness-function of phenotype

$S(I_i)$, and W_{ij} indicates the probability of reproducing I_j by replicating I_i.:

$$
\begin{aligned}
I_i &\xrightarrow{f[S(I_i)] \cdot W_{ij}} I_i + I_j \\
I_i + I_k &\xrightarrow{g[S(I_i), S(I_k)] \cdot W_{ij}} I_i + I_j + I_k \qquad (4) \\
I_i &\xrightarrow{\quad \Phi \quad} \emptyset
\end{aligned}
$$

Thus the $f[S(I_i)]$'s refer to the level of phenotypes whereas the W_{ij}'s indicate the genotypes dynamic. The $g[S(I_i), S(I_k)]$'s denote the rate of the catalyzed reaction. By decoupling both levels from each other yields following schema (Fig. 3):

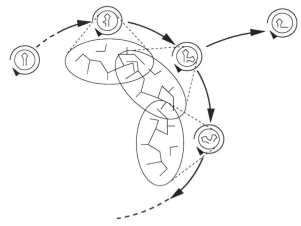

Figure 3: Population-Support-Dynamics of a hypercyclic organization with a parasite. Each phenotype — sketched by secondary structures — induce a corresponding compatible set and an embedded neutral net. The parasitic phenotype profits by a hypercyclic phenotype only without providing support.

Important for the dynamical characteristics of the system are the reaction-graphs of phenotypes and the error-prone replications on the level of genotypes. The topologies of the underlying neutral nets assure that there are couplings between each two of them. Parts of the population can switch from one net to the other and thereby cause a stabilizing effect for the hypercycle.

3.3. Hypercycles without Parasites

The stochastic process describing the hypercyclic coupled networks exhibits a more complex structure as shown in Fig. 4. We first investigated the time evolution of short hypercycles using the Gillespie algorithm [18]. The underlying stochastic process is closely related to the scheme we introduced in section 3.1 and can be seen as the stochastic analogue of the continuous flow reactor

Hypercycles

N = 1000, p = 0.01

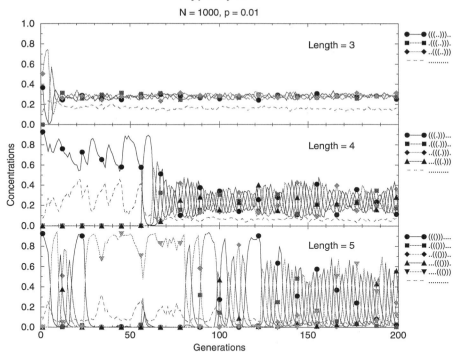

Figure 4: Time evolution of hypercycles of length $n = 3, 4, 5$. In case of infinite population size using theory of nonlinear differential equations there exist a stable inner fixed point for $n \leq 4$. For $n > 4$ this rest point becomes unstable and a stable limit-cycle emerges. Parameters for these simulations: population size = 1000, chain length = 10, reaction rates for catalyzed replication 10× faster than autocatalytic background replication.

Hypercycles with Parasite

N = 100, p = 0.01

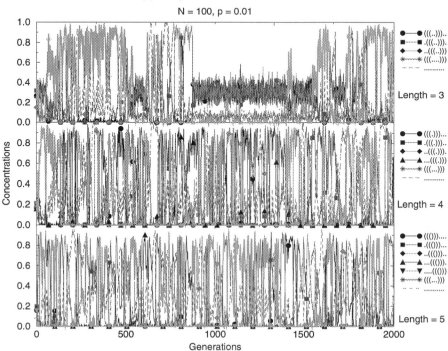

Figure 5: Time evolution of hypercycles with a parasite of length $n = 3, 4, 5$. Parameters for these simulations are the same as in Fig. 4 except for the population-size which is 100. The replication of the parasite is catalyzed by phenotype ● with the same reaction rate as hypercyclic catalysis. Solid symbols denote members of the hypercycle, ∗ indicate the parasite, and the dashed line is the background.

usually modeled by differential equations. Phenomena like the transition between two neutral nets as monitored in section 2.4 show that it is adequate to model these systems fully stochastic. We were particularly interested to compare the time evolution of three- to five-phenotype hypercycles with the corresponding results from differential equation theory. The results are as follows:

For infinite populations we distinguish the following scenarios:

$n \leq 4$: There exists a stable inner fixed point.

$n > 4$: Via a supercritical Hopf-Bifurcation the inner rest point becomes instable and a stable limit-cycle emerges.

3.4. Hypercycles with Parasites

Interesting questions arise by introducing a competing parasite (Fig. 6). Recalling the results for hypercycles in case of infinite populations we would expect the following [21]: depending on the ratio of the reaction rates of the competitors and of the initial concentrations either the hypercycle or the parasite will survive at the expense of the other.

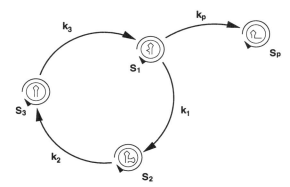

Figure 6: Hypercycle with three phenotypes and one parasite. S_i are the corresponding structures and k_i refer to the reaction rates of catalyzed replication $i = 1, 2, 3$, and p for the parasite.

Another approach has been studied by Boerlijst & Hogeweg [5] who investigated hypercycles with parasites using cellular automata and partial differential equations. On a two dimensional grid the authors observed spirals stabilizing the hypercycles versus the competing parasite. In the stochastic formulation we observe the following:

In contrast to homogeneous models with infinite population size the competing behavior between parasite and hypercycle is not a drastic *live and let die* scenario. Both competing systems can coexist for a long time. Due to the (transient) periodic behavior of hypercycles with four and more elements the parasitic concentration exhibits periodic variations which cannot be observed in deterministic, homogeneous systems (Fig. 5).

4. Discussion

The mathematical model of sequence to structure maps allows to study catalytic reaction networks on the level of RNA secondary structures in a realistic framework. Neutral nets with respect to secondary structures come close in sequence space and exhibit a topology that induces a diffusing populations. Transitions between these neutral nets of equal fitness have been observed. Further studies indicate that there is a strong evidence that these transition-phenomena also occur in more complex landscapes. By designing autocatalytic reaction networks as multi-layer dynamics we have two levels of dynamical systems:

- Level of Phenotypes
- Level of Genotypes

Both levels are correlated by a genotype-phenotype-mapping. Thus genotypic changes of the population will influence the characteristics of interactions between phenotypes in a certain extend. Due to the neutral properties of this mapping we will expect a "smooth" response and a "drifting" of catalytic networks in the space of genotypes.

In this paper we have studied hypercyclic coupling of autocatalytic phenotypes. The results obtained by computer simulations of the underlying stochastic process show a different behavior compared to the case of infinite population size. Using theory of nonlinear differential equations for $n \leq 3, 4$ there exists a stable inner fixed point and for $n = 5$ there exists a stable limit cycle [9]. The permanence of the limit cycle [20] is a nontrivial mathematical result and uses explicitly the compactness of the concentration simplex. The simulations of a corresponding stochastic process show substantial deviation from the predictions of the theory of differential equations. The computer experiments support that in the case of a hypercycle without parasites there is no convergence of random variables, whose states are the numbers of the population located on one particular neutral net, to a stationary distribution.

In case of hypercycles with parasites we observe that even when the parasite has a higher fitness the fraction of sequences located on neutral nets belonging to the hypercycle is significantly higher than a random one. There exists even a coexistence of parasite and hypercycle to a certain extent if the reaction rates of catalyzed reaction for both the hypercycle and the parasite are in the same magnitude.

Those preliminary results suggest a formulation of an analytical theory in terms of stochastic processes. As proposed by Peter Schuster [30] such a theory has to include the graph structure of the support —the neutral networks— and the sequence to structure mapping explicitly. In particular this theory could make nontrivial prediction on chemical reaction systems in biotechnology. Present day *in vitro* techniques are already capable to perform crucial parts of the work presented here. Recent experiments [17, 16] raise the hope that a system for powerful selection of catalysts are within reach of exploration.

Acknowledgments

Fruitful discussion with Walter Fontana, Michael Gebinoga and Peter Schuster are gratefully acknowledged. Special thanks to Jacqueline Weber who supplied unpublished material for Fig. 2. Part of the work has been done at the Santa Fe Institute, Santa Fe, NM in October 1995. Christian Forst thanks the institute for a great stay and the researchers for a stimulating atmosphere.

References

[1] M. A. Andrade, J. C. Nuño, F. Morán, F. Montero, and G. J. Mpitsos. Complex dynamics of a catalytic network having faulty replication into error-species. *Physica D*, 63:21–40, 1993.

[2] R. J. Bagley and J. D. Farmer. Spontaneous emergence of a metabolism. In C. G. Langton, C. Taylor, J. D. Farmer, and S. Rasmussen, editors, *Artificial Life II*, volume X of *Santa Fe Institute Studies in the Science of Complexity*, chapter Origin/Self-Organization, pages 93–141. Addison Wesley, Redwood City, 1992.

[3] R. J. Bagley, J. D. Farmer, and W. Fontana. Evolution of a metabolism. In C. G. Langton, C. Taylor, J. D. Farmer, and S. Rasmussen, editors, *Artificial Life II*, volume X of *Santa Fe Institute Studies in the Science of Complexity*, chapter Origin/Self-Organization, pages 141–158. Addison Wesley, Redwood City, 1992.

[4] C. K. Biebricher, M. Eigen, and W. C. Gardiner Jr. Kinetics of RNA replication: Competition and selection among self-replicating RNA species. *Biochemistry*, 24:6550–6560, 1985.

[5] M. C. Boerlijst and P. Hogeweg. Spiral wave structure in pre-biotic evolution: Hypercycles stable against parasites. *Physica D*, 48:17 – 28, 1991.

[6] J. A. Doudna and J. W. Szostak. RNA catalysed synthesis of complementary-strand RNA. *Nature*, 339:519–522, 1989.

[7] M. Eigen. Selforganization of matter and the evolution of biological macromolecules. *Die Naturwissenschaften*, 10:465–523, 1971.

[8] M. Eigen, J. McCaskill, and P. Schuster. The molecular Quasispecies. volume 75, pages 149 – 263. J. Wiley & Sons, 1989.

[9] M. Eigen and P. Schuster. *The Hypercycle: a principle of natural self-organization*. Springer, Berlin, 1979 (ZBP:23493).

[10] J. D. Farmer, N. H. Packard, and A. S. Perelson. The immune system, adaptation and machine learning. *Phsica*, 22 D:187–204, 1986.

[11] R. A. Fisher. *The genetical theory of natural selection*. Oxford: Clarendon Press., 1930.

[12] W. Fontana and L. W. Buss. "The Arrival of the Fittest": Towards a theory of biological organization. *Bull. Math. Biol.*, 1994. in press.

[13] W. Fontana, W. Schnabl, and P. Schuster. Physical aspects of evolutionary optimization and adaption. *Physical Review A*, 40(6):3301–3321, 1989.

[14] W. Fontana and P. Schuster. A computer model of evolutionary optimization. *Biophysical Chemistry*, 26:123–147, 1987.

[15] C. V. Forst, C. Reidys, and J. Weber. Evolutionary dynamics and optimization: Neutral Networks as model-landscape for RNA secondary-structure folding-landscapes. In F. Morán, A. Moreno, J. Merelo, and P. Chacón, editors, *Advances in Artificial Life*, volume 929 of *Lecture Notes in Artificial Intelligence*, Berlin, Heidelberg, New York, 1995. ECAL '95, Springer.

[16] M. Gebinoga. Hypercycles in biological systems. *J. Endocyt.*, 1995. submitted.

[17] M. Gebinoga and F. Oehlenschläger. Comparison of self-sustained sequence replication reaction systems. *Eur. J. Biochem.*, 1995. accepted.

[18] D. Gillespie. Exact stochastic simulation of coupled chemical reactions. *J. Chem. Phys.*, 81:2340–2361, 1977.

[19] J. Hofbauer. On the occurance of limit cycles in the Lotka- Volterra equation. *Nonlinear Analysis*, 5:1003–1007, 1981.

[20] J. Hofbauer, J. Mallet-Paret, and H. Smith. Stable periodic solutions for the hypercycle system. *J. Dyn. Diff. Equ.*, 3(3):423, 1991.

[21] J. Hofbauer and K. Sigmund. *The Theory of Evolution and Dynamical Systems*. Cambridge University Press (Cambridge), 1988.

[22] S. A. Kauffman. Autocatalytic sets of proteins. *J. Theoret. Biol.*, 119(1):1–24, 1986.

[23] M. Nowak and P. Schuster. Error tresholds of replication in finite populations, mutation frequencies and the onset of Muller's ratchet. *Journal of theoretical Biology*, 137:375–395, 1989.

[24] J. C. Nuño, M. A. Andrade, and F. Montero. Non-uniformities and superimposed competition in model of an autocatalytic network formed by error-prone selfreplicative species. *Bull. Math.Biol.*, 55:417–449, 1993.

[25] J. C. Nuño, M. A. Andrade, F. Morán, and F. Montero. A model of an autocatalytic network formed by error-rone self-replicative species. *Bull. Math. Biol.*, 55:385–415, 1993.

[26] S. Rasmussen. Toward a quantitative theory of the origin of life. In C. G. Langton, editor, *Artificial Life*, volume VI of *Santa Fe Institute Studies in the Sciences of Complexity*, pages 79–104, Redwood City, 1989. Addison Wesley.

[27] S. Rasmussen, C. Knudsen, and R. Feldberg. Dynamics of programmable matter. In C. G. Langton, C. Taylor, J. D. Farmer, and S. Rasmussen, editors, *Artificial Life II*, volume X of *Santa Fe Institute Studies in the Sciences of Complexity*, pages 211–254, Redwood City, 1991. Addison Wesley.

[28] C. Reidys, C. V. Forst, and P. Schuster. Replication on neutral networks of RNA secondary structures. *Bull. Math. Biol.*, 1995. almost submitted (since Oct. 1994).

[29] C. Reidys, P. F. Stadler, and P. Schuster. Generic properties of combinatory maps and neutral networks of RNA secondary structures. *Bull. Math. Biol.*, 1995. submitted.

[30] P. Schuster. Artificial life and molecular evolutionary biology. In F. Morán, A. Moreno, J. Merelo, and P. Chacón, editors, *Advances in Artificial Life*, Lecture Notes in Artificial Intelligence, Berlin, Heidelberg, New York, 1995. ECAL '95, Springer.

[31] P. Schuster, W. Fontana, P. F. Stadler, and I. L. Hofacker. From sequences to shapes and back: A case study in RNA secondary structures. *Proc.Roy.Soc.(London)B*, 255:279–284, 1994.

[32] J.-P. Serre. *Linear Representations of Finite Groups*. Springer, 1977.

[33] P. F. Stadler, W. Fontana, and J. H. Miller. Random catalytic reaction networks. *Physica D*, 63:378, 1993.

[34] P. F. Stadler, W. Schnabl, C. V. Forst, and P. Schuster. Dynamic of small autocatalytic reaction networks – II. Replication, mutation and catalysis. *Bull. Math. Biol.*, 57(1):21–61, 1995.

[35] M. S. Waterman. Secondary structure of single - stranded nucleic acids. *Studies on foundations and combinatorics, Advances in mathematics supplementary studies, Academic Press N.Y.*, 1:167 – 212, 1978.

[36] J. Weber. Transitions between two neutral networks. private communication, 1996.

Propagation of Information in Populations of Self-Replicating Code

Johan Chu[1] and Chris Adami[2,3]

[1]Department of Physics 114-36
California Institute of Technology, Pasadena, CA 91125
jchu@cco.caltech.edu

[2]W. K. Kellogg Radiation Laboratory 106-38
[3]Computation and Neural Systems 139-74
California Institute of Technology, Pasadena, CA 91125
adami@krl.caltech.edu

Abstract

We observe the propagation of information in a system of self-replicating strings of code ("Artificial Life") as a function of fitness and mutation rate. Comparison with theoretical predictions based on the reaction-diffusion equation shows that the response of the artificial system to fluctuations (e.g. velocity of the information wave as a function of relative fitness) closely follows that of natural systems. We find that the relaxation time of the system depends on the speed of propagation of information and the size of the system. This analysis offers the possibility of determining the minimal system size for observation of non-equilibrium effects at fixed mutation rate.

1   Introduction

Thermodynamic equilibrium systems respond to perturbations with waves that re-establish equilibrium. This is a general feature of statistical systems, but it can also be observed in natural populations, where the disturbance of interest is a new species with either negligible or positive fitness advantage. The new species spreads through the population at a rate dependent on its relative fitness and some basic properties of the medium which can be summarized by the diffusion coefficient. This problem has been addressed theoretically [1] and experimentally (see e.g. [2] and references therein) since early this century. The application of the appropriate machinery (diffusion equations) to the spatial propagation of *information* rather than species, is much more recent, and has been successful in the description of experiments with *in vitro* evolving RNA [3, 4].

Systems of self-replicating information (cf. the replicating RNA system mentioned above) are often thought to represent the simplest living system. They offer the chance to isolate the mechanisms involved in information transfer (from environment into the genome) and propagation (throughout the population), and study them in detail.

It has long been suspected that living systems operate, in a thermodynamical sense, far away from the equilibrium state. On the molecular scale, many of the chemical reactions occurring in a cell's metabolism require non-equilibrium conditions. On a larger scale, it appears that only a system far away from equilibrium can produce the required diversity (in genome) for evolution to proceed effectively (we will comment on this below).

In the systems that we are interested in – systems of self-replicating information in a noisy and information-rich environment – the processes that work for and against equilibration of information are clearly mutation and replication. In the absence of mutation, replication leads to a uniform non-evolving state where every member of the population is identical. Mutation in the absence of replication, on the other hand, leads to maximal diversity of the population but no evolution either, as selection is absent. Thus, effective adaptation and evolution depend on a balance of these driving forces (see, *e.g.* [7, 8]). The relaxation time of such a system, however, just as in thermodynamical systems, is mainly dictated by the mutation rate which plays the role of "temperature" in these systems [8]. As such, it represents a crucial parameter which determines how close the system is to "thermodynamical" equilibrium. Clearly, a relaxation time larger than the average time between (advantageous) mutations will result in a non-equilibrium system, while a smaller relaxation time leads to fast equilibration. The relaxation time may be defined as the time it takes information to spread throughout the entire system (*i.e.* travel an average distance of half the "diameter" of the population). A non-equilibrium population therefore can always be obtained (at fixed mutation rate) by increasing the size of the system. At the same time, such a large system segments into areas that effectively cannot communicate with each other, but are close to equilibrium themselves. This may be the key to genomic diversity, and possibly to speciation in the absence of niches and explicit barriers.

The advent of artificial living systems such as tierra [5, 7] and avida [10, 11] have opened up the possibility of checking these ideas explicitly, as the evolutionary pace in systems both close and far away from equilibrium can be investigated directly. As a foundation for such experiments, in this paper we investigate the dynamics of information propagation in the artificial life system sanda, a variant of the avida system designed to run on arbitrarily many parallel processors. This is a necessary capability for investigating arbitrarily large populations of strings of code. The purpose of our experiments is two-fold. On the one hand, we would like to "validate" our Artificial Life system by comparing our experimental results to theoretical predictions known to describe natural systems, such as waves of RNA strings replicating in $Q\beta$-replicase [3, 4]. On the other hand, this benchmark allows us to determine the diffusion coefficient and velocity of information propagation from relative fitness and mutation rate. Finally, we arrive at an estimate of the minimum system size which guarantees that the population will not, on average, equilibrate.

In the next section we briefly describe sanda and its main design characteristics. The third section introduces the reaction-diffusion equation for a discrete system and

analytical results for the wavefront velocity as a function of relative fitness and mutation rate. We describe our results in the subsequent section and close with some comments and conclusions.

2   The Artificial Life System "Sanda"

Like avida, sanda works with a population of strings of code residing on an $M \times N$ grid with periodic boundary conditions. Each lattice point can hold at most one string. Each string consists of a sequence of instructions from a user-defined set. These instructions, which resemble modern assembly code and can be executed on a virtual CPU, are designed to allow self-replication. The set of instructions used is capable of universal computation.

Each string has its own CPU which executes its instructions in order. A string self-replicates by executing instructions which cause it to allocate memory for its child, copy its own instructions one by one into this new space, and then divide the child from itself and place it in an adjacent grid spot. The child then is provided with its own virtual CPU to execute its instructions.

When a string replicates, it places its child in one of the eight adjacent grid spots, replacing any string which may have been there. Which lattice point is chosen can be defined by the user. In our experiments, we have used both random selection and selection of the oldest string in the neighbourhood. As we shall see, the selection mechanism has a significant effect on the spread of information.

It should be noted that this birth process, and indeed all interactions between strings, are local processes in which only strings adjacent to each other on the grid may affect each other directly. This is important as it both supplies the structure needed for studies of spatial characteristics of populations of self-replicating strings of code, and allows longer relaxation times – making possible studies of the equilibration processes of such systems and their nonequilibrium behavior.

This process of self-replication is subject to mutations or errors which may lead to offspring different from the original string and in most cases non-viable (*i.e.* not capable of self-replication). Of the many possible ways to implement mutations, we have used only copy errors — every time a string copies an instruction there is a finite chance that instead of faithfully copying the instruction, it will instead write a randomly chosen one. This chance of mutation is implemented as a mutation rate R – the probability of copy-error per instruction copied. A mutation rate R for a string of length ℓ will therefore lead to a fidelity (probability of the copied string being identical to the original) $\alpha = (1 - R)^\ell$. This then, allows us to evolve a very heterogeneous population from an initially homogeneous one. The resulting evolution, co-evolution, speciation etc. have been and continue to be studied. [6, 7, 8, 9, 10, 11]

What decides whether one particular sequence of instructions (or genotype) will increase or decrease in number are the rate at which it replicates, and the rate that it is replaced at. In our model, the latter is genotype independent (the "chemostat" regime). Accordingly, we define the former (*i.e.* its average replication rate) as the genotype's fitness. In other words, fitness is equal to the inverse of the time required to reproduce (gestation time).

To consistently define a replication rate, it is necessary to define a unit of time. Previously, in tierra and avida, time has been defined in terms of instructions executed for the whole population (scaled by the size of the population in the case of avida). In sanda, we define a physical time by stipulating that it takes a certain finite time for a cell to execute an instruction. This base execution time may vary for different instructions (but is kept constant in all experiments presented here). The *actual* time a cell takes to execute a certain instruction is then increased or decreased by changing its "efficiency". Initially, each cell is assigned an efficiency near unity, $e = (1 + \eta)$, where η represents a small stochastic component. In summary, the time it takes a cell to execute a series of instructions depends on the number of instructions, the particular instructions executed, and the cell's efficiency.

Self-replication consists of the execution of a certain series of instructions by the cell. Thus, the fitness of the cell (and its respective genotype) is just the rate at which this is accomplished and depends explicitly on the cell's efficiency. We can assign better (or worse) efficiency values to cells which contain certain instructions or which manage to carry out certain operations on their CPU register values. This allows us to influence the system's evolution so as to evolve strings which carry out allocated tasks. A cell that manages a user-defined task can be assigned a better efficiency for accomplishing it. Such cells, by virtue of their higher replication rate, would then have an evolutionary advantage over other cells and force them into extinction. At the same time, the discovery that led to the better efficiency is propagated throughout the population and effectively frozen into the genome.

In addition to the introduction of a real time, sanda differs from its predecessors in its parallel emulation algorithm. Instead of using a block time-slicing algorithm to simulate multiple virtual CPUs, sanda uses a localized queuing system which allows perfect simulation of parallelism.

Finally, sanda was written to run on both parallel processors and single processor machines. Therefore, it is possible, using parallel computers, to have very large populations of strings coevolving. This permits studies of extended spatial properties of these systems of self-replicating strings and holds promise of allowing us to study them away from equilibrium.

3 Diffusion and Waves

Information in sanda is transported mainly by self-replication. When a string divides into an adjacent grid site, it is also transferring the information contained in its code (genome) to this site. We have looked at the mode and speed of this transfer in relation to the fitness of the genotype carrying the information, the fitness of the other genotypes near this carrier, and the mutation rate.

Consider what happens when one string of a new genotype appears in an area previously populated by other genotypes. We will make the assumption that the fitness of the other viable (self-replicating) genotypes near the carrier are approximately the same. This holds for cases where the carrier is moving into areas which are in local equilibrium. We will use f_c for the fitness of the newly introduced (carrier) genotype and f_b for the fitness of the background genotypes. If $f_c < f_b$, obviously the new genotype will not survive nor spread.

In the following, we have studied three different cases: diffusion, wave propagation, and wave propagation with mutation.

The diffusion case represents the limit where the fitness of both genotypes are the same. It turns out that this can be modelled as a classical random walk. On average, if the carrier string replicates it will be replaced before it can replicate again. This is effectively the same as the carrier string *moving* one lattice spacing in a random direction chosen from the eight available to it. The random walk is characterized by the disappearance of the mean displacement and the linear dependence on time of the mean squared displacement:

$$\langle r \rangle(t) = 0 \qquad (1)$$
$$\langle r^2 \rangle(t) = 4Dt \qquad (2)$$

where D is defined as the diffusion coefficient.

For our particular choice of grid and replication rules, we find for the diffusion coefficient of a genotype with fitness f,

$$D^{(b)} = \frac{3}{8}a^2 f \qquad (3)$$

where a is the lattice spacing. This holds for a "biased" selection scheme where we select the oldest cell in the neighbourhood to be replaced. (See below.)

If $f_c > f_b$ then we find that instead of diffusion we obtain a roughly circular population wave of the new genotype spreading outward. We are interested in the speed of this wavefront.

Let us first treat the case without mutation. If the radius of this wavefront is not too small we can treat the distance from the center of the circle r as a linear coordinate. We define $\rho(r,t)$ as the mean normalized population density of strings of the new genotype at a distance r from the center at a time t measured from our initial seeding with the new genotype. We assume that the ages of cells near each other have roughly the same distribution and that this distribution is genotype independent, ensuring that the selection of cells to be replaced does not depend on genotype either.

Then, we can write a flux equation (the reaction-diffusion equation) which determines the change in the population density $\rho(r,t)$ as a function of time

$$\frac{\partial \rho(r,t)}{\partial t} =$$

$$\left[\frac{3}{8}\rho(r-a,t) + \frac{1}{4}\rho(r,t) + \frac{3}{8}\rho(r+a,t) \right] f_c \left(1 - \rho(r,t)\right)$$

$$- \left[\frac{3}{8}(1 - \rho(r-a,t)) + \frac{1}{4}(1 - \rho(r,t)) \right.$$

$$\left. + \frac{3}{8}(1 - \rho(r+a,t)) \right] f_b \rho(r,t) . \qquad (4)$$

Since we are interested in the speed of the very front of the wave, we can assume ρ to be small. Also, from physical considerations we assume ρ is reasonably smooth. Then, we can use a Taylor expansion for $\rho(r \pm a, t)$ and keep the lowest order terms to obtain

$$\frac{\partial \rho(r,t)}{\partial t} = \frac{3}{8}a^2 f_c \frac{\partial^2 \rho(r,t)}{\partial r^2} + (f_c - f_b)\rho(r,t) . \qquad (5)$$

This can be solved for the linear wavefront speed $v^{(b)}$ yielding [12]

$$v^{(b)} = a \sqrt{\frac{3}{2}} \sqrt{f_c(f_c - f_b)} \qquad (6)$$

$$= 2\sqrt{D_c^{(b)}(f_c - f_b)} \qquad (7)$$

where $D_c^{(b)}$ is the diffusion coefficient of the carrier genotype when using a biased (by age) selection scheme.

To study the case of wave-propagation with mutation we shall make the assumption that all mutations are fatal. We can then calculate a steady state density of non-viable cells δ,

$$\delta = 1 - \alpha^{1/8} \qquad (8)$$

where the fidelity α is the probability that a child will have the same genotype as its parent (i.e., not be mutated). As mentioned earlier, the fidelity is related to the mutation rate R by

$$\alpha = (1 - R)^\ell \qquad (9)$$

where ℓ is the length of the particular string. Modifying our previous flux equation to take into account these new factors and repeating our previous analysis gives us

$$v^{(b)} = 2\alpha\sqrt{D_c^{(b)}(f_c - \alpha^{1/8}f_b)} . \qquad (10)$$

Let us now consider the effects of different selection schemes for choosing cells to be replaced. The relations we derive above hold true for the case in which we replace the oldest cell in the 8-cell neighbourhood when replicating ("age-based" selection). Another method of choosing a cell for replacement is to choose a random neighbouring cell regardless of age. This scheme, which we term "random selection" as opposed to the biased selection treated above, effectively halves the replication rate of all cells. It follows that the diffusion coefficient is also halved,

$$D^{(r)} = \frac{3}{16}a^2 f \qquad (11)$$

$$= \frac{1}{2}D^{(b)} \qquad (12)$$

and for the velocity of the wavefront (with no mutation) we find

$$v^{(r)} = 2\sqrt{D_c^{(r)}\frac{(f_c - f_b)}{2}} . \qquad (13)$$

In Fig.1, we show a histogram of the number of offspring that a cell obtains before being replaced by a neighbour's offspring, for the biased selection case (left panel) and the random case (right panel). As expected from general arguments, half of the cells in the random selection scenario are replaced before having had a chance to produce their first offspring (resulting in a reduced diffusion coefficient), while biased selection ensures that most cells have exactly one child.

4 Results

We carry out our experiments by first populating the grid with a single (background) genotype of fitness f_b. Then, a single string of the carrier genotype with fitness f_c is placed onto a point of the grid at time $t = 0$. We then observe the position and speed of the wavefronts formed, the mean squared displacement of the population of carrier genotypes, and various other parameters as a function of time.

With f_b kept constant[1], we have varied f_b/f_c from 0.1 to 1.0 in increments of 0.1. Also, the mutation rate R was varied from 0 to 14×10^{-3} mutations per instruction, in increments of 1×10^{-3}.

A comparison of the theoretical vs. measured mean square displacement as a function of time for a genotype with no fitness advantage compared to its neighbours ($f_b/f_c = 1$) is shown in Fig.2. The data were obtained from approximately 1500 runs. The solid lines represent the (smoothed) averages of our measurements (for biased and random selection schemes), while the dashed lines

---

[1]The gestation time was approximately 330,000, where the base execution time for each instruction was (arbitrarily) set to 1000: $f_b = \frac{1}{330000}$

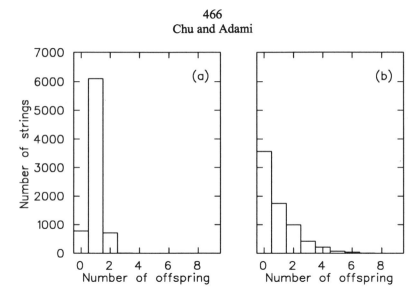

FIG. 1   Distribution of number of strings generating different numbers of offspring, for the biased selection case [panel (a)] and the random selection scenario (b).

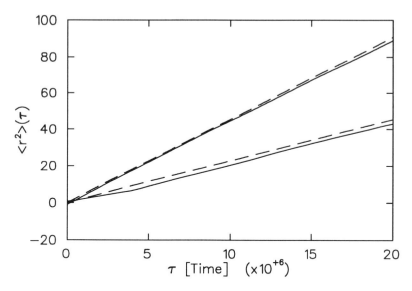

FIG. 2   Mean squared displacement of genome as a function of time due to diffusion. Solid lines represent experimental results obtained from 1500 independent runs. Dashed lines are theoretical predictions. The upper curves are obtained with the biased selection scheme while the lower curves result from the random selection scenario.

are the theoretical predictions obtained from the diffusion coefficients (3) and (11) respectively. The slopes of the measured and predicted lines agree very well confirming the validity of our random walk model and the diffusion coefficient predicted by it (without any free parameters). The slight discrepancy between the experimental curves and the predicted ones at small times is due to a finite-size effect that can be traced back to the coarseness of the grid.

Fig.3 shows the measured values of the wavefront speed for cases where $f_c > f_b$ and without mutation, with the corresponding predictions. Again, the higher curve is for biased and the lower for random selection. Note that the wavefront speed gain from an increase in fitness ratio is much better than linear. Note also that all predictions are again free of *any* adjustable parameters.

The dependence of this curve on the mutation rate is shown in Fig.4. Increasing the mutation rate tends to push the speed of the wave down. It should be noted, however, that because we have only used copy mutations there is no absolute cutoff point or error threshold α_c where all genotypes cease to be viable, with $\alpha_c > 0$. Rather, genotypes can spread until α is very close to the limit $\alpha_c = 0$.

Finally, we plot the dependence of the wavefront speed on the mutation rate for a fixed value of the fitness ratio ($f_b/f_c = 0.6$) in Fig.5. Data were obtained from an average of four runs per point in the biased selection scheme. Again, the prediction based on the reaction-diffusion equation with mutation agrees well (within error bars) with our measurements.

5 Discussion and Conclusions

Information propagation via replication into physically adjacent sites can be succinctly described by a reaction-diffusion equation. Such a description has been used in the description of *in-vitro* evolution of RNA replicating in Qβ-replicase [3, 4], as well as the replication of viruses in a host environment [13]. The same equation is used to describe the wave behavior of different strains of *E. Coli* bacteria propagating in a petri dish [14], even though the means of propagation in this case is motility rather than replication.

We have constructed an artificial living system (sanda) based on the avida design which allows the investigation of large populations of self-replicating strings of code, and the observation of non-equilibrium effects. The propagation of information was observed for a broad spectrum of relative fitness, ranging from the diffusion regime where the fitnesses are the same through regimes where the difference in fitness led to sharply defined wavefronts propagating at constant speed. The dynamics of information propagation led to the determination of a crucial time scale of the system which represents the average time for the system to return to an equilibrium

state after a perturbation. This relaxation time depends primarily on the size of the system, and the speed of information propagation within it. Equilibration can only be achieved if the mean time between (non-lethal) mutations is larger than the mean relaxation time. Thus, a *sufficiently* large system will never be in equilibrium. Rather, it is inexorably driven far from equilibrium by persistent mutation pressure.

For artificial living systems such as the one we have investigated, it is possible to formulate an approximate condition which ensures that it will (on average) never equilibrate, but rather consist of regions of local equilibrium that never come into informational contact. From the timescales mentioned above, we determine that the number of cells N in such a system must exceed a critical value:

$$ N > \left(\frac{2\,v(f)}{R_\star\,a} \right)^{2/3} , \qquad (14) $$

where $R_\star$ is the rate of *non-lethal mutations*, $v(f)$ the velocity of information waves, and a the lattice spacing (assuming a mean time between non-lethal mutations $t_\star \approx (N R_\star)^{-1}$).

Beyond the obvious advantages of a non-equilibrium regime for genomic diversity and the origin of species, such circumstances offer the fascinating opportunity to investigate the possibility of non-equilibrium pattern formation in (artificial) living systems. However, the most interesting avenue of investigation opened up by such artificial systems is that of the study of the fundamental characteristics of life itself. Since it is widely believed that many of the processes that define life, including evolution, occur in a state which is far from equilibrium, to study such processes it is necessary to have systems which exhibit the properties of life we are interested in and that can be quantitatively studied in a rigorous manner in this regime. The availability of artificial living systems as experimental testbeds that can be scaled up to arbitrary population sizes on massively parallel computers is a step in this direction.

Acknowledgements

J.C. would like to thank Mike Cross for continued support, and Roy Williams, Than Phung and the Center for Advanced Computing Research at Caltech for their help. C.A. was supported in part by NSF grants PHY94-12818 and PHY94-20470. This research was performed in part using the CSCC parallel computer system operated by Caltech on behalf of the Concurrent Supercomputing Consortium. Access to this facility was provided by Caltech.

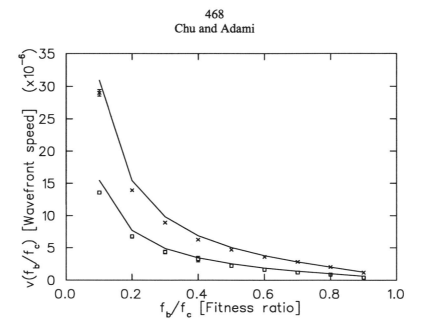

FIG. 3 Wavefront speed of a genotype with fitness f_c propagating through a background of genotypes with fitness f_b, averaged over four runs for each data point. Upper curve: biased selection, lower curve: random selection. Solid lines are predictions of Eqs. (7) and (13).

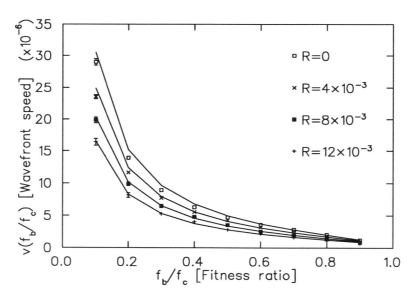

FIG. 4 Measured wavefront speeds versus fitness ratio for selected mutation rates R (symbols) are plotted with the theoretical predictions from Eq. (10) (for the biased selection scheme only).

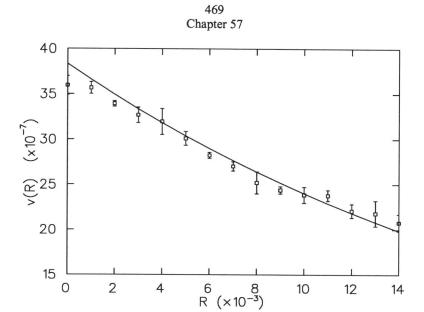

FIG. 5 Wavefront speed of a genotype (biased selection) with relative fitness $f_b/f_c = 0.6$ as a function of mutation rate (symbols). Solid line is prediction of Eq. (10).

References

[1] R.A. Fisher, Ann. Eugen **7** (1937)355.

[2] Th. Dobzhansky and S. Wright, Genetics **28** (1943)304.

[3] G.J. Bauer, J.S. McCaskill, and H. Otten, Proc. Natl. Acad. Sci. USA **86** (1989)7937.

[4] J.S. McCaskill and G.J. Bauer, Proc. Natl. Acad. Sci. USA **90** (1993)4191.

[5] T. S. Ray, in *Artificial Life II:* Proceedings of an Interdisciplinary Workshop on the Synthesis and Simulation of Living Systems, Santa Fe Institute Studies in the Sciences of Complexity, Proc. Vol. 10, edited by C. G. Langton et al., Addison-Wesley, Reading, MA, p. 371 (1992).

[6] T. S. Ray, Physica **D 75** (1994)239; Artificial Life **1** (1994)195.

[7] C. Adami, Physica **D 80** (1995)154.

[8] C. Adami, Artificial Life **1** (1994)429.

[9] C. Adami, Phys. Lett. **A 203** (1995)23.

[10] C. Adami and C.T. Brown, In R.A. Brook and P. Maes (Eds.), *Artificial Life IV*: Proceedings of the Fourth International Workshop on the Synthesis and Simulation of Living Systems, p. 377. MIT Press, Cambridge, MA (1994).

[11] C. Adami, C.T. Brown, and M. Haggerty, Proc. of 3rd Europ. Conf. on Artificial Life, June 4-6, 1995, Granada, Spain, Lecture Notes in Computer Science p.503, Springer Verlag (1995).

[12] M. C. Cross and P.C. Hohenberg, Rev. Mod. Phys. **65** (1993)851.

[13] J. Yin and J.S. McCaskill, Biophys. J. **61** (1992)1540.

[14] K. Agladze et al., Proc. Roy. Soc. Lond. B, **253** (1993)131.

CA, Biological Networks

The Application of Cellular Automata to Network Externalities in Consumer's Theory: A Generalisation of Life Game

Sobei H. Oda, Ken Kiura & Kanji Ueda

S.H. Oda: Faculty of Economics, Kyoto Sangyo University, Motoyama, Kamigamo, Kita-ku, Kyoto 603, Japan. E.mail: oda@cc.kyoto-su.ac.jp

K. Miura: Faculty of Engineering, Kobe University, 1-1 Rokkodai-cho, Nada-ku, Kobe 657, Japan. E.mail: miura@mi-2.mech.kobe-u.ac.jp

K. Ueda: Faculty of Engineering, Kobe University, 1-1 Rokkodai-cho, Nada-ku, Kobe 657, Japan. E.mail: ueda@ mech.kobe-u.ac.jp

Abstract

To buy a suit, an antique, or a computer, one may consider how many other people purchase the same product. If a person's decision depends on the number of those who make the same decision, it is said that there are network externalities. This paper develops a model of cellular automata to describe such markets with network externalities. The basic idea regards each cell as a person whose reservation price for a commodity, the maximum price he or she may pay for the commodity, depends on the number of his or her neighbours who purchased the product in the previous period. Simulations reveal some patterns of diffusion: (1) If all are conformists who prefer doing as their neighbours do, an equilibrium state where individuals cease to change their decisions is usually attained after some periods, but the number of those who buy the product depends on the initial conditions. (2) The situation is reversed if some are so snobbish that they hate to follow their neighbours: although individuals do not cease to change their decisions, the number of purchasers usually fluctuates around a value which is independent of the initial conditions with small amplitude.

1. Introduction

It is usually assumed in economic theories that a consumer's utility depends only on his or her own consumption: a person's preference is not affected by other people's behaviour. However, this is not always the case; to buy a suit, an antique, or a computer, one may consider how many other people have the same product. If a person's optimal decision depends on the number of those who make the same decision, economists say there are network externalities. In this paper we shall develop a model of cellular automata to describe markets where network externalities are observed.

Not a few theoretical and empirical studies have been done about network externalities among consumers since Liebenstein (1948) presented the concept: recent related studies are Choi (1994), Church & King (1993), Curien & Gensollen (1990), Ducan (1990), Kesteloot (1992), Liebowitz & Margolis (1994), etc. However, theoretical analysis has been developed mainly to express network externalities within the framework of equilibrium theories, which presumes that no transactions are made until a consistent set of all transactions is discovered. In Section 2 we shall review it, mentioning why it can only inappropriately express the market dynamics generated by network externalities.

In Section 3, we shall formulate a cellular automata model to describe a market with network externalities. The basic idea regards cells as those who may or may not buy a product according to its price and the number of their neighbours who purchased the product last time. By doing so, in contrast to the equilibrium approach, we can describe a market where people repeatedly gather local information, do a small calculation to make a decision, and put it into practice.

In Section 4, we shall explain some results from the simulations of our model. In the first half of this section, supposing that all are conformists who prefer doing as their neighbours do, we analyse the population dynamics generated by globally uniform birth and death rules. In the second half of this section, by assuming that some are so snobbish that they hate to follow their neighbours, we analyse the population dynamics generated by locally different birth and death rules. Being cautious about deriving general statements only from simulations, we could say that in both analyses the long-run equilibrium - if there exists such a situation - can differ from the one defined in Section 2.

Last, in Section 5, we shall briefly discuss some aspects of our analysis as a cellular automata model and an economic/marketing theory.

2. Equilibrium analysis

Pindyck and Rubinfeld (1990, pp. 113-117) explains the simplest equilibrium analysis of the market with network externalities in the following way.

Suppose that Consumer k buys a commodity if, and

only if, its price P does not exceed a certain level:

$$X_k \begin{cases} = 1 & \text{if } P \leq P_k \\ = 0 & \text{otherwise} \end{cases} \quad (1)$$

where X_k stands for Consumer k 's demand for the commodity.[1] If there is a network externality,

$$P_k = f_k (N_k) \quad (2)$$

where N_k stands for the number of purchasers of the commodity which Consumer k believes. Consumer k is called a *conformist* (*snob*) if f_k is an increasing (decreasing) function of N_k. In the circumstances X_k is a function of P and N_k:

$$X_k = F_k (P, N_k) . \quad (3)$$

The pair of price and quantity (P^*, X^*) defines an equilibrium if no one wants to alter his or her decision if the set is realised.

$$\begin{aligned} X^* &= \sum_{\text{all } k} F_k (P^*, X^*) \\ X^* &= S (P^*) \end{aligned} \quad (4)$$

where $X = S (P)$ stands for the market supply curve function. Since $X = \sum_{\text{all } k} F_k (P, X)$ is an implicit expression of the market demand curve $X = D (P)$ derived on the supposition that every buyer correctly expects the market demand: $N_k = X$, (4) implies that neither sellers (producers) nor purchasers (consumers) have reason for changing their decision if $P = P^*$ and $X = X^*$. Under some conditions (4) determines a unique equilibrium set of price and quantity. Figure 1 illustrates such a case where all are conformists.

However, the existence of equilibrium in itself does not imply that it is realised. Economic theories often assume auction so that commodities are neither sold nor bought till all sellers and buyers fix their decisions: first (P^*, X^*) is discovered by auction and then X^* units of the commodity are produced to be sold at the price of P^*. This is the dichotomy of information processing (communication and calculation) and economic activities (selling and buying). Rarely is it the case in the real world. As an example, consumers may find a type of suit being in fashion when they see someone wearing it on the street. In the

circumstances a person's economic activity (to buy and put on a suit) generates information (which suit is in fashion) and affects other persons' economic activity (which suit they purchase). Information processing and physical activities interact with each other in the real economy.

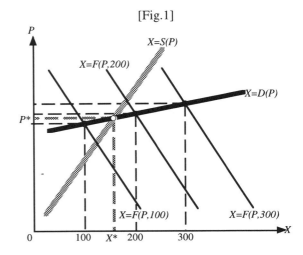

[Fig.1]

3. Cellular automata model

Let us imagine a peaceful village where people go for a walk every weekend. The only concern of the villagers during weekdays is whether they will go out with a rose on the coming weekend. Apart from the price of a rose and one's own preference (some may like roses more than others), one may consider whether those who may be seen during the walk put on a rose; a person may be delighted by seeing a neighbour wearing a rose, while another person may be disappointed by it.

Let us suppose that the village which is divided into B^2 squares like a chessboard and that a person lives in each square. We designate the villager living in the (i, j) square as V_{ij} and define his or her neighbours as

$$N_{ij} (R_{ij})$$

$$= \left\{ V_{mn} \begin{array}{l} \max (1, i - R_{ij}) \rfloor m \lfloor \min (B, i + R_{ij}) \\ \max (1, j - R_{ij}) \rfloor n \lfloor \min (B, j + R_{ij}) \\ V_{mn} \neq V_{ij} \end{array} \right\} \quad (5)$$

Let us also assume that to wear a rose on the Saturday of the t th week ($1 \leq t$), one must buy a rose at the price of P on the previous day and that if V_{ij} purchases and wears a rose, his or her utility increases in money terms by

$$\dot{P}_{ij} \left[1 + \alpha_{ij} \sigma_{ij} (t) \right] - P \quad (6)$$

---

1 Here P_k is called the reservation price of Consumer k and it is presumed that no consumer purchases more than one units of the commodity even if it is very cheap; this is usually the case if it is a consumer durable, say a refrigerator.

where $\dot{P}_{ij}$ is a positive constant; α_{ij} is a constant which is positive (negative) if V_{ij} is a conformist (snob); $\sigma_{ij}(t)$ represents the local ratio of rose-wearers which V_{ij} observes on the Saturday of the t th week:

$$\sigma_{ij}(t) = \frac{\sum_{V_{mn} \in N_{ij}} X_{mn}(t)}{E_{ij}(i)E_{ij}(j) - 1} \quad (7)$$

where the numerator of the right-hand side stands for the number of the V_{ij}'s neighbours who put on a rose on the weekend while the denominator represents the number of the V_{ij}'s neighbours:

$$X_{mn}(t) \begin{cases} = 1 & \text{if } V_{mn} \text{ puts on a rose} \\ & \text{on the Saturday of the } t\text{th week} \quad (8) \\ = 0 & \text{otherwise} \end{cases}$$

$$E_{ij}(k) \begin{cases} = B & \text{if } B \leq 1 + 2R_{ij} \\ = 1 + R_{ij} + k & \text{if } k - R_{ij} < 1 \\ & \text{and } k + R_{ij} \leq B \\ = 1 + R_{ij} + B - k & \text{if } 1 \leq k - R_{ij} \quad (9) \\ & \text{and } B < k + R_{ij} \\ = 1 + 2R_{ij} & \text{otherwise} \end{cases}$$

The difficulty which villagers may feel on every Friday is that they must decide whether they buy a rose or not without knowing how many of their neighbours will wear a rose on the next day. In the circumstances V_{ij} could not but determine $X_{ij}(t)$ according to his or her expectation on $\sigma_{ij}(t)$:

$$X_{ij}(t) = F_{ij}(P, \hat{\sigma}_{ij}(t)) \quad (10)$$

where $\hat{\sigma}_{ij}(t)$ stands for the V_{ij}'s expectation on $\sigma_{ij}(t)$ and

$$F_{ij}(P, \hat{\sigma}) \begin{cases} = 1 & \text{if } P \leq \dot{P}_{ij}(1 + \alpha_{ij}\hat{\sigma}) \\ = 0 & \text{otherwise} \end{cases} \quad (11)$$

As to the determination of $\hat{\sigma}_{ij}(t)$ we assume the following simple rule:

$$\hat{\sigma}_{ij}(t) = \sigma_{ij}(t-1) \quad (12)$$

As to the initial condition, we define the central part of the village as the C^2 square at the centre of the B^2 square village ($0 < C \leq B$). We assume that at the initial point in

time ($t = 0$), no one wears a rose outside the central part while everyone living in the central part may put on a rose independently at the probability of s ($0 < s \leq 1$); consequently, approximately $100s$ percent of the central inhabitants put on a rose in the 0th week: $s = \sigma(0)$.

On all the above-mentioned assumptions and conditions, the overall ratio of rose-wearing people:

$$\sigma(t) = \frac{\sum_{j=1}^{B}\sum_{i=1}^{B} X_{ij}(t)}{B^2} \quad .(13)$$

is uniquely determined.

Following the definition in the previous section, we can define an equilibrium as a situation where no one regrets. On the Saturday of the t th week V_{ij} does not regret the previous day's decision if he or she sees $\sigma_{ij}(t)$ is such that $X_{ij}(t) = F_{ij}(P, \sigma_{ij}(t))$. Hence the set of X_{ij}^* defines an equilibrium if the following is satisfied for all i and j:

$$X_{ij}^* = F_{ij}(P, \frac{\sum_{V_{mn} \in N_{ij}} X_{mn}^*}{E_{ij}(i)E_{ij}(j) - 1}) \quad .(14)$$

Checking this for all the 2^{B^2} possible combinations of X_{ij}^*, we can either say that there is no equilibrium or obtain every equilibrium set of X_{ij}^*.

The equilibrium ratio of rose-wearing people is defined by

$$\sigma^* = \frac{\sum_{j=1}^{B}\sum_{i=1}^{B} X_{ij}^*}{B^2} \quad .(15)$$

However, since finding the equilibrium set of X_{ij}^* may require a very large computational quantity for large B, we regard such $\sigma^\#$ that satisfies

$$\frac{\sum_{j=1}^{B}\sum_{i=1}^{B} F_{ij}(P, \sigma^\#)}{B^2} - \sigma^\# = 0 \quad (16)$$

as the approximation of σ^*. In fact $\sigma^\#$ represents the precise value of σ^* if everyone's neighbourhood is the whole village (then everyone is a neighbour of everyone else): $\sigma^\# = \sigma^*$ if $B \leq 1 + 2R_{ij}$ for all i and j. Since (16) is essentially the same as (3), this is presumed in the analysis of the previous section.

We shall make a few simulations in the following section. Since we shall use some variations of the above-mentioned basic model, let us conclude this section by mentioning some variations of the above-mentioned basic model.

First, we may assume that no villager can be original enough to recognise the habit of rose-wearing without seeing someone wearing a rose:

$$X_{ij}(t) = 0 \text{ if } \sigma_{ij}(u) = 0 \text{ for all } 0 \le u \le t-1 . \quad (17)$$

As we shall see in the next section, this additional assumption can be significant if C is small.

Secondly, we may replace (7) with

$$\sigma_{ij}(t) = \frac{X_{ij}(t) + \sum_{V_{mn} \in N_{ij}} X_{mn}(t)}{E_{ij}(i) E_{ij}(j)} \quad (18)$$

and modify (13) accordingly. This replacement implies that villagers take their previous decision into the calculation of the local ratio of rose-wearing people. Scarcely does this modification affect the qualitative properties of the model. As we shall see in the next section, however, if is R_{ij} small, the difference between (7) and (18) may be large enough to affect the dynamics considerably in quantitative terms.

Thirdly, we can suppose that the village lies on the surface of a torus by combining opposite edges of the square village. On this periodic boundary condition, the village has no periphery; for example V_{1j}'s northern neighbour is V_{Bj} while V_{i1}'s western neighbour is V_{B1}. Hence the number of V_{ij}'s neighbours is always $\min\left[(1+2R_{ij})^2, B^2\right] - \frac{1}{2} \pm \frac{1}{2}$; for example if $R_{11} = 1$, V_{11} has in all eight or nine neighbours: V_{BB}, V_{B1}, V_{B2}, V_{1B}, V_{12}, V_{2B}, V_{21}, V_{22} (and V_{11} if $\sigma_{ij}(t)$ is of (18) type). Since this is useful to see how the dynamics develop in a hypothetical market which has no central point, we shall often use this variant in the following section.

4. Simulations

4.1 Cases where consumers are homogeneous

Let us stat with the cases where all villagers are conformists of the same type while the price of a rose is between the minimum and the maximum reservation price of villagers:

$$R_{ij} = R, \quad \dot{P}_{ij} = \dot{P}, \quad \alpha_{ij} = \alpha$$
$$\text{and } \dot{P} < P < \dot{P}(1+\alpha) \text{ for all } i \text{ and } j . \quad (19)$$

As is readily checked there exist three equilibrium values of $\sigma(t)$:

$$\sigma_1^{\#} = 0, \quad \sigma_2^{\#} = \frac{1}{\alpha}\frac{P - \dot{P}}{P} \text{ and } \sigma_3^{\#} = 1 .^2 (20)$$

Nevertheless, in most simulations $\lim_{t \to \infty} \sigma(t) = 0$ or $\lim_{t \to \infty} \sigma(t) = 1$.

We can immediately see why it is rarely observed that $0 < \lim_{t \to \infty} \sigma(t) < 1$ if we see Figure 2, where the return map of

$$s(t) = \frac{\sum_{i=1}^{B} \sum_{i=1}^{B} F_{ij}(P, s(t-1))}{B^2} \quad (21)$$

is shown. If R is large enough, the return map fully governs the dynamics of $\sigma(t)$: if $B \le 1 + 2R$, $\sigma(t) = s(t)$ for all $t \ge 1$; consequently $\sigma(t) = 0$ for all $t \ge 1$ if $\sigma(0) < \sigma_2^{\#}$, while $\sigma(t) = 1$ for all $t \ge 1$ if $\sigma(0) > \sigma_2^{\#}$. This instability is basically maintained if $1 + 2R < B$ in our simulations: even for smaller R the range of $\sigma(0)$ where $\sigma(t)$ does not converge to zero or unity is rather short; it is still shorter for larger R.

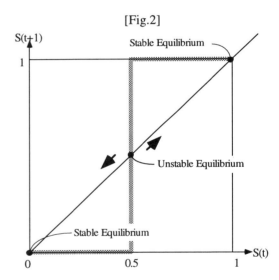

[Fig.2]

We can see why $\sigma(t)$ rarely converges between zero and unity even if R is small. See Figure 3, where two cases are compared. (In this and the following maps of the village white points represent rose-wearers while black points stand for non-rose-wearers.) Two initial conditions

---

2 Strictly speaking, $\sigma_2^{\#}$ does not satisfy (16); because if $\hat{\sigma}_{ij}(t) = \sigma_2^{\#}$ for all i and j, (10) implies that $X_{ij}(t) = 1$ for all i and j so that $\sigma(t) = 1 \ne \sigma_2^{\#}$. The fact is that $\sigma_2^{\#}$ is an equilibrium only if villagers may or may not buy a rose whose price equals their reservation price. However, having checked that no simulation in the text is affected if the first condition of (11) is replaced with $P < \dot{P}_{ij}(1 + \alpha_{ij}\hat{\sigma})$, we ignore this throughout the analysis.

are so similar (actually out of 10000 $X_{ij}(0)$ only one is not common to both conditions) that the development of the black-white pattern is apparently undistinguishable till $t = 50$, when the pattern ceases to change in most areas of the village. However, the initial small difference survives so that the lower large white area connects with the middle area in a case while they remain separate in the other case. Although all the other areas are identical and remain unchanged in both cases, the connected white area grows to cover all over the village so that $\sigma(t)$ reaches unity in the former case.[3]

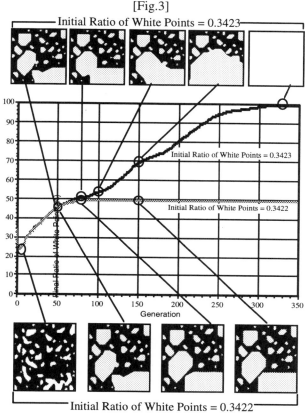

[Fig.3]

(B = C = 100 without boundary condition, $P = 0.9$, $\sigma_{ij}(t)$ is defined by (7), $\dot{P}_{ij} = 1$, $\alpha_{ij} = 1$ and $R_{ij} = 1$.)

Let us now consider the final distribution of rose-wears, or the final black-white patters. In our simulations, even if $0 < \lim_{t \to \infty} \sigma(t) < 1$, the black-white pattern always becomes stable except for the borders of the white areas: all or most $X_{ij}(t)$ remains the same value for large enough t. Perfectly stable patterns are often observed if the village has no boundary and villagers take into their own account the calculation of the local ratio of rose-wearing people.

See Figure 4, where three cases with different $R_{ij} = R$ are compared. Obviously the greater R is, the larger the pattern is. The reason is that those who live near by have common neighbours. If R increases, the number of common neighbours increases in relation to that of all neighbours; V_{ij} and V_{ij+1} share four persons among each eight neighbours (50 percent) if $R = 1$, while they share eighteen persons out of each twenty four neighbours (75 percent) if $R = 2$. The greater the ratio of common neighbours, the more likely they are to have a closer local ratio of rose-wearing people and thus make the same decision.[4]

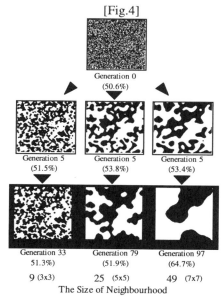

[Fig.4]

(B = C = 150 with boundary condition, $P = 1$, $\sigma_{ij}(t)$ is defined by (18), $\dot{P}_{ij} = 1$ and $\alpha_{ij} = 1$.)

---

3 In the example of Fig.3 a person buys a rose only if more than three out of his or her eight neighbours purchased a rose last week. In the circumstances the randomly distributed initial white points are first reduced to small separating groups (this is why $\sigma(t)$ once decreases in the figure) which cannot grow boundlessly without being connected with other groups. If P is so small that a person purchases a rose if three out of his or her eight neighbours do, a small white area such as a 2×3 rectangular expands limitlessly even if there are no other white points. As a result $\lim_{\sigma(t) \to \infty} \sigma(t) = 1$ is often predictable only from local information and the probability that $\lim_{\sigma(t) \to \infty} \sigma(t) = 1$ increases to unity as B increases.

4 Another effect of a larger R is, as is shown in Figure 4, that it usually takes longer until the final black-white pattern appears.

Although what is stated in the previous paragraph applies to almost most cases, it is not always so. Let us mention an exceptional case at the end of the analysis of the cases where all villagers are conformists. Figure 5 shows the development of the black-white pattern under the same condition that is assumed in the first case of Figure 4 except that $\sigma_{ij}(t)$ is defined by (18). Although the size of neighbourhood is small ($R = 1$), the final black-white patterns are rather large.

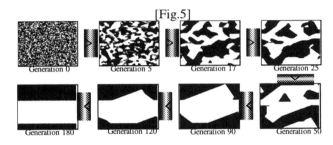

[Fig.5]

Generation 0   Generation 5   Generation 17   Generation 25

Generation 180   Generation 120   Generation 90   Generation 50

4.2 Cases where consumers are heterogeneous.

Let us consider those cases where there live two types of villagers: a type of conformist and a type of snob. As an example we show simulations of the following case: where $B = C = 100$ with boundary condition, $P = 1$ and $\sigma_{ij}(t)$ is defined by (18); forty percent of the villagers are conformists with $\dot{P}_{ij} = 1.1$ and $\alpha_{ij} = 0.3$, while the other sixty percent are snobs with $\dot{P}_{ij} = 1$ and $\alpha_{ij} = -0.3$; conformists and snobs are randomly distributed. The return map of $s(t)$ is shown in Figure 6.

[Fig.6]

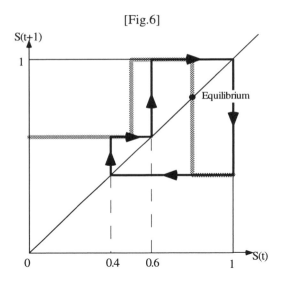

Here we see a unique equilibrium value: $\sigma^{\#} = 0.8$. By the same reason mentioned in Figure 2, however, this unstable equilibrium point does not seem to attract $\sigma(t)$. It is, as is shown in Figure 7, it is actually the case. If anything, the three-period limit cycle: $0.6 \rightarrow 1.0 \rightarrow 0.4 \rightarrow 0.6 \rightarrow \ldots$ may affect the dynamics of $\sigma(t)$. In fact mathematically it is obvious that $\sigma(t)$ falls into the limit cycle from the beginning if $\sigma(t) = s(t)$ (i.e. if $B \leq 1 + 2R$). In addition in all simulations $\sigma(t)$ soon starts to repeat the cycle precisely if $R \geq 5$.

For $R < 4$, however, a somewhat different three-period cycle is observed or something like the three-period limit cycle is observed only for enough small t. The value

of $\sigma(t)$ continues to fluctuate with small amplitude around 0.72 in the long run. This seems to be related not to the unstable equilibrium value 0.8 but to the average value for the three-period limit-cycle: $\frac{0.4 + 0.6 + 1}{3} = 0.67$. Since R is so small that $\sigma_{ij}(t)$ can be significantly different from one another, the first limit cycle from the initial value $\sigma(0)$ must gradually be divided into many local quasi three-period different phased cycles.

Let us see the case where $R = 2$ more closely. See Figure 7, where Line k represents the number of points whose colour (black or white) at time t is the same as it was at time $t - k$. The value of Line $t - k$ is always zero if the same black-white pattern appears every k times, while the value of every line is about 5000, or the half of population, if every point changes colour independently at the probability of fifty percent. Hence we can see the following. Although the aggregate black-white ratio fluctuates with small amplitude, about fifty percent of all points change colour every time. The above-mentioned three-period limit cycle soon disappears and more complicated dynamics emerges. Unlike in the case where all villagers are homogeneous, the black-white pattern does not cease to change, which is so involved that it is virtually unpredictable.[5]

However, again unlike in the previous case, the long-run average of $\sigma(t)$ is quite stable even for considerable changes in $\sigma(0)$. The dynamics of $\sigma(t)$, as it were, thermodynamically stable in the sense that though it fluctuates around a stable value with small amplitude, the value of individual $X_{ij}(t)$ does not cease to change in a complicated manner. It should however be remarked that this thermodynamical stability comes not from homogeneity but from heterogeneity in villagers' rules of behaviour.

It is well known in economic literature that only 0 and 1 are stable equilibrium values if all people are conformists of the same type while there may exist a stable equilibrium otherwise; for example Dixit and Nalebuff (1991, pp.231-238) explains why and how QWERTY keyboard layout dominates the market with a graph similar to Fig. 2 and Fig.6. However, though being free from our criticism on the dichotomy of information processing and economic

---

5In figure 8 the value of Line 24 is lower than 100 (one percent of population) for all large enough t. Hence if a point is white at $t = 100$, you can safely say that it will be white at $t = 124$, which statement is correct at the probability more than ninety-nine percent. In fact the black-white pattern at $t = 100$ is similar to the pattern at time $t = 124$, which is similar to the pattern at time $t = 148$, which is similar to the pattern at time $t = 172$. .... Nevertheless the black-white pattern at $t = 1300$ may be quite different from the pattern at $t = 100$; actually we have checked that Line k ($k < 100$) does not approaches a lower level than Line 24.

activities, this aggregate dynamic model ignores that locally available information differs from person to person. By taking this into account, we have shown that $\sigma(t)$ may be attracted by a value which differs from any stable or unstable equilibrium value.[6]

[Fig.7]

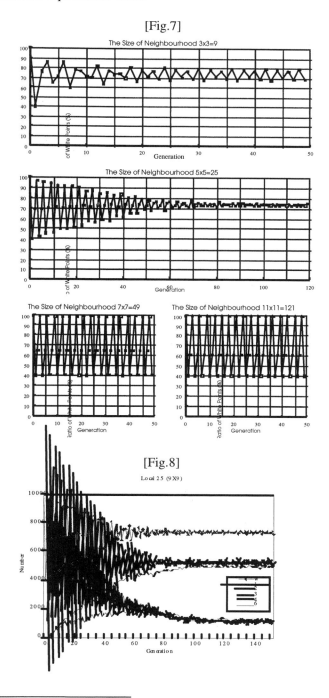

[Fig.8]

Local 2.5 (9 X9)

4.3 Macroscopic and microscopic stability of the diffusion process

Rogers (1962) and other marketing theorists claim that consumers can be classified according to when they purchase a new product; for example Rogers and Shoemaker (1971) classify them as innovators (2.5 percent), early adopters (13.5 percent), early majority (34 percent), late majority (34 percent) and laggards (16 percent) according to the timing of purchasing a new product. From our viewpoint, however, the timing of purchasing does not correspond to the type of consumers; two consumers of the same type may make a different decision if their local condition is different.

In addition, why the diffusion curve, or the curve to show the current or cumulative sales or quantity of a new product, is like a logistic curve is explained by the heterogeneity of consumers: different types of consumers buy a new product at different points in the diffusion process. As Figure 3 suggests, however, an S-shaped diffusion curve is obtainable if consumers are all homogeneous but locally available information may differ from person to person. From our viewpoint, the heterogeneity of consumers is necessary not for the existence of an S-shaped diffusion curve but for its stability. If all consumers are homogeneous, our cellular automata model becomes a cellular automata model where the birth and death rules are not locally different. Once a pattern from which white points spread boundlessly is formed in a small neighbourhood - even if white points can grow nowhere else - it can spread all over the world. However, if heterogeneous consumers are seeded randomly, whether the number of white points (rose-wears) grows or not is locally different. In other words, whether white points spread or not cannot be determined by local initial conditions. They spread only if it is possible globally and as a result the diffusion process becomes robust.

[Fig.9]

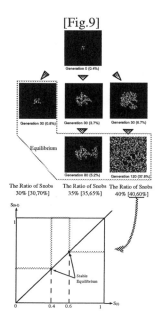

6At the end of this subsection let us mention another function of snobbish people. It is diffusing new information. Let us examine how rose-wearing fashion spreads on the supposition that only those who live in the small center square initially know it. See Figure 9. If the number of snobs is small, the fashion is not popularised. This is quite natural; conformists, who buy a rose only when they see sufficiently many of their neighbours wear a rose, cannot spread the new fashion.

5. Concluding remarks

Let us review our analysis from a more general viewpoint. We believe that our model can be seen from three different points: as an economic theory, a marketing theory and a model of cellular automata. Let us reconsider this order at the end of this paper.

As an economic theory, the analysis shows how the actual market process can be distorted by the dichotomy of information process and physical activities. This tradition, which describes economic activities on the supposition that no physical transactions are put into practice until all necessary communication and calculation for optimisation are perfectly done, has diffused into economic theories so widely and deeply that it is rarely mentioned - to say nothing of being criticised - explicitly; two important exceptions are Hicks (1939) and Kornai (1971). It is certain that assumptions are carefully chosen in equilibrium theories so as to assure the existence of an equilibrium (hopefully with its uniqueness and stability); examples are most assumptions about differentiability and convexity. Nevertheless, what is crucial is not such explicit mathematical assumptions but the dichotomy that presumes that the real world can be predicted or simulated perfectly, which cannot be maintained from the viewpoint of computational quantity and the complicity of the real world. Even if the benefit of decentralised decision-making in the market economy may be basically explained by the present equilibrium theories, the merit and robustness of interactive information process and economic transactions in ever-changing economies is yet to be analysed. We hope our model could make some contribution to develop economic theories upon this direction.

As a marketing theory this may give a microeconomic foundation to the theory of the diffusion process of new products. Rogers (1962) and other marketing theorists claim, based numerous empirical studies, that since the valuation of new products and the locally available information differ from person to person, consumers adopt in such different time lag that the quantity of a new product grows along with a S-shaped curve (something like a logistic curve). As far as we know, however, the relation among heterogeneity of purchasers, difference in locally accessible information and the shape of the diffusion curve has not been examined explicitly in terms of mathematics or simulation. Our model and analysis could have some meaning in the circumstances; simulations suggest that the diffusion curve is unstable if purchasers are homogeneous conformists while it is stable if purchasers consist of conformists and snobs.

As a model of cellular automata our model is a generalisation of the conventional life game (see Poundstone 1985). Our birth and death rules (to live or die if the number of neighbours is more or less than a certain number) is simpler and less interesting than the standard ones (to be able to live only if the number of neighbours is neither too large nor too small). However, the introduction of locally different rules will be able to create a number of applications of cellular automata in various fields, complicating the return map of $s(t)$ and consequently the dynamics of $\sigma(t)$.

References

Bass, F.M. (1969):"A new product growth model for consumer durables", in *Management Science*, vol.15, pp. 215-227.

Choi, J.P. (1994): "Competitive choice and planned obsolescence", in *Journal of Industrial Economics*, vol.42, pp.167-182.

Church, J. & King, I. (1993): "Bilingualism and network externalities", in *Canadian Journal of Economics*, vol.26, pp.337-345.

Curien, N. & Gensollen, M. (1990): "Network externality: its impact on growth and pricing of the telephone service", in P. Champsaur et-al eds. Essays in Honour of Edmond Malinvaud, MIT. Press.

Dixit, D. and Nalebuff, B. (1991): *Thinking Strategically: The Competitive Edge in Business, Politics, and Everyday Life*, Norton.

Ducan, G.M. (1990): "The effect of probabilistic demands on the structure of cost functions", in *Journal of risk and uncertaincy*, vol.3, pp.211-220.

Hicks, J.R. (1939): *Value and Capital; an inquiry into some fundamental principles of economic theory*, Oxford University Press.

Kesteloot, K. (1992): "Multimarket cooperation with scope effects in demand", in *Journal of Economics*, vol.55, pp.245-264.

Kornai , J. (1971): *Anti-equilibrium; on economic systems theory and the task of research*, North Holland.

Liebenstein, H. (1948): "Bandwagon, snob, and Veblen effects in the theory of consumers' demand", in *Quarterly Journal of Economics*, vol.62, pp.165-201.

Liebowitz, S.J. & Margolis, S.E. (1994): "Network externality: an uncommon tragedy", in *Journal of Economic Perspectives*, vol.8, pp.133-150.

Pindyck, R.S. & Rubinfeld, D.L. (1990): *Microeconomics*, Macmillan.

Poundstone, W. (1985): *The Recursive Universe; cosmic complexity and the limits of scientific knowledge*.

Rogers, E.M. (1962): *Diffusion of Innovation*.

Rogers, E.M. & Shoemaker (1971): *Communication of Innovation*.

MODELLING NANOSCALE PHENOMENA WITH CELLULAR AUTOMATA:

Some Chemical-Physics Observations

Edward A. Rietman

Bell Laboratories

600 Mountain Ave., Murray Hill, NJ 07974, ear@allwise.att.com

ABSTRACT

Molecules undergo only a finite number of possible chemical reactions. They can therefore be modeled as finite state machines and an array of them in a cellular automata can be used to study molecular dynamics and self organization at the nanotechnology scale. The cellular automata rule-table is, in essence, a map to molecular architecture. We discuss the possibility for using genetic algorithms to evolve cellular automata rule-tables that map to nanotechnology building blocks. In this paper we present some empirical studies for the above conjecture. We demonstrate that we can extract from the cellular automata rule-table, thermodynamics and macro-scale information.

INTRODUCTION

We start this paper with a review of the literature where others have used cellular automata to model molecular phenomena. The bulk of the literature has focused on solidification models, crystal growth and defect formation, and etching and deposition processes. We have extended, what has been reported in the literature, in the domain of etching and deposition, to show that crystal surface roughness, entropy and crystal surface etch/growth rate can be extracted from the cellular automata rule-tables. We literally have a map from probabilistic rule-tables to surface roughness and etch/growth rate. Knowledge of the surface roughness and rate of change of the surface are important parameters for designing nano-scale devices. Surface structure is also important for molecular recognition and molecular information processing (cf. Lehn, 1995). In the last part of the paper we argue that with genetic algorithms, cellular automata rule-tables for "molecular-scale automata" can be developed. With that tool it should be possible to design molecular nanotechnology building blocks.

SOLIDIFICATION MODELS

The vast majority of published literature on cellular automata models of molecular phenomena are concerned with dendrite growth, crystallization, and grain boundary studies. Crisp (1985) demonstrated the growth of defects in anthracene (C14H10) with a simple 2-state, 5-cell neighborhood array. The focus of the study was the mechanisms of defect formation as a result of photodimerisation. Packard (1986) and his colleagues studied lattice models of solidification and aggregation. Packard used a 2-state, 7-cell neighborhood (hexagonal lattice, center cell and 6 neighbors) to study lattice models for solidification and crystal growth. The model considers flow of heat by adding a continuous variable, temperature, at each lattice site. The time evolution of the temperature field follows a classical equation for heat flow. The change in temperature at each site is given as a function of the temperature of the neighbors. The Gibbs-Thompson effect (solidification at curved surfaces) is taken into consideration. The model is thus a hybrid of continuum and discrete elements. In two other papers, by Packard and his colleagues, Meyer et al. (1988) and Richards et al. (1990) use a genetic algorithm to find the automaton rule-table for the cellular array to model the growth of dendrites. They show how it is possible to use the genetic algorithm with experimental data to model a real world dendrite growth process.

Rappaz and Gandin (1993), Gandin et al. (1993), Cortie (1993) and Spittle and Brown (1994) all use cellular automata to model solidification processes of one and two component systems.

A rather unique application was presented by Kier and Cheng (1994a, b). In these two papers the authors model the dynamics of aqueous solutions. Their modeled relations of viscosity and vapor pressure relations are in excellent agreement with observations from experimental data. Their array was an extended neighborhood of 9 cells on a 55 X 55 square grid.

Jackson et al. (1994) report on a microsegration far from equilibrium with a discrete space-time model that is essentially a cellular automata model. (The primary difference between a cellular automata model and a lattice Monte Carlo model is that the sites in a CA are updated in parallel while those in a LMC model are updated asynchronously.) Their focus of the study is the equilibrium distribution coefficient. The model is compared with laser melting thin films of bismuth on silicon single crystal surfaces. The model is in excellent agreement with the experimental observations.

ETCHING MODELS

One of the earliest, discrete lattice models of etching was given by Blonder (1985), who makes several important observations. These models can be used to study the dynamics of molecular processes well below 1000A and that they would provide excellent tools for the study of technologically important issue involving microstructure manufacturing. He simulates both isotropic and anisotropic etching where the focus of the study is on the fractal nature of the etching surface. The fractal dimensionality for his two-dimensional model is 1.333. Blonder does not mention that his model is essentially a cellular automata.

Toh et al. (1992) model the multi-atom pits formed from sputter etching a surface. They use a 2-state 5-cell neighborhood cellular automata. The focus of the work is on demonstrating the surface roughness after removal of different size clusters. The only other paper in the open literature on etching models is by Than and Buttgenbach (1994). They use a three-dimensional model to examine the anisotropic etching of (100) silicon. Their probabilistic cellular automata rules are derived from experimental measurements of etch rate for the appropriate crystal face.

The primary literature, on studying these type of phenomena on crystal surfaces, consists of analysis of the fractal nature of the surface (cf., Barabasi and Stanley, 1995). The work we have done differs from all of the above in that we are not focusing on studying the surface etching/growth and relating fractal surfaces. Rather we are concerned with predicting the surface roughness from the automata rule-table. We desire to predict the rate of etch/growth from the automata rule-table. Thus our basic conjecture differs from other workers in that we claim that the molecular phenomena can be modeled with automata and we show how the rule-table of the automata can map directly to the surface properties. From that we can obtain the well known physics already discussed in the literature. Our demonstration is thus at a further level of abstraction and more removed from physical modeling.

MAPPING RULE-TABLES TO ROUGHNESS AND GROWTH

For a 2-state, 5-cell neighborhood the rule-table can be described by a 32 element vector. In the etching/growth studies this vector was composed of 32 probability numbers between zero and one. Each cell in the array is in one of two states $s_i \in \{0, 1\}$. The probability of jumping from state 0 to state 1 is given by considering the current state and the states of the nearest neighbors in the von Neumann Neighborhood.

The rate of a molecule jumping from lattice site i to an adjacent site j, in a molecular crystal is given by,

$$r(i, j) = \nu \exp\left(-\frac{\Delta E}{kT}\right) \qquad \text{(EQ 1)}$$

where ν is the vibrational frequency; ΔE includes binding energy and chemical potential, and T is the temperature in Kelven. For the programmable matter in cellular automata we have different rates for many of the 32 configurations in the rule-table, just as we would have many rates in the various crystal planes in real crystal lattices. In a real crystal the neighbor configurations need to be take into account along with the vibrational frequency, the binding energy and the chemical potential. Dividing the rates by the maximum rate we get a probability number that represents the probability of a jump.

The probability of a molecular or atomic jump resulting in a condensation on a crystal surface is given by

$$P(c) = \frac{\exp(\Delta\mu/kT)}{1 + \exp(\Delta E/kT)} \qquad \text{(EQ 2)}$$

and the probability for a desorption (etching) is given by

$$P(d) = \frac{1}{1 + \exp(\Delta E/kT)} \qquad \text{(EQ 3)}$$

In the cellular automata space we don't have control of the temperature, T; binding energy, ΔE; or chemical potential, $\Delta\mu$ at least not directly. What we can control is the probabilities, P(c) and P(d). So the probability space for the molecular processes become the probability elements in the cellular automata rule-table and the 32 element rule-table will have 16 P(c) elements and 16 P(d) elements. If we examine the ratio P(c)/P(d) we can deduce if the process is driven by P(c) or P(d). The natural logarithm of the ratio of the two probabilities in Eq [3] and Eq [4] is a function of the chemical potential.

$$\ln\left[\frac{P(c)}{P(d)}\right] = \frac{\Delta\mu}{kT} \qquad \text{(EQ 4)}$$

The initial configuration of the cellular array consists of a large rectangular region defined as the crystal. On this crystal surface etching or growth will occur. All cells in the crystal are in state 1 and those in the surrounding regions are in state 0. The growth occurs by ballistic deposition with surface diffusion of the molecules. In pure ballistic deposition, without any surface diffusion, the resulting surface would have deep pits with vertical side walls. Surface diffusion will tend to smooth out the surface. The crystal etch is also essentially the reverse of ballistic deposition. Without surface diffusion the etch would be anisotropic with deep pits and vertical side walls.

The data recorded during each time instant of the cellular automata run were: time (i.e. iteration), mass loss/gain of the crystal, number of cells with only one neighbor (N1), number cells with only 2 neighbors (N2), number of cells with only 3 neighbors (N3), number of cells with only 4 neighbors (N4), and surface area or roughness (R = 3*N1 + 2*N2 + N1).

In order to maintain crystal integrity certain elements in the rule-table were held fixed. Others were changed by hand and the results recorded in a data file for later analysis. Table 1 shows the actual rule-table identifying those elements, their probability and their state transition. This table indicates for element 0: if center cell is in state 0 and all neighbors are in state 0 then the update rule is go to 0. Similar transitions are to be interpreted for the other rule-table elements. Table 1 also shows the state transition rules for a "standard vector," that is, a rule-table that results in no changes in the cellular automata space for all time. This standard vector is used in computing metrics to describe the rule vectors. These metrics are then used in mapping to the physics of the process. One metric used is simply to find the cosine of the angle between the standard vector and the vector (or rule-table) of current interest. The angle between the standard vector U and the vector of interest V is given by

$$\cos(\theta) = \frac{UV}{|U||V|} \qquad \text{(EQ 5)}$$

where $|X|$ is understood to be the magnitude of the vector.

A second metric is the eigenvalue of the column matrix V^T. The vector's transpose is found and this column matrix is then manipulated by a Singular Value Decomposition (SVD). An M X N matrix, A, with M rows > N columns can be written as a product of an M X N matrix B, and N X N diagonal matrix, W and a transpose of an N X N matrix C.

$$A = B \bullet W \bullet C^T \qquad \text{(EQ 6)}$$

The matrices B and C are orthogonal. The diagonal elements of W are the singular values. Stewart (1973) and Basilevsky (1983) are excellent sources for detailed discussion of SVD. Press et al. (1988) give an algorithm and the SVD is part of the mathematical operations available in Mathematica (cf.

Wolfram, 1991).

Usually in cellular automata the mapping from rule-table space to configuration space is injective or surjective (cf. Durando, 1994). By using both the singular value of the rule-table and the cosine of the angle between the rule-table of interest and a standard rule-table, the mapping becomes bijective. The relation between the cosine of the angle and the singular value of the vector, from a linear regression is

$$\cos(\theta) = \frac{VU}{|V||U|} = -0.0671 + 0.1918W \qquad \text{(EQ 7)}$$

with a correlation of 0.9698. In this expression V is the vector or rule-table of interest, U is the standard vector, and W is the singular value of the column matrix from the rule-table. There are rare exceptions where the singular values of two column matrices will be identical (cf. Press et al, 1988).

From the collected data we can perform a linear regression relating the deposition rate to the functional in Eq. (4). This results in the relation

$$rate = 98.9 + 101.7\left(\frac{1}{kT}\right) \qquad \text{(EQ 8)}$$

The correlation for this linear fit is R=0.9398 and Figure 1 shows the, so called, Arrhenius plot for this reaction. The slope of 101.7 is the "chemical potential," in units of kT, for the system. This clearly indicates that the basic conjecture is reasonable. We can use cellular automata as programmable matter.

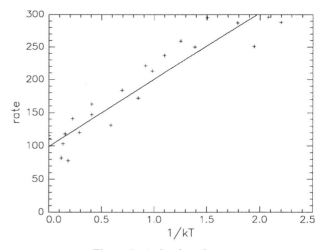

Figure 1. Arrhenius plot

The above two metrics describing the rule-vectors enable us to find the mapping from this rule-table space to the observed physics properties. A plot of the rate of change in the surface (etching or growth) with respect to cosine of the angle, or with respect to the eigenvalue, gives a scatter plot from which it becomes clear that a third dimension will be needed to shatter the two-dimensional space. Figure 2 is a diagram of the functional relation between the rate of change in the crystal surface (i.e. the velocity of the growth front), the eigenvalue of the rule-vector and the cosine of the angle of the vector. Given a cosine of an angle and the eigenvalue we can read from the surface-plot the expected growth/etch rate. Similar graphical studies can be done on changes, as a function of time on N1, N2, N3 and N4 (defined above).

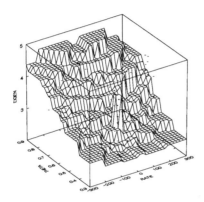

Figure 2. Surface plot of rate data.

Given the expected etch/growth rate we can find the expected roughness of the crystal surface. Figure 3 shows N(i) rate distributions related to the etch/growth rate. These figures show significant instability. However, the basic trend for the maximum of the smoothed envelope functions clearly shows that as the rate increases from negative to more positive we can expect an increase in the generation of the number of cells with fewer neighbors. This indicates that the surface is becoming more rough and the surface entropy is increasing.

In this paper, we have demonstrated the basic conjecture that dynamics of cellular automata can be used to model nano-scale phenomena. The next logical phase in the project is to examine 3-state, 5-cell neighborhoods; 2-state, 9-cell neighborhoods and 3-state, 9-cell neighborhoods. These will have 243, 512 and 19683 elements, respectively in their rule-tables. The first two systems can be done with hand coding. For the third system an automatic method to discover

useful rule-tables will be used. Similar studies of polymer folding on a lattice can be done with cellular automata. In this case the objective should be to find a mapping of the automata rule-table to the physics of the folded polymer and a description of the folded shape.

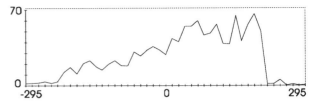
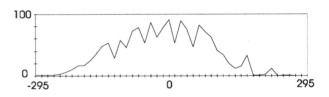
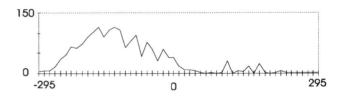
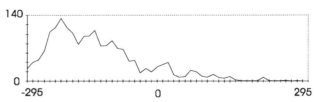

Figure 3. Distributions of the number of cells with N(i) neighbors as a function of rate of change in the crystal mass.

SOME BLUE-SKY POSSIBILITIES

As the number of devices on integrated circuit chips increase and the size of the devices shrink the next logical technology, as discussed by Drexler (1992) will be at the molecular scale. With an Avogadro number of components programming and assembly will be prohibitive. If we copy the basic methodology of Darwinian evolution we can begin now to design basic building blocks or nanotech LEGOs for a molecular nanotechnology. (LEGO is a registered trade mark of LEGO Systems Inc.) The scheme we are working on involves the basic fact that a molecule will undergo a finite number of types of reactions. When these molecular state changes are coded as a look-up table, and the look-up table coded as a bit string (or character string) we can manipulate this string as if it were a chromosome undergoing Darwinian evolution. If the state changes of a molecule are represented as a string, than a flask of molecules can be represented as a 3-dimensional array of these strings. New strings can be evolved by means of a genetic algorithm involving chromosome cross-over and mutation.

It is well known that cellular automata can self-organize to various structures (cf. Toffoli and Margolus, 1987). The difficulty in developing any specific structure lies in programming the cellular automata. One approach, first suggested by Meyer et al. (1989) and Richards et al. (1990) is to use a genetic algorithm to find the rule-set for the cellular automata to produce the desired structures within the CA space. This same approach was later suggested by Sims (1991) and de Garis (1992) to grow complex shapes. The best results for target shapes has been reported by Saitou and Jakiela (1994). For an excellent reference to genetic algorithms see Goldberg (1989).

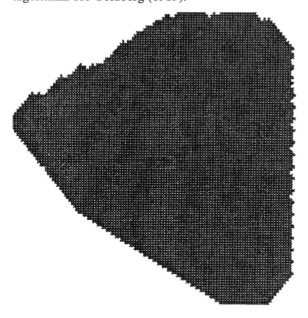

Figure 4. Cellular automata growth of a triangular shaped object on a square lattice.

We are attempting a similar approach to build structures in a cellular automata space. We use a genetic algorithm to develop the rule-table for a population of cellular automata. As an example of how the cellular automata can be used to grow objects, examine Figure 4. This figure is a screen dump of an attempt to evolve triangular objects in the cellular automata space (square lattice). Two rule-tables were concatenated together into a larger chromosome for a genetic algorithm (GA) manipulation and the effects of these two rule-tables on the phenotype is easily seen in the figure. The south-east edge of the triangular object shows two distinct growth phases. These two segments of the chromosome are known as operons and the entire chromosome is a differentiable chromosome, as discussed by Wilson (1988) and de Garis et al. (1992). Each operon is used to evolve a different "segment" of the structure being grown in the cellular automata space. Thus the object growth is analogous to growing an artificial embryo (cf. de Garis, 1992).

Extending the above object growth ideas and the molecular automata ideas it should be possible to design any molecular structure. Several approaches could be tried for realistic object growth. One approach involves a problem similar to protein folding and packing (cf. Richards, 1977; Richardson et al. 1992; and Creighton, 1992). These artificial proteins could be modified as described by Drexler (1994). A second approach is essentially a template-directed growth mechanism (cf. Ponder, 1987 and Heywood and Mann,. 1994). Yet a third method involves self-organization from solution (cf. Cram, 1986, Service, 1994). Once the appropriate rule-table has been developed, than a mapping from this rule-table to a set of molecular species must be found.

We expect the major difficulty with the above scheme is the mapping from the rule-table to a molecular hyperspace. The above section on mapping rule-tables to etch/growth rate suggest that this can be done by carefully selecting the representation for the rule-table. As Horvath (1992) points out there are millions of organic compounds. But, by using topological constraints (cf. Merrifield and Simmons, 1989) and the principle of molecular similarity (Johnson and Maggiora, 1990) we can reduce this to a set of compounds within a class of realistic molecular species. The chromosome, or rule-table, should be constructed with molecular rules that represent known chemistry and physics. Principles of molecular topology and molecular similarity as well as principles of molecular folding and intermolecular dynamics should be included. Wagener and Gasteiger (1994) give an excellent example of how to construct a chromosome for a genetic algorithm to "construct" a target molecular structure. Without these included the chance of finding the mapping from the rule-table to a real-world molecular hyperspace would be quite low.

The cellular automata analogy may prove to be too

complex from a rule-set perspective and too restrictive from a molecular topology perspective. It may be necessary to model the system on a lattice with molecular dynamics and molecular mechanics replacing the cellular automata dynamics but, there is no obvious reason that the cellular automata approach would not work (cf. Doolen et al. 1990). Chou et al. (1994) has, with appropriate dynamics changes, used a cellular automata to model self- replicating autocatalytic oligonucleotides. With the appropriate transition rules we should be able to "grow" any desired structure including Drexler's (1992) rod logic and Carter's (Carter et al., 1987) soliton switches.

Acknowledgments

I thank Jim Mitchell (Bell Labs) for support of this research. I thank George Gilmer and Matthew Marcus (both at Bell Labs) for many stimulating conversations on etching and deposition and/or cellular automata. I thank Dale Ibbotson (Bell Labs) for his support, early in the project and I thank Mark Andrews (McGill Univ.) for proof reading an early version of the manuscript and for all his encouragement. I thank Katsunori Shimohara (ATR, Kyoto, Japan) for his encouragement and support of the project and for inviting me to present these ideas at ATR in December '94. I thank the organizers of the Canadian Society of Chemistry for inviting me to present these ideas at the CSC meeting in Guelph, Canada, in May '95.

References

1. Barabasi, A.-L. and Stanley, H. E., FRACTAL CONCEPTS IN SURFACE GROWTH, Cambridge University Press, New York, NY (1995)

2. Basilevsky, A., APPLIED MATRIX ALGEBRA IN THE STATISTICAL SCIENCES, North-Holland, New York, NY (1983)

3. Blonder, G. E., "Simple Model for Etching" Physical Rev. 33B, 6157-6168 (1985)

4. Carter, F. L. Schultz, A. and Duchworth, D. "Soliton Switching and its Implications for Molecular Electronics", MOLECULAR ELECTRONIC DEVICES II, F. L. Carter (Editor), Marcel Dekker, New York, NY (1987)

5. Chou, H.-H., Reggia, J. A. Navarro-Gonzalez, R. and Wu, J. "An Extended Cellular Space Method for Simulating Autocatalytic Oligonucletides", Computers Chem. 18(1), 33-43 (1994)

6. Cortie, M. B., "Simulation of Metal Solidification Using a Cellular Automaton", Metallurgical Trans. 24B, 1045-1053 (1993)

7. Cram, D. J. "Preorganization-From Solvents to Spherands", Angew. Chem. Int. Ed. Engl. 25, 1039-1057 (1986)

8. Creighton, T. E. (editor), PROTEIN FOLDING, W. H. Freeman, New York, NY (1992)

9. Crisp, G. M., "A Cellular Automaton Model And Defects in Crystal Growth, I Anthracene", Chemical Physics, 97, 321-330 (1985)

10. de Garis, H. "Artificial Embryology: the Genetic Programming of an Artificial Embryo" in Soucek, B. and the IRIS Group, DYNAMIC, GENETIC, AND CHAOTIC PROGRAMMING: The Sixth Generation, John Wiley, New York, NY, 1992

11. de Garis, H., Iba, H. and Furuya, T., "Differentiable Chromosomes: The Genetic Programming of Switchable Shape-Genes", in Manner, R. and Manderick, B. (Editors) PARALLEL PROBLE SOLVING FROM NATURE, Elsevier Science Publishers, BV (1992)

12. Doolen, G. d., Frisch, U., Hasslacher, B., Orszag, S. and Wolfram, S. (editors), LATTICE GAS METHODS FOR PARTIAL DIFFERENTIAL EQUATIONS, Addison-Wesley, Redwood City, CA (1990)

13. Drexler, K. E. NANOSYSTEMS: MOLECULAR MACHINERY, MANUFACTURING AND COMPUTATION, Wiley, New York (1992)

14. Drexler, K. E. "Molecular Nanomachines: Physical Principles and Implementation Strategies", Annu. Rev. Biophys. Biomol. Struct. 23, 377-405 (1994)

15. Durand, B., "The Surjectivity Problem for 2D Cellular Automata", J. of Computer and System Sciences, 49, 718-725 (1994)

16. Gandin, Ch.-A., Rappaz, M. and Tintillier, R., "Three-Dimensional Probabilistic Simulation of Solidification Grain Structures: Application to Superalloy Precision Castings", Metallurgical Trans. 24A, 467-479 (1993)

17. Goldberg, D. E. GENETIC ALGORITHMS IN SEARCH, OPTIMIZATION & MACHINE LEARNING, Addison- Wesley, Redwood City, CA (1989)

18. Horvath, A. L., MOLECULAR DESIGN CHEMICAL STRUCTURE GENERATION FROM THE PROPERTIES OF PURE ORGANIC COMPOUNDS, Elsevier, Amsterdam (1992)

19. Heywood, B. R. and Mann, S. "Template-Directed Nucleation and Growth of Inorganic Materials", Adv. Mater. 6(1), 9- 20 (1994)

20. Jackson, K. A., Gilmer, G. H., Temkin, D. E. and Beatty, K. M., "Microsegration Far From Equilibrium", Submitted (1994)

21. Johnson, M. A. and Maggiora, G. M. (editors), CONCEPTS AND APPLICATIONS OF MOLECULAR SIMILARITY, Wiley, New York, NY (1990)

22. Kier, L. B. and Cheng, C.-K., "A Cellular Automata Model of Water", J. Chem. Inf. Comput. Sci., 34, 647-652 (1994)

23. Kier, L. B. and Cheng, C.-K., "A Cellular Automata Model of an Aqueous Solution", J. Chem. Inf. Comput. Sci., 34, 1334-1337 (1994)

24. Lehn, J.-M., SUPRAMOLECULAR CHEMISTRY: CONCEPTS AND PERSPECTIVES, VCH Publishers, New York, NY (1995)

25. Merrifield, R. E. and Simmons, H. E., TOPOLOGICAL METHODS IN CHEMISTRY, Wiley, New York, NY (1989)

26. Meyer, T. P., Richards, F. C. and Packard, N. H., "Learning Algorithm for Modeling Complex Spatial Dynamics", Phys. Rev. Letter, 63, 1735-1738 (1989)

27. Packard, N. H., "Lattice Models for Solidification and Aggregation", Science on Form: Proceedings of the First International Symposium for Science on Form, Kato, Takaki and Toriwaki, (editors), 95-101 (1986)

28. Ponder, J. W. and Richards, F. M. "Tertiary Templates for Proteins Use of Packing Criteria in Enumeration of Allowed Sequences for Different Structural Classes", J. Mol. Biol. 193, 775-791 (1987)

29. Press, W. H., Flannery, B. P., Teukolsky, S. A. and Vetterling, W. T., NUMERICAL RECIPES IN C: THE ART OF SCIENTIFIC COMPUTING, Cambridge U. Press, New York (1988)

30. Rappaz, M. and Gandin, Ch.-A. and Rappaz, M. "Probabilistic Modelling of Microstructure Formation in Solidification Processes", Acta. Metall. Mater., 41(2), 345-360 (1993)

31. Richards, F. C., Meyer, T. P. and Packard, N. H. "Extracting Cellular Automata Rules Directly From Experimental Data", Physica, 45D, 189-202 (1990)

32. Richards, F. M. "Areas, Volumes, Packing, and Protein Structure", Ann. rev. Biophys. Bioeng., 6, 151-176 (1977)

33. Richardson, J. S.; Richardson; D. C. Tweedy, N. B.; Gernert, K. M.; Quinn, T. P.; Hecht, M. H.; Erickson, B. W.; Yan, Y.; DcClain, R. D.; Donlan, M. E. and Surles, M. C. "Looking at Proteins: representations, Folding, Packing, and Design" Biophys, J. 63, 1186-1209 (1992)

34. Saitou, K. and Jakiela, M. J., "Meshing of Engineering Domains by Meitotic cell Division", ARTIFICIAL LIFE IV Proceedings of the Fourth International Workshop on the Synthesis and Simulation of Living Systems, R. Brooks and P. Maes (editors), 289-294 MIT Press, Cambridge, MA (1994)

35. Service, R. F. "Self-Assembly Comes Together", Science 265, 316-318 (1994)

36. Sims, K. "Interactive Evolution of Dynamical Systems" TOWARD A PRACTICE OF AUTONOMOUS SYSTEMS, Proceedings of the First European Conference on Artificial Life, MIT Press, Cambridge, MA (1991)

37. Spittle, J. A. and Brown, S. G. R., "A 3D Cellular Automaton Model of Coupled Growth in two Component Systems", Acta. Metall. Mater., 42(6), 1811-1815 (1994)

38. Stewart, G. W., INTRODUCTION TO MATRIX COMPUTATIONS, Academic Press, New York, NY (1973)

39. Than, O. and Buttgenbach, S. "Simulation of Anisotropic Chemical Etching of Crystalline Silicon Using A Cellular Automata Model", Sensors and Actuators, 45A, 85-89 (1994)

40. Toffoli, T. and Margolus, N. CELLULAR AUTOMATA MACHINES, MIT Press, Cambridge, MA (1987)

41. Toh, Y. S., Nobes, M. J. and Carter, G. "A Cellular Automata Simulation Study of Surface Roughening Resulting from Multi-Atom Etch Pit Generation During Sputtering", Nuclear Instruments and Methods in Physics Research, 67B, 586-589 (1992)

42. Wagener, M. and Gasteiger, J. "The Determination of Maximum Common Substructures by a Genetic Algorithm: Application in Synthesis Design and for the Structural Analysis of Bilogical Activity", Angew. Chem. Int. Ed. Engl. 33(11) (1994)

43. Wilson, S. W., "The Genetic Algorithm and Simulated

Evolution", in Langton, C. G. (editor) ARTIFICIAL LIFE, Addison-Wesley Pub. Redwood City, CA (1988)

44. Wolfram, S., MATHEMATICA A System For Doing mathematics by Computer, Second Edition, Addison-Wesley Publishing Co., Redwood City, CA (1991)

Table 1. If (rand() < p) then state indicated, otherwise opposite state. Note: Numerical values indicate fixed probabilities.

typical vector   standard vector

A Simple Self-Reproducing Cellular Automaton with Shape-Encoding Mechanism

Kenichi Morita and **Katsunobu Imai**
Faculty of Engineering, Hiroshima University
Higashi-Hiroshima-shi, 739 Japan
E-mail: {morita, imai}@ke.sys.hiroshima-u.ac.jp

Abstract

We propose a new self-reproducing model of a 12-state cellular automaton SR_{12} in which various objects called Worms and Loops can reproduce in a very simple manner. In this model, conversions (i.e., encoding and decoding) between the shape of an object and its description can be performed directly and symmetrically in both directions. Hence, objects need not have their static descriptions to perform reproduction. By this method, complexity of self-reproducing configurations is greatly reduced: the minimum number of cells is only 4 for the Worm, and 8 for the Loop. This model also has a large tolerance to the variety of objects' shapes, and in fact, a Worm or a Loop of arbitrary shape (but satisfying some minor condition) can self-reproduce in this cellular space.

1 Introduction

After the famous work of von Neumann [8], many studies on self-reproducing machines used the framework of a cellular automaton (CA). One of the reasons of using CA is that a self-reproducing mechanism (or algorithm) and the machine itself can be described precisely with the mathematical rigor.

When giving a definition of self-reproduction, von Neumann supposed the computation- and construction-universality as the condition for a self-reproducing machine to exclude passive or trivial replication of patterns in a cellular space. But, because of this condition, the early models [2, 8] needed huge configurations.

Instead of the above condition, Langton [5] posed a new criterion only requiring that the construction of a daughter configuration should be actively directed by the parent configuration, and that information stored in the configuration must be treated in two different manners, i.e., "interpreted" and "uninterpreted". Along this line, he designed a very simple self-reproducing CA in a modified 8-state model of Codd [2]. After that, several variants and simplified models appeared [1, 3, 7, 9, 10]. For example, Byl [1] showed a 6-state CA model in which a configuration consisting of 10 cells can self-reproduce, reducing both the numbers of states and cells.

Although von Neumann's self-reproducing machine was very complex, his essential idea was elegant and useful. Hence, most models after von Neumann have employed his method. In his model, a self-reproducing machine possesses its description as a "gene" besides the body itself. And self-reproduction is carried out by interpreting the description to construct a body, then copying and attaching it to the daughter.

However, if the machine can encode its shape into a description by checking its body dynamically, there is no need to keep the entire description. In fact, there proposed a few models that performs self-reproduction in such a manner [3, 4, 7]. Ibánes et al. [3] showed a 16-state model in which sheathed loops can reproduce by using a self-inspection method. Morita and Imai [7] also gave this kind of method independently. In the latter model, it is further shown that such a type of self-reproduction can be realized in a "reversible" cellular space.

Reversible cellular automaton is a backward deterministic CA, in which every configuration has at most one predecessor. It can be regarded as a model of a space that reflects physical reversibility. To design a reversible CA, a framework of "partitioned CA" (PCA) is useful (see [6, 7] for the detail). A PCA with von Neumann neighborhood is a special type of CA whose cell is divided into five parts. In our previous work [7], a reversible PCA having 8 states in each part (thus one cell has 8^5 states) was given. It was shown that various configuration called Worms and Loops can reproduce in its reversible space (Figs. 1 and 2).

In this study, we show a new 12-state self-reproducing CA SR_{12} having no static description. Though the shape-encoding method employed here is essentially the same as our previous model, we could obtain much simpler one by removing the reversibility constraint. The number of states is not so small as compared with others (e.g., [1, 5, 9]), but it has the following advantages:

1. Complexity of a self-reproducing configuration is very low. For example, a Worm with only 4 cells, and a Loop with only 8 cells can self-reproduce. Other self-reproducing configurations are also simple.

2. A Worm or a Loop of an *arbitrary* shape (but satisfying some condition) can self-reproduce. Thus, self-reproducing ability of an object is relatively robust against distortion or change of a configuration.

3. Since shape-encoding and decoding are performed directly and symmetrically, their mechanisms can be easily understood.

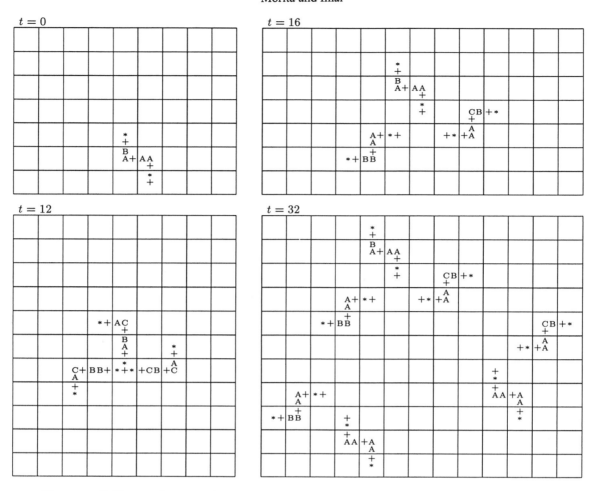

Figure 1: Self-reproduction of a Worm in a *reversible* PCA space (Morita and Imai [7]).

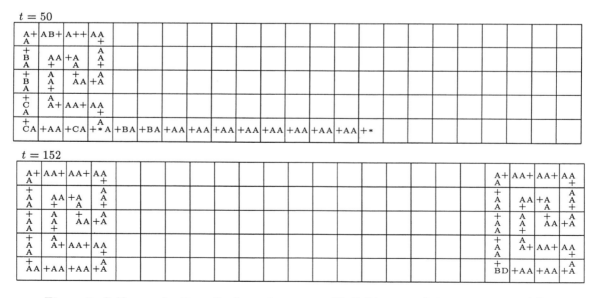

Figure 2: Self-reproduction of a Loop in a *reversible* PCA space (Morita and Imai [7]).

2 Designing a Simple Self-Reproducing CA with Shape-Encoding Mechanism

We design here a 12-state CA SR_{12} in which various configurations can self-reproduce in a simple way by using a shape-encoding method. SR_{12} is a CA with von Neumann neighborhood, and has the following state set.

$$Q = \{\#, \uparrow, \rightarrow, \downarrow, \leftarrow, S, L, R, B, *, \bullet, +\}$$

The state $\#$ is a quiescent state, and indicated by a blank in the following. The four states $\uparrow, \rightarrow, \downarrow, \leftarrow$ are called signal transmission states. The states S, L, R, B are mainly used as signals to encode the shape of an object. The states $*, \bullet$ are the ones to control various processes in reproduction including encoding and decoding . The state $+$ is used when a branching occurs at an end of a transmission line.

Formally, the local transition function is a mapping $f : Q^5 \rightarrow Q$ that determines the state transition of each cell, depending on the present states of five neighbor cells (i.e., center, upward, rightward, downward, and leftward cells). Thus, the transition relation $f(c, u, r, d, l) = c'$ or a "rule" can be depicted as follows.

$$\begin{array}{c} \boxed{u} \\ \boxed{l}\,\boxed{c}\,\boxed{r} \\ \boxed{d} \end{array} \mapsto \boxed{c'}$$

The function f constructed here is rotation symmetric (i.e., isotropic) but in a *weak* sense, because in a rotated rule the directions of arrows of $\uparrow, \rightarrow, \downarrow, \leftarrow$ must be also rotated. In the following, we do not describe the function f itself, but show examples of transitions of configurations of the cellular space to explain how SR_{12} works.

2.1 Transmission of Signals

A signal transmission line is a configuration formed by placing transmission states and signal states alternately as shown in Fig. 3. Appropriately setting the transition function, signals propagate along the line to the direction of arrows one cell per step. Note that a transmission line must not touch itself.

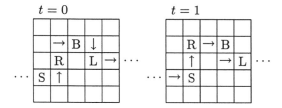

Figure 3: A signal transmission line in the cellular space of SR_{12}.

2.2 Decoding and Execution of Commands

If signals S, L, R, and B are once interpreted (i.e., decoded), they act as "commands" for extending or branching a transmission line. Table 1 shows the commands and their operations. Decoding and execution of

Command	Operation
S	Advance the head of a transmission line straight ahead
L	Advance the head of a transmission line leftward
R	Advance the head of a transmission line rightward
B	Branch the head of a transmission line in three ways

Table 1: Four commands S, L, R and B.

commands are taken place at the head of a transmission line.

A *head* is an end cell of a transmission line to which signals flow, and a *tail* is an end cell from which signals flow. Four commands shown in Table 1 are decoded and executed at the head. Fig. 4 shows how advance commands are decoded and executed. It takes three steps to execute an advance command. (Branch command B will be explained later.)

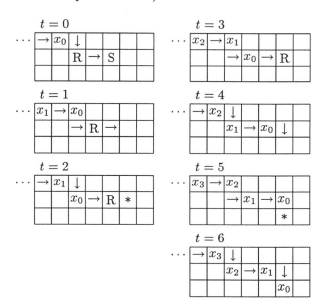

Figure 4: Execution of advance commands S and R at the head of a transmission line ($x_i \in \{S, L, R, B\}$).

2.3 Encoding the Shape into Commands

Encoding is in fact a reverse process of decoding, and here, its operation is carried out at the tail of a transmission line. Namely, if the tail is straight (or left-turning, right-turning, respectively) in its form, the command S (L, R) is generated. The tail then retracts by one cell. In such a manner, the shape of a transmission line can be converted into a command sequence, and it is sent to the direction of the head. It also takes three steps per one cell to encode the shape. Fig. 5 shows an example of an encoding process.

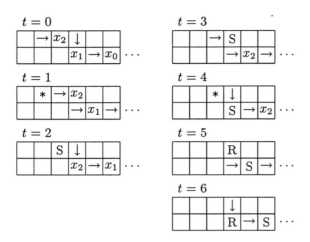

Figure 5: Encoding the shape of a tail into commands S and R ($x_i \in \{S, L, R, B\}$).

2.4 A Worm

A *Worm* is a simple transmission line with open ends, thus has a head and a tail. As mentioned above, decoding and encoding are taken place at the head and the tail, respectively. Since encoded signals are sent to the head, a Worm crawls like a caterpillar in the cellular space. Fig. 6 shows the behaviors of three Worms.

It is easily seen that the length (i.e., the number of cells) of a Worm does not vary if it contains only advance commands and never touches itself. Hence the same configuration must appear infinitely many times if we identify translated configurations as the same ones. Thus, we can classify such Worms into two categories: "cycling" and "travelling". A Worm is called *cycling* iff its configuration appears at the same position after some time steps. A Worm is called *travelling* iff its translated configuration appears after some time steps, thus it moves away in some direction. In Fig. 6, the uppermost Worm is a cycling one, and the other two are travelling.

2.5 Self-Reproduction of a Worm

The signal B is a command that creates three-way branches at the head of a transmission line (or a Worm). Once a branch has been made, signals coming to this point are copied and then propagate in three ways. If the tail of the Worm reaches the branching point, the Worm is split into three objects. Therefore, by giving a branch command, *every* travelling Worm can self-reproduce indefinitely in the two-dimensional plane, provided that it does not touch itself in the branching process. In this model, only the center daughter (among three daughter Worms) inherit the ability of self-reproduction. By this, collisions of Worms are avoided. Note that, if we give a branch command B to a cycling Worm, collisions will occur. Figs. 7 and 8 show self-reproducing processes of Worms.

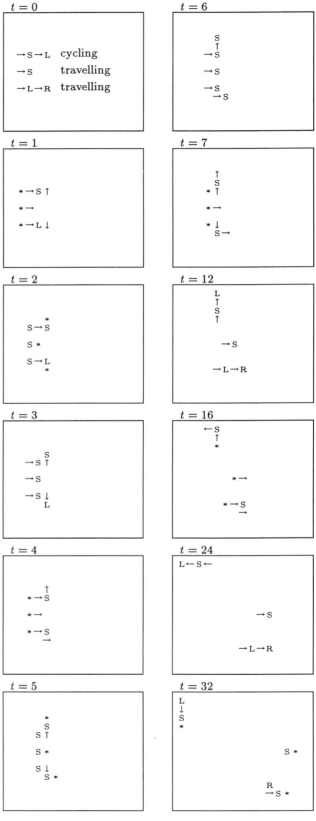

Figure 6: Behaviors of one cycling and two travelling Worms in SR_{12}.

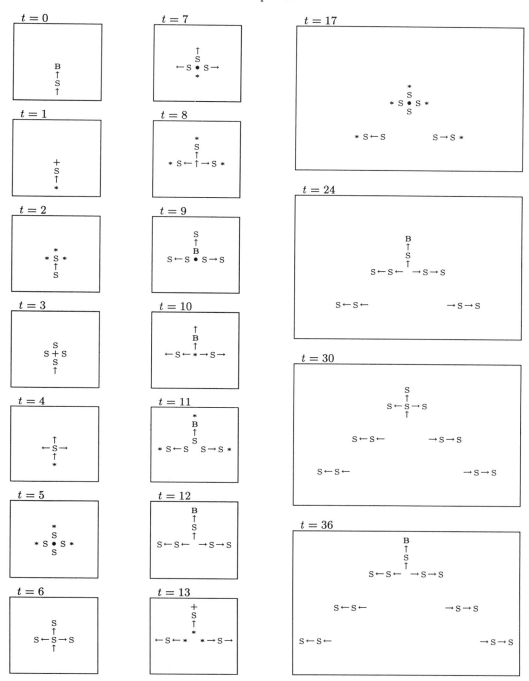

Figure 7: The smallest self-reproducing Worm in SR_{12}.

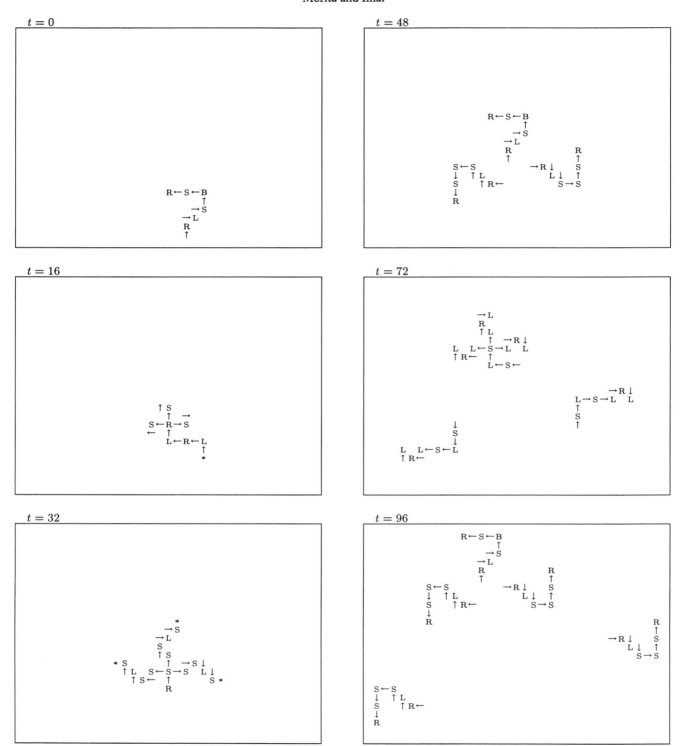

Figure 8: Other example of a self-reproducing Worm in SR_{12}.

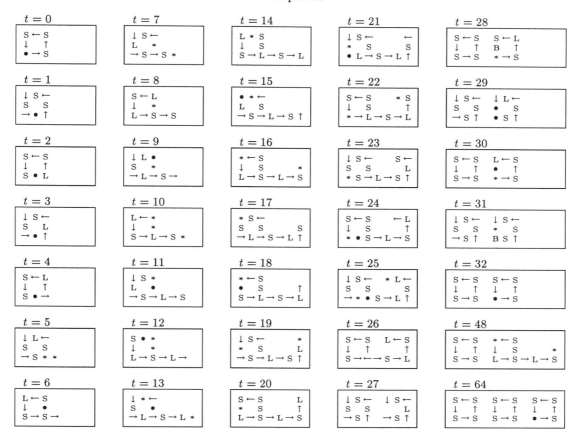

Figure 9: Self-reproducing process of the smallest Loop in SR_{12}.

2.6 Self-Reproduction of a Loop

A *Loop* is a simple closed transmission line, thus has neither a head nor a tail. If a Loop contains only usual signals S, L, R, or B, they simply rotate in the Loop and self-reproduction does not occur. By replacing a signal at some appropriate position by a control state •, it begins to reproduce itself.

When the state • reaches to a corner, it first makes an "arm" to construct a daughter Loop. After that, the shape of the mother Loop is encoded into a sequence of advance commands. This encoding process is essentially the same as the one occurring at the tail of a Worm (but there are some differences). It is controlled by states * and •, which are generated when the arm is created. If these control signals go through all the cells of the mother Loop, and return back to the branching point again, the encoding process terminates, and then the arm is cut off. The arm cut off from the mother Loop acts just like a Worm. But its head will eventually meet its tail to form a Loop, and this will become a daughter Loop identical to her mother. Figs. 9 and 10 show the processes of self-reproduction of Loops. By putting • at an appropriate position, *every* Loop having only S signals can self-reproduce in this way, provided that the arm touches neither the mother Loop nor itself.

3 Concluding Remarks

In this paper, we designed a new CA SR_{12} that supports simple self-reproduction. The numbers of states and rules of SR_{12} are 12 and 2204, respectively, where the latter includes rotated rules but not quiescent rules (i.e., rules where the next-state becomes the quiescent state). In the cellular space of SR_{12}, a large variety of objects have the ability to handle with command sequences, a kind of programs: i.e., creating a command sequence by checking its body, interpreting and executing it to construct a body, and copying it (at a branch point). This ability makes it very easy for various objects to reproduce themselves.

Computer simulation results of self-reproducing processes can be seen as QuickTime Movies via WWW at the following URL.

http://kepi.ke.sys.hiroshima-u.ac.jp/projects/ca/sr/

Files of transition rules of SR_{12} are also available at the above URL.

References

[1] J. Byl, Self-reproduction in small cellular automata, *Physica D*, **34** (1989) 295–299.

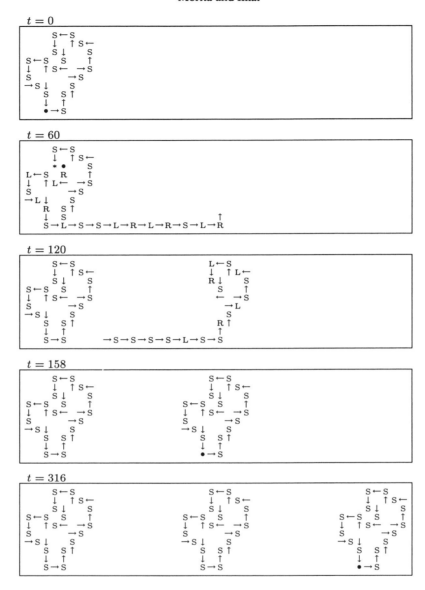

Figure 10: Self-reproduction of a more complex Loop in SR_{12}.

[2] E.F. Codd, *Cellular Automata*, Academic Press, New York (1968).

[3] J. Ibáñez, D. Anabitarte, I. Azpeitia, O. Barrera, A. Barrutieta, H. Blanco, and F. Echarte, Self-inspection based reproduction in cellular automata, in *Advances in Artificial Life* (eds. F. Moran et al.), LNAI-929, Springer-Verlag (1995) 564–576.

[4] R. Laing, Automaton models of reproduction by self-inspection, *J. Theor. Biol.*, **66** (1977) 437–456.

[5] C.G.Langton, Self-reproduction in cellular automata, *Physica*, **10D** (1984) 135–144.

[6] K. Morita, and M. Harao, Computation universality of one-dimensional reversible (injective) cellular automata, *Trans. IEICE Japan*, **E72** (1989) 758–762.

[7] K. Morita, and K. Imai, Self-reproduction in a reversible cellular space, International Workshop on Universal Machines and Computations, Paris (1995) (to appear in *Theor. Computer Science*). http://kepi.ke.sys.hiroshima-u.ac.jp/projects/rca/sr/

[8] J. von Neumann, *Theory of Self-reproducing Automata* (ed. A.W.Burks), The University of Illinois Press, Urbana (1966).

[9] J.A. Reggia, S.L. Armentrout, H.H. Chou, and Y. Peng, Simple Systems that exhibit self-directed replication, *Science*, **259** (1993) 1282–1287.

[10] G. Tempesti, A new self-reproducing cellular automaton capable of construction and computation, in *Advances in Artificial Life* (eds. F. Moran et al.), LNAI-929, Springer-Verlag (1995) 555–563.

Frustration and Clustering in Biological Networks

Hugues Bersini
IRIDIA- CP 194/6
Universite Libre de Bruxelles
50, av. Franklin Roosevelt - 1050 Bruxelles
Belgique
email: bersini@ulb.ac.be

Abstract

Researches in Alife often call upon computer simulations of biological network to understand and mimic the natural dynamics exhibited by the units of these networks in reality. Among the most studied networks are: Hopfield Neural Networks (HNN) and Idiotypic Immune Networks (IIN). Despite their different mathematical characterization, the two networks share among others two salient structural aspects: the de-stabilizing effect of frustrated connectivities and the autonomous tendency to fragment the whole network into small clusters of units showing similar dynamics. In this paper, results of computer simulation are presented and explained to illustrate these common properties.

1 Introduction

Among its different assignments, ALife serves as a regular and convenient forum for researchers interested in theoretical biology and in the functionalist side of life to exchange their views and to realize how similarly some of their models appear to behave. One intensively studied structure, common to a large part of ALife developments, is a network of units indexed by i, varying with time $a_i(t)$, and interconnected by means of a connectivity or affinity matrix m_{ij} where m_{ij} indicates the strength of the connection between units i and j. In general the evolution in time of this network is given by means of a system of differential equations: $da_i/dt=F(m_{ij},a_j)$ or, in a time-discrete form: $a_i(t+1)= F(m_{ij},a_j(t))$, where F captures how the units mutually interact. This interaction can take very different mathematical forms, from the simplest: a linear sum $\sum_j m_{ij}a_j$ to more complicated non linear forms including multiplicative, quadratic, polynomial or sinusoidal type of relationship. Among the most famous instances of these biological networks one can find: 1) Ecological networks, either in their linear version [13], [25] or in their non-linear version like in the Lokta-Volterra type of networks [32] - 2) Boolean networks [35] [19] with relation among the units of a logical type, binary interaction and binary state. Regulatory genetic network is the type of

biological reality that these models aim at better grasping - 3) Hopfield Neural Networks [15] [2] - 4) Coupled map lattice [17] [18] [8] for the study of spatiotemporal chaos, in which the units, showing intrinsic chaotic activity, are situated on a lattice and interact with a suitably chosen set of other units - 5) Network of oscillators [34] [9] which, for important coupling strength, exhibit macroscopic mutual entrainment which reminds a variety of rhythmic behaviour observed in biological clocks, in many physiological organisms and in the synchronization of insects collective behaviour - 6) Immune idiotypic network [5] [10] [11] [12] [29] [33] [37] [38].

When simulating such biological networks a lot of similar features have already been detected as for instance the behavioural sensitivity the network with respect to the way any unit is updated at each time step: synchronously or asynchronously [4] [23]. Intuitively some structural aspects are likely to be responsible for common behavioural characteristics whatever particular network under study. As a preliminary attempt to point out these common structural sensitivities, this paper will focus on only two of these networks: Hopfield Neural Network (HNN) and Immune Idiotypic Network (IIN).

Suppose a network of interconnected Boolean units and that this network is further constrained such that two units being connected means that unit 1 in one state can only co-exist with unit 2 in the anti-state. A two unit networks can settle in only two possible configurations. Then take a three unit network and connect these units in an open chain: unit 1 is connected only to unit 2 which in turn is connected only to unit 3. Here again two configurations are possible with the 1-2 couple as well as the 2-3 couple each containing two units settled in reverse states. The problem gains particular interest by closing the chain, then getting a odd loop, connecting unit 3 back to unit 1 (see fig.1). We now have three couples which must each independently complies with the imposed constraint: the state/anti-state pairing. Looking at the Moebius triangle in fig.2 you observe a very similar type of impossible global configuration despite three possible local coupling. No global configuration turns out to be possible: the couples mutually compete for reaching their state/anti-state configuration. In the modeling of spin glasses, this well-known phenomenon, designated by the term frustration [30], is responsible for preventing spin glasses from relaxing to their minimal energy level, but equally for enlarging the set of intermediary solutions among which the network can choose to settle.

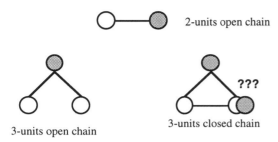

Fig.1: The frustration phenomenon

Fig.2: A Moebius triangle is a frustrated figure

A frustrated network gives rise to two types of phenomenon: first an enlargement of the repertoire of possible equilibrium configurations and then, in some further cases, the network wanders around all these possible configurations without stopping in one of them. More precisely the frustrated network dynamical regime always increments its degree of complexity with respect to the non-frustrated one: from fixed point to oscillations and from oscillations to chaos. The next sections will show that in HNN, the presence of frustrated loops de-stabilizes fixed point to generate oscillations and, in IIN, the presence of odd feedback loops is responsible for bringing forth a new type of random itinerancy called frustrated chaos. The section three will discuss why this frustrated chaos might be an original type of regime with respect to the classical stretch-and-fold type of chaos. This behavioral sensitivity to the presence of frustration can be perceived as a precious addition in any biological network since, as a result of a tiny structural change, it increases the diversity of "meaningful" stationary regimes to be self-selected by the network and offers this same network the possibility to present a large repertoire of potential responses to external interactions.

Regarding the second aspect, i.e. fragmentation of the network in small clusters of oscillatory units, a dilute type of connectivity in HNN is very likely to make the network self-organise in such a way. Besides the brain is well known for presenting weak interconnectivity: more or less several thousand synapses per neuron. In ecosystems also, species do not interact with all others and restrict their interaction to a very small subset. Immune cells are very specific and present affinity with very few other cells. In Kauffman's Boolean networks, this local interactivity was originally shown to entail the formation of structural clusters which exhibit oscillatory dynamics all together but in

different locations of the network. These clusters are uncoupled and separated by "neutralizing" zones which limit their mutual influence. The behaviour of the network taken as a whole presents then a sufficient diversity obtained by multiplying all local diversities and a greater stability or robustness due to the limited propagation of perturbation. We will see that this clustering effect remains true for HNN with the exception that, in contrast to Boolean Network, when their degree of connectivity exceeds the small threshold, HNN (in agreement with May's [25] and Amari's [1] theoretical analysis) tends to stabilize instead of getting chaotic.

IIN also tend to fragment into small networks of oscillatory or chaotic units. However in contrast with HNN, this clustering occurs whatever degree of connectivity so that low degree of connectivity turns out to be a consequence and no longer a condition of this clustering effect. In both networks, this clustering by fragmentation is also a direct consequence of the regular NK nature of the connectivity while, in randomly connected network, although the oscillations persist, the organisation of the network in small clusters isolated by "resting" units is harder to perceive. Either all units oscillate or the clusters travel through the network. Clustering can be seen as one possible way, proposed by the network, to make meaningful any external interaction. The following organisation of the paper is straightforward. In the next section, we will illustrate and discuss the frustration and clustering phenomena in HNN while the successive section will be dedicated to these same phenomena but in IIN.

2 Frustration and Clustering in Hopfield Neural Networks

2.1 Frustration

Let's take the simplest case of a Boolean network containing three Boolean units connected in a loop: 1>2>3>1 and turn all connections to be inhibitory i.e. 1 inhibits 2 which inhibits 3 which in turn inhibits 1. One unit inhibits another one when it forces it to settle in the reverse state. It is trivial to see that when updating its units, such a triangular network will eventually oscillate whereas the presence of an even number of negative interactions would force the network to relax in a stable configuration among others. This is the simplest case of a frustrated network. Thomas relies on such simple structures to study genetic regulatory networks [35]. He has shown how the presence of loop in a network, provided it contains an odd number of inhibitory connections, de-stabilizes this same network by triggering oscillations. He negatively judges the presence of negative loops since alternatively the presence of positive loops is responsible for enlarging the repertoire of possible equilibrium configurations, each expressing a particular cell. When frustrated, the network passes through all the possible configurations in a sequential and recurrent way and cannot stop in any of them. This is the simplest illustration of the instability, from fixed point to oscillation, generated by frustrating a network.

In its original conception, symmetric and without self-connection ($m_{ij} = m_{ji}$ and $m_{ii} = 0$), Hopfield network dynamics relaxes to fixed points. Together frustration raises the minimum energy and increases the degeneracy of the ground state. When Hopfield networks are used as a mechanism for associative memory, it is interesting that there be many available fixed points namely an energy function with a lot of equivalent degenerate minima, a situation typically arising in frustrated networks. This is one of the few cases where frustration is judged to be beneficial to the network [2][31].

More interesting for understanding the de-stabilizing effect of frustration is the study of the same Hopfield network but now allowing for asymmetric connectivity (then loosing the proof of convergence to fixed-point attractors) and taken in its continuous form (eq.1):

$$\frac{da_i}{dt} = -\frac{a_i}{t} + \tanh(\sum_{j=1}^{N} m_{ij} a_j);$$ tanh has the classical tangent hyperbolic sigmoid profile and τ is a time constant (simplified to be the same for all neurons and taken to be 100 in our simulations).

Atiya and Baldi [3] have done a detailed analysis on how the units behave when they are interconnected in a loop or a ring, with the asymmetric connection matrix given by

(for the 3-neuron version) : $\begin{bmatrix} 0 & 0 & m_{13} \\ m_{12} & 0 & 0 \\ 0 & m_{23} & 0 \end{bmatrix}$ that is in presence of

an odd inhibitory loops: $m_{12} m_{13} m_{23} < 0$ (they have generalized the study to the presence of any odd number of inhibitory connections). Summarizing their results, if a stability analysis is performed at the origin (a fixed point), the real part of the greatest eigenvalue is given, in the case of a positive loop by: $\lambda = -\frac{1}{\tau} + m_{12} m_{23} m_{31}^{1/3}$, and in the case of a negative loop by: $\lambda = -\frac{1}{\tau} + |m_{12} m_{23} m_{31}|^{1/3} \cos\frac{\pi}{3}$.

So in both cases depending on τ and on the connection values, the system can be stable or unstable at the origin. Now the important difference and the justification for the oscillations appearing in presence of a negative loop is that in that case, although unstable, the origin is the only fixed point. This is easy to show by computing the first dimension of the fixed point: $x_1 = \tau m_{13} f(x_3)$ $= \tau m_{13} f(m_{23} \tau f(x_2)) = \tau m_{13} f(\tau m_{23} f(\tau m_{12} f(x_1))) = F(x_1)$. Due to the presence of the negative loop, x and F(x) can only be of opposite sign, then x_1 can't take negative or positive value but only be equal to 0. In contrast, in case of a positive loop, other additional equilibrium points are possible towards which the network will converge. This analysis confirms a preliminary investigation of Hirsch [15] where it was shown that a necessary condition for the

Hopfield network to oscillate is indeed to exhibit frustration in its connectivity. So in HNN, the de-stabilizing effect of frustration for odd ring connectivity can be theoretically justified and analysed.

2.2 Clustering

We have performed the same type of NK analysis popularized by Kauffman for Boolean Network but now applied to Hopfield Asymmetric network given by eq.1. N is the number of binary units and 2K the number of units with which any unit is interconnected [19]. K reflects the dilute or not dilute nature of the network. The state transition of any unit is randomly extracted from the 2^{2^K} possible transitions. The dynamics of Kauffman's Boolean nets is well known. Two different regimes have to be stressed: one for very dilute network (K=2) and one for fully connected network (K=N). Here again a sharp transition between these two regimes seems to occur at low connectivity. In global network, the regime can be characterized as maximally disordered even chaotic (although this can't be a real chaos due to the finite nature of the network). There are N/e number of cycles. The length of the cycles grows exponentially with K. When K drops to 2, so in presence of very dilute type of connectivity, the properties of the Boolean net change abruptly. The number of cycles is now given by $\sqrt{N}$. The reason why, despite their small number, these cycles keep a short period is due to the fact that the system is partitioned into an unchanging frozen core (this core contains unvarying units) which isolates islands of oscillatory units. This core has several effects: first it blocks the propagation of cyclic behaviour favoring then small cycles, secondly it makes each cyclic attractor stable to most minimal perturbations and endows the local network with precious homeostatic quality. Finally by finely tuning an additional probabilistic parameter but still keeping a low value for K, a phase transition, where the most complex regime is likely to supervene, appears for a critical value of this parameter. The frozen cores melt, and damage spreading from minor perturbations seems to create avalanches on all length scales with a power-law distribution. This new regime has been described as lying somewhere between order and chaos and recently has been endowed with a lot of wonderful qualities (high computational complexity, better adaptive capacity, scale invariance ..).

Let's turn to this same NK analysis applied now to assymetric HNN. Figure 3 shows the synaptic matrix of 10 neurons when K=2. We have done abundant statistics by randomly generating assymetric NK matrix (m_{ij} could only take values 1 or -1). Our results have shown that, in agreement with Kauffman's results, there is a sharp transition of the network behaviour marked at a low level of connectivity i.e K=2 for N=30, K=3 for N=60, K=4 for N=100. So the threshold for K seems to increase and decrease with N. Below it there is a high probability to find the network into an oscillatory behaviour with, like in Kauffman's net, small clusters of oscillating neurons separated by large zone of resting neurons. Above it the network nearly almost falls into a fixed point. This is an important difference with Kauffman's results since strongly connected networks behave very simply as fixed point to be contrasted with the more complicated dynamics of Boolean nets. Amari [1] has shown why for large random networks with global connectivity, you can apply the law of large number and assimilate the HNN to a set of disconnected and isolated networks which then become all convergent. However we think that such a threshold effect can be better explained by relying on the results obtained for linear networks.

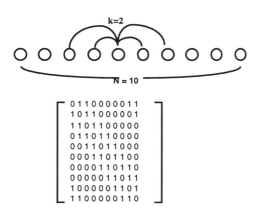

Fig.3 : A NK (10-2) Hopfield Network

20 years ago, Gardner and Ashby [13] followed by May [25], all three interested in the behaviour and the stability of large ecosystems, have accomplished a seminal preliminary investigation simply by analyzing the stability conditions of a linear network: $\dfrac{da_i}{dt} = \sum_j m_{ij} a_j$

In general the stability of any system of differential equation can be studied by restricting this study to the behaviour of the linearized system at an equilibrium point. The three authors reached the same non obvious conclusion that large networks with randomly fixed connection matrix are stable up to a certain degree of connectivity. Beyond this degree, scaling linearly with the number of units, there is a sharp transition and divergent dynamics characterize the network behaviour. In brief, local networks i.e. when the degree of connectivity (for a given interconnectivity strength) is below a well-defined threshold are stable while global ones are unstable.

The relation between fixed point behaviour in HNN and divergent behaviour in linear system comes from the fact that a positive eigenvalue (easier to obtain with global network) would be responsible for a fixed point in Hopfield net: If $\lambda a_i = \sum_j m_{ij} a_j$ with λ the eigenvalue, then

$\lambda a_i^2 = \sum_j m_{ij} a_j a_i$ and since a fixed point implies $\sum_j m_{ij} a_j a_i \geq 0$, the fact that $\lambda \geq 0$ has higher probability for global network implies also a greater probability of fixed point for global connectivity.

For randomly connected networks, there is still a connectivity threshold which separates oscillatory behaviour (for dilute networks) from fixed points (above the connectivity threshold). However, the clustering effect is harder to observe since very few units don't oscillate. The large part of neurons is involved in longer and thus more complicated cyclic attractors. There is no longer the presence of Kauffman's frozen zone separating among themselves the cluster of oscillatory units. Then the possibility rises that such a clustering by fragmentation reduces to an artifact of the NK regularity of the connectivity structure and that any observation of the network which aim at detecting and isolating groups of units in random networks requires other type of measurements. The detection of units synchronously oscillating, like performed by Kaneko for characterizing his Coupled Map Lattice [17][18], could be a viable alternative. Also synchronization in NN has received increasing attention these last years as a way of explaining labeling, segmenting and variable binding mechanisms. Indeed such explanations get rid with any need for structural neighbouring to perform neurons regrouping. The clustering by fragmentation has to be substituted by a more subtle but richer clustering by synchronization mechanism.

3 Frustration and Clustering in Immune Idiotypic Network

3.1 Frustration

The possibility that frustration turns an homeostatic idiotypic network into an oscillatory one was already observed with circumspection by Hiernaux [14]. He believed that this remarkable sensitivity of the dynamics of the network to its connectivity ought to make questionable the idiotypic network structure of the immune system, another negative perception of the frustration effect. In this section, the next qualitative transition will be investigated: from oscillations to chaos. The system of coupled ODE's showing this interesting frustration induced phenomenon was originally meant to study the dynamics of one particular immune idiotypic network first proposed by Varela et al. [37], Stewart and Varela [33] and largely studied and described in the literature [5] [7] [12] [33] [37] [38].

The interest for the dynamical behaviour of the immune network arose from the observation that the concentration of natural antibodies displays fluctuation patterns that are believed to be related to the connectivity of the immune cells instead of the result of encounters with external antigens. Moreover these antibodies in normal and auto-immune individuals have been shown to fluctuate in a different way, and hypothetically this might suggest to relate these two regimes with different structures of connectivity and to explain the disease by a structural alteration. Up to date, the most interesting dynamical pattern exhibited by the network simulations is an oscillatory regime (some of the fluctuation patterns observed in biological experimental data have in fact a strong oscillatory tendency [38]) in which the units always separate in two groups oscillating in counterphase. As a consequence, this type of network turns out to be susceptible to a frustration phenomenon that we indeed observed in the presence of odd loops.

The immune idiotypic network model under study contains N units (i=1..N) (such a unit is often called a clone in the immune literature). In contrast with other more familiar biological structures like neural networks, a unit is representative of two different immune cells: the antibody f_i and its associate producer the B lymphocyte b_i. On account of the very high specificity of B lymphocytes, which only produce antibodies sharing this same specificity, a unique index i serves as reference mark to one type of antibody and its B lymphocyte associate producer. For each clone i, the system of ODE's accounts for B lymphocyte proliferation and maturation, antibody production, the formation and subsequent elimination of antibody-antibody complexes, the natural "death" of antibodies and B lymphocytes and finally a supply of B lymphocytes (named the "source") coming from the bone marrow. Antibody-antibody and antibody-B lymphocyte interactions are determined by a so-called affinity matrix m, which is symmetric and reflects the network structure of the model. An entry m_{ij} is called the affinity between clone i and j and, for the present study, only takes value 1 if affinity exists between clone i and j and 0 if not. The evolution in time of the concentration of the clone i two immune actors f_i and b_i is described by the two differential equations (eq.2):

$$\frac{df_i}{dt} = -k_1 \sigma_i f_i - k_2 f_i + k_3 mat(\sigma_i) b_i$$

$$\frac{db_i}{dt} = -k_4 b_i + k_5 prol(\sigma_i) b_i + k_6 \qquad i = 1..n$$

k_1 to k_6 are six time constants. The extent to which two clones interact in the network is thus determined by m and the concentration of the antibodies. The integral impact of the whole network on a specific clone i is measured by a value σ_i which is called the field: $\sigma_i = \sum_{j=1}^{j=n} m_{ij} f_j$; mat and prol are two log-normal functions which determine how B lymphocytes mature and proliferate upon activation by the field:

$$mat(\sigma_i) = exp\left\{-\left(\frac{\ln(\sigma_i/\mu_m)}{s_m}\right)^2\right\} \quad prol(\sigma_i) = exp\left\{-\left(\frac{\ln(\sigma_i/\mu_p)}{s_p}\right)^2\right\}$$

The parameter values for the simulations described in this paper are: $k_1=0.0016[conc^{-1}d^{-1}]$; $k_2=0.02[d^{-1}]$; $k_3=2.0[d^{-1}]$; $k_4=0.1[d^{-1}]$; $k_5=0.2[d^{-1}]$; $k_6=0.1[d^{-1}]$; $\mu_m=80[conc]$; $s_m=0.5$; $\mu_p=120[conc]$; $s_p=0.5$.

The biological motivations behind such a modeling is outside the scope of this paper (see [38] for these motivations). Also the value for each parameter was determined in agreement with biological data which need not be discussed here. Basically the parameters were tuned so as to obtain an oscillatory behaviour for the simplest possible network containing 2 complementary clones with the affinity matrix given by: $\begin{bmatrix} 0 & 1 \\ 1 & 0 \end{bmatrix}$ with one clone concentration oscillating in counterphase with the complementary one.

We limit the parametric bifurcation analysis to the obtainment of limit cycle behaviour for the two-clone network, the departure point of our study. As shown in [33], this oscillatory behaviour is very robust and strongly prevails for a large range of parameter values.

In order to produce frustration in the structure of connectivity, attention is paid only to affinity matrix which reflects the complementarity of the clones (two complementary clones which can be seen as two opposite spins), thus in the absence of self-affinity ($m_{ii}=0$) and with affinity restricted to complementary clones ($m_{ij}= m_{ji}$ takes its value in [0,1]). Such a structure will indeed lead to the open and closed chains which are precisely our objects of interest. Three cases are worth of focus. The respective affinity matrixes are: 2-clone $\begin{bmatrix} 0 & 1 \\ 1 & 0 \end{bmatrix}$, 3-clone open chain $\begin{bmatrix} 0 & 1 & 0 \\ 1 & 0 & 1 \\ 0 & 1 & 0 \end{bmatrix}$ and 3-clone closed chain $\begin{bmatrix} 0 & 1 & 1 \\ 1 & 0 & 1 \\ 1 & 1 & 0 \end{bmatrix}$.

For both the two-clone and the non frustrated three-clone situation (open-chain) the regime is clearly periodic. Interestingly enough the 3-clone open chain situation is very close to the 2-clone situation when substituting one of the clones in the 2-clone case by a couple of them in the 3-clone case. It is remarkable to see for the 3-clone situation and for whatever number of clones in general how much the 2-clone dynamics prevails and the attractive effect it exerts on all other configurations. In the 3-clone open chain situation, described by six differential equations, the network behaves nearly in the same way as in the 2-clone case with clones 1 and 3 oscillating in perfect synchronization so as to form a double-clone equivalent to one of the two clones in the 2-clone case (except for the amplitude which is not surprisingly half the value of clone 2 equal to each of the clones of the 2-clone case). Since taken individually clone 1 and 3 are in a situation indistinguishable from the 2-clone situation i.e. they present affinity with one and only one clone (i.e. clone 2), they tend to behave just like in the 2-clone situation with as direct consequence their mutual coupling and the appearance of the double-clone.

When closing the chain (1<-->2<-->3<-->1) and so doing obtaining the very same frustrated triangle already encountered in the section dedicated to Hopfield networks, the periodic regime switches to an aperiodic one. Since now, taken individually, each clone presents the same local connectivity (they are all connected to two neighbors) and then appears indistinguishable from the others, none of them can assume the privilege to oscillate alone (then differently) in counterphase with the double-clone. Accordingly, the double-clone is continuously and erratically changing the nature of its members. This perfect clonal equivalence is obviously a very basic reason and original feature of the complicated regime which typifies the closed chain case. As expected this type of aperiodicity disappears for four clones and in general for an even number of clones. In the 4-clone either closed or open chain, the two double clones oscillate in counterphase, in contrast with the 5-clone closed chain where the aperiodic regime reappears. We have extended the observation of how chains of interconnected clones (only the neighbouring elements of the diagonal of the connectivity matrix are non-zero) behave up to 19 clones. As we expected, first return maps and the calculated power spectra indicate the presence of chaos for any odd loop while even chains are responsible for oscillatory behaviour.

An important question to be addressed in this paper is the nature of the 3-clone closed chain regime. The computer experiments of the dynamics show strong evidence of an aperiodic behaviour. A simple reasoning may help to eliminate some well-known possible regimes intermediary between chaos and periodicity like a toroidal attractor. Indeed this type of attractor is generally due to the merging of distinct periodicities, each associated to different variable actions. However, the main characteristic of the 3-clone closed chain is the perfect equivalence among the three clones and their respective concentration. It is indeed this same equivalence which is responsible for inducing the frustration phenomenon and the resulting aperiodicity. In previous papers [5] [6], we have performed and described technical analysis: power spectrum, first return Poincaré map, Lyapunov exponents, symbolic dynamics with all results converging to testify the presence of chaos in the time series.

Although this dynamics presents the typical signs of chaos, it is hard to fit it into the well known chaotic regimes. Intuitively, the network perfect clonal equivalence i.e. the homogeneity in the variables dynamics makes the classical stretch-and-fold interpretation characterizing the largest family of chaotic dynamics more delicate to apply here. Rather the frustrated chaos behaviour is a succession of attempts to decouple the system in two groups of oscillators, an impossible achievement making the dynamics rambling over very brief and successful configurations. Since each cyclic behaviour shows fractal basin boundaries, the switching among these cyclic attractor is beyond all predictability. You can't predict when a point in the phase space will be attracted by one of the three cycles since the attractive regions have frontiers themselves impossible to draw with finite precision. This is an on-line and continuous manifestation of the final state sensitivity [28] which characterizes systems with multiple attractors separated by fractal frontiers. This form of random itinerancy among brief cyclic behaviour presents important similarities with Kaneko's chaotic itinerancy [17][18]. Each form of cyclic attractor switching is likely to present an intrinsic form of unpredictability due to the fractality of the basins of attractions. However in Kaneko's CML a chaotic background is responsible for the de-stabilizing effect while in the idiotypic network such a continuous de-stabilizing does not need any exogenous chaos.

3.2 Clustering

Always aiming at a better characterization of how the three-clone dynamical regimes scale up when increasing the network size, together with Detours and Calenbuhr [12] we have recently launched a systematic study which again was largely inspired from Kauffman's NK analysis for Boolean networks. A complete study of the results is under progress but so far some general tendencies can be drawn. Chaos is found for most of the N-K values and a significant outcome appears to be the fragmentation of the network into clusters of 2,3 or sometimes 4 activated clones separated by resting clones. The number of separating resting clones is related to the degree of connectivity. Clusters of 2 and 4 clones are oscillating and clusters of 3 clones shows the frustration chaos presented above. The clones within the clusters fluctuate with an average of $f_i=40$ whereas the resting clones separating the clusters fluctuate around mean concentration three orders of magnitude less. So like in the HNN case, clustering by fragmentation is a natural self-organised tendency of large IIN networks.

Notice however that in order to obtain such a fragmentation, the network needs not be diluted from the very beginning, quite the contrary is true, the dilution comes to be a consequence, and no longer a necessary condition, of the fragmentation. During its time evolution, the idiotypic network spontaneously tunes its connectivity to low value. It is known that the embrionnary idiotypic network shows larger connectivity than the adult one. This is indeed found also in simulations together with a reinforcement of the selectivity of the new clones to be recruited in the network.

The works of Gardner, Ashby and May discussed above seem to suggest that a biological ecosystem in order to be stable must be organized into a set of separated sub-networks where species in one sub-network are insulated from interactions with species in another sub-network. This self-selection for local type of connectivity was also observed in a coupled-map-lattice computer simulation of ecosystems [32] where again the degree of interconnectivity appeared as an emergent property regulated by the network itself on the road to its equilibrium states. Compartmentalization of species communities into independent clusters were experimentally validated by Stuart Pimm [30] [20] and seems to be characteristic of animal communities. In their natural quest for stability the ecological network tunes autonomously their connectivity to low threshold value.

Again, like for HNN, this clustering phenomenon is highly sensitive to the regularity of the connectivity. A randomly connected network shows re-organisation tendency more complicated than local clustering. Although there are still clones whose concentration is order of magnitude less than others, the way they regroup is harder to characterize and much more experimental analysis is needed.

4   Conclusions

The main motivation of this paper was a qualitative overview of two biological networks modeling in an attempt to spot similar form of dynamical sensitivity to structural aspects. These biological networks are Hopfield Neural Network and Immune Idiotypic Network. The two structural influences we observed are the great sensitivity the networks dynamics present to frustrated connectivity and the tendency for regularly connected networks to fragment into small clusters. Frustrated connectivity is, in few cases, responsible for enlarging the diversity of equilibrium regimes but, more generally, for provoking unstability in network: fixed points turn into oscillation while oscillation turns into chaos. This unstability is due to the "wavering" of the network unable to settle into one of the equally possible equilibrium regime. As a benefic outcome of frustration, the network is able to recurrently propose a large repertoire of potential behaviors which can be triggered in response to external interaction.

It has been shown in [7] how, when coupled to an auto-antigen, the frustrated chaotic attractor degenerates into one of the three periodic regimes and how the network realizes then a form of tolerant response to this auto-antigen. The presence of the auto-antigen stops the frustration by making the concentration of the clone with which it presents affinity to vanish. This is a very simple illustration of a particular idiotypic network showing tolerance towards auto-antigen without the need for ad hoc mechanisms that prevent an immune response. Moreover the resulting two-clone oscillatory network, when having one of its clone connected with an auto-ag (like done before), will see its connected clone to grow exponentially in a way which reminds the classical immune reaction against an external antigen. This two stages phenomenon obtained by two successive antigenic encounters: first tolerance with a three-clone network and then immune reaction with the two-clone network resulting from the first interaction, can be seen as a low scale qualitative replica of the two consecutive lives of the immune system: tolerant in its embryonary state and defensive in the adult state.

The tolerance phenomenon presents also interesting similarities with the control of chaos [28] since it is by perturbing the dynamics that the system is trapped into one of the oscillatory attractors that it was recurrently visiting. This new regime is the one which gives sense or label the external perturbation. In the field of neurophysiology and referring to works of Lourenço and Babloyantz [22], neural net can exploit frustrated chaos for the generation of an enormous repertoire of attractors. Indeed frustrated chaos can very easily be provoked by slightly modifying the connectivity structure. This can be the result of adding a new unit in the network. What simpler way nature could have chosen to generate chaos in a network ? Afterwards, it is the encounter with an external stimulus that will turn the chaotic regime into an oscillatory one. Return to chaos can again be provoked by a de-stabilizing frustration effect.

The fact that frustration has been detected in the great majority of physical and biological networks studied so far: spin glass [36], genetic [35], neural [2][31][24][3], oscillatory [9] and immune [5][6], whose mathematical description can be quite different, is pleading for the understanding of frustration as dependent just upon the structure of connectivity. Such a generic phenomenon should not be restrictively construed as an insignificant artifact of our mathematical and computer modeling but rather as a real biological effect, playing yes or not a benefic role (if not a natural way to un-frustrate the network must exist), that further investigation will have for goal to better characterize.

This ubiquity is also true for the clustering effect that we observed when both networks were regularly connected. First we have shown that in case of a sharp behavioural transition in increasing the HNN network connectivity, a dilute form of connectivity is often responsible for more interesting regimes. As a matter of fact, as far as our knowledge of natural networks go, dilute type of connectivity, simpler and more economical, appears to be the rule in nature. We need to distinguish further between two forms of clustering: "clustering by fragmentation" and "clustering by synchrony". We have shown that clustering by fragmentation is likely to occur only in regularly connected network. Clustering by synchrony could substitute for it in networks randomly interconnected and thus more realistic. Clustering is important as a way of assigning a label or a meaning to any form of external interaction. For instance, clustering by synchrony seems to be of great interest in neural networks to support cognitive mechanisms such as labeling and variable binding. On the other hand, in immunology some authors are convinced that immune memory and locality are unseparable aspects [26].

Which type of clustering gives any network more capabilities is a critical question, hard to answer with our current knowledge. This alternative between coding by some form of spatial distribution or coding by dynamics homogeneity goes not without reminding a similar debate in the connectionnist community between local or distributed type of representation. Today more information on the general functions of clustering in real biological networks turn to be of first necessity to hope a beginning of answers to these important interrogations. The use of frustration to easily generate diversity together with clustering for labeling any interaction should deserve increasing attention in the future.

Acknowledgments: Thanks to V. Calenbuhr and V. Detours for their essential contribution in shaping the ideas that are presented in this paper.

References

[1] Amari, S. 1972. Characteristics of random nets of analog neuron-like elements. In IEEE Transactions on Systems, Man and Cybernetics - Vol SMC.2, No 5., pp. 643-657.

[2] Amit, D.J. 1989: Modelling Brain Function: *The World of Attractor Neural Networks* - Cambridge University Press - Cambridge

[3] Atiya, A. and P. Baldi. 1989: Oscillations and Synchronization in Neural Networks: An exploration of the Labeling Hypothesis - *International Journal of Neural Systems* - Vol.1, No 2 - pp. 103-124 (1989)

[4] Bersini, H. and V. Detours. 1994: Asynchrony induces stability in Cellular Automata Based Models - In *Artificial Life IV* - Eds Brooks R. and P. Maes - MIT Press - pp. 382-387.`

[5] Bersini, H. and V. Calenbuhr. 1995 Frustration Induced Chaos in a System of Coupled ODE's - *Chaos, Solitons and Fractals* - Vol.5 - No.8 - pp. 1533-1549.

[6] Bersini, H. and V. Calenbuhr. 1995 - Frustration in Biological Networks: A Source of Diversity, Instability and Chaos - In *revision for Physica D.*

[7] Calenbuhr, V., Bersini, H., Stewart, J. and F.J. Varela. 1995: Natural Tolerance in a Simple Immune Network - Submitted to *J. Theoretical Biology.*

[8] Chaté H. and P. Manneville. 1992: Collective behaviors in coupled map lattices with local and non local connections - *CHAOS* 2 (3) - pp.307 - 313

[9] Daido H. 1992: Quasientrainment and Slow Relaxation in a Population of Oscillators with Random and Frustrated Interactions - *Physical Review Letters* - VOl. 68, No 7 - pp. 1073-1076

[10] De Boer, R.J. and A. Perelson. 1991: Size and Connectivity as Emergent Properties of a Developing Immune Network - In *J. Theoretical Biology* - 149 -pp. 381-424.

[11] De Boer, R.J., A. S. Perelson and I. G. Kevrekidis. 1993: Immune Network Behaviour - I. From Stationary States to Limit Cycle Oscillations - *Bulletin of Mathematical Biology* , Vol. 55, No 4, pp. 745-780.

[12] Detours, V., Calenbuhr, V. and H. Bersini. 1995: Clustering phenomena in idiotypic network - *IRIDIA Internal Technical Report.*

[13] Gardner, M.R. and W.R. Ashby. 1970: Connectance of Large Dynamic (Cybernetic) Systems: Critical Values for Stability - *Nature* Vol. 228 - p.784.

[14] Hiernaux, J. 1977: Some Remarks on the Stability of Idiotypic Network - *Immunochemistry*, Vol. 14 - pp. 733-739. Pergamon Press.

[15] Hirsch, M.W. 1987: Convergence in neural networks - in *Proc. 1987 Int. Conf. Neural Networks,* San Diego, CA.

[16] Hopfield J.J. 1982: Neural networs and physical systems with emergent collective computational abilities - In *Proc. Nat. Acad. Sci. USA* - vol. 79 - pp. 2554 - 2558.

[17] Kaneko, K. 1989: Pattern Dynamics in Spatiotemporal Chaos - *Physica D* 34 - pp. 1-41.

[18] Kaneko, K. 1992: Overview of coupled map lattices - *CHAOS* 2 (3) - pp. 279-282.

[19] Kauffman S.A. 1989: Principles of Adaptation in Complex Systems - *Lectures in the Sciences of Complexity* - SFI Studies in the Sciences of Complexity - Ed. D. Stein - Addison-Wesley - pp. 619-712.

[20] Keley, K. 1994: *Out of Control. The rise of neo-biological civilization* - Addison Wesley.

[21] Lewis, J.E. and L. Glass. 1992. Nonlinear Dynamics and Symbolic Dynamics of Neural Networks - in *Neural Computation* - Vol.4 - No 5.

[22] Lourenço, C. and A. Babloyantz. 1994. Control of Chaos in Networks with Delay: A Model of Synchronization of Cortical Tissue - *Neural Computation* 6 - pp. 1141-1154.

[23] Lumer, E.D. and G. Nicolis 1993: Synchronous versus asynchronous dynamics in spatially distributed systems - to appear in *Physica D.*

[24] Marcus, C.M., F.R. Waugh and R.M. Westervelt. 1991: Nonlinear dynamics and stability of analog neural networks - in *Physica D* 51 - pp. 234-247.

[25] May, R.M. 1972: Will a Large Complex System be Stable? - Nature Vol. 238 - pp. 413- 414

[26] Neumann, A.U. and G. Weisbuch. 1992. Dynamics and Topology of Idiotypic Networks - Bulletin of Mathematical Biology - Vol. 54 - No 5 - pp. 699-726.

[27] Omata, S. and Y. Yamaguchi. 1988. Entrainment among coupled limit cycle oscillators with frustration - Physica D 31 - pp. 397-408.

[28] Ott, E., Sauer, T. and J.A. Yorke. (Eds.) 1994. Coping with Chaos - Wiley Series in Nonlinear Science - John Wiley and Son, Inc.

[29] Perelson, A.S. 1990: Theoretical Immunology - In *Lectures in Complex Systems* - SFI Studies in the Sciences of Complexity, Lect. Vol. II, Edited by Erica Jen, Addison-Wesley.

[30] Pimm Stuart. 1991. The Balance of Nature - University of Chicago Press.

[31] Sherrington, D. 1990: Complexity Due to Disorder and Frustration - *Lectures in the Sciences of Complexity - SFI Studies in the Sciences of Complexity* - Lect. Vol. II, Ed. Erica Jen - Addison-Wesley - pp. 415-455.

[32] Solé, R.V., Bascompte, J. and J. Valls. 1992: Nonequilibrium dynamics in lattice ecosystems: Chaotic stability and dissipative structures - in *CHAOS* 2 (3) -pp.387-395.

[33] Stewart, J. and F. Varela. Dynamics of a class of immune networks. II. Oscillatory activity of cellular and humoral components. *Journal of Theoretical Biology.* 144, pp. 103-115 (1990).

[34] Strogatz, S.H., Mirollo, R.E. and P.C. Matthews. 1992: Synchronization of Pulse-Coupled Biological Oscillators - in *SIAM Journal on Applied Mathematics* - vol. 50, No 6, pp. 1645-1662.

[35] Thomas, R. 1991: Regulatory Networks Seen as Asynchronous Automata: A Logical Description - J. Theor. Biol. 153 - pp. 1-23.

[36] Toulouse, G. 1977:*Commun. Phys.* 2 - 115.

[37] Varela, F.J., Coutinho, A., Dupire, B. and N.N. Vaz 1988. Cognitive networks: immune, neural and otherwise - In *Theoretical Immunology, Part Two*, edited by A.S. Perelson. SFI Studies in the Sciences of Complexity, vol. 3, Reading, MA: Addison-Wesley, 377-401.

[38] Varela, F.J. and A. Coutinho. 1991: Second Generation Immune Network - in *Immunology Today* - Vol. 12 No 5.

Dynamical networks which depend on each other

J.N.Yoshimoto

Graduate School of Human Informatics, Nagoya University, Nagoya 464-01, Japan
e-mail address: gba02073@niftyserve.or.jp or 100475.1076@compuserve.com

Abstract

A new model of communicating objects is proposed in order to study the emergent phenomena in communication. Here, the "object" is made up of a dynamical network which can store the semantic memory, an encoder which expresses the network information, and a decoder which interprets the expression sent from the other network. Information stored in each network is exchanged between objects and the network alters its own structure according to the interpretation made by its decoder. The model is constructed to be as simple as possible without introducing any fixed task nor target in their performance. Dynamical patterns of communication were analyzed and importance of topological effects was found. Self-organized feed-back loops are origins to make communication complex. Roles of communication in evolutionary systems are discussed.

1   Introduction

In many situations in studies of biology or cognitive science, we encounter the problem of communication between objects. Here, with the term "objects" we mean the structured units such as biological cells, networks or agents which have the ability to change their own structure according to the information perceived. These problems of communicating objects should share the following three features in common: First, the information transmittance between objects is not perfect. When one object tries to express its own status, the whole information of the status could not be sent but only the fragment of it should be sent. Examples of fragmented information are chemical substances emitted from cells and words spoken in the human conversation. Objects perceive such partial information, which may result in the unexpected chain of perceptions and reactions. Second, the each object should change dynamically without a static fixed structure. In general we could not expect the fixed target or the answer within the system of communicating objects, unlike the classical problems treated with the back-propagation or the Hopfield neural networks [1]. Thus, dynamical change of objects is an emergent behavior without answers provided. Third, different information is stored in different objects and is exchanged among them. The action of the object may affect the other object and trigger off its large dynamical

change. Then, the information obtained from the affected object should reflect the structure of the first object. The first object can learn its own structure in the past through such perception-reaction loop. In this way feed-back loops can emerge when different information is stored in different objects. Such "self-reference" interactions should be most prominent when the degree of freedom of each object is in the same order.

A simplest problem these features can be seen is communication between two objects. We shall refer to such communication as "conversation". In the present paper I offer a new simple model of conversation between two dynamical networks. It is examined how the above three features, incompleteness of the information transmittance, dynamical change of the partner, and the self-organized feed-back and self-reference effects appear in the conversation.

Conversation or dialogue with the human natural language has been extensively studied by researchers of cognitive science and the game and the process of mutual understanding have been studied from pragmatical points of view [2, 3, 4, 5, 6]. Also in the field of artificial intelligence, communication between agents has been attracted much interest [7]. These studies aiming at the concrete human phenomenon or the technological idea should lead to the deeper understanding of the human knowledge structure [8]. They often depend, however, on complex situations of their own contexts and are refined to give answers to their specific problems. In this paper, instead, we develope the model to be as simple as possible to analyze patterns in the artificial conversation between two dynamical networks and to reveal the underlying fundamental structure in a quantitative way. Data thus obtained in this constructive approach provide a basis to study the further complex conversations among many networks and their social behavior.

2   Model

The model of artificial conversation is schematically shown in Fig.1. Each object is made up of network, encoder, and decoder. The network is represented by a directed graph which consists of N nodes and $N(N-1)$ links. The strength of the link is a dynamical variable which should be changed in the course of conversation. Our network resembles to the semantic network which was used to study how the semantic information is stored in the human brain [9]: A node corresponds to a symbol or some compact and segmented information. Only one node is visited at one time by the encoder or by the decoder. A link designates the next node to be visited. Thus, by sequentially visiting nodes, the sequence of symbols is generated (encoded). This sequence is what is spoken out in the conversation. To keep the model as simple as possible, however, we do not attribute any specific meaning to each node. The structure of the generated sequence of such abstract symbols and associated dynamical change of links are investigated in order to study the emergent phenomena in conversation.

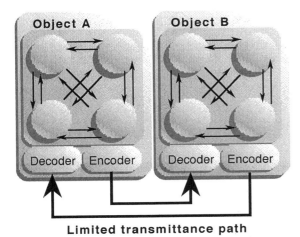

Limited transmittance path

Fig.1: Schematic representation of the conversation between two objects. Each object is composed of network, decoder, and encoder.

Link is an arrow originating from the "source node" and pointing to one of $N-1$ other nodes. The source node is the node visited by the encoder or by the decoder at some specific instance. Link does not point the source node itself. In order to make the model dynamically flexible, we treat the strength of link as a fuzzy parameter varying over some finite range. In the present simulation, we use integer ranging from 0 to 255 to express the strength of link. (We did not use the floating point variable for the reason of the computational efficiency.) The "destination node'", which is the node visited at the next time, is chosen by comparing the strength of $N-1$ links. The network status at some instance is thus defined by a "link matrix" whose elements represent strength values of links. In Fig.2 an example for the case $N=4$ is shown. Two networks, S1 and S2, are making conversation. The element $S1^{ij}$, for example, is the strength of the link originating from the source node i and pointing to the node j in the network S1. In Fig.2 links with strength 179, 247, and 113 are originating from the source node 3 and pointing to the node 1, 2, and 4, respectively.

$$
\begin{pmatrix} 0 & 1 & 85 & 8 \\ 91 & 0 & 137 & 50 \\ 179 & 247 & 0 & 113 \\ 27 & 178 & 144 & 0 \end{pmatrix} \rightleftharpoons \begin{pmatrix} 0 & 208 & 175 & 195 \\ 211 & 0 & 56 & 109 \\ 243 & 214 & 0 & 207 \\ 115 & 154 & 169 & 0 \end{pmatrix}
$$
$$\text{S1} \qquad\qquad\qquad\qquad \text{S2}$$

Fig.2: An example of the conversation between $N=4$ networks, S1 and S2. Strength of the link is the element of 4x4 link matrices.

How to communicate

Two networks making conversation are defined to have the same set of nodes. Initial values of two link matrices are randomly produced. Thus, two networks have the same set of symbols but have different semantic memory (different link matrices). The network which are sending information to the other network is called the speaker and the network receiving information is the hearer. The conversation sequence is proceeded with the following steps:

1. One of two networks is chosen as the speaker and the other is to be the hearer.
2. Some node in the speaker and in the hearer is chosen arbitrarily as the source node at the first step.
3. The encoder of the speaker chooses the destination node by comparing the strength of $N-1$ links originating from the source node in the speaker. The rule to determine the destination node is explained in detail in the subsection, **encode**.
4. The speaker speaks the number of node visited by the encoder (the destination node).
5. The hearer hears the spoken node (the destination node of the speaker) and compared it to the hearer's status. This process is to **decode** the spoken word.
6. Then, the hearer alters its link matrix by following one of the optimization rules explained in the subsection, **optimization**.
7. The speaker and the hearer change their roles: The hearer becomes the speaker of the next talk. Here we refer to the cycle from the step 3 to the step 7 as "talk". The node spoken in the step 4 is the source node of the new speaker .
8. Go to the step 3 and begin the next talk.

Thus generated sequence of spoken nodes (sequence of talks) is the conversation. The encoder encodes the semantic memory and speaks one particular node. The decoder decodes the spoken information and compare it to its semantic memory. The conversation results in the sequence of visited nodes. The whole conversation was examined many times by changing initial source node and initial link matrices.

Encode

The semantic memory is encoded by the encoder and the encoded information is decoded to the semantic memory by the decoder. In general there should be cases that the method of encoding and the method of decoding are not consistent with each other. Such inconsistency should lead the conversation to the loop of misunderstanding. Here, in order to emphasize such misunderstanding phenomena, we realize inconsistency by introducing two different types of encoder. One type of the encoder is referred to as the positive encoder. The positive encoder always chooses the strongest link (the link which has the largest strength value) and chooses the destination node to be the one pointed by the strongest link. We call the network which has the positive encoder the type P network. The other type is referred to the negative encoder (the type N network). The type N is opposite to the type P: The negative encoder always chooses the destination node to be the one pointed by the weakest link. One could use an analogy to human conversation; the type P network an honest person and the type N network a perverse person. The destination node visited by the encoder is spoken as the "outer information"

Suppose the network S1 in Fig.2 is a speaker and the node 3 is the source node. If S1 is the type P network, the strongest link with the strength 247 is chosen. Then, the destination node is the node 2. If S1 is the type N network, the weakest link with the strength 113 is chosen. Then, the destination node is the node 4. The number of node, 2 (for the type P) or 4 (for the type N), is spoken as the outer information.

Decode

In the first step, the decoder generates the inner information and in the second step, the decoder compares the inner and the outer information and sends the result to the optimizer.

Since the source node of the speaker is already known to the hearer, the decoder in the hearer can choose its destination node by consulting the hearer's link matrix. Here, we define only a single type of the decoder. The decoder chooses the destination node pointed by the strongest link originating from the source node. Both the type P and the type N networks were defined to have this positive decoder. Thus chosen destination node in the hearer is the inner information which is never spoken out to the other network. The inner information is used only within the hearer.

Then, the outer information spoken by the speaker and the inner information generated inside the hearer are compared. The decoder is supposed to be unable to distinguish whether the partner network is type P or type N. The decoder always assumes that the other network is type P. Therefore, if the outer and the inner information agree with each other, then the decoder sends the message to the optimizer that there is no need to optimize the hearer's link matrix. If the outer information and the inner information designate different nodes, on the other hand, the decoder sends the message to the optimizer that the speaker's semantic memory is different from that of the hearer and that the hearer's link matrix should be changed by using the optimization rule to

understand the speaker and to harmonize the conversation. Of course there are other possible combinations of positive and negative encoders and decoders. Though it is interesting to examine these varieties of combination, we adopt, in this paper, the minimal set (two extreme encoders and the single decoder) to observe the nontrivial behavior in the simple model.

In Fig.2 the decoder of the hearer S2 compares links with the strength 243, 214, and 207 when the source node is the node 3. The decoder chooses the destination node to be the node 1. When the outer information (the number of the node spoken by S1) is 1, then the decoder tells the optimizer that there is no need to optimize links. When the outer information is other than 1, then the decoder tells the optimizer to change the strength of links.

Optimization

The optimizer is a daemon which changes the link matrix of the hearer, $S(hearer)^{ij}$. When the optimizer received the message from the decoder that the outer information designates k, and the inner information designates l as destination nodes originating from the source node i with $k \neq l$, then the optimizer changes the link matrix by using one of the following three optimization rules:

rule I: $S(hearer)^{ij}$ for all j except k is reduced and $S(hearer)^{ik}$ is increased as

$$S(hearer)^{ij} \rightarrow S(hearer)^{ij} - \delta^j \qquad \text{for } j \neq k,$$
$$S(hearer)^{ik} \rightarrow \min\left(S(hearer)^{ik} + \sum_{j \neq k} \delta^j , 255 \right), \qquad (1)$$

where $\delta^j = \min\left(\delta, S(hearer)^{ij} \right)$ and δ is a constant positive integer. min(A, B) is the smaller of A and B. Eq.(1) is iteratively applied until $S(hearer)^{ik}$ becomes the largest of $S(hearer)^{ij}$ for $j = 1 \sim N$. In this rule order of strength of $S(hearer)^{ij}$ for j except k is preserved.

rule II: $S(hearer)^{jk}$ for all j except i is reduced and $S(hearer)^{ik}$ is increased as

$$S(hearer)^{jk} \rightarrow S(hearer)^{jk} - \delta^{\prime j} \qquad \text{for } j \neq i,$$
$$S(hearer)^{ik} \rightarrow \min\left(S(hearer)^{ik} + \sum_{j \neq i} \delta^{\prime j} , 255 \right), \qquad (2)$$

where $\delta^{\prime j} = \min\left(\delta, S(hearer)^{jk} \right)$. Eq.(2) is iteratively applied until $S(hearer)^{ik}$ becomes the largest of $S(hearer)^{ij}$ for $j = 1 \sim N$. In this rule order of strength of $S(hearer)^{jk}$ for j except i is preserved.

rule III: This rule is the combination of the rule I and the rule II;

$$S(hearer)^{ij} \to S(hearer)^{ij} - \delta^j \qquad \text{for } j \neq k,$$
$$S(hearer)^{jk} \to S(hearer)^{jk} - \delta^{ij} \qquad \text{for } j \neq i,$$
$$S(hearer)^{ik}$$
$$\to \min\left(S(hearer)^{ik} + \sum_{j \neq k} \delta^j + \sum_{j \neq i} \delta^{ij}, 255 \right). \qquad (3)$$

Eq.(3) is iteratively applied until $S(hearer)^{ik}$ becomes the largest of $S(hearer)^{ij}$ for $j = 1 \sim N$. In this rule order of strength of $S(hearer)^{ij}$ and $S(hearer)^{jk}$ except the i k element is preserved.

In the rule II, care should be taken when $S(hearer)^{il}$ =255. Since $S(hearer)^{il}$ is not decreased by the rule II, the optimization will end up with $S(hearer)^{il} = S(hearer)^{ik}$ =255. A subsidiary rule has to be added to decrease $S(hearer)^{il}$ in this case. In the simulation explained in the next section, however, this situation did no take place within the examined set of initial conditions. Thus, we do not go into this detail furthermore.

All these rules are designed to satisfy approximate conservation laws: In the rule I the change of $\sum_{j=1}^{N} S(hearer)^{ij}$ is suppressed to be as small as possible, in the rule II the change of $\sum_{j=1}^{N} S(hearer)^{jk}$ is suppressed, and in the rule III the change of $\sum_{j \neq k} S(hearer)^{ij} + \sum_{j \neq i} S(hearer)^{jk} + S(hearer)^{ik}$ is suppressed. Without these conservation laws, the link strength decreases or increases too rapidly and the conversation is terminated with short sequence. In the simulation we used the value $\delta = 2$ for the rule I and II and $\delta = 1$ for the rule III.

Consider the example in Fig.2. When the source node is 3 and S1 is type P, the speaker S1 speaks the destination node to be the node 2. The inner information of S2 is the node 1. Then $S2^{ij}$ is changed with the optimization rule. Results after optimization are shown in Fig.3.

$$\begin{pmatrix} 0 & 208 & 175 & 195 \\ 211 & 0 & 56 & 109 \\ 243 & 214 & 0 & 207 \\ 115 & 154 & 169 & 0 \end{pmatrix} \xrightarrow{\text{rule I}} \begin{pmatrix} 0 & 208 & 175 & 195 \\ 211 & 0 & 56 & 109 \\ \mathbf{233} & \mathbf{234} & \mathbf{0} & \mathbf{197} \\ 115 & 154 & 169 & 0 \end{pmatrix}$$

$$\begin{pmatrix} 0 & 208 & 175 & 195 \\ 211 & 0 & 56 & 109 \\ 243 & 214 & 0 & 207 \\ 115 & 154 & 169 & 0 \end{pmatrix} \xrightarrow{\text{rule II}} \begin{pmatrix} 0 & \mathbf{192} & 175 & 195 \\ 211 & \mathbf{0} & 56 & 109 \\ 243 & \mathbf{246} & 0 & 207 \\ 115 & \mathbf{138} & 169 & 0 \end{pmatrix}$$

$$\begin{pmatrix} 0 & 208 & 175 & 195 \\ 211 & 0 & 56 & 109 \\ 243 & 214 & 0 & 207 \\ 115 & 154 & 169 & 0 \end{pmatrix} \xrightarrow{\text{rule III}} \begin{pmatrix} 0 & \mathbf{202} & 175 & 195 \\ 211 & \mathbf{0} & 56 & 109 \\ \mathbf{237} & \mathbf{238} & \mathbf{0} & \mathbf{201} \\ 115 & \mathbf{148} & 169 & 0 \end{pmatrix}$$

Fig.3: Different three rules of optimization. The link matrix before the optimization is left and the one after the optimization is right. Bold figures are links which are altered by the optimization.

Termination of communication

When the outer and the inner information disagree with each other and the optimizer alter the link matrix of the hearer, the hearer obtains the new information that can not be generated by itself. We call such a talk the "significant" talk. Here we define a talk as a series of procedures from the step 3 through the step 7 of the subsection "how to communicate". When the optimizer did not work, on the other hand, we call that talk the "gibberish" talk. Thus the conversation is the sequence of significant talks and gibberish talks.

In all the conversations simulated with $N = 16$, optimization ceased after some transient sequence of significant and gibberish talks. Conversations fell into the periodic loop of gibberish talks. The number of talks contained in the gibberish loop (the length of the gibberish loop) must be less than N. Therefore, when N successive gibberish talks appeared, then the conversation was terminated. The number of significant talks appeared before termination can be used as a parameter that characterizes the conversation.

3 Simulation

Networks with the number of nodes, $N = 16$, are used in the simulation. The network character is assumed to be either of type P or type N. Thus, 4 types of conversation, PP, PN, NP, and NN are considered. In the PN-conversation the first speaker is type P and in the NP-conversation the first speaker is type N.

The initial link matrix was randomly produced. 17 different networks were prepared in this way and a pair of networks were chosen from 17 networks to make conversation. All possible pairs were matched, so that 16x17 matches were examined. All 16 nodes were chosen one by one as the source node at the first talk. Thus $16 \times 16 \times 17 = 4352$ conversations were examined for each type of conversation. Three rules of optimization were applied and compared.

Networks before conversation are written as $S1_{initial}$ and $S2_{initial}$, and networks after conversation are written as $S1_{final}$ and $S2_{final}$. At the starting point of the conversation S1 is the speaker and S2 is the hearer. The similarity between networks is measured by distance, d. The distance between $S1_{final}$ and $S2_{final}$ is, for example, defined as

$$d(S1_{final} - S2_{final}) = \sqrt{ \frac{1}{N(N-1)} \sum_{i=1}^{N} \sum_{j=1}^{N} \left(S1_{final}^{ij} - S2_{final}^{ij} \right)^2 }, \quad (4)$$

where $S1_{final}^{ij}$ and $S2_{final}^{ij}$ are $S1^{ij}$ and $S2^{ij}$ after the conversation. Five other distances are defined in similar ways. See Fig.4. We also use notations like $d(S1_{final} - S2_{final}; PN)$ to represent the distance $d(S1_{final} - S2_{final})$ for the case S1 is the type P network and S2 is the type N network.

We also measured the difference between networks by

using inner products, such as $\sum_{i=1}^{N} \sum_{j=1}^{N} S1_{final}^{ij} S2_{final}^{ij}$. Results obtained from the inner product measurement, however, gave the same qualitative information as given by d.

In Table 1 results of conversations, distances and the number of significant talks are shown for the each type of conversation and for different optimization rules. From Table 1 we can see that the averaged number of significant talks in PP, PN, NP, and NN type conversation, N^{sig} (PP), N^{sig} (PN) and so on are

$$N^{sig} (PP) < N^{sig} (NN) < N^{sig} (PN) \approx N^{sig} (NP). \qquad (5)$$

The averaged distance between S1 and S2 after conversation, $d(S1_{final} - S2_{final})$ is

$$d(S1_{final} - S2_{final} ; PP) < d(S1_{initial} - S2_{initial}), \qquad (6)$$

$$d(S1_{initial} - S2_{initial})$$
$$< d(S1_{final} - S2_{final} ; PN) \approx d(S1_{final} - S2_{final} ; NP)$$
$$< d(S1_{final} - S2_{final} ; NN). \qquad (7)$$

The averaged distance between the network before conversation and the same network after the conversation, $d(S1_{initial} - S1_{final})$ or $d(S2_{initial} - S2_{final})$ is

$$d(S1_{initial} - S1_{final} ; PP)$$
$$< d(S1_{initial} - S1_{final} ; NN) \approx d(S1_{initial} - S1_{final} ; PN)$$
$$< d(S1_{initial} - S1_{final} ; NP), \qquad (8)$$

$$d(S2_{initial} - S2_{final} ; PP)$$
$$< d(S2_{initial} - S2_{final} ; NN) \approx d(S2_{initial} - S2_{final} ; NP)$$
$$< d(S2_{initial} - S2_{final} ; PN). \qquad (9)$$

Though the fluctuation among samples is large, clear relations among averaged values, Eqs.(5-9), hold independently of which optimization rule is used.

It is easy to interpret Eq.(6): After the conversation, two P networks come closer to each other and the mutual understanding is increased. This is because each network learns the other one in a straightforward and consistent way.

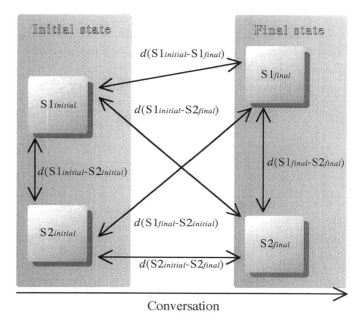

Fig.4: Distances between networks before and after conversation.

Table 1: Number of significant talks and network distances in conversations between 16 nodes networks.

Conversation type	Rules of optimization	Number of significant talks	$d(S1_{final}\text{-}S2_{final})$	$d(S1_{initial}\text{-}S1_{final})$	$d(S2_{initial}\text{-}S2_{final})$	$d(S1_{initial}\text{-}S2_{final})$	$d(S1_{final}\text{-}S2_{initial})$
P-P	I	5.14±2.21	101.8±4.0	12.9±6.0	14.5±5.8	102.7±4.0	102.9±4.0
	II	5.40±2.36	101.9±4.0	13.8±6.4	15.5±6.2	102.8±4.0	103.0±4.0
	III	5.25±2.24	101.8±4.0	13.2±6.2	14.8±5.9	102.8±4.0	103.0±4.0
P-N	I	7.50±4.74	104.6±4.0	15.8±7.3	18.7±8.3	102.5±4.0	106.5±4.4
	II	8.06±5.61	104.7±3.9	17.0±8.2	20.4±9.5	102.6±4.0	106.7±4.5
	III	7.87±5.38	104.6±3.9	16.2±7.8	19.4±9.1	102.5±3.9	106.6±4.5
N-P	I	7.48±4.70	105.0±3.9	17.8±8.7	16.9±7.1	106.8±4.4	102.7±4.0
	II	7.97±5.55	105.1±3.9	19.3±9.9	18.1±7.9	107.0±4.5	102.8±3.9
	III	7.80±5.34	105.0±3.9	18.4±9.5	17.3±7.5	106.9±4.5	102.7±3.9
N-N	I	6.61±3.18	108.9±4.5	15.1±6.4	16.3±6.2	106.6±4.1	106.3±4.1
	II	7.19±3.82	109.2±4.8	16.4±7.1	17.7±6.8	106.8±4.2	106.4±4.2
	III	6.92±3.53	109.1±4.7	15.6±6.7	16.8±6.5	106.7±4.1	106.4±4.1

Initial distance between networks, $d(S1_{initial}\text{-}S2_{initial})$ was 103.9±4.0 in all conversations. Results are averaged over 4352 conversations with different initial conditions.

When the type N network is involved in the conversation, on the other hand, this consistency is broken. Eq.(7) shows that after the conversation, two networks separate from each other. This is more evident in the NN-conversation than in the PN- or NP-conversation. More inconsistency is found in the former case than in the latter case.

This argument is not enough to explain Eqs.(5), (8), and (9) requiring more detailed consideration. The length of the significant talks is larger in the PN- or the NP-conversation than in the NN-case. Thus, in the PN- or the NP-conversation, both the type P and the type N networks are rewritten many times in one conversation and two networks drift together without making $d(S1_{final} - S2_{final})$ not so large. This drift results in the large values of $d(S1_{initial} - S1_{final})$ and $d(S2_{initial} - S2_{final})$. Eq.(8) and Eq.(9) show that the type N network is more rewritten than the type P network.

These circumstances are graphically represented in Figs5, 6, and 7. In these figures nodes sequentially visited by the encoder are expressed by alphabets, A,B, C, ... Fig.5 shows trivial examples of the PP-conversation. In Fig.5a the conversation ends up with the length-3 gibberish loop. In Fig.5b the length-4 loop is formed. Both odd and even number length of gibberish loops are possible after small number of optimizations.

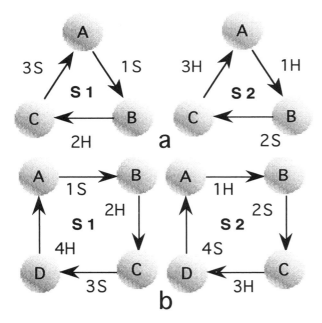

Fig.5: Examples of conversation between S1 (type P) and S2 (type P); **a**, conversation ends up with a closed loop of odd number of nodes and **b**, a closed loop of even number of nodes. Solid arrows are strongest links. Number on the arrow indicates the number of talk in which the arrow is consulted. The arrow designated with "S" is used when the network plays a role of the speaker, and "H" a role of the hearer. For example, "3S" indicates that the arrow is used in speaker's side at the 3rd talk.

Fig.6 shows the more complex cases in the NN-conversation. Fig.6a represents that the length-3 gibberish loop is impossible and the conversation should be lead to the longer loop. After the 3 significant talks of BCA, B can not be spoken and some other node, D, must be the next destination node. As shown in Fig.6b, however, it is easy to fall in the even-number length of gibberish loop.

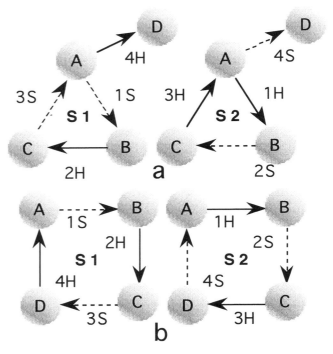

Fig.6: Examples of conversation between S1 (type N) and S2 (type N). Doted arrows are weakest links and solid arrows are strongest links. Other symbols have the same meaning as in Fig.5. **a**: From the topological reason, it is impossible to make a loop closed among odd number of nodes and the conversation is extended to the node D. **b**: The conversation ends up with a closed loop of even number of nodes.

In the NP- or PN-conversation, it is also impossible to form the length-3 gibberish loop. Fig.7 is an example in the PN-conversation. The situation is more complex than in the NN-conversation. In the 4th talk the weakest link in S1, which was used in the 1st talk, is optimized to be the strongest one. This is a simplest example of the feed-back effect self-organized in the conversation. The word spoken by S1 affects S2. Then, S1 has to be modified through the loop BCAB. The reason of this modification originates from S1's own action at the first time. The loop of the link is , thus, "twisted" (the weakest link is turned into the strongest one after the traverse of the loop). This twist is found in the type N network: Thus, the type N network has to pay more effort (modification) than the P type network. If one could use a human analogy, this would be the case that the liar must keep to extend his (or her) own lie, or that more efforts are needed to the liar than to the honest person. The twist of the loop is a seed to elongate the conversation and to enlarge $d(S1_{initial} - S1_{final})$ or $d(S2_{initial} - S2_{final})$.

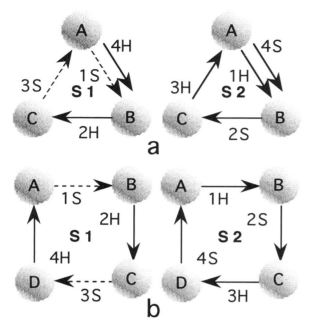

Fig.7: a: Twist of the conversation graph and **b**: a closed loop of even number of nodes in conversation between S1 (type N) and S2 (type P). Symbols have the same meaning as in Fig.6. In **a**, the link A→ B in S1 is changed from the weakest to the strongest at the 4-th talk. This rewriting of the link strength is a simplest example of the self-organized feed-back efect. This self-reference does not take place in the PP- or NN- conversations.

Thus, the present simulation of conversation revealed the importance of the topological point of view: The odd- and even-numbered loops play different roles in each type of conversation. In the PN- and NP- conversation, the self-reference is realized as an emergent phenomenon in the conversation and is represented as a "twist" in the loop of nodes.

4   Discussion

It may be possible to interpret the optimization as the cost that has to be paid by the network. To decrease its own cost, the network has to behave as type P irrespectively of whether the partner or the environment is type P or type N. If the optimization is a merit that could increase the flexibility of the network, on the other hand, then the network should behave as type N irrespectively of whether the partner or the environment is type P or type N. Thus, it is possible to construct a game theoretic model if we count the change of the link matrix as a point lost or gained by the network. Also we can consider a genetic algorithm (GA) if we select the network according to the counted points and make its network type inherit to the next generation. Simulations like the present

model, thus, provide a basis how the rules of the game or the GA strategies emerge from the sub-level structure and dynamics. In the present research I intended to examine a simple model that can offer a basis of such rules. Though the random number and the fixed target are commonly used in GA strategies, in the present model, random numbers were only used to give initial conditions and all the rules of the system dynamics are deterministic and no signal from the supervisor outside the system was used.

All the conversations found in the present simulation were terminated in a finite length. There is neither chaotic nor infinitely lasting significant talks in the present model. The typical length and structure of conversation, however, should depend on the precise rules adopted in the simulation. In fact, many other variant rules are possible. In actual human conversation, for example, many words could be spoken from the speaker at once before roles of the speaker and hearer are altered. This irregularity of the length of spoken words should be a universal feature found in many other areas of communication than human conversation. If we incorporate this irregularity in the model, the topological consideration valid in the present model might lose its sense. Thus we do not claim that the present model should be a good explanation of the human conversation or any other specific biological communication. Rather, we aimed at constructing a model of artificial communication to focus on the general aspects underlying the human and biological communications.

Any life must live in its environment. The environment, however, is not fixed nor static but is dynamic and is altered by the life itself. Thus the self-reference emerged from interactions between lives and the environment is an essential feature of what is to live. In this sense, there is no fixed answer which can be taught from outside but each life has to change without supervision. The simplest example of "environment" is the partner, which is defined to be the same life-form as "self". The "partner" and the "self" have the same structure but has different information. In this case the "self" is an environment by looking from the side of the "partner". A pair of mutually dependent dynamical networks which exchange information give an example of the "self" and the "partner" which affect each other by sharing their histories and contexts.

We should stress two main features of the present model: First, different information is stored in different objects and each object changes its structure by receiving the information sent from the other one. Second, by repeatedly exchanging the information through different ways of signal processing (different encoders in the present model), the initial information each network possessed should be replaced by the erroneous but new one. Such features are common in evolving systems and we could consider the possibility that these two features are important driving forces to evolve the system. This is an example of the "deterministic error" [10] which could change constituents of the system without the help of external noise given from the outside of the system. By revealing the mechanism how the simple events generated by simple interacting networks bring about the complex sequences of information, we could find new structures and laws underlying the emergence of complex behaviors. Such efforts should give a step toward the goal of researches on complexity and artificial life.

Acknowledgment

I would like to thank Masaki Sasai for logical discussions and suggestion on English expressions.

References

1. John Hertz, Anders Krogh, and Richard G. Palmer, *Introduction to the theory of neural computation*, (Addison-Wesley, 1991).
2. Takashi Mutoh, p.161-189 in *Gendaikiso-shinrigaku VII*, ed. by Takashi Sakamoto, (Tokyo university press, 1983).
3. Gabriella Airenti, Bruno G. Bara, and Marco Colombetti, *Cogniive and behavior games in the pragmatics of dialogue*, Cognitive Science **17**, 197-256(1993).
4. James A. Levin and James A. Moore, *Dialogue-games: Metacommunicaton structures for natural language interaction*, Cognitive Science **1**, 395-420(1977).
5. Roger C. Schank, *Rules and topics in conversation*, Cognitive Science **1**, 421-441(1977).
6. Roger C. Schank, *Language and memory*, Cognitive Science **4**, 243-284(1980).
7. *Multi argent and cooperative computation II*, ed. by Kyoh Ishida, (Kindai-kagakusya, 1993).
8. Marvin Minsky, *The society of mind*, (Simon & Schuster, 1986).
9. M. Ross Quillian, p.227-270 in *Semantic information processing*, ed. by Marvin Minsky, (The MIT press, 1968).
10. Takashi Ikegami and Takashi Hashimoto, *Coevolution of machines and tapes*, p.234-245 in *Advances in Artificial Life*, ed. by F. Moran et al, (Springer, 1995).

Evolution of Intricate Long-Distance Communication Signals in Cellular Automata Using Genetic Programming

David Andre

Visiting Scholar
Computer Science Dept.
Stanford University
860 Live Oak Ave, #4
Menlo Park, CA 94025 USA
andre@flamingo.stanford.edu

Forrest H Bennett III

Visiting Scholar,
Computer Science Dept.,
Stanford University
Stanford, California 94305
fhb3@slip.net

John R. Koza

Computer Science Dept.,
Stanford University
Stanford, California 94305-9020
koza@cs.stanford.edu
http://www-cs-
faculty.stanford.edu/~koza/

Abstract

A cellular automata rule for the majority classification task was evolved using genetic programming with automatically defined functions. The genetically evolved rule has an accuracy of 82.326%. This level of accuracy exceeds that of the Gacs-Kurdyumov-Levin (GKL) rule, all other known human-written rules, and all other rules produced by known previous automated approaches.

Our genetically evolved rule is qualitatively different from other rules in that it utilizes a fine-grained internal representation of density information; it employs a large number of different domains and particles; and it uses an intricate set of signals for communicating information over large distances in time and space.

1. Introduction

Local rules govern the important interactions of many animate and inanimate entities. The study of artificial life often focuses on how the simultaneous execution of a single relatively simple rule at many local sites leads to the emergence of interesting global behavior (Langton 1989). These studies often also deal with the question of how entities that receive information only about their immediate local environment can engage in the long-distance communication necessary to coordinate intricate global behavior. Sometimes, these issues are posed in terms of how complex computations can be performed over great distances in time and space using rules that operate only with data that is nearby in time and space.

2. Automatic Programming of Cellular Automata

Cellular automata are an abstract way of studying and analyzing the simultaneous execution of local rules. Complex overall behavior is often produced by cellular automata as the result of the repetitive application (at each cell in the cellular space) of the seemingly simple transition rules contained in each cell (Burks 1970; Farmer, Toffoli, and Wolfram 1983; Wolfram 1986; Gutowitz 1991).

A cellular space is a uniform array of cells arranged in a certain topological arrangement in a certain number of dimensions. In a *cellular automaton* (CA), each cell in a cellular space is occupied by an identical automaton. The next state of each individual automaton in the cellular space depends on its own current state and on the current states of the other automata in a specified local neighborhood around the individual automaton. The state of each automaton at time 0 is called its *initial condition*.

For a one-dimensional cellular automaton, the cellular space is a linear arrangement of identical automata. The next state of each individual automaton might depend, for example, on the current state of that automaton and the current states of its six neighbors at distances up to 3. We denote these seven neighbors as X (for the automaton at the center), W (the adjacent automaton to the west), E (the adjacent automaton to the east), WW (the automaton at distance 2 to the west), EE, WWW, and EEE. A cellular space is said to have *periodic boundary conditions* when the cellular space is toroidal. If the automaton located in each cell has only two states, the state-transition function of the automaton is a Boolean function of its own current state and the states of its neighbors at a specified distance.

It is extremely difficult, in general, to design a single state-transition rule that, when it operates in each cell of the cellular space, produces a desired behavior.

Genetic algorithms (Holland 1975) operating on fixed-length character strings have been successfully used to evolve the initial conditions and state-transition rules for cellular automata (Meyer, Richards, and Packard 1991). Genetic programming (Koza 1992, 1994a, 1994b; Koza and Rice 1992) has been used for automatic programming of cellular automata randomizers (Koza 1992).

3. The Majority Classification Problem

The majority classification problem is one vehicle for exploring how complex calculations can be performed over large areas using rules of interaction that operate over a relatively small distance. In one commonly studied version of this problem, there is a one-dimensional linear arrangement of 149 two-state automata whose update rule operates on information within a distance of three. The initial states of the 149 automata (called the *initial configuration*) are the inputs to the calculation. If all 149 automata relax to a common state (0 or 1) after a certain amount of time, the common state is considered to be the binary output of the calculation. For the majority classification task, 149 0's constitute the correct answer if a majority of the 149 initial bits are 0 and a 149 1's are correct if a majority of the bits are 1. Thus, to solve this problem, a seven-argument Boolean transition rule must be found such that when it is situated at all 149 cells of a one-dimensional cellular automaton, the automaton converges to the correct configuration of 149 0's or 149 1's after 600 time steps. The fitness of a rule is measured by its ability to correctly do this computation for a random initial configuration.

It is difficult to construct a two-state, seven-neighborhood cellular automata rule that performs this majority classification task reasonably well on a 149-bit input configuration. Seven bits cannot store an integer as large as 149 (if, for example, one were storing and transmitting a signal communicating a locally observed excess of 0's or 1's). It is unknown whether a perfect solution to this problem exists.

The difficulty that human programmers have had with this task is indicated by its history. In 1978, Gacs, Kurdyumov, and Levin developed a two-state, seven-neighbor rule for the purpose of studying reliable computation under random perturbations. This Gacs-Kurdyumov-Levin (GKL) rule performs the majority classification task reasonably well. The GKL rule is successful on 81.6% of the inputs consisting of a configuration of 149 bits (each chosen independently with 50% probability). Gonzaga de Sa and Maes (1992) showed that this system does indeed relax to a common state.

The majority classification task has been the subject of extensive study (Mitchell, Hraber, and Crutchfield 1993; Das, Mitchell, and Crutchfield 1994; Mitchell, Crutchfield, and Hraber 1994; Crutchfield and Mitchell 1995; Das, Crutchfield, Mitchell, and Hanson 1995; Mitchell 1996).

Lawrence Davis (1995) cleverly modified the GKL rule and created a rule that achieved slightly better accuracy than the GKL rule. His rule has an accuracy of about 81.8%. In 1993, Rajarshi Das (1995) created another rule that achieved an accuracy of about 82.178%. Since several of these rules have not been previously published, we show them in table 1. The last row in this table shows the genetically evolved rule described later in this paper. The 128 bits are presented in the natural order that they would appear in a state transition table starting with state 0000000 and ending at state 1111111.

Das, Mitchell, and Crutchfield (1994) evolved rules using a version of the genetic algorithm operating on fixed-length strings. These evolved rules sometimes exhibited qualitatively the same behavior as the GKL rule; however, none of the rules evolved using the genetic algorithm operating on fixed-length strings were as accurate as the original GKL rule. As Das, Mitchell, and Crutchfield (1994) reported, the genetic algorithm usually found only relatively uninteresting block-expanding rules that score in the range of 65-70% accuracy. The best result from their studies had 76.9% accuracy. This reported performance may have been the consequence of factors such as the small population size employed.

Land and Belew (1995) suggested that the standard representation of the cellular automata rule as a chromosome string of length 128 used in most previous work in evolving one-dimensional cellular automata using the genetic algorithm may hinder evolution. They suggest that higher-level representations (such as condition-action pairs) may aid the evolutionary process because of the higher degree of locality in the condition-action pairs.

Given Land and Belew's (1995) findings, the tree representation employed by genetic programming seems well suited for this task because it permits the size and shape of the ultimate solution to undergo evolution. The search strategy employed by genetic programming (and the genetic algorithm) is also important for this problem. Although many Boolean problems can be trivially solved by hillclimbing methods in a variety of representations, such methods work only when the fitness cases (i.e., the 2^7 lines in the truth table) are independent. When a Boolean function is used for a cellular automata rule, there is no correct answer for a given set of inputs that is independent from the answers for the other inputs. Also, genetic programming supports automatically defined functions, whereas the conventional genetic algorithm operating on fixed-length strings does not have a similar facility for exploiting regularities, symmetries, homogeneities, and modularities of the problem environment.

4. Preparatory Steps

The runs reported here used standard genetic programming with automatically defined functions (Koza 1994a) as summarized in table 2. The problem (coded in ANSI C) was run on a medium-grained parallel Parystec computer system consisting of 64 Power PC 601 80 MHz processors arranged in a toroidal mesh with a host PC Pentium type computer.

Table 1   The succession of "best" cellular automata rules for the majority classification task.

Rule	State Transitions
GKL 1978	00000000 01011111 00000000 01011111 00000000 01011111 00000000 01011111 00000000 01011111 11111111 01011111 00000000 01011111 11111111 01011111
Davis 1995	00000000 00101111 00000011 01011111 00000000 00011111 11001111 00011111 00000000 00101111 11111100 01011111 00000000 00011111 11111111 00011111
Das 1995	00000111 00000000 00000111 11111111 00001111 00000000 00001111 11111111 00001111 00000000 00000111 11111111 00001111 00110001 00001111 11111111
GP 1995	00000101 00000000 01010101 00000101 00000101 00000000 01010101 00000101 01010101 11111111 01010101 11111111 01010101 11111111 01010101 11111111

Table 2   Tableau for the majority classification problem for one-dimensional cellular automata.

Objective:	Find a seven argument Boolean function that performs the majority classification problem for a 149-width one-dimensional cellular automata.
Architecture of the overall program with ADFs:	One result-producing branch and one 2-argument automatically defined function, ADF0, and one 3-argument automatically defined function, ADF1. ADF1 can refer to ADF0.
Terminal set for the RPB:	X, E, EE, EEE, W, WW, and WWW.
Function set for the RPB:	AND, OR, NAND, NOR, NOT, IF, XOR, ADF0, and ADF1.
Terminal set for ADF0:	X, E, EE, EEE, W, WW, WWW, ARG0, and ARG1.
Function set for ADF0:	AND, OR, NAND, NOR, NOT, IF, and XOR.
Terminal set for ADF1:	X, E, EE, EEE, W, WW, WWW, ARG0, ARG1, and ARG2.
Function set for ADF1:	AND, OR, NAND, NOR, NOT, IF, XOR, and ADF0.
Fitness cases:	• 1,000 149-bit initial configurations were used as in-sample fitness cases. These initial configurations were created randomly, with no bias (i.e., 0 and 1 each have an independent 50% probability of being chosen). Thus, the distribution of densities of the initial state vectors was a binomial distribution centered at 0.50. • The out-of-sample fitness cases consisted of 1,000,000 (and later 10,000,000 and 15,000,000) similarly created initial configurations.
Raw fitness:	1,000 minus the number of fitness cases for which the system relaxes to the correct configuration after 600 time steps.
Standardized fitness:	1,000 minus raw fitness.
Hits:	Raw fitness.
Parameters:	• Population size, M, is 51,200 (64 times 800). • Maximum number of generations to be run, G, is 51. • 89% crossovers, 10% reproductions, and 1% mutations were used on each generation. • A maximum of 500 points (functions and terminals) for the result-producing branch and 250 points for each automatically defined function was allowed. • Structure-preserving crossover with branch typing was used. • The other parameters for controlling the runs of genetic programming were the default values specified in Koza (1994a).

The so-called *distributed genetic algorithm* or *island model* for parallelization was used. That is, subpopulations (*demes*) were situated at the processing nodes of the system. Population size was $Q = 800$ at each of the $D = 64$ demes for a total population size of 51,200. The initial random subpopulations were created locally at each processing node. Generations were run asynchronously on each node. After a generation of genetic operations was performed locally on each node, four boatloads, each consisting of $B = 3\%$ (the migration rate) of the subpopulation (selected on the basis of fitness) were dispatched to each of the four toroidally adjacent nodes. Details of the parallel implementation of genetic programming can be found in Andre and Koza 1996.

5. Emergent Properties of the Most Successful Run

We made five runs of genetic programming on this problem. Each run produced hundreds of individuals that behaved in a manner reminiscent of the GKL rule. Each of the five runs produced numerous individuals that score well above the best accuracy of 76.9% produced by the genetic algorithm operating on fixed-length character strings.

The best-of-run individual from one of these five runs scores a higher accuracy than any other known rule (table 1), including the GKL rule, all other known human-written rules, and all rules produced by all known previous automated approaches.

An examination of the most successful run illustrates the emergence of many interesting entities prior to the creation of the best individual.

The best individual program from the initial random generation indiscriminately classifies all fitness cases as having a majority of 1's . Since 525 of the 1,000 randomly created fitness cases on this particular run happened to have a majority of 1's , this best of generation 0 scores 525 hits.

The best individual of generation 1 scores 650 hits. The activity of a one-dimensional cellular automata can be presented as a two dimensional grid in which the top horizontal row contains the states (0 or 1) of the 149 automata at a time 0 (i.e., the initial configuration of the system) and in which each successive row represents the states of the 149 automata at successive time steps. Figure 1 shows a small part of such a diagram for this individual. In the space-time diagram, we see large areas dominated by solid blocks of repeated simple regular patterns, called *domains*, where a given domain is specified by a regular expression. The two domains shown in figure 1 are the domain denoted by the regular expression 1^* and the domain denoted by the expression 0^*. The space-time diagrams in this paper display 1's as black, and 0's as white. Thus we call the 1^* domain black (designated by (**B**)) and the 0^* domain white (designated by (**W**)).

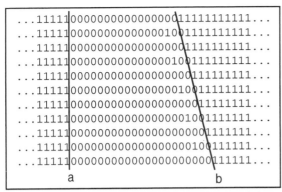

Figure 1. Eleven time steps of the partial space-time behavior of the best individual of generation 1 on one fitness case showing the spread of the zero domain.

The domains of this generation 1 individual interact in various ways. When a domain consisting of a solid block of 1's is to the left of a domain consisting of a solid block of 0's , the interface consists of ...111000... and the corresponding positions at the next time step also consist of ...111000... (where the underlined digit represents the same automaton). Because these particular two domains do not move left or right over time, this particular domain interface is said to have a velocity of zero.

Following Das, Mitchell, and Crutchfield (1994), we describe such an interface between two domains as a particle, denoted P(xy), where x is the domain on the left and y the domain on the right. Particles are one of the ways that information is communicated across large distances in time and space in a cellular space.

In figure 1, line a shows the path of the P(BW) particle with a velocity of 0 and line b shows the path of the P(WB) particle with a velocity of 1/2.

This evolved automata from generation 1 overpredicts a majority of 1's and underpredicts a majority of 0's . This individual is an example of what Mitchell et al. (1993) called a *block-expanding rule* (i.e. a rule that converges to a state unless a sufficiently large block of adjacent or nearly adjacent instances of the opposite state exists in the input).

The best program of generation 6 scores 706 hits on the 1,000 in-sample fitness cases. A portion of its space-time behavior is shown in figure 2. The behavior of this individual is similar to the individual of generation 1. However, it scores slightly better because it has modified the conditions under which it expands a block. The interaction between the domain of zeros on the left and ones on the right is quite complex in this individual, and the interface between the two domains is quite large. The particle P(WB) travels at a velocity of 2/7.

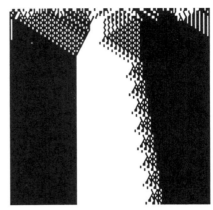

Figure 2. Partial space-time behavior of the best individual of generation 6 on one fitness case. Black represents 1's , white 0's .

The best individual of generation 15 scores 815 hits. Its behavior (see figure 3) is somewhat similar to that of the GKL rule, although it scores less than 80% on out-of-sample fitness cases. Like the GKL rule (figure 7), this rule separates white on the left from black on the right with a gray domain that grows into both black and white. When black is to the left of white, a zero-velocity particle characterizes their interaction. The combination of these two concepts yields the basic mechanism that both GKL and this generation 15 individual use to compute global measures of density. If the domain of all white is larger, it will win out over black, and vice versa.

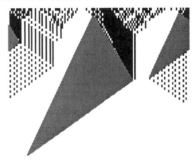

Figure 3. Space-time behavior of the best individual of generation 15 on a typical initial state vector.

Although similar to GKL, the rule of generation 15 has several new gray domains that are not quite the same as the gray domain in the GKL rule's behavior. The new domains interact, as can be seen in figure 4. In this example, the zero and one domains do not enter into the computation until the very end – all of the primary computation is performed by the new gray domains. At this point, however, the new gray domains do not interact particularly well – the rule fails often when it performs computation with the new gray domains.

The best individual of the run emerged on generation 17. The 36-point result-producing branch of the evolved Boolean expression is shown below:

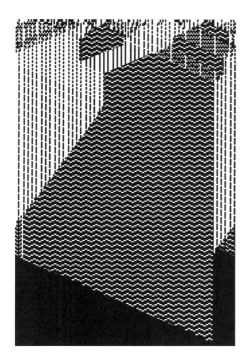

Figure 4. Space-time behavior of the best individual of generation 15 where there are no all black or all white domains until the end.

```
(nand (xor (or (adf0 X (not WWW)) (not WWW))
(adf0 (adf0 E X) (or E W))) (or (nand (if EEE E
X) (if EEE W (and EE WWW))) (adf1 (nand W E)
(xor WWW W) E))).
```

The 10-point automatically defined function ADF0 is

```
(if (nor (or X X) (nor arg1 arg0)) EEE WWW).
```

The 44-point automatically defined function ADF1 is

```
(xor W (xor (adf0 (adf0 (if (or (not W) (adf0
WWW arg2)) (xor (adf0 WWW X) (nor WW WWW)) (nand
(xor X X) (or X WW))) (nor (or (if arg2 EEE
arg2) (nor arg2 arg1)) (not (xor W E)))) (xor W
(not arg2))) EEE)).
```

This rule scores 824 hits on the 1,000 in-sample fitness cases, and scores 82.4% accuracy over 100,000 out-of-sample cases. It scores 82.326% accuracy over 10,000,000 additional cases. This accuracy is slightly better than the score of the GKL rule. We are aware of two human-coded

Table 3. Out-of-sample comparison.

Rule	Accuracy	Number of test cases
Best rule evolved by genetic algorithm (Das et al 1994)	76.9%	10^6
GKL human-written	81.6%	10^6
Davis human-written	81.8%	10^6
Das human-written	82.178%	10^7
Best rule evolved by genetic programming	82.326%	10^7

rules that also are better than the GKL rule, the Davis rule (1995) and the Das rule (1995). All four rules are shown in table 1. Table 3 shows the results of testing (on the same out-of-sample fitness cases) the three human-written rules, the best rule produced by the genetic algorithm, and the best rule evolved by genetic programming. As can be seen, the best rule evolved by genetic programming is slightly better than all the other rules. Non-parametric c2 tests with one degree of freedom were performed; the probability(p) that the pairwise differences between the best rule evolved by genetic programming and each of the other three rules were attributable to chance was less than 0.001. (i.e. the differences are statistically significant, $p < 0.001$).

6. The Best Rule Evolved by Genetic Programming

Why does the genetically evolved rule score better than the best known rules written by humans? First, the evolved rule has more domains than the GKL rule. These eleven domains, shown in table 4, classify the density of 1's into finer levels of gray than do the domains found in the GKL rule's behavior as discussed by Das, Mitchell, and Crutchfield (1994). The domains in the GKL rule's behavior are black, white, and checkerboard gray, corresponding to the regular expression $(10)^* \cup (01)^*$ (Das, Mitchell, and Crutchfield 1994). In addition, the evolved rule's computation uses a larger number of particles. The genetically evolved rule discovered 10 particles which are identical to the particles (Das, Mitchell, and Crutchfield 1994) in the GKL rule; however, it also discovered at least 40 additional particles which involve the new gray domains. All the new particles have velocity 0, +3, or -3.

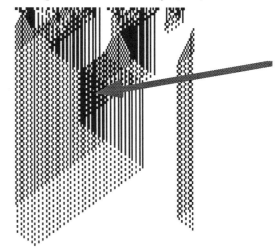

Figure 5. Space-time diagram showing the behavior of the best evolved rule. The differences between the shades of gray are crucial, especially in the area pointed to by the arrow, as otherwise the automata would not converge in this example.

Having more domains would be purely a superficial difference if the new domains did not participate in the computation. However, it appears that the new gray domains are crucial to the computations being performed by the genetically evolved rule. In the behavior shown in figure 5, for example, the distinct behavior of the new grays is critical to the success of the rule. If all the grays acted identically, then the automata would not converge in this example. The interactions of the new gray domains in the area indicated by the arrow allow the white domain to escape and encroach to the left.

In addition, there are time periods in the behavior of the evolved rule where none of the GKL-like domains exist; the computation is carried out entirely by the new gray domains. Figure 6 shows such a space-time diagram.

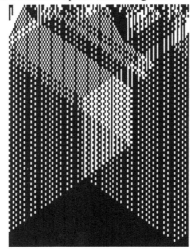

Figure 6. The behavior of the best evolved individual on one set of initial states.

Even though it is apparent that the new gray domains take part in the computation, one might question whether they account for any part of the difference in score between the best evolved rule and the GKL rule. However, the behavior of both rules shown in figure 7 indicates that the finer levels of gray do give the evolved rule some advantage. On the left of the initial state vector, there are two fairly large regions of white (0's) separated by a region of black

(1's) marked in the diagrams by the arrows. Under the GKL rule, the black area is eliminated by the two adjacent white domains. Under the evolved rule, these two white areas get classified as light gray domains, and the black area becomes a dark gray domain (all shifted to the right slightly). Because it can make use of extra domains, the evolved rule can keep the information that there is a significant density of black (1's) in the vicinity of the arrow until more global information can resolve the local dispute.

The basic mechanism of the evolved rule is similar to that of the GKL rule in that there is a race among the black, white, and gray areas (Das, Mitchell, and Crutchfield 1994). Figure 8 shows a space-time diagram of the behavior of the evolved rule.

In the evolved rule, a white domain (**W**) is separated on the right from a black domain (**B**) by a growing domain of checkerboard gray (**6**). The white domain (**W**) is separated on the left from the black domain (**B**) by one or both of the separator domains, (**3**) and (**8**), which are domains whose interactions with either white or black have zero velocity. In the case shown in figure 8, the (**B**) domain is larger, and the gray (**6**) domain cuts off the white domain (**W**), allowing the black domain (**B**) to break through. In this case, the extra gray domains of (**7**) and (**9**) are not important, but they play a role in other fitness cases.

The mechanism discussed above is sufficient for many cases, but fails to handle the case when the black and white domains are of approximately equal size. In this circumstance, the gray (**6**) domain cuts off both the white and black domains. In the behavior of the GKL rule, when there is such a 'tie', after a brief transition, the black and white domains seem to 'swap' places, separated again by a new growing gray domain.

In the behavior of the best evolved rule such collisions occur slightly differently and yield different behavior after the collision. Under the evolved rule, the black (**B**) and white (**W**) domains are separated by a potentially larger distance by one or both of the separator domains (**8**) and (**3**). If there is a tie, new domains emerge after the collision, and there is no immediate gray separator domain.

The new gray domains of (**7**) and (**9**) appear to represent the continuation of the black (**B**) domain, whereas the (**2**) and (**1**) domains appear to represent the continuation

Table 4 The domains of the best evolved rule.

Regular Domain	Domain Name	Color
0*	W	White
(000001)*∪(100000)*∪(010000)*∪(001000)*∪(000100)*∪(000010)*	1	Very Light Gray
(000101)*∪(100010)*∪(010001)*∪(101000)*∪(010100)*∪(001010)*	2	Light Gray
(001)*∪(100)*∪(010)*	3	Light Gray
(001101)*∪(100110)*∪(010011)*∪(101001)*∪(110100)*∪(011010)*	4	Gray
(x001011)*∪(100101)*∪(110010)*∪(011001)*∪(101100)*∪(010110)*	5	Gray
(01)*∪(10)*	6	Gray
(011101)*∪(101110)*∪(010111)*∪(101011)*∪(110101)*∪(111010)*	7	Dark Gray
(011)*∪(101)*∪(110)*	8	Dark Gray
(011111)*∪(101111)*∪(110111)*∪(111011)*∪(111101)*∪(111110)*	9	Very Dark Gray
1*	B	Black

of the white (**W**) domain. Thus, when there is a tie in the evolved rule, the original domains of black and white disappear completely, and the computation is carried out entirely by the gray domains.

In the circumstance shown in figure 9, the black (**B**) and white domains (**W**) are separated by the (**3**) domain. When the checkerboard gray (**6**) domain cuts off the (**B**) domain, a new domain (**1**) is created that encroaches on both the (**6**) domain and the (**3**) separator domain. As it happens, the (**6**) domain cuts off the white (**W**) domain just as the particle $P_{(13)}$ reaches the (**W**) domain. As a result, the dark gray domain (**7**) begins to encroach on the gray (**6**) domain and creates a vertical wall with the (**1**) domain. Then, when the dark gray domain (**7**) reaches the very light gray domain (**1**) on the right, the gray (**5**) domain is formed.

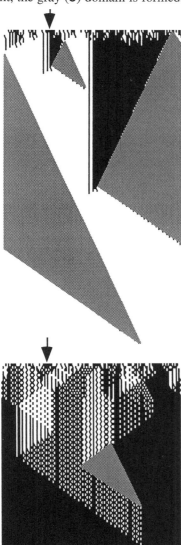

Figure 7. The space-time behavior of the evolved rule (bottom) and the GKL rule (top) on the same initial state vector. The ability of the evolved rule to classify domains of the input as intermediate gray values allows it to avoid the 'round-off' error that the GKL makes.

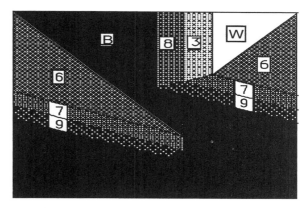

Figure 8. Abstracted Space-Time domain diagram for the best evolved rule.

This domain (**5**) serves a similar purpose as the checkerboard gray domain (**6**), in that it separates a dark domain (**7**) from a very light domain (**1**). When the gray domain (**5**), which grows to the left into the (**7**) domain, reaches the very light gray domain (**1**), the very light gray domain (**1**) begins to expand to the right. As might be expected, when the very light gray domain (**1**) hits a very light gray domain (**1**), a pure white domain (**W**) is created.

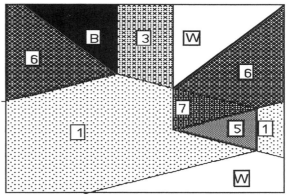

Figure 9 The best evolved rule's abstracted space-time domain behavior on a tie where the answer is white (W).

One problem that a rule utilizing zero-velocity particles can have is that the initial state vector could either be in a state or relax to a state where convergence does not take place. If the automata either starts in or reaches a state where the automata is filled with domains that have zero-velocity interactions with the adjacent patterns, the automata cannot converge. Thus, one potential downside to the evolved rule is that because it utilizes more domains in its computation that have zero-velocity particles, it may be more likely to be trapped in a non-convergent steady-state. We found only one such input pattern in our testing (see figure 10). Given that the evolved rule scores better than any other known rule, however, it is possible that the occasional non-convergence represents a strategic tradeoff rather than a defect.

7. Conclusions

The success of genetic programming on this problem suggests that genetic programming might be useful for other problems where emergent computation is sought.

A cellular automata rule for the majority classification task was evolved using genetic programming with automatically defined functions. The genetically evolved rule has an accuracy of 82.326%. This accuracy exceeds that of the Gacs-Kurdyumov-Levin (GKL) rule, all other known human-written rules, and all other known rules produced by previous automated approaches. The genetically evolved rule is qualitatively different from these rules. The genetically evolved rule utilizes a very fine internal representation of density information; it employs a large number of different domains and particles; and it uses an intricate set of signals for communicating information over large distances in time and space.

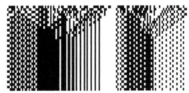

Figure 10. The behavior of the evolved rule on an initial state vector where the automata does not converge.

Acknowledgements

The authors gratefully thank Lawrence Davis, Melanie Mitchell, and James Crutchfield for helpful discussions and for reviewing a draft of this paper and Simon Handley for reviewing a draft of this paper.

Bibliography

Andre, David and Koza, John R. 1996. Parallel genetic programming: A scalable implementation using the transputer architecture. In Angeline, Peter J. and Kinnear, Kenneth E. Jr. (editors). *Advances in Genetic Programming 2*. Cambridge, MA: MIT Press.

Burks, Arthur W. 1970. *Essays on Cellular Automata.* Urbana, IL: University of Illinois Press.

Crutchfield, J. P. and Mitchell, Melanie. 1995. The evolution of emergent computation. *Proceedings of the National Academy of Sciences, USA*. 92 (23).

Das, Rajarshi, Mitchell, Melanie, and Crutchfield, J. P. 1994. A genetic algorithm discovers particle-based computation in cellular automata. In Davidor, Yuval, Schwefel, Hans-Paul, and Maenner, Reinhard (editors). 1994. *Parallel Problem Solving from Nature - PPSN III.* (Lecture Notes in Computer Science, Volume 866). Berlin: Springer-Verlag. 344-353.

Das, Rajarshi, Crutchfield, J. P., Mitchell, Melanie, and Hanson, J. E. 1995. Evolving globally synchronized cellular automata. In Eshelman, Larry J. (editor). *Proceedings of the Sixth International Conference on Genetic Algorithms.* San Francisco, CA: Morgan Kaufmann Publishers.

Das, Rajarshi. 1995. Personal communication.

Davis, Lawrence. 1995. Personal communication.

Farmer, Doyne, Toffoli, Tommaso, and Wolfram, Stephen (editors). 1983. *Cellular Automata: Proceedings of an Interdisciplinary Workshop, Los Alamos, New Mexico, March 7-11, 1983.* Amsterdam: North-Holland Physics Publishing. Also in *Physica D*, volume 10.

Gacs, P., Kurdyumov, G. L., and Levin, L. A. 1978. One dimensional uniform arrays that wash out finite islands. *Problemy Peredachi Informatsii.* 12(1978) 92 – 98.

Gonzaga de Sa, P. and Maes. C. 1992. The Gacs-Kurdyumov-Levin automaton revisited. *Journal of Statistical Physics.* 67(3/4) 507–522.

Gutowitz, Howard (editor). 1991. *Cellular Automata: Theory and Experiment.* Cambridge, MA: MIT Press. Also in *Physica D* 1990.

Holland, John H. 1975. *Adaptation in Natural and Artificial Systems.* Ann Arbor, MI: University of Michigan Press. The 1992 second edition was published by MIT Press.

Koza, John R. 1992. *Genetic Programming: On the Programming of Computers by Means of Natural Selection.* Cambridge, MA: MIT Press.

Koza, John R. 1994a. *Genetic Programming II: Automatic Discovery of Reusable Programs.* Cambridge, MA: MIT Press.

Koza, John R. 1994b. *Genetic Programming II Videotape: The Next Generation.* Cambridge, MA: MIT Press.

Koza, John R., and Rice, James P. 1992. *Genetic Programming: The Movie.* Cambridge, MA: MIT Press.

Land, Mark and Belew, Richard K. 1995. In McDonnell, John R., Reynolds, Robert G., and Fogel, David B. (editors). *Evolutionary Programming IV: Proceedings of the Fourth Annual Conference on Evolutionary Programming.* Cambridge, MA: MIT Press. Pages 403–434.

Langton, Christopher G. (editor). 1989. *Artificial Life, Santa Fe Institute Studies in the Sciences of Complexity.* Volume VI. Redwood City, CA: Addison-Wesley.

Meyer, Thomas P., Richards, Fred C. and Packard, Norman H. 1991. Extracting cellular automaton rules directly from experimental data. In Gutowitz, Howard (editor). *Cellular Automata: Theory and Experiment.* Cambridge, MA: MIT Press.

Mitchell, Melanie. 1996. *An Introduction to Genetic Algorithms.* Cambridge, MA: MIT Press.

Mitchell, Melanie, Crutchfield, J. P., and Hraber, P. T. 1994. Dynamics, computation, and the "edge of chaos": A re-examination. In G. Cowan, D. Pines, and D. Melzner (editors). *Complexity: Metaphors, Models, and Reality.* Santa Fe Institute Studies in the Sciences of Complexity, Proceedings, Volume 19. Reading, MA: Addison-Wesley.

Mitchell, Melanie, Hraber, P. T., and Crutchfield, J. P. 1993. Revisiting the edge of chaos: Evolving cellular automata to perform computations. *Complex Systems.* (7) 89-130.

Wolfram (editor). 1986. *Theory and Applications of Cellular Automata.* Singapore: World Scientific.

Analysis of Cycles in Symbolic Chemical System based on Abstract Rewriting System on Multisets

Yasuhiro Suzuki, Shusaku Tsumoto, and Hiroshi Tanaka

Department of Information Medicine

Medical Research Institute,Tokyo Medical and Dental University

1-5-45 Yushima, Bunkyo-ku Tokyo 113 Japan

Email: {suzuki.com, tsumoto.com}@mri.tmd.ac.jp, tanaka@cim.tmd.ac.jp

Abstract

One of the most essential temporal structure in life systems is a cycle, which can be observed in any hierarchy of living things, such as TCA cycle in cytoplasmic level, the cell cycle in cell division, and the life cycle of living things. In this paper, an abstract rewriting system on a multiset is introduced to model a chemical reaction as a symbolic rewriting system acting on a multiset. By use of this model, the condition of a cycle emergence, its robustness and how this system works under the probabilistic condition are examined. The results show not only that a cycle will emerge even under a simple initial condition, but also that complex behavior of a cycle, such as fusion of several cycles, is observed when input randomness is introduced. Furthermore, the formal analysis of ARMS leads to two theorems on the termination of this system, where the interaction between the order of rules and inputs plays an important role.

1 Introduction

One of the most essential temporal structure in life systems is a cycle, which can be observed in any hierarchy of living things. For example, in metabolic pathways inside the cell, TCA cycle is used to extract energy from organic chemicals, which plays an important role in cell metabolism[14]. Also, the cell cycle in cell division is important for the growth of life systems, and the life cycle can be observed in all living things[14].

Thus, a cycle can be viewed as a universal structure in all the hierarchies of complex systems, especially in living things, whose importance has been pointed out by several researchers of complex systems, such as Eigen's hypercycle[3], Maturana's autopoiesis[12], Kauffman's NK network[9], and Fontana's Algorithmic Chemistry[4, 5]. However, these researches do not focus on the conditions under which such a cycle will emerge and the process in which it becomes stable.

In this paper, we introduce a new abstract rewriting system on multiple sets (ARMS) in order to examine the conditions of cycle emergence and the algebraic characteristics of the obtained cycle. In this model, a multiset [1] is taken as a role of a test tube, which contains "symbols", which correspond to chemical compounds. Then, rewriting rules, corresponding to product of chemical reaction formulae, act on this multiset, and the applied symbols are transformed into other symbols, corresponding to chemical reactions. Furthermore, we assume that the specific symbol a is input to this multiset. Interestingly, it is easily shown that even such a simple structure give rise to a cycle, although the structure of rules is strongly constrained to do that.

Then, we further examine the condition of emergence of a cycle, such as the effect of inputs and that of the order of rule application. The results show not only that a cycle will emerge even under a simple initial condition, but also that complex behaviors of a cycle, such as fusion of several cycles and period-doubling are observed when the initial condition is perturbed during the simulation. These results suggest that randomness of input is one of the principal factors on complex behavior of a cycle. The paper is organized as follows: Section 2 shows our abstract rewriting system. Section 3 presents a computational model using the abstract rewriting system which acts on multisets. Then, Section 4 gives experimental results, and Section 5 discusses their meaning. Section 6 describes related work, and finally, Section 7 concludes this paper.

2 Abstract Rewriting System

Our computational model is based on the abstract rewriting system because of the following three reasons. First, chemical reactions, which are important in our model, can be viewed as rewriting rules. For example, $\frac{1}{2}O_2 + H_2 \rightarrow H_2O$ is a kind of a rewriting rule. Thus, the abstract rewriting system gives a formal model of chemical reactions. Second, abstract rewriting system does not need a specific architecture like turing machine[7] and cellular automata[15]. Finally, third, we can apply

---

[1] A multiset is defined as a set which is allowed to include the same elements. For example, $\{a, a, b, c\}$ is not a set, but a multiset, while $\{a, b, c\}$ is both a set and a multiset.

the results of researches on the abstract rewriting systems, such as those on rewriting pathways, and rewriting rules.

In this section, we first introduce what is rewriting calculus, then, we introduce an abstract rewriting system and its examples.

2.1 Rewriting Calculus

Rewriting is one of the fundamental structure of calculus, which transforms complicated symbols into understandable ones. For the limitation of space, we discuss the following two typical examples: formal grammar[7] and λ-calculus[1]. For further information, readers could refer to [2].

Formal Grammar Formal grammar can be viewed as a rewriting system. For instance, the following rule: $S \to aSb$, $S \to ab$ can generate a sequence of characters, such as $S \to aSb \to aaSbb \to aaabbb$.

It is well known that this kind of rewriting system is applied to description of morphogenesis in L-system[6]. The main difference between L-system and our abstract rewriting system is that our model focuses on temporal behavior of chemical system rather than pattern formation, which is discussed later in Section 6.

λ-calculus The λ-calculus is also classified into a rewriting system. Let V denote a set of variables and $\Sigma = \{\lambda, (,)\} \cup V$ denote an alphabet of λ-calculus. Then, reduction(β), which calculates the value of a function, can be viewed as a rewriting rule. Then, an obtained pair (Σ, β) is an abstract rewriting system. For example, rule S, K and I are defined as: $S \equiv \lambda x.x$, $K \equiv \lambda xy.x$, $I \equiv \lambda xyz.xz(yz)$, respectively. Using these rule, we can reformulate SKK as follows: $SKK \to \lambda yz.Kz(yz)K \to \lambda z.KzKz \to \lambda z.z (\equiv I)$.

In fact, λ-calculus is closely related with rewriting system. For further information, readers could refer to [10].

2.2 Abstract Rewriting System

An abstract rewriting system abstracts the algebraic characteristics of calculus, whose example is shown in the above subsection, focusing on rewriting. Introducing this formal structure, several characteristics of rewriting can be discussed in the common framework. Thus, this concept is applied to various formal methods in mathematics and computer science, such as proof theory[8], algebraic description of computer software[13], and automated deduction[11].

Let us first begin with the definition of the abstract rewriting system.

Definition 1 (Abstract Rewriting System) *An abstract rewriting system is defined as a pair (A, R), where A and R denotes a set and a set of binary relations, respectively.* □

Next, the final result of rewriting calculus, called normal form, and finitely terminating are defined as follows.

Definition 2 (Normal Form) *If there does not exist b such as $a \to b$ and $b \in A$, then $a \in A$ is called normal form.* □

Definition 3 (Finitely Terminating) *If the all rewriting pathways are finite, it is said that this system satisfies the finitely terminating property.* □

3 ARMS

3.1 Definition of ARMS

Using the concepts of abstract rewriting system, we introduce a new abstract rewriting system on multisets (ARMS) in order to examine the conditions of cycle emergence and the algebraic characteristics of the obtained cycle. ARMS is defined as follows.

Definition 4 *Abstract rewriting system on multisets is defined as a quintuplet (A, R, O_R, C, I), where A, R, O_R, C and I denote a set of symbols, a set of rewriting rules, rule order, a multiset of symbols, and a set of input strings, respectively.*

In this model, a multiset C is used as "a test tube", which contain "symbols" in A, which correspond to chemical compounds. Then, rewriting rules R, corresponding to chemical reactions, act on this multiset, and the applied symbols are transformed into other symbols. Moreover, for simplicity, we assume that no character outputs from a multiset C, whose problem will be discussed in Section 5.

For example, let us consider a case where R is equal to:

$$aa \to e : r_1, \quad b \to c : r_2,$$
$$d \to e : r_3$$

and C is equal to $\{\}$. Then, when I is equal to $\{b\}$, that is, when b is input to C ($C = \{b\}$), r_2 can be applied, and C is transformed into $\{c\}$. That is, $\{b\} \to \{c\}$.

However, when I is equal to $\{e\}$, C will not be transformed, because no rule in R can be applied to C. Thus, these examples suggest that the relation between R and I should constraint the characteristics of calculus in C, unless C is infinite, which is discussed later in Section 5.

In this paper, we also focus on the effect of finiteness of a test tube, thus we assume that C is finite. Especially, for simplicity, the cardinality of C, $|C|$ is set to 10 ($|C| = 10$) in our experiments. Then, normal form can be defined as follows.

Definition 5 (Normal Form in ARMS) *If no rule in R can be applied to C and if no string in I can be input to C, then it is said that C is in normal form.* □

Thus, normal form corresponds to the steady state, or the death of living things.

procedure ARMS Rewriting Step (*integer k, list R,*
list C(k), var list C(k + 1))
/* k: State Number,   R: Rule set $\{r_1, r_2, \cdots, r_n\}$ */
/* C(k): Multiset in State k (Input),
C(k + 1): Multiset in State k + 1 (Output)*/
var
   i : *integer*;   D : *list*; /* i: Counter   D: Multiset */
begin
   $i := 0$; $D := C(k)$;
   while ($i < |R|$) **do**
     begin
      if ($|D| < 10$) **then**
        Input "a"
        if (r_i can be applied) **then**
          Rewrite D using r_i ; $C(k + 1) := D$;
      else if (r_i can be applied) **then**
          Rewrite D using r_i ; $C(k + 1) := D$;
     end
   $i := i + 1$;
end {ARMS Rewriting Step}

Figure 1: An Algorithm for ARMS

3.2 How ARMS works

For experiments, we specify the characteristics of ARMS in the following way.

Initial Condition   As to the initial condition, A and I is set to $\{a, b, c, d, e\}$ and $\{a\}$, respectively. Then, the cardinality of $|C|$ is set to 10, because of the following two reasons. First, even in this small space, ARMS shows the complex behavior, as shown in the next section. Second, although we have already checked the behavior of ARMS with respect to $2 \le |C| \le 100$, each behavior in the large cardinality is very similar to the behavior when $|C|$ is equal to 10. Finally, rewriting is applied for 5005 steps, which is equal to the total size of search space of C.

Initial State and Final State   Initial state of C is set to an empty set ($C = \{\}$). On the other hand, final state is defined as a normal form defined in the above subsection. That is, *if no rule in R can be applied to C and if no string in I can be input to C, then C is in a final state.*

Order of Rules   In ARMS, we assume that one rule is applied in each rewriting step unless no input is allowed based on a given rule order O_R. For example, let us consider the case when $R = \{r_1, r_2, r_3\}$ and $O_R = \{r_1 \to r_2 \to r_3\}$. Then, each rule is applied in the following way. In Step 1, r_1 is applied. In the next steps, Step 2 and 3 , r_2 and r_3 are applied, respectively. In Step 1, r_1 is applied again. Thus, transition of the order in each step can be viewed as a "shift" operation on a bit string.

Based on this order, an algorithm for rewriting steps in ARMS is described as shown in Fig. 1.

An Example   In this example, we assume that a will be input after each rewriting step. Let R be a set of the following rules:

$$aa \;\to\; e \;:r_1, \quad b \;\to\; c \;:r_2, \quad d \;\to\; e \;:r_3$$

The initial state is set to $\{\}$.

$$State1 : \{\}$$

A rule r_1 is applied, but it fails, so only input of symbol "a" will be done in this step. Then, the next state is set to $\{a\}$ after the input.

$$State2 : \{a\}$$

In this state, ARMS tries r_2, but it fails, so only input of symbol a will be done again.

$$State3 : \{a, a\}$$

ARMS tries r_3, but it fails again, so only a will be input.

$$(State4) : \{a, a, a\}$$

In State 4, r_1 is applied again, and it succeeds. Thus, this state is transformed into:

$$State4 : \{b, a, a\}$$

It is notable that in State 3, r_1 can be applied, but ARMS do not so, because only one rule is applied in each rewriting step.

4 Experimental Results

Throughout the experiments, R is set to $\{r_1, r_2, r_3, r_4, r_5, r_6\}$, where each rule is described as the following formulae,
$$\{a\,a\,a \to b : r_1, \; b\,a \to c : r_2, \; c \to d\,d : r_3,$$
$$d\,e \to a : r_4, \; d \to e : r_5, \; d \to c : r_6\}.$$

4.1 Rule Order and Emergence of Cycles

Experimental Results   We, first, examine the relationship between rule order and emergence of cycles. In the above rule set R, the total number of rule order is equal to $6! = 720$. For each order, we assume that a will be input after each rewriting step and check whether cycles will emerge or not.

Surprisingly, in only 9.4 per cent(68/720) of 720 kinds of order, cycles emerge, and in the rest, 90.6 per cent, rewriting calculus is terminated. In 68 kinds of order where cycles emerge, steps needed to generate a cycle are 15 to 22 steps, and its average and its standard deviation is 19 and 3.3 steps, respectively. The average of the period length of cycles is 5.5 steps, whose standard deviation is 0.49 steps.

As to terminated cases, the average of steps needed for termination is 39 steps, and its standard deviation is 6.48 steps.

Typical Examples In this paragraph, we present two examples [2] which illustrates the importance of rule order. The first example is a typical case which generates a cycle. This typical example has the following rule order:

$$O_{R1} = \{r_1 \to r_2 \to r_3 \to r_4 \to r_5 \to r_6\},$$

whose state transition is shown below. After 18 steps, the system is stable in forming a cycle, whose period length is 5 steps.

1. $\{\}$
2. $\{a\}$
    $\downarrow$ 16 steps
18. $\{a, a, a, a, a, b, c, e\}$
19. $\{a, a, a, a, a, c, c, e\}$
20. $\{a, a, a, a, a, a, c, d, d, e\}$
21. $\{a, a, a, a, a, a, a, c, d\}$
22. $\{a, a, a, a, a, a, a, a, c, e\}$
23. $\{a, a, a, a, a, b, c, e\}$
24. $\{a, a, a, a, a, c, c, e\}$
25. $\{a, a, a, a, a, a, c, d, d, e\}$
26. $\{a, a, a, a, a, a, a, c, d\}$
27. $\{a, a, a, a, a, a, a, a, c, e\}$
        $\cdots$

The next example is a typical case, which terminates in 42 steps. Although ARMS applies the same rules, r_1 to r_5 for state transition, the obtained result is completely different, as shown below. This example has the following rule order:

$$O_{R2} = \{r_3 \to r_1 \to r_2 \to r_4 \to r_5 \to r_6\}$$

Then, the state transition is given as follows:

1. $\{\}$
2. $\{a\}$
    $\downarrow$ 16 steps
18. $\{a, a, a, a, a, a, a, c, c\}$
19. $\{a, a, a, a, a, b, c, c\}$
20. $\{a, a, a, a, a, c, c, c\}$
21. $\{a, a, a, a, a, a, c, c, c\}$
22. $\{a, a, a, a, a, a, a, c, c, c\}$
23. $\{a, a, a, a, b, c, c, c\}$
24. $\{a, a, a, a, c, c, c, c\}$
25. $\{a, a, a, a, a, c, c, c, c\}$
26. $\{a, a, a, a, a, a, c, c, c, c\}$
        $\cdots$
    $\downarrow$ 16 steps
42. $\{a, a, c, c, c, c, c, c, c, c\}$

In the next subsection, we further examine the effect of inputs and rule order. For this purpose, we adopt the above two kinds of order, O_{R1} and O_{R2}, because of the following two reasons: first, the behavior of O_{R1} is a typical cycle structure in 68 cases. Second, the behavior of

---

[2] It is notable that these two orderings provide illustrative examples on the formal property of about non-termination of ARMS, which is discussed in Section 5.

O_{R2} is completely different from the above one, although ARMS applies the same rules in these two cases.

4.2 Effect of Inputs and Rule Order

In the above section, we assume that "a" is input after each rewriting step, with rule order fixed. Then, we examine the effect of rule order over the whole permutation of rule order. In this subsection, we only adopt the above two orderings: O_{R1} and O_{R2} and examine the effect of random inputs. After that, we introduce randomness in rule order and examine the effect of rule order randomness.

Characteristic Function In order to incorporate randomness, we introduce characteristic function as follows.

Definition 6 (Characteristic Function) *Let x be a uniform random number selected from $[0, 1)$. Then a characteristic function $h_\delta(x)$ is defined as:*

$$h_\delta(x) = \begin{cases} 1 & (x < \delta) \\ 0 & (x \geq \delta), \end{cases}$$

where δ denotes a threshold from the following set, $\{0.1, 0.2, 0.3, 0.4, 0.5, 0.6, 0.7, 0.8, 0.9\}$. □

For example, when δ is equal to 0.9, then the frequency, with $h_\delta(x)$ positive, is equal to 0.9. Thus, when this function is applied to inputs, a will be input for nine of ten rewriting steps, which also means that no input will be done in one of ten steps. On the other hand, when the characteristic function is applied to rule order, the rule order will not be perturbed in nine of ten rewriting steps, which means that rule order is perturbed in one of ten steps. For example, let us consider a case of O_{R1}. When the sixth step in ten rewriting steps is perturbed, rule is applied as shown in the following sequence: r_1, $r_2, r_3, r_4, r_5, r_2(r_6), r_1, r_2, r_3, r_4$, where r_6 is changed to r_2. Thus, both input randomness and rule randomness is equal to $1 - h_\delta(x)$.

Experimental Results Using the above two kinds of order, we make the following three kinds of experiments: (1) Decrease the frequency of input, with rule order fixed, (2) Introduce randomness in rule order, with inputs in every step, and (3) Decrease the frequency of input, and introduce randomness in rule order.

In each case, we perform 100 trials, each of which consists of 5005 rewriting steps, and measure the effect on emergence of cycles, extinction of cycles, and steps needed for termination.

Decrease Frequency of Input, with Rule Order Fixed In the above three kinds of experimental results, the most interesting one is cases when the frequency of input is decreased, with the rule order fixed. In the cases

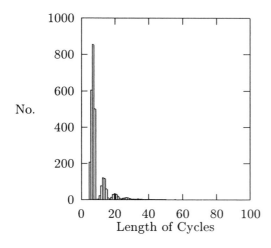

Figure 2: An Illustrative Example in O_{R1}

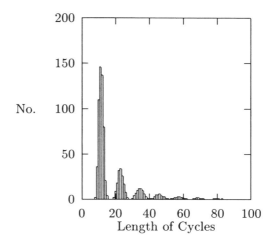

Figure 3: An Illustrative Example in O_{R2}: Frequency of Input: 0.4, with Rule Order Fixed.

Table 1: Relation between Frequency of Inputs (δ) and Termination of Calculus

δ	0.7 $\geq$	0.6	0.5	0.4	$\leq$ 0.3
O_{R1}	0	0	0	0	0
O_{R2}	100	100	98	13	0

Rule Order: Fixed

of rule order O_{R1}, rewriting steps are not terminated in all the trials, and cyclic structure also emerges. Interestingly, the period length of cycle varies over 7 to 30 steps, and period-doubling of cycles is observed. Fig.2 shows an illustrative example in the experiments, whose frequency of inputs is 0.2. Vertical axis shows the number of cycles which emerge in 100 trials, and horizontal axis shows the period length of cycles. In this figure, the peaks of the period length of cycles are located around 7, 13, 20, and 28 steps, which shows period-doubling. As discussed later in Section 5, for each period-doubling, fusion of cycles is observed. On the other hand, in the cases of rule order O_{R2}, unstable cycles emerge and rewriting steps are terminated while the threshold is larger than 0.5. However, when the threshold is equal to 0.4, almost the all rewriting trials are not terminated, where cycles become stable. Moreover, at this point, the variability of the period length of cycles is largest among the all trials. Fig.3 shows the distribution of the period length of cycles, whose notation is the same as Fig.2. The peaks of the period length of cycles is located around 11, 23, 34, 46, 57, and 67 steps, which shows period-doubling. We closely examine these experiments in Section 5, which shows that several kinds of cycle fusion is observed.

If the threshold is less than 0.3, all the trials are stable, similar to the cases of rule order O_{R1}. These results are summarized into Table 1.

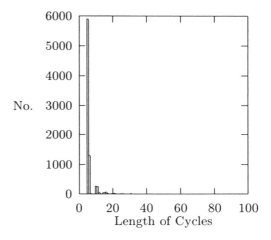

Figure 4: An Illustrative Example in O_{R1}: Input: Fixed, Randomness of Rule Order: 0.2.

Randomness in Rule Order, with Inputs in Every Step In these experiments, as to rule order O_{R1}, cycles become unstable and period-doubling is observed in O_{R1} when randomness of rule order is low. Fig. 4 shows the distribution of the period length of cycles when randomness of rule order is equal to 0.2, whose notation is the same as Fig. 2.

However, as randomness of rule order grows large, the number of emerging cycles decreases exponentially. Table 2 shows this tendency, the relation between randomness of rule order and the number of cycles emerging in 100 trials. When the randomness is larger than 0.5, almost the all trials generate only one cycle in general.

On the other hand, the behavior of cycles in O_{R2} is different. As shown in Table 2, the number of emerging cycles decreases exponentially, as randomness of rule order grows large. However, the behavior of cycles when randomness of rule is higher than 0.5 is different from

Table 2: Relation between Randomness of Rule Order $(1 - \delta)$ and Number of Emerging Cycles

$1 - \delta$	0.1	0.3	0.5	0.9
O_{R1}	1300(5)	325(5)	106(5)	23(5)
O_{R2}	1269(11)	1118(5)	335(3)	300(3)

A(B) : A and B denote the number of emerging cycles, and the median of the period length of cycles, respectively.

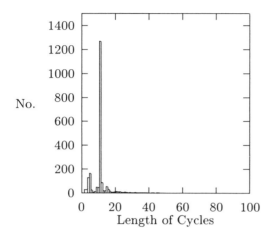

Figure 5: An Illustrative Example in O_{R2}: Input: Fixed, Randomness of Rule Order: 0.1.

that when the randomness is lower than 0.3: the median of the period length of cycles in the latter cases half smaller than that in O_{R1}, while that in the former cases is equal to or twice than that in O_{R1}. Interestingly, trials in the case of O_{R2} have two phase transitions: one is between 0.1 and 0.2, and the other is between 0.3 and 0.5.

Fig. 5 shows the distribution of the period length of cycles in O_{R2} when randomness of rule order is equal to 0.1. It is notable that the cycles whose period length is 11.0 are dominant over those whose period length is 5.0.

Decrease Frequency of Input and Increase Randomness in Rule Order In the final cases when the frequency of input is decreased and randomness is introduced in rule order, the obtained results are straightforward. In the cases when randomness is introduced in rule order with an input in every step, cycles become unstable in O_{R1}, and only unstable cycles emerge in O_{R2}. However, in both cases, the number of emerging cycles decreases exponentially, as randomness of rule order grows large. Interestingly, the behavior of cycles in O_{R1} is very similar to that in O_{R2}, except when the frequency of input is very high and randomness of rule order are very low. In the exceptional cases, both cases are very similar

to the cases in Subsection 4.1, except for emergence of cycles in the case of O_{R1}.

5 Discussion

5.1 Balance in ARMS

In this rewriting system, we assume that there is no output from a multiset C, for simplicity. Therefore the balance between the number of characters used in a rewriting step(n_u), that of input character(n_i), and that of generated characters(n_g) is an important factor by which rewriting steps do not terminate. That is, if the sum of n_u is equal to or less than the sum of n_i and n_g, then the calculus will not stop. If this balance breaks and the input flow($n_i + n_g$) is larger than (n_u), then its rewriting will terminate when input is impossible.

Definition 7 (Balance) *Let $|\alpha_k|$ and $|\beta_k|$ denote the length of the kth left hand side α_k of a rule r_k, and that of right hand side β_k, respectively. The balance $\triangle B$ in ARMS is defined as:*

$$\triangle B = \sum_{k=1}^{n} |\alpha_k| + m - \sum_{k=1}^{n} |\beta_k|,$$

where let n and m denote the number of rules which an ARMS system uses, and the number of sum of input symbols. □

The following lemma is obtained definition. For the limitation of a space, the proof of the following theorems is not provided below, although each proof is simple.

Lemma 1 *When the balance $\triangle B$ is not equal to 0, the ARMS system terminate.* □

Furthermore, in order to discuss the halting prosperity of ARMS, we need to define strict completeness.

Definition 8 (Strict completeness) *Let R_s and I_n denote a complete rule set which ensure the unique normal form and a set of input respectively. If a pair (O_{R_s}, I_n) dose not generate any cycle, it is said that the pair is strictly complete.*

For example, when $O_{R_1} = \{ab \rightarrow b : r_1\}$ and $I_1 = \{b\}$, $\{ab\}$ be rewritten as $\{b\}$, which is the normal form with an input "b". Thus the pair (O_{R_1}, I_1) is strictly complete. However, when we use O_{R_1} and $I_2 = \{a\}$, the above state $\{b\}$ will become $\{ab\}$ with an input of "a", where r_1 can applied. Thus, this input generates a cycle and the pair (O_{R_1}, I_2) is not strictly complete. On the basis of the balance $\triangle B$ and the strict completeness, the following theorems are derived by using the formal properties of an abstract rewriting system.

Theorem 1 (Non Termination of ARMS) *If a pair (O_{R_s}, I_n) is not strictly complete and the balance of the pair is equal to 0 ($\triangle B = 0$), then an ARMS does not terminate.* □

The following theorem is derived with the define of strict completeness and lemma1.

Theorem 2 (Termination of ARMS) *If the balance of the pair is not equal to 0 ($\triangle B \neq 0$), else if the balance of the pair is equal to 0 ($\triangle B = 0$), and a pair (O_{R_s}, I_n) is strictly complete then, an ARMS terminate.* □

Let us illustrate these theorem by using O_{R1} and O_{R2}, which is introduced in Section 4.

(1)O_{R1} The balance of O_{R_1} is equal to zero and $(O_{R_1}, \{a\})$ is not strictly complete, because two rules r_1 and r_4 contribute to the emergence of a cycle in the following way: the right hand side $r_4 : de \rightarrow a$ is equal to the left hand side of $r_1 : aaa \rightarrow b$. Thus, the pair $(O_{R_1}, \{a\})$ generates a cycle.

(2)O_{R2} The balance of O_{R_2} is equal to zero, and $(O_{R_2}, \{a\})$ is strictly complete, because the ARMS system only use two rules: r_2 and r_3 in the state transition. Thus, the pair do not generate a cycle.

Although this model is one kind of idealization with no output, the behavior of ARMS is interesting enough: Even if any output is assumed, the complex behavior of cycles, such as period-doubling, fusion of cycles, is observed.

Thus, the most important contribution of output is that it relaxes the condition of finitely terminating, since output supports the elimination of characters unused in rewriting step. Therefore, it may contribute to maintenance of a multiset with any output.

5.2 Fusion of Cycles

As discussed in Section 4, a special case in rule order O_{R2}, with the frequency of input 0.4, generates complex behavior of cycles. Closer examination shows that a core cycle generates first and that other cycles around this cycle fuse into a core cycle in rewriting steps.

The generated core cycle c_8 is given as follows:

$$c_8 : 8 \rightarrow 9 \rightarrow 10 \rightarrow \cdots \rightarrow 18 \rightarrow 8 : (11steps),$$

where each number denotes the number of rewriting steps. Around the c_c, the following cycle c_{54} is also observed:

$$c_{54} : 54 \rightarrow 55 \rightarrow 56 \rightarrow \cdots \rightarrow 66 \rightarrow 54 : (13steps),$$

It is impossible to transit from State 8 to State 54 and State 66 to State 11, with input fixed, but it will become possible when randomness of input is introduced. Then, c_8 fuses into c_{11}, and a new cycle will be generated as follows:

$$c_c : 8 \rightarrow 54 \rightarrow \cdots \rightarrow 66 \rightarrow 11 \rightarrow \cdots \rightarrow 8 : (21steps)$$

Thus, fusion of cycles depends on randomness of input: randomness of input influences the application of rules, and then change of application of rules causes the change of structure of a multiset, then it opens the hidden pathway to fusion of cycles.

Although the mechanism of fusion of cycles is not fully studied, it is notable that even such a simple structure emerges a complex behavior of cycles. Further research on fusion, such as classification of cycles, will be a future work.

6 Related Work

6.1 L-system

The most famous application of rewriting system to computational model on living things is L-system[6], which models the morphogenesis of living things, such as the growth of trees. This system formalizes the process of morphogenesis as firing of rewriting rules and is defined as a formal language system (Σ, P, ω), where Σ, P, and ω, denotes a set of states, a set of rewriting rules, and a type of cell at initial state, respectively.

For example, let Σ be equal to $\{1, 2, 3, 4\}$, and P be equal to:

$$P = \{1 \rightarrow 42, \quad 2 \rightarrow 23, \quad 3 \rightarrow 1(2), \quad (\rightarrow (, \quad) \rightarrow)\}.$$

Then the process of morphogenesis can be viewed as the following rewriting process:

$$S1 = 1 \rightarrow S1 = 42 \rightarrow S1 = 4223 \rightarrow S1 = 4221(2)$$

The most important difference between L-system and ARMS is that ARMS focuses on the temporal aspects of rewriting processes, rather than the spatial aspects. In fact, ARMS does not include any spatial information on a multiset, but models temporal behavior of chemical systems.

6.2 Algorithmic Chemistry

Fontana introduces an abstract model, called λ-gas[4], where a new chemical is generated by interactions between existing chemicals, using λ-calculus. This model is described by a set of functions which correspond to molecules. Two functions are randomly selected, and they interacts with each other, which is represented as a compound of function $f(g)$. Then, different functions will be generated when the environment of a system is changed, provided the condition in which no limitation is given to interaction,

Although this model also focuses on characteristics of chemical reaction, the main difference between λ-gas and ARMS is that our interest is in temporal aspects of emergence of cycles. Furthermore, Fontana also discusses the difference between λ-calculus and abstract rewriting system as follows[4].

With some ingenuity the observer will further derive all laws supplied by the uncovered group structure(Knuth and Bendix, 1970: Huet and Oppen, 1980). If read as rewrite rules, the equations thus obtained will enable the

observer to exactly describe(and predict) each and every collision product in the system - without any knowledge about λ-calculus. The observer will, then, have discovered a perfectly valid theory of that organization, without reference to its underlying micromechanics (from: [4, p.22]).

6.3 Cellular Automata

Using the concepts of abstract rewriting system, cellular automata[15] can be formalized as rewriting system with spatial information. In cellular automata, rewriting rules correspond to local rules. For example, the following local rules,

000	001	010	100	101	110	111
0	1	0	1	0	1	0

can be viewed as rewriting rules, such as $000 \to 0$. Thus, from the above local rules, we obtain the following rewriting rules:

$$000 \to 0, \quad 001 \to 1, \quad 010 \to 0, \quad 011 \to 1,$$
$$100 \to 1, \quad 101 \to 0, \quad 110 \to 1, \quad 111 \to 0.$$

The most important differences between cellular automata and ARMS are the following two points. First, ARMS do not use any spatial information. Rewriting rules are global, rather than local in cellular automata. Thus, although cellular automata focus on local interactions between neighbors, ARMS focuses on the interaction of rules with a given multiset. Second, our interest is in formal characteristics of rewriting calculus, rather than pattern formation in cellular automata.

7 Conclusion

In this paper, we introduce a new abstract rewriting system on multisets, and model chemical reactions as a symbolic rewriting system which acts on a multiset, which can be viewed as a test tube. Using this model, we examine the condition of cycle emergence, its robustness and how this system works under the probabilistic condition. The results show not only that a cycle will emerge even under a simple initial condition, but also that complex behavior of a cycle, such as fusion of several cycles, is observed when the initial condition is perturbed during the simulation. Furthermore, the formal analysis of ARMS leads to two theorems on the termination of this system, where the interaction between the order of rules and inputs plays an important role.

Acknowledgments

This research is supported by Grants-in-Aid for Scientific Research No.07243203 from the Ministry of Education, Science and Culture in Japan.

References

[1] H. P. Barendregt, The Lambda Calculus, North-Holland, 1985.

[2] N. Dershowitz and J. P. Jouannaud, Rewrite Systems, in Handbook of theoretical computer science 245-309, Elsevier. 1990.

[3] M. Eigen and P. Schuster, The Hypercycle, Springer-Verlag, 1979.

[4] W. Fontana and L. W. Buss, The Arrival of the fittest: Toward a Theory of biological organization, Bulletin of Mathematical Biology, Vol.56, No.1, 1-64, 1994.

[5] W. Fontana, Algorithmic Chemistry, Artificial Life II, 160-209, Addison Wesley, 1994.

[6] D. Frijtyers and A. Lindenmayer, L system, Lecture Note In Computer Science, vol. 15, Springer Verlag, 1994.

[7] J. E. Hopcroft and J. D. Ullman, Introduction to Automata theory, Languages and Computation, Addison-Wesley, 1979.

[8] G. Huet and D. C. Oppen, Equations and rewrite rules, Formal Language Theory, 349-405, Academic Press, London, 1980.

[9] S. A. Kauffman, The Origins of Order, Oxford University Press, 1993.

[10] J. W. Klop, Term Rewriting System, Handbook of Logic in Computer Science, 3-62, Clarendon Press, 1992.

[11] D. E. Knuth and P. B. Bendix, Simple word problems in universal algebras, North-Holland, 1985.

[12] H. R. Maturana and F. J. Varela, Autopoiesis and Cognition, D. Reidel Publishing Company, 1980.

[13] M. J. O'Donnell, Computing in system described by equations, Lecture Note in Computer Science, Vol.58, Springer Verlag, 1977.

[14] J. D. Watson, N. H. Hopkins at el, Molecular biology of the gene, The Benjamin/Cummings publishing Company, Inc, 1992.

[15] S. Wolfram, Cellular Automata and Complexity, 1994.

AUTHOR INDEX